Impression

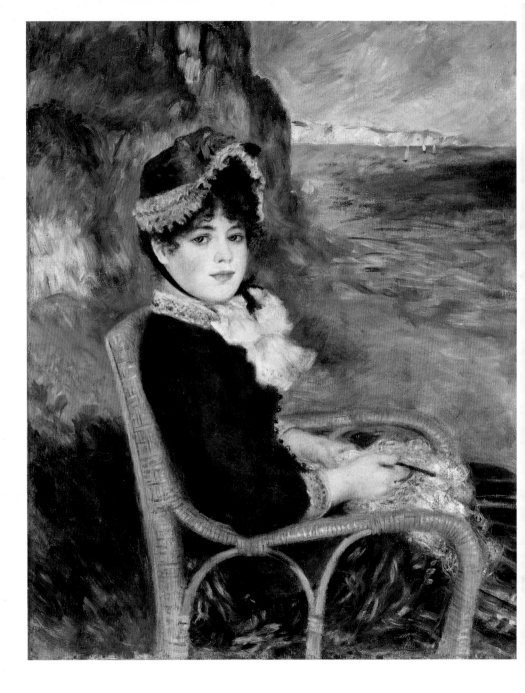

IMPRESSIONISM

1860–1920

Edited by Ingo F. Walther

Part I

IMPRESSIONISM
IN FRANCE

by

Peter H. Feist

TASCHEN

HONG KONG KÖLN LONDON LOS ANGELES MADRID PARIS TOKYO

"To treat a subject for the colours and not for the subject itself, that is
what distinguishes the Impressionist from other painters."
GEORGES RIVIERE, 1877

Illustration page 2:
Pierre-Auguste Renoir
By the Seashore, 1883
Au bord de la mer
Oil on canvas, 92 x 73 cm
New York, The Metropolitan Museum of Art

Illustration page 402:
Childe Hassam
Fifth Avenue at Washington Square, 1891
Oil on canvas, 56 x 40.6 cm
Lugano, Thyssen-Bornemisza Collection

This work was originally published
in two volumes.

To stay informed about upcoming TASCHEN titles, please request our
magazine at www.taschen.com/magazine or write to TASCHEN America,
6671 Sunset Boulevard, Los Angeles, CA 90028,
USA; contact-us@taschen.com; Fax: +1-323-463-4442.
We will be happy to send you a free copy of our magazine,
which is filled with information about all of our books.

© 2012 TASCHEN GmbH
Hohenzollernring 53, D–50672 Köln
www.taschen.com

Original edition: © 1993 Benedikt Taschen Verlag GmbH
© 2012 for the reproductions: VG Bild-Kunst, Bonn,
and the estates of the artists
Edited and produced by
Ingo F. Walther, Alling/Munich
English translation: Michael Hulse
Cover design: Sense/Net Art Direction, Andy Disl and Birgit Eichwede, Cologne
www.sense-net.net

Printed in Singapore
ISBN 978–3–8228–5053–4

Contents

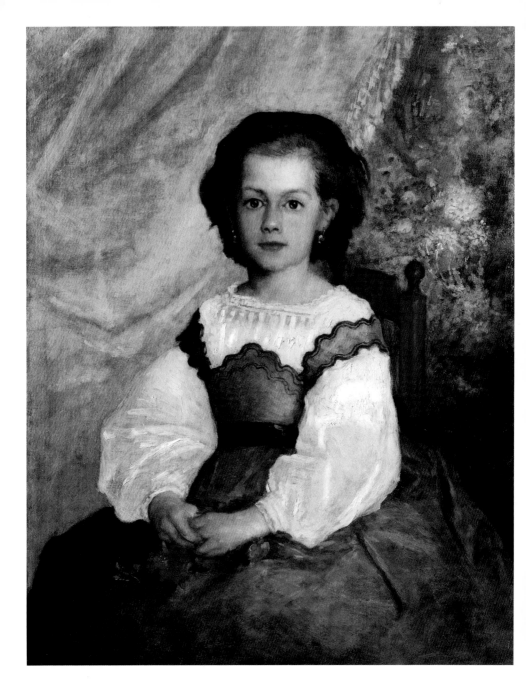

Editor's Preface

On 15 April 1874 an exhibition featuring 30 artists opened in the Paris studio of Nadar the photographer. They had joined for the express purpose of presenting their work to the public as a group. It was the first group exhibition to be mounted without state intervention or the jurying process. And it was also the birth of Impressionism – an avant-garde event, a revolution that was to be of great significance for all the movements that followed, in Modernist art and after.

And the art that went on display was avant-garde and revolutionary too: landscapes, cityscapes and other subjects from everyday life, in light, luminous colours, full of atmosphere, the brushwork consisting merely of brief strokes and dabs. The paintings had partly been done *sur le motiv*, in the open. It was a protest against the dusty studio art of the time with its lofty historical and mythological subjects, its colours predominantly gloomy and earthy, its light chosen purely to suit the artist.

Impressionist painting has remained the most fascinating product of modern art – and the most popular, as has been shown in recent years by spectacularly successful exhibitions of Degas, Gauguin, van Gogh, Manet, Monet or Renoir. Their work fetches record prices. The critical literature on them fills libraries. And yet some aspects of Impressionism have not been sufficiently researched, while several of the painters and their works have remained unknown, or have been forgotten.

This study describes the history of Impressionism, and of Neo- and Post-Impressionism, in France; it also affords an overview of related artistic developments elsewhere in Europe and in North America.

Volume I deals with France. The book aims not only to deal with the illustrious names – Monet, Renoir, Manet, Pissarro, Sisley, Degas, Cézanne, Gauguin, van Gogh, Seurat, Signac – but also to present little-known artists who were important for Impressionism, among them Gustave Caillebotte, a significant painter whose work was not "discovered" till a century after his death. The monograph includes 17 of his paintings. Others included are Bracquemond, Cross, Forain, Gonzalès, Guillaumin, Lebourg, Lépine, Luce, Morisot, Raffaëlli and Vignon.

Volume II deals with painting elsewhere in Europe and in North America that was inspired by French Impressionism or evolved parallel to it. Though this art may not always be strictly Impressionist, it nonetheless owed a debt to the French artists even when their style was translated into a different national artistic idiom. Volume II also features a reference section including brief biographies, bibliographies and photographs of 236 artists, as well as numerous entries on other movements, critics, publications and locations.

Pierre-Auguste Renoir
Mademoiselle Romaine Lacaux, 1864
Oil on canvas, 81 x 65 cm
Cleveland (OH), Cleveland Museum of Art

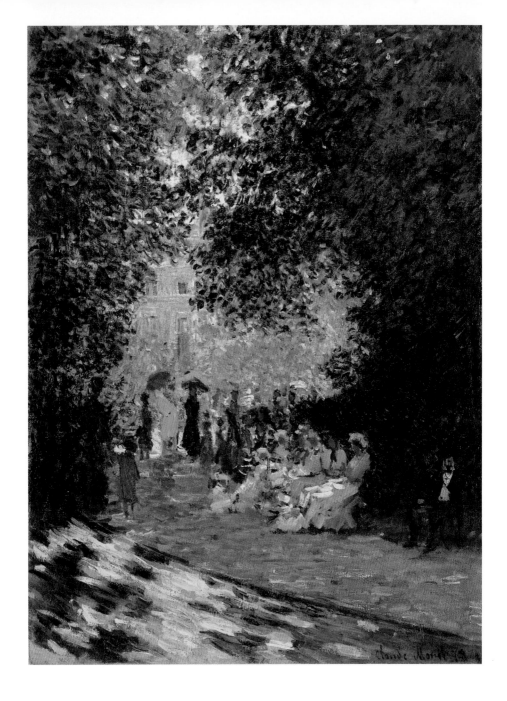

I Appraising Impressionism

Impressionist paintings are today among the most admired of all artworks. They are the pride of every public and private collection. As a rule they offer a visual feast, and possess a magic of their own that captivates the practised connoisseur and the less experienced art lover alike. Countless reproductions have made many Impressionist works familiar worldwide. And the flood of publications is growing continually, making available all the information we ever wanted to have on both the works and the artists.

Nevertheless, the debate on the aesthetic standing of Impressionist art and its place in art history is not over. Like any dispute over value judgements, it never will be. Nowadays, new questions are being raised concerning the forces that power historical developments in art, and the relations of Impressionism to other artistic movements. Many of these questions are being broached because art historians, for a good thirty years at least, have been charting a more complete and nuanced map of 19th-century art history.[1] For a long time it was widely thought that for decades only the Impressionists produced art that was of value and noteworthy as a gauge of the *Zeitgeist*; but this view must now be amended, even if eminent scholars of Impressionism such as John Rewald have been angrily condemning the recent revaluation of Salon art.[2]

There is a point to such anger as long as market considerations are in the foreground and conservative nostalgia takes precedence over careful aesthetic evaluation. But we must clear the way for a discriminating critical look at Impressionism and at the limits of Impressionist art's capacity to grasp and render the world artistically and to satisfy ever-changing aesthetic needs. Outstanding art moves and impresses us; but this should not obscure our realization that even the greatest masterpiece can never be "absolute", can never fulfil every conceivable expectation. Indeed, its impact may derive from a quality of emphatic one-sidedness.

The term "Impressionist" primarily describes a particular way of painting, drawing or working in graphics. There are comparable approaches in sculpture, literature and music. In relatively early days, when the Impressionist movement was still just one controversial strand in the art scene and at the same time a readily-surveyed aspect of recent art history (which younger artists were already critically rejecting), a young German art critic by the name of Richard Hamann wrote "Impression-

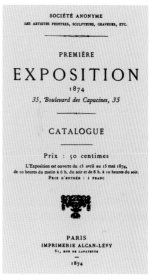

SOCIÉTÉ ANONYME
DES ARTISTES PEINTRES, SCULPTEURS, GRAVEURS, ETC.

PREMIÈRE

EXPOSITION
1874
35, *Boulevard des Capucines, 35*

CATALOGUE

Prix : 50 centimes

L'Exposition est ouverte du 15 avril au 15 mai 1874,
de 10 heures du matin à 6 h. du soir et de 8 h. à 10 heures du soir.
PRIX D'ENTRÉE : 1 FRANC

PARIS
IMPRIMERIE ALCAN-LÉVY
61, RUE DE LAFAYETTE
1874

Catalogue of the first Impressionist exhibition, 1874

Claude Monet
Monceau Park, 1878
Le parc Monceau
Oil on canvas, 73 x 54 cm
Wildenstein 466
New York, The Metropolitan Museum of Art

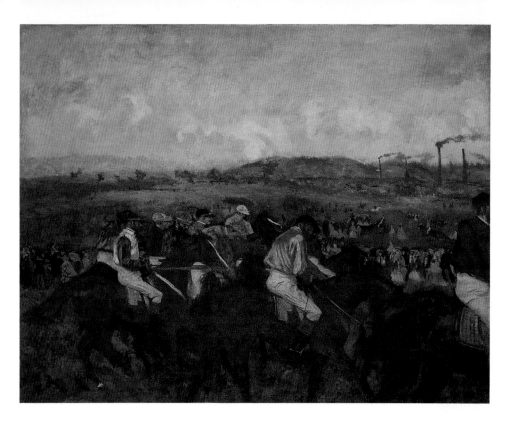

Edgar Degas
Gentlemen's Race. Before the Start, 1862
Course de gentlemen. Avant le départ
Oil on canvas, 48.5 x 61.5 cm
Lemoisne 101. Paris, Musée d'Orsay

ismus in Leben und Kunst" (1907).³ Hamann saw the distinctive qualities of Impressionist principles as deriving from a contemporary feel for life itself, from kinds of sensibility and behaviour that could be encountered as much in everyday life, philosophy and science as in art. But another German art critic of about the same age, Werner Weisbach, who had been lecturing on Impressionist painting at the University of Berlin since 1904, took a different approach in the two volumes of his "Impressionismus: Ein Problem der Malerei in Antike und Neuzeit" (1910/11).⁴ In linking Impressionist art to the aesthetics of antiquity, Weisbach was seeking to give the new art a respectable ancestry and to explain its principles as fundamentals that were always available to the art of painting. This approach has not been ignored, but scholars today prefer to see Impressionism as one particular artistic type of evolution unfolding alongside others in a historical, cultural and aesthetic situation that was unique. American and British art historians in particular – critics such as Robert L. Herbert, Albert Boime or Timothy J. Clark – stress the decisive part played by cultural and social circumstances in art history, rather than individual aesthetic or formal strategies on the part of the artists themselves.⁵ "The New Painting. Impressionism 1874–1886", edited by Charles S. Moffett, provides invaluable documentation of these interrelations.⁶ Moffett's title comes from an 1876 essay by the critic Edmond Duranty, "to draw attention to the entire spectrum of the modern movement rather than restricting it to one or another ism."

Impressionism represents the grand finale of a particular way of appropriating the world through painting or drawing. This method, often termed realism, evolved in Europe in the dawn of the modern era. But Impressionism also established various features that were preconditions and characteristics of 20th-century art. For this reason, critics have tended to see Impressionism as either an end or a beginning – or both.

Most of the movement's principles reveal Impressionism to have been a summation of earlier views and intentions, a conclusion, a peak. What struck most contemporaries as rebellious modernity was in fact closely linked to tradition. Many people today respond to traditionalism of this kind, and with good reason, without being conservative in any narrower

Pierre-Auguste Renoir
Oarsmen at Chatou, 1879
Les canotiers à Chatou
Oil on canvas, 81 x 100 cm
Daulte 305
Washington, National Gallery of Art

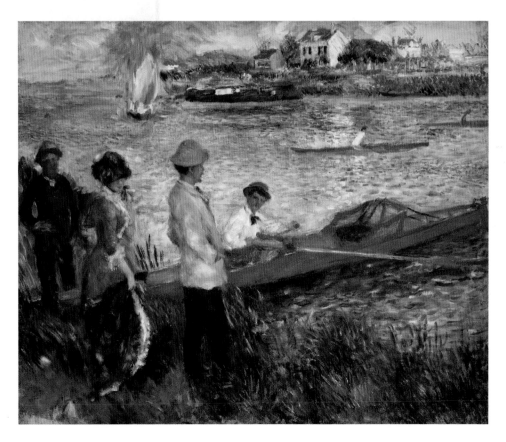

sense of the word. It was not until Post-Impressionism that a fundamental aesthetic upheaval and breakthrough occurred with the "end of scientific perspective" (Fritz Novotny)[7], when artists departed from an approach long taken for granted, the view that art should reproduce what was actually seen. Taken as a whole, though, Impressionism remains astoundingly contemporary: people today are still struck by the arresting specifics of the paintings. There can be no other explanation for the spectacular numbers that turn out to exhibitions of Impressionist art or for the continuing popularity of Impressionist works with collectors. But since one and the same painting – or "text", in modern analytic semiotics – can be "read" differently at different times by people with different interests, the present study will include a look at differing ways of reading, then and now.

The Impressionist style of painting first emerged as a definable, shared approach among a small group of young French artists, and it was these artists who were meant by the term – which was originally coined disparagingly. In any account of the movement, the work of Edouard Manet (1832–1883),[8] Edgar Degas (1834–1917),[9] Claude Monet (1840–1926),[10] Pierre-Auguste Renoir (1841–1919),[11] Camille Pissarro (1830–1903),[12] Alfred Sisley (1839–1899),[13] Frédéric Bazille (1841–1870)[14] and Berthe Morisot (1841–1895)[15] must occupy the central position.[16] These artists produced work over careers of varying lengths. Others who were also involved with the movement deserve more attention than they generally get, however – artists such as Armand Guillaumin (1841–1927),[17] Gustave Caillebotte (1848–1894)[18] or Eva Gonzalès (1849–1883).[19] The Post-Impressionist Paul Cézanne (1839–1906),[20] the key figure in the transition from 19th-century to 20th-century art, occupies a special position of his own.

The history of Impressionism would not be complete without the distinctive work of the Neo-Impressionists Georges Seurat (1859–1891),[21] Paul Signac (1863–1935)[22] and their fellows,[23] or of the Post-Impressionists Paul Gauguin (1848–1903),[24] Vincent van Gogh (1853–1890)[25] and Henri de Toulouse-Lautrec (1864–1901).[26] A delightful late afterglow of Impressionism came with the *intimisme* of Pierre Bonnard (1867–1947)[27] and Edouard Vuillard (1868–1940).[28]

But the history of Impressionism is not merely a French one. It is European, indeed global, as was demonstrated in 1990 by authors from around the world in "Impressionismus: Eine internationale Kunstbewegung 1860–1920", edited by the American art critic Norma Broude.[29] Impressionism did not derive from French preconditions and circumstances alone, nor would its rapid international spread be explicable if comparable tendencies had not already existed elsewhere.

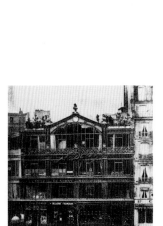

Photographer Gaspard-Félix Tournachon Nadar's house at Boulevard des Capucines 35. The first Impressionist exhibition of 1874 was held in his studio.

Pierre-Auguste Renoir
The Walk, 1870
La promenade
Oil on canvas, 80 x 64 cm
Daulte 55. Private collection

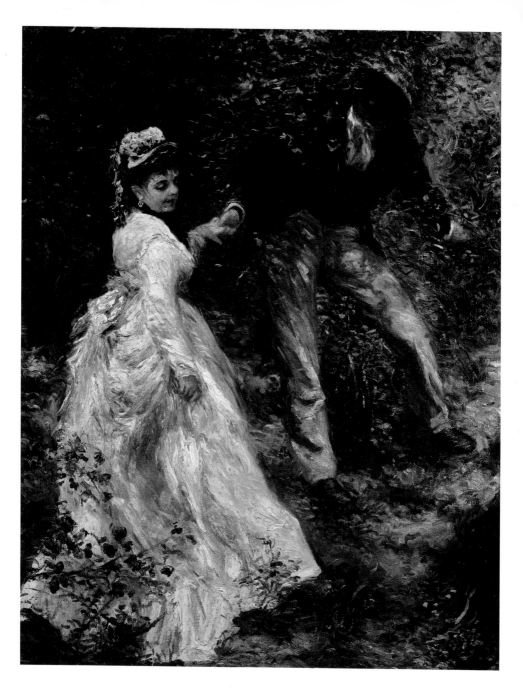

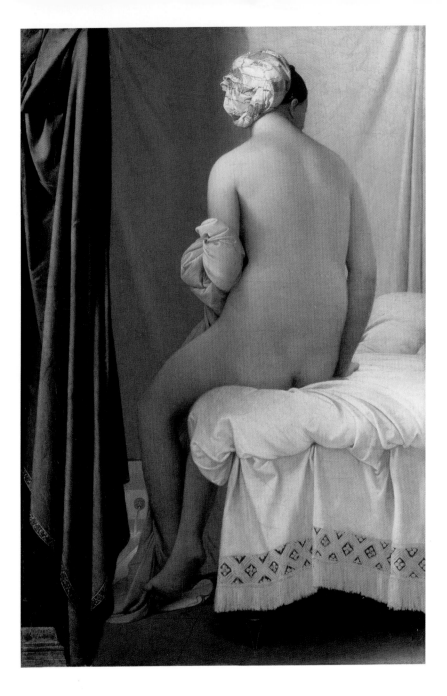

2 The Prehistory of Impressionism

We shall be examining the Impressionist conception of art and its roots in greater detail presently, but first it is useful to take a look at what went before. To do so will explain why Impressionism, though its origins were not only French, first emerged in France. France offered the best soil in which the movement could grow and achieve form and energy. Since the late 17th century, the political and artistic status quo had meant – to put it simply – that some of the most important decisions concerning the future course of European art were made in Paris. If French absolutism under Louis XIV, the *roi soleil*, had made France a model to be followed, the French Revolution of 1789 in turn brought worldwide class upheavals in its train. The evolution of middle-class society in the 19th century – including the evolution of that society's arts – advanced a little earlier and more consistently in France than in other countries. Despite the fact that England's production levels and capital resources had made it the "workshop of the world", in the visual arts – across the entire spectrum of exhibitions, dealers and the creation of taste – the 19th-century capital was Paris. The genesis and dissemination of Impressionism required the lifestyle and cultural climate of Paris.

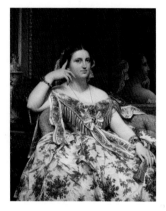

Jean Auguste Dominique Ingres
Portrait of Madame Inès Moitessier, 1856
Portrait de Madame Inès Moitessier
Oil on canvas, 120 x 92.1 cm
London, National Gallery

Throughout the arts, particularly in the modern era, we can observe divergent artistic ideas and the resultant approaches to creative work co-existing. This is what we might term stylistic polyphony. In part it derives from the fact that arists of different generations are at work at the same time. When they are young they are shaped by their various situations, and subsequently remain true to the views they then formed or else adapt them in ways that differ from their coevals. The diversity is also caused by the fact that society (and, within society, groupings and levels that may be radically at odds) makes – or indeed insists on – various requirements of art. These requirements ensure that artworks are made for various purposes and to satisfy a variety of interests (and at the same time attempt to oust or obstruct work conceived along contrary lines).

Three strands in French painting in the first two thirds of the 19th century that were of particular significance for the subsequent emergence of Impressionism should be emphasized. To some extent they followed upon each other, and to some extent they overlapped chronologically. Of course we should not forget the attitudes and approaches from which the initially small group of Impressionists set themselves apart, at a criti-

Jean Auguste Dominique Ingres
The Bather of Valpinçon, 1808
La baigneuse de Valpinçon
Oil on canvas, 146 x 97.5 cm
Paris, Musée du Louvre

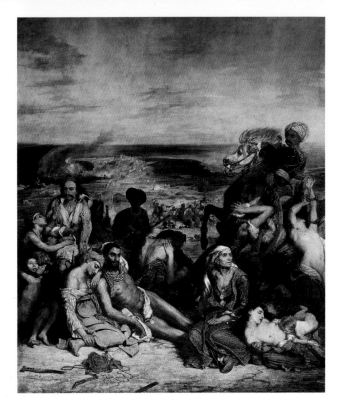

Eugène Delacroix
The Massacre on Chios, 1824
Le massacre de Scio
Oil on canvas, 417 x 354 cm
Robaut-Chesneau 91. Paris, Musée du Louvre

cal distance. This is complex territory, since the distinctions and polarities are not always clearly defined; there was shared ground too, and
reciprocal influences.

The weightiest tradition was that of Classicism, involving a valuing of
ancient Greek and Roman art and their exemplary qualities above all
else. Classicism recognised the authority of the formal idiom and choice
of subjects of great art of the past – and implied the imitation of that art.
Those who espoused it shared the conviction that works of art should be
beautiful, noble and instructive. They believed there were definite criteria
for beauty and rules governing the way it should be created. The classical
view placed the idea above reality. The artist, in this view, was inspired

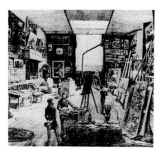

Delacroix' studio in Paris, Rue Notre-Dame-de-
Lorette

with an idea of perfection, and his task was to correct the chance imperfections of given reality by means of his style and shaping skills. The
study of exemplary works of antiquity, and obedience to formal rules,
took precedence over the study of Nature.

It is true that Classicism served the French Revolution, and subsequently, with shifts of emphasis, the *Style Empire* of Napoleon. But it
remains true, nonetheless, that Classicism, with its tendency to immunize

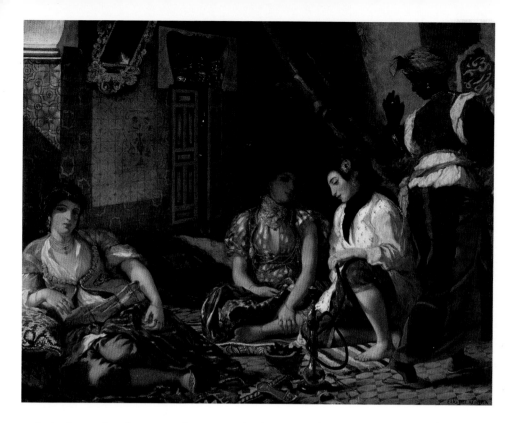

societal values against change, was the aptest mode of expression for those with a conservative interest in preserving the social status quo. In terms of the politics of the arts, Classicism was represented by the Academy and by its art college, the Ecole des Beaux-Arts.[10] The foremost Classical painter was Jean Auguste Dominique Ingres (1780–1867),[11] whose patriarchal authority was still making itself felt when the Impressionists first made an attempt to put their views on art before the public. Though these views were diametrically opposed to Classicism in every important respect, some of the younger painters did have a regard for certain qualities in the work of Ingres, and were later to rethink the basic principles of Classicism.

Ingres was a draughtsman of the first rank. He had an absolutely sure hand in drawing a line, and specifically in drawing the outlines of figures – which Classicism saw as the crux in formulating and conveying an idea. The compositional disposition of figures had to be harmonious and clear, as in a relief, and constitute a unified and well-ordered whole. Calmness and leisureliness inform the figures' gestures and poses. A good example is Ingres' first lifesize nude, *The Bather of Valpinçon* (p. 14), so

Eugène Delacroix
The Women of Algiers, 1834
Femmes d'Alger dans leur appartement
Oil on canvas, 180 x 229 cm
Robaut-Chesneau 482. Paris, Musée du Louvre

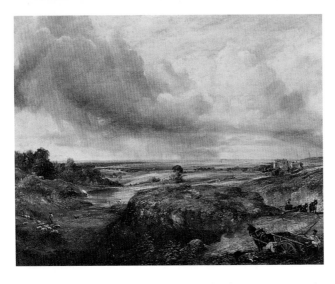

John Constable
Hampstead Heath, 1824
Oil on canvas, 60 x 77 cm
Winterthur, Oskar Reinhart Collection

called after the man who commissioned it. This fine painting's simple, tranquil mood made an impression on those who came after, not least for its careful observation of the gentle play of light upon the woman's body. Ingres primarily worked in the mode that the doctrines of Classicism rated highest, histories – showing mythological or historical scenes, events from the Bible or the lives of the saints, or perhaps the histories of the kings of France. But he was also fond of the "oriental" subject matter that was particularly the domain of the Romantics – scenes of harem life, for instance.

Moreover, Ingres was a first-rate portraitist, as we can see in the psychologically persuasive *Portrait of Madame Inès Moitessier* (p. 15), which also conveys an opulent sense of the sitter's wealth. The artist worked on this portrait for twelve years, till, at the age of sixty-six, he finally felt satisfied. Ingres influenced the course along which art evolved not only through his own work but also through his teaching, in Paris and at the Académie Française department in Rome, where all who won the coveted Prize of Rome furthered their own training before accepting chairs in Paris and preaching the doctrines of a late Classicism that was in steady decline.

For decades, Ingres' very antithesis seemed to be Eugène Delacroix (1798–1863).[32] A painter of true genius, Delacroix was one of the most temperamental artists in the history of European art. To him, colour and not the line was the all-important formal means – and so the Classicists at the Académie Française barred him election to their hallowed ranks no fewer than seven times before he finally joined in 1857. From the very start, Delacroix startled the public and the critics alike with his fully-toned, sensuous use of colour, his passionate and highly personal interpretations of his material, and his eccentric choices of new subjects. He

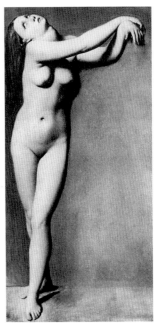

Jean Auguste Dominique Ingres
Angélique, 1819
Oil on canvas, 84.5 x 42.5 cm
Paris, Musée du Louvre

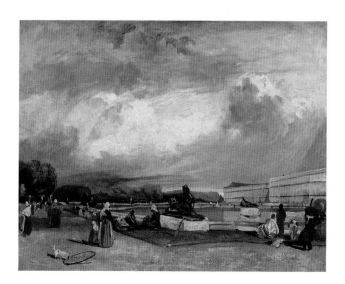

Richard Parkes Bonington
Water Basin at Versailles, c. 1826
Le parterre d'eau à Versailles
Oil on canvas, 43 x 54 cm
Paris, Musée du Louvre

felt that not only the dramatic and tragic events of antiquity but also those of his own times merited a place in art.

The prime early example of this is his large-scale painting *The Massacre on Chios* (p. 16). In 1822, the Greek inhabitants of the island of Chios had mounted a rebellion against their Turkish overlords, whereupon twenty thousand of them had been butchered. Many western Europeans felt deeply involved in the Greek struggle for liberty. In his picture, Delacroix has grouped his figures relief-style as in a classical composition, but the rich modelling of the colours harks back to Peter Paul Rubens (1577–1640). Ingres, by contrast, forebade his pupils to study the great Baroque master. The painter Antoine-Jean Gros (1771–1835) shared Ingres' tastes and, horrified by Delacroix's painting, dubbed it "the massacre of painting". From a Classicist point of view, it hardly helped that Delacroix had lightened and loosened the colours of the landscape background shortly before the exhibition opened; he had seen *The Hay Wain* (p. 20) by the English painter John Constable (1776–1837)[33] – the painting that presently won the exhibition Gold Medal. *The Hay Wain* came as a revelation to Delacroix, encouraging him to be more responsive to light and colour values, and to record his impressions with greater spontaneity. It was no accident that his eye lit upon that painting.

English Antecedents

Since the 18th century, English painters and those who bought their work had displayed a particular interest in landscape – which the doc-

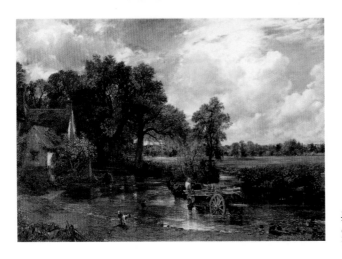

John Constable
The Hay Wain, 1821
Oil on canvas, 130.2 x 185.4 cm
London, National Gallery

trines of Classicism rated low. Owing to the distinctive evolution of English society and the nation's economy, England had originated a fundamentally new approach to landscape: the landscape garden.[34] From the third quarter of the 18th century on, the principles of the English garden were assiduously imported by continental clients and artists of modern taste – as were the numerous other economic, technical, practical and intellectual advances the Industrial Revolution had brought. England was especially blessed with gifted artists, in watercolour and oils, who gave their attention almost exclusively to native or foreign landscapes (including townscapes, harbour scenes and seascapes). The distinctive landscape atmospheres and moods established by different kinds of weather or light offered an important aesthetic attraction in this kind of work; the precision with which they were recorded decided its value as art. The public and the buyers wanted the pictures to make the same impression on them, if at all possible, as the landscape itself might make.

From the 1820s on, three painters in particular introduced significant innovations which the Impressionists were later to draw upon: J. M. W. Turner (1775–1851),[35] Constable, and Richard Parkes Bonington (1801–1828).[36] Turner took his bearings in part from the 17th-century Dutch seascape tradition and from dramatic 18th-century shipwreck scenes which we can consider an early stage in Romantic art. While Romanticism in general was to leave the Impressionists fairly unmoved, Turner's leaning towards a profoundly meditative, historical-cum-philosophical approach to pictorial content offered a variant of Romantic art that remained important. His idiosyncratic version of the Romantic view of Nature included a unique eye for the expressive atmospherics of light and colour phenomena.

In fact, Turner concentrated so intensely on these effects that the late paintings of sunlight seen breaking through haze or mist could often

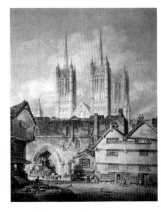

J. M. W. Turner
Cathedral Church, Lincoln, 1795
Watercolour over crayon, 45 x 35 cm
London, British Museum

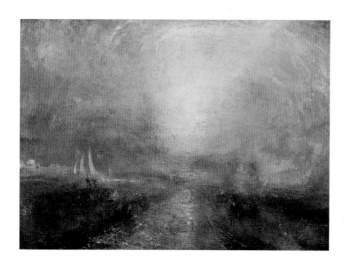

J. M. W. Turner
Yacht Approaching the Coast, c. 1838–1840
Oil on canvas, 102 x 142 cm
London, The Tate Gallery

J. M. W. Turner
Rain, Steam and Speed – The Great Western
Railway, 1844
Oil on canvas, 91 x 122 cm
London, National Gallery

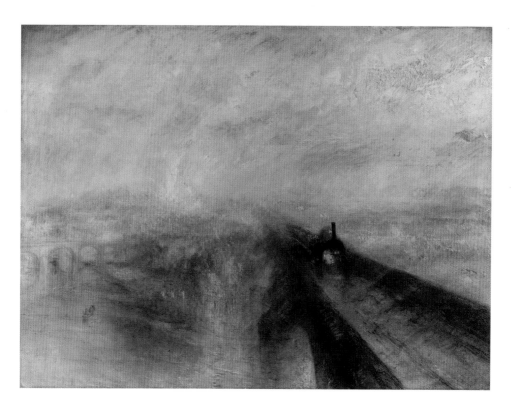

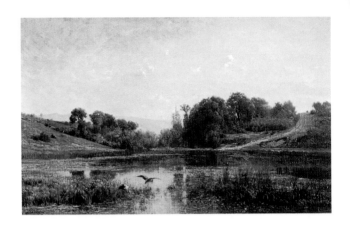

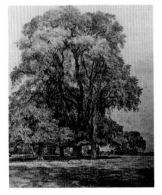

become almost non-representational, abstract constructs of loose, amorphous whirls and smears of colour (p. 21). The visionary, supra-real character of such works was matched by their titles; in other paintings (and again in their detailed, descriptive titles) Turner was aiming at a quality of reportage (one thinks of his famous experience of a storm on shipboard, for instance), or else displayed his alertness to the latest technology of his times. One of the latter works is *Rain, Steam and Speed – The Great Western Railway* (p. 21). Since their invention there, steam railways had been revolutionizing the transport of freight and people in England; the same was true in other countries too from the 1830s on. A new era of communications had dawned. Trains raced along their tracks at speeds that had previously been impossible, smoking and steaming, crossing viaducts, cutting through country that used to be peaceful and idyllic. The experience was a new one, and many – such as Wordsworth – were shocked. Painters tended to be fascinated by the railways as subjects for art. The picture Turner painted when he was almost seventy uses superlative composition and technique to express the spatial sovereignty and speedy thrust of the new technology, both its audacity and its danger. To many contemporaries, paintings such as this – which shares the visionary use of colour and form so characteristic of Turner's mature and late work – could often seem the incomprehensible extravagance of a madman.

The earlier innovations of a Constable were certainly more accessible. This painter, by no means universally esteemed in England during his lifetime, almost exclusively painted the landscape and villages of his home, Suffolk, and the outlying areas of London (p. 18). While his work was in many respects a continuation of 17th-century Dutch art, Constable did take a significant step forward in the core sensuousness of art taken from life, by recording the colour impressions that his subjects made upon him in meticulous nuances, though with a sketcher's disregard for exact detail; above all, he introduced brighter light. Simple

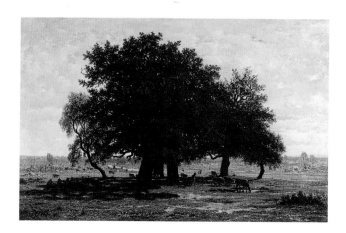

Théodore Rousseau
Clump of Oaks, Apremont, 1852
Groupe de chênes, Apremont
Oil on canvas, 63.5 x 99.5 cm
Paris, Musée du Louvre

motifs, things accessible to everyone, were being more highly valued by
the aesthetics of the time, and in his choice of undramatic subjects Constable was squarely in line with this key development in 19th-century art.
In France too, where Constable's work became familiar from the 1820s
on, younger artists were astounded and delighted to see how freshly and
with what subtle nuances a green, say, might be painted.

Bonington, who died young, lived mainly in Paris. His art represented
the earliest English component in the prehistory of Impressionism, in
terms of a broad influence on taste. Principally a watercolourist and
lithographer, he was one of a loose association of English and French
artists. Their landscapes and townscapes, as well as their historical genre
scenes (i.e. everyday life in times past), were popular with a largely
middle-class clientele on both sides of the Channel. Bonington's work,
in the tradition of English watercolour art which in the same period
produced John Sell Cotman and John Varley, was prized for its light
touch and spontaneity, and also for its brightness: *Water Basin at Versailles* (p. 19) is a fine example. It is an art that involves the observer more
closely and directly in the individual experience of the artist and the
specifics of a particular visual experience. Bonington was encouraging
the public to value a personal viewpoint, the effects of colour made
possible by seemingly unimportant objects or unexpected juxtapositions
of objects, and the idiosyncratic qualities of a personal signature. As
early as 1824, the conveying of an optical illusion was seen by Parisians
as the "English method".[37]

Gros and Corot were struck by Richard Parkes Bonington's work, and
Delacroix was already his friend when in 1818 he saw John Constable's
Hay Wain. Delacroix saw Bonington, and possibly Turner, Constable
and others, when he travelled to London in 1825 in order to study English innovations more closely. It was the English influence on Delacroix's
art in particular that made his paintings so interesting to the Impressionists.

Art and Reality

In subject matter and approach, Delacroix had much in common with the Romantic school that was being established in his day; but differences in their ideas of what art was, as well as in the quality of work produced, prompted him to keep his distance. The solitary genius declined to be associated with a movement that achieved rapid success and popularity. The Romantics painted historical and literary scenes full of effects and moving touches; their picturesque landscapes and imaginary folklore subjects were done in smooth colours with fine-pointed brushes.[38] The Impressionists were having none of this. Only the history and genre painter Ernest Meissonier (1815–1891) achieved a higher level, in his hyper-precise and often small-format pictures, which were soon fetching exorbitant prices (p. 27).

Another broad, predominant current in 19th-century art was steadily gaining ground, though widely differing emphases were placed within the movement. The only word we have to describe this current is the rather tired word "realism".[39] Realist painters trusted the evidence of their own eyes and aimed to open a window on the world; given this aim, it was easy to link epistemological, ethical, social or political factors. For the realists, there was no doubt that what could be seen was real. The visible world was the given reality, and works of art were supposed to present a copy of it, a copy that was "true to Nature". The fidelity that produced verisimilitude had to be learnt, and achieving it required hard work in every individual case. And seeing itself, though a universal human capacity, called for practice if finer skill were to be acquired. Draughtsmen and painters found that in working on their art they developed new ways of seeing: the images they made of Nature taught them to look at Nature in new ways.

For the evolution of realism, the landscape and genre painters of the Barbizon School were of the greatest importance.[40] The use of the term "school" alluded to the museum terminology for grouping older works of art linked by regional origin – though the word had of course also been used in other senses by then (the "Romantic school"). In point of fact it was only in retrospect, in 1890 for the first time, that critics and art dealers referred to a Barbizon School. At times they also spoke of the "generation of 1830". In the 1830s, younger artists tended with ever greater frequency to do their studies from Nature in the woods near the palace of Fontainebleau, some sixty kilometres south-east of Paris. There lay the village of Barbizon.

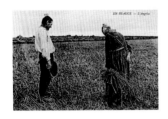

"The Angelus". Postcard after Millet's painting (right), 1905

It was gently undulating country, with boggy hollows, gnarled oaks and curious rocky outcrops: landscape spartan but various, and of that identifiably northern character that supplied the early 19th century with aesthetic and emotional values to be used as a counterbalance to "classical" Italy. As early as 1800, the landscape painter Pierre-Henri de Valenciennes (1750–1819), a member of the Paris Academy of Art, had published a textbook in which he contrasted faithful "landscape portraiture" with "historical [or] pastoral landscapes" that tended to be liter-

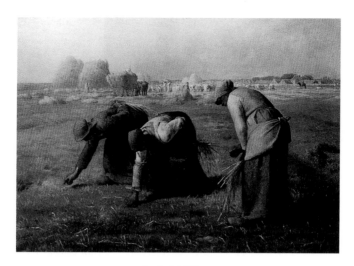

Jean-François Millet
Gleaners, 1857
Les glaneuses
Oil on canvas, 83.5 x 111 cm
Paris, Musée d'Orsay

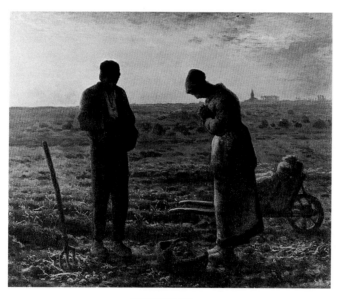

Jean-François Millet
The Angelus, c. 1859/60
L'angélus
Oil on canvas, 55.5 x 66 cm
Paris, Musée d'Orsay

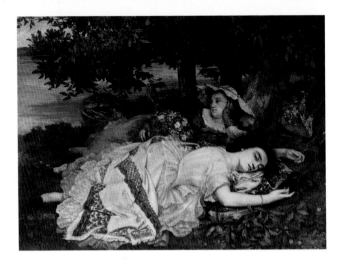

Gustave Courbet
Girls on the Bank of the Seine, 1857
Les demoiselles des bords de la Seine
Oil on canvas, 173.5 x 206.5 cm
Fernier 203. Paris, Musée du Petit Palais

ary in conception and were largely imaginary. In making the contrast he took 17th-century Dutch and Flemish art as the model to be followed, rather than Italian art or the work of the French classical artist Nicolas Poussin (1593–1665).

Observing Nature closely inevitably drew the attention of painters to shifting conditions of light and their relevance to colour. An interest in these matters was almost universal in Europe in that period. We have already seen that English artists made a contribution of particular significance. In the decades that followed, though, a new landscape art came into being in the woods at Fontainebleau, at Barbizon, and in a small number of other places. Taking simple motifs, and emphasizing fidelity to the appearance of things, this new realistic landscape art was to exert a far-reaching influence on the history of art, partly because the artists working (often together) in these places were extremely gifted, but mainly because of the proximity to Paris, which was further consolidating its position as the art capital of Europe.

If young French artists took to the Fontainebleau woods, it was partly because of their dissatisfaction with political and social conditions under the July Monarchy that followed the revolution of July 1830. The regime of Louis Philippe, known as the bourgeois monarch, was corrupt. Many an artist felt that "back to Nature" was the better, more sensible alternative. By 1857, Jules-Antoine Castagnary (1830–1888), the critic, felt that the revival of landscape art reflected the fact that society, dissatisfied with itself, was seeking out the tranquillity of the forests and fields.[41] This retreat from the principal arena of modern social conflict was accompanied by the fight against the Academy's classical doctrine of art. For the Academy, realistic landscape art remained the lowest aesthetic denominator, so to speak; the same applied to scenes of everyday life featuring ordinary people – and in particular the peasants, farmers,

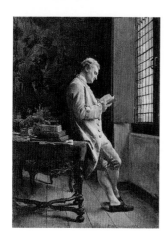

labourers and herdsmen living around Barbizon. In art they could only be the *petit genre* – or, as it came to be called, genre painting. Human fellow-feeling or compassion with the socially underprivileged might well play a part in the artist's choice of subject; if it did so, however, it would merely be seen as expressing traditional curiosity, and the product would be dismissively labelled "picturesque".

The core of the Barbizon school consisted of Théodore Rousseau (1812–1867) and his friend Jules Dupré (1811–1889), Charles-François Daubigny (1817–1878), the Spanish painter Narcisse Diaz de la Peña (1807–1876), the animal painter Constant Troyon (1810–1865) and the presiding elder spirit, Camille Corot (1796–1875).[42] There was also Jean-François Millet (1814–1875),[43] who arrived at Barbizon with his rather curious companion Charles Jacque (1813–1894) as late as 1847. Rousseau's clumps of trees, craggy rocks in forest clearings and extensive river landscapes viewed in gentle, muted light have a serious emotional charge, verging on piety, in such works as the 1852 *Clump of Oaks, Apremont* (p. 23). Daubigny loved plains, fields seen in bright light, and, above all, pond water (p. 22) and the tranquil banks of the Seine and the Oise, which he painted from his boat, Le Botin, from 1856 onwards.

Corot had visited the woods at Fontainebleau as early as 1822 to paint studies. He then spent three years in Italy, brightening his palette and taking a calm, essentially middle-class and private look at the great historical buildings of the country. After his return to France, he regularly went to the villages and small towns near the Fontainebleau woods to paint. He used a silvery shimmer to endow the trees and houses with an understated magic – a magic that steadily cast its spell on fellow-artists and connoisseurs of art throughout Europe (pp. 29 and 30).

Millet met the Rousseau group in the period after 1846, and at Barbizon in 1849 he finally found the most eloquent backdrop for his scenes of decent hard work and the life of poor farmers and labourers. Figures and compositions such as the *Gleaners* or the couple at prayer in *The Angelus* (p. 25) presented a passionately held socio-philosophical aesthetic in a pointed, almost confrontational manner; as time went by, they

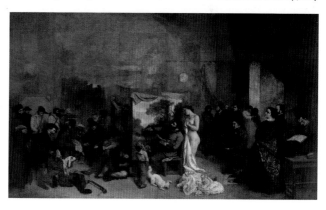

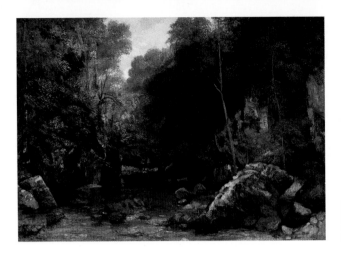

came to be seen worldwide as models for an agrarian art with ethical roots in the soil of home.

In many respects, Millet's approach to art overlapped with that of Gustave Courbet (1819–1877).[44] His was the most invigorating contribution to the evolution of 19th-century realism in painting, and it also had the most far-reaching consequences. Courbet's personality and his preferred range of subjects were rooted in the farming lower classes and in the craggy, wooded landscape of his home parts on the fringes of the Jura mountains. Later, however, he also turned to the coast of Normandy (p. 31) and (unlike the Barbizon painters) to certain aspects of city life in Paris, seen in *Girls on the Bank of the Seine* (p. 26). He was a pugnacious man, with strong republican convictions, and a vehement advocate not only of his own views on art but also of their social and political implications: for him, art was ultimately political in function. Through his own work, he definitively made realism a central concept in artistic debate, and for a lengthy period he established the term as the description of a particular style. Although Courbet himself did not always abide by the precept, he asserted that only the reality seen by the artist could be the point of departure, and evaluative criterion, for a work of realist art. For this reason he excluded historical, mythological and religious art – indeed all art of purely imaginary origin – from his definition of realist art.

Courbet's paintings are milestones in the history of 19th-century art, thanks to his core artistic vision, the physical power of his heavy, earthy paint (substantially applied, at times with a spatula) and the provocative, plebeian force that informs many of the figures in his works. His most important paintings include the immense *Burial at Ornans* (1849/59; Paris, Musée d'Orsay); *The Stone Breakers* (1849; formerly Dresden, Gemäldegalerie, but lost in the War); the rather enigmatic programmatic

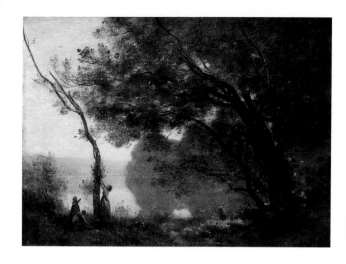

Camille Corot
Memory of Mortefontaine, 1864
Souvenir de Mortefontaine
Oil on canvas, 65 x 89 cm
Robaut 1559. Paris, Musée du Louvre

picture *The Artist's Studio* (p. 27); *Girls on the Bank of the Seine* (or, to be exact, whores); various versions of *The Wave* (about 1870); and his paintings of the French Channel coast, such as *The Cliff at Etretat after the Storm* (p. 31). Courbet's work fascinated many younger artists, and differing views of art were necessarily defined in relation to his.

Art in Paris around 1860

The influence of these artists on the Paris art scene at the beginning of the 1860s varied. Aesthetic positions of every description, as well as shares in the art public's attention and respect and in the market, had to be competed for and constantly reasserted. The conditions that prevailed in the art world,[45] reflecting conditions in general and the frequent shifts in various social and political groupings' power and interests, were not normally favourable to those who espoused reality, Nature and light.

In France, the economic and social structures of capitalism evolved rapidly and forcefully. The Second Empire – created in 1852 when Napoleon's nephew Charles Louis Napoléon Bonaparte (1808–1873), who had been elected President of the French republic in 1848, proclaimed himself Emperor Napoleon III of France – sought to create the best possible political atmosphere for capitalism. Development of the means of production and the overall acceleration of industrialization affected life profoundly. In Paris, the most striking change was in the city's urban structure, brought about by the Prefect of the Seine Département, Georges Haussmann (1809–1891). In terms of foreign policy, Napoleon III hoped to augment French power and global influence, with a competitive eye on the position of Britain.

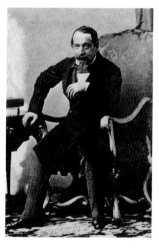

Emperor Napoleon III, Charles Louis Napoleon Bonaparte (1808–1873). Photo: Disdéri

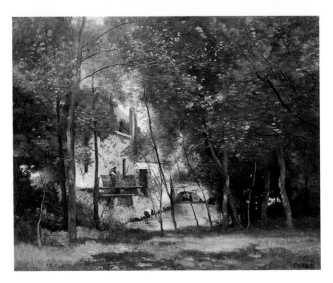

Camille Corot
The Mill at Saint-Nicolas-les-Arras, 1874
Le moulin de Saint-Nicolas-les-Arras
Oil on canvas, 65.5 x 81 cm
Robaut 2184. Paris, Musée d'Orsay

In 1855, to enhance the standing of France and the French economy, a World Fair was held in Paris, the second of its kind following the success of the Great Exhibition in London in 1851.[46] At the Paris fair, the programme included a large-scale art exhibition, with the aim of consolidating the international significance of French art, the market for that art, and the status of Paris as an art centre and an arbiter of taste and style. From then on, the great world fairs – the next were again in London (1862) and Paris (1867) – were also events in the ongoing history of art; and that first French *Exposition universelle* in 1855 was an art event in a number of ways.

Over five thousand paintings, as well as sculptures and other works, afforded the visitor a comparative overview of contemporary European art. In the French section, the two rivals Ingres and Delacroix were juxtaposed. The panel of assessors, dominated by Academy classicists and historicists, accepted only a very few works by Corot, the other Barbizon painters, and particularly Millet; as for Courbet, he was so seriously underrepresented that he decided to put his work on show independently, near the exhibition centre. This was by no means usual; it was also a costly, risky business. The traditional approach was for artists to make a major new work, or a small selection of works, accessible to public view in their own studios.[47] Courbet, however, had a pavilion built especially for his own work, and called the show quite simply: "Realism. Gustave Courbet".

The centrepiece of the show was *The Artist's Studio*, a huge programmatic painting. It is a complex work. Its iconography is multivalent, and the aesthetic programme advanced in it has been variously interpreted and evaluated; to this day, it remains one of the most debated 19th-

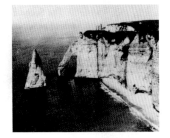

The cliffs at Etretat. Photograph, c. 1910

century pictures. Neither the impenetrable full title – *The Artist's Studio, a Real Allegory, Covering a Period of Seven Years in My Artistic Work* – nor the explanatory accounts Courbet offered a number of friends makes an unambiguous interpretation feasible. In the present context it is of particular importance that in this painting Courbet – who generally preferred to advance his concept of realism in connection with figural work – shows the artist (who quite clearly bears his own features) at work on a landscape. In doing so, he is emphasizing the significance of landscape art for realism, and he is assigning to Nature (as an aesthetic category) a central place in his aesthetic programme – which in turn was a component of an overall utopian view of culture and society. "To paint out in Nature, amongst natural people, in a natural way" – as the German painter Wilhelm Leibl (1844–1900) put it[48] a quarter of a century later – became a fundamental article of faith for realist artists everywhere. In Courbet's picture, the natural people are those seen taking the first look at the new landscape being painted: the model, an ordinary woman presented in natural nakedness, and a child, bearing the hopes of the future.

Gustave Courbet
The Cliff at Etretat after the Storm, 1870
La falaise d'Etretat après l'orage
Oil on canvas, 133 x 162 cm
Fernier 745. Paris, Musée d'Orsay

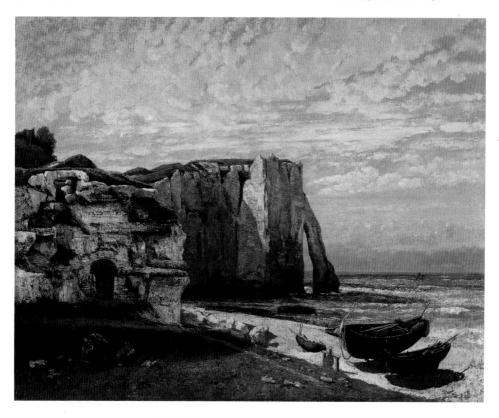

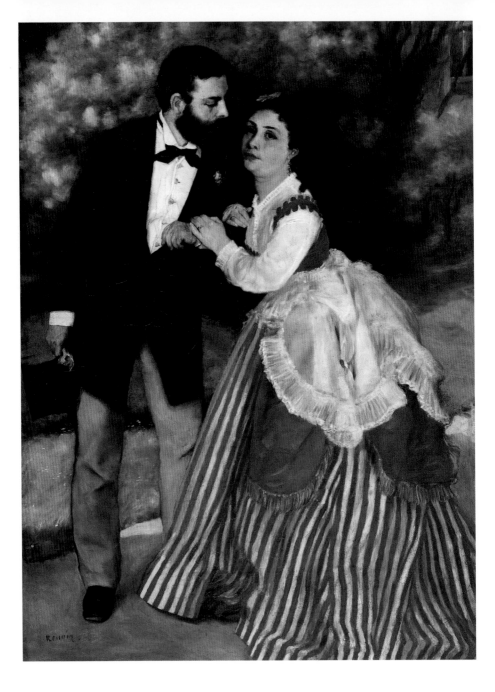

3 A New Generation

The World Fair and the Courbet exhibition naturally attracted the attention of the artists who were later to be the Impressionists, or at least those who were old enough to take an interest. Over the next few years, all of them were to embark on a life in art; they met and established their own creeds as artists.

Pissarro was the eldest. Subsequently the most unwavering of them all in his advocacy of the original principles of Impressionism, he was also the only one to show work at every one of their group exhibitions. He was the son of pious Jewish parents who had moved from southern France to the West Indies. There Camille was born at Charlotte-Amalie on Saint-Thomas, an island in the Antilles, then a Danish colony. His father intended the lad to go into business too, and sent him to school in the Paris suburb of Passy from 1842 to 1847, where Camille drew from Nature and visited museums. Back on Saint-Thomas, he became the friend of Fritz Melbye, a Danish painter, and in 1852 together with him he fled his father's business world to lead an artist's life in Caracas. Pissarro senior finally acceded to his son's professional wishes, and in 1855 sent him to receive proper training in Paris, where he was supported by another branch of the family. Pissarro did not embark on serious art study, though, preferring to make occasional use of the facilities of the Académie Suisse on the Quai des Orfèvres, from about 1859 on. Charles Suisse had himself modelled for artists, and now earned a living by putting a studio and nude models at the disposal of artists for a modest fee. No tuition was offered; but painters who proposed to do figural work needed to study the nude in various positions, and hiring models for one's own use was expensive, so a fair number of artists did make use of Suisse's facilities. By doing so they also met other artists and benefitted from advice. At the Académie Suisse, Pissarro presently met Monet, Guillaumin and Cézanne.

He painted landscapes at a number of villages outside Paris, preferring the banks of the Seine, Marne and Oise. In his style he followed Corot, whose work he had admired at the 1855 World Fair and with whom he had sought personal contact. Courbet influenced him too, in his coloration. In 1859 he submitted work to the Salon for the first time, and was accepted. In the early 1860s he moved in with Julie Vellay, the daughter of a wine-grower in Burgundy who was working as a maid for his par-

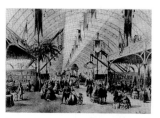

The Machine Hall at the World Fair, Paris, 1855.
Lithograph

Pierre-Auguste Renoir
Alfred Sisley and his Wife, 1868
Les fiancés
Oil on canvas, 105 x 75 cm
Daulte 34. Cologne, Wallraf-Richartz-Museum

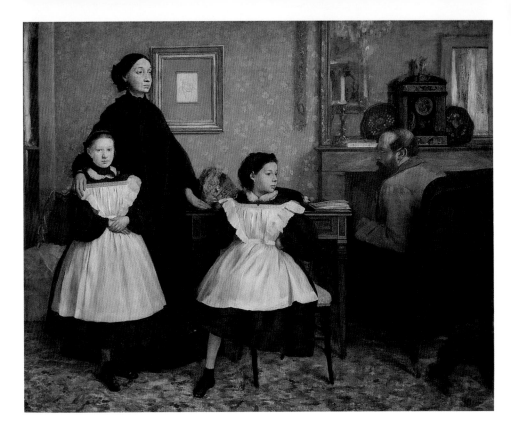

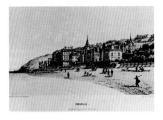

The beach at Trouville. Lithograph by Adolphe
Maugendre, 1867

ents. Their first son, Lucien, who was to become a talented graphic artist
as well as a painter in his own right, was born in 1863. Pissarro and Julie
married in 1871, by which time three of their eight children had already
been born. It was a large family, and for a long time they lived in decidedly modest circumstances.

Manet's beginnings as an artist were altogether different. He came of
a well-to-do family, its menfolk civil servants and army officers. He went
to a good school, and grew up in cultivated *haute bourgeoisie* surroundings. His father was opposed initially to Manet's wish to become a
painter, but then from 1850 to 1856 he was permitted to study under
Thomas Couture (1815–1879)[49] at the Ecole des Beaux-Arts. The latter
was a gifted neo-Renaissance painter; though himself a business-minded
"reluctant *bourgeois*" (Pierre Vaisse),[50] he held society in moral disdain.
Manet was to retain a certain respect for his teacher his whole life long,
although in his own art he struck out in quite different directions, but he
suffered under Couture's method of instruction, which called for an im-
personal sense of the ideal, while Couture's poisonous attacks on Dela-

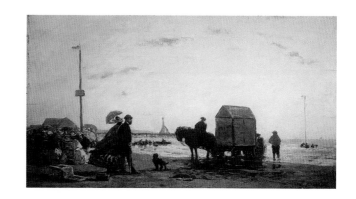

Eugène-Louis Boudin
Beach Scene, Trouville, 1863
La plage à Trouville
Oil on panel, 25.4 x 45.8 cm
New York, The Metropolitan Museum of Art

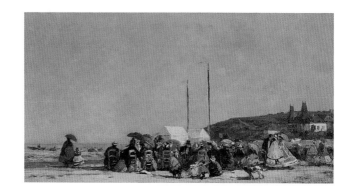

Eugène-Louis Boudin
Beach Scene, Trouville, 1864
La plage à Trouville
Oil on panel, 26 x 48 cm
Schmit 258. Paris, Musée d'Orsay

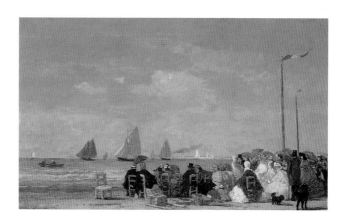

Eugène-Louis Boudin
Beach Scene, Trouville, 1863
La plage à Trouville
Oil on panel, 34.9 x 57.8 cm
Schmit 274
Washington, National Gallery of Art,
Mr. and Mrs. Paul Mellon Collection

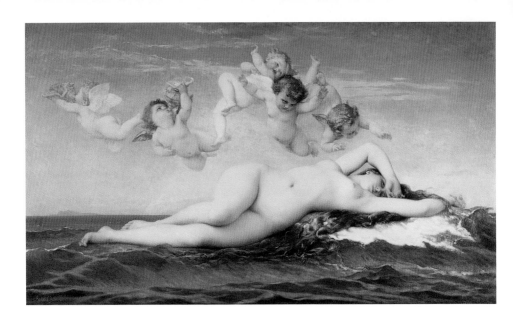

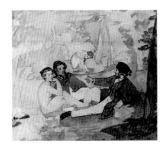

Alexandre Cabanel
The Birth of Venus, 1863
La naissance de Vénus
Oil on canvas, 130 x 225 cm
Paris, Musée d'Orsay

Edouard Manet
Le déjeuner sur l'herbe (study), 1862/63
Watercolour, pencil, pen and ink,
37 x 46.8 cm
Rouart/Wildenstein II,306
Oxford, The Visitors of the Ashmolean Museum

croix, Rousseau or Courbet repelled him. The artificial light in the studio and the equally artificial poses of the models only made matters worse. "I paint what I see, and not what others choose to see", was Manet's response to academic doctrine; and his emphasis on the legitimacy of a subjective viewpoint was as important as the stress he placed on looking rather than acquiring conventions and rules. Still, from today's perspective what links Manet to Couture (who is seen as representing eclecticism or historicism) is his high regard for the humanist legacy of figural painting with a moral message, and the use of visual quotations from the art of the past. When Manet had completed his studies he moved into a studio of his own, and visited the great museums of Holland, Germany and Italy. In 1852 his son by a Dutch piano teacher, Suzanne Leenhoff, had been born; Manet and Leenhoff married in 1863, when his father's death left Manet financially independent and indeed affluent. For public purposes, the son, Léon-Edouard Leenhoff, who often served as a model for Manet, was described as Suzanne's little brother and the artist's godson.

In his early paintings, Manet applied the paint with a thick, even pastose richness, using dark backgrounds and compositional components that recalled Dutch and, above all, Spanish art of the 17th century. A "Spanish" approach became fashionable among realistic and historical painters alike, its influence consolidated by Napoleon III's Empress, Eugénie, who was a Spanish countess and did much to promote the music, dance and dress fashions of Spain.

There was a recognisably Spanish flavour to the *Absinth Drinker*

(1858; Copenhagen, Ny Carlsberg Glyptotek) which Manet submitted to the Salon in 1859 (his first submission) and which was turned down by the jury over Delacroix's vote in favour. Couture reprimanded his former student for making a character from the twilit fringes of society the subject of a full-figure, almost life-size portrait. "Is one really to paint such repugnant subjects? My dear friend, you yourself are the absinth drinker. You are the one who has lost his hold on morality."[51] Before Impressionism had properly begun, in other words, the coming aesthetic debate on individual rebellion, the use of pictorial conventions for material hitherto considered inappropriate, and the interconnections of aesthetic with moral (and ultimately socio-political) values had already been sketched in.

Manet had hit upon a procedure that was to characterize much of his subsequent work: by adapting available visual figures and their expressive values to contemporary reality he was able to experiment with the productive contrasts and incompatibilities that became apparent. He made copies of 16th- and 17th-century art in order to master its strategies and roamed Paris, which was in a state of rapid change, prob-

Edouard Manet
Le déjeuner sur l'herbe, 1863
Oil on canvas, 208 x 264.5 cm
Rouart/Wildenstein I,67. Paris, Musée d'Orsay

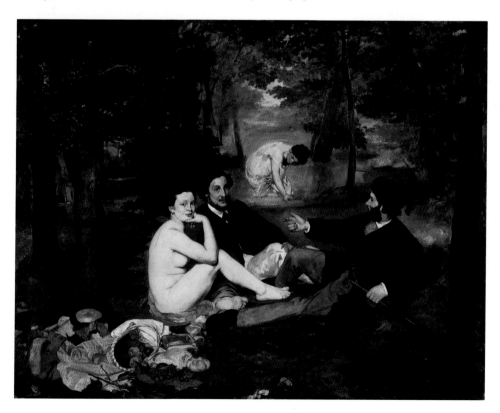

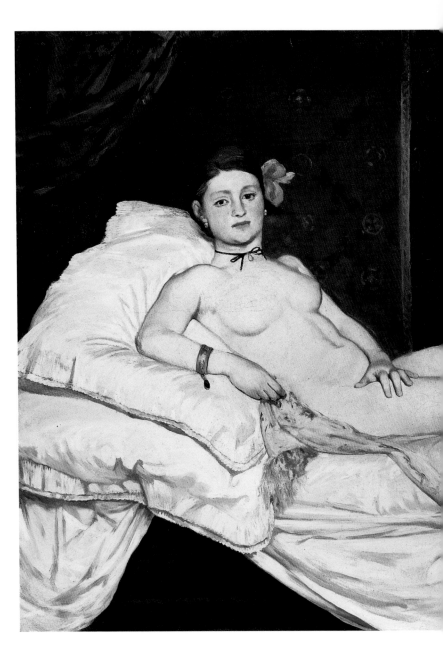

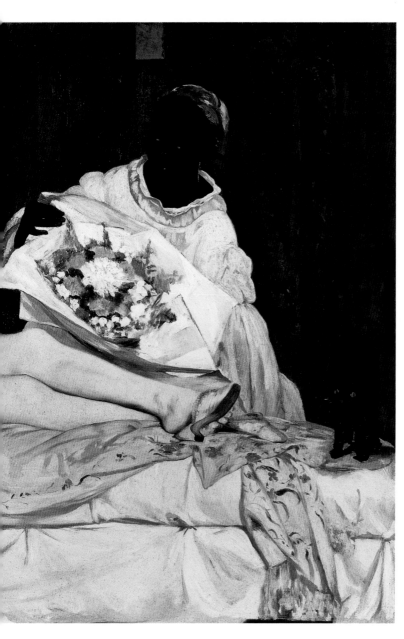

Edouard Manet
Olympia, 1863
Oil on canvas,
130.5 x 190 cm
Rouart/Wildenstein I,69
Paris, Musée d'Orsay

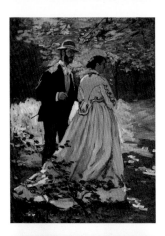

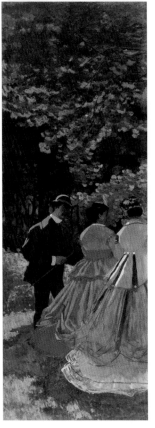

ing the city's subtlest secrets. He became a flâneur – that new type of man about town later so profoundly analysed by Walter Benjamin. The flâneur accepts the workings of chance. Himself moving in his own irregular way, he is the observer of a world in constant flux. He is attentive but remains uninvolved at heart. He is unprejudiced and does not leap to judgemental conclusions. Antonin Proust (1832–1905), Manet's former schoolmate and his lifelong friend, later (with the benefit of culturally enriched hindsight) left an account of their strolls as flâneurs as the 1860s arrived. Along the boulevards, he reported, Manet would draw in his notebook "nothing at all: a profile, a hat – in a word, a fleeting impression". He saw white-clad demolition workers seen in a cloud of white dust against a white wall as "the symphony in white that Théophile Gautier refers to".[52] Gautier (1811–1872), the poet and novelist, was also an art critic, an influential man with government contacts. And *Symphony in White* (cf. Volume Two, p. 573) was the innovative title the American painter James Abbott McNeill Whistler (1834–1903), an acquaintance of Manet's, gave to a portrait of a girl which attracted attention in Paris in 1863.

Manet made his debut appearance in the Salon in 1861 with a painting that was still Spanish in style but which found favour and indeed was given an honourable mention (the lowest distinction available). His portrait of the Spanish dancer *Lola de Valence* (p. 47) was of a similar kind. Her costume, painted in bold, solid colours, doubtless constituted the main attraction of the task for the artist. In March 1863 he held his first solo exhibition at Louis Martinet's gallery on the Boulevard des Italiens. One picture that drew on his flâneur observations, *Music at the Tuileries* (p. 43), met with a poor response. At that time, with the imperial palace of the Tuileries still intact, society people would flock to the gardens to see and be seen. A military band (not in Manet's painting) would be playing and people would meet there to talk, among them Manet himself, who often went there after lunch at Tortoni's, with his new friend the poet Charles Baudelaire (1821–1867),[53] spent the afternoons drawing, and later showed his studies to friends – artists, writers and critics alert to his work – back at Tortoni's. This was also the period when Manet and Degas became friends.

Parts of *Music at the Tuileries* are sketchily painted or indeed left unfinished. The crowd of people is only partly resolved into isolated groups engaged in conversation. There are neither a central focus in the composition nor any main figures. The cropping of figures at the edges – the figure cropped at left is Manet himself, seen behind his equally stylish fellow-painter Albert de Balleroy (1828–1873) – emphasizes that what we are seeing is a slice of life. It was an approach that flew in the face of established ideas of unity. Garden chairs and a parasol are given prominent positions in the foreground. The picture is bright, but no light source can be identified. The paint is applied everywhere with equal vigour and generosity, though the definition of shapes does slacken from the left of the canvas to the right. People in the art scene would recognise some of those portrayed in the picture: the man standing somewhat to

Claude Monet
Le déjeuner sur l'herbe (study), 1865
Oil on canvas, 130 x 181 cm
Wildenstein 62
Moscow, Pushkin Museum of Fine Art

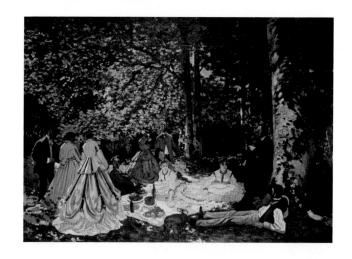

Claude Monet
Le déjeuner sur l'herbe (centre section), 1865
Oil on canvas, 248 x 217 cm
Wildenstein 63B
Paris, Musée d'Orsay

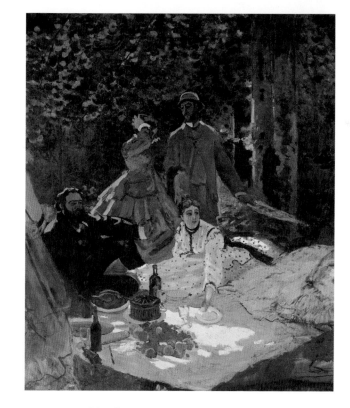

Left:
Claude Monet
The Walkers (Bazille and Camille), 1865
Les promeneurs (Bazille et Camille)
Oil on canvas, 93 x 69 cm
Wildenstein 61
Washington, National Gallery of Art,
Ailsa Mellon Bruce Collection

Claude Monet
Le déjeuner sur l'herbe (left section), 1865
Oil on canvas, 418 x 150 cm
Wildenstein 63A. Paris, Musée d'Orsay

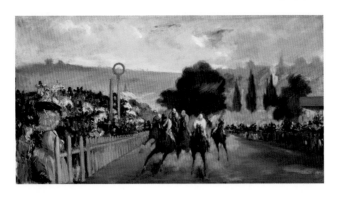

Edouard Manet
The Races at Longchamp, c. 1865–1867
Courses à Longchamp
Oil on canvas, 43.9 x 84.5 cm
Rouart/Wildenstein I,98
Chicago, The Art Institute of Chicago

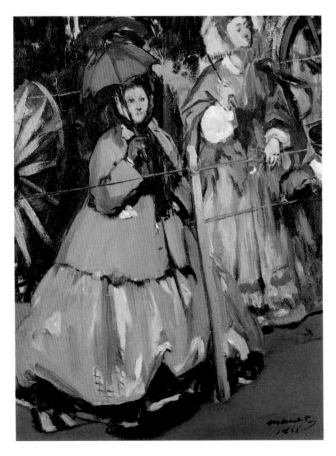

Edouard Manet
At Longchamp Racecourse, 1864
Champ de courses à Longchamp
Oil on canvas, 42.2 x 32.1 cm
Rouart/Wildenstein I,95
Cincinnati, Cincinnati Art Museum

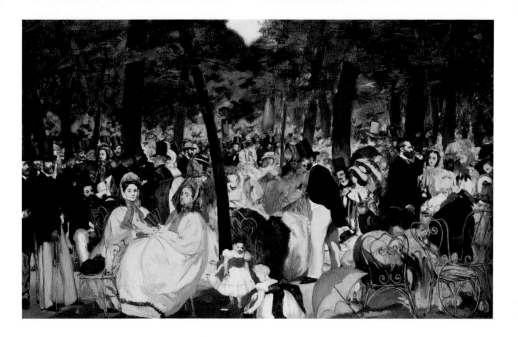

the right of centre is Manet's brother Eugène (1833–1892), and the man
sitting behind him, in front of a tree, is the composer Jacques Offenbach
(1819–1880), who had just scored his first great hit with "Orphée aux
enfers" (1858), a delicious spoof on classicism and the Second Empire.
The group behind the two seated ladies at left includes Baudelaire and
Gautier, whose opinions Manet valued, and a third person who has not
been definitely identified but may be the Franco-Irish art patron Baron
Isidore Taylor (1789–1879), one of the finest connoisseurs of Spanish
art. *Music at the Tuileries*, which apparently remained unsold till 1882,
resembles Courbet's *The Artist's Studio* in offering a programmatic view
of a young artist's identification with a specific socio-cultural situation.
In its compositional approach it opened up one of the various routes
subsequently to be followed by the Impressionists.

Degas was close to Manet in terms of their social status, education and
attitude to art. He was more of a figure painter than Manet, and took
only a very occasional interest in landscapes. The natural light of open
spaces was not for him; he preferred artificial light. As a result, some art
historians have difficulty fitting him (and Manet) into a more narrowly
conceived definition of Impressionism; but the fact is that he was a dedicated driving force behind the movement. It would not be possible to
describe the new, Impressionist approach to art and reality in its full
complexity without reference to Degas.

He was born into a well-to-do upper middle-class family with aristocratic connections; till 1873 he spelt his name in its original way, de Gas.

Edouard Manet
Music at the Tuileries, 1862
La musique aux Tuileries
Oil on canvas, 76.2 x 118.1 cm
Rouart/Wildenstein I,51
London, National Gallery

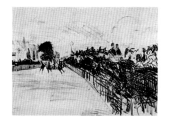

Edouard Manet
Horse Race, 1864
Course de cheveaux
Lithograph, 36.5 x 51 cm

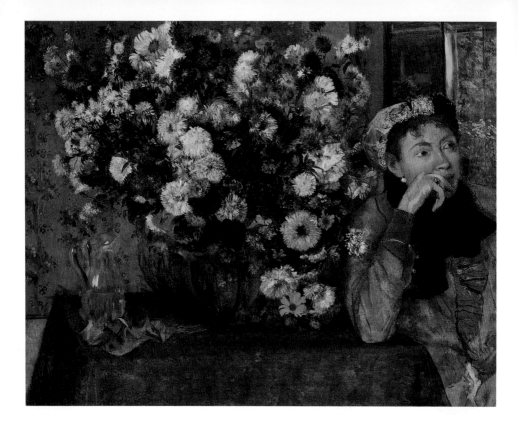

Edgar Degas
Woman with Chrysanthemums, 1865
Femme aux chrysanthèmes
Oil on canvas, 73.7 x 92.7 cm
Lemoisne 125
New York, The Metropolitan Museum of Art

His grandmother was Italian, his mother a Creole – that is, a French-woman born in America, in New Orleans (a French possession till 1803). He was educated to a high standard at the Lycée Louis-le-Grand, and while he was still at school his father, who was interested in art, allowed him to set up a studio at home. After briefly reading law, from 1853 on he studied under various artists, including Louis Lamothe, a pupil of Ingres, and for a short time was at the Ecole des Beaux-Arts. His guiding light was not Delacroix but the master draughtsman Ingres. He studied the art of the old masters closely in museums and on several visits to Italy. Where Manet rediscovered the attitudes of figures in older art in his contemporaries, however, Degas took the opposite approach, introducing a more modern and relaxed note into the figures in his history paintings.

Making copies of old masters in Italy, Degas was already outlining a programme of Impressionist representation of contemporary life in his diary. Unpublished till 1921, these entries, begun in 1859, included a list of subjects that he considered it important to study: musicians with

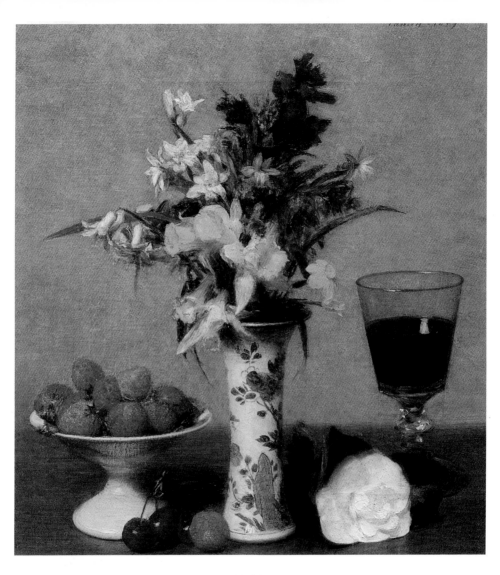

Henri Fantin-Latour
Still Life with Flowers and Fruit, 1865
Nature morte aux fleurs et fruits
Oil on canvas, 64 x 57 cm
Fantin-Latour 276 bis
Paris, Musée d'Orsay

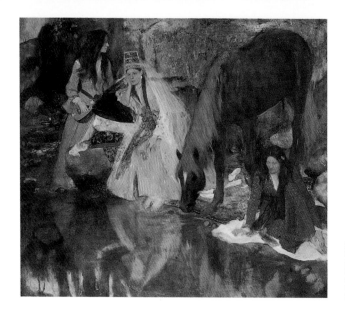

Edgar Degas
Mlle Eugénie Fiocre in the Ballet "La Source",
c. 1867/68
*Mlle Eugénie Fiocre à propos du ballet de
«La source»*
Oil on canvas, 130 x 145 cm
Lemoisne 146. New York, The Brooklyn Museum

various instruments, the smoke from cigarettes and from locomotives or steamships, "mourning" (a series using every kind of black), or "dancers of whom one can see only their bare legs, caught in mid-movement, or having their hair dressed; countless impressions; cafés in the evening with gas lamps turned up brighter or lower, the light reflected by mirrors..."[54] All of these motifs were to occur either in his own work or in that of others.

The subject of mourning was in Degas's mind when he painted the Bellellis in mourning in Florence in the late 1850s. *The Bellelli Family* (p. 34) is the earliest Impressionist masterpiece. Baron Gennaro Bellelli was an opponent of the Bourbons and a revolutionary of 1848, exiled from his Neapolitan home. The painting shows him with his wife Laura, the artist's aunt and daughter of the late Don Ilario de Gas, a banker in Naples; it also includes the couple's daughters. At twenty-four, Degas was already in full command of the portraitist's art. His interest was in the psychological state his subjects were in; compositionally, he opted (as he was to do so often in the future) for an arrangement that was all the more striking for being unfamiliar. At left we see the baroness, composed and dignified – although her hand makes a hard, nervous impression on the tabletop. Her daughter Giovanna's hands are clasped modestly before her as in Hans Holbein's *Anne of Cleves*, which Degas had copied in the Louvre just a short while previously. Solemnity is avoided, though, by the more relaxed position of her feet. As we look further to the right, the dignified front put up by this lifesize group becomes less persuasive. Giulietta, seated in the middle and occupying the most prominent posi-

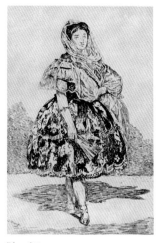

Edouard Manet
Lola de Valence, 1863
Etching and aquatint, 23.5 x 16.1 cm

tion in the painting, has a slightly coquettish air; she has drawn one leg up under her, so that it even looks as if she were one-legged. Degas's figures in later work often convey this impression. The girl is facing to the right, where her father, assigned a surprisingly minor role in the layout, is seen with his back to us, offering a shoulder and a profile half in shadow. He has been jammed in among furniture and a medley of interesting and colourful objects on the mantelpiece, where the interplay of real and mirror images provides a teasing conundrum.

At that date, marginalizing the father and head of the family in this way was the height of unconventionality. It was also unusual to undermine the seriousness of a family portrait by using relaxed poses. Degas was subverting the conventions. His group portrait has become a simple everyday scene. Though the people's gestures may suggest that they are indeed a family, belonging together, they are not looking at each other: their gazes go in different directions, their facial expressions are cool, and contact between them and us is thus minimalized. This casual coolness was to be a hallmark or leitmotiv throughout the figural work of Degas and the other Impressionists. Through it, the artists were articulating their responses to a prevailing mood of social austerity. They preferred

Edouard Manet
Lola de Valence, 1862 (to post–1867)
Oil on canvas, 123 x 92 cm
Rouart/Wildenstein I,53. Paris, Musée d'Orsay

Edouard Manet
The Fifer, 1866
Le fifre
Oil on canvas, 161 x 97 cm
Rouart/Wildenstein I,113. Paris, Musée d'Orsay

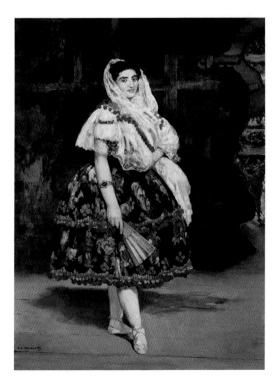

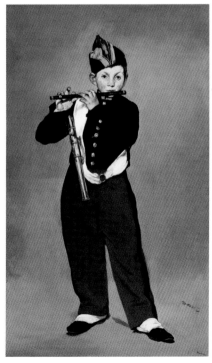

to show things as they truly saw them, and would not veil the facts by superimposing a sham emotional demonstrativeness. In the Bellelli picture, the inanimate objects in the room, the weighty tokens of wealth, furthermore have an oppressive presence. For instance, Degas has placed a hard gold picture frame right by the mother's head: it is a subtle and subtly disquieting effect, giving the picture-within-a-picture, a mere red chalk drawing on the wall, almost greater significance than a main character in the portrait. Degas worked on the painting over a lengthy period, not completing it till after his return to Paris in 1860; he kept it in his own possession till his death. It plainly had family as well as aesthetic meaning for him – and he had no financial need to sell it.

He made his first Salon submission in 1865. It was one of the five history paintings he did in all, but at the same time he had hit upon a modern subject that was to hold his interest for thirty years – horse racing. In 1861 he had gone to the races at Mesnil-Hubert with the Valpinçons, family friends, and in 1862 he continued his observations at Longchamp, a track laid out near Paris in 1854, where the first *Grand Prix* was being run that year. Both racing and its use as a subject for art had been imported from England over the past thirty years as a pastime for the aristocracy. In England, Théodore Géricault (1791–1824), one of the pre-eminent French Romantic artists of the early 19th century, had painted horses at the gallop in 1821, showing them in a way that had been accepted as correct since antiquity, with all four legs outstretched off the ground. In Degas's time, though, people had begun to wonder whether horses really did have all four legs simultaneously in the air. It was the photographer Eadweard Muybridge who supplied final proof in his motion studies done between 1872 and 1877 (p. 71).[55] At first Degas

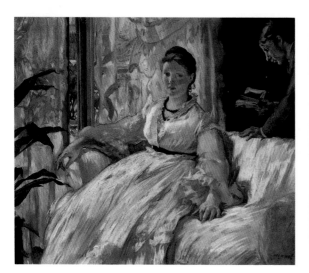

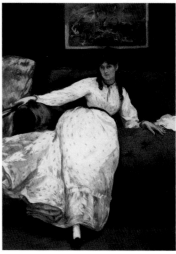

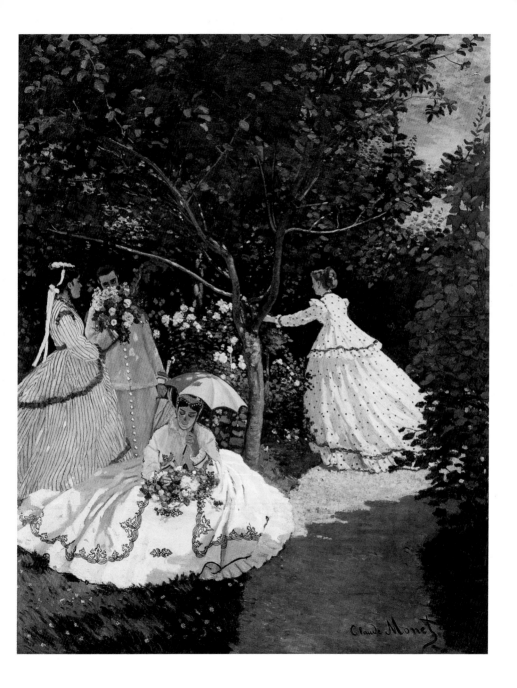

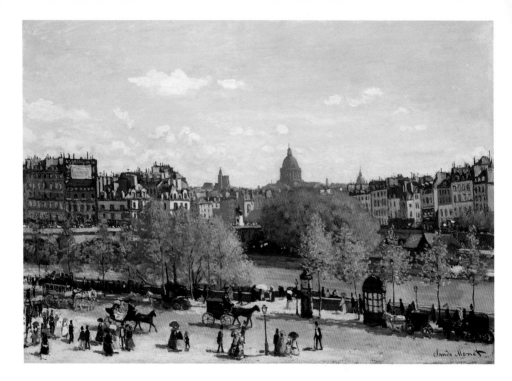

was interested in the process of getting ready to start; he liked watching
the horses and riders in various states of tension and relaxation; and he
was interested in racetrack society, from ladies in carriages to the jockeys
in their colourful shirts. His paintings (cf. p. 10) used a restless patterning of colour patches and combined a precision rendering of positions
with sketchy brushwork – especially for the background, where smoking factory chimneys or a glimpse of a railway train suggested the
proximity of a modern city. Degas cropped his figures brusquely as if to
emphasize that the picture could convey no more than a spatial and
temporal section of a larger scene and continuing motion.

Monet, six years Degas's junior and ten years Pissarro's, had not yet
found his way as an artist at this point. The eldest son of a Parisian
shopkeeper who had moved to Le Havre for business reasons when
Monet was five, he had to overcome financial and family obstacles in
making art his life. At school his caricatures earned him fame and even
a modest income, which he used in 1859 to pay for studies in Paris when
his application for a state grant was turned down. He was confirmed in
his wish to study art by an aunt who was an amateur artist, and above
all by Eugène Boudin (1824–1898), a landscape painter who worked in
Le Havre and along the coast of Normandy and whom Monet had met
the year before.[56]

Claude Monet
Quai du Louvre, 1867
Oil on canvas, 65 x 93 cm
Wildenstein 83
The Hague, Haags Gemeentemuseum

Right:
Claude Monet
The Garden of the Infanta, 1867
Le jardin de l'infante
Oil on canvas, 91 x 62 cm
Wildenstein 85
Oberlin (OH), Allen Memorial Art Museum

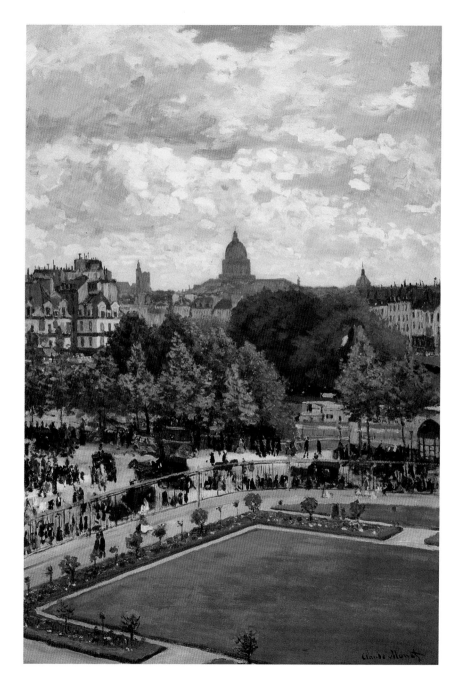

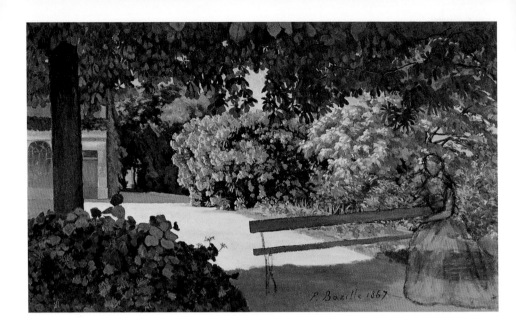

Frédéric Bazille
The Terrace at Méric (Oleander), 1867
Terrasse à Méric (Les lauriers-roses)
Oil on canvas, 56 x 98 cm
Daulte 26. Cincinnati, Cincinnati Art Museum

Boudin, the son of a Honfleur sailor, spent most of his life in seaside towns and concentrated on painting landscapes by the sea, everyday coastal scenes. The tradition he was following was primarily an English one; though Boudin did not paint ships at sea. Rendering precisely observed slices of Nature, and in particular the changing colour values of things seen in the open, sufficed for him aesthetically. Little by little the public began to respond to his work. The pictures he painted over the years in his loose, sketchy way did not, strictly speaking, possess any central subjects. Even his market or beach scenes present an extensive panorama of colour and economically deployed line accentuation. The atmosphere is bright, moist and highly sensitively registered (p. 35). Corot in old age was inevitably delighted, for his "meteorological beauties" he dubbed Boudin the "king of the skies". At first Monet, then young, was repelled; but work together on the spot opened his eyes and convinced him that (as Boudin put it) "one must be extraordinarily stubborn in abiding by the *impression primitive*".[57] Much later, Monet was to say: "If I became a painter it was thanks to Boudin."[58]

Monet had been intended for conventional Parisian academic training. Instead he merely frequented the Académie Suisse, meeting Pissarro and others there. The military service he had to see through in Algeria interrupted his studies for a few months; but then a severe bout of typhoid fever brought Monet home. Returned, he resumed work with Boudin and with the Dutch painter Johan Barthold Jongkind (1819–1891), who specialized in beach scenes. He even subsequently referred to Jongkind

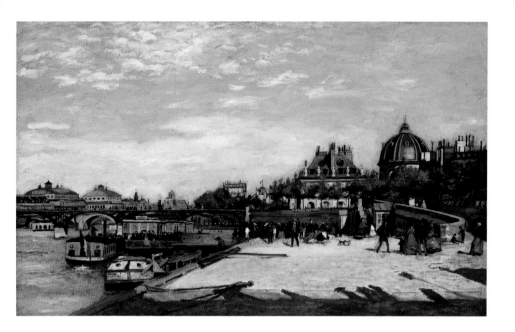

as his "true teacher".[59] Monet's aunt bought him out of service (which had lasted seven years in all) and he now turned to more serious study at the College of Fine Art in Paris and particularly in the private studio of the Swiss professor Charles Gleyre (1806–1874).[60] The studio could accommodate several dozen students for a whole day's life drawing or painting at a time; and twice a week, unpaid, Gleyre would make corrections and offer his thematic or compositional recommendations. At one time, Gleyre himself had practised his skills at the Académie Suisse and learnt watercolour techniques under Bonington, before developing his own classic-cum-Romantic eclecticism. Fidelity to the real appearance of things left him indifferent, as did "non-ideal" genre and landscape painting. What he was out to teach his students was an appreciation of lofty subjects, style and ideal beauty. His personal modesty, his long experience of poverty and humiliatingly dependent circumstances, and his assertive republicanism prompted respect among his students, even among those who rebelled against his views on art. These latter included Monet: realistic still lifes he did at this period have survived. They also included Bazille, Sisley and Renoir. The four became friends.

Bazille was the son of a wealthy wine-producer and notary in Montpellier. His circumstances were quite different from Monet's. Since 1862 he had been studying in Paris: medicine, but mainly painting under Gleyre.

Sisley was the son of an English merchant living in Paris, and remained a British citizen. He spent four years in London training for a business

Pierre-Auguste Renoir
The Pont des Arts, Paris, 1867
Le Pont des Arts
Oil on canvas, 62 x 102 cm
Los Angeles, Norton Simon Foundation

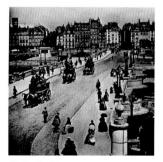

The Pont Neuf, Paris. Photograph, 1855

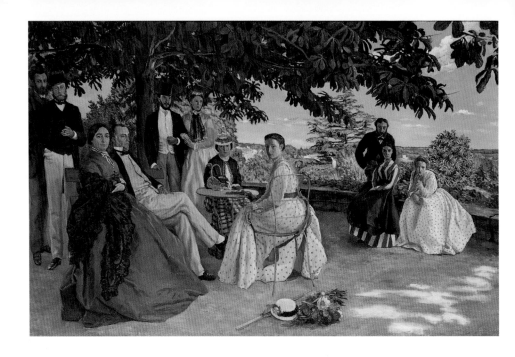

Frédéric Bazille
Family Reunion, 1867
Réunion de famille
Oil on canvas, 152 x 230 cm
Daulte 29. Paris, Musée d'Orsay

career, but art was already the greater attraction. In October 1862 he entered Gleyre's studio, and thus a life as the somewhat less successful fellow-traveller or indeed imitator of his friend Monet.

Renoir had a little more professional experience than his companions. His family – his father was a tailor in Limoges – had moved to Paris when the boy was four. The young Renoir's artistic gift was initially put to use in a china pottery where he worked as an apprentice, spending his lunch breaks drawing in the Louvre nearby. When the manufacturer bought a machine that printed rococo motifs onto china plates, Renoir lost his job. He earned a living painting blinds, then church drapery for overseas missionaries. By April 1862 he had saved enough to enter the Ecole des Beaux-Arts and to work at Gleyre's studio.

That year, a southern Frenchman named Cézanne was at the Académie Suisse, as he had been the previous year. He was an idiosyncratic, vehement man, though his self-confidence was unsteady; he was trying (in vain) to prepare for the Ecole's entrance exam. His father was something of a tyrant, who had risen from being a hatter to joint proprietor of a bank and was insisting, at least initially, that the youth who would one day inherit study law. But Cézanne's imaginative school-friend Emile Zola (1840–1902), now living in Paris and destined to become the foremost French writer of the late 19th century, had played a particularly influential part in confirming Cézanne's artistic leanings.[61] At that time,

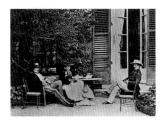

On the terrace. Photograph, c. 1870

the only common ground between Cézanne's art and what was to be Impressionism was the rejection of prescriptive aesthetic rules; but Pissarro became his friend, as did Armand Guillaumin, a poor railway worker who painted in his spare time and had been at the Académie Suisse since 1861.

It was at this time that Renoir met Henri Fantin-Latour (1836–1904),[62] a friend of Manet and Whistler who liked painting poetic floral still lifes (p. 45). In 1861, together with the copper engraver Félix Bracquemond (1833–1914),[63] a friend of Degas, Fantin-Latour placed two young amateurs, Edma and Berthe Morisot, with Corot, who was to teach them landscape painting. Thus by the early sixties all of the links had been forged that were in time to create the Impressionist community.

Developments were stimulated from 1863 on by spectacular events on the Paris art scene, and particularly at the Salon.

The Salon and Rejection

We have already had occasion to refer to the Salon, and shall be doing so again. The history of Impressionism cannot in fact be grasped without reference to it.[64] In terms both of an overall aesthetic evolution and of the

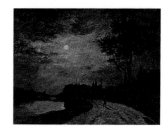

Pierre-Isidore Bureau
Moonlight at L'Isle-Adam, 1867
Clair de lune sur les bords de l'Oise à L'Isle-Adam
Oil on canvas, 33 x 41 cm
Paris, Musée d'Orsay

Frédéric Bazille
Portrait of Pierre-Auguste Renoir, 1867
Portrait de Pierre-Auguste Renoir
Oil on canvas, 62.2 x 50.8 cm
Daulte 22. Algiers, Musée des Beaux-Arts

Frédéric Bazille
Self-Portrait with Palette, 1865
Autoportrait à la palette
Oil on canvas, 108.5 x 72.6 cm
Daulte 10
Chicago, The Art Institute of Chicago

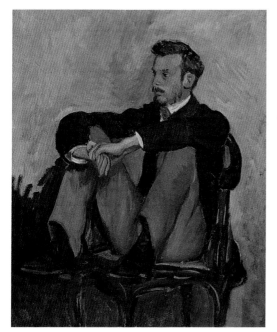

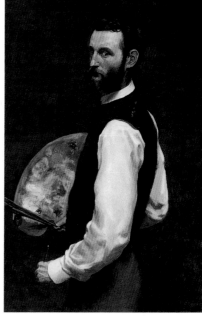

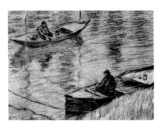

Claude Monet
Angling in the Seine at Pontoise, 1882
Black crayon on card, 25.6 x 34.4 cm
Cambridge (MA), Fogg Art Museum,
Harvard University

Claude Monet
The Beach at Sainte-Adresse, 1867
La plage de Sainte-Adresse
Oil on canvas, 75.8 x 102.5 cm
Wildenstein 92
Chicago, The Art Institute of Chicago

Claude Monet
The Regatta at Sainte-Adresse, 1867
Les régates à Sainte-Adresse
Oil on canvas, 75 x 101 cm
Wildenstein 91
New York, The Metropolitan Museum of Art

lives of individual artists, the ways that artworks and the "clients" are brought together are invariably of germane importance. In the course of time, these processes have varied. In the 19th century, public exhibitions were finally established as the crucial, indispensable means of putting the producers and consumers of art in touch. Social, economic and cultural evolution had produced a situation in which art was mainly made by independent people who were neither the servants of princes nor the slaves of guild guidelines. As independent artists, they made their living by selling on the art market to clients who might be anybody at all.

This was the rule, despite exceptions such as employment of artists by colleges, the direct commissioning of works, or the fact that an occasional artist might have inherited enough money not to need to sell his work. An increasingly important intermediate role was played by art dealers, too, whose ongoing commercial gallery shows made contact possible. From 1862 to 1865, for instance, Louis Martinet gave permanent space at his gallery to the Société Nationale des Beaux-Arts under the chairmanship of Gautier. This group included Corot, Daubigny and Manet, among others. Martinet's major rival, Francis Petit, made space available to the Cercle de l'Union Artistique at his Rue Choiseul gallery. Martinet also published a magazine, the *Courrier artistique*, to publicize the work he handled. At a later date, the linking of exhibitions and periodical publications was to become a regular feature of the art and media market.

For the artists, finding exhibition space was absolutely vital to survival. Their efforts to do so became a driving force in art history. Impressionism occupies a key position in the history of galleries and exhibitions; indeed, that history would be scarcely comprehensible were it not for the Impressionists' struggle to circumvent rejection.

In France, the Paris Salon was the exhibition space *par excellence*. The country had long been centralized both in political and in cultural terms, and aesthetic criteria were laid down in the capital. The political and cultural clout of France, and the achievements of French artists, had made the Paris art scene a major centre of international weight ever since the 17th century. Since 1673 there had been regular exhibitions by members of the Royal Academy of Art. These exhibitions were known as the Salon after the great hall at the Louvre where they were held. Following the 1789 revolution, non-members of the Academy were permitted to exhibit in the show as well, as of 1791. In 1848, another year of revolution, the exhibition was mounted without the intervention of a selection committee, for the first time – with the result that a full 5,180 works were put on display. From 1855 to 1863 the Salon was held every other year; after that it became what it had sometimes been already, an annual event. A panel selected the works. Till 1863, this committee consisted of members of the Académie des Beaux-Arts, itself a division of the Institut de France, the premier instrument of state arts policy. From 1864 on, three quarters of the committee members were elected by artists who had already been awarded a medal of distinction and could therefore exhibit without submitting to the selection panel (*hors concours*).

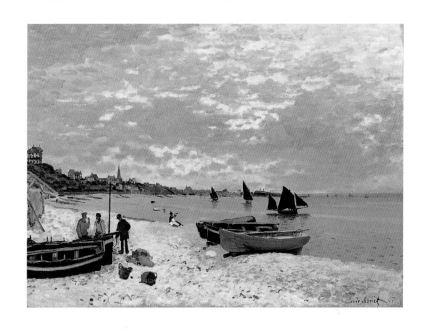

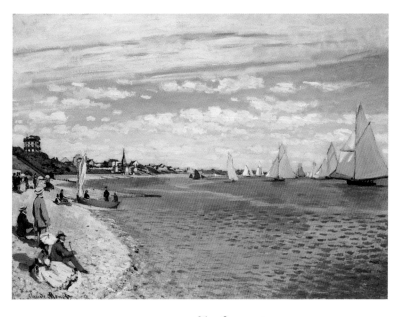

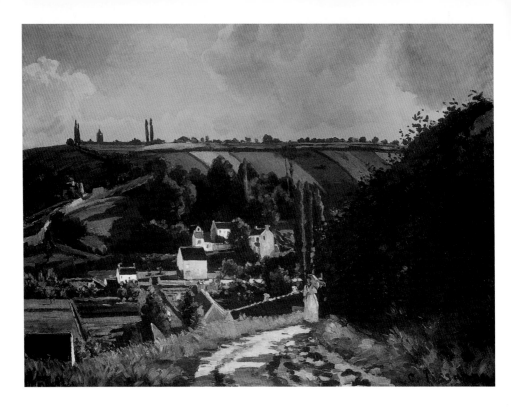

Camille Pissarro
Jallais Hill, Pontoise, 1867
La Côte du Jallais, Pontoise
Oil on canvas, 89 x 116 cm
Pissarro/Venturi 55
New York, The Metropolitan Museum of Art

And in 1869 *all* the artists who had ever exhibited at the Salon became eligible to elect two thirds of the committee.

In 1881 the government devolved its control of art's public access to the artists themselves, and from that date on the Société des Artistes Français, consisting of artists who had already exhibited at the Salon, chose the panel. In other words, the presiding forces in French art were always recruited via the Salon. Its role in the dissemination of art can be readily grasped from the statistics. In 1863 alone, over 4,000 works were rejected. In 1874 a total of 3,657 works were exhibited. In 1876 the number of paintings alone was 2,500. In 1880, 2,586 artists exhibited a range of work that included 3,957 paintings and some 2,000 drawings. The works were hung right up to the ceilings, and there was little hope that visitors to the Salon would be invariably equal to the strain on their concentration. Many a small or unspectacular picture would inevitably be overlooked. Even so, the Salon was intended to provide information on the art officially considered worthy of respect and purchase. In 1875, no fewer than 51,509 copies of the Salon catalogue were sold – which suggests that the number of actual visitors must have been considerably greater.

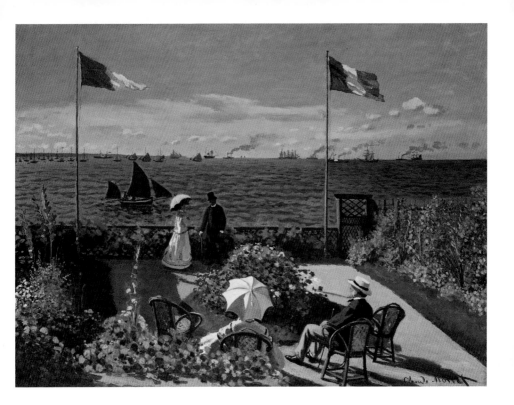

The Salon was a constant target of attack by artists. It was cursed; it was disdained out of pride, or eschewed out of despair, by artists who felt the works were not properly exhibited. Nevertheless, the great French jamboree of art – which also attracted foreign submissions – remained crucial to artists for the time being. If they were to secure a place in the scene, and establish new aesthetic approaches, they had to crack the Salon.

Art criticism in the daily and weekly press, and in the art journals (sometimes distinctly short-lived), dealt at particular length with the Salon. There were also pamphlets, broadsheets and cartoons. Artists were compelled to woo the critics and to organize their own promotion. And still the fact remained that most of the public preferred not to make up their own minds and simply relied on the committee's expert opinion, while a painting that carried the mark of rejection on its stretcher would only rarely find a buyer.

Attempts were repeatedly made to put art before the public in other ways. Commercial art galleries were soon to become the most important alternative. As this process took its course, artists competing with each other were also involved in the competition among dealers, and found

Claude Monet
Terrace at Sainte-Adresse, 1867
Terrasse à Sainte-Adresse
Oil on canvas, 98 x 130 cm
Wildenstein 95
New York, The Metropolitan Museum of Art

their careers depended on the outcome of those competitions. As we have seen, since the late 18th century artists had tended to open their studios for a day or so in order to show one or more new works; but for an unknown beginner occupying some shabby garret, this was hardly a viable solution to the problem. And Courbet's maverick pavilion of 1855, the first large-scale solo show on a freelance basis, was not a financial success.

The committee that selected the 1863 Salon was especially difficult to please. Of over 5,000 works submitted by about 3,000 artists, they rejected about 4,000. The resulting discontent among artists and in the press was so great that Napoleon III visited the Palais de l'Industrie to view the exhibition himself. He consulted the committee chairman, Comte Alfred-Emilien de Nieuwerkeke (1811–1892), a sculptor and Director General of National Museums, who in 1855 had commented on Millet's work: "This is the painting of democrats, of people who don't change their linen, who want to deceive men of the world. It is an art which displeases and disgusts me."[65] The emperor decided that the artists should have the option of putting their rejected works on public show elsewhere in the exhibition building.

This liberal gesture, which gave offence to Napoleon III's academic art politicians, was part of his manoeuvring to combat unpopularity: once an adherent of the ideas of the utopian socialist Claude-Henry Comte de Saint-Simon (1766–1825), the emperor was now suffering from a signal lack of success. Turbulent social events – and not least property speculation during the redevelopment of Paris – had left many people feeling insecure, and had exacerbated political tensions. In 1863, only the Republican opposition candidates were returned to the Chamber of Deputies in Paris. To show largesse in the arts was a safe but effective way of soothing public feeling.

Napoleon III's own notion of good art was illustrated when he promptly bought *The Birth of Venus* (p. 36) by Alexandre Cabanel (1823–1889) for 40,000 francs for his personal collection. Though the classicizing title gave the work Salon respectability, the woman's seductive pose was "titillatingly ambivalent" (Werner Hofmann)[66] in a way typical of the "female nudes then invading the exhibition halls" (Max Osborn).[67] Classical and rococo traditions were co-present in this fairly cool, brightly coloured, smoothly painted work, and it proved so successful that Cabanel painted numerous versions of it. That same year he was made a member of the Academy and a professor at the Ecole des Beaux-Arts.

Of course the Salon also featured fairly true-to-life genre and history paintings. There were also works by Courbet, who had just been engaging in joint landscape work with Corot, and Millet – though a provocative Courbet showing drunken priests was even turned down for the Salon des Refusés, on political-cum-ethical grounds. There were works in the Salon des Refusés that had been rejected not for thematic reasons but because of their style or quality. Among these were paintings by Cézanne, Fantin-Latour, Guillaumin, Jongkind, Pissarro, Whistler, and

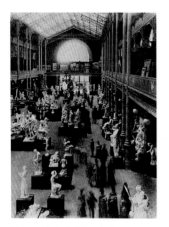

The 1855 Salon in the Palace of Industry

Frédéric Bazille
View of the Village of Castelnau-le-Lez, 1868
Vue de village Castelnau-le-Lez
Oil on canvas, 51 x 35 cm
Daulte 36. Montpellier, Musée Fabre

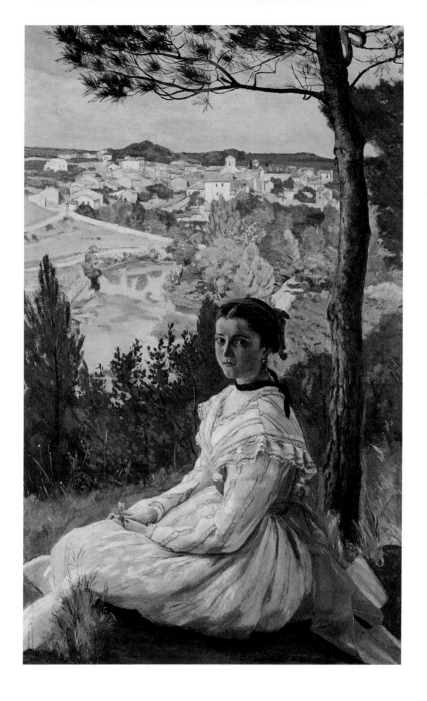

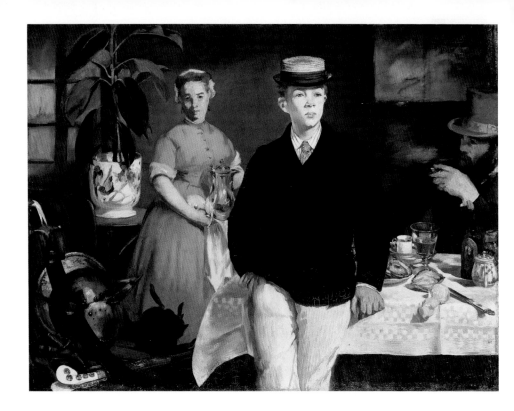

particularly Manet. The latter's *Le déjeuner sur l'herbe* (p. 37) – originally titled *Bathing* – was a *succès de scandale*, and twenty-three years later Zola immortalized the debate it provoked, the scorn and derision, in his novel *The Masterpiece* (1886), a fictionalized history of the Impressionist movement.[68]

The verisimilitude of Manet's painting was not, of course, flawless. We see two fully dressed Paris bohemians out on a summer's day (Manet's models were his brother Gustave and Ferdinand Leenhoff, who became his brother-in-law that same year). They are reclining on the grass in a woodland clearing by a pond or stream where their two women companions have been bathing. One of them (Victorine Meurent, who was modelling for Manet at the time) is sitting naked with the men, who are deep in talk. Her discarded clothing is beside her, by the luncheon basket, and she is gazing evenly out of the canvas and straight into our eyes. The figures, and especially the still life objects in the foreground, are lovingly detailed, and the natural surroundings are landscaped in with a generous hand. There are distinct areas of brightness, even though no specific light source or even an interplay of sun and shade is definable.

Edouard Manet
Luncheon in the Studio, 1868
Le déjeuner dans l'atelier
Oil on canvas, 118 x 153.9 cm
Rouart/Wildenstein I,135
Munich, Bayerische Staatsgemäldesammlungen,
Neue Pinakothek

Right:
Edouard Manet
The Balcony, c. 1868/69
Le balcon
Oil on canvas, 170 x 124.5 cm
Rouart/Wildenstein I,134
Paris, Musée d'Orsay

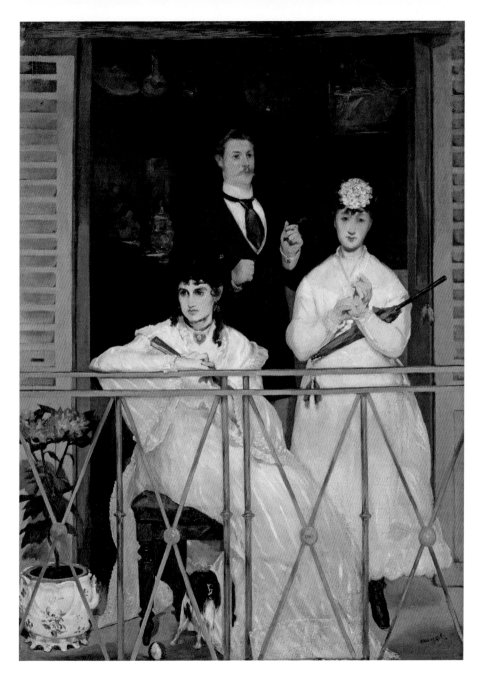

The subject of the picture threw many of those who saw it. Almost everyone was familiar with the masterpiece of the Venetian High Renaissance which hung in the Louvre and to which Manet was alluding in order (as he supposedly observed to Proust) "to make it new in a transparent atmosphere"[69] – Giorgione's *Country Concert* (possibly completed by Titian). In that work, we see two dressed gentlemen and two naked women sitting in the open by a fountain, playing music. Manet's contemporaries were perfectly ready to enjoy poetic eroticism in the garb of a distant age (or in the pseudo-ancient look Cabanel gave it); but if the setting was the Bois de Boulogne or Argenteuil in modern times, they were outraged by the indecency of it.

Manet was in fact aiming to rediscover the noble bearing of a cultured tradition in his contemporaries. To this end he also incorporated in his composition the physical gestures of reclining river gods in an engraving done by Marcantonio Raimondi from a drawing by Raphael. This fell on stony ground at the time. And later, indeed, art historians of a Modernist persuasion accused Manet of lacking compositional imagination of his own. As many have remarked, the picture lacks unity – in spatial, gestural and colour terms. From our present point of view, this very fact is eloquent of Manet's forward-looking modernity; and the inconsistencies in the work as a whole, the cracks that the artist has not papered over, the painting's montage and quotation quality, accurately convey the state of culture in his own era. It is a stock-taking, coolly assessing work, free of moralizing. The artist's own gaze is as even as naked Victorine's. The relationship between the gentlemen (possibly artists) and their lady friends (perhaps models) is one of inequality; it is economic and pragmatic in character rather than emotional. The people's gazes do not meet, and the classic, formulaic gesture of the man reclining on the right evokes no response in the woman, who makes a sovereign, isolated impression.

The scandal prompted by the Salon des Refusés – an experiment which the government declined to repeat – merely served to accelerate artistic evolution and stimulate debate. Manet's painting, and those he had previously shown at Martinet's, brought younger artists flocking to him. In their admiring eyes he was a confident force for the new. It was not till 1866, though, that Monet, Pissarro and Cézanne personally met Manet.

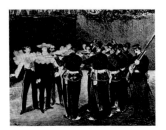

Edouard Manet
The Execution of Emperor Maximilian, 1868
L'exécution de l'Empereur Maximilien
Lithograph, 33.3 x 43.3 cm

Edouard Manet
The Execution of Emperor Maximilian (four fragments), 1867
L'exécution de l'Empereur Maximilien
Oil on canvas, 19 x 16, 99 x 59, 89 x 30 and 35 x 26 cm
Rouart/Wildenstein I,126
London, National Gallery

Edouard Manet
The Execution of Emperor Maximilian, 1868
L'exécution de l'Empereur Maximilien
Oil on canvas, 252 x 305 cm
Rouart/Wildenstein I,127
Mannheim, Kunsthalle Mannheim

Establishing a Position

Seven years lay between the Salon des Refusés and the trauma of the Franco-Prussian War, which brought France defeat, the end of imperial rule, and the experience of the Paris Commune. For the artists we are concerned with, they were seven years of quest, and of alternating success and failure. The period ended with the establishment of a common artistic personality and of Impressionism as a joint movement. Most of the artists submitted regularly to the Salon (now held annually). As a rule

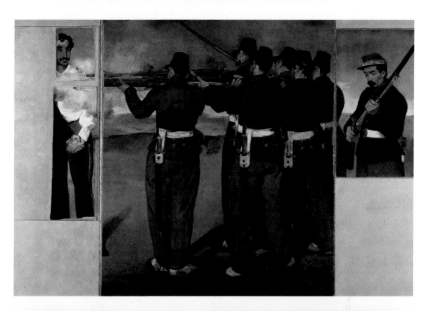

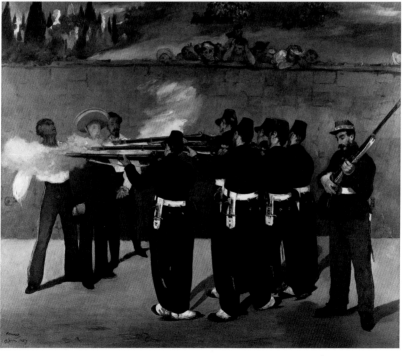

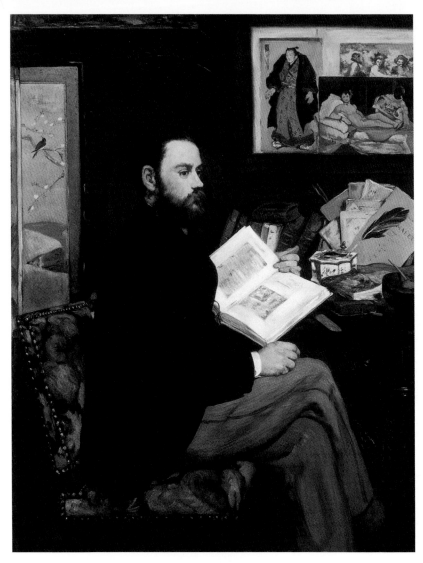

Edouard Manet
Portrait of Emile Zola, 1868
Portrait d'Emile Zola
Oil on canvas, 146.5 x 114 cm
Rouart/Wildenstein I,128
Paris, Musée d'Orsay

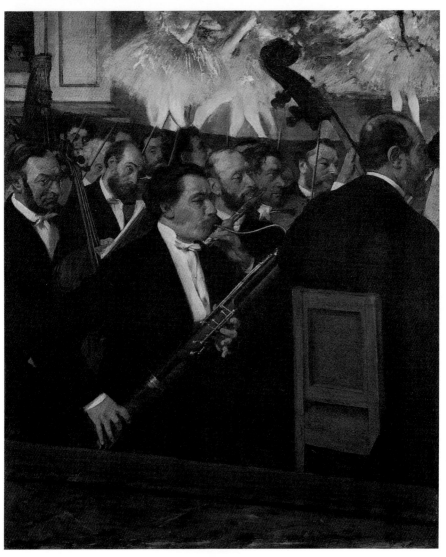

Edgar Degas
The Opera Orchestra, c. 1868/69
L'orchestre de l'Opéra
Oil on canvas, 56.5 x 46.2 cm
Lemoisne 186
Paris, Musée d'Orsay

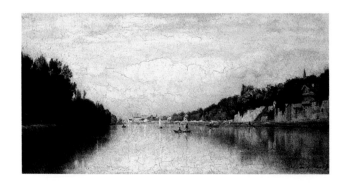

Stanislas Lépine
Banks of the Seine, 1869
Bords de la Seine
Oil on canvas, 30 x 58.5 cm
Paris, Musée d'Orsay

they were accepted at their first try, as were Renoir and Morisot in 1864, Monet and Degas in 1865, Bazille and Sisley in 1866, Gonzalès in 1870. At times they also had work rejected subsequently. Cézanne's work was too uncompromising ever to find favour with the selection panel. The sifting of Salon art was particularly thorough in 1867, when a further World Fair held in Paris prompted the thought of an independent group show, paid for by the group; but the idea was abandoned, not least for lack of funds – though Manet did have a pavilion built for a solo show during the Fair, as did Courbet once again.

The painters were tireless in their search for motifs, new ideas and stimuli, contacts and friendships. Some worked together for periods. They debated their aesthetics, among themselves and with critics; of the latter, Zola was to be of particular importance for them. From 1866 on he was vigorous on their behalf, contributing criticism of their art to a shortlived periodical called "L'Evénement". For those who had no money behind them, the financial situation could often be very difficult, and at times they lived in penury. Bazille gave Monet occasional support. Pictures had to be sold at giveaway prices if there was a chance of a sale at all. It did not make matters easier if wives and children had to be supported: Pissaro and Manet had families, and Monet and Sisley followed them in 1866.

In aesthetic terms, the problems facing the group lay in certain definable areas. They all wanted to take up the realism practised by Courbet and the Barbizon school and take it further, adapting it as they went. For this continuation of the line, Zola used the term "naturalism" from 1865 on; it had been coined two years earlier by the Republican art critic Castagnary, a friend of Courbet's.[70] For Zola, the Renaissance metaphor of a painting as a window through which reality could be seen still applied. Similarly, he saw the picture or even the artist as a screen or window pane on which phenomena that originated in reality could be seen. However, Zola importantly added that every artist was an individual medium in his own right, clouding or refashioning the phenomena in his own peculiar way or breaking them up prismatically, as it were. This, in fact, is how the artist transforms what is given into a work of art. In

Right:
Armand Guillaumin
A Path in the Snow, 1869
Chemin de creux, effet de neige
Oil on canvas, 66 x 55 cm
Serret/Fabiani 5. Paris, Musée d'Orsay

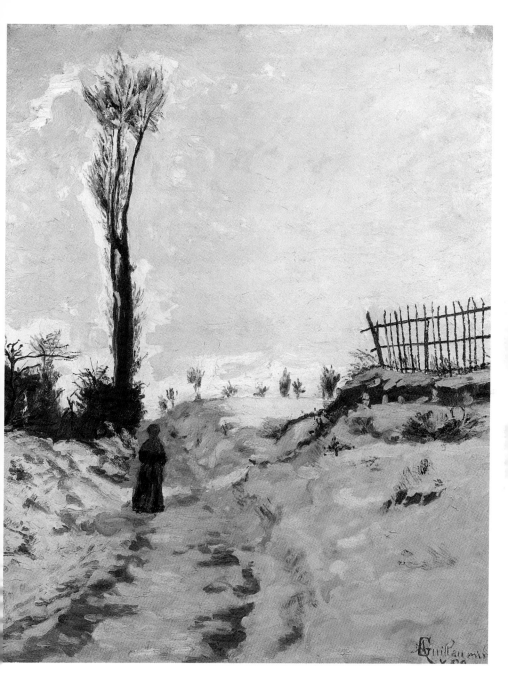

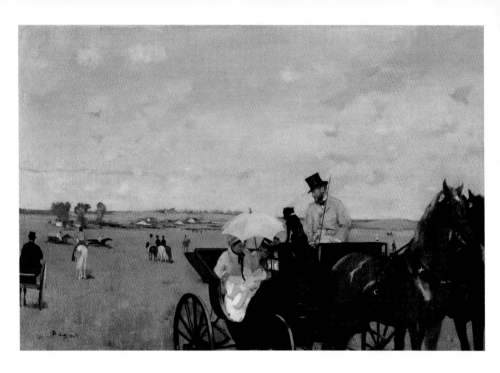

Edgar Degas
A Carriage at the Races, c. 1869–1872
Aux courses en province (La voiture aux courses)
Oil on canvas, 36.5 x 55.9 cm
Lemoisne 281. Boston, Museum of Fine Arts

1867, Zola put this with classic simplicity: "A work of art is a corner of creation seen through a temperament."[71]

Plural objective reality was taken as a valid given. This meant that the artists were debarred from pursuing preconceived ideals – say, in the representation of human figures. Partly for oppositional political reasons, the realists, for their part, had hitherto preferred to portray people from the lower classes or fringes of society. Renoir and Monet, wanting Salon space and portrait commissions, were divided between the undaunted quest for truth and conformity to prevailing aesthetic ideals or social norms.

For most of the artists, following realism or naturalism meant going into the country to paint in outlying villages or on the coast of Normandy – where the optical qualities of light and atmospherics that fascinated them, and the colour values, could be studied even better than in the forests or beside rivers. When their master, Gleyre, closed his school in 1864 for reasons of old age, Monet, Renoir, Bazille and Sisley took to systematic forays into the country. In 1863 they had already gone to the Fontainebleau woods; Renoir met Diaz, who advised him to paint lighter, and Pissarro and Morisot met Corot. In 1864, Monet and Bazille worked at Honfleur, on the coast, where they met Boudin and Jongkind. Manet too began to take an interest in harbour scenes and ships at sea (The Departure of the Folkestone Boat, p. 77).

As well as landscape and light, what particularly interested the new artists was modern life. They were forever identifying subjects of striking contemporaneity, and establishing their right to a place in art; increasingly, though, a new way of seeing and representing motifs came to occupy the foreground of their attention. They set out to convey movement and flux. Life in the new cities was marked by an accelerated tempo and the loosening of old ties and hierarchies, and they wanted to get these changes into their work. The artist became an observer, alert but uninvolved, recording interesting but randomly selected moments in a process he simply happened to be witnessing, from a standpoint occupied by chance rather than design.

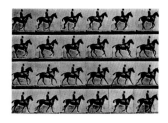

Motion study: canter. Documentary photographs by Eadweard Muybridge, c. 1878

More than the rest, Manet liked painting scenes of current affairs. A major one is *The Execution of Emperor Maximilian* (p. 65).[71] Chasing imperial expansion, France had sent a military force to Mexico in 1863, and the young Austrian Archduke Maximilian had accepted the Mexican throne. When American pressure obliged the French to withdraw their troops, Napoleon III's protégé was left to fend for himself, and was presently executed with two of his generals, on 19 June 1867, at Queré-

Edgar Degas
Race Horses in Front of the Stands, c. 1869
Le défilé (Chevaux de courses, devant les tribunes)
Thinned oil on paper on canvas, 46 x 61 cm
Lemoisne 262. Paris, Musée d'Orsay

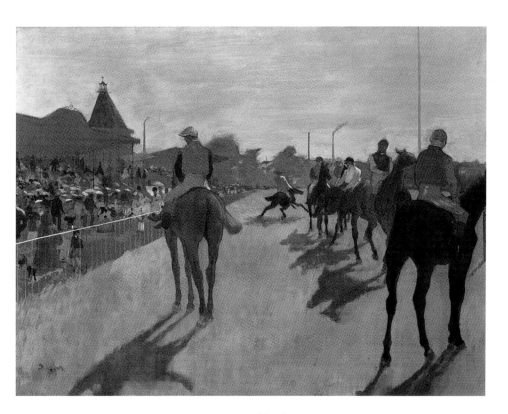

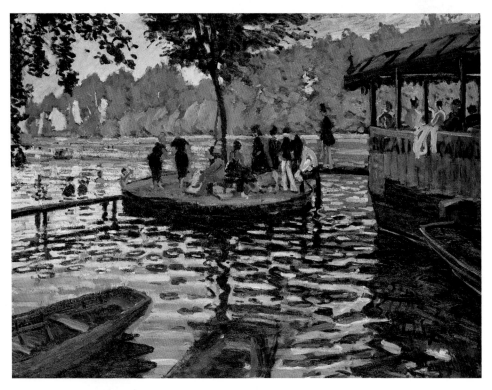

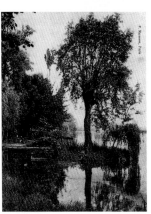

La Grenouillère

taro. Manet, drawing on news reports and press pictures, set about re-creating the event, which had been a humiliating blow to Napoleon III's ambitions. He put the firing squad in French uniform – partly because he was working from model soldiers an officer friend lent him. Four versions of the painting and a lithograph (p. 64) resulted; distribution of the latter was banned for political reasons, as was exhibition of the first, small version of the painting at Manet's World Fair pavilion. The final version, now in Mannheim, was painted in early 1868. Manet has done the lifesize figures in bold colours, making the uniforms into an almost decorative pattern. What we see is the working of a faceless military machine – which does not fit actual events in Mexico. The gun barrels are the dominant compositional horizontal; they do not in fact point in correct perspective at the victims. A remarkable, dispassionately neutral calm broods upon the scene. Though Manet was doubtless attempting a personal response to events, his own creed of impersonality proved an obstruction.

He had already painted a *View of the World Fair* (Oslo, National

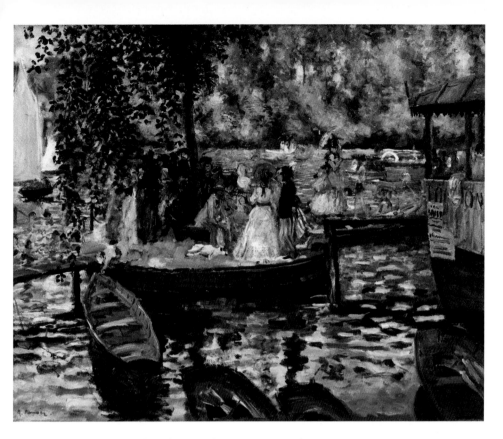

Gallery) in which a number of solo figures and groupings appeared on a rise near the Fair, seeming curiously unrelated to each other. And as early as 1864/65 he had engaged in friendly competition with Degas to paint the races and the ladies in the crowd (p. 42). Manet's method was to render the overall impression with a sketchy use of patchy colourwork, rather than trying to detail the bearing of figures. In his last racecourse picture (p. 42), the horses are galloping straight towards us – which has the optical effect of arresting movement entirely.

Following the scandal of Le déjeuner sur l'herbe, Manet prompted an even more violent controversy with Olympia (pp. 38/39), painted the same year and shown at the Salon in 1865. The lifesize nude quotes Titian's famed Venus of Urbino in the Uffizi, Florence, which Manet had copied in 1865. Manet well knew that in painting portraits of Venus, Titian would be portraying a lover of the prince who commissioned the picture. Manet's contemporaries were well aware of this too; but they could not accept the translation of a Renaissance goddess into a woman who was plainly a highly-paid Paris prostitute and who paraded her lofty

Claude Monet
La Grenouillère, 1869
Oil on canvas, 74.6 x 99.7 cm
Wildenstein 134
New York, The Metropolitan Museum of Art

Pierre-Auguste Renoir
La Grenouillère, 1869
Oil on canvas, 66 x 81 cm
Stockholm, Nationalmuseum

name as defiantly as her nakedness. In Manet's conception of the picture, a gap yawned wide between the Titianesque mood and drapes, the "Romantic" black servant and the cat, and, on the other hand, the astringently contemporary coolness of the woman, reclining with a certain angular coarseness and giving us a calculating, businesslike look. Manet's contemporaries were affronted.

Of course the look on the woman's face was Manet's doing more than his model Victorine's. He used light colours and no warm shadows. The painting was so flat that Courbet dismissively compared it with a playing card. The vivid personality and verisimilitude present in *Olympia* produced an immediacy and truthfulness that were shocking right across Napoleon III's Second Empire, regardless of individual ideological persuasions. Manet was aware that he had produced something of significance. His whole life long he kept the painting in his own possession. When his widow, needing money, proposed selling it to an American in 1888, Monet collected funds – primarily from artists – to ensure that a work rightly regarded as a milestone in modern French art could be acquired for the Louvre. (In 1890, it is true, the *Olympia* was initially only accepted into the contemporary art collection of the Palais Luxembourg.)

Manet demonstratively placed a small study for the painting behind his sitter in his portrait of Zola, who was doing so much on his behalf in essays and a pamphlet (p. 66).[73] The pamphlet can be seen to the right on the writer's desk. Zola himself makes a well-groomed rather than bohemian impression. The portrait also includes other programmatic material important to Manet: a reproduction of a painting by Diego Velázquez (1599–1660), whose work Manet admired more than ever following his visit to Spain in 1865, and Japanese artworks – a painted screen, and a coloured woodcut.

Japanese art and crafts, and "Japonaiserie", were then newly in fashion throughout western Europe.[74] In part this was an extension of the 18th-century "Chinoiserie", which had linked the aesthetic interest of things exotic to an enlightened admiration for the wisdom and philosophy of the Far East (and also of Islam and the Near East). The Japanese vogue represented an active, historicizing interest in older or remoter art forms that could be used for one's own rethinking; and its influence continued to be potent into the 20th century. Long closed off to the outside world, Japan had been "opened" to the USA and Europe since 1854. Two years later, the Parisian etcher Bracquemond, who partly exhibited with the Impressionists, discovered and bought a volume of woodcuts by Hokusai (1760–1849; see left). He was impressed by the realistic precision and compositional ease of the art in which Hokusai, a late figure in an urban-cum-folk strain in Japanese painting, recorded his observations of everyday life. One of those infected by Bracquemond's enthusiasm was Whistler, who exhibited a portrait of a young woman in Japanese costume at the 1865 Salon. The picture hit the taste of the time: since 1862 a Paris store known as "La Porte Chinoise" had been doing brisk trade in oriental goods, and the London

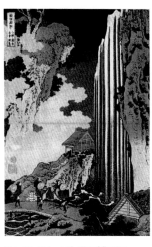

Katsushika Hokusai: The Waterfall at Ono, c. 1823–1830. Coloured woodcut, 37.2 x 25.2 cm

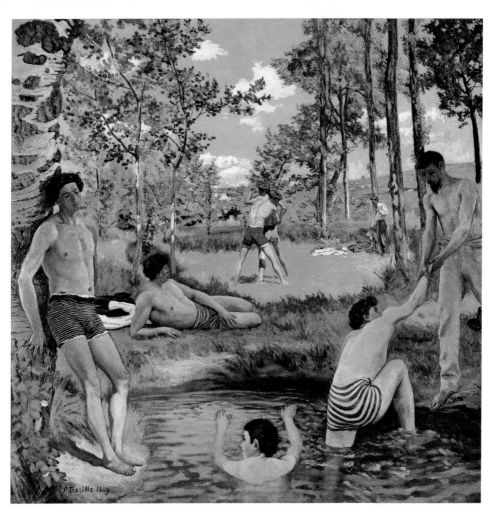

Frédéric Bazille
Bathers (Summer Scene), 1869
Scène d'été
Oil on canvas, 158 x 159 cm
Daulte 44
Cambridge (MA), Fogg Art Museum,
Harvard University

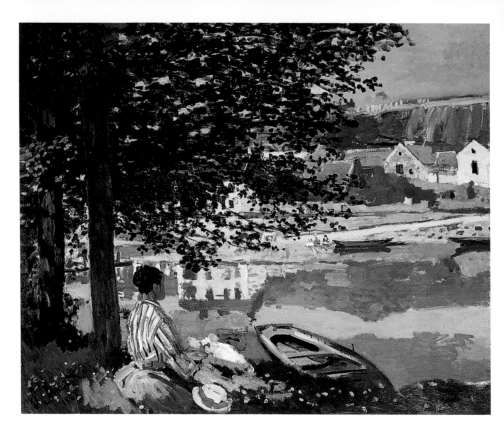

Claude Monet
The River, Bennecourt, 1868
Au bord de l'eau, Bennecourt
Oil on canvas, 81.5 x 100.7 cm
Wildenstein 110
Chicago, The Art Institute of Chicago

World Fair of that year had featured a broad selection of Japanese crafts. The trend was confirmed at the Paris World Fair in 1867.

Initially, Manet was not altogether impressed by the Japanese talent for adopting unusual perspectives, cropping in striking ways, and evoking the fleeting moment. Instead, what interested him was the decorative potential of generously, sweepingly outlined individual figures, seen against barely spatial, almost monochrome backgrounds – as can be seen from his *Fifer* in National Guard uniform (p. 47). This was a commonplace enough motif; however, it was rendered here in a demanding format, and predictably enough, the Salon committee of 1866 turned it down.

At the close of the decade Manet painted a number of masterpieces. *Reading* (p. 48), a small genre portrait of Manet's wife and their son Léon, is of particular note for its place in the evolution of the artist's style. In this private work, Manet gave himself full rein to pursue all the nuances of white he could see. The true subject of this "interior open-air picture", claims Denis Rouart, Manet's grand-nephew and author of the

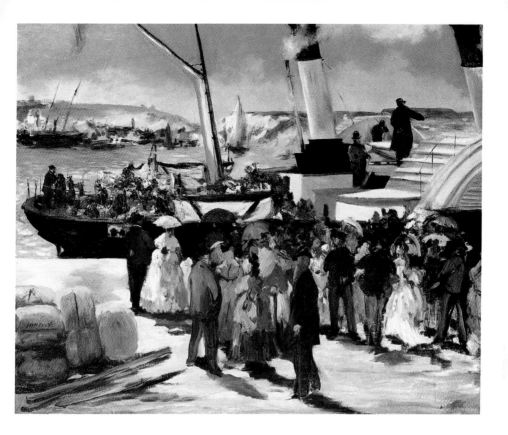

most recent *catalogue raisonné* of his works, is "the finely modulated play of the light".[75]

Delicacy of touch, a relish for whites, as well as a real respect for the sitter, are also apparent in *Repose* (p.48), a full-figure portrait of the young painter Berthe Morisot, whom Manet met in 1868. Reclining on the settee, she seems at once relaxed and tense, somewhat distanced yet attracted to the artist and something of a siren. She may have a stylish look in our eyes; contemporary cartoonists dismissed her as vulgar.

Manet's conception of the visual image was most plainly evidenced in two large pictures that were both shown in the 1869 Salon. In *Luncheon in the Studio* (p.62), the main figure is Léon. Only the still life of old weapons, the props of the history painter, suggests that this might be a studio scene. A second still life is on the table: the painter is demonstrating his capacity for conveying the sensuous qualities of things in paint. There is no action in the picture, no talk, not even eye contact; in fact, there seems no explanation for the scene we are offered, and this is what creates its peculiarly unsettling air. In essence, it is not a scene at all. In

Edouard Manet
The Departure of the Folkestone Boat, 1869
Le départ du bateau de Folkestone
Oil on canvas, 59 x 71 cm
Rouart/Wildenstein I,147
Philadelphia (PA), Philadelphia Museum of Art

defiance of custom, Manet was not out to tell a tale at all. He was simply painting.

The Balcony (p. 63) has an even greater quietness, a greater ceremony of presence, and a more exacting use of spatial values. It was the first occasion that Berthe Morisot sat as a model; beside her is the violinist Fanny Claus, their friend the landscape artist Antoine Guillemet, and, barely visible in the background, Léon. A painting by Francisco de Goya (1746–1828), which Manet may have been familiar with from a copy in a Paris collection, conceivably influenced the arrangement, though Manet, surprisingly, had a low opinion of Goya. The uncommunicative isolation of the figures is striking; their expressionlessness and apparent lack of emotion confounded Manet's contemporaries. Almost a century later, in 1949/50, the Belgian Surrealist René Magritte (1898–1967) painted a version of the picture (Ghent, Musée des Beaux-Arts) in which he substituted coffins for the people, thus highlighting the lifeless effect. For Manet, the structural issues at stake were worth considerable attention, however, and he placed special emphasis on the strongly coloured shutters and the balcony rail that separates us from the group in the picture.

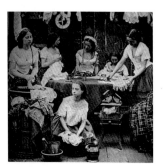

Laundresses in Paris, c. 1870

In the later 1860s, Manet became the most highly regarded of the artists, writers and aficionados who met with some regularity, usually on Friday evenings, at the Café Guerbois, 11 rue des Batignolles (now 19 avenue de Clichy). Manet, whose flat and studio were in the street, was now seen as the leader of the new school, widely dubbed the Batignolles School. In 1864, in his *Hommage à Delacroix* (Paris, Musée d'Orsay), Fantin-Latour had portrayed a group of ten artists, including Manet, with a portrait of Delacroix, whom they all revered. Now it was Manet's turn to be at the centre of attention. *A Studio in the Batignolles Quarter* (p. 81) shows Manet at work. The studio space accommodates objects of classical and Japanese art, the two traditions he was stressing. Manet is being respectfully watched by (from left to right) the German painter Otto Scholderer (1834–1902), who had arrived in Paris in 1868; Renoir; sculptor, poet and art critic Zacharie Astruc (1835–1907); Zola; his friend Edmond Maître; and Bazille and Monet.

Degas, who was particularly close to Manet in artistic terms, did not go out of his way to keep company with the other artists, whom he met about 1865 at the Café Guerbois. From 1865 to 1870 he submitted to the Salon every year, and had work accepted; thereafter he never submitted again. He worked hard at psychologically precise, realistic portraits, observing light and colour very closely, but his interest in new compositional approaches and subjects that would convey a specifically modern spirit was even greater. *Woman with Chrysanthemums* (p. 44), which probably depicts one Madame Hertel of whom we know nothing more, may well be the earliest example of so radical a displacement of a portrait sitter from the centre of a composition.[76] But then, is this picture of a woman somewhat absently, nervously putting her hand to her lips and gazing sideways at some person or thing unknown actually or primarily a portrait? It seems far more of a lavish floral still life. Our picture

Edgar Degas
Woman Ironing, c. 1869
La repasseuse
Oil on canvas, 92.5 x 74 cm
Lemoisne 216
Munich, Bayerische Staatsgemäldesammlungen,
Neue Pinakothek

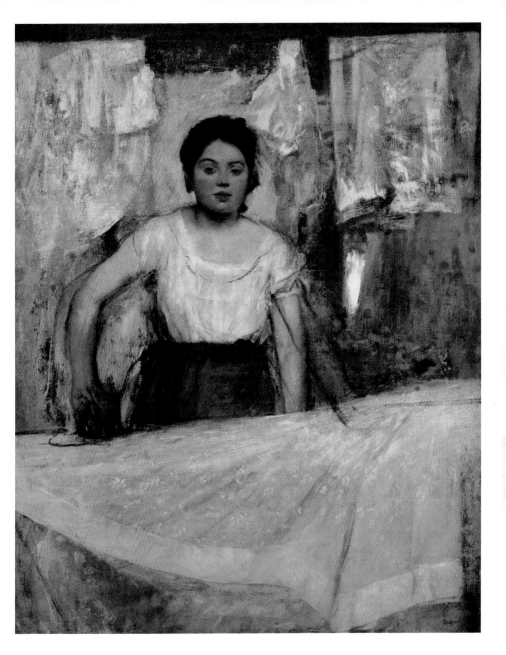

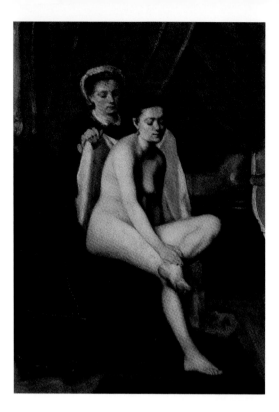

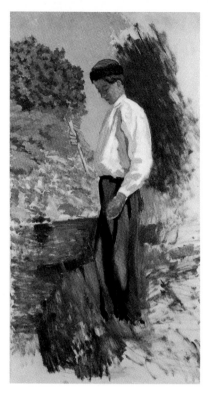

Frédéric Bazille
After the Bath, 1870
Sortie de bain
Oil on canvas, 41 x 30 cm
Daulte 49. Private collection

Frédéric Bazille
Louis Auriol Fishing, 1870
Louis Auriol pêchant à la ligne
Oil on canvas, 103 x 55 cm
Daulte 58. Private collection

categories may need to be flexible. The subjects in Degas's works – person or plant, glove or water jug – are on a par with each other, as they are in Manet's works too. In every portrait he painted, Degas opted for a different pose. It almost invariably recorded a fleeting moment, showing the subject feeling restless or uncertain about his or her relations with the world outside or with his or her own real self. The novel approach of these portraits probably influenced Manet in portraits such as that of Zola (p. 66).

Following his Salon debut with a history painting, Degas exhibited a racetrack scene there in the following year, 1866. At the same time he entered fully into the thematic world that was to be the hallmark of his art: theatre, dance and music. The world of entertainment, and the lifestyle of the affluent city classes, provided him with the perfect pretext to concentrate on the conscious act of seeing, of unbiassed observation. In the 1868 Salon he exhibited a painting of Eugénie Fiocre in a scene from the ballet "La Source", premièred in 1866 (p. 46). Compared with Degas's later dance scenes, this one makes a placid impression, like an illustration to a fairy tale. Of greater importance is *The Opera Orchestra* (p. 67), which is in some respects a work of striking novelty. Degas portrayed the

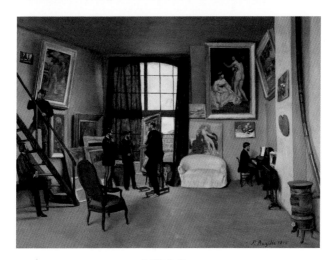

Frédéric Bazille
The Artist's Studio, Rue de la Condamine, 1870
L'atelier de Bazille, rue de la Condamine
Oil on canvas, 98 x 128.5 cm
Daulte 48. Paris, Musée d'Orsay

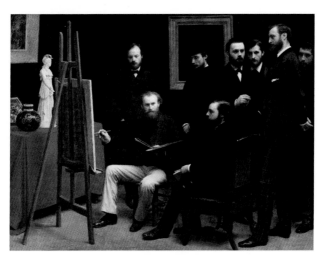

Henri Fantin-Latour
A Studio in the Batignolles Quarter, 1870
Un atelier aux Batignolles
Oil on canvas, 204 x 273.5 cm
Fantin-Latour 409. Paris, Musée d'Orsay

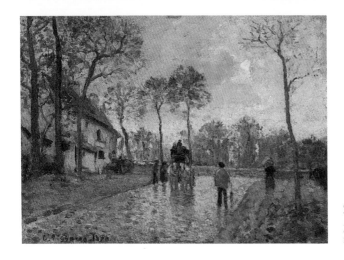

Camille Pissarro
The Mailcoach at Louveciennes, 1870
La diligence à Louveciennes
Oil on canvas, 25.5 x 35.7 cm
Pissarro/Venturi 80. Paris, Musée d'Orsay

musicians – among them the bassoon player Désiré Dihau, a friend to whom he gave the finished painting – as seen from the front row of the stalls, complete with croppings dictated by chance. The point of view that he chose also meant presenting the ballerinas on stage as no more than a disorderly tangle of legs and colourful tutus, minus their heads. This picture contained the seeds of a lifetime's work on related subjects.

Degas only rarely ventured beyond his own social sphere, but at this period he also first broached a theme that was later to engage him a number of times, albeit less fully than it interested others: women ironing. From 1865 on, the women who toiled at their ironing in the basic, steamy, hothouse rooms of the laundries featured regularly in Salon paintings.[77] Zola famously took one of them as a main character, Gervaise in his 1877 novel "L'Assommoir". As early as 1867, in his novel of artistic life, "Manette Salomon", Edmond de Goncourt took ironers and dancers as the two women's professions that (as he put it in his diary) "offer an artist the most appealing models of contemporary femininity".[78] The literary and artistic attractiveness of laundry women lay partly in the fact that they were widely perceived as loose-living, since their miserable pay forced many of them into prostitution. Not that this is apparent in Degas's earliest studies, which in 1869 resulted in an unfinished lifesize painting, *Woman Ironing* (p. 79). It is a delicate, arresting portrait of an unknown woman seen in a fragrantly sketched setting of whites, greys and pale pinks.

At this time, as a number of portraits show, Degas was fascinated by Yves Morisot (who became Madame Gobillard in 1867). She was the elder sister of Berthe, who had attracted Manet's attention. Berthe Morisot was the daughter of a top-ranking civil servant and the great-niece of the eminent rococo painter Jean-Honoré Fragonard (1732–1806). With her other sister, Edma (who abandoned painting when she married in

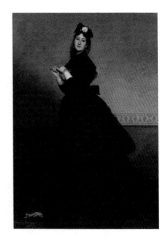

Emile-Auguste Carolus-Duran
Lady with Glove
(Madame Pauline Carolus-Duran), 1869
La dame au gant (Mme Pauline Carolus-Duran)
Oil on canvas, 228 x 164 cm
Paris, Musée d'Orsay

Right:
Camille Pissarro
The Road from Versailles at Louveciennes, 1870
La route de Versailles à Louveciennes
Oil on canvas, 100 x 81 cm
Pissarro/Venturi 96
Zurich, E.G. Bührle Collection

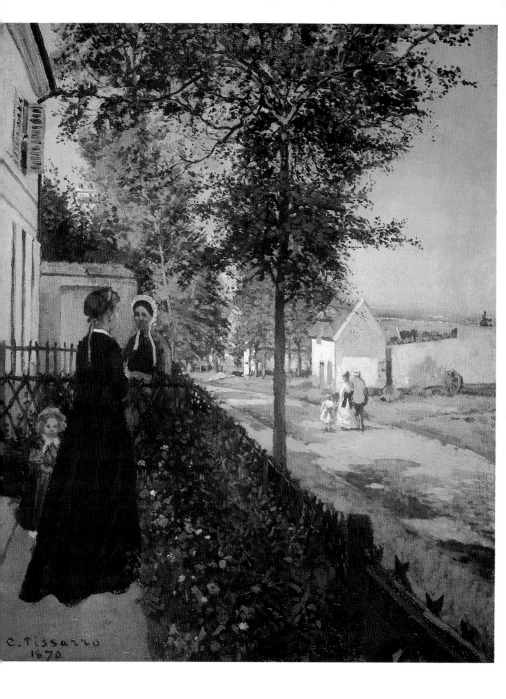

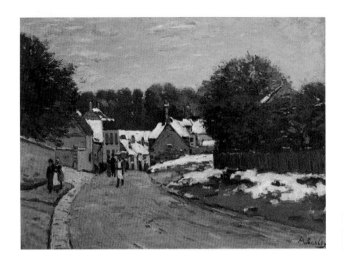

Alfred Sisley
First Snow at Louveciennes, c. 1870/71
Premières neiges à Louveciennes
Oil on canvas, 54 x 73 cm
Daulte 18. Boston, Museum of Fine Arts

1869), she had taken private tuition, mainly from Corot, and from 1864 on she regularly exhibited landscapes at the Salon. A double portrait (p. 88) shows her mother reading and her sister Edma on a settee, listening or thinking; the picture was not merely reminiscent of Manet's approach (cf. p. 48) but was in fact so heavily reworked by him (she now regarded Manet as her teacher) that she withdrew it from the 1870 Salon, where it had been accepted – no longer feeling sure of it. For a young woman at that time it was not easy to balance the willingness to learn with self-confidence, liking for a man with professional self-esteem, in a society dominated by men. Furthermore, Manet was also giving a good

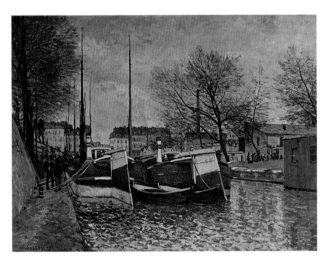

Alfred Sisley
Saint-Martin Canal in Paris, 1870
Le canal Saint-Martin à Paris
Oil on canvas, 54.5 x 73 cm
Daulte 17. Winterthur, Oskar Reinhart Collection

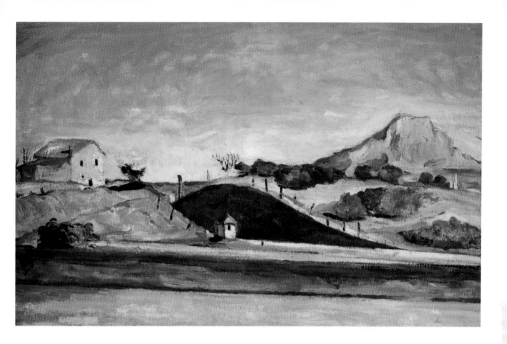

Paul Cézanne
The Railway Cutting, c. 1870
La tranchée
Oil on canvas, 80 x 129 cm
Venturi 50
Munich, Bayerische Staatsgemäldesammlungen,
Neue Pinakothek

deal of attention to another student, Eva Gonzalès, and submitted a large and rather stiff portrait of her (1870; London, National Gallery) to the same Salon.

Bazille too, the well-off medical student, who was spending more and more of his time painting, was combining a new approach to figural work with energetic attention to colour values in the open. In the few years still left to him before his early death, he could still seem rather unassured, yet at the same time his new aesthetic was evolving in astonishingly bold and versatile ways. On two occasions, four years apart, he tackled open-air portraiture, doing a young woman dressed in light colours, with a view of the village of Castelnau-le-Lez rising upon a gentle slope in the background. The 1868 painting (p. 61) was exhibited at the Salon the following year.

Between these two solo portraits came his most ambitious work, the large *Family Reunion* (p. 54), which was taken by the Salon in 1868. It shows Bazille's parents and relations on the terrace at Méric (cf. p. 52), their country residence near Castelnau in the Lez valley. The picture conveys a sense of family and of social status, a particular lifestyle, and a fresh response to Nature and light; in painting it, Bazille was also out to convince his family of his ability as an artist. This "masterpiece of the bourgeoisie" (François Daulte)[79] would repay sociological study. The postures of the figures alone speak volumes. They are coolly presented in a silence innocent of event. None of them is looking at the others. The

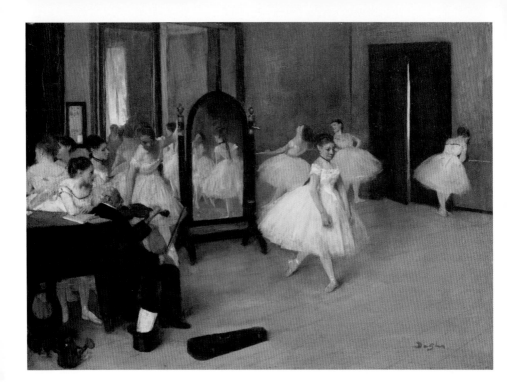

scene is not one that the artist has observed unnoticed; rather, the artist (and so we too) and the subjects are taking a calm, even, assessing look at each other, from a careful distance.

The little picture Bazille painted of himself with his Batignolles artist friends a short time later (p. 81) is rather different. He had shared his studio with Monet and Renoir (and did a portrait of the latter: p. 55). He had also given them financial support in other ways. Then in 1868 he moved to a new studio not far from the Café Guerbois. We see him in the studio, showing a new work to Manet (who painted Bazille, the tall figure by the easel, himself) and Monet; his good friend Maître is playing the piano; on the stairs, probably Zola and either Renoir or Sisley are talking. It is a scene of friendship, artistic work, and intellectual give and take: animated, easy-going, and without apparent hierarchical ranking.

The previous summer at Méric, Bazille had painted one of his most striking works, one that gained acceptance by the 1870 Salon. *Bathers* (p. 75) shows a number of youths in a grove of birches, fooling about and bathing in a pool. There is an occasional clumsiness in the rendering of the bodies, the foreshortening of perspective, and the painting of the water. The lighting of the figures is uneven, and they do not seem to be lit by the same sources as the setting. (This issue was to preoccupy Renoir

Edgar Degas
The Dancing Class, c. 1872
La classe de danse
Oil on panel, 19.7 x 27 cm
Lemoisne 297
New York, The Metropolitan Museum of Art,
H.O. Havemeyer Collection

Right:
Edgar Degas
Musicians in the Orchestra, 1870/71
Musiciens à l'orchestre
Oil on canvas, 69 x 49 cm
Lemoisne 295
Frankfurt am Main, Städelsches Kunstinstitut
und Städtische Galerie

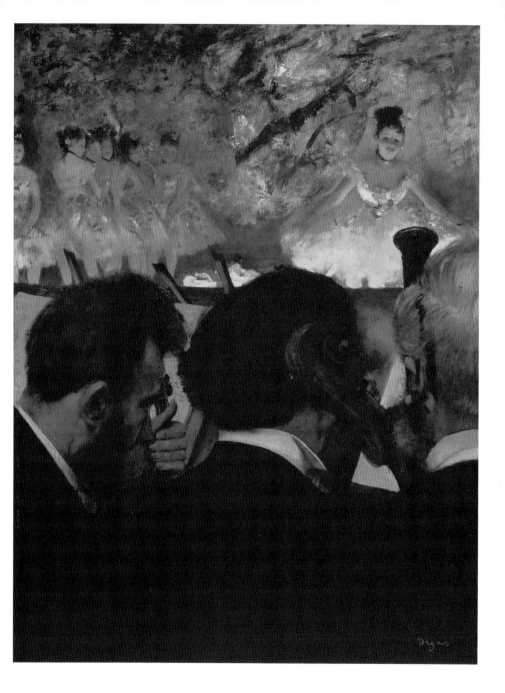

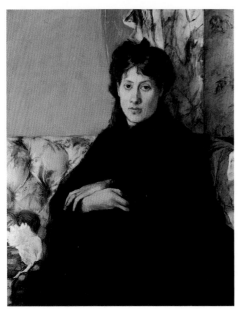

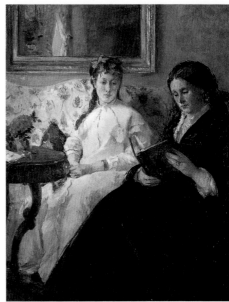

Berthe Morisot
Portrait of Madame Pontillon, 1871
Portrait de Madame Pontillon
Pastel on paper, 81.3 x 64.1 cm
Bataille/Wildenstein 419
Paris, Musée du Louvre, Cabinet des Dessins

Berthe Morisot
The Mother and Sister of the Artist (Reading),
c. 1869/70
Portrait de Mme Morisot et de sa
fille Mme Pontillon (La lecture)
Oil on canvas, 101 x 81.8 cm
Bataille/Wildenstein 20
Washington, National Gallery of Art,
Chester Dale Collection

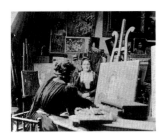

Berthe Morisot in her Paris studio

and Monet some years later.) But what is arresting in this picture by a man still in his twenties is its view of life and of man, and its determination (which perhaps owed something to Manet) to rediscover the figurative values of the old masters in modern everyday life: the man leaning against the tree at left resembles a St. Sebastian (say, by Antonello da Messina), the reclining youth an ancient river deity. And the helpfulness of the man at right may recall Christ helping the damned up out of purgatory.

Pissarro, and particularly Sisley, concentrated on landscapes, including atmospheric scenes of street life in small towns or life on the Paris waterways. They met regularly, and worked together with Monet and Renoir. In 1866, 1868 and 1870 Sisley exhibited at the Salon, but in 1867 and 1869 he was turned down. Sisley's work (pp. 84 and 96–99) showed his interest in the colour impressions of trees and buildings and particularly in the shifting play of light and cloud on a landscape.

In 1866, Pissarro settled at Pontoise with his family, then moved to Louveciennes in 1869; but he had an apartment in Paris too, and sometimes used it as a base when he went to the Café Guerbois evenings. On several occasions he joined Monet to work on the same view. The motifs he chose and his treatment of them show how systematically he was working on presenting spatial depth while retaining a firm structure in the visual surface, and how carefully he aimed to record gradations of colour under the influence of changing light. Apart from 1867, he was regularly accepted by the Salon, though he sold little as a result. Only

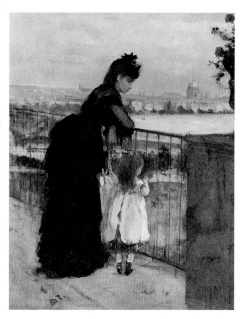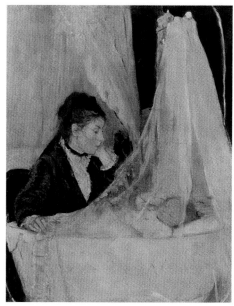

one unimportant dealer took an interest in his work. In 1868, together with Guillaumin, he tried to make a little money painting shop signs and doing other work of a similar kind.

He had more experience as a painter, compared with Monet, Renoir or Sisley, and in consequence his pictures possessed a greater maturity (pp. 58, 82, 83). His colours became visibly brighter, though Pissarro also had a penchant for muted shades beneath an overcast sky. He was particularly adept at nuancing shades of green and using the modulations to suggest depth without impairing the unity of impact. In the main he chose and handled his subjects so that the linear and the physical, plastic qualities would abet the marriage of spatiality and surface structure. Straight roads, often lined with trees, plunging into the depths at an angle and inscribing a dynamic sense of movement into a tranquil landscape, as well as *routes tournantes* twisting a gentle way through undulating country, are characteristic features in his work. The colouring and construction create a sense of structural interaction that looks almost Cubist – with hindsight. This quality, which was even more strikingly present in the work of his sometime follower Cézanne, has led to a higher valuation now being placed on Pissarro's work than was once the case.[80]

Renoir's aims were broader in scope, though his aesthetics were less secure than Pissarro's. Trying to carve out a place for himself in the Paris art scene, and at the same time having to sell pictures to make a living, he was not always clear in his own mind about the direction he was moving in. He was close to his Café Guerbois associates, particularly to

Berthe Morisot
On the Balcony, c. 1871/72
Sur le balcon
Oil on canvas, 60 x 50 cm
Bataille/Wildenstein 24. Private collection

Berthe Morisot
The Cradle, 1873
Le berceau
Oil on canvas, 56 x 46 cm
Bataille/Wildenstein 25
Paris, Musée d'Orsay

Bazille and Monet. In his application of paint he at first had a heavier touch than Manet, for instance, tending more to the manner of Courbet, who gave him personal advice and encouragement in 1865. About 1866 he began to lighten his palette, to dispense with underpainting in darker shades, and to study light in the open closely. To this end, in 1865 and 1866, with his painter friend Jules Le Cœur, he repeatedly went to Marlotte in the Fontainebleau woods or took long boat rides on the Seine with Sisley and Bazille. In spring 1867 he painted Paris city scenes with Monet. His view of the recently built *Pont des Arts* (p. 53), which spans the Seine between the Louvre and the Academy of Fine Arts, is a broad, panoramically structured scene that includes the bustle at a steamer landing stage and a lively interplay of light, shadow and clouds of various colours.

His main artistic aim became apparent in numerous genre portraits of his girl-friend, Lisa Tréhot, the daughter of a post office clerk. One life-size open-air portrait of her, exhibited at the 1868 Salon and now in the Folkwang Museum, Essen, had what Zacharie Astruc called a compelling "rightness of effects, finesse of colour shading, unity and purity of impression".[81] The bright light and transparent shadows found particular favour. The critic Théophile Thoré (1824–1869), who advocated *art social* under the pseudonym Wilhelm Bürger, found them "so naturally and exactly observed that people will think the whole thing wrong since they are used to imagining Nature in conventional colours".[82] The double portrait of Sisley and his newly wed wife Marie Lescouzec (p. 32) which Renoir painted a year after the picture of Lise is a winningly persuasive presentation of real feeling, made all the more attractive by the brilliant colourfulness of the dress; in this picture, though, the couple are not seen in uniform exterior light.

In summer 1869, Renoir changed his ways of painting, indeed of viewing his subjects, when he and Monet spent time on leisure-time pursuits of the Parisians. La Grenouillère was a bathing and boating lake with a bar and restaurant, on the island of Croissy in the Seine at Bougival. It was "widely known as a popular place for middle-class Parisian men to meet ladies of the *demi-monde*".[83] There were dealers who wanted paintings on this kind of subject,[84] so Renoir and Monet set about painting them – though the pictures they produced lacked sufficient precise detail and did not have the required anecdotal flavour. Their paintings (pp. 72, 73) were more like studies towards further works: they registered what they saw in compositions that were open-ended at the sides and seemed almost to shake and pitch as much as the boats and jetties. They painted rapidly and vigorously, in a way well suited to the bustle of people noisily enjoying themselves and to the shifting lights and colours on the agitated surface of the water. That favourite word in artistic debates at the Café Guerbois and in the Fontainebleau woods, "impression", was the very term for what the two artists were trying to capture. In their Grenouillère pictures they established something that had yet to wait five years for its name: Impressionism.

Monet was the most consistent of all the artists then questing in similar

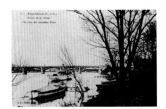

The bank of the Seine at Argenteuil, with the new bridge in the background. Postcard, c. 1900

Claude Monet
Riverside Path at Argenteuil, 1872
La promenade d'Argenteuil
Oil on canvas, 50.4 x 65.2 cm
Wildenstein 223
Washington, National Gallery of Art

Claude Monet
The Harbour at Argenteuil, 1872
Le bassin d'Argenteuil
Oil on canvas, 60 x 80.5 cm
Wildenstein 225. Paris, Musée d'Orsay

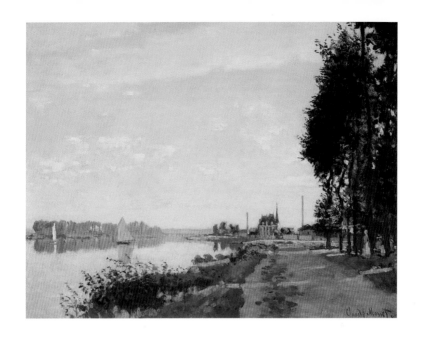

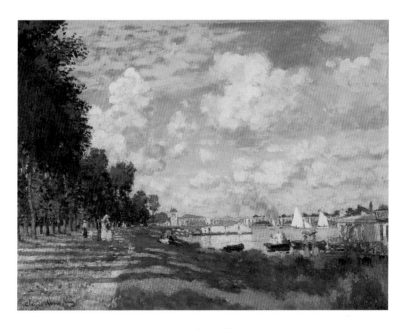

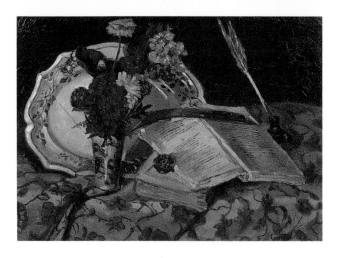

Armand Guillaumin
Still Life: Flowers, Faience, Books, 1872
Nature morte: fleurs, faïence, livres
Oil on canvas, 32.5 x 46 cm
Serret/Fabiani 14. Paris, Musée d'Orsay

directions through similar experiments. His life was a hard one, particularly so when he married in defiance of his family and had a wife to look after. He and Camille Doncieux had had a first son in 1867; they married in 1870. To succeed with female portraits such as he was then painting, he would have had to paint them more like *Lady with Glove* (p. 82), say – with a casual coquettishness yet an inscrutable modesty of gesture. This brilliantly painted work took a prize at the 1869 Salon. The young artist Charles Durand, known as Carolus-Duran (1837–1917), had painted his young wife. A dazzling career as a portrait painter lay before him.

Monet was interested in the problems posed by groups of several figures in the open. He wanted to outdo Manet's *Le déjeuner sur l'herbe* (p. 37) both in terms of consistent *plein-airisme* and indeed in format: in

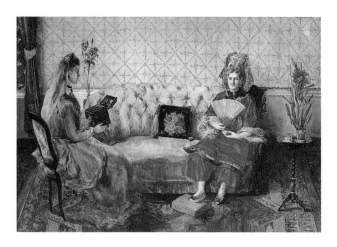

Zacharie Astruc
The Chinese Gifts, c. 1873
Les présents chinois
Watercolour on paper, 38 x 55 cm
New York, Sharon Flescher Collection

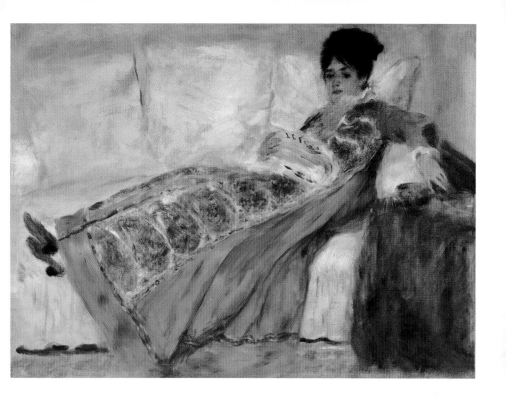

the late summer of 1865, at Chailly in the Fontainebleau woods, he painted his own picture of the same title, a group of twelve on a huge canvas measuring over four and a half by six metres and requiring a special and complicated easel. His wife, Camille, and various painter friends, among them Bazille and, at the centre, Courbet, modelled. Needless to say, Monet painted preliminary studies; the generous swathes of colour, often contrasting violently and varying greatly in brightness, have an almost Fauvist look to them. Though Monet continued work that winter in his Paris studio, however, the painting remained unfinished. He was unable to submit it to the 1866 Salon; later, rolled up, it spoiled, and all that remains now are a few impressive fragments (pp. 40, 41). Fortunately a study to which the date 1866 was subsequently added, in which some of the dresses are different colours and Courbet is not yet present, has survived to show what the composition was to look like as a whole.

Other comparable but less ambitious paintings, such as *Women in the Garden* (p. 49), painted in summer 1866, were completed. Monet did them at his new home closer to Paris, at Ville-d'Avray; Bazille paid for the materials; and the Salon committee, particularly hard to please in

Pierre-Auguste Renoir
Madame Monet Reading "Le Figaro", 1872
Madame Monet lisant «Le Figaro»
Oil on canvas, 54 x 72 cm
Lisbon, Fundação Calouste Gulbenkian Museu

World Fair year 1867, rejected them. When Monet looked at Paris, he saw visitors from all over the world, with potential purchasers among them, and doubtless with them in mind he painted a number of views from the windows of the Louvre (pp. 50, 51). All of them attest his admiration for the French capital's bustling energy, diversity and pride. That summer he visited his parents on the coast of Normandy and pressed on with what he had learnt from Boudin and Jongkind. He experimented with various points of view, and contrasted the fishermen's walks with the holidaymakers' promenades. In one painting in particular, *Terrace at Sainte-Adresse* (p. 59), he essayed a presentation of middle-class holiday behaviour amidst luscious flower beds and atmospheric beauty, in a light far brighter than in the woods near Paris. Monet's relish for powerful colours, and his numerous modern motifs, compensated for the lack of imagination or tension in the composition.

Over the next few years he overcame his compositional weakness. In his beautiful *The River, Bennecourt* (p. 76), the Grenouillère pictures (p. 72), and his Trouville beach scenes, his new attitude to Nature, a greater sense of dramatic tension in the visual image, and a stronger and more spontaneous use of colour were all happily forged into a new unity. Monet's eye for the beauties of this world, and his evident desire to pass on to viewers and buyers the pleasure he took in it, notably recorded his remarkable fundamental approach to life and art as an artist who said a big yes to life, despite constant hardship which placed him in frequent financial dependence on Bazille or the scarcely better-off Renoir. It was not his current circumstances but his vision of a better, more harmonious state that lay at the heart of Monet's art. At the same time, he insisted on painting only what he saw and felt himself, and abiding entirely by the imperatives of momentary appearances.

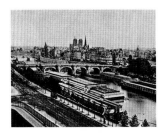

The Ile de la Cité, Paris

Impressionism

By the late 1860s, though no one could have distinguished the fact at the time, everything that was shortly to constitute Impressionism was already present in powerful early form. It is not easy to define Impressionism, though. It was the art of a small group of fairly young artist friends who spent a great deal of time in each other's company; but this is a purely external feature. The aesthetic aims and approaches of the group by no means invariably dovetailed. Friendship, and mutual strategies to secure positions in the art world, linked them to artists whose styles were not Impressionist at all. Every individual trait in the style had its roots and antecedents in pre-Impressionist art, and parallels in non-Impressionist art.

To paint in an Impressionist way meant representing a seen, given reality as it appeared to the eye. Everyday reality was foregrounded, particularly that of the artist's own social class, especially if it was engaging and attractive. Leisure activities made preferable subjects to

Berthe Morisot
View of Paris from the Trocadéro, 1872
Vue de Paris des hauteurs du Trocadéro
Oil on canvas, 45 x 81 cm
Bataille/Wildenstein 23
Santa Barbara (CA), The Santa Barbara Museum of Art

Edouard Manet
The Railway, Gare Saint-Lazare, c. 1872/73
Le chemin de fer, Gare Saint-Lazare
Oil on canvas, 92.7 x 114.3 cm
Rouart/Wildenstein I,207
Washington, National Gallery of Art

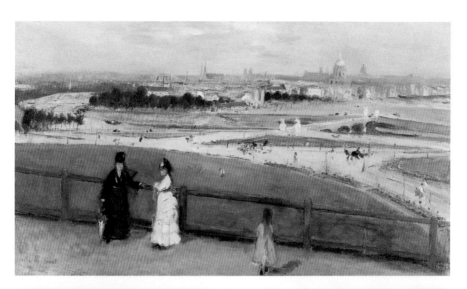

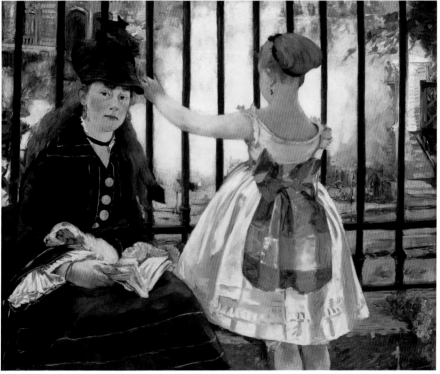

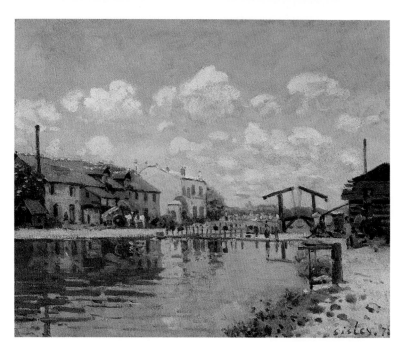

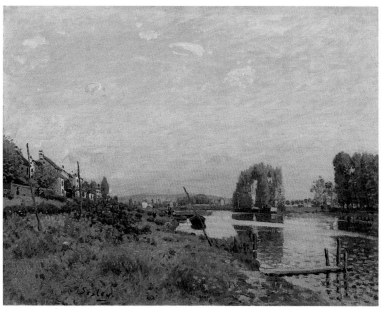

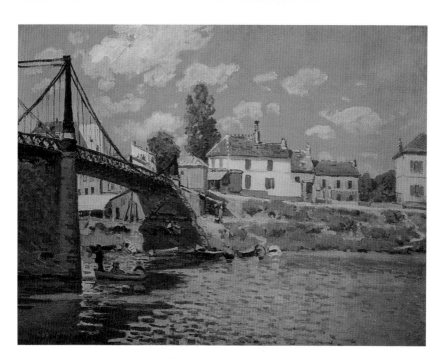

Alfred Sisley
The Bridge at Villeneuve-la-Garenne, 1872
Le pont de Villeneuve-la-Garenne
Oil on canvas, 49.5 x 65.5 cm
Daulte 37
New York, The Metropolitan Museum of Art

Left:
Alfred Sisley
The Saint-Martin Canal, 1872
Le canal Saint-Martin
Oil on canvas, 38 x 46.5 cm
Daulte 35. Paris, Musée d'Orsay

Alfred Sisley
The Island of Saint-Denis, 1872
L'Île Saint-Denis
Oil on canvas, 50.5 x 65 cm
Daulte 47. Paris, Musée d'Orsay

worktime. Country, sea and sky were seen from their appealing sides. These were not unusual motifs by any means, and matched public taste well enough to mean sales. The Impressionists were particularly interested in dynamic aspects of the real, in anything that spoke of speedy flux. Indeed, the sense of change and movement was crucial – including the change and movement of light and colour. The Impressionists viewed the world exclusively through their own eyes as painters, and insisted that they were ahead of their contemporaries in terms of correct seeing. They were for more light and brighter colours; and the fact is that they really did grasp earlier or more emphatically than others what effect colour contrasts in a painting have, how the colour of a thing changes according to its surroundings and the conditions of light, and that shadows are of different colours. They also realised that a stronger or brighter impact can be achieved by a colour if dabs of various un-mixed colours are applied adjacently on a canvas, mixing optically only when they are registered by the onlooker's eye. Experiments aimed at a new way of seeing struck them as germane, a vital legitimation of artistic endeavour; and for this reason they occasionally declared that it was of no importance what subjects happened to be painted.

Impressionism was important in art history for three reasons. The first was that, in terms both of colour and of the cropping of sections of reality, the truth of a picture was relative because it depended on the person who did the seeing and painting and applied only at a specific

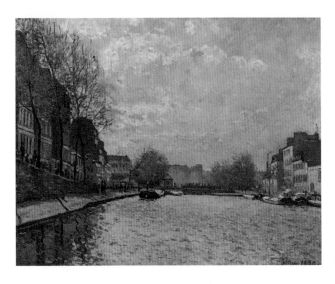

Alfred Sisley
The Saint-Martin Canal in Paris, 1870
Vue du canal Saint-Martin, Paris
Oil on canvas, 50 x 65 cm
Daulte 16. Paris, Musée d'Orsay

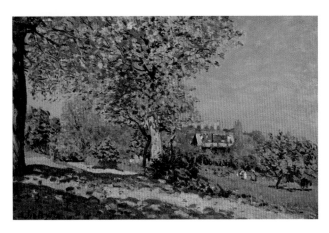

Alfred Sisley
Landscape at Louveciennes, 1873
Paysage à Louveciennes
Oil on canvas, 54 x 81 cm
Daulte 49
Tokyo, National Museum of Western Art

moment in specific circumstances. This idea was underlined by the openness of pictorial form in Impressionist art: the image was an excerpted section of space and time, to be recorded in rapid sketches.

The second reason was that the relativity of the image, and its open form, prompted those who looked at them to look and feel for themselves in new ways, and in so doing to complete the visual image and message. The individual picture was no longer an authoritative, incontestably valid source of instruction – though of course the artists had a natural interest in having their own ways of seeing and painting accepted by as many people as possible as correct and persuasive.

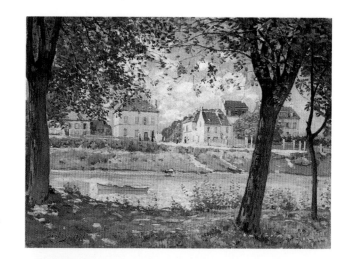

Alfred Sisley
Villeneuve-la-Garenne on the River Seine, 1872
Villeneuve-la-Garenne sur Seine
Oil on canvas, 59 x 80.5 cm
Daulte 40. St. Petersburg, Hermitage

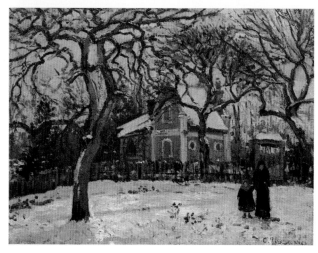

Camille Pissarro
Chestnut Trees at Louveciennes, c. 1872
Châtaigniers à Louveciennes
Oil on canvas, 41 x 54 cm
Pissarro/Venturi 146
Paris, Musée d'Orsay

The third reason why Impressionism was important was that, regardless of the representational value of the pictures, the act of painting as a pleasurable venture in itself, and the artwork as its enduring record, became established as intellectual values in their own right. This autonomy of creativity enabled the doctrine of *l'art pour l'art*, long in the offing, to gain ground. The view that an artist painted because he happened to want to and had the skill became widespread: the entire meaning and cultural significance of a picture might now consist solely in the fact that it was a picture rather than anything else.

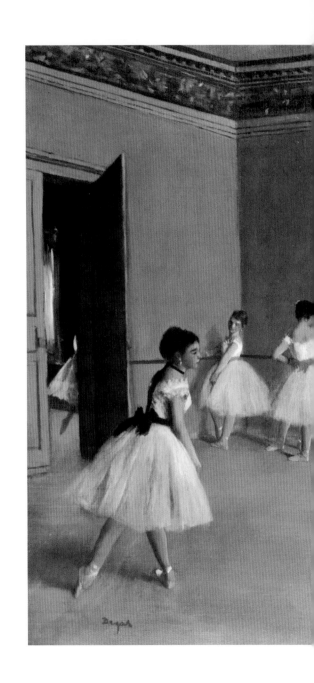

Edgar Degas
Dance Studio of the Opera, Rue Le Peletier, 1872
Le foyer de la danse à l'Opéra, rue Le Peletier
Oil on canvas, 32 x 46 cm
Lemoisne 298. Paris, Musée d'Orsay

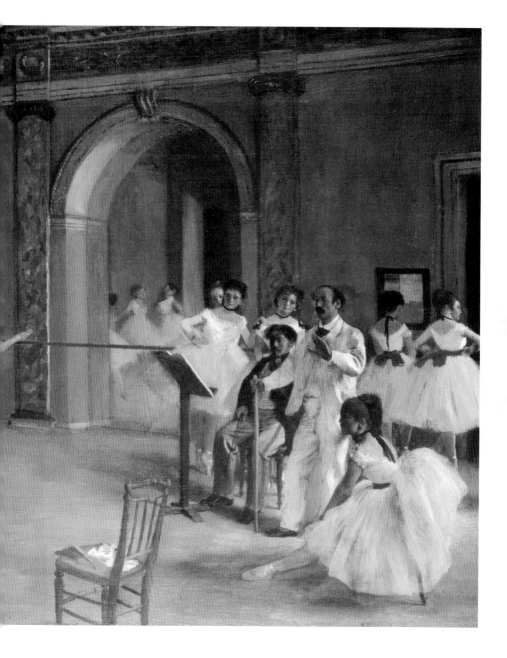

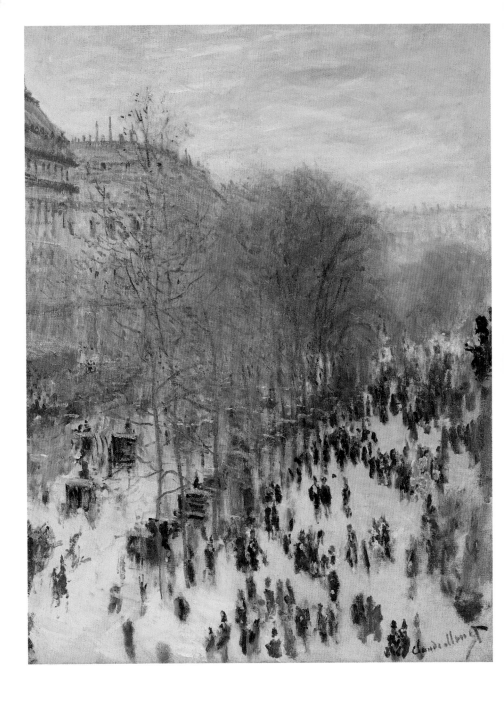

4 Getting there

For the small group of artists aged between thirty and forty, with their new ideas of Nature and art, the chances were good that they would establish their position with a growing proportion of the critics, the public, and art institutions, as the Barbizon painters had done some years before. "The landscape of France," it was said, "looks more like Corot's pictures with every year that passes" – and the witticism aptly reflected the influence the Barbizon artists had had on ways of seeing. But profound political changes were to deflect the normal course of aesthetic evolution.

War and Dispersal

In summer 1870, in a manner that was characteristic of the 19th century, France went to war with Prussia and certain other German states. France emerged defeated. Napoleon III capitulated at Sedan on 2 September and was taken prisoner by the Prussians; and two days later his opponents at home in Paris proclaimed France a republic. Bismarck's Prussia continued the war till the ceasefire of 28 January 1871 and the peace of 10 May. Under the Treaty of Frankfurt France surrendered Alsace and most of Lorraine to the new German Empire, which had been proclaimed on 18 January at the Palace of Versailles (of all places). The unstable fledgling republic of France was rocked by the Commune: in Paris, surrounded by German troops, a central committee of the lower classes established a more or less socialist commune of a kind familiar from precedent, from March to May. French troops put down this Commune (which had attracted the support of various artists, including Courbet) in a week of bloody and cruel fighting in May 1871.

The artists with whom we are concerned were affected by these events in various ways. Bazille enlisted in the Zouaves and was killed in a skirmish at Beaune-la-Rolande on 28 November 1870. Renoir too joined the army, but served in southern France, far from the front. He fell ill, received his discharge, and returned to Commune Paris, where Guillaumin and others were too. Manet, a Republican of firm conviction, joined the National Guard in Paris after the fall of the monarchy. Like Bracque-

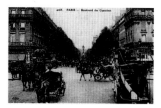

Boulevard des Capucines, Paris

Claude Monet
The Boulevard des Capucines, 1873
Le Boulevard des Capucines
Oil on canvas, 79.4 x 59 cm
Wildenstein 293
Kansas City (MO), Nelson-Atkins Museum of Art

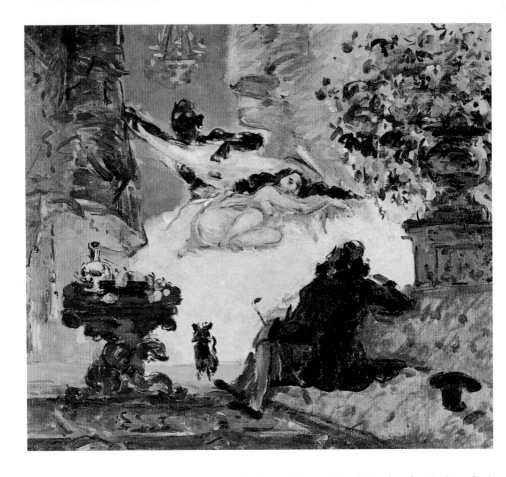

Paul Cézanne
A Modern Olympia, c. 1873
Une moderne Olympia
Oil on canvas, 46 x 55.5 cm
Venturi 225. Paris, Musée d'Orsay

mond, Carolus-Duran, Tissot and the delicate late classicist Pierre Puvis de Chavannes (1824–1898), who was subsequently to play an important part in Post-Impressionism, he was under the command of Meissonier. Manet observed the misery in besieged Paris, and the defeat of the Communards, attentively, and was deeply shocked and moved. Degas, by no means a Republican, also served in the National Guard; like the others, he never actually saw active service. All of them still had enough free time to continue painting, drawing and frequenting the Café Guerbois. Morisot was living in Paris, and withdrew to the country, like Degas, only during the months of the Commune. Sisley had British nationality and was thus not directly affected by the war and its upheavals; he remained at Louveciennes, but the economic decline resulting from the war, and his father's death, made him a poor man. Pissarro, a Danish citizen and thus a foreigner too, left Louveciennes (which was not far from the theatre of war) and fled via Britanny to London. His house was looted, by the French and especially the Germans. Hundreds of paintings which he had left behind were destroyed.

Monet spent the summer of 1870 on the coast again and, no friend of the Empire, avoided military service by going to London too, where he met Pissarro and Daubigny. The latter introduced him to the Parisian art dealer Paul Durand-Ruel (1833–1922), whose gallery in Rue de la Paix (and since 1870 in Rue Laffitte) had helped establish the Barbizon painters and was now acquiring a second house in London, in New Bond Street. There, Durand-Ruel now placed a number of works by Monet and Pissarro on show. Both found themselves with an opportunity to view various English paintings more closely, and Constable's landscapes in particular confirmed them in their views. Returning to France in 1871,

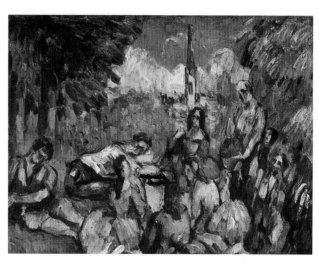

Paul Cézanne
Le déjeuner sur l'herbe, c. 1873–1875
Oil on canvas, 20.8 x 27 cm
Venturi 238. Paris, Musée de l'Orangerie

Monet stopped in Holland for his first visit of any duration, to see the museums and study new motifs. In 1869 Cézanne had begun an affair with Hortense Fiquet, a bookbinder's assistant and part-time model; after the outbreak of war he found her lodgings at L'Estaque near Marseilles, where he secretly visited her from Aix-en-Provence and painted. It was imperative that his strict and narrow-minded father, who disapproved of his son's art, know nothing of Hortense, since he might otherwise discontinue the 150 francs monthly allowance to Paul.

Manet was the only one whose art evidenced the traces of those turbulent times. Drawings and graphics which he did not dare publish recorded the defeat of the Commune, through motifs similar to those in *The Execution of Emperor Maximilian.* We know that Manet, as well as Degas, was profoundly affected by the butchery in Paris; a letter written to Berthe Morisot by her mother provides eloquent evidence.[85]

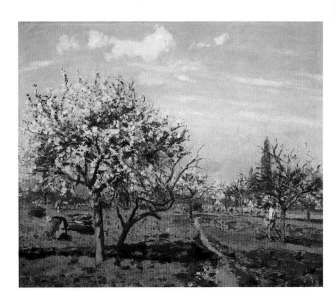

Camille Pissarro
Orchard in Blossom, Louveciennes, 1872
Verger en fleurs, Louveciennes
Oil on canvas, 45 x 55 cm
Pissarro/Venturi 153
Washington, National Gallery of Art,
Ailsa Mellon Bruce Collection

The temporary émigrés tried hard to extend their repertoire of motifs. Monet painted views of London and of Dutch canals and houses. In Pissarro's case it is striking that his interest in viewing unfamiliar sights went hand in hand with the continuity of a personal way of seeing. What he chose to paint in London suburbs was not unlike the village scenery of Louveciennes and environs, right down to the lanes leading to the distance and the gentle light.

The art of Cézanne, on the other hand, underwent a radical transformation during this period. Hitherto, all he had really had in common with the others had been ambition, an urge for innovation, and a rebellion against academic norms. In a letter of 1866 he had declared, "I shall have to decide to paint only in the open from now on"; initially, however, the deed did not follow upon the word. Both thematically and formally, Cézanne's art was more lacking in unity than that of his fellows. Unlike Monet, he poured his violent shifts of mood and response, and indeed his sexual obsessions, into his choices of subjects and the ways he rendered them. Self-taught, he struggled with difficulties in figural work and perspective spatiality. But he was also prone to give his temperament full rein, laying total and provocative claims to subjectivity.

Cézanne's paintings covered a broad range of subjects. One showed his father frontally, sitting on an armchair as on a throne and reading a newspaper. Originally the paper was the anti-imperial "Siècle"; but Cézanne overpainted its title, substituting "L'Evénement", the short-lived journal where Zola had published his first impassioned defence of Manet and other innovative artists in April and May 1866. These essays were

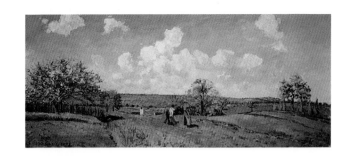

Camille Pissarro
The Four Seasons: Spring, 1872
Les quatre saisons: Le printemps
Oil on canvas, 55 x 130 cm
Pissarro/Venturi 183. Private collection

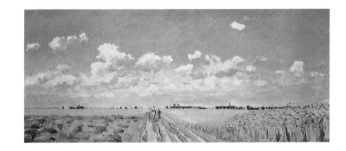

Camille Pissarro
The Four Seasons: Summer, 1872
Les quatre saisons: L'été
Oil on canvas, 55 x 130 cm
Pissarro/Venturi 184. Private collection

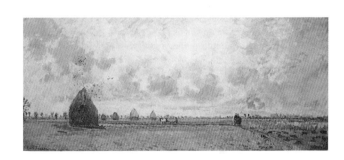

Camille Pissarro
The Four Seasons: Autumn, 1872
Les quatre saisons: L'automne
Oil on canvas, 55 x 130 cm
Pissarro/Venturi 185. Private collection

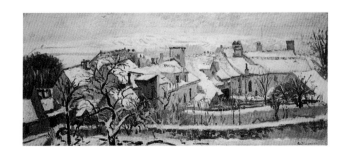

Camille Pissarro
The Four Seasons: Winter, 1872
Les quatre saisons: L'hiver
Oil on canvas, 55 x 130 cm
Pissarro/Venturi 186. Private collection

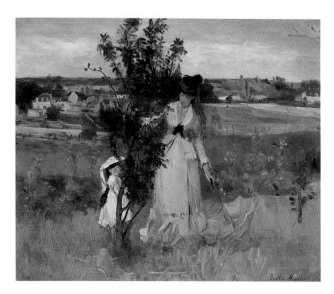

Berthe Morisot
Hide and Seek, 1873
Cache-cache
Oil on canvas, 45 x 55 cm
Bataille/Wildenstein 27
New York, Mrs. John Hay Whitney Collection

collected in pamphlet form as "My Salon" - and dedicated to his friend
Cézanne (though there was no article on Cézanne's art in the colection).[86]
Though Zola's views on art were unlikely to sway Cézanne *père*, Paul's
visual allusion was meant as an argument: he wanted his father, who was
grudgingly paying the allowance to his son, to register the fact that the
art public were taking note of Paul Cézanne the artist. In 1870 and 1871,
at Aix and L'Estaque, Cézanne (as he later related) decided, following an

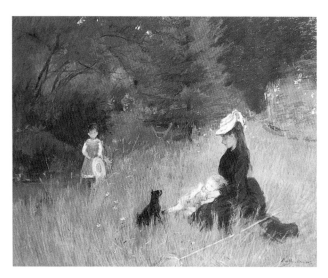

Berthe Morisot
In the Grass, 1874
Sur l'herbe
Pastel on paper, 73 x 92 cm
Bataille/Wildenstein 427
Paris, Musée du Petit Palais

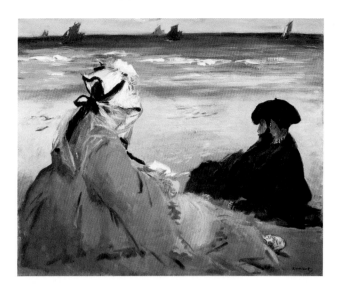

inner upheaval that he did not describe, to abide absolutely by Nature in his future art.[87]

Cézanne painted the landscape of his home parts, beneath the mighty Mont Sainte-Victoire, a mountain heady with ancient legend. He registered the incursions of modern life into the eternal face of Nature in works such as *The Railway Cutting* (p. 85). His aim was to experience and understand Nature by looking at it with appropriate humility and

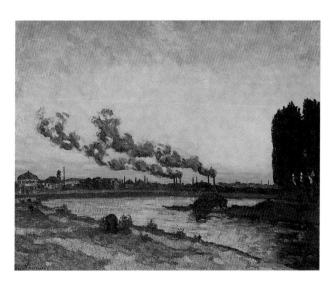

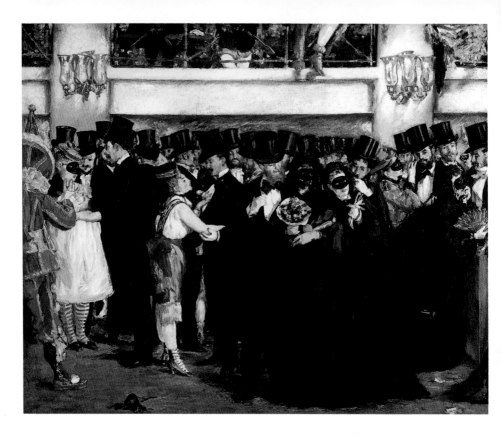

Edouard Manet
The Masked Ball at the Opera, c. 1873/74
Le bal masqué à l'Opéra
Oil on canvas, 59 x 72.5 cm
Rouart/Wildenstein I, 216
Washington, National Gallery of Art

attention. If he was out to create a photographic reproduction, though, he was nonetheless approaching Nature with his own ideas in mind, and looking in a way that his own views had delimited. Forms were simplified, and he worked sketchily, in powerful pastose colours, painting brightly. Henceforward, objectivity and interpretation were to be balanced in his work, a certain reticence together with a passionate involvement of his own self in the subject. He could never be entirely an Impressionist; but from 1871 on his art did have a fundamentally Impressionist tenor.

The Barrier of Mistrust

In the years that followed, the artists continued to work hard in the style they had struck out in. They were now certain of their ideas, and their efforts were directed at a more systematic solution of the structural prob-

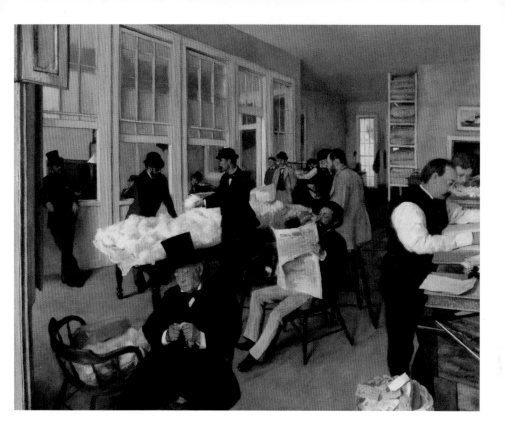

lems they encountered during their work. Arts policy during the Second Empire had impeded their progress, and some of them had been politically opposed to the old regime too, so they now expected that greater recognition and better sales would come their way. But in this they were to be sorely disappointed.

The new republic was an insecure thing. Despite the reparations payments exacted by Germany, economic recovery was surprisingly prompt; but one of the first economic slumps of global proportions stifled this recovery in 1873. Power structures had by no means been clarified: President Adolphe Thiers was followed in office by Marshal Patrice MacMahon in 1873, with Victor Duc de Broglie as head of government. These two men aimed to restore a parliamentary monarchy under the old Bourbon dynasty; but the monarchists were divided, and there were adherents of imperial Bonapartism still to be reckoned with. In 1875, albeit by a majority of only one, a Republic constitution was adopted by the National Assembly that was to remain in force till 1940.

What matters for our present purposes is that the state of profound

Edgar Degas
The Cotton Exchange at New Orleans
(Portraits in an Office), 1873
Le bureau de coton à La Nouvelle-Orléans
(Portraits dans un bureau)
Oil on canvas, 73 x 92 cm
Lemoisne 320. Pau, Musée des Beaux-Arts

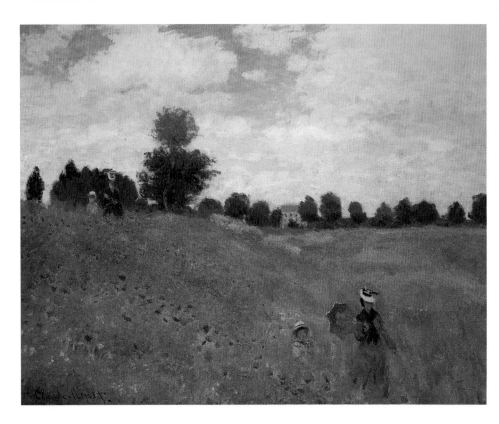

Claude Monet
Red Poppies at Argenteuil, 1873
Les coquelicots à Argenteuil
Oil on canvas, 50 x 65 cm
Wildenstein 274. Paris, Musée d'Orsay

social shock that followed the Paris Commune produced an intellectual climate in which innovation or aesthetic revolution were viewed with fear, distrust or even loathing. For a considerable time to come, a cliché view of the Impressionists insisted on seeing them as "Communists", regardless of whether the painter in question happened to have sympathized with the Communards or not. For the first post-war Salon, in 1872, the jury was once again elected by artists who had been awarded a Salon distinction. In 1873 Paul Alexis (1847–1901), a friend of Zola and Cézanne and a regular at the Café Guerbois, wrote in a newspaper article that there were quite a few artists who, for this reason, longed for the Empire only recently so despised and vilified, and for the days of the Comte de Nieuwerkerke.[88]

On the other hand, a socio-cultural development continued that has remained important in art to this day. Art dealers were becoming more and more significant. The public fell into various unrelated sectors; there were only loose links between aesthetic positions, tastes or artistic preferences, and social status, worl-views, or political attitudes and interests; so the artists began to stress that the response of the expert was all

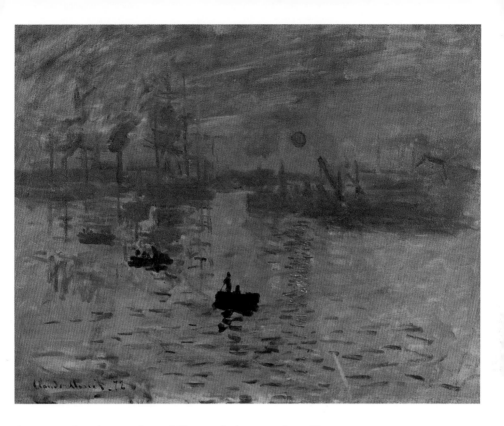

that mattered to them. Understandably enough, however, they still hoped to capture a wider and wider public.

At first, for the Impressionists, one dealer was of paramount importance: Durand-Ruel. He gave them confidence, despite the fact that even decades later he still preferred the Barbizon painters, who were more to his personal taste. As a dealer, he gambled that his clientele's aesthetic requirements would continue to develop. When the new movement finally got off to its proper start, his part was considerable. In January 1872 he bought everything he could lay his hands on in Manet's studio, and then works by almost all the other artists of the new Batignolles school. In 1873 he published a lavish three-volume sales catalogue with an introduction by the writer Armand Silvestre (1837–1901), who was intimate with the artists of the Café Guerbois. This catalogue, titled "Recueil d'estampes", featured 300 reproductions of works in Durand-Ruel's keeping. There were over twenty pictures each by Delacroix, Corot, Millet and Rousseau; seven each by Courbet and Manet; and a smaller number of works by Pissarro, Monet, Sisley and Degas. Durand-Ruel had also already bought work by Renoir and offered it for sale in

Claude Monet
Impression: Sunrise, 1873
Impression, soleil levant
Oil on canvas, 48 x 63 cm
Wildenstein 263. Paris, Musée Marmottan

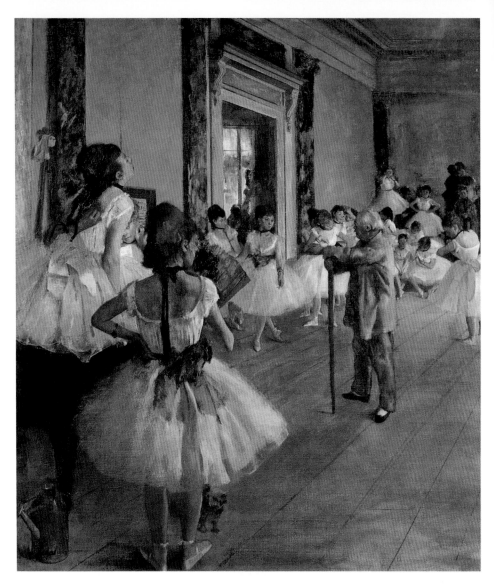

Edgar Degas
The Dance Class, 1874
La classe de danse
Oil on canvas, 85 x 75 cm
Lemoisne 341. Paris, Musée d'Orsay

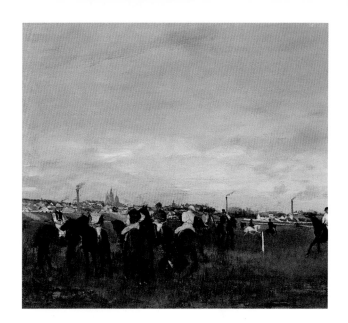

Edgar Degas
The Races. Before the Start, before 1873
Le champ de courses. Avant le départ
Oil on canvas, 26.5 x 35 cm
Washington, National Gallery of Art

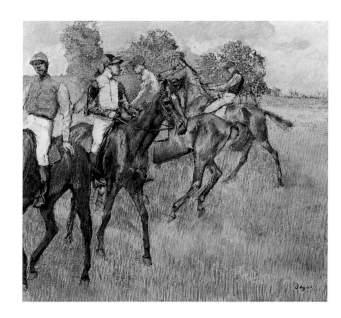

Edgar Degas
Race Horses, c. 1873
Chevaux de courses
Pastel, 57.5 x 65.4 cm
Lemoisne 755
Cleveland, The Cleveland Museum of Art

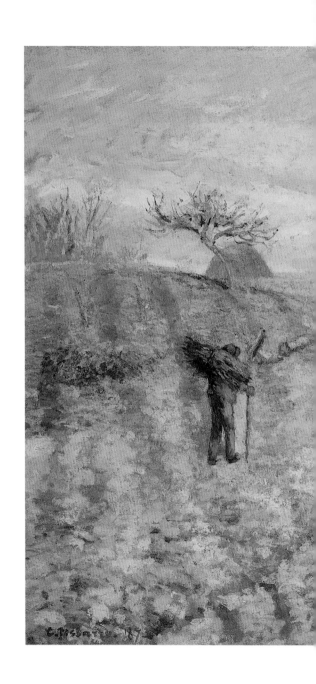

Camille Pissarro
Hoarfrost, 1873
Gelée blanche
Oil on canvas, 65 x 93 cm
Pissarro/Venturi 203
Paris, Musée d'Orsay

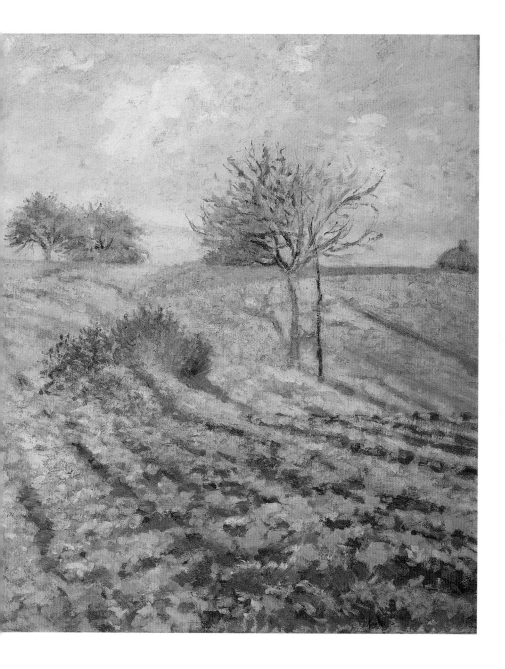

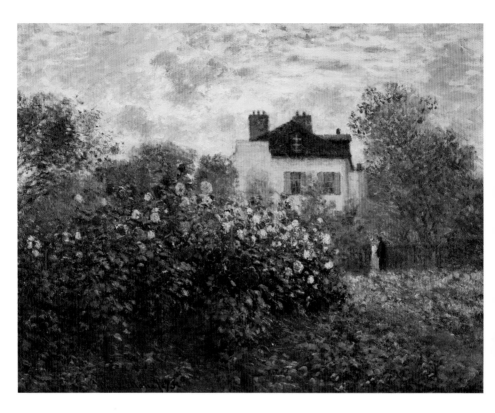

Claude Monet
Monet's Garden at Argenteuil, 1873
Le jardin de Monet à Argenteuil
Oil on canvas, 61 x 82 cm
Wildenstein 286. Private collection

his London rooms. In the following year, though, the financial effects of
the slump forced him temporarily to suspend the purchase of paintings
that provided him no return in the short term.

In the debates on the best market strategy, Manet was one of those
who considered that the real decisions on public stature were taken at
the Salon. In 1873 he had a certain success there with his stylish portrait
of Berthe Morisot (p. 48), painted three years earlier. Other paintings
from that same productive year show that he was not only trying to
extend his ideas of modern subject matter but also aiming at a brighter,
more fluid and open manner of painting. *The Masked Ball at the Opera*
(p. 110) is suggestive of his ironic delight in the behaviour of the
gentlemen in tails and top hats, providing him with an opportunity to
shine at black, and the gaiety of the colourful girls. The top edge of the
painting emphasizes the cropped nature of this sectional view. The work
was bought by the Impressionists' first generous collector and patron,
the wealthy opera singer Jean-Baptiste Faure (1830–1914). He also
bought *The Railway, Gare Saint-Lazare* (p. 95), begun in 1872, shown

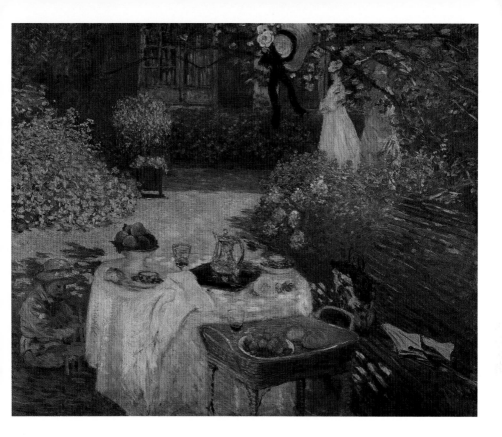

at the Salon in 1874, and in reality a genre portrait of Manet's model Victorine and the daughter of his friend Alphonse Hirsch, in whose Paris garden near the station the picture was painted. The true subject is the exclusion of women from the new dynamics of modern life. In the summer of 1873, Manet was energetically tackling the problems posed by figures in the open. He painted in Paris, in the garden of his successful painter friend Alfred Stevens; or on holiday at Berck-sur-Mer on the coast, producing works such as *On the Beach* (p. 109).

Degas, free of the need to sell pictures in order to live, pursued his interest in people, their characters and temperaments, their faces and body language. The way they behaved struck him as remarkably eloquent of the conditions they led their lives in. He painted uncommissioned portraits or had his acquaintances present situations that conveyed typical behaviour. Crowds at racetracks (pp. 70, 71) and the lean, diminutive jockeys on their delicate, nervy horses (p. 115) supplied him with open-air motifs. He was relatively unconcerned with the play of sunlight; but he was all the more drawn to the curious colour effects

Claude Monet
The Luncheon, 1873
Le déjeuner; panneau décoratif
Oil on canvas, 160 x 201 cm
Wildenstein 285. Paris, Musée d'Orsay

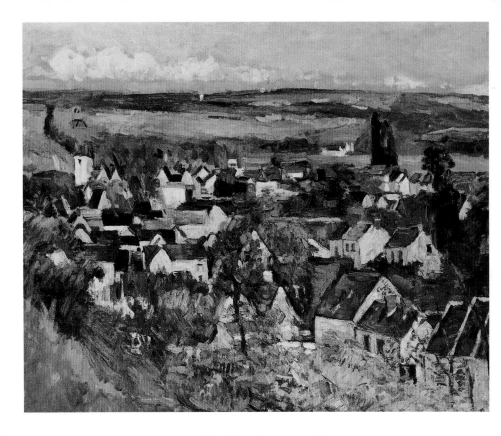

Paul Cézanne
View of Auvers, c. 1874
Auvers, vue panoramique
Oil on canvas, 65.2 x 81.3 cm
Venturi 150
Chicago, The Art Institute of Chicago

produced by cool, incisive gaslight. Gas was increasingly being used for lighting in theatres, restaurants and other public places, as well as homes. And ballet became the main focus of Degas's artistic interest, an inexhaustible source of interesting postures and movements.

Yet Degas rarely drew, much less painted, directly from a model. Rather, he used and developed his gift for exact observation, for memorizing details and then, in the studio, freeing what he had seen and resolving it in a composition. Degas's approach contrasted greatly with that of the open air painters; he was against their spontaneity, in fact. He insisted on the artist's right to transform and clarify what he has seen in a visual form of his own making. What appealed to him most in observed reality was the chance element, things that might appear meaningless at first. For him as a sceptical observer free of illusions, messages consisted primarily in permitting the individual to act with neither meaning nor result. There were no overall, lucid, causal contexts. Today, given the further development of given reality and of art, Degas may well strike us as especially "modern" on account of this sceptical pessimism.

In *Musicians in the Orchestra* (p. 87) he went in even closer to the heads of the orchestra musicians than in his earlier approach to the subject (p. 67). The spatial and colourist ensemble, with the dancers' limbs and faces lit strangely by the limelight from below, emphasizes unclarity or polarities.

From 1872 on, Degas devoted most of his attention to ballerinas practising under their master (pp. 100/101) or rehearsing on stage, where occasionally gentlemen would be looking on and would afterwards express a wish to take one of the girls home with them (p. 129). These scenes provided Degas with an opportunity to record the beauty of dance steps and the sheer effort that went into them, but also the bored weariness of ballerinas killing time as they waited to go on, stretching or scratching. He studied the girls' lean bodies; they tended to come from the poorer classes. Positioning their feet delicately had become second nature with them. Degas clearly perceived the contrast between their fairylike grace and their wretched social circumstances. He could see that ballet meant speedy, formalized movement, solo but especially in groups,

Paul Cézanne
Six Women Bathing, c. 1874/75
Baigneuses
Oil on canvas, 38 x 46 cm
Venturi 265
New York, The Metropolitan Museum of Art

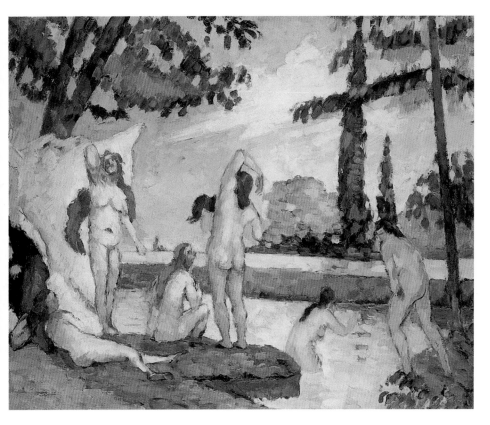

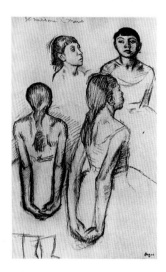

Edgar Degas
Four Studies of a 14-year-old Dancer, 1879
Pencil on paper, 48 x 30 cm
Paris, Musée du Louvre, Cabinet des Dessins

Edouard Manet
The Monet Family in the Garden, 1874
La famille Monet au jardin
Oil on canvas, 61 x 99.7 cm
Rouart/Wildenstein I, 227
New York, The Metropolitan Museum of Art

Berthe Morisot
Chasing Butterflies, 1874
La chasse aux papillons
Oil on canvas, 46 x 56 cm
Bataille/Wildenstein 36
Paris, Musée d'Orsay

across an extensive, empty space. He devised ever new compositions in order to establish the greatest possible motion and spatiality in a fixed, immobile, flat scene.

The approaches taken in Japanese woodcuts prompted Degas to try out a degree of asymmetry hitherto unknown in European art. He juxtaposed crowded figures and vacant spaces, cropped figures or overlaid them with objects that happened to be standing around, and generally heightened the sense of chance at work. This seeming chaos, though, was networked with barely perceptible linear interrelations and parallel repetitions in the figures and the architectural backgrounds, and the visual structure was cemented by consonances and counterpoints of colour. The sizes of his pictures varied, gradually increasing; his approach as draughtsman and as painter evolved from a miniaturist, old-master delicacy to a more generous, relaxed largesse.

The circumscribed but artistically striking world of ballet and dance theatre afforded Degas an aesthetically structured model for relations and behavioural patterns in a society that indulged in such luxuries. There, as he put it, he found "the movements of the ancient Greeks united in one place",[89] but he also found an internally inconsistent union of art, work and business, and an unemotional manufacture of feeling. Author Joris-Karl Huysmans (1848–1907) presently wrote that "Degas [...] unremittingly dethroned the mercenary girl rendered stupid by her mechanical strutting and monotonous leaps..."[90] It is primarily the attractive colours of the pictures that tell us how susceptible Degas was to the magic of theatre. But his view of his own role as sceptical observer compelled him to strip away the magic from these idols of the entertainment world, of a social stratum hungry for pleasures.

Degas had an acute eye for everyday behaviour presented in a psychologically precise way, and for the critical moments in life that are expressed in mutual silence. *The Cotton Exchange at New Orleans* (p. 111) was kin thematically and stylistically to a fairly familiar kind of genre realism; for that reason, it was the first Degas to be acquired by a French museum, and for a long time indeed the only one. Degas's uncle Michel Musson – the elderly gentleman checking the product quality in the foreground – ran a cotton exchange in America, and Degas had gladly used this found subject, with its various autonomous and unrelated components, when he visited New Orleans. For pictures such as this, Degas at times used a photo he had himself taken as a starting point instead of preliminary studies;[91] this was the origin of Impressionist Realism in the representation of social reality. Degas himself, it is true, was not consistent in pursuing this line further, although he encouraged others to do so.

For financial reasons, Renoir inevitably needed sales and success more than Degas did. His attempt to lighten his palette and loosen his formal idiom was apparent not only in city scenes and landscapes but also in his small private portrait, *Madame Monet Reading "Le Figaro"* (p. 93). It would seem he surprised her at home in Argenteuil, lying on the sofa reading the paper; without troubling to adopt any more formal pose, she is gazing calmly at the artist (and at us) with her fine, dark eyes. This was

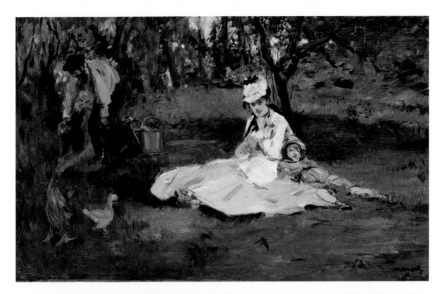

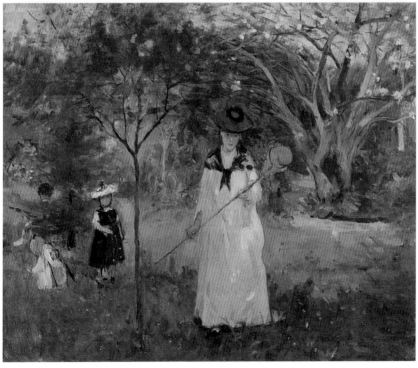

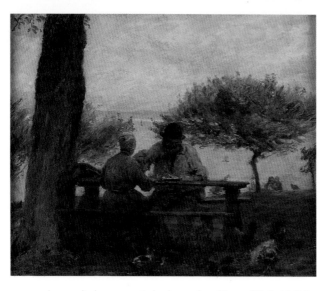

Adolphe-Félix Cals
Luncheon at Honfleur, 1875
Le déjeuner à Honfleur
Oil on canvas, 44.5 x 53.5 cm
Paris, Musée d'Orsay

a natural, unstudied scene precisely observed; and it was filled with light, a thing of fragrance, sketchily done in thin paint. It was an *hommage*, tenderly done, without the sarcasm that was usually evident in Degas.

In Pissarro's case we see the maturity and assurance of a copious output. Living at Pontoise, in hilly country among vegetable growers, where industrialization was still in its infancy, he had all the motifs he needed

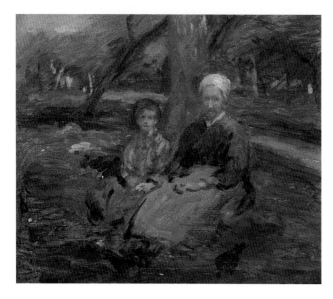

Adolphe-Félix Cals
Woman and Child in the Orchard, 1875
Femme et enfant dans un verger
Oil on canvas, 31.5 x 37.5 cm
Paris, Musée d'Orsay

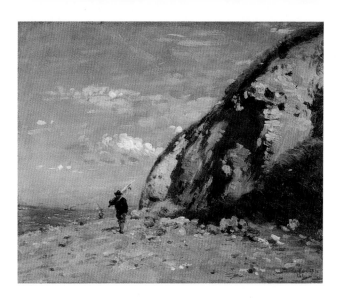

Adolphe-Félix Cals
Fisherman, 1874
Pêcheur
Oil on canvas, 25 x 31 cm
Paris, Musée d'Orsay

for his notions of artistic subjects and formal strategies. Nature cultivated by human toil and thus made accessible to the emotions, the tensions and harmonies of the terrain with its natural vegetation and man-
made buildings and artefacts – these were sufficient to keep his responses
on the alert and his eye registering constructively and noting formal
solidities. The world recorded in his paintings is a tranquil, peaceful
place and a makeweight to the hectic, profiteering reality that was in
many ways becoming uglier elsewhere.

Edouard Béliard (1835–1902), of whose art we know next to nothing
(p. 155), painted with Pissarro, as did Guillaumin, who worked night
shifts in order to paint by day. From Pissarro he took the structure and
composition of street views with figures (p. 154) and the creation of
spatial depth by the use of twisted lanes. But he also had a somewhat
romantically coloured view of modern industry of his own. In one work
(p. 109) we see smoke billowing from factory chimneys in the Paris suburb of Ivry, like triumphant banners fluttering against a ruddy golden
evening sky: is this some new impression, a positive view of technological
progress and French economic power, or is it a warning against the
destruction of the natural environment and of a fine riverscape? If Pissarro himself occasionally painted a new alcohol factory in Pontoise, for
instance, it seemed he saw a certain dignity in a place of work and felt it
was not at odds with the landscape, even if he was not entirely happy
about it.[92]

For Pissarro, the most important contact was his genuinely productive
work with Cézanne. The latter had settled in Pontoise in late 1872 to
receive guidance from his mentor. Pissarro introduced him to the paint
and art dealer Julien "Père" Tanguy (1825–1894), who had fought with

the Communards and now supplied Cézanne with paints and canvases in exchange for paintings (which initially he could not sell). It was similarly intellectual affinity that took Cézanne in early 1873 to Auvers, a village not many kilometres from Pontoise, where Dr. Paul Gachet (1828–1909), who had his practice in a working-class district of Paris but did not live there, put lodging, a studio and an etching printing press at his disposal, as well as buying occasional pictures. Gachet was a homoeopathic doctor, a freethinker and socialist who had been an army doctor during the Commune. He was interested in modern art, dabbled in painting himself, and frequented the Café Guerbois. For years he had been a friend of Pissarro and Guillaumin.

Near to Pissarro, and indeed often painting the same motif (though not at the same time), Cézanne adopted an Impressionist way of painting. And he in turn evidently strengthened Pissarro's desire for a constructivist visual structure and a sense of spatial depth achieved purely by gradation of colour values without changes in the planar qualities of the picture. His vehemence of old, and his oddly strained relations with Manet, whose well-groomed elegance and respect for the Salon repelled him, issued in his parodic paraphrase of Manet's controversial nude – *A Modern Olympia* (p. 104). Gachet bought it. His little *Le déjeuner sur l'herbe* (p. 105), on the other hand, with its crowd of sketchy figures and the verticals of trees and spire, is closer to Pissarro's work. The same is true of the crystalline patterning of *View of Auvers* (p. 120). These were contributions to the overall evolution of Impressionism, no doubt, and justify the view "that Pissarro and Cézanne, between 1870 and 1880, jointly laid the foundations of modern art"[93] – that is, of the view that pictorial values are autonomous, a view that gained ground from the late 19th century on.

For the moment, though, the main line of the new art was dictated by the quest for a new articulation of impressions and sensations conveyed by the flux of natural phenomena. To be precise, it was a matter of finding ways to express a positive, primarily hedonistic revelling in the natural and cultivated world, a setting with which humanity was conceived and shown to be in harmony. This was Pissarro's intention. Others such as Morisot (p. 95), Guillaumin or Sisley (pp. 96–99), partly under Manet's influence, placed a greater emphasis on city life in their work, or took people out in the open as their central subjects rather than as an excuse for landscapes.

Delight in the beauty of Nature accompanied a desire to juxtapose pure and contrasting colours, such as red and green or blue and yellow. Contrasts of this kind produced decorative effects that led Monet in particular to paint a great profusion of floral and blossom scenes. Glinting water on the Seine or one of its tributaries, beneath a blue sky studded with white clouds, and with a few cheerful sailing boats on the waves, prompted a more generous, relaxed, pastose application of paint.

For his resplendent large painting *The Luncheon* (p. 119), which he exhibited in 1876 under the telling title *Decorative Mural*, Monet hit upon a characteristic visual idea. Into a flower garden scene, where the

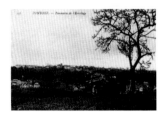

The Hermitage near Pontoise. Postcard c. 1890

Camille Pissarro
A Cowherd at Pontoise, 1874
Gardeuse de vache sur la route du Chou, Pontoise
Oil on canvas, 55 x 92 cm
Pissarro/Venturi 260
New York, The Metropolitan Museum of Art

Camille Pissarro
The Hermitage at Pontoise, 1874
Un coin de l'Ermitage à Pontoise
Oil on canvas, 61 x 81 cm
Pissarro/Venturi 262
Winterthur, Oskar Reinhart Collection

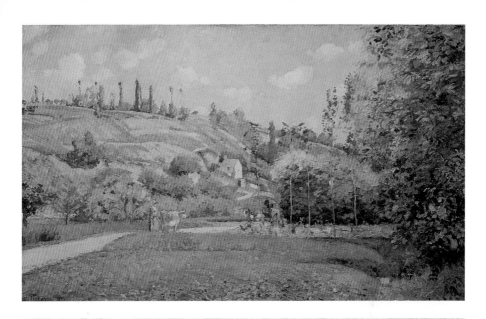

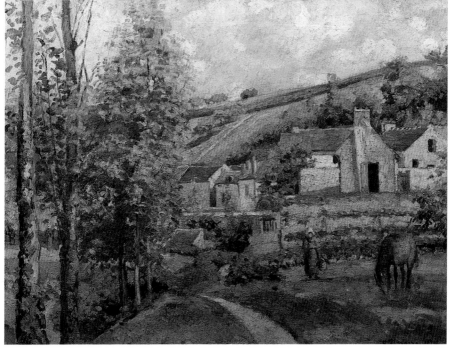

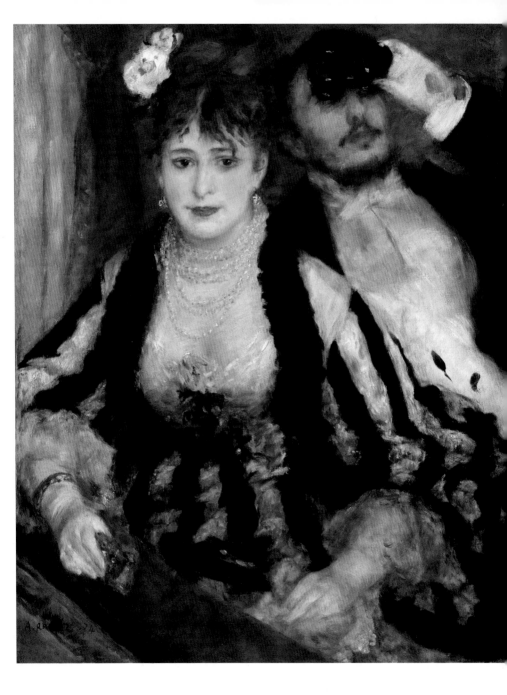

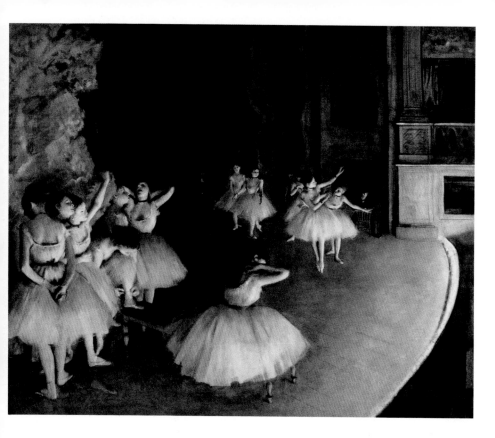

Edgar Degas
Rehearsal of a Ballet on Stage, 1874
Répétition d'un ballet sur la scène (Salle de danse)
Oil on canvas, 65 x 81 cm
Lemoisne 340. Paris, Musée d'Orsay

Left:
Pierre-Auguste Renoir
The Theatre Box, 1874
La loge
Oil on canvas, 80 x 63.5 cm
Daulte 116
London, Courtauld Institute Galleries

interplay of sunlight and blue shadows is dominant, he introduced the human cast (his family) primarily through the objects they had left behind, via a kind of still life. In this way he was able to take as his true subject a situation that in fact already lay in the past. The angled view of the abandoned table and seat, and the overlaying of the figures glimpsed in the background, suggest that the person viewing the scene has only just happened upon it; and this motif of departure constitutes an experiment with motion and with a dimension that is strictly speaking inaccessible to painting, the dimension of time. Degas was not the only one to find painting the passing of time become a central issue. It was to be a problem for Impressionism in general, and indeed subsequently for all of Modernism.

Movement, and the presence of crowds indistinguishable as individuals, as well as the atmospheric appeal of a winter's day at carnival time, prompted Monet to paint two pictures of the *Boulevard des Capucines* (p. 102). Monet clearly had an intuitive sense of the essence of modern city life. He was also a master of the sensuous effect that derives from

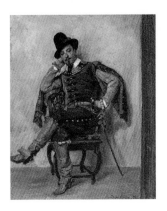

Marcellin Desboutin
Portrait of Jean-Baptiste Faure, 1874
Portrait de Jean-Baptiste Faure
Oil on canvas, 40.8 x 32.7 cm
New York, Wheelock Whitney and Company

Edgar Degas
At the Beach, 1876
Bains de mer
Thinned oil on paper on canvas, 46 x 81 cm
Lemoisne 406. London, National Gallery

this diagonal view downward and into a deep perspective. The canvas is meshed with short brushstrokes, some thin and abrupt, others thick and pastose, in fairly light shades. We almost imagine we can hear the sounds of carriages, horses' hooves, and people walking and talking. It is a record of reality in a state of busy flux.

Around 1800, Paris already had a population of about 550,000. By 1850 it was a million, but by 1870 the figure had climbed to almost 1.9 million. In those two decades, the formative years for the Impressionists, the city's population increased annually about six times as fast as it had done in the first third of the century. In his novel "The Spoils", written from 1869 to 1871, Zola described the ruthless land speculation when the new boulevards were being laid out, when "the old Paris was being ploughed under, the quarter of rebellions and barricades" (from 1789 to 1848) – the very term Haussmann had himself used.[94] But he also described a new, positive feeling towards the changed city: "The two lovers had a genuine passion for the new Paris... their eyes gazed affectionately on the vast, broad, grey ribbons of pavements with their benches, columns papered with colourful posters, scrawny trees. That bright track, growing ever narrower till it reached a rectangle of vacancy at the far horizon... the crowds of people pouring by, and the sound of their footfall and voices, gradually filled the two of them with unqualified and unmixed joy, with a sense of the excellence of street life."[95]

And then in 1873, on one of his visits to home parts at Le Havre, Monet painted a picture (which he later inscribed with the earlier date of 1872) of the old harbour. Hastily sketched in strong blue-green, violet,

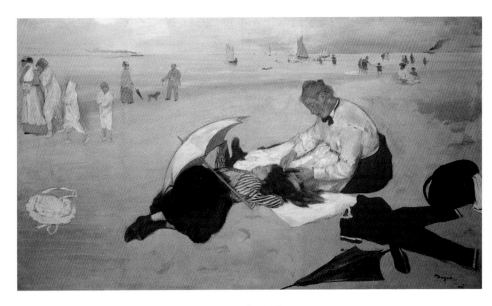

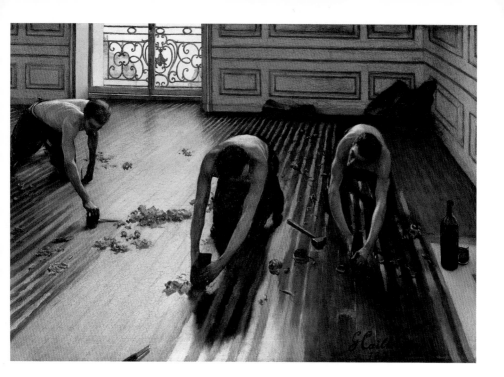

grey and reddish orange, it shows shipping, wharfs and dockland factories veiled in morning haze. It is an unromantic sunrise, effectively
structured in obedience to the golden section (p. 113). When a title was
needed in a hurry for the catalogue of the exhibition we shall presently
be discussing, Monet supposedly suggested simply *Impression*, and the
catalogue editor, Renoir's brother Edouard, added an explanatory *Sunrise*. The artist was not to know that in this way – via dismissive criticism
which seized upon the first word – he had given the entire movement its
name, and had made the painting itself a key, pivotal work in the history
of modern art.

Gustave Caillebotte
The Floor Strippers, 1875
Les raboteurs de parquet
Oil on canvas, 102 x 146.5 cm
Berhaut 28. Paris, Musée d'Orsay

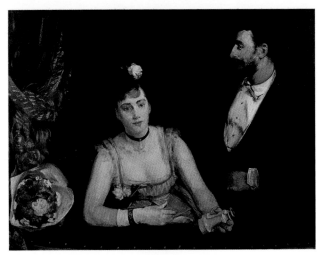

Eva Gonzalès
A Box at the Théâtre des Italiens, c. 1874
Une loge aux Italiens
Oil on canvas, 98 x 130 cm
Paris, Musée d'Orsay

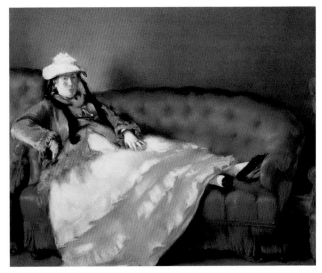

Edouard Manet
Madame Manet on a Divan, 1874
Mme Manet sur un divan
Pastel on paper on canvas, 65 x 61 cm
Rouart/Wildenstein II,3
Paris, Musée du Louvre, Cabinet des Dessins

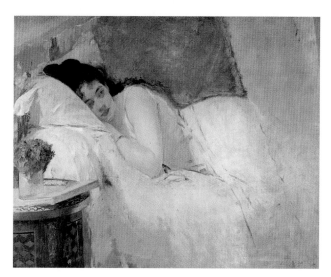

Eva Gonzalès
Morning Awakening, 1876
Le réveil
Oil on canvas, 81.5 x 100 cm
Bremen, Kunsthalle Bremen

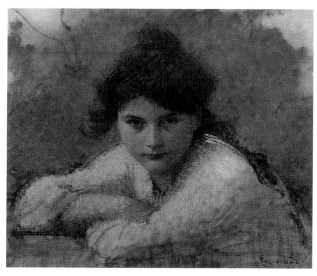

Eugène Vidal
Girl Resting on her Arms
Jeune fille accoudée
Oil on canvas, 47 x 59 cm
Private collection

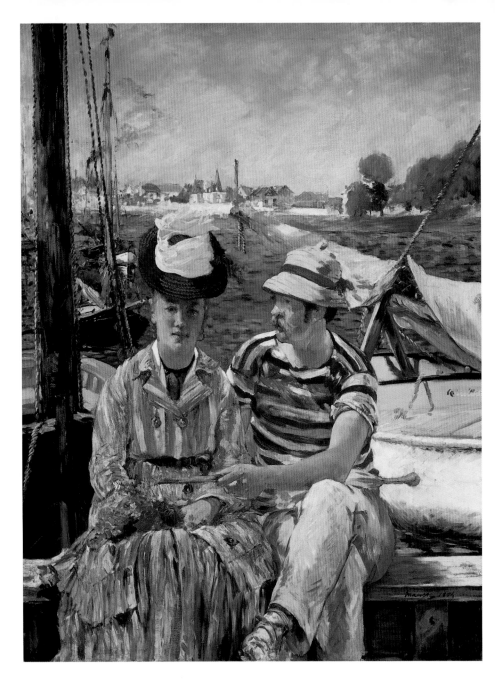

5 A Group Show and a Name

Only a few of our artists submitted paintings to the 1873 Salon. Of these few, only Manet and Morisot were successful. The Salon des Refusés was repeated that year; but the more important development was that the thought of making one's way independently of the Salon was gaining substantial ground. Durand-Ruel's interest, and his catalogue, fed the hope that dealers would establish the new art. Monet, for example, had had a good year in 1872. Durand-Ruel had bought at least 29 pictures from him, and there were other buyers too, bringing his total income to 12,000 francs. Monet now employed a gardener to tend the flower beds he painted, and he no longer needed to starve his appetite for good food and drink.[96]

The economic crisis of 1873 muted the artists' hopes, despite the fact that good prices were still being paid for paintings in early 1874. In the latter half of 1873 they returned in heated debates to the old idea of an independent exhibitors' association. Certain artists such as Manet and critics such as Théodore Duret (1838–1927), who had started to advocate the new art, still considered the struggle for a place in the Salon to be the crux. Others, among them the politically left-wing critic Castagnary, argued the case for autonomous shows that bypassed the jury system. Renoir drew upon his experience working for the crafts trade when they discussed organizational and financial issues. Pissarro made enquiries into the statutes of a bakers' co-operative in Pontoise. These statutes ultimately served as a model for those of the new co-operative, the Société anonyme des artistes (or, as it was given on the cover of the first exhibition catalogue, the Société anonyme des artistes-peintres, sculpteurs, graveurs, etc.). The society was constituted on 27 December 1873, registered with the relevant authorities, and announced to the public in "La Chronique des Arts et de la Curiosité" of 17 January 1874.

Every member had to pay at least 60 francs a year. This fee earned the right to exhibit two works, the hanging of which would be decided by lot. Ten per cent of sales proceeds were to be returned to the co-operative's capital. The group busily sought further members to strengthen the financial base, and even placed advertisements using the names of artists who in the event declined to join. Names that were recognised by the Salon and valued by the public were particularly welcome, to consolidate the co-operative's credibility. This was a quite new strategy for bringing

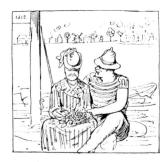

"We thank M. Manet for introducing a touch of humour into this rather dismal Salon." Cartoon by Bertall in "L'Illustration", 29 May 1875

Edouard Manet
Argenteuil, 1874
Oil on canvas, 148.9 x 115 cm
Rouart/Wildenstein I,221
Tournai, Musée des Beaux-Arts

art to the public's attention. There was no joint programme in writing, nor was there ever to be one. Degas suggested calling the group "La Capucine" (nasturtium) – from the seven or eight exhibition rooms at 35 Boulevard des Capucines – but the proposal was not adopted. The exhibition space belonged to Félix Tournachon called Nadar (1820–1910), the highly-regarded photographer, who had recently transferred his business to other premises. It is not altogether clear whether he gave the group the use of the rooms gratis or for a fee of 2,020 francs; since he himself was in financial straits, the latter is the likelier alternative.

On 15 April 1874, a fortnight before the official Salon opened, the Société's exhibition opened for a month, from 10 a.m. to 6 p.m. as well as 8 till 10 p.m. Admission cost one franc, as it did to the Salon, and the inaccurate catalogue half that amount. Thirty-one artists exhibited, and the catalogue ran to 165 entries, some of them multiple. Contrary to the Société's statutes, all of the artists exhibited more works than they had paid to exhibit. The show was well attended, by about 3,500 people in all, and earned a slight profit, at least on first inspection; at the end of the year, however, every member would have had to pay in at 184.50 francs to cover debts and restock the co-operative's capital; and so, on 17 December 1874, the thirteen members present at a general meeting agreed to wind up the Société. It had not been a successful form of organization. Its fame in the history of art was assured, though. And in the short term it confirmed the artistic resolve and persistence of the most important artists.[97]

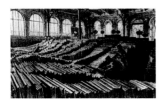

The paintings rejected by the Salon jury in 1863 were deposited in the Palace of Industry

Half of the Société artists (sixteen) did not repeat the experiment. Apart from Monet's old father-figure Boudin, and a delicate follower of Corot, landscape painter Stanislas Lépine (1835–1892), whose paintings (pp. 68, 202) had long since found an audience, these were all artists who, despite subsequent Salon exhibition, were to earn no places of any significance in the story of art; and, above all, they did not paint in an Impressionist way. Among them were Antoine Attendu (1845–1905), a painter of still lifes; landscape painters Louis Latouche (1829–1884), Auguste de Molins (1821–1890), Mulot-Durivage (1838–1944) and Léopold Robert; and the enamel painter Alfred Meyer (1832–1904). Astruc, the painter and sculptor, poet and art critic, had a good dozen works in the show, mainly watercolours, several of them dealing with the fashion in orientalism (p. 92). Gustave Colin (1828–1910), whose subjects followed the Spanish vogue, had been consigned to the Salon des Refusés along with Manet in 1863, and had been praised by Zola for his lighting effects. The show included sculpture by the aged Louis Marie Ottin (1811–1890), who exhibited there because he was an inveterate anti-establishmentarian. In the days of the Commune he had been on the committee of the Paris Artists' Association led by Courbet. Another aged painter, the realistic genre artist Adolphe-Félix Cals (1810–1880), a working-class Parisian now living in Honfleur and associated with Boudin (pp. 124, 125), also had progressive views on politics and art.[98] He remained loyal to the exhibition venture.

Certain painters and graphic artists took part for reasons of personal

Claude Monet
The Road Bridge at Argenteuil, 1874
Le pont routier, Argenteuil
Oil on canvas, 60 x 79.7 cm
Wildenstein 312
Washington, National Gallery of Art

Claude Monet
The Bridge at Argenteuil, 1874
Le pont d'Argenteuil
Oil on canvas, 60 x 80 cm
Wildenstein 311. Paris, Musée d'Orsay

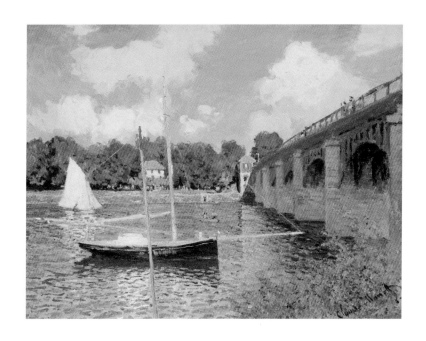

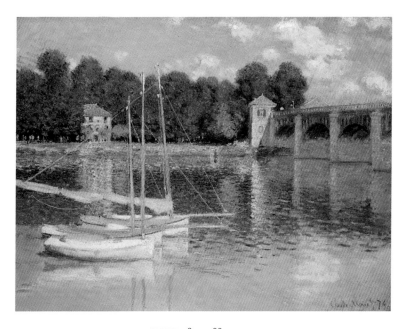

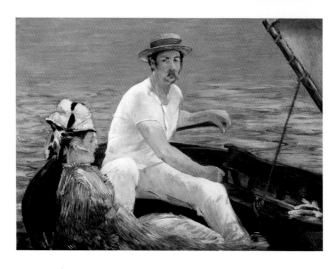

Edouard Manet
Boating, 1874
En bateau
Oil on canvas, 97.2 x 130.2 cm
Rouart/Wildenstein I,223
New York, The Metropolitan Museum of Art

loyalty. One of those recruited by Degas was Giuseppe De Nittis, a successful Italian who happened to be vexed at official art and his dealer, Goupil, at the time. When his Salon success returned, he no longer saw any point in participating in an obscure venture. The versatile genre and landscape painter, etcher and sculptor Vicomte Ludovic-Napoléon Lepic (1839–1889), whose portrait Degas painted more than once, stayed with the group for the second exhibition, as did Béliard, the Pontoise landscape artist, whom his friend Pissarro had won over.

In 1874, the painters who were to remain the essential core of the exhibition group put characteristic works in the show, works typical of the new art's approach. Some of these are today considered major Impressionist works, such as dance and racecourse scenes (pp. 70, 86, 114) and women ironing by Degas. Monet had landscapes (p. 112) and street scenes (p. 102), as well as the famous *Impression: Sunrise* (p. 113). Morisot had some of her finest early works (pp. 88, 89, 108), paintings light in touch that show a relaxed yet attentive, meaningful quality in human conduct. Her first teacher, the old Joseph Guichard, found fault with her pictures for their light transparence; he told her that oil was unsuitable for kinds of work best done in watercolour; and he felt she would be ruining what she had hitherto accomplished, the respect she had earned, if she exhibited in Société company. Like Sisley, Pissarro was not represented by his strongest work (pp. 116/117); and Cézanne prompted widespread indignation with *A Modern Olympia*. Guillaumin and Degas's old school friend Henri Rouart (1833–1912), an engineer and talented amateur artist who played a leading part in the co-operative and exhibited his work (on which too little research has yet been done)[99] in the later Impressionist exhibitions too, also exhibited landscapes. Among Renoir's work in the show was *The Theatre Box* (p. 128), done in opulently nuanced colours, a freshly felt homage to female beauty. Doubtless

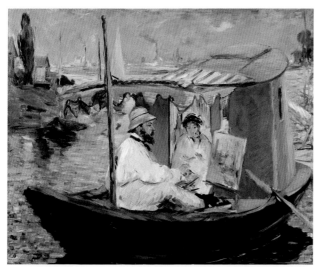

Edouard Manet
Claude Monet and his Wife in his Studio Boat, 1874
Claude Monet et sa femme dans son studio flottant
Oil on canvas, 82.5 x 100.5 cm
Rouart/Wildenstein I,210
Munich, Bayerische Staatsgemäldesammlungen,
Neue Pinakothek

Claude Monet
The Studio Boat, 1874
Le bateau-atelier
Oil on canvas, 50 x 64 cm
Wildenstein 323
Otterlo, Kröller-Müller Museum

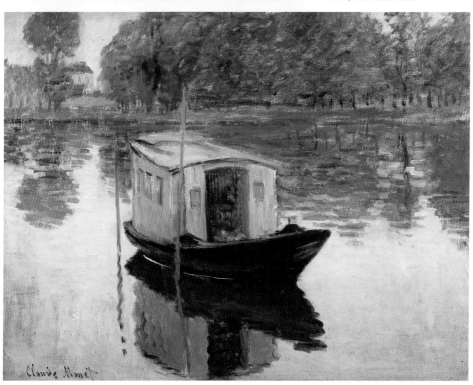

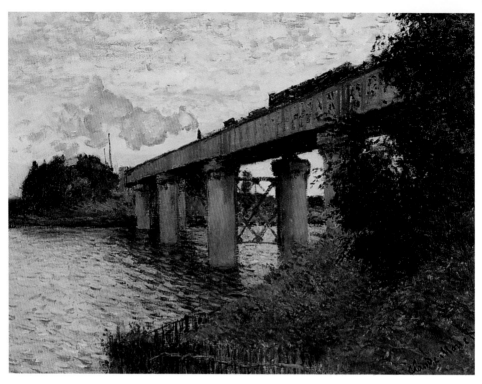

Claude Monet
The Railway Bridge, Argenteuil, 1873
Le pont du chemin de fer, Argenteuil
Oil on canvas, 54 x 71 cm
Wildenstein 319. Paris, Musée d'Orsay

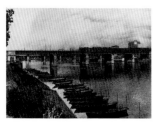

The Railway Bridge over the Seine at Asnières,
before 1900

Renoir was glad to be paid 425 francs for this painting by Père Martin, a paint and picture dealer; Renoir urgently needed the money to pay rent arrears. By way of comparison, a curious little picture by Academy member Jean-Léon Gérôme (1824–1904) was extremely successful at the Salon and earned Goupil the dealer 45,000 francs.

The exhibition on the Boulevard des Capucines was noted to some extent by the critics, especially in left-wing or opposition, republican publications.[100] Most of the conservative press preferred not to give a platform to the opponents of official arts policy. Naturally the significant stylistic differences amongst the exhibitors were remarked on, but the greatest amount of attention was given to the new aesthetics, be it in praise or damnation. Silvestre, who had written on them the previous year in Durand-Ruel's catalogue, used the political term "revoltés" of them in the republican "L'Opinion Nationale" (22 April). A week later, in the widely read conservative "La Presse" (29 April), Emile Cardon seized upon this and went on to deride the artists as a "School of the impression". The famous Salon des Refusés (did he mean 1863 or 1873?) had been a veritable Louvre in comparison, he declared.

The term "Impressionists" was first used four days earlier (25 April 1874) in the heading of an article in the satirical magazine "Le Charivari".

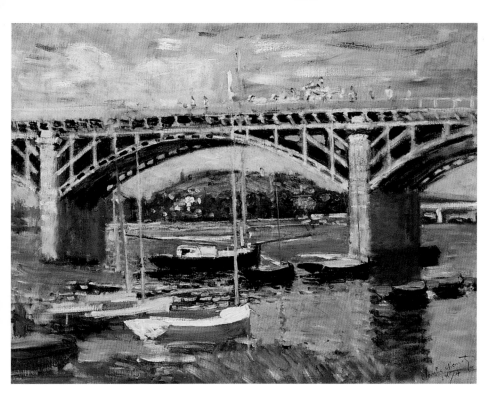

Claude Monet
The Bridge at Argenteuil, 1874
Le pont d'Argenteuil
Oil on canvas, 60 x 81.3 cm
Wildenstein 313
Munich, Bayerische Staatsgemäldesammlungen,
Neue Pinakothek

The great Honoré Daumier (1808–1879) had published lithographs in the magazine till he went blind in 1872. Now it was the elderly copper engraver, genre painter and popular playwright Louis Leroy (1812–1885) who scoffed at the exhibition. He claimed to have visited the show with a pupil of Ingres who, confronted with Monet's *Impression: Sunrise* and still more his *Boulevard des Capucines* and the work of Cézanne, had regularly gone out of his mind. Crying, "Eheu, I am an impression on legs, the avenging palette knife", he did a (barbaric!) Indian dance, Leroy reported. Of greater weight than the squib that earned Leroy his immortality was Castagnary's approving critique in "Le Siècle" four days later (29 April). Castagnary singled out as "Impressionists" (in the heading, too) Pissarro, Monet, Sisley, Renoir, Degas and Morisot, carefully differentiating their individual styles. For him, they were Impressionists "in the sense that they do not reproduce a landscape but rather convey the sensation produced by the landscape". This, he said, was the reason why the word "landscape" was replaced by the word "impression" in titles.

The term, which remains "in itself imprecise" (Rewald), has been repeatedly challenged or newly defined, but it has stuck. It is a label of convenience, a useful and flexible convention that has long since become indispensable, like most terms that describe movements or styles in art.

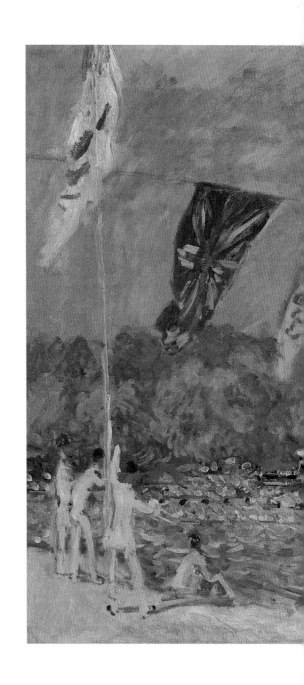

Alfred Sisley
The Regatta at Molesey, 1874
Les régates à Molesey
Oil on canvas, 66 x 91.5 cm
Daulte 126. Paris, Musée d'Orsay

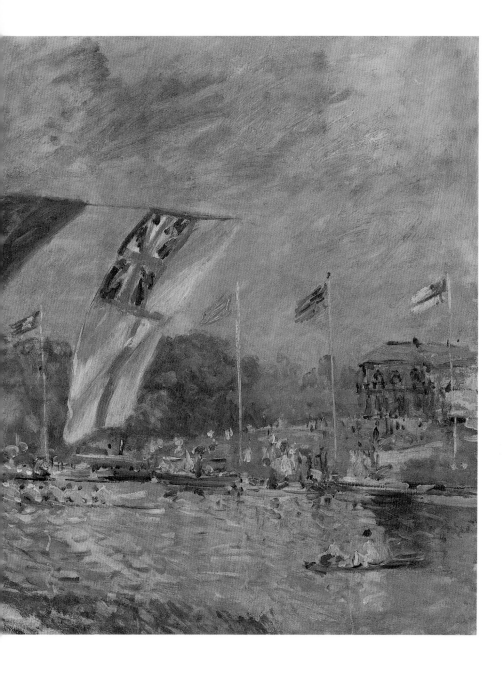

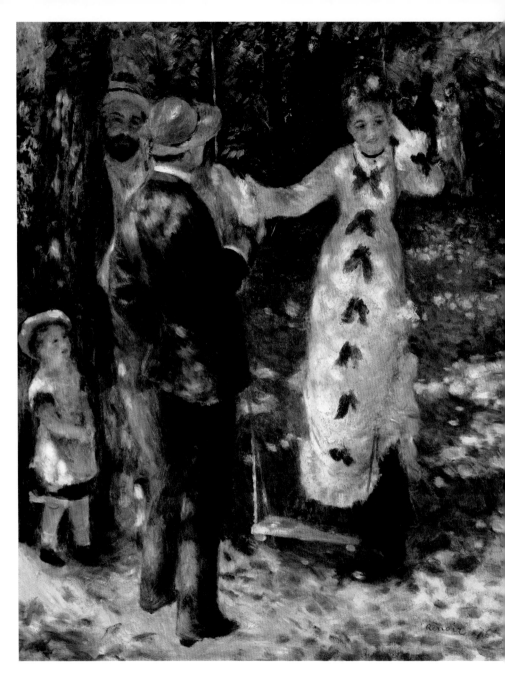

6 From Self-Confidence to Doubt

The core of the shortlived Société, most of them in their mid-thirties, had reason to feel satisfied with the attention they had attracted. They would not be deflected from their ideas by dismissive criticism. And indeed they found that Manet was coming closer to their own position, although in terms of exhibition strategy he agreed to differ. Zealously they went to work, and were impressively productive; though, generally speaking, their financial position deteriorated. The debates concerning approaches that were likeliest to succeed did not cease; and the Impressionists were not spared the problems all artistic groups have had to face in modern times, negotiating compromises between individuality, competitiveness and a group spirit.

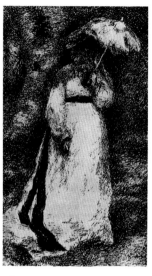

Pierre-Auguste Renoir
Lise with a Parasol, 1867
Lise à l'ombrelle dans la forêt
Pen and ink on paper
Whereabouts unknown

Evolving a New Style

Following their show in Nadar's rooms, the Impressionists continued to paint energetically in the style they had adopted, and in the next few years they explored all the possibilities of their approach. Their attention centred on the colours of objects in open-air light, and ways of conveying those colours by juxtaposing dabs (*taches*) of paint as unmixed and bright as possible. The artists definitively parted company with the idea that there was a value distinction to be drawn between completed paintings and sketches. Indeed, they considered the sketch more truthful and better because of its spontaneous freshness. From later comments we know they wanted the painter to be "only an eye", to do nothing but see, and not to think. They neither wished to be constrained by rules nor did they care for contextual and evaluative processes that concerned their subjects as parts of a reality beyond the painting.

This conception of the meaning of what an artist does was of course not universally shared among them, nor did it remain uninfluenced by other considerations of the didactic functions of art. The realisation that the quality of a work of art was independent of its subject – articulated in the 1860s and defiantly asserted against academic hierarchical views of subject matter – by no means implied that artists were not free to make a selection of specific themes and motifs. And in fact Impressionism did

Pierre-Auguste Renoir
The Swing, 1876
La balançoire
Oil on canvas, 92 x 73 cm
Daulte 202. Paris, Musée d'Orsay

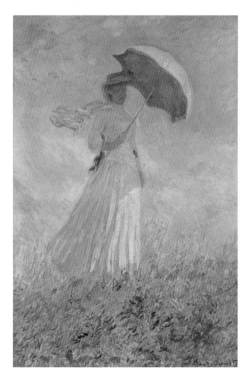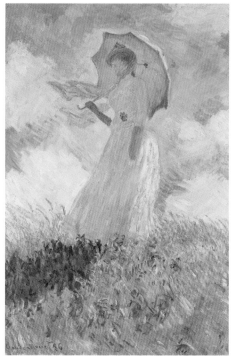

Claude Monet
Lady with Parasol (facing right), 1886
La femme à l'ombrelle (vers la droite)
Oil on canvas, 131 x 88 cm
Wildenstein 1076. Paris, Musée d'Orsay

Claude Monet
Lady with Parasol (facing left), 1886
La femme à l'ombrelle (vers la gauche)
Oil on canvas, 131 x 88 cm
Wildenstein 1077. Paris, Musée d'Orsay

Right:
Claude Monet
The Walk. Lady with Parasol, 1875
La promenade. La femme à l'ombrelle
Oil on canvas, 100 x 81 cm
Wildenstein 381
Washington, National Gallery of Art,
Mr. and Mrs. Paul Mellon Collection

have an iconography of its own. The artists naturally knew that for most people the subjects of artworks are a vital part of the whole, and affect their accessibility and saleability. It is all the more remarkable, then, that they made so few concessions on fundamentals.

Pissarro persisted in painting the same unprepossessing views of Pontoise and the vicinity: the Hermitage, the Côte des Bœufs, or the track that led through Le Chou, on the banks of the Oise, to Auvers (p. 174). On a number of occasions he stayed for some time with his painter friend Ludovic Piette (1826–1877) at his farm, Montfoucault, near Melleray, in the quite different landscape of the Mayenne. Piette did a small gouache portrait of Pissarro that gives a vivid sense of how the latter worked: gazing with attentive concentration, his whole body tensed, he is standing in the open at an easel shaded by a small parasol. Piette, who was to die shortly, painted in a manner similar to Pissarro's, but with a more meticulous attention to detail and without Pissarro's structural energy. Pissarro recruited him for the third Impressionist exhibition.

Cézanne and Guillaumin regularly consulted Pissarro for his advice. Their approach was closer to his insistence on constructing a picture out of colour, linear, and plastic or spatial components. Cézanne would depart radically from this line from time to time, painting imaginary figural

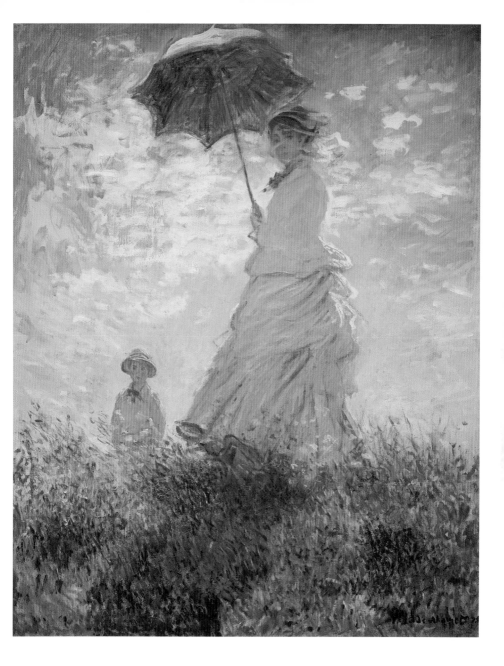

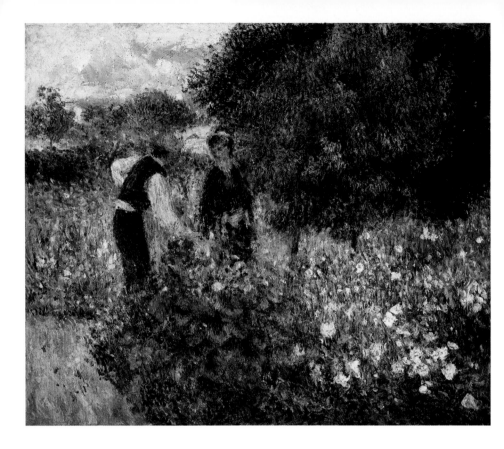

Pierre-Auguste Renoir
Conversation with the Gardener, c. 1875
La cueillette des fleurs
Oil on canvas, 51 x 63 cm
Chicago, The Art Institute of Chicago

scenes or indulging his sexual obsessions. At that period he also copied a painting by his old fellow-student Guillaumin, a scene showing workers shovelling building sand on the Quai de Bercy in Paris.[101] Guillaumin's way of working was more relaxed and dexterous than Cézanne's, and more geared to the fleeting moment.

Pissarro's achievement in terms of the artistic appropriation of given reality can be nicely seen in two views of the same subject that he curiously did not exhibit in a group show (pp. 174, 175). They are landscapes in late winter or early spring, gentle and bright, the dabs of paint evoking a veil of moist freshness, the middle ground consisting of whitish yellow and red houses and roofs positioned like crystals on a slope. In the foreground, a network of thin trees and branches stabilizes the visual surface and creates optical distance. The verticals are emphatic in the vertical-format picture, while in the other curved lines lean to the sides. Pissarro has harmonized his two concerns – to convey his powerful impression of Nature persuasively, and to establish a picture structured by human

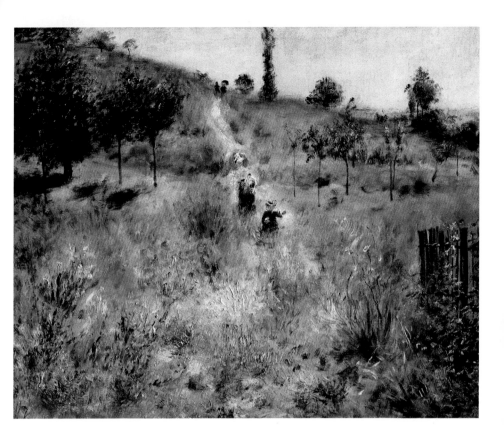

Pierre-Auguste Renoir
Country Footpath in the Summer, c. 1875
Chemin montant dans les hautes herbes
Oil on canvas, 60 x 74 cm
Paris, Musée d'Orsay

hand as an autonomous and complementary addition to visible reality – and he has done so in exemplary fashion.

And Pissarro was at that time in serious financial need, frequently depressed and insecure about his art, despite the collectors who took an interest. One of these was a friend of Guillaumin's youth, Eugène Murer (1845–1906), who was a pâtissier in Paris. In 1876/77 he invited his artist friends to dinner at his restaurant every Wednesday; they included Renoir, Sisley, Pissarro, Monet and Cézanne, as well as critics and free-thinking friends such as Tanguy and Gachet. On one occasion he tried to help Pissarro by raffling off paintings among his customers.

Till 1878 Monet lived at Argenteuil; then for three years he moved to Vétheuil, some fifty kilometres further from Paris, also on the Seine. The river landscape at Argenteuil and then Vétheuil was his favourite motif; his paintings of that landscape are probably the first we think of when we hear the word Impressionism. From 1872 on, Monet had painted on the river bank at Argenteuil, looking either up- or downriver (p. 91).

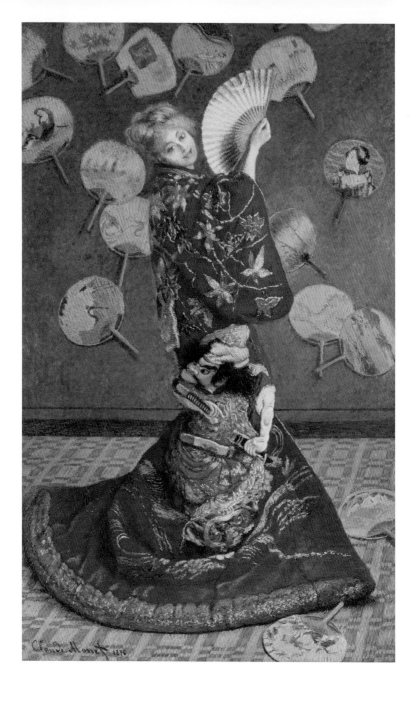

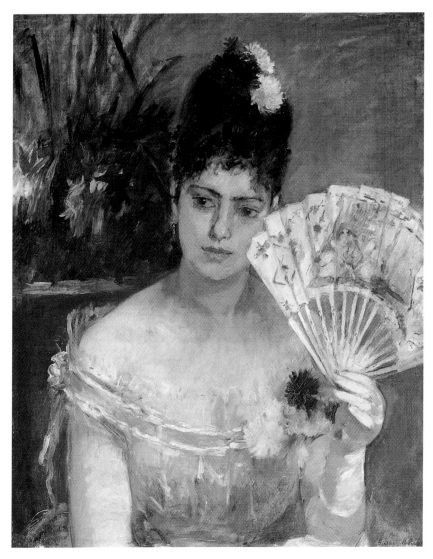

Left:
Claude Monet
Madame Monet in Japanese Costume, 1875
La Japonaise (Camille Monet)
Oil on canvas, 231 x 142 cm
Wildenstein 387
Boston, Museum of Fine Arts

Above:
Berthe Morisot
At the Ball, 1875
Jeune fille au bal
Oil on canvas, 62 x 52 cm
Bataille/Wildenstein 60
Paris, Musée Marmottan

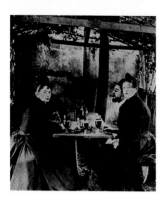

In the garden of the Moulin de la Galette:
Henri de Toulouse-Lautrec with friends

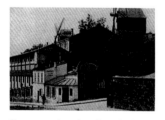

The entrance to the garden at the Moulin de la
Galette, Rue Lepic, c. 1885

Pierre-Auguste Renoir
Le Moulin de la Galette, 1876
Oil on canvas, 78.7 x 113 cm
Daulte 208. Tokyo, private collection

Pierre-Auguste Renoir
Le Moulin de la Galette, 1876
Oil on canvas, 131 x 175 cm
Daulte 209. Paris, Musée d'Orsay

According to which way he chose, the trees cluster as verticals at the left or right edge, their shadows on the path parallel horizontals. Together with the upright masts of sailing boats, and horizontal brush strokes or a bridge on the horizon (generally intersecting the visual space at a position consonant with the golden section), this Monet riverbank system evolved its own simple set of coordinates to create a firm pictorial structure. Within this structure, dabs of paint or individual brush strokes might be positioned in a more relaxed way, to recreate the motion of light on a landscape, the adumbrated figures of walkers, or the drift of white clouds across a blue sky. The two road and rail bridges rebuilt after the war were another subject Monet repeatedly painted, and here he could experiment with the spatial effects of diagonals (pp. 137, 140, 141). Engineering achievements using iron, and steaming railway trains or the flow of traffic across a road bridge, also introduced an element of modernity into Monet's landscape. On just one occasion he introduced a variation on the bridge theme, painting the Asnières road bridge in dim grey light, and in front of it workers unloading coal barges (1875; Paris, private collection). But this excursion into social realism remained "une note à part", as Monet himself later put it – a motif he did not pursue further in his artistic view of the world and creative strategy.[101]

Monet was naturally more drawn to scenes of walking in Nature (p. 147) or family bliss in a garden of flowers (p. 219). But he did not allow Paris to disappear from his view. In 1877 he decided to explore the visual attractions of a railway station filled with smoke and steam. There are amusing anecdotes describing Monet, then far from well off and harshly treated by the critics, turning up stylishly dressed and self-assured to talk the stationmaster at the Gare Saint-Lazare into having locomotives generate more steam, or even keeping trains waiting so that the pictures he, Monet, painted would be more atmospheric (pp. 170, 171). And then on 30 June 1878 a new and intoxicating mass of colour presented itself to his eyes. On that day, a further World Fair was opened in Paris, a first occasion for national celebration since the humiliation of 1871. Monet painted the flags and banners in Rue Saint-Denis (p. 177); the slogans "Vive la France" and "Vive la République" will surely have found an answering echo in his own bosom.

Renoir was especially close to Monet, both personally and in his aesthetics. For him, though, the human figure rather than landscape was always the main focus of attention. He lived in Paris and liked visiting his friend in Argenteuil. Often he would idle among the trippers and rowers at La Grenouillère, between Bougival and Croissy, or on the nearby Seine island of Chatou. There he particularly enjoyed stopping by to see Fournaise the innkeeper and his beautiful daughter. His glowing, relaxed paintings, visibly prompted by a moment actually experienced and carefully observed, recorded that world as a place where happiness and harmony were attainable. His people look contented. For his female models he always sought out girls of ampler proportions in his Montmartre neighbourhood, many of them sempstresses by trade. They liked posing, and had nothing against indulging a lover who could pay,

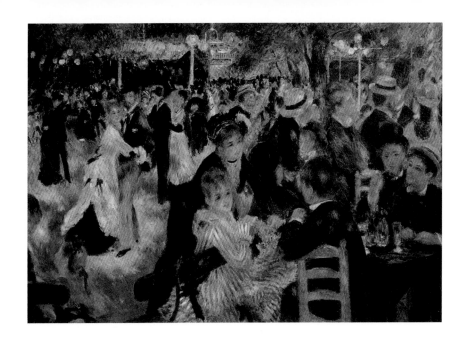

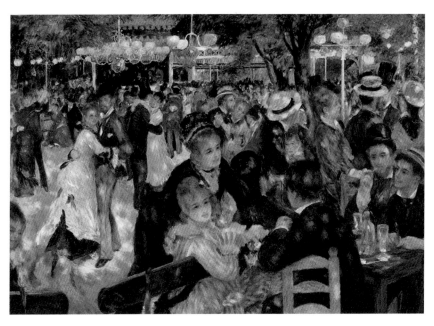

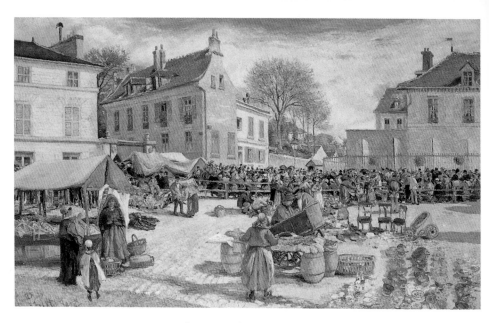

Ludovic Piette
The Market outside Pontoise Town Hall, 1876
Place de l'hôtel de ville à Pontoise, un jour
de marché
Oil on canvas, 111 x 186 cm
Pontoise, Musée Pissarro

either. Renoir liked them. Without troubling over questions of morality or society, he glorified the beauty and sensuality he saw in them.

His admiration for French 18th-century masters such as Jean-Antoine Watteau (1684–1721), François Boucher (1703–1770) and Fragonard –

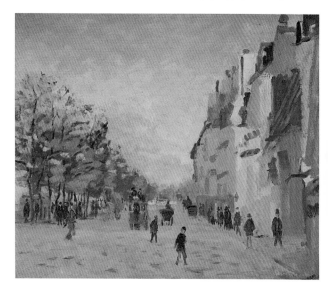

Armand Guillaumin
Quai de la Gare, Snow (Quai de Bercy), c. 1875
Quai de la Gare, effet de neige (Quai de Bercy)
Oil on canvas, 50.5 x 61.2 cm
Serret/Fabiani 29. Paris, Musée d'Orsay

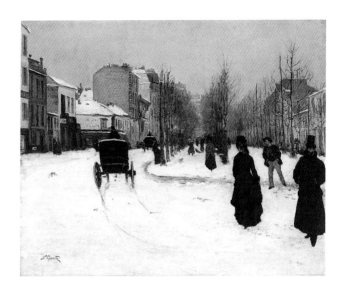

Norbert Goeneutte
The Boulevard de Clichy under Snow, 1876
Le Boulevard de Clichy sous la neige
Oil on canvas, 60 x 73.5 cm
London, The Tate Gallery

whom he had copied in his own youthful days as a porcelain painter –
lay behind erotic pictures such as *Anna* (p. 163). This nude is entirely
natural, neither coquettish, nor provocative, nor with that cool lasci-
viousness with which Gérôme invested his enamel-sleek odalisques in
oriental harem scenes at about the same time. Renoir's colourist subtlety
tenderly recorded nuanced shades in the flesh of this woman sitting on
the edge of a lilac patterned armchair in front of a sketchy background
of what seem to be white undergarments against darker plum black. The

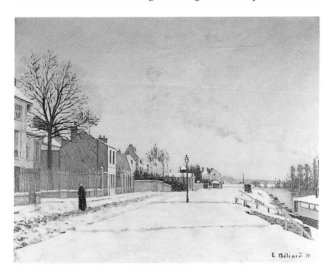

Edouard Béliard
Banks of the Oise, 1875
Bords de l'Oise
Oil on canvas, 72 x 91 cm
Etampes, Musée Municipal d'Etampes

interplay of lighter and darker areas is as important in lending the composition its baroque dynamism as are the turned and arrested position of the body or the red highlighting on the chair, lips and the corners of the eyes. In summer 1875, in his garden, Renoir had already painted the same model (who also appears in Manet's *Nana*, p. 160, as well as in pictures by other painters such as Gervex). In the earlier painting, the woman, wearing a ring and bracelet, has been enhanced aesthetically: Renoir shows her in the posture of the famed Aphrodite of Knidos. His eye was mainly concerned with the shimmering effects of light and coloured shadow falling through the foliage. This is humanity seen in harmony with Nature but simultaneously mythologized by the allusion to antiquity. For contemporaries, this style of painting was so innovatory that the influential critic Albert Wolff (1835–1891) raged in "Le Figaro" (3 April 1875) that the picture showed a piece of rotting flesh with the green and violet signs of putrefaction upon it.

That same year, in a somewhat larger canvas peopled with a large number of figures, Renoir presented the social gaiety and Parisian lifestyle that he endorsed as an artist. *Le Moulin de la Galette* (p. 153) shows a beer and dance garden in Montmartre: two disused windmills had been converted into bars, and gas lighting installed in the garden. Ordinary working people, young artists, and men down from the city to find a girl, would go there at weekends or in the evenings. Renoir's picture has all the charm of a chance impression but is in fact well composed and planned out. The figures in the space, which is marked off at the front by seat backs, form circular groups. Their gazes connect them or link us in the outside world into their world. The white lanterns mesh a grid of coordinates across the canvas. Even dabs of colour establish correspondences across the composition, and thus unity in the carefree confusion. In the blue, pink and white striped dresses of some of the girls we see a revival of 18th-century fashion – just as the entire scene is reminiscent of a *fête galante* by Watteau. In order to paint the scene as he conceived it, Renoir posed a number of his friends and models. They helped him carry his cumbersome easel and large canvas from the nearby studio to the gardens, where he then painted on the spot, in the open.

A large, unforced sketch (Copenhagen, Ordgrupsgaard Samlingen) served to fix the composition. The order in which two further versions were done is still subject to dispute.[103] A sketchier version of medium size (p. 153, top) initially belonged to Renoir's new admirer, Victor Chocquet; in 1990, it was sold at Sotheby's in New York for US$ 78, 100, 100 to the Japanese paper manufacturer Ryoei Saito – the second-highest price ever paid for a work of art at that date. In almost every detail it matches the larger version, which was quickly bought by Caillebotte and later passed to the French state with his estate. It seems unlikely that Renoir needed to paint a version in an intermediate size in order to establish the final, large painting. At that time his efforts were all directed to fixing open-air impressions, and work on the big version at a later date, in the winter, in his studio (as has been suggested), would have run counter to those endeavours. Nor would he have needed the help of

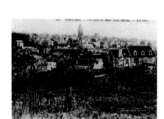

Pontoise. Postcard, c. 1890

Camille Pissarro
Harvest at Montfoucault, 1876
La moisson à Montfoucault
Oil on canvas, 65 x 92.5 cm
Pissarro/Venturi 364. Paris, Musée d'Orsay

Camille Pissarro
Rye Fields at Pontoise, Côte des Mathurins, 1877
Les seigles, Pontoise, Côte des Mathurins
Oil on canvas, 60 x 73 cm
Pissarro/Venturi 406. Japan, private collection

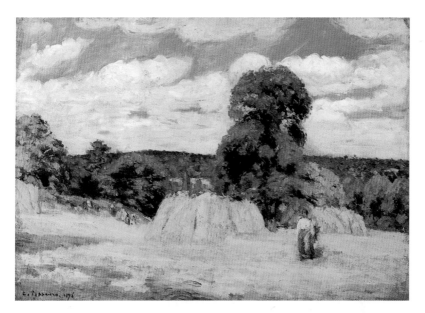

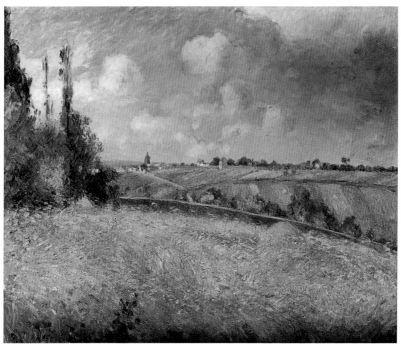

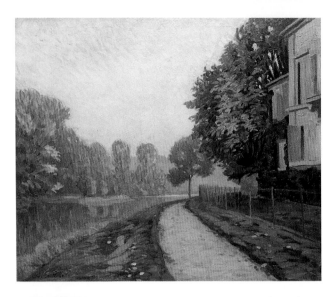

Gustave Caillebotte
Riverbank in Morning Haze, 1875
Bord de rivière, effet de brume matinale
Oil on canvas, 65 x 46 cm
Berhaut 18. Private collection

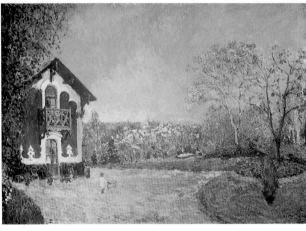

Alfred Sisley
Louveciennes, 1876
Vue de Louveciennes
Oil on canvas, 65 x 92 cm
Daulte 208
New York, The Metropolitan Museum of Art

others to move his picture and easel (a recorded fact) if he had been engaged on the small painting. So the likeliest assumption must be that he did a repeat copy of the big painting in a sketchier format for Chocquet, in a size that was better suited to hanging in Chocquet's home. Paintings on this subject of friendly chat or lovers' talks and open-air conviviality were to recur in Renoir's work of the late 1870s (p. 144), alongside portraits for a growing circle of patrons and genre work.

In the 1881 painting *The Luncheon of the Boating Party* (p. 220) we have the crowning work in Renoir's series on social occasions and

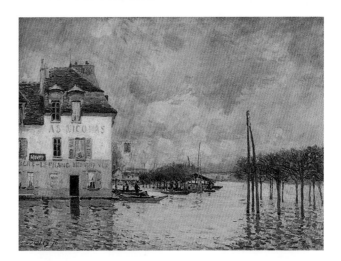

Alfred Sisley
Flood at Port-Marly, 1876
L'inondation à Port-Marly
Oil on canvas, 60 x 81 cm
Daulte 240. Paris, Musée d'Orsay

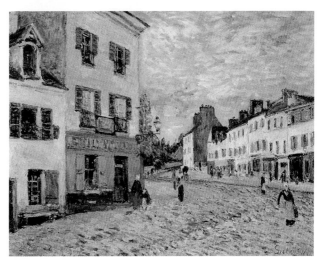

Alfred Sisley
Market Place at Marly, 1876
Place de marché à Marly
Oil on canvas, 50 x 65 cm
Daulte 199. Mannheim, Kunsthalle Mannheim

leisure. Renoir's old friend from military days, Baron (formerly Captain) Barbier, assembled the models for this festive scene at Fournaise's. Once again the assembly of people dressed either for sport or as city pleasure-seekers resolves into small groups, couples, or solo figures apparently lost in thought. The positioning of the figures gathers upon a diagonal line from bottom left to top right. Unconsciously, we always register this line as an active, rising thing in paintings; it is this diagonal that arrests our gaze and leads us into the picture. But Renoir wants a unified surface impression, and so he also ensures that there is a greater ease in the

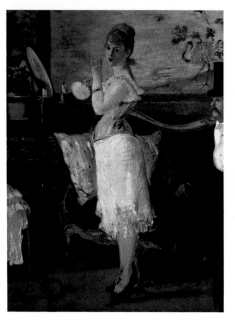
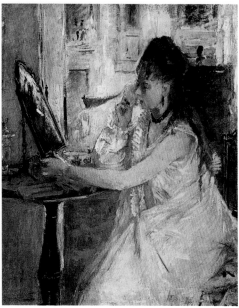

foreground figures and their postures; together with the luscious still life on the table, we feel we are in the presence of a superabundance of fine things, pleasant people and brilliant painting. The awning produces a diffused light in the picture instead of light from a single source. Renoir has forgone his dappled patchwork of sunlight and shadow. But even without the moulding possible to light effects, the two men in the fore-ground are solidly three-dimensional, without the sketchiness of Im-pressionist figures. It was the advent of a new approach in Renoir, to which we shall be returning.

In the summer of 1874, after the first Impressionist exhibition, Manet visited Monet and his family at Argenteuil. He painted the family: Monet busy gardening in the background, his wife Camille and their seven-year-old son Jean on the grass centre-picture. It is a relaxed composition, painted with the unstrained air of a sketch. Renoir was present too, and painted the same scene (Washington, National Gallery of Art). The story goes that Manet found Renoir's picture terrible and said the younger artist would never produce anything worthwhile; supposedly he even suggested to Monet that he ought to talk his friend out of painting. It is notable proof of the lack of homogeneity in the new movement, and the different qualities of personal relations among them, as well as of the mistakes artists can make when assessing each other's work.

Ironically enough, at that time Manet was entering fully into the Im-pressionist spirit of *plein-airisme*. He did a portrait of Monet with his wife on his blue-and-green-painted *bateau-atelier*, painting the banks of

Edouard Manet
Nana, 1877
Oil on canvas, 154 x 115 cm
Rouart/Wildenstein I,259
Hamburg, Hamburger Kunsthalle

Berthe Morisot
Young Woman Powdering Herself, 1877
Jeune femme se poudrant
Oil on canvas, 46 x 39 cm
Bataille/Wildenstein 72
Paris, Musée d'Orsay

Right:
Edgar Degas
At the Café-Concert: the Song of the Dog,
c. 1876/77
La «Chanson du Chien»
Gouache and pastel over monotype on paper,
57.5 x 45.4 cm. Lemoisne 380
New York, The Metropolitan Museum of Art

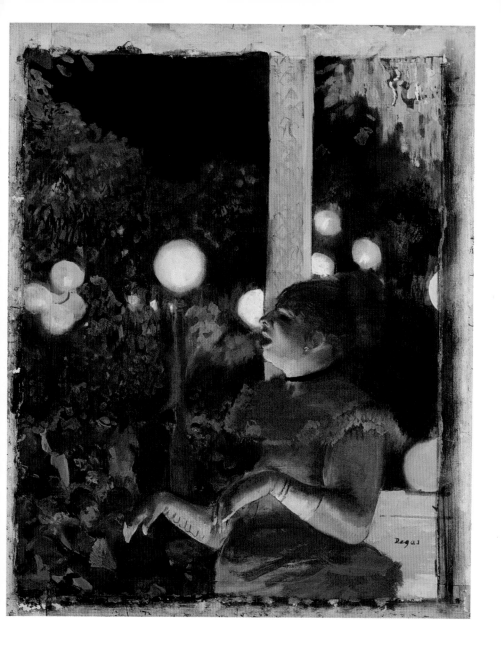

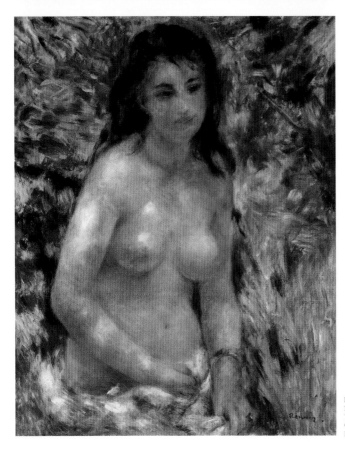

Pierre-Auguste Renoir
Nude in the Sunlight, c. 1875/76
Torse de femme au soleil
Oil on canvas, 81 x 64.5 cm
Daulte 201. Paris, Musée d'Orsay

the Seine and the boats (p. 139). The mast, slightly off the vertical, and the curves of the boat and awning convey a sense that the boat is rocking slightly in the water; the water itself, like the figures and bank, is painted in a light, open manner. Two other, larger canvases that show the figures from a closer position – open-air genre portraits rather than landscape paintings, in which the people establish eye contact with us – bring home the intense dedication Manet brought to his work that August in Argenteuil, a location that had normally (since 1869) been primarily Monet's and Renoir's domain. The vertical-format painting, the larger of the two (p. 134), is structurally the tighter thanks to its linear components, and is also the richest in motifs and forms. The sketchy horizontal-format picture (p. 138) uses large spaces of glowing colour. We do not know who the women in these paintings are; the man was either Manet's brother-in-law, the Dutch painter Rodolphe Leenhoff, or Baron Barbier, whom we have mentioned in connection with Renoir.

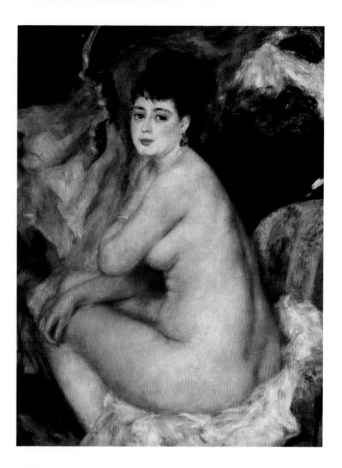

Pierre-Auguste Renoir
Female Nude (Anna), 1876
Nue (Anna)
Oil on canvas, 92 x 73 cm
Daulte 213
Moscow, Pushkin Museum of Fine Art

Manet was now committed to Impressionism and was a strong advocate of Monet in particular. In 1875, together with Duret, an art critic friend, he debated secretly buying ten or twenty of Monet's paintings without the latter knowing the identity of the purchasers; he was so short of money that he was offering his work for a mere 100 francs a canvas. It would help Monet, and might well be a profitable deal for Manet and Duret. In 1877 he tried (albeit in vain) to convince another critic, Wolff, of the value of Monet's art and that of his associates. In the course of this attempt he even painted a portrait of Wolff, though there were differences of opinion over the picture.

The following year, Manet's long-standing interest in modern city life prompted him to make a proposal for a major work of public art. He wrote to the mayor of Paris suggesting that the council chambers in the new town hall be painted with a variety of compositions "representing the belly of Paris, to use a current expression that describes my aim nicely

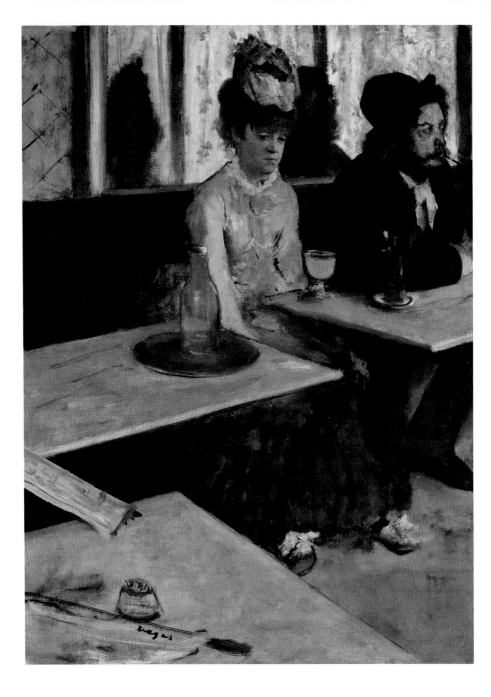

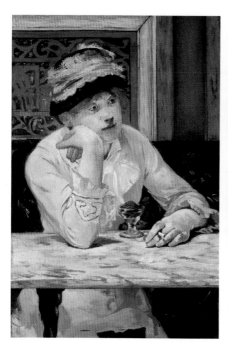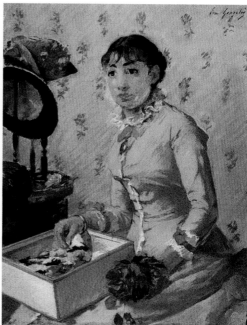

Edouard Manet
Plum Brandy, c. 1877/78
La prune
Oil on canvas, 73.6 x 50.2 cm
Rouart/Wildenstein I,282
Washington, National Gallery of Art

Eva Gonzalès
The Milliner, c. 1877
La modiste
Gouache and pastel on canvas, 45 x 37 cm
Chicago, The Art Institute of Chicago

Left:
Edgar Degas
The Absinth Drinker, 1876
L'Absinthe (Au café)
Oil on canvas, 92 x 68 cm
Lemoisne 393. Paris, Musée d'Orsay

– the various pursuits and trades that are plied here and their milieus: in brief, the public and social life of our times. I would propose Paris market halls, Parisian railways, the bridges of Paris, subterranean Paris [the sewage system], racetrack Paris, and public gardens. The ceiling could have a gallery of living dignitaries, in poses that befit their position, whose role in civilian [not military] life has contributed to the greatness and wealth of Paris."[104] Manet received no reply to his proposal.

In 1877 Manet's *Nana* (p.160) prompted a further controversy. Turned down by the Salon, it was exhibited in the window of "a well-known shop that sold knick-knacks in the Boulevard des Capucines" – in other words, presented virtually "on the pavement" to a broad public with no interest in art (Werner Hofmann).[105] This fresh, lifesize, full-length portrait of a young woman in her underthings, making up in her boudoir while a top-hatted gentleman waits, explores the Parisian themes of lifestyle and subculture that Manet was taking a closer look at. It was an exploration that put him in Degas's company. But it also continued the subtle analysis of relations between the sexes, glimpsed in fleeting moments, that was visible in the Argenteuil boat scenes as well.[106] The rejection of the picture by the Salon was probably due to the fact that Manet's model, Henriette Hauser, was currently having an affair with the Prince of Orange[107] – and the authorities did not want to insult him. The title, as with *Olympia* merely a woman's name (but an eloquent

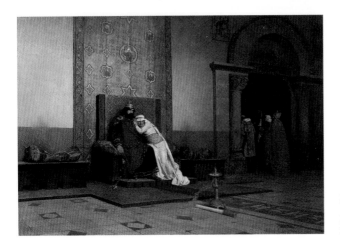

one), establishes a literary link that has been much debated in recent scholarship.

Manet was working on his painting for weeks during the autumn and winter of 1876/77. At the same time, a new novel by his friend Zola, "L'Assommoir", was being serialized in a newspaper, "La République des lettres", and was published in book form early in 1877: that year alone it went through 38 impressions. Nana the whore, who later became the titular heroine of another novel (in 1879), made her appearance in a chapter that was printed in November 1876, when Manet was already at work on the picture. But Zola had of course outlined the subjects and main characters of his Rougon-Macquart novel cycle years before; and Manet may have been familiar with Zola's plans. Literature, at any rate, gave him a striking title that would draw even more attention to his painting. The circumstances are unusual in the annals of art; for purposes of our present assessment of the painting, though, they are of course of secondary importance. It is an enchanting work from Manet's most avowedly Impressionist phase, a precise and realistic analysis of one aspect of the social and cultural scene, and first-rate proof of Manet's skills in orchestrating visual material. Its motifs and structures bear the imprint of distance; the partnership shown is one of cool unemotionality; and the woman, though she has something of the sensual temptress, seems also unapproachable – merchandise and cultic statue at once.

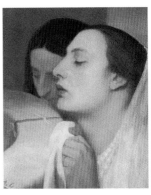

Manet then did a number of restaurant paintings, such as *Plum Brandy* (p. 165), which one critic recently described as disquieting on account of its unresolved mood and message. In Manet's day, the woman could only be a prostitute. At the Brasserie de Reichshoffen in the Boulevard Rochechouart – which served bock beer from Alsace and had women dancing for (and largely ignored by) its customers, a true cross-section of Parisian society – Manet hit on the idea of painting a panoramic survey of modern society. He began work on it in his studio in

1878, using models; but then cut it into separate canvases, some of which he painted further versions of (pp. 178, 179). The use of female waitresses in brewery pubs that offered music and entertainment was a new departure at the time. Manet's rapidly painted studies experimented in various kinds of eye contact between the characters, some of them people who simply happen to witness a moment; and he tried out the presentation of people who remain strangers to each other – a worker in his blue shirt, gentlemen in top hats and coats, bored girls. The graphic artist Henri Guérard, who had just married Eva Gonzalès, and the actress Ellen Andrée were among Manet's models.

The following year Manet was out in the open again, to paint *In the Garden Restaurant of Père Lathuille* (p. 195). Père Lathuille's was a suc-

Jules Bastien-Lepage
Haymaking, 1877
Les foins
Oil on canvas, 180 x 195 cm
Paris, Musée d'Orsay

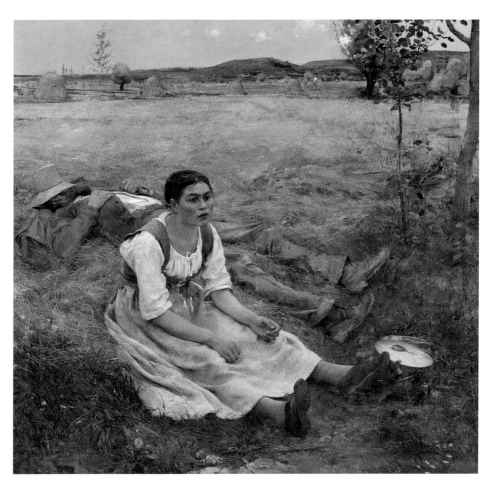

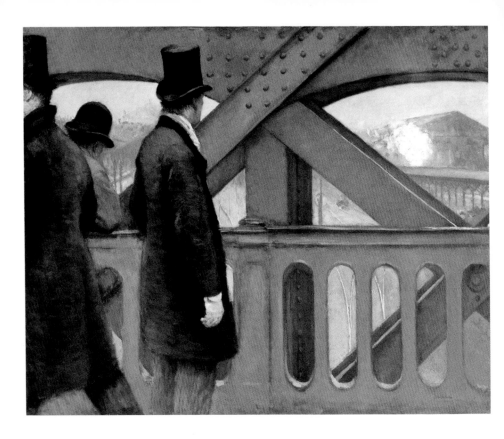

Gustave Caillebotte
Le pont de l'Europe, 1877
Oil on canvas, 105 x 130 cm
Berhaut 46. Fort Worth, Kimbell Art Museum

cessful restaurant in the Avenue de Clichy. In the picture, the proprietor's son is making up to a stylish lady; the eye contact is of an unusually intimate quality for Manet. This scene, thoroughly Impressionist in treatment, has a unity which has struck certain recent critics as crude, and uncomfortably kin to the mannerisms of anecdotal, narrative, academic genre painting. But then, Manet was not averse to tradition and the conventions of middle-class art. He was out to beat the opposition on their own territory, the Salon, and to prove to the public that what it expected in art could (and must) be done satisfactorily using modern painting techniques. That said, though, Manet's customary preference for detached observation, for the stance of *impassibilité* approved by Flaubert, and his aversion to unsubtly explicit narrative content in a picture, were graphically expressed in the silent couple in *In the Conservatory* (p. 195), painted at the same time.

Manet's pupil Eva Gonzalès has had little success with art lovers and critics to this day. Assuredly her modest output is uneven – though the same can be said of her more famous fellows. Her concepts and tech-

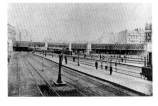

The Pont de l'Europe in Paris

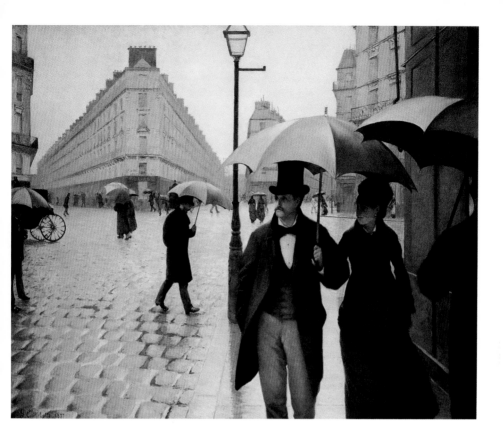

Gustave Caillebotte
Paris, the Place de l'Europe on a Rainy Day, 1877
La Place de l'Europe à Paris, temps de pluie
Oil on canvas, 212.2 x 276.2 cm
Berhaut 52. Chicago, The Art Institute of Chicago

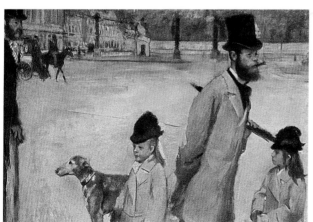

Edgar Degas
Place de la Concorde
(Comte Lepic and his Daughters), 1876
La Place de la Concorde
(Le Comte Lepic et ses filles)
Oil on canvas, 79 x 118 cm
Lemoisne 368
Formerly Berlin, Oskar Gerstenberg Collection
(presumed destroyed in the Second World War)

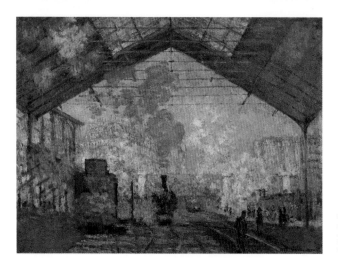

Claude Monet
Gare Saint-Lazare, Paris, 1877
Intérieur de la Gare Saint-Lazare à Paris
Oil on canvas, 75.5 x 104 cm
Wildenstein 438. Paris, Musée d'Orsay

niques were decisively influenced by Manet, whom she greatly admired; her first teacher had been the successful Salon artist Charles Chaplin (1825–1891). *A Box at the Théâtre des Italiens* (p. 132) – probably rejected by the 1874 Salon and not accepted till 1879, when it still remained unsold – suffers if compared with Renoir's painting of the same date on the same subject (p. 128), in terms of composition, colouring, and the warm, insinuating magic of the model. Nor does it have the elusive expressiveness of Manet's figural groups. The dry energy of its structure, though, perhaps appeals more to the tastes of an era after Impressionism than it did to contemporaries. By contrast, the sponta-

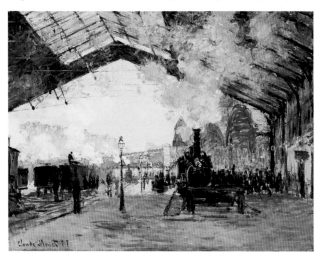

Claude Monet
Gare Saint-Lazare: the Train from Normandy, 1877
La Gare Saint-Lazare: le train de Normandie
Oil on canvas, 59.6 x 80.2 cm
Wildenstein 440
Chicago, The Art Institute of Chicago

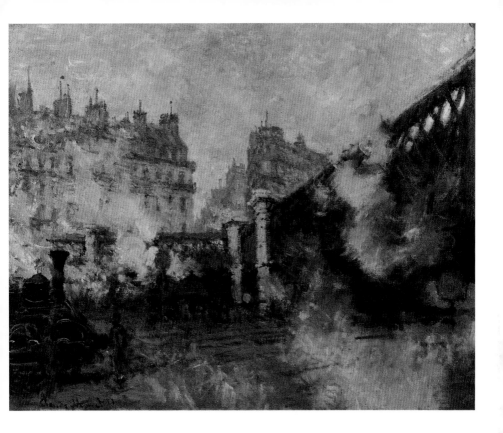

neity with which *Morning Awakening* (p. 133) has been seen and caught, and the sheer poetry of its sensibility, are superbly in line with Impressionism as Manet understood it at the time. Plainly Gonzalès was still hesitant to proceed wholeheartedly down the Impressionist path, no doubt partly through the influence of Guérard, whom she married at some point between 1878 and 1880 (the date is unclear). Her little study of a milliner (p. 165) has a distinct charm, though, and its psychological expressiveness is not unlike what Degas could achieve. Eva Gonzalès – herself still mourning Manet, who had died not long before – died in 1883 aged only thirty-four, shortly after giving birth to her first child.

Her rival, Berthe Morisot, enjoyed a lengthy and successful career. Free of material worries, though not of the duties of a wife and (from 1878 on) mother, she was able to paint essentially as she pleased. But she set great store on measuring up to public scrutiny. Though in artistic and social terms she had an affinity with Manet, whose younger brother Eugène she married in late 1874, she stopped submitting to the Salon (where she had scored successes) and committed herself to the Impres-

Claude Monet
Le pont de l'Europe, Gare Saint-Lazare, 1877
Oil on canvas, 64 x 81 cm
Wildenstein 442. Paris, Musée Marmottan

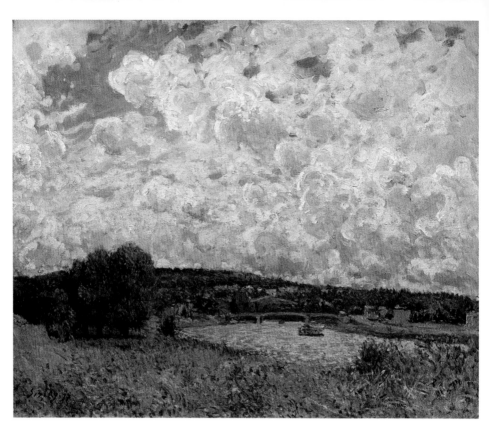

Alfred Sisley
The Seine at Suresnes, 1877
La Seine à Suresnes
Oil on canvas, 60.7 x 73.7 cm
Daulte 267. Paris, Musée d'Orsay

sionist group. She was very active on their behalf, in financial and other ways. Her paintings, which became increasingly unstrained in style, were predominantly impressions of happy family life or togetherness, or of the cultured, stylish life of her family and friends (pp. 123, 160, 192). She preferred light, tender colours, had a precise eye, and took an interest in the psychological state expressed by her models. A particularly fine use of colour distinguishes *At the Ball* (p. 151), with its slightly asymmetrical structure and the young woman's attentive sideways look. Morisot's artistic and human qualities amply account for the high regard in which she was held by fellow painters as different in character as Renoir and Degas, Monet and Puvis de Chavannes, as well as such writers as the poet Mallarmé.

Sisley's career evolved along idiosyncratic and in part tragic lines. Criticism has tended to sideline him in its presentations of Impressionism, partly through dependence on art market forces. The pictures he painted are Impressionism of an outstanding order, yet from the connoisseurs' point of view he was never more than a member of the movement

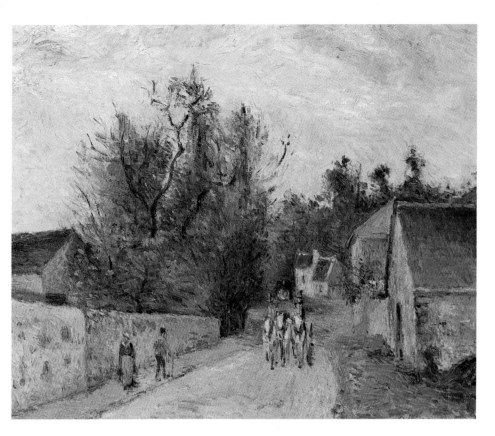

who painted like Monet. He was also prey to personal misfortune; to the
end of his life he never quite managed to put his financial difficulties
behind him, nor did he live to see his art enjoy wider recognition. The
fact is that Sisley conveys no strong sense of an artistic personality. His
range of subjects is not great: he painted landscapes only, with an occasional figure. His art in total lacks subjects, techniques or qualities peculiarly his. And so, for example, the personal collection Monet left at his
death included only one Sisley, but three Pissarros, five Morisots and no
fewer than twelve Cézannes (though only one Degas and nothing by
Manet). Yet Sisley's paintings are things of beauty and light, done with
ease, the expression of a positive spirit. His unspectacular landscape
work alternates between distant and closer views, like the intimate landscapes of the Barbizon school (pp. 99, 158). He painted the waters of the
Seine at Bougival or Marly (p. 96) as sensitively as the nuances of snow
colour in Pissarro's beloved lanes and gardens of Louveciennes (pp. 84,
183). Till 1877 he lived at Marly, where on one occasion flooding provided him with unusual and appealing subject matter (p. 159). Then he

Camille Pissarro
The Mailcoach. The Road from Ennery to the
Hermitage, 1877
La diligence. Route d'Ennery à l'Ermitage
Oil on canvas, 46.5 x 55 cm
Pissarro/Venturi 411. Paris, Musée d'Orsay

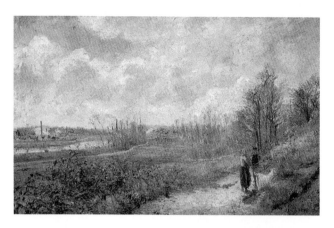

Camille Pissarro
Path at "Le Chou", 1878
Le sente du Chou
Oil on canvas, 50 x 92 cm
Pissarro/Venturi 452
Douai, Musée des Beaux-Arts de la Chartreuse

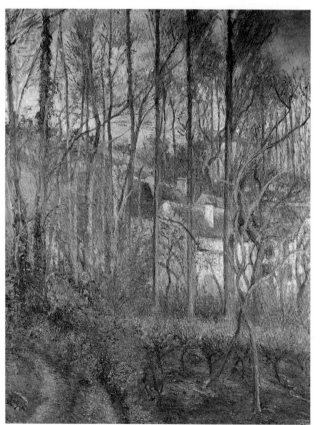

Camille Pissarro
La Côte des Bœufs at the Hermitage near Pontoise,
1877
La Côte des Bœufs à l'Ermitage près de Pontoise
Oil on canvas, 114.9 x 87.6 cm
Pissarro/Venturi 380. London, National Gallery

Right:
Camille Pissarro
Vegetable Garden and Trees in Blossom, Spring,
Pontoise, 1877
Printemps à Pontoise, potager et arbres en fleurs
Oil on canvas, 65.5 x 81 cm
Pissarro/Venturi 387. Paris, Musée d'Orsay

Camille Pissarro
The Red Roofs, 1877
Les toits rouges, coin de village, effet d'hiver
Oil on canvas, 54.5 x 65.6 cm
Pissarro/Venturi 384. Paris, Musée d'Orsay

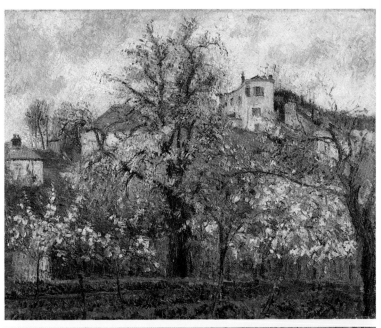

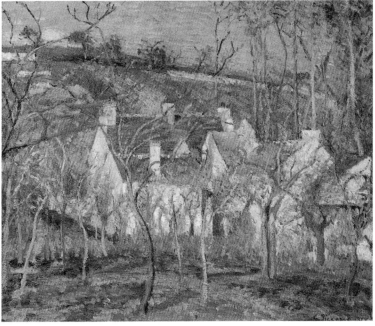

moved to Sèvres, where he got into financial difficulty with landlords and was evicted, before a patron finally came to his rescue.

Caillebotte's position was entirely different. He was financially independent, and the aesthetic lack of bias which is the advantage of the amateur inclined him to experiment. Of a well-to-do family, he studied at the Academy of Art in Paris for a short time in 1873 but then turned to marine engineering, sailing and rowing. In 1874, he met Degas, Renoir and other artists exhibiting in the Boulevard des Capucines. Degas won him over, and the following year Caillebotte bought his first paintings by his new friends and took to painting as often as he could with them, and like them. He was especially interested in light in the open, and fleeting impressions of a kind hitherto not considered proper subjects, while he was drawn thematically to human figures and aspects of urban life. His view of Impressionist realism was closest to that of Degas; however, he was also more open than the others to the world of hard physical work, and more emphatic in his willingness to take it as his subject.

He painted two versions of *The Floor Strippers* (p. 131), exhibiting both at the second Impressionist show in 1876. It was work he had seen at his parents' home. This was an aspect of Courbet's and Millet's realism – the latter's *Gleaners* comes to mind – adapted to the Impressionist idiom. He emphasized effects of light; the action presented in the painting is that of a moment; and the composition uses novel, "Japanese" perspective. Caillebotte subsequently brightened his palette considerably and relaxed his brushwork, yet never adopted fragmentary or sketchy approaches that might have dispelled the illusion of three-dimensionality or interfered with the exact definition of things in a painting. His pictures remained primarily discoveries of new aspects of contemporary reality, *tranches de vie*, unexpected slices of modern life. When Caillebotte's paintings were first publicly displayed, at the second Impressionist exhibition, the critics were taken aback by his "bizarre perspectives", the photographic character of his work, and its three-dimensionality. They were struck by his art's forceful modernity even as they registered the simultaneous use of traditional methods of representation.

Pont de l'Europe (p. 168), which crops passers-by on the bridge spanning the Gare Saint-Lazare's track approach, is interesting not least for the alert regard Caillebotte the engineer had for the new technology. He did several meticulous studies towards two versions of the painting. The lines of receding perspective in Caillebotte's work can often draw us with a disquieting violence into a picture's spatial depth: his perspective recalls the designer's drawing board. This is true of his large, atmospheric painting of the Place de l'Europe on a rainy day as well (p. 169). Renoir was to paint a similar scene some years later (p. 239), but his canvas presented a graceful throng of beautiful women and children; Caillebotte's painting, by contrast, uses wide, open spaces and figural tensions. His people straightforwardly want to get somewhere. The division of the composition into particular zones recalls Manet or Degas. The man in the foreground, so close that he is about to step out of the canvas and has had

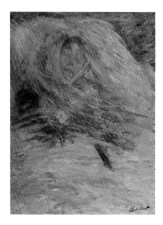

Claude Monet
Camille Monet on her Deathbed, 1879
Camille Monet sur son lit de mort
Oil on canvas, 90 x 68 cm
Wildenstein 543. Paris, Musée d'Orsay

Claude Monet
Rue Saint-Denis, Festivities of 30 June, 1878, 1878
La rue Saint-Denis, fête du 30 juin 1878
Oil on canvas, 76 x 52 cm
Wildenstein 470. Rouen, Musée des Beaux-Arts

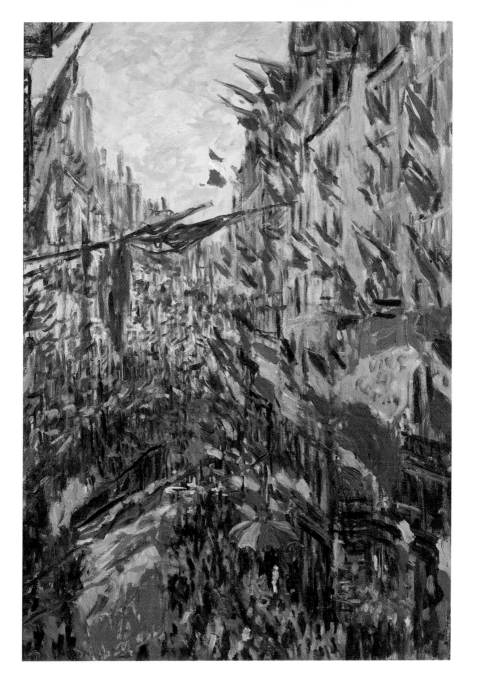

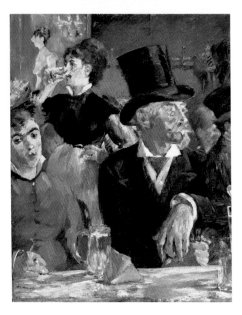

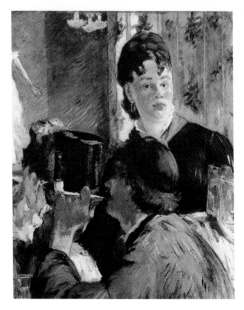

Edouard Manet
Bock Drinkers, 1878
Buveurs de bocks
Oil on canvas, 47.5 x 30.2 cm
Rouart/Wildenstein I,280
Baltimore (MD), The Walters Art Gallery

Edouard Manet
The Waitress, 1878/79
La serveuse de bocks
Oil on canvas, 77.5 x 65 cm
Rouart/Wildenstein I,312
Paris, Musée d'Orsay

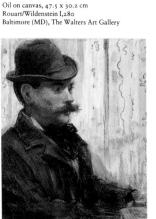

Edouard Manet
Man in a Round Hat (Alphonse Maureau), 1878
Homme au chapeau rond (Alphonse Maureau)
Pastel on paper, 54.7 x 45.2 cm
Rouart/Wildenstein II,6
Chicago, The Art Institute of Chicago

to be cropped below the knee, has the look of a conqueror, the woman on his arm a companion with the air of an afterthought despite her prettiness.

Caillebotte's subject matter included almost the entire Impressionist range: rooftops, town squares, gardens, oarsmen, sailors, swimmers, portraits, landscapes and still lifes (pp. 168, 182, 184, 185, 201 etc.). He often found his subjects near the family home by the River Yerres. In 1880 an acquaintance modelled for his lifesize portrait of a café regular (p. 209). The subject, technique, colouring, use of space, and subtle deployment of the mirror, all have something of Manet or Degas. But Caillebotte outdid Manet in expressing an entire social psychology in this portrait of a good-humoured, unfooled, slightly crafty man of the lower middle class. The moment, though one that recurs every day, is unique, and is brought before us with great clarity, in all its colours, sounds, even – we fancy – smells. Though he was extremely traditional in his approach, Caillebotte seems even more Impressionist in this painting than his fellow artists and mentors.

Degas's personality was riddled with paradoxes. His art's importance for the 20th century has been better understood in the wake of post-modern views that highlight the value of coupling a sense of tradition with innovation. Degas was a difficult, solitary man and a sickly hypochon-

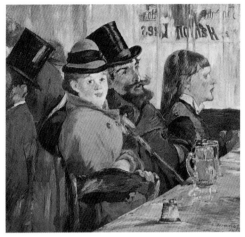

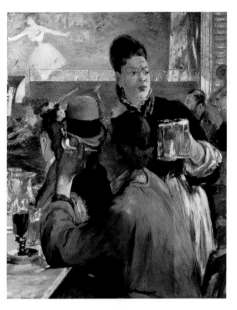

Edouard Manet
At the Café, 1878
Au café
Oil on canvas, 78 x 84 cm
Rouart/Wildenstein I,278
Winterthur, Oskar Reinhart Collection

Edouard Manet
The Waitress, 1879
La serveuse de bocks
Oil on canvas, 97.1 x 77.5 cm
Rouart/Wildenstein I,311
London, National Gallery

driac, but he always put his views crisply and lucidly in public forums. The more Impressionism acquired a defined sense of direction, the more emphatically he denied that he was a member of the movement. And yet for years (and from the very outset) he was one of the most active organizational talents in the group. He remained a friend – albeit with a certain aloofness – of most of the Impressionists, and never flinched from criticism, ridicule or even quarrels. He was rightly proud of his abilities as an artist; they were the product of untiring endeavour and a tenacious desire to improve. Like any important artist, he was repeatedly tormented by depressing self-doubt and despondency.

Degas was against landscape work, and particularly *plein-airisme*: his aim was not to paint spontaneously but to retain a sense of form and intellectual control, and not to "lose one's wits when confronted with Nature", as he once put it. Ironically enough, his only solo show during his lifetime, at Durand-Ruel's in 1893, was of landscape pastels done from impressions on a journey made in summer the year before. When a friend later asked if the landscapes were transcripts of mental or spiritual states (which would have satisfied the demands then being made by Symbolism), Degas brusquely put him right: "No, states of vision." He added: "We don't use such high-flown terms." By "we" he meant the painters of his generation and circle who had set out to paint realistically

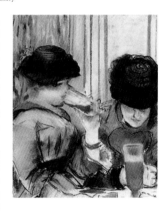

Edouard Manet
Two Women Drinking Bocks, 1878
Buveuses de bocks
Pastel on paper, 61 x 50.8 cm
Rouart/Wildenstein II,7
Glasgow, Burrell Collection

and considered themselves as workers or craftsmen rather than as on a par with writers.

In the 1870s, though, Degas did do the occasional landscape study, particularly racetrack scenes and crowd pictures – all painted in the studio, as it happens. In 1875 or 1876 he painted an outdoor group portrait centred on a fellow artist, Vicomte Lepic, who had exhibited at the first two group shows, with his two daughters. *Place de la Concorde: Comte Lepic and his Daughters* (p. 169) is one of the most curious paintings of families and people out walking – all of the people in it are completely ignoring each other. It was most recently known to be in the possession of the Berlin collector Oskar Gerstenberg, and is presumed to have been destroyed in the Second World War. About 1876 Degas did a beach scene that was equally unusual (p. 130). In this painting, the clearly defined clothes and accessories seem to be leading some odd life of their own.

Degas continued to be mainly interested in dance on stage and during rehearsals. He was so devoted to the theatre that in 1877 he designed the set of a comedy, "La Cigale", by his friends Ludovic Halévy and Henri Meilhacs, in which a modern "intentionalist" painter (one of the labels by which the Impressionists were also known) was lampooned because his paintings could just as well be hung upside down (in which case they showed a different subject).

Degas sometimes painted women ironing (pp. 79, 242), but he was interested above all in people, various configurative juxtapositions, effects of light and colour, and confusing perspective in restaurants or cafés-concert (pp. 161, 181). Like Manet after him (p. 221), he recorded the remarkable visual juxtaposition of contrary or different things, and the lack of communication between people who happen to occupy the same space. On occasion he deliberately established this effect, using models. A fine example (p. 164) is his picture of actress Ellen Andrée and the copper engraver, painter and good-natured bohemian Marcellin Desboutin (1823–1902), who had had work in the second Impressionist exhibition. The two people are seen in Café de la Nouvelle-Athènes, where Degas and his friends often went in the 1870s.

The painting is an ingenious composition. The marble table tops keep the two people in their places, both literally and metaphorically. They appear marginalized. It seems as if we happen to be seeing them from another table. At the same time, the painting analyses human fate with a seriousness unusual in Degas. We sense his compassion with this dismally hopeless woman, ignored by her companion and gazing with cool resignation into vacancy while he draws at his pipe. The picture – which (it is worth repeating) was set up in this way rather than observed – became a centrepiece of the new Impressionist critical realism on the strength of this analysis. The somewhat moralistic title, *The Absinth Drinker* (that is to say, the woman with her milky-green drink), was first given at a much-criticized exhibition in London in 1893. Suggestions that it was in the second group exhibition in 1876, under the title *In the Café*, do not seem convincing, given that none of the numerous reviews

Jean-Louis Forain
In the Wings, 1878
Dans les coulisses
Gouache, watercolour and coloured crayon on paper, 36.2 x 26 cm. Private collection

Edgar Degas
Singer with a Glove, 1878
Chanteuse de café (Chanteuse au gant)
Pastel and tempera on canvas,
52.8 x 41.1 cm. Lemoisne 478 bis
Cambridge (MA), Fogg Art Museum,
Harvard University

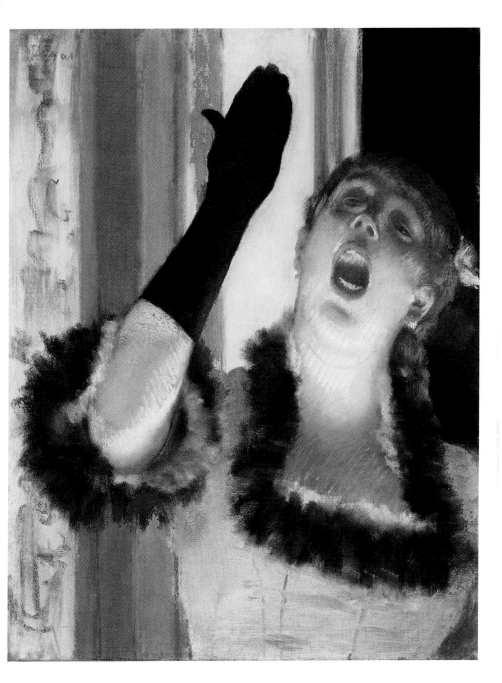

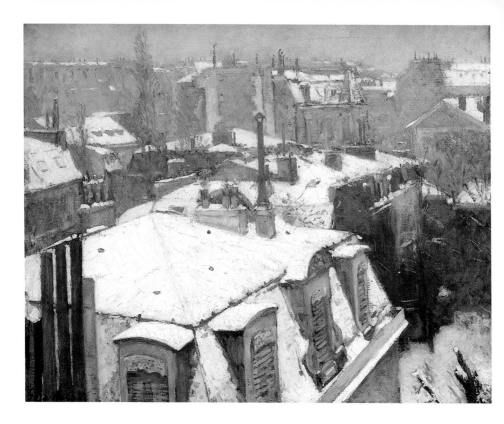

Gustave Caillebotte
Snow-covered Roofs in Paris, 1878
Toits sous la neige, Paris
Oil on canvas, 64 x 82 cm
Berhaut 107. Paris, Musée d'Orsay

of the show mentioned it. The picture was immediately bought, though, by Henry Hill, a tailor who had bought numerous works by Degas and lived in Brighton, where it was exhibited in September 1876 and censured by some because of its subject. In 1892/93 it rapidly changed owners, no fewer than three times.[108]

Degas used pastel with growing frequency for the many studies of singers – gesturing and fashionably tricked out – that he did in the cafés-concert. Pastel permitted fleeting impressions, a mere breath of an effect; but its granular, grainy quality had a physical presence of its own, giving the surface of a picture a sensuous interest independent of the subject and encouraging us to read this new creation as the work of a human hand. With his chemist friend Luigi Chialiva (1842–1914), Degas discovered a fixative that made pastel indelible. Degas often printed a black and white monotype first and then drew over the outline in pastel, a technique he himself had invented. At other times, he would defamiliarize and consolidate the colour texture by combining the pastel drawing with oils thinned with turpentine. The paint dried faster, which

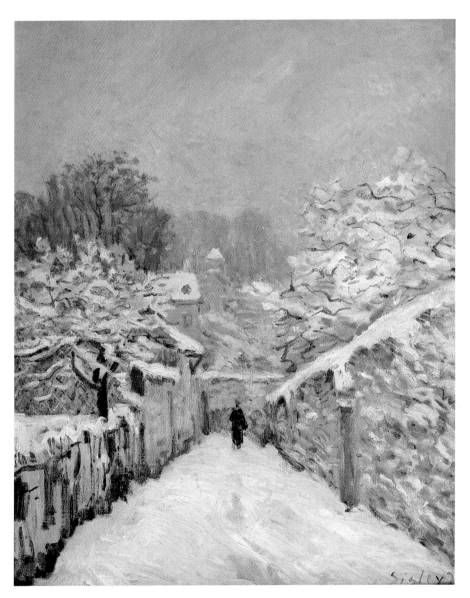

Alfred Sisley
Snow at Louveciennes, 1878
La neige à Louveciennes
Oil on canvas, 61 x 50.5 cm
Daulte 282. Paris, Musée d'Orsay

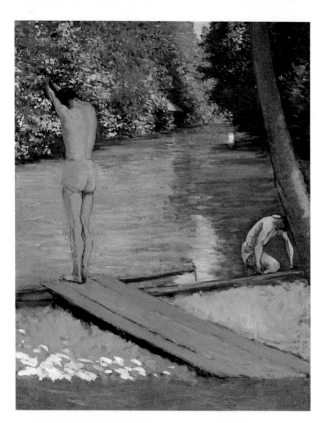

Right:
Gustave Caillebotte
Canoeing, 1878
Les périssoires
Oil on canvas, 157 x 113 cm
Berhaut 91. Rennes, Musée des Beaux-Arts

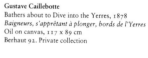

Gustave Caillebotte
Bathers about to Dive into the Yerres, 1878
Baigneurs, s'apprêtant à plonger, bords de l'Yerres
Oil on canvas, 117 x 89 cm
Berhaut 92. Private collection

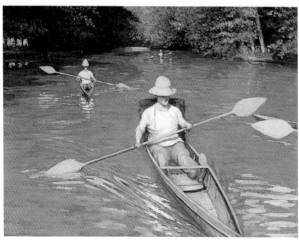

Gustave Caillebotte
Canoeing on the Yerres, 1877
Périssoires sur l'Yerres
Oil on canvas, 89 x 115.5 cm
Berhaut 95. Upperville (VA),
Mr. and Mrs. Paul Mellon Collection

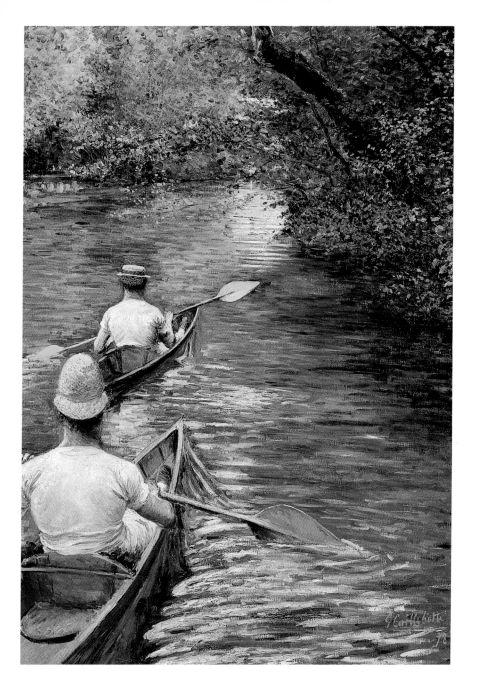

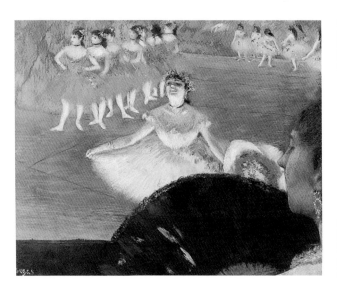

Right:
Edgar Degas
The Star or Dancer on the Stage, c. 1876–1878
L'étoile ou Danseuse sur la scène
Pastel over monotype on paper, 58 x 42 cm
Lemoisne 491. Paris, Musée d'Orsay

Edgar Degas
Dancer with Bouquet, c. 1878–1880
Danseuse au bouquet
Pastel on paper, 40 x 50 cm
Lemoisne 476
Providence (RI), Museum of Art,
Rhode Island School of Design

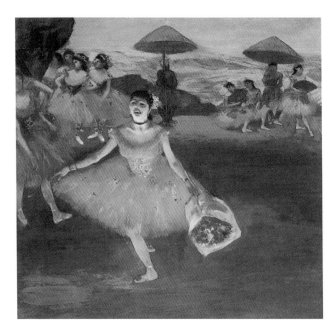

Edgar Degas
Dancer with Bouquet (Curtseying), c. 1877/78
Danseuse au bouquet saluant
Pastel on paper, 72 x 77.5 cm
Lemoisne 474. Paris, Musée d'Orsay

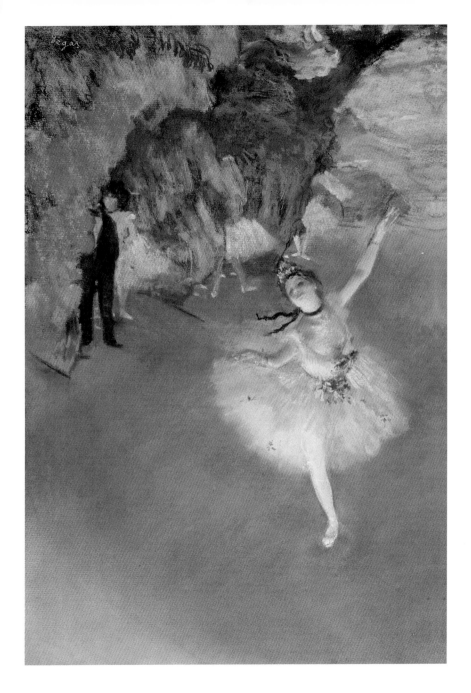

permitted more rapid work and produced a pastel-like effect of the fleeting moment.

Degas continued to be absorbed by unusual angles of vision. His exacting eye would isolate unusual, delicate postures that occurred during a continuum of motion. He noted colour changes produced by light or the proximity of other colours. He saw how the cold white gaslight used for stage lighting distorted the usual look of palely made-up faces when it lit them from below. His variations on a single theme, differing only slightly, repeatedly document Degas's Impressionist view of the equal appeal and value of individual moments in an infinite time sequence; they also, of course, show an artist tenaciously at work, unsatisfied by any one of the solutions he finds to his task.

An exchange of contemptuous glances between characters in a picture could be used to signal the theme of prostitution. Degas kept this in mind when observing dancers, too. The body language of singers, as he well knew, was also under intermittent police observation; singers might be examined by a psychiatrist on court orders, or even confined in an asylum for "hysteria". Degas's friend Jules Claretie once defended a woman he had drawn, Mademoiselle Bécat from the Café des Ambassadeurs, in court.[109]

William-Adolphe Bouguereau
The Birth of Venus, 1879
La naissance de Vénus
Oil on canvas, 300 x 215 cm
Paris, Musée d'Orsay

William-Adolphe Bouguereau
Bathers, 1884
Baigneuses
Oil on canvas, 200.7 x 129 cm
Chicago, The Art Institute of Chicago

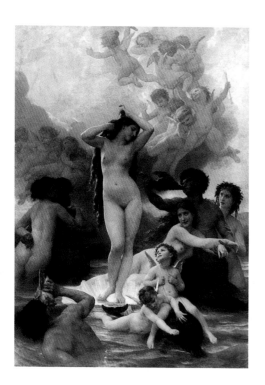

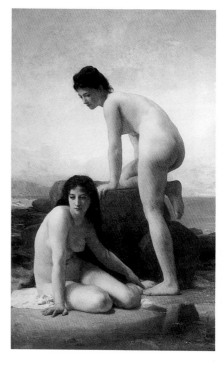

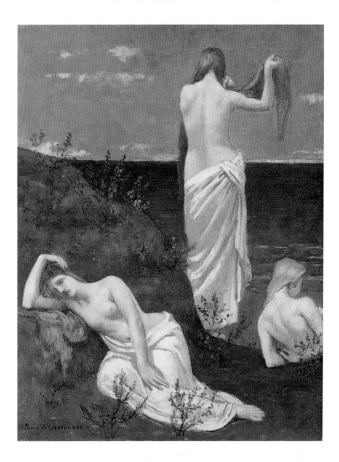

Pierre Puvis de Chavannes
Young Women on the Seashore, 1879
Jeunes filles au bord de la mer
Oil on canvas, 205 x 154 cm
Paris, Musée d'Orsay

For Degas, who was plagued at an early stage in life with worries about his failing eyesight, and who ceaselessly trained his visual memory, seeing was the crucial sense, and it provided an inexhaustible supply of subjects for pictures. He came to be on close terms with the American painter Mary Cassatt (1845–1926; see vol. II), who had been living in Europe since 1868 and was rejected by the Salon in 1875 and 1877 after initial minor successes; she was a younger fellow artist willing to be inspired by his ideas, and a stylish model as well. Accompanying her through the Louvre or to the milliner's, Degas paid careful and constant attention to her unforced American self-assurance, which was founded on wealth (p. 238). He persuaded her to exhibit in the Impressionist shows, and she became one of the earliest and most important advocates of the new art in the USA.

Observation of a relatively secret nature, and the public showing of scenes normally private and unseen, played a part of growing importance

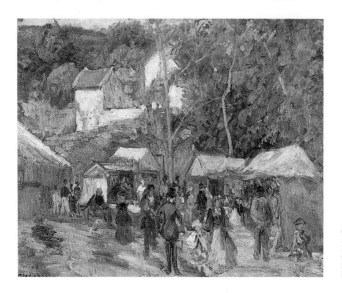

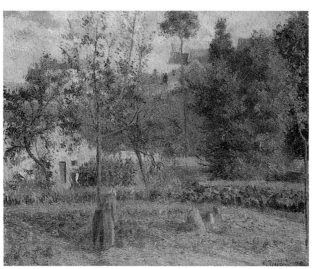

in Degas's later work from 1877 on, till this voyeurish strain became dominant. Disputes still rage over whether his female nudes washing and drying themselves in tubs and rooms should be filed under "brothel" and "prostitution". It is certain that the models Degas was able to observe, by employing them in his studio, were beyond the middle-class pale of moral normality by virtue of their willingness to pose; and we know from Renoir's models that models often sold their sexual favours. These works

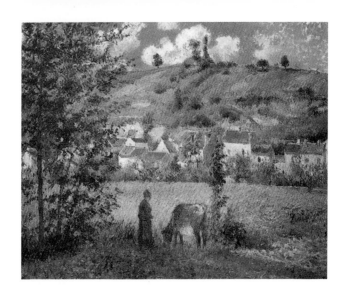

Camille Pissarro
Landscape at Chaponval, 1880
Paysage à Chaponval
Oil on canvas, 54.5 x 65 cm
Pissarro/Venturi 509. Paris, Musée d'Orsay

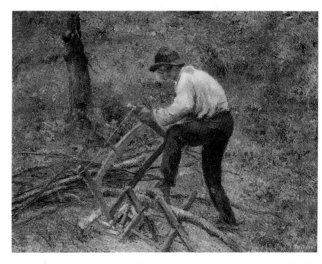

Camille Pissarro
The Woodcutter, 1879
Le scieur de bois
Oil on canvas, 89 x 116.2 cm
Pissarro/Venturi 499
Perth, The Robert Holmes à Court Collection

are at the heart of the unending debates over Degas's supposed misogyny, and equally over the nature of representational realism in Impressionism.

In March 1875, not long after the Société anonyme was wound up, Monet, Morisot, Renoir and Sisley had 73 works auctioned off at the Hôtel Drouot. The writer Philippe Burty (1830–1890) noted in his introduction to the catalogue that the paintings were "like small fragments of

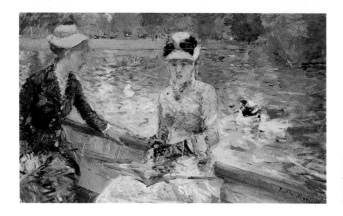

Berthe Morisot
Summer Day (Bois de Boulogne), 1879
Jour d'été (Le lac du Bois de Boulogne)
Oil on canvas, 45.7 x 75.2 cm
Bataille/Wildenstein 79
London, National Gallery

a mirror of life as a whole", reflecting "fleeting, colourful, subtle, appealing things" that merited admiration.[110] But the police were obliged to restrain an unruly public at the auction, to protect the painters and those who took their part. The prices the pictures fetched – some were sold, either back to the artists themselves or to patrons such as Duret and Caillebotte – averaged only half what they had once been. Victor Chocquet (1821–1891) made his first appearance there. He was a true lover of art, impelled by his love of beauty rather than by art-market speculation. A civil servant of modest means, he spent all he could on works of art. In 1877, despite financial troubles, he retired in order to devote his time to collecting. Chocquet was particularly susceptible to the shapes and colours of 18th-century bric-à-brac, and the continuation of a sensual approach to art in Delacroix. He bought a considerable number of Delacroix's paintings and sketches. Renoir, he felt, had an affinity with the elder painter; and Renoir led him in turn to Cézanne, Monet, Pissarro and others.

On 30 March 1876 the second Impressionist exhibition opened in three rooms of Durand-Ruel's galleries at 11, Rue Le Peletier. This time there were only nineteen exhibitors rather than thirty-one; but the catalogue ran to 252 items as against the previous 165, many of them multiple entries. Six of the artists were newcomers; Durand-Ruel's financial situation was difficult, and the show had to be financed by the group themselves once again. (This time it paid them a closing dividend, albeit of only three francs a head.) The organization of other activities was largely done by Caillebotte and the faithful Charles Tillot (1825–1895), an older landscape and flower painter who lived on the skirts of the Barbizon woods and had been recruited by Degas. His delicate floral still lifes (p. 264), which recall Fantin-Latour, cannot be described as Impressionist. Nor can the work of other acquaintances of Degas such as Desboutin (who never experienced difficulty exhibiting at the Salon). His small portrait of the baritone Jean-Baptiste Faure (p. 130) – who was a collector of Manet, Degas, Monet and Sisley and indeed funded Sisley's

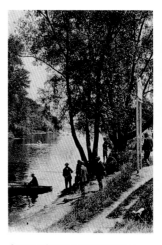

Oarsmen and anglers in the Bois de Boulogne,
Paris. Postcard, c. 1900

visit to England in 1874 – could just as easily have been hung in the Salon, even if it has the flavour of a study. Desboutin's picture portrays Faure in an appropriately affected pose in character for a Meyerbeer opera.

Many of the paintings in the show were already the property of collectors. Most of the Monets, for instance, belonged to Faure, and one to Chocquet. Of Renoir's 18 canvases, six were Chocquet's, and only five were still for sale. Sisley's paintings chiefly belonged to art dealer "Père" Martin (c. 1810–c. 1880). The aim of the exhibition, in other words, was partly to provide Impressionism with a platform and to legitimate its credentials with possible future collectors by demonstrating that buyers of repute already owned such works.

The show provoked a lively response from the critics. Their attention was particularly caught by two paintings that were not Impressionist in the narrower sense. Monet's *Madame Monet in Japanese Costume* (p. 150), a lifesize portrait of his wife, was a decorative *tour de force* in which the artist demonstrated his ability to handle what had long been in fashion among the middle classes. The blonde hair of his would-be Japanese subject, her exaggerated coquettishness, the grotesque gown,

Pierre-Auguste Renoir
The Seine at Asnières, c. 1879
La Seine à Asnières
Oil on canvas, 71 x 92 cm
London, National Gallery

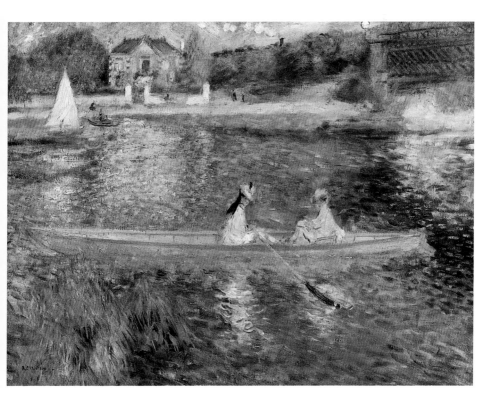

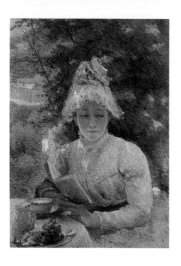

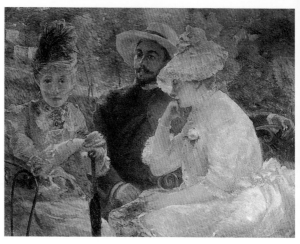

and the many fans, add up to a surfeit that may be meant ironically. Monet sold the painting to the Comte de Rossi right away, for the pleasantly high price of 2,000 francs. Degas would have liked to exhibit his *Portraits in an Office (New Orleans)* (p. 111) – thus the catalogue title – in Manchester too. "If any of the mill owners there ever needs a painter, he can try me," he wrote to his friend Tissot.[111] The painting prompted a surprising range of differing responses, demonstrating how taken aback the critics were by the subject, approach and compositional technique – and how blind critics can be. Zola found the precise draughtsmanship unclear and histrionic, and doubted whether Degas's brushwork would ever be genuinely creative.

Works painted in a manner that recorded brief impressions were the backbone of the exhibition, however. This was recognised, and influential critics such as Wolff attacked paintings such as Renoir's *Nude in the Sunlight* (p. 162) accordingly. The very headings given many of the reviews included the word "Impressionist" or "Impressionalist" – or even, in some cases, "Intransigent", a word which carried a negative political charge for conservatives. Given the prevailing censorship conditions, anti-MacMahon republican papers tended to remain vague when pointing out that artistic truthfulness, the modernity and authenticity of subject matter, the individuality of certain ways of seeing, and the unconventional nature of the aesthetic approaches adopted by the new artists, were all intrinsically connected with democratic, egalitarian ideals of freedom.

The most detailed analysis was a 38-page pamphlet by writer and art critic Louis Edmond Duranty (1833–1880), titled "La Nouvelle Peinture". A print run of 750 copies was published at the author's own expense while the exhibition was still on and probably sent to a number of newspaper editors. In 1946 it was reprinted, and in 1986 the English

Marie Bracquemond
Tea Time (Portrait of Louise Quivoron), 1880
Le goûter (Portrait de Louise Quivoron)
Oil on canvas, 81.5 x 61.5 cm
Paris, Musée du Petit Palais

Marie Bracquemond
On the Terrace at Sèvres, 1880
Sur la terrasse à Sèvres (La terrasse de la villa Brancas)
Oil on canvas, 88 x 115 cm
Geneva, Musée du Petit Palais

Right:
Edouard Manet
In the Garden Restaurant of Père Lathuille, 1879
Chez le Père Lathuille
Oil on canvas, 92 x 112 cm
Rouart/Wildenstein I,291
Tournai, Musée des Beaux-Arts

Edouard Manet
In the Conservatory, 1879
Dans la serre
Oil on canvas, 115 x 150 cm
Rouart/Wildenstein I,289
Berlin, Neue Nationalgalerie, Staatliche Museen zu Berlin, Preußischer Kulturbesitz

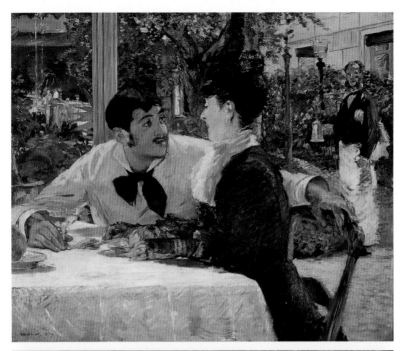

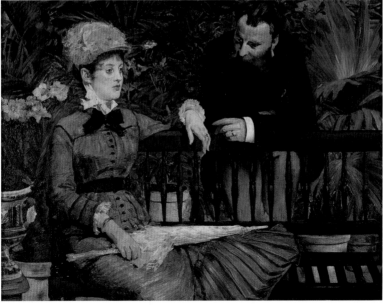

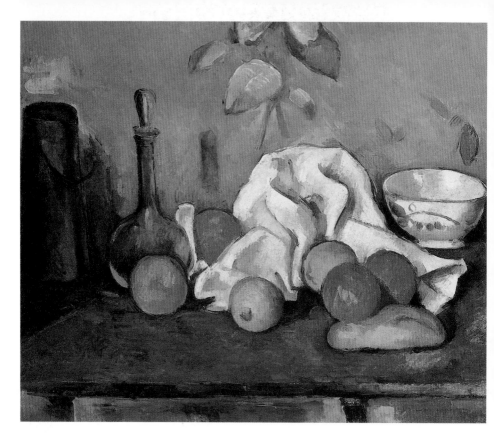

Paul Cézanne
Still Life with Fruit, 1879/80
Nature morte aux fruits
Oil on canvas, 45 x 54 cm
Venturi 337. St. Petersburg, Hermitage

translation was the centrepiece in a retrospective show and major publication.[112] Duranty had been an advocate of literary realism as a young man in 1856, and in 1877 he was to publish a novel about contemporary artistic life, "Louis Martin the Painter", heavily laced with theory. Duranty talked over "La Nouvelle Peinture" with Degas; some, indeed, supposed Degas its true author. The pamphlet took the unusual step of identifying none of the exhibiting artists or works by name (though containing references to other artists). Instead, Duranty sketched a thumbnail history of the new realism and made a programmatic call for its further development. Duranty was wholeheartedly on Degas's and Manet's side, but he was no partisan for Monet's, Sisley's or Pissarro's landscape art. Like Degas, he refused to adopt the term Impressionism, which had been widely current since 1874. Duranty would have preferred the new art to evolve along different, more realistic lines. It is only correct to consider Impressionism – or, not the same thing, the history of the eight group shows – by Duranty's lights (emphasizing

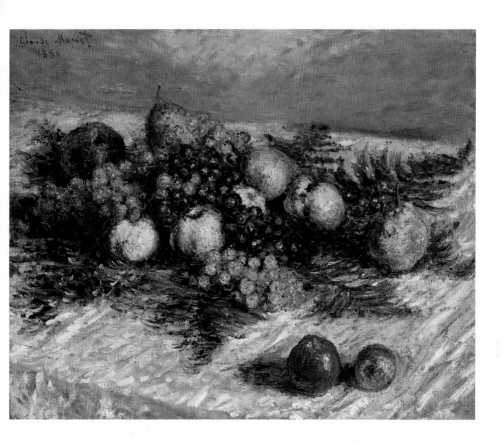

newness) if we view Degas as an Impressionist too. Or, to put it differently: the criterion of newness was very soon to be applicable to other,
non-Impressionist painting as well.

Claude Monet
Still Life with Pears and Grapes, 1880
Nature morte avec poires et raisins
Oil on canvas, 65 x 81 cm
Wildenstein 631. Hamburg, Hamburger Kunsthalle

The second group exhibition left the painters dissatisfied. The French
economy was not in the best of states. It is true that in the summer of
1876 Monet worked at Rottenbourg, the Montgeron residence of the
collector Ernest Hoschedé (1837–1891), painting decorative open-air
pictures for the home there, which Hoschedé's wife, Alice, had inherited
a few years before. Manet, rejected by the Salon, was also a guest at
Rottenbourg. Hoschedé, however, the director of Au Gagne Petit (a department store), was so avid a collector that he was twice compelled to
sell off paintings by auction. His foolhardiness led to his dismissal from
the firm, and in 1878, with debts of 82,500 francs at Durand-Ruel's and
Petit's, he went bankrupt. So Monet found himself selling works for
prices of 100 to 200 francs to others, such as the Paris-based Rumanian
doctor Georges de Bellio (1828–1894). A homoeopath like Gachet, he

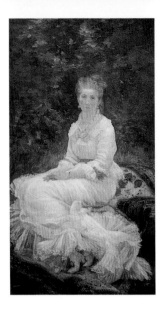

Marie Bracquemond
The Lady in White, 1880
La dame en blanc
Oil on canvas, 181 x 100 cm
Cambrai, Musée de la Ville de Cambrai

had recently started collecting Impressionist paintings, which in due course his daughter inherited; she and her husband left them to the Académie Française. Monet, acutely short of money, would even beg two or three hundred francs off rich art lovers. (This was admittedly only a financial shortage by the standards of middle-class people who expected to lead a cultural life. A sempstress would earn only one or maybe two francs for a twelve-hour day, and would be unemployed for several months a year; a milliner might earn twice that sum. Monet's earnings from the portrait of Camille would have represented three to six years' wages for working women.)

In April 1877 there was another Impressionist exhibition, organized and arranged by Caillebotte this time. Today it is viewed as the best and most homogeneous of the Impressionist shows, the pinnacle of the movement's achievement in terms of the original conception. It was Caillebotte's exhibition; he himself paid for the hire of spacious rooms on the second floor of 6, Rue Le Peletier, opposite Durand-Ruel's galleries.[113] The building was in the heart of Parisian business and cultural life, only a few paces from the Hôtel Drouot auction rooms and near the Bourse and the magnificent new opera house designed by Charles Garnier (1825–1898). Eighteen artists were involved in the exhibition. Among them was Cals, in his late seventies, who had been a participant since the first exhibition. He sent his small, tranquil, warm-hued, easily painted, plein-airist genre paintings of fishing folk and farmers from Honfleur (pp. 124, 125). The approach Cals took to art resembled that of Daubigny and Boudin. Renoir had brought in two friends, Frédéric Cordey (1854–1911) and Pierre Lamy (Franc-Lamy; 1855–1919), who were re-

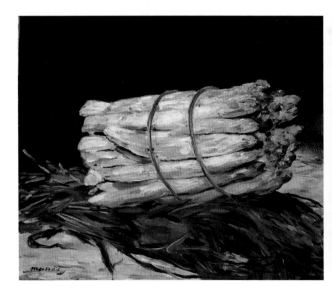

Edouard Manet
Bundle of Asparagus, 1880
Une botte d'asperges
Oil on canvas, 46 x 55 cm
Rouart/Wildenstein I,357
Cologne, Wallraf-Richartz-Museum

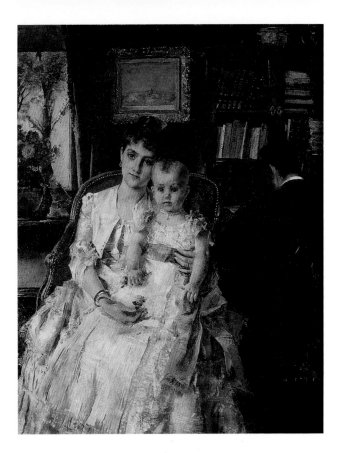

Alfred Stevens
Family Scene, c. 1880
Scène familiale
Oil on canvas, 65.3 x 51.5 cm
Paris, Musée d'Orsay

belling against the art college and had served him as models for *Le Moulin de la Galette*. The future was to find neither of them creative, nor did they participate in further group shows. The same applied to Degas's friend Alphonse Maureau, who had a meticulously proportioned small study (p. 289) on display, revealing him to have affinities with Monet. Pissarro brought in his Pontoise friend Ludovic Piette (1826–1877; p. 154). However, the exhibition, notable for its careful hanging, was dominated by Caillebotte, Monet, Pissarro and Renoir. For the first time, works were presented in plain white frames, works such as Renoir's aforementioned masterly painting of pleasure gardens in Montmartre, or Monet's and Caillebotte's stylistically very different railway scenes of the nearby *Gare Saint-Lazare* (p. 171) and the *Pont de l'Europe* (p. 168). As critic Richard Brettell has recently stressed, Caillebotte failed, despite all his efforts, to present Manet's *Nana*, which the Salon had turned down and which Manet was displaying, as we have seen, in a shop window (p. 160).

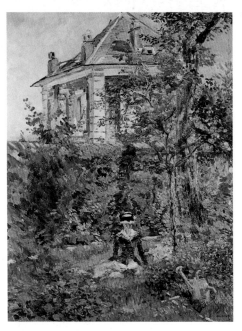

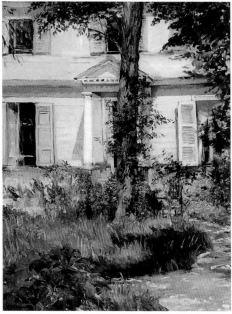

The paintings of Cézanne constituted a special feature of the exhibition. Their subject matter, and the artist's close attention to Nature, placed him with Pissarro and Guillaumin, with whom he debated artistic creeds. But the difficulties with Nature that he told friends of, and his as yet unformed desire to create paintings that were firm structures with their own internal laws, meant that in the eyes of most contemporaries his work appeared ponderous or even unbearably crude. The portrait of his new admirer, Chocquet, turned out so grim a complex of thick paint streaks that one critic dubbed the sitter "the chocolate murderer". Cézanne's position was at an ever greater remove from mainstream Imprressionism. The critics dealt harshly with him, and the daylong efforts of Chocquet, who owned almost everything Cézanne was exhibiting, to talk people round were of no avail. Cézanne was an irritable, mistrustful, antisocial person, and easily discouraged; he never again participated in an Impressionist show, allowing his contacts with his old friends to lapse. As the 1870s closed, though, he did (somewhat later than his fellows) locate his own personal style – a style which was to play a decisive role in the visual idiom of art after Impressionism.

The hanging and the impressive number of works by each of the leading painters made the 1877 show a programmatic group exhibition. But the artists were also visibly individuals who offered points of meaningful comparison. Their aesthetic aims could be clarified in this way and the eye could be attuned to an understanding of the new art. The Salon, by

Edouard Manet
Girl in the Garden at Bellevue, 1880
Jeune fille au jardin de Bellevue
Oil on canvas, 92 x 70 cm
Rouart/Wildenstein I,347
Zurich, E.G. Bührle Collection

Edouard Manet
House at Rueil, 1882
Maison de Rueil
Oil on canvas, 92 x 73 cm
Rouart/Wildenstein I,406
Melbourne, National Gallery of Victoria

Right:
Gustave Caillebotte
Square at Argenteuil, 1883
La promenade d'Argenteuil
Oil on canvas, 60.5 x 70.5 cm
Berhaut 246
Los Angeles, The Armand Hammer Collection

Gustave Caillebotte
Farmhouse at Trouville, 1882
La chaumière, Trouville
Oil on canvas, 54 x 65 cm
Berhaut 196
Chicago, The Art Institute of Chicago

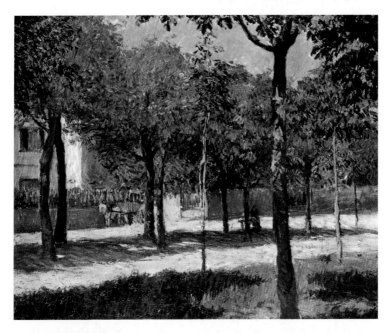

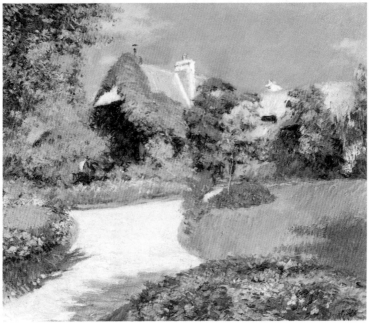

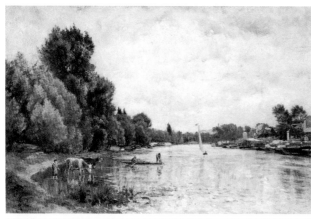

Stanislas Lépine
The Seine near Argenteuil
La Seine près d'Argenteuil
Oil on canvas, 38 x 69.3 cm
Private collection

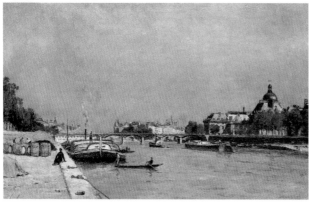

Stanislas Lépine
Paris, Pont des Arts, c. 1878–1883
Oil on canvas, 39.5 x 60 cm
Private collection

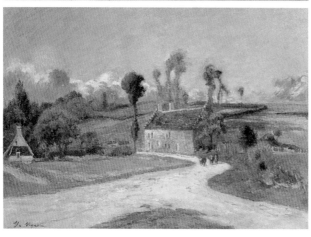

Paul-Victor Vignon
The Crossroads
La croisée des chemins
Oil on canvas, 33 x 46.5 cm
Beverly Hills (CA), Louis Stern Galleries

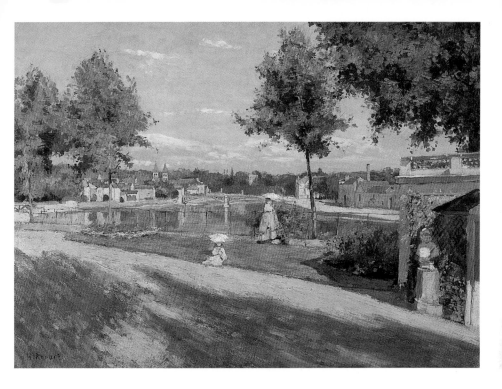

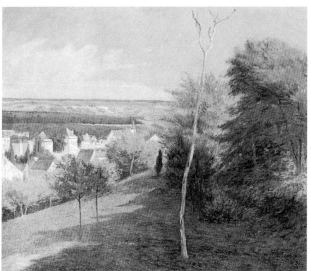

Henri Rouart
Terrace on the Banks of the Seine at Melun, c. 1880
La terrasse au bord de la Seine à Melun
Oil on canvas, 46.5 x 65.5 cm
Paris, Musée d'Orsay

Paul-Victor Vignon
The Hills at Triel, c. 1881
Les hauteurs de Triel
Oil on canvas, 46.4 x 55.4 cm
Beverly Hills (CA), Louis Stern Galleries

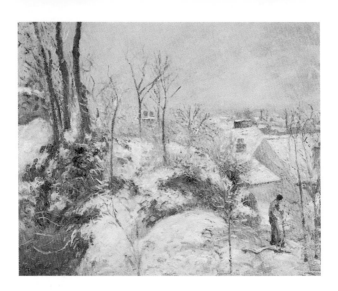

Camille Pissarro
Cottage at Pontoise in the Snow, 1879
La Garenne à Pontoise, effet de neige
Oil on canvas, 59 x 72 cm
Pissarro/Venturi 478. Chicago, The Art Institute of Chicago

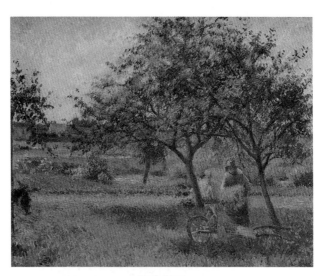

Camille Pissarro
The Wheelbarrow, c. 1881
La brouette, verger
Oil on canvas, 54 x 65 cm
Pissarro/Venturi 537. Paris, Musée d'Orsay

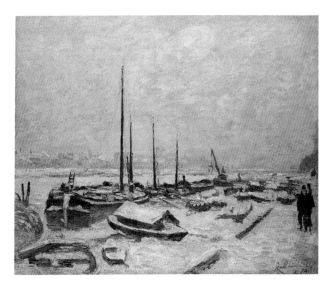

Armand Guillaumin
The Seine in Winter, 1879
La Seine pendant l'hiver
Oil on canvas, 14 x 25 cm
Private collection

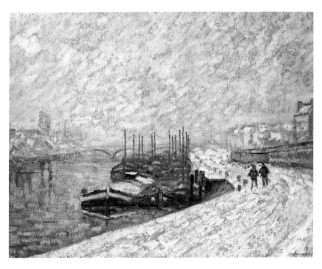

Armand Guillaumin
Barges in the Snow, 1881
Remorqueurs dans la neige
Oil on canvas. Bayonne, Musée Bonnat

contrast, only ever showed a very few submissions by any artist, and hung them insensitively. Too many works were presented in alphabetical order of artist's name, or by format, or following some other extrinsic principle, regardless of what other works might be alongside.

At Degas's insistence, the show was not described as an "Impressionist" exhibition. But Georges Rivière (1855–1943), a young tax official who was also a journalist in his spare time, published at Renoir's prompting four issues of a journal called "L'Impressionniste" while the exhibition was on, assessing the art on display. This sealed the term – though others, such as "Intentionalism", were still heard for a time, while politically charged labels such as "Intransigent" also survived for a period. (Claretie had even proposed that the technique of the Impressionists be known as the telegram style.) A year later, in 1878, when another exhibition (which did not come off) was planned, Manet's friend Duret published a monograph, "Les Peintres impressionnistes", in which he attempted an overview and history of the movement. In the same year, the term entered the Larousse encyclopaedia.

Quite apart from its name, this new phenomenon in art was a talking point of the day, as various things suggest. In far-off Basle, for instance, the historian and art historian Jacob Burckhardt (1818–1897), lecturing on Rembrandt in 1874 and 1877, brusquely dismissed any overvaluation of light and colour by "daubers and sketchers, whether of genius or not". He condemned them for subordinating the true subjects of art to the "mighty elements of light and air" and for taking them as a mere pretext for "trickery".[114] In this – and in his attack on unattractive draughtsmanship and composition and on common, unimposing figure models (an attack he aimed at Rembrandt too) – Burckhardt did not necessarily mean Manet, Monet or Degas, whose works he can hardly have been familiar with, but a broad current since Courbet and the Barbizon school which had been flowing internationally in the major exhibitions. In terms of the central art of the day, Impressionism was simply the most "intransigent", heretical, radically avant-garde option.

The critical response to the Salon exhibitions reflected an ongoing debate between historical art, still lauded by the academicians as the loftiest art, and genre, still-life and landscape art, which was increasingly being bought by well-to-do collectors for their own homes. The controversy over ways of seeing and representation, over the exemplary status given particular historical styles, over the degree to which new forms of expression were appropriate to the modern era, was part of the same debate.[115]

Talented painters schooled on the old masters, such as Jean-Paul Laurens (1838–1921), who was of the same generation as the Impressionists, were interested in seeking out the less familiar moments in mediaeval history, since they would impress a jaded public with the force of novelty. One such moment was the excommunication of Robert the Pious (p. 166). The details, and the textural, material qualities of the things we see, have been meticulously reproduced. It is like a snapshot of a single moment, with the church delegation leaving the royal couple

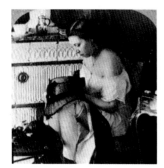

Milliner. Photograph, 1861

Paul Gauguin
Study of a Nude. Suzanne Sewing, 1880
Etude de nu ou Suzanne cousant
Oil on canvas, 111.4 x 79.5 cm
Wildenstein 39
Copenhagen, Ny Carlsberg Glyptotek

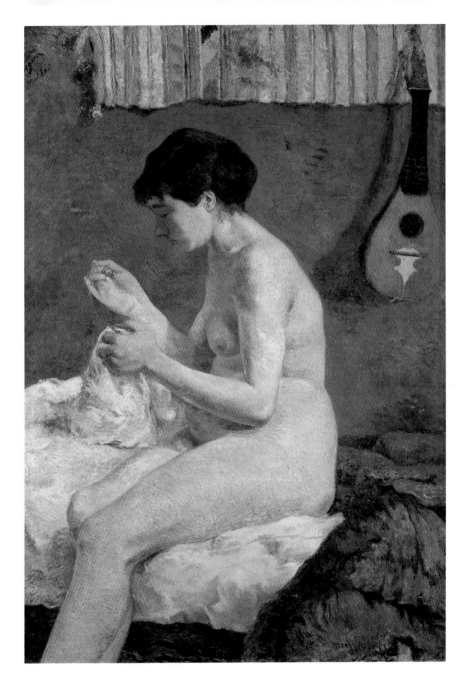

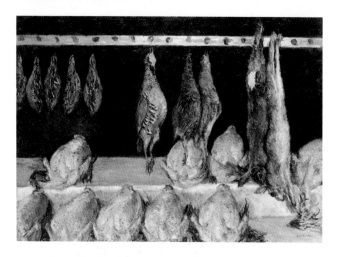

Gustave Caillebotte
Still Life: Chickens, Pheasants and Hares, 1882
Nature morte: poulets et gibiers à l'étalage
Oil on canvas, 76 x 105 cm
Berhaut 220. Private collection

staring despondently at the symbolically extinguished candle. This record of a single moment, the oblique angle on vacant space, and the candle smoke, all play a role similar to that in Degas. Later, younger history painters such as Georges-Antoine Rochegrosse (1859–1938) were to achieve even more startling shock effects in what the critic Karl Woermann has called their "art of terror". Archaeological, historical or ethnographic precision – when even fictional biblical narrative was being reconstructed (following the Pre-Raphaelites' example) – was combined with a realistic, atmospheric *plein-airisme* that introduced greater amounts of light into Salon pictures.

The most common form of historicism that reused styles of past ages, often in eclectic combinations, was the sensual, seductive, stylish portrayal of beautiful women; the supposed subject could be taken from Christianity, or from Greek or Roman myth. William-Adolphe Bouguereau (1825–1905), an Academy member since 1876, was one of the foremost artists of this kind (p. 188). A devout Catholic, he was out to oppose traditional ethical values to the materialism of the world about him, but all he managed was the frisson of superficial delights. There was an unbridgeable gap between his art and that of Renoir (p. 162) or indeed Cézanne (p. 121); the gap remained even when Bouguereau attempted a subject such as bathers, which had no ideological strings attached.

The intriguing aesthetic problem of the period lay in the relations between – on the one hand – realism, naturalism, and the new Impressionist art (widely criticized, and spurned by the Salon), and – on the other hand – similar styles of art which, though they did not escape uncriticized, earned widespread esteem and recognition by the state. Moral, political, aesthetic and technical grounds for rejection or critical dismissal were asserted in a fairly cavalier fashion. Today, in contrast, paintings will be approved unseen, so to speak, as long as the artist in question was a member of the Impressionist movement.

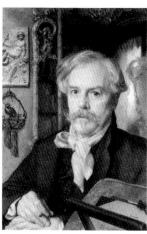

Félix Bracquemond
Portrait of Edmond de Goncourt, 1880
Portrait de M. Edmond de Goncourt
Charcoal on canvas, 55 x 37.9 cm
Paris, Musée du Louvre, Cabinet des Dessins

Right:
Gustave Caillebotte
In a Café, 1880
Dans un café
Oil on canvas, 155 x 115 cm
Berhaut 134. Rouen, Musée des Beaux-Arts

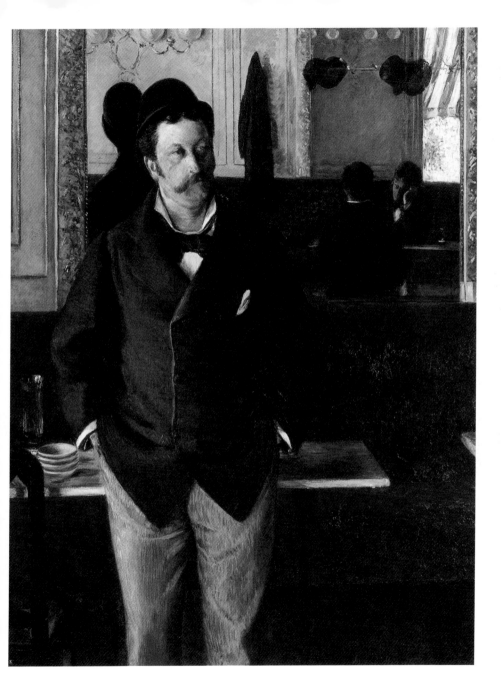

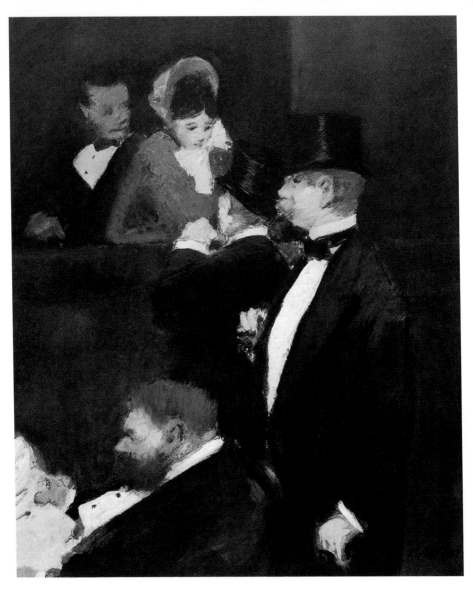

Jean-Louis Forain
A Box at the Opéra, c. 1880
Une loge à l'Opéra
Gouache and oil on card, 31.8 x 26 cm
Cambridge (MA), Fogg Art Museum,
Harvard University, Bequest of Annie Swan Coburn

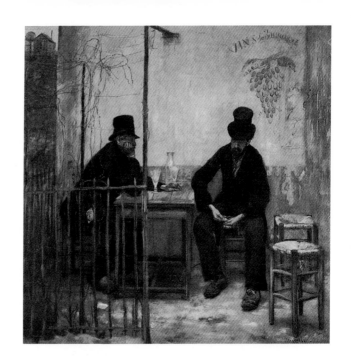

Jean-François Raffaëlli
The Absinth Drinkers, 1881
Les buveurs d'absinthe
Oil on canvas, 110.2 x 110.2 cm
Private collection

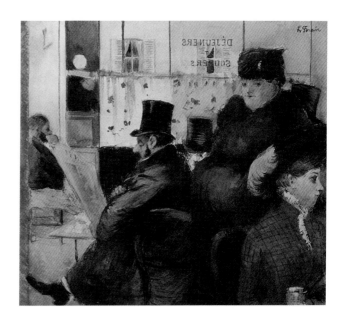

Jean-Louis Forain
In the Café de la Nouvelle Athènes, 1879
Au café de la Nouvelle Athènes
Watercolour, 35.3 x 39.1 cm
Paris, Musée du Louvre, Cabinet des Dessins

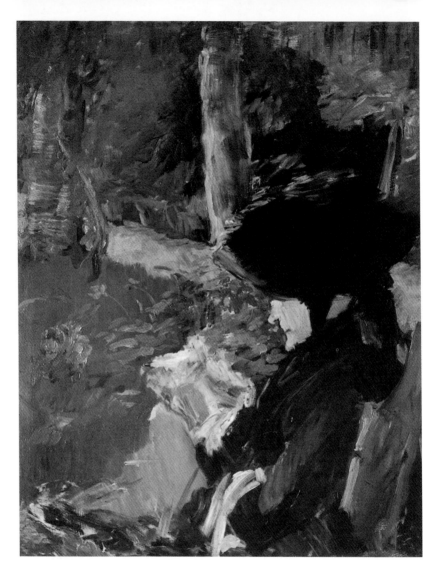

Edouard Manet
Manet's Mother in the Garden at Bellevue, 1880
La mère de Manet dans le jardin de Bellevue
Oil on canvas, 82 x 65 cm
Rouart/Wildenstein I,346. Paris, private collection

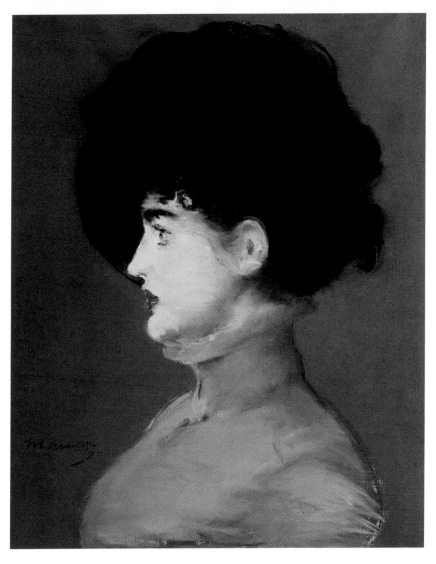

Edouard Manet
The Viennese: Portrait of Irma Brunner in a Black Hat, 1880
La Viennoise (Dame au chapeau noir: Irma Brunner)
Pastel on paper, 54 x 46 cm
Rouart/Wildenstein II,78
Paris, Musée du Louvre, Cabinet des Dessins

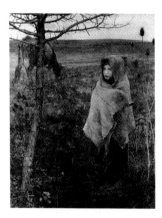

Jules Bastien-Lepage
Poor Fauvette, 1881
Pauvre Fauvette
Oil on canvas, 162.5 x 112.5 cm
Glasgow, Glasgow Art Gallery and Museum

Pierre-Auguste Renoir
On the Terrace, 1881
Sur la terrasse
Oil on canvas, 100.2 x 81 cm
Chicago, The Art Institute of Chicago

Naturalism was clearly gaining ground in pictures such as those of Jules Bastien-Lepage (1848–1884), a farmer's son. At the 1878 Salon his *Haymaking* (p. 167) attracted a good deal of attention. His sister modelled for the somewhat plain, dull woman in the painting. The view of agricultural labour as exhausting toil was derived from Courbet and Millet, but Bastien-Lepage brought it up to date by painting a dynamic, asymmetrical composition, in light colours, with an airy landscape in the background. In 1884 the German critic Adolf Rosenberg dismissed a similar picture as "fleeting photography". In his later historical and genre work too – which earned him Degas's sarcastic soubriquet "the Bouguereau of Naturalism"[116] – Bastien-Lepage remained stronger and more serious than other famous contemporary painters of peasant life, such as Jules Breton (1827–1906).

Landscape art at the Salon was becoming increasingly bright and sketchy, and as early as 1876 it was criticized as being too Impressionistic. Boudin's little coastal scenes (p. 35) were for many years the best of this kind of art. The rest mainly comprised views of Paris, scenes of city life, and excursions into the surrounding country, subjects which were not necessarily far removed from Impressionism. One conservative critic warned in 1879 in the "Gazette des Beaux-Arts": "Bougival is a dangerous model."

De Nittis, who briefly worked with the Impressionists in 1874 and may have been inspired by Degas to work in pastel in 1877, painted the most distinctive scenes capturing life in the boulevards and squares. His work was in great demand. The young Norbert Goeneutte (1854–1894) had a less relaxed hand than Sisley but a delicate sense of tonalities and the optical effects of snow surfaces against which figures become silhouettes. The anecdotal connections he established between figures avoided the mischievous absurdities Degas tended to like (p. 155). Much the same can be said of Jean Béraud (1849–1936) and his stylish, sometimes extremely small pictures (p. 371). They are bright, taut compositions that capture fleeting moments in everyday life. They always include brief episodes that can be retold in greater detail than, say, paintings by Renoir with similar subject matter. Painters such as Béraud did not want this thematic interest (often described as literary) vanquished by the "mighty elements of light and air" or subjected to autonomous colour structures. The representational and narrative aspect of pictures, increasingly emphasized at that time by graphic illustrations in magazines and by photographs, is always more accessible to the wider public than questions of form; and so painters were always tempted to pander to expectation, and earn the status and profit that would quickly result. The detailed and humorous *Autumn Regatta at Argenteuil*,[117] painted in 1879 by Paul Renouard (1854–1924), was highly thought of, and one critic warned against confusing this fine painter with another, a dauber called Renoir, whose name happened to sound similar.

One of the most successful painters of modern life was an associate and acquaintance of the Impressionists proper, the Belgian artist Alfred Stevens (1823–1906; p. 199). As early as 1871, the Morisots said he

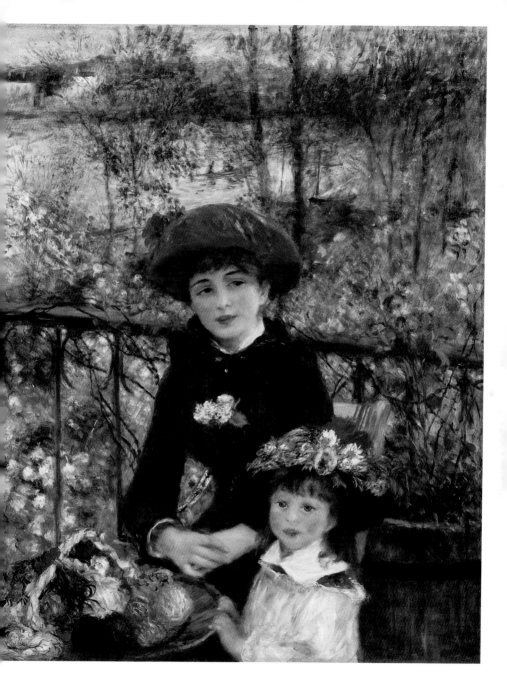

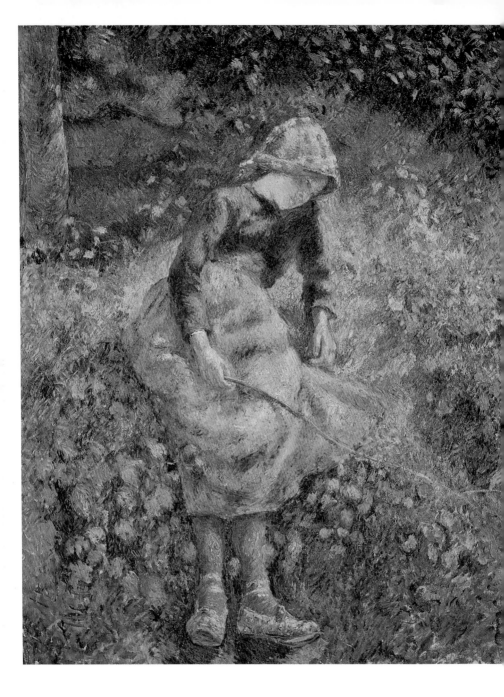

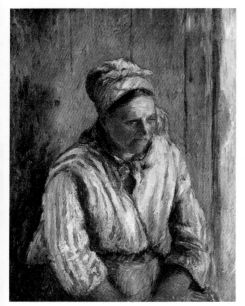
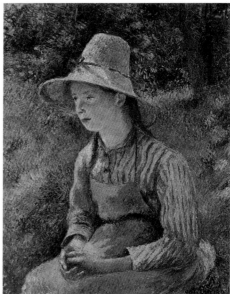

Camille Pissarro
Mère Larchevêque (the Washerwoman), 1880
La mère Larchevêque (La laveuse)
Oil on canvas, 73 x 60 cm
Pissarro/Venturi 513
New York, The Metropolitan Museum of Art

Camille Pissarro
Young Peasant Girl Wearing a Hat, 1881
Jeune paysanne au chapeau
Oil on canvas, 73.4 x 59.6 cm
Pissarro/Venturi 548
Washington, National Gallery of Art,
Ailsa Mellon Bruce Collection

Left:
Camille Pissarro
The Shepherdess, 1881
La bergère (Jeune fille à la baguette)
Oil on canvas, 81 x 64.7 cm
Pissarro/Venturi 540. Paris, Musée d'Orsay

would be earning over 100,000 francs that year with his graceful, delicately draughted and painted pictures. Jacques Tissot (1836–1902), a friend of Degas, was said by the same source to have made 300,000 francs in one sale in England in 1875. (In England he called himself James.) Since 1859 he had been exhibiting at the Salon. Because of his involvement in the Commune he spent over a decade in England, from where he travelled to Venice in 1874 to summer with the Manets. He returned to Paris in 1882. He put on a large-scale solo exhibition and embarked on a fifteen-part sequence of paintings, *Women of Paris*, which went on show in 1885. His paintings and pastels were invariably meticulously drawn, dryly painted, yet often effectively composed, and charmingly anecdotal (pp.241, 251). Recently they have enjoyed a revival on the art market and among scholars.[118]

Debating Content and Strategies

1878, the year of the next World Fair in Paris was a year of setbacks for the Impressionists. The preceding year, France had finally consolidated its political status as a republic, and it now needed to re-establish its full international standing. This required that the cultural image be cleansed of all traces of radicalism, especially in view of revived unrest in the workers' movement. Thus in 1878 Manet was rejected by the

Catalogue of the fourth Impressionist exhibition, 1879

Claude Monet
Monet's Garden at Vétheuil, 1881
Le jardin de Monet à Vétheuil
Oil on canvas, 150 x 120 cm
Wildenstein 685
Washington, National Gallery of Art

Salon, and the plan for a group exhibition by the Impressionists was dropped.

The fourth exhibition was held in April/May 1879 in a flat at 28 Avenue de l'Opéra. Sixteen artists exhibited some 260 works. This time Renoir, Sisley, Morisot and Guillaumin were conspicuous by their absence, not to mention Cézanne, who did not rejoin the group. Monet never went to see the show, partly because of his difficult personal circumstances at the time. In addition to a few new paintings, he had several older works and many that had already been sold in the show. The exhibition was coordinated by Degas, who also organized the fifth, in spring 1880, which again lacked Renoir and Sisley, and this time Monet too. It was on the mezzanine of a building at 10, Rue des Pyramides which was still under construction, and the rooms were filled with noise and dust. This happened again at the sixth exhibition in April 1881, which was held at the same address as the famed first, 35 Boulevard des Capucines, though this time in a poorly lit flat at the back of the building. With thirteen artists exhibiting something over 170 works, it was the smallest of all the group shows.

In regard to the generous exhibition of 1879, which attracted over 15,400 visitors (four times as many as in 1874), a number of works were added while the show was running, with the result that the catalogue is unreliable. At the 1880 exhibition, Degas intended to exhibit his remarkable first sculpture, the coloured lifesize wax figure of a fourteen-year-old ballerina, dressed in real pieces of clothing, but in the event he left the display case empty, which must have produced a veritably surreal effect. The dancer was first seen by the public at the 1881 exhibition. The 1880 poster used the expression *Artistes Indépendants*, while the catalogue refrained from using the phrase. All of these things were symptoms of insecurity, compared with the carefully prepared and staged exhibition of 1877.

There were various causes for these symptoms. In Renoir's and then Monet's case, it is apparent that they wanted to abandon the image of rebellious outsiders, not least in order to improve their finances. Their aim was to reconcile "official" and "modern" art. This was in line with the prevailing political climate. Traumatic memories of the Commune were fading away, and, following a partial amnesty in 1879, a general amnesty was offered to Communards in prison or exile in July 1880. Three days later, 14 July was celebrated as a national holiday for the first time, recalling the fall of the Bastille in 1789. A moderate radicalism could dominate the political scene as long as it remained moderate. And finally, the media and market system afforded new opportunities which could take the place of a cooperative-style exhibition collective.

One of Renoir's new acquaintances was a diplomat, Paul Bérard (1833–1905), who repeatedly invited the painter to Wargemont, his country residence in Normandy, and commissioned portraits. Renoir had met Bérard at the home of Charpentier, who exerted a strong influence on the fate of the Impressionists at that time. Georges Charpen-

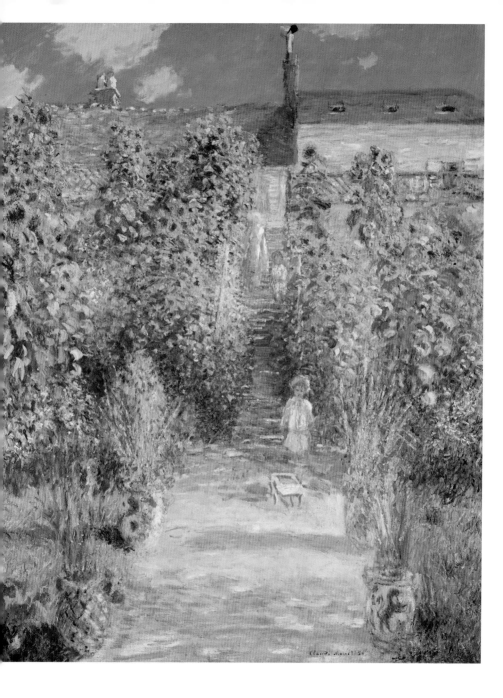

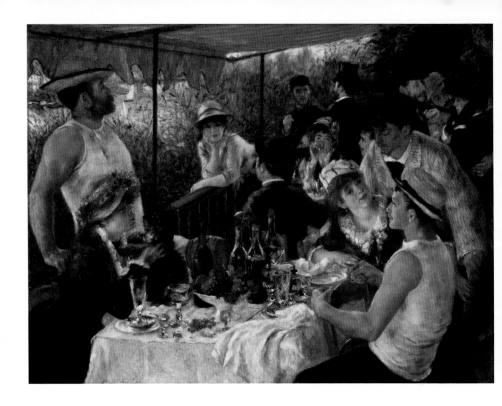

Pierre-Auguste Renoir
The Luncheon of the Boating Party, 1881
Le déjeuner des canotiers
Oil on canvas, 129.5 x 172.7 cm
Daulte 379
Washington, The Phillips Collection

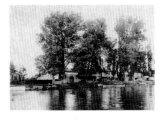

The rowing club at Bougival on the Seine, setting of
"The Luncheon of the Boating Party"

tier (1846–1905), somewhat younger than Renoir, was the successful publisher of Zola, Maupassant and Daudet. Since 1875 he had been host to politicians, intellectuals and artists of every persuasion at his magnificent home. His patronage rapidly expanded to include the entire group. Renoir painted Madame Marguerite Charpentier with her daughter, son and dog in her Japanese salon; the group portrait excited considerable interest at the 1879 Salon. From that year on, at the instigation of his cultured and ambitious wife, Charpentier published a new illustrated literary and art magazine, "La Vie moderne": Armand Silvestre edited the art section. It reported in an unstrained style on contemporary art of various kinds that was relatively accessible. A special feature was the provision of rooms named after the magazine, where Renoir's younger brother Edmond (1849–1943), a journalist, had the task of organizing a monthly series of small exhibitions. This gallery was intended to afford readers and the educated public an insight into one artist's studio at a time, as it were. The second of these exhibitions, understandably successful, featured the well-known De Nittis; the fifth was devoted to Renoir, mainly his pastels. Manet, Monet (1880) and Sisley (1881) followed before very long.

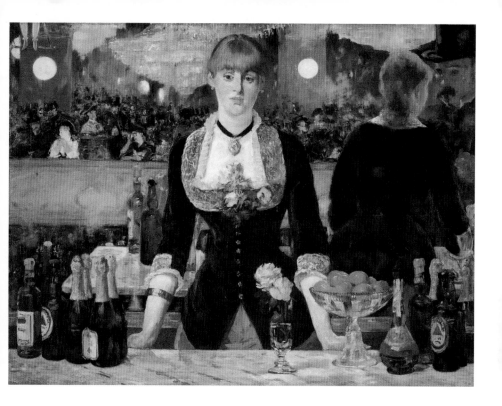

Edouard Manet
A Bar at the Folies-Bergère, c. 1881/82
Un bar aux Folies-Bergère
Oil on canvas, 96 x 130 cm
Rouart/Wildenstein I,388
London, Courtauld Institute Galleries

Renoir had successfully submitted to the Salon in 1878, and Monet followed him in 1880, though Sisley was turned down in 1879. Manet's brand of Impressionism was on view at the 1879 Salon with *Boating* (p. 138), a light, boldly cropped and strongly coloured work painted five years before. It was bought direct from the Salon by a collector. Manet's political convictions were reflected in his vigorous portrait of Georges Clemenceau (1841–1929), the new leader of the republic radicals (1879/80; Paris, Musée d'Orsay).

Degas was furious at the "renegades" who had joined the Salon. Caillebotte and the gentle-spirited Pissarro, who was already acquiring the air of an elderly patriarch, tried hard to maintain good relations. Caillebotte became resigned in 1881; Degas was pursuing other artistic goals too, and no new agreement could be reached. At the fourth exhibition, Degas had included figure painters, among them Cassatt and Marie Bracquemond (1841–1916). The latter notably had open-air work in the 1880 show that used colour in an Impressionist way and was flooded with light yet was also conspicuously exact in its draughtsmanship (pp. 194, 198). Like Degas, the youthful Jean-Louis Forain (1852–1931) had a preference for theatre and restaurant motifs (pp. 210, 211). Similar

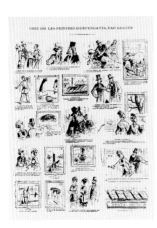

Cartoon by Draner (Jules Renard) on the fourth
Impressionist exhibition, from "Le Charivari",
23 April 1879

Pierre-Auguste Renoir
Two Girls, c. 1881
Deux jeunes filles
Oil on canvas, 80 x 65 cm
Moscow, Pushkin Museum of Fine Art

subjects appeared in the work of Eugène Vidal (1847–1907) and the Italian Federico Zandomeneghi (1841–1917), formerly of the Florentine pleinairist "Macchiaioli" school. There were also the moderately Impressionist landscape painters Albert Lebourg (1849–1928; pp. 313, 383) and Paul-Victor Vignon (1847–1909; pp. 202, 203) and, only once, the fairly fashionable graphic artist and painter Henry Somm, i.e. François Sommier (1844–1907; p. 263).

With Cassatt, Forain was the strongest artistic personality among Degas's followers. The son of a scenery-painter, he wanted art that was critical, satirical and committed. Under the influence of Goya and Daumier he mainly did graphic work as magazine and book illustrations or in series. As a painter he had mastered Impressionist techniques, having a precise touch for light conditions and a subtle flair for the structural division of a visual space. His small-format scenes of the entertainment world used distinctive contrasts of dark and light or of strong, glowing colour, and combined sketchy adumbrations with more substantial blocks of solid colour that had their own patchwork, asymmetrical values. This owed something to Manet. His caricatural overdrawing of figures contrasted starkly with the treatment of similar material by Renoir, Morisot or Cassatt, though, and tended to look rather superficial. The details in his works did not always possess that sense of inevitability that we associate with details in Degas before him, or Toulouse-Lautrec after.

Of comparable standing was Jean-François Raffaëlli (1850–1924), whom Degas had been trying to recruit since 1878. A former bookkeeper and singer, essentially self-taught, he essayed various thematic areas, and alternated between the Salon and other exhibition strategies. Raffaëlli was a follower of Millet, the "poet of the humble" (as Wolff, an admiring critic, put it). In 1884 he was to score so solid a financial success with a large private solo exhibition that he lost interest in the Impressionists. His contact with them in 1880 and 1881 was in any case merely loose, and consisted partly in a shared interest in social fringe groups. At first he painted Breton peasants, then urban alcoholics and rag-and-bone collectors. He also shared the Impressionists' concern with the persuasive atmospherics of sketchy pictorial spatial contexts. *The Absinth Drinkers* (p. 211), a semi-lifesize canvas exhibited in 1881 as *The Down and Outs*, would have appealed to Degas for the canvas structure and the subject of lonely outsiders, but also the delicately nuanced colouring. Raffaëlli's later *Waiting Wedding Guests* (p. 240) has an almost grotesque sense of the fleeting moment: the figures are squeezed out to the side and the setting is the dominant subject. Raffaëlli became a major figure in a Europe-wide artistic concern with the urban poor that extended well into the 20th century. This movement took only a few elements from Impressionism: the cropping, the flexible structures, and the sketchy application of paint.

Another newcomer in this very loose grouping was Paul Gauguin (1848–1903), who was to be important later. The son of a republican journalist and a Peruvian creole whose father had been a socialist, Gau-

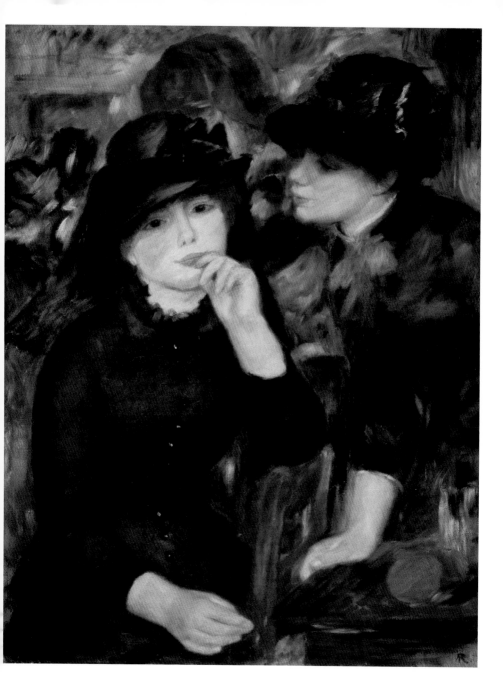

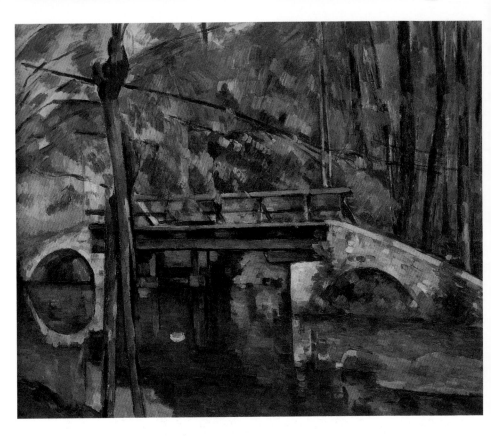

Paul Cézanne
The Bridge at Maincy, c. 1882–1885
Le pont de Maincy
Oil on canvas, 58.5 x 72.5 cm
Venturi 396. Paris, Musée d'Orsay

guin was in the merchant navy before working as a stockbroker and painting in the manner of Corot in his spare time. In 1876 he was accepted by the Salon. Gauguin used the money he made on the stock exchange to buy paintings. Pissarro, whom he met in 1874, probably through Pissarro's patron Arosa, taught him Impressionist landscape techniques and a sense of composition. The paintings he did at this period, such as those of the Seine banks in Paris, strongly resemble those of Guillaumin, another protégé of Pissarro and the Pontoise school. In 1879 Gauguin had a sculpture in the Impressionist exhibition, submitted late and not listed in the catalogue, and again exhibited sculptural work in 1880 and 1881 but also – indeed, mainly – landscapes, painted in relatively dark colours with a great many blue shadows executed with brief, tiny brush-strokes. His striking lifesize *Study of a Nude. Suzanne Sewing* (p. 207) combined a number of technical strategies and was a major feature of the 1881 show. Huysmans likened it to Rembrandt and hailed it as the most realistic nude in contemporary painting. The heavy flesh of this big-boned pregnant woman, together with her everyday

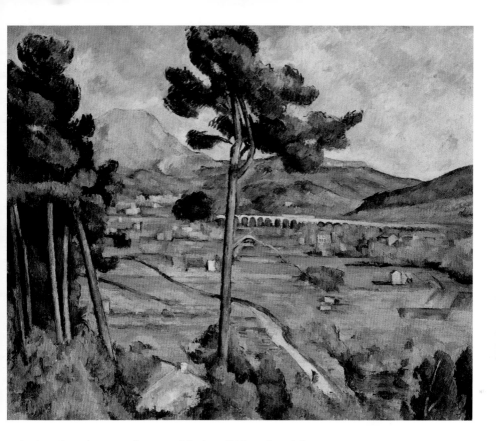

Paul Cézanne
Mont Sainte-Victoire seen from Bellevue,
c. 1882–1885
La Montagne Sainte-Victoire, vue de Bellevue
Oil on canvas, 65.5 x 81 cm
Venturi 452. New York, The Metropolitan
Museum of Art

task, share the realistic eye of Degas, while the still-life quality of the setting and the overall conception of the picture suggest Manet's approach. The fine brushwork of the nuanced colouring of light, and the blue and green shadows on the woman's skin, recall Renoir and even more Pissarro, who was just beginning to paint figures. For some years, Gauguin was to move with the Impressionist current. To Impressionism he owed his independence of convention, his feel for light in the open, the glowing force of his colours, and his unstrained and flexible sense of pictorial structure.

For a long time, and in the customary academic manner, the critics accused the new artists of renouncing not only traditional values and ennobling beauty but also the more demanding subjects. As in the first half of the 19th century, the supposed decline of art was ascribed to its "industrialization", which allegedly led to mass production. Thus Claretie for instance, who had found in connection with the 1874 Salon (not the concurrent Impressionist show) that landscape artists were contenting themselves with mere impressions and, indeed, that paintings

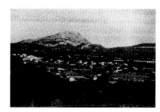

Mont Sainte-Victoire and the railway viaduct.
Photograph, c. 1935

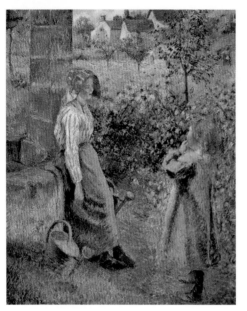

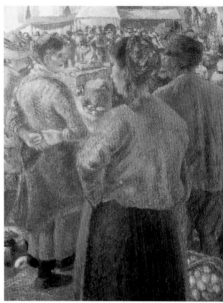

were being influenced by photography.[119] Those advocating a new art were divided. Some, such as Duranty, put their weight behind a realistic or naturalistic representation of modern life;[120] others, such as Rivière, defined Impressionism as a movement that portrayed a subject not for its own sake but for the colour values which it provided an opportunity to observe.[121] Those who espoused narrative genre painting, frequently taking their bearings from literature, could be astoundingly insensitive to artistic differences in painting techniques, and to specifically painterly qualities. They often preferred more accessible semi-Impressionists such as De Nittis, Béraud, Goeneutte or Gervex.

The critical judgements made by Huysmans in reviews from 1879 to 1881 fluctuated strikingly.[122] He drew interesting parallels with contemporary architecture (such as the new railway stations and market halls), much in line with Zola's "Le Ventre de Paris" (1873). His sympathies were initially with Manet and Degas, and particularly Raffaëlli, Forain and Caillebotte; the colourist techniques of the Impressionist pleinairists, and especially their blue and purple shadows, he called hysterical. He accused the painters (as Zola increasingly did) of not achieving the aims they set themselves and leaving unfulfilled the hopes they had at first aroused. Given the political climate of France after 1870/71, it was remarkable that Huysmans chose to highlight the realistic quality of a German painter, Max Liebermann (1847–1935). He even wished that Monet's railway station scenes shared the full interest in working life that characterized the art of Adolph von Menzel (1815–1905) as seen in his

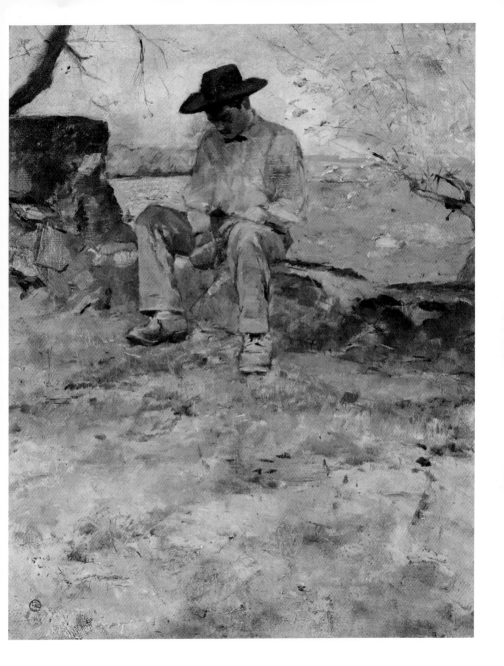

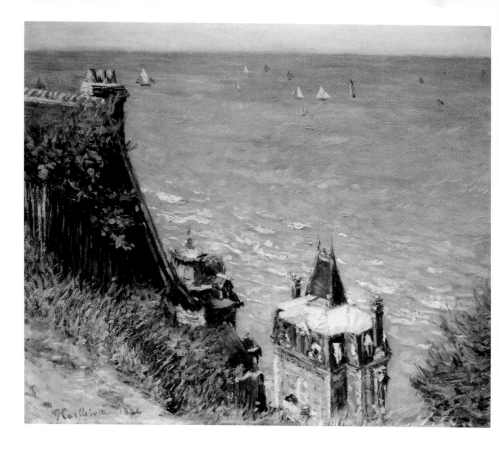

Gustave Caillebotte
The Pink Villa, Trouville, 1884
La villa rose, Trouville
Oil on canvas, 60 x 75 cm
Berhaut 271. Private collection

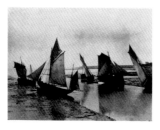

Yachts at La Rochelle. Photo: Atget, 1896

1875 painting *The Iron Rolling Mill*. In 1881, on the other hand, Huysmans found the Impressionism of Pissarro persuasive, and declared that he had taken that strain to maturity.

The position of one lone outsider proved controversial. Pierre Puvis de Chavannes was to play an important part in artistic movements over the next two or three decades. Largely self-taught as a painter, he had a taste for murals, and combined allegories in a classical tradition with growing brightness, sensitivity to landscape and atmosphere, and attention to the fate and dignity of "simple" people (in a manner distantly reminiscent of Millet – the more so since Puvis put his figures arrested in slow, straightforward gestural attitudes or simply froze them). In this, Puvis' art was fundamentally different from the radically naturalistic, sensation-seeking moments captured by other painters of histories. His *Young Women on the Seashore* (p. 189) had affinities with Impressionism not only through the motif and brightness; what matters in the painting is not so much the reproduction of a particular subject as the wealth of diverse sensations the picture may prompt in us, and the sense that this is the true aim of artistic endeavour. As early as 1874, Castagnary had largely defined Impressionism through its emphasis not on landscape as such but rather on the sensations caused by it.

The 1882 Salon struck critics as more modern. The review in the "Gazette des Beaux-Arts" was written by Manet's friend Proust. The year before, the Salon had for the first time no longer been under state control, being organized instead by a committee elected by artists who had already been accepted by the Salon in the past. This committee drew up the statutes of a Société des Artistes Français, which was founded in 1882 and organized the Salon from that date on.[123] The state – and this remained true of the new society too – had been unable to solve the problem of reconciling the exhibition requirements of a growing number of artists with the ideal and qualitative demands implied in making a representative selection that would be ideologically sound and educative. In any case, since 1879 the state had been a changed thing, making greater concessions to democratic ideas, personal liberty, and a liberal interplay

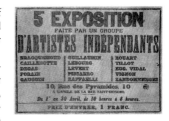

Poster for the fifth Impressionist exhibition, 1880

The Harbour at Argenteuil, 1882
Le bassin d'Argenteuil
Oil on canvas, 65 x 81 cm
Berhaut 230. Private collection

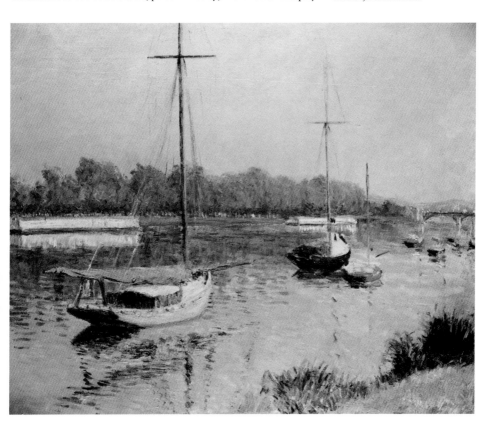

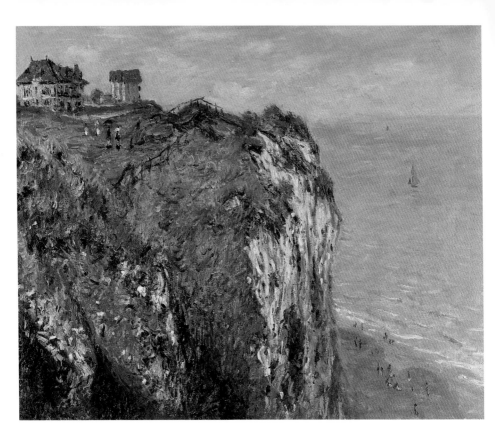

Claude Monet
Cliffs near Dieppe, 1882
La falaise à Dieppe
Oil on canvas, 65 x 81 cm
Wildenstein 759
Zurich, Kunsthaus Zürich

of competing forces. Towards the end of 1881, Antonin Proust became Minister for the Arts. The 1880 Salon included paintings with political, republican subjects, among them work by Gervex and the great *Miners' Strike* by Alfred Roll (1846–1919). The jury, chaired by Bouguereau, debated awarding Manet a medal; the award was in fact not made till 1881, under the new order.

At the same time, Durand-Ruel had weathered his financial crisis of 1880/81 and was again buying significant numbers of Impressionist paintings (though the collapse of a bank that supported him, the Union générale, brought new difficulties in 1882). In Georges Petit (c. 1835–1900) he now had a serious competitor. Petit organized appealing "expositions internationales", and from 1880 on put pressure on Monet to submit to the Salon again. In 1882, to clear his stock, Durand-Ruel organized what was billed as the seventh exhibition of independent artists, hung by Caillebotte and Pissarro and located on the top floor of 251 Rue Saint-Honoré. On the ground floor, a panoramic view of the battle of Reichshofen in Alsace (in 1870) was displayed, a detailed over-

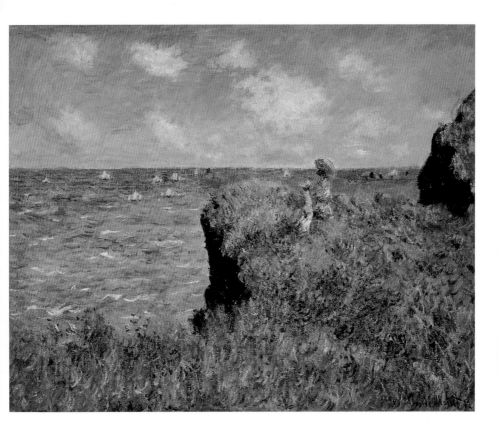

Claude Monet
Clifftop Walk at Pourville, 1882
La promenade sur la falaise, Pourville
Oil on canvas, 66.5 x 82.3 cm
Wildenstein 758
Chicago, The Art Institute of Chicago

view of the kind then popular with the public, sometimes including real objects illusionistically built in. It was a curious meeting of two fundamentally different kinds of art, both dependent on sense impact for their effect. Only one of them was popular, though – that on the ground floor. This was the more ironic since the group work upstairs was thematically harmless and thoroughly suitable for hanging on the wall at home.

Three quarters of that work consisted of landscapes. The figural work, particularly Pissarro's shepherdesses or peasant women (pp. 216, 217) or Renoir's *The Luncheon of the Boating Party* (p. 220), the exhibition's *pièce de résistance*, was thoroughly appealing too. This time Monet, Renoir and Sisley were again in the show, as was Morisot, while Degas and his followers in critical realism remained without. Cassatt and Rouart refused to participate for this reason. For Renoir, concerned to retain customers and in any case not a man inclined to controversy, Pissarro – with his friends and his anarchist leanings – represented quite enough in the way of risk. Partly for health reasons, Renoir was spending

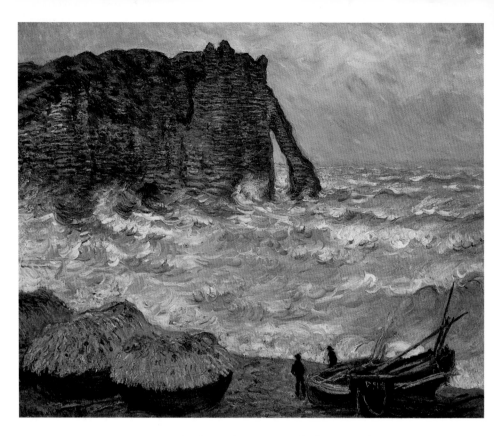

Claude Monet
Rough Sea at Etretat, 1883
Etretat, mer agitée
Oil on canvas, 81 x 100 cm
Wildenstein 821. Lyon, Musée des Beaux-Arts

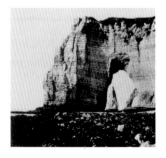

La Manneporte at Etretat, c. 1910

his time in the warmer South of France, and twice indeed sojourned in Algiers; he mainly left the exhibition of his work to Durand-Ruel. Tetchy after a bout of pneumonia, he wrote to the dealer on 26 February 1882 from L'Estaque, where he was visiting Cézanne: "To exhibit with Pissarro, Gauguin and Guillaumin is like exhibiting with simply anybody. Soon we'll be having Pissarro invite Lavrov, the Russian, or some other revolutionary. The public do not like things that smell of politics, and at my age I do not want to be a revolutionary. To remain along with the Israelite Pissarro is revolution. Get rid of these people and give me people like Monet, Sisley, Morisot etc. and I'm with you, because then it is no longer a political issue, it's art pure and simple."[124] But he did wish to go on with Degas, whom he found "incomprehensible".[125] Renoir's anti-semitic remark did not put an end to good working relations, though. Renoir – like Monet, who thought similarly – had only a precarious grasp of political current affairs. Their interest was in their art and their lives as artists. Many years later, Renoir, speaking of Durand-Ruel and his political views, told his son Jean: "We needed a reactionary to defend

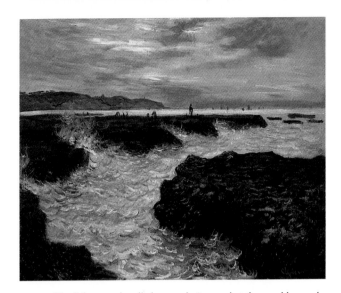

our art. The Salon people called us revolutionary, but they could scarcely shoot him as a Communard."[126]

Manet, whom the independent artists repeatedly and vainly tried to recruit for exhibition purposes, was approaching the end of his life as an artist. He spent the summer of 1880 in a rented house at Bellevue, for health reasons, and summer 1881 at Versailles. His last residence was a villa in Rueil. When a narrow majority of the Salon jury awarded him their medal (second class), he called on his fellow artists to thank them

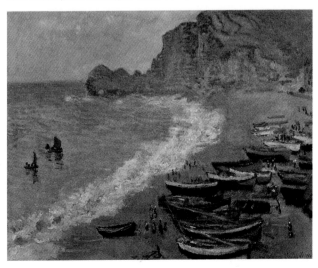

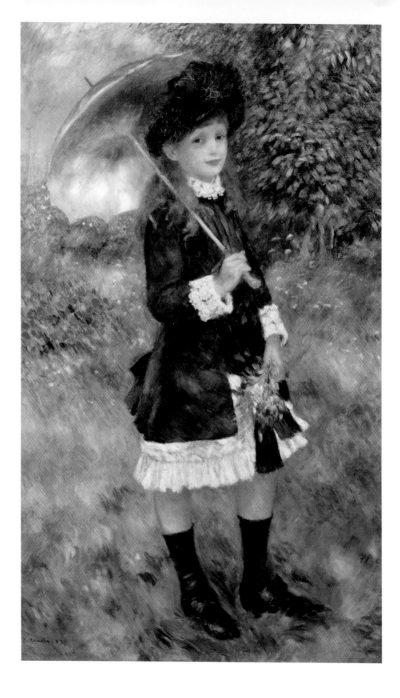

– Carolus-Duran, Cazin, Gervex, Guillemet, Roll, and others who were in no sense in his artistic league. Some months later, thanks to Minister Proust, he was awarded the cross of the Legion of Honour. When the Comte de Nieuwerkerke, formerly the imperial art panjandrum, congratulated him, Manet wrote in a surprisingly resigned tone to a friend: "He could have conferred an award on me. He would have made me very happy. Now it is too late to make up for twenty years without success."[127]

Manet was painting uneven scenes and portraits and still struggling for the uncertain recognition the art scene can grant, which in his case remained inseparable from the unhappy Salon. On the other hand, in late 1881 he was still planning to paint engine drivers and stokers in a locomotive, the "modern heroes" he admired as much as Zola (who had written a novel using this material nine years before). But primarily he was painting a series celebrating the sensual charms and challenges offered by beautiful women. These works, partly in pastel, sometimes showed ladies of the *demi-monde*. He intended four of them to make a series on the four seasons (p. 213), but this remained unfinished. As he was consumed by the disease that was to kill him, Manet also turned to the lush summer delights of gardens at Bellevue and Rueil, bringing a quality of humble observation to his work, as if the exacting delicacy of his brushwork might delay the extinction of life. The sectional views he painted were limited at every side, as if his horizon were literally becoming invisible (p. 200).

In the winter of 1881/82 Manet painted a picture that can stand as a summation of his art: *A Bar at the Folies-Bergère* (p. 221). Now exempt (as an award winner) from the jury process, he exhibited it at the 1882 Salon. The critic Julius Meier-Graefe later unfathomably called it "the weakest work Manet ever painted",[128] but most recent scholars have rightly been fascinated by the qualities of the painting and the intensity and diversity of Manet's renewed analysis of part of the society he lived in. The colours are rather subdued, it is true (which may be intended to convey the smoky somnolence of the pleasure palace), but on the other hand Manet gives us first-rate proof of his still-life talent in the foreground. The hard, cold quality of the white light globes is perfectly caught; they are like buttons on the canvas. Manet's pastose brushwork creates a unified tapestry of colour correspondences and contrasts across the various spatial levels.

Those levels themselves are intentionally confusing; most of what we see is a reflection in the bar mirror behind the woman. The laws of perspective are broken in a fashion that was a radical departure at the time. The woman's back, and the customer facing her (in whom we are invited to see ourselves), are reflected at an angle. The barwoman, whose tightly girded midriff seems wrongly drawn, seems on offer for consumption like the bottles and fruit before her, with her deep, flower-adorned decolleté. Only the roses in the wine glass seem an expression of tenderness towards her. With her weary, vacant, slightly sideways gaze, she has the inimitable Manet *impassibilité*. Only her attractive public front is participating in her work in the Parisian world of entertainment; the full

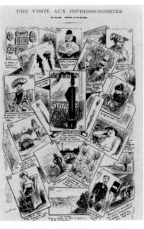

"A Visit to the Impressionists": cartoon by Draner (Jules Renard) on the seventh Impressionist exhibition, from "Le Charivari", 9 March 1882

Pierre-Auguste Renoir
Young Girl with a Parasol (Aline Nunès), 1883
Jeune fille à l'ombrelle (Aline Nunès)
Oil on canvas, 130 x 79 cm
Paris, David-Weill Collection

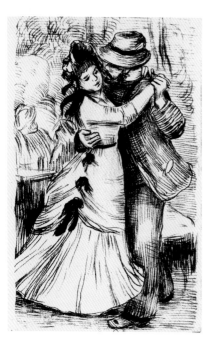

Pierre-Auguste Renoir
Dance in the Country, 1880
Danse à la campagne
Etching, 21.8 x 13.4 cm

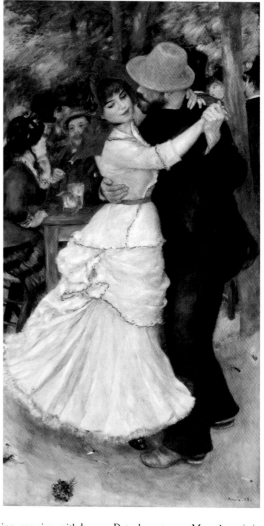

Pierre-Auguste Renoir
Dance at Bougival (Suzanne Valadon
and Paul Lhote), c. 1882/83
La danse à Bougival
Oil on canvas, 182 x 98 cm
Daulte 438. Boston (MA), Museum of Fine Arts

human being remains withdrawn. Detachment was Manet's artistic method (not to be confused with a lack of feeling in the man), and so his scene records what he saw (and pondered) impassively, levelling no grand accusations. "But for that very reason his pictures objectively constitute a more biting critique of society than any socio-critical caricature could achieve."[119]

Finally, already partly paralysed, Manet painted a number of small still lifes such as *Bundle of Asparagus* (p. 198), which became well known in Germany because Liebermann, a great admirer of Manet, once

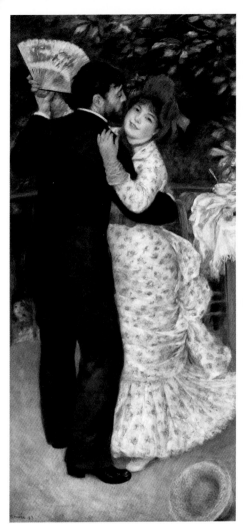

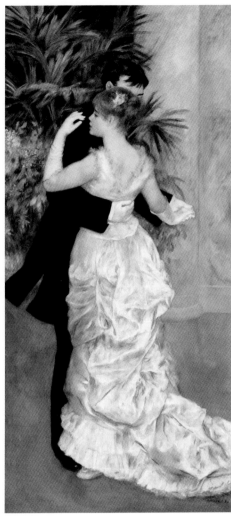

owned it. Manet also painted endless variations on the theme of flowers in vases. It is moving to look at these enchanting impressions of the loveliness of the natural world, given what we know of the advanced state of Manet's illness when he painted them. In April 1883 he had a foot amputated; a few weeks later he died in considerable pain. At his grave, Proust observed, punning in Latin: "Manet et manebit." (He remains and he will remain.)

Degas was persistent in his art, concentrating all the more intensely on ever fewer thematic areas. About 1882, with Cassatt, he discovered a

Pierre-Auguste Renoir
Dance in the Country (Aline Charigot and Paul Lhote), c. 1882/83
La danse à la campagne
Oil on canvas, 180 x 90 cm
Daulte 441. Paris, Musée d'Orsay

Pierre-Auguste Renoir
Dance in the City (Suzanne Valadon and Eugène-Pierre Lestringuez), 1882
La danse à la ville
Oil on canvas, 180 x 90 cm
Daulte 440. Paris, Musée d'Orsay

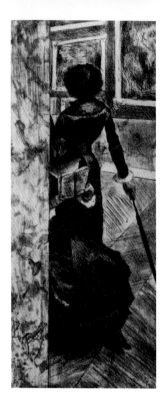

Edgar Degas
Mary Cassatt at the Louvre, 1879/80
Mary Cassatt au Louvre
Etching, 36.3 x 26.6 cm

Pierre-Auguste Renoir
Les Parapluies, 1883
Oil on canvas, 180.3 x 114.9 cm
Daulte 298. London, National Gallery

new subject in milliners and their shops, finding it possible to discover the offbeat beauties of modern life through this material. His studies of jockeys and horses now tended to foreground curious patterns of brightly coloured jockeys' clothing and edgy horses. His *Women Ironing* (p. 242) reminds us why Degas wanted to recruit a painter such as Raffaëlli to the independent group. Degas's meticulous preparatory studies, and the variations he did on the theme, show how seriously he took it. The element of the grotesque in one tired woman's yawn is no more absurd, no likelier to diminish the woman's dignity, than the poses in which we see weary dancers massaging their aching feet, something Degas observed time and again. His ballet scenes, bar a few exceptions, now lost the anecdotal component introduced by ballet masters, watching gentlemen, or mothers (or procuresses) reading papers. Degas was more and more interested in individual physical gestures, the consonance of groups, and above all the colour impact of a total view, which he now made into the dominant sense appeal in pictures done for preference in grainy pastel. Another new subject area that significantly engaged him – women about their toilet – will be discussed below in connection with issues of public presentation.

Monet was also changing his subjects or emphases. Despite his disagreements with Degas over exhibition strategies or work methods, the formless, iridescent patches of colour on the ice of his winter river landscapes, say, reveal similarities with Degas's increasingly colourful pictures from the world of ballet. Monet, the leader of the true Impressionist core, left Argenteuil in 1878 and settled at Vétheuil, fifty kilometres further from Paris. At the end of 1881 he moved again, to Poissy, but failed to be inspired by any subjects there and in spring 1883 moved yet again, and finally, to Giverny, a village of 280 inhabitants, situated like the others on the Seine. Often he lived in real penury. Since his time at Vétheuil he had been living with Alice Hoschedé (and her six children), who had separated from her bankrupt art-collector husband. In 1892, following Hoschedé's death, Alice became Monet's second wife. Camille, his first, had died in 1879 after a long illness. Monet did a pale pink and blue study of her on her deathbed, the evanescent fluidity of which seems to articulate the slipping away from life of the loved one (p. 176). He later told Clemenceau that he had been struck by the various colours in his dead wife's face and had been horrified to realise how much a prisoner of his visual experience he was, impelled by instinct to paint and nothing but.[130] The loving husband had almost been supplanted by the painter. The issue of unfeeling, detached observation versus the conquest of grief by customary artistic work was one that recurred in the literature and art of the time.[131]

Vétheuil, with its church seen across the river, provided Monet with a motif he painted exhaustively in countless variations. He frequently combined it with lush poppy fields in the foreground, with Alice and her children occasionally to be seen picking flowers. More than in comparable work of the 70s, Monet would now do the red flowers as a massed agglomerate of dabs. Despite continuing financial insecurity, he

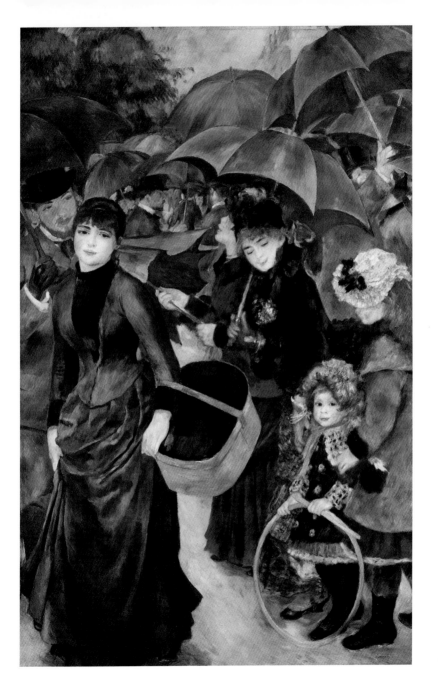

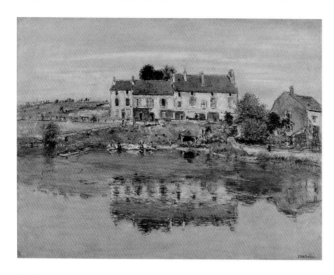

Jean-François Raffaëlli
Houses on the Banks of the Oise
Petites maisons au bord de l'Oise
Oil on card, 65 x 85 cm
Paris, Musée d'Orsay

liked to go to his home parts in Normandy in summer or winter, from 1881 on; later he would join Renoir when the latter visited Cézanne in Provence, or travel to the Italian Riviera. Monet was forever questing for new landscape motifs. Every walk, as witnesses reported, afforded an opportunity to size up views and angles of vision. When confronted with paintings that are almost identical, we can now no longer say which versions were attempts at improvement, which captured different impressions, or which were copies of successful paintings.

Sisley likewise went tirelessly in search of motifs along the Seine and

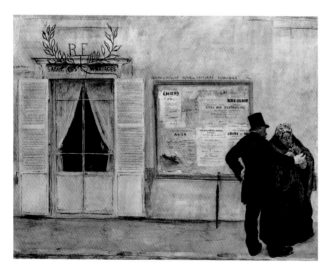

Jean-François Raffaëlli
Waiting Wedding Guests, 1884
Les invités attendant la noce
Oil on panel, 52.5 x 68.5 cm
Paris, Musée d'Orsay

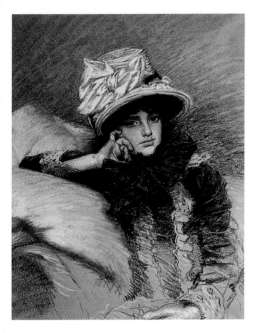

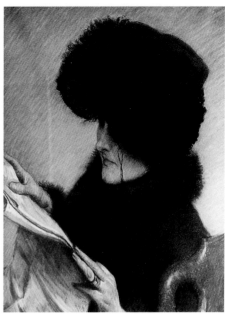

its tributaries; he looked no further. He abided by views of village streets or of interesting groups of buildings; he would be drawn to an old stone bridge, the kind of subject that had fascinated painters since Corot. In unprepossessing patches of gardens or meadows, landscapes on the skirts of towns or along river banks, he could often discover the most arresting colour or light effects (pp. 313, 339).

Pissarro's art entered a period of change, though he never abandoned his principle of fidelity to what the eye saw. At the end of 1882 he moved to Osny (near Pontoise), then in spring 1884 to Eragny on the River Epte, where he, his wife, and their six children remained for the rest of their lives. As well as simple landscapes, generally with an amount of additional interest (p. 275), he painted Paris street scenes for the first time, and in 1883 views of Rouen, where he visited his old patron Murer in his hotel. But these new motifs were only to bear their full fruit later. The most striking of his new departures concerned his market scenes featuring a larger number of figures (p. 226), and particularly open-air or indoor scenes in which farmers or maids are given dominant roles to play. The landscape painter had become a figure painter.

Degas, as was suspected at the time, had a hand in the diagonal or top views and the slant tensions introduced into some of the pictures. In Pissarro, though, perspectives of this kind remained notably gentler. Even if he generally looked (literally) down on his models, even on seated half-length figures, there was no sarcasm in his gaze, but rather fellow

James Tissot
Berthe, 1883
Pastel on paper, 73 x 59 cm
Paris, Musée du Petit Palais

James Tissot
The Newspaper, 1883
Le journal
Pastel on paper, 63 x 50 cm
Paris, Musée du Petit Palais

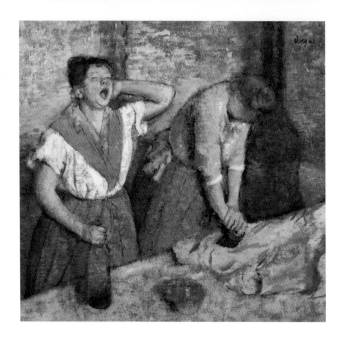

Edgar Degas
Women Ironing, c. 1884
Les repasseuses
Oil on canvas, 76 x 81.5 cm
Lemoisne 785. Paris, Musée d'Orsay

feeling (p. 217). The large, rounded shapes of the figures and the patterning of areas they establish, as well as the lassitude expressed in movement so slow as to be barely perceptible, influenced Gauguin's idea of visual images significantly; he was in Pissarro's circle, and was a contributory factor in Pissarro's tensions with Renoir and Monet.

Pissarro generally painted very brightly, utilizing a good deal of green and yellow, and even rather sweet shades and strong contrasts that had now become distinctly removed from the subtle nuances of Corot. Above all, he employed brush-strokes that grew ever briefer, and mere dabs. A spatial structure established by houses and the sinuous curves of roads and paths was superseded by an interwoven fabric of equal parts of pigment across a visual area. Cézanne, who sometimes went to see Pissarro, was struck by this; so was Guillaumin, though for the time being he adhered to an older solution to the problem of spatial and surface qualities and of paint application (p. 205). The young artist Charles Angrand (1854–1926) painted in a style that closely resembled Pissarro's.

Morisot's life, with summers in Bougival and winters in Nice, was a carefree, happy one, even if looking after her daughter and supervising the building of a Paris house made demands on her. Her Impressionist style achieved its full bloom in this period, in light open-air or interior scenes of family contentment or domestic tasks, painted with notable ease, or portraits of lovely young people. Caillebotte chose his subjects

Right:
Henri de Toulouse-Lautrec
The Laundress, 1884–1886
La blanchisseuse
Oil on canvas, 93 x 75 cm
Dortu 346. Paris, private collection

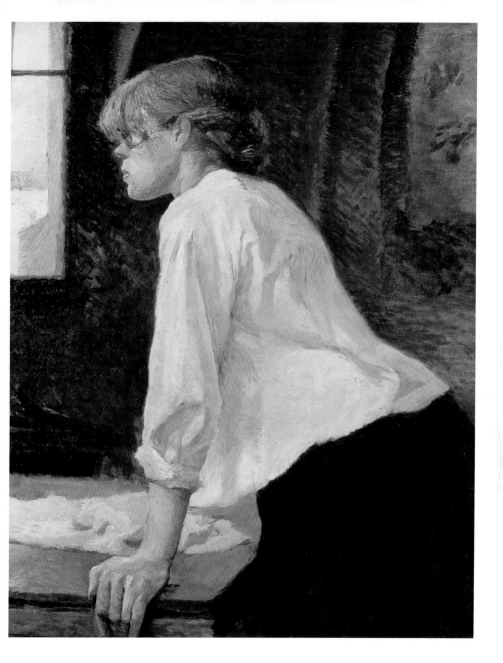

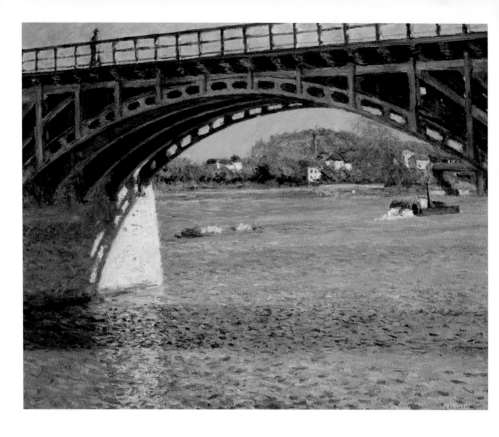

Gustave Caillebotte
The Bridge at Argenteuil and the Seine, 1885
Le pont d'Argenteuil et la Seine
Oil on canvas, 65 x 82 cm
Berhaut 310
Lausanne, Samuel Josefowitz Collection

as he pleased, painting oarsmen on the Seine, people in the country, or scenes in his home in Paris or in cafés.

Renoir was one of those artists who on the one hand were determined not to throw away their mounting success on the art scene and market but on the other hand grew insecure about their way of painting. Despite his landscapes and city scenes, Renoir was at heart a (female) figure painter, and he never lost the high regard he had for the great classical traditions. At an early stage, when his friends were damning academic classicism outright, he had "let them go on talking and had silently admired the belly of Ingres' *Source*." In old age he sardonically remarked: "I do not know if I would have become a painter if God had not created the female bosom."[132] Sales permitted him to travel to the south for the first time in 1881; in the spring he went to Algeria, in Delacroix's footsteps, as it were; in the autumn and winter to Italy; and then to L'Estaque to see Cézanne. His enthusiasm for the controversial music of Richard Wagner, an enthusiasm he shared with many modern artists positioned between realism and symbolism, prompted him to solicit a portrait

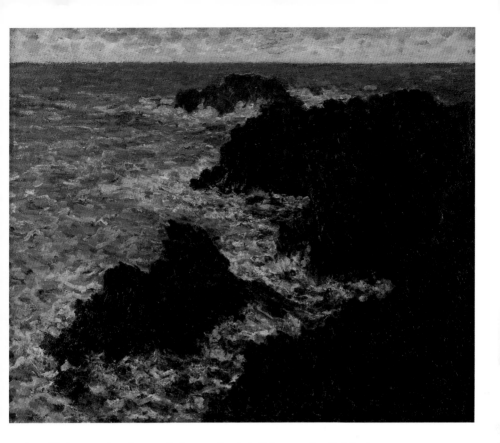

Claude Monet
The Rocks of Belle-Ile (Rough Sea), 1886
Les rochers de Belle-Ile (La côte sauvage)
Oil on canvas, 65 x 81.5 cm
Wildenstein 1100. Paris, Musée d'Orsay

session with the ungracious Saxon, who happened to be in Palermo and would spare only 35 minutes for a hasty sketch. Above all, Renoir was filled with admiration for the work of Raphael and the ancient frescoes of Pompeii, which reminded him of Corot's graceful nymphs.

Renoir was now disquieted by what he later referred to as the "traps of sunlight".[133] Never again would he resolve the three-dimensionality of flesh so fully into dabs of light and shadow and colour as in *Nude in the Sunlight* (p. 162), which had so angered the venomous Albert Wolff. First he took to carefully drawing and modelling seated female nudes in the open, all of whom he described as bathers. His eye for heavy volumes and clear outlines, for curves and smooth surfaces, could at times be sculptural, and was connected with Renoir's sense of having exhausted Impressionism and arrived in a cul de sac. Painting in the open, from Nature, merely produced momentary effects, he now felt. It was a real creative crisis accompanying three main and distinct developments. One was that Renoir, aged forty and gradually achieving success, was settling down. In 1880 he met a young sempstress from the country, Aline Cha-

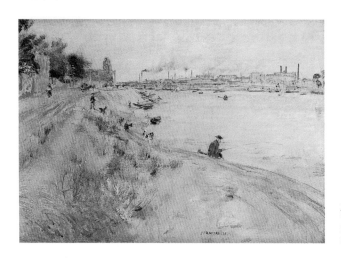

Jean-François Raffaëlli
Fisherman on the Bank of the Seine
Pêcheur sur la rive de la Seine
Oil on canvas, 25.7 x 35.6 cm
Private collection

rigot (1859–1915). They moved in together in 1882 and married in 1890, when their first son was already five. A second aspect was the changed character and climate of French society and culture. Renoir could cope, though without full consent; his enthusiasm was only for the lost values of the past. As a subject for art, contemporary reality receded, displaced by timeless idylls of undefinable location. The third factor was the arrival of the next, young generation of artists, who as always were partly continuing available lines in novel ways and partly bent on substituting something new and incomprehensible.

There were observers who lamented Renoir's changed method as the destruction of twenty years of achievement. Renoir was meticulous: he spent three years, longer than ever before, working on *The Bathers* (p. 304), completing it in 1887 and ending a dry spell in his productivity. The figures are a curious cross between momentarily glimpsed, uninhibited Paris street girls (Paul Jamot, 1923) and the creatures of a stylized, classicized composition. In contrast to Renoir's long-standing attempts to blend figures optically into their surroundings, the women seen in this work stand out clearly against the landscape. In parts the landscape is done with precision; in parts it is almost naive (and the water clumsily done). The women's bodies are modelled in fine, bright nuances of light and shadow. The restless body language of these bathers, and the additive, patchwork quality of the composition, heighten the contrariety in this picture and, though it remains fascinating, they ultimately diminish its value.

Another major painting also bore the signs of years of work and rework: *Les Parapluies* (p. 239). Changing fashions have even been identified in the clothes the people are wearing; and the changeover from a relaxed technique to tauter modelling is self-evident. Renoir's eye for female beauty, cute children and tender gazes is at work here, and the motifs are additively ranged in the Impressionist manner. Chance move-

Right:
Armand Guillaumin
The Fishermen, c. 1885
Les pêcheurs
Oil on canvas, 81 x 66 cm
Serret/Fabiani 122. Paris, Musée d'Orsay

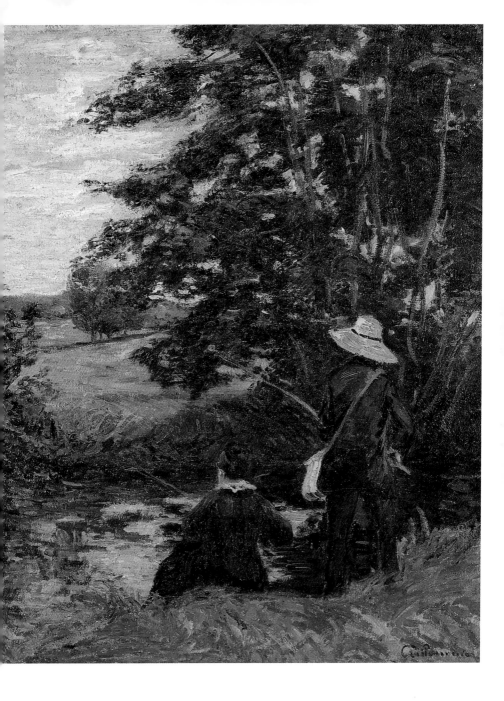

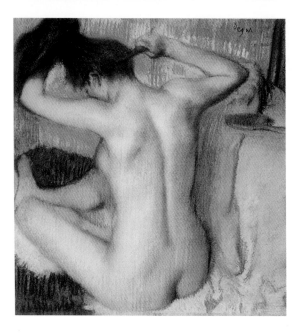
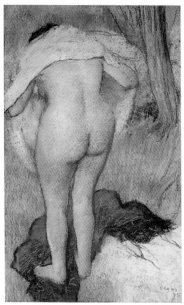

Edgar Degas
Woman Combing her Hair, c. 1885
Femme se peignant
Pastel on card, 53 x 52 cm
Lemoisne 898. St. Petersburg, Hermitage

Edgar Degas
After the Bath. Woman Drying Herself, 1885
Après le bain. Femme s'essuyant
Pastel on paper, 80 x 51.2 cm
Lemoisne, supplement 113
Washington (DC), National Gallery of Art

ments and the overlapping of figures combine with the statuesque, ancient air of the milliner with the hatbox and with the abstract three-dimensional pattern of the umbrellas that give the canvas its title. Good as this impression of street bustle is, finely as the blue-grey and silvery moist atmosphere with its dull gold patches of light has been caught, what we see is the conflict between truth to a visual experience and the linear, decorative patterning that articulates the artist's imposition of form-giving will.

Before *Les Parapluies*, Renoir completed three other scenes of Paris life (pp. 236, 237). Durand-Ruel had commissioned three high-format panels for his dining room. As with the *Moulin de la Galette*, Renoir had two fellow painters – Lhote and Lestringuez – pose for these dance paintings, as well as the model Suzanne Valadon and his beloved Aline. (Suzanne Valadon – actually Marie-Clémentine Valade, 1867–1938 – later became a gifted artist herself and the mother of the painter Maurice Utrillo, 1883–1955.) The body language, the overall visual rhythm, the materiality of the clothing and the colouring all set the more restrained city ball scene apart from the tender togetherness at a country inn or the conviviality of a boating party at Bougival. The happy, appealing smile of Aline in one painting is the nucleus of the composition.

At that time, Cézanne sought close contact with his associates of the early years, and in his art he approached very close to one fundamental Impressionist tenet: to concentrate entirely on what was seen. But at the same time he moved on from Impressionism, in order "to make of it

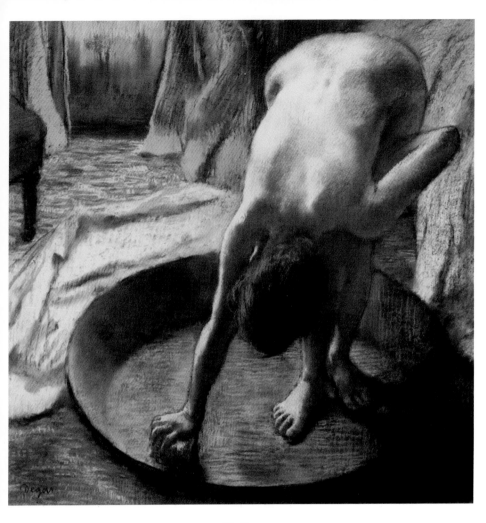

Edgar Degas
The Tub, 1885/86
Le tub
Pastel on paper, 70 x 70 cm
Lemoisne 876
Farmington (CT), The Hill-Stead Museum

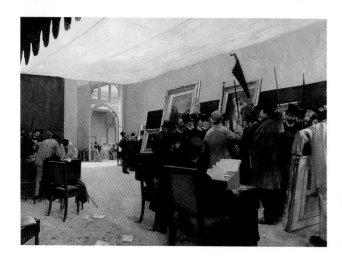

Henri Gervex
The Salon Jury, 1885
Une séance du jury de peinture, Salon des artistes français
Oil on canvas, 299 x 419 cm
Paris, Musée d'Orsay

something as solid and lasting as the art in the museums" and not remain content with the mere recording of an impression.[134] He was living mostly in Aix and the vicinity, but between 1879 and 1885 he paid several visits to the friend of his youth, Zola, in Médan (not far from Paris), as well as to Pissarro at Pontoise. In 1882 and 1883 (the second time with Monet), Renoir was his guest in Provence and painted with him at La Roche-Guyon, on the Seine near Giverny, in 1883. In 1882, just once, he succeeded in placing a painting in the Salon. Rejected once more in 1884, he finally abandoned the "battle for Paris".

The Bridge at Maincy (p. 224), near Melun, surrounded by slender trees in glowing emerald depths, was one of the first masterpieces of a mature personal style that was to have implications of great consequence for future art. There is an inner dynamic and a dimension of time to the painting, as if it expressed a process of becoming. This derives from the unstrained and unfinished brushwork and from the gently swaying lines that demarcate colour boundaries. Adjoining patches of colour are always balanced, however delicately. The interwoven overall *gestalt* invariably meant more to Cézanne than the unambiguous representation of details. He created that *gestalt* through an idiosyncratically tentative approach, continually comparing the impression of the natural scene with the organic pictorial image and trying to bring the two into line.

In addition to portraits or studies of his partner Hortense Fiquet (1850–1918), and still lifes, Cézanne also tackled one of Impressionist art's main subjects, the human figure, and specifically open-air nudes (usually described as bathers). In Cézanne, nudes could always assume another character – romantically literary, or dramatically related to the psychology of sex. Cézanne was a shy person, and Aix a prudish, philistine town, so that painting naked women in the open was quite out of the question. He therefore sketched copies of paintings he admired by old masters such as Titian or Rubens when he was in the Louvre in Paris. He also used reproductions or photographs of paintings at home, and nude photographs that were available to artists. He only ever drew single figures in complicated poses, though, and never entire compositions. Again, in this work he would dissect the subject into fragments and sectionalize movement. His whole life long, dissatisfied and often aware of failure, his aim was to put the pieces back together in a meaningful overall structure.

Cézanne's main work was done in landscapes. He painted the river valleys of the Ile-de-France and, above all, his beloved hard, bright, sun-baked Provence. His dream was that someone who looked at his paintings might smell the characteristic scents of the region and feel the mistral blowing. Over the course of decades he never tired of walking the hills in order to paint the majestic profile of Mont Sainte-Victoire, often with the valley of the Arc in the foreground and the impressive intrusion of a lengthy new railway viaduct (p. 225). Later he was to define his method by saying, "I merely try to convey perspective by means of colour."

Albert Besnard
Portrait of Madame Roger Jourdain, 1886
Portrait de Mme Roger Jourdain
Oil on canvas, 200 x 155 cm
Paris, Musée des Arts Décoratifs

James Tissot
The Painters and their Wives, c. 1885
Les peintres et leurs femmes
Oil on canvas, 146 x 101.7 cm
Norfolk (VA), The Crysler Museum

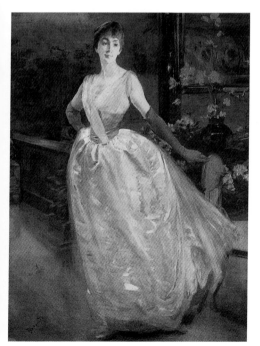

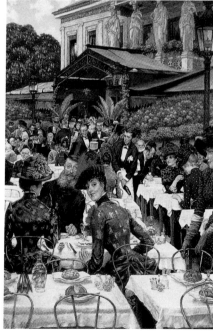

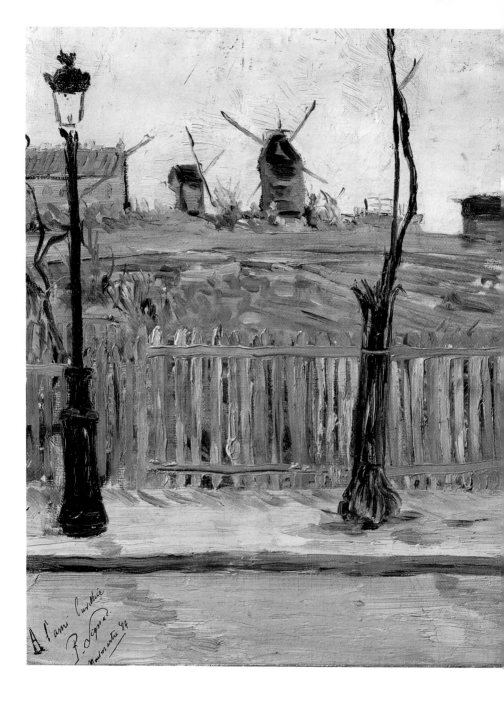

7 Neo-Impressionism and Post-Impressionism

While Pissarro, Renoir and Cézanne were painting the pictures we have just been discussing, the arts in France were witnessing events that changed the parameters for the Impressionists. By the time of the eighth and last group exhibition in May/June 1886, which reviews almost unanimously labelled Impressionist, the front line where new or controversial aesthetics were fought out had moved. (Of course such controversies were always only the concern of an avant-garde minority on the fringe of the mainstream art perceived and wanted by the majority of people with any interest at all in such matters – not to mention the many who took no interest at all.)

Despite its new circumstances, under the guidance of the Société des Artistes Français, the Salon continued its policy of exclusion. Since the jury was elected by artists who had previously been honoured with a Salon medal, it retained its distrust of new rivals. For this reason, 1884 saw the establishment of a second annual Salon by some 400 dissatisfied members of the Société des Artistes Indépendants. There was to be no jury assessment of artists' work. The idea was Albert Dubois-Pillet's (1846–1890); an amateur artist and freemason who was a gendarme by profession, he became the secretary and vice-president of the association. Odilon Redon (1840–1916) chaired the debates on the society's statutes. He was a friend of Corot and Fantin-Latour who had become known primarily for his drawings and graphics in the years since 1879. His easeful, sometimes asymmetrical, enigmatic and even fantastic little works had already been showcased in Charpentier's "La Vie moderne" and elsewhere. Guillaumin was actively involved. The young Georges Seurat (1859–1891), who had been so disenchanted with his studies at the Ecole des Beaux-Arts that he broke them off in 1879, preferring to paint in the manner of Renoir, met Paul Signac (1863–1935) through the debates; Signac shared his views. In December 1884 the first unjuried show by the Indépendants was then held.

The foundation of this group of Indépendants inaugurated the era of what came to be known as secessions. At the turn of the century, secessional offshoots and splinter groups were time and again to prove the main innovatory force in art throughout Europe, America and even Japan. The Indépendants mounted a second exhibition in 1886. By 1890/91 they were experiencing the usual fate of dissatisfied groups who

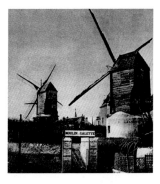

The mills of Montmartre, with the Moulin de la Galette on the right, c. 1840

Paul Signac
Rue Caulaincourt: Mills on Montmartre, 1884
Rue Caulaincourt: Moulins à Montmartre
Oil on canvas, 35 x 27 cm
Paris, Musée Carnavalet

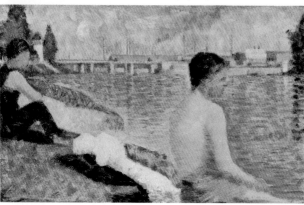

Georges Seurat
Horses in the Seine
(Study for "Bathing at Asnières"),
c. 1883/84
Cheval blanc et cheval noir dans l'eau
Oil on canvas, 15.2 x 24.8 cm
Dorra/Rewald 88; De Hauke 86
London, Courtauld Institute Galleries

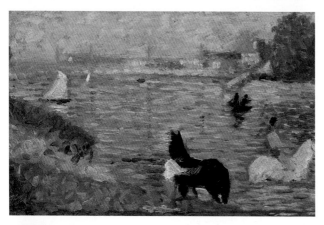

Georges Seurat
Bather (Study for "Bathing at Asnières"), c. 1883/84
Baigneur assis
Oil on canvas, 17.5 x 26.4 cm
Dorra/Rewald 96; De Hauke 84
Kansas City (MO), Nelson-Atkins Museum of Art

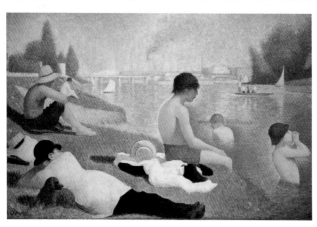

Georges Seurat
Bathers at Asnières, 1883/84
Une baignade à Asnières
Oil on canvas, 201 x 300 cm
Dorra/Rewald 98; De Hauke 92
London, National Gallery

take things into their own hands: under the guidance of Meissonier, now an old man, they set up the Société Nationale des Beaux-Arts (known as the Nationale) and re-introduced a jury system. Unassessed exhibitions certainly guaranteed the freedom of the artist; unfortunately, though, they afforded no protection against self-important people with not an ounce of talent. This proved counterproductive in terms of the needs of genuinely innovatory art.

But the confrontation of official and secessional Salons was no longer the only problem. The official Salon still held the promise of a reputation and distinction, improved prospects of public commissions, or professorial chairs. The difficulty was that people were already drawing a distinction between traditional "academic" art and a stylistically more plural "official" art. Mainstream artists who borrowed from realism and Impressionism could now achieve fame and good sales, as Gervex, De Nittis, Raffaëlli and others demonstrated.[135] The Salon, and public commissions, were becoming more important for art in ideal terms and for the financial conditions of artists' lives. Now, artists tended rather to need to define their position in the face of a new cultural power: the dealers.[136]

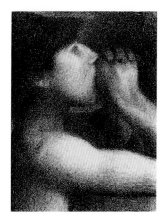

Durand-Ruel had been the most important dealer for the Impressionists, and was to be even more important in the years ahead. He had organized the seventh group exhibition in 1882, and smaller shows for Boudin, Monet, Renoir, Pissarro and Sisley in 1883. That year he also exhibited modest collections of their works at associated commercial galleries in London, Boston, Rotterdam and Berlin. The Berlin show was at Fritz Gurlitt's gallery, which he had opened in 1880. Menzel annihilatingly found the paintings "terrible". In 1886, Durand-Ruel and his American colleague James Fountain Sutton embarked on an ambitious measure to conquer a market which was indeed soon to prove decisive in the future fortunes of Impressionism but which was problematic because of drastic customs duty increases in 1882: they mounted a huge sales exhibition in the US, under the auspices of the American Art Association.

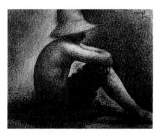

His most successful and wideawake rival was Georges Petit, not least with his *expositions internationales*, held annually from 1882 on, where the work of academicians, leading genre painters, realists and pleinairists was as thoroughly mixed as in Charpentier's "Vie moderne" shows. In 1885, Monet exhibited ten landscapes at Petit's alongside work by Albert Besnard (1849–1934), Cazin, Gervex, Raffaëlli, Stevens, Liebermann and others. In 1886 he, Renoir and Raffaëlli were again in the show; and in 1887 he, Renoir, Raffaëlli, and his coeval, the sculptor Auguste Rodin (1840–1917), who was soon to become a good friend, joined the hanging committee, selecting Morisot, Pissarro and Sisley, among others. Monet placed his influence with his friends behind his belief that dealers were the decisive factor in making reputations and success. The Impressionists, he felt, ought not to seem Durand-Ruel's pet group, but should occupy a variety of positions. It was some years before Durand-Ruel felt able to accept this view.

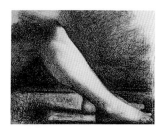

In the mid–1880s, one of the most successful dealers in paintings and graphics, who already had an international presence, began to take an interest in the Impressionists. Adolphe Goupil (1806–1893) had established the firm with a partner in 1827; from 1875, as a result of his grand-daughter's marriage (she was a daughter of Gérôme the painter) to a Monsieur Valadon, the firm traded as Goupil, Boussod et Valadon. One of the partners was the uncle of Vincent van Gogh (1853–1890), and the employee who started acquiring Pissarros for the gallery from 1884 on, and then Sisleys, Monets and Renoirs, was the Dutch painter's younger brother, Theo (1857–1891). Ten years later, the enterprising dealer and publisher Ambroise Vollard (1867–1939) was also to play a part in spreading the fame of the Impressionists, though he came to be interested primarily in the Post-Impressionists.

In 1886, following protracted discussion, the eighth Impressionist exhibition was held not at Durand-Ruel's but in five rooms rented by the artists at 1 Rue Lafitte, above the Maison Dorée, a chic restaurant. It was a five-minute walk from either Durand-Ruel's gallery or his rival's,

Georges Seurat
Watering Can, 1883
L'arrosoir
Oil on canvas, 24.4 x 15.5 cm
Dorra/Rewald 65; De Hauke 57
Upperville (VA), Mr. and Mrs. Paul
Mellon Collection

Georges Seurat
Houses at Le Raincy, c. 1882
Maisons au Raincy
Oil on canvas, 24.5 x 15.5 cm
Dorra/Rewald 36; De Hauke 17
Paris, private collection

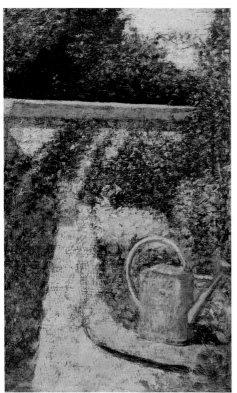
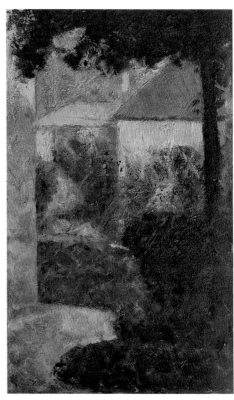

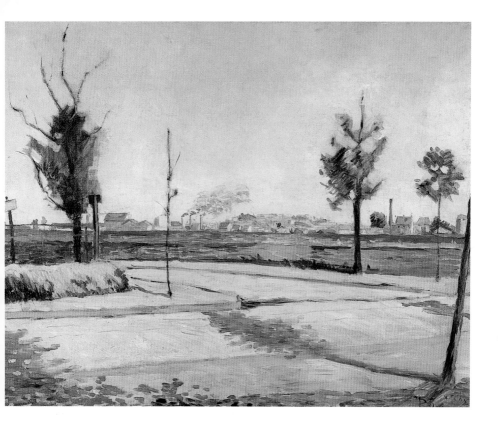

Petit's, and was in a district frequented by well-to-do people with an interest in art.[137] Seventeen artists were in the show; the catalogue listed 246 items. Five of the artists had been in the first show twelve years earlier, and six others had participated at least three times. But Monet, Renoir, Sisley and Caillebotte refused to exhibit because Degas had again smuggled in "his" associates – Bracquemond, Cassatt, Forain and Zandomeneghi – and Pissarro was also introducing protégés they did not care for.

Among other things, Forain displayed irreverent pastels, modishly chic *demi-monde* scenes. Degas perplexed the public partly with his milliner's shop scenes but mainly with ten pastels that carried the curiously meticulous, archivist title, *Series of Female Nudes, bathing, washing, drying, cleansing, combing their hair or having it combed.* The level detachment Degas brought to his pictures of women at their toilet, some of them seemingly coarse or plump, in postures at times awkward or even grotesque as they went about intimate business in which they would normally be unobserved, was interpreted as an iconoclastic attack on the

Paul Signac
Outskirts of Paris: the Road to Gennevilliers, 1883
Faubourg de Paris: La route de Gennevilliers
Oil on canvas, 72.9 x 91.6 cm
Paris, Musée d'Orsay

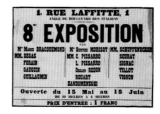

Poster for the eighth Impressionist exhibition, 1886

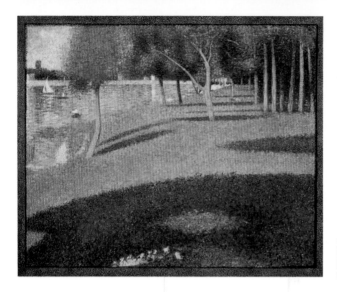

Right:
Georges Seurat
A Sunday Afternoon at the Ile de la Grande Jatte, 1885
Un dimanche après-midi à l'Ile de la Grande Jatte
Oil on canvas, 70.5 x 104 cm
Dorra/Rewald 138; De Hauke 142
New York, The Metropolitan Museum of Art

Georges Seurat
L'Ile de la Grande Jatte, 1884
Oil on canvas, 81.5 x 65.2 cm
Dorra/Rewald 116; De Hauke 131
New York, Mrs. John Hay Whitney Collection

19th century's sacrosanct idol of female beauty, and an expression of the unmarried Degas's personal misogyny. With the possibility of legal consequences under the obscenity laws in mind, the critics refrained from suggesting that women who consented to be drawn in bath tubs and the like, in tiny rooms with floral-pattern furniture, must surely be prostitutes in cheap brothels.

In addition to Guillaumin (who exhibited village landscapes from Damiette in the Ile-de-France) and Gauguin, Pissarro introduced one of the latter's acquaintances, the bank clerk and amateur artist Emile Schuffenecker (1851–1934), as well as Seurat and Signac. The "fantastic visions" (as one critic put it) of Redon, mainly drawings, were stylistically odd ones out at the show. No one could detect any link with the Impressionists at all. Doubtless it was because Redon was one of the leaders of the Indépendants that he was invited to exhibit (and accepted). Seurat's *Bathers at Asnières* (p. 254), begun in autumn 1882 and the product of numerous preparatory studies, had been refused by the 1884 official Salon and shown at the first Indépendants exhibition. There it was seen by Signac, who introduced Pissarro and Seurat the following year, when the latter had almost completed *A Sunday Afternoon at the Ile de la Grande Jatte* (pp. 260/261). Pissarro was so impressed that he immediately adopted the dot method, a technique later labelled Neo-Impressionist. He also gave the younger painter welcome advice. Pissarro's son Lucien, who mainly worked in graphics, joined them, and the four exhibited together in one room. Their techniques were so similar that visitors to the show reputedly could not tell them apart. The *Grande Jatte* painting was the most striking in the Maison Dorée show. Signac exhibited *Two Milliners, Rue du Caire* (p. 266). That August, he and Seurat

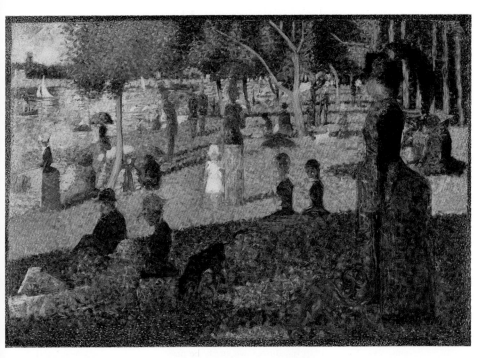

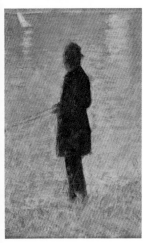

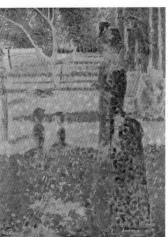

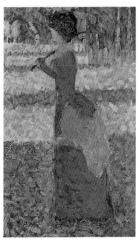

Georges Seurat
Angler (Study for "A Sunday Afternoon at the
Ile de la Grande Jatte"), 1884–1886
Oil on panel, 24 x 15 cm
Dorra/Rewald 132; De Hauke 115
London, Courtauld Institute Galleries

Georges Seurat
Couple (Study for "A Sunday Afternoon at the
Ile de la Grande Jatte"), 1884–1886
Oil on canvas, 81 x 65 cm
Dorra/Rewald 136; De Hauke 138
England, private collection

Georges Seurat
Woman with Parasol (Study for "A Sunday
Afternoon at the Ile de la Grande Jatte"), 1884
Oil on canvas, 25 x 15.5 cm
Dorra/Rewald 133; De Hauke 153
Zurich, E.G. Bührle Collection

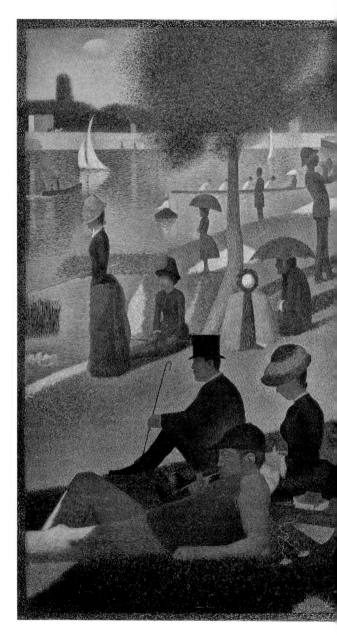

Georges Seurat
A Sunday Afternoon at the Ile de la
Grande Jatte, 1884–1886
*Un dimanche après-midi à l'Ile de la
Grande Jatte*
Oil on canvas, 206.4 x 305.4 cm
Dorra/Rewald 139; De Hauke 162
Chicago (IL), The Art Institute
of Chicago

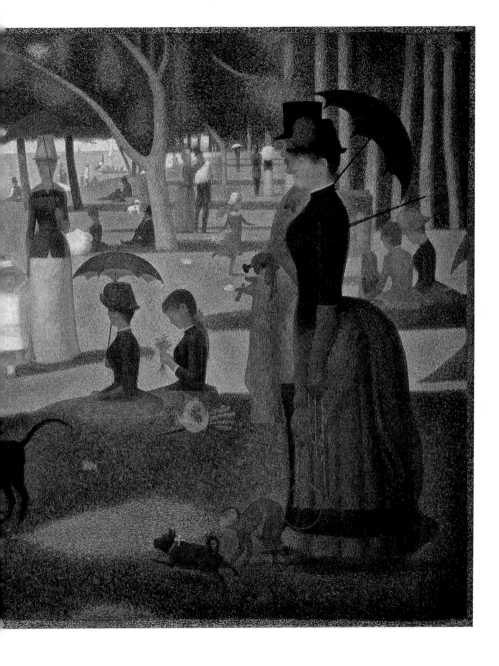

again showed their main works at the Indépendants. The use of dots won over other painters too, among them the jolly Norman Louis Anquetin (1861–1932), while Vincent van Gogh and Henri de Toulouse-Lautrec (1864–1901) used the brief and even brush-strokes Pissarro and Cézanne had employed before them.

Van Gogh, son of a Dutch vicar, was familiar with French and English art through his work for branches of Goupil & Cie. in The Hague and London and at the Paris head office of the dealership from 1869 to 1876. He had also been a lay preacher in England and Belgium before finally deciding in 1880, after years of drawing, to be a painter. In spring 1886 he went to Paris to study in the independent atelier of naturalist history painter Fernand Cormon (1845–1924). There he met Anquetin, Toulouse-Lautrec and Emile Bernard (1868–1941), among others. His brother Theo, being in art dealing, quickly put Vincent in touch with Pissarro and the other Impressionists. This, and the new exhibitions he saw that year, prompted van Gogh to abandon the melancholy, darkly brooding scenes of toilsome peasant and weaver life, and landscapes whose sketchiness and colour range placed them in the company of the Barbizon painters. He took to brighter work using strong, pure colours and more relaxed brushwork. City scenes, still lifes and portraits replaced his earlier subject matter. As early as 1887, though, he was telling his friends that he had to go beyond Impressionism. He took a close

Jean-Louis Forain
Ball at the Paris Opera, c. 1885
Un bal à l'Opéra
Oil on canvas, 74 x 61 cm
Moscow, Pushkin Museum of Fine Art

Edgar Degas
Six Friends of the Artist, 1885
Six amis de l'artiste
Pastel on paper, 113 x 70 cm
Lemoisne 824
Providence (RI), Museum of Art,
Rhode Island School of Design

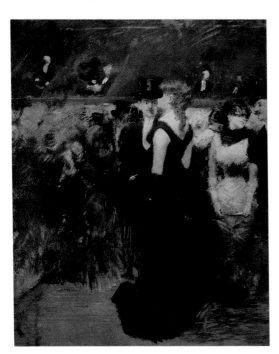

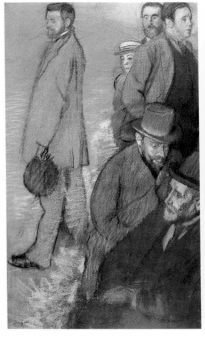

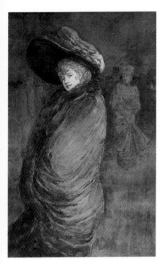

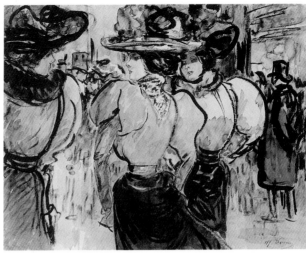

Henry Somm
The Red Overcoat
Le manteau rouge
Watercolour on paper
Rouen, Musée des Beaux-Arts

Henry Somm
Stylish Ladies in the Street
Elégantes dans la rue
Watercolour and ink on paper on card,
48.3 x 62.3 cm. Private collection

interest in Japanese coloured woodcuts, and together with Anquetin, Bernard, Gauguin and Toulouse-Lautrec (calling themselves the Painters of the Little Boulevard, as opposed to Monet, Pissarro and company of the Great Boulevard) he exhibited a large number of pictures at La Fourche, a restaurant in the Avenue de Clichy. In February 1888, after two fertile years in Paris, van Gogh went south, moving to Arles in Provence. His attitude to colours and their expressive potential had been transformed, and he was thirsting for stronger colours in brighter light.

Henri Marie Raymond de Toulouse-Lautrec-Monfa to give him his full name) came of ancient aristocratic stock in south-west France. He had painted and drawn skilfully at an early age; in Paris, he first took private tuition, then lessons with Bonnat and then (1882 to 1886) Cormon. His health was poor and broken legs had not healed, so that he was already a dwarfish cripple with short legs, unable to participate in riding, hunting, dancing or the love affairs of high society. He had no financial worries, though, and was able to take an independent, bitingly sarcastic view of the world around him. He was a hedonist given to alcoholic over-indulgence; his physical state doubtless drove him to this, as it did to mental deterioration. Forain strongly encouraged him at first, and from the early 1880s on his art had the brightness and the brief, easy brushwork of Impressionism (p. 227). For him, a generation junior to Degas, Impressionist technical and structural approaches were already part of the available repertoire from which to proceed onward.

The extent to which Impressionism could already be considered a finished chapter in art history, open to criticism from various points of view, can be gauged from Zola's novel "L'Œuvre", published in that fateful year of 1886. The novel was part of Zola's Rougon-Macquart series, and its hero was an artist to whom Zola gave the features of his

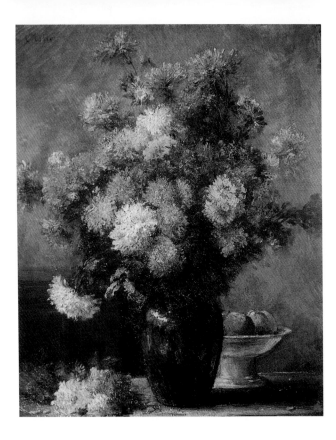

Charles Tillot
Still Life with Flowers
Nature morte aux fleurs
Oil on canvas, 81.5 x 65 cm
New York, private collection

friend Cézanne, together with aspects of Manet's career (such as the scandal concerning *Le Déjeuner sur l'Herbe*) and that of Monet (his penury, and his portrait of his dead wife). This hero painted in an Impressionist style – and was a failure. Zola, the good Naturalist, believed Impressionism was incapable of making a powerful creative response to modern social realities. Cézanne, deeply hurt, broke off their friendship.

Simultaneously a new aesthetic confrontation hit the art scene. On 18 September 1886, Jean Moréas (originally Papadiamantopoulos, 1856– 1910), a writer of Greek extraction, published his Symbolist manifesto in the much-read "Figaro littéraire". This gave a name to a movement that had been palpable for some years in literature, the visual arts, music and theatre. In contrast to the naming of Impressionism, this time there was no ridicule involved; it was a positive, programmatic term. Of course it was open to varying interpretation. Symbolism was also to become a rallying-point for various new trends that played an important role in the next few years. One major literary Symbolist was the poet Stéphane Mallarmé (1842–1898), who had taken Manet's part in 1874 and had his portrait painted by him in 1876 – a wonderful portrait, nervy, wary, at odds with intimacy. He was now particularly close to Morisot. Redon was a typical example of a Symbolist artist.

Behind the new aesthetics lay the shift from positivist, materialist theories of the exact scientific knowability and governability of Nature and society to various brands of idealism, a broad range that included a revival of religious belief. Scepticism concerning technological and scientific progress and its consequences for civilization undermined optimistic emphasis on progress and the belief in an earthly paradise.

The existence of an objective reality was being questioned – or at least its epistemological verifiability and the possibility that it could be represented. Perceptions registered on the senses, it was felt, provided no information on anything that really existed. One could be content – impressionistically – with recording the diversity of those perceptions. Otherwise, the only alternative (now considered the better option) was to see the evidence of the senses, or the image conveyed by the subject, as a symbol that pointed the way, so to speak, to the thing meant, however circuitously – the way to a reality that ultimately retained its mys-

Paul Gauguin
The Four Breton Girls, c. 1886
La danse des quatre Bretonnes
Oil on canvas, 72 x 91 cm
Wildenstein 201
Munich, Bayerische Staatsgemäldesammlungen,
Neue Pinakothek

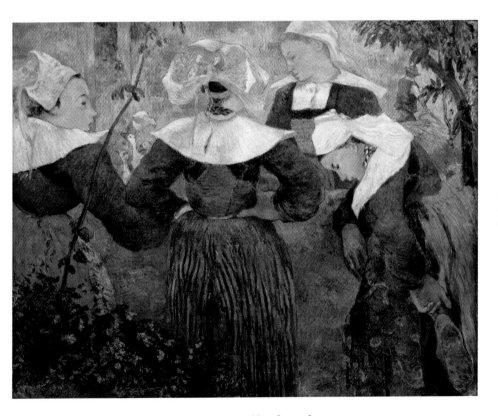

tery. Many of the typical terms appeared in an 1888 essay: "In painting and literature, representation of Nature is sheer delusion... on the contrary, painting and literature aim to convey an apprehension of things using the means specific to painting and literature. What ought to be expressed is not a representational image [of the subject] but its character. Whyever should one pursue the thousand insignificant details registered by the eye? One ought to seek out the essence and reproduce that, or rather: produce it... Using the smallest possible number of characteristic lines and colours, the painter will capture the essence of the chosen object and thus escape the charge of photographic imitation. Primitive and folk art are symbolist in this sense, as is Japanese art... To confuse line and colour implies that one is unable to grasp their peculiarities as expressive means: the line expresses what abides, colour what is of the passing moment. The line is an almost abstract symbol and conveys the character of the object, while the unity of colour conditions

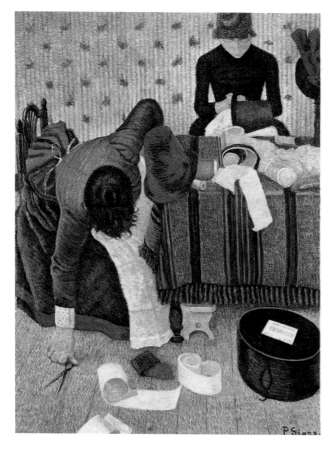

Paul Signac
Two Milliners, Rue du Caire, c. 1885/86
Apprêteuse et garnisseuse, rue du Caire
Oil on canvas, 111.8 x 89 cm
Zurich, E.G. Bührle Collection

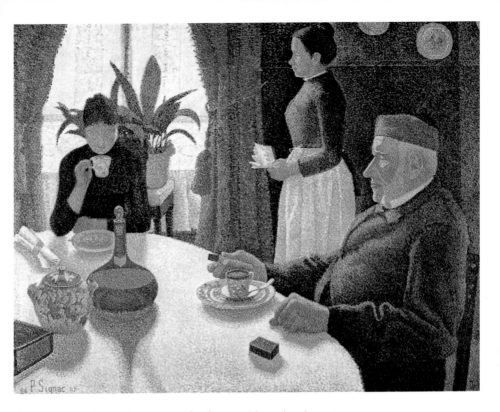

Paul Signac
Breakfast (The Dining Room), c. 1886/87
Le petit déjeuner ou La salle à manger
Oil on canvas, 89 x 115 cm
Otterlo, Kröller-Müller Museum

the overall atmosphere and the emotional realm..."[138] This makes clear the points of disagreement with the Impressionist emphasis on what the eye saw and on momentary colour phenomena, on the prior value of colour dabs over the line, on the part played by chance, and (in Degas's case, at least) on the possibilities opened up by photography. While the Impressionists were still fighting the academic wing, they were now being attacked on a new front as well.

Little magazines, often short-lived and publishing poetry, prose, graphics, and essays on aesthetics, art, culture theory and politics, were increasingly playing a part in the making of art history. The critics tended to be young men who wrote alongside other jobs, men such as Félix Fénéon (1861–1944), Gustave Kahn (1859–1936), Roger Marx (1859–1913), Octave Mirbeau (1848–1917) and the novelist Gustave Geffroy (1855–1926), who worked for Clemenceau's newspaper "La Justice" and was made director of the famous state-run tapestry manufactory under Clemenceau's government.

In 1884, when the Indépendants were forming their society, the "Revue Indépendante" was also started, a magazine first edited by Fénéon and responsible after 1887 for small-scale exhibitions too. Politically it was anarchist. The dream of a society free of rule was an old one. Modern artists – of necessity individualists – were particularly prone to dream it. Courbet's friend Pierre-Joseph Proudhon (1809–1865) coined the term. Another friend, the Russian nobleman Mikhail Bakunin (1814–1876), stood alongside Richard Wagner in the revolution in Dresden in 1849. His successor as leader of the anarchists in western Europe was the Russian aristocrat Petr Kropotkin (1842–1921). Pissarro read the latter's books, much to Renoir's dismay, as we have seen. A magazine he edited from Geneva, "La Révolte", was continued from 1887 in Paris by his former secretary Jean Grave (1854–1939). Pissarro did illustrative work for this and similar publications from 1889 on.

On 1 May 1885, under the pseudonym Trublot, Paul Alexis, a friend of Zola, Renoir, Pissarro and Seurat, wrote in the popular left-wing paper "Le Cri du Peuple", edited by the ex-Communard Jules Vallès (1832–1885): "The Impressionists stand for the same thing in painting as the Naturalists in literature and the socialists in politics... Following the overall movement of the century, alert to the natural sciences and to truth, they share a concern to unsettle privilege, deference and pedantry, to unseat those who cling to establishment opinions, and to startle the stupidity of the bourgeoisie."[139]

The "Revue Wagnérienne", which began in 1885, not only celebrated Wagner as the creator of a new, sensuous, nervy music, and as the founder of a new artistic synthesis of poetry, music, drama, decor and festival theatre, but also dealt with "Wagnerian painting". This supposedly included Puvis de Chavannes and Redon, as well as Monet, Cézanne and Degas, because their pictures offered an enigmatic evocation of reality rather than merely representing it.

"Le Décadent" was published for a short period in 1886. The authors and readers valued an individual blend of cultured address, luxurious extravagance, inactive and meditative solitude, exquisite pleasures and vices, sadism, and the longing for death. This blend, they averred, was only possible in the closing phase of a long cultural history; it had been thus with the decay and decadence of ancient Rome. Sophisticated art, they claimed, was a response to universal collapse and the spiritual shallowness of the times. One of the most thorough presentations of the decadent attitude and its aesthetics appeared in Huysmans' novel "A rebours" (Against Nature, 1884). In that work, Huysmans turned away from his previous enthusiasm for realistic portrayals of modern life; his art criticism was consistent with his new position.

Only a few decades earlier, the widely-touted goal had been to champion modern life, rejecting the classical, academic legacy of the past. Now, however, capitalism was beginning to cause concern. Many felt a certain abhorrence at the phenomena and processes that left the imprint of modernity on the times. As a result, there was a tendency to seek ways of escape. The vague hope of some future paradise was sustained mainly by the quest for other, lost paradises; and, as in the Romantic era, there were those who supposed they could find them among peoples who lived in simpler, pre-technological and pre-societal conditions.

Paul Signac
The Railway at Bois-Colombes, 1886
L'embranchement de Bois-Colombes
Oil on canvas, 33 x 47 cm
Leeds, Leeds City Art Gallery

Paul Signac
Gasometers at Clichy, 1886
Les gazomètres à Clichy
Oil on canvas, 64.8 x 81 cm
Melbourne, National Gallery of Victoria

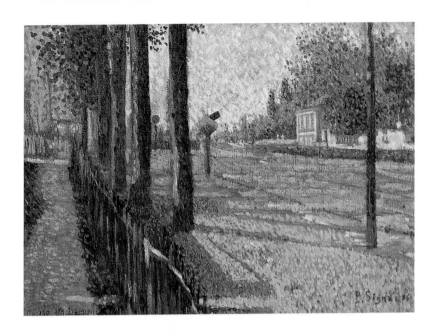

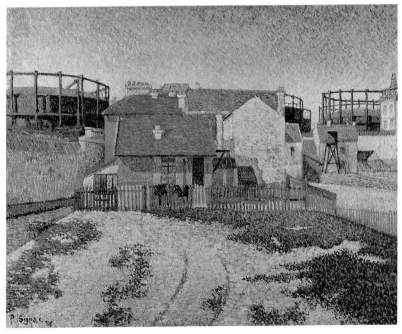

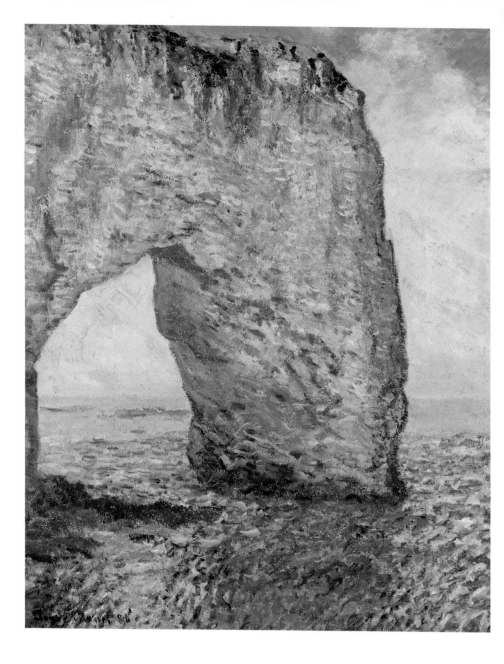

Georges Seurat
The Beach at Bas-Butin near Honfleur, 1886
La plage de Bas-Butin, Honfleur
Oil on canvas, 67 x 78 cm
Dorra/Rewald 165; De Hauke 169
Tournai, Musée des Beaux-Arts

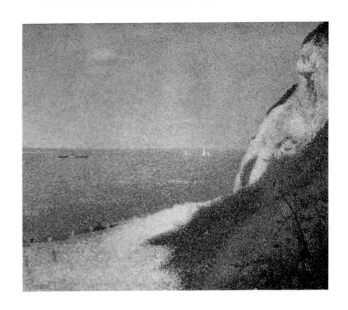

Georges Seurat
Bec du Hoc, Grandcamp, 1885
Le Bec du Hoc, Grandcamp
Oil on canvas, 66 x 82.5 cm
Dorra/Rewald 153; De Hauke 159
London, The Tate Gallery

Left:
Claude Monet
La Manneporte near Etretat, 1886
La Manneporte près d'Etretat
Oil on canvas, 81 x 65 cm
Wildenstein 1052
New York, The Metropolitan Museum of Art

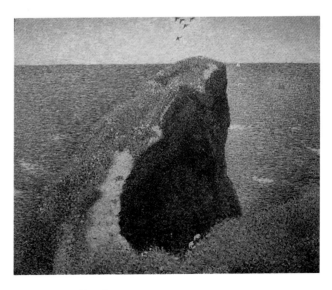

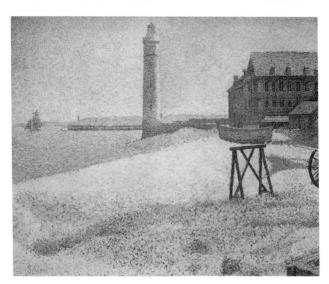

Georges Seurat
The Lighthouse at Honfleur, 1886
L'hospice et le phare à Honfleur
Oil on canvas, 66.7 x 81.9 cm
Dorra/Rewald 168; De Hauke 173
Washington (DC), National Gallery of Art,
Mr. and Mrs. Paul Mellon Collection

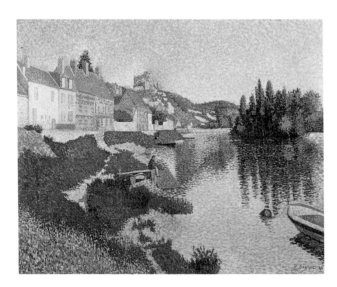

Paul Signac
The River Bank, Petit-Andely, 1886
La berge, Petit-Andely
Oil on canvas, 65 x 81 cm
Paris, private collection

Georges Seurat
The "Maria", Honfleur, 1886
La Maria, Honfleur
Oil on canvas, 53 x 63.5 cm
Dorra/Rewald 169; De Hauke 164
Prague, Národní Gallery

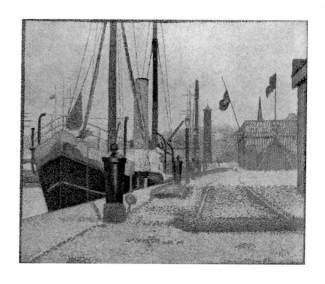

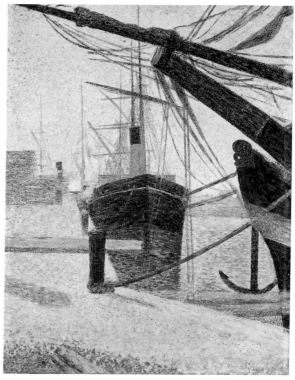

Georges Seurat
The Harbour at Honfleur, 1886
Le port d'Honfleur
Oil on canvas, 79.5 x 63 cm
Dorra/Rewald 166; De Hauke 163
Otterlo, Kröller-Müller Museum

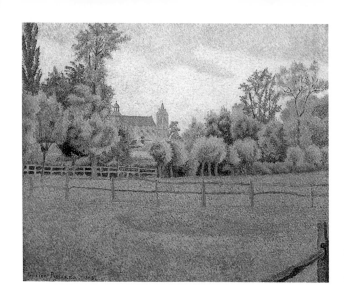

Lucien Pissarro
The Church at Gisors, 1888
L'église de Gisors
Oil on canvas, 60 x 73 cm
Thorold 24. Paris, Musée d'Orsay

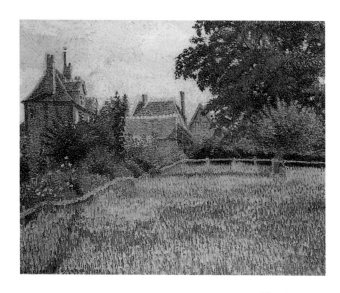

Lucien Pissarro
The Deaf Woman's House, 1888
La maison de la sourde
Oil on canvas, 58 x 72 cm
Thorold 9
Oxford, The Visitors of the Ashmolean Museum

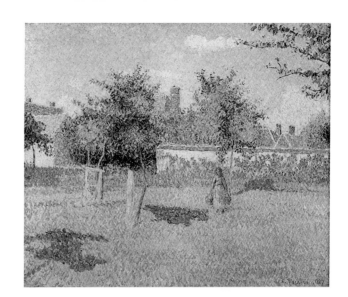

Camille Pissarro
Woman in an Orchard. Spring Sunshine
in a Field, Eragny, 1887
Femme dans un clos. Soleil de printemps
dans le pré à Eragny
Oil on canvas, 54 x 65 cm
Pissarro/Venturi 709. Paris, Musée d'Orsay

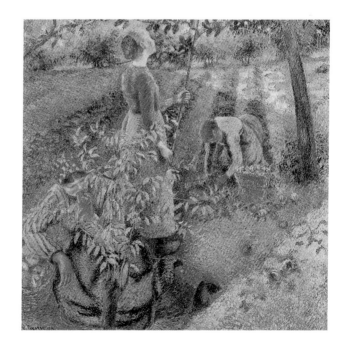

Camille Pissarro
Apple Picking, 1886
La cueillette des pommes
Oil on canvas, 128 x 128 cm
Pissarro/Venturi 695
Kurashiki, Okayama (Japan),
Ohara Museum of Art

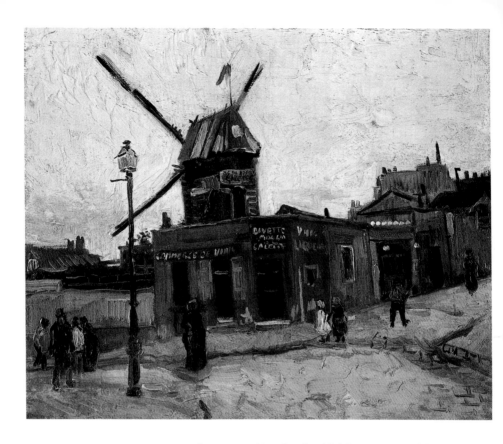

Vincent van Gogh
Le Moulin de la Galette, 1886
Oil on canvas, 38.5 x 46 cm
F 227, JH 1170, Walther 189
Otterlo, Kröller-Müller Museum

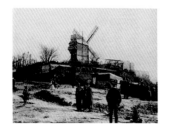

The Moulin de la Galette, Montmartre

In summer 1886, after the eighth Impressionist exhibition, Gauguin went for the first time to the Breton fishing village of Pont-Aven, on the Atlantic coast, to paint the landscape and people. At the same time, at nearby Kervilahouen, Monet found a new subject in the "wild" and "terrible" cliffs and spray of Belle-Ile. The following year, Gauguin ventured into the tropics, to the French Caribbean colony of Martinique. In spring 1888, though, he returned to Pont-Aven, where he was presently a member of the new Pont-Aven School of artists. There had been occasional groups of this kind decades earlier; even so, the Pont-Aven painters were one of the first and most famous rural artists' colonies. The phenomenon quickly spread throughout Europe; one well-known colony was at Worpswede in Germany. In summer 1888 Emile Bernard went to Pont-Aven, introducing an idea he and Anquetin had had for a new, decorative style highlighting contained colour spaces, which he called cloisonnism. The name and method came from the time-honoured technique of *émail cloisonné*, in which a very fine metal partition separated the colour zones. Gauguin used the approach in 1888 for his *Vision after*

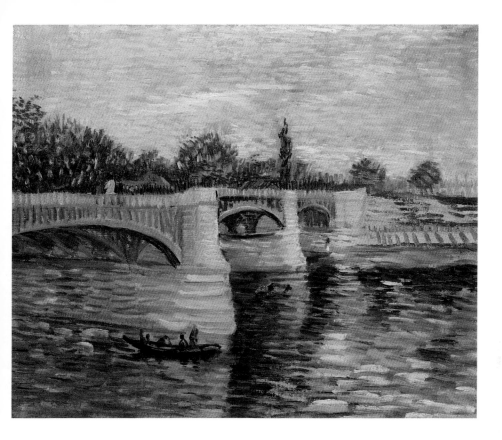

the Sermon (p. 303), his first attempt to introduce a purely imaginary scene into a visual world which, since Courbet, had been exclusively governed by the evidence of the painter's own eyes.

Another young painter who was still studying in Paris at the Académie Julian was Paul Sérusier (1864–1927). Under Gauguin's guidance he painted a small wooden panel (p. 320) at the Bois d'Amour near Pont-Aven, using strong, luminous strokes. The representational character of the brushwork had almost disappeared; instead, the strokes produced a strong, wild colour accord such as the Fauves and the Expressionists were to use routinely twenty years later. The young symbolist and decorative painters who organized an exhibition of "synthetic" painting, with Gauguin, at the Café Volpini in Paris in 1889 saw Sérusier's picture as their talisman. Synthesis, and unified totality of effect, were the new watchwords, instead of the Impressionist analysis of light and dissection of colour. The Café Volpini was opposite the entrance to the art pavilion at the Paris World Fair – bigger than ever – which marked the centenary of the French Revolution. The exhibition of "A Century of French Art"

Vincent van Gogh
Pont de la Grande Jatte, 1887
Oil on canvas, 32 x 40.5 cm
F 304, JH 1326, Walther 273
Amsterdam, Van Gogh Museum,
Vincent van Gogh Foundation

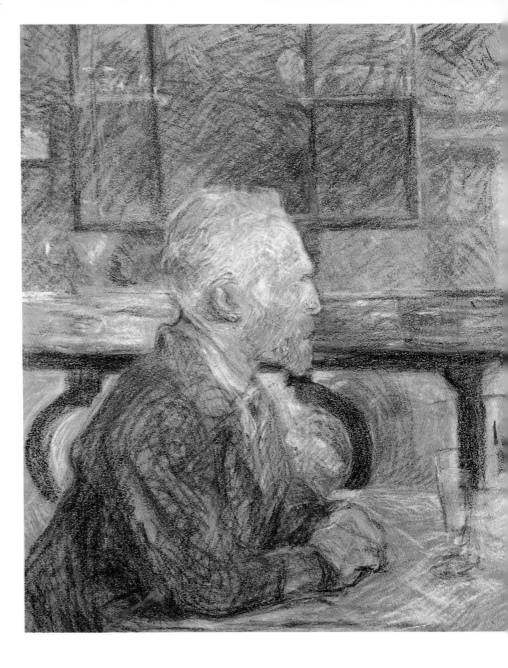

included Manet and Monet; Renoir had expressly refused to be included since he did not want his paintings hung alongside conventional work. Now it was the turn of the next generation to stake their claims.

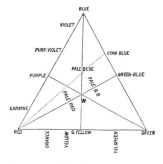

Chromatic triangle by Ogden N. Rood. From: "Modern Chromatics", 1879

The Colour of Light: Pointillism

While the idealist, symbolist line in thought was producing critical reservations concerning exact explanations and rules, "scientific Impressionism" (Camille Pissarro) was simultaneously being conceived. If the two lines were at odds, that fact did not prevent the sharing of certain things, nor did it stop painters from being friends and exhibiting together. After all, it was still fashionable to link art with the exact sciences. A few years before, in 1879, Zola had coined the term "experimental novel" for his objective, naturalist analyses of social and mental states.

Seurat's aim was to found his art on an incontestable system. Studying under a pupil of Ingres, he had conducted a careful examination of pictures by Delacroix which struck him as being not altogether consistent in their use of colour. He also read a great deal. He happened upon a publication from 1839 by a chemist, one Eugène Chevreul (1786–1889) – "De la Loi du contraste simultané des couleurs et de l'assortiment des objets colorés" – together with a later study by the same author, "Des Couleurs et de leur application aux arts industriels à l'aide des cercles chromatiques" (1864). There were also more modern investigations of complementary colours and the optical laws governing their perception. "Modern Chromatics" (1879), by the New York physicist Ogden Nicholas Rood (1831–1902), was published in French translation in 1881. In 1880 David Sutter (1811–1880) published a series of articles on phenomena of vision in the magazine "L'Art". And from 1886 on, Seurat found his views conclusively endorsed by Charles Henry (1859–1926), who was working as a librarian at the Sorbonne. Henry was a man familiar with many disciplines – mathematics, biology, literature, music and psychology – and gave popular evening lectures. In 1885 he had published an "Introduction to Scientific Aesthetics". In colours and in the directions of lines, Henry proposed a distinction between the "dynamogenic" (i.e. creating momentum and pleasure) and the "inhibiting" (i.e. retarding, and causing pain). Seurat and Signac drew their own circular colour scheme in order to clarify the spiritual relations of colours in their own minds.

In a letter written to Durand-Ruel in 1886, Pissarro gave an economical description of the technique Seurat had been the first to use after thorough study of the scientific theories: "The aim is to substitute optical mixing for the mixing of pigments, or, to put it differently, to analyse colour tonalities into their fundamental components."[140] Science had found that colours reached the eye in the form of light of differing wavelengths, and were mixed in the eye to establish the colour that corresponded to the object seen. If a painter juxtaposed tiny dots of unmixed

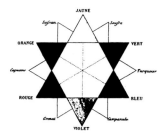

Chromatic diagram by Charles Blanc (1813–1882)

Henri de Toulouse-Lautrec
Portrait of Vincent van Gogh, 1887
Portrait de Vincent van Gogh
Pastel on card, 54 x 45 cm
Dortu 278
Amsterdam, Van Gogh Museum,
Vincent van Gogh Foundation

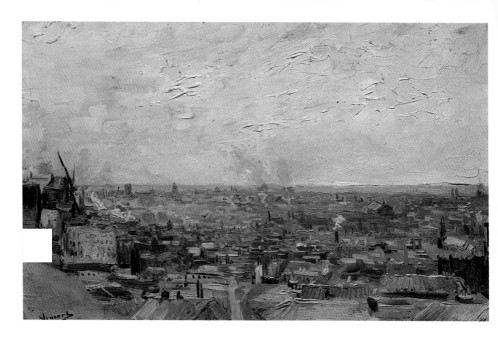

Vincent van Gogh
View of Paris from Montmartre, 1886
Oil on canvas, 38.5 x 61.5 cm
F 262, JH 1102, Walther 182
Basle, Öffentliche Kunstsammlung Basel,
Kunstmuseum

primary colours in the right way, the eye would perceive them as the desired colour tone when looking from a certain distance; and that tone would appear lighter than if it had been mixed in the conventional way, on the palette or the canvas. For instance, blue and yellow dots juxtaposed would produce green. Furthermore, the intensity of colours would be greater if the eye perceived them through simultaneous contrast, together with a context of a different colour. Seurat had called this procedure "chromoluminarism" but then settled on "divisionism". The term that gained currency, though, and by which the technique is still known today, was Signac's "pointillism". Fénéon came up with the more historically coloured term Neo-Impressionism, which Signac subsequently accepted.

In 1881 and 1882, Seurat concentrated on drawing. Indeed, capturing nuances of light and dark was always to be of great significance for him. He almost invariably used Conté chalk on Michallet paper, the surface of which is so grainy that the white still glimmers through even the deepest black (p. 255). In his tiny oils too, done in sketchy brush-strokes on wood panels, he strikingly often used dark figures silhouetted against light backgrounds, and linear elements to structure his space (p. 259). Seurat's subjects were chosen preponderantly from the work and leisure of ordinary people in the outer suburbs of Paris, where the social changes and construction created by industrialization were at their most noticeable. The English art critic Richard Thomson has pointed out that Seurat, like the intellectual anarchists in whose circles he moved, registered

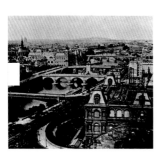

Paris and the Seine bridges seen from Saint-Gervais
church tower

these socio-cultural phenomena with a clear critical awareness, and deliberately took them as his themes.[141]

Bathers at Asnières (p. 254), at two by three metres a demonstratively large work, was his first programmatic picture. The location was not far out, like Argenteuil or Bougival, but close to newly built factories. There was no restaurant, and those who bathed there went because the rail fare to Argenteuil was too expensive. Fourteen surviving oil studies and a number of drawings show how meticulously Seurat prepared the painting (p. 254). The atmosphere is one of hazy brightness; the sky and water almost constitute a single colour continuum, which powerfully diminishes the spatiality of the work. The figures look exhausted; their three-dimensionality has an inflated look, and the outlines of the colour zones are sharp. These outlines are not marked by actual lines, though, but solely by the different colours of the tiny brush-strokes or by an aura of light. The boy at right who has entered the water is tooting a call into the silence through his cupped hands much like the conch-blowing Tritons in roughly contemporaneous symbolist art by Arnold Böcklin (1827–1901). The scientifically precise rendering of the colours of this carefree genre scene and sunny landscape admittedly introduces a disquieting note of ornamentality, involving as it does the uncompromising use of a technique that has no time for unimportant details.

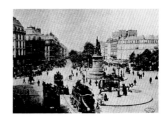

The Place de Clichy in the Batignolles quarter.
Photograph, 1900

Paul Signac
The Boulevard de Clichy under Snow, 1886
Le Boulevard de Clichy, la neige
Oil on canvas, 46.5 x 65.5 cm
Minneapolis (MN), The Minneapolis
Institute of Arts

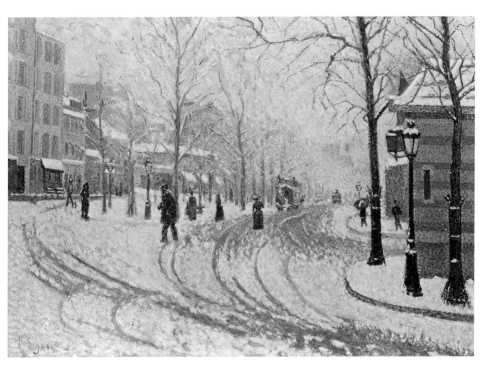

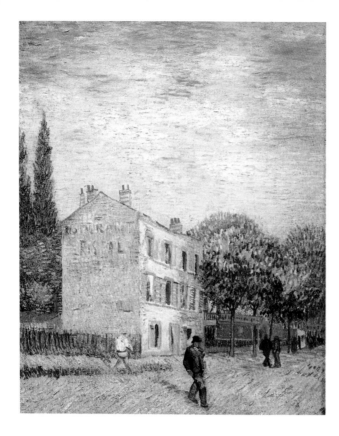

The urge to establish a specific form that obeyed strict internal laws won out over faithful reproduction of what the eye saw – as became more apparent in the painting Seurat shortly began work on, *A Sunday Afternoon at the Ile de la Grande Jatte* (pp. 260/261). These people are enjoying their sunny leisure on an island in the Seine near the Neuilly Bridge to Courbevoie, a place convenient for the city and not far from the modern quarter of La Défense. The picture continues Seurat's analysis of the new encounters of different social strata. Symbolic motifs such as the monkey on a lead – in Parisian slang, a monkey was a prostitute – and the formal allusions to dolls and tin soldiers introduce a grotesque note. While he was working on this large canvas, Seurat practised painting landscapes drenched in light by doing form and colour studies of fields of flowers near Paris and curious cliff formations on the coast of Normandy, such as the *Bec du Hoc* (p. 271). Above all, he used oil studies of segments of the work, and of the total composition, to establish the overall harmony of the painting. The picture is done entirely in tiny dots, including the strip around the painting proper.

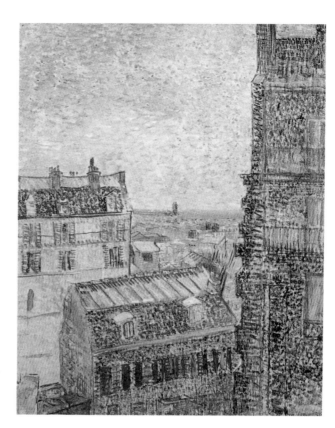

Vincent van Gogh
Paris Seen from Vincent's Room in the Rue Lepic,
1887
Oil on canvas, 46 x 38 cm
F 341, JH 1242, Walther 222
Amsterdam, Van Gogh Museum,
Vincent van Gogh Foundation

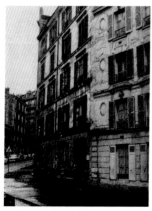

54 Rue Lepic, where Vincent van Gogh lived in
1886 as a subtenant of his brother Theo

Contemporaries have left accounts of the concentration and stamina Seurat brought to his work, on a ladder before the huge canvas, scrutinizing the various subjects in light or shade and patiently selecting his colour dots. He worked in his studio every afternoon and evening, completing a small section every day, like a fresco painter or mosaic artist. Impressionist analysis of the passing moment, the slice of life in motion, had become an artificial, synthetic *gestalt*. It was to prove as enduring – like the quite different style Cézanne evolved – as the art already in the museums. Seurat wanted the modern people in his paintings to move with the same free, ceremonial grace as Phidias's figures on the Parthenon frieze from the Acropolis in Athens.[142] He paid close attention to work that Puvis de Chavannes was painting at the same time, and found the neo-classical symbolist confirmed him in his approach. And indeed, the first critics to applaud Seurat described him as a "materialist" or "modernized" Puvis.

After the *Grande Jatte* painting, *Bec du Hoc* and various others had been exhibited, Seurat only had five years to live; he died of diphtheria

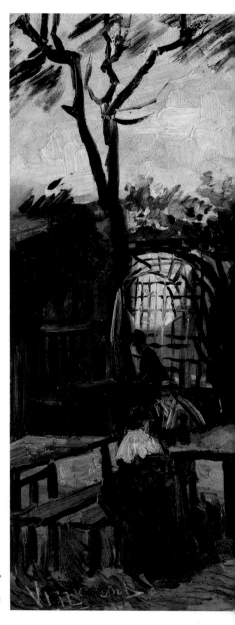

Vincent van Gogh
Terrace of a Café on Montmartre,
1886
Oil on canvas, 49.5 x 64.5 cm
F 238, JH 1178, Walther 190/191
Paris, Musée d'Orsay

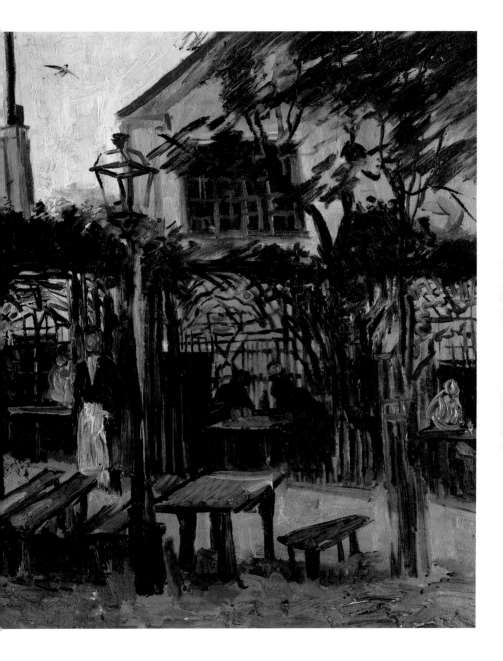

in March 1891.[143] During that time he largely abandoned painting in the open. He was trying to make his system even more exact; in 1890 he wrote it down. He became self-importantly proud, and went into voluntary isolation from his hordes of imitators. The *Grande Jatte* was exhibited at the 1886 Impressionist show, then with the Indépendants, and again in 1887 in Brussels with Les Vingt, a prominent artists' association founded in 1884. Les Vingt, with their lawyer and art-critic leader Octave Maus (1856–1919), played a very important part in the international dissemination of Impressionism, but particularly in that of Neo-Impressionism, Symbolism and Post-Impressionism.

In *The Models* (pp. 298, 299, 301) Seurat affords a glimpse of his studio and the artist's work. Waiting amidst discarded clothing, or dressing, these lean and altogether unerotic nudes are related to the completed *Grande Jatte*, which is partly to be seen on the studio wall. The situation, quite free of the anecdotal, has a quality of chance that recalls Manet; it is monumentalized into lifesize and has the air of a relief. It might be seen as an ironic paraphrase of the classic motif of the Three Graces. It is also a totally serious attempt to establish normal postures of standing or sitting, using frontal, profile and rear views, as Puvis and the German painter Hans von Marées (1837–1887) had been doing at the same time. Seurat was struggling to assert a new classicism outside the tired conventions of the academic variety. Time and again he embarked on studies recording impressions and then developed them using his systematic "divisionism".

At the same time Seurat was working on *The Circus Parade* (p. 300), followed by *Le Chahut* (p. 318) and the not quite finished *Circus* (p. 329). He also painted a buxom young woman powdering herself (p. 319) – his lover, Madeleine Knobloch, of whose existence only his closest friends were aware. It was a Degas world, but quite differently handled. The effects of stage lighting, overlapping and cropped foreground figures, and a certain malice in the grotesque way types of people or posture were presented, were certainly not unrelated to Degas, but the differences were greater: a sense of ceremony accompanied by distortions and grimaces, motion arrested in mechanical parallel attitudes, a strict patterning of spaces, and an emphatically enigmatic flavour despite the seemingly straightforward attention-getting. The core note is struck by display, by the noisy, colourful, made-up and costumed world of tinsel illusion. Revue theatre provided Seurat with a means of criticizing a society engrossed in mean, witless gaping (the figure at bottom right in *Le Chahut*) and becoming steadily desensitized. The skill of the circus artiste in animated suspension, like that of the dancers and musicians, obeys the whip of a ringmaster or conductor or impresario – always the same suave moustached character. The clown in the foreground of *The Circus* is yelling out, revealing the truth, as the court jesters and fools used to do and artists now do. This late work gives us the full disquieting, emblematic legacy of a painter who had set out to find a scientific method of reproducing colour.

Signac was the most devoted follower and propagandist of Seurat's

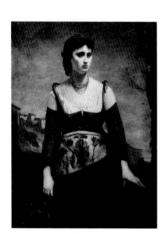

Agostina Segatori modelling for Corot's painting "Agostina", c. 1866

Vincent van Gogh
Agostina Segatori in the Café du Tambourin, 1887
Oil on canvas, 55.5 x 46.5 cm
F 370, JH 1208, Walther 206
Amsterdam, Van Gogh Museum,
Vincent van Gogh Foundation

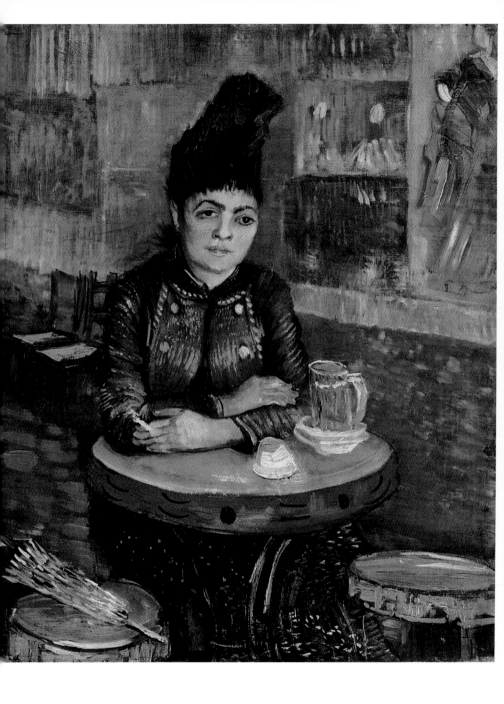

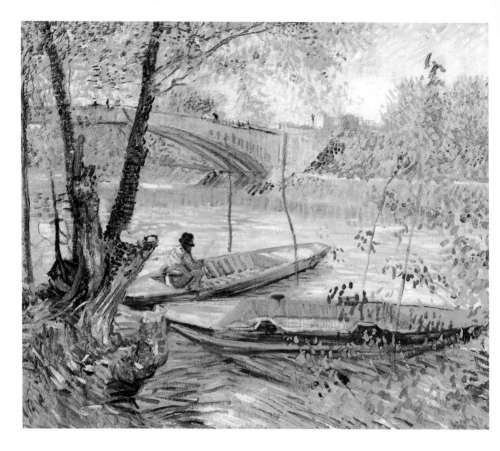

Vincent van Gogh
Fishing in Spring, Pont de Clichy, 1887
Oil on canvas, 49 x 58 cm
F 354, JH 1270, Walther 237
Chicago, The Art Institute of Chicago

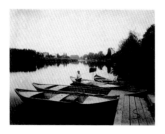

Boats on the Marne. Photo: Atget, 1903

method. In various interior genre scenes he tried his hand at a new presentation of physical volume and striking gestures (p. 267). If a milliner bent to pick up the scissors she had dropped, it became a loaded dramatic gesture eloquent of weary toil. Influenced by his friend Guillaumin, Signac began painting suburban and industrial landscapes (pp. 257, 269). From 1882 – a keen yachtsman himself – he repeatedly painted sunny seaside landscapes and harbours bobbing with boats. From 1892 he was a regular visitor to Saint-Tropez. His watercolours in particular had an airy verve; but in his oils, too, his pointillism was always fresher, more generous and radiant, than in the increasingly austere and sombre Seurat. He dabbed his strong though oddly sickly-sweet colours onto his canvases in rectangular patches of equal size.

His most distinctive blend of scientific Impressionism, Symbolism and Japanese decorative spatial approaches came in his Uncle Sam portrait of Fénéon, the Neo-Impressionists' energetic spokesman, who always made a rather droll impression (p. 321). The picture – ironic, theatrical,

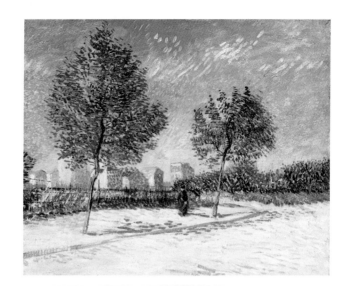

Vincent van Gogh
On the Outskirts of Paris, 1887
Oil on canvas, 38 x 46 cm
F 351, JH 1255, Walther 252
USA, private collection

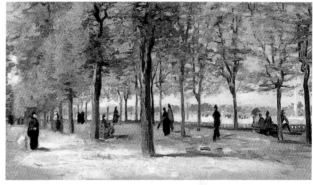

Vincent van Gogh
In the Jardin du Luxembourg, 1886
Oil on canvas, 27.5 x 46 cm
F 223, JH 1111, Walther 157
Williamstown (MA), Sterling and Francine
Clark Art Institute

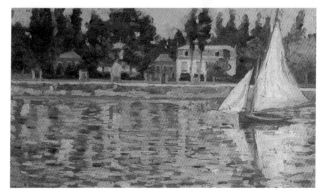

Alphonse Maureau
Banks of the Seine, c. 1877
Bords de la Seine
Oil on panel, 14.5 x 24 cm
Florence, Galleria d'Arte Moderna

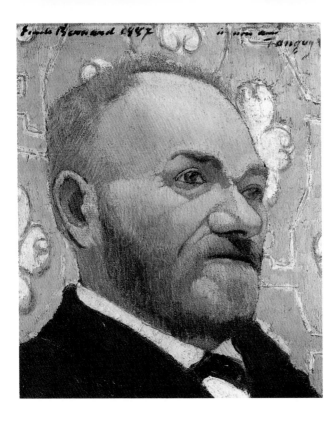

Emile Bernard
Portrait of Père Tanguy, 1887
Portrait du Père Tanguy
Oil on canvas, 36 x 31 cm
Lüthi 72. Basle, Öffentliche
Kunstsammlung Basel, Kunstmuseum

poster-like – was exhibited with the Indépendants in 1891. Signac gave it the cumbersome but exact title *Portrait of Félix Fénéon in Front of an Enamel of a Rhythmic Background of Measures and Angles, Shades and Colours*. At that time, in 1890, he was working closely with Henry, illustrating his theoretical writings. He was convinced that, using Henry's aesthetic tables, one could compute the measures and angles in a picture and check shapes for harmony. This struck him as being "of great social importance" for the aesthetic education of those active in the applied arts. Fénéon, painted pointillistically, is holding a cyclamen in fingers of a neo-Gothic delicacy that was presently to be a hallmark of certain Symbolists (such as the Swiss artist Ferdinand Hodler, 1853–1918). The "enamel" background, based on the design on a Japanese kimono, emphasizes dynamic curves in a way that looks forward to another style soon to break – Art Nouveau.

Pointillism or divisionism did not permit strong personal styles. Thus the artists have to be assessed primarily through the slight differences in their subject matter, the degree to which they blended their aesthetic aims

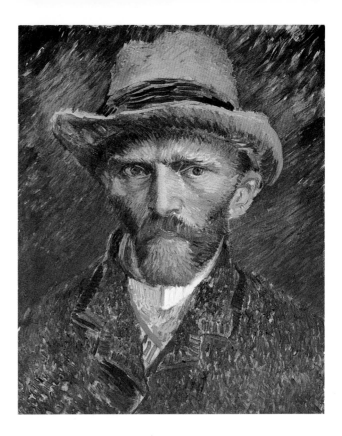

Vincent van Gogh
Self-Portrait in a Grey Felt Hat, 1887
Oil on card, 41 x 32 cm
F 295, JH 1211, Walther 211
Amsterdam, Stedelijk Museum
(on loan from the Rijksmuseum)

with realistic or Impressionist or indeed Symbolist leanings, and, of course, the energy they brought to visual structures of their own and the work of creating persuasive images with them.

Dubois-Pillet, an active Indépendant, died young in 1890. He painted atmospheric landscapes and city scenes (p. 311). Angrand, one of Seurat's first followers, moved on from vigorous and spontaneous brushwork (p. 295) to a dense fabric of points. His working-class couple out walking (p. 307) have their own simple dignity, and are well established in the light ochres of the clearly structured street scene. In the 1890s, linear styles and Symbolism prevailed over pointillism, and Angrand eventually moved on once more. Anquetin's tie with divisionism was of even briefer duration. As early as 1888, Bernard's friend (and rival) had begun to seem the quintessential new Symbolist (p. 306). Towards the end of 1891, interviewed on the occasion of an "Impressionists and Symbolists" exhibition at Le Barc de Boutteville galleries, he stressed that he espoused neither ism. Mirbeau had recently criticized him tartly for his traditionalist horrors.

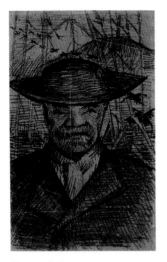

Vincent van Gogh
Portrait of Père Tanguy, 1887
Pencil on paper, 21.5 x 13.5 cm
Amsterdam, Van Gogh Museum,
Vincent van Gogh Foundation

Vincent van Gogh
Portrait of Père Tanguy, 1887
Oil on canvas, 92 x 75 cm
F 363, JH 1351, Walther 282
Paris, Musée Rodin

Henri-Edmond Cross (1856–1910), whose actual name was Delacroix, had exhibited in the Salon before turning to Impressionism via Monet. Then in 1884 he joined Seurat and Signac, and adhered till his death to a radiantly bright pointillism. He was most attracted to subjects in the south of France, in Venice, and elsewhere in Italy. Cross did not solely use unmixed prime colours for his pictures, which aspired to use spatial areas decoratively. The poetically titled *The Golden Isles* (p. 323), painted in 1891/92 and showing the Mediterranean islands of Hyères, suggests with particular vividness where the potential of Neo-Impressionism lay. From this point, the path led either to the decorative Symbolism and sophisticated opulence of the Vienna Secession artist Gustav Klimt (1862–1918) or to non-representational, abstract art dependent on colour accords alone.

Maximilien Luce (1858–1941), just beginning a long life and a tremendous output of paintings, drawings and posters, was a close friend of the anarchist leader Grave from 1887 on, and the friendship played a decisive part in his outlook. In style a pointillist from that year, he frequently painted streets and buildings in his home city of Paris (pp. 295, 374, 375). In figure work he retained a realistic approach to social actuality. Neo-Impressionist technique later constituted only one of the visual options he combined with his exact draughtsmanship.[144]

The young Lucien Pissarro (1863–1944) had a flair for brief brushstrokes combined with very light, dustily pale points. He used his technique to paint humanized landscapes of a kind his father liked to do (p. 274). He counterbalanced spatial depth with a tendency to emphasize surfaces which went hand in hand with his preference for graphic and illustrative work. After 1883 he went repeatedly to England, settling there for good in 1890; he married a Jewish Englishwoman and became a British citizen in 1916. His Eragny Press (established 1894), named for his home village, became one of the most highly respected small publishers in the new European movement of printed book art. In 1919, with the Belgian Théo van Rysselberghe (1892–1926) and the Englishman James Bolivar Manson, later director of the Tate Gallery in London, he founded the short-lived Monarro Group to promote the influence of the French Impressionists on English art. Pissarro was well regarded by various points on the art spectrum. For some years he alternated between pointillism and old-style Impressionism. His whole life long he painted attractive, if not especially inspired, English and French landscapes, the views always free of tension and sometimes seeming a little clumsy.

In his divisionist work, his father, Camille Pissarro, retained his scenes of land under cultivation, mostly tranquil farm or garden work or river landscapes, almost all near his new home at Eragny-sur-Epte or in Paris. He preferred minimal strokes to Seurat's dots. Whenever he pictured buildings, fields and trees together, as in the view from his window (p. 312) or his intriguing misty scene at Rouen harbour (p. 312), his old penchant for firm linearity and cubic compositional components became apparent. Pissarro preferred a constructive visual structure, even if the light was flickering and the section chosen seemingly random.

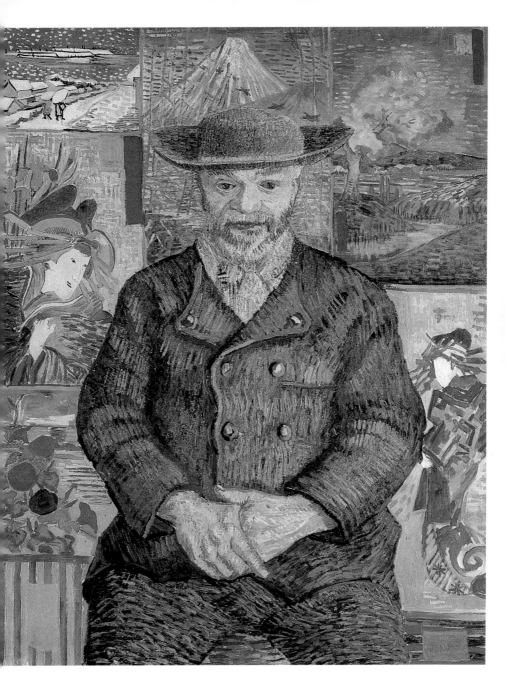

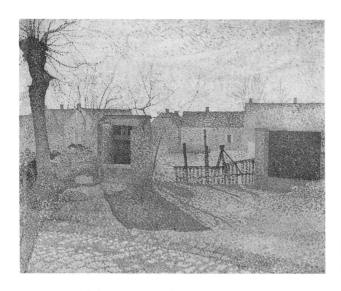

In 1890 – with the impressions of a visit to England fresh in his mind, and prepared by a visit to Holland in 1889 which had reawoken his love of Nature and his admiration of Monet, Degas, Renoir and Sisley[145] – Pissarro put the "systematic divisionism of our friend Seurat" behind him. Looking back in 1896, he wrote to the Belgian architect, painter and designer Henry van de Velde (1863–1957) that the "so-called scientific theory" of Seurat was "an aesthetic diametrically opposed" to life and movement. It had made it impossible for a man of his temperament to remain true to what he felt: that is, "to convey life and movement, or

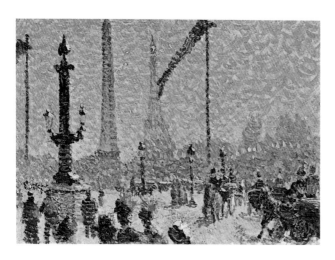

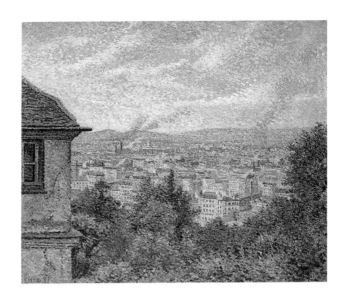

Maximilien Luce
Paris Seen from Montmartre, 1887
Paris vu du Montmartre
Oil on canvas, 54 x 63 cm
Bazetoux 161. Geneva, Musée du Petit Palais

the wonderful way Nature simply happens to look... Fortunately, it turned out that I was not the man for this kind of art, which makes an impression of deadly monotony on me."[146]

Pointillism remained central for only a few painters. As a style in its own right, it was a brief transitional phase in the history of art, yet releasing the hitherto unknown luminous force of pure colours by "dividing" them optically was to prove important for much that followed.

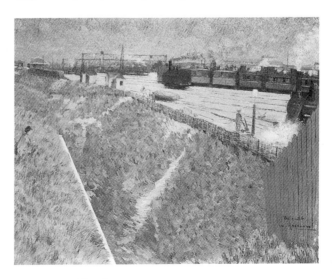

Charles Angrand
The Western Railway Leaving Paris, 1886
La ligne de l'ouest à sa sortie de Paris
Oil on canvas, 75 x 92 cm
Lausanne, Samuel Josefowitz Collection

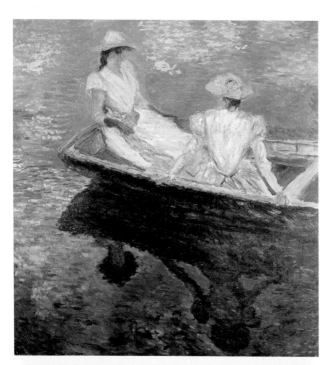

Claude Monet
Young Girls in a Boat, 1887
Jeunes filles en barque
Oil on canvas, 145 x 132 cm
Wildenstein 1152
Tokyo, National Museum of Western Art,
Matsukata Collection

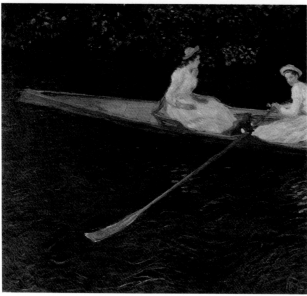

Claude Monet
Boating on the River Epte, 1890
En canot sur l'Epte
Oil on canvas, 133 x 145 cm
Wildenstein 1250
São Paulo, Museu de Arte de São Paulo

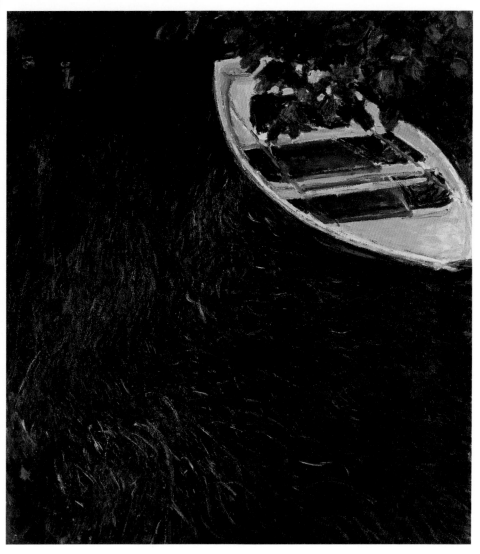

Claude Monet
The Boat, 1887
La barque
Oil on canvas, 146 x 133 cm
Wildenstein 1154
Paris, Musée Marmottan

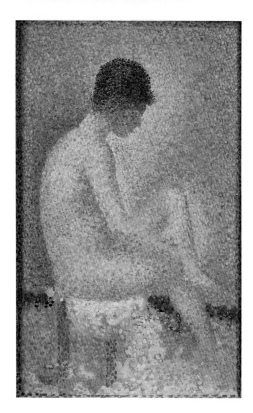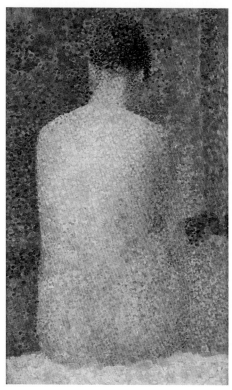

Georges Seurat
Seated Female Nude
(Study for "The Models"), c. 1886/87
Poseuse de profil
Oil on panel, 25.4 x 16.2 cm
Dorra/Rewald 175; De Hauke 182
Paris, Musée d'Orsay

Georges Seurat
Model from Behind
(Study for "The Models"), c. 1886/87
Poseuse de dos
Oil on panel, 24.5 x 15.5 cm
Dorra/Rewald 176; De Hauke 181
Paris, Musée d'Orsay

Despite the overall monotony of the exacting system, stripping artists of their individuality, the personal achievement of Seurat remains. The tenacious consistency with which he structured his visual ideas was arresting, as was the unflinching intensity he brought to his labours.

The Synthetist Moment

In the late 1880s, a number of young artists rejected Impressionism and Neo-Impressionism alike after first being fellow travellers for a time. Certain characteristics of Impressionism remained in their techniques, which may be called Post-Impressionist. One formal feature was a stronger emphasis on two-dimensional surface spaces, and greater freedom with colour and line. Representation of what the eye saw was displaced by the tonal harmonies inherent in the picture itself.

This principle of space had already interested Manet, and was apparent in Monet's loose brushwork and especially the uniform dots of Seu-

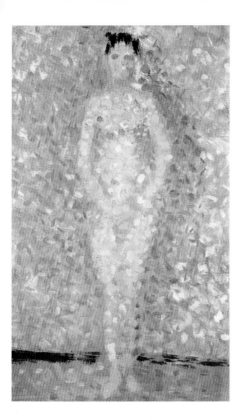

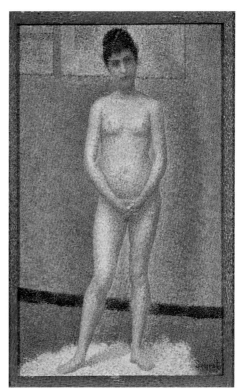

rat. But now the new artists were interested in larger, homogeneously coloured zones enclosed in their own contours (the *cloisons*). The picture was to be a synthesis, a coherent and autonomous entity, and not an analysis of reality, motion and phenomena of colour and light. Accordingly, the subjective establishment and interpretation of subjects was rated higher than looking at Nature through an individual temperament.

Every new movement finds it *de rigueur* to appeal to a historical tradition. In this case, the line was traced back to the very beginnings, to the primitive. The endeavour was comparable with the responses of Rousseau and the Romantics to the decline of absolutism and the startling beginnings of the industrial revolution in the later 18th century, and it took its place in a varied current of Neo-Romanticism. The new artists struck a distinctive note in the high value they placed upon the decorative, and their openness to the applied arts. They admired the way older cultures, where the makers of art had been craftsmen, took it for granted that utility objects could be decorated. A decorative pattern of shapes and colours could possess an autonomous beauty all its own, they felt – a beauty that was aesthetically perfect and sensuously enhanced the

Georges Seurat
Standing Female Nude
(Study for "The Models"), 1887
Poseuse de face, debout
Oil on panel, 25.4 x 16.2 cm
Dorra/Rewald 173; De Hauke 179
Paris, private collection

Georges Seurat
Standing Female Nude
(Study for "The Models"), 1887
Poseuse de face, debout
Oil on panel, 25 x 16 cm
Dorra/Rewald 174; De Hauke 183
Paris, Musée d'Orsay

quality of life. In other words, these artists too were rebelling against the academic hierarchies.

Gauguin became the central figure in this movement, even if certain other painters practised its preachings more doggedly, and his work alone came to be accorded the highest place in the history of Post-Impressionist art. In early 1891, the critic G.-Albert Aurier (1865–1892) took Gauguin's work as his point of reference for an account of Symbolist aesthetics, writing a second article on the subject shortly before his early death. The new art, he declared, "aims not to picture objects, as even Impressionism did (which was merely a variant of realism)... but rather to articulate ideas by putting them into a particular idiom." Objects were no more than "signs" for artists, who then recorded them in simplified form. The work of art should instead be "ideational", since its sole ideal was to express ideas; "symbolic", because it expressed them through shapes; and "synthetist", because the object was not grasped *qua* object but as a sign standing for an idea. And for these reasons it should also be "decorative", since truly decorative painting – as with the Egyptians, and probably the Greeks and primitive painters too – was an artistic creation at once subjective, synthetist, symbolic and ideational. To this tautological position Aurier added his assessment of Gauguin as

Georges Seurat
The Circus Parade, c. 1887/88
La parade de cirque
Oil on canvas, 99.7 x 150 cm
Dorra/Rewald 181; De Hauke 187
New York, The Metropolitan Museum of Art

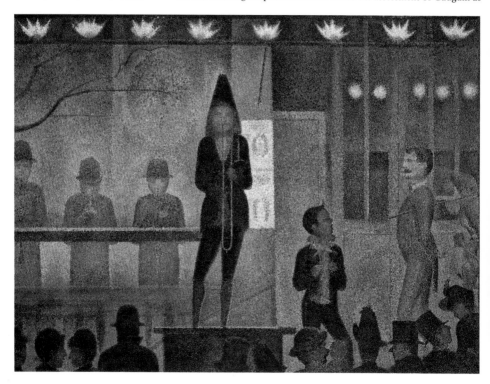

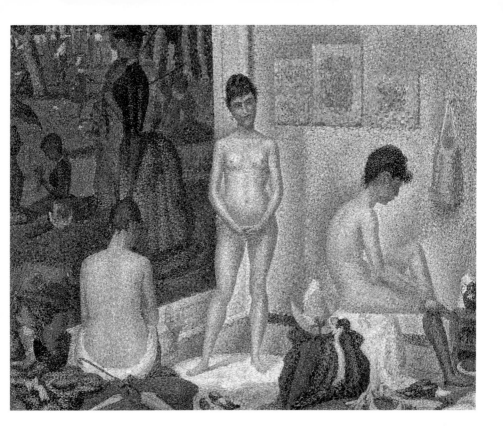

a savage (recalling the "noble savage" of 18th-century utopias). He concluded with the demand that the walls of public buildings be placed at the disposal of this artist of genius, Gauguin, for the painting of enormous decorative murals.[147] (Cézanne too hankered after commissions for mural work some time later, but his wishes were similarly in vain.)

Gauguin esteemed Cézanne's art but rejected Seurat's pointillism. Till his first stay at Pont-Aven in 1886 he painted similarly to his mentor, Pissarro, and afterwards too he continued to use Impressionist techniques intermittently. Even his motifs – rural genre scenes, landscapes, animals and even still lifes – tended to remain within the traditional Impressionist compass. *The Four Breton Girls* (p. 265), though, heralded a decorative spatial rhythm that evoked movement and song in a way that went beyond representation. There is a radical distinction to be drawn between this veritably ceremonial presentation of unfamiliar gestures and old-style folklorish art.[148] Gauguin's aim was to return, through learning, to roots that he felt to be of greater value.

A key painting was the 1888 *Vision after the Sermon: Jacob Wrestling*

Georges Seurat
The Models (small version), 1888
Les poseuses
Oil on canvas, 39.4 x 48.7 cm
Dorra/Rewald 179; De Hauke 184
Paris, Heinz Berggruen Collection
(On loan from the National Gallery, London)

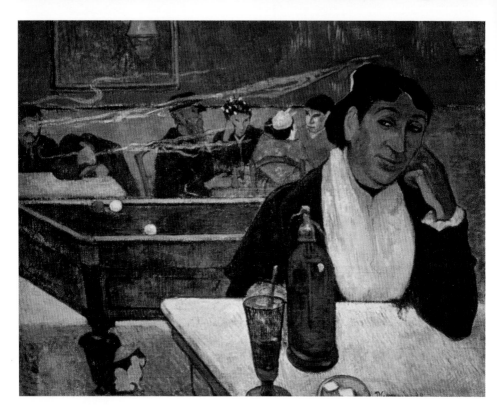

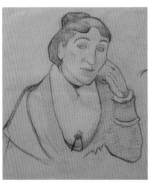

Paul Gauguin
L'Arlesienne (Madame Ginoux), 1888
Crayon and charcoal on paper, 56.1 x 49.2 cm
San Francisco, The Fine Arts Museum,
Achenbach Foundation

with the Angel (p. 303). The Breton women returning home from church, and the priest, are foreground onlookers as in Degas's theatre paintings. What they are witnessing is about as far away from them as Degas's dancers would be from a theatre box, and the two spatial levels are as uncompromisingly juxtaposed. But here what they see – the vision recorded in Genesis 32, 24–29 – appears to their mind's eye alone. The biblical scene is kept apart from them by a tree trunk (the diagonal clearly influenced by Japanese art), the spatial position of which remains unclear, and the ground is an unreal and overwhelming glow of red.

This painting, which was too innovative to be accepted by many contemporaries, broke new stylistic ground, along with Sérusier's talisman painting *The River Aven at Bois d'Amour* (p. 320) and the work of Anquetin (p. 306). In fact it was Anquetin (who later lapsed into a traditionalism of no interest) who reconciled Impressionism and an almost surreal use of spatial decorativeness in his grand painting *A Gust of Wind on the Seine Bridge* (1889; Bremen, Kunsthalle Bremen). Gauguin was expressly seeking after stylized rather than mirror images. "This year I have sacrificed everything, technique, colour, to style," he observed – meaning

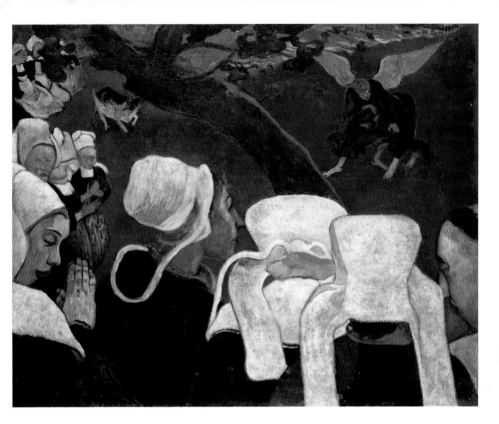

an autonomous uniform order of shapes. The emphasis on style was a core feature of Symbolism.

In late 1888, Gauguin and van Gogh made their famous attempt to work together in Arles and learn from each other (p. 302). The Dutch painter was the more committed to the enterprise, which foundered on differences of temperament and aesthetics. In 1891 Gauguin set out for the South Seas, to Tahiti (a French colony). The artistic fruits of that journey, exhibited during his return stay in France from 1893 to 1895, did not bring him the success he hoped for. Till his death in 1903 he then remained first on Tahiti and then finally on Hiva-Oa (Dominique), one of the Marquesas Islands. Full of inner contradictions, complicated in his behaviour, fighting for fame and against the colonial authorities, and a victim of syphilis in the end, he made a genuine attempt to understand the world-view and mythology of the native peoples. In his poeticized autobiographical account, *Noa Noa*, first published in the *Revue blanche* in 1897, he sought to bring his alien realm closer to a Europe that was not without a taste for the exotic. But his utopian notion that he could become a child of Nature like the indigenous women he lived

Left:
Paul Gauguin
Night Café in Arles (Madame Ginoux), 1888
Au café (Mme Ginoux)
Oil on canvas, 72 x 92 cm
Wildenstein 305
Moscow, Pushkin Museum of Fine Art

Paul Gauguin
Vision after the Sermon: Jacob Wrestling with the Angel, 1888
La vision après le sermon ou La lutte de Jacob avec l'ange
Oil on canvas, 73 x 92 cm
Wildenstein 245
Edinburgh, National Gallery of Scotland

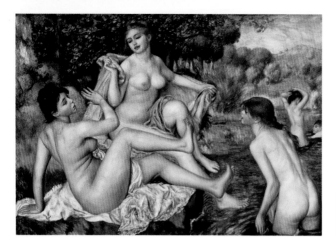

Pierre-Auguste Renoir
The Bathers, 1887
Les grandes baigneuses
Oil on canvas, 118 x 170 cm
Philadelphia (PA), Philadelphia Museum of Art

with was a delusion as long as he continued to draw money transfers from the Paris agent who handled his art (ranting all the while against capitalism and bourgeois culture).

His paintings, though, brought honest integrity and a real appreciation to bear on the beautiful "golden bodies" of the indigenous people and on the resplendent colours of Nature in the tropics (pp. 334/335). The Polynesian titles he gave his paintings were intended (in line with his Symbolist views) to deepen their mysterious allure. The poses in which we see his nude or semi-nude people – relaxed, about their everyday business, pictured realistically – are eloquent of peace and tranquillity; it is, however, a peace that is often examined psychologically, and clouded by sadness or the fear of demons. These people harmoniously occupy an environment that is rendered in flat, ornamental terms. The outlines, proportions and details are all subject to the simplification and some-what awkward coarseness characteristic of primitive art. Gauguin also quoted the hallmarks of ancient Egyptian art (p. 333). The gravity and enigmatic otherness of certain attitudes transform commonplace poses into cultic images of magical force (pp. 332, 352). Gauguin's simple brushwork and intensely contrastive colours largely retain the Impressionist approach to three-dimensionality through shadow, patches of light and an extensive use of green.

Gauguin hoped that Bernard would accompany him to the South Seas. Bernard's work included a vigorous, concentrated portrait of Père Tanguy (p. 290), the indefatigable supporter of innovatory artists. But the two artists fell out. Bernard was shortly to return to a traditional, historical technique. So too was Sérusier, who had enrolled at the independent Académie Julian with several others in 1888. A group of friends was established who were ardent adherents of synthetism, sought the symbolist advice of Redon, and revered both Puvis and Cézanne. The group of young artists were semi-seriously seized by religious and mys-

Right:
Pierre-Auguste Renoir
After the Bath, 1888
Après le bain
Oil on canvas, 65 x 54 cm
Tokyo, private collection

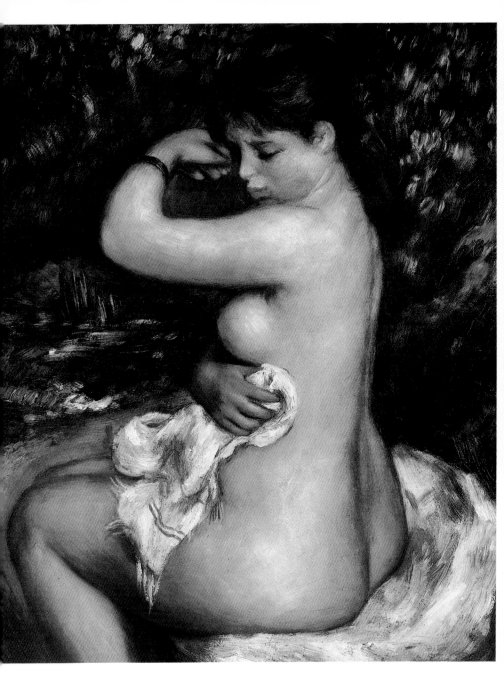

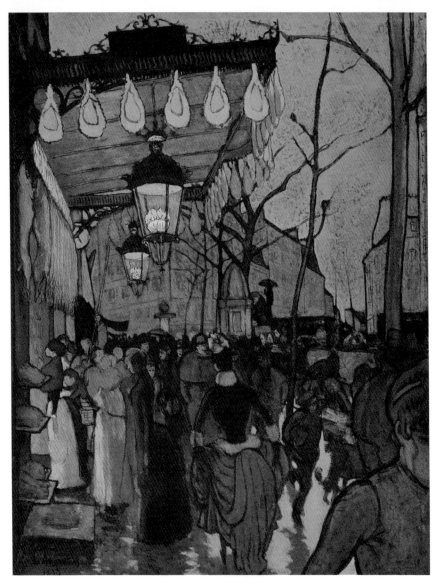

Louis Anquetin
Avenue de Clichy – Five O'Clock in the Evening, 1887
Avenue de Clichy – cinq heures du soir
Oil on canvas, 69 x 53.5 cm
Hartford (CT), Wadsworth Atheneum

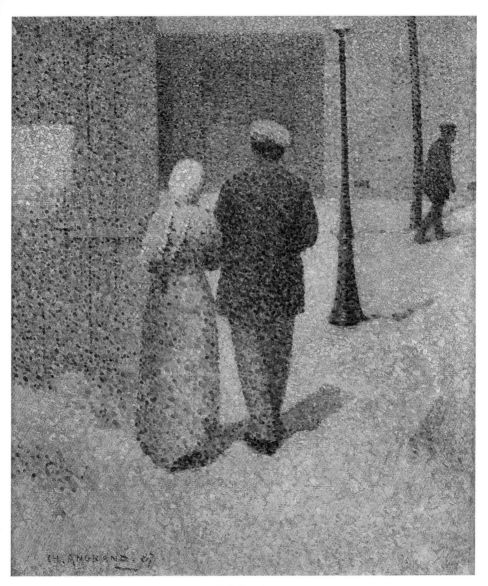

Charles Angrand
Man and Woman in the Street, 1887
Couple dans la rue
Oil on canvas on card, 38.5 x 33 cm
Paris, Musée d'Orsay

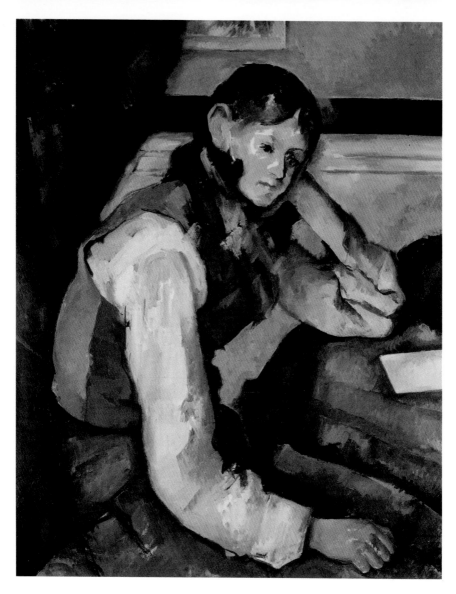

Paul Cézanne
Boy in a Red Waistcoat, c. 1888–1890
Garçon au gilet rouge
Oil on canvas, 79.5 x 64 cm
Venturi 681
Zurich, E.G. Bührle Collection

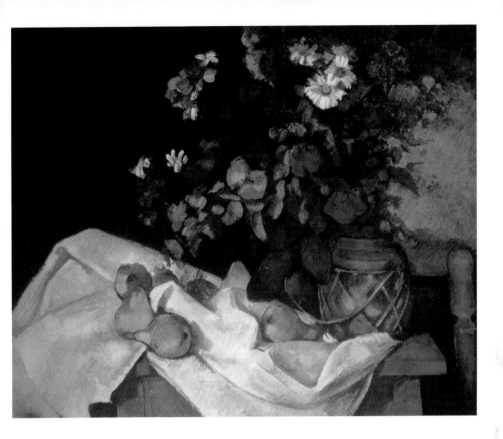

Paul Cézanne
Still Life with Flowers and Fruit, 1888–1890
Nature morte aux fleurs et fruits
Oil on canvas, 65 x 81 cm. Venturi 610
Berlin, Alte Nationalgalerie, Staatliche Museen
zu Berlin – Preußischer Kulturbesitz

tical feeling, but were equally intent on provocative media impact; Sérusier gave them the Hebraic name Nabis (prophets), and indeed their
regular meeting place in the home of one member was declared a temple.
One of their number, the Dutchman Jan Verkade (1868–1946), took
monastic orders not long after. From 1891 the Nabis exhibited at Le Barc
de Boutteville, the gallery which had previously promoted the Neo-Impressionists and Symbolists. Several of the artists attempted to meet Aurier's demand for an all-embracing synthesis of art forms by designing
stage sets for small avant-garde theatres, posters, and tapestries.

One of their leading theorists was Maurice Denis (1870–1943), who
was influenced by Gauguin and subsequently played an important part
in religious art. *The Muses* or *In the Park* (1893; p. 341) is a good
example of how an open-air Impressionist genre scene can be transformed into a rhythmic, decorative tapestry. The ethereally slender, sensitive, ivory-pale figures are established in soft, flowing lines; their manner has a ceremonial remoteness, so that they seem supernatural beings
in some mysterious sacred grove. This, certainly, was a triumph of style,

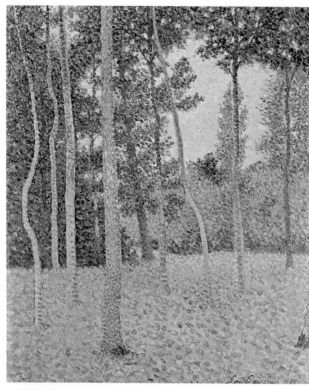

Léo Gausson
Undergrowth, 1888
Sous-bois
Oil on panel, 31.7 x 26.7 cm
Michigan, private collection

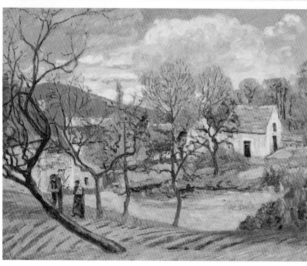

Armand Guillaumin
Outskirts of Paris, c. 1890
Environs de Paris
Oil on canvas, 74 x 93 cm
Serret/Fabiani 210
USA, Mrs. Lyndon Baines
Johnson Collection

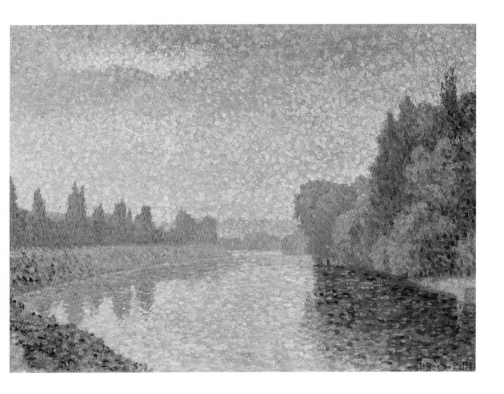

Albert Dubois-Pillet
The Marne at Dawn, 1888
La Marne à l'aube
Oil on canvas, 32 x 46 cm
Paris, Musée d'Orsay

overlaid on the legacy of the preceding generation. Denis did later use a sprightly, pallid, bright Impressionist technique of dabs, though.

In 1890, aged just twenty, he had published an article in a little magazine which dealt with "Neo-Traditionalism", it is true, but in its preamble calmly stated what was to be a central creed of Modernism: "One must bear in mind that before a painting is a warhorse, a naked woman or an anecdote, it is essentially a flat surface covered with colours arranged in a particular way."[150]

Light for the World

In 1888 Gauguin, van Gogh and Bernard painted portraits of each other, and self-portraits, to seal their artistic brotherhood.[151] It was for this group that van Gogh hoped the yellow house in Arles (p. 315) – which he had used a modest legacy to fit out and paint – would serve as home and studio; he proposed to hang pictures of sunflowers there in such a

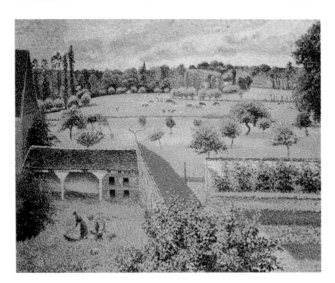

Camille Pissarro
View from the Artist's Window at Eragny,
c. 1886–1888
Vue de ma fenêtre, Eragny sur Epte
Oil on canvas, 65 x 81 cm
Pissarro/Venturi 721
Oxford, The Visitors of the Ashmolean Museum

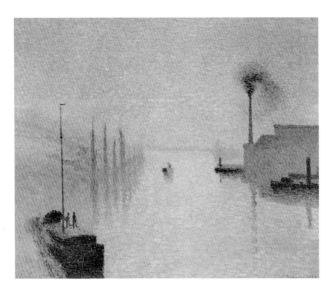

Camille Pissarro
Lacroix Island, Rouen, in Fog
L'Ile Lacroix, Rouen, effet de brouillard
Oil on canvas, 46.4 x 55.6 cm
Pissarro/Venturi 719
Philadelphia (PA), Philadelphia Museum of Art,
John G. Johnson Collection

Albert-Charles Lebourg
Road on the Banks of the Seine at Neuilly in
Winter, c. 1888
Route au bord de la Seine, à Neuilly, en hiver
Oil on canvas, 50 x 73 cm
Bénédite 963. Paris, Musée d'Orsay

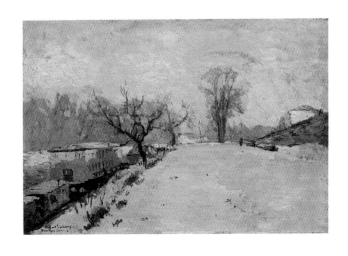

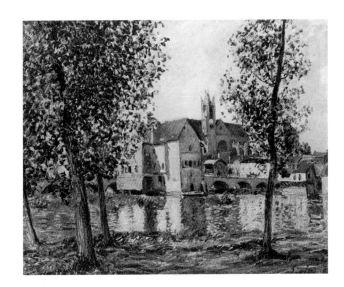

Alfred Sisley
Moret-sur-Loing in Morning Sun, 1888
Vue de Moret-sur-Loing, soleil du matin
Oil on canvas, 60.5 x 73.5 cm
Daulte 678. Private collection

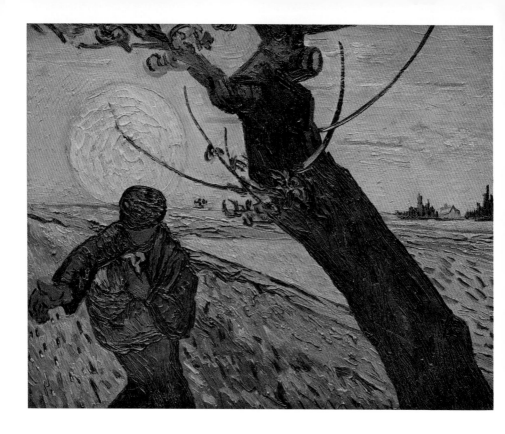

Vincent van Gogh
The Sower, 1888
Oil on canvas, 32 x 40 cm
F 451, JH 1629, Walther 453
Amsterdam, Van Gogh Museum,
Vincent van Gogh Foundation

way as to recall an altar.[152] Many things met in this hope: a realistic appropriation of visible reality; a wish to use art for democratic, Christian or missionary, and anarcho-socialist ends; decorative beautifying of the place one lived in; and a Symbolist approach to the deeper significance of things and the emotional impact of colour and form harmonies.

Van Gogh adopted these views, and particularly the Impressionist and pointillist techniques, from 1886 to 1888 in Paris. He devoured the Impressionists' subjects. He schooled his sense of colour by painting countless floral still lifes, and did at least fifteen paintings of the old Moulin de la Galette (p. 276), which may have reminded him of Holland – though he had never painted a windmill when he was there. His views of the city, of walkers in the park, the Seine, or avenues (pp. 277, 280, 289) were among the best that Impressionism produced – even if an undisciplined brushwork or a confrontational approach to objects and forms could sometimes mar the effect. *Fishing in Spring, Pont de Clichy* (p. 288) affords an instructive comparison with Monet's tranquil *The River* (p. 76) painted twenty years earlier. Van Gogh painted countless

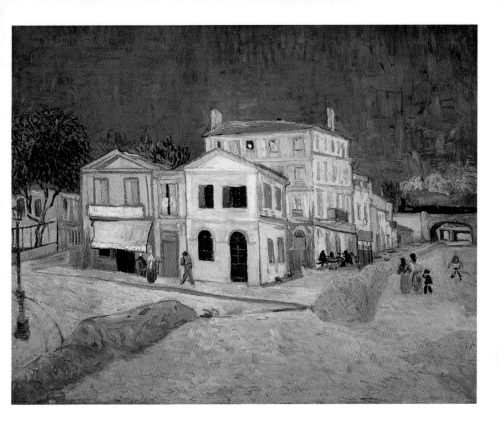

self-portraits, and in his portraits of ordinary people his fellow feeling led him to emphasize their sadness, dignity and kindness. The *Portrait of Père Tanguy* (p. 293) is a good example.

In February 1888 he moved to Arles, where the light was brighter and the colours more luminous. He was tireless in his quest for subjects that would provide the happiest accord between things seen and his own sensations. He changed his colours, made them more robust, and composed in contrasts. Van Gogh wanted his pictures to serve humankind, to bring them light; at the same time, he was determined to make no concessions where his artistic aim of honest self-expression was concerned, despite the fact that his brother, Theo, was unable to sell his work in Paris. In material terms, Vincent was totally dependent on Theo, who believed in his brother's artistic vision. Van Gogh quoted revered realists such as Millet in works like *The Sower* (p. 314). Hours on end spent painting in the open almost gave him sunstroke. He wanted to sow light for the world; painting had become identical with life itself.

At Christmas 1888 the failure of his venture with Gauguin (who

Vincent van Gogh
Vincent's House in Arles (The Yellow House), 1888
Oil on canvas, 72 x 91.5 cm
F 464, JH 1589, Walther 423
Amsterdam, Van Gogh Museum,
Vincent van Gogh Foundation

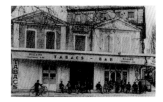

Van Gogh's "yellow house" in Arles, where he lived from May 1888 till April 1889

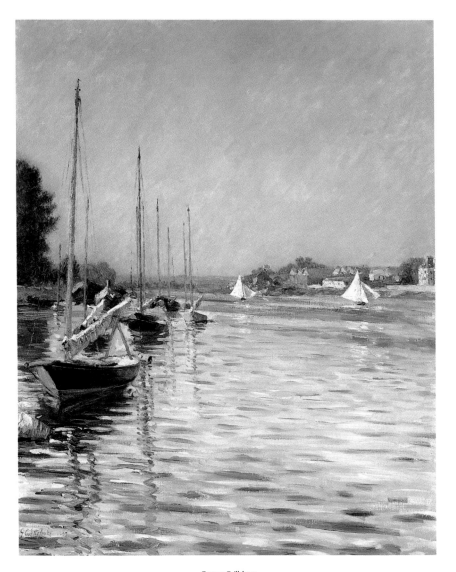

Gustave Caillebotte
Boats on the Seine at Argenteuil, 1892
Bateaux sur la Seine à Argenteuil
Oil on canvas, 73 x 60 cm
Berhaut 413
London, Richard Green Gallery

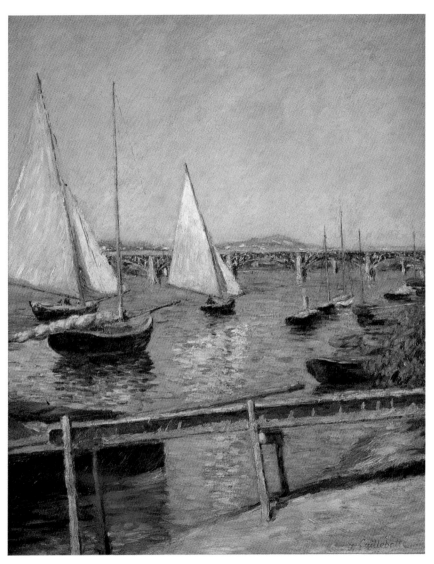

Gustave Caillebotte
Sailing Boats at Argenteuil, c. 1888
Voiliers à Argenteuil
Oil on canvas, 65 x 55.5 cm
Berhaut 359. Paris, Musée d'Orsay

thought in more businesslike ways) prompted van Gogh's symbolic act of self-mutilation: he cut off an earlobe. In dedicating his act to a prostitute, the marginalized and humiliated artist (who could still be used for pleasure) was associating himself with her in his own philosophy. At that point van Gogh had nineteen months to live, and spent some of that time under psychiatric treatment. When finally Dr. Gachet at Auvers, the old friend of the Impressionists, decided to look after him, Vincent shot himself in the very fields he had so often painted. In those nineteen months he had painted about 255 further pictures, the subjects, angles, colours and free brushwork of which went notably beyond Impressionism. Indeed, the intense colours and the dramatic shapes (as in his flamelike cypress trees and swirling stars) anticipated Expressionism. But it is fair to assume that the pleasure the Impressionists took in the things of the world, their accessibility, and the beauty of their colours, played a significant part in putting paintings by the impoverished van Gogh at the top of today's art price range.[153]

Georges Seurat
Le Chahut, c. 1889/90
Oil on canvas, 171.5 x 140.5 cm
Dorra/Rewald 199; De Hauke 199
Otterlo, Kröller-Müller Museum

The Pain of Pleasure

Georges Seurat
Dancers on Stage (Study for "Le Chahut"), 1889
Danseuses sur la scène (Etude pour «Le Chahut»)
Oil on panel, 21.8 x 15.8 cm
Dorra/Rewald 197; De Hauke 197
London, Courtauld Institute Galleries

Toulouse-Lautrec was not yet twenty when in 1882, already in full command of Impressionist techniques and ways of seeing, he painted his port-

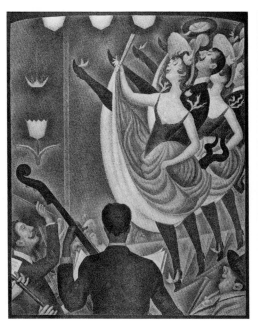
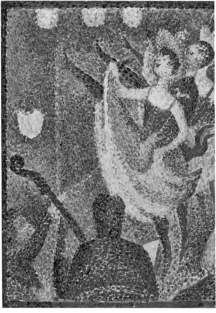

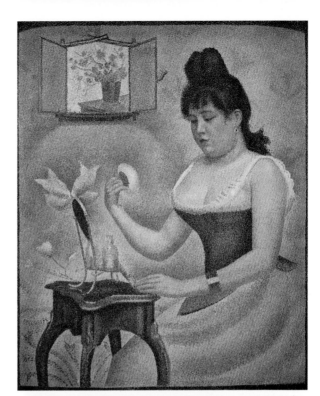

Georges Seurat
Young Woman Powdering Herself, c. 1889/90
Jeune femme se poudrant
Oil on canvas, 95.5 x 79.5 cm
Dorra/Rewald 195; De Hauke 200
London, Courtauld Institute Galleries

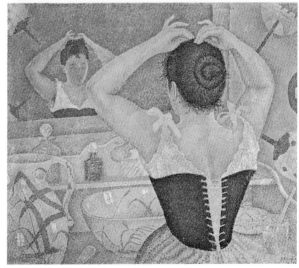

Paul Signac
Woman Taking up Her Hair, 1892
Femme se coiffant
Oil on canvas, 59 x 70 cm
Paris, Collection Mme Gachin-Signac

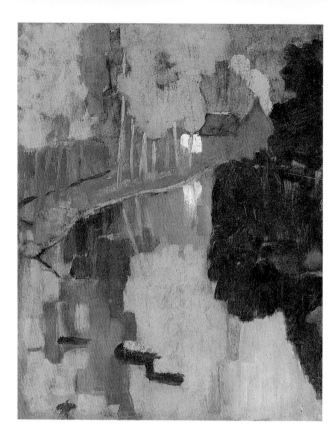

Paul Sérusier
The River Aven at Bois d'Amour (The Talisman),
1888
L'Aven au Bois d'Amour (Le talisman)
Oil on panel, 27 x 21.5 cm
Guicheteau 2. Paris, Musée d'Orsay

rait *Young Routy* (p.227). At Cormon's studio he met the Post-Impressionists, subsequently exhibiting with them at the Indépendants and the Brussels exhibitions of Les Vingt. But he was not the man for binding group ties. He wanted companions to talk to or drink with, and that was all. He was quick to adopt the cloisonnists' large, strong colour spaces with their defined linear boundaries in his own formal idiom. For Toulouse-Lautrec, though, an expressive, swinging line like a whiplash (such as soon became the hallmark of Art Nouveau) was more important than it would ever be for his friend Anquetin or for Gauguin. Above all, he retained to the end a light, nervy sketchiness in his painting technique; a delight in capturing grotesque movement and the effects of artificial light; and an interest in unusual sectional views and plunging depth perspective of a kind he had admired in Forain and especially Degas. He did an airy but firmly structured pastel portrait of van Gogh, whom he had met at Cormon's (p.278), showing him at the Café du Tambourin, run by Agostina Segatori (cf. van Gogh's portrait of her, p.287). The grainy paper had much the same effect of loosening up the pastel as it had had when Seurat tried the same approach.

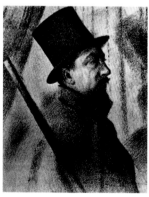

Georges Seurat
Portrait of Paul Signac, 1890
Conté crayon on paper, 34.5 x 28 cm
De Hauke 694. Private collection

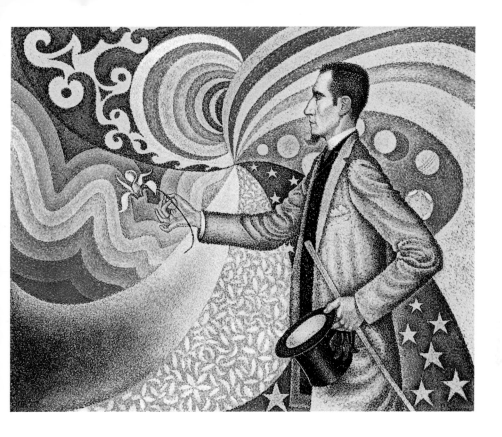

Paul Signac
Portrait of Félix Fénéon in Front of an Enamel of a
Rhythmic Background of Measures and Angles,
Shades and Colours, 1890
Portrait de Félix Fénéon sur l'émail d'un fond ryth-
mique de mesures et d'angles, de tons et de teintes
Oil on canvas, 73.5 x 92.5 cm
New York, The Museum of Modern Art

Van Gogh doubtless liked the interest in people and their fates that
Toulouse-Lautrec attested in his outstanding portraits and genre scenes
from those years. Toulouse-Lautrec was a skilful draughtsman, far better
able than van Gogh to capture character, temperament and the momentary mood of a person in facial expression, gestures and – most of all –
body language, and, through these, that person's social situation. The
realism of Courbet or Zola survived in Toulouse-Lautrec with an intensity alien to his Symbolist contemporaries. He painted Carmen Gaudin, a
blonde working woman who often modelled for him, as a tired laundress
(p. 243) gazing with longing out of her top floor window at the wide
world without. We see her very slightly from below, so that the woman,
propped firmly on her arms, shoulders and back tensed, makes a more
rebellious impression than any similar figure between Degas and the
young Picasso, or any of the other figures at windows that had been a
19th-century visual stock in trade ever since the Romantics.[154]

As a wealthy aristocrat, Toulouse-Lautrec was hardly destined by
birth to be alert to the social issues that were growing more acute in his

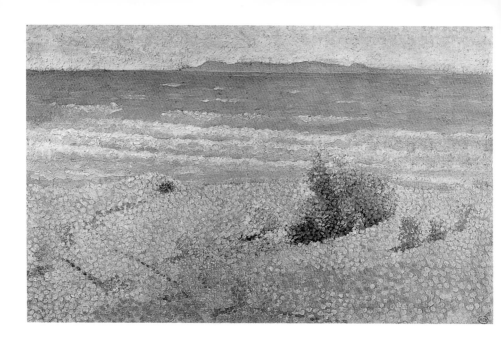

Henri-Edmond Cross
Beach on the Mediterranean, c. 1891/9
La plage en Méditerranée
Oil on card, 38 x 61 cm
France, private collection

day. But his own physical misfortune had made him more sensitive to the lot of others. Of course he was a rich man going to the theatres and revues and cafés-concert[155] in quest of entertainment; but his dwarfish stature meant the cost was twice as high for him. He developed an acute sense of the polarity between the professional life of dancers and prostitutes, and the simple humanity they preserved in what private life remained to them. He did psychologically penetrating *plein-air* portraits of some of them in the garden of Père Forest's Montmartre inn, where he was living from 1884.

Toulouse-Lautrec's subject matter, including most of his situation portraits, was drawn from the theatre, variety shows and the circus, from restaurants, horse racing and brothels. Some of his best work showed the Moulin Rouge (pp. 324, 325) in the Boulevard de Clichy, which had been opened in late 1889, the year of the World Fair. Those who went there were doubtless upright middle-class citizens, but the dancing was eccentric and challenging, of a kind associated with robuster folk entertainment. One of the establishment's stars was the temperamental La Goulue (Louise Weber, 1870–1929), another the lean Valentin (Jules Renaudin), nicknamed Le Désossé (boneless) for his agility. The sectional views, spatial sense, alternation of light and dark and of colours and lighting effects, as well as his sketchy technique, all reveal Toulouse-Lautrec's debt to the Impressionists in these works; the contour lines that define his almost silhouetted figures, on the other hand, are synthetist.

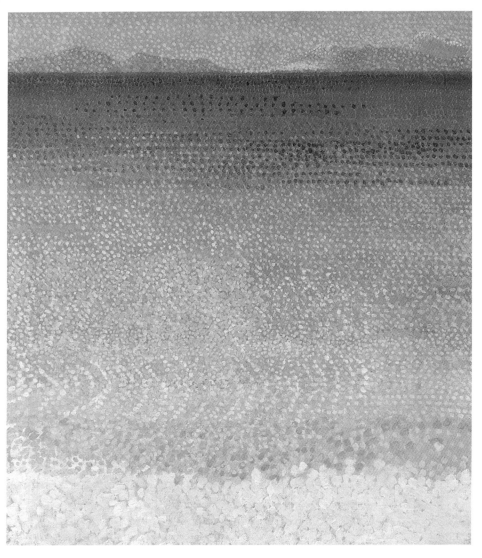

Henri-Edmond Cross
The Golden Isles, 1891/92
Les Iles d'Or
Oil on canvas, 59 x 54 cm
Compin 36. Paris, Musée d'Orsay

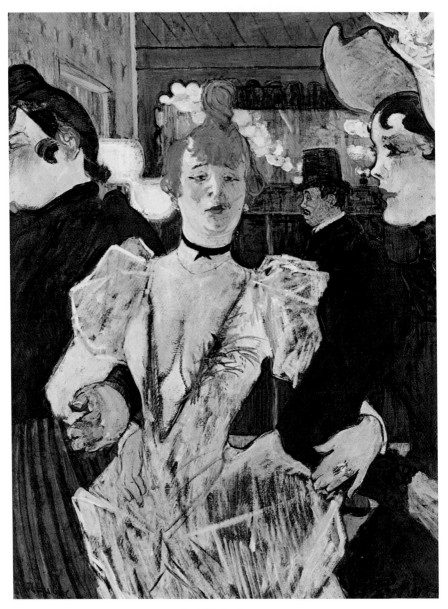

Henri de Toulouse-Lautrec
La Goulue Entering the Moulin Rouge, 1892
La Goulue entrant au Moulin Rouge, accompagnée de deux femmes
Oil on card, 79.4 x 59 cm. Dortu 423
New York, The Museum of Modern Art, Gift of Mrs. David M. Levy

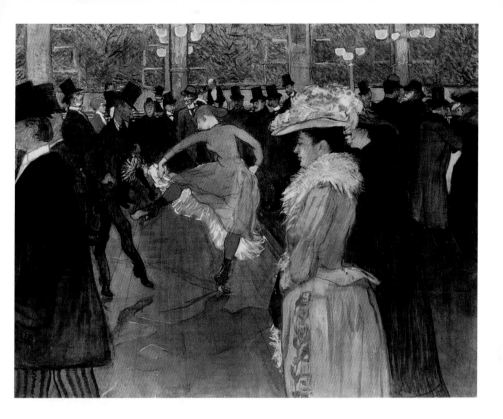

The owner of the Moulin Rouge realised that this new customer who could hold his drink had a novel, provocative style in art that could make attractive advertising for the establishment – better, certainly, than the sickly-sweet small posters done hitherto by Jules Chéret (1836–1933). In October 1891 Toulouse-Lautrec's first poster was on the walls of Paris, a large colour lithograph that emphasized blocks of space. Along with the France-Champagne poster by the young Pierre Bonnard (1867–1947), a member of the Nabis, this inaugurated a new era in poster graphics. Thanks to its openness to applied arts conceived as a mass product for a mass audience, advertising henceforth became a medium well suited to daring graphic experiment. Toulouse-Lautrec did another thirty lithographic posters for literary cabarets, chanson singers and publishers. On several occasions (including superlative portraits) his subject was the dancer Jane Avril (1868–1943), who performed on a variety of stages. The structure of the picture showing her at the Jardin de Paris (p. 327) is clearly a variation on themes by Degas. The bold elegance of the singer Aristide Bruant (p. 327), or the almost demonic idiosyncrasy perceived in a violinist in another poster, went beyond Impressionism.

Henri de Toulouse-Lautrec
A Dance at the Moulin Rouge, 1889/90
La danse au «Moulin Rouge»
Oil on canvas, 115.5 x 150 cm
Dortu 361
Philadelphia (PA), Philadelphia Museum of Art

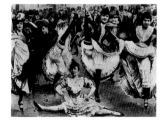

At the Moulin Rouge. La Goulue is on the floor

The self-assurance and charisma of La Goulue fascinated Toulouse-Lautrec. In 1895, when she had put on so much weight (her nickname meant "glutton") that she only appeared in a dive of her own, he painted wall drapes of coarse canvas showing her in several of her famous numbers, for the premises. He had already painted her provocative if nervous entry into the Moulin Rouge, with her sister and a fellow performer (p. 324), and had conveyed something of the psychological pressure show business exerts on its stars. In all his work, men – including his friend and cousin, Dr. Gabriel Tapié de Céleyran (1869–1930) – tended to be subject to spiteful caricaturist swipes; prostitutes in brothels, on the other hand, though shown in unbeautiful coarseness, prompted a warm fellow feeling in him. He was interested in the way they behaved to each other outside their work, and in their lesbian relations, a private emotional realm which they opposed to their business world of sex (pp. 344, 345). In fact Toulouse-Lautrec sometimes even lived in brothels. His economical, assured, "unfinished" studies recorded the movements of models who were altogether uninhibited. To his painter's eye, hungry for form, they seemed more natural and thus lovelier than professional models with their polished poses.

Toulouse-Lautrec was increasingly indifferent to the offence his family took at his descent into a nether world of vice. From 1893 on he also chose not to enter works for any juried exhibition. His old school friend Maurice Joyant (1864–1930) was working for Goupil's as Theo van Gogh's successor, then partner, and finally sole proprietor of the gallery. It was he who set up the first solo exhibition for Toulouse-Lautrec in

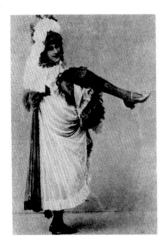

Jane Avril. Photograph

Louis Anquetin
Girl Reading a Newspaper, 1890
Jeune femme lisant un journal
Pastel on paper on card, 54 x 43.5 cm
London, The Tate Gallery

Louis Anquetin
In the Theatre Foyer, 1892 (Au foyer du théâtre)
Oil on canvas. Private collection

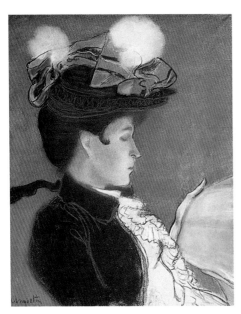

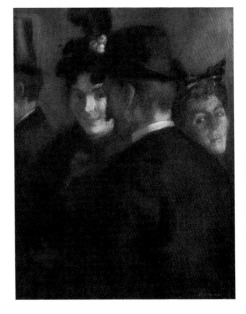

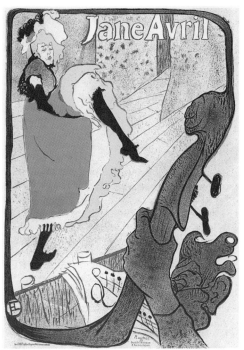

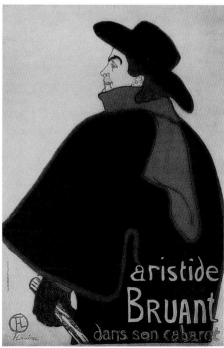

1893, which brought the artist a certain recognition from Degas. Joyant it was as well who received the rights to Toulouse-Lautrec's artistic estate from the artist's father, now a stranger to his wayward son. Alcohol, syphilis contracted in 1888, and sheer disgust at life, were driving Toulouse-Lautrec increasingly to distraction. In February 1899 he collapsed in the Rue des Moulins brothel and was taken to an asylum. Before long he was able to make the escorted journey to Bordeaux, where he set up in a studio and painted his relentlessly forceful final theatre pictures, such as *Messalina with Two Extras* (Zurich, Collection E. G. Bührle). For the last three weeks of his life he was tended by his beloved mother at Château Malromé, where he died two months before his thirty-seventh birthday. Through this idiosyncratic offshoot, something of the Impressionist heart had continued to beat into the 20th century.

Henri de Toulouse-Lautrec
Jane Avril at the Jardin de Paris, 1893
Jane Avril au «Jardin de Paris»
Lithograph, 124.5 x 89.5 cm
Wittrock 11. Private collection

Henri de Toulouse-Lautrec
Aristide Bruant at his Cabaret, 1892
Aristide Bruant dans son cabaret
Lithograph, 137 x 96.5 cm
Wittrock 6. Private collection

8 The Fruits of Persistence

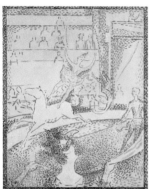

Georges Seurat
Study for "The Circus", 1891
Etude pour «Le cirque»
Oil on canvas, 55 x 46 cm
Dorra/Rewald 210; De Hauke 212
Paris, Musée d'Orsay

Georges Seurat
The Circus, 1891
Le cirque
Oil on canvas, 185.5 x 152.5 cm
Dorra/Rewald 211; De Hauke 213
Paris, Musée d'Orsay

By the late 1880s and early 1890s, Impressionism was a firmly established feature of the art landscape, familiar even outside France, and was continually attracting new followers. Its fate was that of every modern creative concept: on the one hand, traditionalists continued to combat the movement, accusing it of abandoning aesthetic norms and, in the broadest of political terms, of undermining the existing order; on the other hand, Impressionism had itself become the target of newer movements with their own new scales of values. Any style is necessarily one-sided and will offer opponents a purchase if they choose to highlight its shortcomings. The Impressionists no longer saw any point in compromising with academic views in order to gain entry to the Salon. Indeed, certain aspects of the Impressionist programme had meanwhile influenced the art that was given official support.

The "reflex responses made by Impressionism"[356] to the alternative aesthetics of younger artists were a quite different matter. The major Impressionist masters never held academic positions and had no pupils worth mentioning, with the exception of Pissarro, who gave advice and encouragement to his juniors over many years. But they did take a close look at whatever tempting innovations the younger artists might have hit upon after first trying to paint in the usual Impressionist ways. And the *zeitgeist* had in any case changed; the aesthetic climate had been transformed. Symbolist and decorative approaches modified the late phase of Impressionism. For that reason, the movement offered no resistance to interpretations of its original intentions made under the influence of Post-Impressionism by well-meaning young critics.

Impressionist art was no longer the domain of a group (and anyway, the group had never been entirely unified or homogeneous from the outset). Rather, the individual artists – even if they were linked by friendships or often exhibited together – were now concerned to conquer the upper reaches of the market and assure their positions in art history. Their exhibitions at commercial galleries in and outside France were of greater importance than the Salons, where they might go unnoticed in the crowd. Changes in prices occasioned by auctions of private collections (generally when the collector died) affected the prices the artists' new works fetched. And they continued the struggle to have the Impressionist contribution to the glorious annals of French art recognised. In

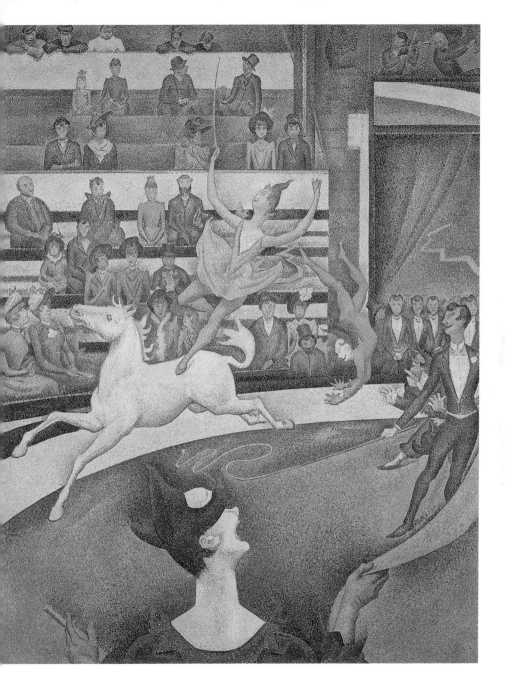

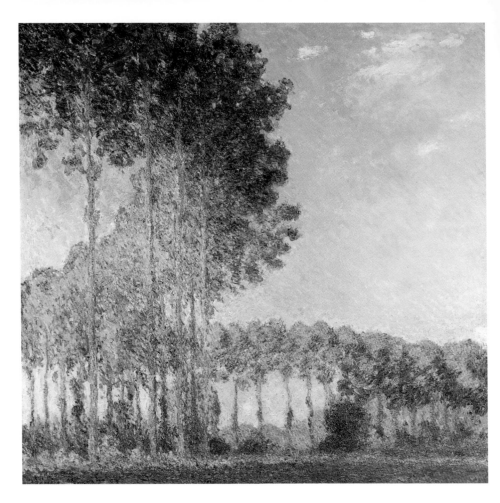

this struggle, their old collective spirit, friendship and mutual esteem stood firm.

The inclusion of 15 Manets in the 1889 World Fair boosted the fame of the artist. His widow, who was in financial straits, still owned important works, such as the epoch-making *Olympia*. When it seemed likely that the painting would be sold to an American, Monet organized a collection to keep the picture in France, for the Louvre. A great many art lovers, intellectuals and artists contributed. Some were too poor to do so. Manet's old friend Zola refused, on the rather strange grounds (for him) that he did not want to be involved in pushing prices up, for the sake of the owners of other Impressionist pictures. Yet the proposed 20,000 francs for *Olympia* were nothing to the 336,000 francs that had

Claude Monet
Poplars on the Banks of the Epte, 1891
Peupliers au bord de l'Epte
Oil on canvas, 88 x 93 cm
Wildenstein 1312. USA, private collection

Right:
Claude Monet
Haystack in the Snow, Morning, 1890
Meule, effet de neige, le matin
Oil on canvas, 65.4 x 92.3 cm
Wildenstein 1280. Boston (MA), Museum of Fine Arts

Claude Monet
Haystack in the Snow, Overcast Weather, 1891
Meule, effet de neige, temps couvert
Oil on canvas, 66 x 93 cm. Wildenstein 1281
Chicago (IL), The Art Institute of Chicago

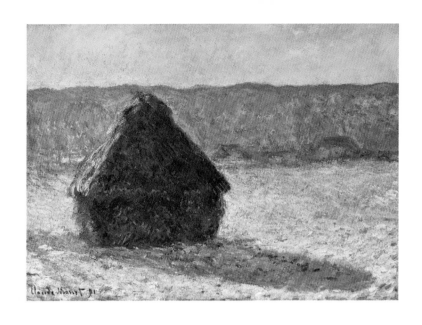

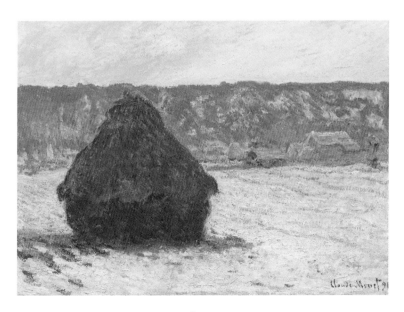

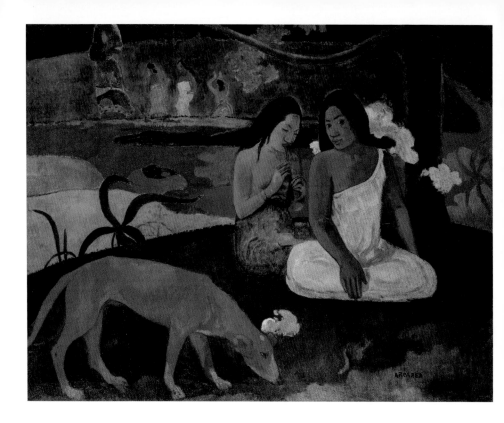

Paul Gauguin
Pastime ("Arearea"), 1892
Joyeusetés
Oil on canvas, 75 x 94 cm
Wildenstein 468. Paris, Musée d'Orsay

been paid in New York in 1887 for a Meissonier, for instance. At the beginning of 1890, *Olympia* was bought for 19,114 francs and donated to the nation. It was placed not in the Louvre, in the event, but in the Palais de Luxembourg, where contemporary art was exhibited.

Individual works by Renoir and Morisot acquired by the state were also added to the Luxembourg's holdings, in particular the legacy of Caillebotte. The controversy is notorious, and was in fact the last hurdle that had to be cleared before the triumph of Impressionism was finally assured.[157] Caillebotte, who died in 1894, had appointed Renoir the executor of his will. On the advice of Léonce Bénédite (1859–1925), director of the Luxembourg, the museum's committee and the Minister of the Arts accepted Caillebotte's bequest of 67 paintings by Manet, Monet, Renoir, Pissarro, Sisley, Degas and Cézanne, and Caillebotte's own *The Floor Strippers*. But then the press intervened, at a delicate political moment. Anarchist unrest had peaked on 24 June 1894 with the assassination of President Sadi Carnot. Following this, anarchist intellectuals such as Luce and Fénéon were arrested, and Pissarro thought it prudent to spend a few months in Belgium. The Dreyfus affair also began in 1894

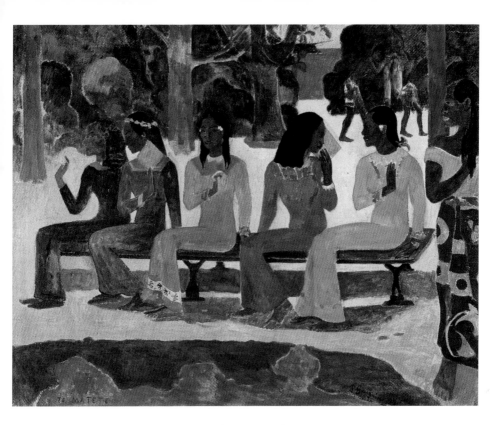

(October), when the Jewish Captain Alfred Dreyfus was wrongly court-martialled for treason, prompting a wave of anti-semitism (which directly affected Pissarro) and deeply dividing French society, including the Impressionists. Degas broke off his contacts with Jewish friends. The ministry now considered that the Luxembourg's bulk accession of works by controversial painters posed a problem. Tough negotiations resulted in the rejection of 29 of the pictures in the legacy, among them 11 by Pissarro alone, though none by Degas. This spoke volumes about government tactics; but the controversy became really fierce when the Caillebotte collection was exhibited in early 1897. The Academy of Fine Arts, on a majority of 18 to 10, passed a protest against the insult to French painting. The aged Gérôme gave an interview in which he sounded off against the state for supporting such "rubbish". When a self-important, stupid senator raised the issue in the National Assembly, Henri Roujon (1853–1914), head of the fine-art section of the ministry, replied with calm aptness: "Though most of us will not consider Impressionism to have said the last word on art, we nonetheless agree that it is a viable form of art... and that the evolution of Impressionism, which

Paul Gauguin
We Shall not Go to Market Today
("Ta matete"), 1892
Le marché
Oil on canvas, 73 x 91.5 cm
Wildenstein 476. Basle, Öffentliche
Kunstsammlung Basel, Kunstmuseum

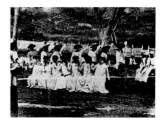

Old photograph which, together with an ancient Egyptian bas-relief, inspired "We Shall not Go to Market Today"

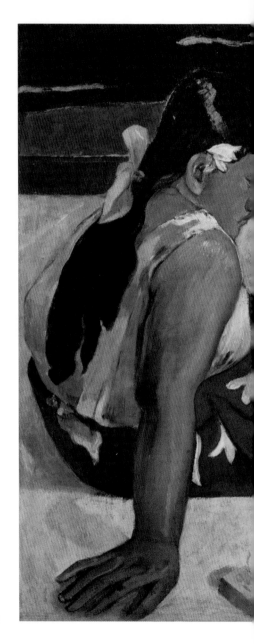

Paul Gauguin
Two Women on the Beach, 1891
Femmes de Tahiti ou Sur la plage
Oil on canvas, 69 x 91.5 cm
Wildenstein 434. Paris, Musée d'Orsay

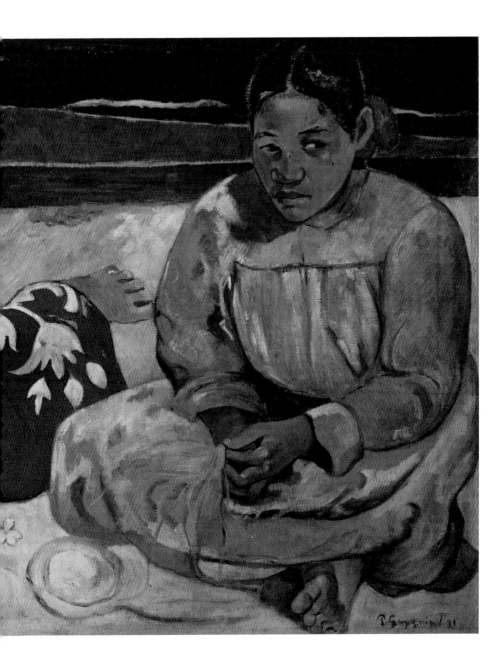

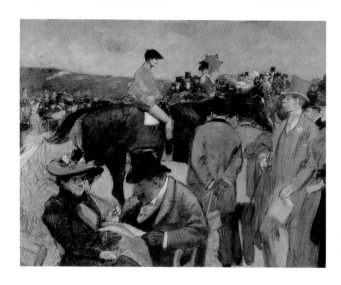

Jean-Louis Forain
At the Races, c. 1890
Aux courses de chevaux
Oil on canvas, 38 x 45 cm
Moscow, Pushkin Museum of Fine Art

does interest some people, constitutes a chapter in the history of contemporary art which we are in duty bound to exhibit on the walls of our museums."

At the 1900 World Fair in Paris, which marked the dawn of the new century, the Impressionists were crammed into a side room; but at the Centennale, the retrospective exhibition of a century of French art, they could not be denied space, especially since the critic Roger Marx (1859–1913) – who had written on Bernard, Gauguin and others and was now responsible for provincial museums – was hanging the show.

Impressionist approaches had spread to the works of other landscape, genre and portrait painters in various ways. Renouard, a painter and graphic artist prized for his fashionable, skilful, inventive city and theatre scenes and portraits, was perceived together with Forain, Chéret and "the great master, Degas".[158] Lebourg – recruited by Degas for the Impressionist exhibitions in 1879 and 1880 – was a member of the Société Nationale who now painted French landscapes in which he chose typical Impressionist motifs and deployed their atmospheric effects (pp. 313, 383). Much the same can be said of the younger Gustave Loiseau (1865–1935), a self-taught painter who experimented with pointillism around 1884, sojourned in Pont-Aven, and then, on his many travels, painted landscapes, mainly featuring rivers and the coast (pp. 378, 379). He was dubbed "the historian of the Seine" because he was adept at what Impressionism was best suited to: recording and celebrating shifting conditions of light and the changes made in a landscape by human hand. He was contracted to Durand-Ruel in 1897. Charles Durand-Ruel, the young boss, saw Loiseau as the most gifted of the second-generation Impressionists.[159]

There were also older painters, such as Louis-Hilaire Carrand (1821–1899) from Lyons, who were tempted into adopting Impressionist viewpoints and techniques. In the mid–80s, Roll, who had caused a furore in 1880 with his *Miners' Strike*, was painting very fine, sensitive, lifesize open-air portraits. A founder member of the Nationale, in 1905 he became its president. That position was previously occupied by Albert Besnard (1849–1934), who had won the Prix de Rome in 1874 and subsequently in London absorbed Pre-Raphaelite influences and tightened the precision of his draughtsmanship. From 1884 on he made skilful use of the Impressionist eye for light, for bright colours, for the presentation of motion, and for motifs happened upon by chance. From 1887, his decorative talent brought him major commissions for ceiling and mural paintings. As the 20th century began he was being seen by some as the finest French painter since Delacroix.[160] When in 1905 he was asked his opinion on the situation of art, he stressed the role of Nature, and particularly of its rhythm; he criticized Impressionism for lacking concentration and thought, but assessed the movement – thanks to Monet, Renoir and Pissarro – as a "glorious period of the past".[161]

Camille Pissarro
The Chat, 1892
La causette
Oil on canvas, 89 x 165 cm
Pissarro/Venturi 792
New York, The Metropolitan Museum of Art

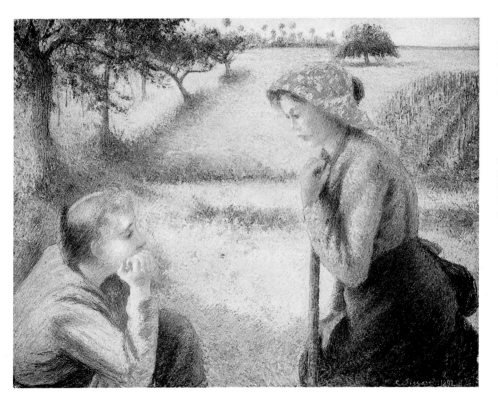

Renoir had tried to discipline his work by aiming at a classical note. In this he was the first to respond to the anti-sensuous Neo-Traditionalism of the *zeitgeist* as the century ended, and of younger artists' endeavours. Towards 1890, after his dry spell, he returned to colour in full bloom, light brushwork, and, above all, unconditional commitment to what the eye experienced. He was commissioned to paint portraits, which he did in amiable styles with an occasional touch of dramatic life, overlapping with genre work. He frequently stayed at Essoyes in Burgundy, the home town of Aline, whom he married in 1890. The way of life and the people there appealed to him. It was not only because they cost less than professional Parisian models that he liked to paint the young women of Essoyes as laundresses. He had a strong intuitive sense of their healthy physical rapport with the natural surroundings and their time-honoured task, and it was that harmony that he was painting. Criticism of the toilsomeness of their labour, such as we find in the laundresses and women ironing by Degas and Toulouse-Lautrec (pp. 242, 243), was not at all Renoir's purpose. He travelled widely, visited friends, and liked to go to the sea. In 1897 in Essoyes he broke his right arm in a bicycle accident, as he had done once before, in 1880. This produced rheumatoid arthritis, which, together with the partial atrophy of a nerve in his left eye, confined him to a wheelchair from 1902 to 1905.

Since the late 1880s, Renoir had enjoyed the company of Morisot (Madame Eugène Manet). She in turn frequently visited Monet and Sisley, and often included Mallarmé among her own guests. Her first solo exhibition in 1892, at Galerie Boussod & Valadon (run by Toulouse-

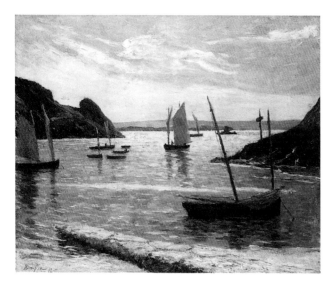

Maxim Maufra
Ile de Bréhat, 1892
Oil on canvas, 60 x 72 cm
Private collection

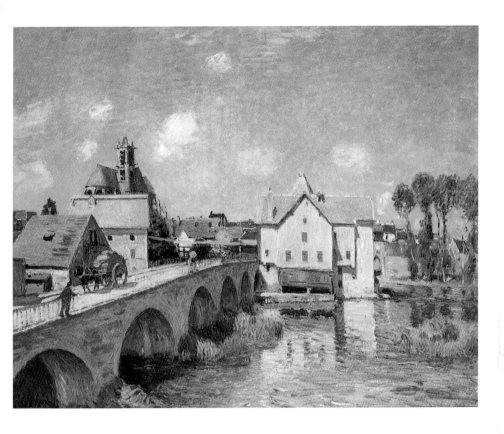

Alfred Sisley
The Bridge at Moret, 1893
Pont de Moret
Oil on canvas, 73.5 x 92.5 cm
Daulte 817. Paris, Musée d'Orsay

Lautrec's friend Joyant) and with a catalogue introduction by Geffroy, was a success – one clouded, however, by her husband's death not long before. The following year she also lost her sister, Yves Gobillard (1838–1893). She was especially fond of Yves' daughter Jeanne (Nini) and frequently painted her, at times together with her own daughter, Julie. In 1900 Jeanne Gobillard married the poet Paul Valéry, and Julie Manet married the painter Ernest Rouart (1874–1942), son of Henri Rouart, who had exhibited at seven of the Impressionist shows (p. 203). In 1894, through the offices of Mallarmé, the state acquired its first Morisot, *Young Girl in a Ball Gown* (Paris, Musée d'Orsay), from the collection which Duret was then having to sell. The intelligent, sensitive, highly gifted Morisot died of pneumonia in 1895, aged just 54.

Her art, to which she always referred in modest and highly self-critical terms, was exclusively an art of personal happiness at the grace and beauty of those who were close to her, particularly girls, seen in the available light of gardens or drawing rooms. "She painted only what her eye actually saw, and not what her reason told her she saw," her grand-

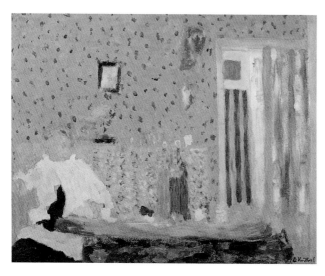

son Denis Rouart observed.[161] Her style underwent a change around 1889. Instead of short brush-strokes she now tended to use lengthy strokes in sweeping arabesques. Together with her concentration on essentials. this produced a gently melodic, atmospheric overall effect. Her elegiac feel for the past happiness of youth and the dangers to traditional civilized values now outweighed the physiognomic scruple, and the precision with which she recorded the passing moment, that had characterized her earlier paintings.

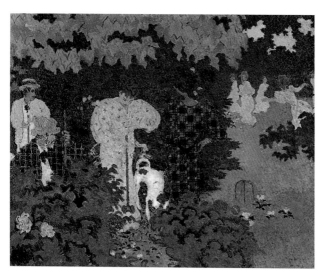

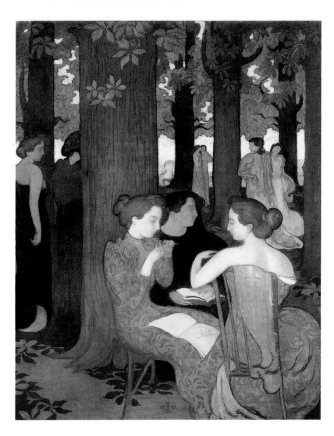

Maurice Denis
The Muses or In the Park, 1893
Les Muses ou Dans le Parc
Oil on canvas, 171.5 x 137.5 cm
Paris, Musée d'Orsay

The baroque château of Mesnil near Nantes, which Morisot had bought in 1892, and the little house near the church at Moret-sur-Loing which Sisley rented in 1889 as the last but one of his many homes, were separated by a distance not only geographical but also social. Sisley never succeeded in putting his straitened financial circumstances behind him. The few times he travelled were made possible by individual patrons such as François Depeaux, a Rouen ship owner. Sisley became embittered and withdrawn, preferring not to see even his old fellows. He did, however, ask Monet to his deathbed, in order to take his farewell before he died a painful death of cancer in his sixtieth year. From 1890 he regularly exhibited with the Société Nationale des Beaux-Arts, which he had joined at Roll's prompting. Durand-Ruel and Boussod & Valadon both represented his work, and in 1897 Petit organized a large exhibition of his finest work. But the press ignored the show almost completely, and nothing at all was sold. Sisley, who was already ill but had recently revisited his English homeland in quest of motifs, was exhausted.

That his light, peaceful landscapes and many views of the houses, old

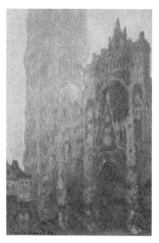

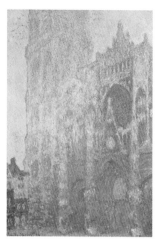

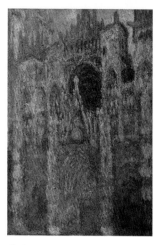

Claude Monet
Rouen Cathedral in the Morning, 1894
*La cathédrale de Rouen. Le portail et la tour
Saint-Romain à l'aube*
Oil on canvas, 106.1 x 73.9 cm
Wildenstein 1348. Boston (MA), Museum
of Fine Arts

Claude Monet
Rouen Cathedral in the Morning Sun.
Harmony in Blue, 1894
*La cathédrale de Rouen. Le portail,
soleil matinale. Harmonie bleue*
Oil on canvas, 91 x 63 cm
Wildenstein 1355. Paris, Musée d'Orsay

Claude Monet
Rouen Cathedral in the Morning. Harmony in
White, 1894
*La cathédrale de Rouen. Le portail et la tour Saint-
Romain, effet du matin. Harmonie blanche*
Oil on canvas, 106 x 73 cm
Wildenstein 1346. Paris, Musée d'Orsay

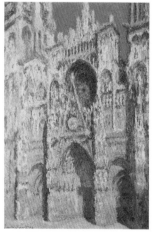

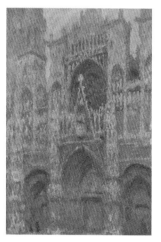

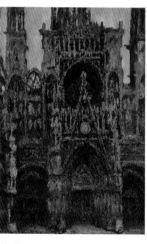

Claude Monet
Rouen Cathedral in Bright Sunlight. Harmony in
Blue and Gold, 1894
*La cathédrale de Rouen. Le portail et la tour Saint-
Romain, plein soleil. Harmonie bleue et or*
Oil on canvas, 107 x 73 cm
Wildenstein 1360. Paris, Musée d'Orsay

Claude Monet
Rouen Cathedral in Overcast Weather.
Harmony in Grey, 1894
*La cathédrale de Rouen. Le portail, temps gris.
Harmonie grise*
Oil on canvas, 100 x 65 cm
Wildenstein 1321. Paris, Musée d'Orsay

Claude Monet
Rouen Cathedral. Frontal View. Harmony in
Brown, 1894
*La cathédrale de Rouen. Le portail vu de face.
Harmonie brune*
Oil on canvas, 107 x 73 cm
Wildenstein 1319. Paris, Musée d'Orsay

Right: cf. caption bottom left this page

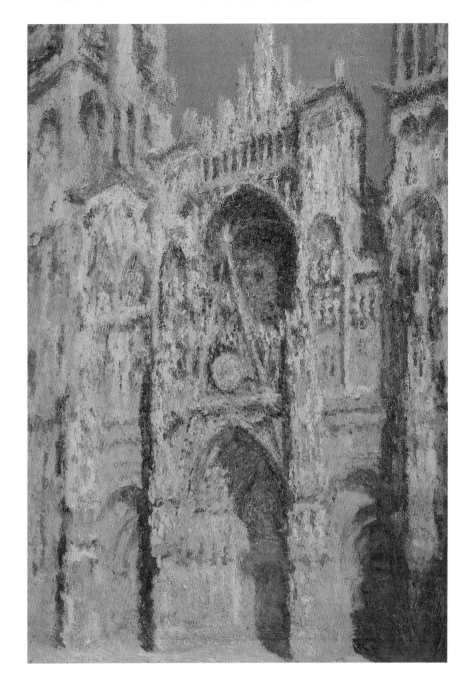

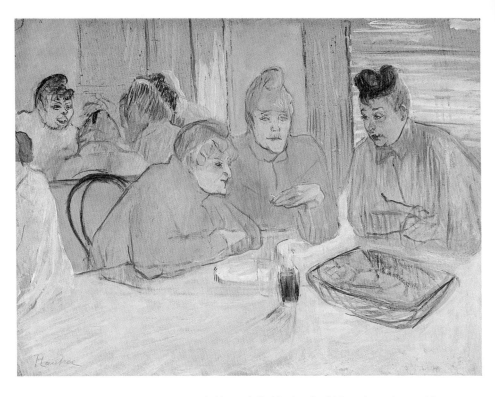

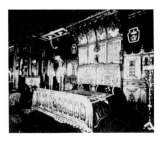

Henri de Toulouse-Lautrec
Women in a Brothel, c. 1893/94
Ces dames au réfectoire
Oil on card, 60.3 x 80.5 cm
Dortu 499. Budapest, Szépművészeti Múzeum

The Knight's Room in the Rue des Moulins brothel

stone bridge and Gothic church of Moret (p. 339) met with so poor a response, and that the prices for them did not rise until after his death (though they then rose steeply), is not altogether difficult to understand. Sisley never attempted to bring his style into line with the taste for symbolist or synthetist work. His motifs and view of Nature placed him too plainly as an emulator of Monet; and he had no material distinctly his own that could have asserted his own individuality. This became most apparent when in 1893/94, parallel to Monet's Rouen cathedral series (pp. 342, 343), he painted about 15 views of the church at Moret, twelve of which we now have knowledge of.[163] Like all Sisley's later works, they are firmly painted, and evidently aim to give a rather ordinary sense of the appearance of the building instead of the veils of light and colour impressions Monet registered when looking at his cathedral. Sisley's work focussed on the thing seen; but art was evolving towards a more subjective emphasis on configurations of colours and shapes. Monet's cathedrals were already fetching 15,000 francs at that time, while in 1896, when one of Sisley's church views was resold, it was for a mere 305 francs.

Guillaumin, in their mutual friend Murer's judgement, did not paint

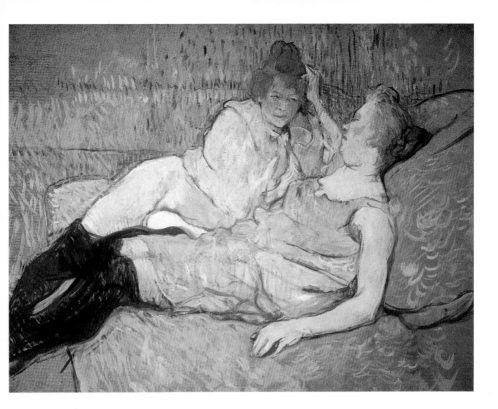

with the finesse and agility of Sisley. In the 1890s he was slower than the rest to abandon views of the Paris Seine docks with barges. He lived long, till 1927, and on his travels around France and its coasts he painted characteristically Impressionist motifs. He used a rather violent, brusque brush-stroke that already, in the 1890s, anticipated Fauvism. His colours were vigorously contrasted and luminous, and sometimes became decoratively, almost campily patterned (p. 351). In 1891 he won 100,000 francs in the Loterie Nationale, which enabled him to give up his job with the road and canal building department and devote his time to painting. In 1894 Durand-Ruel mounted Guillaumin's first solo exhibition, which was quite successful.

Pissarro, who had played a key role in Guillaumin's early development, highlighted the problems of Impressionism anew in his late period. He had given up pointillism, though to the very end he still used small dots of colour. The pleasure he took in landscape painting remained, and he went on repeated short journeys around the Ile-de-France and Normandy looking for new subjects. He painted farm women at work, talking (pp. 216, 217, 226) or, in 1894/95, bathing and washing their feet in a woodland stream.

Henri de Toulouse-Lautrec
The sofa, 1895
Le sofa
Oil on card, 63 x 81 cm
Dortu 601
New York, The Metropolitan Museum of Art

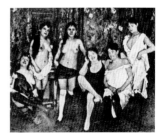

The ladies of the Rue des Moulins

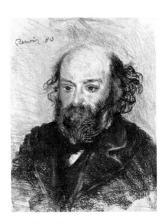

Pierre-Auguste Renoir
Portrait of Paul Cézanne, 1880
Portrait de Paul Cézanne
Pastel on paper, 53.5 x 44.4 cm
Private collection

Paul Cézanne
The Smoker, 1895–1900
Le fumeur
Oil on canvas, 91 x 72 cm
Venturi 686. St. Petersburg, Hermitage

Pissarro's health and an eye complaint obliged him to paint less in the open, where it was windy, and more indoors, from the window. But this was only one of the reasons why, after his short-lived attempts in 1883, he now developed an interest in the city that only Monet and Caillebotte had shared to the same extent. In Paris (1893, 1897/98, 1902), Rouen (1896 and 1898), Dieppe (1901) and Le Havre (1903) he rented rooms from which he enjoyed dynamic perspectives of squares and boulevards (pp. 356, 357), the city and the river or harbour and bridges (p. 355). He painted variations and repeated views in order to capture various atmospheric moods and also to have something to offer to as many buyers as possible. His old skills in spatial structure were visibly still with him, even if a certain tiredness or lack of tension are sometimes apparent. Doubtless this return to city material was prompted by the wish to record the new contemporary realities, which had always been a plank in the Impressionist platform. "The revolting, brand new, glittering station, a number of chimneys... with swathes of smoke... the working-class district, as far as the iron Pont Boieldieu, in the morning, in gentle sunshot mist," was not, he felt, banal, as some critics had claimed, but "as beautiful as Venice, of an extraordinary character... It is art, seen with my own innermost feelings." [164]

That the revolting or ugly was beautiful was a paradoxical, provocative, defiantly anti-academic article of Naturalist faith, one echoed in the aesthetics of the Primitivists and the Fauves. In Pissarro, it was a view that went hand in hand with social and political convictions that set him apart from his fellow Impressionists. Unlike Renoir, who lamented the decline of beauty in the industrial age, Pissarro criticized society with an eye to the future. In his letters he raged at neo-Gothic historicism and "religious Symbolists, religious Socialism, ideational art, occultism, Buddhism" – all of which he saw as the devious reactionary ploys of the bourgeoisie. Alas, he even went so far as to detect this aberration in *Vision after the Sermon* (p. 303) by his former protégé Gauguin, and in Gauguin's circle generally. [165] By contrast, what he admired in genuine Gothic, such as the statues at Rouen Cathedral, was the harmony of Nature and decorative values.

There is a plunging spatial depth in his cityscapes. They pulsate with the flow of traffic along tree-lined avenues amidst a solid architectural frame. Their structures use cubic, towering buildings or draw our gaze disquietingly into a restless throng. The light is usually leaden and muted, a wintry light, or indeed we see the gleam of gaslight on wet roads at night. "All I see," wrote the 73-year-old Pissarro in 1903, the year of his death, "is dabs [*taches*] of colour. When I begin a painting, the first thing I try to fix is the accord... The great problem that has to be solved is... to bring everything into line with the overall harmony, with that accord I have spoken of." [166]

Pissarro's situation was at once typical and an exception. He was no longer very short of money, but he still had no sense of financial security and occasionally had to trim his children's allowances. Sometimes, though, Monet (who earned more) would borrow money from him to

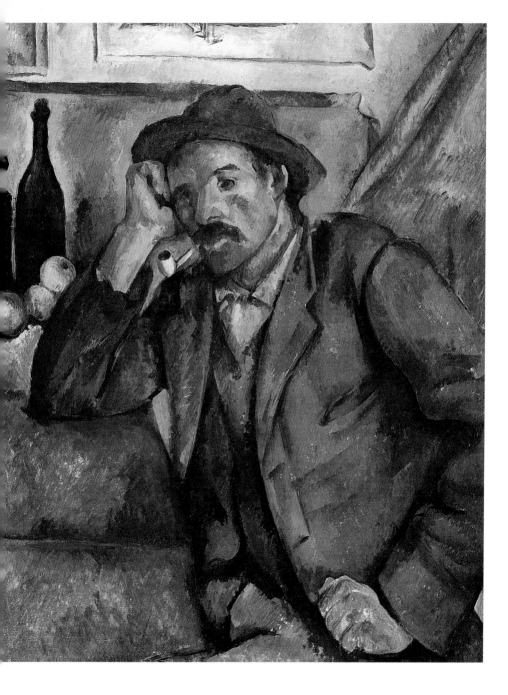

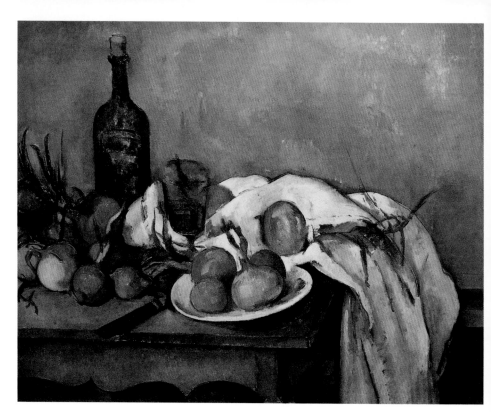

Paul Cézanne
Still Life with Onions, 1895–1900
Nature morte aux oignons
Oil on canvas, 66 x 82 cm. Venturi 730
Paris, Musée d'Orsay

bridge a financial crisis. In 1892 Durand-Ruel became Pissarro's sole gallery agent, arranging a large and successful solo show followed by a number of smaller exhibitions in the next few years. With Durand-Ruel's approval, Pissarro also sent small batches of work to dealers abroad – in 1894 to Berlin, for instance, where he was a member of the Secession, and to Dresden. It angered him if it was only by chance that he heard of a museum acquisition of one of his paintings, as was the case with the Berlin National Gallery; and he had a fundamental distrust of dealers, who thought in terms of storehouse space and market forces and agreed among themselves to keep his prices below Monet's. His rivalry with Monet played a part in an exhibition at Durand-Ruel's in 1898, where he showed series of works, including twelve Paris avenue scenes and seven or eight of avenues and boulevards. Pissarro believed he was being disadvantaged because of his political views; but it was probably his fidelity to realistic principles of vision that the public no longer felt comfortable with. It was this that made him and Sisley – as he pithily put it in a letter of 24 February 1895, somewhat resigned but faithful to his artistic stance – "the rearguard of Impressionism".

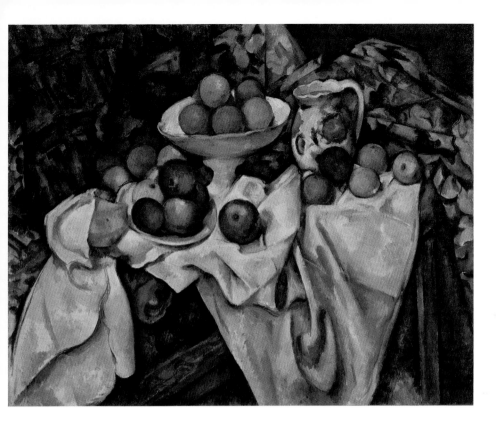

Paul Cézanne
Still Life with Apples and Oranges, c. 1895–1900
Nature morte aux pommes et oranges
Oil on canvas, 74 x 93 cm
Venturi 732. Paris, Musée d'Orsay

And what of Monet, the vanguard of the movement, one of whose paintings had given Impressionism its name? With great consistency he continued to develop a response to reality which was anchored in Impressionism: in order fully to capture changing conditions, he painted entire series of pictures, transforming (as the titles of studies recently published have it) Nature into art.[167]

Monet had enough self-confidence to act independently of the dealers. He played Petit and Durand-Ruel off against each other, but worked mainly with the latter; and he sold his large output via a number of galleries, especially Bernheim's. Monet too had to put up with Durand-Ruel's urging him to keep painting the sun rather than stormy seas; and the dealer would push him to paint more of the subjects that sold well, and paint them faster. Only with misgivings did Monet go along with these wishes.

At Argenteuil, Vétheuil and the Gare Saint-Lazare, Monet had already probed the various aspects of a single subject, and had exploited effective views by painting them more than once. In the mid–80s he began a systematic analysis of the effects of changing light. This work ran paral-

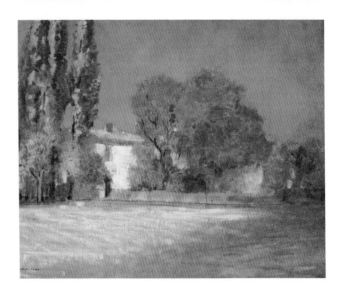

Odilon Redon
Peyrelebade, c. 1896/97
Oil on canvas, 36.5 x 45 cm
Paris, Musée d'Orsay

lel, in his own way, to that of Seurat. In 1885, Guy de Maupassant observed him at the coast, at Etretat: "Often I would follow Monet as he searched for impressions. The truth is that he was no longer a painter; he was a hunter. He would set out followed by children carrying his canvases, five or six canvases showing the same motif at different times of day and in different conditions. He would take one after another, set it up for work and put it aside, depending on how the sky changed."[168] Others observed the same working habits in later years. At Etretat in Normandy, where in 1869 Courbet had already painted a number of coastal landscapes (p. 31), Monet was fascinated by the sheer cliffs and the bizarre shape of the Manneporte, an arch of rock (p. 270). He returned to the subject over several years, and to the jagged crags and stormy Atlantic at Belle-Ile-en-Mer in Britanny (p. 245). Using Impressionist dabs to establish an irregular pattern was almost as important in such work as recording a striking view.

The same essentially applies to Monet's last figural work worth mentioning. The three pictures of a woman with a parasol (pp. 146, 147) do of course record an impression on a walk with his stepdaughter-to-be, Suzanne Hoschedé, whose face is obscured by her fluttering scarf. The pictures showing the two Hoschedé girls in a boat (p. 296) are also scenes of that everyday life which the Impressionists had made a fit subject for art. But these works were doubtless painted primarily because Monet's eye was captivated by particular colour accords, effects of reflection, and the "Japanese" angle of vision from above.

It was in Giverny in 1884 that Monet was first struck by the haystacks. In 1890/91 he painted a series of 18 pictures (p. 331), 15 of which he exhibited at Durand-Ruel's; every one was immediately sold for prices

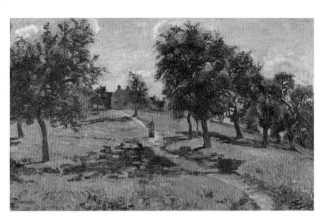

Armand Guillaumin
Landscape in Normandy: Apple Trees, c. 1887
Paysage en Normandie: Les pommiers
Oil on canvas, 60.5 x 100 cm
Paris, Musée d'Orsay

Armand Guillaumin
View of Agay, 1895
Vue d'Agay. Pointe du Dramont
Oil on canvas, 73 x 92 cm
Serret/Fabiani 340. Paris, Musée d'Orsay

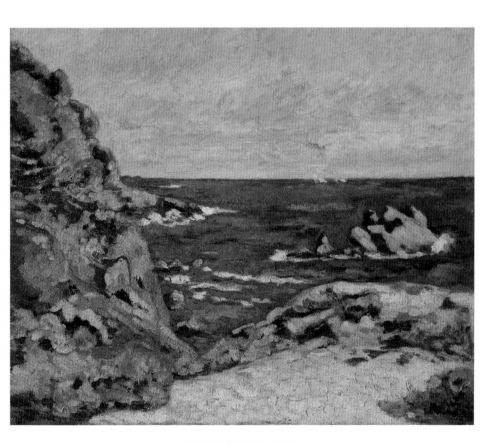

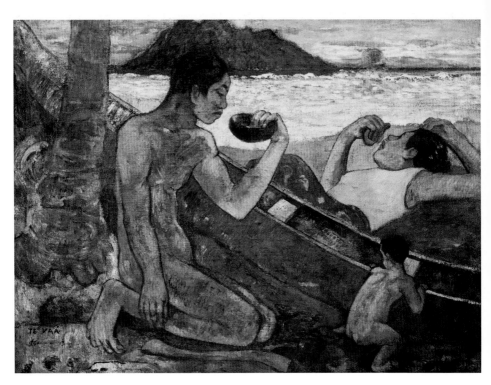

Paul Gauguin
The Dug-Out ("Te vaa"), 1896
La pirogue
Oil on canvas, 96 x 130 cm
Wildenstein 544. St. Petersburg, Hermitage

from 3,000 to 4,000 francs. Morning and evening, in late summer and in winter, in sunny or overcast conditions, he stood at the selfsame spot, watching how the light changed the world. His brushwork was energetic and dense. The irregular *taches*, not standing for any specific detail, glowed in contrasted juxtaposition, so pastose that the thickness had a rough, relief-like impact. The crusts of thick paint gleamed in the light or even cast tiny shadows of their own. People had meanwhile acquired a more practised eye for such effects (and therefore came to value it where they had previously overlooked it, in late Titian or Rembrandt).

When one of Monet's haystacks was exhibited in Moscow in 1895, it was seen by Wassily Kandinsky (1866–1944). Kandinsky had completed law studies, and the following year began to study art in Munich. He later wrote: "The catalogue told me that it was a haystack. I could not recognise it as such myself... I vaguely felt that the subject was missing from the picture... But what was completely clear to me was the un-dreamt-of power of the palette, which I had previously known nothing of... I had a sense that painting itself was the subject."[169] For Kandinsky, this encounter was a decisive impulse on his own way forward to ab-stract, "absolute" painting some 15 years later. Monet, though, is said to have laughed aloud when he heard of Kandinsky's reaction. He him-

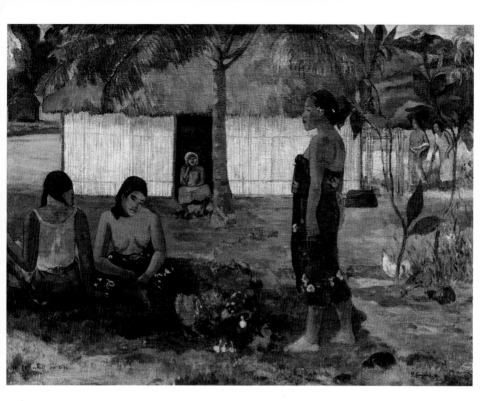

Paul Gauguin
"Why are you angry?" ("No te aha oe riri?"), 1896
«Pourquoi es-tu fâchée?»
Oil on canvas, 95.3 x 130.5 cm
Wildenstein 550
Chicago (IL), The Art Institute of Chicago

self was still primarily interested in impressions made on him by something he had actually seen.

In 1892 he exhibited about 15 pictures of poplars, and in 1895 twenty views of Rouen Cathedral. These were the finest and most unified of his series. Subsequently he did 24 pictures of the cliff coastline at Varengeville in Normandy (1896), 18 morning scenes by the Seine (1897), over 37 views of the Thames in London (1899–1904) and 29 paintings of Venice (1908/09). The poplars, on the banks of the Epte near Giverny, Monet painted from spring to autumn 1891. He paid a wood merchant (who had just bought them for timber) not to fell them till he had painted them from his boat (p. 330). The freshness of his rendering of an easeful natural scene, and the delicacy of his colours, are such that we imagine we can sense the breeze soughing in the trees. The trees, the sky, and the reflections in the water, form a unified whole. The surface structure is linear and harmoniously proportioned. These qualities make Monet's poplars supremely subtle blends of impressions, poetry and decorative values with lithe structure, the manifest traces of the artist's work, and the overflow of feeling.

The cathedral series is more dramatic, radical and charged with mystery (pp. 342, 343). Monet visited Rouen in 1893 at the expense of the

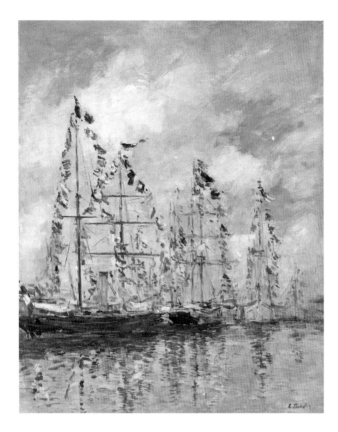

Eugène-Louis Boudin
Sailing Ships at Deauville, c. 1895/96
Deauville. Le bassin
Oil on panel, 45.8 x 37.1 cm
Washington (DC), National Gallery of Art,
Ailsa Mellon Bruce Collection

collector Félix Depeaux (who also supported Sisley), and painted the intricate Gothic façade from his hotel window. The given date of 1894 indicates that, as with other paintings, Monet continued work on the canvases at home, making the interrelations exact. His son Michel swore that his father only ever worked straight from the subject; of course Monet's practice is in fact simply a responsible artist's perfectly understandable desire to arrive at the best possible visual form. The series abides by the old Impressionist principle of the sectional view dictated by chance. It offers fragmented views of the façade rather than a conventionally informative architectural overview. The details are lost in a total impression of colour, light and shadow playing upon an intricate surface. The subject is not explained; it is rendered mysterious, a thing of wonder. The fact that the subject is a venerable cultural legacy of the Middle Ages only heightens its symbolic appeal. Monet emphasized the browns and reddish golds that he saw in the shadows and the morning light, at noon and in the dusk.

The general drift of the series was in line with prevailing philosophical

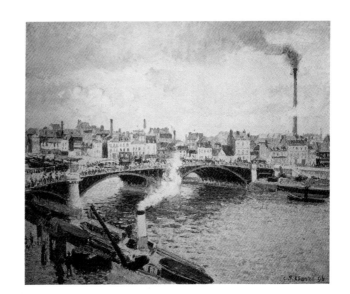

Camille Pissarro
Morning, Overcast Weather, Rouen, 1896
Matin, temps gris, Rouen
Oil on canvas, 54 x 65 cm
Pissarro/Venturi 964
New York, The Metropolitan Museum of Art

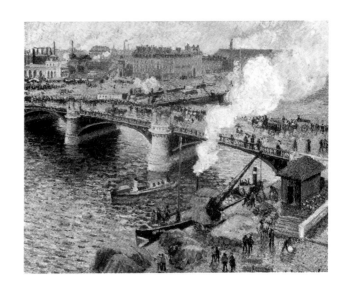

Camille Pissarro
Pont Boieldieu in Rouen in a Drizzle, 1896
Le Pont Boieldieu à Rouen, temps mouillé
Oil on canvas, 73.3 x 91.4 cm
Pissarro/Venturi 948
Toronto, Art Gallery of Ontario

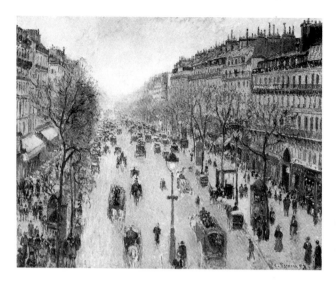

Camille Pissarro
The Boulevard Montmartre on a Cloudy Morning,
1897
Boulevard Montmartre, matin, temps gris
Oil on canvas, 73 x 92 cm
Pissarro/Venturi 992
Melbourne, National Gallery of Victoria

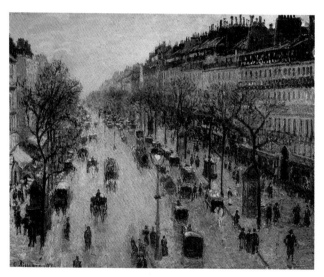

Camille Pissarro
The Boulevard Montmartre on a Winter Morning,
1897
Boulevard Montmartre, matin d'hiver
Oil on canvas, 65 x 81 cm
Pissarro/Venturi 987
New York, The Metropolitan Museum of Art

currents of the time, especially the empirio-criticism of Ernst Mach
(1838–1916). According to Mach, it was not things but colours and
other sensations that constituted the "true elements of the world".
Monet's paintings state that Rouen Cathedral cannot be said to *be* a
particular colour. Rather, it appears to us in various, changing colours,
all of them legitimate in their way. This represented a quite extraordinary
licence for artistic subjectivity, and gave it a task. The total meaning of

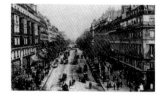

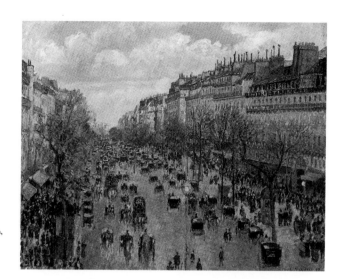

Camille Pissarro
The Boulevard Montmartre on a Sunny Afternoon,
1897
Boulevard Montmartre, après-midi, soleil
Oil on canvas, 74 x 92.8 cm
Pissarro/Venturi 993. St. Petersburg, Hermitage

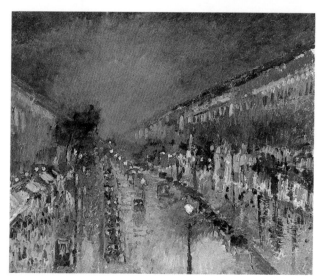

Camille Pissarro
The Boulevard Montmartre at Night,
1897
Boulevard Montmartre, effet de nuit
Oil on canvas, 53.3 x 64.8 cm
Pissarro/Venturi 994. London, National Gallery

these works, though, was only apparent on the one unique occasion
when they were all exhibited together. They were then sold to individual
collectors, and it was not till long after that smaller groups could be
assembled by certain museums.

Left: The Boulevard Montmartre.
Photograph, c. 1900

Monet and Cézanne respected each other, and ultimately there was more shared ground in their art than is commonly realised. The two painters, of course, led quite different lives. In 1886 Cézanne inherited about 400,000 francs after his father's death, which made him financially independent, indeed affluent. Only a few months before he had married Hortense Fiquet, by whom he already had a 14-year-old son; Cézanne had concealed both from his father for fear of having his allowance (a man in his forties!) cut. He was unable to live on the proceeds of his art, but now he was his own man. On the rare occasions when he had exhibited in Paris he had reaped only ridicule. A few of his paintings remained on show in Père Tanguy's famous back rooms. Young painters who saw them there were not quite sure if the artist was even still alive – despite the fact that every year till 1899 Cézanne spent some time in Paris, painting, studying old paintings and sculptures in the Louvre, and drawing copies of them. Mainly he lived at Aix, where the provincial eye saw him as an odd-man-out and a failure. An irascible man, mistrustful even of his friends, he became increasingly wary of contact with people. Even his wife, who did not understand his art, became a stranger to him. For all this, Cézanne would have liked to lead a conventional middle-class life. In 1894, when he met Clemenceau, Geffroy and Rodin at the home of Monet (who was now an established figure with contacts), Cézanne was deeply moved when Rodin, whose sculpture had earned numerous awards, shook his hand. Even at a later date he was still wishing he would be commissioned to paint murals in order to reach "ordinary people" rather than simply painting "some rubbish or other" for rich Americans.

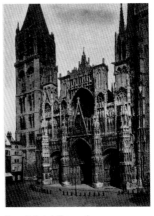

Rouen Cathedral. Photograph, c. 1900

Sales had picked up ever since Vollard, newly established in Paris galleries, put on Cézanne's first major solo show in 1895. Further small exhibitions followed, and in 1899 Vollard bought everything that was available in Cézanne's studio. In 1900 Roger Marx included three Cézannes in the Centennale at the World Fair. Cézanne's final recognition came through repeated exhibition with the Indépendants, and subsequently in the new autumn salon (where the Fauves were concentrating their forces), and through exhibitions abroad. Cézanne's extraordinary impact on younger artists became clear with the memorial retrospective in 1907, the year after his death. In 1901 Denis had exhibited a large *Homage to Cézanne* (1900; Paris, Musée d'Orsay, Gift of André Gide) at the Indépendants – though the dark and indiscriminately spaced painting had little in common with Cézanne's approach. It shows a lifesize group, Denis and nine other painters dressed in black, and Vollard, solemnly contemplating a Cézanne still life.

Cézanne had direct contact with some of his young admirers following the 1895 exhibition. The writer Joachim Gasquet (1873–1921), son of one of the painter's schoolfriends, familiarized himself with Cézanne's views from 1896 to 1900 and then wrote them up in 1912/13 in the form of three imaginary conversations (published 1921). Gasquet partly drew

Camille Pissarro
The Old Market-Place in Rouen and the Rue de l'Epicerie, 1898
Les anciennes halles à Rouen et la rue de l'Epicerie
Oil on canvas, 81 x 65 cm
Pissarro/Venturi 1036
New York, The Metropolitan Museum of Art

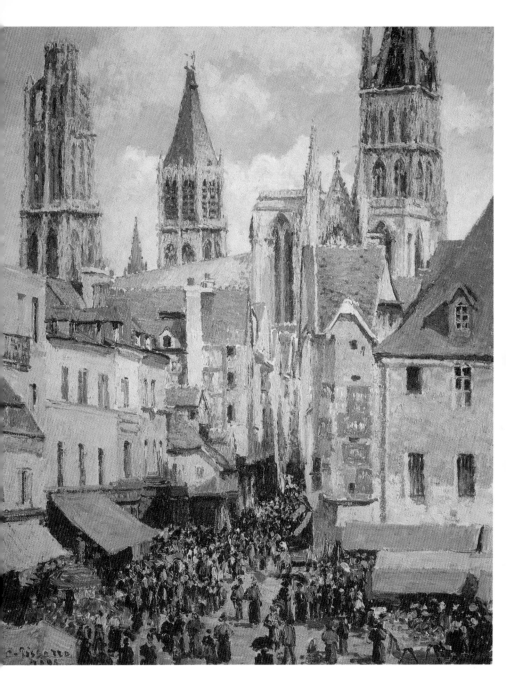

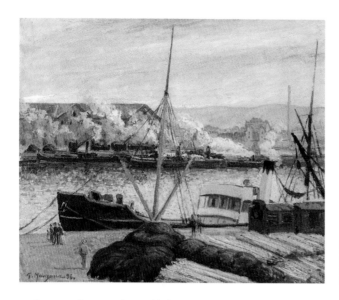

Manzana (Georges Pissarro)
The Harbour at Rouen, 1898
Le port de Rouen
Oil on canvas, 55 x 65 cm
Paris, Galerie Etienne Sassi

on Cézanne's letters and on published memoirs by others. Some of the statements put into Cézanne's mouth seem coloured by the symbolist philosophy of Gasquet, but the gist is corroborated by the letters, and helps gain a purchase on understanding Cézanne's bulky but magnificent late work.

He concentrated on portraits and figure paintings of family, friends, and ordinary people he could persuade to sit for him; and on landscapes, still lifes, and open-air nudes that were labelled, in the customary way, "bathers". These subjects may not seem entirely promising, but for Cézanne they were laden with philosophical significance, and contained messages related to the improvement of life and the world. These messages, though, were immanent in the works, a specific function of painting, distinct from anything that might have been known or said previously. And they made their impact quite independently of the brouhaha of the market place, of opinion-mongering and art dealing, and without concurrent political positions being adopted as Cézanne's mentor Pissarro did.

Cézanne wanted to create images of the subjects he took, images that would become a subordinate part of Nature, images which (as Courbet and the Impressionists had both preached and practised) were drawn from careful observation. In this respect Cézanne, like Monet and Renoir, likened himself to children who see with eyes free of the distortions caused by education and conditioning, or to a camera fixing the image of reality and nothing but. The individual temperament, he felt (contrary to Zola's definition), should not be interposed like a prism splitting up rays. On the other hand, Cézanne always referred to powerful feelings, especially for his home parts, which he hoped would be communicated

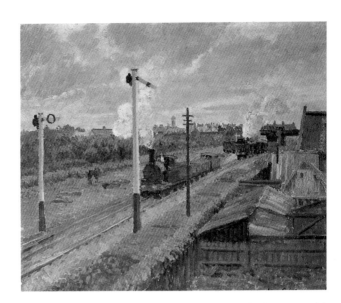

by his paintings. This twofold truth, both objective and subjective, could only be established if the appearance of phenomena was not reproduced but represented – by colour equivalents. Spatial distances, and three-dimensionality, had to be suggested by perspectives of colour in Cézanne's creed – by the sense of spatiality conveyed by various colour values which appear to the eye either to advance or to recede. The use of shadow for three-dimensionality was wrong; the colours had to be modulated. The work of art (thought Cézanne) was an autonomous product created in contact with reality by looking, by theory, and by an

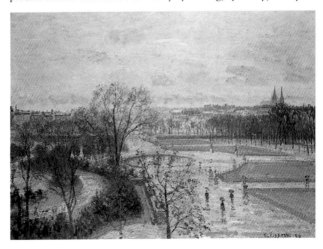

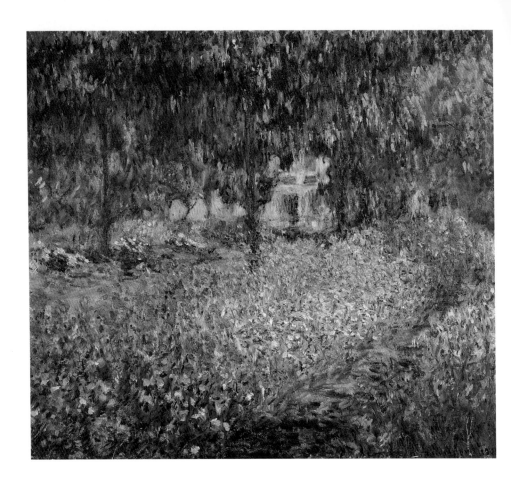

Claude Monet
Monet's Garden, the Irises, 1900
Le jardin de Monet, les iris
Oil on canvas, 81 x 92 cm
Wildenstein 1624. Paris, Musée d'Orsay

assured craftsmanly hand. He saw it as a "harmony parallel to Nature".
For Cézanne, Nature – including all its contrary movements of growth
and death, structure and decay, inertia and motion – was a cosmos, and
thus had its own order. To record this in the microcosm of a painting
required the hardest of work. The fruits of that toil almost never satisfied
Cézanne. And so it was that friends would witness the artist in old age
weeping as he stamped on unfinished canvases, dissatisfied with the way
he had recorded his perceptions.

An exact dating of Cézanne's paintings is very difficult. He never considered his works finished, and many indeed show clear signs of being
more unfinished than even a high Impressionist regard for sketchiness
would permit; so he signed only a very few, and then at the request of
the buyer. At times, mementoes or wallpaper that Cézanne's biographers

Claude **Monet**
The Houses of Parliament, London, c. 1900/01
Le parlement, ciel orageux
Oil on canvas, 81.6 x 92.1 cm
Wildenstein 1605. Lille, Musée des Beaux-Arts

have traced to one of his homes can provide a clue. Thus, for instance, if the *Boy in a Red Waistcoat* (p. 308) – a young Italian Cézanne painted four times in relaxed poses – was done in a Paris flat on the Quai d'Anjou, the date must have been between 1888 and early 1890. But arguments have been advanced for a date in the early Nineties too. What does seem incontestable is that Cézanne's sitter was at ease in the world, as his pose suggests. For purposes of compositional balance, Cézanne felt justified in making the youth's right arm unnaturally long.

Still lifes provided him an opportunity to paint things in accordance with his conception of form, and he could subject them to lengthier scrutiny than he could human sitters. In still lifes he could explore ways of establishing visual harmony and three-dimensionality more thoroughly. It is clear to the attentive eye that he used colours both to signal

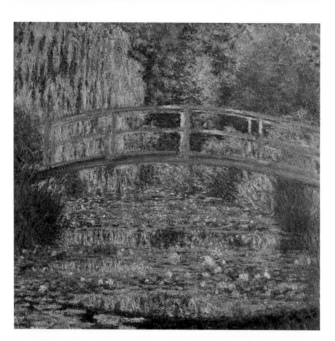

Right:
Claude Monet
The Japanese Bridge, 1899
Le bassin aux nymphéas
Oil on canvas, 92.7 x 73.7 cm
Wildenstein 1518
New York, The Metropolitan Museum of Art

Claude Monet
The Japanese Bridge, Harmony in Green, 1899
Le bassin aux nymphéas, harmonie verte
Oil on canvas, 89 x 93.5 cm
Wildenstein 1515
Paris, Musée d'Orsay

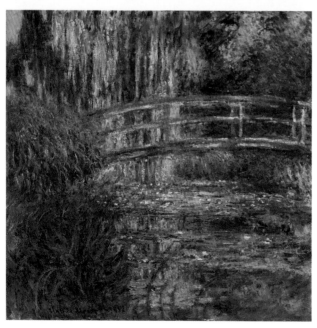

Claude Monet
The Japanese Bridge, 1900
Le bassin aux nymphéas
Oil on canvas, 89.2 x 92.8 cm
Wildenstein 1630
Boston (MA), Museum of Fine Arts

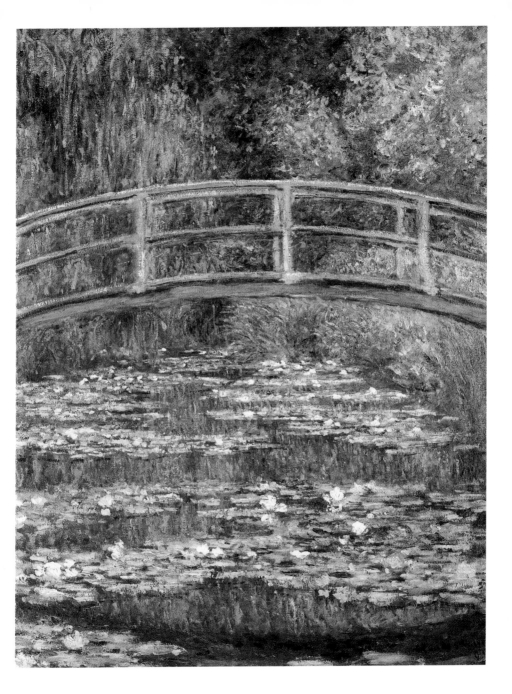

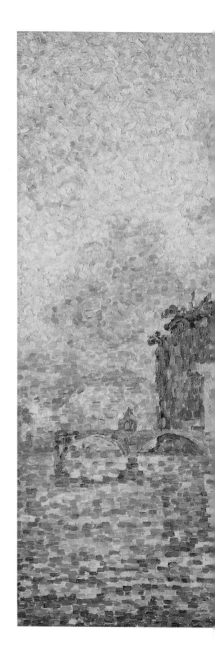

Paul Signac
The Papal Palace at Avignon, 1900
Le château des Papes à Avignon
Oil on canvas, 73.5 x 92.5 cm
Paris, Musée d'Orsay

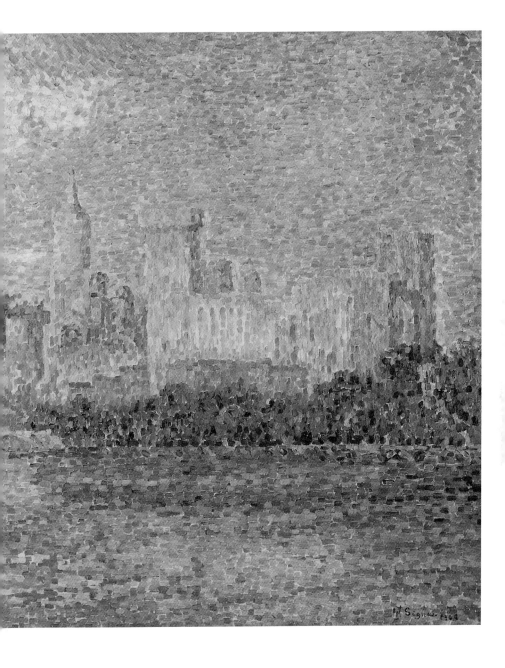

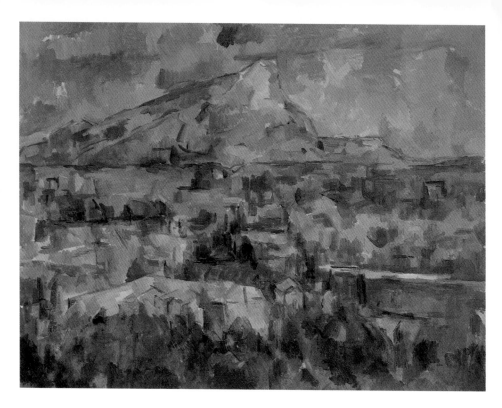

Paul Cézanne
Mont Sainte-Victoire, 1904–1906
La Montagne Sainte-Victoire
Oil on canvas, 73 x 91 cm
Venturi 798. Philadelphia (PA),
Philadelphia Museum of Art

the boundaries of different objects and to establish an overall visual continuum, to convey three-dimensionality even as they remained parts of a surface pattern. Cézanne never outlined subjects as the cloisonnists did. In the latter half of the Nineties, after his successful exhibition at Vollard's, he increasingly did more opulent, spatially more dynamic, indeed baroque compositions (pp. 348, 349). These pictures are far removed from the straight representation of a laid table. No one would pile crockery, fruit, a brocade drape and a crumpled tablecloth on a chest in this way (p. 349). This is painting for its own sake, with its own rules.

In old age, Cézanne still tirelessly walked the country around Aix in order to paint the ensemble effect of earth, vegetation and ordinary houses, in a manner at once organic and crystalline. He was particularly fond of painting his revered Mont Sainte-Victoire, towering over the valley as in a vision (p. 368). In October 1906, out painting, he contracted pneumonia, from which he then died. Almost all of his late works have that distinctive, generous formal assurance which we associate with the late periods of the masters; yet Cézanne, whose principle it was only to work *sur le motif*, would pause for a long time over a brush-stroke if he was not absolutely certain of the colour, even preferring to leave the

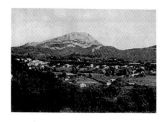

View of Mont Sainte-Victoire
from Bellevue

space blank. This gives his paintings the appearance of work in progress, in the process of becoming – an inner dimension of time that had originated in the Impressionist alertness to movement and change but had led to a new conception of the relativity of visual statements.

From the outset, Cézanne had painted oils and watercolours and done drawings of nudes in the open. There has recently been a major exhibition and publication on this area of his work.[170] From 1895 Cézanne's attention to this theme, which doubtless touched on psychological problems within himself, was summed up in three large-format groups of bathers that were to occupy him till he died (p. 369). The throng of female nudes, altogether unerotic, are caught in attitudes which are partly unclear and seem to have cultic rather than bathing or games-playing significance. Some of the poses, despite the heaviness, can be traced to ancient sculpture or to Renaissance or baroque painting. The shapes are crudely simplified. They have a primitive expressive power, which meant more to the artist than accuracy or beauty. Away beyond, Nature glows a "sacred blue". This tense vision, which was incapable of completion, provided a point of departure for Matisse, Picasso, the Expressionist painters of the Brücke, and generations of artists down to the present day.

Cézanne's art was and remains of such extraordinary consequence

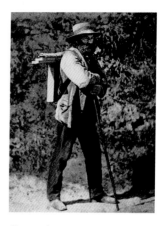

Cézanne setting out to paint

Paul Cézanne
The Bathers, 1900–1905
Les grandes baigneuses
Oil on canvas, 126 x 196 cm
Venturi 721. London, National Gallery

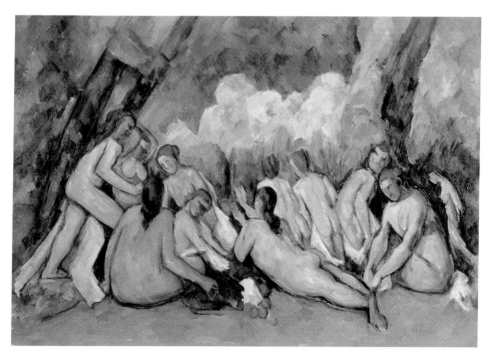

because it doggedly confronted a paradox. It aimed to be both representational image and invention, objective and subjective, a moment and all eternity, and all this in harmonious equilibrium. At the turn of the century, Cézanne's art was doing a balancing act, so to speak, with the dominant aesthetic fundaments of the 19th and the 20th centuries.

The Wisdom of Age

When Cézanne died in 1906, the last of the founding fathers of 20th-century art, who took Impressionism and transformed it into something new, was gone. These four founding fathers, according to the influential Austrian critic Werner Hofmann,[171] were Seurat, who systematically took colour apart (died 1891); van Gogh, who heightened expressiveness (died 1890); Gauguin, who established a new synthesis of colour and formal tonalities (died 1903); and Cézanne, who persistently based everything on the accuracy with which phenomena were observed. In 1905, the year before Cézanne died, a number of young artists exhibited work at the Paris autumn salon (a further splinter system that had been in operation for two years) in which they already went beyond these founding fathers. The critic Louis Vauxcelles labelled these painters – who included Henri Matisse (1869–1954) and Georges Braque (1882–1963) – "Fauves" (savages). At the same time in Dresden, four architecture students established an artists' group (soon to include other members) known as the Brücke (bridge). The style of these painters rapidly attracted the label Expressionist.

But three of the artists who created Impressionism continued to paint for a decade or even two beyond that time (not counting Guillaumin, their fellow traveller since the start, or the American Cassatt, who had joined at an early stage). These three were Degas, Renoir and Monet, and they continued to create masterpieces despite the onset of old age and infirmity.

Degas was hit earliest and hardest. In various ways he remained a special case. He had fought for independent exhibition space for himself and others, but latterly proved indifferent to showing his work. He was rich, which meant that access to the art market meant nothing to him. But this did not prevent him from making scathing comments on the profits dealers or collectors made by reselling his works, comparing them to stable owners growing rich by selling horses they had merely fed a little hay to. In 1912 he was present when a picture by his friend Rouart, painted in 1876/77, fetched the staggering price of 430,000 francs. From 1886 he himself sold solely through Durand-Ruel, who in 1893 organized Degas's only solo exhibition in France in his lifetime.

Degas remained with his favourite subjects: situation portraits, jockeys, ballet dancers, and above all women (prostitutes) at their toilet, works such as he had shown as a series at the last Impressionist exhibition in 1886. He gave up painting in oils (not, as recent scholarship has found, in 1890 but much later) in favour of his preferred pastels, and

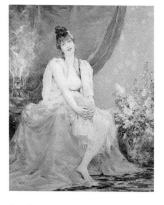

Franc-Lamy
An Exotic Beauty
Une beauté exotique
Oil on canvas, 73.5 x 61 cm
Private collection

Jean Béraud
On the Boulevard, 1895
Sur le boulevard
Oil on canvas, 33 x 25 cm
Paris, Musée Carnavalet

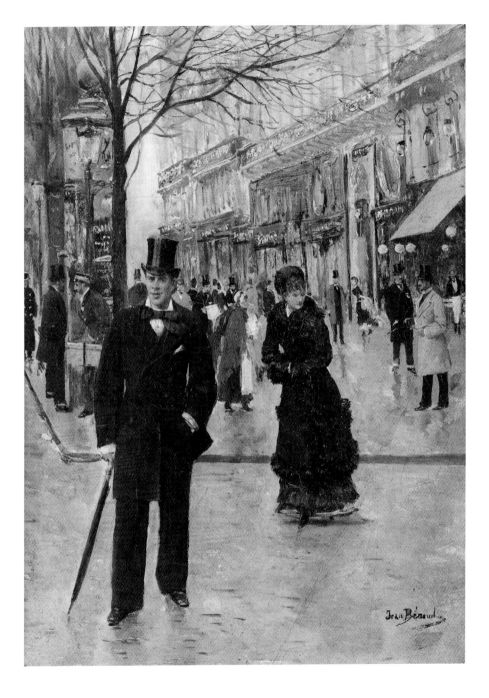

Jean Béraud

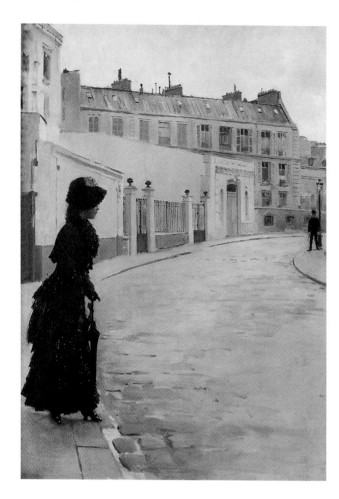

Jean Béraud
Waiting, Paris, Rue de Chateaubriand, c. 190
L'attente. Rue de Chateaubriand, Paris
Oil on canvas, 56 x 39.5 cm
Paris, Musée d'Orsay

charcoal drawings. A major reason for this change was the failure of his sight. We cannot say quite how blind he was. His friend Halévy said in 1894 that he was nearly blind,[172] but Degas went on drawing till about 1910. He was also a keen photographer. He photographed nude women washing, as preliminary and complementary studies for his drawings and pastels. These photographs include some of the finest in the history of nude photography.[173] When arranging group photos he could be a bully to his friends if they were slow to adopt the poses he wanted them in. His failing eyesight did not prevent him from buying pictures by Delacroix, Gauguin, van Gogh, Cézanne and others at auctions. "I buy, I buy, I can't help myself," he told Halévy in 1895[174]. He also went to exhibitions, dispensing his characteristic sarcasm: Monet's landscapes, he said, with their light and agitated atmosphere, made him feel there must be a draught in the exhibition room – he felt like putting up his collar.

His late bathers and dancers were mainly large-format. The charcoal sketches in particular were largely simplified and at times coarsely drawn variations on unusual, expressive poses he had hit upon. His pastel and mixed techniques produced a rough, relief-like texture reminiscent of the pigmented dust (and vulnerability) of a butterfly's wings. It is as if there were space between the individual particles of colour for light or darkness. There is an unfinished, vibrant sense of movement in these works that destabilizes them, as in Cézanne or Monet. Towards the end, as Degas's blindness deepened, all he could record were shapes and colours from a remembered repertoire, much as the deaf Beethoven worked with remembered chords. He would now draw thicker outlines to structure the turbulence of the colours. His eyes could no longer see delicate lines.

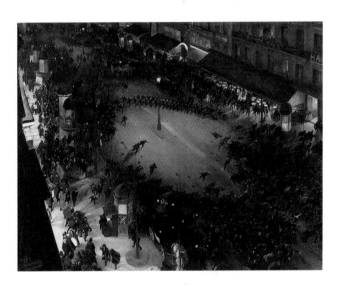

André Devambez
The Charge, 1902
La charge
Oil on canvas, 127 x 162 cm
Paris, Musée d'Orsay

He took to using tracings to repeat and adapt figures, in variable groupings. He was drawing on a lifetime's store of observation and draughtsmanship. Obsessed with a concept of form that had become quite detached from subject, persisting in his experiments, he left 20th-century artists a legacy that pointed the way forward for many. "With absolute consistency he had investigated whatever was unfinished, rudimentary and fragmentary in his world of forms, and his radical simplifications of form; and brusque, disruptive material idiom, had effectively countered the triumphant style of the times with its melodic lines, Art Nouveau."[175]

From the 1880s, Degas also sculpted dancers and bathers in wax and clay. In the 20th century, sculpture done by painters was to become a significant branch of artistic endeavour. For Degas, so preoccupied with

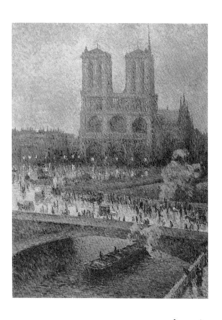

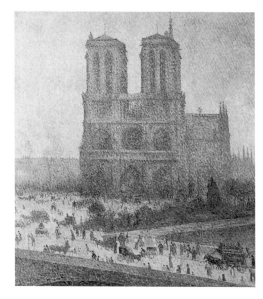

Maximilien Luce
Notre-Dame, 1900
Oil on canvas, 81.2 x 60.3 cm
Bazetoux 146
Private collection

Maximilien Luce
Notre-Dame, 1901
Oil on canvas, 85 x 79.4 cm
Bazetoux 148
New York, Mr. and Mrs. Arthur G. Altschul
Collection

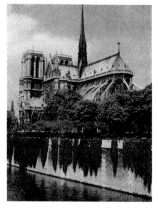

Notre-Dame, Paris. Photograph, c. 1900

forms in motion and their spatial relations, it was an unsurprising field of further experiment. The audacious sketchiness and delicacy of his sculptures even went beyond that of his drawings. Once blindness no longer permitted drawing, all that was left was to work with his fingers. After his death in 1917, some 150 partially wax or clay figures were found in his studio, some of them damaged or broken. Hebrard later cast 74 of them in bronze.

Renoir too turned to sculpture in old age, though the few pieces he made remained more traditional. They were done between 1913 and 1917 at a time when a young pupil of Aristide Maillol's (1861–1944), the Catalan Richard Guino (1890–1973), placed his hands at Renoir's disposal; for, if Degas could no longer see, Renoir's hands could no longer grip. They were so gnarled by arthritis that his brush had to be jammed between his fingers for him. Guino modelled the sculptures following Renoir's instructions or his indications with a cane.

Since 1905, Renoir had been living at Cagnes-sur-Mer, where he built a house on the Les Colettes estate, moving into it in 1908. On occasion he also stayed at Essoyes. He lost a good deal of weight and from 1910 was confined to a wheelchair, in continous pain. Even in bed he needed wire guards to keep the covers off his twisted and hypersensitive body. At the very opening of the First World War, his sons Pierre (1885–1952) and Jean (1894–1979) were seriously wounded. Their mother, Aline, selflessly tended by Jean, died in 1915. After the war ended in 1918, Renoir, now 78, was honoured with a visit to the Louvre, to see the paintings he loved best; a small one of his own had temporarily been hung beside a magnificent Veronese. His art had earned its place in Eu-

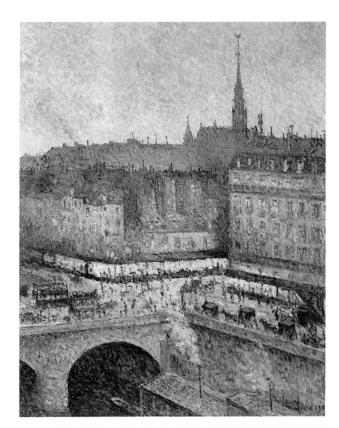

Maximilien Luce
La Sainte-Chapelle, Paris, 1901
Oil on canvas, 63 x 53 cm
Bazetoux 265
San Francisco (CA), Montgomery Gallery

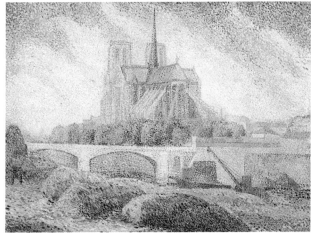

Hippolyte Petitjean
Notre-Dame, c. 1895
Oil on canvas, 54.3 x 70.8 cm
Private collection

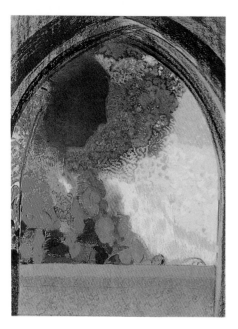

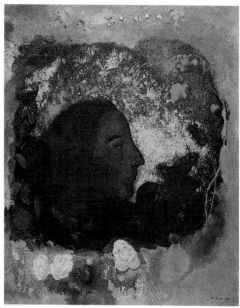

ropean culture, in the continuation of which he defiantly believed. Five months later he was buried beside his wife in Essoyes.

To an almost incredible extent, Renoir's late work remained a celebration of beauty, healthful vigour, and *joie de vivre*. His unflagging desire to paint erected a protective barrier of hundreds of paintings, against pain, against the woes of reality. Working in his house, his garden, and the glassed studio he had built in 1915 in order to paint as if in the open, he recorded his impressions of trees, shrubs, flowers and people in large-format and smaller pictures using light brushwork and dabs. The colours became less real, sometimes indeed cloyingly bright. An unnatural brightness of light irradiated his canvases. Painting was life for Renoir. To repeat the pleasure he had taken in some unanticipated use of colour struck him as perfectly in order; and thus the paintings which collectors now hungered after were sometimes without real vigour or critical self-discipline, and might not be valued very highly today were it not that they bear Renoir's signature.

Renoir's most powerful inspiration was still derived from the sensual, rosy, fleshy bodies of young women. To his son Jean (later a film director of the first water), to young artists who visited and later wrote on him, such as Albert André (1869–1954) and the American Walter Pach, to his old friend Rivière or the art dealer Vollard, he expressed his unchanged views time and again. Ultimately he assessed his women models purely according to how well their skin took the light. Any intellectual capacities they might possess left him cold. When he was occasionally talked into doing portraits, he was generally unsuccessful at conveying mental qualities, and his presentation of sophisticated style could likewise easily become mere accessories and a vacant facial expression.

But when he painted the maid, Gabrielle, transforming her into the very epitome of female youth, bloom and happiness, the full magic of his art came into its own (p. 390). We see her in a flimsy négligée at an 18th-century dressing table, pleased to see how jewellery and a rose in her hair enhance her own beauty. Such works were "a feast for the eyes" (as Delacroix once said art should be) – and also, quite simply, celebrations of the sensual beauty of women. Gabrielle Renard (1879–1959) was a cousin of Aline's who joined the household in 1894 as Jean's nanny and did not leave till she married an American painter in 1914. Possibly she did not really possess the grace we see in her. Perhaps Renoir was following his own ideal rather than visible fact. The inner rhythm of these paintings was now calmer and less capricious. In Matisse, who visited him in 1917 and whose paintings he respected, Renoir saw a worthy successor, one who would adopt in his own changed way Renoir's view of the visual image and his dream of harmony.

Paul Gauguin
Sunflowers on a Chair, 1901
Tournesols dans un fauteuil
Oil on canvas, 73 x 91 cm
Wildenstein 603. St. Petersburg, Hermitage

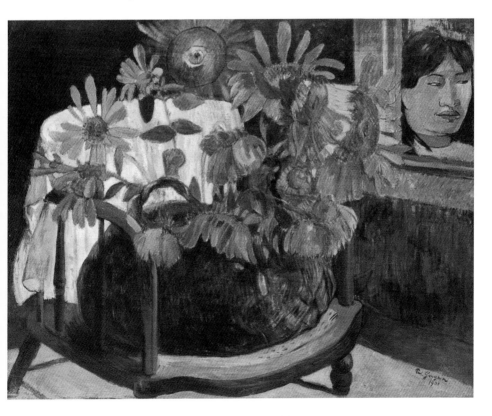

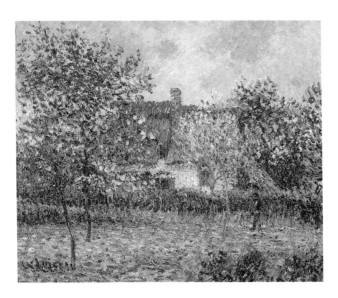

Gustave Loiseau
Orchard in Spring, c. 1899–1900
Le verger au printemps
Oil on canvas, 38.4 x 46 cm
Private collection

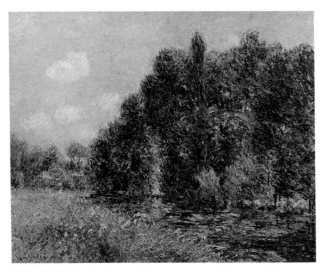

Gustave Loiseau
Banks of the Seine, 1902
Bords de la Seine
Oil on canvas, 65 x 81.5 cm
Private collection

In 1883 Monet had moved into a house at Giverny which he subsequently bought. That home became the centre of his existence, from
which he rarely went on forays for new subjects. Instead he preferred to
invite old friends, new admirers, and dealers who were awaiting paintings, to visit. At the turn of the century he travelled once again to London, where from his hotel window he painted the Thames, the bridges
and the Houses of Parliament in the autumn and winter mists (p. 363).

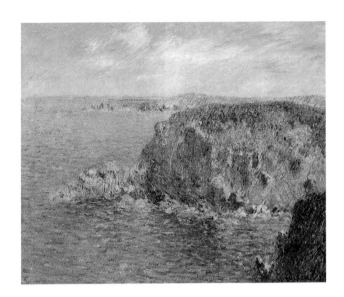

Gustave Loiseau
Cape Fréhel and "La Teignouse" Cliffs, 1906
Cap Fréhel, le rocher «La Teignouse»
Oil on canvas, 60 x 73 cm
Private collection

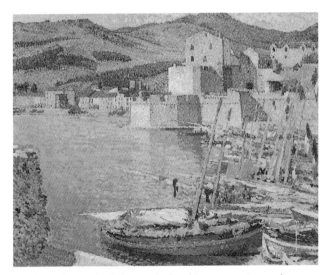

Henri Martin
The Harbour of Collioure
Le port de Collioure
Oil on canvas, 75.5 x 93.5 cm
Private collection

Scholars today are divided as to whether this concentration on the amorphous was prompted by new thinking and aesthetic concepts or by the old Impressionist delight in specific atmospheric effects.[176] The sole reason Monet gave for travelling to London was the fog. His paintings are tightly-woven fabrics of short brush-strokes. The palpably material texture of oils and canvas is greater than that of the subjects, which seem insubstantial in the haze. Monet subsequently attuned the colours of the

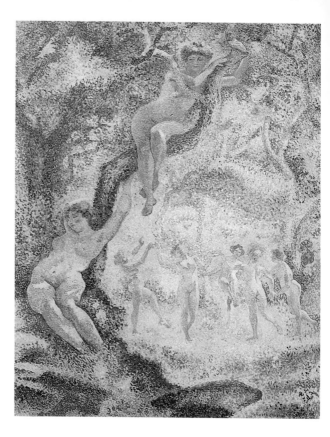

Henri-Edmond Cross
The Clearing, c. 1906/07
La clairière
Oil on canvas, 162 x 130 cm
France, private collection

various pictures in his studio, and exhibited them as a series at Durand-Ruel's in 1904.

But ultimately Giverny sufficed Monet. It gave him all he needed in order to demonstrate his concept – and mastery – of painting. It also afforded him the pleasure of gardening: not merely painting Nature, but shaping it with his own hands. "All I can do is gardening and painting," he told the art critic Maurice Kahn in 1904, who reported the observation in the large-circulation paper "Le Temps".[177] In 1893 Monet had bought an adjoining plot of land and received permission to dam the Ru, a tributary stream of the Epte, in order to create a pool. Across this he had a "Japanese" wooden bridge built. It was hard to convince neighbouring farmers that neither the altered course of the stream nor the waterlilies he planted in the pool would be harmful to agriculture. Using a troop of gardeners, he laid out and tended his famous garden over the next thirty years. There were two garden studios in it.

The death of his wife Alice in 1911 was such a blow that for three years he did not paint. And in 1914 his son Jean died. But Monet's friend

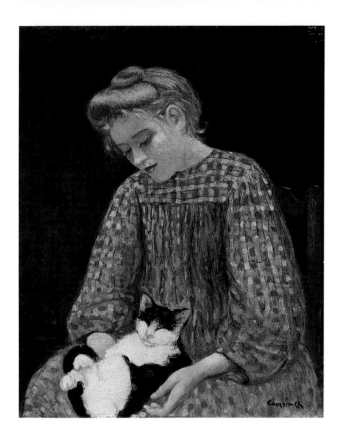

Charles Camoin
Girl with a Cat, c. 1904
La fille au chat
Oil on canvas, 65 x 54 cm
Private collection

Clemenceau succeeded in persuading the 74-year-old to return to his art. Jean's widow, Blanche, née Hoschedé (1865–1947), at once Monet's daughter-in-law and step-daughter and herself starting to paint, became his housekeeper. The day after the First World War ended, Monet's patriotic feelings prompted him to offer Clemenceau, then Prime Minister, two paintings as a gift to the nation. Six days later, Clemenceau visited Monet, with Geffroy, and seized upon an ambitious idea Monet himself had long had for a building devoted to Monet's *paysages d'eau* - as the first *Nymphéas* (waterlilies) series had been titled when exhibited at Durand-Ruel's in 1900.[178] When the Tiger (as Clemenceau was nicknamed) was defeated at the polls in 1920, and retired from political life, it seemed this plan would come to nothing. But a journalist, François Thiébault-Sisson, made the proposal public, and the state took it up. A contract signed in 1922 envisaged the Orangerie of the Tuileries as a site for Monet's art, over 100 square metres of which (much still to be completed) he gifted to the nation in return for the state's assurance of a permanent exhibition professionally handled.

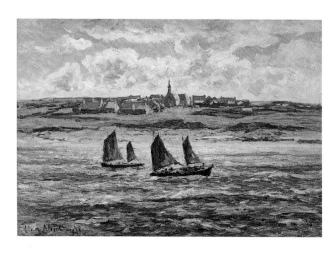

Henry Moret
The Village of Paulgoazec, 1906
Village de Paulgoazec
Oil on canvas, 38.2 x 55 cm
Paris, Galerie Bruno Meissner

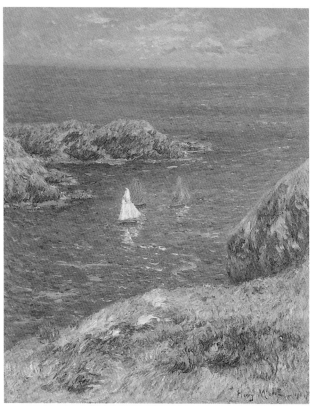

Henry Moret
Ouessant, Calm Seas, 1905
Ouessant, jour de calme
Oil on canvas, 93 x 74 cm
Private collection

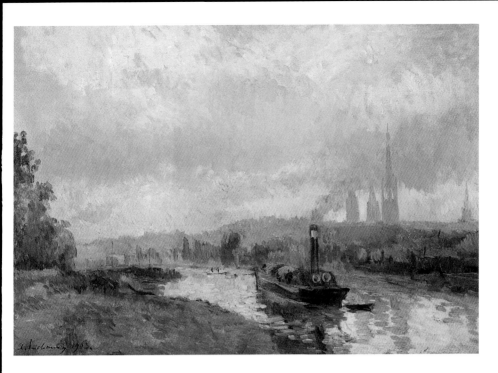

What was so special about this "Sistine Chapel of Impressionism" – as the artist André Masson (1896–1987) termed it – was that it involved neither the decoration of a space used (like the Pope's chapel) for non-artistic purposes, nor a patriotic or historical national Pantheon, nor the representation of modern life such as Manet had in mind for the Paris city hall or Cézanne for other public spaces. Rather, the Orangerie became a temple of pure vision, where we look at art in which an aged painter has expressed his responses to plants, water and light. Till the age of 86, Monet performed demanding physical work in order to master the vast areas involved, also painting countless large and small variations on his themes on the side, in order to assess and structure his visions. From 1912 he had cataracts in both eyes, and in 1923 had to have an operation on the right eye. It was some time before he could be provided with genuinely helpful spectacles, and he had to rely on his own knowledge of paint and the effects of mixed colours, and of consonance and contrast, when placing colours on his surface according to the label on the tube or their position on his palette. He was no longer able to judge with his own eyes the relation of details to the whole. Thus some of the results were blurred and streaky pictures, disappointing in their colours; art historians are still reluctant to pronounce their opinions on these works. Monet did not live to see the opening of the Orangerie permanent exhibition in May 1927, having been buried by

Albert-Charles Lebourg
Barges at Rouen, 1903
Remorqueurs à Rouen
Oil on canvas, 50 x 73.5 cm
Bénédite 1371. Paris, Musée d'Orsay

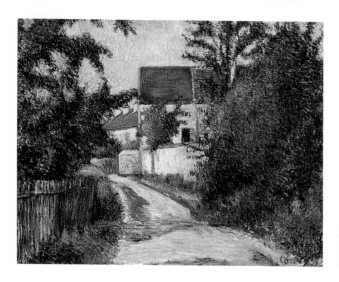

his closest friends five months before; at his own wish it was not a state funeral.

The roughly square *paysages d'eau* showing the Japanese bridge, among the very first pictures Monet had painted of his earthly paradise a quarter century before (pp. 364, 365), are exemplary variations on a theme in different conditions of light. The Japanese influence survives in them. Monet's brushwork at that date was still more intent on capturing

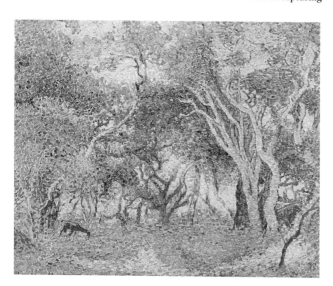

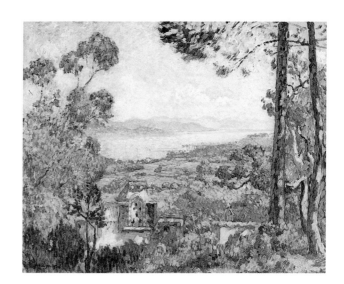

Henri Lebasque
View of Saint-Tropez, 1906
Vue de Saint-Tropez
Oil on canvas, 73 x 92 cm
Private collection

form than Cézanne's. The water, waterlilies, grasses, trees and bridge give structure and spatial differentiation to the visual space. The way waterlily stems moved below the water's surface, and the reflections of trees, fascinated Monet.

Elsewhere in his garden he painted the lush opulence of flowers, shrubs, overhanging trees and patchwork light (p. 362). There is no horizon to our field of vision, and this, with the tapestry of dabs and *taches*,

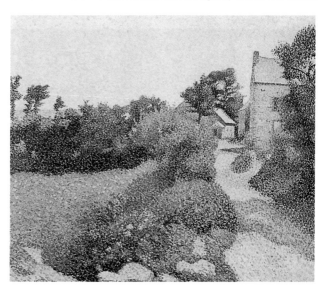

Henri Delavallée
Sunny Street, c. 1887
La rue ensoleillée
Oil on canvas, 45.7 x 55.2 cm
Indianapolis (IN), Indianapolis Museum of Art,
Mr. and Mrs. W.J. Holliday Collection

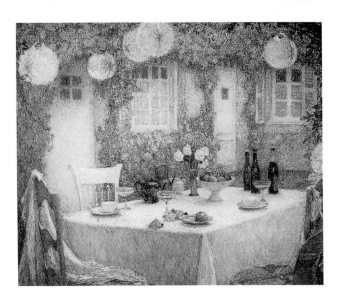

Henri le Sidaner
Table beneath Lanterns, Gerberoy, 1924
La table aux lanternes, Gerberoy
Oil on canvas, 125 x 150 cm
Farinaux-Le Sidaner 535
Chicago (IL), M. Sternberg Gallery

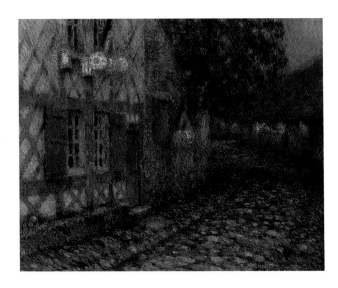

Henri Le Sidaner
14 July, Gerberoy, 1910
Le 14 juillet, Gerberoy
Oil on canvas, 82 x 100 cm
Farinaux-Le Sidaner 201
Private collection

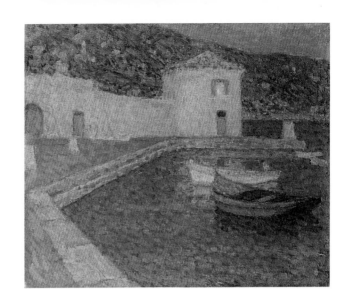

Henri Le Sidaner
House by the Sea at Dusk, 1927
La maison de la mer au crépuscule
Oil on canvas, 46.3 x 56 cm
Farinaux-Le Sidaner 620
Private collection

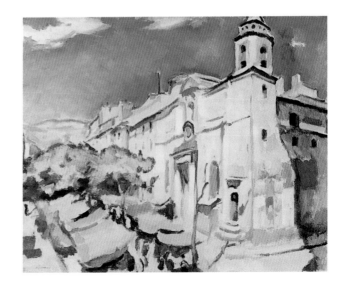

Charles Camoin
The Market Place, Toulon, c. 1908
La Place du Marché, Toulon
Oil on canvas, 65 x 81 cm
Private collection

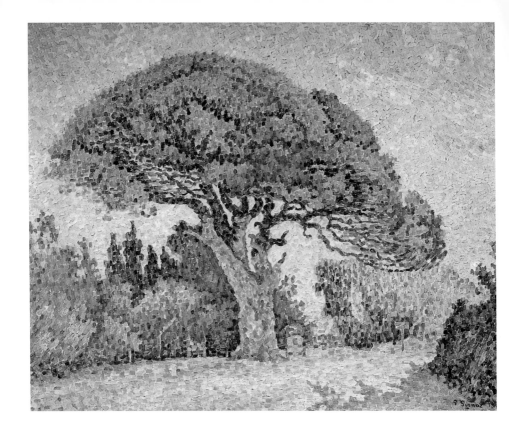

Paul Signac
Pine Tree at Saint-Tropez, 1909
Pin à Saint-Tropez
Oil on canvas, 72 x 92 cm
Moscow, Pushkin Museum of Fine Art

perpetuates the abiding Impressionist ambition to harmonize spatial depth and surface. Versions of the same subject painted twenty years later, though, emphasized the surface patterning almost exclusively. The *Nymphéas* pictures done from 1904 on, entering a second stage of development around 1916, were mainly what Monet termed "landscapes of reflection". Their vitality derives from the poetic spell which the moist, succulent, sexually symbolic open calyxes of the waterlily blossoms – adrift on the dangerous dark depths of the marshy waters – cast on Symbolist poets and their public alike. The vigorous, pastose curls of paint that sketch the flowers fall into tenderly spatial arabesques reminiscent of Art Nouveau. The floating islands of colour are intermingled with sky colour and the hanging weeping willows and their reflections, in like intensity of colour.

These tantalizing images of motifs with reflections become hypertrophied in the large essays and variations Monet did in the early 1920s for the Orangerie walls (p. 393). Against a blue in which the pink and yellow

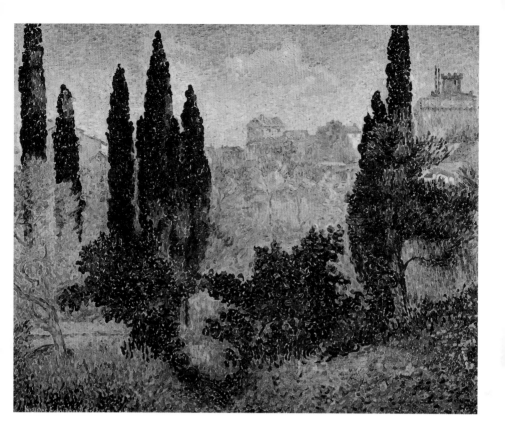

reflections of clouds gleam we see the floating carmine flowers, with willow depending from above and irises entering the field of vision from below. The relish Monet brought to his lavish, sometimes impurely coloured work remains permanently evidenced: this spontaneous record of impressions has become a gestural, absolute kind of painting such as was to be rediscovered in the Tachism and action painting of the Twenties. Wistaria hanging down above the water (pp. 394/395) becomes an almost completely non-representational exercise in colour accords, authoritatively reversing traditional views of visual priorities in composition. Impressionism had come a long way since the youthful artists retorted to their furious teachers: "I paint what I see the way I see it."

Henri-Edmond Cross
Cypresses at Cagnes, 1908
Les cyprès à Cagnes
Oil on canvas, 81 x 100 cm
Compin 212. Paris, Musée d'Orsay

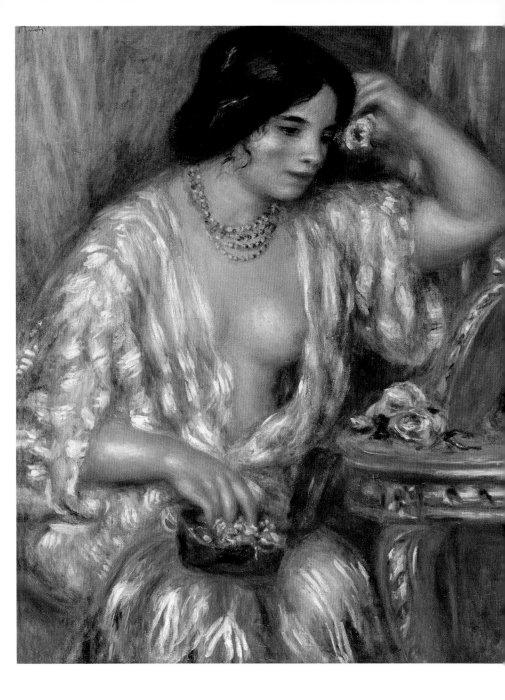

9 "The Masters will last"

Since the end of the 19th century, Impressionism had become established worldwide, not only in France, among artists and in terms of public expectation. Slowly but surely, the number of those who saw Impressionism as a genuine and notably contemporary way of registering experience of the world grew. It is true that in 1905 Durand-Ruel offered 315 first-rate paintings by all the main Impressionists at Grafton Galleries in London – the best and biggest overview anywhere before 1945 – only to have not a single work sold.[179] However, more and more painters were availing themselves of the structural and formal approaches Manet, Monet, Degas and the others had evolved in the 1860s.

Some used them for subjects the founding Impressionists had avoided. Thus André Devambez (1867–1944) painted the gendarmerie breaking up a demonstration in the Boulevard Montmartre at night (p. 373). The slant angle from above of the street and the crowds, the rapid movement, the dramatic spaces, the unusual lighting, all drew on the Impressionist idiom, though the detail was exacter than in comparable street scenes done not long before by Pissarro (pp. 356, 357). Whenever a precision image of actuality was the aim, later artists tended to use Impressionist methods only with reservations. But when artists and the public want a life-asserting, beautiful, light and energetic version of the visible world, Impressionism has stood its ground worldwide to this day, even if many subsequent movements have long since superseded its claim to be avant-garde.

Two painters who moved back from Post-Impressionist, decorative, symbolist styles to Impressionism, and are sometimes referred to as Intimists for their subjects and for the exquisite delicacy of their colour harmonies, afford attractive proof of the vitality of Impressionism. As a student, Bonnard had designed a poster that impressed Toulouse-Lautrec, and displayed a sensitive touch for decorative effects in paintings exhibited with the Indépendants (p. 340). Bonnard painted his father, sister and brother-in-law playing croquet in the grounds of the family home in south-east France – an old favourite among Impressionist subjects. The overall effect, though, is of a decorative tapestry using Art Nouveau shapes and an elegiac evening mood. Around 1900 Impressionism gained the upper hand in his work, bringing him more into line with Renoir, Monet and Signac; later he was to alternate between Fauvist

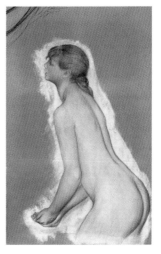

Pierre-Auguste Renoir
Study for "Bathers", c. 1884
Etude pour «Les Baigneuses»
Red, black and white chalk, 98.5 x 64 cm
Chicago (IL), The Art Institute of Chicago

Pierre-Auguste Renoir
Gabrielle with Jewels, c. 1910
Gabrielle aux bijoux
Oil on canvas, 82 x 65.5 cm
Private collection

intensity and a rather trite representational copying of views. Bonnard was best at interior nudes drenched in light, or festive family scenes in the open, when he could celebrate the beauty of things and the pleasure of seeing them in bright, lightly dabbed brushwork.

Edouard Vuillard (1868–1940) was in agreement with him in his love of detail, or rather of a luxurious copiousness, and in his concentration on everyday life, portraits of friends, interiors and landscapes – in a word, a typically Impressionist range of subject matter. Vuillard too had a taste and talent for the decorative, and among his early work were stage-set designs. He was closely associated with the magazine "Revue blanche", which was of such importance for the Post-Impressionists and was edited from 1889 to 1903 by Thadée Natanson. Natanson and his beautiful, capricious Franco-Polish wife Marie (Misia), née Godebska – who was portrayed by Toulouse-Lautrec, Vuillard, Renoir and Bonnard, among others – were the heart of an active circle. Vuillard was captivated by the atmosphere. Till the end of his days, elected to the Académie des Beaux-Arts, he retained a highly sensual but cultured approach to seeing and painting. A small early study (p. 340) is a good example, with its dynamic structure, balanced asymmetry and enjoyment of a world that offers beautiful things.

How does Impressionism weigh in the balance of critical, historical and aesthetic judgement? What do people feel on leaving the galleries throughout the world that cherish their French Impressionist holdings as particularly popular and costly treasures? A number of painters, en-dowed with an intuitive sense many years ahead of most of their contem-poraries, discovered important aspects of life and reality in middle- and lower-class circles in highly civilized, modern industrial society, and made art of what they saw. They expressed what they saw in apt and innovatory artistic form, producing among the public, in the course of time, attitudes and ways of seeing to match. Building on realism that was true to appearances and using open-air techniques, the artists painted pictures which many people to this day feel to be images of a world where they themselves would like to live. Unlike various contemporaries and successors, the Impressionists thought nothing of work that dwelt on problematic, distressing or depressing aspects of reality; they painted only the sides of life, and the moments, that asserted pleasure, *joie de vivre*, a feast of the senses. This was in line with their temperaments and convictions, which they adhered to even in the most difficult of personal circumstances, and also accorded with a rather naive optimism concern-ing the society they lived in. To various, individually differing degrees they were intelligent and sensitive enough to acquire greater critical de-tachment from the world about them as the years went by. Thus many of their pictures recorded reservations they felt, or inner tension, or of-fered alternative visions by appealing to the past or to timeless utopias. Though this meant their paintings ran the overall risk of too complais-antly striving for harmony, the works thus had an inner consistency and truthfulness. And this alone can assure works of art a long-term validity and relevance; this alone can make them moving masterpieces.

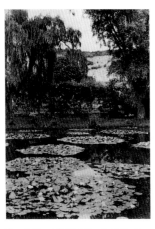

The waterlily pond in Monet's garden at Giverny, c. 1933

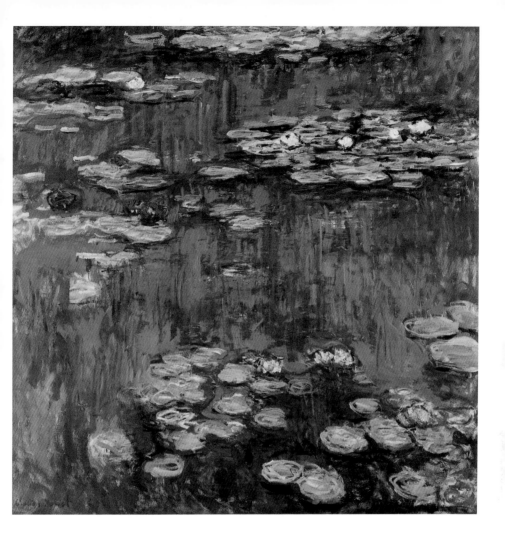

The Impressionists set great store by their craft, and by new and attractive styles of form. In this they were audacious, and their work bore fruit in the further evolution of art too. The claim that subject matter was unimportant in assessing artistic quality was of course first and foremost a youthful protest against tired old subjects. Of graver consequence was their rejection of the philosophical or literary. However, their belief (one they held with regret) was that their culture as a whole was losing the great ideas and traditions it had lived by. Other artistic movements that were philosophically, religiously or politically motivated to connect with

Claude Monet
Waterlilies, 1914
Nymphéas
Oil on canvas, 200 x 200 cm
Wildenstein 1800
Tokyo, National Museum of Western Art

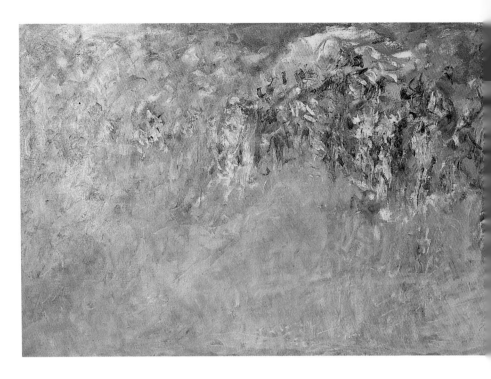

those traditions enjoyed only limited success. The resignation with which
a Degas would concentrate on what was pragmatically possible was
expressed in his dry remark: "Two hundred years ago I would have
painted Susannah and the Elders, the biblical subject, but now what I
paint is women washing in bathtubs."[180] Like many others, he realised
that modern praxis was incompatible with mythology, with the "uncon-
scious artistic processing" of reality in a folk imagination, which is so
much more favourable to artistic creativity than modern rationality.[181]

Impressionist technique significantly enriched the repertoire of art.
The Impressionists introduced ways of suggesting motion through
sketchy, open composition and brushwork; used evocatively unusual
sectional views taken from a spatial and chronological continuum; discovered how dependent colour was on light, and established a hitherto
unknown brightness, purity and vigour in colours; found new ways of
relating painted surface, spatial illusion and three-dimensionality in visual structures; and asserted a new autonomous value for both the materials out of which art is made and for the visible traces of the artist's
own work. All of this proved a fertile legacy for 20th-century artists of
various persuasions. Sometimes this circumstance has meant that Impressionist art is automatically seen as more diverse in its aesthetic ap-

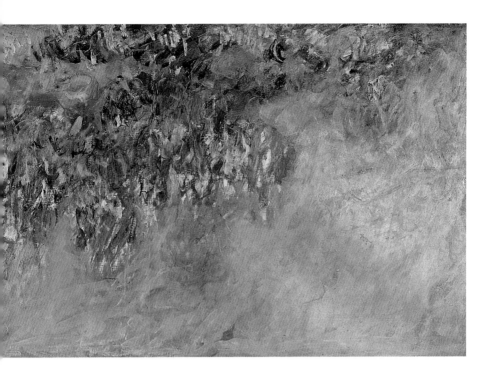

proach to visible reality, and intellectually richer, than what came later. Hofmann has summed up the historical significance and fertility of Impressionism by seeing it as the "watershed" of the 19th and 20th centuries – which implies the reaching of a peak.[182]

Zola was a shrewd judge, though his opinions were controversial. Writing in "Le Figaro" in 1896 on the Salon, he recalled his own beginning and that of his friends thirty years earlier.[183] He had hoped that their art would go in a different, more critical and realistic direction. He was appalled at the way light had become a modish and superficial component in art, and horrified at the Symbolism prevalent in the mid–90s. His contemporaries who were still painting took offence at his view of them as pioneers of a better future art who in their own achievement remained imperfect. Like many a later art historian, they failed to note that he still approved wholeheartedly of their audacious beginnings. Writing of Manet, Monet and Pissarro, he declared: "The masters will last."

Claude Monet
Wistaria, 1919/20
Glycines
Oil on canvas, 100 x 300 cm
Wildenstein 1904. Paris, Musée Marmottan

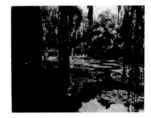

Monet's waterlily pond at Giverny, c. 1933

Acknowledgements and Picture Credits

The editor and the publisher would like to thank the museums and public collections, the galleries and private collectors, the archives and photographers, and all others who have assisted in the preparation of this two-volume monograph. Particular gratitude is due to Mrs Claudia Brigg, Christie's Colour Library, London, and Mrs Eve Boustedt, Impressionist and Modern Art Department, Sotheby's, London, for varied and diverse supportive cooperation. Thomas Jaworek, Durham, prepared numerous photographic reproductions especially for this publication, and we owe him special thanks, as we do the editor's assistants, Antje Günther and Matthias Feldbaum, both Munich.

Unless otherwise individually indicated, the copyright for the reproduced works is held by the heirs of the respective artists or their legal successors: Balla: © VG Bild-Kunst, Bonn, 2012. Benson: © Gerold Wunderlich & Co., New York. Bonnard: © VG Bild-Kunst, Bonn, 2012. Camoin: © VG Bild-Kunst, Bonn, 2012. Delavalle: © VG Bild-Kunst, Bonn, 2012. Denis: © VG Bild-Kunst, Bonn, 2012. Devambez: © VG Bild-Kunst, Bonn, 2012. Ensor: © VG Bild-Kunst, Bonn, 2012. Gagnon: © Estate of Clarence A. Gagnon, VIS-ART Copyright, Inc. Gallen-Kallela: © Pirkko Gallen-Kallela, Helsinki. Grabar: © VG Bild-Kunst, Bonn, 2012. Knight: © John Farquharson Ltd, London. Martin: VG Bild-Kunst, Bonn, 2012. Miller: © Goldfield Galleries, Los Angeles. Munch: © The Munch Museum/ The Munch Ellingsen Group/ VG Bild-Kunst, Bonn, 2012. Sickert: © VG Bild-Kunst, Bonn, 2012. Trübner: © Henry Trubner, Seattle.

The locations and owners of the works are listed in the captions to the illustrations, except for those cases where they wished to remain anonymous or were not known to the editor. The editor and the publisher would greatly appreciate any information regarding incomplete or incorrect details. Key to the abbreviations: l = left, t = top, r = right, b = bottom.

AMHERST, Massachusetts, Mead Art Museum: 621.– ANTELLA, Scala, Istituto Fotografico Editoriale: 533, 540, 544.– BARCELONA, Museu Nacional d'Art de Catalunya: 555, 564, 566 b, 567.– BELGRAD, Narodni Muzej: 530 l, 530 r, 531.– BERLIN, akg images: 207 (Photo: Erich Lessing), 265, 302 t, 302 b (Archives CDA), 303, 332 (Photo: Erich Lessing), 333 t, 334/335 (Photo: Erich Lessing), 352, 353, 377, 434 t.– BERLIN, Bildarchiv Preußischer Kulturbesitz: 434 b, 448.– BEVERLY HILLS, California, Louis Stern Galleries: 202, 203.– BOSTON, Museum of Fine Arts: 602 t, 610.– BRUSSELS, Musee d'Ixelles: 424 t.– BRUSSELS, Musees Royaux des Beaux-Arts: 431.– BUDAPEST, Magyar Nemzeti Galéria (Photo: Mester Tibor): 500, 520, 521 l, 521 r, 523 t, 524 t, 524 b.– CAMBRIDGE, Fogg Art Museum, Harvard University: 210.– CAPE TOWN, South African National Gallery: 586.– CHICAGO, The Art Institute of Chicago: 618.– CHICAGO, R.H. Love Galleries: 622.– CHICAGO, Terra Museum of American Art, Daniel J. Terra Collection: 611, 615, 635.– COPENHAGEN, Den Hirschsprungske Samling (Photo: Hans Petersen): 493.– COPENHAGEN: Statens Museum for Kunst (Photo: Hans Petersen): 472, 481 b, 486 b, 495.– CRACOW, Muzéum Narodówe Krakowie (Photo: Tadeusz Szklarczyk): 512, 513 b, 515.– DETROIT, Detroit Institute of Art, Manoogian Collection (Courtesy Richard A. Manoogian): 614 b, 630 t, 618 t.– DRESDEN, Staatliche Kunstsammlungen, Gemäldegalerie Neue Meister: 439.– ECUBLENS, Archiv André Held: 35 t, 58, 69, 83, 92 t, 96 t, 96 b, 97, 127 t, 127 b, 132 t, 156 t, 158 b, 159 b, 160 r, 211 b, 300, 329, 337, 355 t, 356 b, 359, 378 b, 459, 599.– ETAMPES, Musée d'Etampes: 155 b.– EUERBACH, Schloß Obbach, Sammlung Georg Schäfer: 447.– FORT WORTH, Amon Carter Museum: 620.– GOTHENBURG, Göteborgs Konstmuseum: 476, 483, 486 t, 488.– HELSINKI, Valtion Taidemuseo (Photo: Matti Routsalainen): 466, 478, 484.– INDIANAPOLIS, Indianapolis Museum of Arts: 634 l.– LAREN, Singer Museum: 416 b.– LINCOLN, Usher Art Gallery: 570.– LINZ, Neue Galerie der Stadt, Wolfgang-

Gurlitt-Museum: 444.– LIVORNO, Museo Civico Giovanni Fattori: 537.– LONDON, The Bridgeman Art Library: 580, 583 b, 584.– LONDON, Christie's Colour Library: 133 b, 180, 246, 263 r, 370, 375 b, 387 b, 416 t, 427 b, 549.– LONDON, Fine Art Society: 582.– LONDON, Pyms Gallery: 587.– LONDON, Richard Green Gallery: 316.– LONDON, Sotheby's: 202 b, 203 b, 316, 338, 360, 375 t, 378 t, 379, 381, 382, 384 t, 385 t, 539.– LONDON, The Tate Gallery: 572, 576, 583 t, 589, 590, 597.– LONDON, University of London, Courtauld Institute Galleries: 221.– LUGANO, Fondazione Thyssen-Bornemisza: 402.– MADRID, Centro de Arte Reina Sofía: 562.– MADRID, Museo del Prado, Cason del Buen Retiro: 552, 556, 557, 558, 559, 563, 565, 568, 580.– MALMÖ, Malmö Museer: 474 t.– MANCHESTER, Manchester City Art Gallery: 581, 585.– MILWAUKEE, Milwaukee Art Museum: 616 b.– MONTREAL, The Montreal Museum of Fine Arts (Photo: Brian Merrett): 632.– MUNICH, Archiv Alexander Koch: 61, 212.– NEW YORK, Coe Kerr Gallery: 634.– NORRKÖPING, Norrköpings Konstmuseum: 473 b.– OSLO, Nasjonalgalleriet (Photo: Jacques Lathion): 469, 470, 474 b, 475, 479, 481 t, 497.– OTTAWA, The National Gallery of Canada: 579, 626, 627 t.– OTTERLO, Kröller-Müller Museum: 419.– PARIS, Galerie Bruno Meissner: 382 t.– PARIS, Galerie Etienne Sassi: 360.– PARIS, Gilles Néret: 202 o, 205 t.– PARIS, Guy Loudmer: 386 b.– PARIS, Photographie Giraudon: 134, 151, 174 t, 209, 252, 371.– PARIS, Réunion des Musées Nationaux: 10, 14, 16 t, 17, 19, 23, 27 t, 28, 29 t, 30 t, 31, 34 t, 36 t, 37, 38/39, 45, 54 t, 63, 66, 67, 68, 71, 81 t, 82 t, 82 b, 89 r, 100/101, 109 t, 114, 116/117, 123 b, 124 t, 124 b, 125, 129, 131, 142/143, 166 t, 167, 172, 173, 175 t, 182, 183, 189, 190 b, 199, 203 t, 204 b, 213, 216, 240 t, 240 b, 247 t, 274 t, 275 t, 298 l, 298 r, 299, 307, 311, 313, 317, 320 t, 323, 339, 340 t, 340 b, 341, 350, 351 t, 351 b, 366/367, 372, 373, 376 r, 383, 389, 411, 427 t.– PHILADELPHIA, The Pennsylvania Academy of the Fine Arts: 623 t, 631.– PONTOISE, Musée Pissarro: 154 t.– POZNAN, Muzéum Naródowe (Photo: Pietraszak): 514.– PRAGUE, Národní Galerie (Photo: Milan Posselt, Oto Palán): 516, 517 t, 517 b, 518 t, 518 b, 519.– PROVIDENCE, Museum of Art, Rhode Island School of Design (Photo: Cathy Carver): 536 b, 609, 630 b.– QUEBEC, Musée du Québec (Photo: Patrick Altman): 636, 637.– ROCHESTER, New York, Memorial Art Gallery of the University of Rochester: 624.– ROTTERDAM, Museum Boymans-Van Beuningen: 417.– SAINT LOUIS, The Saint Louis Art Museum: 640.– SAN FRANCISCO, Montgomery Gallery: 375 t.– SKAGEN, Skagens Museum (Photo: Svend Thomsen): 473 t, 477, 494, 499.– SOUTH HADLEY, Massachusetts, Mount Holyoke College Art Museum: 605.– SOUTHAMPTON, New York, The Parrish Art Museum (Photo: Noel Rowe): 619.– STOCKHOLM, Nationalmuseum: 482.– STOCKHOLM, Prins Eugens Waldemarsudde: 480.– STOCKHOLM, Thielska galleriet: 489.– THE HAGUE, Haags Gemeentemuseum: 408 t, 413 l, 413 r.– TOLEDO, The Toledo Museum of Art: 603 b, 604 t.– TORONTO, Art Gallery of Ontario: 607 (Photo: Larry Ostrom), 627 b (Photo: Carlo Catenazzi).– TOURNAI, Musée des Beaux-Arts: 195 l.– TURKU, Turun Taidemuseo: 487.– UTRECHT, Centraal Museum Utrecht, Stichting Van Baaren Museum: 408 b, 412 t.– WALTHAM, Massachusetts, Rose Art Museum, Brandeis University: 633.– WASHINGTON, National Gallery of Art: 613.– WASHINGTON, The Phillips Collection: 612 b.– WEILHEIM, Artothek: 260/ 261, 432, 435, 438, 442 t, 443, 445, 457, 561. ZAGREB, Moderna Gallerija (Photo: Fedor Vucemilovic): 528.– Documentation Wildenstein Institute: 52, 80 l, 80 r, 158 t, 184 t, 208 t, 228, 229 b, 379 t, 387 t. All other master copies may be found in the collections cited in the captions; the archives of the editor or of the former Walther & Walther Verlag, Alling, or the archives of Benedikt Taschen Verlag, Cologne; or else were specially photographed by Thomas Jaworek for this work.

Notes

1 W. Hofmann: Das irdische Paradies. Kunst im neunzehnten Jahrhundert. Munich 1960; R. Zeitler: Die Kunst des 19. Jahrhunderts (Propyläen Kunstgeschichte, II). Berlin 1966; H.G. Evers: Vom Historismus zum Funktionalismus (Kunst der Welt. Die Kulturen des Abendlandes, 21). Baden-Baden 1967; R. Rosenblum, H.W. Janson: 19th Century Art. Painting and Sculpture. New York and London 1984.

2 J. Rewald. In: Camille Pissarro. Hayward Gallery, London; Grand Palais, Paris; Museum of Fine Arts, Boston. London et al. 1981, pp. 9–12 (exhibition catalogue).

3 R. Hamann: Der Impressionismus in Leben und Kunst. Cologne 1907.

4 W. Weisbach: Impressionismus. Ein Problem der Malerei in der Antike und Neuzeit. 2 volumes. Berlin 1910/11.

5 A. Boime: Thomas Couture and the Eclectic Vision. New Haven and London 1980; T. J. Clark: The Painting of Modern Life. Paris in the Art of Manet and His Followers. London 1985; R.L. Herbert: Impressionism. Art, Leisure and Parisian Society. New Haven and London 1988.

6 C.S. Moffett (ed.): The New Painting. Impressionism 1874–1886. The Fine Art Museum of San Francisco et al. Oxford and Geneva 1986 (exhibition catalogue).

7 F. Novotny: Cézanne und das Ende der wissenschaftlichen Perspektive. Vienna 1938.

8 The following contains lists of works and selected monographs, together with those exhibition catalogues important for recent research. – D. Rouart and D. Wildenstein: Edouard Manet. Catalogue raisonné. 2 volumes. Lausanne and Paris 1975; A.C. Hanson: Manet and the Modern Tradition. New Haven and London 1977; K. Adler: Manet. Oxford 1986.

9 P.A. Lemoisne: Degas et son œuvre. 4 volumes. Paris 1946–1949; P. Cabanne: Edgar Degas. Munich 1958; Degas. Grand Palais, Paris; Metropolitan Museum, New York; Musée des Beaux-Arts, Ottawa. Paris et al. 1988 (exhibition catalogue).

10 D. Wildenstein: Claude Monet. Biographie et catalogue raisonné. 4 volumes. Lausanne and Paris 1974–1985; Hommage à Claude Monet. Grand Palais, Paris 1981 (exhibition catalogue); R. Gordon and A. Forge: Claude Monet. Paris 1983; J. House: Monet. Nature into Art. New Haven and London 1986; K. Sagner-Düchting: Claude Monet, 1840–1926. The Triumph of the Eyes. Cologne 1992.

11 F. Daulte: Renoir. Catalogue raisonné de l'œuvre peint, volume 1: Figures 1860–1890. Lausanne and Paris 1971; W. Pach: Pierre-Auguste Renoir. Cologne 1958; Renoir. Hayward Gallery, London; Grand Palais, Paris;

Museum of Fine Arts, Boston. Paris et al. 1985 (exhibition catalogue); P.H. Feist: Pierre-Auguste Renoir, 1841–1919. A Dream of Harmony. Cologne 1991.

12 L.R. Pissarro and L. Venturi: Camille Pissarro. Son art, son œuvre. 2 volumes. Paris 1939; Pissarro. Hayward Gallery, London; Grand Palais, Paris; Museum of Fine Arts, Boston. London et al. 1981 (exhibition catalogue); C. Lloyd: Camille Pissarro. Geneva 1981; R.R. Bretell: Pissarro and Pontoise. The Painter in a Landscape. New Haven and London 1990.

13 F. Daulte: Alfred Sisley. Catalogue raisonné de l'œuvre peint. Lausanne and Paris 1959.

14 F. Daulte: Frédéric Bazille et son temps. Geneva 1952.

15 G. Wildenstein and M.-L. Bataille: Berthe Morisot. Catalogue des peintures, dessins, aquarelles. Paris 1960; D. Rouart (ed.): Correspondance de Berthe Morisot avec sa famille et ses amis Manet, Puvis de Chavannes, Degas, Monet, Renoir et Mallarmé. Paris 1950.

16 L. Venturi: Les Archives de L'Impressionnisme. 2 volumes. Paris and New York 1939; J. Rewald: Die Geschichte des Impressionismus, Cologne 1965; L. Venturi: De Manet à Lautrec. Paris 1953; O. Reuterswärd: Impressionisterna inför publik och kritik. Stockholm 1952; J. Leymarie: Impressionismus. 2 volumes. Geneva 1955; P. Pool: Die Kunst des Impressionismus. Berlin 1970; M. and G. Blunden: Der Impressionismus in Wort und Bild. Geneva 1979; A. Bellony-Rewald: Le monde retrouvé des impressionnistes. Paris 1977; S. Monneret: L'Impressionnisme et son époque. Dictionnaire international illustré. 4 volumes. Paris 1978–1981; D. Kelder: Die Großen Impressionisten. Munich 1981; Französische Impressionisten und ihre Wegbegleiter. Neue Pinakothek, Munich 1990 (exhibition catalogue).

17 G. Serret and D. Fabiani: Armand Guillaumin, 1841–1927. Catalogue raisonné de l'œuvre peint. Paris 1971.

18 M. Berhaut: Caillebotte, sa vie et son œuvre. Catalogue raisonné des peintures et pastels. Paris 1978; K. Varnedoe: Gustave Caillebotte. New Haven and London 1987.

19 C. Roger-Marx: Eva Gonzalès. Saint-Germain-en-Laye 1950.

20 L. Venturi: Cézanne. Son art, son œuvre. 2 volumes. Paris 1936; K. Badt: Die Kunst Cézannes. Munich 1956; W. Rubin (ed.): Cézanne. The Late Work. The Museum of Modern Art, New York, New York 1977 (exhibition catalogue); L. Gowing (ed.): Cézanne. The Early Years, 1859–1872. Royal Academy of Arts, London et al. London 1988 (exhibition catalogue); J. Rewald: Cézanne.

Biographie. Cologne 1986; H. Düchting: Paul Cézanne, Biographie. 1839–1906. Nature into Art. Cologne 1991.

21 H. Dorra and J. Rewald: Seurat. L'œuvre peint. Biographie et catalogue critique. Paris 1959; C.M. de Hauke: Seurat et son œuvre. 2 volumes. Paris 1961; R. Thomson: Seurat. Oxford 1985.

22 Signac. Musée du Louvre, Paris 1963/64 (exhibition catalogue); Paul Signac, 1863–1935. Paintings, Watercolors, Drawings and Prints. New York 1977 (exhibition catalogue).

23 J. Rewald: Le post-impressionnisme. De van Gogh à Gauguin. Paris 1961; J. Sutter: Die Neoimpressionisten. Berlin 1970.

24 G. Wildenstein and R. Cogniat: Gauguin. Catalogue des tableaux. Volume 1, Paris 1964; G.M. Sugana: L'opera completa di Gauguin. Milan 1972; W. Jaworska: Gauguin et l'école de Pont-Aven. Paris 1971; F. Cachin: Gauguin. Paris 1988; I.F. Walther: Paul Gauguin, 1848–1903. The Primitive Sophisticate. Cologne 1992; Paul Gauguin. Grand Palais, Paris 1989 (exhibition catalogue).

25 J.-B. de la Faille: The Works of Vincent van Gogh. Amsterdam and New York 1970; J. Hulsker: Van Gogh en zijn weg. Het complete werk. Amsterdam 1977; I.F. Walther and R. Metzger: Vincent van Gogh. The Complete Paintings, 2 volumes. Cologne 1990.

26 M. Joyant: Henri de Toulouse-Lautrec, 1864–1901. 2 volumes. Paris 1926/27; M.G. Dortu: Toulouse-Lautrec et son œuvre. 6 volumes. New York 1971; M. Arnold: Henri de Toulouse-Lautrec, 1864–1901. The Theatre of Life. Cologne 1992.

27 J. and H. Dauberville: Bonnard. Catalogue raisonné de l'œuvre peint. 4 volumes. Paris 1965; Pierre Bonnard. Städelsches Kunstinstitut, Frankfurt am Main 1985 (exhibition catalogue).

28 J. Russel (ed.): Edouard Vuillard, 1868–1940. Toronto and London 1971 (exhibition catalogue).

29 N. Broude (ed.): Impressionismus. Eine internationale Kunstbewegung 1860–1920. Cologne 1990; cf. Landschaft im Licht. Impressionistische Malerei in Europa und Nordamerika 1860–1910. Wallraf-Richartz-Museum, Cologne 1990 (exhibition catalogue).

30 A. Boime: The Academy and French Painting in the Nineteenth Century. London 1971; N. Pevsner: Academies of Art. Past and Present. New York 1973; P. Grunchec and J. Thuillier (eds.): La peinture à l'Ecole des Beaux-Arts. Les concours des Prix de Rome, 1797–1863. 2 volumes. New York 1984/85 (exhibition catalogue).

31 G. Wildenstein: Ingres. London 1954; G. Picon: Ingres. Geneva 1980.

32 R. Huyghe: Delacroix. Munich 1967; P. Georgel and L. Rossi-Bortolatte: Tout l'œuvre peint de Delacroix. Paris 1975; Eugène Delacroix. Gemälde. Zurich and Frankfurt am Main 1987/88 (exhibition catalogue).

33 M. Rosenthal: Constable. The Painter and His Landscape. New Haven and London 1983; G. Reynolds: The Later Paintings and Drawings of John Constable. 2 volumes. New Haven and London 1984.

34 J.D. Hunt and P. Willis (eds.): The Genius of the Place. The English Landscape Garden 1620–1820. London 1975; A. v. Buttlar: Der Landschaftsgarten. Munich 1980.

35 W. Hofmann (ed.): William Turner und die Landschaft seiner Zeit. Kunsthalle Hamburg, Munich 1976 (exhibition catalogue); A. Wilton: J.M. Turner. Leben und Werk. Munich 1979; M. Butlin and E. Joll: The Paintings of J. M. W. Turner. 2 volumes. New Haven and London 1984.

36 J. Ingamells: Richard Parkes Bonington. London 1979; C. Peacock: Richard Parkes Bonington. London 1979.

37 M. Pointon: The Bonington Circle. English Watercolor and Anglo-French Landscape 1790–1855. Brighton 1985, p. 80.

38 Cf. "Equivoques". Peintures françaises du XIXᵉ siècle. Musée des Arts décoratifs, Paris 1973 (exhibition catalogue); A. Celebonovic: Peinture kitsch ou réalisme bourgeois. Paris 1975; Un autre XIXᵉ siècle. Peintures et sculptures de la collection de M. et Mme Joseph M. Tanenbaum. Galerie Nationale du Canada, Ottawa 1978 (exhibition catalogue); C. Ritzenthaler: L'Ecole des Beaux-Arts du 19ᵉ siècle. Les pompiers. Paris 1987.

39 J.C. Sloane: French Painting between the Past and the Present. Artists, Critics and Traditions from 1848 to 1870. Princeton 1951; L. Nochlin: Realism. Harmondsworth 1971 (Style and Civilization, edited by J. Fleming and H. Honour); G.P. Weisberg (ed.): The European Realist Tradition. Bloomington 1982; W. Klein: Der nüchterne Blick. Programmatischer Realismus in Frankreich nach 1848. Berlin and Weimar 1989.

40 R.L. Herbert: Barbizon revisited. Essay and Catalogue. New York 1962; J. Bouret: L'Ecole de Barbizon et le paysage français au XIXᵉ siècle. Neuchâtel 1972; Zurück zur Natur. Die Künstlerkolonie von Barbizon, ihre Vorgeschichte und Auswirkung. Kunsthalle Bremen, Bremen 1977/78 (exhibition catalogue); H.-P. Bühler: Die Schule von Barbizon. Französische Landschaftsmalerei im 19. Jahrhundert. Munich 1979; L'Ecole de Barbizon. Maîtres français du XIXᵉ siècle. Ghent, The Hague, Paris 1985/86 (exhibition catalogue).

41 J. Castagnary: Salons 1857–1870. Paris 1892, p. 17.

42 A. Robaut: L'œuvre de Corot. Catalogue raisonné et illustré. 5 volumes. Paris 1904–1906; A. Schoeller and J. Dieterle: Corot. Supplément au catalogue de l'œuvre par Robaut et Moreau-Nélaton. Paris 1948; J. Selz: Camille Corot. Courbevoie 1988.

43 A. Fermigier: Jean-François Millet. Geneva 1977.

44 R. Fernier: La Vie et l'œuvre de Gustave Courbet. Catalogue raisonné. 2 volumes. Lausanne 1977/78; T.J. Clark: Image of the People. Gustave Courbet and the Second French Republic 1848–1851. London 1973; L. Nochlin: Gustave Courbet. A Study of Style and Society. New York 1976; Gustave Courbet (1819–1877), Grand Palais, Paris 1977/78 (exhibition catalogue; cf. H. Toussaint: Le dossier de "L'Atelier" de Courbet, pp. 241–272); K. Herding (ed.): Realismus als Widerspruch. Die Wirklichkeit in Courbets Malerei. Frankfurt am Main 1978; S. Faunce and L. Nochlin: Courbet Reconsidered. New Haven and London 1988; M. Fried: Courbet's Realism. Chicago 1989.

45 Kunstverhältnisse. Ein Paradigma kunstwissenschaftlicher Forschung. Wissenschaftliches Kolloquium, Institut für Ästhetik und Kunstwissenschaften der Akademie der Wissenschaften der DDR. Berlin 1988. – The expresssion "Kunstverhältnisse", used in the German text and translated here as "the conditions that prevailed in the art world", was formed by the author following R. Rosenberg's use of the expression "Literaturverhältnisse" ("prevailing literary conditions") in the title of his work: Literaturverhältnisse im deutschen Vormärz. Berlin 1975.

46 J. Allwood: The Great Exhibitions. London 1977; W. Friebe: Vom Kristallpalast zum Sonnenturm. Eine Kulturgeschichte der Weltausstellungen. Leipzig 1983; G. Maag: Kunst und Industrie im Zeitalter der ersten Weltausstellungen. Munich 1986; P. Mainardi: Arts and Politics of the Second Empire. The Universal Exhibitions of 1855 and 1867. New Haven and London 1987.

47 From K.W. Luckhurst: The Story of Exhibitions. London and New York 1951, p. 55, in 1781, the "one-picture-shows" began in London with "The Death of Chatham" by J.S. Copley. In France J.L. David exhibited his "Sabine Women" from 1799 to 1804, reaping considerable financial award. It was the contemporary relevance and sensational quality of the subject matter on view which proved the decisive factor in this and other, later cases. Short-term exhibitions free of admission held in the respective artist's studio were coming in at this time. The artist's studio as exhibition and sales gallery was to be encountered particularly in the second half of the century.

48 W. Leibl: Letter to his mother from 18ᵗʰ March, 1879. In: J. Mayr: Wilhelm Leibl. Sein Leben und Schaffen. Munich 1935, p. 78.

49 A. Boime: Thomas Couture and the Eclectic Vision. New Haven and London 1980.

50 P. Vaisse: Thomas Couture ou le bourgeois malgré lui. In: "Romantisme. Revue du dix-neuvième siècle" 17/18 (1977), pp. 103–122.

51 E. Moreau-Nélaton: Manet, raconté par lui-même. Volume 1. Paris 1926, p. 26.

52 A. Proust: Edouard Manet. Souvenirs. In: "La Revue blanche" 8 (1897), No.88–93. – In 1897, Degas disputed Daniel Halévy's claim that Manet had already used pleinair-ist impressions in the 1860s.

53 J. Mayne (ed.): Art in Paris 1845–1862. Salons and other Exhibitions reviewed by Charles Baudelaire. London 1965; C. Baudelaire: Le peintre de la vie moderne. Essais, "Salons", journaux intimes.

54 First edition in 1921. Cf. J. Rewald: see note 16, p. 116

55 Eadweard James Muybridge (1830–1904) had been experimenting since 1872 with – among others – photographs of galloping horses taken using twelve cameras, so-called "chronophotography". His photographs were published in 1878 in "La Nature". It is highly probable that Degas attended a slide show given by Muybridge in Paris in 1881. Cf. Degas. Grand Palais, Paris; Musée des Beaux-Arts, Ottawa; The Metropolitan Museum, New York. Paris 1988, p. 459 (exhibition catalogue).

56 R. Schmit: Catalogue raisonné de l'œuvre peint d'Eugène Boudin. 2 volumes. Paris 1973; J.Selz: Boudin. Paris and New York 1982.

57 Note from a sketchbook of Boudin; J. Rewald: see note 16, p. 30.

58 Monet in an interview. F. Thiébault-Sisson: Claude Monet. Un entretien. In: "Le Temps". Paris, 27ᵗʰ November, 1900. J. Rewald: see note 16, p. 30; K. Sagner-Düchting: Claude Monet. Cologne 1992, p. 11.

59 From the same interview. Rewald, ibid. p. 47; Sagner-Düchting, ibid. p. 16. For Jongkind cf. V. Hefting: Jongkind. Sa vie, son œuvre, son époque. Paris 1975.

60 Charles Gleyre ou les illusions perdues. Winthertur, Lausanne, Aarau, Marseilles, Munich, Kiel 1974/75 (exhibition catalogue).

61 Cézanne et Zola. Paris 1936. Rewald's dissertation marked the beginning of his study of Impressionism. – E. Zola: Salons. Recueillis, annotés et présentés par F. W. J. Hemmings and R.J. Niess. Geneva and Paris 1959; E. Zola: Œuvres critiques, III. Préfaces de G. Besson, H. Mitterand and G. Picon, notices et notes de H. Mitterand (Œuvres complètes. Edition établie sous la direction de H. Mitterand, 12). Paris 1969; E. Zola: L'œuvre; P.H. Feist: Zolas Kritik am Impressionismus in der Malerei. In: Realismus und literarische Kommunikation (Sitzungsberichte der Akademie der Wissenschaften der DDR, Gesellschaftswissenschaften, no.8/G). Berlin 1984, pp. 45–51.

62 Fantin-Latour. Grand Palais, Paris; Galerie Nationale du Canada, Ottawa; Fine Arts Museum, San Francisco. Paris et al. 1982 (exhibition catalogue).

63 J.-P. Bouillon (ed.): Félix and Marie Bracquemond. Mortagne-Chartres 1972.

64 No comprehensive history of the Paris "Salon" and its later splitting-up exists; all that is available is a multitude of individual studies and references in the literature. Cf. P. Vaisse: Salons, Expositions et Sociétés d'artistes en France 1871–1914. In: Saloni, gallerie, musei e loro influenza sullo sviluppo dell'arte dei secoli XIX e XX. (edited by F. Haskell) Bologna n.d., pp. 141–155, and further contributions in this vein. – Cf. K.W. Luckhurst: The Story of Exhibitions. London and New York 1951; E. Mai: Expositionen. Geschichte und Kritik des Ausstellungswesens. Munich 1986.

65 J. Rewald: see note 16, p. 16.

66 W. Hofmann. In: Courbet und Deutschland. Kunsthalle, Hamburg, and Städelsches Kunstinstitut, Frankfurt am Main 1978/79, p. 603 for no. 779 (exhibition catalogue).

67 M. Osborn. In: A. Springer: Handbuch der Kunstgeschichte. Volume 5, Leipzig ⁹ 1925, p. 175.

68 See note 61. – In detail: P. Brady: "L'Œuvre" de Emile Zola. Roman sur les arts, manifeste, autobiographie, roman à clef. Geneva 1967; R.J. Niess: Zola, Cézanne, and Manet. A Study of "L'Œuvre". Ann Arbor 1968.
69 J.L. Vaudoyer: Edouard Manet. Paris 1955.
70 W. Klein: Der nüchterne Blick. Programmatischer Realismus in Frankreich nach 1848. Berlin and Weimar 1989, p.240.
71 E. Zola: Mes haines. Paris 1867.
72 An extensive study of the work's history may be found in N.G. Sandblad: Manet. Three Studies in Artistic Conception. Lund 1954. Manet had the final version of the picture exhibited as a one-work show in Philadelphia, New York and Boston in 1879 through the mediation of travelling friends; inevitably, this proved unsuccessful.
73 Previously working for a publishing house, Zola became a freelance writer and critic in 1866. In 1867, he published a large-scale study on Manet, in whom he saw an ally in the fight for a modern realism.
74 G.P. Weisberg et al. (eds.): Japonisme. Japanese Influence on French Art 1854–1910. Museum of Art, Cleveland 1975; S. Wichmann: Japonismus. Ostasien – Europa. Begegnungen in der Kunst des 19. und 20. Jahrhunderts. Herrsching 1980; K. Berger: Japonismus in der westlichen Malerei 1860–1920. Munich 1980.
75 D. Rouart and D. Wildenstein: Edouard Manet. Catalogue raisonné. Lausanne and Paris 1975, Volume 1, p.5.
76 P. Jamot in: "Gazette des Beaux-Arts" 1918, p.152.
77 E. Lipton: The Laundress in Late Nineteenth-Century French Culture. Imagery, Ideology and Edgar Degas. In: "Art History" 3 (1980), pp.295–313.
78 Edmond de Goncourt, 13th February, 1874. Journal des Goncourt, 5, 1891, p.111f.
79 F. Daulte: Frédéric Bazille et son temps. Geneva 1952, p.135.
80 F. Daulte wrote, back in 1957 in the catalogue for the Pissarro exhibition organized by the Berne Kunstmuseum, of the need for a new consideration of the artist's output. This has now been achieved, above all through C. Lloyd, R.R. Bretell (see note 14), R.E. Shikes and P. Harper: Pissarro. His Life and Work. London 1980; R. Thomson: Camille Pissarro. Impressionism, Landscape, and Rural Labour. Birmingham and Glasgow 1990 (exhibition catalogue). Cf. C. Lloyd (ed.): Studies on Camille Pissarro. London 1986.
81 Z. Astruc quoted from L. Venturi: Les archives de l'Impressionnisme. Volume 1. Paris and New York 1939, p.31.
82 T. Thoré: Salons. Volume 2. Paris 1870, p.531.
83 K. Adler: Wiederentdeckte Impressionisten. Oxford 1988, p.95.
84 Ibid. p.96.
85 D. Rouart (ed.): The Correspondence of Berthe Morisot. London ² 1959, p.63. (5th June, 1871). Cf. recently J. Baas: Edouard Manet and "Civil War". In: "Art Journal" 44 (1985), pp.36–42.
86 J. Rewald: Cézanne and His Father. In: J. Rewald: Studies in Impressionism. Paris 1985, pp.69–101, especially pp.78–89.
87 For J. Gasquet cf. P. Cézanne: Über die Kunst. Reinbek 1957, p.98.

88 In: "L'Avenir National", Paris 5th May, 1873; J. Rewald: Histoire de l'Impressionnisme. Paris 1955, p.187.
89 Degas to Mrs. Havemeyer. In: D.C. Rich: Degas. Cologne 1959, p.19.
90 J.-K. Huysmans: Certains. Paris ³ 1898, p.23.
91 P. Cabanne: Degas. Munich 1957, p.29.
92 Cf. R.R. Bretell: Pissarro and Pontoise. The Painter in a Landscape. Thesis (unpublished) Yale University, New Haven 1977.
93 C. Lloyd: Camille Pissarro. Geneva 1981, p.72.
94 E.R. Curtius: Die französische Kultur. In: E.R. Curtius and A. Bergsträsser: Frankreich. Volume 1. Stuttgart 1930, p.165.
95 E. Zola: La Curée. Paris 1986, p.256.
96 A. Bellony-Rewald: Die verlorene Welt der Impressionisten. Berlin 1978, p.132f.
97 The details concerning the exhibition and its past history are to be found in many reminiscences and publications, among them J. Rewald: Histoire de l'Impressionnisme; D. Wildenstein: Claude Monet. Biographie et catalogue raisonné. Volume 1. Lausanne 1974, as well as in the exhibition catalogues Centenaire de l'Impressionnisme, Grand Palais, Paris 1974, and C.S. Moffett (eds.): The New Painting. Impressionism 1874–1886. Washington and San Francisco, Geneva 1986 (see note 6).
98 J. Rewald: see note 16, pp.201 and 358, note 35.
99 Henri Rouart had studied painting under Millet, and previously under Edouard Brandon (1831–1897) and Jean-Baptiste-Léopold Levert (b.1828), among others; it is possible that, through his mediation, they took part at least in the 1874 exhibition.
100 Most of the relevant articles were reprinted in the exhibition catalogue Centenaire de l'Impressionnisme. Paris 1974, with the curious exception of that by A. Silvestre. An analysis was undertaken by O. Reuterswärd in his Swedish thesis: Impressionisterna inför publik och kritik, Stockholm 1952. The language barrier would appear to be the reason why this thorough work is so seldom mentioned. The most recent relevant study may be found in P. Tucker and S.F. Eisenman in: C.S. Moffett (ed.): The New Painting. Geneva 1986.
101 J. Rewald: Cézanne and Guillaumin (first published in 1975). In: Studies in Impressionism. London 1985, pp.103–119, especially pp.106–109.
102 D. Wildenstein's localization of the motif and dating of the picture, refuting earlier suppositions: Claude Monet. Catalogue raisonné. Volume 1. Lausanne and Paris 1974, no. 364. Cf. for the critique T.J. Clark: The Painting of Modern Life. London 1985, p.190f. and colour plates XVIII and XIX.
103 J. Rewald (ed.): John Hay Whitney Collection. New York; Tate Gallery, London 1960/61, no. 47; F. Daulte: Auguste Renoir. Catalogue raisonné de l'œuvre peint. Volume 1. Lausanne 1971, no. 207–209.
104 D. Rouart and D. Wildenstein: Edouard Manet. Catalogue raisonné. Volume 1. Lausanne and Paris 1975, p.20f. Cf. M.L. Bataille: Briefe Edouard Manets. In: "Kunst und Künstler" 32 (1933) p.10–20.
105 W. Hofmann: Nana. Mythos und Wirklichkeit. Cologne 1973.
106 Ibid. p.42.

107 Ibid. p.17. Other authors are of the opinion that the model is identical with Renoir's "Anna", despite the differing bodily posture and colour of hair.
108 R. Pickvance: "L'Absinthe" in England. In: "Apollo" (London), May 1963, pp.395–398; D. Cooper: The Courtauld Collection. London 1954, p.42, note 3 and p.60f.; C.S. Moffett (ed.): The New Painting. Geneva 1986, p.161.
109 H. Dawkins: Degas and the Psychogenesis of Modernism (Critique to C. Bernheimer: Figures of Ill Repute, Representing Prostitution in Nineteenth-Century France. Cambridge (MA) 1989). In: "Art History" 13 (1990), pp.580–585, especially pp.583 and 585, note 13.
110 J. Rewald: see note 16, p.209.
111 T. Reff: Degas. The Artist's Mind. New York 1976, p.182.
112 Duranty: La nouvelle peinture. A propos du groupe d'artistes qui expose dans les galeries Durand-Ruel. Paris 1876 (new edition by M. Guérin, Paris 1946); C.S. Moffett: The New Painting, Impressionism 1874–1886. Geneva 1986.
113 R.R. Bretell: The "First" Exhibition of Impressionist Painters. In: C.S. Moffett: The New Painting. Geneva 1986, pp.189–202, especially p.190.
114 J. Burckhardt: Kulturgeschichtliche Vorträge. Edited by R. Marx. Stuttgart 1941, pp.60 and 112f.
115 About the predominant painting see among others P. Vogt: Was sie liebten … Salonmalerei im XIX. Jahrhundert. Cologne 1969, and also the studies mentioned in note 38.
116 K. McConkey: The Bouguereau of the Naturalists: Bastien-Lepage and British Art. In: "Art History" 1 (1978), pp.371–382.
117 Reproduced in a wood engraving and commented upon in T.J. Clark: The Painting of Modern Life. London 1985, repr. 96, p.190.
118 M. Wentworth: James Tissot. Oxford 1984. His rediscovery began with an exhibition in Providence (RI) and Toronto in 1968.
119 J. Claretie: L'Art et les artistes français contemporains. Paris 1876, pp.207–209.
120 Duranty: Réflexions d'un bourgeois sur le Salon de peinture. In: "Gazette des Beaux-Arts" 19 (1877). Cf. Duranty's novel, "Le peintre Louis Martin", published at the same time, the portrait of a painter marked by the impression that modern Parisian life makes upon him.
121 G. Rivière. In: "L'Impressionniste", Paris, 6th April, 1877, p.4, quoted from J. Rewald: see note 16, p.204 and C.S. Moffett: The New Painting. Geneva 1986, p.201.
122 J.-K. Huysmans: L'Art moderne. Paris 1883.
123 P. Vaisse in the title mentioned in note 64.
124 L. Venturi: Les Archives de l'Impressionnisme. Volume 1. Paris 1939.
125 Ibid. p.120 (letter from 24th February).
126 J. Renoir: Mein Vater Auguste Renoir. Frankfurt am Main 1965, p.136.
127 D. Rouart and D. Wildenstein: Edouard Manet. Catalogue raisonné. Volume 1. Lausanne 1975, p.23.
128 J. Meier-Graefe: Edouard Manet. Munich 1912; reprint in W. Teubner, ed.: Meier-Graefe: Das Fest der Farben. Berlin 1986, p.208.
129 K.H. Usener: Edouard Manet und die Vie

Moderne. In: "Marburger Jahrbuch für Kunstwissenschaft" 19 (1974) pp. 9–32, quotation p. 32 (Paper from 1959).

130 G. Clemenceau: Claude Monet. Paris 1928, p. 19 f. J Rewald: see note 16, p. 248.

131 E. de Goncourt: La Faustin. Paris 1882; E. Zola: L'Œuvre. Paris 1886. Alexandre Robert (1817–1891) had painted "Luca Signorelli Painting His Dead Small Son" back in 1848.

132 According to the reminiscences of A. André: Renoir, Paris 1923, and J.-E. Blanche: Propos de peintre. De David à Degas. Paris 1919.

133 J. Renoir: Mein Vater Auguste Renoir. Frankfurt am Main 1965, p. 99.

134 Passed on as a remark made by Cézanne to Maurice Denis in March 1905. M. Denis: Cézanne. In: "L'Occident" (Paris), September 1907; P.M. Doran (ed.): Conversations avec Cézanne. Paris 1978, p. 170.

135 For the distinction between academic and official art, see the sociological study on the art of M.-C. Genet-Delacroix: Vie d'artistes: art académique, art officiel et art libre en France à la fin du XIXe siècle. In: "Revue d'histoire moderne et contemporaine" 33 (1986), pp. 40–73.

136 H.C. and C.A. White: Canvases and Careers. Institutional Change in the French Painting World. New York 1965. Also M. Ward: The Rhetoric of Independence and Innovation. In: C.S. Moffett: The New Painting. Geneva 1986, pp. 421–442.

137 Cf. M. Ward, see note 136.

138 E. Dujardin: Le Cloisonisme. In: "Revue indépendante", 19th May, 1888, quoted following J. Rewald: Le Post-impressionnisme. De van Gogh à Gauguin. Paris 1961, p. 98. This is the most comprehensive work to deal with the problems raised here.

139 According to R. Thomson: Seurat. Oxford 1985, p. 95.

140 M. and G. Blunden: see note 16, p. 177.

141 See note 139, also J. Sutter and R.L. Herbert: Die Neoimpressionisten. Berlin 1970; A. Boime: George Seurat's "Un Dimanche après-midi à la Grande Jatte" and the Scientific Approach to History Painting. In: E. Mai and A. Repp-Eckert (eds.): Historienmalerei in Europa. Mainz 1990, pp. 303–333.

142 According to G. Kahn in the discussion of an exhibition by Puvis de Chavannes at Durand-Ruel's in late 1887. R. Thomson: see note 139, p. 116.

143 The 100th anniversary of his death was celebrated in Paris and New York by the most comprehensive exhibition to date of those works which, while less well known, are most significant within the history of art. Cf.: The Grande Jatte at 100. In: "The Art Institute of Chicago. Museum Studies" 14 (1989) no.2.

144 The artist, anticapitalist and with an ongoing commitment against war, was always interested in a realistic manner in the particular character of localities, working processes, and movements of the body, for example those performed by bathers or wrestlers. He exhibited regularly from 1889 on at the Société des Artistes Indépendants, whose president he became in 1891. Cf. D. Bazetoux and J. Bouin-Luce: Maximilien Luce. Catalogue de l'œuvre peint. 2 volumes. Paris 1986.

145 Cf. letter to his son Lucien, November 1889.

146 J. Rewald: Le Post-impressionnisme. De van Gogh à Gauguin, Paris 1961, p. 254.

147 Ibid. pp. 482 f. and 518 f. The articles by Aurier were published in the "Mercure de France", March 1891, and in the "Revue Encyclopédique" 1st April, 1892. Cf. W. Rasch: Fläche, Welle, Ornament. Zur Deutung der nachimpressionistischen Malerei und des Jugendstils. In: Festschrift Werner Hager. Recklinghausen 1966, pp. 136–160, especially p. 144.

148 For example Adolphe Leleux (1812–1891) "Un Mariage en Bretagne", 1863, Musée des Beaux-Arts, Quimper. In: Le Musée du Luxembourg en 1874. Paris 1974, no. 157 (exhibition catalogue).

149 R. Hamann and J. Hermand: Stilkunst um 1900. Berlin 1967.

150 Reprint in M. Denis: Théories, 1890–1910. Du Symbolisme et de Gauguin vers un nouvel ordre classique. Paris 1912.

151 J. Rewald: Le Post-impressionnisme. De van Gogh à Gauguin, Paris 1961, pp. 113 ff. with reproductions.

152 K. Hoffmann: Zu van Goghs Sonnenblumenbildern. In: "Zeitschrift für Kunstgeschichte" 31 (1968) pp. 27 ff. – On van Gogh in general, see the extensive study by I.F. Walther and R. Metzger: Vincent van Gogh. The Complete Paintings. 2 volumes. Cologne 1990.

153 In 1987, one version of the "Sunflowers" was sold for 250 million francs; in the same year, "The Irises" went for 300 million francs and in 1990 a version of the "Portrait of Doctor Gachet" for 450 million francs.

154 J.A. Schmol called Eisenwerth: Fensterbilder. Motivketten in der europäischen Malerei. In: Beiträge zur Motivkunde des 19. Jahrhunderts. Munich 1970, pp. 13–165.

155 M. Arnold: Henri de Toulouse-Lautrec in Selbstzeugnissen und Bilddokumenten. Reinbek 1982, pp. 37 ff. For greater detail, see W. Barthelmess: Das Café-Concert als Thema der französischen Malerei und Graphik des ausgehenden 19. Jahrhunderts. Thesis Berlin 1987.

156 W. Haftmann: Malerei im 20. Jahrhundert. Munich 1954, p. 46 f. – The book was seminal for the concept of modernist art in the German-speaking sphere of art history.

157 The process, which impossible to authenticate in every detail, is described in the light of research conducted by M. Berhaut in G. Bazin: Les Trésors de l'Impressionnisme. Paris 1958.

158 A. Dayot: Exposition des œuvres de Paul Renouard aux Galeries du Théâtre d'Application. Paris n.d., p. 13.

159 Gustave Loiseau. Didier Imbert Fine Art. A la mémoire de Durand-Ruel. Paris 1985 (exhibition catalogue). A catalogue raisonné is in preparation.

160 Thus the article by F. Monod in Thieme-Becker: Allgemeines Künstlerlexikon. Volume 3. Leipzig 1909, pp. 528–530.

161 G. Mourey: Albert Besnard. Paris 1906, pp. 123–125 (reprint of an interview with C. Morice in "Mercure de France", 1st September, 1905).

162 D. Rouart, preface to: Berthe Morisot. Zeichnungen, Pastelle, Aquarelle, Gemälde (edited by I. Moskowitz). Hamburg 1961.

163 O. Reuterswärd: Sisley's "Cathedrals". A Study of the "Church at Moret" Series. In: "Gazette des Beaux-Arts" 94, 6. per. 39 (1952) pp. 193–202, and the catalogue raisonné by F. Daulte, Lausanne and Paris 1959.

164 J. Rewald (ed.): Camille Pissarro. Letters to his son Lucien. Paris 1953 (Letter from Rouen, 2nd October, 1896).

165 Letters of the 20th April and 13th May, 1891, ibid. pp. 197 and 208 f.

166 L.R. Pissarro and L. Venturi: Camille Pissarro. Son art, son œuvre. Volume 1. Paris 1939, p. 69.

167 J. House: Monet. Nature into Art. New Haven and London 1986; H. Keller: Ein Garten wird Malerei. Monets Jahre in Giverny. Cologne 1982.

168 G. de Maupassant: La Vie d'un paysagiste. In: "Le Gil Blas", Paris 28th September, 18 1886.

169 W. Kandinsky: Rückblick 1901–1913. Berl 1913.

170 M.L. Krumrine (ed.): Paul Cézanne. Die Badenden. Kunstmuseum, Basle 1989 (exhibition catalogue).

171 W. Hofmann: Grundlagen der modernen Kunst. Eine Einführung in die symbolischer Formen. Stuttgart 1966, pp. 190–229.

172 D. Halévy: Degas parle. Paris 1960, p. 77.

173 B. Bernard (ed.): The Impressionist Revolution, London 1986, p. 85 for a photograph from c. 1896 (Malibu, J. Paul Getty Museum), which I believe to have been utilized in this year for several paintings and pastels; Degas. Grand Palais, Paris; Musée des Beaux-Arts, Ottawa; The Metropolitan Museum of Art, New York. Paris et al. 1988, no. 340, p. 549 (exhibition catalogue).

174 See note 172, p. 86.

175 G. Adriani: Edgar Degas. Pastelle, Ölskizzen, Zeichnungen. Cologne 1984, p. 96.

176 P. Tucker: Monet in the '90s. The Series Paintings. Museum of Fine Arts, Boston et al. New Haven and London 1989 (exhibition catalogue). Cf. the review of this exhibition by E. Parry Janis in: "Burlington Magazine" 132 (1990), no. 1053, pp. 887–889.

177 D. Wildenstein: Claude Monet. Catalogue raisonné et biographie. Volume 4. Paris 1985, p. 41.

178 K.H. Usener: Claude Monets Seerosen-Wandbilder in der Orangerie. In: Wallraf-Richartz-Jahrbuch 14 (1952), pp. 216–225.

179 J. Rewald: Depressionist Days of the Impressionists. In: J. Rewald: Studies in Impressionism. London 1985, pp. 203 ff.

180 Passed on by P. Borel in his edition of J. Fèvre's reminiscences: Mon oncle Degas. Geneva 1949, p. 52.

181 K. Marx in his manuscript in preparation of an introduction to the "Grundrisse der Kritik der politischen Ökonomie" from 1857. K. Marx and F. Engels: Werke. Volume 42. Berlin 1983, p. 44.

182 W. Hofmann: Grundlagen der modernen Kunst, Stuttgart 1966, p. 181.

183 E. Zola: Peinture (Le Salon de 1896). In: "Le Figaro", 2nd May, 1896. In: H. Mitterand (ed.): E. Zola: Œuvres complètes; Œuvres critiques, III, Paris 1969, pp. 1047–1052.

Part II

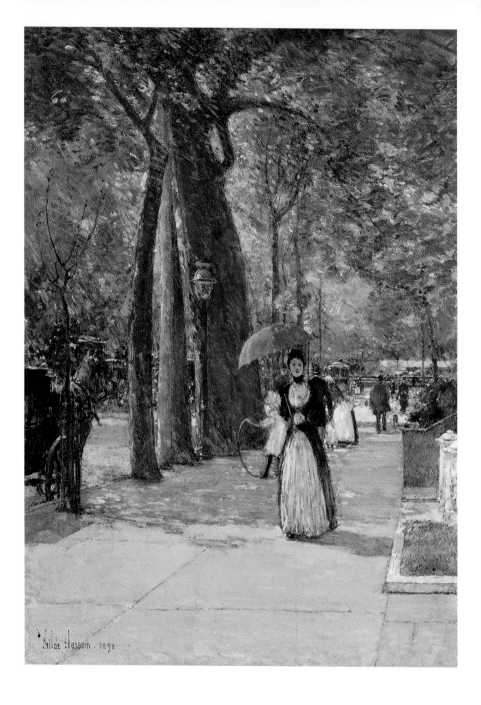

Part II

IMPRESSIONISM IN EUROPE
AND NORTH AMERICA

by

Beatrice von Bismarck,
Andreas Blühm, Peter H. Feist,
Jens Peter Munk, Karin Sagner
and Ingo F. Walther

Brief Biographies of the Authors

PETER H. FEIST, born in Varnsdorf (Czechoslovakia) in 1928, studied art history, history and archaeology in Halle, where he was assistant lecturer from 1952–1958, receiving his doctorate in 1958. 1958–1981 at the Humboldt University, Berlin, from 1968 as Professor of Art History. 1982–1990 Director of the Institute for Aesthetics and Art Studies of the GDR Academy of Sciences in East Berlin. Member of the Leibniz Society. Numerous publications on the history and theory of art, including the *Metzler Kunsthistoriker-Lexikon*. Feist's monograph on *Renoir* was published by TASCHEN. He wrote the text for "Impressionism in France" and the chapter on eastern and south-eastern Europe.

BEATRICE VON BISMARCK, born in Wiesbaden in 1959, studied art history in Freiburg im Breisgau, London and Berlin, completing a doctorate on the art-critical French reception of Gauguin in 1989. 1989–1993 research assistant at the Städelsches Kunstinstitut, Frankfurt am Main. Since 2000, Professor of Art History and Picture Studies at the Hochschule für Grafik und Buchkunst in Leipzig, of which she has been Pro-rector since 2003. Publications on art history, art criticism and art theory in the 19th and 20th centuries. Wrote the contribution on North America.

ANDREAS BLÜHM, born in Berlin in 1959, received his doctorate in 1987 on the iconography of the Pygmalion myth from the Free University of Berlin. 1988–1990 post at the Museum für Kunst und Kulturgeschichte, Lübeck, where he organized exhibitions on Ulrich Hübner and Johann Friedrich Overbeck. Exhibition director since 1990 at the Museum Ostdeutsche Galerie, Regensburg. 1993–2005 exhibition director at the Van Gogh Museum in Amsterdam, where he was responsible for the highly successful *Van Gogh and Gauguin* exhibition (2002/03). Since 2005 Director of the Wallraf-Richartz Museum, Fondation Corboud, in Cologne. Numerous publications on art history. He wrote the chapter on Germany.

JENS PETER MUNK, born in Ry in 1951, studied art history in Copenhagen and Rome from 1971–1981 and taught at the University of Copenhagen. 1984/85 curatorial assistant at the Ordrupsgaardsamlingen and Den Hirschprungske Samling. Working since 1988 as curator at the Ny Carlsberg Glyptotek, Copenhagen. 1995–2002 curator at Den Hirschsprunske Samling. Since 2002 Administrator of Public Monuments for the city of Copenhagen. Numerous publications on 19th-century art in Scandinavia and France. He wrote the contribution on Scandinavia.

KARIN SAGNER, born in Erlabrunn-Steinheidel (Erzgebirge) in 1955, studied art history and history of literature in Munich. In 1983, she completed a doctorate on Monet's water-lily paintings. Research assistant at the Bayerische Staatsgemäldesammlungen in Munich until 1988. Freelance author since 1989. Freelance exhibition curator since 1995, including "Monet and Modernism" (2001/02). Her study *Claude Monet 1840–1926. A Feast for the Eyes* was published by TASCHEN. Wrote the contributions on the Netherlands and Belgium, Italy, Spain and Great Britain.

INGO F. WALTHER (1940–2007) was born in Berlin and studied literature, medieval studies, literature and art history in Frankfurt am Main and Munich. His publications for TASCHEN include *Vincent van Gogh. The Complete Paintings* (in collaboration with Rainer Metzger), *Pablo Picasso 1881–1973* (in collaboration with Carsten-Peter Warncke) and *Codices illustres. The World's Most Famous Illuminated Manuscripts*. He was the editor and compiled the directory of Impressionism.

Contents

10 Painting in the Netherlands and Belgium in the Impressionist Period

Tradition and Modernity:
The Hague School and the Amsterdam Impressionists

Dutch 17th-century art made its exciting impact not only on the French pre-Impressionist Barbizon painters, who saw the landscapes of a Salomon van Ruysdael (1600–1670) as modern in flavour (compared with the idealized landscapes of academic art) and as expressing a view of Nature in line with their own endeavours. The French Impressionists themselves also recognised those qualities. In addition, the art of Frans Hals (c. 1583–1666) and Jan Vermeer (1632–1675) increasingly attracted their interest in the 1860s. What they valued in Hals was particularly the freedom of his broad brush-strokes, while in Vermeer they admired his colourist virtuosity.

The French artists approached the Dutch old masters they esteemed not only by copying paintings in the Louvre but also through contemporary writings such as those of the critic Théophile Thoré (1824–1869). Furthermore, the personal contacts between French and Dutch artists were many. Thus Monet named the Dutchman Johan Barthold Jongkind (1819–1891) as his most important mentor (beside Boudin), to whom he owed a new and more intense view of Nature. Monet first met Jongkind in 1862, though like many of his contemporaries he had already admired his work – primarily seascapes and beach scenes – at the Paris Salon. Jongkind's highly sensitive use of colour, and his subtle rendering of atmospherics and effects of light on water or snow, were of particular interest. His airy landscapes, flooded with light and established with relatively economical and free brushwork, made Jongkind a significant precursor of Impressionist art.

Jongkind illustrates in a special way the distinctive relations and mutual influences of Dutch and French art, relations that were of such consequence for Impressionism. He first studied in The Hague under the landscape artist Andreas Schelfhout (1787–1870). In Paris, where he continued his studies in 1855 and worked in the studio of Eugène-Gabriel Isabey (1803–1886), the marine artist, Jongkind took a close interest in the art of the Barbizon school, whose view of Nature seemed to tend in the direction he was himself pursuing. That same year, disappointed by his failure to win an award at the Paris World Fair, he

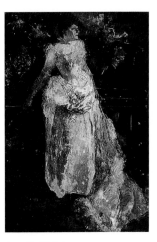

George Hendrik Breitner
Portrait of Mrs. Theo Frenkel-Bouwmeester, 1887
Portret van vrouw Theo Frenkel-Bouwmeester
Oil on canvas, 217 x 152 cm
Amsterdam, Stedelijk Museum

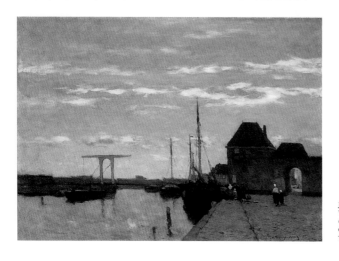

Johannes Hendrik Weissenbruch
View of Haarlem
Gesicht op Haarlem
Oil on canvas, 72 x 102 cm
The Hague, Haags Gemeentemuseum

returned to Rotterdam. When he next visited Paris in 1860, with water-colours and wintry or moonlit landscapes he had done in Holland, he was so great a success with his fellow artists and the critics that he decided to concentrate on the sought-after Dutch motifs of his home parts every summer from then on. Paintings such as the *View of Rouen* (p. 409) date from the decade (up to 1870) of his artistic breakthrough. His palette lightened at this time. His brushwork was bold, uncon-strained and sketchy, revealing his interest in recording the mood and atmospherics of the moment.

Inspired by Jongkind and the Dutch old masters, several of the French Impressionists travelled at various times to the Netherlands, to study in museums and paint the landscape. It was the paintings of windmills and canals Monet did on his stay in Zaandam in 1871 that prompted Boudin to view him as the future leader of the Impressionist movement. Dutch artists in the later 19th century, in their turn, were led by the Barbizon

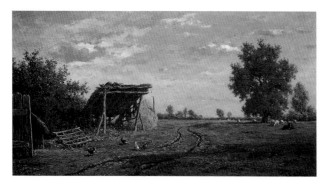

Willem Roelofs
Summertime, 1862
Zomer
Oil on panel, 27 x 49.2 cm
Utrecht, Centraal Museum, on loan from
the Van Baaren Museum Foundation

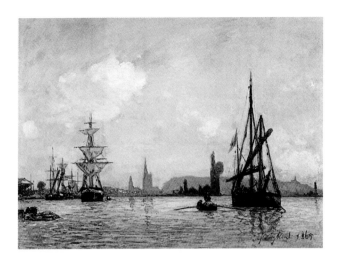

Johan Barthold Jongkind
View of Rouen, 1865
Oil on canvas, 41.9 x 56.2 cm
Hefting 336. Private collection

school's example to introduce greater tensions into their work. This produced a more searching scrutiny of Nature, and a more comprehensive sense of their own nation's art.

The Hague School was of signal importance in this context. Its heyday ran from the 1860s to the 1880s, and the achievement of those years earned 19th-century Dutch art a new respect and reputation. Johannes Warnardus Bilders (1811–1890) had already withdrawn in the 1850s to Oosterbeek, the "Dutch Barbizon", a wooded region where he painted from Nature; and soon he had attracted a number of pupils, among them Anton Mauve (1838–1888). In the summer months they were joined by the brothers Jacob Hendricus (1837–1899), Matthijs (1837–1917) and Willem Maris (1844–1910), and by Willem Roelofs (1822–1897), Jozef Israëls (1824–1911) and Johannes Hendrik Weissenbruch (1824–1903). Most of these artists had already had first-hand experience of Barbizon art; moreover, Dutch art dealers were frequently offering works by the Barbizon school for sale at that period.

In 1871, a number of these painters settled in the Hague. It was a charming small town then, still largely untouched by industrialization. That move, and their joint exhibition at the academy of art there in 1875, marked the birth of the Hague School. Contemporary critics were quick to highlight their realistic bent, the relatively new ways of seeing and representation, and the grey tonalities of their paintings; the emphasis of tonality over colour sometimes supplied grounds for adverse criticism. The Hague painters, in freeing their brushwork and establishing a more intense relation with Nature, cited their great Dutch predecessors, particularly Rembrandt, Vermeer, Hals and the 17th-century realists; this rather blunted the point of hostile criticism, given that the status of these artists was no longer contested. Nonetheless, the Hague School was not a unified movement, nor did its coherence last: there were signs that it was breaking up as early as the mid-1880s, when landscape began to change under expanding industrialization. The artists had largely contented themselves with seascapes and views of mills in the idyllic region around The Hague and Scheveningen. They also painted tranquil interiors and genre pieces. Israëls – along with Mauve, the brothers Maris, Roelofs and Weissenbruch – was the foremost representative of this line. During studies in Paris he had met Jongkind and the Barbizon painters, and, beginning with a romantic, historicizing style, had quickly developed an arresting approach that at times owed a palpable debt to the tragic realism of Rembrandt. His subject matter, which earned him success throughout Europe, was mainly the life of ordinary people – peddlers, tailors, fishermen. Among his many admirers were the young Liebermann and van Gogh.

While Weissenbruch's teacher, Schelfhout, had placed little value on painting in the open, for Weissenbruch and other artists of the Hague School, with their knowledge of Dutch 17th-century art and the Barbizon school, *plein-airisme* became fundamental. Taking Daubigny's floating studio, "Le Botin", as their model, Weissenbruch and Roelofs regularly went out in boats. Roelofs' pasture, windmill and canal landscapes – of which *Summertime* (p. 408) is a fine example – use lighting effects that express a painterly freedom comparable with Daubigny's. Weissenbruch's spacious Dutch scenes, such as *View of Haarlem* (p. 408), contrast in their use of bolder and broader brushwork. In their own specific, lyrical way, drawing foremost on the colourist juxtaposition of silvery blues and greens with warmer shades, Weissenbruch's paintings nicely captured the moist atmosphere that lies upon Dutch landscapes.

Jacob Maris, another prominent figure in the Hague School, initially painted figural work, and subsequently landscapes. Six years in Paris gave him ample opportunity to study French art, and he especially admired Courbet and the atmospheric panoramic views of Daubigny. Back home, painting his native Dutch landscapes with a muted palette that registered subtly intimate nuances of light and hue, he evolved a distinctively Dutch style in works such as *Allotment Gardens near The Hague* (p. 413). His brother Matthijs was exposed to various influences during his studies in the Hague, Paris and London. He espoused the sensitive realism of the Hague School in figural work, landscapes (such as *Quarry at Montmartre*, p. 413) and portraits; but the impact of the later German Romantics and of the English Pre-Raphaelites also produced in Matthijs Maris a strong tendency towards dreamy, fairy-tale realms. Willem Maris in his turn, who was in fact a student under his brothers at The Hague Academy, was more fully Impressionist. He assigned a dominant role to effects of shimmering light, concentrating on the Dutch landscape (*Dusk*, p. 412) and paintings of animals.

Though they viewed an immediate response to Nature as the essential prerequisite for landscape art, studies painted on the spot, with a fresh and spontaneous air to them, mainly served the Hague artists purely as preparation. The final oil was painted in the studio from the preliminary

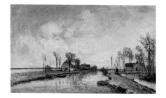

Johan Barthold Jongkind
Dutch Landscape, 1862
Landschap
Oil on canvas, 34.5 x 56.6 cm
Hefting 230. Private collection

Johan Barthold Jongkind
Rue de l'Abbé-de-l'Epée and Church
of Saint James, 1872
*La rue de l'Abbé-de-l'Epée et l'église
Saint-Jacques du Haut-Pas*
Oil on canvas, 47 x 33.5 cm
Hefting 580. Paris, Musée d'Orsay

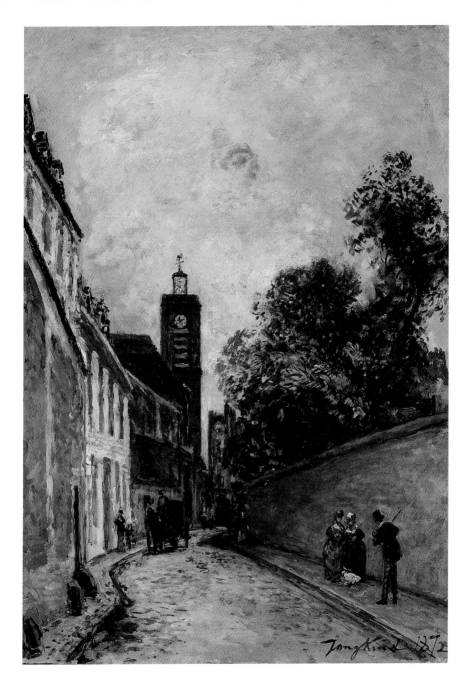

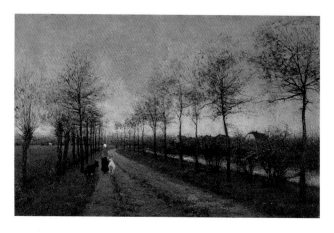

studies. This fact, with their subject matter and their (initially) tonality-dominated palettes, constituted signal differences from the contemporaneous major phase of French Impressionism. The artists of the Hague School are better described as realists of a pre-Impressionist cast than as Impressionists of a distinctive – and distinctively Dutch – kind.

Once The Hague began to lose its appeal for them, Roelofs and Weissenbruch preferred to paint in the polders. Mauve moved to Laren, where Albert Neuhuys (1844–1914), another member of the Hague School, had settled in the meantime. Soon there was talk of a Laren School and a new "Dutch Barbizon", but in fact it was thematically more or less a continuation of the Hague art. Mauve, a cousin of van Gogh (whom he often advised on his art), was primarily drawn to pasture landscapes and street scenes of considerable colourist sophistication. His contemporaries were not slow to admire the wonderfully silvery and

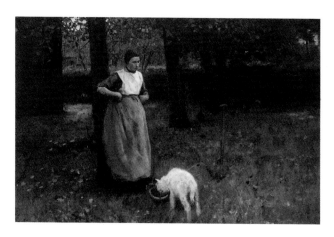

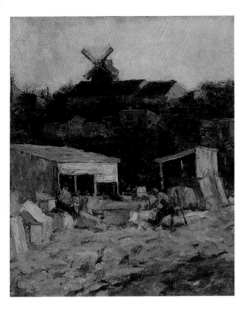

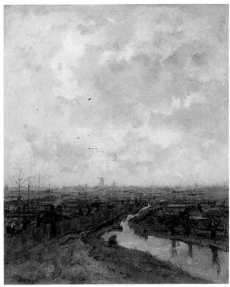

diffuse light in his paintings, his relaxed brushwork, and his atmospherics (as in *Laren Woman with Goat*, p. 412).

For younger artists such as George Hendrik Breitner (1857–1923) and Isaac Israëls (1865–1934), son and pupil of Jozef, The Hague soon felt like a backwater. They preferred the city life of Amsterdam, where the 1880s saw a large number of artists working in Impressionist modes and attempting to cut loose from the Hague School. Certainly, the Hague artists were abandoning their grey tonalities during the decade, lightening their palettes, using stronger colours, and relaxing their brushwork. But the major subject for the Amsterdam Impressionists was now city life. Closer to the French Impressionists in their thematic concerns, they painted scenes of modern life, and the simple pleasures of city people, consciously working social components into their art. The Amsterdam group – which included Breitner, as its leader, Israëls, and Floris Hendrik Verster (1861–1927) – took a great interest in Naturalist literature. Indeed, Breitner was nicknamed the "Zola of Amsterdam". After van Gogh, with whom he was in touch in 1882 and 1883, he was assuredly the most important Dutch Impressionist. A pupil of Willem Maris, he studied in Paris in the 80s, and painted Barbizon-inspired work in Cormon's studio. The examples of Manet (whose 1884 retrospective he saw), of Monet, Pissarro and Degas, and of Japanese art, were crucial to his future development.

Even so, Breitner's pastose interiors with their audacious brushwork, and his full-length portraits, retained their visible links with specifically national traditions. Dutch qualities reminiscent of a Rembrandt or Ver-

Matthijs Maris
Quarry at Montmartre, c. 1871
Steengroeve bij Montmartre
Oil on canvas, 55 x 46 cm
The Hague, Haags Gemeentemuseum

Jacob Hendricus Maris
Allotment Gardens near The Hague, c. 1878
Slatuintjes bij The Hague
Oil on canvas, 62.5 x 54 cm
The Hague, Haags Gemeentemuseum

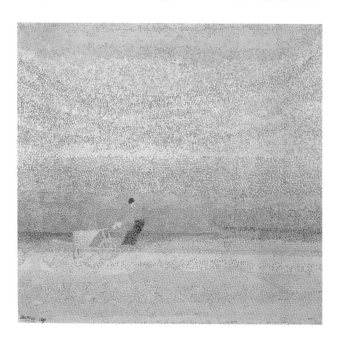

Jan Toorop
Shell Gathering on the Beach, 1891
Schelpenvisser op het strand
Oil on canvas, 61.5 x 66 cm
Otterlo, Kröller-Müller Museum

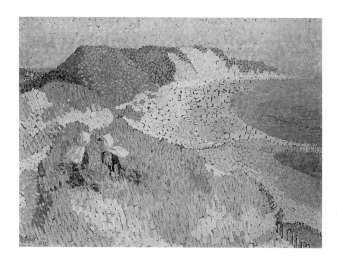

Jan Toorop
The Dunes and the Sea at Zoutlande, 1907
Duinen en zee te Zoutlande
Oil on canvas, 47.5 x 61.5 cm
The Hague, Haags Gemeentemuseum

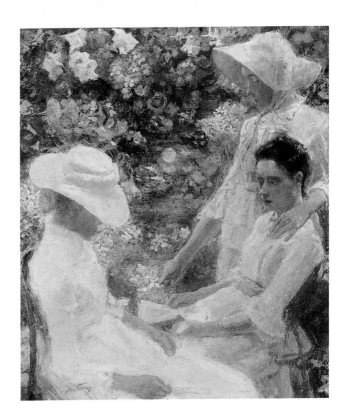

Jan Toorop
Three Women with Flowers, c. 1885/8
Trio fleuri
Oil on canvas, 110 x 95 cm
The Hague, Haags Gemeentemuseum

meer are apparent in the loving presentation of fabrics, furniture and tiled floors in his interiors, for instance. *The Earring* (p. 417), painted in Breitner's most prolific period between 1886 and 1901, is characteristic of his reduced and understated palette using only a few colours such as black, white and brown, and done with a spatula. His preference for dark colours earned his idiosyncratic style the sobriquet Black Impressionism. In works such as *The Dam* (p. 416), Breitner successfully drew out the poetry in everyday life. In later work, he had a predilection for scenes of old Amsterdam seen at dusk or on overcast winter days. His range of subjects also included working life in the city; this was an interest he shared with Verster and Israëls, in such works as their pictures of servant girls.

Verster's Impressionist eye for reflections and for blocks of colour informed not only the landscapes he painted, mainly around Leiden, but also still lifes squarely in the great Dutch tradition. Israëls betrayed a frequent stylistic proximity to Breitner in his Amsterdam years from 1885 to 1903; inspired by Zola, he tackled city subjects such as factory workers, sailors' bars, prostitutes and cabarets. This led him to join the

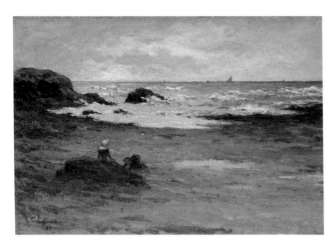

rival Amsterdam artists' group, the Tachtig. At Scheveningen he met Liebermann. From the mid-80s he worked in the open, painting scenes that make a very spontaneous impact; his tonally harmonic palette and transparent coloured shadows marvellously caught atmospheric phenomena that he had carefully observed. In later years, particularly following his sojourn in Paris from 1903 to 1904, his technique became looser and sketchier. Israëls steadily became a pre-eminent Dutch Impressionist (p. 419).

The generation of Willem Bastiaan Tholen (1860–1931) and Willem de Zwart (1862–1931) combined the Hague School and Amsterdam Impressionist approaches by deliberately rejecting the "grey school" and tackling modern, urban subject matter. Tholen did this in unusual butchers' and slaughterhouse paintings. Willem Witsen (1860–1923)

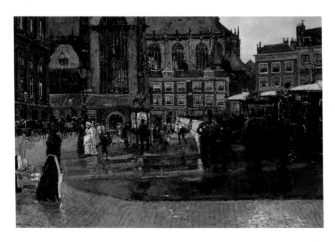

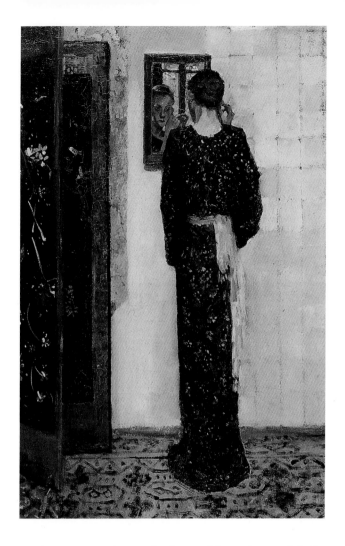

George Hendrik Breitner
The Earring, c. 1893
Het oorringetje
Oil on canvas, 84.5 x 57.5 cm
Rotterdam, Museum Boymans-Van Beuningen

struck a more narrative note in pictures of Amsterdam canals in the snow, or the bridges and squares of London in the fog.

The foundation of the Hague Art Circle also reflected the new developments in art. Jan Theodorus Toorop (1858–1928), who ran the painting section, established contact with the internationalist Les Vingt in Belgium, which smoothed the Dutch artists' way to a prompt assimilation of French and Belgian Neo-Impressionism. Toorop studied at the Amsterdam Academy and subsequently in Brussels, where his most important teacher was James Ensor (1860–1949). He and Ensor became friends and visited Paris together, where Toorop's appreciation of French art, and particularly Manet, became substantial. A visit to England left him with a taste for Whistler. In the 1880s, Toorop shared with the Brussels artists an interest in Neo-Impressionism. The work he painted, exhibited with Les Vingt and elsewhere, used muted tonal harmonies influenced by Whistler, as well as a systematic division of brushwork and a pointillist use of colour dots derived from the Neo-Impressionists (pp.414, 415). In the 90s, Toorop turned increasingly to Art Nouveau and to the arts and crafts revival, quickly becoming a major figure in Belgian Art Nouveau. His work of that period was highly stylized in draughtsmanship and thematically prone to symbolist reverie.

Dutch artists such as Hendrik Pieter Bremmer (1871–1956) and, for a while, van Gogh, also followed the pointillist or divisionist line. Nevertheless, the dominance of the Hague School was to remain till the First World War, with even Piet Mondrian (1872–1944) following the example thus set in his early years. In 1892, Mondrian entered the Rijksakademie in Amsterdam, where he met Breitner and, questing for

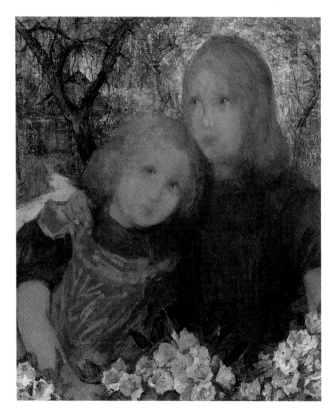

Piet Mondrian
Idyll, c. 1900
Lente Idylle
Oil on canvas, 73.5 x 62 cm
Seuphor 227. Private collection

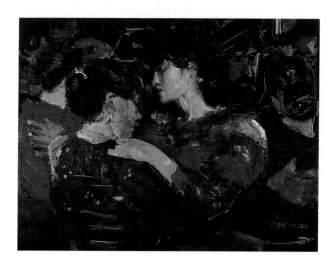

Isaac Israëls
In the Dance Hall, 1893
In het danshuis
Oil on canvas, 76 x 100 cm
Otterlo, Kröller-Müller Museum

new means of expression, showed a growing interest in Impressionism –
which thus had an influence on developments that were to go much
further (*Idyll*, p. 418).

Impressionism in Belgium

Belgium became an independent kingdom in 1831 following the nationalist revolt of the previous year. Related feelings of national autonomy
were manifest in Belgian art of the time. From 1863 on, the writer Camille Lemonnier (1844–1913) repeatedly insisted on the distinctness of
the Belgian nation's art and literature. Belgian art shared the fine traditions of the Low Countries, and in the Flemish painters Peter Paul
Rubens (1577–1640) and Pieter Breughel the Elder (1525/30–1569)
numbered some of the greatest European artists in its ancestral line. In
the second half of the 19th century, though, Belgian art was strongly
under the influence of neighbouring France. The art scene there opened
up options that seemed already available or adumbrated in local art.
History painting, highly esteemed, fitted this pattern most obviously; the
leading artists in this genre were Ferdinand Pauwels (1830–1904) and
Louis Gallait (1810–1887).

In the later 19th century, Belgium was economically one of the most
advanced countries in Europe. The social problems which this involved
were reflected in a committed art that dealt with the world of the poor;
and it is scarcely surprising, then, that realism was so successful in 19th-
century Belgium. In Flemish and Dutch art alike, realism had a significant tradition that could look back to a Breughel or an Adriaen Brouwer

(1605/06–1638). In the 1860s and early 1870s this background produced an admiration of the new French art, in particular that of Courbet and Millet. One of the foremost Belgian artists in this line was Constantin Meunier (1830–1905), whose landscapes and scenes of everyday life presented the hard life of workers and miners with a true-to-life realism that yet contrived to include symbolist touches. The interest aroused by this style of art was such that in 1867 the Société libre des Beaux-Arts was founded.

French Impressionism met with a warm welcome in Belgium. Among the upper middle classes of Brussels and Ghent there were many affluent collectors of an open-minded, cosmopolitan kind, and the art of Degas

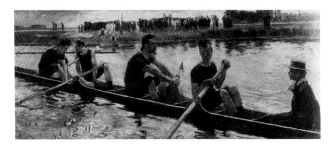

Guillaume van Strydonck
The Oarsmen, 1889
Les canotiers
Oil on canvas, 84.5 x 201.9 cm
Tournai, Musée des Beaux-Arts

and Manet had its following there at a fairly early stage. Nonetheless, Impressionism made only a gradual impact on Belgian art. The Tervueren School played an important part in gaining its entry. Tervueren, a village in Brabant, had attracted a number of artists who made the first Belgian attempt to deal extensively with the subject matter of the Barbizon artists; and so Tervueren was quickly dubbed "the Flemish Barbizon". One of the most important of these painters was Isidore Verheyden (1846–1905), who combined the Barbizon style (familiar to Flemish artists from their sojourns at Fontainebleau) with an Impressionist interest in fleeting atmospheric effects, an interest that appeared mainly in his landscapes and coastal scenes. Verheyden, who was a founder member of Les Vingt in Brussels in 1884, was sceptical in regard to the ultimate implications of Impressionism, though, and later left the group. Around 1880, his enthusiasm for light and *plein-airisme* was also shared by artists such as Joseph Adrien Heymans (1839–1921), working at Termonde near Ghent, and prompted luminous, brighter, clearer use of colour. One of Verheyden's best known pupils was Anna Boch (1848–1936), who had a perceptive grasp of the problems and currents in modern art. At an early date she bought works by Seurat and Gauguin, among others, as well as the only painting van Gogh sold in his lifetime. Boch too was a member of Les Vingt; the group played a decisive role in the Belgian reception and dissemination of Impressionism.

Les Vingt, like the Indépendants in Paris, existed in order to promote new, innovatory art. The twenty members (either Belgian or resident in

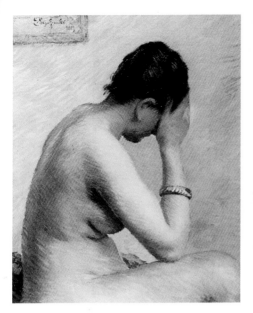

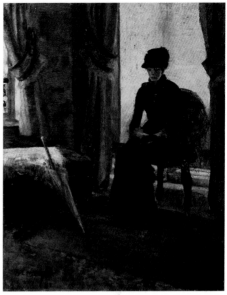

Emile Schuffenecker
Female Nude Seated on a Bed, 1885
Femme nue assise sur un lit
Oil on canvas, 65 x 45 cm
Private collection

James Ensor
The Dejected Lady, 1881
De sobere dame
Oil on canvas, 100 x 81 cm
Brussels, Musées Royaux des Beaux-Arts
de Belgique

Belgium) included Georges Lemmen (1865–1916), Guillaume Vogels (1836–1896), Alfred William Finch (1854–1930), Théo van Rysselberghe (1862–1926), Fernand Khnopff (1858–1921), Henry van de Velde (1863–1957), Toorop, and Ensor, among others. They planned annual exhibitions at which the twenty members and the same number of invited artists at home and abroad would show work. There were also concerts and poetry readings. The very first exhibitions featured Impressionist art from France and Britain. The secretary and leader of the group was a lawyer, Octave Maus (1856–1919). When Les Vingt was disbanded in 1893, it was Maus who created La Libre Esthétique, an association that provided an internationally recognised forum for modernist aesthetics and ideas up till the First World War, thus assuring Brussels its role as an avant-garde centre around the turn of the century. Together with Edmond Picard (1836–1924) and the writer Emile Verhaeren (1855–1916), Maus used the new weekly magazine "L'Art Moderne" to profile both the aims of Les Vingt and the international art scene in general.

The magazine's Paris correspondent was Fénéon, a writer who (as we have seen in Volume I) was closely associated with Neo-Impressionism in France. Indeed, it was Fénéon who first coined the term Neo-Impressionism in "L'Art Moderne" in 1886, in an article on Signac and Seurat, who were exhibiting for the first time that year at the eighth Impressionist exhibition and were prompting controversy. Interestingly, this new offshoot style was rapidly adopted by Les Vingt: replacing the line by the point or dot was the very kind of liberation from conventional norms

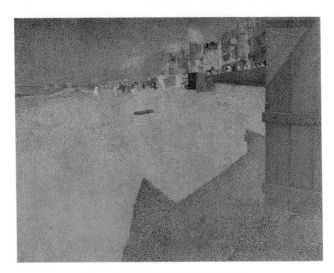

Henry van de Velde: Bathing Huts at Blankenberge, 1888
Strand med badhokjes in Blankenberge
Oil on canvas, 71 x 100 cm
Billeter/Hammacher 18. Zurich, Kunsthaus Zürich

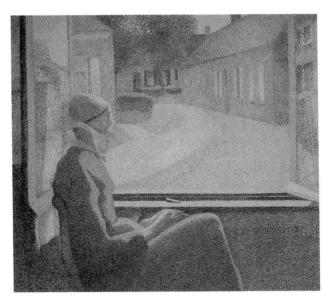

Henry van de Velde: Woman at the Window, 1889
Zittende vrouw voor een venster
Oil on canvas, 111 x 125 cm. Billeter/Hammacher 20
Antwerp, Musée Royal des Beaux-Arts

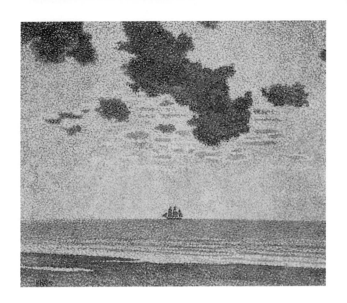

Théo van Rysselberghe
Heavy Clouds, Christiania Fjord, 1893
Grote wolken, Christiania Fjord
Oil on canvas, 50.8 x 63 cm
Indianapolis (IN), Indianapolis Museum of Art

that Belgian artists were calling for. Thus Seurat's famous picture *A Sunday Afternoon at the Ile de la Grande Jatte* (pp. 260/261) – the first work in which the artist applied his new divisionist principles of colourism – was exhibited with Les Vingt as early as 1887. The interchange between French and Belgian artists was constant and active.

Flemish artists, though ready in their reception of Impressionism, adopted the approach in a more structured form; this was apparent in their greater emphasis on draughtsmanship and chiaroscuro features. This resulted in the occasional juxtaposition of native Flemish styles with imported Impressionist styles that derived from the French. The more Flemish version was to be found in the work of Vogels (who began in Tervueren); Albert Baertsoen (1866–1922), one of whose finest paintings was *Ghent, Evening* (p. 431); Ferdinand Willaert (1861–1922); and the early Ensor. The major exponents of the more French-oriented line were Emile Claus (1849–1924), who painted in the style of Monet; Henri Evenepoel (1872–1899), a friend of Toulouse-Lautrec; and the foremost Belgian Neo-Impressionist, Rysselberghe. Other artists active between 1880 and 1918, who made the Impressionist period in Belgium so notable, included Guillaume van Strydonck (1861–1937); Willy Schlobach (1864–1951), who was inspired by Turner and Monet; Rodolphe (1860–1927) and Juliette Wytsman (1860–1925), a married couple both of whom were painters; and the self-taught Marcel Jefferys (1872–1924), who was also inspired by Monet.

Claus did not start out as a painter. As a student at Antwerp, he rebelled against the academic instruction of his Romantic tutor, Narcisse de Keyser (1813–1887). A stay in Paris, and the art of Bastien-Lepage,

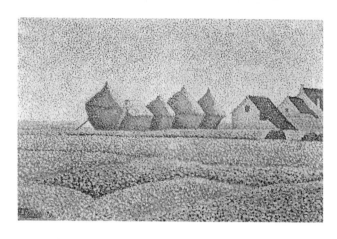

Alfred William Finch
Haystacks, 1889
Les meules de foin
Oil on canvas, 32 x 50 cm
Brussels, Musée d'Ixelles

prompted work that echoed the social concerns of Zola. Claus spent the winters of 1889 to 1892 in Paris and – though draughtsmanship of an academic kind always remained fundamental in his view – he steadily adopted more of the Impressionist techniques and subjects, moving further and further from the earthy tonalities of the Antwerp school. Paintings such as Sunshine and A Corner of my Garden (p. 427) show how intensely he grappled with the phenomenon of light and different atmospheric conditions. His subjects, frequently landscapes, recall Monet. At his home, "Zonneschijn", near Astène – restructured by van de Velde – Claus entertained numerous artist and writer friends such as Verhaeren, on whom he exerted a considerable influence. His active presence on the Belgian art scene also included membership of Les Vingt and the Libre

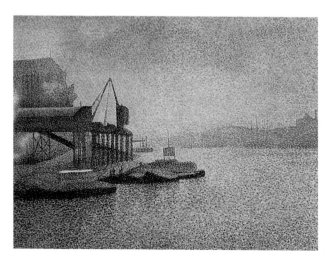

Georges Lemmen
View of the Thames, 1892
Vue de la Tamise
Oil on canvas, 61 x 86.7 cm
Providence (RI), Museum of Art,
Rhode Island School of Design

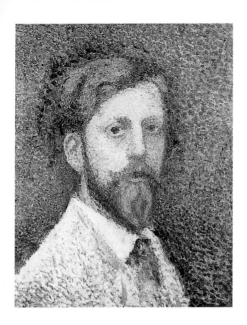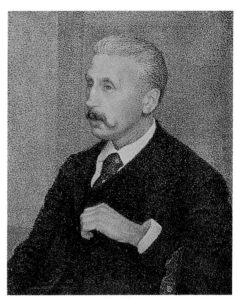

Esthétique. In 1904, with Ensor, Lemmen, Boch and others, he founded the Cercle vie et lumière. Claus was extremely successful, both at home and abroad. His numerous pupils, among them Georges Morren (1868–1941), constituted a fairly homogeneous group within Belgian Impressionism. Claus's significance was unjustly eclipsed by the rise of Belgian Expressionism.

Evenepoel, resident in Paris from 1892, took an enthusiastic interest in Montmartre life in his paintings, posters and illustrative work. In the late 1890s – his most productive period, brought to an abrupt end by the artist's early death – he painted portraits, street scenes and interiors. Evenepoel studied in Moreau's studio, where (by his own report) he learnt that "every brush-stroke must be guided by feeling", and that colour must be at once thought and dreamt if it is to render Nature imaginatively. This conviction led Evenepoel to a highly personal brand of Impressionism. *Sunday in the Bois de Boulogne* (p. 428) and *Veterans' Festival* (p. 429) demonstrate his flair for unusual composition. His Sunday walkers in the Bois de Boulogne seem to be walking out of the canvas to right and left, at different speeds, as in a snapshot. The left edge of the picture is audaciously cropped, and left of centre there is an empty space that seems to be pushing the actual movement out to the sides. Compositionally, this highly idiosyncratic picture recalls Toulouse-Lautrec, while the colours, featuring Evenepoel's preferred ochres, owe more to Moreau. Evenepoel's colourism and expressive brushwork constitute a meeting of Impressionism and Fauvism, and make his art one of the finest

Georges Lemmen
Self-Portrait, 1890
Zelfportret
Oil on canvas, 43 x 38 cm
Lausanne, Samuel Josefowitz Collection

Théo van Rysselberghe
Portrait of Auguste Descamps, the Painter's Uncle, 1894
Portrait d'Auguste Descamps, l'oncle du peintre
Oil on canvas, 64 x 53 cm
Geneva, Musée du Petit Palais

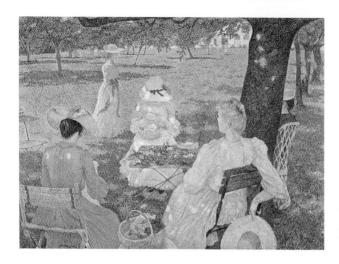

Théo van Rysselberghe
Family in an Orchard, 1890
Famille assemblée dans un verger
Oil on canvas, 115.5 x 163.5 cm
Otterlo, Kröller-Müller Museum

achievements in late 19th-century painting. He himself was a friend of both Impressionists and Fauvists; one friend he had made during his apprentice years in Paris was Matisse, who esteemed him highly.

Rysselberghe too was close to Fauvism in his later years. Like his friends Maus and Verhaeren, he was a member of Les Vingt, and played a decisive part in disseminating French and British avant-garde art in Belgium. His earliest work showed a strong interest in portrait painting, and he naturally enough received his first Impressionist influences primarily from the portrait work of Manet, Degas and Whistler. He was also impressed by Spanish art and by Hals. This fascination was reflected in his relaxed but powerful brushwork and his strongly contrastive effects of light. In 1886 Rysselberghe made contact with Seurat and Signac, and his style evolved in a Neo-Impressionist direction. From that time on he regularly exhibited at Neo-Impressionist shows in Paris. His pointillist *Heavy Clouds, Christiania Fjord* (p. 423), painted in 1893, is largely based on complementary contrasts of blue and orange, and of yellow and violet; the central coupling of blue and yellow establishes the most powerful contrast in terms of light and dark and of warm and cold. This serves to highlight the heaviness of the rainclouds, their irregular shapes making them stand out all the more above the calm line of the watery horizon. This picture is Rysselberghe at his most Seuratian, his technique deploying effects of colour, contour and shape in ways that were squarely in line with the cognitive psychology of the time.

As well as van de Velde, Rysselberghe ventured into the applied arts, which were undergoing a notable international revival at the turn of the century. The Arts and Crafts movement in England had provided the main spur, rejecting modern mass production and calling for a return to cottage ideals of craft. This implied involving art in every area of life

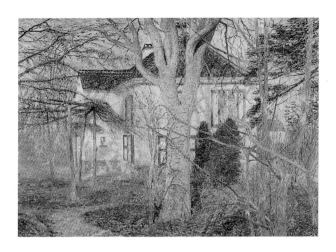

Emile Claus
Sunshine, 1899
Zonneschijn
Oil on canvas, 80.5 x 116.5 cm
Paris, Musée d'Orsay

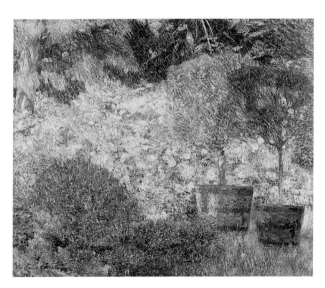

Emile Claus
A Corner of my Garden, 1901
Un coin de mon jardin
Oil on canvas, 60 x 74 cm
Private collection

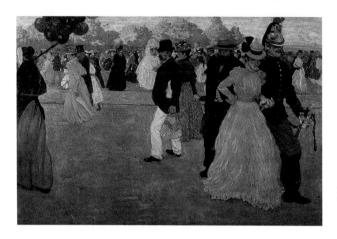

Henri Evenepoel
Sunday in the Bois de Boulogne, 1891
Zondag in het Bois de Boulogne
Oil on canvas, 59 x 90.2 cm
Antwerp, Musée Royal des Beaux-Arts

and experience, and in this respect the ideal resembled that of the "Ge-samtkunstwerk". Integration of this kind was widely considered an es-sential prerequisite if societal conditions were to be radically changed. Les Vingt were quick to espouse these ideas. Rysselberghe did illustra-tions for literary works (especially those of the Belgian symbolist writers), made posters, and designed catalogues and furniture. His true talent, though, was nevertheless as a painter. His art began to undergo a change after 1898, following a visit to Paris, and he turned increas-ingly to nudes and open-air scenes, done in relaxed, Impressionist brushwork. About 1908 he abandoned the Neo-Impressionist approach altogether.

Briefly, between 1889 and 1892, Finch also tried his hand at Neo-Impressionist techniques, under the influence of his meetings with Seurat and Pissarro, and works such as *Haystacks* (p. 424) resulted. In 1897 Finch settled in Finland, and after 1900 he was primarily important in the applied arts, into which he tried to import Neo-Impressionist theories of colour and proportion. Like many of his contemporaries, Finch be-lieved art could expand to include other areas of experience and thus effect a fundamental improvement in life; social utopianism of this kind often appeared in aesthetics at that date. In Helsinki he became professor of ceramics and established the Septem group, which successfully intro-duced Impressionism – and particularly Neo-Impressionism – into Fin-land. Like his friend Ensor, Finch had studied at the Academy in Brussels; both were founder members of Les Vingt.

Finch's friend Lemmen, a richly talented and unjustly forgotten painter, was also quick to be fired by Impressionist innovations, and published articles on the subject in "L'Art Moderne". He repeatedly criticized Belgium's public exhibition facilities. Influenced by Rysselber-ghe and his own friendship with Seurat and Signac, Lemmen adopted a Neo-Impressionist technique, locating his own personal, poetic version

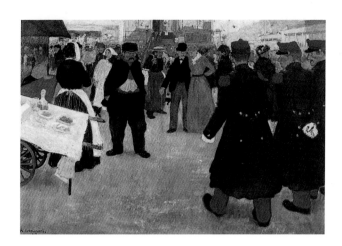

Henri Evenepoel
Veterans' Festival, 1898
La fête aux invalides
Oil on canvas, 80 x 120 cm
Brussels, Musées Royaux des Beaux-Arts
de Belgique

of pointillism in such works as his *View of the Thames* (p. 424). Though
he was successful at exhibitions (including the Indépendants in Paris)
with his Neo-Impressionist paintings, and particularly with his portraits,
Lemmen began to change his position again from 1895 on, tending increasingly towards an espousal of the more traditional views of Claus
and Heymans – together with whom he would create the Cercle vie et
lumière in 1904. The artists of this circle were known as the Luminists,
and included those who had been trying to find suitable ways of presenting light since the Termonde School. Lemmen's intimate works, such as
the *Self-Portrait* (p. 425), which surely best expressed the artist's reticent,
introspective nature, now became suggestive of Renoir or Bonnard. But
Lemmen also played a significant part in the foundation of the L'Art
group, which contributed to the applied arts revival in Belgium. He himself did posters, tapestries, ceramics, and book illustrations, as well as
watercolours and drawings; yet to this day he has largely been denied his
due recognition.

Van de Velde was also associated with the circle of Claus and Heymans after attending the Antwerp Academy and Carolus-Duran's studio
in Paris. He was one of the most important and influential artists at the
turn of the century, albeit less in painting than in architecture and the
Arts and Crafts movement. Van de Velde's predilection for motifs from
farming life was reflected in his high opinion of Millet's and Pissarro's
art. In 1887 he first saw Seurat's *Grande Jatte*, which influenced his own
style, with the result that in 1889, as one of Les Vingt, he exhibited
Neo-Impressionist paintings such as *Bathing Huts at Blankenberge* and
Woman at the Window (p. 422), which are among his best known
works. From 1890 van de Velde's attention was increasingly on other
artistic fields, and around 1894 he abandoned painting for good. For
many artists, Impressionist or Neo-Impressionist styles were simply a
transitional phase on the way to Symbolist or Expressionist art of a kind

that has often been explained in terms of a "mystical" tendency in Flemish painting.

Symbolism evolved alongside Impressionism. The major Belgian Symbolists were Khnopff and Ensor, but the style was also evident in the mysticism of the first Sint Martens Laten School – the "Flemish Pont-Aven" near Ghent – where Gustaaf van de Woestijne (1881–1947) and others established the link with Flemish Expressionism. The artists of this group had all started out in Impressionism and then moved on to Expressionism. Ensor's work exemplifies the development: from *The Dejected Lady* (p. 421) he moved on to carnival scenes, ghosts, monsters, and the masks for which he is famous, evolving a highly idiosyncratic realistic-cum-symbolist style that in some ways echoed the fantastic tradition of Hieronymus Bosch (1450–1516) and Breughel – in other words, the great heritage of Flemish and Dutch art. In sum, it can be said that the new, autonomous, individualist approach that distinguished Belgian art between 1884 and 1913 owed a crucial debt to the Impressionist breakthrough – which indeed ultimately made modern art in Belgium possible.

KARIN SAGNER

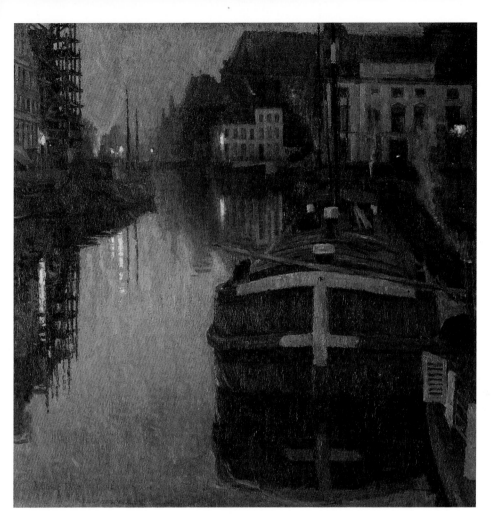

Albert Baertsoen
Ghent, Evening, 1903
Gand, le soir
Oil on canvas, 151 x 155 cm
Brussels, Musées Royaux des Beaux-Arts de Belgique

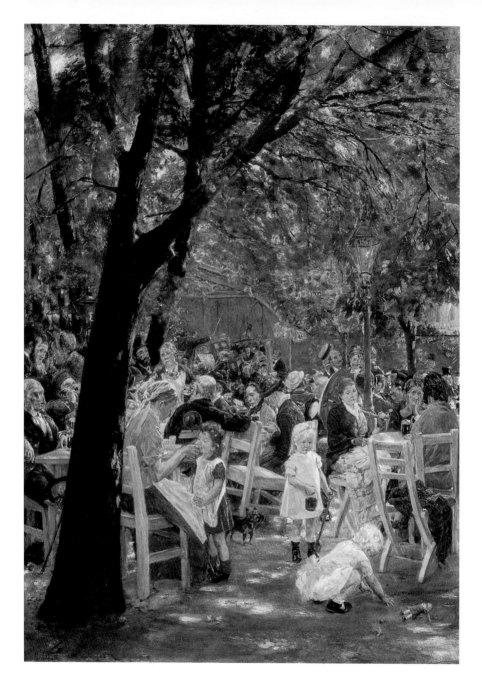

11 "The light of freedom": Impressionism in Germany

German and French Impressionism

"The division of colour is all nonsense. I have just
seen it once again: Nature is simple and grey."
MAX LIEBERMANN

French Impressionism remains the yardstick by which Impressionism in other countries is judged, and this naturally applies to Germany too. The achievements of forerunners such as Karl Blechen (1798–1840), Carl Gustav Carus (1789–1869), Johann Georg Dillis (1759–1841), Wilhelm Leibl (1844–1900), Adolph von Menzel (1815–1905), Carl Schuch (1846–1903) or Johannes Sperl (1840–1914) were crucial to the subsequent development of *plein-airist* painting. And yet, regardless of the specifically national tradition that lay behind German Impressionism, the fact remains that the younger artists increasingly had to make their way in the international market, judged by international critics. And that meant Paris.

The French capital had superseded Rome as a place of artistic pilgrimage. The academies and private art schools, as well as the world fairs held there since 1855, had only consolidated the position of Paris, and the list of German painters who duly went there resembles a who's who of German Impressionism: Max Liebermann (1874–1935), Gotthard Kuehl (1850–1915), Fritz von Uhde (1848–1911), Lesser Ury (1861–1931), Lovis Corinth (1858–1925), Heinrich von Zügel (1850–1941), Max Slevogt (1868–1932), Wilhelm Trübner (1851–1917), Leo von König (1871–1944) and Albert Weisgerber (1878–1915). Scholars have justifiably wondered what these artists were looking for in Paris – and what they found. Critics often emphasize that the German artists knew little of the new developments in art. Some point out that the Germans tended no longer to be young, and indeed to be well advanced in their technical grasp, by the time they first encountered French Impressionism. Others deny there was any connection whatsoever.

What the artists themselves said tends to be not very informative. Familiarity with the new French art generally cannot be documented till the 1890s. Since the recorded responses largely dovetail, it is fair to assume that the artists were not merely trying to safeguard their own work's claims to originality. To what extent the legacy of enmity between the Germans and French following the Franco-Prussian War played a part is a moot point. Corinth, whose stinting political view of the world was in line with the prevailing patriotic mood, reported that

Max Liebermann
Munich Beer Garden, 1884
Münchner Biergarten
Oil on canvas, 95 x 69 cm
Munich, Bayerische Staatsgemäldesammlungen,
Neue Pinakothek

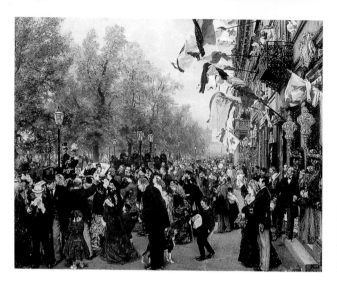

Adolph von Menzel
Departure of King Wilhelm I for the Front,
31 July 1870, 1871
Abreise König Wilhelms I. zur Armee
am 31. Juli 1870
Oil on canvas, 63 x 78 cm
Berlin, Staatliche Museen zu Berlin –
Preußischer Kulturbesitz, Nationalgalerie

German artists in France would deny their national origins for fear of local hostility. By the same token, the artist who was perceived in Germany as an imitator of the French was ill-advised, to say the least.

In their own country, the founding fathers of Impressionism had to wait till the close of the century for official approval. Their exhibitions were private in character and did not reach a wider public. The Salon was still seen as the major platform for those who wanted public attention and criticism based on comparison. Leibl was noticed there in 1870, and in 1874 Liebermann exhibited *Plucking Geese* (p. 434), a painting

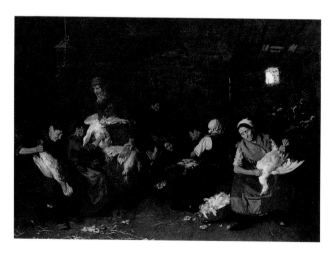

Max Liebermann
Plucking Geese, c. 1870/71
Die Gänserupferinnen
Oil on canvas, 172 x 118 cm
Berlin, Staatliche Museen zu Berlin –
Preußischer Kulturbesitz, Nationalgalerie

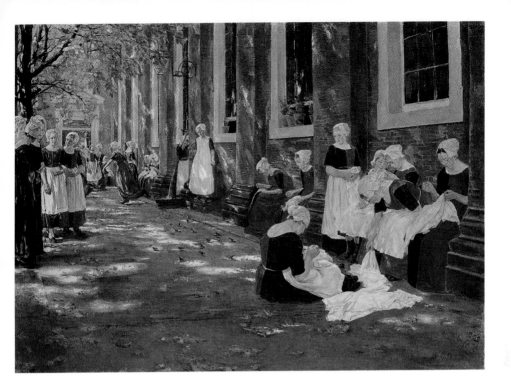

that used the earthy heaviness of his early work and had been damned two years earlier in Berlin as representing "the absolute in ugliness". Liebermann later owned paintings by Manet, including *Bundle of Asparagus* (p. 198). His own interest was in the Barbizon School; and Courbet, Leibl's friend, still attracted the admiration of German painters of a progressive disposition.

In 1880 Uhde exhibited his *Chanteuse* (Munich, Neue Pinakothek) at the Salon. The painting strongly recalls Franz Defregger (1835–1921). In 1884 Corinth submitted his *Conspiracy* (whereabouts unknown), which had won a bronze medal in London. In this painting and those done in Paris, no influence of French Impressionism is detectable, which is scarcely surprising, given that he was studying at the Académie Julian under Bouguereau, the academic Salon painter. Could it be that the reservations younger French artists had concerning the venerable Salon and its celebrated artists had not yet reached German ears?

Our first evidence of German acquaintance with the Impressionists dates from 1883, when Gurlitt's in Berlin put Carl and Felicie Bernstein's collection on view. The public had no idea what to make of what they saw. The writer and critic Jules Laforgue (1860–1887), one of the early advocates of Impressionism, was at the court in Berlin at that time, em-

Max Liebermann
The Orphanage at Amsterdam, c. 1881/82
Freistunde im Amsterdamer Waisenhaus
Oil on canvas, 78.5 x 107.5 cm
Frankfurt am Main, Städelsches Kunstinstitut und Städtische Galerie

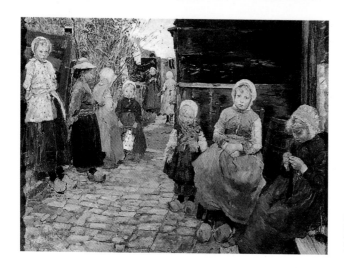

Fritz von Uhde
Fisher Children in Zandvoort, 1882
Fischerkinder in Zandvoort
Oil on canvas, 60 x 80 cm
Vienna, Neue Galerie in der Stallburg

ployed to read to the German Empress; and the exhibition did not escape his keen notice. "If Berlin acquires even a modicum of insight into art, it will be the doing of Herr Gurlitt", he observed. But the public response did not encourage a repeat show, and the Bernstein collection was to remain an exception for some time.

By the turn of the century, Gauguin and Denis had been exhibited in Germany and French Impressionism, though not yet fully established there, was becoming familiar. The critics set about discovering simi-larities with modern German art – which provided opponents with a weighty argument, the accusation that the German artists were "aping" the French. This hit the Germans where it hurt; for all their admiration for the French achievement, they did not want their own work dismissed as imitative.

Once it had been levelled, the accusation prompted intense efforts to show how German Impressionism (now thus described) differed stylisti-cally from French. The artists never tired of defining their own auton-omy. Liebermann's famous assertion that Nature is grey, quoted at the head of this chapter, was meant programmatically, and illustrates a di-lemma that confronts art criticism to this day when it has to label the style of the period in Germany

According to Horst Imiela, the term "Impressionism" was first applied to German painting by the dealer Paul Cassirer (1871–1926). Imiela cites Corinth's wife as his source. But surely the earliest description of a Ger-man painting as "Impressionist" came from Laforgue's pen. In his mem-oirs of Berlin he noted that Menzel's *Coronation of King Wilhelm I at Königsberg* (Hanover, Niedersächsisches Landesmuseum), painted in 1861–1865, featured "an attempt at Realism, indeed at Impressionism, remarkable in official art".

Menzel's *Departure of King Wilhelm I* (p. 434) depicted the Berlin street bustle with a virtuoso yet free brushwork, and a disdain for the draughtsman's minutiae, that anticipated later solutions of this thematic problem. Menzel's subject is so displaced from the centre that we do not indeed see it till we look more closely. What matters more to him is the difficult task of conveying a crowd's enthusiastic mood, which he does through the accumulation of details. It is not without irony that, of the relatively few German paintings that deal with contemporary public affairs, there is this one that employs Impressionist technique even before the term was in currency. Though Menzel's colourist method may seem related to that of the Impressionists, his relation to the movement was, however, a tarnished one, and he told the Bernsteins his poor opinion of the French paintings they hung in their home in no uncertain terms.

The formal affinities which the art of Liebermann, Corinth and Slevogt (to name only the three leading figures) bore to French Impressionism naturally obscure the differences which emerge on closer inspection. The most signal criterion in differentiating between German and French Impressionism is the way the paint is applied. Liebermann was not alone in his aversion to the scientific division of appearance into the colours of the spectrum. Juxtaposing almost unmixed colour tonalities was not for the Germans. We can see how the attitudes compare if we consider a subject whose very changeability invites experiment, a subject which is indeed intimately associated with the origins of Impressionism as a

Fritz von Uhde
Two Daughters in the Garden, 1892
Zwei Töchter im Garten
Oil on canvas, 145.5 x 116.5 cm
Munich, Bayerische Staatsgemäldesammlungen, Neue Pinakothek

Fritz von Uhde
Big Sister, 1885
Die große Schwester
Oil on card, 48.5 x 33 cm
Munich, Städtische Galerie im Lenbachhaus

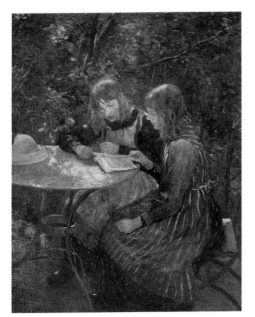

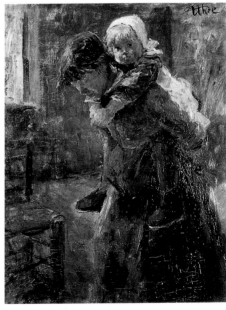

term: water – or, to be exact, the surface of moving water with the shifting play of light on it. Monet's revolutionary treatment of sunlight on water in the 1872 landmark painting *Impression: Sunrise* (p. 113) had had so little influence, twenty-two years later, on the well-informed and deliberate artist Leopold von Kalckreuth (1855–1928), that the German artist felt no need to go beyond the linear drawing of waves in his painting *Returning Dockworkers on the Elbe* (Hamburg, Hamburger Kunsthalle).

This comparison shows how representationally fixated on their subject German artists remained during the act of painting. Yet both principles open up new directions. And both options – which could be interpreted as a striving for greater truthfulness in recording what was seen, and thus as a higher objectivity – opened the door to a new subjectivity. Where Monet and his successors liberated colour, the Germans drew their growing strength from an ever more relaxed handling of the line, which was gradually permitted a life independent of the subject, a presence that expressed an individual signature. The development of Corinth's art affords the best example of this.

In their approach to composition there were similarities and differences between the Germans and French. The latter usually gave equal attention to every part of a composition, whereas the Germans might place emphases, as Liebermann's *Woman with Goats* (p. 442) nicely shows. In this picture, the major interest lies in the contrast between the heroic compositional treatment and the everyday nature of the motif.

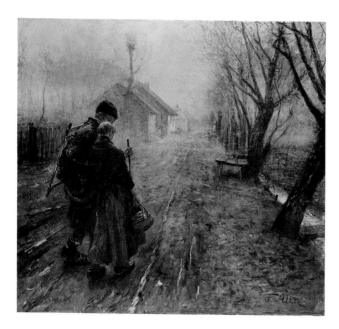

Fritz von Uhde
Walking to Bethlehem, c. 1890
Der Gang nach Bethlehem (Schwerer Gang)
Oil on canvas, 117 x 126 cm
Munich, Bayerische Staatsgemäldesammlungen,
Neue Pinakothek

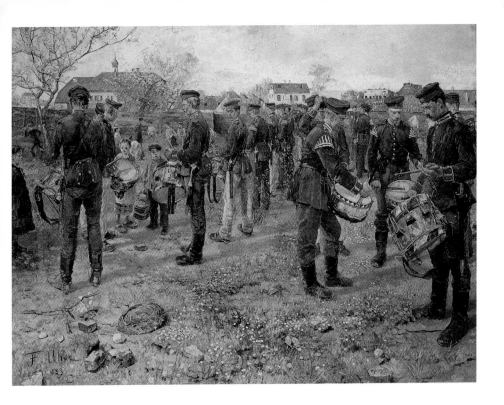

Of greater weight was the contrast between the French and German Impressionists' choices of subjects. Germany abounded in genre paintings of everyday life and leisure, but the German Impressionists' use of their new style for narrative or history paintings would have been unthinkable among the modern French artists. This feature of German Impressionism has often been ignored by critics, or dismissed as a false start, on the grounds that it had nothing in common with Impressionism as conceived by the French.

Turn-of-the-century neo-classicism, and the triumphant achievements of Arnold Böcklin (1827–1901) and Max Klinger (1857–1920), demonstrated that as the 19th century closed it was still usual to treat abstracts such as happiness, love and peace in allegorical fashion. The leaning towards history painting discernible in Corinth and Slevogt, in Trübner, and occasionally even in Liebermann, suggests that the German Modernists were not out to break with academic tradition. Rather, they tried to adapt it to their own preferences. Corinth's history paintings might be described as realistic idealism. At all events, they are far removed from any principle of art for art's sake. Still, Impressionist history painting constituted a more drastic assault on habitual ways of seeing than a focus

Fritz von Uhde
Bavarian Drummers, 1883
Die Trommelübung (Bayerische Trommler)
Oil on panel, 72 x 95 cm
Dresden, Gemäldegalerie Neue Meister

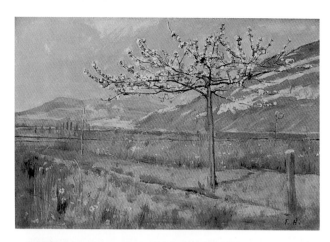

Ferdinand Hodler
Apple Tree in Blossom, c. 1890
Blühender Apfelbaum
Oil on canvas, 26.5 x 40 cm
Winterthur, Oskar Reinhart Collection

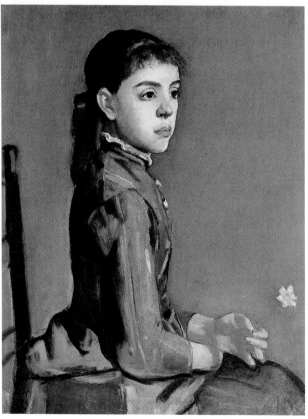

Ferdinand Hodler
Portrait of Louise-Delphine Duchosal, 1885
Bildnis Louise-Delphine Duchosal
Oil on canvas, 55 x 46 cm
Zurich, Kunsthaus Zürich

on landscape could have done. The inherent contradiction between grave subjects and light styles could not always be overcome. And only painters prepared to compromise, such as Hugo Vogel (1855–1934) or Ludwig Dettmann (1865–1944), won official commissions and painted murals on public buildings. This might be placed under the heading of what Karl Scheffler (1896–1951) termed "Salon Impressionism".

Of course the label "Impressionism" was not uncontroversial or capable of unambiguous interpretation in France. Whether masters such as Manet or Degas can properly be included in the group is debatable. Scheffler, a leading apologist of German turn-of-the-century Modernism, retrospectively attempted a definition that concentrated on the intellectual background of the style and has a certain across-the-board validity: "When every object is dissolved in an atmosphere, and the aim is to present light, air and motion, the painter can only use means of representation that pass over the detail in favour of the overall impression perceived by the eye and nothing else." If everything is reduced to this common denominator, it is no longer of great moment that Monet and Pissarro render light in juxtaposed, unmixed brush-strokes while Liebermann and Slevogt continue their attempt to capture the specific shade or tonality of an object. Their differing methods of dissection and sketching basically establish a similar effect, that of something visually registered in an instant – an impression.

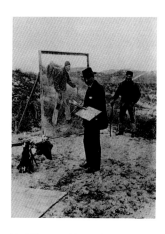

Max Liebermann and his model at work in the open on "Peasant Walking" (destroyed 1945). 1894

A Brief History of German Impressionism

In 1907 art historian Richard Hamann (1879–1961) published his study "Der Impressionismus in Leben und Kunst", in which he attempted a retrospective overview. The title of his book promised to deal with Impressionism in life and art, and implied a programmatic extension of the term across the genre divides, an aim which may not strike us as audacious or indeed questionable. Hamann proposed criteria by which Impressionism could be identified in various areas. In music, it was anti-logical and expressed a neurasthenic awareness; in poetry, it was atmospheric and given to repetition; in philosophy, it was subjective and vivid. Characteristically for his period, he felt that the crux was "a feverish longing for spontaneity, for the free movement of light in open spaces, such as the creative moment offers: in its entire uniqueness, in a constant state of flux within its own laws, yet subject to chance as well."

This view, which seems to suit Expressionism better, may not immediately appear apt to the serious toil that went into German Impressionist works, which often make a less radical impression than works by French contemporaries. But the new stress on the artist's individual achievement was undoubtedly relevant to the Germans too. Realism, and the principle of truth, were the soil that nourished German Impressionism; but they were superseded by the painter's autonomy. It was only through *plein-airisme* that Liebermann's "imagination in painting" became possible.

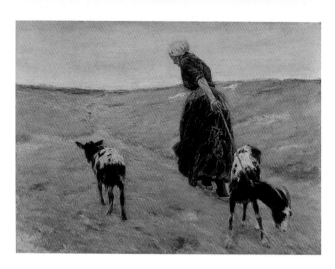

Max Liebermann
Woman with Goats, 1890
Frau mit Ziegen
Oil on canvas, 127 x 172 cm
Munich, Bayerische Staatsgemäldesammlungen,
Neue Pinakothek

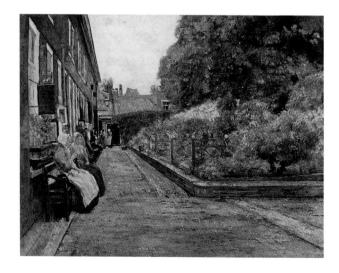

Max Liebermann
St. Steven's Foundation, Leyden, 1889
Stevenstift in Leiden
Oil on canvas, 78 x 100 cm
Berlin, Staatliche Museen zu Berlin –
Preußischer Kulturbesitz, Nationalgalerie

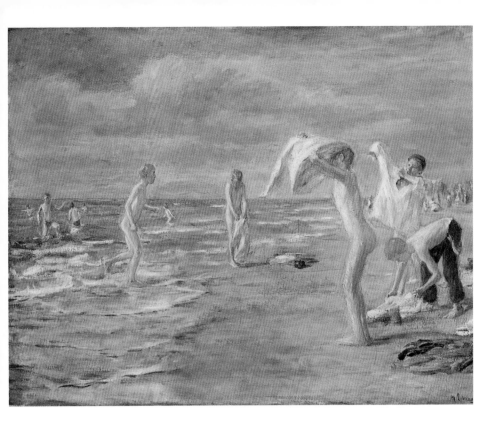

Max Liebermann
Boys Bathing, 1898
Badende Knaben
Oil on canvas, 122 x 151 cm
Munich, Bayerische Staatsgemäldesammlungen,
Neue Pinakothek

Painting in the open had been established decades before, by various painters. At the great centennial exhibition at the Nationalgalerie in Berlin in 1906, when Impressionism was at its peak, the public was bewildered to find that much that had been supposed a revolutionary innovation was already there in the work of artists long since canonical. The "Impressionist" Menzel was discovered. Names such as Blechen or Christian Morgenstern (1805–1867) were remembered, and the value of the oil study as a genre in its own right was registered. German art, partitioned into schools, had come up with stunning achievements; and work had often been done in parallel, at various places, in mutual ignorance. The art colleges at Karlsruhe, Munich and (from 1860) Weimar had demonstrated a more tolerant flexibility than those at Düsseldorf and Berlin. The struggle for realism, and for a higher estimation of landscape art, had flared up anew in the 1850s and 1860s. In contrast to France, though, the debate did not spread beyond academic circles.

Liebermann, born in 1847, was the eldest of the leading German Impressionists. Like Leibl, he had roots in realism. Like most of his fellow travellers, he had enjoyed academic training; but even his choice of the new art college at Weimar, modern in outlook, was indicative of his leanings. In 1871 he met Mihály von Munkácsy (1844–1900), and the impact of the Hungarian's art confirmed Liebermann in his wish to paint a scene of everyday life in the earthy brown so prized by the realists. This picture was *Plucking Geese* (p. 434), a meticulous composition for all its vigorous brushwork. Its success was mixed; one critic damned Liebermann as the "apostle of ugliness", and his subject and technique alike bewildered the public, but he did find a purchaser for his first major work, Strousberg, a railway magnate and philanthropist.

We must pass over the factors that decided Liebermann for realism, such as his reading of Ferdinand Lassalles (1825–1864); social progress in Holland, where he travelled for the first time in 1871; or his observation of farm labour, of which Hans Rosenhagen left an account. Lieber-

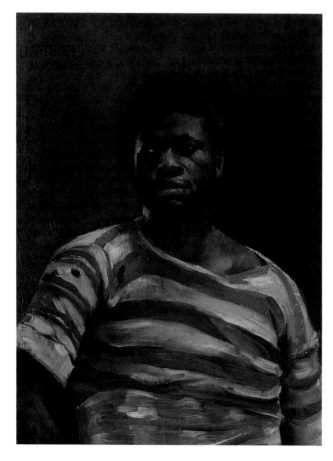

Lovis Corinth
"Othello" the Negro, 1884
Neger "Othello"
Oil on canvas, 78 x 58.5 cm
Berend-Corinth 19
Linz, Neue Galerie der Stadt Linz,
Wolfgang-Gurlitt-Museum

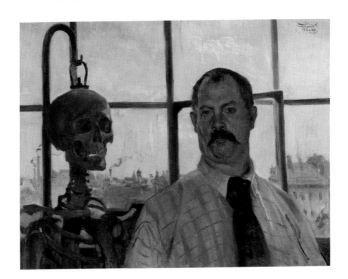

Lovis Corinth
Self-Portrait with Skeleton, 1896
Selbstbildnis mit Skelett
Oil on canvas, 66 x 86 cm
Berend-Corinth 135
Munich, Städtische Galerie im Lenbachhaus

mann's love of the simple life probably derived less from political conviction than from his own well-to-do middle-class background and his
childhood in the heart of Berlin. It is important to bear in mind that his
use of subjects drawn from working life was not a reflection of the new
German Empire's boom years, but rather a reflection of a pre-industrial
state.

In 1872, a year after the Franco-Prussian War, Liebermann spent his
first fortnight in Paris; other sojourns were to follow. He wanted to see
the masterpieces of realist art, and was especially anxious to see Barbizon, the famous home of *plein-air* art, with his own eyes. But of greater
moment for German Impressionism were his visits to Holland, which
had lost its position as the centre of art over the centuries. In 1871 and
subsequently, he repeatedly visited Holland, some of his stays there being
lengthy – even before "Les maîtres d'autrefois" by Eugène Fromentin
(1820–1876) sparked off a fashion for Holland. It is impossible to say
what fascinated Liebermann most – the undramatic landscape with its
distinctive colours; Rembrandt, Hals, and other old masters whose
painterly liberty he felt kin to; or the works of contemporaries such as
Mauve or Jozef Israëls. In a painting on a Dutch subject, *The Orphanage
at Amsterdam* (p. 435), painted in 1881/82, Liebermann began to put the
blacker shades of his early realism aside, and to brighten up his palette.
For the first time he rendered sunlight falling through trees perfectly. It
is a truly Impressionist perception; but it was not the fruit of any spontaneous inspiration, nor a sketch hastily set down. As Günter Busch
rightly stresses, this composition – which seems so effortless and unde-
liberate – was the result of careful thought and months of hard work.
What may be even more surprising is that maturer works of this kind

were not done in the open at all, but were studio paintings done in the traditional manner from sketches.

The Dutch period in Liebermann's work was followed by the Menzel period. Adolph von Menzel's virtuoso use of colour inevitably influenced his German Impressionist successors. Liebermann's *Munich Beer Garden* (p. 432) most strikingly reveals his debt to Menzel. This convivial scene of folk life, with its even brushwork, is still far removed from the major form of *Woman with Goats* (p. 442). Despite continuing spiteful criticism, Liebermann was now to score his first successes. His *Old Men's Home in Amsterdam* (private collection), painted in 1881, brought him the first French award made to a German painter since the Franco-Prussian War.

The other modern German painter to enjoy international success was Uhde. Born the year after Liebermann in 1848, he began studies at the Dresden Academy in 1866 but soon broke them off in order to serve as a soldier for the next ten years. In 1877/78 he settled in Munich and became a pupil of Munkácsy, with an interruption when he visited Paris in 1879/80. The pictures of the largely self-taught Uhde drew on the legacy of realism, and their narrative lyricism placed them squarely within the cliché conceptions of sentimental German sensibility in art. His pastose, patchy application attests the formal freedom now won by artists; but Uhde himself would never have embraced the full experimentalism of the French. Rather, the impact of his art derived from the tension between stylistic openness and expressive content – even if this conflict was generally neutralized in some form.

Bavarian Drummers (p. 439), painted in 1883, is set on a Munich parade ground. Uhde stresses the random positioning of his numerous figures – though it required meticulous study and endless preliminary sketching before he was satisfied with the arrangement. Both monumental and as incidental as a snapshot, the painting baffled the public. Uhde was more successful with *Walking to Bethlehem* (p. 438), painted around 1890. This

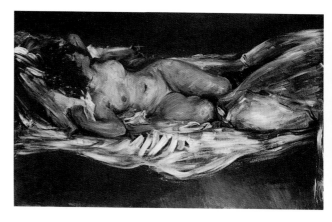

Lovis Corinth
Reclining Nude, 1899
Liegender weiblicher Akt
Oil on canvas, 75 x 120 cm
Berend-Corinth 179
Bremen, Kunsthalle Bremen

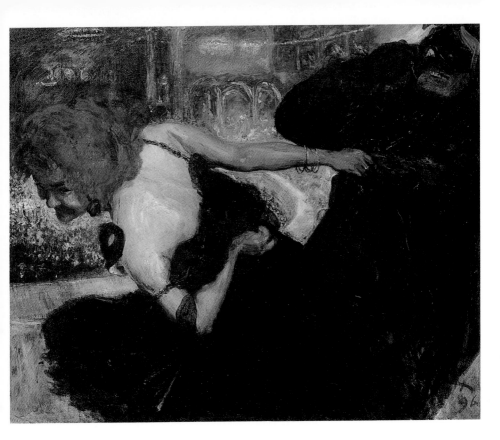

translation of Mary and Joseph's journey to Bethlehem into contemporary costume and a familiar environment was immediately accessible.

More Impressionist in subject and colouring was the 1892 *Two Daughters in the Garden* (p. 437). Though the subject is carefree, the painting is not without melancholy. The Impressionist style – which Uhde has not unreservedly embraced – retains its function of characterizing the girls. Admittedly Uhde has essayed a sense of the random moment and image, such as are essential to the Impressionist style; but his figures do not occupy their space with the disregard and independence of figures in Degas' work.

Trübner, born in 1851, was also of Liebermann's and Uhde's generation. The Munich International Art Exhibition of 1869, and meetings with Leibl, Courbet and Schuch, made a deep impression on him, and he used his new-found freedom to develop a highly individual style in representing the natural world (pp. 449, 461). Trübner's brushwork was notable for its deliberation, and he juxtaposed and contraposed colours, albeit without dividing them. Like the German Impressionists generally, he respected the

Max Slevogt
Dance of Death, 1896
Totentanz
Oil on canvas, 102 x 123 cm
Nuremberg, Germanisches Nationalmuseum,
Georg Schäfer Collection

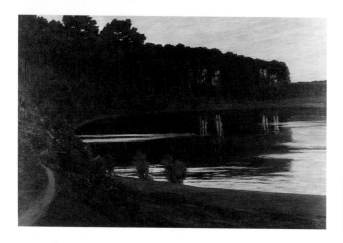

Walter Leistikow
Sundown at Lake Grunewald, 1898
Sonnenuntergang über dem Grunewaldsee
Oil on canvas, 167 x 252 cm
Berlin, Staatliche Museen zu Berlin –
Preußischer Kulturbesitz, Nationalgalerie

given colours of objects. While the group around Monet and Pissarro established an airy atmosphere by separating brush-strokes, Trübner's landscapes had a tactile three-dimensionality to them. His influence on the next generation in Germany cannot be exaggerated. Many younger artists, including those who did not study under him, admired him unreservedly and gladly acknowledged that they had learnt the most from him.

The most famous of them was Corinth, who met Trübner in Munich. Corinth had already spent several years at the extremely conservative Königsberg Academy, which was under the influence of Berlin, before moving to the Bavarian capital in 1880. There he studied under Defregger and Ludwig von Löfftz (1845–1910). In the early years, Corinth's development as artist was not untypical. His early portraits used the brown shades that had been preferred from Leibl to Franz von Lenbach (1836–1904). In 1884 he went to Paris and studied at the Académie Julian. As a German, he was not particularly popular; but he was proud of the praise of his tutor Bouguereau, the academic painter (p. 188). Like so many others, Corinth was torn between striking out in new directions and striving after official recognition, and he submitted to the Salon; but in 1887, when every one of his paintings was turned down, he returned to Germany a disappointed man. Not till 1890 did he receive the longed-for honourable mention for his *Body of Christ* (whereabouts unknown). His most forward-looking work of the period was *"Othello" the Negro* (p. 444), a portrait painted in Antwerp in 1884. In this picture, Corinth was free of narrative or anecdotal ballast; and the model is seen not only for painterly qualities but also with considerable empathy.

In the 1880s, Munich was the uncontested art centre of Germany, though by then its splendour as a royal city was fading. Slevogt, then aged just seventeen, moved there in 1885 to study at the Academy under Wilhelm von Diez (1839–1907). The following year, King Ludwig II, a devoted art lover, died; Slevogt drew him when the body was lying in

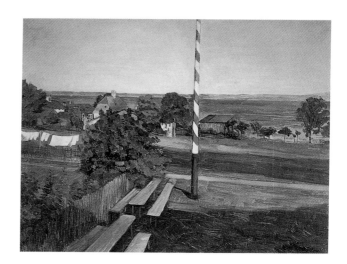

Wilhelm Trübner
The Pub on Fraueninsel, 1891
Das Wirtshaus auf der Fraueninsel
Oil on canvas, 48 x 65 cm
Winterthur, Oskar Reinhart Collection

state. It was a moment in which one might emblematically see the change-over from one era to the next, or the co-presence of polar opposites.

The importance of the Munich Academy and its liberal approach is underlined by the impressive list of major German Impressionists who studied there before subsequently coming into their own. But the Munich Academy and its exhibition system were not at the sole service of the modern; the Piloty School was still dominant. Conflicts simmered between the various convictions and interests. Controversy over artists'

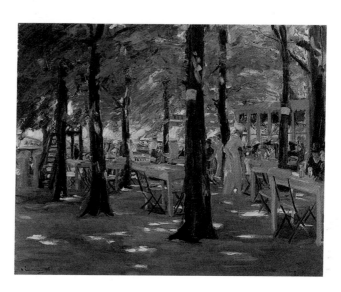

Max Liebermann
"De Oude Vinck" Restaurant, Leyden, 1905
Das Gartenrestaurant "De Oude Vinck"
in Leiden
Oil on canvas, 71.7 x 88 cm
Zurich, Kunsthaus Zürich

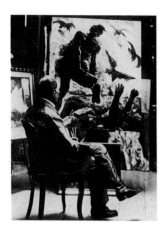

Lovis Corinth in his Berlin studio. 1917

participation in shows, and the constitution of juries, led to the first German Secession in Munich in 1892. The names of the founding members are a reminder of how various were the styles of those who felt the new group was the better home. The realists and Impressionists included Trübner, Uhde, Corinth, Slevogt, Zügel and Kuehl. Their first exhibition included works by Liebermann, and Degas and Monet too.

Berlin, the rapidly expanding new capital of a unified Germany, gradually began to outpace Munich as an art centre. In 1892, it is true, there was not yet a Secession group there; but the tensions between traditionalist and more progressive artists were unmistakable. In 1892 the Group of XI was formed there; among the members were Ludwig von Hofmann (1861–1945), Walter Leistikow (1865–1908) and Liebermann. Laforgue, a keen observer of the Berlin scene, had acutely noted in 1887 that the need for a change in the prevailing artistic climate was universally apparent. He even saw a connection between Modernist hopes and impending changes in the national leadership. Expectations of Emperor Friedrich III, who was seen as liberal, had been disappointed because he had reigned for only a short time, and his son Wilhelm II, despite his ostentatious enthusiasm for the arts, was in fact no friend of the innovatory. The foundation of the Group of XI was prompted by what became known as the Munch affair. At the recommendation of Uhde, the Norwegian artist Edvard Munch had been invited by the Association of Berlin Artists to exhibit; but when the show was opened and the members saw his work, they cancelled their invitation – an insult that prompted outrage among the moderns and liberals.

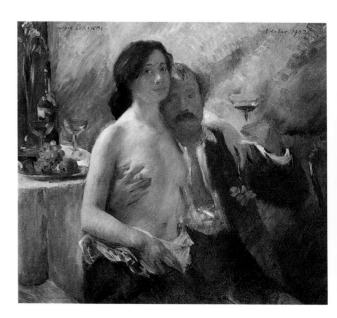

Lovis Corinth
Self-Portrait with his Wife and a Glass
of Champagne, 1902
Selbstbildnis mit seiner Frau und Sektglas
Oil on canvas, 98.5 x 108.5 cm
Berend-Corinth 234. Private collection

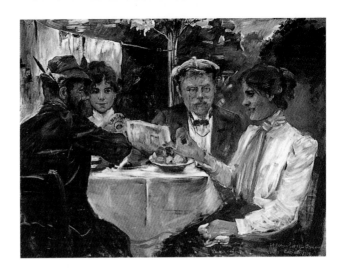

Lovis Corinth
In Max Halbe's Garden, 1899
In Max Halbes Garten
Oil on canvas, 75 x 100 cm
Berend-Corinth 185
Munich, Städtische Galerie im Lenbachhaus

Liebermann had been awarded the small Gold Medal in 1888, his first official recognition, and from then on refused to participate in Academy exhibitions. He forfeited his chances of political patronage in Germany by taking up a doggedly cosmopolitan stance. In 1889, when the French Republic took the centenary of the Revolution as the main theme for the Paris World Fair, the German Reich declined to take part in an anti-mon-archical event. In response, Liebermann organized private participation by German artists, with two aims in view: it was an opportunity for himself and fellow artists to have their work seen by an international public, and it was also a chance to bypass academic juries and put together a freely chosen selection of modern German art for viewing in France. He was subsequently awarded the Order of the Legion of Honour, but the Prussian government forbade him to accept the honour. Now the conflict was out in the open – and there were many who eagerly adopted it and made it a public issue.

It is important to bear in mind that even in the 1890s Impressionism was not yet established in Germany, and in fact never became the single dominant movement there. In France, the Impressionists were largely alone in their resistance to relatively pure academicism – and their last group show was held in 1886. The German Impressionists, however, emerged parallel with a number of modern movements. Interaction was inevitable.

The Munich Secession's umbrella for artists of very different kinds, and the triumph of Böcklin and Klinger, led to a kind of Art-Nouveau-cum-Impressionism after 1892. Coming from their different points of departure, Corinth, Slevogt and Hofmann adopted formal features which did not – strictly speaking – belong together. Hofmann's lyrical reveries were expressed in an Art Nouveau idiom which used not the linear, graphic emphasis on contrast that was usual but the pastose brushwork of Impressionism. Corinth, in his 1892 *Portrait of Otto Eckmann* (Hamburg, Hamburger Kunsthalle), deliberately emphasized ornamental aspects of the picture's structure. The portrait, of one of German Art Nouveau's leading book and textile designers, uses brushwork that can only be described as decorative in its flourishes. Slevogt's *Dance of Death* (p. 447), painted in 1896 and entirely *fin de siècle* in mood, lacks any intermediate zone between foreground and background, and highlights colour contrast; art of this kind would have been inconceivable without the international poster art of the period.

In 1894, Corinth and Slevogt joined the Munich Free Association, a splinter group within the Secession that was soon dubbed the Megalomania Association. It included Trübner, Hans Olde (1855–1917), Thomas Theodor Heine (1867–1948), Otto Eckmann (1865–1902) and Peter Behrens (1868–1940), and thus both Impressionist and Art Nouveau artists. Both movements were active in "Simplicissimus", a leading periodical of the time. Böcklin's presence was great; Corinth's 1896 *Self-*

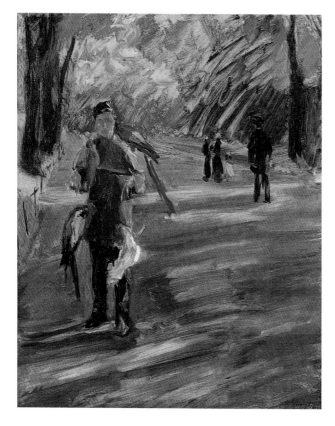

Max Slevogt
Man with Parrots, 1901
Der Papageienmann
Oil on canvas, 81.5 x 65.7 cm
Hanover, Niedersächsisches Landesmuseum

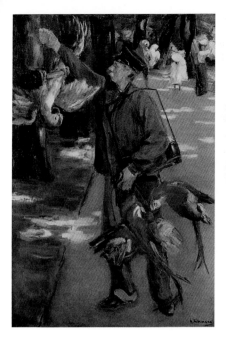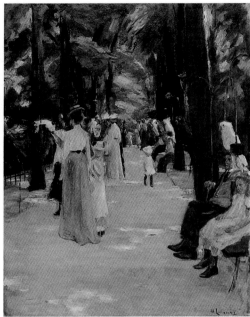

Portrait with Skeleton (p. 445) was a variation on the Swiss artist's approach to the traditional memento mori theme. The two pictures, referring to a long lineage in portrayals of life's vanity, are thematically comparable, but the differences in approach are striking: where Böcklin uses colour nuances, and the proximity, facial expressions and gestures of the protagonists, seen against an undefinable background, to create a mysterious atmosphere, Corinth deliberately avoids all unclarity whatsoever. The skeleton on its hook is plainly an anatomical model. The painter is beside it, but no relation is established between him and the skeleton. Corinth does not pressure us into any specific interpretation; rather, we are left alone to ponder dry bones and a fleshy painter. A stock in trade of Symbolist anecdote has become a sober record of things as they are.

In his study "Der Subjektivismus in der Malerei" (1892), Hugo Ernst Schmidt claimed that the triumph of Impressionism had been total: "Liebermann and Uhde are in all the state galleries. Peaceloving citizens are momentarily disquieted at this state of affairs, then they think: ah, so this is a new period in art, and they turn over and go back to sleep." But talk of an Impressionist victory was premature optimism. As late as 1895, Woldemar von Seidlitz regretfully noted that Liebermann, whom he revered, still appalled exhibition visitors. In the years before the Berlin Secession too was founded – which finally ensured a breakthrough for German Impressionism – many of the works now considered to be the

Max Liebermann
Man with Parrots, 1902
Der Papageienmann
Oil on canvas, 102.3 x 72.3 cm
Essen, Museum Folkwang

Max Liebermann
The Parrot Walk, 1902
Die Papageienallee im Zoo von Amsterdam
Oil on canvas, 88 x 72.5 cm
Bremen, Kunsthalle Bremen

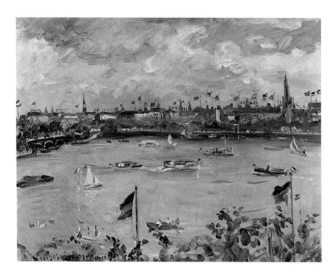

Lovis Corinth
Emperor's Day in Hamburg, 1911
Kaisertag in Hamburg
Oil on canvas, 70 x 90.5 cm
Berend-Corinth 483
Cologne, Wallraf-Richartz-Museum

movement's major achievements were painted. Liebermann put dark colours and melancholy portrayals of rural toil behind him. Following the 1889 *Mending the Nets* (Hamburg, Hamburger Kunsthalle) and the 1890 *Woman with Goats*, which earned him a major Gold Medal in Munich and was bought by the Pinakothek there, he turned to lighter subject matter (and for his trouble was later deemed by art historians to have abandoned social commitment in order to pander to middle-class taste). Stylistically, the lightening of Liebermann's palette and his more rapid completion of work brought him closer to the French. Degas, who had already been struck by the controversial history painting *Christ in the Temple* (Hamburg, Hamburger Kunsthalle), praised the 1898 *Boys*

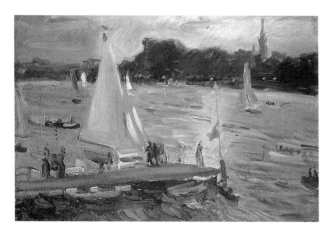

Max Slevogt
The Alster at Hamburg, 1905
Blick auf die Alster bei Hamburg
Oil on canvas, 59 x 76 cm
Berlin, Staatliche Museen zu Berlin –
Preußischer Kulturbesitz, Nationalgalerie

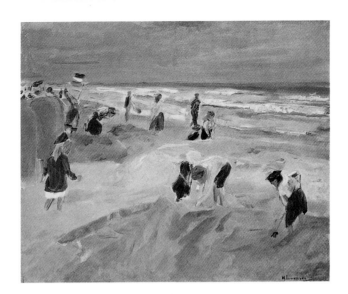

Max Liebermann
The Beach at Nordwijk, 1908
Strandszene in Nordwijk
Oil on canvas, 66 x 80.5 cm
Hanover, Niedersächsisches Landesmuseum

Bathing (p. 443). Their respect was mutual; that same year, Liebermann published an article on Degas in the periodical "Pan". Slowly but surely, official recognition followed. In 1896 Liebermann was belatedly allowed to accept his Order of the Legion of Honour, which indicated that Franco-German détente was proceeding; and the following year a large exhibition and his appointment to a chair at the Royal Academy of Fine Art in Berlin confirmed that he had finally arrived.

Corinth differed from Liebermann, not only in temperament. He moved on from his occasionally stiff adoptions of Leibl and Art Nouveau, and in 1899 his *Reclining Nude* (p. 446) demonstrated a thoroughly natural use of Impressionist style for figure painting. German Impressionism's major works tended to be painted not in the landscape area (as with the French) but rather in nudes and portraits. While Liebermann always retained a sense of distance when approaching his models, Corinth took greater liberties and penetrated deeper into the inner soul. His 1899 portrait of Rosenhagen the critic's mother (Berlin, Nationalgalerie) anticipated his later arrestingly characterful portraits; the study goes far beyond a record of facial features and includes the relation of the figure to the surrounding space in its interpretation of personality.

The growing interest in Impressionism was connected with the shift in the art centre from Munich to Berlin. German art, previously splintered into many little schools, seemed to have found its focal base in the expanding metropolis, and in this respect was in line with political developments in the new empire. Liebermann, born in Berlin, was now the patriarch whose organizational talent was marked by a tolerance and understanding of younger artists, and soon many who had turned their backs on Munich were gathering about him. One after another quit

Bavaria – from Corinth, whose *Salome* (Leipzig, Museum der bildenden Künste) had been turned down by a Munich jury in 1899, to Slevogt, who had his first solo show at Cassirer's in Berlin in 1899.

The Berlin Secession, founded relatively late, provided an umbrella for new and established, German and foreign artists. Though they espoused no single aesthetic, the group had the aura of an avant-garde. Its establishment was prompted in 1898 by a controversy over a picture by Leistikow that brings home how powerful the "enemies" (Peter Paret) of modern art were in Germany. The jury of the grand Berlin Art Show had rejected his *Sundown at Lake Grunewald* (p. 448). It is difficult now to imagine why so innocuous a painting should have

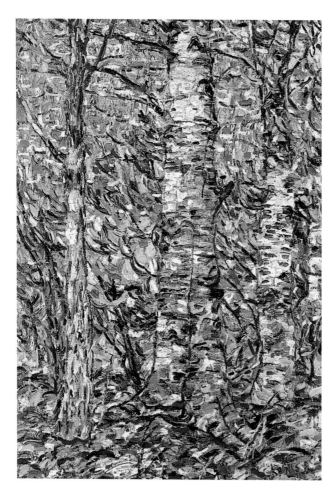

Christian Rohlfs
Birch Wood, 1907
Birkenwald
Oil on canvas, 110 x 75 cm
Essen, Museum Folkwang

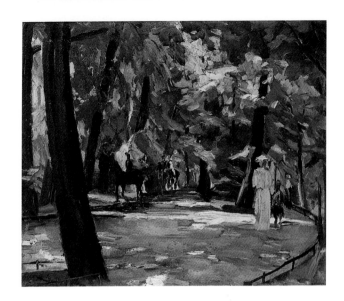

Albert Weisgerber
Riding in the English Gardens, Munich, 1910
Ausritt im Englischen Garten in München
Oil on canvas, 60 x 70.5 cm
Saarbrücken, Saarländisches Landesmuseum

sparked a row; but the academicians' veto was felt to be particularly outrageous because Leistikow's elegiac impression combined the atmospherics of Nature with Art Nouveau characteristics and was thus squarely in line with a late Romantic tradition. Subsequently the painting was privately bought and donated to the Nationalgalerie. When the director of the gallery, Hugo von Tschudi, showed the painting to Kaiser Wilhelm II not long after, in order to show that contemporary German art was going its own way, he was brusquely informed that the picture did not record Nature as it truly was – after all, he was familiar with the Grunewald area from his hunting outings. The Kaiser's (poor) adviser and mouthpiece in questions of art was Anton von Werner (1843–1945), president of the Academy and the artist who painted the proclamation of the German Reich. The opposition of the Kaiser and von Werner had the unintended effect of encouraging the new aesthetics and consolidating Berlin's position as the centre of German Modernism. The time to cast off the yoke of academic tutelage had come. Liebermann became president of the Berlin Secession and Leistikow first secretary. Curt Herrmann (1854–1929), Ludwig Dettmann, Otto Heinrich Engel (1866–1949), Oscar Frenzel (1855–1915) and later Franz Skarbina (1849–1910) were all in the committee, which put Impressionist painters in a dominant position. Leistikow was seen as the motor behind the movement. The sixty-five members quickly prepared their first exhibition. First they demanded their own, separate, unjuried rooms at the Berlin Art Show – their main principle being the freedom to choose the work by which they were represented themselves, through an independent hanging committee.

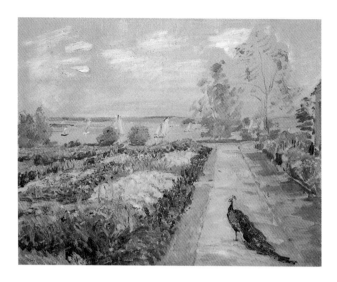

We should not underestimate the economic importance of the annual exhibitions. The Secessionists were primarily hoping for liberalized competition on an open and flourishing art market. No compromise could be reached, nor was it realistic to suppose that it could be. On 20 May 1899 the first Secession exhibition was opened, in purpose-built premises financed by donations. The opening was a social occasion that rippled far beyond the circumscribed circles of the connoisseurs and patrons of avant-garde art.

That first exhibition included work by Secession members and other Berlin artists, but also took as its avowed aim the presentation of a broad range of contemporary German work, including that of Böcklin, Leibl and Hans Thoma (1839–1924). In future years, the Secession vindicated its international stance by exhibiting such foreign artists as Bonnard, Cézanne, Gauguin, Ferdinand Hodler (1853–1918), Toulouse-Lautrec, van Gogh and others (without establishing any discrimination according to country of origin). Hodler, the Swiss artist, was represented by the strongly linear work characteristic of his art. His realistic, Impressionist phase, seen in such paintings as *Apple Tree in Blossom* or *Portrait of Louise-Delphine Duchosal* (p. 440), was already a thing of the past.

Twenty-seven years after Impressionism was born in the Société anonyme's exhibition in Nadar's rooms, the principle of disinterested pleasure as a criterion for assessing art now seemed established, and the arduous struggle for the freedom of art was bearing fruit. Yet the artists and their backers were as unable as ever to stay out of political controversy. Politics across the entire spectrum, from right to left, assumed it had proprietary rights in art. Whether they wished it or not, artists were drawn into politics. This process began in art criticism, which often, lacking formal arguments, vilified art of an unwelcome political persuasion through innuendo. Secessionists were seen as social democrats, revolutionaries, or even anarchists, while academic artists were considered good monarchists loyal to the Kaiser. Again, Wilhelm II was largely to blame. In a notorious speech on the opening of Berlin's Siegesallee in 1901, he accused modern art of merely presenting wretchedness in an even more miserable light than it normally appeared in. It was an art of misery and the gutter, he declared; and the terms stuck, being used in particular of the Secessionist line in Impressionism.

The first ten years following the founding of the Berlin Secession in 1899 may be considered the heyday of German Impressionism. Important works included Liebermann's *Man with Parrots* and *The Parrot Walk* (p. 453), both painted in 1902, and numerous beach scenes (p. 455); Corinth's 1902 *Peter Hille* (Bremen, Kunsthalle), his 1905 *Childhood of Zeus* (Bremen, Kunsthalle) and his 1906 *Rudolf Rittner Playing Florian Geyer* (Wuppertal, Von der Heydt-Museum); Slevogt's studies done at Frankfurt Zoo (*Man with Parrots*, p. 452) as well as his pictures of the singer Francisco d'Andrade as Don Giovanni; and the major works of the minor artists. Many of the minor artists have been unjustly forgotten, and we do well to recall some of them. Of the elder

Max Liebermann
At the Races, 1909
Pferderennen in den Cascinen
Oil on panel, 52.5 x 74 cm
Winterthur, Kunstmuseum Winterthur

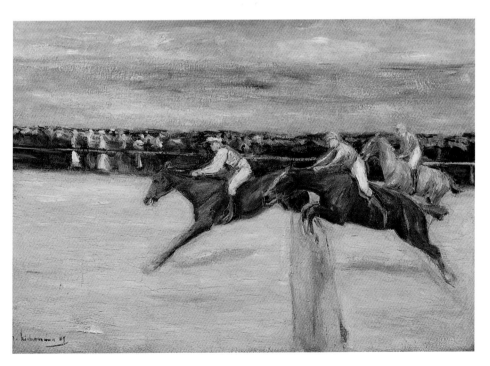

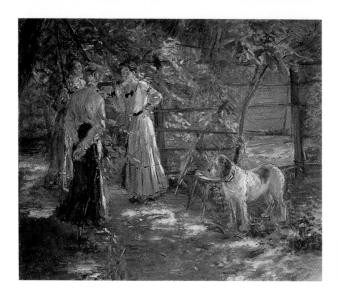

Fritz von Uhde
In the Garden (The Artist's Daughters), 1906
Im Garten (Die Töchter des Künstlers)
Oil on canvas, 70 x 100 cm
Mannheim, Kunsthalle Mannheim

generation whose Impressionism was of a moderate kind there were
Kalckreuth and Kuehl, as well as the "Salon" Impressionists Ulrich Hübner (1872–1932), Skarbina, and Karl Hagemeister (1848–1933), who
emphasized effects that were easy on the eye. Ury, whose painting of
streets wet after rain had made his name, was a more versatile painter
than these. Paul Baum (1859–1932) and Curt Herrmann were too much
under the influence of the French, and especially of the Pointillists and
Post-Impressionists; Christian Rohlfs (1849–1938; p. 456) was an eclectic in whom all the styles met; and Oskar Moll (1875–1947) and Weisgerber (p. 457) were already betraying the influence of the Fauves.

The achievements of those years may tempt us to forget that Impressionism was not the sole predominant movement in Germany. A younger
generation was already emerging, anxious to go beyond Impressionism.
They built on the freedom that had been won in order to state aesthetic
positions that expressed different, more turbulent temperaments as well
as different goals. The Impressionists, who had once been the rebels
fighting institutionalized, academic intransigence, were now themselves
seen as the Establishment. Their mounting irritation at the Expressionists
was primarily a product of a generation gap and the resulting conflict.

In 1906, when Wilhelm II had once again refused to approve an
Academy exhibition in Liebermann's honour, the latter himself turned
down Young Men at the Sea (Weimar, Schloßmuseum), which Max
Beckmann (1884–1950) had submitted for the next Secession show. The
grand master of German Impressionism, hitherto so generous to younger
artists, was quick to see that the painting could be interpreted as a deliberately antithetical response to Liebermann's own more cultivated art.

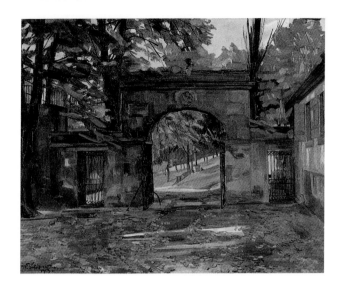

And Corinth's uncomprehending reaction to his juniors was even crasser. His execration of Matisse was couched in language that scarcely bears quotation and is in no wise more restrained than the dismissals he himself had once had to endure.

The Berlin Secession presently hit an internal crisis. In 1908, Leistikow died. He had been the mainspring and spirit of the group; and now the differences in the members' views became irreconcilable. Among them

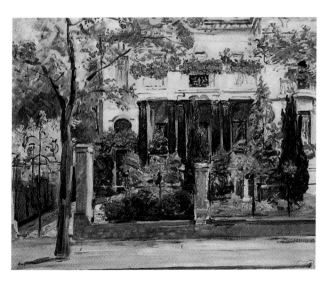

now were Lyonel Feininger (1871–1956), Erich Heckel (1883–1970), Wassily Kandinsky (1866–1944), Ernst Ludwig Kirchner (1880–1938), Paul Klee (1879–1940), Emil Nolde (1867–1956), Max Pechstein (1881–1955) and Karl Schmidt-Rottluff (1884–1976) – painters who no longer had much in common with either Art Nouveau or Impressionism. The rejection of Beckmann was symptomatic. In 1910, the year before the "Brücke" Expressionist group was founded, the committee excluded 27 painters in the selection process – the younger ones whose art the elder did not understand. Nothing could prevent the Secession from falling apart now. In 1911 Liebermann resigned his presidency, and began to lead a more private life, a decision which was of course reflected in his art. From now on he mainly painted his garden or beach scenes, with the occasional commissioned portrait.

There was a caesura in Corinth's creative life too. Not long after Liebermann's resignation from the shaky Secession, he had a stroke, in December 1911, which threatened to limit his ability to paint. Corinth steeled himself to control the shaking of his hands; and his new physical state was so far from crippling his style (as was later disagreeably claimed) that a comparison of later works (p. 463) with *Emperor's Day in Hamburg* (p. 454), painted in August 1911, shows no falling off whatsoever in his sovereign command of the fleeting effect. It is true, though, that his struggle to paint did cost him a certain lightness; and it is all the more admirable that in his *Portrait of Julius Meier-Graefe* (p. 463) he

Max Liebermann
Self-Portrait, 1911
Selbstbildnis
Oil on canvas, 81 x 65 cm
Private collection

Max Slevogt
Portrait of Mrs. C., 1917
Bildnis Frau C.
Oil on canvas, 71 x 52 cm
Private collection

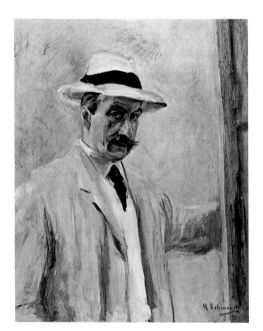

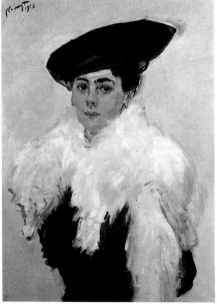

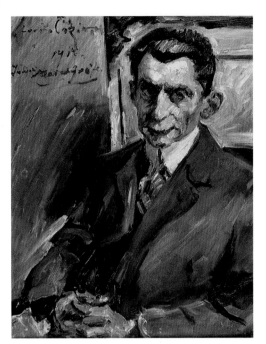

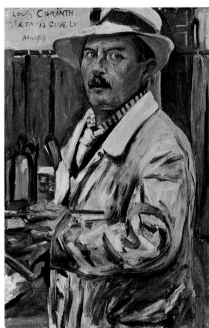

harmonized colour and form without any sense of untruthfulness to the sitter.

    As a member of the Berlin Secession committee, Slevogt had never played a particularly prominent part in organizational matters. The south German Slevogt is a curiously elusive character, compared with Berlin's intellectual, disciplined Liebermann or the sanguine, melancholy East Prussian Corinth. After the disintegration of the Secession, he used the time up to the outbreak of the First World War to paint some of his finest lyrical pictures. No other German Impressionist achieved the lightness of touch that distinguishes his Neu-Cladow (1912) and Egyptian (1913/14) paintings.

    If the Franco-Prussian War had clouded relations between the two peoples for some time, the renewed military conflict put an abrupt stop to the productive interchanges of younger artists. Widespread national hysteria even infected the more level-headed Impressionists, who in 1911 had defended Gustav Pauli (curator of the Bremen Kunsthalle) against charges that his buying policy neglected German art in favour of French.

    Robert Sterl (1867–1932) and Slevogt became war artists. The fighting stopped the promising career of Weisgerber, who had been finding an individual path of his own between Impressionism and Expressionism, and also lost the more famous August Macke (1887–1914) and Franz Marc (1880–1916) to art. Most of the major Secession artists were too

Lovis Corinth
Portrait of Julius Meier-Graefe, 1917
Bildnis Julius Meier-Graefe
Oil on canvas, 90 x 70 cm
Berend-Corinth 688. Paris, Musée d'Orsay

Lovis Corinth
Self-Portrait in a Straw Hat, 1913
Selbstbildnis mit Strohhut
Oil on canvas, 98 x 66 cm
Berend-Corinth 576
Wuppertal, Von der Heydt-Museum

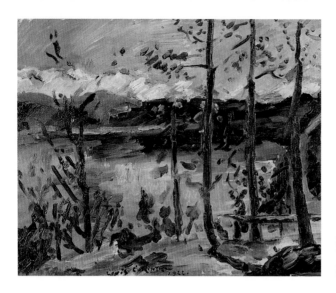

Lovis Corinth
Easter at Lake Walchen, 1922
Ostern am Walchensee
Oil on canvas, 60.5 x 80 cm
Berend-Corinth XVI. Private collection

old to fight, but they contributed to Cassirer's "Kriegszeit", a crudely propagandist publication that used Impressionist graphics. In 1915 Liebermann painted a portrait of Field Marshal von Bülow; Corinth, failing to win Hindenburg for a sitting, made do with Admiral von Tirpitz (Berlin, Deutsches Historisches Museum). Slevogt's penchant for narrative produced a cycle of works dealing with Fernando Cortez, viewing war and conquest through the lens of history painting.

Patriotic art of this kind, together with the public's increasing familiarity with Impressionism (which now seemed almost academic beside the incomprehensible art of the younger Expressionist and Cubist painters), finally produced the long-desired recognition in the highest quarters. In 1917, on the artist's 70th birthday, Liebermann was awarded the Order of the Red Eagle, third class, by the Kaiser, and given a major exhibition at the Berlin Academy of Fine Arts. That same year, Slevogt was put in charge of a master class, and the following year, on his 60th birthday, Corinth was appointed to a chair.

In 1918 Corinth paid his first visit to the Walchensee, a lake in Upper Bavaria. In a manner comparable with Liebermann's Wannsee pictures or Monet's waterlilies, Corinth painted a series of compositions, over the next few years, in which the representation of what he actually saw became less and less important, and the autonomy of painting itself became the true subject (p. 464). The painter of the actual became a painter of the metaphysical, as the art historian Wilhelm Hausenstein (1882–1957) noted; or, in Kirchner's words, "He began mediocre and ended great." The Expressionist's words are respectful but convey only insufficiently how much the following generation owed to Impressionism.

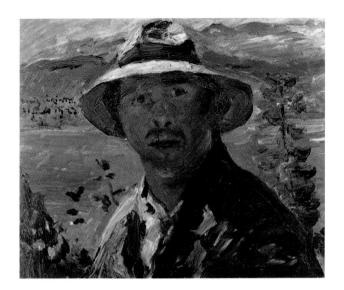

Lovis Corinth
Self-Portrait in a Straw Hat, 1923
Selbstbildnis mit Strohhut
Oil on card, 68.5 x 84 cm
Berend-Corinth 925
Bern, Kunstmuseum Bern

Without the art of their predecessors, the Expressionist achievement would have been inconceivable.

The years of the Weimar Republic marked the end of German Impressionism. They had prompted a great deal of change, and now viewed the new styles with suspicion and adhered to their own. Free of financial worries, painting whatever subjects they chose, they created late masterpieces in the 1920s, even if they no longer established the image of the period. To the very end, Corinth and Slevogt tried to reconcile Impressionism and history painting. It was no coincidence that the subject of Corinth's great painting of 1925 was *Ecce Homo* (Basle, Kunstmuseum) and that Slevogt worked till his death in 1932 on the *Golgotha* fresco in the Church of Peace in Ludwigshafen.

The barbarism that clouded the arts in the years ahead, culminating in the notorious 1937 exhibition of "degenerate" art, even made posthumous attacks on Corinth, who had not failed to love the fatherland. The Nazi ideologues arrived at a medical compromise, as it were, damning the work Corinth painted after his stroke of 1911 as "degenerate". Liebermann lived to see the changes the Nazis implemented. The eldest of the three great German Impressionists, he was also the only Jew in the group. He had been given the freedom of the city of Berlin in 1927, but after the Nazis came to power he was out of favour, and there were no official regrets when he resigned from the Academy (of which he had been Honorary President since 1932). He had helped to fire "the light of freedom" (Hermann Uhde-Bernays), and now lived to see it extinguished.

ANDREAS BLÜHM

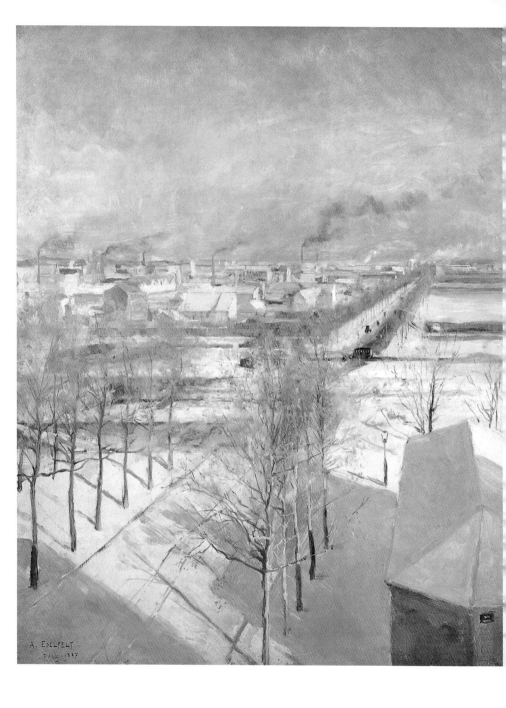

12 The New Reality: Impressionism in Scandinavia

Scandinavian Artists in Paris

Around 1870, growing numbers of Scandinavian artists took to visiting Paris, the modern metropolis with its many-sided art scene. Travel abroad had long been a tradition among artists once they graduated from the Academy, and the intense light of the south exerted its old attraction on the new generation too, not least since this was the heyday of *plein-airisme* (and studio work from open-air sketches). The artists who travelled in the 1870s and 1880s were not only questing for new experiences and new horizons, though; what was new about their journeyings was their wish for guidance in the private schools and studios of Paris. The artists financed their travels partly from public funds and partly through affluent private patrons. Typically, a Scandinavian artist's period abroad would last two or three years, allowing time to go to a college and to travel outside Paris, frequently to Italy or Spain. In some cases, artists remained in France for a whole decade. During the same period, numerous artists also attended German colleges of art in Berlin, Karlsruhe, Munich and Düsseldorf.

We shall be looking at about 35 Danish, Finnish, Norwegian and Swedish artists who extended their technical skills in Paris. We shall give equal attention to all four nationalities, though in fact the Swedes were somewhat in the majority, doubtless because there was a Swedish artists' colony at Grèz-sur-Loing.

A large number of northern artists attended the school of Léon Bonnat (1833–1922). Among them were Laurits Tuxen (1853–1927), Theodor Esbern Philipsen (1840–1920), Peder Severin Krøyer (1851–1909), Helene Schjerfbeck (1862–1946), Hans Olaf Heyerdahl (1857–1913), Harriet Backer (1845–1932), Edvard Munch (1863–1944) and Prince Eugene (1865–1947). Some, such as Albert Edelfelt (1854–1905), Schjerfbeck and Ernst Abraham Josephson (1851–1906), were tutored by Gérôme; others went to the Académie Julian, among them Akseli Gallen-Kallela (1865–1931) and Eero Järnefelt (1863–1937); still others, such as Richard Bergh (1858–1919), Hanna Pauli (1864–1940), Nils Kreuger (1858–1930), Anna Ancher (1859–1935) and Maria Wiik (1853–1928), attended the Académie Colarossi, where they were able to work under the guidance of various artists – the last three, for instance,

Albert Edelfelt
Paris in the Snow, 1887
Paris i snö
Oil on panel, 46 x 37 cm
Helsinki, Ateneumin Taidemuseo

taking classes with Puvis de Chavannes. Though some of the French tutors are no longer assigned an important role in art history, at the time they were well respected in the Salon milieu. Tuition at Bonnat's stressed formal aspects rather than colourism. The study of *valeurs* was important (the significance of light in the overall impact of a picture). Though the watchword was *simplicité*, artists were unlikely to learn colourist freedom at Bonnat's. Painting in the open offered a great challenge; it had been made usual around 1830 by the Barbizon painters (Rousseau, Daubigny, Corot) and was a crux for the Impressionists. The examples Scandinavian artists followed in figure painting were those of realist painters such as Bastien-Lepage, Millet and Breton, with their sentimental scenes of lower-class life. Work with a clear social message was not always conducive to the evolution of distinctively painterly qualities, but in this respect the Impressionists were able to offer new solutions in regard to both subject matter and the approach to colour and light.

The Encounter with Impressionism

None of the artists we are concerned with seems to have had any closer personal contact with any of the Impressionists; and we have only sporadic, chance information concerning the Scandinavian artists' response to the new style. In 1882, Erik Werenskiold (1855–1938) wrote a perceptive account of the new aesthetics in an article on the Impressionists in the "Nyt Tidsskrift". One thing he emphasized was the Impressionists' aim to present the visible world not only as we suppose we know it but also as it really appears. To Werenskiold's way of thinking, the movement's breakthroughs lay in the painting of movement and of daylight.

That same year, the Norwegian Lorentz Dietrichson wrote a polemical retort to Werenskiold; his article was published in 1884 in "Norsk Maanedsskrift for Literatur, Kunst og Politik". Dietrichson felt that the Impressionists did not reproduce Nature as they saw it, but rather created an abstract image of it, by dividing colours into component parts and by using colourist rather than formal means to convey motion. He drew attention to technological and scientific developments, and stressed photography's ability to record the passing moment as one of the many preconditions that had made Impressionism possible.

In 1886 Werenskiold summarized the Impressionist influence in self-assured, categorical terms in the Oslo newspaper "Aftenposten": "Many have come under their influence, but unless I am much mistaken only Krohg and myself have made Impressionism their own central artistic principle... There may be one or two others among the younger generation." Christian Krohg expressed things more diffidently in a lecture on "Art and Culture" delivered the same year to a student association. He commented: "We, the present generation of Norwegian painters that includes myself, are not Impressionists – alas! All we can do is stand on the mountain gazing into the Promised Land."

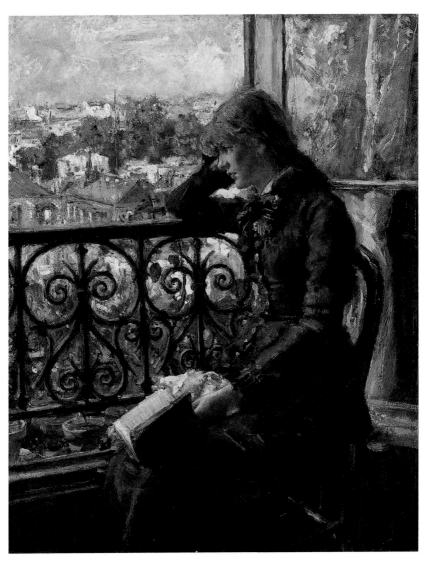

Hans Olaf Heyerdahl
At the Window, 1881
Ved vinduet
Oil on panel, 46 x 38 cm
Oslo, Nasjonalgalleriet

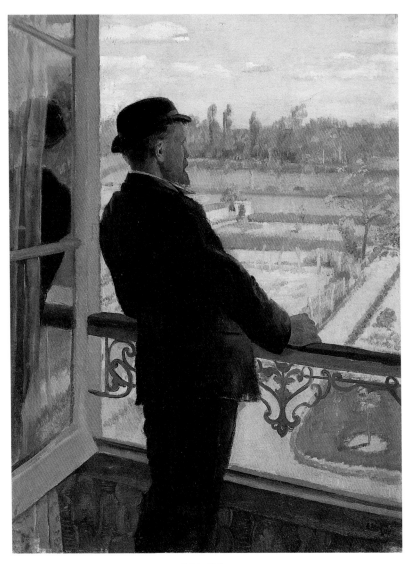

Christian Krohg
Portrait of the Artist Karl Nordström at Grèz, 1882
Maleren Karl Nordström, Grèz
Oil on canvas, 61.5 x 46.5 cm
Oslo, Nasjonalgalleriet

When he was first in Paris from 1876 to 1879, studying under Gérôme, the Danish painter and art historian Karl Madsen encountered Impressionist art at the second of their exhibitions. He was dismissive: "I have never seen such junk. All that paint, all that perfectly good canvas, all those expensive frames – wasted on such muck." Some years later, though, he reconsidered, and in the "Dagsavisen" of 22 and 23 October 1882 he wrote a thorough analysis of Impressionism, perhaps under the influence of Werenskiold's article, which he quoted. Somewhat apologetically, he began: "Arguably the movement is in many respects too assertively modern. Nevertheless, it is too large and important, and in recent years has extended its influence too considerably, to be dismissed." Madsen was clear on the Impressionist intention to record reality as directly as possible, and noted the methods that they used (cool colours, blue shadows, eccentric "Japanese" or "photographic" composition, sketchy form). He stressed the rational, dispassionate relation of Impressionist art to the environment: "They are not moralists. Even less are they panegyrists of beauty as a commodity." Above all, he felt, the modernity of Impressionism was rooted in contemporary city life: "Paris is more cosmopolitan than ever. It is the city where the essence of modern life can be experienced in its most powerful form." Madsen shared the French artists' interest in Japanese art, of which he himself possessed a notable collection, and in 1885 he published his study of Japanese painting, a work which was widely noticed, particularly by Danish artists. In short, Scandinavia was not lacking in insight into the distinctively modern features of Impressionist art. Not everyone, though, was as sure as Werenskiold or Krohg of how to respond to Impressionism in their own work.

In 1885, Krøyer, Liebermann, the Finnish artist Edelfelt, and 18 other artists of various nationalities, as well as Krøyer's former teacher Bonnat, were invited to exhibit at the fourth "Exposition internationale" at Georges Petit's gallery. Monet had ten paintings in the show. The Danish artists Viggo Johansen (1851–1935) and Julius Paulsen (1860–1940) were in Paris at the time, and their enthusiasm for Monet doubtless stemmed from that exhibition at Petit's.

Gauguin was in Copenhagen in 1884/85; he had married a Danish wife, Mette, and was planning to settle there. Though he in fact returned to Paris before a year was out, he did exhibit with the Art Association from 1 to 6 May 1885. Despite his work being on view for only a very short period, it still managed to confound Copenhagen art lovers accustomed to quite different fare. The press completely ignored the exhibition; but artists who had been to Paris or knew of the new aesthetics in other ways took a great interest in it. In 1889 the same venue presented an exhibition titled "Nordic and French Impressionism", which primarily featured paintings in Gauguin's own collection which he had deposited with his wife when he left Denmark. It included work by Guillaumin, Manet, Degas, Forain, Cézanne, Pissarro, Sisley and Angrand, as well as by Gauguin himself and the American Mary Cassatt. Side by side with these works were hung paintings by Gauguin's friend Philipsen, and by Johansen, Werenskiold, Krohg, and Krohg's wife, Oda. The previous year, Impressionist work by Manet, Monet and Sisley had been seen in Copenhagen – a modest selection included amidst Salon art in a show of French painting sponsored by Carl Jacobsen, the brewer. On the whole, though, Jacobsen, who later founded the Ny Carlsberg Glyptotek, was no great friend of Impressionism, and did not include their work in his own large collection of French art. Krøyer, who had been sent to Paris in his capacity as exhibition curator, tried in vain to introduce the new art.

Then in 1893 the artists' association Den frie Udstilling mounted the most important show of Gauguin and van Gogh to be seen outside France at that date. The Danish public had the chance to view 51 Gauguins and 29 van Goghs. Generally speaking, there were ample opportunities for Copenhagen artists and art lovers to familiarize themselves with recent French art. Monet, whose works had not been included in the 1889 show, visited Norway in 1895, to see his son-in-law Jacques Hoschedé in Christiania (Oslo). He spent a peaceful working retreat at Bjørnegården with Jenny Bjørnson, the first wife of Bjørnstjerne Bjørnson (1832–1910), the great poet and dramatist. The Bjørnegården estate was at Sandviken, some 15 kilometres from the capital, and there Monet defied the cold to paint a series of snowy landscapes. Krohg was of course one of the many artists (up to 20 every day) who paid their respects to Monet at the Grand Hotel in Christiania when he spent a few days there before returning home. Prince Eugene was also there, together with his servants and retinue.

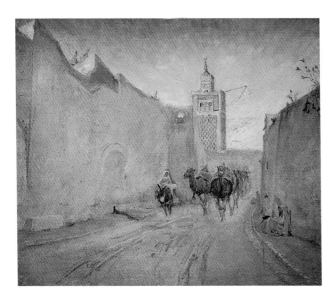

Theodor Esbern Philipsen
Street in Tunis, 1882
En gade i Tunis
Oil on oilcloth, 40 x 47 cm
Copenhagen, Statens Museum for Kunst

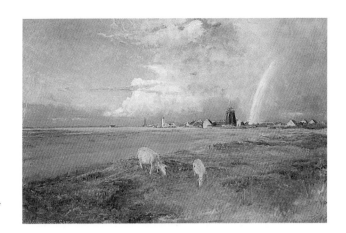

Viggo Johansen
Near Skagen Østerby after a Storm, 1885
Udkanten af Skagen Østerby efter en tordenbyge
Oil on canvas, 95 x 147 cm
Skagen, Skagens Museum

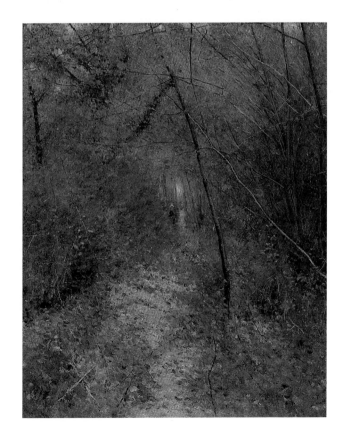

Karl Frederik Nordström
A Clearing in the Woods at Grèz, 1882
Skogsgläntan, motiv från Grèz
Oil on canvas, 114 x 92 cm
Norrköping, Norrköpings Konstmuseum

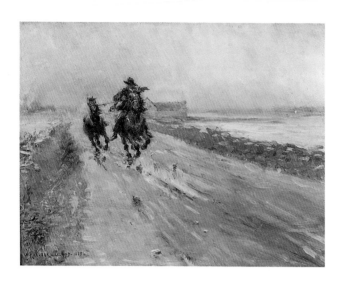

Nils Edvard Kreuger
Gypsy on Öland, 1885
Tattare på Öland
Oil on panel, 32 x 41.5 cm
Malmö, Malmö Museer

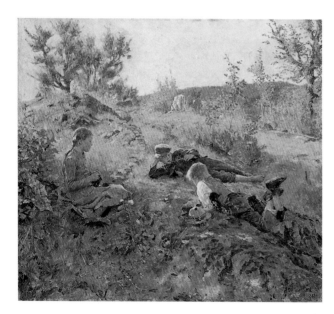

Erik Werenskiold
Shepherds on Tåtøy, 1883
Gjitere. Tåtøy
Oil on canvas, 59 x 65 cm
Oslo, Nasjonalgalleriet

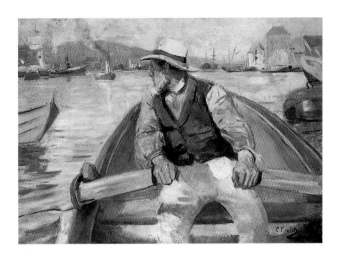

Artists' Colonies

When summer arrived and tuition ceased at the private schools in Paris, the artists deserted the city. The coast of Brittany was especially popular for painting holidays. Krøyer, Schjerfbeck and Wiik worked at Concarneau, Järnefelt at Veneux-Nadon, and Munch at Saint-Cloud. In the 1880s, there was a Swedish artists' colony at Grèz-sur-Loing, by the Fontainebleau woods. Among the regular visitors were Kreuger, Bergh, Karl Nordström (1855–1923), Carl Olof Larsson (1853–1919), Bruno Liljefors (1860–1939) and Anshelm Leonhard Schultzberg (1862–1945). Krohg was there too, in 1882.

In due course they took the idea of the artists' colony back to Scandinavia with them. The most famous of the northern colonies was at Skagen. Many artists went straight there after their periods abroad, and its importance as a place where new ideas were absorbed and transmitted, helping the further development of northern art, must be stressed. Among those who used Skagen were Krøyer and Krohg, and other Danish, Norwegian and Swedish artists returned there every summer, to paint in the fine northern light in the company of friends old and new.

Plein-air Painting

Studies in Parisian academies were one thing, independent work in the summer countryside another thing altogether. The wish for Salon acceptance prompted many artists to defer to prevailing taste for four-square academic formal discipline – which ran utterly counter to attempts at a direct presentation of the real. To what extent artists were satisfied with immediate responses to Nature was a question of individual disposition, but the Impressionist example certainly exerted a strong influence on Scandinavian artists. Brief brush-strokes like commas, and a light, un-mixed palette – both hallmarks of Impressionist art – made little impact on northern artists, though, even if a few of them did see the advantages of the technique.

One of these few was Johansen, as can be seen from his *Near Skagen Østerby after a Storm* (p. 473), painted with Monet's influence still fresh. Sheep are grazing in the foreground, while on the horizon, which divides the picture in two, we see Skagen with its mill, light-house, and the yellow-painted houses with their red tiled roofs. The

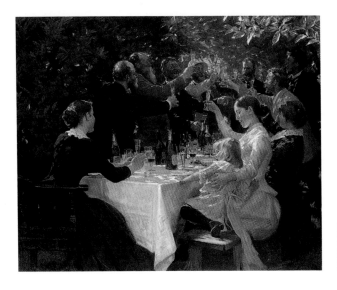

Peder Severin Krøyer
Hip Hip Hooray! An Artists' Party at Skagen,
c. 1884–1888
Hip, hip, hurråa! Kunstnerfest på Skagen
Oil on canvas, 134.5 x 165.5 cm
Gothenburg, Göteborgs Konstmuseum

painting lacks compositional tension, but the observation of Nature is exact: the crystal clear air after the downpour seems to put a greener sheen on the grass, while a delicate rainbow still stands out against the fading blue-black storm clouds and the massive white cumulus clouds on their heels. The lighter clouds have caught a hint of pink and brown from a low sun, which is also giving the sheep a touch of gold. In *St. John's on Tisvilde Beach* (p. 481) Paulsen presents a dra-matic natural scene. His unusual freedom of colour and technique in-troduces a dynamic feel to the fleeting moment; once again we sense the presence of Monet.

Of the Danish landscape painters, it was unquestionably Philipsen who had the soundest grasp of Impressionism and most consistently adopted its views on light, colour and brushwork. His speciality was in fact animal paintings, but his pictures of spring or autumnal landscapes

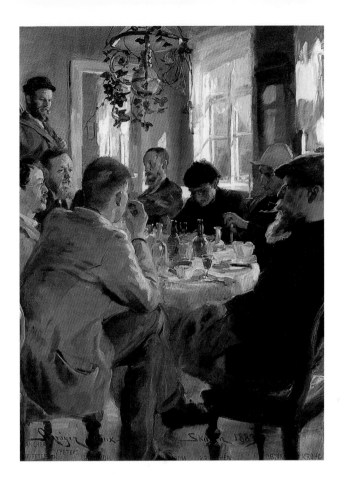

Peder Severin Krøyer
Artists at Breakfast, 1883
Ved frokosten
Oil on canvas, 82 x 61 cm
Skagen, Skagens Museum

near Copenhagen shared the distinctive mood of Pissarro and Sisley. The shadows of trees and fenceposts in *A Lane at Kastrup* (p. 486) were done in the bluish violet characteristic of Impressionism. The colours are cool, and soft, yellowish light veils the red rooftops in the background.

Nature and Civilization

In spring 1888, during his first sojourn in France, Westerholm painted *The Seine at Paris* (p. 487). The cloudy sky, the river diagonally crossing the canvas, and the tree that anchors the composition, were all in line with classic landscape art. But the picture also betrays a modern eye which makes its important, non-idyllic contribution to the visual struc-

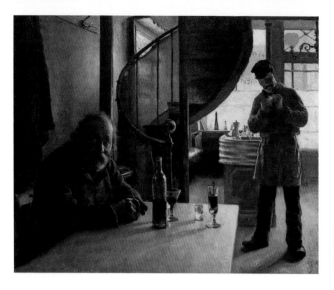

Eero Järnefelt
Lefranc the Wine Merchant, Boulevard Clichy,
Paris, 1888
Fransk vinstuga
Oil on canvas, 61 x 74 cm
Helsinki, Ateneumin Taidemuseo

ture. The three factory chimneys positioned as counterpoints to the tree, and the iron bridge marking the divide between water and sky, document the relentless advance of modern civilization. If Westerholm's choice of subject naturally included an awareness of the Impressionist eye for light and atmospherics, it also emphasized the collision of industrialization with unspoilt Nature – a recurring motif in Impressionism, and one which we shall encounter repeatedly in various guises.

Man and Nature

In his first summer working at Grèz, Nordström was totally under the influence of the seventh Impressionist exhibition. A Clearing in the Woods at Grèz (p. 473) does not seem fully committed to Impressionist technique, though; the filigree of the slender tree trunks retains a linear clarity. The leafage and ground, on the other hand, are a shimmering fabric of green, blue and ochre brush-strokes such as might satisfy even the most orthodox of Impressionists. The female figure near the point where the path vanishes may seem to have been positioned by chance, but in fact she has her specific spatial and narrative part to play in the overall composition.

Werenskiold too attended the Impressionist exhibition in spring 1882. Later that year, on Tåtøy, an island off Norway's Sørland coast, he painted Shepherds on Tåtøy (p. 474). The influence of Pissarro is again apparent; a large proportion of the 35 works the French artist exhibited in 1882 depicted farm girls and shepherdesses. His figures, seen resting,

Christian Krohg
Portrait of the Artist Gerhard Munthe, 1885
Maleren Gerhard Munthe
Oil on canvas, 150 x 115 cm
Oslo, Nasjonalgalleriet

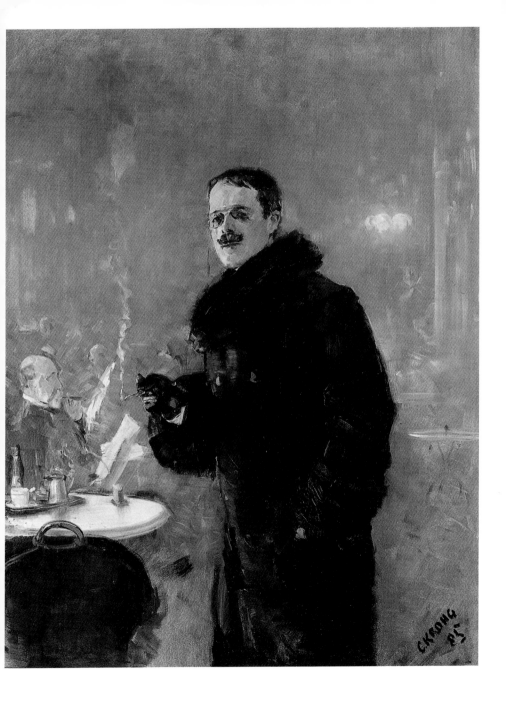

talking or knitting, typically seem organic parts of the natural setting, an impression that Pissarro emphasized through his brushwork, outlining both the figures and the landscape features in short, pastose strokes using mainly unmixed colours. The total impact was reinforced by placing the horizon very high in the picture, or eliminating it altogether, so that the landscape seems to mantle the figures. Werenskiold has adopted this approach in placing his three children, who, supposedly looking after the cattle grazing in the background, have in fact sought the shade of trees on a hot afternoon in late summer. None of the three is positioned above the horizon; rather, they seem embedded in the landscape. The brushwork is Impressionist only in part, without the determined consistency of Pissarro's. The treatment of the figures strikes us as more a result of Bonnat's tuition, which involved the detailed study of models and work on *valeurs*.

Effects of Light

The mid-1870s saw the peak of Renoir's experiments with the effect of sunlight falling through foliage and dappling figures and objects with a patchwork of shadow and light. His paintings *Nude in the Sunlight* (p. 162), *The Swing* (p. 144), and *Le Moulin de la Galette* (p. 153) provided first-rate, striking examples of this effect. For painters elsewhere, this was a novelty and a breakthrough. Pauli's *Breakfast* (p. 482) may have been inspired by Monet's 1873 *The Luncheon* (p. 119). Both pictures feature a laid table with garden seat and chairs in the shade. In Monet's, lunch has just been finished and the table left; in Pauli's, breakfast is about to begin. The central motif in both paintings is the laid table and the white cloth, while the figures – in the one, a boy playing and

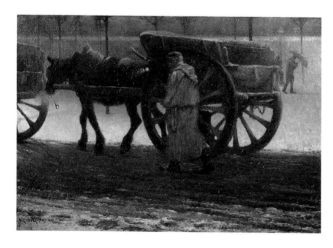

Nils Edvard Kreuger
Snowy Weather, Paris, 1885
Snöväder i Paris
Oil on canvas, 127 x 184 cm
Stockholm, Prins Eugens Waldemarsudde

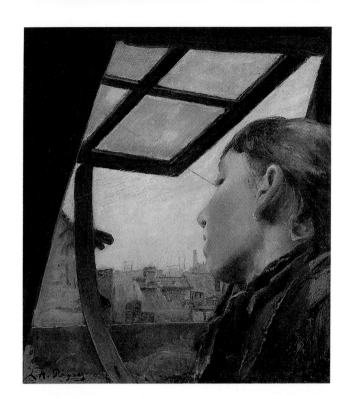

Laurits Andersen Ring
Girl Looking out of a Skylight, 1885
Ung pige, der ser ud af et tagvindue
Oil on canvas, 33 x 29 cm
Oslo, Nasjonalgalleriet

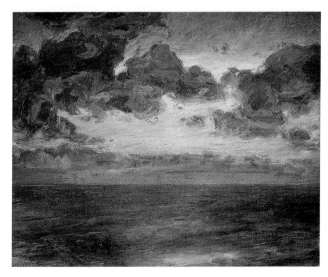

Julius Paulsen
St. John's on Tisvilde Beach, 1886
Sankt Hans nat ved Tisvilde strand
Oil on canvas, 63 x 75.5 cm
Copenhagen, Statens Museum for Kunst

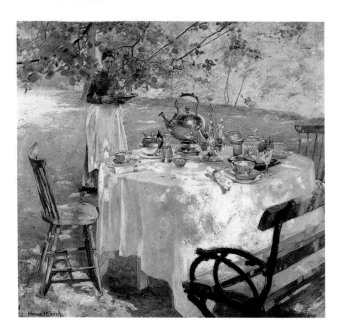

Hanna Pauli
Breakfast, 1887
Frukostdags
Oil on canvas, 77 x 107 cm
Stockholm, Nationalmuseum

ladies strolling in the background; in the other, a servant with a tray –
make an incidental impression and serve merely to amplify the narrative
content. Pauli's cloth is dappled with light and shadow, and the glasses,
china and metal pots are catching the light that is falling through the
foliage.

Krøyer tackled a similar motif in *Hip, Hip, Hooray! An Artists' Party
at Skagen* (p. 476). The composition was based on a photograph taken
in summer 1884. The party was in the garden of the Anchers (husband
and wife were both artists) at Skagen. We see the artists raising their
champagne glasses in a toast. Among those present are Johansen, Krohg,
the Anchers themselves, Oscar Björck (1860–1929) and Thorvald Niss
(1842–1905). The motif of movement captured in the male group is
nicely complemented by the tranquillity of the seated women and the
child.

Josephson pursued similar effects of light in Brittany, in a painting on
a different subject, *Autumn Sunlight* (p. 489). The composition assigns
equal value to the old woman in the doorway and the whitewashed wall,
on which shadows of trees and pale sunlight play. The dapples are also
on the woman's dark skirt and the white cloth she is holding. It is a
picture that has turned away from parties, joys and feasts: here, the
painter's emphasis on fleeting effects is inseparable from a perception of
the transience of human life.

Plein-airisme and the Interior

There is a direct continuity from *plein-airisme* of the true outdoor kind to interiors that record the immediate effects of sunlight. The Skagen painters were particularly fond of this effect. Krøyer's *Artists at Breakfast* (p. 477), painted in 1883, was a logical development of motifs he had worked on in France, such as *Artists at Breakfast in Cerney-la-Ville* (1879) and *Passengers on a Seine Boat* (1881; both Skagen, Skagens Museum). The Skagen painting portrays Danish, Norwegian and Swedish artists at table. The objects on the table stand out in the strong sunlight in red and green against the white cloth. The light effectively glows in Krohg's bushy gingery beard and catches the sleeve of Charles Lundh's jacket. The loose brushwork and inexact outlines highlight the sense that a lively and significant moment has been captured.

Anna Ancher was a mistress of interior light and colour. Unlike Krøyer, she generally used her effects to establish a quiet, contemplative mood. The sensitivity and gifted colourism of her paintings created soulful, intimate atmospheres. In *Sunlight in the Blue Room. Helga Ancher Knitting in her Grandmother's Room* (p. 494), she uses the contrast of sunlight and the silhouettes of potted plants and window crossbars on

Hugo Birger
Scandinavian Artists Breakfasting at the Café Ledoyen, Paris, on Salon Opening Day, 1886
Skandinaviska konstnärernas frukost i Café Ledoyen, Paris, fernissnigsdagen
Oil on canvas, 183.5 x 261.5 cm
Gothenburg, Göteborgs Konstmuseum

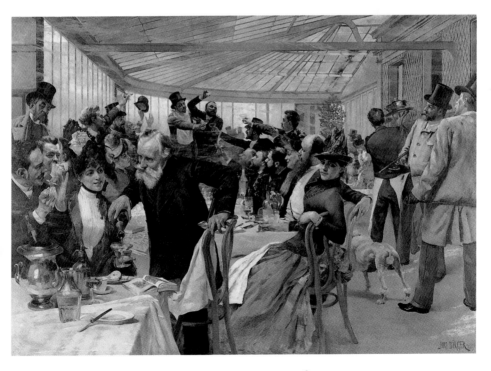

the wall and floor. Her colour scheme is based on the contrasting blue of the wall and upholstery and the yellow of the curtains, an effect that is replicated in the blue smock and blonde hair of the girl sitting by the window. *The Artist's Mother, Anna Hedvig Brøndum* (p. 499) is far more of a true portrait, of course; and yet this frontal view of a seated woman with a pillow at her back, snoozing in the sun, depends on its palette of rose, violet, white, yellow and blue shades.

Järnefelt strikes a decidedly Parisian note in *Lefranc the Wine Merchant, Boulevard Clichy, Paris* (p. 478). The milieu is characteristically that of a city. But formally, too, the artist has used a compositional approach that was typical of Caillebotte and Degas, just as his gleaming brushwork recalls Manet. Considerable emphasis is placed on the various kinds of light. The backlighting and the effects that it creates in the semi-dark room are dramatic, from the foreground, where detailed attention has been paid to the play of light on the glasses and bottle with their various contents and on the features of the elderly man, via the silhouetted merchant and the brass newel head at the foot of the spiral

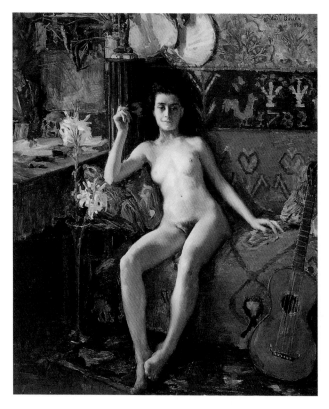

Akseli Gallen-Kallela
Démasquée, 1888
Oil on canvas, 65 x 55 cm
Helsinki, Ateneumin Taidemuseo

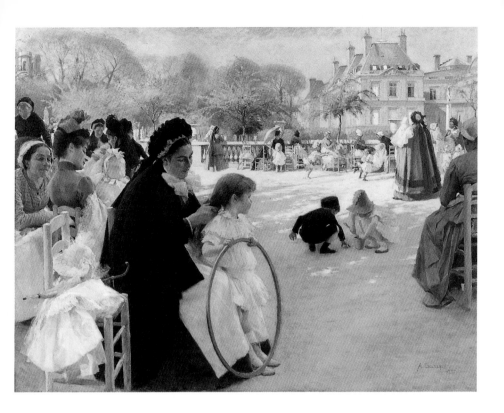

staircase, to the metal cladding of the counter. The banister of the stairs is covered in red canvas rendered translucent by a window beyond, which casts a reddish gleam on the wall and table, a gleam that is reflected by the counter cladding too. Furthermore, the merchant is lighting his pipe with a match, thus providing another source of light that illuminates his face and hands with a warm glow. The use of *contrejour* in a dark interior, and the arrested movement, reflect the experiments that Caillebotte in particular was making in the mid–1870s. We might, for instance, compare the white backlighting and the resulting reflections on the floor and elsewhere to be observed in the French artist's *The Floor Strippers* (p. 131). In Järnefelt's painting, the spatial composition is firm, with an emphasis on verticals and horizontals; however, the spiral stair is unusual, and attracts attention by virtue of the fact. The spatial tension it establishes contrasts with the simplicity of the tabletop's disappearance into the fore perimeter.

Social realism of the kind espoused by Millet, Courbet and Bastien-Lepage often entered the work of Scandinavian artists. Unlike the elder generation, who often took their subjects from farming and the life of

Albert Edelfelt
In the Luxembourg Gardens, 1887
I Luxembourgträdgården i Paris
Oil on canvas, 144 x 188 cm
Helsinki, Ateneumin Taidemuseo

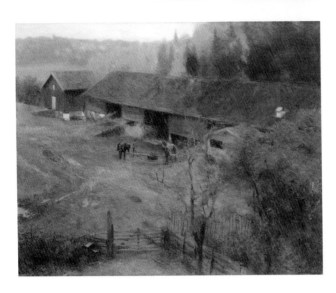

Erik Werenskiold
Autumn, 1891
Høst
Oil on canvas, 120 x 151 cm
Gothenburg, Göteborgs Konstmuseum

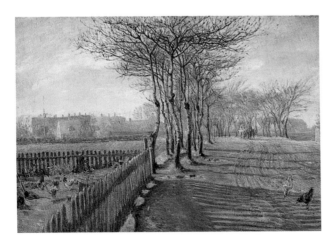

Theodor Philipsen
A Lane at Kastrup, 1891
En allé i Kastrup
Oil on canvas, 55 x 82 cm
Copenhagen, Statens Museum for Kunst

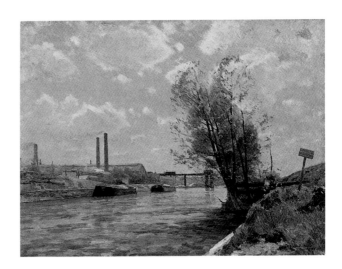

Victor Westerholm
The Seine at Paris, 1888
Seine invid Paris
Oil on canvas, 60.5 x 81.5 cm
Turku, Turun Taidemuseo

craftsmen, the younger artists turned to industrial work, where large numbers of people could be seen going about their bustling business in confined spaces. This crowded and busy atmosphere accorded with the pulsating rhythm of modern life that so preoccupied the Impressionists. Anders Zorn (1860–1920) painted a series of scenes from a Stockholm brewery. *In a Brewery* (p. 488) shows a number of women sitting working in a row in a room the wet floor of which glistens with light reflected from ceiling lighting. Zorn's brushwork is broad and rapid, and his gold, brown and black provides an effective context for the strong red of one woman's blouse.

Point of View and Composition

Two crucial points of departure for compositional structure in Impressionist art were photography and Japanese art. Photographic technique called for a sense of the passing moment, for images that recorded movement in a seemingly random fashion, for points of view often dictated by chance. Abrupt cropping fragmented subjects as in a snapshot – though the effect also occurred in 18th-century Japanese woodcuts. Japonisme (as the imitation of Japanese styles was known) introduced a clear-cut and decorative sense of space and image to pictures.

One distinctive Impressionist theme was the view from a window. Just as Monet, Pissarro and Caillebotte had painted crowds on Paris boulevards as seen from high windows, Krohg in 1883 painted *Von Eidsvolds Square (Impression of Karl Johan Street)*. In 1882 Krohg had seen the seventh Impressionist exhibition, and would have noticed work of a related kind by Caillebotte. His painting used a high, acute angle of vision to look down on the bustle in Christiania's most elegant street. Free of any specific narrative content, the picture simply conveys "a milieu in the great image of the age", as the artist put it in an 1886 lecture.

Munch was in close touch with Krohg and his circle in the 1880s. In 1889, and repeatedly in the Nineties, he visited Paris, where for a brief time he was much taken with Impressionism, as paintings such as *Spring on Karl Johan* (p. 492) or *Rue Lafayette* (p. 491) show.

Werenskiold transposed the Impressionist point of view to a quite different context in *Autumn* (p. 486), that of a Norwegian farm. He had visited Paris most recently in 1889, and in the autumn of that year he had participated in the Copenhagen show of Gauguin's own work and paintings from his collection of Impressionist art. The muted and somewhat melancholy colours familiar from Gauguin's Impressionist phase are here again in Werenskiold's painting. The view, which seems to have been chosen at random, admits fencing and a barn at an unusual angle (much as certain things might feature in a Paris street scene); the throng of passers-by we might expect in a city scene is replaced here by two horses at work.

Caillebotte's 1880 *Balcony, Boulevard Haussmann* (Paris, private collection) made its clearest impression on two Norwegian artists. Krohg came closest to the Frenchman's concept in his *Portrait of the Artist Karl Nordström at Grèz* (p. 470). Nordström himself left an account of how the picture came to be painted: "We had both recently studied Impressionist art at an exhibition in Paris, and our hearts were brimful of powerful new impressions. Afterwards, Krohg one day observed me standing at the open window of my room, wearing my navy suit, with the park in the background. He asked me with some eagerness to stay just as I was, ran off to fetch a canvas and the necessary

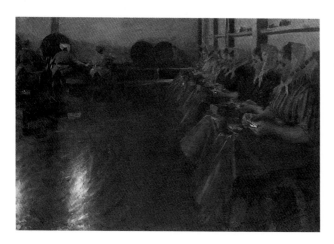

Anders Zorn
In a Brewery, 1890
Stora bryggeriet
Oil on canvas, 100 x 68 cm
Gothenburg, Göteborgs Konstmuseum

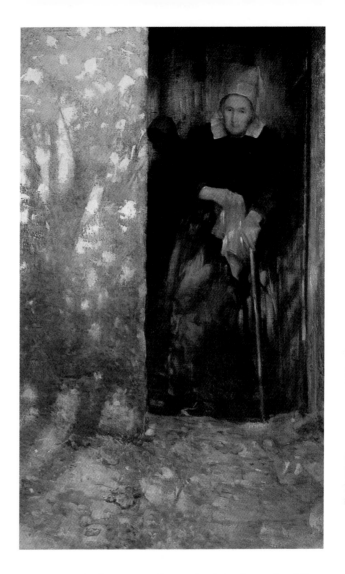

Ernst Josephson
Autumn Sunlight, 1896
Höstsol
Oil on canvas, 130 x 82 cm
Stockholm, Thielska Galleriet

equipment, and within moments he was already hard at work . . ." Despite the differences in setting and pictorial structure, there can be no doubt that Caillebotte's painting provided the direct inspiration for Krohg's. In both cases the subject is resting on an ornamental wrought-iron railing, and both are reflected in an open window. Heyerdahl too had tried his hand at a similar motif the year before, in *At the Window* (p. 469). Like Caillebotte, he presented a city scene in strong light viewed from a balcony, though here the main subject is a seated woman rather than a standing man, pausing for a moment in her reading to gaze ahead, lost in thought. She recalls women we often see in Manet or Morisot. The stylistic affinity to Morisot's limpid colours and freedom in brushwork is striking.

It is uncertain whether there were any direct French influences on *Girl Looking out of a Skylight* (p. 481), which Laurits Andersen Ring (1854–1933) painted in 1885. At that time, the artist had not yet visited Paris; however, the impact of Japonisme on the decorative structure is unmistakable. Ring was at that time a close friend of Madsen, who was working on his study of Japanese art. The subject and the presentation of the passing moment are rendered in a very confined space, one that permits of no narrative extras. The girl's half-averted face and the view of the city rooftops are both linked and kept separate by the play of depth and space created by the slant opening and by the angles and crossbars of the skylight.

Paulsen's *Under the Pont des Arts, Paris* (p. 495) is at once Impressionist and "Japanese". The picture is plainly related to the Impressionists' countless Seine landscapes; and the bridge arch that dominates the foreground recalls Japanese woodcuts, as well as Monet's Japanese bridge in his garden at Giverny. The very title of the painting has an Impressionists' flavour. The freshness of the colours and the intensity of the light confirm the French feel of the work.

In winter 1887, Edelfelt painted *Paris in the Snow* (p. 467) from the window of his suburban studio. The view, though it has a flavour of the fortuitous, is deliberately, tautly structured, and the subject, though scarcely oriental, is yet done *à la japonaise*. The lane crosses the image and the real space toward the horizon, its course rhythmically underpinned by trees and, further off, carriages and a tram. In the foreground, a snow-covered rooftop is cropped by the right edge. The shadows of this and the neighbouring building (from which Edelfelt is presumably viewing the scene) join the shadows of the trees to establish a contrapunctal diagonal dynamic. The smoke from the factory chimneys, blown from left to right across the horizon, adds to the effect.

Snowscapes both rural and urban were a staple of the Impressionist repertoire. They afforded an opportunity to examine the pure effect of light and shadow, reflections and colours, on the snow's gleaming surface. In *Snowy Weather, Paris* (p. 480) Kreuger tackled the motif at street level, in winter 1885. The horse-drawn wagon is seen in typical winter atmospherics. It is twilight, and the white of the snow appears blue in the glow of the streetlamps. The snowy weather is interposed like a filter between us and the things we see; but the snowfall itself is visible, especially in the orange light from the wagon lamp. The horse's breath blurs the outline of the wheel of the wagon ahead, which is abruptly cropped in a way suggestive of movement. In the background, discreetly positioned but with eloquent effect on our sense of a counter-movement, a man can be seen making his way into the falling snow, shielded by an umbrella.

Edvard Munch
Rue Lafayette, 1891
Oil on canvas, 92 x 73 cm
Oslo, Nasjonalgalleriet

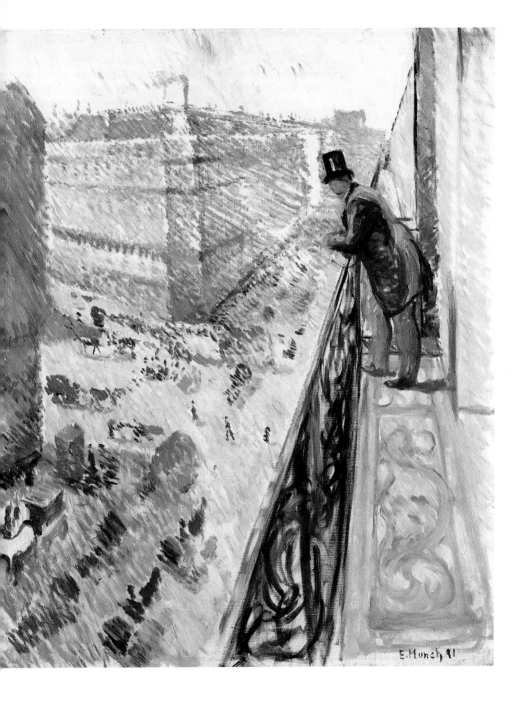

E.Munch 91

The Sense of Movement

Light broken on waves, a swell, or the surface of water, together with reflections of the sky, plus local colour, naturally constituted a favourite Impressionist subject. In 1892, Krøyer painted a handful of modestly-sized canvases of Danish beaches, paying tribute to the pleasures people took in the summer. In *Bathing Children* (p. 493) he gave his attention to light on the sea, capturing a fleeting moment as a boy runs into the water, splashing showers of spray.

Boating on the Seine was another motif that continually engaged the Impressionists. In 1877, Caillebotte painted an imaginative variation on the theme in *Canotier en chapeau haut de forme*. In this work, the cropping plays a decisive part: the boat and oars are only partly visible, as are the rower's legs. Krohg copied this approach in *Look ahead. The Harbour at Bergen* (p. 475), but also contrived to heighten the illusion that we are witnessing a snapshot moment: the rower is turning briefly to check his course and avoid a collision with other boats, not least the

Edvard Munch
Spring on Karl Johan, 1891
Vår på Karl Johan
Oil on canvas, 80 x 100 cm
Bergen, Bergen Billedgalleriet

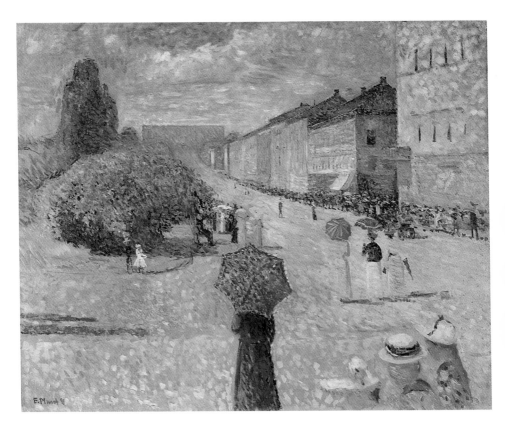

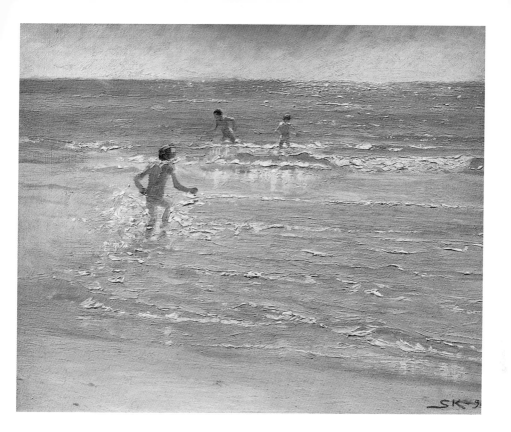

steamer in the background. This movement has the effect of transferring the energy apparent in the foreground to the horizon. The sunlight also enables Krohg to paint the reflections in the water.

Peder Severin Krøyer
Bathing Children, 1892
Badende børn
Oil on canvas, 33 x 40.5 cm
Copenhagen, Den Hirschsprungske Samling

Philipsen's *Street in Tunis* (p. 472) recalls a journey to Tunisia in 1882. Along a shady, cool lane between high white walls, a herd of camels are approaching us, raising dust and thus obscuring the animals to the rear. A rider on an ass, making slow progress and having to move aside, is casting a long shadow on the wall. The distinctive movement of camels is precisely captured in economical browns. The sun is gilding a white tower, and the sky is a yellowish green. Kreuger's *Gypsy on Öland* (p. 474) is an equally evocative study of motion. The horseman is riding at a gallop, leading a second horse behind him. It is raining, and the horses' hooves are splashing water from puddles. The wind is ruffling their manes and the man's clothing.

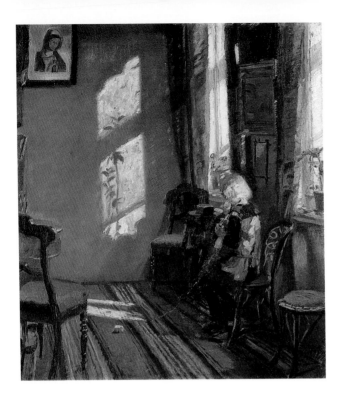

Anna Ancher
Sunlight in the Blue Room. Helga Ancher
Knitting in her Grandmother's Room, 1891
*Solskin i den blå stue. Helga Ancher
ved strikketøjet i bedstemors stue*
Oil on canvas, 65 x 59 cm
Skagen, Skagens Museum

"La Vie Moderne"

Though the new, modern, optimistically progressive style of middle-class culture associated with the new industrial heyday was apparent in other European cities too, the range of connotations implicit in the phrase "la vie moderne" is suggestive of the Paris experience. The Paris scene was often one of factory chimneys, new architecture, and busy crowds on the boulevards, on foot or in vehicles. Closer to, we witness bourgeois and bohemian lifestyles alike: the pillars of society are there, industrialists and speculators, and so are the artists, independent if financially insecure, leading their tempting life of outdoor leisure and sport and indulging in a broad variety of colourful entertainments. There were theatre shows and exhibitions, horse races and restaurants, balls, salons, and – for bohemians and sempstresses alike – the *grisettes*, dance clubs and bars of Montmartre. By day one could take lunch in the greenery, read a paper in the park, or take a boat trip on the Seine. At night a café-chantant or café-concert offered amusement, as did the brothels. Krohg's *Portrait of the Artist Gerhard Munthe* (p. 479) suggested that Bohemia was alive and well in Christiania too. We have to guess at the nature of this smoky interior, the poorly lit Grand Café, with its gentlemen reading the papers and smoking cigars. In the foreground is an uncleared, deserted table. The subject has just come in from the street. He is clearly a dandy, wearing a dark coat with a voluptuous fur collar and sporting a moustache and eyeglasses. In his gloved right hand he holds a burning cigarette, the swirl of smoke drifting into the bluish haze of the room.

Bohemian ways were usual in the artists' private realms too. In *Démasquée* (p. 484), Gallen-Kallela afforded a glimpse of his own milieu and thus of his attitude to his role as artist. The picture was painted in Paris in 1888. The model is just taking a break from posing, and the portrait has captured her at rest – in an unpretentious yet sensual relaxed position, free of attitudinizing yet also challenging, and, of course, lightly mocking. The artist has caught her weary smile, the way she is rubbing her hurting feet, the negligent gestures of her hands and arms on the sofa-top blanket, and a black half-mask she is holding in her right hand. The painting is unmistakably a homage to the odalisques of Ingres, and to Goya's Maya. But this woman is a modern contemporary, and if she

Julius Paulsen
Under the Pont des Arts, Paris, 1910
Under Pont des Arts, Paris
Oil on canvas, 46 x 55 cm
Copenhagen, Statens Museum for Kunst

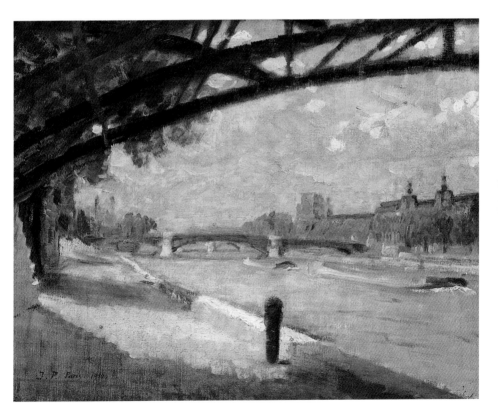

is *démasquée* it means she is seen stripped of literary, moral or historical veils – like Manet's *Olympia* (pp. 38/39), which drew on similar sources. A Buddha and two Japanese fans, a guitar and mask from Spain, and the colourful Finnish woven blanket, attest the importance of exotic accoutrements to Gallen-Kallela. The white lilies as a symbol of chastity, the crucifix, and the skull, suggest that the young woman has been posing as a penitent Magdalene. The present confronts the past; but the picture leaves us in no doubt as to which emerges on top.

The annual Salon provided the Scandinavian artists in Paris, too, with an occasion for festivities, especially if at least one of their number had submitted successfully. Hugo Birger (1854–1887) commemorated one such party in 1886 in *Scandinavian Artists Breakfasting at the Café Ledoyen, Paris, on Salon Opening Day* (p. 483). There is nothing Impressionist about the brushwork, but the subject and composition clearly owe something to Manet, Renoir or Degas. Swathes of smoke are drifting beneath the café's glass roof. The people's bodies, heads and hats provide the rhythmic spatial dynamics. No one person is highlighted; rather, the artist presents a sense of convivial bustle. First, perhaps, we notice the Swedish painter Hugo Salmson pouring champagne into a lady's glass. But our attention is also caught by Birger's Spanish wife, seated right of centre, who has turned to look straight at us. Beyond her we see a row of profiles taking us deeper into the space; the two men conversing at right perform the same function, the very direction of their gaze pointing our attention to the rear left, where some jovial toast is plainly just being offered.

Edelfelt's *In the Luxembourg Gardens* (p. 485), painted in 1887, uses a similar structure. Artists frequently took an interest in social life in parks. The light on the greenery, the flower beds and colourful dresses of the ladies, the children at play, all helped make park scenes interesting to painters. Manet's *Music at the Tuileries* (p. 43) had pointed the way, showing how a single focus of attention could be avoided. Figures stood where they happened to be; sometimes they were harshly cropped, so as to underline the impression of a chance glimpse. Edelfelt has grouped the children with their nannies along the edges, and they are looking in every direction. Spatial depth seems to open up almost by accident, yet the picture in fact features a carefully established transition from the shade beneath the trees to the sunlit promenade. As with Birger, the eye is invited to travel along a particular route: from bottom left, we follow the furled parasol across to the girl's hoop and on to the two children stooping at play, and then fetch up at the rear view of a lady in the middle distance. Beyond her, we follow the frieze of white-clad children in the background to the parasol of a woman in black, where our gaze is anchored in the replication of shape in a black article of clothing on the back of a chair, at the centre of the picture. The basic colours (as so often in Manet) are black, white, grey and ochre; the one standing lady is highlighted by the long red ribbon that falls down her cape, from her hat almost to the ground. This red is echoed in the paler red hat of a young woman at left.

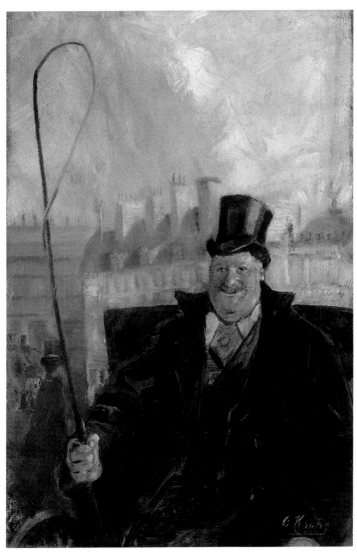

Christian Krohg
Paris Hackney Cab Driver, 1898
Pariserkusk
Oil on canvas, 43 x 29 cm
Oslo, Nasjonalgalleriet

Krohg's portrait of a *Paris Hackney Cab Driver* (p. 497) shows another side of modern life. The city streets are briefly suggested with a few sketchy façades, and in the background are a top-hatted man and a horse-drawn carriage; but the foreground is entirely occupied by the jovial cabman, more a type than an individual. We are shown just enough of the cab to be in no doubt that he is seated on the box; and the raised whip is absolutely unambiguous. Krohg's social commitment is as palpable in this portrait of the kind of proletarian usually ignored by polite society as it is in his writings.

The examples noted here of Scandinavian art produced under the influence of French Impressionism by no means tell the whole tale of Scandinavian art of the period in question. Impressionism exerted only a brief influence, and that on only a few artists. All the artists who had contact with the Paris art scene experimented with the new aesthetics and techniques; but as soon as they were again far from the French source, their work shortly regained its native, traditional character, and was coloured by the distinctive qualities of their own countries and countrymen. Even so, there can be no doubt that the path to greater freedom in the handling of light and colour, the essentials of the painter's art, and also to a new concept of reality, led via Paris.

JENS PETER MUNK

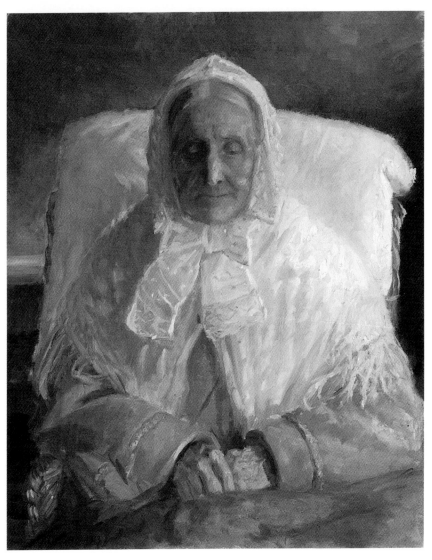

Anna Ancher
The Artist's Mother, Anna Hedvig Brøndum, 1913
Kunstnerindens moder, fru Anna Hedvig Brøndum
Oil on canvas, 79 x 63 cm
Skagen, Skagens Museum

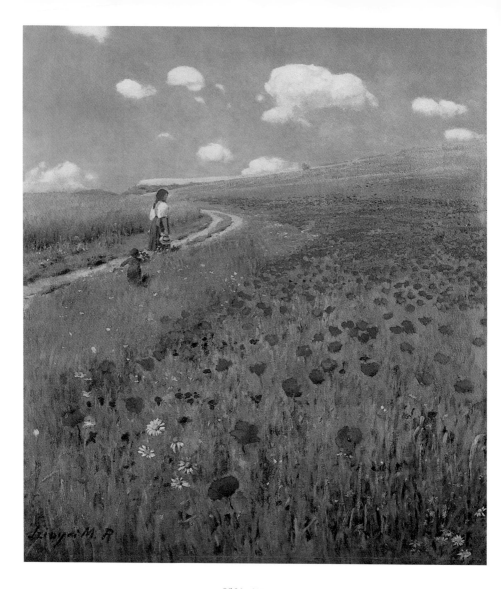

Pál Szinyei Merse
A Field of Poppies, 1902
Pipacsos mező
Oil on canvas, 88.5 x 79.7 cm
Budapest, Magyar Nemzetí Galéria

13 Homelands and Europe: East and Southeast European Impressionists

Impressionist painting arose in eastern central Europe, eastern Europe and southeast Europe for two reasons. Artists in regions ruled by the Russian Czar or the Austro-Hungarian Dual Monarchy, or in states that had recently fought for their liberation from the Ottoman Empire, were changing their techniques in obedience to the selfsame inner logic as their counterparts in western and central Europe. At the same time, they were under the influence of France, and, because that influence was subject to a certain "time lag", it took complex forms in the East.

Two phenomena were of importance. First, the insistence of realist, Impressionist and Post-Impressionist artists on the subjective truth of their paintings, and thus on their right to individual free creativity, was linked closely and for a long time with non-artistic, social struggles and, above all, with campaigns for national liberation. Ideas of an art both committed and instructive remained vibrant longer in eastern Europe, and were more widespread than in the West. Secondly, problems that appeared purely aesthetic sometimes acquired a greater political sensitivity than was the case in, say, the French debates on the relations between Impressionism and anarchism.

Russia

The standing conflict in Russia was that between the defenders of the Slavic, orthodox culture and those who were prepared to learn and take their bearings from the West. Since Peter the Great, Russian art had been in step with west European aesthetic principles and stylistic developments. Academic training and the criteria by which artists were evaluated proceeded from the same classical base as in Paris. But in Russia, too, outside officially sanctioned art, an interest was growing in the simple life and the landscape of the homeland, as well as in outdoor light, such as we see in the limpid, poetic paintings of Alexei Gavrilovich Venezianov (1780–1847).

In 1863 – which happened to be the year of the first Paris Salon des Refusés – 14 St. Petersburg Academy students who favoured realism rebelled against Academy regulations. They were promptly expelled,

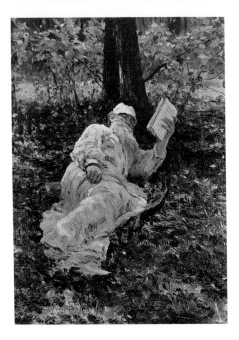

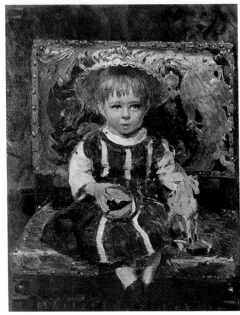

Ilya Yefimovich Repin
Tolstoy Resting in the Woods, 1891
Lev Nikolajevitsch Tolstoj se odmara u sumi
Oil on canvas, 60 x 50 cm
Moscow, State Tretyakov Gallery

Ilya Yefimovich Repin
Portrait of the Artist's Daughter Vera, 1874
Portret V.I. Repine
Oil on canvas, 73 x 60 cm
Moscow, State Tretyakov Gallery

and founded their own association. Together with members of the Moscow College of Art, which was socially and aesthetically progressive, this group became the Travelling Exhibitions Cooperative, which was established in 1870 and mounted its first public show in 1871 – in the St. Petersburg Academy, of all places, before it went on to Moscow and, in particular, provincial towns. The Peredvishniki (Wanderers), as these artists were called, mainly concentrated on realistic genre and landscape works; like the French artists grouped about Monet, there were a number of insignificant traditionalists among these Russian painters. Art by the Peredvishniki constituted the core of the most important collection of modern Russian art, that of the Moscow businessman Pavel Mikhailovich Tretyakov (1832–1898). A collector since 1856, he had opened a gallery beside his own home to the public in 1881, and in 1892, true to an idea he had had in 1860, he donated the collection to the city of Moscow for a national gallery. The Tretyakov Gallery contains the most important collection of Russian art, and has had an abiding influence on perceptions of Russian art history.

Scenes of village life, of poverty and toilsome work, or of social contrasts, were controversial both aesthetically and politically, just as Courbet's or Millet's were in France. In Russia, though, the arduous lot of the peasants, and debates on the role traditional village ways of life should play in the national identity, were of much greater importance.

This factor could endow genre painting with an instructional, societal weight that verged on agitprop; and this circumstance encouraged the adoption of the "literary" qualities Manet had introduced. Landscape paintings also focussed more on people's ways of life, on society, and on the people themselves. Russian painters (and their public) inclined to Romantic or Symbolist views, rather than to sober realism or the Impressionist obsession with questions of perception such as engaged the west European mind. Ivan Nikolaievich Kramskoy (1837–1887), the intellectual leader of the Peredvishniki, put into words a polarity that was repeatedly to cause misunderstanding and alienation on both sides: "With us content, with them form. With us, the idea is the main thing, with them, the technique."[1]

Thus Impressionist technique, often of a very high calibre, tended to be only one aspect of Russian painters' art. Ilya Yefimovich Repin (1844–1930) was a case in point. Graduating from the St. Petersburg Academy at the age of 29, he helped assure the international repute of Russian art with *Volga Boatmen* (1870–1873; St. Petersburg, State Russian Museum), which had taken him three years to complete. It was immediately exhibited at the 1873 Vienna World Fair, at a time when painters such as Monet were still being routinely turned down by the Paris Salon. Repin then spent the years from 1873 to 1876 in western Europe, including France, exhibiting at the 1875 Paris Salon. He was not taken with the sketchiness of Impressionism, and found only Manet to

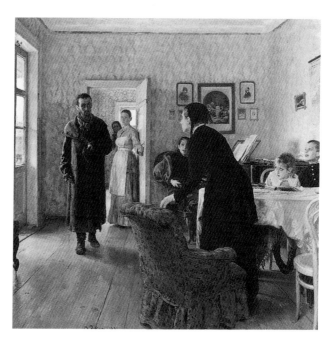

Ilya Yefimovich Repin
They did not expect him, 1884
Ne ždali
Oil on canvas, 160.5 x 167.5 cm
Moscow, State Tretyakov Gallery

his taste. Even so, his technique acquired a fresh ease in private studies such as the portrait of his little daughter Vera (p. 502).

His paintings of the 1880s that were important for their focus on social problems included *They did not expect him* (p. 503), which presents the early return home of a political exile. The sensitive colouring and atmospherics of this truthful picture are convincing, as are the spatial tensions, the snapshot recording of movement, and the precise rendering of facial expressions. In 1890 Repin left the Peredvishniki, and four years later was appointed professor at the Academy, which had now been reformed. Impressionism was acquiring a weightier presence at that point; but if Repin portrayed Lev Nikolaievich Tolstoy (1828–1910) in a remarkably "unofficial" pose, reclining in the grass, reading, wearing a peasant smock, in a painting notable for its generous, sketchy brushwork and its attention to effects of light and shadow (p. 502), then the contemporary beholder was intended to concentrate more on the content than he might in the case of Manet's relaxed portrait of Mallarmé, say. From 1880 on,

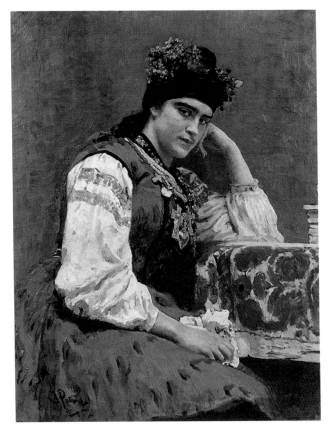

Ilya Yefimovich Repin
Portrait of Sofia Mikhailovna Dragomirova, 1889
Oil on canvas, 98.5 x 78.5 cm
St. Petersburg, State Russian Museum

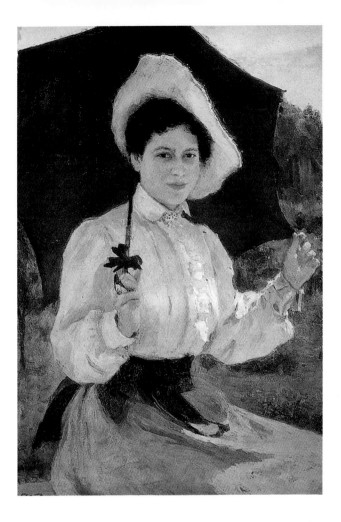

Ilya Yefimovich Repin
In the Sun, 1900
Na solnce
Oil on canvas, 94.3 x 67 cm
Moscow, State Tretyakov Gallery

Tolstoy became a sharp critic of the status quo, a social reformer for whom peasant life was the model.

Repin's journey to France in 1873 had been made with an aristocrat of his own age, Vassili Dimitrievich Polenov (1844–1927). In 1878, Polenov's *A Yard in Moscow* (p. 507) helped ease his admission to the Peredvishniki, whose leader he became following the death of Kramskoy. The picture's emphasis lies not on the perfectly presentable home of well-to-do people but on the bare grass and sandy paths in the yard and particularly the wonderful light flooding the whole scene, including the church in the background. It is an "intimate landscape" of the kind Daubigny and other Barbizon artists had established, only much brighter, its col-

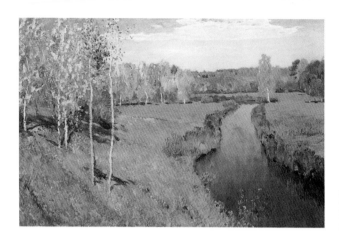

Isaac Ilyich Levitan
Golden Autumn, 1895
Zolotaja osen
Oil on canvas, 82 x 126 cm
Moscow, State Tretyakov Gallery

ours more intense. From 1892 to 1895 Polenov taught landscape painting at the Moscow College of Art, and his work of the Nineties was
particularly notable for spacious, atmospheric landscapes.

One of his pupils was Isaac Ilyich Levitan (1860–1900), a Jew from a
poor background. Levitan was a friend of his coeval, the writer Anton
Pavlovich Chekhov (1860–1904), later to achieve world fame. He exhibited with the Peredvishniki but was not able to visit western Europe
till 1890. Finally he became his own teacher's successor as head of the
Moscow College of Art's landscape school. He was unequalled in his
ability to evoke a veritably pantheist sense of the vastness of landscape,
or the dappling of light in a *Birch Grove* (p. 506) with its rhythmic,
delicately structured colour harmonies. Levitan, who rejected the Impressionism of Monet, was *par excellence* one of those who established
a continuity from pre-Impressionist, lyrical responses to Nature through
to Symbolist or Neo-Romantic Post-Impressionism. Nonetheless, his

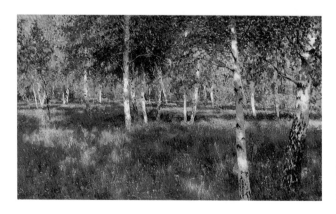

Isaac Ilyich Levitan
Birch Grove, c. 1885–1889
Erezovaja rosa
Oil on paper on canvas, 28.5 x 50 cm
Moscow, State Tretyakov Gallery

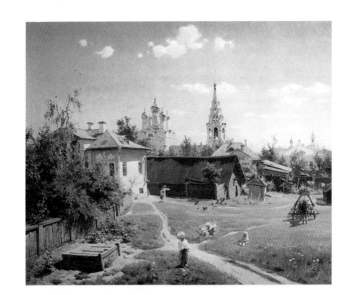

Vassili Dimitrievich Polenov
A Yard in Moscow, II, 1878
Moskovskij dvorik, II
Oil on canvas, 64.5 x 80.1 cm
Moscow, State Tretyakov Gallery

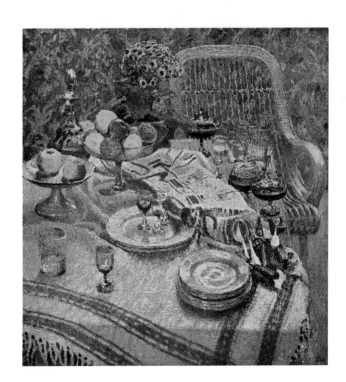

Igor Emmanuilovich Grabar
After Lunch, 1907
Nepribrannyj stol
Oil on canvas, 100 x 96 cm
Moscow, State Tretyakov Gallery

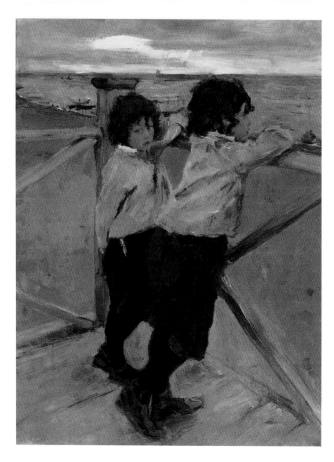

Valentin Alexandrovich Serov
The Children. Sasha and Yurra Serov, 1899
Deti. Saša i Jura Serovi
Oil on canvas, 71 x 54 cm
St. Petersburg, State Russian Museum

paintings reveal a thoroughly Impressionist sensitivity to phenomena of light and the autonomy of pure, strong colours.

Igor Emmanuilovich Grabar (1871–1960) was a somewhat younger artist who studied under Repin and in Munich and was soon to be a signal presence as a historian of Russian art and especially as director of the Tretyakov Gallery. A more textbook Impressionist himself, he was skilful in capturing colour phenomena that accompanied surprising seasonal change, as in *Winter* (p. 509), but this spontaneous kind of Impressionism was to be only a passing phase in his own evolution as an artist.

Valentin Alexandrovich Serov (1865–1911) defies pigeon-holing too. He was one of the foremost Russian artists around the turn of the century, and as a young man he had already painted one of the loveliest pictures of the 19th century, *Girl with Peaches* (p. 511). Serov was one of the Rasnotshinz intelligentsia (non-aristocrats exempt from taxation) who were so important in intellectual life and social progress, and who

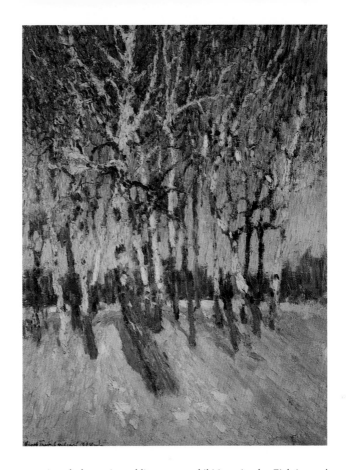

Igor Emmanuilovich Grabar
Winter, 1904
Zima
Oil on canvas, 75 x 54.5 cm
St. Petersburg, State Russian Museum

constituted the main public at art exhibitions in the Eighties and Nineties. His father was a composer who died young, his mother a pianist, and Serov himself was a child prodigy. Aged about nine, he was tutored in Paris by Repin, continued his studies in Moscow, and transferred to the Petersburg Academy at the age of 15. He then travelled repeatedly to western Europe. He was a regular in the illustrious circle of artists who frequented the Abramcevo estate 60 kilometres north of Moscow. The theatre-mad railway tycoon Savva I. Mamontov was the centre of the group, and it was his daughter Vera who sat for Serov's *Girl with Peaches* in 1887. The picture won a first prize in portrait painting from the Art Connoisseurs' Association. Its delight in light and colour, the ease of its brushwork and handling of outline, the ordinariness of the situation, the chance arrangement of objects in the background and the still life in the fore, are all qualities the painting shares with a Manet or Renoir of the previous decade. But Serov is also precise in his attention

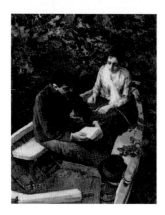

Constantin Alexeievich Korovin
Couple in a Boat, 1887
Para v lodke
Oil on canvas, 53 x 43 cm
Moscow, State Tretyakov Gallery

to facial expression, and for his sitter's character and emotional profile. That is to say, he introduces a human dimension that interested Degas alone of the French Impressionists, and in his case only in a sceptical, somewhat aloof way. Serov, who taught at the Moscow College of Art from 1897 to 1909, was later to be a high-society portrait artist, painting aristocrats and intellectuals. He had a firm grasp of the fleeting moment, and a bravura sense of colour. These qualities, and the nervous tensions or decorative zest of his outlining, made his works highly evocative.

His somewhat older friend Constantin Alexeievich Korovin (1861–1939) was surely the purest Russian Impressionist, the closest to the French spirit, which his several visits to western Europe after 1885 familiarized him with. He too was one of the Abramcevo group, and with Serov he exhibited with the World of Art association, founded in 1900 as an offshoot of the periodical of the same name (published 1899–1904) by the editor Sergei Diaghilev (1872–1929), later famous as a ballet impresario. In the early years of the century, this periodical played a leading part in establishing links with France, Britain and Germany, and creating an international, Secessionist art that blended Impressionism, decorative Art Nouveau, and a Neo-Romantic art that stressed the values of home regions. Korovin's Paris street scenes (p. 510), lush still lifes, and pictures of holidaymakers on the Crimean coast or a young couple in a

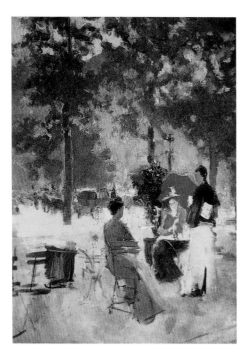

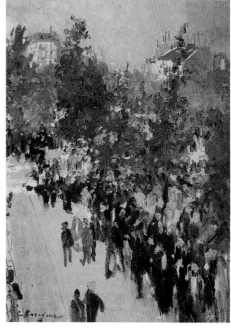

Valentin Alexandrovich Serov
Girl with Peaches, 1887
Devočka s persikami
Oil on canvas, 91 x 85 cm
Moscow, State Tretyakov Gallery

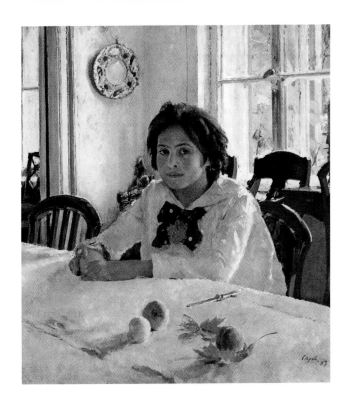

Kasimir Malevich
Flower Girl, 1903
Cvetounica
Oil on canvas, 80 x 100 cm
St. Petersburg, State Russian Museum

Left:
Constantin Alexeievich Korovin
Café in Paris, c. 1890–1900
Parizskoe kafe
Oil on canvas, 50 x 61 cm
Moscow, State Tretyakov Gallery

Constantin Alexeievich Korovin
Boulevard des Capucines, Paris, 1906
Pariž, Bul'var Kapucinok
Oil on canvas, 73.3 x 60.2 cm
Moscow, State Tretyakov Gallery

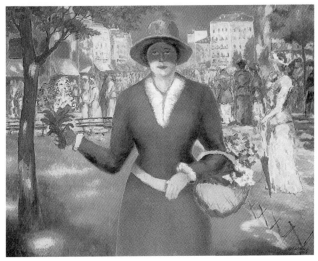

rowing boat (p. 510), all show him to have been in love with the colours and beauty of the world, with the evidence of the eye. More than any previous artist except arguably his teacher Polenov, he made the sketchy rendering of colourful impressions a viable form of finished artwork in Russian painting, too. His early works (such as those reproduced here) were nonetheless closer to the precise draughtsmanship and narrative interest of a Caillebotte or Forain than to Monet, twenty years his senior. One fact marks a difference from the French Impressionists, though: the man in the rowing boat is the artist himself, seen together with the artist Maria W. Yakunchikova. To the French way of thinking, this would not have qualified as something the artist himself had seen; they did not paint self-portraits in developed, narrative contexts.

Poland

Polish art had existed in a country that had been under the yoke of three foreign powers since the late 18th century: Prussia, Austria-Hungary and, to the largest extent, Czarist Russia. This historical condition produced a strain of patriotism that was passionate and given to sad nostalgia for past grandeur and remembrance of tragic defeats. The nation's intellectual life largely took its bearings from France, and this was reflected in the ideas and organizational structures that prevailed in Polish art. Poland's powerful interest in nationhood, the country's struggle for a culture of its own, and the time lag apparent in aesthetic developments compared with France, all meant that Impressionism in landscape, genre

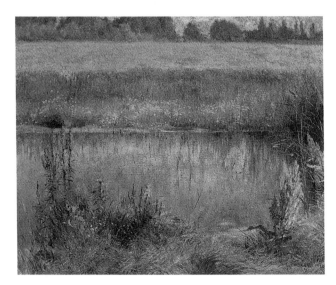

Władysław Podkowiński
Field of Lupins, 1891
Pole lubinu
Oil on panel, 49.5 x 61.5 cm
Cracow, Muzéum Narodówe

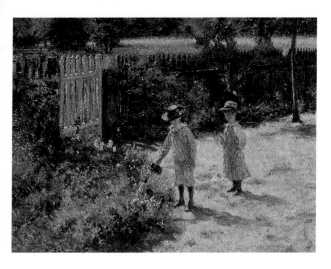

and portrait painting was initially a mere phase, quickly superseded by Post-Impressionist or Symbolist tendencies. On the other hand, a powerful influence of French Impressionism was still palpable as late as 1930.[1]

In 1889, Władysław Podkowiński (1866–1895) and Józef Pankiewicz (1866–1940) of the Warsaw College of Art visited Paris for the World Fair. There they encountered Impressionism, and, through Theo van Gogh, the paintings of Cézanne. The exhibition of their own work in Warsaw in 1890 signalled the beginning of Impressionism there. In the few years that remained to Podkowiński in his short life, he used very bright and sometimes strongly contrastive colours, split in accordance with divisionist principles, to paint typical Impressionist landscape and garden subjects (pp. 512 and 513). Pankiewicz helped make Cracow (part of the Austro-Hungarian Empire till 1918) the leading centre of Polish Secessionism and a constant rival of Warsaw. The Sztuka (Art) Association was founded in Cracow in 1897, and in 1899 the new bearings in art earned the label Young Poland. In 1900 the Cracow College of Art was elevated to Academy status, and there Pankiewicz taught from 1906 till 1914 and again from 1919 till 1923 (though he repeatedly visited western Europe in the same periods). He too combined Impressionist and various Post-Impressionist approaches. In the Nineties he brought an equal intensity to sunlight and to nighttime scenes with the light of city streetlamps (p. 514). For Polish purposes, Pankiewicz adapted Cézanne's handling of colour, and his programmatic view that art should be "a harmony parallel to Nature", into Polish "Colourism", which was to remain influential till after 1945. From 1925 till his death he ran a Paris wing of the Cracow Academy, where a number of younger painters from Cracow constituted the Komytet Paryski (Paris Committee). Their version of late or Post-Impressionism is generally known as "Kapism" from the initials (K.P.) of the group.

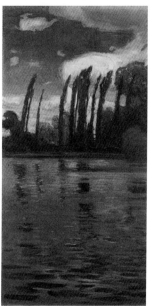

Polish painting in that period was polarized between pre-Impressionist traditions committed to communicating thematic messages and Post-Impressionist or Symbolist strategies. We can see this well in the Cracow professors Leon Wyczółkowski (1852–1936) and – especially – Jan Stanisławski (1860–1907). The latter lived for many years in Paris, painted pointillist work on occasion in Poland and his Ukrainian homeland, and then, as professor of landscape art and co-founder of the Sztuka, became a major figure in the Cracow art revival. He adopted Monet's poplar motif (p. 330) – a frieze-like, decorative product of the Nineties – and developed it further in the stylized, linear, melancholy manner of Art Nouveau (p. 513), reworking the same subject in lithographs and woodcuts too. Olga Boznańska (1865–1940) lived in Paris from 1895 till her death, settling for a style derived from early Impressionism, delicately painted, with atmospherics reminiscent of Manet or Whistler, while for Władysław Ślewiński (1854–1918), who lived and

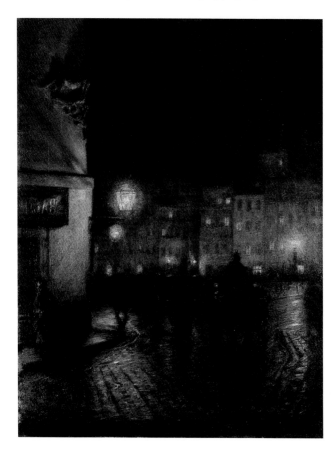

Józef Pankiewicz
The Old City Market, Warsaw, at Night, 1892
Rynek Starego Miasta w Warszawie Noça
Oil on canvas, 61 x 45.5 cm
Poznan, Muzéum Narodówe

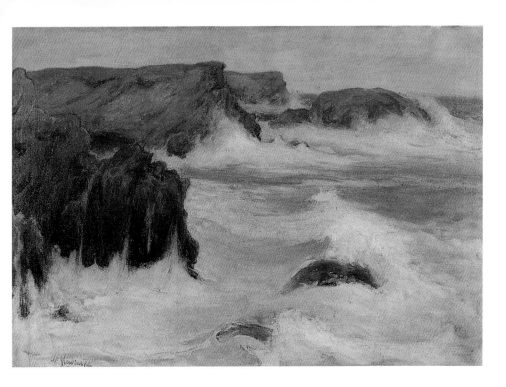

worked in Paris and Brittany from 1888 to 1905 and again from 1910 on, the decisive note was set by the spatial flatness and symbolic innuendos of Gauguin and the Nabis. His art too, of course, was not without its Impressionist roots (p. 515).

Władysław Ślewiński
Rough Sea at Belle-Ile, 1904
Morze (Fale nadbrzezne)
Oil on canvas, 57.5 x 82 cm
Jaworska 138
Cracow, Muzéum Narodówe

For many Poles, a variety of Romanticism that aimed at psychological interpretation continued to set the tone in aesthetics, social and intellectual conduct, and attitudes to history. This cast of mind blessed Poland with close interaction between painting, literature and the theatre. There were a large number of talents with both literary and artistic gifts in the Modernist period, and artists often had a notable rapport with music and with traditional folk art.[5]

Bohemia and Moravia

The Czech sense of nationhood evolved in more self-assured and unproblematic ways under the Habsburgs than did Poland's under the Czars. Artistic contact with Vienna and Munich was good, and the influence of French art, apparent from the 1860s on, was indicative of the underlying logic of European cultural development rather than of politically conditioned responses. In 1863, the year of the Paris Salon des

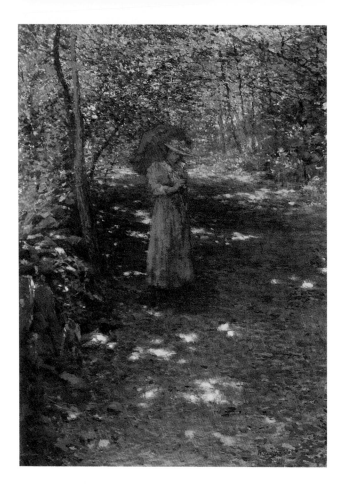

Antonín Slavíček
Walking in the Park, 1897
V parku procházce
Tempera on card, 69.5 x 52.8 cm
Prague, Národní Gallery

Refusés, the Umělecká Beseda (Artists' Association) was established in Prague, for artists working in every field. In 1887 the first modern artists' organization running exhibitions of its own was founded, taking its name from Josef Mánes (1820–1871), pioneer of national art and co-founder of the Beseda, and publishing the periodical "Volné smery" (Free Directions).

In Bohemia too the struggle for a national culture and a historical tradition of one's own was so important that late Romanticism and emotional historicism (such as characterized the Prague National Theatre's opulent indulgences of the 1880s) were not perceived as being irreconcilably at odds with the new aesthetics, as they were in France in the same period. An intimate realism that discovered the landscape of the homeland in a Barbizon spirit could easily be accommodated to national his-

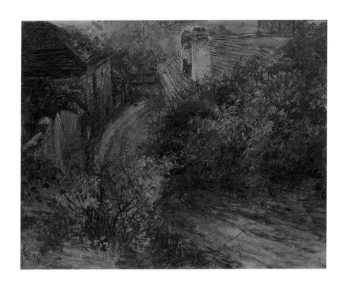

Otakar Lebeda
Lilac. Village Path, 1899
Šeřík. Cesta vesnicí
Mixed media on card, 66 x 79 cm
Prague, Národní Gallery

torical art. The Prague College of Art was the centre of this accommo-
dation. It was an approach that enabled artists to adapt their aesthetic
approaches to the task in hand – in a manner that has repeatedly baffled
west European critics. An Impressionist handling of light and colour, for
Czech artists, was not the statement of an aesthetic creed; rather, it was
a use of available methods that had been tested for their suitability for
the evolution of a national art of the homeland.

Otakar Lebeda (1877–1901), who spent a year working in France and
shot himself at the age of 24 following a nervous disorder, painted landscapes now sad, now turbulent, which show him essentially locating an
Impressionist style, though he also shared the fractured mood of the

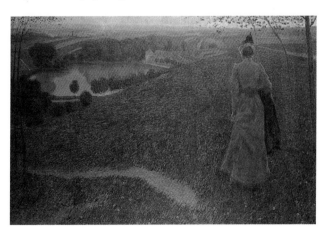

Antonín Hudeček
Quiet Evening, 1900
Večerní ticho
Oil on canvas, 120 x 180 cm
Prague, Národní Gallery

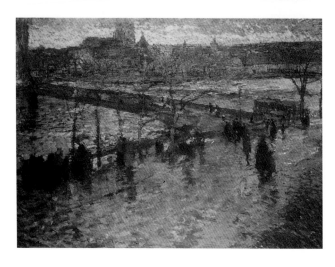

Symbolist Nineties (p. 517). Antonín Slavíček (1870–1910) was the closest to Impressionism of a French kind, though it was not till 1907 that he visited France. He was a pupil of Julius Mařák (1832–1899), a leading painter of patriotic landscape art. From the 1890s on, Slavíček's subject matter, relaxed brushwork, bright colours, and even structures were strongly reminiscent of Pissarro (pp. 516 and 518).

Quiet Evening (p. 517) was painted by his friend Antonín Hudeček (1872–1941), a fine talent who has regrettably remained relatively unsung. Hudeček was soon to adopt a more expressive strategy, influenced by Munch. *Quiet Evening* is pointillist in its handling of the grassy slope but Neo-Romantic in its atmospherics, which inform the composition

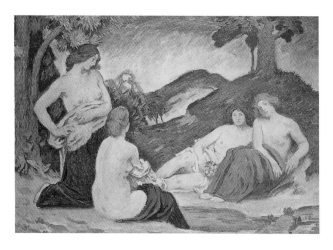

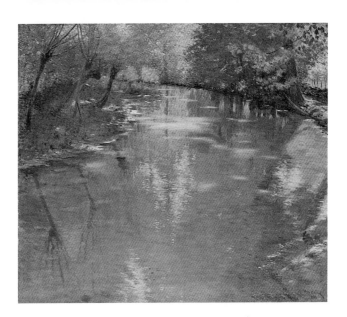

Antonín Hudeček
A Stream in Sunshine, 1897
Potok ve slunečním svitu
Oil on canvas, 81 x 90 cm
Prague, Národní Gallery

and colours and insist on a rhythm of curves (as in the tree reflections in the lake, or the slender tree trunks at left) such as was characteristic of heavily stylized European art at the turn of the century. Other works by Hudeček give their full attention to effects of light (p. 519).

The art of Jan Preisler (1872–1918) was of a late Impressionist kind, and underwent change thanks first to the example of Gauguin and then to Fauvism and Expressionism. For some time this style was of greater moment than Impressionist art itself, though an Impressionist delight in Nature remained a fundamental of Czech painting. In 1902 Preisler visited Italy with Hudeček, not travelling to France (and the Low Countries) till 1906. In 1913 he became professor at the Prague Academy. Picture such as *Bathers* (p. 518) record his interest in Renoir and Cézanne.

Hungary

The proud Hungarians had been deeply humiliated by the defeat which met their revolt against the Habsburgs in 1848/49. An agricultural country where the land was parcelled into vast estates, Hungary was socially and economically far behind western Europe, and this was not without implications for art. Attempts to establish a national historical tradition culminated in the millennial celebrations of the Magyar settlements in 1896, with great festivities and artworks. The discovery and valuation of distinctive Hungarian landscapes and folk ways of life were vital sources of motivation for Hungarian artists. Like all smaller nations

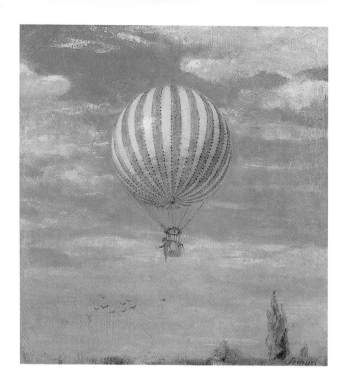

Pál Szinyei Merse
The Balloon, 1878
Léghajó
Oil on canvas, 41.5 x 39 cm
Budapest, Magyar Nemzeti Galéria

disadvantaged by history, Hungary was torn in two directions, wanting to keep up with what the leading European art centres considered modern and interesting, but at the same time wanting to preserve their own distinctive appeal.[4]

Mihály Munkácsy (i.e. Michael Lieb, 1844–1900) belonged to the generation of Monet and Liebermann. He achieved an international name in Düsseldorf and particularly Paris, where he lived from 1872 to 1896, marrying a wealthy baroness. In 1878 he was himself given a title. His own brand of realism was forceful, and contrived to retain the broad thematic range and effects beloved of the Salon. His paintings dealt with religious or philosophical material, society life in opulent interiors (comparable to similar work by the Belgian artist Stevens), and also scenes of social drama and the enduring fight for liberty. In Munkácsy's work, light and colour are not those of a pleinairist, and, as is so often the case, it was only his studies that had any impulsive spontaneity or freshness.

His friend László Páal (1846–1879) studied in Munich and then spent his short, hard life in Paris and the woods of Fontainebleau, where he introduced the Barbizon school's principles to Hungarian landscape art. He tended to paint tracks, village streets or the fringes of peaceful forests (as on p. 521), with lofty or crooked tree trunks bathed in gentle sunlight, the silvery green and sandy brown subtly nuanced, and highlighting afforded by a whitewashed house or the clothing of an old woman in the middle distance. Mildly elegiac moods mattered more to him than visual structure or the division of colours.

In Munich at about the same time, a member of Leibl's circle, Paul von Merse, likewise one of the country gentry, who had named himself Pál Szinyei Merse (1845–1920) after his home town in what is now Slovakia, undertook a valiant lone attempt at bright *plein-air* painting. His sketches make a relaxed, spontaneous impression, but in the paintings he did from them he preferred detailed precision presentation and a draughtsman's emphasis on subject matter. His strong interest in the Swiss artist Böcklin is unmistakable. In 1873 he painted his best known picture, *Luncheon on the Grass (The Picnic)* (p. 523). It recalls outings young artists and their girlfriends made near Munich, but was in fact painted in the studio. The subject and treatment would have been considered modern at the time. The poses of the reclining men and of the man squatting in the foreground are deliberately unconventional, conceived as snapshot records of a moment, though the group as a whole has been meticulously related to the overall composition. The scene is bathed in bright sunshine, yet the brightness does not seem the product of genuinely close observation. The colours have not been analytically split to intensify their luminous impact, nor has the problem of presenting figures at one with the natural setting in a dapple of light and shadow been tackled here. In other words, Szinyei Merse's treatment of light and

László Páal
Path in the Woods of Fontainebleau, 1876
Ut a Fontainebleau-i erdöben
Oil on canvas, 65 x 46 cm
Budapest, Magyar Nemzeti Galéria

Károly Ferenczy
October, 1903
Október
Oil on canvas, 126 x 107 cm
Budapest, Magyar Nemzeti Galéria

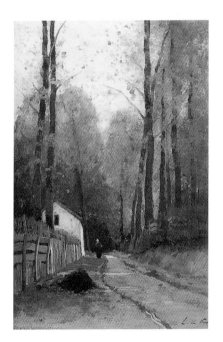

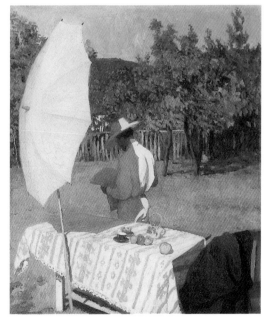

colour is of a non-Impressionist order (such as Renoir occasionally approximated to in the late Eighties). *The Balloon* (p. 520), painted five years later, a delightful picture showing a red and yellow balloon and combining an interesting subject with an unusual visual effect, has attracted symbolic interpretation.[5] Following failures at exhibitions in Vienna and Budapest, Merse ceased painting till 1894. He subsequently was rediscovered as a forerunner of Hungarian Modernist art and returned to painting landscapes. In 1905 he was appointed principal of the Budapest College of Art. Even when painting subjects that had always appealed to the Impressionist eye, such as poppy fields (pp. 500 and 523), he never abandoned his Böcklinesque approach, so that ultimately he lagged behind the direction art was taking in his time.

In 1896, the year of the millennial celebrations, an artists' colony was established in hilly eastern Hungary at Nagybánya (now Baia Mare in Rumania). This followed the Alföld group, artists of the Hungarian plains, who had studied peasant life and landscape at Szolnok in particular. The Nagybánya painters grouped about the colony's initiator, Simon Hollósy (1857–1918), almost all found their way there via Munich. They worked in a variety of styles, from an almost transcendent realism à la Bastien-Lepage to a Symbolist form of Art Nouveau, though always retaining an overriding interest in the homeland and its people. Károly Ferenczy (1862–1917), later professor at the Budapest Academy and tutor to a great many students, was notably consistent in his deployment of an Impressionist sense of light and of the colour harmonies between

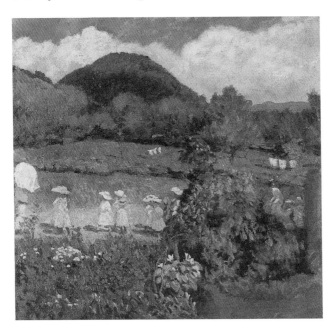

Károly Ferenczy
Summer Day, 1906
Nyári nap, Majális
Oil on canvas, 100 x 103.2 cm
Budapest, Magyar Nemzeti Galéria

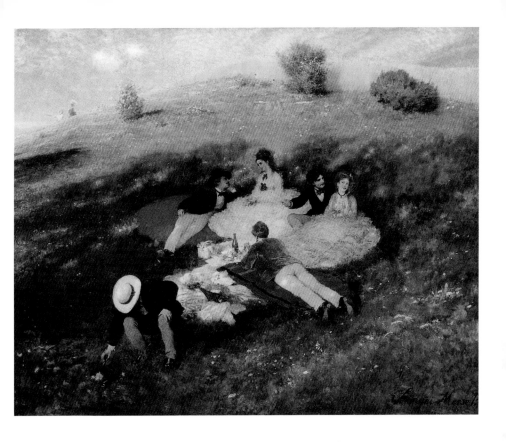

Pál Szinyei Merse
Luncheon on the Grass (The Picnic), 1873
Majális
Oil on canvas, 123 x 161.5 cm
Budapest, Magyar Nemzeti Galéria

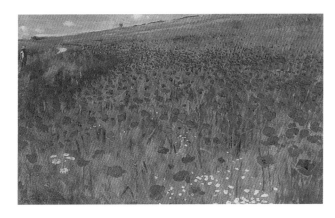

Pál Szinyei Merse
A Field of Poppies, 1896
Pipacsos mező
Oil on canvas, 39 x 63.2 cm
Budapest, Magyar Nemzeti Galéria

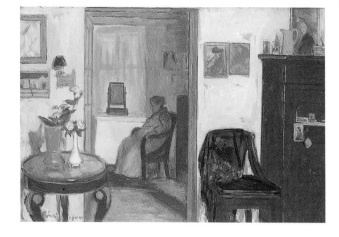

József Rippl-Rónai
Living on Memories, 1904
Amikor az ember visszaemlékezéseiből él
Oil on card, 70.5 x 103 cm
Budapest, Magyar Nemzeti Galéria

József Rippl-Rónai
Lady in a Polka-Dot Dress, 1889
Nő fehérpettyes ruhában
Oil on canvas, 187 x 75 cm
Budapest, Magyar Nemzeti Galéria

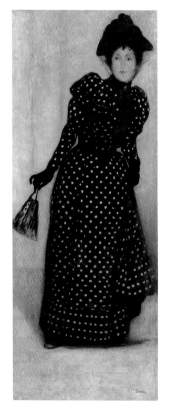

people and their surroundings. *October* (p. 521), with its still strong autumnal light, is a fine example of his ability to simulate a spontaneous response to the fortuitous moment. It is a pleasingly unusual, asymmetrical composition including a garden table at an angle, with a breakfast still life, the sunshade of a *plein-air* painter, and a man standing and glancing through the newspaper.

József Rippl-Rónai (1861–1927) was a special case because he was involved in the evolution of Post-Impressionism in Paris.[6] He too tended to oscillate rapidly between various techniques. After studying in Munich, he gained a Hungarian state scholarship to Paris in 1887, where he became the assistant of the overworked Munkácsy and painted pictures which the latter signed with his own name. The first work he painted in his own right, the 1889 *Lady in a Polka-Dot Dress* (p. 524), was quite different in style, suggesting the influence of Whistler. The lifesize figure is caught frontally in mid-movement, painted in a relaxed, sketchy manner but with firm, curving outlines and a decorative use of spatial areas. The whole is informed by the indefinable appeal of the woman's veiled, somewhat earnest and meditative, yet pretty face. These were very much the kind of qualities that inspired Bonnard and Vuillard too.

As Rippl-Rónai's personal style developed, he betrayed changing preferences in colourist technique, and an Art Nouveau linearity and use of larger decorative spaces was superseded by a mosaic pointillism and then by powerful Fauvist colours in what he himself called his "maize cob style". Elements of Impressionism persisted in his work, and particularly of the intimate late Impressionism of his friend Vuillard. A good example is the symbolically-titled interior *Living on Memories* (p. 524), with the old mother deep in the remoter, gloomier parts of a bright picture. The pieces of furniture, cropped by the edges, establish a compositional rhythm and, painted in a loose manner, are atmospherically comforting in the accord of their colours.

Romania

For decades Hungary and Turkey, and at times Russia, fought out a tug-of-war over Romania. About half of the country's present territory, Transylvania, was Hungarian till 1918. The Danubian principalities of Moldavia and Wallachia adopted the name "Romania" through union in 1862, attaining independence of Turkey. From 1866 this new principality was ruled by a Hohenzollern. In 1878 its sovereignty was guaranteed by the major European powers, and in 1881 Romania became a kingdom. Cultural continuity with developments elsewhere in Europe was inevitably affected by time lag. The fact that the country spoke a Romance language heightened the tendency of artists to take their bearings from France. The art colleges founded in 1860 at Jassy in Moldavia and in 1864 in the capital, Bucharest, adopted western European teaching methods and views, especially those of the French academies.

Nicolae Grigorescu (1838–1907), who started out as a painter of icons, moved on from the Bucharest College to Paris for further training from 1861 to 1869. Though he did not entirely abandon patriotic historical subject-matter, he was the first Romanian artist to break with academic tradition by adopting *plein-air* landscape styles. He made repeated visits to France, and his technique acquired an ease that places them scarcely second, in the freshness of the treatment, to the early work of Pissarro or Sisley (p. 526).

One case eloquent of eastern Europe's difficult entry into Modernism was the tragically short life of Ion Andreescu (1850–1882). The son of a brandy merchant with a great many children, he graduated from the Bucharest Art College and became a teacher of drawing and calligraphy

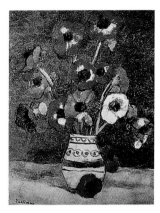

Stefan Luchian
Anemones
Oil on canvas, 44.5 x 35 cm
Bucharest, Muzeul de Artă, Galeria Naţională

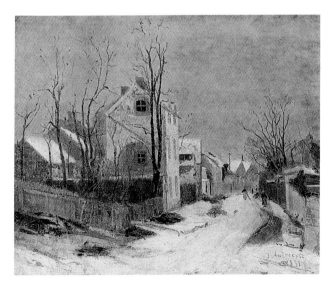

Ion Andreescu
Winter at Barbizon, 1881
Iarna da Barbizon
Oil on canvas, 54 x 65 cm
Bucharest, Muzeul K.H. Zambaccian

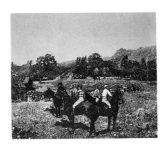

Stefan Luchian
The Last Race, 1892
Ultima cursa de toamna
Oil on canvas, 58 x 67 cm
Bucharest, Muzeul de Artă, Galeria Natională

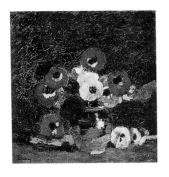

Stefan Luchian
Anemones, 1908
Oil on canvas, 42.5 x 43 cm
Bucharest, Muzeul de Artă, Galeria Natională

at a provincial grammar school. In 1874, the year the Impressionists made their first joint public appearance in Paris, Andreescu exhibited a delightfully fresh still life of a few blackcurrants and nothing but, his first appearance in a Bucharest show. In 1878, already suffering from the tuberculosis that was to kill him, he was awarded a travel scholarship to France, where he spent two years at the Académie Julian. At Barbizon he was tutored by Grigorescu. He exhibited small landscapes in the 1879, 1880 and 1881 Paris Salons. He was acquainted with Georges de Bellio (1828–1894), a Romanian doctor and art collector who lived in Paris, and will presumably have shared his liking for Impressionist art. Andreescu's pictures were almost invariably small-format, designed to satisfy old-fashioned tastes, and were sold in Bucharest via Alexis Gebauer, who was in the music trade. In spring 1882 he had some 60 paintings in a rather poorly attended exhibition. Since his works had been exhibited at the Paris Salon though, he was not without purchasers in Bucharest, and one painting was acquired by the state. Only a few months later, however, he was dead.

Andreescu's pictures tend to suggest fresh delight in the beauty of Nature, relish of its colours. He was forever trying to create fresh, harmonious art out of what he saw. The rich colours of grass, foliage, rocks and sky, and the structural appearance of trees in the woods at Fontainebleau, exerted a continual attraction (p. 527), but he was also proficient at intricately nuanced whites, greys and light ochres in a village scene such as *Winter at Barbizon* (p. 525), exhibited at the 1881 Salon. If these paintings bore the signature of Pissaro, and were anywhere but in a remote gallery far from the highways of the international museum-going public and the predilections of art historians, they would long since have enjoyed a just esteem.

It was to be some time yet before Impressionist views on art made any headway in Romania. That they did so was mainly thanks to Stefan

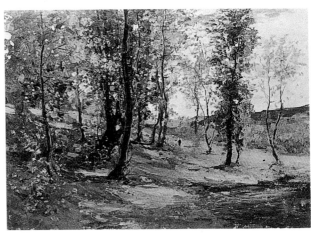

Nicolae Grigorescu
A Clearing, c. 1885
Luminis
Oil on canvas, 54.5 x 81.5 cm
Bucharest, Muzeul de Artă, Galeria Natională

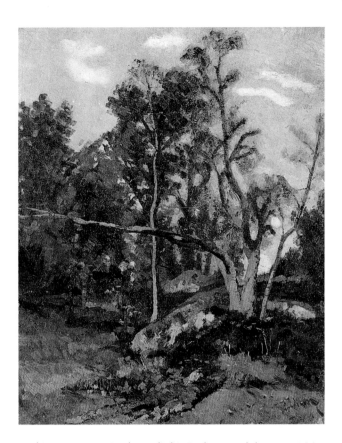

Ion Andreescu
Edge of the Forest, c. 1880
Margine de pădure
Oil on canvas, 61 x 50.5 cm
Bucharest, Muzeul de Artă, Galeria Naţională

Luchian (1868–1916), who studied in Bucharest and then (1889) Munich before going to the Académie Julian in Paris (1890–1892). He then returned home, where he co-founded an independent art show in 1896 and, in 1902, the Tinerimea artistica (Artistic Youth) association. In Paris, the example of Manet and Degas had prompted him to tackle such subjects as horse races (p. 526), and he had absorbed a first influence of Post-Impressionism. He was the first Romanian artist to develop a real feel for cityscapes. For fellow Romanian artists, though, he was primarily important as a master of autonomous colour and of thick, pastose and spontaneous brushwork.

Following Grigorescu and Andreescu, it was Luchian who played a key part in establishing Impressionist choices of subject matter, ways of seeing, and techniques (albeit often modified by intense Fauvist colourism or simplified form), as a tradition that would extend well into the 20th century. It may well have been thanks to these artists that, the greatest successes achieved by Impressionism outside its native France were reached in Romania.[7]

Among the Yugoslav peoples of the Balkans, the difficulties and tragedies of modern history long delayed the evolution of recognisably modern culture. From the Middle Ages till 1918, Slovenia, with its major city of Ljubljana, belonged to Habsburg Austria. In the same period, Croatia, with the city of Zagreb, was also under Habsburg and Hungarian control, and did not achieve any measure of autonomy till 1868. Serbia, with its capital in Belgrade, achieved independence between 1867 and 1878, after four centuries of Turkish rule. This success made Serbia a model for other southern Slavic liberation movements; but in the case of Bosnia (with Sarajevo as capital) and Herzegovina, all that could be accomplished in 1878 was to exchange the Turkish master for an Austro-Hungarian. In 1918 these and other territories became a Serbian-dominated kingdom, which adopted the name Yugoslavia in 1929. Individual endeavours to create a new, more true-to-life aesthetic as well as national cultural institutions and artistic associations inevitably went hand in hand with attempts to escape the hegemony of Vienna or Budapest, and to locate alternative examples to follow, in Munich, Paris or Russia.

In 1904, the first South Slav Art Exhibition was held (including Bulgaria). The organizers intended it as a first demonstration of the cultural unity of Yugoslavia and of the distinctive ways that culture differed from other cultures. Further exhibitions of this kind followed in Sofia in 1906, in Zagreb in 1908, and again in Belgrade in 1912. A historical assessment penned in 1968 concluded that "Impressionism was the first call to arms in modern Yugoslav art".[8] As in all eastern Europe, Impressionism was obliged to compete with more emotional, Neo-Romantic, Symbolist renderings of Nature, which were more effective as vehicles for patriotic ideas. At the same time, Impressionism also became intermingled with other internationally disseminated, decorative forms of Post-Impressionist Modernism.

From about 1880, individual Yugoslav painters were becoming acquainted both with academic and with realistic and, above all, *plein-air* approaches in art, in Paris and, more often, in Munich. The private academy founded in Munich in 1891 by the Slovenian realist Anton Ažbè (1862–1905) played a vital part in this process. The Russian artist Grabar taught there from 1896, and the academy numbered Kandinsky among its students. In Belgrade, the Slovak Kirilo Kutlik (1847–1900) ran a school he had founded in 1895. In Croatia, an artists' organization was set up in 1897 to promote both a national school in art and Modernism in general. In these aims, though, specifically Impressionist ways of seeing and of handling colour – such as are evident in the delicate *Trees in Snow* (p. 528) by the tragic young genius Slava Raškaj (1877–1906) – constituted only one stylistic strand.

Full-blown Impressionism did eventually become apparent in a number of locations in the opening decade of the 20th century. In Slovenia, where a first national art show was held in 1900 at Ljubljana, Ivan Grohar (1867–1911), after first experimenting with other styles, took to

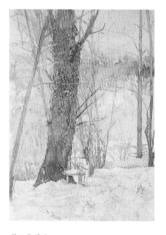

Slava Raškaj
Trees in Snow, 1900
Stablo u snijegu
Watercolour on paper, 43.3 x 59 cm
Zagreb, Moderna Galerija

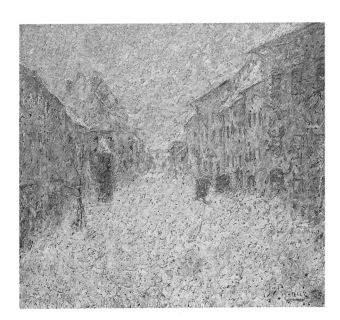

painting landscapes that combined precise atmosphere with vibrant and coherent brushwork. It is this union of mood and technique that makes *Snow in Škofja Loka* (p. 529) so appealing. On the advice of his friend Rihard Jakopić (1873–1918), Grohar had attended Ažbè's academy in Munich, and with Jakopić, Matija Jama (1872–1947) and Matej Sternen (1870–1949) – who all studied at Ažbè's, too – founded an artists' group named after the River Sava.

This Slovenia Sava group made a strong impression on young Serbian painters when they exhibited at the 1904 Belgrade show. Several of these, who were to make significant contributions to Serbian Impressionism, had been to Kutlik's school or to Ažbè's in Munich. After Kutlik died in 1900, the realist Rista Vukanović (1873–1918) and his German wife Beta (Babette Bachmayer, 1872–1927) took over his school, which became a state establishment in 1905.

The 1904 Yugoslav exhibition led Marko Murat (1864–1944), who had been trained in Munich and had received an award for an immense history painting at the 1900 Paris World Fair, to start an artists' association known as Lada (Harmony). This association survived till the Second World War. Murat, who evolved a subtle approach to open-air painting early in his career, later painted pure Impressionist work, mainly in Dubrovnik, where he worked in conservation from 1919 to 1932. On the other hand, though, in the decade after 1908 he espoused the strongly nationalist ideology of the Medulić group (so called after the Croatian Renaissance artist Andrija Medulić, called Andrea Schiavone). The leader of the Medulić group was the sculptor Ivan Meštrović (1883–1962).

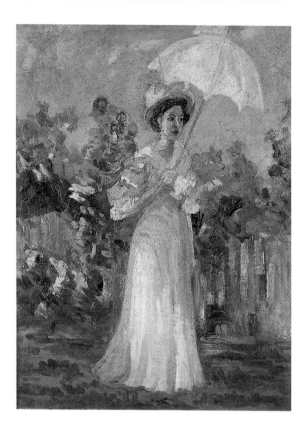

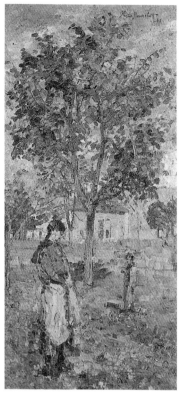

Nadežda Petrović
Lady with a White Parasol, c. 1910
Figura sa belim šeširom
Oil on canvas, 90.2 x 65 cm
Belgrade, Narodni Muzej

Kosta Miličević
Spring, 1913
Proleće
Oil on canvas, 102 x 50.3 cm
Belgrade, Narodni Muzej

Three Serbian painters a decade younger, born at a time when French Impressionism was already in full bloom, painted very fine work in a style influenced by Monet and his closer associates. All three studied at Kutlik's and Ažbè's academies; two of them also spent time in Paris. They were members both of Lada and of the Medulić group, and in the First World War they served against Austria-Hungary with patriotic fervour. Milan Milovanović (1876–1946) returned from Paris in 1906 a convert to Impressionism. He used the style in 1907 when he visited the Orthodox monasteries of Serbia, Macedonia, and Mount Athos. He subsequently became committed to national, historical art, and was then a war artist. In 1917, while convalescing from an injury, he was transferred to Capri, where his happiness at having survived is expressed in the visual relish with which he recorded the strong colours of his new surroundings (*The Blue Door*, p. 531). From 1920 on he taught at the Belgrade College of Art, although no longer painting himself. Kosta Miličević (1877–1920) taught for several years at the school run by Vukanović. His landscape works, such as *Spring* (p. 530), are notable for their harmony, brightness and ease; in subject matter and style they recall Pissarro.

The most arresting of the younger Serbian artists was Nadežda Petrović (1873–1915), whose practice as painter and writings as critic were alike aimed at furthering the cause of Modernism as vigorously as possible. Petrović studied under Kutlik, then under Ažbè, and then at a private summer course taught in Munich by the Secessionist Julius Exter (1863–1939). She exhibited at the 1904 Belgrade show, and was impressed by Grohar and his group. The following year she organized the first Serbian artists' colony, at Sičeva in the country. In 1906 she had work in the first Lada exhibition, and later joined Medulić. She spent the years from 1910 to 1912 in Paris, meeting the Fauves and exhibiting, like them, at the autumn Salon. Some years before, though, in Munich, Petrović had already been painting the intensely colourful and dynamically structured *Trees in a Wood* (1902; Belgrade, Narodni Muzej), in a manner that would reappear some years later, in the same place, in the work of Kandinsky and the Blaue Reiter Expressionists. In contrast to such excursions, pictures Petrović later painted back in Serbia, such as the bright, generously sketched, resplendent *Lady with a White Parasol* (p. 530), are Impressionism of a fine, pure order.

PETER H. FEIST

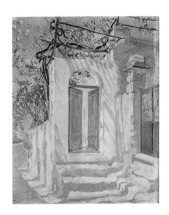

Milan Milovanović
The Blue Door, 1917
Plava vrata
Oil on canvas, 48 x 39 cm
Belgrade, Narodni Muzej

1   N.A. Dmitrieva: "Peredvishniki and Impressionists". In: *Russian Art in the Second Half of the 19th Century and Early 20th Century*, Moscow, 1978, pp. 18–39 (in Russian). Cf. D.W. Sarabianov: "On the Distinctive Character of Russian Impressionism". In: *Russian 19th-Century Art and the European Schools*, Moscow, 1980, pp. 166–181 (in Russian). Cf. also the comparisons with French art in O.A. Liaskovskaia: *Plein-airisme in Russian 19th-Century Painting*, Moscow, 1966 (in Russian).

2   See Z. Kempiński: *Impresjonizm polski*, Warsaw, 1961 (with a German synopsis) and T. Dobrovolski: *Malarstwo polskie ostatnich dwustu lat* (Polish Art of the Last Two Hundred Years), Breslau etc., 1976.

3   Cf. the exhibition catalogue *Romantyzm i Romantyczność w sztuce polskiej XIX i XX wieku* (Romanticism and Romantic Approaches in Polish 19th- and 20th-Century Art), Warsaw, 1975.

4   A recent survey is provided in J. Szabó: *A XIX. század festészete Magyarországon* (19th-Century Hungarian Painting), Budapest, 1985.

5   A. Szinyei Merse: *Bildgattungen und Themen im Jugendwerk von Pál Szinyei Merse* (Genres and Themes of Pál Szinyei Merse's Early Work). In: *Acta Historiae Artium* 27 (1981) no. 3/4, pp. 287–361. For biographical and stylistic reasons, the date assigned varies between 1878 and 1882.

6   K. Keserü: *József Rippl-Rónai*, Budapest, 1982.

7   M. Deac: *Impresionismul în pictura românească. Precursori, maeştri, influenţe*, Bucharest, 1976 (with a French synopsis), p. 112.

8   L. Trifunović, in the exhibition catalogue *Serbische Malerei zwischen den Weltkriegen, 1918–1939* (Serbian Art between the World Wars, 1918–1939), National Museum, Belgrade, and Gemäldegalerie Neue Meister, Dresden, 1968, p. 8.

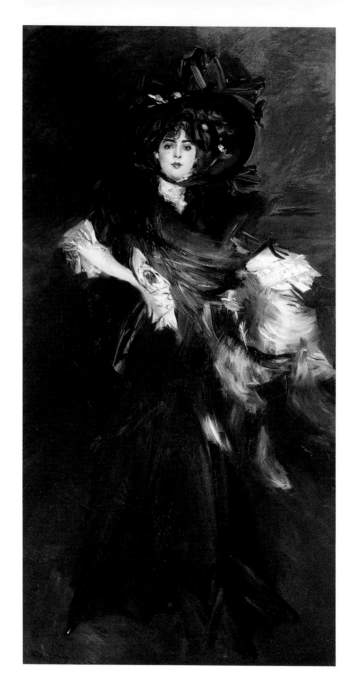

14 Impressionism and Italian Painting in the Latter Half of the 19th Century

The mid–19th century in Italy was the period of the Risorgimento, the movement that culminated in Italian unification free of Bourbon or Austrian rule. That movement provided the political and cultural backdrop for one of the most important and influential groups in Italian art in the second half of the 19th century: the Macchiaioli. This group of landscape, portrait and genre painters, flourishing from about 1850 to 1880, was based on Florence, which had become one of the most cosmopolitan cities in Italy in the 19th century thanks to liberal Habsburg/Lorraine rule. Florence was a place where revolutionaries and those who had fought in the liberation movement did not need to go in fear. Among these were many artists who had been volunteers in the 1848 and 1859 wars of liberation. In 1864 Florence became the provisional capital of the four-year-old kingdom of Italy, though in 1870, when Rome became the capital, Florence again lost its leading position and lapsed back into provincial status. These two dates mark the heyday of the Macchiaioli.

Despite the great differences between the Macchiaioli and the French Impressionists, the two groups were and still are the subject of comparison. Misleading tags such as "Italian Impressionism" merely suggest that the French movement has supplied the yardstick for assessing the Italian. This can partly be traced back to contemporary Italian critics such as Diego Martelli (1838–1896). Though the French and Italian artists shared certain ideas – such as a sketchiness in technique, modernity, and an interest in photography and Japanese woodcuts – the two schools nonetheless emerged from quite different cultural and social origins.

Unlike France with its Paris-oriented centralism, Italy had for centuries enjoyed a plural evolution in numerous regional art centres such as Florence, Rome, Milan, Naples and Turin. Moreover, the Macchiaioli movement began ten years before French Impressionism. Its openly revolutionary character constituted a signal difference from Impressionism, which occasionally made a point of avoiding political conflict; we need only recall the French artists who went into exile during the Franco-Prussian War. The Macchiaioli were working in a country predominantly agricultural, its infrastructure rural in temper. It was not till after unification that the Italian ecomomy gradually emerged from the doldrums around the turn of the century. In France, by contrast, industrialisation was already well advanced by the latter half of the 19th century.

Giovanni Boldini
Portrait of Mlle Lantelme, 1907
Ritratto di Mlle Lantelme
Oil on canvas, 227 x 118 cm
Rome, Galleria Nazionale d'Arte Moderna

Most of the Impressionists were from middle-class, town backgrounds, and this affected their subject matter and approach; along with landscapes they painted the city, scenes of industrial progress, and moments in modern life. For the Macchiaioli, political and social commitment largely precluded the painting of leisure and pastimes such as the Impressionists favoured. Thus the art of the Macchiaioli did not share the cheerfulness of mood established in so many Impressionist works by the subject matter and use of colour.

In other words, their situation was altogether different from that of the French artists. Nevertheless, there were points of resemblance. The age of liberation in Italy had produced an emphasis on *il vero* in art – a truthful, realistic fidelity to what the eye saw. Painting in the open and the study of light were as essential to this endeavour as an acceptance of

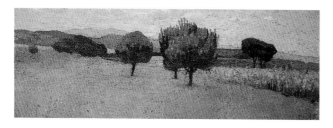

Giuseppe Abbati
Landscape at Castiglioncello, 1863
Campagna di Castiglioncello
Oil on panel, 10 x 30 cm
Florence, Galleria d'Arte Moderna

modern subject-matter in art. The core of the Macchiaioli consisted of eleven painters born between 1824 and 1838 (a somewhat elder generation than the French Impressionists). The most important of them were Giovanni Fattori (1825–1908), Silvestro Lega (1826–1895), Serafino De Tivoli (1826–1892) and Vincenzo Cabianca (1827–1902), among the older painters, and Giuseppe Abbati (1836–1868), Adriano Cecioni (1836–1886), Raffaelo Sernesi (1838–1866) and Telemaco Signorini (1835–1901) of the younger. The Venetian landscape artist Guglielmo Ciardi (1842–1917) was associated with the group, as were also, to varying extents, Giuseppe De Nittis (1846–1884), Federico Zandomeneghi (1841–1917) and Giovanni Boldini (1842–1931), who con-

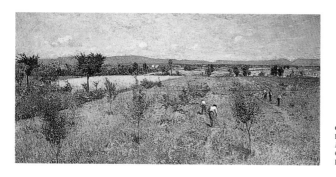

Guglielmo Ciardi
Harvest, 1883
Messi d'oro
Oil on canvas, 132 x 275 cm
Rome, Galleria Nazionale d'Arte Moderna

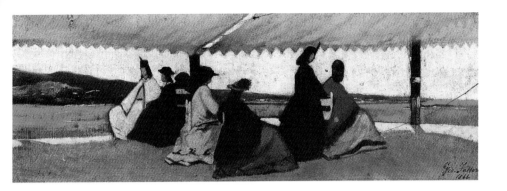

centrated on society-portrait art. These last-named three all took their bearings from France, and eventually moved to Paris.

The individual efforts of these artists differed so greatly that talk of a movement or group is in fact not genuinely tenable. Their backgrounds were quite different, though all were involved in various degrees in the Risorgimento. They were familiar with the liberal but romantically religious ideas of Giuseppe Mazzini (1805–1872), the leading ideologue of the Italian national movement. In 1831, while abroad, Mazzini had founded the Young Italy society to fight for the freedom, independence and unity of Italy, and he was associated with Giuseppe Garibaldi (1807–1882) in his war of independence. Though the revolts against foreign rule which Mazzini began in various parts of Italy led to nothing, his liberal ideas, influenced by French socialism and by positivism, had a real impact on the revolutionary movement. Lega painted *Giuseppe Mazzini on his Death Bed* (p. 536), recording the passing of a giant in one of the Macchiaioli's finest achievements. The dying man is seen almost lifesize. He is resting on two pillows and seems no longer aware of what may be going on around him. The cool colours highlight the solemnity and sadness of the mood.

Progressive ideas were aired at the Caffè Michelangiolo in Florence (cf. the photograph on p. 535). Established in 1845 in one of the city's loveliest streets, the Via Larga (now Via Cavour), it had quickly become a preferred avant-garde meeting place, comparable with the Brasserie des Martyrs, the Café Guerbois or the Nouvelles Athènes in Paris. The Florentine revolutionary nationalists under Giuseppe Dolfi met there, as did writers and critics (some of whom were directly involved in the Macchiaioli movement) and painters. "There were two rooms in the café," recalled Cecioni, "one of them decorated with frescos by the artists who frequented it. They would meet there to talk, but there were no meetings of a formal assembly kind." Doubtless political discussion was to the fore at first; but in the 1850s aesthetic debate took pride of place. This development culminated in the sessions led in the 1860s by Martelli, the most important Italian art critic of the time, in which critical assessment

Giovanni Fattori
The Palmieri's Bathing Rotunda, 1866
La rotonda di Palmieri
Oil on canvas, 12 x 30 cm
Florence, Galleria d'Arte Moderna

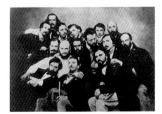

Artists at the Caffè Michelangiolo, 1856. Signorini is in the top row, fourth from left.

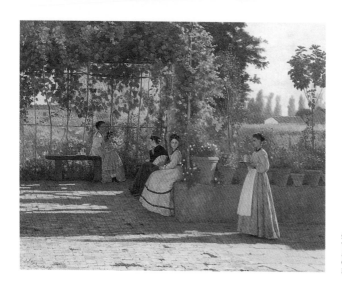

Silvestro Lega
The Pergola, 1868
Il pergolato
Oil on canvas, 75 x 93.5 cm
Milan, Pinacoteca di Brera

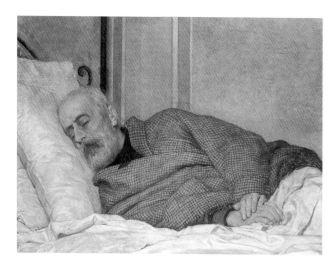

Silvestro Lega
Giuseppe Mazzini on his Death Bed, 1873
Mazzini morente
Oil on canvas, 76 x 96.9 cm
Providence (RI), Museum of Art,
Rhode Island School of Design,
Helen M. Danforth Fund

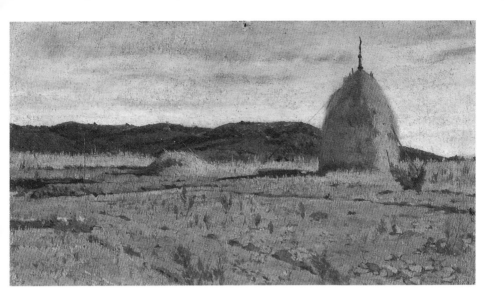

of the new French art, and thus the work of the Barbizon school, was included.

The struggle for national identity inevitably raised questions concerning the position of Italian art in relation both to the country's own history and to contemporary Europe. These questions affected the manner in which Italian culture was perceived, and also the artists' openness to developments elsewhere in Europe. In the mid-Fifties some of the Macchiaioli were already visiting the collection of Count Demidoff in the Villa San Donato in Florence. It included work by the Barbizon painters, Dutch 17th-century and English 18th-century art. Certain of the Caffè Michelangiolo artists had seen Barbizon work at the 1855 Paris World Fair, and shared their knowledge with fellow Italian artists in discussion. De Tivoli was one of them, and presently acquired the nickname *papa della macchia*. Chiaroscuro effects were valued, as was brushwork that involved understated colours and *macchia* – dabs and specks (such as might be found in other artists' preliminary sketches, but only there) – rather than draughtsmanly linearity. Hence the *macchia* technique of sketchily juxtaposed, contrastive dabs that gave its name to the movement. The term also had a secondary connotation with the brigands of *macchia* country, an association that highlighted the wayward approach of these artists compared with academic tradition.

The rejection of academic tradition in Italy grew out of different premisses from that in France. In 19th-century Italy, till unification, art colleges were largely in the control of foreigners. This explains why revolutionary technique was more frequently approved in official quarters: it was seen not so much as a lack of painterly skills, as in France, but as a

Giovanni Fattori
The Haystack, after 1872
Pagliaio
Oil on panel, 24 x 43 cm
Leghorn, Museo Civico Giovanni Fattori

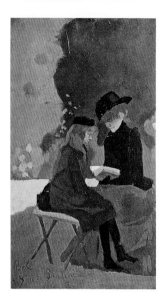

quasi-political offshoot of the Risorgimento. Like many other artists' groups that have initially been misunderstood, the Macchiaioli (to be exact, Signorini) took their name from a tag thought up by an anonymous critic to describe their early work seen publicly for the first time at the first Italian National Exhibition in 1861. That show not only clinched the Macchiaioli's breakthrough but was also a milestone in Risorgimento history, taking as it did Italy past and present and the nation's cultural unity as its theme. Realism was felt to be the best suited strategy for a revival of national art. *Macchia* technique was at once a way of embracing present-day subject matter and of putting the melodramatic, out-of-date tradition of eclectic history painting aside. As Signorini put it: "The *macchia* was initially a way of emphasizing chiaroscuro effects in order to establish a distinction from linear academic art."

This being so, Neapolitan art of a naturalistic persuasion – which ex-students of the Naples Academy such as Domenico Morelli (1826–1901) and later De Nittis introduced to the Caffè Michelangiolo debates – met with a fruitful reception among the Macchiaioli. The Posillippo landscape school, established at Naples around 1820 but with international leanings, was one of Italy's most progressive in the first half of the 19th century. In the second half it was absorbed into the Resina School in Naples; De Nittis was one of its founder members, and he was joined by Cecioni, the main theorist of the Macchiaioli. From 1863 to 1875 the painters of the school consistently advocated *plein-air* work, realism, and a linking of colour and light. Their approach to colour and the curt technique using generous spaces appealed particularly to the early Macchiaioli. In both Naples and Venice, the tradition of veduta painting – topographically precise views of town and country, such as were especially popular in the 18th century and up to the invention of photography and postcards – already presupposed a high degree of realism. That tradition can be seen as one of the key antecedents of the Macchiaioli. And it was small wonder that because of this, and because of the newly awakened love of the mother country, landscape art became central. "Landscape painting is the very epitome of modern art,"

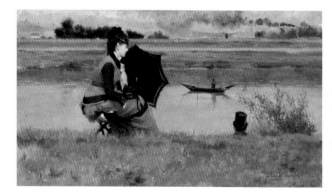

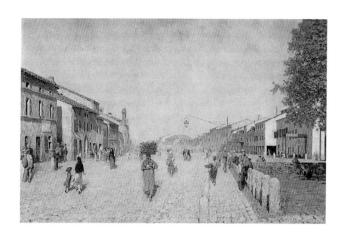

Telemaco Signorini
The Suburb of Porta Adriana, Ravenna, 1875
Borgo di Porta Adriana a Ravenna
Oil on canvas, 66 x 100 cm
Rome, Galleria Nazionale d'Arte Moderna

declared Signorini. "It is the form of expression that defines our century."

This is indirectly linked to responses to academic, foreign-controlled institutions. Italian artists were not able to rebel openly against them, or attack them through their own art, as long as the Austrian or Bourbon hand lay upon them. Thus it was that they turned initially to history painting, patriotically reviewing the past, in order to stimulate national pride and a resentment of foreign rule. Like many writers, artists took up subjects drawn from the greatness of the Italian Middle Ages and Renaissance. This had the effect of underlining the discontinuity between the past and the foreign-dominated present. Such art, most famously exemplified in the work of Francesco Hayez (1791–1881), together with a topographical and geographical precision in the rendering of historical locations, provided a key point of departure for *macchia* painting. In their early work, the Macchiaioli repeatedly painted historical events against the venerable backdrop of Florence, striking a note that related

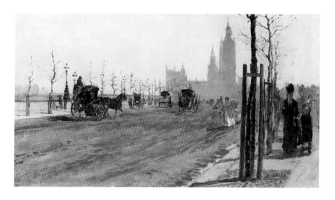

Giuseppe De Nittis
The Victoria Embankment, London, 1875
Oil on canvas, 19 x 31 cm
Piceni II,796. Private collection

to the present. Works by Saverio Altamura (1826–1897) were of this kind, and anticipated the ideas of younger artists by placing an emphasis on topographical details and a contemporary setting; but Abbati's paintings of the great architectural legacy of the Middle Ages were part of the same development.

Awareness of the Italian past extended to the study of the old Italian masters, and especially of the 14th- and 15th-century primitives. From 1848 to 1859, this interest was apparent in the Tuscan Purists, among them Antonio Ciseri (1821–1891). Initially adopting a decidedly anti-classical stance, they had opted for a simple, lucid formal idiom. Certain Macchiaioli painters such as Lega studied under them. Fattori too began to paint historical works in the mid–1850s, and then, with the Italian wars of liberation in mind, military pictures. Fattori's first *macchia* experiments showed him moving on from the academic history painting of his Florentine teacher, Giuseppe Bezzuoli (1784–1855), to a modern style of history painting in which the everyday routine of soldiers' lives could be portrayed shorn of its braggadocio.

Alongside history paintings, the early period of the Macchiaioli notably included the Castiglioncello School's landscape art, of significance in the 1860s in particular. Martelli, who named the school after the Tuscan coastal town of the same name where he owned an estate, invited

Giuseppe De Nittis
Breakfast in the Garden, c. 1884
Colazione in giardino
Oil on canvas, 81 x 117 cm
Barletta, Galleria Giuseppe De Nittis

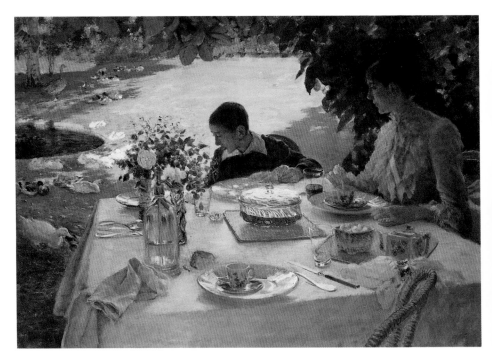

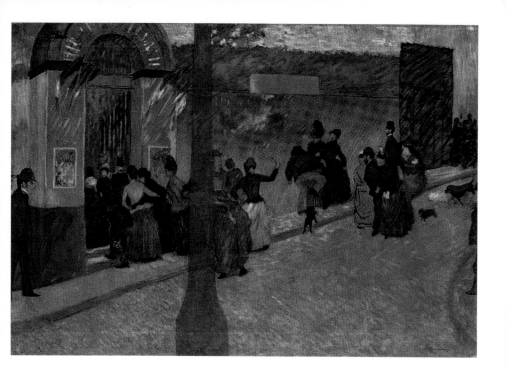

various artists to work in the rough, craggy bush landscape of the Maremma, at irregular intervals – among them Abbati, Odoardo Borrani (1833–1905) and Fattori. These three painters began from similar stylistic positions and constituted a homogeneous subgroup within the Macchiaioli. At first Abbati's art was to the fore, subsequently that of Fattori. Cabianca, Signorini, Cecioni, Boldini and Zandomeneghi were less frequent guests at Castiglioncello. Abbati was very taken with the clear, serene light of that part of the country, and with the colours, and he was the most regular of the visitors. From the early 1860s he was especially close to Martelli. A typical painting of that period was his *Landscape at Castiglioncello* (p. 534). His small-format works, generally painted on wood panels, are characteristic of early Macchiaioli art, with its larger and sometimes geometrically conceived colour zones and its contrasting darker and lighter areas. The chiaroscurist tendencies of the early phase were gradually supplanted by softer, more poetic light. At Castiglioncello, Fattori painted not only a number of highly successful portraits but also enchanting landscape studies such as *The Haystack* (p. 537). The simple compositional structure and his characteristically broad brushwork of the early period are particularly engaging in this painting.

About the same time, in the early 1860s, Signorini and Borrani settled in the Piagentina area east of Florence, to join Lega, who was already

Federico Zandomeneghi
Le Moulin de la Galette, 1878
Il Moulin de la Galette
Oil on canvas, 80 x 120 cm
Piceni 34
Milan, Enrico Piceni Collection

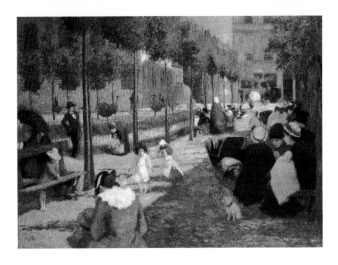

Federico Zandomeneghi
Place d'Anvers, Paris, 1880
Square d'Anvers
Oil on canvas, 100 x 135 cm
Piceni 44
Piacenza, Galleria d'Arte Moderna Ricci Oddi

working there. Compared with the Castiglioncello group, this Piagentina school of essentially these three painters makes a more contemplative impression. After a short time at the Academy in Florence, Lega had joined the army of Tuscany in 1848. Following his return to Florence he had worked in the Purist style, influenced by the teaching of Luigi Mussini (1813–1888) and Ciseri; in the early Sixties he came under the spell of the Caffè Michelangiolo painters, and was increasingly drawn to Macchiaioli realism. He developed an overriding interest in effects of light, an interest he expressed in the *plein-air* Nature studies he painted around Piagentina after 1861. The gentle countryside, and the different temperament of the painters involved, produced a more intimate, emotional art than that of the Castiglioncello painters. Lega, a quiet man, painted simple genre idylls, perhaps influenced by Borrani, who also painted in Piagentina from 1865 on. These idylls used loving detail to record the everyday lives of ordinary rural folk. His draughtsmanship was meticulous and his compositional skill exacting, but what is also astounding is the wealth of narrative detail in the limpid, contrastively arranged zones of darker and lighter colour. At times Lega's approach could resemble the *biedermeier* period in southern German art. One of his finest paintings is *The Pergola* (p. 536), which preserves the flavour of his Purist schooling in its clarity and its compositional balance.

The most productive period for the Piagentina School was the 1860s. Lega subsequently endured a crisis in his creative life. His later work was painted with greater ease and largesse; his last landscapes, done at Gabbro near Leghorn, were darker in character, done in gloomy monochrome. From the early 1870s on Lega was afflicted with a steadily worsening eye condition; at the time of his death in 1892 he was almost blind – and, like most of the Macchiaioli, penniless. Along with Lega,

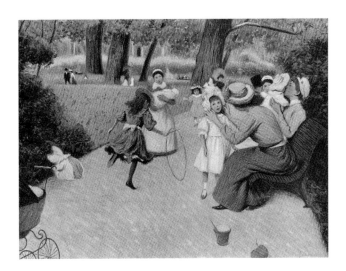

Federico Zandomeneghi
Children's Games in the Parc Monceau
Giochi al Parc Monceau
Oil on canvas, 73 x 92 cm
Piceni 342. Paris, Private collection

Borrani, Abbati and Sernesi, Signorini was also a founder member of the Piagentina School. In addition to being a writer of some power, he also played a leading part in the theoretical and aesthetic discussions at the Caffè Michelangiolo. His views, and the aims of the Macchiaioli, were published in periodicals such as the "Gazettino delle arti del disegno", founded by Martelli in 1867.

Signorini showed an early interest in the sociocritical writings of Pierre-Joseph Proudhon (1809–1865), and in French Positivism. This interest was also expressed in paintings that articulated his social concerns, such as the impressive *Insane Ward at San Bonifacio's, Florence* (p. 544). When it was exhibited in Turin in 1870, the painting sparked violent controversy. Degas, a friend of Signorini since the latter's visit to Paris, responded enthusiastically to its close observation of real conditions. Of the Macchiaioli, only Signorini consistently painted scenes of contemporary urban life. In work such as *The Suburb of Porta Adriana, Ravenna* (p. 539), both Signorini's choice of subject and his bright, fresh technique constituted an affinity with Impressionist paintings of a similar kind. Of all the Macchiaioli, Signorini was the most open to Impressionism. Lega and Fattori barely travelled outside Tuscany, and had no real contact with French Impressionism till after 1879, when Martelli, enthusiastic after a year in Paris, set about introducing the new aesthetics to Italy. Martelli persuaded Degas, Pissarro and others to exhibit in Florence in 1879. Italian artists responded in varying ways to the art they then saw, however. Fattori was not alone in disapproving of what was perceived as the Impressionists' too casual brushwork. Signorini, for his part, travelled widely, spending repeated periods in London and Paris, and the influences to which he was exposed made their way into his own painting.

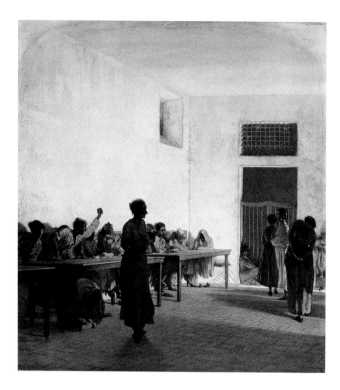

Telemaco Signorini
Insane Ward at San Bonifacio's, Florence,
c. 1866/67
Sala delle agitate a San Bonifacio a Firenze
Oil on canvas, 63 x 95 cm
Venice, Galleria d'Arte Moderna

Interestingly, the nudes and still lifes which so often occur in French Impressionism are almost entirely absent in the work of the Macchiaioli. Their art was deft in managing lighting effects and compositional structure. Unlike their French counterparts, they retained a reliance on line and outline. They created their light effects by means of colour contrasts. This fact, together with their attempts at a simpler formal idiom, and their choices of subject matter, points up the differences in the two movements' aims and concerns. The Italians were distinctly more intellectual in their approach, less interested in spontaneously conveying a sensuous impression of Nature. By the 1870s, the heyday of the Macchiaioli was already over, and developments continued in various directions. Of the early generation, only Lega, Signorini and Fattori retained their importance. From the mid-Sixties on, Italian artists increasingly responded to the pull of Paris. The work of the Macchiaioli had a strong French advocate in Degas, whose Italian family relations and numerous visits to the country had given him a keen interest in Italian art. From 1856 to 1859 he spent a number of periods in Florence, and he too went to Caffè Michelangiolo.

The names of Zandomeneghi and De Nittis are central to the active relations of France and Italy. Till 1863, De Nittis worked in Naples. His

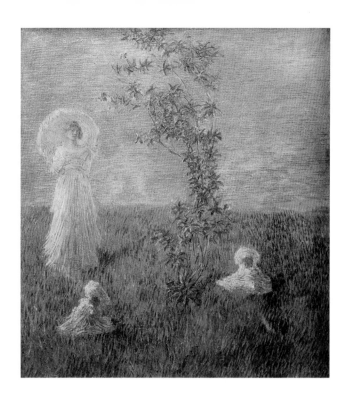

Gaetano Previati
In the Meadow, 1889/90
Sul prato
Oil on canvas, 62 x 56.5 cm
Florence, Galleria d'Arte Moderna

friendship with the Florentine sculptor and critic Cecioni put him in touch with the Macchiaioli in the mid-Sixties, and his style and subject matter were influenced by them. To develop his skills, he went to Paris in 1868, settled there and became established. Thanks to the support of various dealers such as Goupil he achieved a reputation and financial success. Meanwhile, he maintained his contacts with Italian friends and fellow artists via letters and visits. At first, De Nittis was under the influence of Meissonier and Fortuny, painting genre scenes that were successful and sold, or Italian street scenes in which the old Florentine chiaroscuro was still apparent. His relatively unconstrained work, such as his views of Vesuvius, met with no success. In 1873, through Degas, he met the Impressionists, and had five pictures in their first group exhibition in 1874. Though he did not participate in the exhibitions that followed, he continued a friend of Degas, Manet and Caillebotte. De Nittis also had more conventional work in the Salon, where it attracted comment, but his brushwork, composition and technique were steadily coming into line with French Impressionist practice, in paintings such as *The Victoria Embankment* (p. 539) or *Breakfast in the Garden* (p. 540). Draughtsmanship, the precise object, and narrative elements, always remained more important to him than strategies that dissolved things seen into phenomena of light. De Nittis in part painted in obedience to prevailing public taste, and his art thus occupied a position midway between the modish and the avant-garde.

Zandomeneghi was a quite different case. He settled in Paris in 1874, living a reclusive life, and, unsuccessful in his lifetime, was obliged to earn a living doing fashion drawings. He had studied at the Venice Academy, fought under Garibaldi, and been arrested; his influential family intervened for his release. In 1862 he joined the Macchiaioli in Florence, finding their realistic studies of Nature in line with his own ideas on art. He too visited Castiglioncello. Shortly after his arrival in Paris, he wrote to Signorini of his somewhat mixed response to French Impressionism, but gradually, thanks to the advocacy of Martelli, he became more convinced. Zandomeneghi exhibited in the 1879, 1881 and 1886 Impressionist shows. In street scenes such as *Place d'Anvers, Paris* (p. 542) his brushwork was relaxed and sketchy. His portraits (p. 548) sometimes recall Monet.

Zandomeneghi's *Fishing on the Seine* (p. 538) focusses on the life of leisure, showing a fashionably dressed young woman with a parasol on the grassy river bank and a man fishing. Of the man, thanks to the daring composition, we see only a top hat. The painting adopts a highly unusual point of view. Its cropping or overlapping, and the spatial dependence on larger, layered zones of colour, recalls Impressionist art as well as the Japanese woodcuts which were then enjoying so warm a reception. In the background, a smoking factory chimney signals the industrial end of this idyllic world. Realistic breaches of idyllic tones such as this were inconceivable in the academic Salon art of the period, and it shows Zandomeneghi to have been squarely in line with French Impressionism's ideas of painting modern life. His major works were painted in the late 1870s and in the 1880s. Among them were *Le Moulin de la Galette* (p. 541), in which the poster-like figures and spatially flat, simplified forms prompt comparison with the Post-Impressionist work of a Toulouse-Lautrec.

Boldini, who also moved to Paris (in 1871), adopted only certain features of French Impressionism, notably the emphasis on *plein-air* painting. He largely remained a skilful painter of society portraits, something which had been his forte as early as in his Macchiaioli Sixties. In France he relaxed his technique considerably, though to a significant extent he retained the Italian chiaroscuro effects and broad brushwork. Boldini was an acute observer of his fellow beings, and one of his finest works is the virtuoso *Portrait of Mlle Lantelme* (p. 532), with its arrestingly bold, unconstrained brush-strokes.

In the late 1870s, the Florence Macchiaioli seemed to be running out of steam. The older views were now superseded by a more Impressionist strain, promoted by Martelli. This second generation of Macchiaioli included Francesco Gioli (1846–1922) and Armando Spadini (1883–1925), and from the 1880s on its centre was primarily northern Italy. Piedmont had already produced a notable pre-Impressionist in Antonio Fontanesi (1818–1882). Of the Venetians, Ciardi in particular deserves

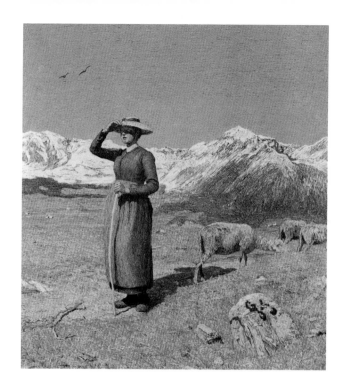

Giovanni Battista Segantini
Midday in the Alps (Windy Day), 1891
Mezzogiorno sulle Alpi (Giornata di vento)
Oil on canvas, 77.5 x 71.5 cm
St. Gallen, Fondazione Otto Fischbacher

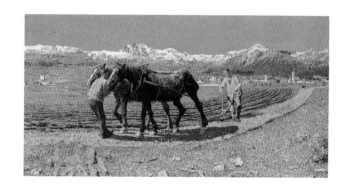

Giovanni Battista Segantini
Ploughing, 1890
L'aratura
Oil on canvas, 116 x 227 cm
Munich, Bayerische Staatsgemäldesammlungen,
Neue Pinakothek

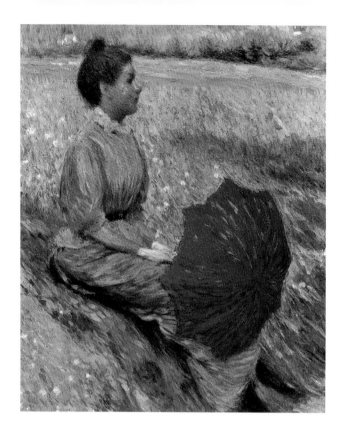

Federico Zandomeneghi
Lady in a Meadow, 1893
Signora nel prato
Oil on canvas, 46 x 38 cm
Piceni 289. Milan, Private collection

mention. His landscapes expressed a profound response to Nature. He had studied at the Venice Academy but had moved on at an early stage to *plein-airisme* and had evolved a style that increasingly shared features with Impressionism. At the end of the 1870s, on Zandomeneghi's advice, he moved to Florence, where he made contact with the Macchiaioli. His structural reliance on effects of light and dark, and his meticulously separated colour zones, constituted an affinity with the group; but he was also open to other aesthetics, and through the Florence debates he became acquainted with the art of the Barbizon painters, of the Neapolitan School, and on the international scene. Canvases such as *Harvest* (p. 534), flooded with light, rendered atmospheric landscapes in a style drawn from the Venetian veduta tradition. These and his views of Venice brought Ciardi great success in his own lifetime.

In the 1880s, Lombardy began to play an active part in Italian art. The movement that originated there declared its loyalty to the great Italian tradition, and was particularly interested in atmospherics of light, colour and texture. In the 1890s, such work came into its own with divisionist

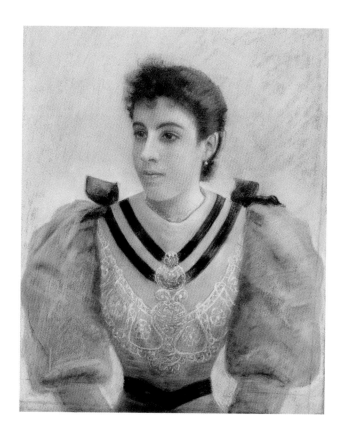

Federico Zandomeneghi
Portrait of a Girl, c. 1893–1895
Ritratto di una giovanetta
Oil on canvas, 60.5 x 73.5 cm
Private collection

or pointillist paintings; the proximity of Lombardy to France and Germany was palpable. Giovanni Carnovali (1804–1873), called Il Piccio, was an important forerunner who departed from the neo-classical tradition and, taking 18th-century Venetian art and Delacroix's use of colour as his points of departure, achieved a freer treatment of light and colour that had a decisive, enabling influence on subsequent developments in art in the Lombard capital, Milan. Il Piccio was one of the many artists, writers and musicians who campaigned in Milan in the 1860s for anti-academic, anti-bourgeois aims and methods in aesthetic work. They felt the hopes which the Risorgimento had aroused had not been fulfilled, and they were opposed to the rapid spread of industrialization in northern Italy in the Nineties, and especially to the growth of Milan's industrial moneyed middle classes. The movement, initially of a mainly literary kind, aimed to liberate art and literature from formalism of any description, and was known as Scapigliatura, or unrestraint. Unlike the Macchiaioli, whose attention was primarily on formal issues, the Scapigliatura group, in close association with writers, developed a brand of ro-

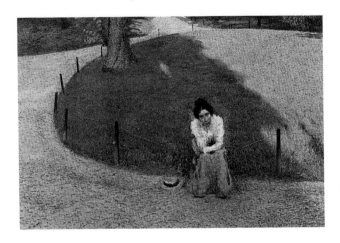

mantic idealism. They were strongly attracted to the poetry of Baudelaire. Medardo Rosso (1858–1928) was the preeminent sculptor in the group, and Daniele Ranzoni (1843–1889) was among the most gifted of the painters. His tiny, divisionist brushwork and dissolved outlines survived in the Neo-Impressionist work of Gaetano Previati (1852–1920; p. 545), Giovanni Segantini (1858–1899), and above all Giuseppe Pellizza (1868–1907).

In the work of Pellizza, the most important Lombard Neo-Impressionist, the goals of the leading French pointillist, Seurat, were most consistently pursued. This was apparent not only in his relinquishing romantic natural scenes such as Impressionism favoured, and preferring an art based upon ideas; he also dispensed with clear outlines, and used strong contrasts of juxtaposed colours. Vittore and Alberto Grubicy, art dealers in Milan, were Italy's most assertive advocates of this style; in the Eighties and Nineties they supported the Scapigliatura artists, and the

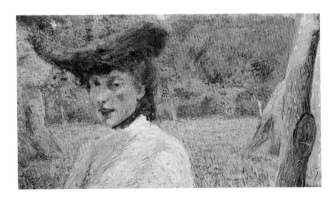

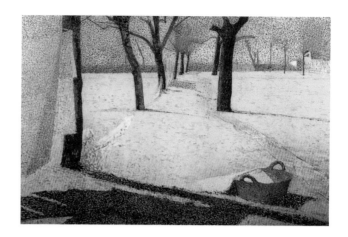

Giuseppe Pellizza da Volpedo
Washing in the Sun, 1905
Panni al sole
Oil on canvas, 87 x 131 cm
Domodossola, Private collection

Italian divisionists such as Pellizza and Segantini. The latter, from 1886 on, developed his own technique for splitting colours, using separate brush-strokes for complementary colour values. Segantini's art concentrated on the light in the mountains, which provided him with a preferred subject which he tended to interpret in strongly Symbolist ways (p. 547). Segantini shared Pellizza's hope that a new world was coming in which artists would play a leading role, their authority no longer derived from academies but from life and the study of Nature.

Industrialization was rapid in Italy in the Nineties, and brought in its train social unrest and strikes, some of which would be bloodily put down. The life of the new working classes provided Pellizza with subject matter for politically committed paintings. His thematic range was great, and included curiously symbolic paintings such as *Washing in the Sun* (p. 551) or work that assigned a pantheistic meaning to light. This in turn pointed forward to Futurist artists such as Giacomo Balla (1871–1958; p. 550) and Umberto Boccioni (1882–1916; p. 550), whose anti-academic stance and visual experiments with light as a bearer of energy and dynamics owed much to the Scapigliatura and the Italian divisionists.

KARIN SAGNER

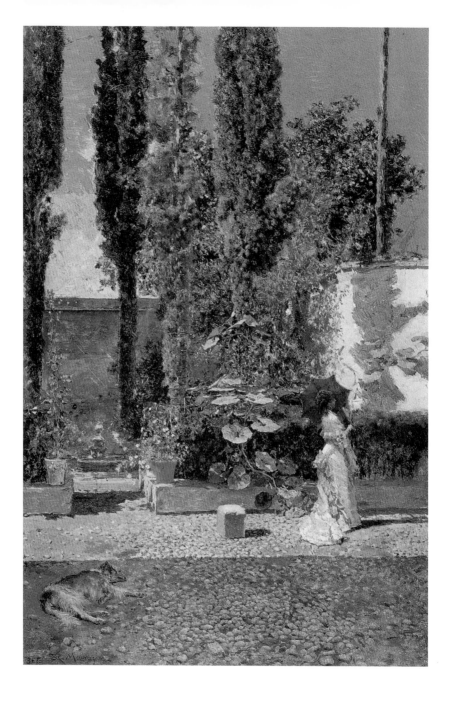

15 Painting in Spain in the Impressionist Period

Spanish art played primarily the role of source and inspiration in the evolution of French Impressionism. The dark tonalities of the 17th century in particular, as in the art of Diego de Silva y Velázquez (1599–1660), Bartolomé Esteban Murillo (1618–1682), Francisco de Zurbarán (1598–1664) and El Greco (1541–1614), as well as Francisco de Goya (1746–1828), aroused great interest among the Impressionists. Manet's admiration for the Golden Age of Spanish painting, and above all for Velázquez, was apparent from about 1860 in his cool colours, his hard, expressive style based on contrasts of light and dark, his relaxed brushwork; and his use of Spanish subject-matter (*The Spanish Singer*, 1860; New York, The Metropolitan Museum of Art). What Manet and other French Impressionists valued in Spanish art was particularly the ease of its brushwork and its handling of colour. We would do well to bear the realistic aspects of Spanish art in mind, too.

Manet had been enthusiastic about Spain long before he first went there in 1865 (his only visit). His love of the country dated back to a friend of his father, the art critic Charles Blanc (1813–1882), whose articles drew the attention of the younger generation of painters to Velázquez in particular. The French interest in Spanish culture and art had been lively since about 1840, partly because of the important collection in the Louvre and partly because of Napoleon III's marriage in 1853 to Duchess Eugenie de Motijo of Spain.

Spain, a country of diversity and contrast, was plagued by unrest in the 19th century until King Alfonso XII came to the throne. Foreign Bourbon rule, revolts against it, separatist movements (especially in Catalonia and the Basque region), colonial wars, and the country's social and economic backwardness and isolation compared with the rest of Europe, had all left their mark on the land.

The many faces of the Spanish landscape – from peaceful Mediterranean beaches to the rocky wilderness of the Costa Verde, from snowy mountains to barren plains to fertile pastures – were all reflected in Spanish art (though without affecting technique). In the 19th century, the wealthiest region was the Mediterranean province of Valencia, while the preeminent cities for cultural life were Madrid in Castile and Barcelona in Catalonia. Though Spanish 19th-century artists were naturally aware of the achievements of Velázquez, El Greco and Goya, they did not

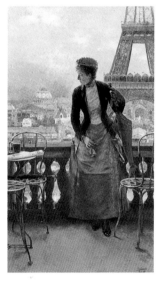

Luis Jiménez y Aranda
A Lady at the Paris World Fair, 1889
Una dama en la Exposición Universal de París
Oil on canvas, 120.6 x 70.2 cm
Dallas (TX), Meadows Museum and Gallery,
Southern Methodist University,
Arthur H. Meadows Collection

Left:
Mariano Fortuny y Carbó Marsal
and Frederico de Madrazo
Fortuny's Garden
El jardín de la casa de Fortuny
Oil on canvas, 40 x 27 cm
Madrid, Museo del Prado, Casón del Buen Retiro

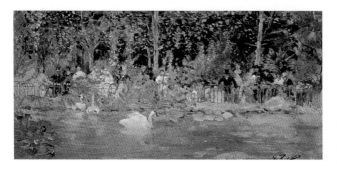

Ignacio Pinazo Camarlench
The Pond
Al borde del estanque
Oil on canvas, 19.5 x 41 cm
Madrid, Museo del Prado, Casón del Buen Retiro

necessarily follow their examples in their own work. Perhaps surprisingly, they made next to no use of the relaxed technique of their "Impressionist" predecessors as a point of departure in their own work; instead, they looked abroad, especially to France.

In the first half of the 19th century, the Madrid classicist José de Madrazo (1781–1859), who painted in the manner of Jacques-Louis David (1748–1825), presided over academic art. Landscape painting was rated low, as was usually the case in the traditional academies. Nevertheless, in Spain, as elsewhere in Europe, there was a growing interest in landscape in the latter half of the century. The Barbizon painters' close observation and rendering of Nature, and their transition from studio work to *plein-airisme* (which paved the way for the Impressionists), met with an increasingly interested reception in Spain. Eugenio Lucas y Padilla (1824–1870), who worked in Madrid and specialized in history painting in the tradition of Meissonier, was a notable figure in this context. His true gift proved to lie in landscape, and his small-format pictures, though still visibly committed to Romantic ways of seeing, had a true-to-Nature verisimilitude and directness.

Mariano Fortuny y Carbó Marsal (1838–1874) also espoused the Meissonier tradition of small-format genre pictures. His brushwork was more relaxed, and he aimed at a lightness of subject matter, rather than the evocative heaviness of the Spanish tradition. His technique was virtuoso, and he took delight in anecdotal detail. Fortuny's paintings, splendid in colour and rich in light effects, were particularly successful in France in the 1870s, where they were thought so modern that in 1875 the Impressionists were bracketed by some critics with the imitators of Fortuny, because of their vigorous brushwork and clear, bright colours. The period of Fortuny's greatest popularity coincided exactly with the rise of Impressionism. The principal difference between Fortuny's approach and the classic Impressionist views of the 1870s lay in his retention of traditional academic chiaroscuro of a kind that preferred blacks, browns and earthy tonalities.

In Spain, one of those who promoted Fortuny was Frederico de Madrazo (1815–1894), whose daughter Cecilia Fortuny married. It was during preparations for the wedding in 1870 that Fortuny had the idea for *At the Vicarage* (p. 555), one of his most famous pictures. Fascinated by light, he painted scenes of Seville, Portici and Granada – genre pictures, nudes, portraits and landscapes of an extraordinary luminous brilliance (p. 552).

But the major momentum in Spanish art in the latter part of the century was provided by Carlos de Haes (1829–1898) and Martín Rico y Ortega (1833–1908). Rico had spent a lengthy period in France and adopted Barbizon approaches. Painting in Venice around the turn of the century, he subsequently did work whose relaxed brushwork and atmospheric use of light strongly recalls Impressionist art (p. 558).

It was Haes, however, who played the key role in disseminating *plein-airist* art and its techniques in Spain. Born in Belgium, the painter had been teaching landscape art at the San Fernando Academy in Madrid since 1857. There his small-format work in the Barbizon manner presented Nature studies free of Romantic effects. The influence he exerted on Spanish landscape art for more than thirty years can scarcely be exaggerated (p. 557).

Some of the most important Spanish Impressionist artists were pupils of Haes. At an fairly early date he was already encouraging Aureliano de Beruete y Moret (1845–1912) and Darío de Regoyos Valdes (1857–1913) to paint studies direct from Nature before doing studio paintings of a relaxed kind from them. Several Spanish Impressionists had

Mariano Fortuny y Carbó Marsal
At the Vicarage, 1870
La vicaría
Oil on panel, 55 x 92 cm
Barcelona, Museu Nacional d'Art de Catalunya

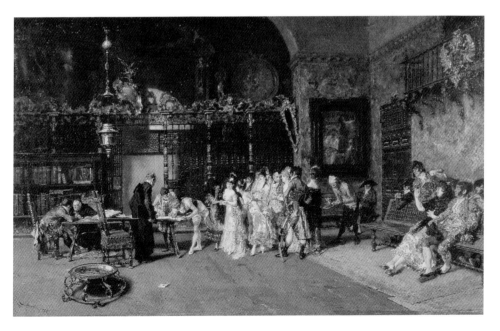

studied in France, Belgium or Germany, though, and many had indeed spent lengthy periods there, which meant that their acquaintance with *plein-airisme* was a result of foreign travel.

Beruete, born in Madrid and mainly active there, studied law and became a member of parliament, travelling abroad on various occasions in that capacity. His art was initially a pastime for his leisure hours; in 1874, however, after meeting Haes, he abandoned his career in politics in order to devote himself fully to art. He followed Haes in his preference for landscape, concentrating on the region around Madrid and Toledo. When the influence of French Impressionism made itself apparent, as in *Hawthorn in Blossom* (p. 556), it was with a Castilian austerity rather than with the light, cheerful touch of the French. His colours used contrasts but retained an earthy quality (*The Manzanares*, p. 559), and his brushwork was coarse, rough and heavy (*Selling the Mule*; Madrid, Museo del Prado). Using this technique he achieved a distinctive success in portraying the qualities peculiar to a given landscape. His brushwork and earthiness ultimately document Beruete's fondness for, and position in, the Spanish tradition, and he also wrote critical, historical works, on the art of the old masters, including the first catalogue raisonné of Velázquez' pictures.

Beruete's artist friends included the Valencian Joaquín Sorolla y Bastida (1863–1923). Sorolla's approach to light and colour was a direct contrast to Beruete's Castilian severity. It was rooted in the idiosyncratic Valencian school, which also included Sorolla's teacher, Francisco Domingo y Marqués (1842–1920) and Ignacio Pinazo Camarlench (1849–1916; p. 554). Pinazo, like most of the Spanish Impressionists, went to Italy after completing his studies at the San Carlos Academy. Scholarships to Italy, or at least a visit to the country, were traditionally *de rigueur* in the training of academic artists, since the classical rules still taught in the 19th century had originally been conceived in Italy. The

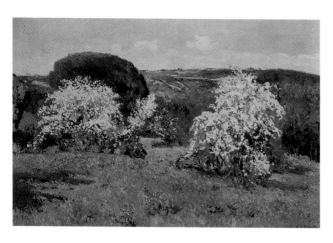

Aureliano de Beruete y Moret
Hawthorn in Blossom, 1911
Espinos en flor (Plantío de infantes)
Oil on canvas, 66 x 100 cm
Madrid, Museo del Prado, Casón del Buen Retiro

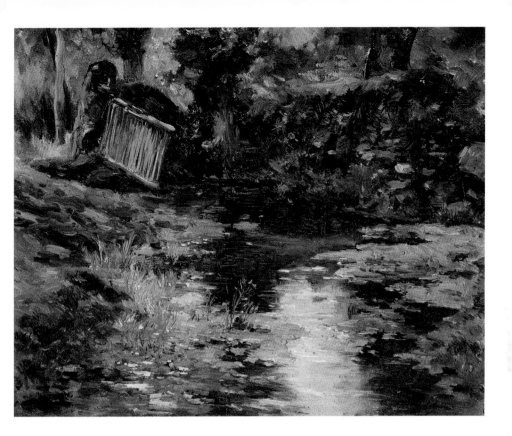

Spanish Impressionists obeyed the prevailing norms far more than their French counterparts in this respect; the French deliberately ventured aside from the straight and narrow of academic doctrine. In Rome, Pinazo took a strong interest in history painting and in landscape art. Back in Spain, he concentrated on the coast of his Valencian home parts, painting in a free and easy, sketchy style (*Luncheon*; Valencia, Museo de Bellas Artes).

Valencian art was notable for its efforts to capture the brief, passing moment by using rapid, unbroken brush-strokes and precision colourism. The vivid *plein-air* scenes, mainly Mediterranean, that the artists recorded in this style nonetheless preserved tonal unities, and might be better described as luminist than Impressionist. That is to say, the persistent survival of earthy colours, and even black, and the generally dark palette, placed them in the tradition of Spanish art.

Sorolla arrived at *plein-airisme* via years as an apprentice and journeyman in Valencia, Rome and Paris. While in Rome, he painted genre

Carlos de Haes
A Stream at Pont-Aven
Un arroyo (Pont-Aven)
Oil on canvas, 31 x 39 cm
Madrid, Museo del Prado, Casón del Buen Retiro

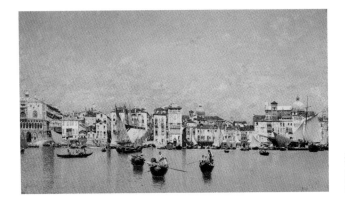

pictures in the realist tradition of Domenico Morelli (1826–1901). During his time in Paris, he came under the spell of Bastien-Lepage. Sorolla satisfied Parisian taste by his religious mood and Parisian subject-matter. Returning to Spain in 1889, he settled in Madrid, where his art began to undergo a stylistic transformation: he attached greater importance to changing conditions of light, and now preferred scenes of Spanish folk life, especially in Mediterranean coastal areas. *The Beach at Valencia* (p. 560) is a good exampe of this kind of work. Even when Sorolla rendered effects of light in an intensified, almost unnatural way, and heightened the expressiveness of his art, his shapes and forms invariably remained identifiable.

The emphasis on form – albeit to varying degrees – constituted a point of difference between Spanish and French Impressionism. The various manifestations of light that played so vital a role in the French idiom were now to be essential in Sorolla's visual approach as well. The dramatic immediacy of *Selling the Catch at Valencia* (p. 561) derives from the gradation of its harmonious palette and the broad, solid forms established by its brushwork. In this painting, Sorolla has captured both the strong light of the south and the everyday life of Spanish fishing folk. In other paintings, his brushwork was often of a more modest yet vibrant order; it is as if his style altered to suit changing conditions of light. His work achieved a freedom of expression rare in Spanish art at that date, and it is small wonder that a museum in Madrid is now devoted entirely to Sorolla's paintings. In the early 20th century he enjoyed enormous international acclaim, and in 1909, for instance, had a solo exhibition in New York that included some 300 works and brought him enthusiastic recognition in the USA.

Another successful artist was the Basque painter Ignacio Zuloaga y Zabaleta (1870–1945). After 1890 he regularly spent periods in Paris, over a number of years, with the result that native Spanish influences and those of French Impressionism and Symbolism blended in his style in a quite distinctive way. His whole life long, Zuloaga was especially attached to the art of Velázquez and Goya, but above all that of El Greco. He was an ardent collector of El Greco's work, buying and renovating the latter's house in order to preserve it for posterity. Zuloaga began his own artistic career copying the old Spanish masters in the Prado, and then, after the obligatory visit to Rome, moved on to Paris, where he enrolled in the studio of Gervex, the friend of Renoir and Manet. This put him in direct touch with the contemporary French avant-garde. He travelled with his new friends Degas and Rodin, and shared a Montmartre studio with Gauguin, who introduced him to Symbolist circles and the poet Stéphane Mallarmé. Though he admired Impressionist art, he nevertheless soon returned in his own paintings to a crisper, more austere style schooled on the Spanish tradition, such as he had adopted in his early work.

Within that tradition, Zuloaga proved every inch a Spanish artist. His dynamic control of line in paintings such as *Celestina* (p. 562) reminds us of his formidable draughtsmanship skills. The emphasis on line and open space, the strong chiaroscuro tendency, and the treatment of the subject, all suggest the presence of Toulouse-Lautrec and Manet, for whom Zuloaga retained his admiration. His specifically Spanish subject-

Aureliano de Beruete y Moret
The Manzanares, 1908
El Manzanares
Oil on canvas, 57.5 x 81 cm
Madrid, Museo del Prado, Casón del Buen Retiro

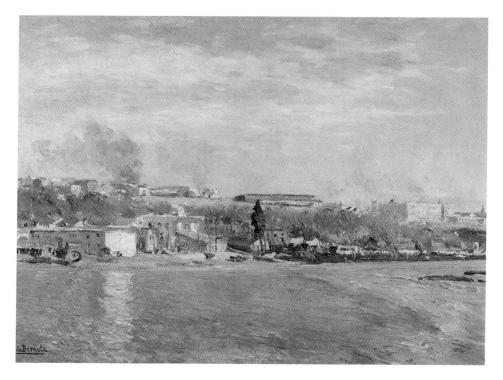

matter included dramatic cliffs and crags, and the sweeping Basque coastline along the Bay of Biscay, where he was frequently to be found despite periods spent in Bilbao, Seville, Granada and Paris. His studio in the little fishing village of Zumaya is now the Casa Museo Ignacio Zuloaga, open to the public.

Zuloaga's pictures, often immense in format, lacked that cheerful note peculiar to Sorolla, though. This was largely true of his scenes of Spanish folk life, too, in which he continued a native tradition of tragic realism by portraying those on the fringes of society – gypsies, beggars, cripples or witches – in distorted, grotesque ways. He also painted portraits of famous contemporaries – musicians, actors, dancers, painters and writers, as well as King Alfonso XIII and various aristocrats. After 1900, thanks mainly to his portraits, he secured a position as an internationally recognised society artist, and, as such, found himself constrained to make concessions to Salon taste, so that in this he resembled Sargent more closely than any of the great French artists.

Of the Spanish artists, Regoyos adopted first Impressionism and later Neo-Impressionism with the most persistent rigour. Born in Asturia, he studied under Haes at the San Fernando Academy in Madrid. In 1880 he went to Paris, where he was to stay a year, entering into a friendship with Luce that would have important consequences. Luce was closely connected with the Belgian art scene, with the result that Regoyos too paid repeated visits to Brussels up to 1889. There he joined the circle of the Neo-Impressionist painter van Rysselberghe, the sculptor Constantin Meunier (1831–1905), the art critic Maus, and Verhaeren the writer. With the last-named, Regoyos undertook the journey through Spain in

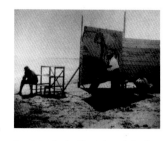

Joaquín Sorolla y Bastida painting on the beach

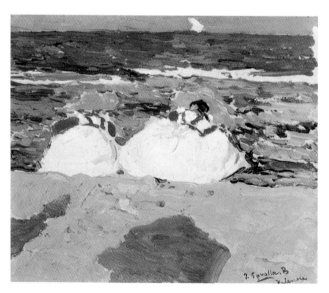

Joaquín Sorolla y Bastida
The Beach at Valencia
Playa de Valencia
Oil on canvas
Madrid, Museo Sorolla

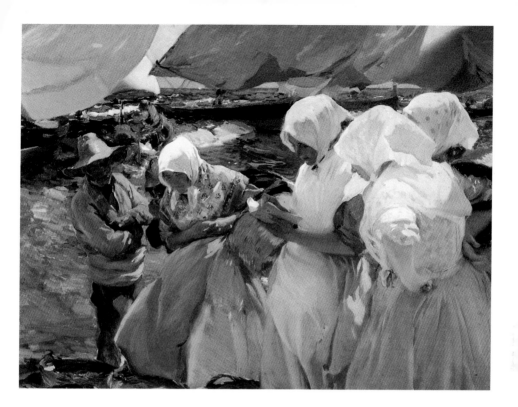

Joaquín Sorolla y Bastida
Selling the Catch at Valencia, 1903
La venta del pescado (Pescadoras valencianas)
Oil on canvas, 93 x 126 cm
Valencia, Diputación Provincial

1888 which prompted Verhaeren's "La España Negra", an exploration of the country's darker sides. In 1883 Regoyos exhibited together in Brussels for the first time, and the following year was a co-founder of Les Vingt, to which group's exhibitions he regularly sent work until it was dissolved. From that time on, Impressionism began to supplant the darker hues of his work.

Regoyos was on the look-out for new modes of expression, and the Neo-Impressionism of Seurat, Signac, Pissarro and Cross aroused his interest. In 1888 he exhibited together with them in the rooms of *La Revue Blanche*, the periodical. For a short time he in fact practised a strict pointillism, as in his portrait of *Dolores Otaño* (p. 563). In 1890, 1892 and 1893 he exhibited with the Indépendants in Paris. From 1900 he was again regularly in Spain, particularly at San Sebastián on the north coast. Ill with cancer, he returned to Spain for good in 1911 and settled in Barcelona. His work met with no success in the official exhibitions there, but the younger avant-garde artists valued it highly. In his subject-matter, Regoyos ranged freely, painting scenes urban and rural, markets and streets, processions and festivals; but his finest work was in landscapes. There he tackled various conditions of light and, unlike most Spanish artists, largely dispensed with the use of black. Avoiding the strong light of the south and the sharp contrasts of light and dark that it produced, he preferred the rich colours of greener northern Spain. His landscapes, painted in light, clear colours with unforced brushwork, re-corded a true emotional rapport with a beloved native country which he never tired of travelling.

It was Catalan art, however, that wholeheartedly adopted Impres-sionism – even if the Catalan preference for greys, violets, ochres and muted greens recalls Whistler rather than a Monet or Renoir. Eliseo Meifren y Roig (1859–1940) was the leading figure here. He studied in Barcelona, then reafter living in Paris for several years, submitting regu-larly to the Salon and selling works through Petit's gallery (where he had a solo show). Meifren worked in France, in Italy, and throughout Spain. In 1916 he journeyed to the USA on the occasion of a solo exhibition of his works in New York. Open to new techniques and new ways of seeing,

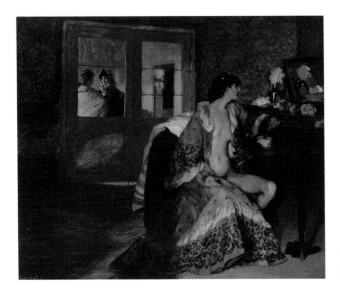

Ignacio Zuloaga y Zabaleta
Celestina, 1906
Oil on canvas
Madrid, Centro de Arte Reina Sofía

he painted in a relaxed, limpid manner, and his pictures have a strongly Impressionist flavour. He liked painting water, the sea and rivers, beaches and fishing ports, seen in various kinds of light. *The Marne* (p. 564) recalls Monet, not least through its view of the opposite bank and a line of poplar trees.

Various painters, such as Nicolas Raurich y Petre (1871–1945), brightened up their palettes under Meifren's influence, and adopted his more spontaneous brushwork. Raurich's taste took him to austere, for-

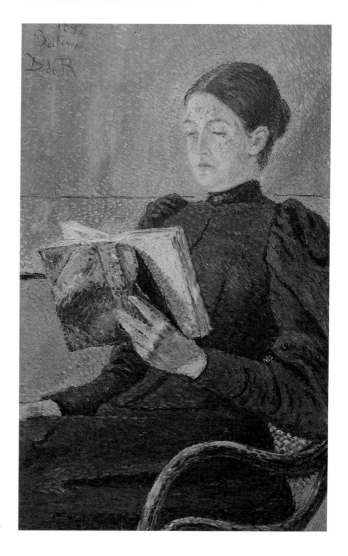

Darío de Regoyos Valdes
Dolores Otaño, 1891
Oil on canvas, 55 x 35 cm
Madrid, Museo del Prado, Casón del Buen Retiro

bidding landscapes such as the Pyrenees or the wild coastline of Catalonia, and he painted them in audacious swathes of colour or with pastose richness (*Solitude*, p. 566). Francisco Gimeno Arasa (1858–1927) also came from Catalonia, and his meeting with Haes in 1884 confirmed him in his own views on landscape painting. Gimeno, who had to earn a living as a house painter and decorator, developed his own turbulent style for pictures of the Spanish countryside. His manner tended to have a broad, almost violent vigour that prompts comparison with the Fauves.

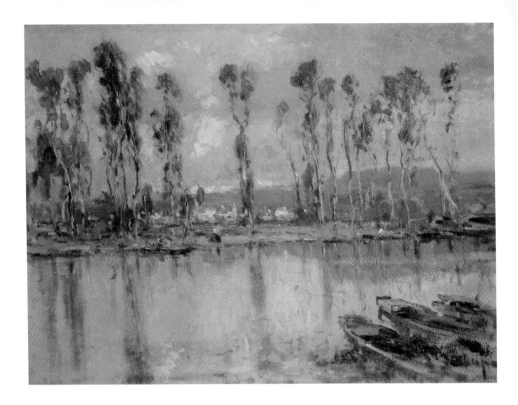

Eliseo Meifren y Roig
The Marne
El Marne
Oil on canvas, 60 x 80 cm
Barcelona, Museu Nacional d'Art de Catalunya

Paintings in this style, such as *Blue Water* (p. 569), recorded typically savage coastlines along the Costa Verde.

Another major Catalan landscape artist who absorbed the example of Impressionism was Santiago Rusiñol y Prat (1861–1931). He was primarily active in Barcelona, where he was an art critic and dramaturgist as well as a painter. Rusiñol began his studies in Spain and continued them in Paris, where in 1891 he exhibited at the Indépendants together with the Impressionists and Symbolists. A friend of Toulouse-Lautrec, he frequented the Café Weber and met the artists who went there, in addition to composers such as Claude Debussy (1862–1918) and writers. Rusiñol paid homage to Impressionism by painting Montmartre. His palette in *The Kitchen of the Moulin de la Galette* (p. 567) was unusually restrained for this most exuberant of colourists, though. His paintings were notable for their precision, their diffuse lighting, and, despite the freedom of Rusiñol's brushwork, their concentration on the subject in hand. In Spain he made his name as the painter of Spanish gardens, some of which dated back to Moorish days. Minute brush-strokes conjured forth all the vibrant magnificence, life and freshness of the gardens of Valencia, Granada, Toledo or Seville; *A Garden in Aranjuez* (p. 565) is a beautiful example. Rusiñol was a contributor to the Barcelona avant-garde periodical "Pél y Ploma" (Brush and Pen), which also featured some of the early drawings with which Picasso first appeared before the public. The first issue of the magazine, edited by Miguel Utrillo, came out in Barcelona in 1899.

At the turn of the century, Barcelona became the capital of the Spanish avant-garde as well as a centre of the anarchist movement. The city was rocked by terrorist assassinations and bombings, its heady, stimulating atmosphere making it a vortex into which many an artist of the period was sucked. "Pél y Ploma" rapidly became the theoretical debating ground of Spanish *Modernismo*. The artists involved were vehement in their calls for Spain to join the main European current and to venture far-ranging social and cultural reform. *Modernismo*, a Spanish form of Art Nouveau, found in Rusiñol not only a committed patron but also an eloquent fellow traveller and spokesman. In 1892, 1893 and 1894 he held "modernist festivals" at Cau Ferrat, his property at Sitges on the Costa Dorada. Among the many artists who attended these festivals was his friend Ramón Casas (1866–1932). Casas similarly contributed to the

Santiago Rusiñol y Prat
A Garden in Aranjuez, 1908
Jardín de Aranjuez
Oil on canvas, 140 x 135 cm
Madrid, Museo del Prado, Casón del Buen Retiro

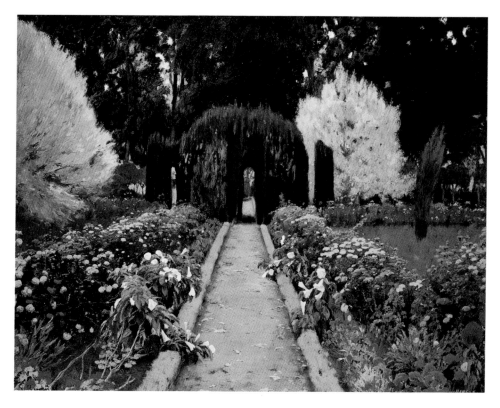

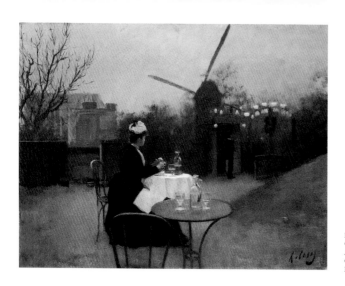

Ramón Casas
Out of Doors, c. 1890/91
Al aire libre
Oil on canvas, 51 x 66 cm
Barcelona, Museu Nacional d'Art de Catalunya

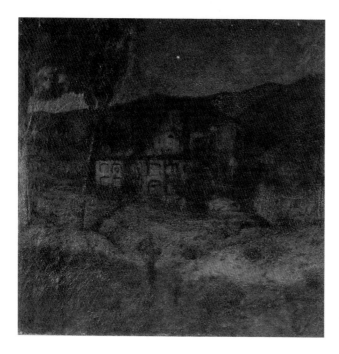

Nicolas Raurich y Petre
Solitude
Solitud
Oil on canvas, 145 x 146 cm
Barcelona, Museu Nacional d'Art de Catalunya

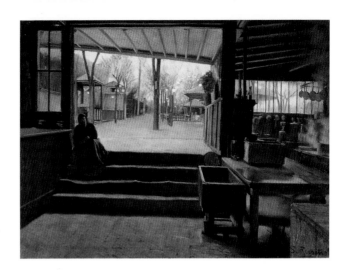

Santiago Rusiñol y Prat
The Kitchen of the Moulin de la Galette, c. 1890
El laboratorio de la Galette
Oil on canvas, 97 x 131 cm
Barcelona, Museu Nacional d'Art de Catalunya

magazines "Pél y Ploma" and "Forma" and, like Rusiñol and many others, had been deeply influenced by a lengthy stay in Paris. The artists of this group significantly prepared the ground for Spain's later reconquest, in the new century, of an autonomous and important position in international art, a process which was decisively initiated by the vitality of the Catalan art scene.

The artistic talent of Ramón Casas was apparent at an early age. As a schoolboy he was already attending the Vincens Academy in Barcelona. In Paris he went to the studio of Carolus-Duran, whose views alternated between academic orthodoxy and Impressionism. In the case of Casas, Impressionism soon gained the upper hand over the methods of his teacher. Even so, *Out of Doors* (p. 566), painted on Montmartre during his Paris years, uses tonalities based on black and it squarely in the main Spanish tradition. The freedom that is reveals especially in the brushwork of the sketchy background, and the spatial flatness with which Casas sidesteps academic perspective, clearly indicate his debt to Impressionism, however. The stark contrast of black and white, and the emphasis on certain lines, give the painting a strongly graphic quality; accordingly, it is hardly surprising to learn that Casas was close to Toulouse-Lautrec and also did posters and graphic work. Of special interest in this context are some two hundred charcoal portraits of famous contemporaries which Casas did and which show him to have been an excellent portrait artist. In Spain he painted both landscapes and folk scenes, though the stress in the latter tended to be on the folklorist elements rather than on effects of colour and light.

The work of Casas, Rusiñol and their fellow artists Joaquín Sunyer (1875–1958), Isidro Nonell (1873–1911) and Joaquín Mir Trinxet

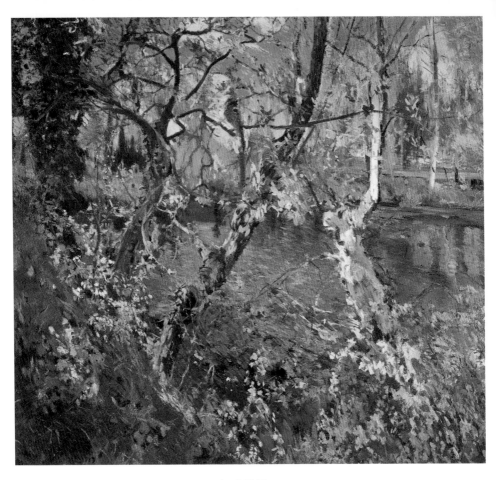

Joaquín Mir Trinxet
The Waters of the Moguda, 1917
Aguas de Moguda
Oil on canvas, 115 x 151 cm
Madrid, Museo del Prado, Casón del Buen Retiro

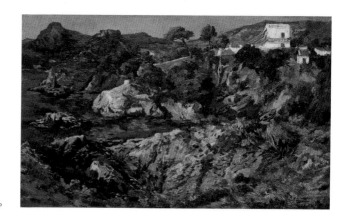

Francisco Gimeno Arasa
Blue Water
Aigua blava (Agua azul)
Oil on canvas, 60 x 98.5 cm
Madrid, Museo del Prado, Casón del Buen Retiro

(1873–1940) was exhibited in Barcelona in a café cabaret which went by the name of Els Quatre Gats (The Four Cats). The establishment had been opened by Pere Romeu in 1897 in imitation of the Chat-Noir in Paris. Every evening, a group of artists influenced by French Impressionism, with Casas and Rusiñol at their centre, would meet there to talk about modern art. It was these artists who were to inspire the young Picasso to strike out in new directions and find his own way of cutting loose from the conventional art and techniques he had learnt from his father, Don José. Thus, Picasso's career had its roots in Catalan Impressionism.

KARIN SAGNER

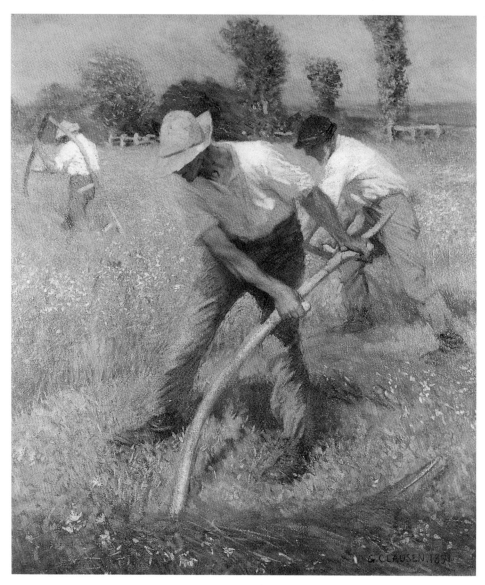

George Clausen
The Mowers, 1892
Oil on canvas, 97.2 x 76.2 cm
Lincoln, Usher Gallery

16 The British Response to French Impressionism

Like many other French artists, Monet and Pissarro were driven into exile in London by the Franco-Prussian War of 1870/71. By their own testimony, what interested them most in English galleries was the landscape art of J. M. W. Turner (1775–1851), John Crome (1768–1821) and John Constable (1776–1837). The sensitivity of these painters toward Nature and the freedom of the artist's expressive means confirmed the French artists in their feelings about new directions in art. English landscape art, and Dutch 17th-century painting, afforded a model for a conscious departure from idealized classical landscapes. Simple rural motifs, the close study of Nature, and an eye for atmospheric phenomena, were all combined and rendered in a brushwork of considerable freedom.

Critics have always rightly stressed the influence of English landscape art on the development of Impressionism; the curious thing is that British painting as a whole did not itself build an innovatory art on the early foundations, in spite of the fact that the English landscape tradition was well represented in Royal Academy exhibitions in the second half of the 19th century. The tradition of Constable could be seen as an ideal vision of unspoilt Nature, and this gratified the wishes of the middle classes, reconciling them to an industrialized increasingly Britain. The industrial revolution had been accomplished first and fastest in Britain, and by the later 19th century the resulting urban explosions were exacerbating the traditional disaffection with the city.

It was not till the turn of the century, when Impressionism had achieved international recognition, that an English revaluation of Turner and Constable ensued, one that would consequently bear fruit with pre-Impressionist English landscape art coming to be seen as a milestone in the evolution of a new style. And it was in this spirit that, in the 1880s, as Impressionism began to catch on in Britain too, its practitioners, such as Wynford Dewhurst (1864–1941), insisted that the British variety was an altogether distinctive native strain. This distinction from French Impressionism (to which the British nonetheless owed the inspiration for their technique) depended primarily on choices of subject-matter. The thematic range was focussed on aspects of contemporary British life. No homogeneous movement evolved in Britain in the closing twenty years of the 19th century; however, an impressive diversity of talent nonetheless did emerge. The British artists often borrowed stylistic features from French Impressionism and also from contemporary Dutch and German art, but they tended to be too inclined to compromise and dilute; accordingly, their significance for English art ultimately resides in their opposition to and defeat of academic conventions, together with their establishment of ties with modern art internationally such as could put an end to British isolation.

The British Impressionists were at first less interested in French landscape art from the 1870s than in the painting of the Eighties – by which time the peak of French Impressionism was past. Most of the British artists, reacting to conditions in Britain, responded more keenly to social content, and assigned major roles in their own work to the human figure. Degas and Manet were therefore in the fore of their interest, while Monet, who had made his name primarily as a landscape artist and had

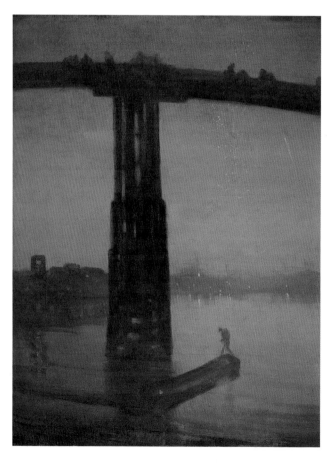

James Abbott McNeill Whistler
Nocturne in Blue and Gold: Old Battersea
Bridge, c. 1872–1875
Oil on canvas, 66.7 x 48.9 cm
London, The Tate Gallery

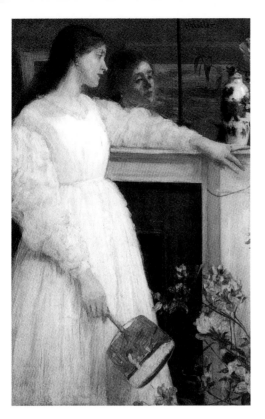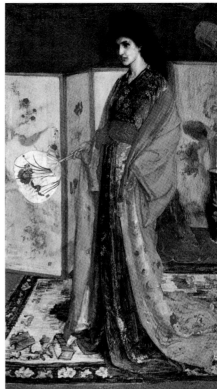

in fact largely dispensed with figures from the 1880s on, was admired for his virtuoso handling of light and colour.

When Monet and Pissarro were in London in 1870/71, their work was still as little known there as elsewhere. Though Durand-Ruel exhibited their paintings there at a relatively early date, it was not till more comprehensive Impressionist shows were mounted in the Eighties that the British reception began in earnest and English collectors started to respond with enthusiasm. At his London branch, Durand-Ruel had first exhibited the Barbizon artists in 1870. Exhibitions and publications were already making a success of the Barbizon school in Britain at that date, and Millet was particularly popular. For various younger British artists, such as George Clausen (1852–1944) or the Scot James Guthrie (1859–1930), Barbizon art retained its allure into the Eighties. A number of British artists went to Paris to shake off the shackles of academic convention such as still prevailed at the Royal Academy and the Royal Scottish Academy. Idealistic Victorian art that glorified the aristocracy, luxury and optimism no longer had anything to say to the times, they felt;

James Abbott McNeill Whistler
The Little White Girl: Symphony in White, No. 2, 1864
Oil on canvas, 76 x 51 cm
London, The Tate Gallery

James Abbott McNeill Whistler
Rose and Silver: The Princess from the Land of Porcelain, 1864
Oil on canvas, 200 x 116 cm
Washington (DC), Freer Gallery of Art, Smithsonian Institution

indeed, its exclusion of contemporary reality was downright undemocratic. Furthermore, neither in England nor more particularly in London was there a cultural and social life that could rival that of Paris in particular and other great European cities in general. In the great economic centre that was London (thus John Ruskin, 1819–1900), naked materialism reigned, of an order that spelt the end of any civilization. Unlike Paris, where the vitality of the arts met with a fairly broad public response, London and its ruling classes had relatively little interest in culture. And so it had to be sought on the continent: in France, Italy, Germany and Holland.

Ironically enough, British artists in France were in closer contact with official Salon art than with the avant-garde. They tended to share the widespread enthusiasm for Bastien-Lepage, who had blended the rural subject-matter of Millet and the Barbizon school with a little social criticism and *plein-airisme* and had scored astonishing successes at the Salon with the result (p. 167). The younger generation were particularly interested in his broad brush-strokes, a new technique which he used (like the Impressionists) for his preliminary open-air sketches before adapting the final, studio product to prevailing taste. If Bastien-Lepage was nonetheless viewed as an Impressionist, it was not least because of the looseness of the criteria then applied to Impressionist art, which could include anything that used a freer technique, open-air studies, and modern subject-matter.

From the Eighties on, Britain's rural *plein-air* naturalism was tightened by the example of Bastien-Lepage and the Barbizon school. In 1883, Clausen was in Paris for several months, working under Bouguereau at the Académie Julian. He met Bastien-Lepage, and then, following a visit to Holland and acquaintances with artists there, followed his own predilection for simple, rustic scenes. Rural subjects remained to the fore in his work, and from the Nineties on he expressed them in his own version of Impressionist techniques. His post-Millet view of Nature and farm work can be seen in *The Mowers* (p. 570), which also exhibits effects of colour and light reminiscent of Monet.

Henry Herbert La Thangue (1859–1929) likewise aimed at a presentation of the simple life led by honest country people. Deeply Romantic in attitude, he had favourite areas in England, Provence and Liguria which he painted in order to establish a pre-industrial image of Nature. Like Clausen, he was strongly influenced by Bastien-Lepage in the 1880s; however, he steadily moved away from the latter's broad brushwork and social criticism alike, and established a structural style that went beyond linear precision, coupled with a more universal subject-matter. La Thangue's understanding of the natural world, as seen in his picture *In the Orchard* (p. 583), painted in the open, might best be compared with that of Pissarro. Pissarro's own art was of course communicated to the British not least by his son Lucien (1863–1944), resident in London since 1883 (p. 274).

From 1883 on, a number of painters gathered, along the lines of their colleagues in Barbizon, at Newlyn in Cornwall. The leaders of the group

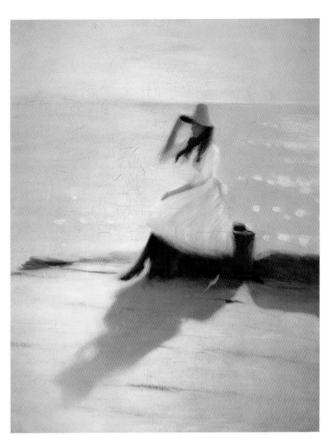

Philip Wilson Steer
Young Woman on the Beach, Walberswick,
c. 1886–1888
Oil on canvas, 125.5 x 91.5 cm
Paris, Musée d'Orsay

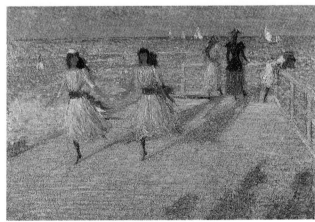

Philip Wilson Steer
Girls Running, Walberswick Pier,
c. 1890–1894
Oil on canvas, 69.2 x 92.7 cm
London, The Tate Gallery

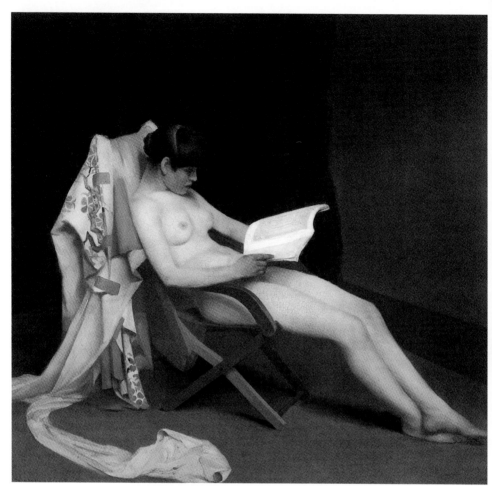

Theodore Roussel
The Reading Girl, 1887
Oil on canvas, 152.4 x 161.3 cm
London, The Tate Gallery

were Stanhope Forbes (1857–1947) and Henry Scott Tuke (1858–1929), and the artists' principal preoccupation was with *plein-air* naturalism, rural subjects, and fishing and coastal scenes. In 1899 Forbes established the Newlyn School of Art. Around the turn of the century, a new generation of artists gathered at the colony, taking their bearings more noticeably from the French Impressionist landscapes of the 1870s. The most striking of these artists was Laura Knight (1877–1972; pp. 586, 587).

In Scotland the 1880s also saw a lively interest in open-air painting. The Glasgow School, numbering some thirty members, was of key importance. Foremost in the group were Guthrie, his fellow Scot William MacTaggart (1835–1910), and the Irish artist John Lavery (1856–1941). They agreed in their opposition to prevailing Victorian taste and the methods of the Royal Scottish Academy. Guthrie's work brought the Glasgow School international recognition. A brief visit to Paris in 1882 left him with the lasting impact of Barbizon *plein-air* painting, which he would adapt to his own landscape art in the years ahead. His colours were delicate, his treatment of light and atmosphere extremely sensitive. In the mid-1880s, Guthrie entered a critical phase which resulted in his almost entirely abandoning landscapes and turning to portraits, interiors and genre work. *The Morning Paper* (p. 582) is one of the finest of his many portraits of middle-class women. Guthrie's pastel technique here and elsewhere seemed to him (as it did to Degas) the aptest means of expression, since it was quick and easy to use and thus ideally suited to recording impressions on the spot. There was great interest in the technique in Britain, as the sheer existence of a Pastel Society in London implies.

Guthrie was a friend of James Abbott McNeill Whistler (1834–1903). He also joined the New English Art Club in London in 1899. This independent, Secessionist movement had been founded in 1885 by Clausen, La Thangue, Forbes, Wilson Steer (1860–1942), Sidney Starr (1857–1925) and Frederick Brown (1851–1941) to promote the new, *plein-air*, sketchy, Impressionist art. The Club was in revolt against the moralizing and anecdotal tone of Victorian art and the teaching methods of the Royal Academy. Its first annual group show was held in 1886, and revealed the members to have espoused aesthetics of various kinds, though a large number had plainly taken the principles of French Impressionism to heart.

Whistler, the friend of Monet and Renoir and, like them, in former times a student at Charles Gleyre's studio in Paris, was instrumental in communicating Impressionism to Britain. Born in America, he had been resident in England since 1863. Scandals such as the Ruskin law suit of 1877 helped make him the idol of the younger artists; more importantly, they discovered in his paintings new possibilities that pointed forward to abstract art. His nocturnes of the early 1870s were pioneering work contemporaneous with Monet's breakthrough (*Nocturne in Blue and Gold: Old Battersea Bridge*, p. 572); it was of these paintings that Ruskin had been so disparaging. In them, Whistler viewed the Thames at night

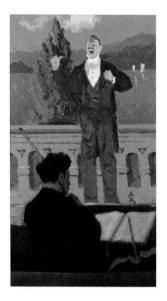

Walter Richard Sickert
Lion Comique, 1887
Oil on canvas, 51 x 31 cm
London, Private collection

in muted, poetic harmonies of hue. What counted was not a precise detail or outline; rather, Whistler was after large, simple, major form. The foreground, middle distance and background were treated in much the same way; conventional perspective was meaningless, given that the canvas was a single colour space. The influence of Japanese art is palpable.

Whistler's structures were of course taken from real observation, but in the studio he adapted what he had seen to an aesthetic ideal, a poetry of vision. It was, despite appearances, a different method from that of the French Impressionists in the 1870s, in other words. Whistler's interest (like that of Degas and Manet) was in the city, modern life of a Baudelairean order. During his short presidency (1886–1888) of the Royal Academy, Whistler not only expounded his aesthetic principles in his 10 o'clock lectures but also promoted French Impressionism and gave it exhibition space in 1886.

Whistler's followers included Theodore Roussel (1847–1926), Paul Maitland (1863–1909), Walter Richard Sickert (1860–1942) and the young Wilson Steer – that is, the artists widely considered the leading British Impressionists. With Starr and Brown they split off from the New English Art Club and sidelined the more rural subject-matter of the Glasgow and Newlyn Schools, or at least exerted a strong influence. Controversy resulted; and between 1886 and 1905, British Impressionism was fought out in the Club – or, by those who resigned, out of it. In 1889 Sickert organized the London Impressionist Exhibition at Goupil's London rooms; a sub-group within the club were using that label. The driving force was Sickert, who possessed a forceful literary skill too and wrote a foreword to the first catalogue in which he outlined the group's aims. He was clearly opposed to official Victorian doctrine, and warned against a decorative art that took its bearings from the Arts and Crafts movement. The task facing British Impressionism, he believed, was to record the magic and poesy that lay all around in everyday life. London, the great metropolis, provided all the stimulating subject-matter that was necessary.

Plainly this did not equally apply to all the London Impressionists, though; and contemporary critics were not slow to voice doubts concerning the unity of the group Sickert insisted existed. A concentration on London subject-matter, for instance, was apparent only in the work of Sickert (p. 588), Starr (p. 579), Roussel (p. 576) and the latter's pupil Maitland (p. 583), and to a lesser extent in that of Steer and Brown. Urban problems resulting from 19th-century expansion in the cities – such as unemployment, poverty, child labour, alcoholism and prostitution – were almost totally absent from this art. The city was being viewed as a predominantly middle-class thing. It was being aestheticized. And still Victorian taste chose to object, precisely because the work of the London Impressionists lacked a moral agenda.

In drawing people's attention to the group's peculiar subject-matter, Sickert had been aiming to pre-empt the criticism that the London Impressionists were merely copying the art of Degas, Monet and Whis-

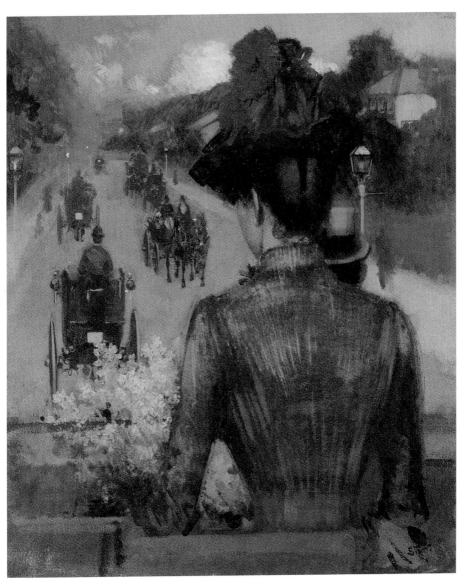

Sidney Starr
The City Atlas, c. 1888/89
Oil on canvas, 60.9 x 50.6 cm
Ottawa, National Gallery of Canada, Gift of the
Massey Collection of English Painting

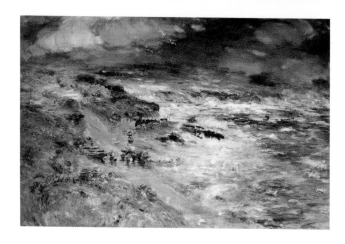

William MacTaggart
The Storm, 1890
Oil on canvas, 121.9 x 183 cm
Edinburgh, National Gallery of Scotland

tler. Lucien Pissarro, however, lecturing at the Club, took a different view. He felt that very few of the English artists, who "painted flat and included black (!) in their palettes", were at all conscious of the principles of Impressionism. He had good words for Steer alone, who, he thought, was the most uncompromising in his adoption of the new style. (Despite these reservations, Lucien Pissarro was to join Sickert's circle some years later.)

Like many another English painter of his generation, Steer, who enrolled at the Académie Julian in Paris in 1882, was initially under the sway of Bastien-Lepage. Back in England, he settled in London, and from 1884 tended to paint at Walberswick on the Suffolk coast. There he painted *Young Woman on the Beach* (p. 575) and similar fresh, outstanding pictures, which he showed at the first London Impressionists exhibition. The fluid style echoed Whistler, while Steer's pastose brushwork (or, indeed, palette knife work) sometimes recalled Courbet or Manet. Subsequently Steer, under the growing influence of French Impressionism, lightened his colours to the point of luminosity, using a technique of visibly separate brush-strokes reminiscent of Monet's boat pictures at Argenteuil (*Summer at Cowes*, p. 581). The additive juxtaposition of strokes of unmixed colour already indicated how much ground brushwork was gaining in Steer's praxis at the expense of formal considerations.

Consistently enough, Steer occasionally came close to pointillism (p. 575). In his clear, simple, sometimes almost linear compositions, Steer had a predilection for backlit figures and shapes and subtly nuanced pastel colours comparable to Monet's work at Antibes and Bordighera. The Neo-Impressionist dissolution of form went unloved in Britain, and for a long time to come its unpopularity was to be a burden on Steer's standing, not only within the Club. Clear form and three-dimensionality remained fundamental in the view of British artists. Steer's approach to a variety of avant-garde lines, from Impressionism via Neo-Impressionism to Symbolism, was reflected in the variety of his own compositional strategies and painting techniques. Thus the more spontaneous of his landscapes and coastal scenes recall Monet and Neo-Impressionism, while his interiors are more in line with Degas, Whistler and John Singer Sargent (1856–1925). It was in the 1880s that Steer painted his most important contributions to British Impressionism. In the mid-Nineties (while teaching as Brown's assistant at the Slade), his style underwent a transformation and he became a romantic eclectic, drawing his subjects increasingly from the landscape art of the 18th and early 19th centuries (Watteau, Constable, Turner), yet all the time keeping his acquired technical resources firmly to hand. In his late period he also painted outstanding watercolours.

Sargent affords an arresting example of just how readily Impressionist elements in the 1880s could be absorbed by a talent that was at heart

Philip Wilson Steer
Summer at Cowes, 1888
Oil on canvas, 50.9 x 61.2 cm
Manchester, City Art Gallery

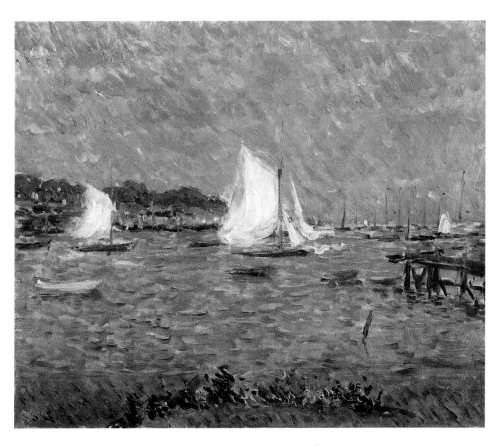

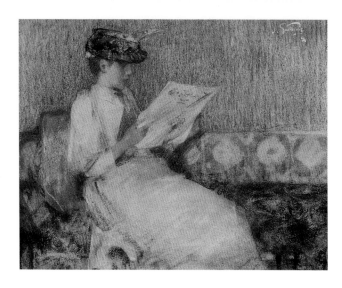

academic. American by birth, he will be examined in greater detail in the chapter "Impressionism in North America" but he should not be forgotten here, since he played a key role in British Impressionism. He was resident in London from the mid-Eighties on, and was one of the foreign painters who repeatedly visited Giverny in order to paint near the revered Monet. Sargent in fact had been a personal friend of Monet's since 1876, and worked at his side in Giverny; and his part in communicating the French master's art to Britain was an important one. Later in his career, Sargent was to be a sought-after society portrait painter of considerable decorative resource; but in his earlier years he had a strong interest in *plein-airisme* and an easy-going technical approach to subjects. The story goes that when they were painting together, Sargent asked for black, which he felt he absolutely needed, but was refused; and the anecdote is richly suggestive of the tradition within which Sargent believed he belonged. In the 1870s in Paris he had not only studied under the academic Carolus-Duran but had also been inspired by dark-toned Spanish art. As with most of the British Impressionists, subject took precedence over form in his eyes. He never accorded the textural substance of a painting an autonomous value, as Monet did in works painted in the same period. In the Eighties, through Monet, Sargent gave more attention to natural effects of light and shadow.

Nevertheless (and this too applied to many of the British Impressionists), the chiaroscurist fundamental principles of academic art based on tonalities remained in the foreground for Sargent. To put those principles aside had been one of the revolutionary achievements of the French Impressionists. Sargent's supposedly Impressionist phase, spent painting in and near Broadway, lasted only from about 1884 to 1889. *Carnation,*

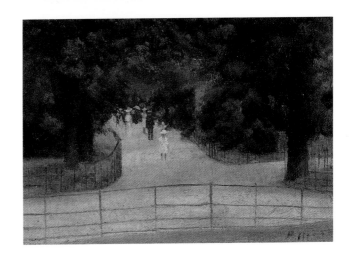

Paul Maitland
Flower Walk, Kensington Gardens, c. 1897
Oil on canvas, 127 x 177.8 cm
London, The Tate Gallery

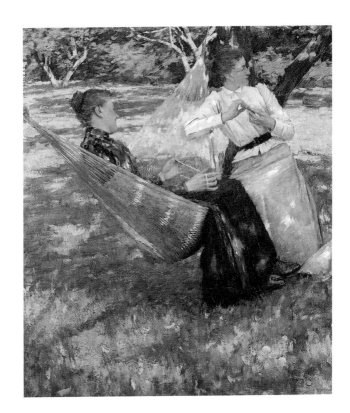

Henry Herbert La Thangue
In the Orchard, 1893
Oil on canvas, 82.9 x 72.4 cm
Bradford, City Art Gallery and Museum,
Cartwright Hall

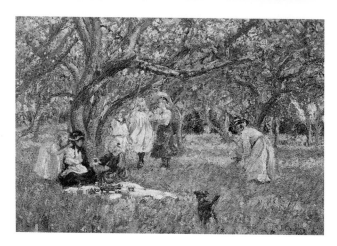

James Charles
The Picnic, 1904
Oil on canvas, 37.5 x 54 cm
Warrington (Cheshire), Museum and Art Gallery

Lily, Lily, Rose (p. 597) was one of his great achievements of that period. The atmosphere and lighting of the painting, exhibited in 1887 at the Royal Academy, made a powerful impact on his fellow artists; Steer was one of those who expressed their enthusiasm, urging Sargent to persuade other members of the Club, such as Clausen and La Thangue, to join the Royal Academy.

By such routes did Impressionist ideas and technical innovations begin to penetrate into the academic institutions. This may well be one reason why the Club began to lose its role as a forum for the new art in the Nineties. The fact that other artists' associations were founded, with Sickert directly involved once again, was merely one further by-product of the process.

Viewed across the entire spectrum of his work, Sickert must surely be regarded as one of the most gifted painters of his age. After studying at the Slade, he visited Degas and Manet in Paris on the recommendation of Whistler. At Dieppe in summer 1885, influenced by Degas, he did pastels and oils of beach scenes and shop fronts, pursuing ideas of pictures in series. The tendency to work in series of paintings was to remain with Sickert. The muted, soft, reticent colours of his early work strongly recalled Whistler, while the sketchiness and the patchwork, broken brush-strokes reflect his experience of France. Following his return to London, Sickert, again with Degas' example in mind, turned to the entertainment world of theatres and music-halls. The famous music-hall pictures which were so successful in England were painted from 1889 on and occupy a central position in his œuvre. Along with his works done in Dieppe (p. 588) and Venice, they constitute one of the three major thematic groups in Sickert's art. One of the first of the music-hall pictures was *Lion Comique* (p. 578). The understated olive green, khaki and (unusually) brownish violet have been lightened, under French influence, with cool greys and ochres. The simple tonal gradation highlights the comedian above the darkness of the orchestra pit. Unlike Degas, Sickert does not trouble with startling cropping or points of view, but, like Degas, he did work in the studio from preliminary studies. Sickert's music-hall paintings are skilful, effective exercises in using the contrast between the bright stage and dark auditorium, in which the human figures seem reduced to puppets or masks, stripped of their individuality. The chiaroscurist leanings in Sickert's work marked him out from the pure, classic Impressionists.

Sickert was active on the Club's behalf till the 1890s. In 1889, he organized a show at Goupil's in Paris at which Starr, Steer, Brown and Roussel exhibited. Durand-Ruel gave him a number of successful shows, and even Neo-Impressionists and Symbolists such as Fénéon and Signac took an interest in his paintings. In 1905 Sickert returned to London, to settle in Camden Town. Up to the First World War he painted highly individual, outstanding works. He was now experimenting more with various techniques, such as overpainting, always proceeding from meticulous draughtsmanship and composition. In this respect his technique was in a direct line of descent from the academic principle of the preliminary *ébauche*. He now concentrated largely on nudes, interiors and genre scenes. From 1908 on, Sickert hosted weekly gatherings of painters at his home in Fitzroy Street, where Lucien Pissarro, Spencer Gore (1878–1914) and Harold Gilman (1876–1919) were among the regulars. In 1911, under Gore's presidency, they held their first public exhibition, calling themselves the Camden Town Group. This was the seed of the influential London Group that would emerge in 1913. The foundation

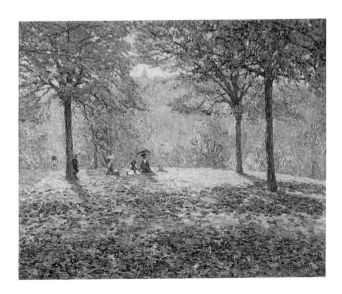

Wynford Dewhurst
Luncheon on the Grass (The Picnic), 1908
Oil on canvas, 82 x 100.7 cm
Manchester, City Art Gallery

of these groups reflected the active reception of Cézanne, van Gogh and Gauguin; Roger Eliot Fry (1866–1934) was in the vanguard of the British critical assessment of Post-Impressionism. Cubist and Futurist work was soon being received too.

Gore was one of the most important English artists in the opening years of the century (p. 590). He studied at the Slade, where he met Gilman and Wyndham Lewis (1884–1957), who were among the first members of the London Group. Gore was also a pupil of Steer, through whom he became acquainted with the work of Monet. In 1903 he met Sickert and Lucien Pissarro; the latter introduced him to the work of his father, Sickert to that of Degas. Gore quickly abandoned the New English Art Club; however, he was not only the first president of the Camden Group, but also – through his friend Lewis – injected Vorticism into the London Group. Vorticism was the British equivalent of Futurism and Cubism.

The president of the London Group was Gilman. From about 1910 on, he worked on an idiosyncratic blend of Signac, van Gogh and Gauguin's styles. He was a careful draughtsman and gave scrupulous attention to preliminaries. Gilman mainly painted landscapes, portraits and interiors with figures, but, in contrast to contemporary French avant-garde painters such as Matisse or Picasso, he always kept the observation of Nature in a firmly central position. In this sense, Gilman considered himself a realist (p. 589).

Sickert's supremely important role consisted not only in assisting the recognition of Impressionism, Whistler, and thus the tradition that lay behind his own work; he also paved the way for a new freedom in artistic

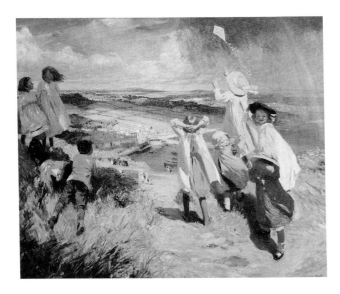

Laura Knight
Flying the Kite, 1910
Oil on canvas, 150 x 180 cm
Cape Town, South African National Gallery

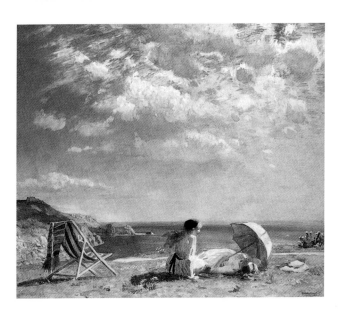

Laura Knight
Wind and Sun, c. 1913
Oil on canvas, 96.5 x 112 cm
London, Pyms Gallery

expression, a freedom that ran parallel to the new sociopolitical mood of the Edwardian decade. If Impressionism in the New English Art Club had been primarily a matter of Sickert and Steer at the beginning of the Nineties, the work of Clausen, La Thangue and Lavery also served to demonstrate that familiarity with the Impressionist achievement was widespread in Britain, and that technical innovations had been adopted not only by the Club but also in the Royal Academy. New associations such as the International Society of Sculptors, Painters and Gravers, founded by Whistler in 1898, quickly outpaced the New English Art Club. Many of its members, of course, were recruited from the ranks of the Club or Sickert's friends.

Clausen, Guthrie and La Thangue now turned increasingly to a pure landscape art that was centred on atmospherics, light and motion. With the old English masters – especially Constable and Turner – in mind, they tended to foreground idylls and Arcadian views of Nature. Perhaps inevitably, *plein-air* painting was superseded once more by studio work, in the output of Clausen and La Thangue and in that of Forbes' turn-of-the-century group at Newlyn. Knight painted curiously heroic-seeming figure compositions and idyllic country pictures, such as *Flying the Kite* (p. 586) and *Wind and Sun* (p. 587). The luminous splendour and the freshness of her work is bewitching to this day. The atmospheric vastness of her sky, and her relatively quiet colours, are reminiscent of the Hague School.

The Glasgow School always tended towards a greater emphasis upon individual personalities than was the case with the Club. In the 1890s, its interest shifted towards the decorative values of Art Nouveau, at the time a new development. The Glasgow avant-garde was fond of a modest symbolism such as linked their work to that of the Nabis and Neo-Impressionists more than to that of Manet or Monet. The preeminent Glasgow artists remained portrait painters, followers of Whistler such as Guthrie.

Monet's influence remained evident in the Edwardian years in paintings by Dewhurst such as *Luncheon on the Grass* (p. 585), which takes Monet's brushwork and some of his style without achieving his compositional unity. Dewhurst saw Monet as the finest of the Impressionists, and put his view in "Impressionist Painting: its Genesis and Development" (1904). In closing, we must mention the Aesthetic movement of the Nineties, a decadent vein parallel to realism and Impressionism. These artists included Charles Condor (1868–1909), William Rothenstein (1872–1945) and William Orpen (1878–1931). This was the second generation of the New English Art Club. They too visited France,

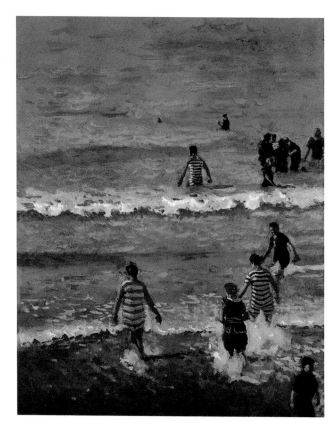

Walter Richard Sickert
Bathers at Dieppe, c. 1902
Oil on canvas, 131 x 104.4 cm
Liverpool, Walker Art Gallery

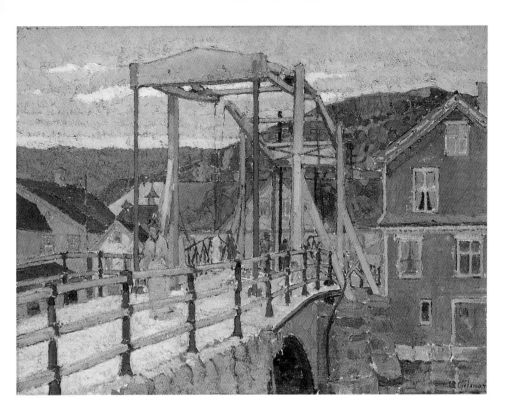

Harold Gilman
Canal Bridge, Flekkefjord, 1912
Oil on canvas, 46 x 61 cm
London, The Tate Gallery

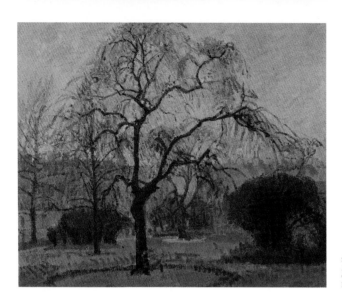

Spencer F. Gore
Mornington Crescent, 1911
Oil on canvas, 63.5 x 76.5 cm
London, The Tate Gallery

and were in touch with Camille Pissarro, Gauguin, the Pont-Aven painters, and Toulouse-Lautrec. Condor and Orpen studied at the Slade, lived in Chelsea, and were friends of Steer. They kept a close eye on developments in French art such as the linear style of the Nabis, the synthetist approach of the Pont-Aven school, or the more expressionist manner of Toulouse-Lautrec.

KARIN SAGNER

17 Impressionism in North America

Origins and Principles of American Impressionism

In 1886 the French Impressionists held their eighth and last joint exhibition in Paris. It was also the year the movement achieved its American breakthrough. At the invitation of the American Art Association in New York, the Paris art dealer Paul Durand-Ruel mounted the most comprehensive exhibition of Impressionist art yet seen in North America at that date, including 23 works by Degas, 17 Manets, 48 Monets, 7 Morisots, 42 Pissarros, 38 Renoirs, and 15 Sisleys. This impressive collection of works ably represented the aims and distinctive characteristics of Impressionism. The show, which opened on 10 April, was so well received that when it closed it moved to the National Academy of Design and on 25 May was re-opened to public view.

Up till this exhibition, Durand-Ruel had contented himself with offering single works or small groups on the American market, and the US had had small opportunity to assess the new art. The first Impressionist painting to be included in an American exhibition was Degas' pastel *Ballet Rehearsal* (1874; Kansas City, MO, Nelson-Atkins Museum of

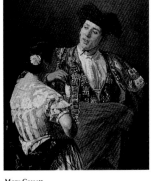

Mary Cassatt
Offering the Panale to the Bullfighter, 1873
Oil on canvas, 100.6 x 85.1 cm
Breeskin 22. Williamstown (MA),
Sterling and Francis Clark Institute

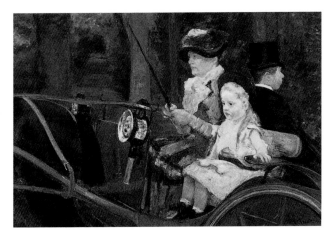

Mary Cassatt
A Woman and Child in the Driving Seat, 1879
Oil on canvas, 89.9 x 130.8 cm
Breeskin 69
Philadelphia (PA), Philadelphia Museum of Art

Art), at the time in an American private collection, which was seen in the American Watercolor Society's annual show in New York in 1878. The following year, Manet's *Execution of Emperor Maximilian* (p. 65) was displayed at the Clarendon Hotel in New York and the Studio Building in Boston. However, another few years were still to pass before anything more than stray works by French Impressionists were seen in America. In 1883, an International Exhibition of Art and Industry (originally conceived as part of an 1881 world fair that never materialized) was held in Boston to show art and crafts from abroad. Durand-Ruel placed a fair number of Impressionist works in this exhibition – about half of all the oils displayed – including 6 Pissarros, 4 each by Renoir and Sisley, and 3 Monets.

The response to the new French aesthetics was initially reserved, and it was not till the 1886 show that a turning point was reached. Private collectors had hitherto been slow to invest; but at the Art Association show Durand-Ruel reputedly took some $40,000. The press reaction was lively, and henceforth contemporary French art featured prominently in art magazines. One commentary in April 1886 declared that the Impressionists possessed "technical skill of a high order", and that the work on show had provided valuable new stimulus for American artists.[1]

The Art Association show marked the true beginning of the reception of Impressionism by American artists. Study in Paris or in rural France became fashionable after 1886, Giverny, where Monet had moved in April 1883, proving particularly popular. In this, American painters were in line with a trend that had been established since the American Civil War (1861–1865). If art in previous decades had been primarily tied to the new sense of nationhood, in the post-war period it acquired a newly cosmopolitan cast. After the Civil War, the US developed a changed, confident view of itself, and the evolution of modern mercantile America can effectively be dated from that time. Its internal unity finally

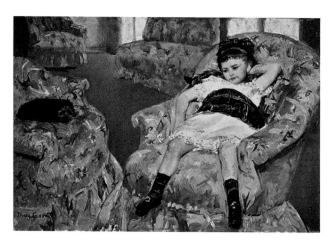

Mary Cassatt
Little Girl in a Blue Armchair, 1878
Oil on canvas, 89.5 x 129.8 cm
Breeskin 56
Washington (DC), National Gallery of Art,
Mr. and Mrs. Paul Mellon Collection

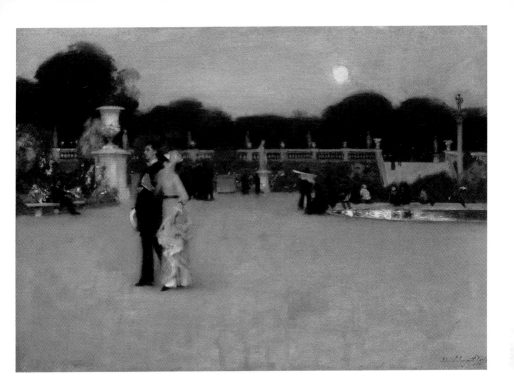

John Singer Sargent
The Luxembourg Garden at Twilight, 1879
Oil on canvas, 64.8 x 91.4 cm
Philadelphia, Philadelphia Museum of Art,
J.G. Johnson Collection

established, the US displayed a new national pride, and displayed it to
all the world. Rather than closing their eyes to outside influences, the
Americans now accepted the challenge to compete; and their strength in
the years ahead was to lie in outdoing the old world in its own fields and
by its own means.

In art, this meant two things. First, American art took to expressing
the nation's achievements and self-confidence. The idealizing tendency
of the American Renaissance, and its display of social status and assurance, were not unlike similar tendencies in European art, and particularly
in Victorian England. Second, if American art had previously been wary
of forfeiting its own identity through contact with art elsewhere, it now
exhibited the sureness and independence of maturity. What mattered
now was to assimilate European traditions and techniques and to transform them into something peculiarly American. American artists took to
attending European academies in greater numbers than had previously
been the case. Düsseldorf had already attracted Americans prior to the
Civil War, and later their German goal was Munich. But it was Paris,
already popular in the 1850s, that became the great magnet for American
art students abroad in and after the 1860s. They matriculated at the
Ecole des Beaux-Arts or at the private schools, the most frequented of

which was the Académie Julian, where they could meet artists from all over Europe.

Paris training was based on life drawing and composition. Tutors followed the canonical wisdom of two centuries of Academy teaching, which assigned a far higher value to history painting, because of its moral dimensions and implications, than to still lifes or landscapes. But of course it was precisely landscape art that had developed a solid tradition of its own in 19th-century America. From the Hudson River School artists Thomas Cole (1801–1848) and Albert Bierstadt (1830–1902) to Luminist artists such as Fitz Hugh Lane (1804–1865) and John F. Kensett (1816–1872), the American line portrayed the specifics of the American landscape. These artists recorded the distinctiveness of Nature in the New World, its vastness, its unspoilt beauty, and its ability to consign Man to a subordinate position.

The Luminists, most active in the third quarter of the century, introduced to American landscape art its powerful atmospherics. As the group's sobriquet implied, they were interested in effects of light. Their compositions were broad in format and tended to position the horizon low in order to paint an immense veil of gauzy sky. The Luminists'

Mary Cassatt
Mother about to Wash Her Sleepy Child, 1880
Oil on canvas, 100.5 x 65.4 cm
Breeskin 90
Los Angeles (CA), Los Angeles County Museum of Art, Mrs. Fred Hathaway Bixby Bequest

Mary Cassatt
Young Woman Sewing in the Garden, c. 1880–1882
Oil on canvas, 92 x 63 cm
Breeskin 144
Paris, Musée d'Orsay

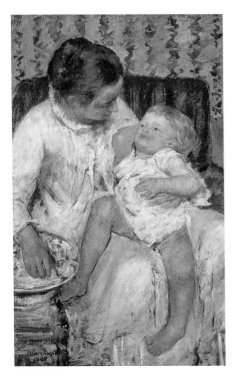
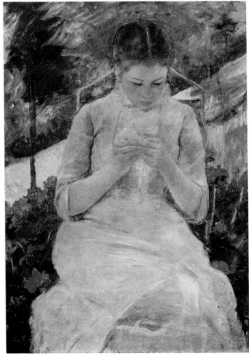

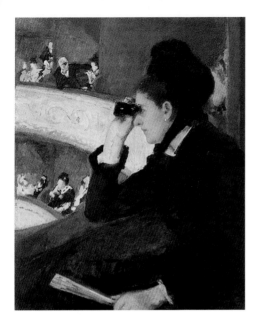

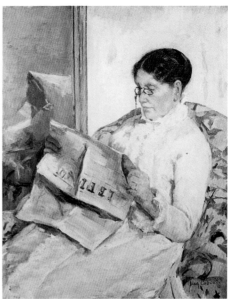

attention to light provided an invaluable seedbed for the adoption of Impressionist techniques by American artists.

Of great importance too was the fact that the new French aesthetics were only one of several artistic options with which Europe confronted the American artists. In terms of the American reception of European art, academic figure-painting and composition, Impressionist brushwork and subject-matter, along with the various principles and approaches of movements that were presently to follow, were contemporaneous and of equal validity. American artists not infrequently combined the most various of influences in their work. By far the majority of those who came to terms with Impressionism retained recognisable continuities with their academic training, preserving firm outlines and forms (especially in figure work) despite their relaxed brushwork. But their structural approaches opened and freshened thanks to landscape art, an area which academic tuition largely ignored. Small wonder, then, that American artists were particularly interested in the pictures of Bastien-Lepage (p. 167), who combined tonally modelled figure work with an unacademic approach to Nature.

Apart from their eclectic way of combining stylistic features, American artists often tended to have only a passing interest in Impressionist aesthetics, using them as a springboard to their own expressive strategies. In those strategies they could draw on the American tradition's tendency to use formats of considerable width with low horizons, for instance. The most important characteristic was the aim to present inner values rather

Mary Cassatt
At the Opera, 1880
Oil on canvas, 80 x 64.8 cm
Breeskin 73
Boston (MA), Museum of Fine Arts,
Charles Henry Hayden Fund

Mary Cassatt
Reading "Le Figaro", 1883
Oil on canvas, 104 x 84 cm
Breeskin 128
Private collection

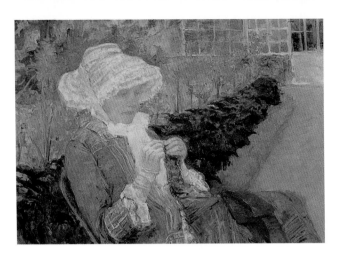

Mary Cassatt
Lydia Crocheting in the Garden at Marly, 1880
Oil on canvas, 66 x 94 cm. Breeskin 98
New York, The Metropolitan Museum of Art,
Gift of Mrs. Gardner Cassatt

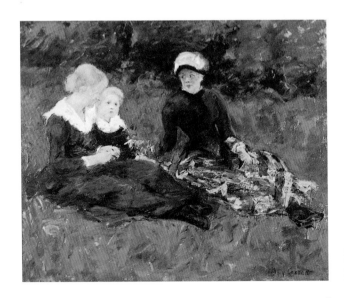

Mary Cassatt
On the Meadow, 1880
Oil on canvas, 54 x 65 cm
Breeskin 93. Private collection

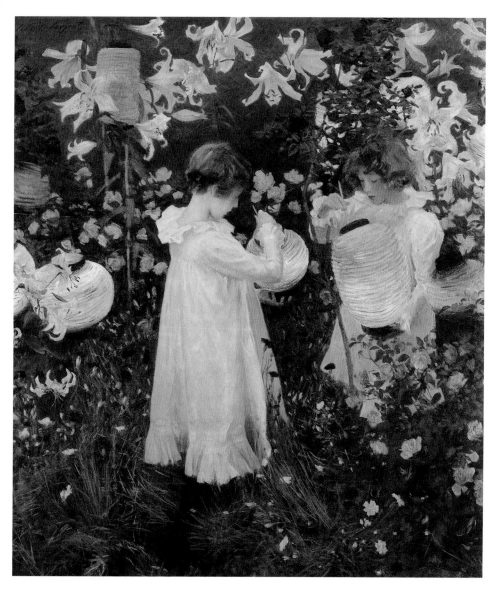

John Singer Sargent
Carnation, Lily, Lily, Rose, 1885/86
Oil on canvas, 174 x 153.7 cm
London, The Tate Gallery

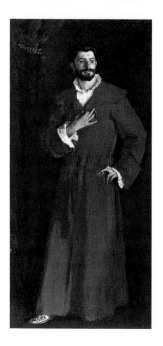

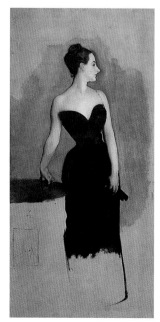

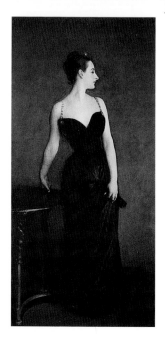

than merely a brief visual impression; French Impressionist technique was felt to be materialist and to neglect ideal values. Fr this reason, the French countermovements of Neo- and Post-Impressionism and Symbolism proved especially attractive to North American artists in the late 19th and early 20th century.

The changes in American responses to French art are a reminder that the Americans primarily saw Impressionism as a thing of formal, aesthetic innovation, and a revolution in brushwork and colourism. Americans did not warm to the French artists' view that their formal departures defined a position not only in the art world but indeed in society at large. Themselves trained in the Paris academic tradition, American artists could see only some secondary significance in the Impressionists' rejection of the academic annual Salon and the structural and cognitive norms that prevailed there. The French Impressionists had tackled thematic areas that had hitherto not been deemed worthy of art: as well as landscapes, they had painted motifs drawn from modern everyday life, often reflecting the societal changes that accompanied industrialization. These subjects were absent from American paintings, which emphasized cheerful rural and urban scenes flooded with light and inhabited by carefree people.

The press responses to the 1886 Art Association exhibition reflected this selective approach. Three points of criticism recurred: Impressionist figure painting was felt to be a brutal, undignified realism; Impressionist technique was too sketchy for true works of art; and deeper qualities such as could not be registered in a first brief glance at subjects were thought to be missing from Impressionist art.

As time went by, only the vehemence with which the charge of sketchiness was levelled was to be abated. It was in fact left standing by developments in American art. In 1878 the Society of American Painters held an exhibition expressly restricted to sketches. In the winter of 1882, the Society of American Painters in Pastel, known as the Pastel Club, was founded, and in four exhibitions from 1884 to 1890 displayed work done exclusively in pastel, a technique customarily reserved for preliminary studies. By the time the Pastel Club was absorbed into the American Watercolor Society and the New York Watercolor Club in 1890, the ground had been thoroughly prepared for the formal, aesthetic innovations of Impressionism. North American artists from McNeill Whistler to Maurice Brazil Prendergast (1861–1924) were to achieve important Impressionist work in pastel and especially in watercolour.

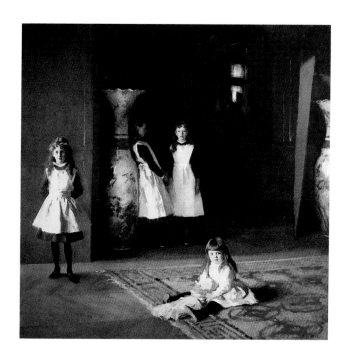

John Singer Sargent
The Boit Daughters, 1882
Oil on canvas, 222.5 x 222.5 cm
Boston (MA), Museum of Fine Arts

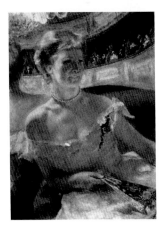

Mary Cassatt
Lydia in a Loge, Wearing a Pearl Necklace, 1879
Oil on canvas, 81.3 x 58.4 cm
Breeskin 64. Philadelphia, Philadelphia
Museum of Art, Bequest of Charlotte
Dorrance-Wright

Mary Cassatt The first two American artists to make a significant contribution to Impressionist painting were Mary Cassatt (1845–1926) and John Singer Sargent (1856–1925). Tellingly, both spent most of their lives in Europe, evolving their Impressionist styles in personal contact with the major French artists of the school.

Cassatt's work was more closely linked with French painting from the 1870s to 1980s than that of any other American. After studying at the Pennsylvania Academy of Fine Arts in Philadelphia, she was one of the first artists to leave after the Civil War, and went to Paris in 1866. There she studied privately with Jean-Léon Gérôme and probably Thomas Couture. The Franco-Prussian War interrupted her stay, but in 1871 she was again in Europe, in Parma, and in the following year in Madrid and Seville. In Spain her art made a distinct change of direction, and, impressed by Velázquez and Murillo, she painted a number of pictures on contemporary Spanish themes, albeit less in the manner of the old masters than that of Manet. The 1873 *Offering the Panale to the Bullfighter* (p. 591) documents this change; Cassatt has chosen a single moment, and her vigorous, contrastive brushwork creates a lively textural structure. Cassatt was subsequently to retain two features present in this composition: the cropping of figures seen close-up, and the absence of anecdotal detail.

In 1873 Cassatt moved to Paris. Degas was soon struck by her work,

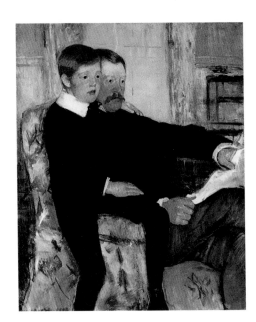

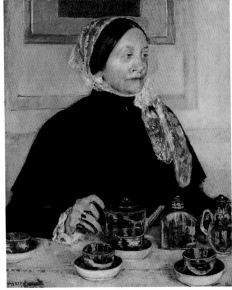

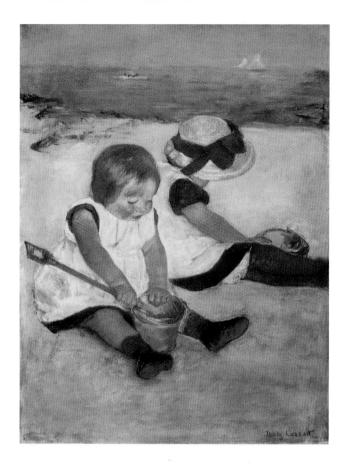

Mary Cassatt
Children on the Beach, 1884
Oil on canvas, 97.6 x 74.2 cm
Breeskin 131
Washington (DC), National Gallery of Art,
Ailsa Mellon Bruce Collection

Left:
Mary Cassatt
Alexander J. Cassatt and his Son Robert
Kelso, 1884
Oil on canvas, 89 x 130 cm
Breeskin 136
Philadelphia, Philadelphia Museum of Art

Mary Cassatt
Lady at the Tea Table, 1885
Oil on canvas, 74 x 61 cm
Breeskin 139
New York, The Metropolitan Museum of Art

while Cassatt in her turn, in 1875, advised her close friend Louisine Elder
– later the wife of Henry Osborne Havemeyer (1847–1907), with whom
she built up the first great Impressionist collection in America – to buy
Degas' 1874 *Ballet Rehearsal.* The professional and personal friendship
of Cassatt and Degas was a close and fruitful one; Degas even added
some touches to Cassatt's *Little Girl in a Blue Armchair* (p. 592). This
painting was rejected by the American section of the Paris World Fair in
the year it was painted, 1878. The girl's relaxed if unbecoming pose, and
the higgledy-piggledy brushwork with which Cassatt captured the patterning of the armchairs and the divan, were presumably to blame for
the rejection. The artist was visibly taking her bearings from Impressionist colourism and from Degas' treatment of the figure. Cassatt joined the
circle of artists under his promotional wing and in 1879 had eleven
paintings, probably co-selected by Degas, in that year's fourth Impressionist exhibition – her first showing with the group. Cassatt exhibited

Childe Hassam
Grand Prix Day, 1887
Oil on canvas, 61 x 86.3 cm
Boston (MA), Museum of Fine Arts,
Ernest Wadsworth Longfellow Fund

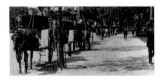

Two-wheel hackney cabs in New York, Fifth
Avenue and Madison Square. About 1900

at all the group shows that were to come except the seventh, when she did not submit out of loyalty to Degas.

One of the paintings Cassatt had on show in that fourth exhibition in 1879 was *Lydia in a Loge, Wearing a Pearl Necklace* (p. 600) – a superlative example of Cassatt's more precisely Impressionist period. As if wishing to emphasize that the American artist was one of the French group, the Parisian press heaped the same harsh critical dismissal on her work as it did on that of the other artists. The light caught on the model's skin, for instance, was damned as a filthy, unreal nonsense. No one so unwashed would even be let into a theatre, said the critics. In fact, the painting is a delight both for its leisurely brushwork and for its spatial construction. Without defining any middle distance, Cassatt places the figure squarely up front, while the mirror in which we see her back reflected (which at first glance seems a background of gallery seats) actually shows us what Lydia herself sees before her. Beside that of Degas we may detect Manet's influence – to be exact, that of *A Bar at the Folies-Bergère* (p. 221).

Cassatt preferred to paint friends and acquaintances. Her sister Lydia

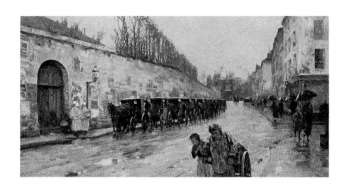

Childe Hassam
Une averse. Rue Bonaparte, Paris, 1887
Oil on canvas, 102 x 196 cm
New York, Hirschl and Adler Galleries

posed frequently. After Lydia died in 1877, Susan – probably a cousin of Cassatt's housekeeper, Mathilde Vallet – made continual appearances, posing for no fewer than nine pictures up to 1883, the last and most mature of which was *Susan on a Balcony Holding a Dog* (p. 628). Another work in this group, *Susan Outdoors in a Purple Hat* (1881; Detroit Institute of Arts, Manoogian Collection), is a good example of Cassatt's rare *plein-air* work. Like Degas, she preferred interiors. And the shrubs and trees in Cassatt's background highlighted the point at which she differed from the main Impressionist landscape painters: what interested her was chiaroscurist effects and the textural structures of brushwork, rather than the glowing effects of light in leafage.

The colouring of the figure, chair and background create flat zones, the ornamental flavour of which anticipates the artist's later style. Influenced by the two-dimensional, clearly-outlined approach and diagonal structures in Japanese woodcuts, Cassatt moved further in the decorative direction in the 1880s. She was also inspired by the mural art of Puvis de Chavannes. Alongside this formal evolution, her central concern with the role of woman also underwent a shift. If her early work had pinned subjects to specific times and situations, her later paintings

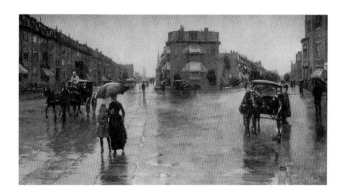

Childe Hassam
Rainy Day, Columbus Avenue, Boston, 1885
Oil on canvas, 66.4 x 121.9 cm
Toledo (OH), The Toledo Museum of Art,
purchased with Funds from the Florence
Scott Libbey Bequest in memory of her father,
Maurice A. Scott

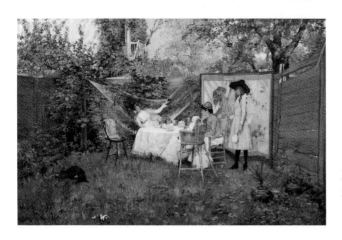

William Merrit Chase
The Open Air Breakfast, c. 1888
Oil on canvas, 95 x 144 cm
Toledo (OH), The Toledo Museum of Art,
purchased with Funds from the Florence
Scott Libbey Bequest in memory of her father,
Maurice A. Scott

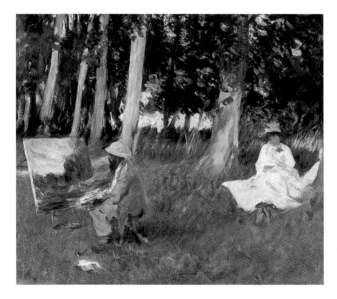

John Singer Sargent
Claude Monet Painting at the Edge of a
Wood, 1887
Oil on canvas, 53 x 64 cm
London, The Tate Gallery

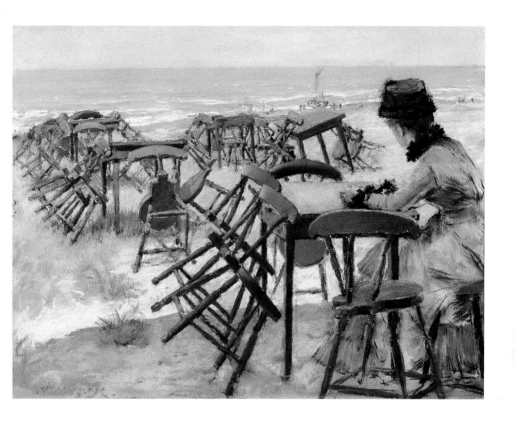

William Merrit Chase
End of the Season, c. 1885
Pastel on paper, 35 x 45 cm
South Hadley (MA), Mount Holyoke
College Art Museum

tended towards a more timeless quality. In the Nineties, her portrayal of women was increasingly coloured by reflections on mutability. In this, Cassatt's development ran parallel to that of most of her French Impressionist fellows, gradually replacing an interest in momentary, fleeting impressions with a quest for more universal messages and content.

John Singer Sargent While Cassatt was acquainted with most of the French Impressionists, and was particularly close to Degas, Sargent's personal and artistic contact with Monet spanned only a brief phase in his creative life. Born in Florence of American parents, Sargent had grown up in Europe. In 1874 he began studying at the Ecole des Beaux-Arts in Paris, and entered Carolus-Duran's studio. He did not pay a first visit to the United States till 1876. Subsequent travels included Madrid, where, like Cassatt, he admired the art of Velázquez. His *Portrait of Madame Gautreau* (p. 598; later retitled *Madame X*) was so poorly received when shown at the Paris Salon that Sargent, hoping for a more favourable welcome, moved to England. There he spent the summer

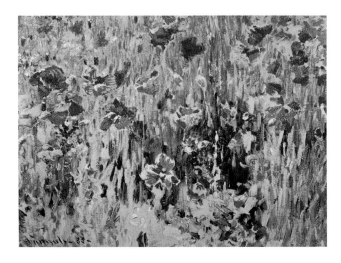

Robert William Vonnoh
Poppies, 1888
Oil on canvas, 33 x 45.7 cm
Indianapolis (IN), Indianapolis Museum
of Art, James E. Roberts Fund

months out of London, in country places such as Broadway, Henley-on-Thames, Calcot and Fladbury.

It was in those working months that Sargent painted the works that marked his brief but intense Impressionist phase. The first composition palpably French in technique was *Carnation, Lily, Lily, Rose* (p. 597), painted at Broadway in the summer and autumn of 1885 and 1886. When the picture was seen at the Royal Academy in London in 1887, he was promptly dubbed the "arch-apostle of the dab and spot school"[1] by one critic; however, in fact, Sargent's Impressionist technique was largely restricted to his painting of the lanterns and flowers. It was not till he visited Monet at Giverny in 1887 that he embraced Impressionism more completely. Sargent's picture *Claude Monet Painting at the Edge of a Wood* (p. 604) records that visit. In this painting, the outlines have become blurred and the brushwork, rather than establishing a perspective three-dimensionality, embeds the figures in a dissolving fabric of colour tonalities. Sargent admired Monet deeply and bought his first of four Monet landscapes in August 1887. In summer 1888 Sargent came closest to Monet's style when painting at Calcot Mill in Oxfordshire. *A Morning Walk* (p. 634) prompts comparison with the paintings Monet did in 1886 of his future stepdaughter, Suzanne Hoschedé, likewise wearing white and carrying a parasol, in the open (p. 146). Sargent's composition is full of bright summer light that produces a dappled effect in the dress and grass.

In contrast to French Impressionist styles, though, the surface of the water and the shade within the parasol are rendered as areas of single colour rather than in broken mosaic fashion. Nor did Sargent sacrifice the exact portrayal of his sister Violet's facial features to an overall impression, as mainstream French tenets would have required. In this fact we are reminded of Sargent's eminence as a portraitist. His portrait skills were the foundation of his fame, and after his Impressionist period (roughly 1884–1889) portrait art was his central concern – though in certain aspects of his work the enriching presence of freer French structural approaches remained alive.

The Evolution of a Distinct American Impressionism

Theodore Robinson When Sargent visited Giverny in 1887, the year after the Art Association Impressionist exhibition in New York, he was not the only American artist who felt the attraction of Monet. Much to Monet's disquiet, painters from various countries set up in Giverny; and the Americans constituted the most sizeable colony among them. There is not yet any agreement as to who was the first of them and can therefore claim to have established Giverny, and the closeness to Monet, in American art.

William Blair Bruce
Landscape with Poppies, 1887
Oil on canvas, 27.3 x 33.8 cm
Toronto, Art Gallery of Ontario,
Purchased with Assistance from Wintario

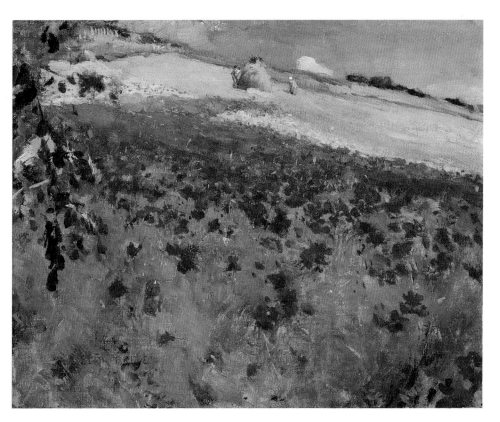

But the historians do agree that in summer 1887 there were seven North American artists at Giverny: the two New Yorkers Theodore Robinson (1852–1896) and Henry Fitch Taylor (1853–1925), Louis Ritter (1854–1892) from Cincinnati, the Bostonians Williard Leroy Metcalf (1858–1925), John Leslie Breck (1860–1899) and Theodore Wendel (1857–1932), and the Canadian William Blair Bruce (1859–1906). These painters are known as the first generation of Givernists, since they initiated the procession of North American artists to the little French town, a phenomenon that lasted into the early 20th century.

This group was important in the history of North American Impressionism for two reasons. First, Breck's solo show at the St. Botolph Club in Boston in 1890 was one of the first exhibitions devoted to an American Impressionist in his home country. Unofficially, the innovatory stylistic skills Breck had acquired at Giverny had been on view to a small

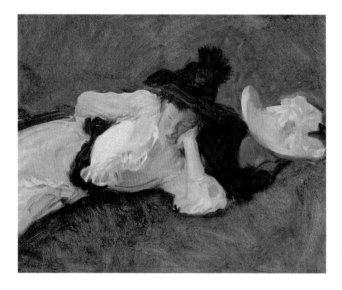

John Singer Sargent
Two Girls on a Lawn, c. 1889
Oil on canvas, 54 x 64 cm
New York, The Metropolitan Museum of Art

public the previous year in the studio of his fellow artist Lilla Cabot Perry (1848–1933). Secondly, in the work of Robinson, North America made its own first influential contribution to Impressionism. Robinson's fellow Americans at Giverny were either slow to grasp the new aesthetics or relied too heavily on the example of Monet. The latter was the case with Breck and with Perry, who visited Giverny no fewer than ten times between 1889 and 1909. Robinson, by contrast, though a good friend of Monet from 1886 on, never became dependent on the Frenchman's style. When he moved into a house near Monet in 1888, he had already been living in France for four years, and before that period he had not been a stranger to Europe; in 1876 he had taken tuition from Carolus-Duran

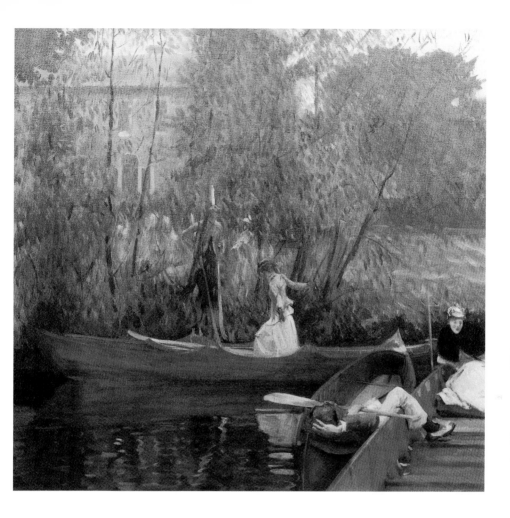

and Gérôme in Paris, and, summering at Grèz, had found in Metcalf and Bruce fellow advocates of a North American espousal of the new European art.

The years Robinson spent at Giverny before finally returning to the US in 1892 fell into two stylistic periods. In the first, he painted figures in landscape settings as well as pure landscapes. These works were firmly structured and use brief, curling, heavy brush-strokes. Though Robinson was close to Monet, it is Pissarro that these paintings most strongly recall. The rural subject matter Robinson shared with another American working at Giverny, Dawson Dawson-Watson (1864–1939), as well as with Perry and Breck, also prompts comparison with Pissarro.

John Singer Sargent
The Boating Party, 1889
Oil on canvas, 87.9 x 92.4 cm
Providence (RI), Museum of Art, Rhode Island School of Design, Gift of Mrs. Houghton P. Metcalf in memory of her husband, Houghton P. Metcalf

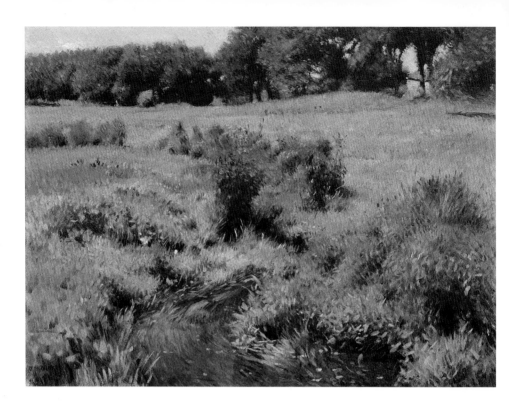

Dennis Miller Bunker
The Pool, Medfield, 1889
Oil on canvas, 45.7 x 61 cm
Boston (MA), Museum of Fine Arts,
Emily L. Ainsley Fund

Not till the early Nineties did Robinson's work enter a second phase of lighter, feathery brushwork. The individual features in a painting were dissolved into highlights of colour that were stripped of contour or detail. *The Wedding March* (p. 615), painted in 1892 for the wedding of the American artist Theodore Earl Butler (1860–1936) and Suzanne Hoschedé-Monet, Monet's stepdaughter, is a fine example of this. At this period, Robinson adopted Monet's practice of painting variations on a theme. Breck had already painted a series of 15 haystack pictures in 1891, following Monet's example of exploring the hidden qualities of a subject by painting it in various lighting and weather, at different times of the year. In the following year, Robinson painted three variations of a view of the Seine valley, using the high vantage point that was so typical of his art. Robinson continued to work in series after he finally left Giverny.

In the US, Robinson was considered one of the pioneers of American Impressionism even before his return in 1892. He had spent every winter in New York, exhibited at the major shows, and from 1889 had displayed his Impressionist work with the Society of American Painters and the National Academy. In 1893, building on his reputation, Robinson taught a summer course at Brooklyn Art School in Napanoch (New York), and taught again the next year at Evelyn College, Princeton (New Jersey).

Robinson's work again importantly changed around 1893. Influenced by Japanese print graphics, which he debated with his friends John Twachtman (1853–1902) and Julian Alden Weir (1852–1919), he began to concentrate on bands of horizontal colour, and this introduced an element of abstraction to his work. This development was in line with his long-standing attempts to combine Impressionist technique with the presentation of values not apparent on the visual surface.

Julian Alden Weir The enthusiasm of Robinson, Twachtman and Weir for the work of Japanese artists such as Katsuschika Hokusai (1760–1849) or Hiroshige (1797–1858) may have been prompted by the tales of their friend and fellow artist Robert Blum (1858–1903), who was in Japan from 1890 to 1892, and by exhibitions of Japanese print graphics

John Leslie Breck
Garden at Giverny, c. 1890
Oil on canvas, 45.7 x 55.5 cm
Chicago (IL), Terra Museum of American Art,
Daniel J. Terra Collection

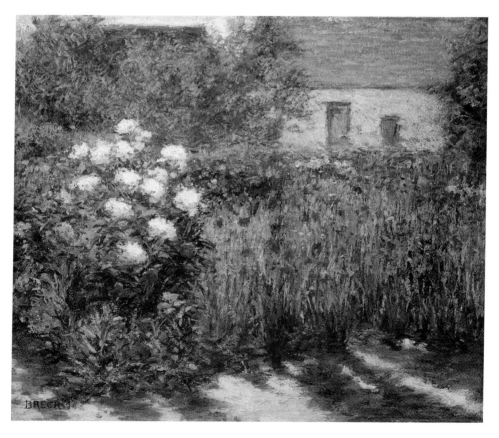

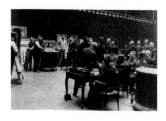

The Society of American Artists exhibition jury, 1906

in America – for instance at the 1893 Chicago World Fair, or at the Museum of Fine Arts in Boston. As the development of a van Gogh or Cassatt showed, in the Eighties and Nineties Japanese art offered many painters a new direction to follow.

One of Weir's most popular works, *The Red Bridge* (p. 623), exemplifies his use of diagonal composition and zones of colour. The bridge, its colour contrasting strongly with the natural setting, opens up decorative possibilities when seen together with its reflection – the two diagonals running in at an angle to each other. The detailed brushwork, a product of Weir's study of Impressionism, loosens the composition without fragmenting it.

Weir was originally one of the few Americans to reject Impressionist technique expressly. A student with Gérôme from 1873, he wrote to his parents from Paris on the occasion of the 1876 Impressionist exhibition: "They do not observe drawing nor form but give you an impression of what they call nature. It was worse than a Chamber of Horrors."[3]

It was not till the late Eighties and early Nineties, while painting near Branchville and Windham in rural Connecticut, that Weir was reconciled to Impressionism; and even then he restricted himself merely to certain aspects of the style. The use of brief, broken brushwork, for example, remained secondary to larger spatial gradations of a few colours. The French influence is more apparent in Weir's choice of subject-matter: in the Windham works, he frequently tackled the modern confrontation of industrial sites and open Nature. Weir's use of the contemporary American scene was in line with the Impressionist requirement of modern motifs.

John Twachtman   Weir's fondness for the landscape of Connecticut was shared by his close friend Twachtman, with whom he exhibited in 1889 and 1893. Of all the American artists who absorbed Impressionism,

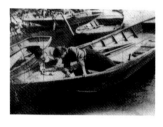

"Two in a boat": photograph by Theodore Robinson, used for his painting (right), 9 x 11.4 cm. About 1890

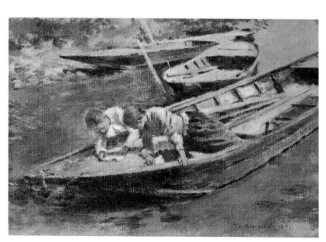

Theodore Robinson
Two in a Boat, 1891
Oil on canvas, 23.8 x 34.6 cm
Washington (DC), The Phillips Collection

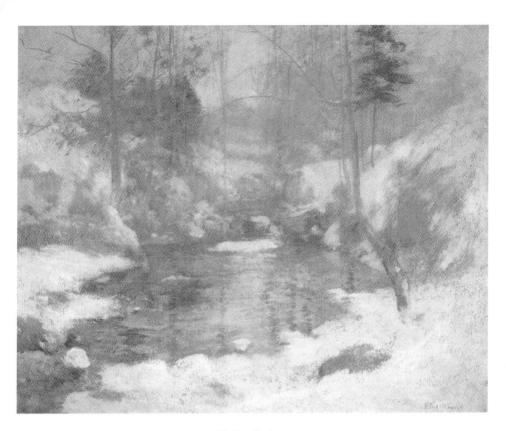

John Henry Twachtman
Winter Harmony, c. 1890–1900
Oil on canvas, 65.3 x 81.2 cm
Washington (DC), National Gallery of Art,
Gift of the Avalon Foundation

Twachtman was probably the most highly regarded both by the critics and by his fellow artists. Indeed, the press response to his work was eloquent of the American reception of Impressionism: the fact that he eschewed the perceived materialism of the French artists earned him special praise. His influence was consolidated by the summer painting school he opened in 1891 at Cos Cob (Connecticut) and by his teaching at the Art Students League in New York.

Twachtman's was the very model of an American career in art. Born in Cincinnati, he trained first at the McKicken School of Design there before studying in Munich from 1875 to 1878, like so many of his

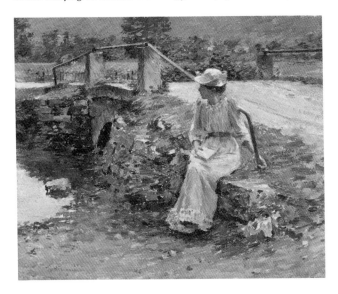

Theodore Robinson
La débâcle, 1892
Oil on canvas, 45.8 x 55.9 cm
Claremont (CA), Scripps College, Gift
of General and Mrs. Edward Clinton Young

countrymen. There he joined the Duveneck Boys, a group of American artists around Frank Duveneck (1848–1919), also from Cincinnati. This group used the realist manner of the Leibl school. In 1882, having already achieved something of a name in America with realist work, Twachtman again left for Europe in search of new aesthetic ideas, this time to Paris. In place of the Munich palette with its prevalent black he now adopted the greys of the French *juste milieu*, which included artists such as Couture and Bastien-Lepage.

Twachtman returned to the US in the winter of 1885, at which time his paintings did not yet bear the traces of an encounter with Impressionism. It was not till the work he painted in Connecticut in the Nineties that the impact began to show. He moved into a Greenwich farmhouse in 1889, and from that time on his palette lightened, albeit typically with a concentration on a few related colours rather than the whole Impressionist spectrum. His softly fluid, proto-abstract forms suggested Post-Impressionist structures anticipating Art Nouveau. His brushwork de-

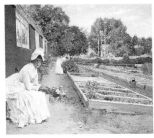

William Merrit Chase
The Nursery, 1890
Oil on canvas, 36.5 x 40.4 cm
Detroit (MI), Detroit Institute of Arts,
Manoogian Collection

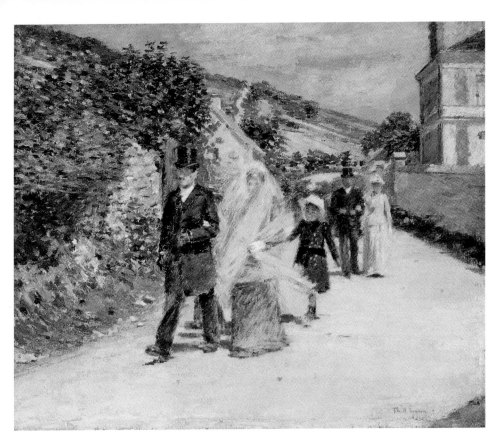

Theodore Robinson
The Wedding March, 1892
Oil on canvas, 56.7 x 67.3 cm
Chicago (IL), Terra Museum of American Art,
Daniel J. Terra Collection

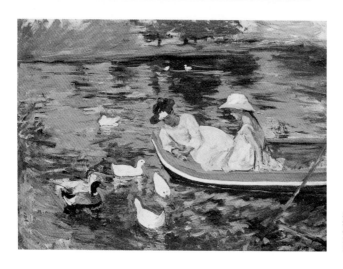

Mary Cassatt
Summertime, 1894
Oil on canvas, 73.4 x 100 cm
Breeskin 240
Los Angeles (CA), The Armand Hammer Collection

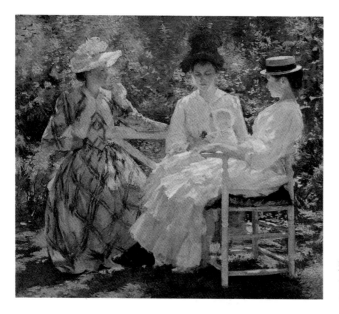

Edmund Charles Tarbell
Three Sisters – A Study in June Sunlight, 1890
Oil on canvas, 89.2 x 102 cm
Milwaukee (WI), Milwaukee Art Museum,
Gift of Mrs. Montgomery Sears, Boston

veloped into a highly personal style, varying from composition to composition, fixing his subjective perceptions with an economical eye to the overall impression. The hills, rivers and lakes near his home gave him enough subject-matter for his paintings, subjects he returned to repeatedly albeit without producing any series in the manner of Monet. His intense scrutiny of Nature was comparable with Monet's, though, and resulted both in landscapes and in close-up views of plant life. His most idiosyncratic and important complex of works concerned the winter landscapes, the best known of which is *Winter Harmony* (p. 613). Painted in whites, greys and blues only, with stray highlighting, works such as this most cogently conveyed the symbolic implications of Twachtman's tendency towards abstraction.

William Merrit Chase Teaching in public or state art schools by artists associated with Impressionism was of central importance in the American dissemination of the new art and its ideas. One of its early advocates was Robert Vonnoh (1858–1933), who taught at the Pennsylvania Academy in Philadelphia from 1891 on. His interpretation of Impres-

Mary Cassatt
The Boating Party, c. 1893/94
Oil on canvas, 90 x 117 cm
Breeskin 230
Washington (DC), National Gallery of Art

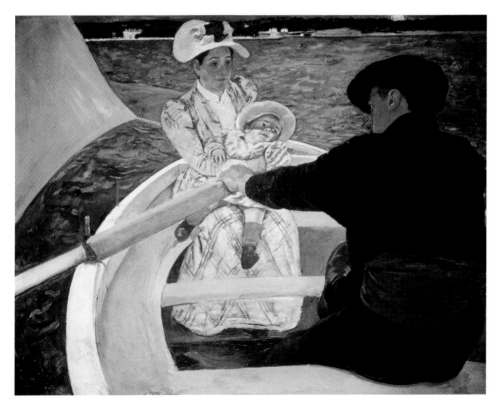

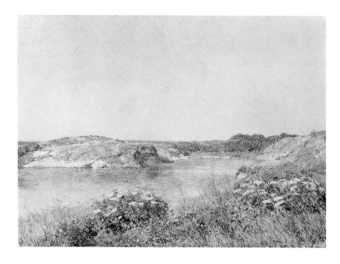

sionism, in works such as *Poppies* (p. 606), emphasized the intensity of colour to an extent that seemingly anticipates the Fauves in France or the German Expressionists. Above all, summer schools devoted to open-air painting (we have already mentioned Robinson's courses at the Brooklyn Art School and Twachtman's at Cos Cob) became established in the 1890s as an integral part of American art teaching. These schools were a response to the need for a national artistic identity distinct from handed-down European doctrine. Surely the most popular and successful of the schools was the Shinnecock Summer School, opened on Long Island in 1891. It was founded by William Merrit Chase (1849–1916), who taught the methods and practice of *plein-airisme* there for twelve consecutive summers. Since Chase also taught at the Art Students League in New York from 1878 to 1895, he can be seen as the most important teacher of his generation.

His own work had a notable stylistic flexibility and openness. He was in Munich from 1872 to 1878, and in 1877 visited Venice with Duveneck and Twachtman; this, though, was his only period of direct contact with European art. His involvement with Impressionist aesthetics, beginning in the 1880s with admiration for Manet, did not grip till he was back in America. A first characteristic group of works were his views of Prospect Park near his Brooklyn home, and later of Central Park in Manhattan, painted from 1886 on. Here his palette was lighter than in his early work, and, with the easier brushwork, attested his conversion to *plein-air* painting. Combining the urban and the natural as they did, these paintings occupied a special position within American Impressionism. They were the first paintings of Frederick Law Olmsted's and Calvert Vaux's parks, which had used deliberately symmetrical lay-outs as a new departure in the American concept of landscape; and the press

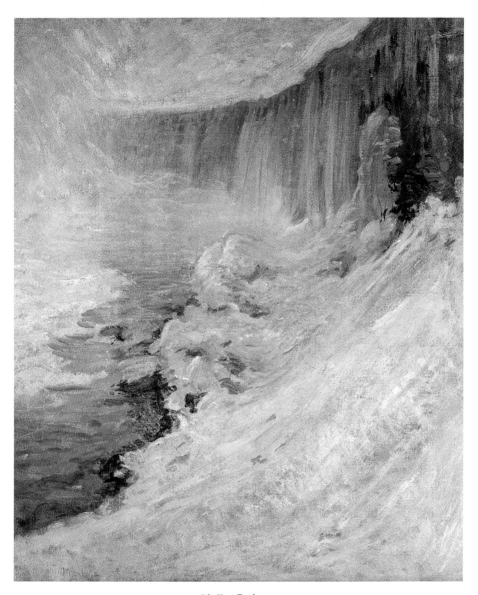

John Henry Twachtman
Horseshoe Falls, Niagara, c. 1894
Oil on canvas, 76.8 x 64.5 cm
Southampton (NY), The Parrish Art Museum,
Littlejohn Collection

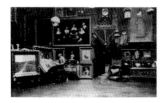

William Merrit Chase's studio in New York.
About 1895

William Merrit Chase
Idle Hours, c. 1894
Oil on canvas, 64.8 x 90.2 cm
Fort Worth (TX), Amon Carter Museum

responded by praising the specifically American subject matter. It was one more proof, if one were needed – declared the critic Kenyon Kox in 1889 – that what America lacked was not subjects but the eyes to see. Kox hoped America had heard the last of artists' complaints that there was no material, given that the subjects were on the doorstep – and the public too, he wrote, would do well to stop inveighing against un-American art, at least until it had seen Chase's wonderful little masterpieces.[4]

The carefree cheerfulness that Chase's canvases emanate became increasingly Impressionist in technique as the Nineties wore on. He became a master of the flickering atmospherics of light set off by blue strips of sea or sky and enlivened by women and children in bright summer dresses. The dunes and beaches of Shinnecock on Long Island provided Chase with his staple material. A particularly fine example of this period in his work is *Idle Hours* (p. 620).

Childe Hassam   Despite his broad influence and high reputation, Chase was not seen as the model Impressionist in America. That role was reserved for Childe Hassam (1859–1935). His Boston and New York cityscapes represented the only American Impressionist art beside Cas-

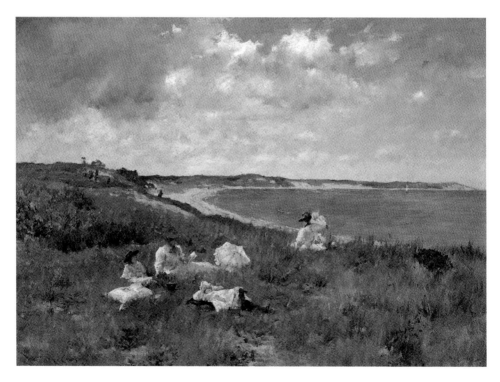

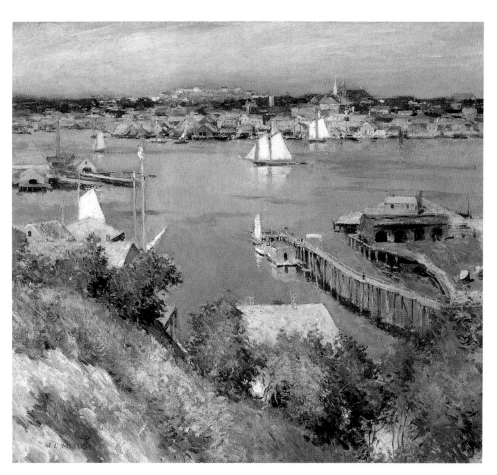

Williard Leroy Metcalf
Gloucester Harbour, 1895
Oil on canvas, 66 x 73 cm
Amherst (MA), Mead Art Museum,
Amherst College, Gift of George D. Pratt

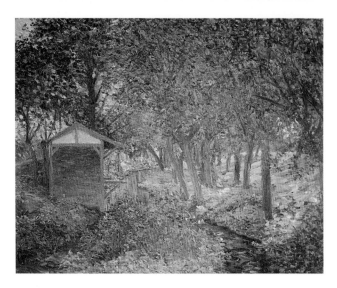

satt's to couple stylistic innovation with contemporary subject-matter. What was more, his career was longer than any other American Impressionist's, extending to a notable willingness to learn new tricks in his late work.

Hassam began in 1876 as an illustrator and engraver, then studied from 1877 to 1878 at the Boston Art Club and the Lowell Institute. By the time he settled in New York in 1884 he had visited England, Holland, Spain and Italy. He began to make a name for himself with rainy or snowy city scenes such as *Rainy Day, Columbus Avenue, Boston* (p. 603). His palette moves in subtle nuances across closely related colours, nicely catching a city atmosphere. Though the choice of colours recalls mainstream American tonalism, the subject prompts comparison with the realistic Paris street scenes of De Nittis or Béraud as well as with Caillebotte's 1877 *Paris, the Place de l'Europe on a Rainy Day* (p. 169).

In 1886, Hassam again went to Europe, this time to Paris. In this period he began to use a more Impressionist technique and colourism. *Grand Prix Day* (p. 602), painted in 1887, is generally cited as the earliest work in his changed style. His palette brighter, his accentual colour contrasts strong, Hassam has turned away from the rain to a sunny summer's day and a crowd on their way to the big June races at Longchamp in the Bois de Boulogne. The well-defined forms and contours which Hassam retained in this painting despite the shorter brush-strokes soon disappeared from the New York scenes which he was paint following his return. For Hassam, the concentration on painting New York street life, which made him famous, was an opportunity to show that American subject-matter was quite as interesting as French. Indeed, he

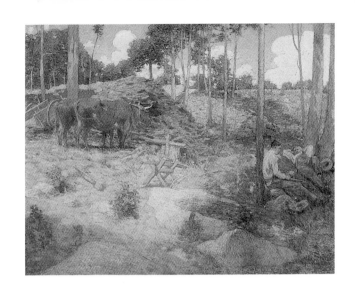

Julian Alden Weir
Midday Rest in New England, 1897
Oil on canvas, 100.6 x 127.9 cm
Philadelphia, The Pennsylvania Academy
of the Fine Arts, Gift of Isaac H. Clothier,
Edward H. Coates, Francis W. Lewis, Robert
C. Ogden and Joseph G. Rosengarten

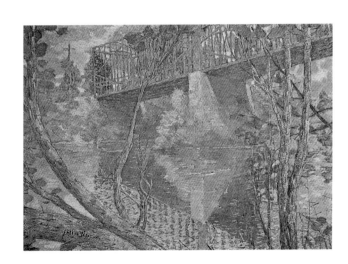

Julian Alden Weir
The Red Bridge, c. 1895
Oil on canvas, 61.5 x 85.5 cm
New York, The Metropolitan Museum of Art,
Gift of Mrs. John A. Rutherford

explicitly averred that Paris boulevards were "not one whit more interesting than the streets of New York. There are days here when the sky and atmosphere are exactly those of Paris, and when the squares and parks are every bit as beautiful in colors and grouping."⁵ Hassam's attention was primarily concentrated on the movement of people and the changing of colours in changing light, as in *Fifth Avenue at Washington Square* (p. 402). His paintings exclude unpleasant details that might suggest social imperfections; this exclusion was something he had in common with his American contemporaries.

Hassam also painted landscapes. He probably first summered on Appledore, an island off the coast of New Hampshire and Maine, in 1884. He had been invited there by his pupil Celia Thaxter, poet and essayist, who ran a summer salon for painters and writers. For many years, the Appledore landscape and Thaxter's luxuriant garden provided Hassam with inspiration. From 1890 till Thaxter's death in 1894, indeed, the area prompted Hassam's finest work. After that caesura, Hassam continued to visit both Appledore and New England coastal towns

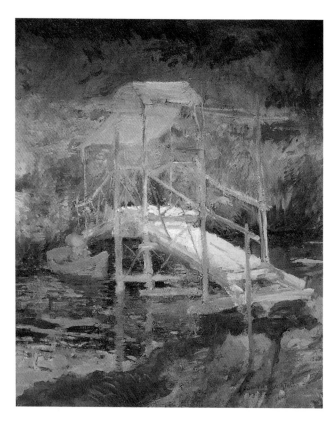

John Henry Twachtman
The White Bridge, c. 1900
Oil on canvas, 76.2 x 63.5 cm
Rochester (NY), Memorial Art Gallery
of the University of Rochester, Gift of
Emily Sibley Watson

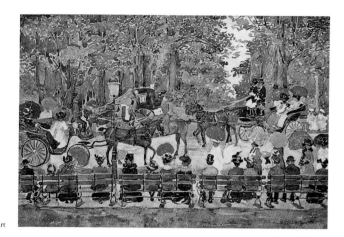

Maurice Brazil Prendergast
Central Park, New York, 1901
Pencil and watercolour on paper, 36 x 55.5 cm
New York, The Whitney Museum of American Art

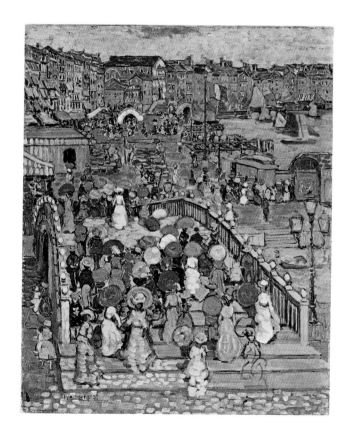

Maurice Brazil Prendergast
Ponte della Paglia, Venice, 1899
Oil on canvas, 71 x 58.5 cm
Washington, The Phillips Collection

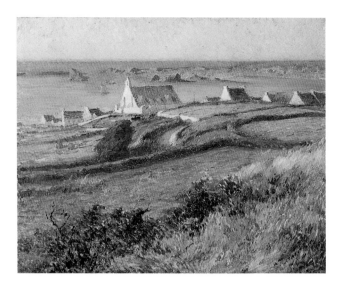

Marc-Aurèle de Foy Suzor-Coté
Port-Blanc in Brittany, 1906
Port-Blanc en Bretagne
Oil on canvas, 64.9 x 81 cm
Ottawa, National Gallery of Canada

such as Newport, Gloucester and Old Lyme in the summers. The seascapes he painted on those visits in the early years of the 20th century introduced a new component into his work. In *Sunset at Sea* (p. 633), for instance, the almost monochrome bands of colour record a vision of the ocean's vastness, in a style that has Symbolist undertones and looks forward to American abstract art.

While Hassam was versatile in his thematic range, at bottom he was always expressing a love of his home country. The series he painted in the second decade of the century are best considered in these terms. They include, for instance, his window paintings – views from an upper floor of a New York building onto streets flanked by high-rise buildings. A second series, comprising the flags paintings, is still more spectacular. Documenting Hassam's patriotic feelings during the First World War, and doubtless in some degree inspired by Monet's *Rue Saint-Denis, Festivities of 30 June, 1878* (p. 177), these pictures transform the flagged buildings of New York into a sea of fluttering colour. Paintings like *Allies Day, May 1917* (p. 639) expressed the confidence of the American war effort in Europe.

Right:
Maurice Galbraith Cullen
Winter at Moret, 1895
Oil on canvas, 60 x 92.1 cm
Toronto, Art Gallery of Ontario,
Gift from the J.S. McLean Canadian Fund

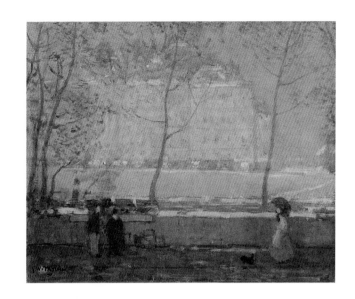

James Wilson Morrice
Quai des Grands-Augustins, Paris, c. 1903/04
Oil on canvas, 50.4 x 61.7 cm
Ottawa, National Gallery of Canada

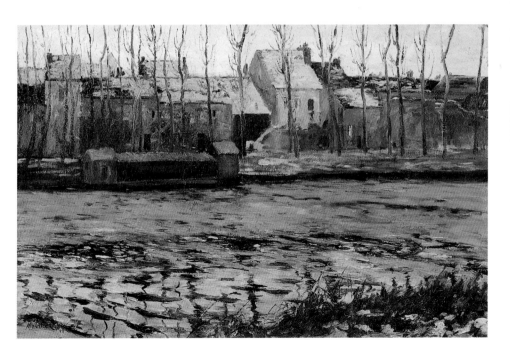

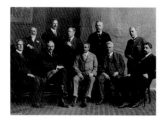

The Ten in Philadelphia in 1908. Standing from left: Chase, Benson, Tarbell, Dewing, De Camp. Seated from left: Simmons, Metcalf, Hassam, Weir, Reid

George Hitchcock
The Bride, c. 1900
Oil on canvas, 76.2 x 61 cm
New York, Private collection

Mary Cassatt
Susan on a Balcony Holding a Dog, 1883
Oil on canvas, 100.5 x 65 cm
Breeskin 125
Washington (DC), The Corcoran Gallery of Art

Establishment and Dissemination: The Second Generation of American Impressionists

The early Impressionist wave in North America, and the major artists – Robinson, Weir, Twachtman, Chase and Hassam – paved the way for the establishment of Impressionism there. New York and Boston, where Impressionist works were regularly on view in exhibitions from the early Nineties, were the twin centres of the new style. From there it gradually spread to other American cities. Chicago first saw works by French Impressionists such as Renoir and Monet in 1888, once again thanks to the industrious Durand-Ruel. They had work at the annual Saint Louis Exposition in 1890 and at the Music Hall Association. A year later, Hassam exhibited 39 pictures there. Also in 1891, there was a French Impressionist show in San Francisco. The great Columbian Exposition at Chicago in 1893 sealed the first phase of hesitancy over the new aesthetics; though the Impressionists were not included in the official French show, there was a special exhibition – a Loan Collection of Foreign Works from Private Galleries in the United States – that afforded a comprehensive overview of their work. Impressionists from a number of countries were included, in fact. Impressionism had become a prominent feature of the American art landscape.

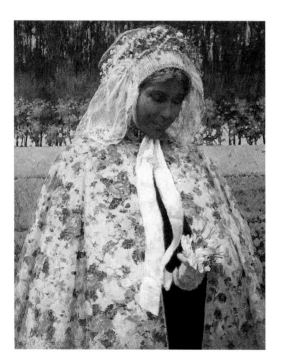

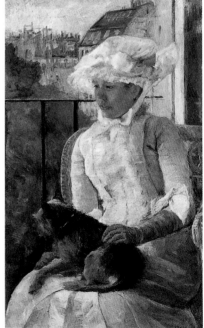

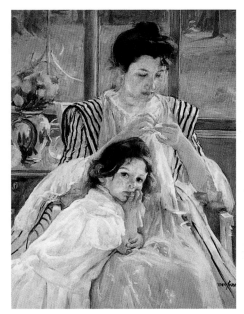

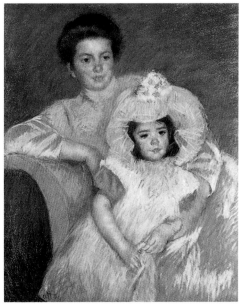

This did not mean that it was unreservedly popular, of course. Indeed, the Columbian Exhibition's emphasis on classical, idealizing work well illustrated the conservatism of the relevant powers in the art world. And the press, though interested, was by no means uniformly well-disposed. Furthermore, the American Impressionists met with resistance in artistic circles, too. Controversy over his teaching methods prompted Chase to resign his presidency of the Society of American Artists in 1895 and to abandon tuition with the Art Students League.

When a group called The Ten American Painters was founded in 1898, it was in response to this climate of rejection. To contemporaries, The Ten (as they were known) were quickly seen as the core of American Impressionism. In point of fact, they were not all equally committed to the new aesthetics; but the group was created by Hassam, Twachtman and Weir (Robinson had died in 1896) – in other words, by the foremost American Impressionists. As well as Chase, who joined in 1902 after the death of Twachtman, The Ten included Metcalf, Edmund Tarbell (1862–1938), Frank Benson (1862–1951), Joseph De Camp (1858–1923), Thomas Dewing (1851–1938), Edward Simmons (1852–1931) and Robert Reid (1862–1929). Most of the members – seven out of ten – were second-generation artists who had only adopted a French Impressionist style in the 1890s. Just as the European Secession movements separated from established institutions, The Ten split off from the Society of American Painters, where they had hitherto exhibited their work. The art shown there, they felt, was too heterogeneous. Their own interest

Mary Cassatt
Young Mother Sewing, 1902
Oil on canvas, 92.4 x 73.7 cm
Breeskin 415
New York, The Metropolitan Museum of Art

Mary Cassatt
Reine Lefèbvre and Margot, c. 1902
Pastel on paper on canvas,
83.2 x 67.5 cm. Breeskin 430
Los Angeles (CA), The Armand Hammer Collection

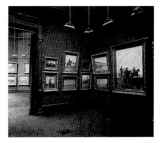

Durand-Ruel's Fifth Avenue gallery in New York.
About 1900

was in the annual public exhibition of work that shared an aesthetic thrust. Usually their choice lighted on the New York galleries of Durand-Ruel and Montross, and the exhibitions then travelled to the St. Botolph Club in Boston, not least because a substantial number of the group – Metcalf, Tarbell, De Camp, Benson and Reid – either came from Boston or had trained there. The Ten survived for almost twenty years till the group was dissolved in 1917, and throughout that period only the members named here participated in group exhibitions.

The Boston School Of the Boston painters, Williard Metcalf was the only one who had also been one of the Givernists who painted in proximity to Monet in 1877. His own work did not turn to Impressionism till the mid–1890s, though, and his fame dated from his membership of The Ten. Metcalf's was an art that celebrated the New England landscape and architecture, familiar from trips he undertook from his New York home. The radiant colours of *Gloucester Harbour* (p. 621), painted

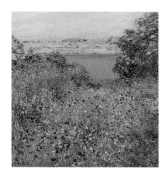

Williard Leroy Metcalf
The Poppy Garden, 1905
Oil on canvas, 61 x 61 cm
Detroit (MI), Detroit Institute of Arts,
Manoogian Collection

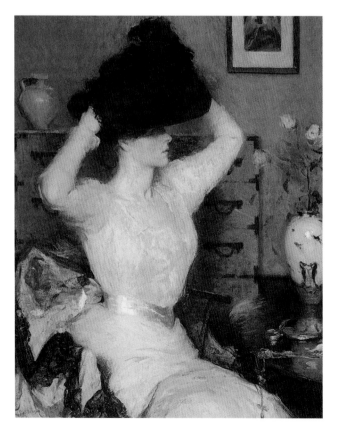

Frank Benson
The Black Hat, 1904
Oil on canvas, 101.6 x 81.3 cm
Providence (RI), Museum of Art, Rhode Island
School of Design, Gift of Walter Callender,
Henry D. Sharpe, Howard L. Chase, William
Gammel, and Isaac C. Bates

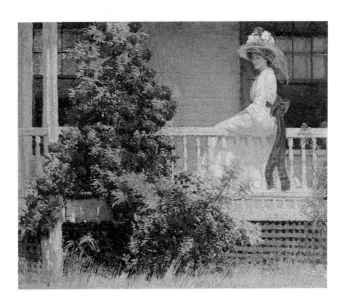

Philip Leslie Hale
The Crimson Rambler, 1908
Oil on canvas, 64.1 x 76.7 cm
Philadelphia, The Pennsylvania Academy
of the Fine Arts, Joseph E. Temple Fund

in 1895 and one of his best known works, show the influence of Impressionism on his art at that date. In style and subject matter, Metcalf was often palpably close to other American artists such as Robinson and particularly Hassam.

Metcalf's predilection for landscape was not typical of the Boston art scene. In contrast to the New York school, 1890s Impressionist art in Boston was primarily concerned with figure painting, and focussed on society ladies in appropriate settings. Tarbell was one of the first to take this direction. His compositions of the Nineties, showing stylish ladies at leisure out of doors, adopted the entire colour spectrum of French Impressionism, and indeed occasionally enhanced it, as in the glows to be seen in his subjects' faces. The choice of theme was mainly responsible for Tarbell's popularity with affluent collectors in Boston. His influence and reputation were also consolidated by years of teaching at the Boston Museum School. People even talked of Tarbellites – that is, other Bostonian figure painters whose technique and approach to their subject-matter betrayed an affinity with his presiding spirit. The foremost of these were Benson, De Camp and Reid, all of whom, like Tarbell, concentrated on portraits.

Philip Leslie Hale (1865–1931) was also seen as one of the Tarbellites. Though not one of The Ten, he was closely associated with its members. Like Tarbell and Benson, he taught at the Boston Museum School, from 1893. Hale brought to Boston figure painting an idiosyncratic variant of the genre that betrayed the influence of Neo-Impressionism. More than his American contemporaries, he tended to dissolve the outlines of white-clad figures, merging them into their settings through a hazy mesh of delicate, pale colours, for preference yellow – as in *The Crimson Rambler* (p. 631).

Hale's art was in essence decorative; it can stand for the prevalence in the work of many a late 19th-century American artist of the oriental influence. The distance the Americans had travelled from the maxims of the French Impressionists up to 1886 can also be guessed from the renaissance of Vermeer in Boston. A monograph on the Dutch master, probably written by Hale, was published in the US in 1904; subsequently, the number of interiors painted by Tarbell, De Camp and Benson rose noticeably. By the early 20th century, *plein-airisme* had lost its stimulative function in Boston.

Impressionism in Canada The reception of Impressionism in Canada ran along broadly similar lines. It did not begin there till about a decade later than in the US: the first public exhibition of pictures by Monet, Sisley, Pissarro and Renoir was held in 1892 in the William Scott Gallery

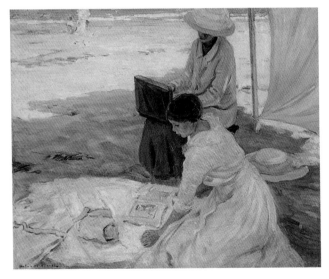

Helen Galloway McNicoll
A l'ombre de la tente, 1914
Oil on canvas, 81.3 x 101.6 cm
Montreal, The Montreal Museum of Fine Arts,
Gift of Mr. and Mrs. David McNicoll

in Montreal, and it was not till 1906 that a comprehensive retrospective of French Impressionism was seen, in Montreal – again featuring paintings loaned by Durand-Ruel. Though the fashion for Canadian artists after 1890 was to study in Paris at the Ecole des Beaux-Arts or the leading private academies and to summer at locations where international artists congregated, it was rare for them to grapple with the technique of Impressionism. When they did, it was either a case of direct imitation of a French model, as with Helen Galloway McNicoll (1879–1915), or – and this applied to the majority – of briefly adopting a style as a transition to other later approaches. For Henri Beau (1863–1949),

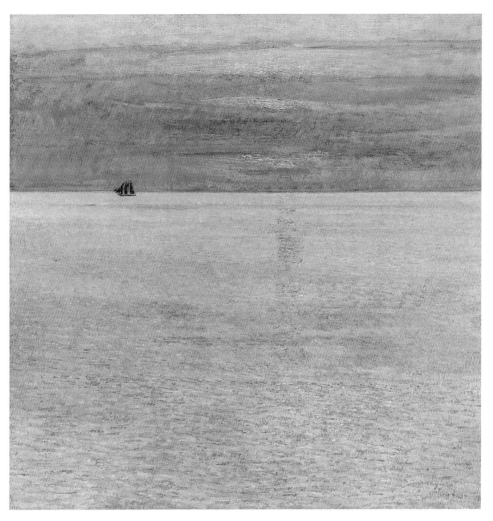

Childe Hassam
Sunset at Sea, 1911
Oil on hessian, 86.3 x 86.3 cm
Waltham (MA), Rose Art Museum, Brandeis University,
Gift of Mr. and Mrs. Monroe Geller

Marc-Aurèle de Foy Suzor-Coté (1869–1937) and James Wilson Morrice (1865–1924), as for the younger William Henry Clapp (1879–1954), Clarence Alphonse Gagnon (1881–1942) and Lawren Harris (1885–1970), the decorative structures and surfaces of Neo- and Post-Impressionism were finally of greater moment than the stylistic achievements of a Monet.

Maurice Galbraith Cullen (1866–1934) was an exception to this rule. He was the first to establish the name and fame of Impressionism in Canada, and was the only one of his generation to adopt an Impressionist style rigorously and arrive at a personal manner of art by that route. Before exhibiting his landscapes for the first time in Canada in 1895, at the newly founded Société Nationale des Beaux-Arts, he studied in Paris from 1888 to 1890 at the Académie Colarossi, the Académie Julian and the Ecole des Beaux-Arts, and was close to his fellow countryman William Bruce. Cullen acquired a love of *plein-air* painting in France which remained with him his whole life long, even in harsh weather. Indeed, it was in his winter landscapes that he evolved the light effects that are unique to his art, in such paintings as *Winter at Moret* (p. 627). Cold, phosphorescent blues predominate, but reddish stray reflections of light radiate a magic warmth. This atmosphere was to become even more

Frank Benson
Sunlight, 1909
Oil on canvas, 82 x 50.8 cm
Indianapolis, Indianapolis Museum of Art,
John Herron Fund

John Singer Sargent
A Morning Walk, 1888
Oil on canvas, 67 x 50.2 cm
The Ormond Family

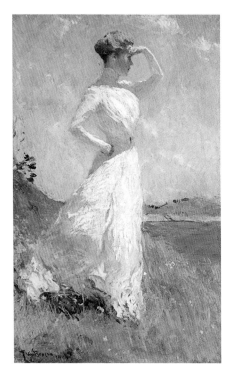

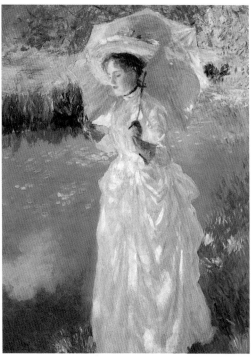

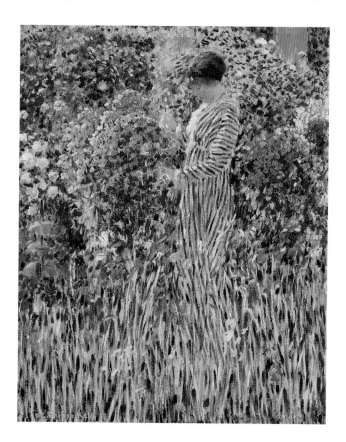

Frederick Frieseke
Lady in a Garden, c. 1912
Oil on canvas, 81 x 65.4 cm
Chicago (IL), Terra Museum of American Art,
Daniel J. Terra Collection

intense in his work after 1906. His late paintings eloquently showed that, for his generation of North American artists, French Impressionism was simply a stage along the way to their own individual, subjective response to the real.

The 20th-Century Aftermath of Impressionism

Impressionism still made its presence felt in the work of artists who did not reach maturity till the early 20th century. What the French example offered comprised first and foremost technical ideas, which could be combined with the strategies of Pointillism, Post-Impressionism and Art Nouveau. By around 1910, Impressionism and its related styles were universal in North America, and had lost their power to provoke. However, they still had significance in catalyzing the formulation by individual artists' groups of their own visual idioms.

The Later Givernists In this respect, the paintings of Frederick Frieseke (1874–1939) and Richard Miller (1875–1943) were an extension of the North American tradition in Impressionist figure painting. Both artists were of the third American generation to paint at Giverny. After the painters of 1887 and shortly thereafter had spent their summers there and returned to the US, there had been a second wave of Giverny tourism in the Nineties. The Americans were drawn less by Monet's art than by the beauty of the countryside, so convenient to Paris, and by the chance of meeting artists from many other countries. The core of the American group was made up of a married couple, Mary (1858–1946) and Frederick MacMonnies (1863–1937). Garden scenes and nudes provided the circle with new motifs that were adopted and adapted by the next, third generation.

The best known of these was Frieseke. Born in Michigan, he trained at the Art Institute of Chicago and in New York before receiving a scholarship to Paris in 1898. Frieseke had begun by painting earthy interiors, but visits to Giverny in and after 1900 led him to abandon them in favour of open-air scenes, of which *Lady in a Garden* (p. 635) is typical. Of the

Henri Beau
Déjeuner sur l'herbe (The Picnic), c. 1905
Oil on canvas, 72.5 x 92.5 cm
Quebec, Musée du Québec

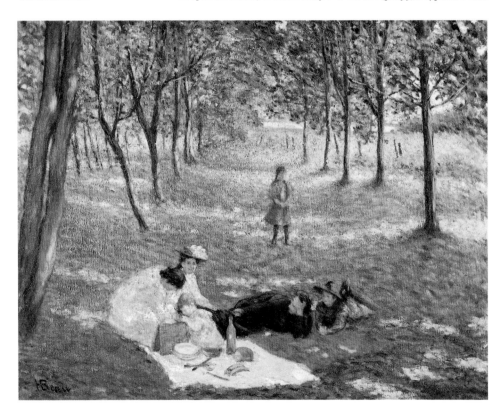

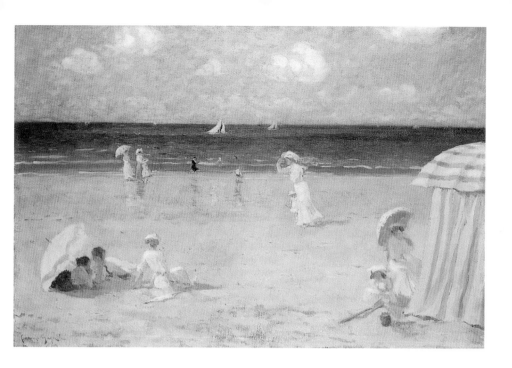

French Impressionists, Renoir in particular must surely have made an impact on him. His presence can be felt in the solidity of Frieseke's women, so different from the women of the Boston School. Effects of sunlight, by the painter's own testimony, were his central concern. His brushwork was only Impressionist in particular areas of his pictures, however – nudes, for instance, he painted in nuanced academic three-dimensionality, while his handling of lush vegetation often acquired a rhythmic, decorative character. The pictures of Frieseke and Miller – whose approach to women was gentler and more intimate (*Reverie*, p. 640) – were exceptionally popular in America. At the 1909 Venice Biennale their works shared a room, representing US art. The Giverny Group (or Luminarists), to which both belonged, was the final fine achievement of Impressionism in America.

The Ash Can School By contrast, when the Ash Can School (or The Eight) came into being, it announced new bearings in 20th-century American art, and superseded the aesthetics and aims of Impressionism. Exhibiting from 1908 on at the Macbeth Gallery in New York, its members on concentrated on the unappealing sides of modern urban life. Ernest Lawson (1873–1939) and Prendergast tried to reconcile this subject matter with a lyrical use of colour derived from Impressionism. The work of these two artists can be taken as representative of the two main

Clarence Alphonse Gagnon
Summer Breeze at Dinard, 1907
Brise d'été à Dinard
Oil on canvas, 54 x 81 cm
Quebec, Musée du Québec

preoccupations in early 20th-century American art: realistic landscape, and an emphasis on formal strategies.

Lawson, born in Canada but resident in the US, brought a rough and ready brushwork to his urban scenes, the realism of which was in line with Ash Can precepts. He shared the group's taste for views of New York from the East, Harlem and the Hudson River. But he preferred landscape work to painting contemporary city life.

In 1891 Lawson was a student of Twachtman's at the Art Students League, and in summer the following year painted at Cos Cob with Twachtman and Weir. His Impressionist leanings were confirmed in 1893 when he met Sisley at Moret. The influence of Twachtman remained apparent even after Lawson's final return from Paris, where he spent most of his time from 1893 to 1896. Like the older painter, he used white for accentual highlights, and his compositions were generally fundamentally lyrical in tone (*Spring Night, Harlem River*, p. 638). Lawson's landscapes, which always betray the proximity of the city, derive their power from luminous colour and solid, pastose brushwork.

The modernity of Prendergast's art did not reside in his subject-matter; it came from the priority he assigned technique over subject. Born in Newfoundland, he grew up in Boston, where the art of Tarbell, Breck and Wendel may have laid the foundation for the colourfulness of his own future work. Studying in Paris, he readily absorbed Post-Impressionist aesthetics after 1890. His views of Paris boulevards and of the promenades at Le Treport, Dieppe, Saint-Malo and Dinard already bore the anti-naturalist hallmark of the Nabis: his figures were simple in form and flat, and the intensity of the colours was independent of spatial depth.

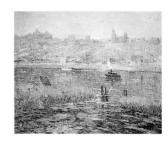

Ernest Lawson
Harlem River, c. 1913–1915
Oil on canvas, 102 x 127 cm
Detroit, Detroit Institute of Arts,
Manoogian Collection

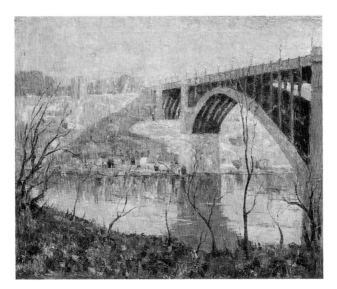

Ernest Lawson
Spring Night, Harlem River, 1913
Oil on canvas on panel, 63.5 x 76.2 cm
Washington (DC), The Phillips Collection

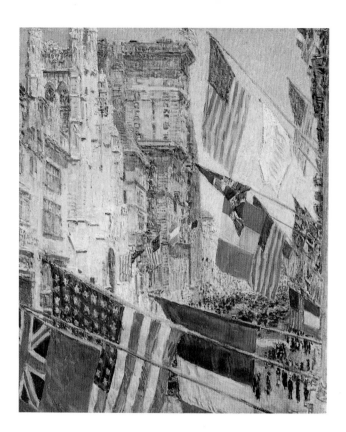

Prendergast's lively compositions guaranteed him success not long after his return to Boston in 1894. His financial circumstances assured, he was able to depart for Europe again in 1898; here he would spend almost two years in France but also in Italy, where he visited Rome, Capri, Siena and – above all – Venice (p. 625). His work, often executed in watercolour, remained distinctively carefree even into the 20th century, at a time when frequent stays in New York had put him in touch with the Ash Can School. The Cézanne exhibition he saw in Paris in 1907 made a profound impression on Prendergast; he was one of the first American artists to value Cézanne and transmit his principles into their own art. The work of Prendergast's maturity attests this influence in its stronger tendency to abstraction, which establishes the sole autonomous reality of the pictorial image: the anecdotal detail of his early work disappears, and spatial gradations are displaced by a single visual level on which brush-strokes are juxtaposed and superposed like solid blocks, leaving the location no longer clearly identifiable. Watercolour was superseded by pastose oil.

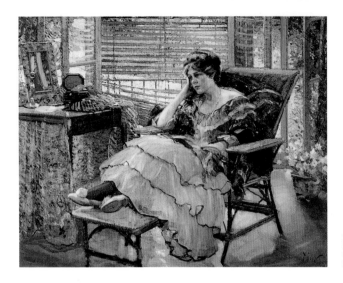

Richard Emile Miller
Reverie, 1913
Oil on canvas, 114.3 x 147.3 cm
Saint Louis (MO), The Saint Louis Art Museum

The artistic development of Maurice Prendergast graphically illustrates the importance of Impressionism for early 20th-century American
painting. Impressionist art was now both widely held in high regard and
prominent in major international exhibitions everywhere; furthermore
the first historical surveys of the movement were beginning to appear,
replacing the initial assessments by art critics. At one time, "The Sun"
newspaper observed in 1916, Impressionism had been controversial, but
now it was ancient history.[6] For artists, it had come to represent a threshold, the crossing of which was a liberation that made access possible to
Neo- and Post-Impressionism and more. The North American discovery
of the more extreme achievements of art after Impressionism – the art of
van Gogh, Gauguin and Cézanne – had barely begun but a new era
dawned. At the Armory Show in New York in 1913, America had its
first sighting of the Cubists, the Fauves and the German Expressionists.
Twenty-seven years after America's first big Impressionist show in 1886,
an exhibition of European art was again to set a milestone in the evolution of American art.

BEATRICE VON BISMARCK

1   Cf. Mariana van Rensselaer, In: *The Independent* 38, 22 April 1886, pp.491 ff., and 29 April 1886,
    pp. 523 ff.
2   Cf. *Art Journal*, 26 June 1887, p.248.
3   Cf. Dorothy Weir Young: *The Life and Letters of J. Alden Weir*, New Haven (CN), 1960, p.123.
4   Kenyon Kox: *William Merrit Chase, Painter*. In: *Harper's New Monthly Magazine*, March 1889,
    p.556.
5   A.E. Ives: *Mr. Childe Hassam on Painting Street Scenes*. In: *Art Amateur*, 27 October 1892, p.117.
6   Cf. *The Sun*, 19 March 1916, part V, p.8.

Directory of Impressionism

with lists of illustrations

The "Directory of Impressionism" contains short biographies of all 236 artists whose work is illustrated in these two volumes, together with their portraits, where these can be traced; it also includes information on writers, critics, art dealers and collectors who were involved in or influenced the development of Impressionism; other entries explain important concepts and localities. Bibliographical details are intended to aid further reading on the subject. Special attention has been given to the lives and works of lesser-known painters. For exhibition catalogues (abbreviated EC), the respective editors, organisers and contributors are listed as editor (ed.), even if they only produced the catalogue or wrote the preface. Page numbers at the end of each entry refer to illustrations reproduced in this book. Many of the following articles, and all the entries on Eastern and South Eastern Europe, are the work of Peter H. Feist; I would like to express my grateful thanks to him and to my colleague, Antje Günther.

I.F.W.

THE ANTECEDENTS OF IMPRESSIONISM

Boime, A.: The Academy and French Painting of the Nineteenth Century. New Haven (CT) and London 1971.– Bouret, J.: L'école de Barbizon et le paysage français au XIXe siècle. Neuchâtel 1972.– Bouret, J.: The Barbizon School. London 1972.– Bühler, H.P.: Die Schule von Barbizon. Munich 1979.– Champa, K.S. (ed.): Barbizon – The Rise of Landscape Painting in France. Corot to Manet. Manchester, New York and Dallas 1991 (EC).– Clark, T.J.: The Absolute Bourgeois: Artists and Politics in France, 1848- 1951. Greenwich (CT) 1973.– Deuchler, F.: Die französischen Impressionisten und ihre Vorläufer: Collectors' catalogues, Vol. I. "Langmatt" Foundation, Sidney und Jenny Brown. Baden 1990.– Nochlin, L.: Realism. New York 1972.– Picon, G.: 1863 – Naissance de la peinture moderne. Paris 1988.– Sloane, J.: French Painting Between the Past and the Present: Artists, Critics and Traditions from 1848 to 1870. Princeton (NJ) 1973.– Thomson, D.: The Barbizon School of Painters. London 1891

IMPRESSIONISM (GENERAL BIBLIOGRAPHY)

Adams, S.: Die Welt der Impressionisten. Weingarten 1990.– Adams, S.: The World of Impressionists. London and New York 1989.– Adhémar, H., J. Adhémar et al.: Chronologie impressionniste: 1863-1905. Paris 1981.– Adhémar, H. and A. Dayez-Distel (eds.): Musée du Jeu de Paume. Catalogue. Paris 1947.– Adler, K.: Wiederentdeckte Impressionisten. Oxford 1988.– Adler, K.: Unknown Impressionists. Oxford 1988.– Bazin, G.: Die Impressionisten. Schöpfer der modernen Malerei. Gütersloh (1985).– Bazin, G.: L'époque impressionniste. Paris 1947.– Bellony-Rewald, A.: The Lost World of the Impressionists. London 1976.– Berger, K.: Japonismus in der westlichen Malerei. Munich 1980.– Bernard, B. (ed.): Die großen Impressionisten. Revolution der Malerei. Munich 1988.– Berson, R. (ed.): The New Painting: Impressionism 1874-1886. Documentation. 2 vols. Seattle (in preparation).– Blunden, M. and G.: Der Impressionismus in Wort und Bild. Geneva 1979.– Blunden, M. et G.: Journal de l'impressionnisme.

Geneva 1970.– Blunden, M. and G.: Impressionists and Impressionism. New York and London 1976.– Bonafaux, P.: Les impressionnistes. Portraits et confidences. Paris 1986.– Bozo, D. and A. Marchais: Sur le motif. Les impressionnistes. Paris 1964.– Brettell, R. et al. (eds.): L'impressionnisme et le paysage français. Los Angeles County Museum of Art, Los Angeles; The Art Institute of Chicago, Chicago; Grand Palais, Paris. Paris 1984 (EC).– Brettell, R. et al. (eds.): A Day in the Country: Impressionism and the French Landscape. Los Angeles County Museum of Art et al. Los Angeles 1984 (EC).– Bromford, D. et al. (eds.): Art in the Making: Impressionism. National Gallery, London 1990 (EC).– Broude, N. (ed.): Impressionismus. Eine internationale Kunstbewegung 1860- 1920. Cologne 1990.– Broude, N. (ed.): Impressionism. The International Movement, 1860-1920. New York 1990.– Cachin, F. (ed.): Europäische Kunst im 19. Jahrhundert. Vol. 2: Realismus – Impressionismus – Jugendstil. Freiburg 1991.– Callen, A.: Techniques of the Impressionists. London 1982.– Callen, A.: Les peintres impressionnistes et leur technique. Paris 1983.– Champa, K.S.: Studies in Early Impressionism. New Haven (CT) and London 1973, New York 1985.– Clark, T.J.: The Painting of Modern Life. Paris in the Art of Manet and his Followers. London and New York 1985.– Cogniat, R.: French Painting at the Time of Impressionists. New York 1951.– Cogniat, R.: Le siècle des impressionnistes. Paris 1976.– Courthion, P.: Malerei des Impressionismus. Cologne 1976, 1981.– Crespelle, J.-P.: La vie quotidienne des impressionnistes: Du Salon des Refusés (1863) à la mort de Manet (1883). Paris 1981.– Crespelle, J.-P.: Guide de la France impressionniste. Sites, musées, promenades. Paris 1990.– Czymmek, G. (ed.): Landschaft im Licht. Impressionistische Malerei in Europa und Nordamerika 1860-1910. Wallraf-Richartz-Museum et al. Cologne 1990 (EC).– Damigella, A.M.: L'impressionismo fuori di Francia. Milan 1967.– Dauberville, J.: La bataille de l'impressionnisme. Paris 1967.– Denvir, B.: The Impressionists at First Hand. London and New York 1987, 1991.– Denvir, B.: The Thames and

Hudson Encyclopaedia of Impressionism. London 1990.– Denvir, B.: Impressionism. The Painters and the Paintings. London 1991.– Distel, A.: Impressionism: The First Collectors. New York 1990.– Distel, A.: Les collectionneurs des impressionnistes. Amateurs et marchands. Paris 1989.– Dukva, J.: Winds from the East. A Study in the Art of Manet, Degas, Monet and Whistler, 1856-1886. Stockholm and New York 1981.– Dunstant, B.: Painting Methods of the Impressionists. New York 1983.– Duret, T.: Die Impressionisten. Berlin 1909.– Duret, T.: Histoire des peintres impressionnistes. Paris 1906.– Farr, D. and J. House (eds.): Impressionist and Post-Impressionist Masterpieces: The Courtauld Collection. The Cleveland Museum of Art, Cleveland; The Metropolitan Museum of Art, New York; The Kimbell Art Museum, Fort Worth; The Art Institute of Chicago, Chicago; The Nelson-Atkins Museum of Art, Kansas City. New Haven and London 1987 (EC).– Francastel, P.: L'impressionnisme, les origines de la peinture moderne de Monet à Gauguin. Paris 1937.– Garb, T.: Women Impressionists. Oxford 1986.– Gaunt, W.: The Impressionists. London 1970, 1990.– Harris, N. (ed.): A Treasury of Impressionism. London, New York, Sydney and Toronto 1979 (EC).– Hartlaub, G.F.: Die Impressionisten in Frankreich. Wiesbaden 1955.– Herbert, R.L.: impressionism. Paris – Gesellschaft und Kunst. Munich 1989.– Herbert, R.L.: Impressionism. Art, Leisure, and Parisian Society. New Haven (CT) and London 1988.– Huyghe, R. et al. (eds.): Centenaire de l'impressionisme. Grand Palais, Paris 1974 (EC).– Impressionism, a Centenary Exhibition. Metropolitan Museum of Art, New York 1974 (EC).– Isaacson, J. et al. (eds.): The Crisis of Impressionism, 1878-1882. The University of Michigan Museum of Art. Ann Arbor (MI) 1980 (EC).– Kelder, D.: Die großen Impressionisten. Munich 1981.– Kelder, D.: The Great Book of French Impressionism. New York 1980.– Kelder, D.: Le grand livre de l'impressionnisme français. Lausanne et Paris 1981.– Kelder, D.: L'héritage de l'impressionnisme. Les sources du XXe siècle. Paris 1986.– Keller, H.: Die Kunst des französischen Impres-

sionismus. Freiburg 1975.– Keller, H.: Aquarelle und Zeichnungen des französischen Impressionismus. Cologne 1980.– Keller, H.: Aquarelles et dessins des impressionnistes français. Paris 1982.– Lassaigne, J.: L'impressionnisme, sources et dépassement, 1850-1900. Geneva 1974.– Laux, W.S. (ed.): Salon und Secession: Zeichnungen und Aquarelle, 1880-1913. Weinheim 1989.– Lemaire, G.-G.: Esquisses en vue d'une histoire du Salon. Paris 1986.– Lengerke, C. and I.F. Walther (eds.): Vom Jugendstil zum Impressionismus. Von Klimt bis Klimt. Munich 1985.– Le Paul, C.-G.: L'impressionnisme dans l'école de Pont-Aven. Lausanne 1983.– Le Pichon, Y.: The Real World of the Impressionists. Paintings and Photographs. 1848-1918. New York 1984.– Les grands boulevards. Paris 1985 (EC).– Léveque, J.-J.: Les années impressionnistes 1870-1889. Paris 1990.– Leymarie, J.: Impressionismus. Biographisch-kritische Studie. 2 vols. Geneva 1955.– Leymarie, J. and M. Melot: Les gravures des impressionnistes: Manet, Pissarro, Renoir, Cézanne, Sisley. Paris 1971.– Leymarie, J.: L'impressionnisme. 2 vols. Geneva 1955.– Martelli, D.: Les impressionnistes et l'art moderne. Paris 1979.– McQuillan, M.: Porträtmalerei der französischen Impressionisten. Rosenheim 1986.– McQuillan, M.: Impressionist Portraits. London 1986.– Milner, J.: The Studios of Paris. The Capital of Art in the Late Nineteenth Century. New Haven (CN) and London 1990.– Moffett, C. S.: Impressionist and Post-Impressionist Paintings in the Metropolitan Museum of Art. New York 1985.– Moffett, C.S. et al. (eds.): The New Painting. Impressionism 1874-1886. The Fine Arts Museums of San Francisco, San Francisco; National Gallery of Art, Washington. Oxford and Geneva 1986 (EC).– Monneret, S.: L'impressionnisme et son époque. 4 vols. Paris 1979-1981.– Nègre, S.: Les impressionnistes de la révolte à la consécration. Fribourg 1985.– Nochlin, L. (ed.): Impressionism and Post-Impressionism 1874-1904. Sources and Documents. Englewood Cliffs (NJ) 1966.– Oberthur, M.: Cafés and Cabarets of Montmartre. Layton 1984.– Passeron, R.: Impressionist Prints. New York 1974.– Pool, P.: Impressionism. New York and London 1967, 1988.– Reff, T. (ed.): Modern Art in Paris 1855-1900. New York and London 1981.– Reuterswärd, O.: Impressionister och purister. Stockholm 1976.– Rewald, J.: The History of Impressionism. New York 1946, London 1980.– Rewald, J.: Histoire de l'impressionnisme. 2 vols. Paris 1955, 1976.– Rewald J.: Die Geschichte des Impressionismus. Schicksal und Werk der Maler einer großen Epoche der Kunst. Zurich 1957, Cologne 1965, 1979.– Rewald, J.: Studies in Impressionism. London and New York 1986.– Rosenblum, R.: Die Gemäldesammlung des Musée d'Orsay. Cologne 1989.– Selz, J.: Kleines Lexikon des Impressionismus. Cologne 1975.– Séruillaz, M.: Les peintres impressionnistes. Paris 1959.– Taylor, B. (ed.): The Impressionists and their World. London 1953.– Taylor, J.R.: Impressionist Dreams. The Artists and the World they Painted. London 1990.– Venturi, L.: Les archives de l'impressionnisme. 2 vols. Paris and New York 1939, 1968.– Venturi, L.: Impressionists and Symbolists. New York 1973.– Venturi, L.: La via d'impressionismo. Turin 1970.– Wadley, N.: Impressionist and Post-Impressionist Drawing. London 1991.– White, B.E. (ed.): Impressionism in Perspective. Englewood Cliffs (NJ) 1978.– Wilson, M.: The Impressionists. Oxford 1983

NEO-IMPRESSIONISM, POST-IMPRESSIONISM

Amann, P.: Post-Impressionismus. Europäische Querverbindungen. Kirchdorf 1986.– Angrand, P.: Naissance des Artistes Indépendants 1884. Paris 1965.– Bowness, A. et al. (eds.): Post-Impressionism: Cross-Currents in European and American Painting. 1880-1906. Royal Academy of Arts, London; National Gallery of Art, Washington. London 1979 (EC).– Cachin, F. (ed.): Félix Fénéon. Au-delà de l'impressionnisme. Paris 1966.– Cogeval, G.: Les années post-impressionnistes. Paris 1986.– Durbe, D.: Il postimpressionismo. Milan 1967.– Frèches-Thory, C. and A. Terrasse: The Nabis. Bonnard, Vuillard and their Circle. Paris 1990.– Gretzner, A. (ed.): Postimpressionism: Two Reactions to French Painting in Great Britain and Ireland. Royal Academy of Painting, London 1979 (EC).– Herbert, E.W.: The Artist and Social Reform. New Haven (CT) 1961.– Herbert, R.L. (ed.): Neo-Impressionists and Nabis in the Collection of Arthur C. Altschul. Yale University Art Gallery, New Haven (CT) 1965 (EC).– Herbert, R.L. (ed.): Neo-Impressionism. The Solomon R. Guggenheim Museum, New York 1968 (EC).– House, John and M.A. Stevens (eds.): Post-Impressionism. Cross-Currents in European Painting. Royal Academy of Arts, London 1979 (EC).– Kelder, D.: The Great Book of Post-Impressionism. New York 1986.– Lee, E.W.: The Aura of Neo-Impressionism. The W.J. Holiday Collection. Indianapolis Museum of Art, Indianapolis 1983 (EC).– Lövgren, S.: The Genesis of Modernism. Seurat, Gauguin, van Gogh and French Symbolism in the 1880's. Uppsala 1959, Bloomington (IN) and London 1971.– Marett, E.: Les peintres luministes. Brussels 1944.– Parson, T. and I. Gale: Post-Impressionism. London 1992.– Rewald, J.: Von van Gogh bis Gauguin. Die Geschichte des Nachimpressionismus. Cologne 1967, 1987.– Rewald, J.: Post-Impressionism. From van Gogh to Gauguin. New York 1956, 1978, 1986.– Rewald, J.: Le post-impressionnisme. De Van Gogh à Gauguin. Paris 1961.– Rewald, J.: Studies in Post-Impressionism. London and New York 1986.– Roskill, M.: Van Gogh, Gauguin and the Impressionist Circle. London 1970.– Shone, R.: The Post-Impressionists. London 1979.– Sillevis, J. et al. (eds.): A Feast of Colour. Post-Impressionists from Private Collections. Noordbrabants Museum, 's-Hertogenbosch. Zwolle 1990 (EC).– Sutter, J.: Les Neo-impressionistes. Neuchâtel 1970.– Sutter, J.: The Neo-Impressionists. Greenwich (CT) and London 1970.– Thomson, B.: The Post-Impressionists. Oxford 1983.– Trente ans d'art indépendant, 1884-1914. Société des Artistes Indépendants, Paris 1926 (EC).– Vom Licht zur Farbe. Nachimpressionistische Malerei zwischen 1886 und 1912. Kunsthalle Düsseldorf, Düsseldorf 1977 (EC).– Wardwell Lee, E. (ed.): Neo-Impressionisten. Seurat tot Struycken. Rijksmuseum Vincent van Gogh, Amsterdam; Indianapolis Museum of Art, Indianapolis. Zwolle 1988 (EC).– Weisberg, G.P.: Beyond Impressionism. The Naturalist Impulse in European Art 1870-1905. London 1992

COLLECTIONS OF SOURCE MATERIAL

Holt, E.G. (ed.): From the Classicists to the Impressionists: Art and Architecture in the 19th Century. New York 1966.– Nochlin, L.: Impressionism and Post-Impressionism, 1874-1904: Sources and Documents. Englewood Cliffs (NJ) 1966.– Venturi, L. (ed.): Les.archives de l'impressionisme, lettres de Renoir, Monet, Pissarro, Sisley et autres, mémoires de Paul Durand-Ruel. 2 vols. Paris 1939 (Reprint: 1969).– White, B.E.(ed.): Impressionism in Perspective. Englewood Cliffs (NJ) 1978

NETHERLANDS AND BELGIUM

Belgian Art 1880-1914. The Brooklyn Museum, New York 1980 (EC).– Bionda, R. et al. (eds.): The Age of Van Gogh. Dutch Painting 1880-1895. Glasgow and Amsterdam 1990 (EC).– Block, J.: Les XX and Belgian Avant-Gardism, 1868-1894. 2 vols. Doctoral thesis, University of Michigan. Ann Arbor (MI) 1980 (Microfilm).– Canning, S.M.: A History and Critical Review of the Salons of Les Vingt, 1884-1893. Doctoral thesis, The Pennsylvania State University. MI Ann Arbor 1990 (Microfilm).– Colin, P.: La peinture belge depuis 1830. Brussels 1930.– Die Haager Schule. Meisterwerke der holländischen Malerei des 19. Jahrhunderts aus Haags Gemeentemuseum. Kunsthalle Mannheim et al. Heidelberg 1987 (EC).– Goyens de Heusch, S.: Het Impressionisme en het Fauvisme in Belgik. Antwerp 1988.– Goyens de Heusch, S.: L'impressionisme et le fauvisme en Belgique. Antwerp and Paris 1988.– Gruyter, J. de: De Haagse School. 2 vols. Amsterdam 1972.– Haagse school: de collectie van het Haags Gemeentemuseum, 's-Gravenhage 1988 (EC).– Hammacher, A.M.: Amsterdamsche Impressionisten en hun Kring. Amsterdam 1946.– Hammacher, A.M. and F.C. Legrand (eds.): Le groupe des XX et son temps. Musée Royale des Beaux-Arts, Brussels; Rijksmuseum Kröller-Müller, Otterlo. Brussels 1962 (EC).– Holländische Impressionisten. Haagsche und Amsterdamsche Schule. Düsseldorf 1950 (EC).– Lemonnier, C.: L'école belge de peinture, 1830-1905. Brussels 1906.– Licht door keel; Nederlandse luministen 1890-1910. Haags Gemeentemuseum. The Hague 1976 (EC).– Loosjes-Terpstra, A.B.: Moderne Kunst in Nederland 1900-1914. Utrecht 1958.– Maret, F.: Les peintres luministes. Brussels 1944.– Maus, O.: Trente années de lutte pour l'art, 1884-1914. Brussels 1926.– Nederlands Impressionisme. Een keuze uit de kollektie van het Rijksmuseum Kröller-Müller, Otterlo. Stadthuis Bolsward 1984 (EC).– The Hague School: Dutch Masters of the 19th Century. Royal Academy of Arts, London 1983 (EC)

GERMANY

Deutsche Impressionisten. Aus dem Niedersächsischen Landesmuseum Hannover. Baden-Baden 1985 (EC).– Franke, E.A.: Publikum und Malerei in Deutschland vom Biedermeier zum Impressionismus. Doctoral thesis, Heidelberg 1934.– Hofmann, W., G. Busch and T. Barollet (eds.): Symboles et Réalités. La peinture allemande 1848-1905. Grand Palais, Paris 1984 (EC).– Huber, J.: Zwischen Harmonie und Aufbruch. Das 19. Jahrhundert. Glattbrugg 1984.– Niemeyer, W.: Malerische Impression und koloristischer Rhythmus. Düsseldorf 1920.– Platte, H.: Deutsche Impressionisten. Gütersloh 1971.– Römpler, K.: Der deutsche Impressionismus. Dresden 1958.– Wichmann, S.: Realismus und Impressionismus in Deutschland. Stuttgart 1964.– Wirth, I.: Berliner Maler – Menzel, Liebermann, Slevogt, Corinth in Briefen, Vorträgen und Notizen. Berlin 1986

SCANDINAVIA

Andreae, R. and M. Kreutzer (ed.): Im Licht des Nordens. Skandinavische Malerei um die Jahrhundertwende. Kunstmuseum Düsseldorf 1986 (EC).– Berg, K., S. Ringbom, B. Lindwall, O. Thue et al.: 1880 – tal i nordikt maleri. Stockholm 1985 (EC).– Dreams of a Summer Night. Hayward Gallery, London 1986 (EC).– Grate, P. and A.G. Hökby: 1880-arene i nordisk maleri. Oslo, Stockholm, Helsinki, Copenhagen 1985 (EC).– Hansen, J.O.: Dänische Malerei 1864-1900. In: "Vor 100 Jahren. Dänemark und Deutschland 1864-1900". Kiel 1981 (EC).– Kent, N.: The Triumph of Light and Nature. Nordic Art 1740-1940. London 1987.– Nasgaard, R.: The Mystic North. Symbolist Landscape Painting in Northern Europe and North America 1890-1940. Toronto 1984.– Reuterswärd, O.: Impressionister och purister. Stockholm 1976.– Robbert, L. (ed.): De drogo till Paris: Nordiska Konstnärinnor pa 1880-talet. Liljvalch Konsthall Stockholm. Stockholm 1988 (EC).– Usselmann, H.: Complexité et importance des contacts des peintres nordiques avec l'impressionnisme. Doctoral thesis, Gothenburg 1979.– Varnedoe, K. (ed.): Northern Light. Realism and Symbolism in Scandinavian Painting 1880-1910. The Brooklyn Museum, New York et al. New York 1982 (EC).– Varnedoe, K. (ed.): Northern Light. Nordic Art at the Turn of the Century. New Haven (CT) and London 1988.– Voss, K.: Die Maler des Lichts. Nordische Kunst auf Skagen. Weingarten 1987.– Wichström, A.: Kvinner ved staffeliet. Kvinnelige malere i Norge for 1900. Oslo 1983

EASTERN AND SOUTH EASTERN EUROPE

Balogh, L.: Die ungarische Facette der Münchner Schule. Mainburg 1988.– Breic, T.: Slowenski impressionizem. Ljubljana 1977.– Cevc, E. and A.: Slowenische Impressionisten und ihre Vorläufer an der Nationalgalerie in Ljubljana. Vienna 1979 (EC).– Cevc, E. and A.: Impressionisti sloveni della Galleria nazionale di Ljubljana. Casale sforcesco, Milan 1981 (EC).– Fjodorow-Dawydow, A.: Russki peisach koza XIX – nacschala XX weka. Moscow 1974.– Jensen, J.C. (ed.): Polnische Malerei von 1830-1914. Kunsthalle Kiel et al. Cologne 1978 (EC).– Karabelnik-Matta, M. and G. Magnaguagno (eds.): Russische Malerei im 19. Jahrhundert. Realismus – Impressionismus – Symbolismus. Aus der Sammlung der Staatlichen Tretjakow-Galerie Moskau und des Staatlichen Russischen Museums Leningrad. Kunsthalle, Zurich 1989 (EC).– Kepinski, Z.: Impresjionizm polski. Warsaw 1961.– Kotalik, J. et al.: Tschechische Kunst 1878-1914. Auf dem Weg in die Moderne. Darmstadt 1985.– Pleiniristi. Narodni Muzeum, Belgrade 1960 (EC).– Salgo, N. et al.: Hungarian Painting. A Century 1850-1950. Washington 1990.– Slowenische Impressionisten aus der Nationalgalerie in Ljubljana. Städtische Galerie, Regensburg 1984 (EC).– Stele, F.: Die slowenischen Impressionisten. Ljubljana 1971.– Sternin, G.: Chudoschestwennaja schisn Rossii na rubesche XIX-XX wekow. Moscow 1970

ITALY

Bellonzi, F.: Il divisionisma della pittura italiana. Milan 1967.– Borgiotti, M.: Genio dei Macchiaioli. Milan 1964.– Borgiotti, M. (ed.): I Macchiaioli. Galleria Narciso. Turin 1965 (EC).– Broude, N.: The Macchiaioli.

Italian Painters of the Nineteenth Century. New Haven (CT) and London 1987.– Bruno, G.: La pittura in Liguria dal 1850 al divisionismo. Avengo 1982.– Calzini, R. and A. Soffici: L'arte dei Macchiaioli. Antologia della critica, scelta di lettere dei pittori macchiaioli e bibliografia. Turin 1977.– Dini, P.: Movimenti pittorici italiani dell'ottocento. I macchiaioli e la scuola napoletana. Milan 1967.– Dini, P.: Dal "Caffè Michelangiolo" al Caffè Nouvelle-Athènes: I Macchiaioli tra Firenze e Parigi. Turin 1986.– Divisionismo romano. Galleria Farnese, Rome 1989 (EC).– Durbè, D. et al. (eds.): Toskanische Impressionen. Der Beitrag der Macchiaioli zum europäischen Realismus. Bayerische Staatsgemäldesammlungen, Haus der Kunst, Munich 1975 (EC).– Durbè, D.: I Macchiaioli, mantres de la peinture en Toscana au XIXᵉ siècle. Paris 1978.– Durbè, D. (ed.): I Macchiaioli – Peintres en Toscana après 1850. Galeries nationales du Grand Palais. Paris 1978 (EC).– Durbè, D. et al. (eds.): The Macchiaioli: Painters of Italian Life, 1850-1900. 1986 (EC).– Durbè, D. and L. Titonel: The Macchiaioli. Masters of Realism in Tuscany. Manchester City Art Gallery. Rome 1982 (EC).– Durbè, D.: La Firenze dei macchiaioli. Rome 1985.– Fiori, T. (ed.): Archivi del Divisionismo. 2 vols. Rome 1969.– Giardelli, M.: I Macchiaioli e l'epoca loro. Milan 1958.– Grada, R. de: I Macchiaioli. Milan 1967.– Lankheit, K.: Von der napoleonischen Epoche zum Risorgimento. Studien zur italienischen Kunst des 19. Jahrhunderts. Munich 1988.– Lavagnino, E.: L'arte moderna dai neoclassici ai contemporanei. 2 vols. Turin 1961.– Matteucci, G. et al. (eds.): Three Italian Friends of the Impressionists: Boldini, De Nittis, Zandomeneghi. Stair Sainty Matthiesen Gallery, New York and Florence 1984 (EC).– Matteucci, E. and P.B. Lande (eds.): I Macchiaioli di Renato Fucini. Florence 1985 (EC).– Monteverdi, M.: Storia della pittura italiana dell'ottocento. 3 vols. Milan 1975.– Naujack, A.: Die Florentiner Macchiaioli. Doctoral thesis, Tübingen 1972.– Quinsac, A.-P.: La peinture divisionniste italienne. Origines et premiers développements 1880-1895. Paris 1972.– Tonelli, E. and K. Hart: The Macchiaioli. Painters of Italian Life, 1850-1900. Seattle 1990

SPAIN

Benet, R.: Impresionismo. [No place of publication] 1952.– El Impresionismo en España. Salas de Exposiciónes de la Dirección General de Bellas Artes, Madrid 1974 (EC).– Fuster, A.: Impresionismo Español. Madrid 1970.– Galvo Seraller, F. and A. González (eds.): Paisaje español entre el Realismo y el Impresionismo. Madrid 1976.– González, C. and M. Martí: Pintores españoles en Paris (1850- 1900). Barcelona 1989.– Pena López, J.: La paisaje español del siglo XIX: Del naturalismo al impresionismo. Doctoral thesis, Madrid 1982.– Rodríguez Alcalde, L.: Los maestros del impresionismo español. Madrid

1987.– Soleil et ombre: l'art portugais du XIXᵉ siècle. Musée du Petit-Palais, Paris 1987 (EC)

GREAT BRITAIN

Baron, W. and F. Farmar: The Painters of Camden Town 1905-1920. London 1988 (EC).– Billcliffe, R.: The Glasgow Boys. The Glasgow School of Painting 1875-1895. London 1985.– Campbell, J.: The Irish Impressionists. Irish Artists in France and Belgium, 1850-1914. National Gallery of Ireland. Dublin 1984 (EC).– House, J. (ed.): Impressionism, its Masters, its Precursors and its Influence in Britain. Royal Academy of Arts, London 1974 (EC).– Flint, K.: Impressionists in England: The Critical Reception. London et al. 1984.– McConkey, K.: British Impressionism. Oxford 1989.– Taylor, H. (ed.): British Impressionism. Castle Museum, Nottingham 1989 (EC).– Watney, S.: English Post-Impressionism. London 1980.– Wortley, L.: British Impressionism. A Garden of Bright Images. London 1988

USA AND CANADA

American Impressionist and Realist Paintings and Drawings from the Collection of Mr. and Mrs. Raymond J. Horowitz. Metropolitan Museum of Art, New York 1973 (EC).– Baur, J.I.H. (ed.): Leaders of American Impressionism. The Brooklyn Museum, New York 1937 (EC).– Bizardel, Y.: American Painters in Paris. New York 1960.– Blaugrund, A. (ed.): Paris 1889: American Artists at the Universal Exposition. Chrysler Museum, Norfolk; Pennsylvania Academy of Fine Arts, Philadelphia; New York 1989 (EC).– Boyle, R.J. et al. (eds.): French Impressionists Influence American Impressionists. Low Art Museum, University of Miami, Miami 1971 (EC).– Boyle, R.J.: American Impressionism. Boston 1974.– Brown, M.W.: American Painting: From the Armory Show to the Depression. Princeton 1970.– Domit, M.M. (ed.): American Impressionist Painting. National Gallery of Art, Washington 1973 (EC).– Fink, L.M.: American Art at the Nineteenth-Century Paris Salons. Washington and Cambridge (MA) 1990.– Gaethgens, T.W. (ed.): Bilder aus der Neuen Welt. Amerikanische Malerei des 18. und 19. Jahrhunderts. Munich 1988 (EC).– Gerdts, W.H. (ed.): American Impressionism. The Institute of Contemporary Art, Boston et al. Seattle 1980 (EC).– Gerdts, W.H.: American Impressionism. New York 1984.– Gerdts, W.H. (ed.): American Impressionismus. Meisterwerke aus öffentlichen und privaten Sammlungen der Vereinigten Staaten von Amerika. Lugano 1990 (EC).– Hiesinger, U.W.: Impressionism in America. The Ten American Painters. Munich 1991.– Hoopes, D.F.: The American Impressionists. New York 1972.– Impressionism and its Influence in American Art. Santa Barbara Museum of Art, Santa Barbara 1954 (EC).– Impressionism in America. University Art Gallery Albu-

querque. Albuquerque 1965 (EC).– Lamb, R.J. (ed.): The Canadian Art Club, 1907-1915. Edmonton Art Gallery, Edmonton 1988 (EC).– Morrin, P., J. Zilczer and W.C. Agge (eds.): The Advent of Modernism: Post-Impressionism and North American Art. High Museum of Art, Atlanta 1986 (EC).– Murray, J. (ed.): Impressionism in Canada 1895-1935. Art Gallery of Ontario, Toronto 1973 (EC).– Novak, B.: American Painting of the Nineteenth Century. New York 1969.– Pierce, P.J.: The Ten. Concord (N.H.) 1976.– Sellin, D.: Americans in Brittany and Normandy: 1860-1910. Phoenix Art Museum, Phoenix 1982 (EC).– Spencer, H., B. Novak et al. (eds.): Impressionnistes américains. Musée du Petit Palais, Paris et al. Paris 1982 (EC).– Weinberg, H.B.: The Lure of Paris: Nineteenth Century American Painters and their French Teachers. New York 1990.– Wilson, R.G., D.H. Pilgrim and R.R. Murray (eds.): The American Renaissance, 1876-1917. The Brooklyn Museum, New York 1979 (EC)

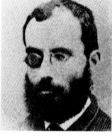

ABBATI Giuseppe
1836 Naples – 1868 Florence
Pupil to his father, Vincenzo Abbati. Studied under Grigoletti at the Venice Academy, where he met Signorini and Vito d'Ancona. 1859 took part in Garibaldi's movement. From 1860 in Florence; frequented the Caffè Michelangiolo; painted plein-air with his friend Martelli in Castiglioncello. Died from the bite of a rabid dog.
CATALOGUE: Dini, P.: A. L'opera completa. Turin 1987
ILLUSTRATION:
534 Landscape at Castiglioncello, 1863

ACADEMIE JULIAN
An art school in Paris, founded in 1868 by Rodolphe Julian (1839-1907), a pupil of Cabanel and Cogniet who himself exhibited in the "Salon des Refusés." The academy prepared pupils for entrance to the Ecole des Beaux-Arts. Once a week, Bouguereau, Boulanger, Ferrier, Fleury, Laurens, Lefèbvre and others corrected the work of their pupils, who included Bonnard, Denis, Corinth, Matisse and Vuillard. In the 1880s there were approximately 600 pupils, and the monthly fee was 60 francs.

ACADEMIE SUISSE
An art school in Paris on the Quai des Orfèvres, founded by Charles Suisse, who had stood as a model for J.-L. David. The academy was attended in its early years by Delacroix, Daumier and Courbet, and later by Cézanne, Pissarro, Monet and Guillaumin, primarily for nude studies. Although it prepared pupils for the Ecole des Beaux-Arts, the school also gave avant-garde artists the chance to try out their new ideas in a relaxed environment without strict control.

AIX-EN-PROVENCE
The old capital of Provence, birthplace of Cézanne, Alexis and Zola. Its attractive countryside was often painted by Cézanne (Mont Sainte-Victoire), Renoir and others. The museums, such as the Musée Granet, galleries and art shops all contributed to make Aix into a centre for art.

ALEXIS Paul
1847 Aix-en-Provence – 1901 Triel
Writer and art critic, early friend of Zola and Cézanne. Moved to Paris in 1869, where his friends introduced him into Impressionist circles. Participated in the meetings at the Café Guerbois and the Nouvelle-Athènes. Became an impassioned defender of the Impressionist view of art, which he linked to Realism in literature. He was a second at the duel between Manet and Duranty. His portrait was painted by Cézanne, Seurat and Zandomeneghi.

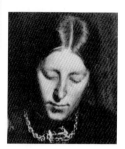

ANCHER Anna
1859 Skagen – 1935 Skagen
Daughter of the Skagen merchant and restaurateur Erik Brøndum. First lessons with K. Madsen. 1875-1878 attended V. Kyhn's drawing school in Copenhagen. Her style influenced above all by Krohg: portraits of fishermen in Impressionist style. In 1889 she studied with Puvis de Chavannes in Paris. 1880 married Michael Ancher. The couple worked at the artists' colony in Skagen, where, since 1870, many Scandinavian artists such as Krøyer and Krohg had moved in order to paint the sea and the simple life of fishing communities. 1882 trip to Berlin and Vienna. 1885 with Krøyer and Johansen in Holland, Belgium and Paris. The most frequent motifs are simple domestic scenes,

young girls in bright, hazy colours and people in rooms filled with sunlight. Painted some very successful portraits of her husband, her old teacher, Kyhn, and her mother. Her father's former hotel is now the museum of the Skagen artists' group.
WRITINGS, DOCUMENTS: Voss, K. (ed.): Letters of A.A. Copenhagen 1984
BIBLIOGRAPHY: Loerges, M.: Et solstrejf i en stue i Skagen. Portræt af A.A. 1980.– Schwartz, W.: A.A. In: "Små Kunstboger", Nr. 27, Copenhagen 1953
ILLUSTRATIONS:
494 Sunlight in the Blue Room, 1891
499 The Artist's Mother, Anna Hedvig Brøndum, 1913

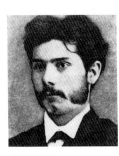

ANDREESCU Ion
1850 Bucharest – 1882 Bucharest
1869/70 Studied at the Bucharest School of Art. 1872-1878 Teacher of drawing and calligraphy in Buzau (Muntenia), influenced by Grigorescu. 1874 his pictures first appeared in an exhibition of contemporary artists in Bucharest. 1879/80 and 1881 with a scholarship at the Académie Julian in Paris; painted under the tutelage of Grigorescu in Barbizon, with three exhibitions. 1881 Return to Bucharest, ill with tuberculosis. 1882 successful exhibition of his small-scale Impressionist landscapes, peasant portraits and still-lifes.
BIBLIOGRAPHY: Bogdan, R.: J.A. 2 vols. Bucharest 1962-1982.– Busuioceanu, A.: A. Bucharest 1936.– Busuioceana, A.: A. Bucharest 1980.– Oprescu, G.: A. Bucharest 1932.– Varga, V. and E. Costescu: A. Bucharest 1978
ILLUSTRATIONS:
525 Winter at Barbizon, 1881
527 Edge of the Forest, c. 1880

ANGRAND Charles Théophile
1854 Criquetot-sur-Ouville (Seine-Maritime) – 1926 Rouen
Son of a country school teacher. First exhibition at the Ecole Municipale des Beaux-Arts in Rouen with Zacharie and Morin; admired Corot. Earned a living at first by coaching. 1875 first trip to Paris. 1882 moved to Paris. Friendly contacts with Seurat, Signac, Luce and Cross; frequented the Café l'Orient and the Café Marengo. Like his friends, he painted in the pointillist style. 1884

and 1886 participated in the "Salon des Indépendants". 1889 joint exhibition with Seurat at Les Vingt in Brussels. The death of his friend Seurat in 1891 was a great blow.

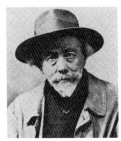

1891-1895 yearly exhibitions, at irregular intervals at the "Salon des Indépendants", too, until his death. From 1896 he led a solitary life in Saint-Laurent in the Pays de Caux. Up to 1900 his painting of form became increasingly pointillist; thereafter he returned to an almost traditional technique with simple forms. 1914 Return to Rouen.
WRITINGS, DOCUMENTS: Lespinasse, F. (ed.): C.A. Correspondance 1883-1926. Lagny-sur-Marne 1988
BIBLIOGRAPHY: C.A. Galeries André Maurice, Paris 1961 (EC).– C.A. 1854-1926. Musée de Dieppe, Dieppe 1976 (EC).– Lespinasse, F.: C.A. 1854-1926. Rouen 1982.– Welsh-Ovcharov, B.: The Early Work of C.A. and his Contact with Vincent van Gogh. Utrecht and The Hague 1971
ILLUSTRATIONS:
295 The Western Railway Leaving Paris, 1886
307 Man and Woman in the Street, 1887

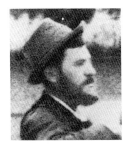

ANQUETIN Louis
1861 Etrepagny (Eure) – 1932 Paris
Settled in Paris in 1882; his apartment on the Avenue de Clichy and his parents' house in Etrepagny became the rendezvous for international artists. Studied under Bonnat and Cormon in Paris, where he met Charles Laval, Toulouse-Lautrec, Bernard and van Gogh. 1883 Continuation of his studies now with Monet in Giverny.

Exhibition 1886/87 with Bernard and Toulouse-Lautrec at the Café Tambourin of pictures in the style of Seurat. 1887 became interested in pointillist theories of colour; developed with Bernard the main principles of cloisonnism. He made the important discovery that certain dominant colours reveal the mood of a picture. 1888 exhibition with Les Vingt in Brussels and the "Salon des Indépendants" in Paris. 1894 travelled with Toulouse-Lautrec through Holland and Belgium. In the Nineties he confronted the realistic techniques of Courbet and Daumier. From 1896, under the influence of Rubens and Delacroix, he developed large figural compositions on ceilings, walls and wall-hangings.
WRITINGS, DOCUMENTS: Anquetin, A.: De l'art. Paris 1970
BIBLIOGRAPHY: L.A. La passion d'être peintre. Galerie Brame & Lorenceau, Paris 1991 (EC)
ILLUSTRATIONS:
306 Avenue de Clichy – Five O'Clock in the Evening, 1887
326 Girl Reading a Newspaper, 1890
326 In the Theatre Foyer, 1892

ARGENTEUIL
Small village, seven miles from Paris on the right bank of the Seine. Accessible by two railway lines and by river boat, it was a popular destination for day-trips from Paris. Once Monet had settled here in 1873 and painted a series of his most beautiful pictures, Argenteuil became an Impressionist centre. Manet, Sisley, Caillebotte and Renoir also met there to paint. Monet set up his studio on a small boat. Argenteuil was a place where artists could work together in a relaxed atmosphere and exchange ideas. In 1878 Monet left Argenteuil and moved to Vétheuil.

ASNIERES
A favourite place with Parisians for day-trips and an important port for river traffic on the Seine. Asnières, along with the island of La Grande Jatte, the Trianon casino, and also the factories of Clichy and Saint-Ouen, offered painters, above all the Neo-Impressionists, a mixture of motifs from modern life, and it acquired the same significance for them as Argenteuil had for the first generation of Impressionists.

ASTRUC Zacharie
1835 Angers – 1907 Paris
Sculptor, painter and art critic. Began as a journalist with several newspapers: 1859 founding of the journal "Le Quart d'heure" and publication of the "14 stations du Salon". In 1855 he met Manet. In 1863, during the exhibition in the Salon, he published the journal "Le Salon feuilleton quotidien". He was also a poet and composer. Member of the Batignolles group; frequented the Café Guerbois and later the Nouvelle-Athènes. In 1874 he was co-founder of the "Société anonyme des peintres, sculpteurs et graveurs" and had six catalogue entries at the first Exhibition of Impressionists. He contributed a bust to the

Salon in both 1876 and 1881. In 1883 one of his sculptures was bought by the French state and exhibited in the Jardin du Luxembourg. In painting he developed a special technique for laying on paint using cotton wool wads instead of brushes. As a critic he was quick to recognize the importance of Courbet and praised Manet, who painted his portrait and portrayed him in "Music in the Tuileries" (p. 43).

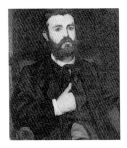

WRITINGS, DOCUMENTS: Astruc, Z.: Le Salon des Refusés. In: "Le Salon", 20. 5. 1863, p. 5
BIBLIOGRAPHY: Flescher, S.: Z.A. Critic and Artist, 1833- 1907. Doctoral thesis, Columbia University. New York 1978.– Flescher, S.: Manet's "Portrait of Z.A.": A Study of a Friendship and New Light on a Problematic Painting. In: "Arts Magazine" 52 (June 1978), pp. 98-105
ILLUSTRATION:
92 The Chinese Gifts, c. 1873

ATELIER CORMON → Cormon, Fernand

ATELIER GLEYRE → Gleyre, Charles

ATTENDU Antoine-Ferdinand
1845 Paris – 1905
Details of his life are unknown. Pupil of Louis Mettling. Landscape and still-life painter active in Neuilly-sur-Seine and Paris. He exhibited between 1870 and 1898 at the Salon and was represented with six works at the first Impressionist exhibition in 1874.

AURIER G. Albert
1865 Châteauroux – 1892 Paris
Poet, critic and painter. Wrote many articles in journals in favour of symbolism and became friends with Bernard. From 1889 he was Chief Editor of "Le Moderniste"; in his later years he became a strong supporter of van Gogh and Gauguin.

AUVERS-SUR-OISE
Village on the Oise, about 18 miles from Paris. As early as the 1850s Daubigny, Daumier and Corot worked here. It later became an important rendezvous for the Impressionist painters. Renoir, Sisley, Cézanne and van Gogh lived there and painted views of Auvers and the surrounding countryside.

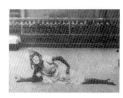

vaert: A.B. Brussels 1910.– Retrospective tentoonstelling A.B., 1866-1922. Museum voor Schone Kunsten, Ghent 1972 (EC)
ILLUSTRATION:
431 Ghent, Evening, 1903

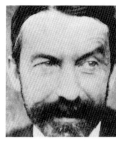

AVRIL Jane
1868–1943
Dancer at the cafés-concert and one of the celebrities of Paris night life. She was a favourite model of Toulouse-Lautrec; her most famous period was the years 1889-1894, when she appeared at the Moulin Rouge (p. 327).

AZBE SCHOOL
The school and studio run by the Slovenian painter Anton Ažbè (1862 Ljubljana – 1905 Munich) founded in Munich in 1891, at which Slovenian painters (Ivan Grohar, Matija Jama, Rihard Jakopić, Matej Sternen), Serbian painters (Miličević, Milovanović, Nadežda Petrović, Rista and Beta Vukanović) and Russian painters (Igor Grabar, A. Javlensky, Wassily Kandinsky) all studied plein-air and Impressionist techniques. Grabar was also there as a teacher from 1896.

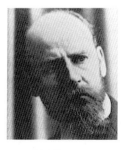

BAERTSOEN Albert
1866 Ghent – 1922 Ghent
Son of a rich Belgian industrialist, studied with G. den Duyts and at the Academy in Ghent with J. Delvin. After a notable success at the Paris Salon in 1887 he stayed for two years at the studio of Roll. 1898 travelled in Italy. 1900 Gold medal at the Paris World Fair. Friendship with Emile Claus. From Realism he developed a characteristic Impressionistic style using short brushstrokes. A favourite motif is his home town, Ghent. He often painted landscapes with grey skies, melancholy in mood. Member of Les Vingt. 1905 influenced by the Fauves and Impressionists. During the First World War he moved to England, where he stayed with John Singer Sargent.
BIBLIOGRAPHY: Eeckhout, P. (ed.): A.B. Ghent 1972 (EC).– Fierens-Ge-

BALLA Giacomo
1871 Turin – 1958 Rome
An important representative of Italian Futurism. Studied at the evening School of Drawing in Turin. Thereafter he settled in Rome, where he worked successfully as a portrait painter. His first Impressionist paintings revealed his interest in colour theory. 1900 stayed in Paris; encountered pointillism and adopted its style of reducing the visible surface to coloured dots. Supported Anarchist ideas, as propounded by certain pointillists like Pissarro. Co-editor of the "Futurist Manifesto of Painting" and, until 1910, painted portraits, landscapes and social themes. 1904 took part in an international exhibition in Düsseldorf. Used pointillist technique for the subject matter of Futurism: dynamism and speed.
WRITINGS, DOCUMENTS: Balla, E.: Con B. 3 vols. Milan 1984-1986
BIBLIOGRAPHY: Barricelli, A.: B. Rome 1966.– Fagiolo dell'Arco, M.: B. pre-futurista. Rome 1968.– G.B. Galleria Civica d'Arte Moderna, Turin 1963 (EC).– G.B. Galleria Nazionale d'Arte Moderna, Rome 1971 (EC).– Robinson, S.B.: G.B. Divisionism and Futurism, 1871-1912. Ann Arbor (MI) 1981
ILLUSTRATION:
550 The Fiancée at the Villa Borghese, 1902

BARBIZON SCHOOL
Group of landscape painters who settled in the village of Barbizon near Fontainebleau, south-east of Paris, and dedicated themselves to plein-air painting. Already an artists' town in the mid-eighteenth century. Achieved its greatest importance in the mid-nineteenth century through its landscape painters, particularly J.-F. Millet and Rousseau, who, with their airy, light-filled pictures, were precursors of the Impressionists. In contrast to the Impressionists, however, they did not paint in the open air, but sketched from nature and then painted their pictures in the studio.

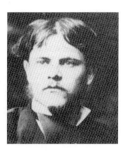

BASTIEN–LEPAGE Jules
1848 Damvillers (Meuse) – 1884 Paris
Came from a country family in northeastern France, where he spent most of his life. 1867 studied at the Ecole des Beaux-Arts in Paris under Cabanel. 1870 Military service; wounded. Exhibited 1870 and 1873-1875 in the Salon. In 1875 he won 2nd place in the competition for the Rome Prize. Close friends with Zola. Painted in a Naturalist style, comparable to that of Courbet and Millet. 1878 notable success in the Salon. 1879-1882 travelled annually to London; contact with Burne-Jones and Clausen. 1881 travelled to Venice and 1884 to Algier, shortly before he died of cancer.
CATALOGUE: Aubrun, M.-M.: J.B.-L. Catalogue raisonné de l'œuvre. Nantes 1985
BIBLIOGRAPHY: Fourcauls, L. de: J.B.-L. Paris 1885.– McConkey, K.: The Bouguereau of the Naturalists: B.-L. and British Art. In: "Art History" (September 1978), pp. 3-17.– Theuriet, A.: J.B.-L. Paris 1885
ILLUSTRATIONS:
167 Haymaking, 1877
214 Poor Fauvette, 1881

BATIGNOLLES
An area of Paris, which was absorbed into the city during the expansion of Paris in 1860. Many artists' studios were to be found there, especially those of the Impressionists. The Café Guerbois in Batignolles was, from 1869, a permanent rendezvous for artists, including Manet, Monet, Renoir, Sisley and Pissarro. The group later to be the Impressionists came to be called the Batignolles School by critics. One of the birthplaces of Impressionism.

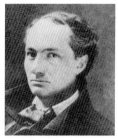

with modernity and introduced the concept of the "heroism of modern life". In 1848 he became for a short period an enthusiastic supporter of the Revolution and edited a revolutionary newspaper with Champfleury. In 1855 he first wrote about Delacroix, whom he particularly admired for the musical effects of his colours and for his surnaturalisme.

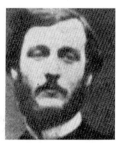

In 1857 the book of poems "Les Fleurs du Mal" was published; due to its alleged immorality it was attacked in the courts. He wrote about caricatures. 1858/59 often at his mother's house in Honfleur. Met Manet, Fantin-Latour, Legros, Whistler and Stevens. Rejected Millet and, only accepted Corot's landscapes; saw photography as a danger to art. 1864-1866 in Belgium. The delayed consequences of syphilis made him lame and unable to speak.

BAZILLE Frédéric
1841 Montpellier – 1870 Beaune-la-Rolande
Came from a rich middle-class Protestant family. 1849-1859 Grammar school in Montpellier. 1859 Began to study medicine in Montpellier. Acquainted with the famous art collector Bruyas. 1862 continued his medical studies in Paris, at the same time attending painting classes at Gleyre's studio, where he met Monet, Renoir and Sisley. Influenced by Manet and Courbet in his painting style. Spent his summers mostly at his parents' country house in Méric. Easter 1863 with Monet in Chailly, in order to paint plein-air in the forest of Fontainebleau. 1864 with his friend Villa he rented a studio in the Rue Vaugi-

BAUDELAIRE Charles
1821 Paris – 1867 Paris
French poet, a friend of painters and one of the most perceptive of art critics in the nineteenth century. Argued for a conception of modernity and subjectivity and emphasised the role of imagination and impassivity (impassibilité). In contrast to classical aesthetics he regarded the bizarre, irregular and unexpected as beautiful. 1842 after some eventful experiences at sea, he settled in Paris. Squandered his inheritance and led an irregular and extravagant life, mostly in poverty. 1845 his first critical article on the Salon; identified Romanticism

rard. June **1864** with Monet in Honfleur, where he met Boudin and Jongkind. Supported Monet financially; gave up his medical studies. **1865** shared a studio with Monet in the Rue de Furstenberg. Exhibited **1866** at the Salon; shared a studio with Renoir in the Rue de la Visconti; shortly afterwards moved to the neighbourhood of the Café Guerbois, where he was a regular customer. Painted numerous portraits of friends and members of his family in the various studios. Exhibited yearly at the Salon. **1869** his picture "Angler with Nets" caused a fierce debate. His quiet. clear landscapes and harmonious family scenes in muted colours made him one of the most significant representatives of Early Impressionism. **1870** fought enthusiastically in the Franco-Prussian War and was killed at Beaune-la-Rolande, before Impressionism had fully developed.
CATALOGUE: Daulte, F.: F.B. et les débuts de l'impressionnisme. Catalogue de l'œuvre peint. Paris 1992
BIBLIOGRAPHY: B. Galerie Wildenstein. Paris 1950 (EC).– Daulte, F.: F.B. et son temps. Geneva 1952.– F.B. and Early Impressionism. The Art Institute of Chicago, Chicago 1978 (EC).– Poulain, G.: B. et ses amis. Paris 1932
ILLUSTRATIONS:
52 The Terrace at Méric (Oleander), 1867
54 Family Reunion, 1867
55 Portrait of Pierre-Auguste Renoir, 1867
55 Self-Portrait with Palette, 1865
61 View of the Village of Castelnaule-Lez, 1868
75 Bathers (Summer Scene), 1869
80 After the Bath, 1870
80 Louis Auriol Fishing, 1870
81 The Artist's Studio, Rue de la Condamine, 1870

BEAU Henri
1865 Montreal – 1949
Autumn **1907** first exhibited at the Paris Salon. His themes were landscapes, flowers, nudes and portraits. Exhibited regularly **1902-1937** at the Salon des Indépendants and at the Société Nationale des Beaux-Arts.
ILLUSTRATION:
636 The Picnic, c. 1905

BELIARD Edouard
1835 Paris – 1902 Etampes
Son of a Paris architect; began his career as a lawyer's assistant and secretary. First painting lessons with Hébert und Cogniet; influenced by Corot; friendly with Proudhon. Travelled to Rome. Exhibited in **1867** at the Salon. A frequent customer in the Café Guerbois. **1870** moved to London. **1872** returned to France, lived in Etampes. **1873** recommended by Alexis to the Société coopérative des peintres et graveurs. Successful participation in the 1st and 2nd Impressionist exhibitions. Mainly painted landscapes; later distanced himself from Impressionist principles. Spent his last years in Etampes.
ILLUSTRATION:
155 Banks of the Oise, c. 1875

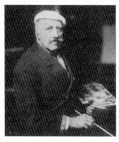

BELLIO Georges de
1828 Bucharest – 1894 Paris
A doctor of Romanian origin, patron and friend of many Impressionist painters, whom he also supported financially. He was a regular customer in their cafés and regularly attended the dinners at the Café Riche. A keen art collector, he bought pictures which otherwise would not have found a buyer. Owned important pictures by Monet ("Impression, Sunrise" p. 113) and Renoir.

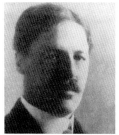

BENSON Frank Weston
1862 Salem (MA) – 1951 Boston
1880-1883 pupil of Otto Grundmann at the Museum of Fine Arts School in Boston. **1883-1885** lived in Paris; studied under Boulanger and Lefèbvre at the Académie Julian. **1885** returned to the USA; lived in Salem (MA); taught art in nearby Portland. One of the first plein-air painters in America, he paved the way for American Impressionism. **1889** moved to Boston, where he taught in his studio; he soon became Professor at the Boston Museum School. Member of The Ten American Painters; annual exhibitions and numerous study trips; in **1903** he received the gold medal in Pittsburgh, in **1904** at St. Louis and in **1906** at Philadelphia.
BIBLIOGRAPHY: Bedford, F.A. et al. (eds.): F.W.B. Berry-Hill Galleries, New York 1989 (EC).– Dodge, E. (ed.): F.W.B., 1862-1951. William A. Farnsworth Library and Art Museum, Rockland (Me.) 1973 (EC).– Morgan, C.L.: F.W.B. New York and London 1931.– Olney, S.F. (ed.): Two American Impressionists: F.W.B. and Edmund C. Tarbell. University of

New Hampshire, Art Galleries, Durham (N.H.) 1979 (EC).– Pfaff, A.E.M.: Etchings and Drypoints by F.W.B. Boston and New York 1917.– Price, L. (ed.): F.W.B. 1862-1951. Essex Institute and Peabody Museum, Salem (MA). 1956 (EC).– Price, L. and F. Coburn (eds.): F.W.B., Edmond C. Tarbell. Museum of Fine Arts, Boston 1938 (EC).– Salaman, M.C.: F.W.B. London 1925.– Wilmerding, J. et al. (eds.): F.W.B.: The Impressionist Years. Spanierman Gallery, New York 1988 (EC)
ILLUSTRATIONS:
630 The Black Hat, 1904
634 Sunlight, 1909

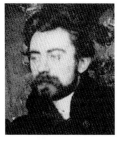

BERAUD Jean
1849 St. Petersburg – 1936 Paris
Born in Russia of French parents. Until **1870.** he studied law in Paris. He then studied art at Bonnat's studio. Friendly with Manet; his favourite themes were people in the city, at first in an Impressionist manner. In **1873** he exhibited for the first time at the Salon. Co-founder of the Société Nationale des Beaux-Arts, took part regularly in exhibitions there **1890-1929**. From **1890** he turned to religious themes in a realistic style, which led to controversial discussions at the Salon.
CATALOGUE: Offenstadt, P.: J.B. Catalogue raisonné (in preparation)
BIBLIOGRAPHY: Un temoin de la Belle Epoque. J.B. (1849-1935). Musée Carnavalet, Paris 1979 (EC)
ILLUSTRATIONS:
371 On the Boulevard, 1895
372 Waiting, Paris, Rue de Chateaubriand, c. 1900

BERNARD Emile
1868 Lille – 1941 Paris
Lived from **1878** in Paris. His initial artistic training was at the Ecole des Arts Décoratifs, then from **1884** at the studio of Cormon. There he met Anquetin, Toulouse-Lautrec and van Gogh. **1885** travelled in Normandy and Britanny, where he met Schuffenecker. Through van Gogh in **1886** he came to know Gauguin, whom he admired considerably. **1888-1891** he worked with Anquetin and Gauguin on the principles of Cloisonnism. After a quarrel about who was the originator of the new style, he broke off all contact with Gaugin in **1891**.

Exhibition at the Salon des Indépendants. **1892** organised the first van Gogh retrospective. In **1893** he left Paris; travelled in Italy and the Middle East; lived in Cairo. **1896** travelled in Spain. **1900** and **1903** visits to Venice. From **1901** he had his own exhibitions in Paris, **1905** at Cassirer's in Berlin and **1908** at the Kunstverein (Society of Arts) in Munich. **1904** returned to Paris. His correspondence with Cézanne was important for the theory of art. **1905** founded the famous journal "La Rénovation Esthétique". His later pictures drew on the style of the Renaissance and were mostly religious themes. The large, heroically conceived figures are filled with expressive pathos.

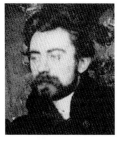

CATALOGUE: Luthi, J.-J.: E.B. Cat. raisonné de l'œuvre peint. Paris 1982
BIBLIOGRAPHY: Cailler, P.: E.B. Geneva 1959.– Cheyron, J. and Z. El Hakim: E.B. 1868-1941. Geneva 1941.– Mornard, P.: E.B. et ses amis. Geneva 1957.– Stevens, M.A. et al. (eds.): E.B. 1868-1941. Ein Wegbereiter der Moderne. Kunsthalle Mannheim and Amsterdam 1990 (EC)
ILLUSTRATION:
290 Portrait of Père Tanguy, 1887

BERNHEIM family
A family of art dealers in the 19th and 20th centuries. Alexandre Bernheim (**1833-1915**) opened an art shop in the Rue Lafitte in Paris in **1863** which was later run by his sons Joseph (**1870-1941**) and Gaston (**1870-1953**; ill.). The family concentrated on Impressionist paintings, especially by Renoir and Monet, who were friends

of theirs. With Durand-Ruel and G. Petit they were the most important Impressionist art dealers. After 1900 the gallery became particularly interested in van Gogh, Cézanne and some of the Post-Impressionists.

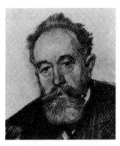

BERUETE Y MORET Aureliano de
1845 Madrid – 1912 Madrid
First studied law, 1867 gained his doctorate. At the same time he attended courses in painting at the studio of Carlos Múgica. 1871/72 active as a politician. 1874 decided on a career as a painter; artistic training with C. de Haes and M. Rico. Co-founder of the Institución Libre de Enseñanza. Travelled frequently in Europe and Spain. One of the most important representatives of Impressionist landscape painting in Spain. In 1878, 1884, 1901 and 1904 he received medals at the National Exhibition of Art in Madrid. 1889 and 1900 member of the international jury for the Paris World Fair. 1900 Chevalier de la Légion d'Honneur. 1898-1909 published an important monograph on the Spanish Baroque painter Velázquez.
WRITINGS, DOCUMENTS: Beruete, A.: Historia de la pintura española en siglo XIX. Madrid 1926
BIBLIOGRAPHY: Lafuente Ferrari, E. et al. (eds.): A.d.B. 1845-1912. Sala de Exposiciones de la Caja de Pensiones, Madrid 1983 (EC)
ILLUSTRATIONS:
556 Hawthorn in Blossom, 1911
559 The Manzanares, 1908

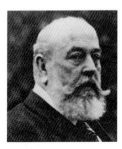

BESNARD Albert
1849 Paris – 1934 Paris
Pupil of Brémont and Cabanel. 1868

exhibited for the first time at the Salon. 1874 winner of the Rome Prize, thereafter 1874-1878 visited Italy, staying in the Villa Medici in Rome. Marriage to the daughter of the sculptor Dubray. Two-year stay in London, where he studied Reynolds, Gainsborough, Lawrence and the Pre-Raphaelites. Return to Paris. Became very quickly an immensely successful portrait painter. Took part in international exhibitions at the gallery of G. Petit. 1893 travelled in England. 1906 travelled to India. Director of the Ecole des Beaux-Arts and the Villa Medici. 1924 became the first painter accepted into the Académie Française. Successful above all in his use of pastels.
BIBLIOGRAPHY: A.B. Radierungen. Galerie zur Mühle. Moosinning/Munich 1981 (EC).– Godefroy, L.: L'œuvre gravé. Paris 1969.– Singer, H.W.: Zeichnungen von A.B. Leipzig 1913.– Coppier, A.-C.: Les Eaux-Fortes de B. Paris 1920
ILLUSTRATION:
251 Portrait of Madame Roger Jourdain, 1886

BING Siegfried (Samuel)
1838 Hamburg – 1905 Vaucresson
Gallery owner, from 1871 in Paris, where he opened a gallery for Far Eastern art, in which he was regarded as a specialist. Also gave opportunities for Impressionist, Post-Impressionist and Symbolist painters to exhibit in his gallery.

BIRGER Hugo
1854 Stockholm – 1887 Helsingborg
1871-1877 studied at the Academy of Art in Stockholm. In 1877 moved to Paris. 1879-1881 shared a studio with Josephson in the Rue Gabrielle. Exhibited from 1879 at the Salon. 1881-1885 travelled in Spain and Morocco; these experiences were transformed into the light-filled atmosphere of his paintings. Executed numerous works in a style accessible to popular taste.
BIBLIOGRAPHY: Strömborn, S.: H.B. Stockholm 1944
ILLUSTRATION:
483 Scandinavian Artists Breakfasting at the Café Ledoyen, Paris, on Salon Opening Day, 1886

BLANC Charles
1813 Castres – 1882 Paris
Influential art critic and art historian,

brother of the Socialist historian and politician Louis Blanc. 1849-1876 wrote a "Histoire des peintres de toutes les écoles" in 14 volumes and founded, in 1859, the "Gazette des Beaux-Arts". 1848 appointed Director of the Académie des Beaux-Arts; President again 1872-1874. 1878 Professor of aesthetics at the Collège de France. His theories of colour influenced the Neo-Impressionists.

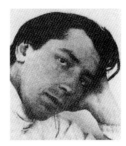

BOCCIONI Umberto
1882 Reggio di Calabria – 1916 Verona
1898-1902 studied in Rome, where he met Gino Severini and Balla. Became acquainted with the painting techniques of Divisionism but developed Neo-Impressionism further and became the leading exponent of Italian Futurism. 1902-1904 stayed in Berlin and Paris. 1907 settled in Milan. 1909 met Marinetti, with whom he composed the Futurist Manifesto in 1910.
WRITINGS, DOCUMENTS: Boccioni, U.: Gli scritti editi e inediti. Milan 1971.– Boccioni, U.: Altri inediti e apparati critici. Milan 1972
CATALOGUES: Bellini, P.: Catalogo completo dell'opera grafica di U.B. Milan 1972.– Calvesi, M. and E. Cohen: L'opera completa di B. Milan 1983.– Palzzeschi, A.: L'opera completa di B. Milan 1969.– Verzotti, G.: B., catalogo completo dei dipinti. Florence 1989
BIBLIOGRAPHY: Argan, G.C.: U.B. Rome 1953.– Birolli, Z.: U.B. Racconto critico. Turin 1983.– B. und Mailand. Kunstmuseum Hannover. Milan 1983 (EC).– B. a Milano. Palazzo Reale, Milan 1983 (EC).– B. prefunturista. Museo Nazionale, Reggio Calabria. Milan 1983 (EC).– Calvesi, M. and E. Coen: B. Milan 1983.– Coen, E. (ed.): B. A Retrospective. Metropolitan Museum of Art, New York 1988 (EC).– Grade, R.: B., il mito del moderno. Florence 1962.– Marchiori, G.: U.B. Milan 1966.– Schulz-Hoffmann, C.: U.B. Volumi orizzontali. Munich 1981
ILLUSTRATION:
550 Portrait of the Artist Adriana Bisi-Fabbri, 1907

BOCH Anna and Eugène
Anna (1848 Saint-Vaast – 1936 Ixelles); Eugène (1855 La Louvière – 1941 Monthyon). Belgian painters of

landscapes and interiors. From a respectable manufacturing family. Painted in Provence, Brittany and Holland. Anna was influenced by van Rysselberghe and Neo-Impressionism, and supported Seurat. She bought a painting from van Gogh, "The Red Vineyard", the only picture he sold in his lifetime. Eugène studied in Paris under Cormon and was friendly with Toulouse-Lautrec, Bernard and van Gogh, for whom he also posed as a model.

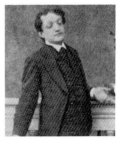

BOLDINI Giovanni
1842 Ferrara – 1931 Paris
First drawing lessons with his father Antonio Boldini, the history and portrait painter. 1862-1865 studied painting at the Academy in Florence with Enrico Pollastrini; became acquainted with the Macchiaioli circle in the Caffè Michelangiolo in Florence. One of the most enthusiastic exponents of plein-air painting. 1866 with Bonti, he travelled to Naples; 1867 trip to Paris. Met Degas again, who had been his neighbour in Florence. 1869 at the invitation of the Duke of Sutherland he went to London; great success as a portrait painter. 1872 moved to Paris; contacts with Goupil; notable successes in the Salon 1874/75. 1880 travelled in England, America, Austria and Germany. 1889 with Degas travelled in Spain. Took part in the international exhibitions at G. Petit's gallery. 1890 Co-founder of the Société Nationale des Beaux-Arts.
CATALOGUES: Camesasca, E. and C.L. Ragghianti: L'opera completa di B. Milan 1970.– Prandi, D.: G.B. L'opera incisa. Reggio Emilia 1970
BIBLIOGRAPHY: B. Musée Jacquemart-André. Paris 1963 (EC).– Cardona, C.: G.B. Genoa 1956.– Cecchi, C.: B. Rome 1962.– Dini, P.: B. Macchiaiolo. Turin 1989.– Doria, V.: B. Inedito. Bologna 1972.– Doria, V.: Il genio di B. Bologna 1988.– G.B., een Italiaan in Parijs. Haags Gemeentemuseum, The Hague 1972 (EC).– G.B. Olii, disegni, incisioni. Genoa 1987 (EC).– G.B. Palazzo della Permanente. Milan 1989 (EC).– Piceni, E. (ed.): B. e Parigi. I aquarelli e disegni. Florence 1959 (EC).– Piceni, E.: B. L'uomo e l'opera. Busto Arsizio 1981.– Sari, G.: B. a Parigi (1871-1931). Alghero 1980
ILLUSTRATION:
532 Portrait of Mlle. Lantelme, 1907

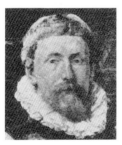

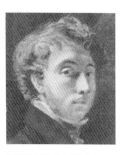

BONINGTON Richard Parkes
1802 Arnold (Nottingham) – 1828
London
1817/18 moved with his family to Calais. Encouraged to take up plein-air painting by the water-colourist Louis Francia. 1818 moved to Paris, met Delacroix. 1821/22 studied at the School of Art with A. Gros and began to paint landscapes and city views on the Seine and on the coast, as well as genre and literary scenes. In 1824 he won the gold medal at the Paris Salon for paintings which, by their fresh colours and sketchy character, contributed to the influence of English painting on French art. 1825 with Delacroix in London. In 1826 went to Venice and other Italian towns. His perception of nature and his style of painting stimulated the painters of the Barbizon school and also Monet (partly through the intermediary influence of E. Isabey, Eugène Boudin and Johan B. Jongkind) to take up Impressionism.
BIBLIOGRAPHY: Cormack, M.: B. Oxford 1989.– Dubuisson, C.E.H.: R.P.B. London 1924.– Ingamells, J.: R.P.B. London 1978.– Ponton, M. (ed.): B., Francia & Wyld. London 1985 (EC).– R.P.B. (1802-1828), Paul Sandby (1730-1809): Wegbereiter der Aquarellmalerei. Städtische Galerie im Prinz-Max-Palais, Karlsruhe 1989 (EC).– R.P.B. On the Pleasure of Painting. New Haven (CT) and Paris 1991 (EC).– Shirley, A.: B. London 1940
ILLUSTRATION:
19 Water Basin at Versailles, c. 1826

BONNARD Pierre
1867 Fontenay-aux-Roses (Seine) –
1947 Le Cannet (Alpes-Maritimes)
1886-1889 studied law in Paris. 1888/89 also studied painting at the Paris art college and at the private Académie Julian. Friendly with Denis, Vuillard and Sérusier, who exposed him to Gauguin's conception of art. Studied Japanese coloured woodcuts. 1889 sold a new style of poster design ("France-Champagne"). 1890 after a short period in military service, he shared a studio with Denis and Vuillard. Co-founder of the Nabis, a Symbolist group of artists. Exhibited 1891-1905 with the Indépendants. Brought out his first poster, became acquainted with Toulouse-Lautrec. 1893 lithographs in "La Revue Blanche". Became friends with its editor, T. Natanson. 1895 Vollard began to

publish his lithographs and book illustrations, which are partly influenced by Redon. He painted scenes of gardens and Paris streets, Impressionist in their composition and brushwork, and close to Degas. 1896 exhibited for the first time in his own at Durand-Ruel. Painted the stage decor for Lugné-Poe's theatre. His style developed into an independent, light-filled Impressionism, which he used for intimate interior scenes (female nudes) and garden scenes. Exhibited 1903 for the first time at the new Autumn Salon. 1906 taught at the Académie Ranson. Used similar motifs to Renoir. 1905 travelled in Spain with Vuillard, and in the following years to Belgium, Holland, England, Italy, Algeria and Tunisia. 1909 in Southern France for the first time. 1912 bought a house in Vernonnet near Giverny. 1913 with Vuillard in Hamburg. 1914-1918 mostly in Saint-Germain-en-Laye. 1918 with Renoir Honorary President of the group "Young French Painting". In 1925 he bought a house at Le Cannet near Cannes. 1926 travelled in the USA. In later years mostly in Le Cannet; until his death he painted landscapes, views from windows, still lifes and nudes in a Fauvist-inspired Impressionist style.

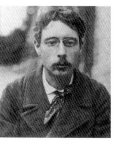

WRITINGS, DOCUMENTS: Clair, J. and A. Terrasse (eds.): B.-Matisse. Correspondance. 1925-1946. Paris 1991
CATALOGUES: Bouret, F.: P.B. L'œuvre gravé. Catalogue complet. Paris and London 1981.– Bouvenne, A.: Catalogue de l'œuvre gravé et lithographié de R.P.B. Paris 1873.– Curtis, A.: Catalogue de l'œuvre lithographié et gravé de R.P.B. London and Paris 1939.– Dauberville, J. and H.: B. Catalogue raisonné de l'œuvre peint. 4 vols. Paris 1966-1974.– Roger-Marx, C.: B. lithographie. Monte Carlo 1958
BIBLIOGRAPHY: Beer, F.J.: P.B. Marseilles 1947.– Cogniat, R.: B. Paris 1989.– Ives, C. et al. (eds.): P.B. The Graphic Art. New York 1989 (EC).– Dubuisson, A. and C.E. Hughes: R.P.B. London 1924.– Gobin, M.: R.P.B. Paris 1950.– Jedlicka, G.: P.B., ein Besuch. Zurich 1949.– Mann, S.: B. Drawings. London 1991.– Natanson, T.: Le B. que je propose. Geneva 1951.– P.B. Kunstmuseum, Basle 1955 (EC).– P.B. Kunsthaus Zürich; Städtische Galerie im Städelsches

Kunstinstitut, Frankfurt am Main; Zurich 1985 (EC).– Raynal, M.: Histoire de la peinture moderne. De Baudelaire à Bonnard. Geneva 1949.– Rewald, J.: P.B. New York 1948.– Rumpel, H.: B. Berne 1952.– Shirley, A.: B. London 1940.– Stokes, H.: Girtin and B. London 1922.– Terrasse, A.: P.B. Paris 1967.– Terrasse, A.: P.B. Leben und Werk. Cologne 1989.– Vaillant, A.: B. ou le Bonheur de Voir. Neuchâtel 1965
ILLUSTRATION:
340 Twilight or The Game of Croquet, 1892

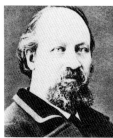

BOUDIN Eugène-Louis
1824 Honfleur – 1898 Deauville
Settled in Le Havre in 1835, where he was an apprentice to a printer. In 1838 he opened an art framer's shop, in which he exhibited paintings by Couture, Millet, Troyon and others. Soon gave up the shop, to dedicate himself wholeheartedly to painting. 1847 travelled to Paris, 1848 visited northern France and Flansers. In 1850 he exhibited two pictures at the Société des amis des arts du Havre, after which the town gave him a scholarship to study at the Ecole des Beaux-Arts in Paris 1851-1853.1855 returned to Honfleur, travelled along the coast. Throughout his life he remained faithful to the Corot tradition and plein-air painting, especially the play of light on water and atmospheric cloud studies. His pastels – exhibited at the Salon in 1859 – were greatly admired by Baudelaire. In 1858 he met Monet and encouraged an equal enthusiasm for plein-air painting. In 1859 he met Courbet and Baudelaire. From 1862 he began to spend holidays at Trouville, where the beach life provided many models. In 1868 he was commissioned to execute a decorative painting for the Château de Bourdainville. During his stay in Brussels 1870/71, new motifs (market scenes) led to a more generous brushwork. Met Durand-Ruel there. 1874 visited Bordeaux, 1876 Rotterdam and 1884 Dordrecht. Showed in the 1st Impressionist exhibition 1874, after which he had considerable success at the Salon. 1889 received the gold medal at the General Exhibition. Based at his home in Deauville, he made various trips to Venice, the Côte d'Azur and elsewhere, which enriched his use of

colour. His pictures of the sea made him one of the forerunners of the Impressionists.
WRITINGS, DOCUMENTS: Knyff, G. de: E.B. raconté par lui-même: Sa vie, son atelier, son œuvre. Paris 1976
CATALOGUE: Schmit, R.: E.B. 1824-1898. Catalogue raisonné. 4 vols. Paris 1973-1984
BIBLIOGRAPHY: Alexandre, A.: L'œuvre d'E.B. Paris 1899.– Benjamin, L.R.: E.B. New York 1937.– Cahen, C.: E.B.: Sa vie, son œuvre. Paris 1900.– Carlo, L.: E.B. Paris 1928.– E.B. Marlborough Fine Art Ltd., London 1958 (EC).– E.B. Kunsthalle, Bremen 1979 (EC).– E.B. in Bretagne. Musée de Rennes. Rennes 1964 (EC).– E.B. 1824-1989. Musée E.B. Honfleur 1992 (EC).– Jean-Aubry, G.: E.B. London 1969.– Jean-Aubry, G. and R. Schmit: E.B. La vie et l'œuvre d'après les lettres et documents inédits. Neuchâtel 1968, 1977.– Les Boudins du Musée Municipal de Honfleur. Honfleur 1956 (EC).– Roger-Marx, C.: E.B. Paris 1927.– Selz, J.: B. Paris 1982
ILLUSTRATIONS:
35 Beach Scene, Trouville, 1863
35 Beach Scene, Trouville, 1864
354 Sailing Ships at Deauville, c. 1895/96

BOUGIVAL
Village 10 miles from Paris in a valley south of the Seine, in extremely attractive and varied landscape, which attracted large numbers of artists in the mid-19th century. Monet stayed here before 1870, and Renoir, Pissarro and Sisley all worked here. Bougival.became famous for the pictures of the "Grenouillère" (Frog Island) which Monet and Renoir painted on the same day in 1869 (pp. 72, 73). Most of the pictures from this area were painted by Sisley, who lived from 1870 to 1877 in the nearby villages of Louveciennes and Marly. Between 1881 and 1884 Morisot lived in Bougival with her family.

BOUGUEREAU William-Adolphe
1825 La Rochelle – 1905 La Rochelle
1846-1850 after attending the School of Art in Bordeaux, he studied at the studio of F. Picot and at the College of Art in Paris. 1850-1854 won the Rome Prize and went to Italy. His participation at the Paris World Fair in 1855 founded his fame and led to commissions that included wall paintings in a graphically exact but idealised late Classical or Neo-Renaissance style. 1875 Professor at the Paris College of Art, later also at the Académie Julian. 1876 member of the

Academy. His Catholic faith was the main principle behind his anti-materialist traditionalism, which meant he also fought against Impressionism; he nevertheless did not flinch from using popular (or even sexual) effects to please his audience. Like Cabanel, he was despised by the Impressionists.

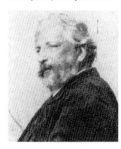

BIBLIOGRAPHY: Isaacson, R.: W.-A.B. Cultural Center, New York 1974 (EC).– Vachon, M.: W.-A.B. Paris 1900.– W.-A.B. Musée du Petit Palais, Paris; Musée des Beaux-Arts, Montreal; The Wadsworth Atheneum, Hartford (CT). Paris 1984 (EC)
ILLUSTRATIONS:
188 The Birth of Venus, 1879
188 Bathers, 1884

BOULOGNE-SUR-MER
Resort and port at the mouth of the Liane on the Channel. **1864** and **1869** a motif for Manet ("The Departure of the Folkstone Boat", p. 77) and Degas ("At the Beach", p. 130).

BOUSSOD ET VALADON, Galerie
Etienne Boussod and Pierre Valadon owned a sumptuous gallery on the Place de l'Opéra in Paris with a branch on the Boulevard Montmartre. They mainly sold Salon paintings. In the 1880s they dealt a great deal in works of the Impressionists (Monet, Sisley, Renoir and Pissarro), after Theo van Gogh had taken over the Montmartre branch in 1879.

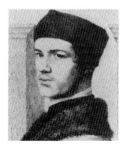

BRACQUEMOND Félix
1833 Paris – 1914 Paris
Real name: Joseph Auguste Bracquemond. Worked first as a circus rider then in a lithographer's workshop.

Gained his artistic training with the painter Joseph Guichard. **1852** exhibited for the first time at the Salon. In **1869** he married the painter Marie Bracquemond, née Quivoran. Neglected painting in favour of graphic art. One of the first to discover the artistic beauty of Japanese wood cuts. Frequented the Café Guerbois and the Café de la Nouvelle-Athènes; his friends included Degas, Manet, Fantin-Latour and Whistler. **1862** Co-founder of the Société des aquafortistes. Became known for his portraits and landscapes as well as his prints of Old Masters. **1872-1879** art manager at the Paris studio of the Limoges porcelain manufacturer Haviland. Participated in the 1st, 4th and 5th Impressionist exhibitions. **1885** published his book "Du dessin et de la couleur". In **1900** he won the Grand Prix de Gravure at the Paris World Fair.
WRITINGS, DOCUMENTS: Bouillon, J.-P.: La correspondance de F.B. In: "Gazette des Beaux-Arts" 82 (December 1973), pp. 351-386.– Bracquemond, F.: Du dessin et de la couleur. Paris 1885.– Bracquemond, F.: Etude sur la gravure et la lithographie. Paris 1897
CATALOGUE: Bouillon, J.-P.: F.B. Le réalisme absolu. Œuvre gravé 1849-1859. Catalogue raisonné. Geneva 1987
BIBLIOGRAPHY: Bouillon, J.-P.: F. et Marie Bracquemond. Mortagne and Chartres 1972 (EC).– F.B. and the etching process. The College of Wooster Art Center Museum, Wooster 1974 (EC)
ILLUSTRATION:
208 Portrait of Edmond de Goncourt, 1880

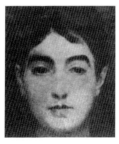

BRACQUEMOND Marie
1841 Morlaix (Finistère) – 1916 Sèvres
Née Quivoron. Grew up in Etampes. Studied at the Ingres studio. Her favourite themes were landscapes, still lifes and interiors; created wall decorations and designs for ceramics. In **1869** she married the graphic artist F. Bracquemond. Taught drawing at a school. **1874** exhibited for the first time at the Salon. **1876** participated at the Exposition de l'Union centrale des arts décoratifs. Exhibited in 1879 at the 4th and in 1880 at the 5th Impressionist exhibitions. With Morisot, Gonzalès and Cassatt she was one of

the greatest female representatives of Impressionism.
BIBLIOGRAPHY: Bouillon, J.-P.: Félix et M.B. Mortagne and Chartres 1972 (EC).– Geffroy, G.: M.B. [no place or date of publication].
ILLUSTRATIONS:
194 Tea Time (Portrait of Louise Quivoron), 1880
194 On the Terrace at Sèvres, 1880
198 The Lady in White, 1880

BRANDON Edouard Emile Pereyra
1831 Paris – 1897 Paris
French painter, graphic artist and art collector. **1849** studied at the Paris College of Art, influenced by Corot. **1856-1863** lived in Rome, where he became friends with Degas. **1861** exhibited for the first time at the Salon. Painted realistic scenes from Jewish life with attentive observation of light phenomena. **1874** took part in the 1st Impressionist exhibition at the invitation of Degas (he owned several paintings by Degas).

BRECK John Leslie
1860 (at sea, near the island of Guam) – 1899 Boston
Son of a naval officer in the service of the East India Society. **1878-1881** moved first to Leipzig, then Munich. Studied there under Sträbhofer at the Academy of Art. **1882** trip to Antwerp, studied under Charles Verlat. **1883** return to America; lived until **1886** in Boston. **1887** moved back to Paris, attending the Académie Julian and painting with Metcalf, Robinson and Bruce in Giverny. Exhibited **1887-1889** in L.C. Perry's studio in Boston. **1889** successful participation at the Paris Salon. **1890** return to Boston, where he exhibited regularly at the St. Botolph Club. **1891/92** travelled in California and England (Kent), contributing to the exhibition at the New English Art Club. **1892-1899** lived in Boston.
BIBLIOGRAPHY: Kimball, B. (ed.): Memorial Exhibition of Paintings by J.L.B. St. Botolph Club, Boston; National Arts Club, New York 1899
ILLUSTRATION:
611 Garden at Giverny, c. 1890

BREITNER George Hendrik
1857 Rotterdam – 1923 Amsterdam
Despite his great talent for drawing, he was apprenticed to a merchant **1871-1874**. **1875-1877** studied art at the Academy in The Hague under J.P. Koelman. Painted histories in the style of Charles Rochussen, but with grater emphasis on the aesthetic effects of colour. **1878/79** taught drawing at evening classes in Leyden. **1880** lessons with the landscape painter W. Maris at the Academy; improved his technique by copying Old Masters (J. Steen, F. Hals and H. Holbein). Became interested in plein-air painting. Became a member of the artists' association Pulchri Studio and worked with others at the Panorama Mesdag. Friends with the Maris brothers; worked for periods at the studio of Willem Mesdag. **1882** taught drawing in the lowest class of the Academy at Rotterdam. Met van Gogh. In **1884** he went to Paris; met Toulouse-Lau-

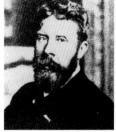

trec and Bernard at the Cormon studio. **1886** settled in Amsterdam. Taught drawing and painting at the Academy near Allebé. Painted urban life in a lively manner with naturalistic perspicacity and delicate colouring. He later reduced his palette to black, white, ochre and brown. **1903-1905** lived in Aerdenhout near Haarlem. Several trips, including Berlin, London, Ghent, Norway and in **1908** Pittsburgh. Beside van Gogh one of the most important Dutch painters of the nineteenth century.

WRITINGS, DOCUMENTS: Hefting, P.H. (ed.): G.H.B. Brieven aan A.P. van Stolk. Utrecht 1970
BIBLIOGRAPHY: Baard, C.W.H.: B. Stedelijk Museum, Amsterdam 1933 (EC).– Centenaire de G.H.B. Institut Néerlandais, Paris 1957 (EC).– G.H.B. Gemälde, Zeichnungen, Fotografien. Rheinisches Landesmuseum Bonn. Cologne 1977 (EC).– Hammacher, A.M. (ed.): B. Museum Boymans-van Beuningen, Rotterdam 1954 (EC).– Hefting, P.H. et al. (eds.): B. als fotograaf. Rotterdam 1956.– Hefting, P.H.: B. Amsterdam 1968.– Hefting, P.H.: B. in zijn Haagse tijd. Utrecht 1970.– Hefting, P.: De foto's van Breitner. The Hague 1989.– Pit, A., W. Steenhoff, J. Veth et al.: G.H.B. Amsterdam 1908-1911.– Pols, I.V.: G.H.B. Doctoral thesis, Amsterdam 1966.– Schendel, A. v.: G.H.B. Amsterdam 1939.– Venema, A.: G.H.B. Bussum 1981.– Veth, J.: G.H.B. 1908
ILLUSTRATIONS:
407 Portrait of Mrs. Theo Frenkel-Bouwmeester, 1887
416 The Dam, c. 1891-1893
417 The Earring, c. 1893

BRETON Jules Adolphe Aimé Louis
1827 Courrières (Pas-de-Calais) – 1906 Paris
Son of a rich farmer. **1847** studied at the Ecole des Beaux-Arts in Paris, after training under G. Wappers in Antwerp. **1849** for the first time at the Salon, he exhibited some paintings of urban poverty. In **1853** he began his portrayals of peasant life, which were to bring him increasing success, for in contrast to Courbet's Realism his scenes of peasant girls gleaning corn reveal, through their noble, almost Classical postures and forms, a "profound feeling for the beauty of the countryside" (Gautier).

1886 Member of the Academy. Also wrote art criticism, memoirs and poetry.
BIBLIOGRAPHY: J.B. and the French Rural Tradition. Joslyn Art Museum, Omaha (NE); Dixon Gallery, Memphis (TN); Clark Institute, Williamstown (MA). Omaha 1982 (EC)

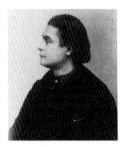

BRUANT Aristide
1851 Courtenay – 1925 Paris
Singer and poet. His cabaret "Le Mirliton" opened in Paris in 1885 and became the meeting place of painters, poets and actors. Two volumes of his chansons were published 1889-1895 with illustrations by Steinlen. Close friends with Toulouse-Lautrec. In 1895 he moved back to Courtenay.

BRUCE William Blair
1859 Hamilton (Ontario) – 1906 Stockholm
After his training at the Academy of Art in Hamilton, he studied in Paris under R. Fleury and Bouguereau. Influenced by Whistler and Cazin. As a plein-air painter, he was fond of beach and harbour motifs. 1888 married the Swedish sculptor Karoline Benedicks-Bruce. Lived in Paris. Spent his last years in Stockholm.
WRITINGS, DOCUMENTS: Murray, J. (ed.): Letters Home: 1859-1906. The Letters of W.B.B. Ontario 1982
ILLUSTRATION:
607 Landscape with Poppies, 1887

BRUYAS Alfred
1821 Montpellier – 1877 Montpellier
Art collector and mason with a remarkable influence on the Impressionists. Known mainly for his support of Courbet. Won over Gachet to contemporary art and was friendly with the parents of Bazilles. He bequeathed his collection to the Musée Fabre in Montpellier.

BUNKER Dennis Miller
1861 New York – 1890 Boston
Pupil of Chase at the National Academy of Design in New York. 1882-1885 studied with Hébert at the Académie Julian and with Gérôme at the Ecole des Beaux-Arts. Influenced by Manet. From 1880 he exhibited at the National Academy of Design. Taught at the Cowles Art School in Boston. 1887 met Sargent. In his last years he developed an increasingly Impressionistic style.

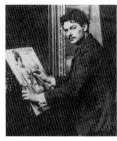

BIBLIOGRAPHY: D.M.B. A Supplementary Group of Paintings and Water Colors Including Some Early Works. Museum of Fine Arts, Boston 1945 (EC).– Ferguson, C.B. (ed.): D.M.B. (1861-1890) Rediscovered. New Britain Museum of American Art, New Britain (CT) 1978 (EC).– Gammell, R.H.I. (ed.): D.M.B. Museum of Fine Arts, Boston 1943 (EC).– Gammell, R.H.I.: D.M.B. New York 1953
ILLUSTRATION:
610 The Pool, Medfield, 1889

BUREAU Pierre-Isidor
1827 Paris – 1880 Paris
Trained as a graphic artist and landscape painter with Jules Dupré. Friendly with Ribot and Boudin. 1865-1876 exhibited landscapes at the Salon. 1873 took part in the Salon des Refusés. In 1874 and 1876 he exhibited work at the 1st and 2nd Impressionist exhibitions.
ILLUSTRATION:
55 Moonlight at L'Isle-Adam, 1867

BÜRGER Wilhelm → Thoré
Théophile

BURTY Philippe
1830 Paris –1890 Parays-par-Astaffort
Art critic, writer and collector. A great supporter of Impressionism, which he admired as a new form of Realism and defended with sensitivity and perspicacity. He particularly favoured Manet, Degas and Renoir. As early as 1874 in his article on the 1st Impressionist exhibition for "La République Française" he recognized the epoch-making importance of the movement. In 1881 he was appointed Inspector of Fine Arts.

CABANEL Alexandre
1823 Paris – 1889 Paris
1840-1845 studied under F. Picot at the Paris Ecole des Beaux-Arts. In 1845 he won the Rome Prize and went to Italy. In 1855 at the Paris World Fair he won the first of his many decorations. 1863 member of the Academy and Professor at the College of Art with an especially large number of students. Served frequently on the Salon jury. He produced precisely drawn, impressive mythological nudes, often in a Neo-Rococo style, and painted portraits and sentimental genre scenes; he was one of the main exponents of the main-

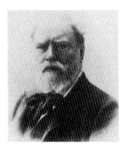

stream of painting in the 2nd Empire and 3rd Republic. Favourite painter of Napoleon III., for paintings like "The Birth of Venus" (p. 36) he was despised by the Impressionists, as also was Bouguereau.

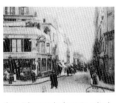

BIBLIOGRAPHY: Dessins d'A.C. 1823-1889. Musée Fabre, Montpellier 1989 (EC)
ILLUSTRATION:
36   The Birth of Venus, 1863

CABARET DE LA MERE ANTHONY
Artists' rendezvous in Marlotte near Fontainebleau, especially in the 1860s. Courbet, Pissarro, Sisley and Monet exhibited their caricatures here. It was the subject of Renoir's painting "The Inn of Mère Anthony" (Stockholm, Nationalmuseum).

CAFE DE LA NOUVELLE-ATHENES
Situated in Montmartre near the Place Pigalle, it was a well- known meeting place for dissidents during the time of Napoleon III; Courbet and Castagnary were also customers. From about 1870, after the Café Guerbois had become too loud for

them, it became the favourite café of the Impressionists. Customers included the artists Manet, Renoir, Degas, Gauguin, Pissarro, Desboutin, Stevens, Forain, Raffaëlli, Zandomeneghi and Caillebotte and the writers Burty, Duranty, Zola, Alexis, Moore and Duret. It was there that Degas painted his picture "The Absinth Drinker", using Desboutin and Ellen Andrée as models (p. 164).

CAFE DES AMBASSADEURS
Popular café-concert, in the gardens of the Champs-Elysées in Paris. Famous singers performed here. In several paintings and lithographs,

Manet, Degas and Henri de Toulouse-Lautrec have left impressions of this café.

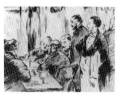

CAFE GUERBOIS
Situated in the Rue des Batignolles 11 (later: Avenue de Clichy), an area in which many artists owned studios. Manet first visited the café in 1866, and soon afterwards it became a favourite meeting place for his friends: Duranty, Duret, Nadar, Silvestre, Zola, Bazille, Degas, Monet, F. Bracquemond, Renoir and Stevens. They were occasionally joined by Pissarro, Cézanne and Sisley for discussion evenings that usually took place on Thursdays. Shortly after the 1st Impressionist exhibition, the artists decided it was too loud for them and changed to the Café de la Nouvelle-Athènes. Zola depicts the atmosphere very nicely in his novel "L'Œuvre".

CAFES-CONCERT
From 1830 there arose in Paris a type of café with varied entertainment. Some of these, such as the Folies-Bergère, are still famous even today. The cafés-concert were at their most popular at the end of the 19th century. For the Impressionists they were centres of that modern life which they aimed to capture in their pictures.

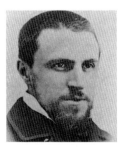

CAILLEBOTTE Gustave
1848 Paris – 1894 Gennevilliers
Son of a middle-class family; in 1887 he inherited his father's fortune and became financially independent for the rest of his life. In 1870 he graduated in law. 1870/71 took part in the defence of Paris during the Franco-Prussian War. 1872 travelled in Italy. 1873 was accepted at the Ecole des Beaux-Arts in Paris; worked irregularly at Bonnat's studio; first contacts with the Impressionists; met Monet; in his style of painting he was chiefly

influenced by Degas. In **1875** he painted his famous picture "The Floor Strippers" (p. 131). His most important subjects were motifs from his immediate surroundings: family, street scenes and working life and scenes from his summer visits to Yerres, especially boat parties. In **1876** he exhibited for the first time at the (2nd) Impressionist exhibition. Helped organise and finance the 3rd, 4th, 5th and 7th exhibitions, where he also exhibited his own work. Became the patron of his artist colleagues Monet, Renoir, Sisley and Pissarro by supporting exhibitions, buying many of the paintings himself, including Renoir's "Le Moulin de la Galette" (p. 153) and "The Swing" (p. 144). In **1882** he retired from public life and only painted still lifes and landscapes. In **1883** he wrote his will, leaving his significant collection of paintings to the French state on the condition that 67 pictures be placed together in the Louvre. After his death from a stroke in **1894** the gift was scandalously hushed up, in particular because of the works by Cézanne. It was only in **1928** that the collection became a part of the Louvre and is now kept at the Musée d'Orsay.

CATALOGUE: Berhaut, M.: G.C., sa vie et son œuvre. Catalogue raisonné des peintures et pastels. Paris 1978
BIBLIOGRAPHY: Berhaut, M.: G.C. Paris 1951.– Maillet, E. (ed.): G.C., 1848-1894. Musée Pissarro, Pontoise 1984 (EC).– Varnedoe, J.K.T.: C.'s Pont de l'Europe: A New Slant. In: "Art International" 18 (1974), No. 4, pp. 28-59.– Varnedoe, J.K.T. and T.P. Lee (eds.): G.C. A Retrospective Exhibition. The Museum of Fine Arts, Houston; Brooklyn Museum, New York. Houston 1976 (EC).– Varnedoe, J.K.T.: G.C. New Haven (CT) and London 1987.– Wildenstein, G. (ed.): G.C. London 1964.– Wittmer, P.: C. au jardin. La période d'Yerres (1860-1879). Saint-Rémy-en-l'Eau 1990
ILLUSTRATIONS:
131 The Floor Strippers, 1875
158 Riverbank in Morning Haze, 1875
168 Le pont de l'Europe, 1877
169 Paris, the Place de l'Europe on a Rainy Day, 1877
182 Snow-covered Roofs in Paris, 1878
184 Bathers about to Dive into the Yerres, 1878
184 Canoeing, 1878
185 Canoeing on the Yerres, 1877
201 Square at Argenteuil, 1883
201 Farmhouse at Trouville, 1882
208 Still Life: Chickens, Pheasants and Hares, 1882
209 In a Café, 1880
228 The Pink Villa, Trouville, 1884
229 The Harbour at Argenteuil, 1882
244 The Bridge at Argenteuil and the Seine, 1885
316 Boats on the Seine at Argenteuil, 1892
317 Sailing Boats at Argenteuil, c. 1888

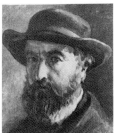

CALS Adolphe-Félix
1810 Paris – 1880 Honfleur
Son of a simple labourer in Paris. 1822 was apprenticed to the engraver Anselin; 1823-1826 apprenticeship with the engraver's firm Pons and Bosq; drawing and modelling lessons. At the same time he studied for one and a half years with Léon Cogniet at the Ecole des Beaux-Arts. Made study trips in the French countryside (Berry, Auvergne). 1835-1848 exhibited in the Salon, but without receiving attention or acclaim. Lived for ten years in various provincial towns. 1858-1869 lived on the Arrouy estate of his patron, Count Doria, and met the art dealer Martin, both of whom supported him. Had exhibitions in 1863 at the Salon des Refusés and in 1865 again at the Salon. In 1864 he painted at Saint-Valéry-en-Caux and in 1869 at Elbeuf-en-Bray. In 1873 he bought a house at Honfleur. 1874 through the intercession of Monet, he exhibited with the later Impressionists at Nadar's. 1876, 1877 and 1879 took part in the 2nd, 3rd and 4th Impressionist exhibitions. Painted melancholy landscapes with stark contrasts of dark and light, and oppressive genre scenes of poverty, fishing communities and the life of workers.
BIBLIOGRAPHY: A.-F.C. 1810-1880. Musée Eugène-Boudin, Honfleur; Musée de Vieux-Lisieux; Musée d'Art et d'Archéologie, Eté, Honfleur 1990 (EC). – Delestre, F.: C. Paris 1975
ILLUSTRATIONS:
124 Luncheon at Honfleur, 1875
124 Woman and Child in the Orchard, 1875
125 Fisherman, 1874

CAMOIN Charles
1879 Marseilles – 1965 Paris
1896 moved to Paris and became the pupil of Gustave Moreau at the Ecole des Beaux-Arts. His fellow students were Rouault, Matisse and Marquet. 1902 travelled in southern France; met Paul Cézanne. 1905 exhibited at the Salon des Indépendants. 1912 travelled through Morocco with Henri Matisse and Marquet. His nudes and landscapes – especially the Côte d'Azur – are influenced less by the Fauves than by Pierre-Auguste Renoir, whom he met during the First World War.

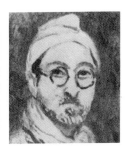

BIBLIOGRAPHY: C.C. Musée des Beaux-Arts, Marseilles 1966 (EC).– Giraudy, D.: C., sa vie, son œuvre. Marseilles 1972
ILLUSTRATIONS:
381 Girl with a Cat, c. 1904
387 The Market Place, Toulon, c. 1908

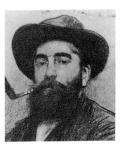

CAROLUS-DURAN Emile-Auguste
1837 Lille – 1917 Paris
Real name: Charles-Emile Auguste Durand. Son of a hotelier, trained at the school of drawing in Lille. In 1855 he moved to Paris, assumed his pseudonym and became friendly, through Zacharie Astruc, with Gustave Courbet and Manet. Attended the Académie Suisse. 1859 first contribution to the Salon. 1862-1866 in Rome with a scholarship from his home town. 1866 first award of a medal from the Salon. Travelled in Spain, admired Velázquez. 1869 began his career as a portrait painter. 1890 co-founder of the Société Nationale des Beaux-Arts and 1899 its President. 1904 joined the Academy. 1904-1913 Director of the French Academy in Rome.
CATALOGUE: Carolus-Duran, J.: C.E. C.-D. Catalogue raisonné (in preparation)
ILLUSTRATIONS:
82 Lady with Glove (Madame Pauline Carolus-Duran), 1869

CASAS Ramón
1866 Barcelona – 1932 Paris
Early training at the Vincens Academy in Barcelona. 1882 studied in Paris under Carolus-Duran. 1883 first exhibition at the Salon. Lived alternately in Paris and Barcelona.

Travelled extensively in the USA, France, Belgium, Italy, Holland and Germany. Worked as an illustrator and designer of posters for the journals Pèl y Ploma and Forma. His portraits and city scenes were influenced by Impressionism. He became an advocate of the avant-garde and a catalyst for the development of modern art in Spain.

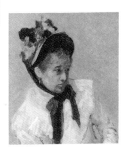

BIBLIOGRAPHY: Ainaud de Lasarte, J.: R.C. Exposición Nacional de Bellas Artes. Madrid 1968 (EC).– Artís A.A.: Retrats de R.C. Barcelona 1970.– Fontebona, R.: R.C. Barcelona 1979, 1982.– Jordi, F.: R.C. pintor. Barcelona 1949.– Rafols, J.F.: R.C., dibujante. Barcelona [no date; post- 1948].– Rafols, J.F.: R.C., pintor. Barcelona 1949
ILLUSTRATIONS:
566 Out of Doors, c. 1890/91

CASSATT Mary Stevenson
1845 Allegheny City (PA) – 1926 Mesnil-Théribus (near Beauvais)
Daughter of a banker; 1851 moved with the family to Paris. 1853-1855 lived in Heidelberg and Darmstadt. 1855 returned to Pennsylvania. Studied 1861-1865 at the Pennsylvania Academy of Fine Arts in Philadelphia. 1866 studied for a short period in the studio of Charles Chaplin in Paris. Self-taught; worked together with Gérôme and Charles Bellay. 1868 exhibited for the first time in the Salon. 1870 Returned because of the Franco-Prussian War. 1871 studied for a time at the Academy Raimondi in Parma; imitated Correggio and Parmigianino, admired Velázquez and Rembrandt. Exhibited 1872 and 1874 in the

Salon. 1873 travelled to Madrid, Seville, Belgium and the Netherlands; copied Velázquez. She finally settled in Paris. In 1877 she met Degas, who advised her to join the Impressionists. Degas and Renoir greatly influenced her style of painting. Her favourite themes are portraits of women and children. From 1890 she also produced prints. Took part in the 4th, 5th, 6th and 8th Impressionist exhibitions. 1891 her first solo show at the Durand-Ruel gallery. 1892 Commissioned to do a mural for the World Fair in Chicago. Spent the summer months at the Château de Beaufresne. 1893 exhibited her work in Paris, 1895 in New York at Durand-Ruel. 1898 travelled in the USA. In 1901 she visited Italy and Spain. 1904 accepted into the Legion of Honour. 1908 last trip to the USA. 1910-1912 travelled extensively in Europe and the Middle East. 1910 became a member of the National Academy of Design in New York. 1914 own exhibition at Durand-Ruel in Paris and award of a gold medal at the Pennsylvania Academy of Art. Her failing eyesight forced her to give up painting. Improved the reception of Impressionist painting in America through her advice and influence on American collectors, including the Havemeyers.
WRITINGS, DOCUMENTS: Mathews, N. (ed.): C. and her Circle: Selected Letters. New York 1984
CATALOGUES: Breeskin, A.D.: M.C. A Catalogue Raisonné of the Oils, Pastels, Watercolors, and Drawings. Washington 1970.– Dohme-Breeskin, A.D.: The Graphic Work of M.C. New York 1948, Washington 1979
BIBLIOGRAPHY: Breeskin, A.D.: The Paintings of M.C. New York 1966.– Breeskin, A.D. (ed.): The Art of M.C. (1844-1926). Isetan Museum of Art (Tokyo) et al., Tokyo 1981 (EC).– Bruening, M.: M.C. New York 1944.– Bullard, E.J.: M.C., Oils and Pastels. New York 1972.– Carson, J.M.H.: M.C. New York 1966.– Getlein, F.: M.C.: Paintings and Pastels. New York 1980.– Getline, F.: M.C. Paintings and Prints. New York 1980.– Hale, N.: M.C. A Biography of a Great American Painter. Garden City (NY) 1975.– Lindsay, S.G. (ed.): M.C. and Philadelphia. Philadelphia 1985 (EC).– Love, R.H.: M.C., The Independent. Chicago 1980.– Mathews, N.: M.C. and the "Rude, Modern Madonna" of the Nineteenth Century. Doctoral thesis, New York University. New York 1980.– Mathews, N.: M.C. New York 1987.– M.C. and the American Impressionists. Dixon Gallery and Gardens, Memphis (TN) 1976 (EC).– McKown, R.: The World of M.C. New York 1972.– Meixner, L.L. (ed.): An International Episode. Millet, Monet and their North American Counterparts. Dixon Gallery and Gardens et al., Memphis 1982 (EC).– Myers E.P.: M.C. A Portrait. Chicago 1971.– Novak, B.: American Painting of the Nineteenth Century. London 1969.– Pollock, G.: M.C. New York 1979.– Segard, A.: Une peintre des en-

fants et des mères, M.C. Paris 1913.– Sweet, F.A. (ed.): Sargent, Whistler and M.C. The Art Institute of Chicago, Chicago 1954 (EC).– Sweet, F.A.: Miss M.C. Impressionist from Pennsylvania. Norman (OK) 1961.– Valerio, E.: M.C. Paris 1930.– Watson, F.: M.C. New York 1932.– Wilmerding, J. et al. (eds.): American Light. The Luminist Movement, 1850-1875. Paintings, Drawings, Photographs. National Gallery of Art, Washington 1980 (EC)
ILLUSTRATIONS:
591 Offering the Panale to the Bullfighter, 1873
591 A Woman and Child in the Driving Seat, 1879
592 Little Girl in a Blue Armchair, 1878
594 Mother about to Wash Her Sleepy Child, 1880
594 Young Woman Sewing in the Garden, c. 1880-1882
595 At the Opera, 1880
595 Reading "Le Figaro", 1883
595 Lydia Crocheting in the Garden at Marly, 1880
596 On the Meadow, 1880
600 Lydia in a Loge, Wearing a Pearl Necklace, 1879
600 Alexander J. Cassatt and his Son Robert Kelso, 1884
600 Lady at the Tea Table, 1885
601 Children on the Beach, 1884
616 Summertime, 1894
617 The Boating Party, c. 1893/94
628 Susan on a Balcony Holding a Dog, 1883
629 Young Mother Sewing, 1902
629 Reine Lefèbvre and Margot, c. 1902

CASSIRER Paul
1871 Görlitz – 1926 Berlin
Art dealer and art critic. One of the first advocates of German Impressionism, he studied art history at Munich and was involved in the founding of "Simplicissimus". In Berlin he founded a publishing house and gallery and supported the artists of the Berlin Secession. From 1902 he edited the journal "Kunst und Künstler".

CASTAGNARY Jules-Antoine
1830 Saintes – 1888 Paris
Art critic and politician, actively supported Realism and Impressionism and was friends with Courbet and Baudelaire. First used the term "Naturalists" for the painters influenced by Courbet.

CEZANNE Paul
1839 Aix-en-Provence – 1906 Aix-en-Provence
1859-1860 studied law in Aix-en-Provence, began to paint "Jas de Bouffan" at his parents' home. 1861 and 1862-1865 attended the Académie Suisse in Paris and his work imitating Old Masters in the Louvre; for a time he returned to Aix as an apprentice in his father's bank; he formed friendships with Pissarro, Bazille, Guillaumin, Monet, Renoir and Sisley; he had known Zola since his school days. 1863 exhibited in the Salon des Refusés. 1865-1870 alternated between Paris and Aix; was continually

rejected at the Salon. 1866 became acquainted with Manet. 1870/71 in Aix and L'Estaque; moved from predominantly fantasy depictions in coarse, mainly dark and heavy colours to painting from nature in the open air, above all landscapes and still lifes, as well as portraits. 1871-1882 mostly in Paris, occasionally in Pontoise and Auvers, where Pissarro introduced him to the Impressionist method; met Gachet and the art dealer Tanguy. Exhibited in 1874 and 1877 with the Impressionists; continued to be rejected by the Salon. 1875 met the collector Chocquet. 1881 developed a Neo-Impressionist style, but still worked "sur le motif". 1882 succeeded in having one picture accepted at the Salon "by a pupil of Guillemet". From 1882 he lived in Aix; annual visits to Paris and its environs, numerous meetings with Zola and Renoir. 1886 quarrelled with Zola over the novel "L'Œuvre"; married his mistress, Hortense Fiquet; death of his despotic father, who left him his fortune and with it financial independence. 1889 at Chocquet's instigation, he exhibited a picture at the Paris World Fair and in 1890 joined the Les Vingt group in Brussels. Visit to Switzerland; contracted diabetes.

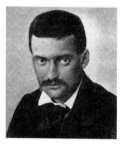

1895 the Paris art dealer Vollard gave him his first large one-man show; as part of the Caillebotte bequest, two of his paintings entered the Musée du Luxembourg. 1896 became friends with the poet Gasquet, who wrote down Cézanne's views on art; stayed at the spa in Vichy. 1897 the Berlin National Gallery was presented with one of his paintings as a gift from a collector. 1899 sale of "Jas de Bouffan"; exhibited with the Independents in Paris. 1900 exhibited in the century retrospective of French art at the Paris World Fair. 1902 built a studio at Aix; met with young artists who admired his work. 1904 his paintings were shown for the first time at the Autumn Salon in Paris; the beginning of his influence on 20th-century painting.
WRITINGS, DOCUMENTS: Bernard, E.: Souvenirs sur P.C. Paris 1921.– Bernard, E.: Sur P.C. Paris 1925.– Cézanne, P.: Correspondance. Paris 1978.– Doran, M. (ed.): Conversations avec C. Basle 1917, Zurich 1991.– Doran, M. (ed.): Conversations avec C. Paris 1978.– Gasquet, J.: C. Paris 1921.– Gasquet, J.: C. Drei Ge-

spräche. Berlin 1948.– Gasquet, J.: Joachim Gasquet's C. A Memoir with Conversation. London 1991.– Graber, H. (ed.): P.C. Nach eigenen und fremden Zeugnissen. Basle 1942.– Guillaud, J. and M.: C. in Provence. New York 1989.– Hess, W. (ed.): P.C.: Über die Kunst. Gespräche mit Gasquet, Briefe. Munich 1980.– Rewald, J. (ed.): P.C. Correspondance. Paris 1937, 1978.– Rewald, J. (ed.): P.C.: Letters. London 1941, Oxford and New York 1976.– Rewald, J. (ed.): P.C. Correspondance. New York 1984.– Rewald, J. (ed.): P.C. Briefe. Zurich 1962, 1979 (New edition: Zurich 1988).– Rivière, G.: Le maître P.C. Paris 1923.– Rilke, R.M.: Briefe über C. Wiesbaden 1952, Frankfurt am Main 1983.– Shiff, R.: C. and the End of Impressionism. Chicago 1980.– Vollard, A.: P.C. Paris 1914.– Vollard, A.: P.C. His Life and Art. New York 1926.– Vollard, A.: En écoutant parler C., Degas et Renoir. Paris 1938.– Vollard, A.: C. Gespräche und Erinnerungen. Zurich 1960
CATALOGUES: Bardazzi, F.: C. Catalogo completo dei dipinti. Florence 1993.– Chappuis, A.: Die Zeichnungen von P.C. 2 vols. Olten and Lausanne 1962.– Chappuis, A.: The Drawings of P.C. A Catalogue Raisonné. Greenwich (CT) and London 1973.– Dunlop, J.: The Complete Paintings of C. London 1972.– Gatto, A. and S. Orienti: L'opera completa di C. Milan 1970.– Orienti, S.: The Complete Paintings of C. London 1972, New York 1972.– Rewald, J.: P.C. The Watercolours. A Catalogue Raisonné. Boston and London 1984.– Rewald, J.: Les aquarelles de C. Catalogue raisonné. Paris 1984.– Venturi, L.: C., son art, son œuvre. 2 vols. Paris 1936 (Reprint: San Francisco 1989)
BIBLIOGRAPHY: Adriani, G.: P.C.: Zeichnungen. Cologne 1978.– Adriani, G.: P.C. Der Liebeskampf. Munich 1980.– Adriani, G.: P.C.: Aquarelle. Cologne 1981, 1982.– Badt, K.: Die Kunst C.s. Munich 1956.– Badt, K.: The Art of C. Berkeley and Los Angeles 1965, New York 1985.– Badt, K.: Das Spätwerk C.s. Constance 1971.– Barskaja, A.: P.C. Leningrad 1983.– Brion, M.: P.C. Paris 1979.– Berthold, G.: C. und die alten Meister. Stuttgart 1958.– Beucken, J. de: C., eine Bibliographie. Munich 1960.– Brion-Guerry, L.: C. et l'expression de l'espace. Paris 1950, 1966.– C.: Les dernières années (1895-1906). Grand Palais, Paris 1978 (EC).– C.: The Early Years 1859-1872. Royal Academy of Arts, London; The National Gallery of Art, Washington; London 1988 (EC).– Chappuis, A.: Album de P.C. Paris 1966.– Cherpin, J.: P.C., l'œuvre gravé. Marseilles 1973.– Cogniat, R.: C. Paris 1939.– Dorival, P.: C. Paris 1948, Hamburg 1949.– Düchting, H.: P.C. 1839-1906. Nature into Art. Cologne 1989.– Elgar, F.: C. New York 1975.– Feist, P.H.: P.C. Leipzig 1963.– Fry, R.: C. A Study of his Development. London and New York 1927.– Geist, S.: Interpreting C. Cam-

bridge (MA) and London 1988.–
Guerry, L.: C. et l'expression de l'espace. Paris 1950.– Gowing, L.: Watercolour and Pencil Drawings by C. London 1973.– Gowing, L.: P.C. The Basel Sketchbooks. New York 1988.– Guerry, L.: C. et l'expression de l'espace. Paris 1950, 1966.– Hoog, M.: L'univers de C. Paris 1971.– Hoog, M.: C. und seine Welt. Paris 1972.– Jean, R.: C., la vie, l'espace. Paris 1986.– Jedlicka, G.: C. Bern 1948.– Kendall, R. (ed.): C. by Himself. London 1988.– Kendall, R. (ed.): P.C. Leben und Werk in Briefen und Briefen. Munich 1989.– Krumring, M.L. (ed.): P.C. Die Badenden. Kunstmuseum, Basle 1989 (EC).– Lem, F.H.: Sur le chemin de la peinture de P.C. Paris 1969.– Leonhard K.: P.C. Mit Selbstzeugnissen und Bilddokumenten. Reinbek 1966.– Lévêque, J.-J.: La vie et l'œuvre de P.C. Paris 1989.– Lewis, M.T.: C.'s Early Imagery. Berkeley (CA) 1989.– Lindsay, J.: C., His Life and Art. New York 1972.– Loran, E.: C.'s Compositions: Analysis of his Form with Diagrams and Photographs of his Motifs. Berkeley 1943, 1963.– Mack, G.: La vie de P.C. Paris 1938.– Martini, A. and R. Negri: C. et le post-impressionnisme. Paris 1976.– McLeave, H.: A Man and his Mountain. The Life of C. London 1977.– Meier-Graefe, J.: P.C. Munich 1910, 1923.– Meier-Graefe, J.: C. London and New York 1927.– Meier-Graefe, J.: C. London und Kreis. Munich 1919, 1922.– Monneret, S.: C., Zola ... La fraternité du génie. Paris 1978.– Muller, J.-E.: C. Paris 1982.– Neumeyer, A.: C.'s Drawings. New York and London 1958.– Novotny, F.: C. Vienna 1937.– Novotny, F.: C. London 1961.– Novotny, F.: C. und das Ende der wissenschaftlichen Perspektive. Vienna 1938.– Perruchot, H.: La vie de C. Paris 1956.– Perruchot, H.: C. Eine Biographie. Eßlingen 1957.– Ponente, N.: P.C. Bologna 1980.– Ramus, C.: C.s Formes. Lausanne 1968.– Raynal, M.: C. Geneva, Paris and New York 1954.– Rewald, J.: C., sa vie, son art, son œuvre, son amitié pour Zola. Paris 1939.– Rewald, J.: C. et Zola. Paris 1936.– Rewald, J.: C. New York 1948.– Rewald, J.: C. Paris 1986.– Rewald, J.: C. Biographie. Cologne 1986.– Rewald, J.: C. A Biography. London and New York 1986.– Rewald, J.: P.C. Sketchbook, 1875-1885. New York 1982.– Rewald, J.: P.C.: The Watercolours. Boston and London 1983.– Rewald, J.: C. and America. Dealers, Collectors, Artists and Critics 1891-1912. London 1989.– Roberts, J.: The World View of P.C. Englewood Cliffs (NJ) 1977.– Rubin, W. et al. (eds.): C. The Late Work. 1895-1906. The Museum of Modern Art, New York 1977 (EC).– Rubin, W. et al. (eds.): C.- les dernières années 1895-1906. Grand Palais, Paris 1978 (EC).– Schiff, R.: Impressionist Criticism. Impressionist Color and C. Doctoral thesis, Yale University, New Haven (CT) 1973.– Schiff, R.: C. and the End of Impressionism. Chicago and London 1984.– Schniewind, C.O.: P.C. Sketchbook. 2

vols. New York 1951.– Shapiro, M.: P.C. Cologne 1956, 1983.– Shapiro, M.: P.C. New York 1952, 1973.– Shapiro, M.: P.C. Paris 1937.– Shapiro, M.: P.C. Paris 1973.– Sherman, H.L.: C. and Visual Form. Columbus (OH) 1952.– Siblik, J.: P.C. Prague 1969.– Taillandier, Y.: C. Paris 1977.– Tompkins Lewis, M.: C.'s Early Imagery. Berkeley, Los Angeles and London 1989.– Uschida, S.: C. Tokyo 1960.– Venturi, L.: C., son art – son œuvre. I-II, Paris 1936.– Venturi, L.: C. Geneva and New York 1978.– Wadley, N.: C. and his Art. London 1975.– Wechsler, J.: C. in Perspective. Englewood Cliffs (NJ) 1975.– Wechsler, J.: The Interpretation of C. Ann Arbor (MI) 1981
ILLUSTRATIONS:
85 The Railway Cutting, c. 1870
104 A Modern Olympia, c. 1873
105 Le déjeuner sur l'herbe, c. 1873-1875
120 View of Auvers, c. 1874
121 Six Women Bathing, c. 1874/75
196 Still Life with Fruit, 1879/80
224 The Bridge at Maincy, c. 1882-1885
225 Mont Sainte-Victoire seen from Bellevue, c. 1882-1885
308 Boy in a Red Waistcoat, c. 1888-1890
309 Still Life with Flowers and Fruit, 1888-1890
347 The Smoker, 1895-1900
348 Still Life with Onions, 1895-1900
349 Still Life with Apples and Oranges, c. 1895-1900
368 Mont Sainte-Victoire, 1904-1906
369 The Bathers, 1900-1905

CHAMPFLEURY Jules Husson
1821 Laon – 1889 Paris
Critic and writer belonging to the circle around Courbet and Baudelaire. Strong advocate of Realism in his theoretical writings "Le Realisme" 1857. His friend Murer introduced him to some of the Impressionists, whose works he collected.

CHARIGOT Aline
1859 Essoyes – 1915 Cagnes
Renoir's favourite model and from 1890 his wife. "Dance in the Country" (p. 237).

CHARLES James
1851 Warrington (near Manchester) – 1906 London
Initial training at Hatherly's School of Art in London. 1872 began his studies at the Royal Academy in London and the Académie Julian in Paris. Exponent of plein-air painting; painted atmospheric, naturalistic landscape and genre pictures. Worked mainly at his country estate of East Ashling House near Chichester; had several stays on Capri. 1875-1906 took part regularly in exhibitions at the Royal Academy; 1897-1905 exhibited occasionally at the Paris Salon.
ILLUSTRATIONS:
584 The Picnic, 1904

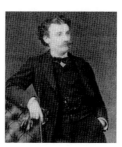

CHARPENTIER Georges
1846 Paris – 1905 Paris
Publisher and art collector. The publishing house he inherited from his father produced works by Flaubert, Maupassant and Zola. The Salon of Charpentier and his wife Marguerite became a meeting place for Naturalist poets, Impressionist painters and socialist politicians. He formed a close friendship with Renoir ("Madame Charpentier and her Children", (New York, The Metropolitan Museum of Art). They supported Renoir and other Impressionists through exhibitions in the rooms of Charpentier's journal, "La vie moderne".

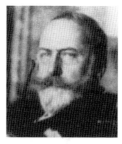

CHASE William Merrit
1849 Williamsburg (IN) – 1916 New York
1867-1869 pupil of the portrait painter Barton S. Hays. 1869-1871 studied at the National Academy of Design in New York. Received a scholarship from business people in St. Louis to travel to Europe. 1872-1876 studied with Piloty at the Munich Academy. 1877 stayed in Venice with Twachtman and Duveneck. 1878 returned to New York. Taught at the Art Students League and the Pennsylvania Academy in Philadelphia. His studio became a rendezvous for young American artists; and he gained a great reputation as a teacher. 1881 travelled to Paris, where he met Stevens. Moved away from a tonal style and turned to brighter colours and plein-air painting. Made frequent trips to Europe. In 1885 became friends with Whistler. 1891 founded the Shinnecock Summer Art School at his summer residence in Shinnecock.

1896 opened the Chase Art School in New York, later famous as the New York Art School. 1903 member of The Ten. 1908 Member of the Academy of Arts and Letters.
BIBLIOGRAPHY: Atkinson, D.S. et al. (eds.): W.M.C.: Summers at Shinnecock, 1891-1902. National Gallery of Art, Washington 1987 (EC).– C. Centennial Exhibition. John Herron Art Museum, Indianapolis 1949 (EC).– Otrange-Mastai, M.L. d' et al. (eds.): W.M.C.: A Retrospective Exposition. The Parrish Museum, Southampton (NY). New York 1957 (EC).– Pisano, R.G. (ed.): The Students of W.M.C. Heckscher Museum Huntington et al., Huntington 1973 (EC).– Pisano, R.G. (ed.): W.M.C. M. Knoedler & Co. New York 1976 (EC).– Pisano, R.G.: W.M.C. New York 1979, 1986.– Pisano, R.G. (ed.): W.M.C. in the Company of Friends. Parrish Art Museum, Southampton (NY). New York 1979 (EC).– Pisano, R.G. (ed.): A Leading Spirit in American Art: W.M.C. 1849-1916. University of Washington, Seattle 1983 (EC).– Roof, K.M.: The Life and Art of W.M.C. New York 1917 (Reprint: New York 1975).– W.M.C. 1849-1916. The Art Gallery, University of California. Santa Barbara 1964 (EC)
ILLUSTRATIONS:
604 The Open Air Breakfast, 1888
605 End of the Season, c. 1885
614 The Nursery, 1890
620 Idle Hours, c. 1894

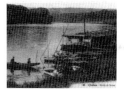

CHATOU
Village on the Seine, 9 miles from Paris. Popular for day trips from Paris and a meeting place for anglers, boating enthusiasts and artists. Renoir worked here between 1879 and 1881 ("The Luncheon of the Boating Party", p. 220) as also did Caillebotte, Monet, Sisley and Degas.

CHESNEAU Ernest
1833 Rouen – 1890 Paris
Writer and art critic. Through his friendship with Nieuwerkerke he became Inspecteur des Beaux-Arts in 1869. He was one of the first to appreciate the artistic importance of Manet, and he compared his "Luncheon on the Grass" with the paintings of Raphael.

CHEVREUL Eugène
1786 Angers – 1889 Paris
A chemist who wrote several treatises on the theory of colour, which became the theoretical basis for many 19th-century painters, from Delacroix to the Pointillists.

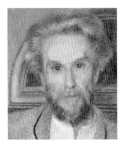

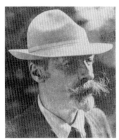

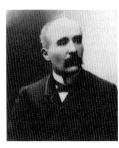

'800 italiano. Galleria Narciso. Turin 1969 (EC).– Perocco, G.: G.C. Bergamo 1958.– Pospisil, M. and F. Pospisil: G.C. Florence 1946
ILLUSTRATION:
534 Harvest, 1883

CHOCQUET Victor
1821 Lille – 1891 Paris
French art collector and civil servant at the Ministry of Finance in Paris. **1875** discovered the Impressionists, in particular Renoir, at the auction in the Hôtel Drouot. Also became a patron of Cézanne. **1876** became acquainted with Monet. Lent six Renoirs, a Monet and a Pissarro to the 2nd Impressionist exhibition. In **1877** retired in order to devote himself entirely to his passion for art. **1882** received an inheritance and in **1890** bought a large house in the Rue Monsigny. On the death of his widow in **1899** the collection was auctioned at G. Petit's for 450,000 francs.

CIARDI Guglielmo
1842 Venice – 1917 Venice
Studied at the Academy in Venice. On trips to France he came to know the Barbizon school. **1868** stayed in Florence; influenced by Signorini and the Macchiaioli group. Trip to Naples; met Domenico Morelli and Filippo Palizzi, whose combination of Romantic painting and Realism influenced him considerably. **1869** successful exhibition of light-filled atmospheric plein-air pictures in Venice, Milan and Vienna. Study tour through Italy, Germany and France. Gained a great reputation at home and abroad as a leading Venetian plein-air painter. **1894-1917** Professor of landscape painting at the Academy in Venice. **1909** one-man exhibition at the Biennale in Venice.

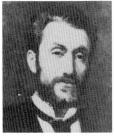

BIBLIOGRAPHY: Disegni inediti di G.C. Padua 1961 (EC).– Menegazzi, L.: G.C. La 'Da Noal, Treviso 1977 (EC).– Omaggio a G.C. Artisti del

CLAUS Emile
1849 Vijve-Saint-Eloi – 1924 Astene
1870-1874 studied at the Academy in Antwerp with the history and portrait painter N. de Keyser and the landscape painter J. Jacobs. **1879** travelled in Spain, Morocco and Algeria. His style of painting is rooted in the Belgian Realist tradition. **1882** exhibited for the first time at the Salon in Paris. **1883** moved to the Villa "Sunshine" in Astene. Spent three winters in Paris. Friendly with Le Sidaner, who introduced him to French Impressionism.He began to use a brighter palette. **1894** exhibition of Impressionist pictures in the rooms of the "Libre Esthétique". Co-founder of the Impressionist artists' association Vie et Lumière. **1914- 1918** emigrated to London; his Thames pictures reveal Divisionist influence.
BIBLIOGRAPHY: Buysse, C.: E.C., mon frère de Flandre. Ghent 1926.– G. Vogels und E.C. Zwei belgische Impressionisten. Wallraf-Richartz-Museum, Cologne 1988 (EC).– Maret, F.: E.C. Antwerp 1949.– Sauton, A.: Un prince du luminisme, E.C. Brussels 1946
ILLUSTRATIONS:
427 Sunshine, 1899
427 A Corner of my Garden, 1901

CLAUSEN George
1852 London – 1944 Cold Ash (Berkshire)
Initially active in interior decoration. He then trained at the Government Art Training School in Kensington. Influenced by the painting style of Bastien-Lepage; mostly painted scenes of country life. **1883** studied under Bouguereau at the Académie Julian in Paris. **1884** exhibited at the Royal Academy and came under severe criticism. Became an active member and co-founder of the "New English Art Club", which aimed to reform the Royal Academy. Influenced by French plein-air painting, he developed his own Impressionist-related style. **1904** Professor of art at the Royal Academy. **1902, 1904** and **1909** successful exhibitions in London.

WRITINGS, DOCUMENTS: G.C.: Six Lectures on Painting. London 1904.–
G.C.: Aims and Ideals in Art. London 1904
BIBLIOGRAPHY: McConkey, K. (ed.): Sir G.C. 1852-1944. Cartwright Hall, London 1980 (EC)
ILLUSTRATIONS:
570 The Mowers, 1892

CLEMENCEAU Georges Benjamin
1841 Moulilleron-en-Pareds (Vendée)
– 1929 Paris
French politician, journalist and art-lover. Studied medicine. Spent time in prison as an opponent of Napoleon III. **1870** began his political career as mayor of Montmartre. **1873** became acquainted with Monet. **1881** founded the newspaper "La Justice", for which G. Geffroy was the art critic. **1895** wrote about Monet's "Cathedrals". **1906-1909** and **1917-1920** President of France, presided over the Versailles peace conference. **1918** Member of the Académie Française. Arranged with Monet the bequest of the "Water Lilies" and the construction of a building to house them.

COLIN Gustave-Henri
1828 Arras – 1910 Paris
1857 exhibited for the first time at the Salon, painted landscapes and genre pictures in the style of the Barbizon school. Knew Delacroix and Corot, travelled frequently in the Basque country. **1863** exhibited at the Salon des Refusés. **1874** took part in the 1st Impressionist exhibition, then again regularly at the Salon. Castagnary admired his attention to light effects. Frequently auctioned pictures at the Hôtel Drouot and was highly esteemed by collectors like Count Doria and Rouart. From **1890** he exhibited regularly at the Société Nationale. **1901** exhibition at the G. Petit gallery.

CONSTABLE John
1776 East Bergholt, Suffolk – 1837 Hampstead, London
1795 moved to London and worked as a topographical illustrator. **1799** studied at the Royal Academy. Influenced by his preference for landscape painting of the 17th and 18th centuries. **1802** exhibited for the first time at the Academy. **1806** visited the Lake District; adopted the principle of a close study of nature. **1811** guest of the Bishop of Salisbury for the first

time. **1819** travelled to Venice and Rome, became an associate member of the Royal Academy. **1820** settled in Hampstead, in the summer mostly in Salisbury or Brighton. **1821/22** painted a series of cloud studies. **1824** gold medal at the Paris Salon; persistent influence on French painting of his view of nature and his use of simple motifs and spontaneous colours. **1827** exhibited again at the Paris Salon. **1829** member of the Royal Academy, although his nature philosophy, unliterary attitude and impressive style was fiercely debated. He made a partial concession to the Romantic search for the Sublime in his combination of landscape with important architectural monuments. **1833** first lectures on landscape painting.
WRITINGS, DOCUMENTS: Beckett, R.B. (ed.): J.C.'s Correspondence. London 1962.– Leslie, P. (ed.): Letters from J.C., R.A., to C.R. Leslie, R.A. London 1932.– Leslie, R.A., C.R.: Memoirs of the Life of J.C., R.A. London 1843 (revised edition, A. Shirley 1937; edited by J. Mayne 1946)
CATALOGUES: Catalogue of the Constable Collection in the Victoria and Albert Museum. London 1960.– Reynolds, G.: The Later Paintings and Drawings of J.C. 2 vols. New Haven (CT) and London 1984

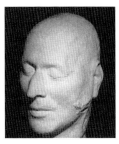

BIBLIOGRAPHY: Badt, K.: J.C.'s Clouds. London 1950.– Beckett, R.B.: J.C. and the Fishers. London 1952.– Cormack, M.: C. Oxford 1986.– Fleming-Williams, I. and L. Parris: The Discovery of C. London 1984.– Fleming-Williams, I.: C. and his Drawings. London 1990.– Hill, D.: C.'s English Landscape Scenery. London 1985.– Holmes, C.J.: C. and his Influence on Landscape Painting. London 1902.– J.C., R.A. New York 1988 (EC).– Parris, L. and I. Fleming-Williams (eds.): C. Tate Gallery, London 1991 (EC).– Reynolds, G. (ed.): J.C. Sketch-book of 1813 and 1814. 3 vols. London 1985.– Rosenthal, M.: C. London 1987
ILLUSTRATIONS:
18 Hampstead Heath, 1824
20 The Hay Wain, 1821
22 Elm Trees at Old Hall Park, East Bergholt, 1817

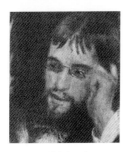

CORDEY Frédéric-Samuel
1854 Paris – 1911 Paris
Studied at the Paris College of Art,
where he protested with Franc-Lamy
about the teaching and called on
Manet – who did not respond – to
found an independent teaching studio. Financially independent, he was
able to devote his time to Impressionist landscape painting. Frequented the
Café de La Nouvelle-Athènes; met
Gachet. 1877 took part in the 3rd Impressionist exhibition. Close friends
with Murer. Painted with Cézanne
and Guillaumin in Auvers, Eragny
and Moret. 1881 with Renoir and
others he travelled in Algeria. 1913
Memorial exhibition at the Choiseul
gallery in Paris.
ILLUSTRATION:
384 Track at Auvers-sur-Oise

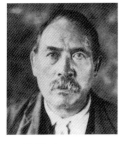

CORINTH Lovis
1858 Tapiau (East Prussia) – 1925
Zandvoort
1876-1880 studied at the Academy of
Art in Königsberg and 1880-1884 in
Munich with Defregger and Löfftz.
Came into contact with the Naturalism of the Leibl group. Classical and
academic influences from studying in
Antwerp with P.E. Gorge and 1884-
1886 at the Académie Julian with
Bouguereau and Robert-Fleury. 1887-
1891 lived in Berlin, then moved to
Munich. 1892 member of the Munich
Secession and the "Freie Vereinigung"
(Free Association). Painted plein-air
in the countryside outside Munich.
1898 spent several months in Berlin;
friends with Liebermann and Leistikow. 1901 moved to Berlin. Successful mostly as a portrait painter. Took
over Leistikow's painting school.

1903 married Charlotte Berend.
Through his contacts with Slevogt
and Liebermann he developed his Impressionist style of painting. 1911
chairman of the Berlin Secession; in
the same year he suffered a stroke.
Visited South Tirol, Rome and the
Riviera. From 1918 he lived mostly at
his country house in Urfeld am Wal-
chensee. 1918 President of the Berlin
Secession. 1925 Honorary member of
the Munich Academy.
WRITINGS, DOCUMENTS: Berend-
Corinth, L.: Mein Leben mit L.C.
Munich 1958.– L.C.: Das Erlernen
der Malerei. Berlin 1908.– L.C.: Ge-
sammelte Schriften. Berlin 1920.–
L.C.: Selbstbiographie. Leipzig 1926
CATALOGUES: Berend-Corinth, C.: Die
Gemälde von L.C. Munich 1958.–
Schwarz, K.: Das graphische Werk
von L.C. Berlin 1922 (Reprint: San
Francisco 1985)
BIBLIOGRAPHY: Berend, C.: Mein
Leben mit L.C. Hamburg 1948.– Bier-
mann, G.: L.C. Bielefeld and Leipzig
1913.– Frick, M.: L.C. Berlin 1976.–
Hahn, P.: Das literarische Figurenbild
bei L.C. Doctoral thesis, Tübingen
1970.– Imiela, H.J.: Die Bildnisse
L.C.s. Doctoral thesis, Mainz 1956.–
Keller, H.: L.C. Walchensee. Munich
and Zurich 1976.– L.C. 1858-1925.
Gemälde und Druckgraphik. Städtische Galerie im Lenbachhaus, Munich 1975 (EC).– Müller, H.: Die
späte Graphik von L.C. Hamburg
1960.– Osten, G.v.d.: L.C. Munich
1950.– Röthel, H.K.: L.C. Zur Feier
seines 100. Geburtstages. Munich
1958 (EC).– Schröder, K.A. (ed.):
L.C. Kunstforum, Vienna; Niedersächsisches Landesmuseum, Hannover.
Munich 1992 (EC).– Uhr, H.: L.C.
Berkeley 1990.– Zdenek, F. (ed.): L.C.
(1858-1925). Museum Folkwang,
Essen et al. Cologne 1985 (EC)
ILLUSTRATIONS:
444 "Othello" the Negro, 1884
445 Self-Portrait with Skeleton,
1896
446 Reclining Nude, 1899
450 Self-Portrait with my Wife and a
Glass of Champagne, 1902
451 In Max Halbe's Garden, 1899
454 Emperor's Day in Hamburg,
1911
463 Portrait of Julius Meier-Graefe,
1917
463 Self-Portrait with Straw Hat,
1913
464 Easter at Lake Walchen, 1922
465 Self-Portrait in a Straw Hat,
1923

CORMON Fernand
1845 Paris – 1924 Paris
Real name: Fernand-Anne Piestre.
Studied in Brussels under J.F. Portaels
and in Paris with Cabanel and
Fromentin. 1870 exhibited a historical painting at the Salon. 1880
achieved success with his large, drastically naturalistic and bright-coloured
"Cain, Fleeing with his Family" (after
Victor Hugo). Professor at the College of Art and popular with students,
who included Toulouse-Lautrec, Anquetin, Bernard, van Gogh and many
others; made them copy paintings in
the Louvre and was liked because he

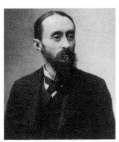

allowed them great freedom. Much
sought after as a portrait and fresco
painter in Paris and Tours. 1898 member of the Academy.

COROT Jean-Baptiste Camille
1796 Paris – 1875 Ville-d'Avray
1822-1825 after an apprenticeship
with a business firm he attended a private school for landscape painting
and nature studies in the open. 1825-
1828 in Italy. Painted studies of landscapes and views of towns that are remarkable for their fresh vitality and
harmonious composition. 1827 exhibited for the first time at the Paris
Salon. 1828 lived in Paris and Ville
d'Avray, later also spent periods in
Arras. Travelled a great deal in
France and visited Italy twice more,
as well as going to Switzerland, England and the Netherlands. 1827 allegorical and religious pictures he occasionally made concessions to contemporary taste. But through his intimate,
light, poetic landscapes and quiet, gra-
cious pictures of women reading or
playing music, he paved the way for a
new and realistic concept of art and
nature – the Barbizon school. 1855 received awards at the Paris World Fair.
A forerunner of the Impressionists,
who wanted him to exhibit at their
first exhibition.

CATALOGUE: Robaut, A.: L'œuvre de
C. Catalogue raisonné et illustré.
Paris 1965
BIBLIOGRAPHY: Baud-Bovy, D.: C.
Geneva 1957.– Clarke, M.: C. and
the Art of Landscape. London 1991.–
Galassi, P.: C. in Italien. Munich
1991.– J.-B.C.C. The Lefevre Gallery,
London 1989 (EC).– Leymarie, J.: C.
Geneva 1979.– Millet, C. and the

School of Barbizon. The Seibu Museum, Tokyo; Museum of Modern
Art, Hyogo 1980 (EC).– Schoeller, A.
and J. Dieterle: Suppléments à
l'œuvre de C. Paris 1956.– Selz, J.: La
vie et l'œuvre de C.C. Courbevoie
1988.– Zimmermann, A.: Studien
zum Figurenbild bei C. Doctoral
thesis, Cologne 1986
ILLUSTRATIONS:
29 Memory of Mortefontaine, 1864
30 The Mill at Saint-Nicolas-les-
Arras, 1874

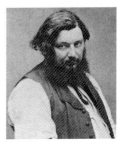

COURBET Gustave
1819 Ornans – 1877 Tour-de-Peilz
(Vevey)
1831 began by drawing from nature.
1839/40 became a mostly self-taught
painter in Paris. 1844 exhibited for
the first time at the Salon; painted
portraits, landscapes, genre scenes
and animals. 1846 travelled in Holland. 1848 friendly with Corot, Daumier and Baudelaire. 1849 first received a medal at the Salon. 1850 exhibited in provincial towns, charging
an entrance fee; subsequently also in
Belgium and Germany. 1855 exhibited at the Paris World Fair; at the
same time he organised his own one-
man exhibition entitled "Realism".
An opponent of the monarchy and
the bourgeoisie, proponent of an anarchist form of socialism, friends with
P.-J. Proudhon. 1861 for a short
period he gave courses in his own studio. 1865 contacts with Whistler and
Monet, controversies with Manet.
1867 once again ran his own exhibition during the Paris World Fair. Influenced and advised the future Impressionists. 1869 acclaimed at an international art exhibition in Munich.
1871 active for artistic affairs during
the Paris Commune, imprisoned afterwards. 1872 Exhibition at Durand-
Ruel's. 1873 held responsible for the
fall of the Vendôme column: flight to
Switzerland. World-wide influence as
a proponent of democratic realism
based on perception through the
senses and dedicated to uncovering
the inner contradictions of reality by
means of formal structure.
CATALOGUE: Courthion, P.: L'opera
completa di C. Milan 1985.– Fernier,
R.: La vie et l'œuvre de G.C. 2 vols.
Lausanne and Paris 1977-1978
BIBLIOGRAPHY: Bazin, G.: C. Biennale. Venice 1956 (EC).– Clark, T.:
Image of the People. G.C. and the

1848 Revolution. London 1973.– Faunce, S. (ed.): C. Reconsidered. New Haven (CT) 1988.– Fernier, J.-J., J.-L. Mayaud and P. Le Nouëne: C. and Ornans. Paris 1989.– Fried, M.: C.'s Realism. Chicago 1990.– G.C. Grand Palais, Paris 1977 (EC).– Léger, C.: C. et son temps. Paris 1948.– Lemonnier, G.: G.C. et son œuvre. Paris 1968.– Les graveurs de C. Musée Courbet 1990 (EC).– Mac Orlan, P.: C. Paris 1951.– Nochlin, L.: G.C. A Study of Style and Society. New York and London 1976.– Riat, G.: C. 1906
ILLUSTRATIONS:
26 Girls on the Bank of the Seine, 1857
27 The Artist's Studio, 1854/55
28 The Shaded Stream, or "Le Puits Noir", 1865
31 The Cliff at Etretat after the Storm, 1870

COUTURE Thomas
1815 Senlis – 1879 Villiers-le-Bel
1831-1839 studied at the Paris Art College with A. Gros and P. Delaroche. 1837 won only second place in the competition for the Rome Prize. 1838 exhibited for the first time at the Salon. Painted history pictures and portraits in the manner of the Venetian Renaissance, always striving to combine allegory with realism, a strict style of drawing and relatively free brushwork. 1847 gained a notable success for his huge impressive picture "The Romans in the Period of Decadence" with its moral criticism aimed at contemporary life. Young painters called on him to open his own school. 1855 despite winning a gold medal, he considered that he had not received the recognition at the World Fair in Paris and did not participate again at the Salon until 1872. 1863 taught at the College of Art emphasising academic precision, attention to brushwork and technique, but also the study of light effects in the open air. His pupils included Manet, Puvis de Chavannes, Anselm Feuerbach and various American artists. An opponent of Courbet's Realism. Wrote a text book on painting. 1869 moved to the country, where his work included genre scenes, mainly for American purchasers.
WRITINGS, DOCUMENTS: Couture, T.: Méthodes et entretiens d'atelier. Paris 1867.– T.C., sa vie, son œuvre, son caractère, ses idées, sa méthode, par lui-même et son petit-fils (preface by C. Mauclair). Paris 1932
BIBLIOGRAPHY: Boime, A. et al. (eds.): T.C. 1815-1879. Musée départemental de l'Oise. Beauvais 1971 (EC).– Boime, A.: T.C. and the Eclectic Vision. New Haven and London 1980.– Enrollment of the Volunteers: T.G. and the Painting of History. Museum of Fine Arts, Springfield (MA); Detroit Institute of Arts, Detroit; Sterling and Francine Clark Art Institute, Williamstown (MA). Springfield 1980 (EC).– L'enrôlement des volontaires de 1792.– T.C. (1815-1879): Les artistes au service de la patrie et danger. Musée départemental de l'Oise, Beauvais 1989 (EC).– T.C. 1815-1879.

Drawings and some Oil Sketches. Shepered Gallery, London 1971 (EC).– T.C. Paintings and Drawings in American Collections. University of Maryland, Art Gallery, 1970 (EC)

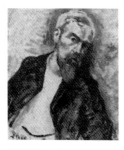

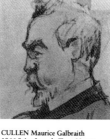

CROSS Henri-Edmond
1856 Douai – 1910 Le Lavandou
Real name: Henri-Edmond Delacroix. British mother. As a child he was tutored by Carolus-Duran. Studied law and attended art school at Lille. From 1876 he was in Paris, studying art with F. Bonvin. 1881 exhibited for the first time at the Salon. Adopted an English name. Altered his style from the dark colours of realism to a brighter Impressionism, especially after his trips in 1883 to the South of France and his meetings with Monet. 1884 Co-founder of the Indépendants, contacts with Seurat and Signac; painted Paris scenes and landscapes. 1888 exhibited with Les Vingt in Brussels. 1891 Vice-President of the Indépendants, change to a pointillist style, moved to southern France. 1894 first individual exhibition with Petitjean. Supported Anarchism through magazine illustrations. 1896 exhibited works of surface decoration and Symbolist expression at the art dealer Bing's Salon de l'Art Nouveau and at Durand-Ruel's, later at other galleries and at the Secessions in Berlin and Dresden. 1903 visited Venice. 1904 worked with Matisse in Saint-Tropez; became friends with Denis. 1908 travelled in Tuscany. The strong colours of his late pictures are close to Fauvism.
CATALOGUE: Compin, I.: H.-E.C. Paris 1964
BIBLIOGRAPHY: Compin, I.: H.-E.C. Paris 1964.– Cousturier, L.: H.-E.C. Paris 1932.– H.-E.C.: Carnet de dessins. Paris 1959.– H.-E.C.: Paysages méditerranéens d'H.-E.C. Musée de l'Amonciade, Saint-Tropez 1990 (EC).– Rewald, J. (ed.): H.-E.C. Fine Arts Associates, New York 1951 (EC)
ILLUSTRATIONS:
322 Beach on the Mediterranean, c. 1891/92
323 The Golden Isles, 1891/92
380 The Clearing, c. 1906/07
384 Undergrowth, 1906/07
389 Cypresses at Cagnes, 1908

CULLEN Maurice Galbraith
1866 Saint-Jean-de-Terre-Neuve – 1934 Chambly-Quebec
Began by studying sculpture with Philippe Hébert. 1889 moved to Paris. 1889-1892 studied painting at the Ecole des Beaux-Arts. 1894/95 exhibited in Paris. Plein-air painting in Pouldu, Moret, Giverny and Venice; achieved much success with his winter landscapes. 1895 returned to Montreal. Spent the summers at Beaupré near Quebec. 1900 and 1902 travelled in Europe again. One of the most important Canadian Impressionists, with a style reminiscent of Sisley.
BIBLIOGRAPHY: Antoniou, S. (ed.): M.C. 1866-1934. Agnes Etherington Art Centre, Queen's University, Kingston (Ontario) 1982 (EC)
ILLUSTRATION:
627 Winter at Moret, 1895

DAGUERRE Louis-Jacques-Mandé
1787 Cormeilles (Val-d'Oise) – 1851 Bry-sur-Marne
Decorative painter and inventor. Worked with Nicéphore Niepce on the development of the first techniques of photography. 1829 experiments to perfect the heliograph. 1835 discovered how to develop a photograph by means of mercury vapour. 1837 discovered how to fix the picture in a solution of common salt. 1838 published his findings through the intercession of the physicist and politician François Arago.

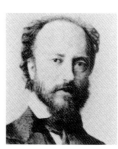

DAUBIGNY Charles-François
1817 Paris – 1878 Auvers-sur-Oise
Trained with his father. 1836 visited Italy. 1838 exhibited for the first time at the Salon. 1840 short period of

study with Delaroche. Became one of the main exponents of realistic landscape and plein-air painting ("Barbizon school"); friendship with Corot and Daumier. 1857 began to paint river landscapes from a boat. 1860 settled in Auvers-sur-Oise. 1866 visited England. Advised and supported the new Impressionist movement – also from his position on the Salon jury. 1870/71 went to London during the war, then to Holland. 1872 advised Cézanne. 1874 the Impressionists wanted him to take part in their first exhibition.
WRITINGS, DOCUMENTS: Moreau-Nélaton, E.: D. raconté par lui-même. Paris 1925
CATALOGUE: Hellebranth, R.: L'œuvre peint de D. Rolle 1976
BIBLIOGRAPHY: C.-F.D. 1817-1878. Dessins, gravures, peintures. Galerie d'exposition de l'Hôtel de Ville d'Aulnay-sous-Bois 1990 (EC).– C. Pissarro, C.-F.D., L. Piette. Musée de Pontoise, Pontoise 1978 (EC).– Fidel-Beaufort M. and J. Bailly- Herzberg: D. Paris 1975
ILLUSTRATION:
22 The Pool at Gylieu, 1853

DEBRAS Louis
1834 Péronne (Somme) – 1917
Exhibited 1843-1866 at the Salon: genre pictures, portraits, landscapes and still lifes. Several stays in Spain. 1874 exhibited four pictures at the 1st Impressionist exhibition.

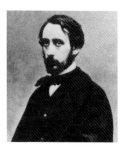

DEGAS Edgar
1834 Paris – 1917 Paris
1852 set up his studio in the house of his father, a cultured banker of aristocratic extraction. 1853-1855 studied with F. Barrias and L. Lamothe and attended the College of Art. 1854-1859 several trips to Italy, some of the time visiting relatives; studied the Old Masters, painted history pictures and realistic portraits. 1861 started his innovative choice of subject matter with his pictures of horse racing. 1862 formed friendships with Manet and Duranty. 1865 his last history picture was exhibited at the Salon; met Renoir, Monet and others; became a frequent customer at the Café Guerbois. 1868 travelled to London with Manet; began to paint scenes from music and dance theatre with unusual points of view and visual angles. 1869 exhibited at the Salon for the

last time; visited Belgium. 1870/71 soldier in Paris; during the Commune he stayed with friends in Normandy; began to have problems with his eyes. 1872/73 visited relatives in New Orleans. 1874 helped organise the 1st Impressionist exhibition; attended meetings at the Café de la Nouvelle-Athènes. 1875 went to Italy. From 1876 to 1881 he took part in the Impressionist exhibitions (2nd to 6th). Led the group of socially critical Realists; became friends with Cassatt; experimented with graphic techniques and with photography. 1878 first purchase of one of his pictures by a museum. 1880 trip to Spain. 1881 exhibited a sculpture at the 6th Impressionist exhibition. 1882 refused to take part in the 7th Impressionist exhibition due to a dispute. 1883 exhibited at Durand-Ruel's in London and New York. 1886 took part in the last group exhibition by the Impressionists. 1889 travelled in Spain and Morocco. 1892 his only one-man exhibition at Durand-Ruel's. The rapid worsening of his eye condition caused him to shun all society; he drew pastels, modelled statues in wax and extended his art collection. 1900 exhibited at the Paris World Fair. 1909-1911 due to failing eyesight, he stopped work completely.
WRITINGS, DOCUMENTS: Fèvre, J.: Mon oncle D. Souvenirs et documents inédits par Pierre Barel. Geneva 1949.– Graber, H.: E.D. nach eigenen and fremden Zeugnissen. Basle 1942.– Guérin, M. (ed.): E.D. Lettres. Paris 1945.– Guérin, M. (ed.): Letters of D. Oxford 1947, New York 1948.– Guillaud, M. et al.: D.: Form and Space. Paris 1984.– Halévy, D.: D. parle . . . Paris 1960.– Halévy, D.: My Friend D. Middletown (CT) 1964.– Reff, T.: The Notebooks of E.D. 2 vols. London 1976, New York 1985.– Reff, T.: D.: The Artist's Mind. New York 1976.– Rivière G.: Mr. D. bourgeois de Paris. Paris 1935.– Valéry, P.: Erinnerung an D. Zurich 1940.– Vollard, A.: D. Paris 1924.– Vollard, A.: En écoutant parler Cézanne, D. et Renoir. Paris 1938
CATALOGUES: Adhémar, J. and F. Cachin: D. Radierungen and Monotypien. Munich 1973.– Adhémar, J. et F. Cachin: E.D. Gravures et monotypes. Paris 1973.– Adhémar, J. and J. Cachin: D. The Complete Etchings, Lithographs and Monotypes. New York 1974, London 1986.– Brame, P. and T. Reff: D. et son œuvre. A Supplement. New York 1984.– Janis, E.P.: D. Monotypes. Catalogue Raisonné. Cambridge (MA) 1968.– Lassaigne, J.: Tout l'œuvre peint de D. Paris 1974.– Lemoisne, P.A.: D. et son œuvre. 4 vols. Paris 1946-1949 (Reprint: New York and London 1984).– Matt, L. v. and J. Rewald: D. Works in Sculpture. His Complete Work. London 1944 and New York 1957.– Matt, L. v. and J. Rewald: Das plastische Werk. Zurich 1957.– Minervino, F. and F. Russoli: L'opera completa di D. Milan 1970.– Minervino, F.: Tout l'œuvre peint de D. Paris 1974.– Minervino, F.: Das Gesamtwerk von D. Lucerne [no date of pub-

lication]. – Parry Janis, E.: D. Monotypes. Cambridge 1968.– Reed, S.W. and B.S. Shapiro: E.D. The Painter as Printmaker. The Complete Prints of E.D. Museum of Fine Arts, Boston 1984 (EC).– Rewald, J.: D.s Complete Sculpture. San Francisco 1944 (Reprint: San Francisco 1990).– Russoli, F.: L'opera completa di D. Milan 1970
BIBLIOGRAPHY: Adriani, G. (ed.): E.D. Pastelle, Ölskizzen, Zeichnungen. Kunsthalle (Tübingen) et al., Cologne 1984 (EC).– Adriani, G. (ed.): D. Pastels, Oil Sketches, Drawings. London and New York 1985.– Adriani, G. (Ed.): D. Pastels, dessins, esquisses. Paris 1985.– Armstrong, C.M.: Odd Man Out. Readings on the Work and Reputation of E.D. Chicago 1991.– studio at auctions. 2 vols. San Francisco 1989 (Reprint).– Boggs, J.S.: Portraits by D. Berkeley 1962.- Boggs, J.S., H. Loyrette, M. Pantazzi et al. (eds.): D. Grand Palais, Paris; Musée des Beaux-Arts, Ottawa; The Metropolitan Museum, New York. Paris 1988 (EC).– Bouret, J.: D. Paris 1965.– Bouret, J.: D. London 1965.– Cabanne, P.: E.D. Paris 1957.– Cabanne, P.: E.D. Munich 1960.– Champigneulle: D. Dessins. Paris 1952.– Cooper, D.: E.D. Pastelle. Basle 1952.– Cooper, D.: Pastels by E.D. New York 1953.– Coquiot, G.: D. Paris 1924.– Dunlop, I.: D. London and New York 1979.– Dunlop, I.: D. Neuchâtel 1979.– Fosca, F.: D. Etude biographique et critique. Geneva 1954.– Gordon, R. and A. Forge: D. London and New York 1988.– Growe, B.: Zur Bildkonzeption E.D.s. Frankfurt am Main 1981.– Growe, B.: D. 1834-1917. Cologne 1991.– Guillaud, M. et al.: D.: Form and Space. Paris 1984.– Hausenstein, W.: D. Bern 1948.– Huyghe, R.: E.H.D. Paris 1953.– Kendall, R. (ed.): E.D. Leben und Werk in Bildern und Briefen. Munich 1988.– Keyser, E. de: D. Réalité et métaphore. Louvain 1981.– Lafond, P.: D 2 vols. Paris 1918-1919.– Lassaigne, E.D. Paris 1945.– Lefèbure, A.: D. Paris 1981.– Lipton, E.: Looking into D. Los Angeles 1986.– Manson, J.B.: The Life and Work of E.D. London 1927.– McMullen, R.: D. His Life, Time and Work. Boston 1984, London 1985.– Meier-Graefe, J.: D. Munich 1920 (Reprint: 1924).– Meier-Graefe, J.: D. London 1923.– Millard, C.: The Sculpture of E.D. Princeton (NJ) 1976.– Pool, P.: D. New York 1963.– Reff, T.: The Artist's Mind. New York 1976.– Rewald, J: D. Sculpture. New York 1951.– Rich, D.C.: D. New York 1951.– Rich, D.C.: D. Cologne 1959.– Rich, D.C.: D. New York 1985.– Roberts, K.: D. Oxford and New York 1976.– Rouart, D.: D., à la recherche de sa technique. Paris 1945.– Rouart, D.: D. In Search of his Techniques. New York and Geneva 1988.– Rouart, D.: D. monotypes. Paris 1948.– Schmid, W. (ed.): Wege zu D. Munich 1988.– Sérullaz M.: L'univers de D. Paris 1979.– Shindoda, Y.: D. Der Einzug des Japanischen in die französische Malerei. Doctoral thesis. Cologne 1957.– Sut-

ton, D.: E.D. Life and Work. New York 1986.– Sutton, D.: D.: Vie et œuvre. Fribourg 1986.– Sutton, D.: E.D. Leben und Werk. Munich 1986.– Terrasse, A.: E.D. Milan 1972.– Terrasse, A.: E.D. Frankfurt am Main, Berlin and Vienna 1981.– Terrasse, A.: D. et la photographie. Paris 1983.– Thomson, R.: The Private D. London 1987.– Thomson, R.: D., the Nudes. London 1988.– Valéry, P.: D., Dance, Drawing. New York 1948.– Vitali, L.: E.D. Milan 1966.– Werner, A.: D. Pastels. New York 1968
ILLUSTRATIONS:
10 Gentlemen's Race. Before the Start, 1862
34 The Bellelli Family, 1858-1860
44 Woman with Chrysanthemums, 1865
46 Mlle Eugénie Fiocre in the Ballet "La Source", c. 1867-68
67 The Opera Orchestra, c. 1868-69
70 A Carriage at the Races, c. 1869-1872
71 Race Horses in front of the Stands, c. 1869
79 Woman Ironing, c. 1869
86 The Dancing Class, c. 1872
87 Musicians in the Orchestra, 1870/71
100 Dance Studio of the Opéra, Rue Le Peletier, 1872
111 The Cotton Exchange at New Orleans, 1873
114 The Dance Class, 1874
115 The Races. Before the Start, before 1873
115 Race Horses, c.1873
122 Four Studies of a 14-year-old Dancer, 1879
129 Rehearsal of a Ballet on Stage, 1874
130 At the Beach, 1876
161 At the Café-Concert: The Song of the Dog, c. 1876/77
164 The Absinth Drinker, 1876
169 Place de la Concorde (Comte Lepic and his Daughters), 1876
181 Singer with a Glove, 1878
186 Dancer with Bouquet, c. 1878-1880
186 Dancer with Bouquet (curtsying), c. 1877/78
187 The Star or Dancer on the Stage, c. 1876-1878
238 Mary Cassatt at the Louvre, 1879/80
242 Women Ironing, c. 1884
248 Woman Combing her Hair, c. 1885
248 After the Bath. Woman Drying Herself, 1885
249 The Tub, 1885/86
262 Six Friends of the Artist, 1885

DELACROIX Eugène
1798 Charenton-St.-Maurice – 1863 Paris
1813 trained at the studio of P. Guérin. 1816 studied at the Paris College of Art. 1822 exhibited for the first time at the Salon – a picture influenced by Gericault and Rubens. Contacts with English water-colour painters. 1824 received acclaim at the Salon. Impressed by Constable, he changed to a brighter use of colour. In 1825 he moved with Bonington to London. 1830 sympathised with the July revolution. 1832 in the service of

the French state in Morocco, where he was particularly impressed; the African light and the motifs were to become subjects for his paintings. 1833 commissioned to do some murals. 1855 exhibited a considerable number of pictures at the Paris World Fair. 1857 after seven attempts, he finally succeeded in gaining admittance to the Academy. In his work, passionate, sensual subjectivity in the choice of subject, composition and use of colour form a highly independent blend of Romanticism and make him one of the most powerful painters of the century. His conception of related colour and emphasis on the total colour effect were an inspiration to the Impressionists.

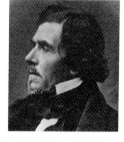

WRITINGS, DOCUMENTS: Delacroix, E.: Œuvres littéraires: Etudes esthétiques; Essais sur les artistes célèbres. 2 vols. Paris 1923.– Guignard, E. (ed.): E.D. Briefe und Tagebücher. Munich 1990.– Joubin, A. (ed.): D. Correspondance. I-V, Paris 1932-1936.– Mittelstädt, K. (ed.): E.D. Dem Auge ein Fest. Aus dem Journal 1847-1863. Frankfurt am Main 1988.– Moreau-Nélaton, E.: D. raconté par lui-même. 2 vols. Paris 1916
CATALOGUES: Escholier, R.: E.D., peintre, graveur, écrivain. 3 vols. Paris 1926-1929.– Huyghe, R.: E.D. London 1963.– Johnson, L.: The Paintings of E.D. A Critical Catalogue. 3 vols. Paris 1986.– Lee, J.: The Paintings of E.D. Oxford 1980-1986.– Robaut, A. and E. Chesneau: L'œuvre complète de E.D. Peintures, dessins, gravures, lithographies, 1813-1863. Paris 1885 (Reprint: New York 1969).– Sérullaz, M.: E.D., dessins. 2 vols. Paris 1984
BIBLIOGRAPHY: Badt, K.: E.D. Werke und Ideale. Cologne 1976.– Bazin, G.: D. Biennale. Venice 1956.– Christoffel, U.: E.D. Munich 1951.– Escholier, R.: E.D. as consolatrice. Paris 1932.– Escholier, R.: E.D. Paris 1963.– Escholier, R.: E.D. Paris 1947.– Joubin, A.: Voyage de D. au Maroc. Paris 1930.– Meier-Graefe, J.: E.D. Munich 1922.– Mémorial de l'Exposition D. au Musée du Louvre. Paris 1964.– Petrova, E.: D. et le siècle romantique. Paris 1990.– Piot, R.: Les palettes de D. Paris 1931.– Rudrauf, L.: E.D. et le problème du romantisme artistique. Paris 1942.– Sérullaz, M.: Les dessins d'E.D. au Musée du

Louvre (1817-1827). Paris 1952.– Sérullaz, M.: Les peintures murales de Delacroix. Paris 1963.– Stuffmann, M. (ed.): E.D. Themen und Variationen: Arbeiten auf Papier. Städelsches Kunstinstitut und Städtische Galerie, Frankfurt am Main 1987 (EC)
ILLUSTRATIONS:
16 The Massacre on Chios, 1824
17 The Women of Algiers, 1834

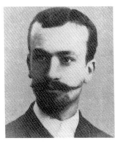

DELAVALLEE Henri
1862 Reims – 1943 Pont-Aven
After university he studied at the college of art in Paris. 1881 visited Pont-Aven, where in 1886 he joined the group of artists influenced by Gauguin, especially E. Bernard. He painted Impressionist, Synthetist and occasionally pointillist paintings, but mainly worked as a graphic artist. 1890 exhibited at Durand-Ruel's. 1891-1901 visited Turkey; became a successful landscape and portrait painter. Thereafter he lived in the Oise valley and at Pont-Aven; had exhibitions at Durand-Ruel's and Vollard's.
ILLUSTRATIONS:
294 Farmyard, 1887
385 Sunny Street, c. 1887

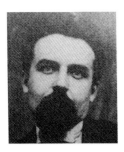

DENIS Maurice
1870 Granville (Manche) – 1943 Saint-Germain-en-Laye
1888 studied at the Paris college of art and at the Académie Julian. Became acquainted with Bernard, Bonnard, Vuillard and Sérusier; the latter introduced him to the Synthetism of Gauguin. 1889 took part in an exhibition at the Café Volpini. 1890 co-founder of the Symbolist group of ar-

tists "Nabis"; he shared a studio with Bonnard and Vuillard, published important articles of art criticism. 1891 exhibited with the Indépendants and with the Nabis at the Le Barc de Bouttevilles gallery. 1892/93 did the decor at the Théâtre de l'Œuvre for a school friend, Lugné-Poe. Beside Impressionist portrait studies and garden scenes, he painted decorative, Art Nouveau and Symbolist works with an increasingly religious content. 1895 the first of several visits to Italy (with Sérusier). 1901 painted a group portrait "Homage to Cézanne". 1903 travelled in Germany, where he visited the former "Nabi" J. Verkade, who had become a monk at the monastery of Beuron. 1906 visited Cézanne in Aix. 1912 published his "Theories". 1919 founded workshops for religious art.
WRITINGS, DOCUMENTS: Blanche, J.-E. (ed.): Correspondance J.-E. Blanche – M.D. (1901-1939). Geneva 1989.– M.D.: Théories 1890-1910. Du symbolisme et de Gauguin vers un nouvel ordre classique. Paris 1912.– M.D.: Nouvelles théories sur l'art moderne et l'art sacré. Paris 1922.– M.D.: Journal (1884- 1943). 3 vols. Paris 1957-1959.– M.D.: Du symbolisme au classicisme: Théories, textes réunis et présentés par Olivier Revault d'Allones. Paris 1964
CATALOGUE: Cailler, P.: M.D. Geneva 1968
BIBLIOGRAPHY: Barazzetti-Demoulin, S.: M.D. Paris 1945.– Brillant, M.: Portrait de M.D. Paris 1945.– Fosca, F.: M.D. Paris 1945.– Jamot, P.: M.D. Paris 1945.– M.D. Orangeries des Tuileries, Paris 1970 (EC).– M.D. Kunsthalle, Bremen 1971 (EC).– M.D. 1870-1943. Fondation Septentrion, Marcq-en-Baroeul 1988 (EC)
ILLUSTRATIONS:
341 The Muses, or In the Park, 1893

DE NITTIS → Nittis

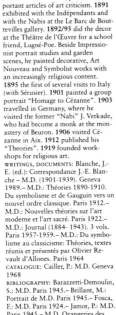

DESBOUTIN Marcellin
1823 Cérilly – 1902 Nice
Came from a rich family; after studying law at Paris he became a pupil of the sculptor Etex in 1845. 1847/48 studied under Couture; foreign trips. 1854-1870 lived in Florence as a painter, engraver and poet. Generous host to many artists, including Degas and De Nittis. 1868 exhibited for the first time at the Salon. Ruined by fi-

nancial speculation; spent several years in Geneva. 1873 settled in Paris; became acquainted with Manet and Degas at the Café Guerbois; exhibited at the Salon again. 1876 frequent customer in the Café de la Nouvelle-Athènes, sat for Degas as model for "The Absinth Drinkers" (p. 164); took part in the 2nd Impressionist exhibition, although he painted exacting character studies and genre scenes in an almost Neo-Baroque style with details. Lived a Bohemian life without means with his wife and eight children. Portrait etchings of his many artist friends. 1881-1888 and 1895-1902 in Nice. 1890 his graphic art was exhibited at Durand-Ruel's with a foreword by Zola. 1890 co-founder of the Société Nationale. 1895 member of the Legion of Honour. 1900 won the grand prize at the Paris World Fair.
BIBLIOGRAPHY: Dupliaux, B.: M.D. Prince des bohèmes. Moulins-Yzeure 1985.– Janin, C.: La curieuse vie de M.D. Peintre, graveur, poète. Paris 1922
ILLUSTRATION:
130 Portrait of Jean-Baptiste Faure, 1874

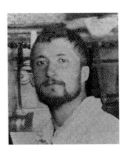

DEVAMBEZ André-Victor-Edouard
1867 Paris – 1944 Paris
Studied at the college of art in Paris; pupil of Constant and Lefèbvre. From 1889 exhibited at the Salon. 1890-1895 in Italy as winner of the Rome prize, later professor at the college of art in Paris and member of the Institut de France. 1900 change of subject matter and style: painted Impressionist-influenced genre pictures of urban crowd scenes such as political demonstrations or theatre audiences. 1910 mural at the Sorbonne. He later painted scenes from the First World War and book illustrations.
BIBLIOGRAPHY: Ménegoz, M. (ed.): A.D. (1867-1944). Musée départemental, Beauvais 1988 (EC)
ILLUSTRATIONS:
373 The Charge, 1902

DEWHURST Wynford
1864 Manchester – 1941 Manchester
Worked first as a journalist and illustrator. In 1891 he began to study art at the Ecole des Beaux-Arts in Paris under Gérôme, Bouguereau and Constant and at the Académie Julian.

Painted Impressionist landscapes of the environs of Paris; admired Monet. In 1897 he exhibited for the first time at the Salon. 1904 and 1907 took part in the London exhibitions of the Society of British Artists and during the following years in international exhibitions at home and abroad. Published articles on Impressionism.
WRITINGS, DOCUMENTS: Dewhurst, W.: Impressionist Painting, its Genesis and Development. London 1904
ILLUSTRATION:
585 Luncheon on the Grass (The Picnic), 1908

DIVISIONISM → Neo-Impressionism

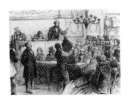

DROUOT, Hôtel
State auction house in the former city residence (Hôtel) of the Napoleonic General Drouot in Paris. The art auctions held there had important indicators of the current asking prices. Whole collections and legacies came under the auctioneer's hammer after the death of an artist or collector or in cases of bankruptcy. Occasionally an artist or collector would have a series of paintings auctioned but might have to buy them back himself to avoid a disastrous fall in price. In 1875 an auction arranged by Durand-Ruel of Monets, Morisots, Renoirs and Sisleys was disrupted by a jeering audience. In 1878 the collections of Jean-Baptiste Faure and Ernest Hoschedé were sold at disastrously low prices.

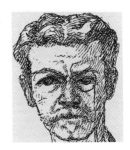

DUBOIS-PILLET Albert
1846 Paris – 1890 Le Puy-en-Velay
Real name: Albert Dubois. 1865 attended the cadet school at St. Cyr, after which he became an officer and amateur painter. 1880 promoted to Captain of the Republican Guard; rejected by the Salon. Spent time with artists and writers in the Café de la

Nouvelle-Athènes. 1884 organizer and first president of the Société des artistes indépendants, where a Naturalist painting influenced by Manet occasioned a furious debate. Encouraged by Seurat, he subsequently began to paint pointillist landscapes, open-air genre scenes and portraits. 1888 and 1890 exhibited with Les Vingt in Brussels. In 1889 he was accused of sympathising with the Bonapartist plot of General Boulanger. He was demoted and transferred to Le Puy as a captain in the gendarmerie; he died of smallpox.

CATALOGUE: Bazalgette, L.: A.D.-P. Catalogue raisonné (in preparation)
BIBLIOGRAPHY: Bazalgette, L.: A. D.-P., sa vie et son œuvre. Villejuif and Paris 1976
ILLUSTRATION:
311 The Marne at Dawn, 1888

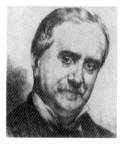

DURAND-RUEL Paul Marie-Joseph
1833 Paris – 1922 Paris
Son of an artist. From 1851 he worked in his parents' gallery, which patronised the painters of the Barbizon school. In 1865 he took over the business from his father. 1869 opened a new gallery in the Rue Le Peletier 11; 1871 first came into contact with Impressionist painters (Pissarro and Monet) in his London gallery. 1872 his first large exhibition of Impressionist works in London. 1871-1873 opened new branches in Brussels. In 1872 he bought all available works by Manet for 32,000 francs; also supported Monet and others. He was the first dealer to commission the total output of artists and secure their livelihood through advance payments. He found, however, that he had to give up purchases. 1876 had little success at the 2nd Impressionist exhibition. 1880 began making purchases again through credit from the banker Feder, but the latter's bankruptcy in 1882 caused renewed financial difficulties. Fierce competition with the artist G. Petit. Supported the 7th Impressionist exhibition, and organised exhibitions by individuals such as Monet; sent pictures to London, Boston, Rotterdam and Berlin (1884), and Brussels (1885). 1886/87 made a breakthrough into new markets through a large Impressionist exhibition in New York. Founded a branch there in 1888 which was managed by his three sons. He had no interest in Neo-

Impressionism or Post-Impressionism; his personal favourites were the artists of the Barbizon school. 1905 large exhibitions in Berlin and London. 1911 left the firm to his sons.

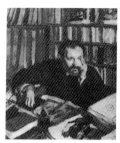

DURANTY Louis Emile Edmond
1833 Paris – 1880 Paris
Founded the short-lived journal "Réalisme" and worked for the "Goncourts". In his copious publications he was a passionate advocate of Impressionist theory. 1876 publication of his book "La nouvelle peinture, à propos du groupe d'artistes qui expose dans les galeries Durand-Ruel".

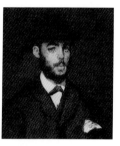

DURET Théodore
1838 Saintes – 1927 Paris
Journalist, art critic and businessman. 1863 travelled round the world for his cognac firm. 1865 met Manet in Madrid. In 1868 he founded a republican newspaper with Zola and others. In 1870 he published his first Salon report, in which he spoke about the Impressionists. 1871 deputy mayor of his region under the Paris Commune and narrowly escaped being shot. Second world trip; collected East Asian art. From 1872 he was in Paris, buying Impressionist pictures and helping with money, but against group exhibitions. 1878 published the first complete history of the movement: "The Impressionist Painters". Visited London frequently; friends with Whistler. In 1882 he wrote the preface to the posthumous exhibition of Manet's works. 1894 financial problems forced him to auction his collection at G. Petit's; never-

theless he began his collections again, which included the Post-Impressionists. 1898 actively supported Dreyfus. 1900 donated works of art to Paris museums, advised collectors and art dealers and published several books on the Impressionists.

ECOLE DES BEAUX-ARTS
College of art in Paris (today: Ecole Nationale Supérieure des Beaux-Arts), the most important art school in the country. Founded in 1796, it had its origins in the Royal Academy of 1648, which had been modelled on Italian lines and trained artists no longer tied to guilds. Until the reform of 1863 it was run by the Institut de France, which retained its influence, as the members of its art section (known as "Academy members") all taught at the Ecole. The professors, seven painters and five sculptors, changing each month, ran the strictly Classical programme of instruction, which consisted of drawing from models and making casts of Classical sculptures, with classes in anatomy, perspective and theory. In addition, the professors ran courses in their own studios. It was not until 1863 that the Ecole set up eleven teaching studios, three of which were for painting, run at first by Cabanel, Gérôme and Pils. Admittance to the Ecole was by entrance examination. There were numerous competitions during the studies, and at the end of the course the competition for the Rome Prize. The subjects given by the college were mythological, historical or Christian. The Rome Prize allowed a student to study for several years at the Académie de France in Rome and opened up interesting prospects for teaching posts and awards.

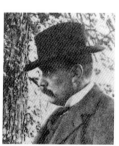

EDELFELT Albert
1854 Kiala – 1908 Haiko
1870 began his art studies at the school of the Finnish Art Society in Helsinki and with the painters B. Lindholm and B. Reinhold. 1871-1873 studied at the Academy of Art in Helsinki, 1873 at the Academy in Antwerp and 1874-1878 with interruptions at the Ecole des Beaux-Arts in Paris under Gérôme. Apart from annual visits to Finland, he lived in Paris. At first he painted history pictures; under the influence of plein-air painting and Bastien-Lepage he

painted Naturalist landscapes and scenes of Finnish farm life. 1876 and 1903 travelled to Italy and 1881 to Spain. As a proponent of Finnish realism, he influenced his younger Scandinavian colleagues, especially Gallen-Kallela. Won great acclaim with the French public for his portraits. In the 1880s and 1890s he exhibited at the Paris Salon, the Salon des Champs-Elysées and the Salon du Champ de Mars. At the Paris World Fair in 1889 he received the Grand Prix d'Honneur. 1904 painted a monumental historical picture for the Academy in Helsinki (now destroyed).

BIBLIOGRAPHY: Berezina, V.N.: A.E. i ego proizvedenija v Gosudarstvennon Ermitaze. Leningrad 1963.– Edelfelt, B.: Ur A.E. pariserbrev till sin mor. Stockholm 1917.– Edelfelt, B.: Ur A.E. brev. Resor och intryck. Stockholm 1921.– Edelfelt, B.: Ur A.E. brev. Liv och arbete. Stockholm 1926.– Edelfelt, B.: Ur A.E. brev. Middagshöjd. Stockholm 1928.– Edelfelt, B.: Ur A.E. brev. Kring sekelskiftet. Stockholm 1930.– Hintze, F.: A.E. 3 vols. Helsinki 1942-1944.– Hintze, F.: A.E. 3 vols. Stockholm 1949.– Hintze, B.: A.E. Porvoo 1953
ILLUSTRATIONS:
466 Paris in the Snow, 1887
485 In the Luxembourg Gardens, 1887

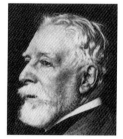

ENSOR James
1860 Ostend – 1949 Ostend
Learned to paint water colours as a child. 1877-1880 studied at the Academy in Ostend and Brussels. His sombre and dramatic interiors, landscapes and portraits mark a departure from traditional ways of seeing and are a deliberate reaction to the art of the academies. The landscapes owe as much to Realism as they do to Impressionism. In 1880 he returned to Ostend. 1882 joined the avant-garde group "L'Essor" and in 1883 was a founder member of Les Vingt in Brussels. There he exhibited his works, which had been rejected by the salons and which were the cause of much debate even in avantgarde circles. 1886-1900 his palette changed to lighter colours. A common motif was the masked figure, and the numerous macabre variations on this theme reveal him to be a precursor of Expressionism and Surrealism. 1926 first exhibition in Paris.

WRITINGS, DOCUMENTS: Ollinger-Zinque, G.: E. par lui-même. Brussels 1976
CATALOGUES: Croquez, A.: L'œuvre gravé de J.E. Geneva 1947.– Taevernier, A.: J.E. Catalogue illustrée de ses gravures, leur description critique et l'inventaire des plaques. Ghent 1973.– Tavernier, A.: Catalogue des gravures. Brussels 1973.– Tricot, X.: J.E. Catalogue Raisonné of the Paintings. Cologne et al. 1992
BIBLIOGRAPHY: Avermaete, R.: J.E. Antwerp 1947.– Croquez, A.: L'œuvre gravé de J.E. Geneva 1947.– Croquez, R.: E. en son temps. Ostend 1970.– Damese, J.: L'œuvre gravé de J. E. Geneva 1967.– Delevoy, R.L.: J.E. Antwerp 1981.– J.E. Württembergischer Kunstverein, Stuttgart 1972 (EC).– J.E. The Art Institute, Chicago; The Solomon R. Guggenheim Museum, New York 1976 (EC).– J.E. Kunsthaus Zürich, Zurich; Koninklijk Museum voor Schone Kunsten, Antwerp 1983 (EC).– J.E. Belgien um 1900. Kunsthalle der Hypo-Kulturstiftung, Munich 1989.– Farmer, J.D.: E. New York 1976.– Fels, F.: J.E. Geneva 1947.– Fierens, P.: J.E. Paris 1943.– Haesaerts, P.: J.E. Brussels 1957, 1973.– Heusinger von Waldegg, J.: J.E. Legende vom Ich. Cologne 1991.– Janssens, J.: J.E. Paris 1990.– Lebeer, L.: J.E.: Aquafortiste. Antwerp 1952.– Legrand, F.-C.: E., cet inconnu. Brussels 1971.– Le Roy, G.: J.E. Brussels 1922.– Lesko, D.: J.E. The Creative Years. Princeton 1985.– Tannenbaum, L.: J.E. New York 1951.– Vanbeselaere, W.: L'Entrée du Christ à Bruxelles. Brussels 1957.– Verhaeren, E.: J.E. Brussels 1908
ILLUSTRATION:
421 The Dejected Lady, 1881

ERAGNY-SUR-EPTE
Village on the River Epte, about 20 miles south of Dieppe. Pissarro lived there from **1884** and painted numerous pictures of the landscape there (pp. 275, 312); Monet also painted here (p. 330).

ESTAQUE (L')
Fishing village near Marseilles. 1870/71 Cézanne lived here with his model Hortense Fiquet and after his depressing stay in Paris discovered his preference for landscape painting. He returned here again and again in later life.

ETRETAT
Fishing village about 15 miles east of Le Havre. The bizarre-looking cliffs of Etretat became a popular motif for artists. Delacroix and Courbet painted here (p. 31), and it was a favourite spot for Monet, who always stayed at Faure's house (pp. 232, 233, 270). Many famous Parisians had their summer residences here, including Maupassant, who watched Monet at work in **1885**.

EVENEMENT (L')
The first newspaper to cover contemporary modern movements; founded in **1848**. 1866 Zola wrote book re-

views and articles on the Salons. His uncompromising defence of modernity led to a scandal. 1872-1896 under its editor Edmond Magnier the paper flourished, reporting daily on artistic events in Paris.

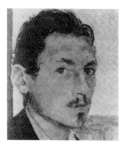

EVENEPOEL Henri
1872 Nice – 1899 Paris
Brought up by nuns after the death of his parents, he trained first in Brussels under B. Garin and then in 1892 at the art college in Paris; worked alongside Matisse and Rouault at Moreau's studio. In 1894 he left Paris to work independently without a teacher. **1897** after years in Algeria and Blida, he died in Paris of typhoid fever, after he had finally made the decision to return to Belgium. Evenepoel worked only five years as an artist and was strongly influenced by Whistler and Manet, yet his work retains its own individual character.
WRITINGS, DOCUMENTS: Hyslop, F.E. (ed.): H.E. Lettres choisies 1892-1899. Brussels 1976
BIBLIOGRAPHY: Bollen, M. and H. Coenen: H.E.s familie. Een reeks Schetsen. Antwerp 1990.– Haesaerts, L. and P.: H.E. Brussels 1932.– Hellens, F.: H.E. Antwerp 1947.– H.E. (1872- 1899). Musée d'Art Moderne, Brussels 1972 (EC).– Hyslop, F.E.: H.E. Belgian Painter in Paris 1892-1899. Pennsylvania 1985.– Lambotte, P.: H.E. Brussels 1908
ILLUSTRATIONS:
428 Sunday in the Bois de Boulogne, 1891
429 Veterans' Festival, 1898

EXHIBITIONS OF IMPRESSIONISTS
1874: 1st Exhibition. "Société anonyme des artistes, peintres, sculpteurs, graveurs, etc. Exposition". 35, Boulevard des Capucines. April 15 – May 15, 10 a.m. – 6 p.m. and 8 – 10 p.m. 30 participants, 167 catalogue entries.
Participants and number of catalogue entries (in brackets): Astruc (4), Attendu (6), Béliard (4), Boudin (6), F. Bracquemond (6), Brandon (5), Bureau (4), Cals (6), Cézanne (3), Colin (5), Debras (4), Degas (10), Guillaumin (3), Latouche (4), Lepic (7), Lépine (3), Levert (3), Meyer (6), Molins (4), Monet (9), Morisot (9), Mulot-Durivage (2), De Nittis (5), A.-L.-M. Ottin (10), L.-A. Ottin (7), Pis-

sarro (5), Renoir (7), Robert (2), Rouart (11), Sisley (5).
1876: 2nd Exhibition. "Exposition de peinture". 11, Rue Le Peletier. April, 10 a.m. – 5 p.m. 19 participants, 252 catalogue entries.
Béliard (8), Bureau (8), Caillebotte (8), Cals (11), Degas (24), Desboutin (13), J. François (8), Legros (12), Lepic (36), Levert (9), J.-B. Millet (10), Monet (18), Morisot (17), L.-A. Ottin (14), Pissarro (12), Renoir (18), Rouart (10), Sisley (8), Tillot (8).
1877: 3rd Exhibition. "3ᵉ Exposition de peinture". 6, Rue Le Peletier. April, 10 a.m. – 5 p.m. 18 participants, 241 catalogue entries.
Caillebotte (6), Cals (10), Cézanne (16), Cordey (4), Degas (25), Guillaumin (12), J. François (2), Lamy (4), Levert (6), Maureau (4), Monet (30), Morisot (12), Piette (31), Pissarro (22), Renoir (21), Rouart (5), Sisley (17), Tillot (14).
1879: 4th Exhibition. "4ᵉ Exposition de peinture". 28, Avenue de l'Opéra. April 10 – May 11, 10 a.m. – 6 p.m. 14 participants, 246 catalogue entries.
F. Bracquemond (4), M. Bracquemond (2), Caillebotte (25), Cals (14), Cassatt (11), Degas (25), Forain (26), Lebourg (30), Monet (29), Pissarro (38), Rouart (23), Somm (3), Tillot (11), Zandomeneghi (5).
1880: 5th Exhibition. "5ᵉ Exposition de peinture." 10, Rue des Pyramides, on the corner of the Rue Saint-Honoré. April 1 – 30, 10 a.m. – 6 p.m. 19 participants, 232 catalogue entries.
F. Bracquemond (3), M. Bracquemond (3), Caillebotte (11), Cassatt (16), Degas (12), Forain (10), Gauguin (8), Guillaumin (22), Levert (20), Levert (8), Morisot (15), Pissarro (16), J.-F. Raffaëlli (36), J.-M. Raffaëlli (1), Rouart (12), Tillot (14), Vidal (9), Vignon (9), Zandomeneghi (8).
1881: 6th Exhibition. "6ᵉ Exposition de peinture". 35, Boulevard des Capucines. April 2 – May 1, 10 a.m. – 6 p.m. 13 participants, 170 catalogue entries.
Cassatt (11), Degas (8), Forain (10), Gauguin (10), Guillaumin (16), Morisot (7), Pissarro (28), J.-F. Raffaëlli (34), Rouart (15), Tillot (10), Vidal (1), Vignon (15), Zandomeneghi (5).
1882: 7th Exhibition. "7ᵉ Exposition des artistes indépendants". 251, Rue Saint-Honoré (Salon du Panorama de Reichshoffen). May 15 – June 15, a.m. – 6 p.m. 9 participants, 203 catalogue entries.
Caillebotte (17), Gauguin (13), Guillaumin (26), Monet (35), Morisot (9), Pissarro (36), Renoir (25), Sisley (27), Vignon (15).
1886: 8th Exhibition. "8ᵉ Exposition de peinture". 1, Rue Laffitte. May 15 – June 15, 10 a.m. – 6 p.m. 17 participants, 249 catalogue entries.
M. Bracquemond (6), Cassatt (7), Degas (15), Forain (13), Gauguin (19), Guillaumin (21), Morisot (14), C. Pissarro (20), L. Pissarro (10), Redon (15), Rouart (27), Schuffenecker (9), Seurat (9), Signac (18), Tillot (16), Vignon (18), Zandomeneghi (12).
Altogether, 56 artists participated in the eight Impressionist exhibitions. Pissarro was the only artist to take

part in all eight shows. Degas, Morisot and Rouart exhibited seven times, Guillaumin and Tillot six times, Monet und Caillebotte five times. The following statistics give the number of exhibitions (1st figure) and the number of catalogue entries (2nd figure): Pissarro (8/176), Degas (7/122), Rouart (7/103), Morisot (7/83), Guillaumin (6/96), Tillot (6/73), Monet (5/121), Caillebotte (5/67), Renoir (4/71), Forain (4/59), Sisley (4/57), Vignon (4/57), Gauguin (4/49), Cassatt (4/45), Cals (4/41), Zandomeneghi (4/40), Levert (4/26), Bracquemond, F. (3/12), Bracquemond, M. (3/11), Raffaëlli, J.-F. (2/70), Lebourg (2/50), Lepic (2/43), Cézanne (2/19), Ottin, L.A. (2/21), Béliard (2/12), Bureau (2/12), François (2/10), Vidal (2/10), Piette (1/31), Signac (1/18), Redon (1/15), Desboutin (1/13), Legros (1/12), Millet (1/10), Ottin, A.-L.-M. (1/10), Pissarro, L. (1/10), Schuffenecker (1/9), Seurat (1/9), Astruc (1/6), Attendu (1/6), Boudin (1/6), Mary (1/6), Brandon (1/5), Colin (1/5), De Nittis (1/5), Cordey (1/4), Debras (1/4), Lamy (1/4), Latouche (1/4), Maureau (1/4), Molins (1/4), Lepine (1/3), Somm (1/3), Mulot- Durivage (1/2), Robert (1/2), Raffaëlli, J.-M. (1/1).

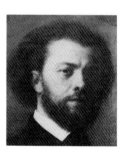

FANTIN-LATOUR Henri
1836 Grenoble – 1904 Buré (Orne)
Son of Théodore Fantin-Latour, the Italian painter and teacher of drawing and a Russian mother. 1841 moved to Paris. Trained first with his father, then 1850-1854 studied drawing at the school of Lecocq de Boisbaudran. After a short period at the Ecole des Beaux-Arts, he did temporary work at Courbet's studio. Copied drawings by Flaxman and paintings by Titian and Veronese in the Louvre. Met Fantin-Latour in 1859 and 1864 he made three visits to England, where he also worked and sold pictures. 1861 exhibited for the first time at the Salon, and thereafter regularly; from 1863 he exhibited in the Salon des Refusés. 1864 after the death of Delacroix he painted his "Hommage à Delacroix", which was exhibited in the Salon in 1865. 1867 showed a portrait of Manet at the Salon. As

well as portraits of artists he painted
numerous landscapes and genre
scenes and a large number of still lifes
with flower motifs, which established
his fame in France. 1870 painted the
famous picture "A Studio in Batignolles" in which he portrayed his colleagues. Despite close contacts with
the Impressionists, he rejected their
theories and never took part in their
exhibitions. A great lover of music, he
was moved by the works of Wagner
to paint opera scenes.
CATALOGUES: Fantin-Latour, V.: Catalogue de l'œuvre complet (1849-
1904) de F.-L. Paris 1911 (Reprint:
Amsterdam and New York 1969.–
Hediard, G.: F.-L. Lithographies.
Geneva 1981
BIBLIOGRAPHY: Abélès, L. (ed.): F.-L.
Coin de table. Musée d'Orsay, Paris
1987 (EC).– F.-L. Grand Palais, Paris
1982 (EC).– Kahn, G.: F.-L. Paris
1926.– Lucie-Smith, E.: F.-L. Oxford
1977.– Sutton, D. (ed.): H.F.-L. Wildenstein & Co, London 1984 (EC).–
Verrier, M.: F.-L. Paris 1978
ILLUSTRATIONS:
45   Still Life with Flowers and Fruit,
1865
81   A Studio in the Batignolles Quarter, 1870

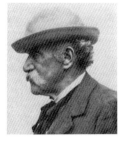

FATTORI Giovanni
1825 Livorno – 1908 Florence
Trained first with Antonio Baldini in
Livorno. 1846-1848 studied at the Accadèmia di Belle Arti in Florence
under Giuseppe Bezzuoli. 1848 interrupted his studies in the revolutionary
years 1848/49 to work in democratic
movements as courier for the Partito
d'Azione. 1850 resumed his studies in
Florence; a regular customer in the
Caffè Michelangiolo, a focal point of
political and later artistic discussion
and debate. 1859 became close
friends with Nino Costa, who encouraged him to paint in a Realist style.
Began to study plein-air. 1861 won
the Concorso Ricasoli prize for the
painting "The Italian Field after the
Battle of Magenta". 1861-1867
mainly in Livorno. The local peasant
life became the subject of his Realist
paintings. 1867 spent the summer in
Castiglioncello with Diego Martelli,
the supporter and theoretician of the
Macchiaioli. 1869 became a teacher
at the Florentine Istituto di Belle Arti.
1872 visited Rome and 1875 Paris,
where he was particularly impressed

by Corot. From 1875 numerous
graphic prints. 1891 wrote a fierce
polemic against the Pointillists. 1900
member of the Accadèmia Albertina
in Turin. One of the main representatives of the Macchiaioli, he
nevertheless retained a life-long aversion to Impressionism.
WRITINGS, DOCUMENTS: Dini, P. (ed.):
Inediti di G.F. Turin 1987.– Errico, F.
(ed.): G.F. Scritti autobiografici editi e
inediti. Rome 1980.– Fattori, G.: Ri-
cordi autobiografici. Florence n.d.
CATALOGUES: Biancaiardi, L. and B.
Della-Chiesa: L'opera completa di F.
Milan 1970.– Malesci, G.: Catalogazione illustrata della pittura a olio di
G.F. Novara 1961
BIBLIOGRAPHY: Baldccini, R.: G.F.
Milan 1949.– Cecchi, E.: G.F. Rome
1933.– Cecconi, A.: G.F. Florence
1914.– Ciaranfi, F.: Incisioni di Fat-
tori. Livorno 1953.– Durbè D. and
M. de Micheli: G.F. Busto Arsizio
1961.– Durbè D.: G.F. Livorno 1953
(EC).– Franchi, A.: G.F. Florence
1910.– G.F. Dipinti 1854-1906. With
contributions by G. Matteucci et al.
Florence and Milan 1988 (EC).– Ghi-
glia, O.: L'opera di G.F. Florence
1913.– Malesci, G.: Catalogazione illustrata della pittura a olio di G.F.
Novara 1961.– Micheli, M. de: G.F.
Busto Arsizio 1961.– Ojetti, U.: G.F.
Milan 1921.– Ommaggio a Fattori.
Artisti del '800 Italiano. Galleria Narciso. Turin 1968 (EC).– Soffici, A.:
G.F. Rome 1921.– Somarè E.: Cento
opere di G.F. nella Collezione Galli.
Milan 1921.– Tinti, M.: G.F. Rome
and Milan 1926
ILLUSTRATIONS:
535 The Palmieri's Bathing Rotunda,
1866
537 The Haystack, after 1872

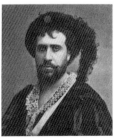

FAURE Jean-Baptiste
1830 Moulins – 1914 Paris
Opera singer, music teacher and composer. One of the first admirers and
collectors of Impressionist paintings;
friends with Durand-Ruel and with
many painters, whose meetings he attended. 1873 bought some pictures
by Manet for a considerable sum, including "Lola de Valence" (p. 46).
Supported Degas, with whom he soon
fell out because Degas failed to produce paintings he had ordered and
paid for. Bought paintings by Monet,
Pissarro and Sisley. 1881 became a
member of the Legion of Honour.

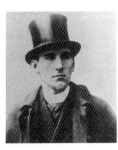

FENEON Félix
1861 Turin – 1944 Châtenay-Malabry
French writer and art critic of Symbolism. 1881 took a post in Paris at the
Ministry of War. 1884 co-founder of
two journals; influenced by Seurat.
1886 became the first art critic to support the Pointillist style, for which he
employed the term "Neo-Impressionism". Published polemical articles of
literary quality, collected under the
title "The Impressionists in the Year
1886". His "Revue indépendante" organised small exhibitions. 1891 his
portrait was painted by Signac
(p. 321). 1894 as a supporter of Anarchism he was arrested and tried for
possession of explosives; defended by
T. Natanson. Until 1903, editorial secretary of Natanson's "La Revue Blanche", for which he organised exhibitions. 1906-1925 Director of the Bernheim-Jeune art gallery. Thereafter he
worked on the catalogue of Seurat.

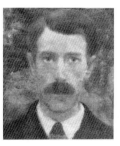

FERENCZY Károly
1862 Vienna – 1917 Budapest
1886 began to paint in Naples and
Rome. 1887-1889 in Paris, under the
tutelage of Bastien-Lepage and others.
1890-1892 in Szentendre on the Danube; painted Realist pictures. 1893-
1896 studied at the Munich Academy
under Herterich, his style becoming
increasingly Impressionist. 1896-1905
mainly in Nagybánya (Baia Mare); became a strong influence on the artists'
colony there. 1901 exhibited for the
first time at the Munich and Berlin exhibitions. 1905-1917 Professor at the
art college in Budapest.
BIBLIOGRAPHY: Die Familie Ferenczy.
Burgschloss Buda, Budapest 1968.–
Genthon, I.: K.F. Budapest 1979.–

Murádin, J.: A.F. müvészcsalád Erdé-
lyben. Bukarest 1981.– Petrovics, E.:
K.F. Budapest 1943.– Réti, I.: A Nagy-
bányai müvésztelep. Budapest 1954
ILLUSTRATIONS:
521 October, 1903
522 Summer Day, 1906

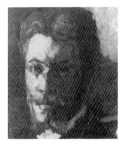

FINCH Alfred William
1854 Brussels – 1930 Helsinki
Known as Willy Finch. 1878-1880 -
studied at the Academy in Brussels,
where he became friends with Ensor.
Around 1880 he painted Realist landscapes and sea views; influenced by
Ensor and Whistler. Co-founder of the
group Les Vingt in Brussels. Frequent
trips to England, where in 1884 he
met Whistler and invited him to take
part the first exhibition of Les Vingt.
1887 and 1888 invited by Whistler to
exhibitions in England. The first
Belgian to adopt Neo-Impressionism –
in 1887 after he had seen Seurat's
"A Sunday Afternoon at the Ile de la
Grande Jatte" (pp. 260/261).
1889 exhibited for the first time with
the Indépendants in Paris. From 1891
he concentrated on ceramics. 1897 in
Finland, where he was appointed
Director of a ceramics concern; introduced Finnish painters to the new
styles of Neo-Impressionism and
worked at the revival of Finnish architecture.
ILLUSTRATION:
424 Haystacks, 1889

FORAIN Jean-Louis
1852 Rheims – 1931 Paris
Made Paris his life-long home. As a
youth he copied the paintings of the
Old Masters in the Louvre. Studied
first with the history painter Jacques-
son de la Chevreuse and later at the
Ecole des Beaux-Arts under Gérôme.
Turned away from history paintings
and became influenced by Manet,
Degas and Japanese woodcuts. 1874
rejected by the Salon. Invited by
Degas to take part in the 4th, 5th, 6th
and 8th Impressionist exhibitions.
1884 and 1885 exhibited in the
Salon. From 1869, influenced by the
graphic art of Goya and the social
criticism of Daumier, he turned almost exclusively to graphic depictions
of modern urban life. From 1876 illustrator for various newspapers and
journals, such as "La Cravache", "Le
Monde Parisien", "Vogue", "Le Figaro" and "Echo de Paris". Famous

for his caricatures, he became one of the most popular artists of his day. 1889 founded the weekly magazine "Le Fifre" and 1898/99 together with Caran d'Ache the journal "Psst!". From 1892 he published his graphic work. In his later years after 1909 he produced mainly religious lithographs and etchings.

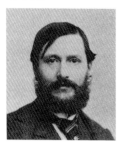

CATALOGUE: Craig-Faxon, A.: J.-L.F.: A Catalogue Raisonné of the Prints. New York and London 1982.– Guérin, M.: J.-L.F. L'œuvre gravé. 2 vols. San Francisco 1980
BIBLIOGRAPHY: Bory, J.-F: F. Paris 1979.– Browse, L.: F. the Painter (1852-1931). London 1978.– Chagnaud-Forain, J. et al. (eds.): J.-L.F., 1852-1931. Musée Marmottan, Paris 1978 (EC).– Faxon, A.C. (ed.): J.-L.F., 1852-1931: Works from New England Collections. Danforth Museum, Framingham 1979 (EC).– Faxon, A.C. and Y. Brayer: J.-L.F.: Artist, Realist, Humanist. Washington 1982 (EC).– Guérin, M.: J.-L.F. lithographe. Paris 1910 (Reprint: San Francisco 1980).– Guérin, M.: J.-L.F. aquafortiste. Paris 1912.– J.-L.F., 1852-1931. Musée Toulouse-Lautrec, Albi 1982 (EC)
ILLUSTRATIONS:
180 In the Wings, 1878
210 A Box at the Opéra, c. 1880
211 In the Café de la Nouvelle-Athènes, 1879
262 Ball at the Paris Opera, c. 1885
336 At the Races, c. 1890

FORTUNY Y CARBO MARSAL Mariano
1838 Reus – 1874 Rome
Brought up in the household of his grandfather, a carpenter and woodcarver. 1850 took drawing lessons at the studio of Domingo Soberanos, then with the miniature painter and silversmith Antonio Bassa. 1852 moved to Barcelona. Attended the Escuela de Artes y Oficios and studied under the sculptor Domingo Talarn. 1853 studied at the art academy of San Jorge; his teachers were Claudio Lorenzale, Milá and Gavarni. 1858-1860 Rome scholarship. 1860 sent to Morocco as a war painter; exhibited his works in Barcelona; returned to Rome via Paris. 1862 went back to Morocco. 1863 his Rome scholarship was extended. 1865 the Duke of Riánsares became his patron. 1867 married the daughter of

the painter Federico Madrazo in Madrid. As a history painter his genre pictures depicting scenes from the 18th century were highly successful, 1870 sensational sale by Goupil in Paris of the painting "At the Vicarage". 1870 lived in Andalusia. 1871 third trip to Morocco. 1872 another visit to Rome.

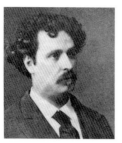

BIBLIOGRAPHY: Alegre Núñez, L.: F. Madrid 1958.– A Remembrance of M.F., 1871-1949. Los Angeles County Museum of Art, Los Angeles 1968 (EC).– F. 1838-1914, Fundación Caja de Pensiones, Madrid 1989.– Gil Fillol, L.: M.F., su vida, su obra, su arte. Barcelona 1952.– González, C. and M. Martí: M.F.M. Barcelona 1990.– M.F. Walters Art Gallery, Baltimore 1970 (EC).– M.F. et ses amis français. Musée Goya, Castres 1974 (EC).– M.F. Museo de Arte Moderno, Barcelona 1974 (EC).– M.F.M. (1871-1949): pinturas, grabados, fotografías, trajes, telas y objetos. Mercado Puerta de Toledo, Madrid 1988 (EC)
ILLUSTRATIONS:
552 Fortuny's Garden
555 At the Vicarage, 1870

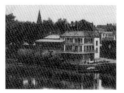

FOURNAISE, Restaurant
A restaurant popular with writers and painters in Chatou, and named after its proprietor. Maupassant, Renoir and Caillebotte were regular customers. Renoir painted "The Luncheon of the Boating Party" (p.220), in which the Fournaise family are pictured with his friends. Renoir painted Fournaise's portrait, and his pretty daughter Alphonsine modelled for him in several paintings, including "La Grenouillère" (p.73).

FRANC-LAMY
1855 Clermont-Ferrand – 1919 Paris
Real name: Pierre Désiré Eugène Franc. Studied at the Ecole des Beaux-

Arts under Pils and Gérôme. Under the influence of Renoir his style moved to Impressionism. 1877 took part in the 3rd Impressionist exhibition with four works of art. Thereafter he returned to a more Classical style. Above all he painted landscapes and portraits, and was active as an illustrator. Member of the Société des Arts Français; from 1880 he exhibited in their salon. 1889 well received at the World Fair and 1900 won a medal. He is depicted in Renoir's painting "Le Moulin de la Galette" (p.153).
ILLUSTRATION:
370 An Exotic Beauty

FRANCOIS Jacques (Jacques-François)
Pseudonym for a woman whose real name has never been discovered. 1876 and 1877 took part in the 2nd and 3rd Impressionist exhibitions.

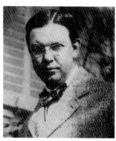

FRIESEKE Frederick Carl
1874 Owosso (MI) – 1939 New York
Studied at the Academy in Chicago, then in Paris with Constant, Laurens and Whistler. Lived alternately in New York and Paris. Member of the Société Nationale des Beaux-Arts in Paris. From 1901 he exhibited regularly in their salon. Concentrated on painting female nudes and portraits, inspired by Whistler, in subdued, hazy colours. Painted some murals in the Wanamaker and Shelbourne hotels in Atlantic City. Exhibited in many international shows in Paris, Venice, Rome, Mannheim, Pittsburgh, Philadelphia. Several awards: 1904 silver medal at the World Fair in Saint Louis (MO) and the gold medal at the international exhibition in Munich; 1935 second Clark Prize at the Corcoran Art Gallery, Washington (DC).
BIBLIOGRAPHY: Chambers, B.W. (ed.): F.C.F. Women in Repose. Berry Hill Galleries, New York 1990 (EC).– F.F. 1874-1939. Telfair Academy of Arts and Sciences, Savannah (GA) 1974 (EC).– A Retrospective Exhibition of the Work of F.F. Maxwell Galleries, San Francisco 1982 (EC).– Weller, A.S.: F.F., 1874- 1939. Hirschl and Adler Galleries, New York 1966 (EC)
ILLUSTRATION:
635 Lady in a Garden, c. 1912

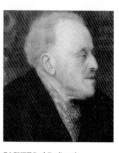

GACHET Paul-Ferdinand
1828 Lille – 1909 Auvers-sur-Oise
French doctor, homoeopath, socialist, art collector, painter and graphic artist. 1848-1855 studied medicine in Paris; made friends with Realist writers and artists. 1855-1859 in Montpellier. From 1859 doctor and homoeopath in Paris, met and painted with artists at such venues as the Café Guerbois and the Nouvelle-Athènes. Held socialist views. 1865-1876 taught anatomy at the state school of art. 1871 military doctor during the Commune. 1872 bought a house in Auvers, where he met and supported Daubigny, Pissarro, Guillaumin and Cézanne. 1874 lent pictures by Cézanne from his own collection to the 1st Impressionist exhibition. Formed a friendship with Renoir. 1890 took on the psychiatric treatment of van Gogh and continued until the latter's death. 1891 exhibited for the first time at the Salon des Indépendants. 1952 Gachet's extraordinary collection of paintings was bequeathed by his son to the French state – now one of the major attractions of the Musée d'Orsay.

GAGNON Clarence Alphonse
1881 Montreal – 1942 Montreal
1897-1900 studied under William Brymner at the Art Association of Montreal. Formed a friendship with W.H. Clapp and shared a studio with him in St. Lawrence. Influenced by Cullen, to whom he owed his change to a brighter-coloured palette. 1904/05 studied at the Académie Julian in Paris under Laurens. Study trips in France, Spain and Italy. 1904 received the bronze medal at an exhibition in Saint-Louis. 1906 exhibited for the first time at the Société des Arts Français in Paris and from 1911 at the salon of the Société Nationale. 1909 returned to Canada. Exhibited at the Canadian Art Club and became a member there in 1910. Stayed mostly in Baie St. Paul, where he painted the landscape of Quebec in the open air. From 1913 he received great acclaim for his winter landscapes. 1915 took part in the World Fair in San Francisco. 1922-1936 second visit to France. Travelled in Italy and Spain.
BIBLIOGRAPHY: Boissay, R.: C.G. Montreal 1988
ILLUSTRATION:
637 Summer Breeze at Dinard, 1907

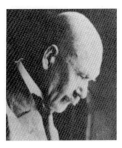

GALLEN-KALLELA Akseli
1865 Pori, Björneborg – 1931
Stockholm
1881-1884 studied at the Finnish Art
Society in Helsinki and the private
academy of A. von Becker. 1884-
1889 in Paris at the Académie Julian
under Bouguereau and at Cormon's
studio. Began realistic plein-air painting under the influence of Bastien-Lepage. 1888 and 1889 exhibited at the
Salon; 1889 first Finnish painter to
become a member of the Société Nationale des Beaux-Arts. 1890 went to
Karelia on the eastern border of Finland. Started the Karelian movement
of Finnish artists. 1888 and 1892
came into contact with Symbolism in
Paris and introduced it into Finland.
1894 designed and built a house and
studio in Ruovesi and at the end of
the year went to Berlin. 1895 became
acquainted with the Arts and Crafts
movement in London. 1897/98 studied fresco technique in Italy. 1900
painted ornamental frescoes of the
Finnish national heroic epic "Kalevala" for the Finnish pavilion of the
World Fair in Paris. 1902 at Kandinsky's invitation he exhibited 36 works
at the "Phalanx IV" exhibition in Munich. In 1903 he was at the Vienna Secession and in 1910 showed with the
"Brücke" in Dresden. 1909/10
travelled in East Africa. 1914 exhibited in San Francisco, New York
and Chicago and travelled through
the USA. He died while working on illustrations for a large edition of the
"Kalevala".
BIBLIOGRAPHY: Juhla-Kanteletar
(ed.): A.G.-K. Helsinki 1984.– Levi-
son, A.: A.G.-K. St. Petersburg 1908.–
Martin, T. and D. Sivén: A.G.-K: National Artist of Finland. Helsinki
1985.– Okkonen, O.: A.G.-K. Elämä
ja taide. Helsinki 1961.– Wietek, Der
finnische Maler A.G.-K. (1865-1931)
als Mitglied der Brücke. In: Brücke-
Archiv 2/3 (1968/69), pp. 3-26
ILLUSTRATION:
484 Démasquée, 1888

GASQUET Joachim
1873 Aix-en-Provence – 1921 Paris
Provençal poet and close friend of Cézanne from 1869 to 1904; his father
Henri had been a childhood friend of
Cézanne. The two kept in close contact by letter and in 1912/13 Gasquet
wrote a book on Cézanne that included conversations with him. Their
friendship was based on deep reli-

gious feelings. Cézanne painted his
portrait and gave him a picture of
Mont Sainte-Victoire.

GAUGUIN Paul
1848 Paris – 1903 Atuona Hiva Oa
(Marquesas Islands)
1849-1855 son of an emigré Republican journalist; grew up in Lima
(Peru), then in Orléans and Paris.
1865-1871 went to sea. 1871-1883
worked as a stock-broker in Paris,
painting in his spare time. 1873 married a Danish woman, Mette Gad; the
couple had five children. 1874 met
Pissarro and other Impressionists and
studied at the Académie Colarossi.
1876 exhibited for the first time at
the Salon. 1879 painted with Pissarro
in Pontoise; exhibited at the 4th Impressionist exhibition. 1880-1886 exhibited at the Impressionist shows
(5th-8th). 1880 at the Salon des Indépendants. 1881 painted with Pissarro
and Cézanne. 1882 moved to Rouen,
then Copenhagen; got into financial
difficulties. 1885 returned to Paris,
leaving the family in Denmark. 1886
went to Pont-Aven for the first time,
met Bernard. Became acquainted with
the van Gogh brothers in Paris and
took part in the 8th Impressionist exhibition. 1887 travelled with the
painter Laval to Panama and Martinique. 1888 with Bernard and
others in Pont-Aven; in his depictions
of Breton customs his style moved towards "Synthetist Symbolism". Exhibited with Theo van Gogh. A stay
with Vincent van Gogh in Arles
ended in disastrous personal conflict.

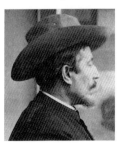

1889 exhibited with "The Twenty" in
Brussels and during the Paris World
Fair at the Café Volpini. Painted in
Pont-Aven and Le Pouldu; exerted influence on Sérusier, Denis and Bonnard. 1890 once more in Le Pouldu
and in the circle of Symbolists in
Paris. 1891 after auctioning his paintings and breaking off with Bernard he
emigrated to Tahiti, to live an alternative life to that of European city civili-
sation. Became ill with syphilis. 1893-
1895 in Paris, Copenhagen and Brittany but had no success trying to sell
his large, symbolic pictures with their
areas of flat, bright colour and scenes
of the South Seas, the epitome of
exotic "Primitivism". 1895-1901 returned to Tahiti, where he also
worked on sculptures, but his health
suffered, partly through alcohol.

1897 published his autobiographical
work "Noa Noa". 1898 suicide attempt and desperate poverty. 1900
commissioned by the dealer Vollard.
1901 moved to the Island of Dominique in the Marquesas Islands.
1902 protested against the policies of
the colonial administration and was
arrested 1903; he died, worn out, at
the age of 54.
WRITINGS, DOCUMENTS: Gauguin, P.:
Vorher und Nachher. Munich 1920.–
Gauguin, P.: Avant et après. Paris
1923, Tahiti 1989.– Gauguin, P.:
Oviri. Écrits d'un sauvage. Paris
1974.– Gauguin, P.: Mon père P.G.
Paris 1938.– Gauguin, P.: My Father,
P.G. New York 1937.– Gauguin, P.: A
ma fille Aline, ce cahier est dédié. 2
vols. Bordeaux 1989.– Guérin, D.
(ed.): P.G. The Writings of a Sauvage,
P.G. New York 1977.– Joachim Gasquet's Cézanne. A Memoir with Conversations. London 1991.– Joly-Se-
galen, A. (ed.): Lettres de G. à Daniel
de Monfreid. Paris 1950.– Loize, J.
(ed.): Noa Noa par P.G. Paris 1966.–
Malingue, M. (ed.): Lettres de G. à sa
femme et à ses amis. Paris 1946.–
Malingue, M. (ed.): P.G. Letters to his
Wife and Friends. Cleveland 1949.–
Merlhès, V.: Correspondance de P.G.
Vol. I. 1873-1888. Paris 1984.– Mittelstädt, P. (ed.): P.G. Der Traum von
einem neuen Leben. Berlin 1991.–
The Intimate Journals of P.G. London
1930.– Wadley, N. (ed.): Noa Noa.
G.s Tahiti. The Original Manuscript.
Oxford 1985
CATALOGUES: Field, S.: P.G. Mono-
types. Museum of Art, Philadelphia
1963 (EC).– Gray, C.: Sculpture and
Ceramics of P.G. Baltimore 1963,
New York 1980.– Guérin, M.:
L'œuvre gravé de G. 2 vols. San Fran-
cisco 1980.– Kornfeld, E., H. Joa-
chim and E. Morgan: P.G. Catalogue
Raisonné of his Prints. Berne 1988.–
Sugana, G.M.: L'opera completa di G.
Milan 1972.– Sugana, G.M.: Tout
l'œuvre peint de G. Paris 1981.– Wil-
denstein, G.: G, sa vie, son œuvre.
Paris 1958.– Wildenstein, G.: G., catalogue. Paris 1964
BIBLIOGRAPHY: Alexandre, A.: P.G.:
Sa vie et le sens de son œuvre. Paris
1930.– Amishai-Maisels, Z.: G.'s Religious Themes. New York and London 1985.– Andersen, W.: G.'s Paradise Lost. New York 1971.– Art of
P.G. National Gallery, Washington;
Art Institute of Chicago; Grand Pa-
lais, Paris 1988/89 (EC).– Bismarck,
B. v.: Die Gauguinlegende. Die Rezep-
tion P.G.s in den französischen Kunst-
kritik 1880-1903. Doctoral thesis,
Berlin 1989.– Boudaille, G.: G. Paris
1963.– Bowness, A.: P.G. London
1971.– Boyle-Turner, C. and S. Josefo-
witz: G. und die Druckgraphik der
Schule von Pont-Aven. Villa Stuck,
Munich 1990 (EC).– Cachin, F.: G.
Paris 1988.– Cachin, F.: G.: The
Quest for Paradise. New York 1990.–
Chassé, C.: G. et le groupe de Pont-
Aven. Paris 1948.– Daix, P.: G. Paris
1989.– Danielsson, B.: G. in the
South Seas. London 1964.– Dorival,
B.: P.G. Carnet de Tahiti. Paris 1954.–
Dovski, L. v.: P.G. oder die Flucht
von der Zivilisation. Berne 1950.–

Dovski, L. v.: Die Wahrheit über P.G.
Darmstadt 1973.– Field, R.S.: P.G.:
The Paintings of the First Voyage to
Tahiti. New York 1977.– Gauguin.
The National Gallery, Washington;
The Art Institute of Chicago, Chi-
cago; Grand Palais, Paris 1988 (EC).–
Gibson, M.: P.G. Recklinghausen
1991.– Gibson, M: P.G. Paris 1990.–
Gray, C.: Sculpture and Ceramics of
P.G. Baltimore 1963, New York
1980.– Gucchi, R.: G. à la Mar-
tinique. Vaduz 1979.– Haase, A. et al.
(eds.): P.G.: Das druckgraphische
Werk. Stuck-Villa, Munich 1978
(EC).– Hoog, M.: P.G. Leben und
Werk. Munich 1987.– Hoog, M.: P.G.
Vie et œuvre. Fribourg 1987.– Hoog,
M.: P.G. Life and Work. London
New York 1987.– Jaworska, W.: G.
et l'école de Pont-Aven. Neuchâtel
1971. (Engl. edition: London 1972).–
Jirat-Wasiutynski, V.: G. in the Context of Symbolism. New York and
London 1978.– Lövgren, S.: The Genesis of Modernism. Seurat, Gauguin,
van Gogh and French Symbolism in
the 1880's. Uppsala 1959, Bloomington (IN) and London 1971.– Le Pichon, Y.: Sur les traces de G. Paris
1986.– Leprohon, P.: P.G. Paris
1975.– Malingue, M.: G., le peintre
et son œuvre. Paris 1948.– Malingue,
M.: La vie prodigieuse de G. Paris
1987.– Mittelstädt, K.: Die Selbstbild-
nisse P.G.'s. Berlin 1966.– Perruchot,
H.: G. Paris 1960.– Perruchot, H.: La
vie de G. Paris 1961.– Pickvance, R.
(ed.): The Drawings of G. London,
New York, Sydney and Toronto 1970
(EC).– Pool, P.: P.G. New York 1978.–
Pope, K.K.R.: G. and Martinique.
Doctoral thesis, The University of
Texas. Austin 1981.– Prather, M. and
C.F. Stuckey (eds.): G. A Retrospec-
tive. New York 1987.– Rewald J.: G.
Paris 1937.– Rewald, J.: G. London
and New York 1938.– Rewald, J.:
G.'s Drawings. New York and Lon-
don 1958.– Roskmaker, H.R.: G.
and the 19th Century Art Theory.
Amsterdam 1972.– Teilhet-Fisk, J.:
Paradise Reviewed: An Interpretation
of G.'s Polynesian Symbolism. Ann
Arbor (MI) 1983.– Thomson, B.: G.
London 1987.– Walther, I.F.: P.G.
1848-1903. The Primitive Sophisticate. Cologne 1988.– Wildenstein,
G.: G. Paris 1964.– Wildenstein, D.
and R. Cogniat: G. Garden City
1974.– Wise, S.: P.G. His Life and his
Paintings. Chicago 1980
ILLUSTRATIONS:
207 Study of a Nude. Suzanne Sewing, 1880
265 The Four Breton Girls, c. 1886
302 Night Café in Arles (Madame Ginoux), 1888
302 L'Arlesienne (Madame Ginoux),
1888
303 Vision after the Sermon: Jacob
Wrestling with the Angel, 1888
332 Pastime ("Arearea"), 1892
333 We Shall Not Go to Market
Today ("Ta matete"), 1892
334 Two Women on the Beach, 1891
352 The Dug-Out ("Te vaa"), 1896
353 "Why are you angry?" ("No te
aha oe riri?"), 1896
377 Sunflowers on a Chair, 1901

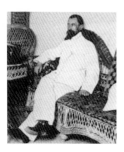

GAUSSON Léo
1860 Lagny-sur-Marne (Seine-et-Marne) – 1944 Lagny-sur-Marne
1883 his interest in art was awakened at an early age in the studio of the graphic artist Eugène Froment, a friend of the family. He began as a wood sculptor, then studied graphics, finally turning to painting. At the Atelier Froment he met Maximilien Luce and Cavallo Peduzzi. Joined the Neo-Impressionists and Symbolists. Influenced by Camille Pissarro, Paul Signac, Luce, van Gogh, Gauguin and Emile Bernard. 1886 exhibited for the first time at the Salon and 1887-1900 at the Salon des Indépendants. Friends with Adolphe Retté, whose books he illustrated; published his own poems under the pseudonym Montesiste. 1899 one-man exhibition at the Théâtre Antoine in Paris. 1900-1910 lived in Africa.
CATALOGUE: Hanotelle, M.: L.G. Catalogue raisonné (in preparation)
BIBLIOGRAPHY: L.G. 1860-1944. Dessins, aquarelles, gouaches, pastels, peintures. Hôtel Drouot, Paris 1979 (EC)
ILLUSTRATION:
310 Undergrowth, 1888

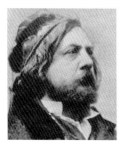

GAUTIER Théophile
1811 Tarbes – 1872 Neuilly-sur-Seine
At first a painter, then poet and critic. Important proponent of Impressionist ideas. 1835 published his famous work "Mademoiselle de Maupin" where he first put forward the concept of "L'art pour l'art", which was to be very significant for the development of aesthetic theory.

GEFFROY Gustave
1855 Paris – 1926 Paris
Novelist, historian and art critic with radical Realist views. Began his career working at Clemenceau's journal "Justice". Frequently in the company of Impressionist painters, he wrote numerous articles about their aims and principles, as well as the introductions to exhibitions by individual artists such as Monet, Pissarro, Rodin and Morisot. 1876 visited Manet at his studio and in 1886 met Monet on Belle-Ile; he later wrote a biography of Monet. In 1894 he published a history of Impressionism in "La vie artistique", and in 1924 "Claude Monet, sa vie, son temps, son œuvre". In his later years he became director of the firm Gobelin.

GENNEVILLIERS
Idyllic spot on the right bank of the Seine near Paris. Manet's family owned a house here and it became a favourite retreat for him, as also for the painter Berthe Morisot after her marriage to Eugène Manet. Caillebotte was a member of the local rowing club and also owned a small house there.

GEROME Jean-Léon
1824 Vesoul – 1904 Paris
From 1841 studied at the Atelier Delaroche. 1843 with his teacher in Rome. 1844 resumed his studies at the same studio, now under Gleyre. 1847 staged his first exhibition, with success, at the Salon. His favourite subjects were scenes drawn from Classical and Oriental mythology, which he depicted in Classical style with realistic precision. 1855 received into the Legion of Honour for his picture "The Age of Augustus". Numerous trips to Germany, 1853 on the Danube and then for five years in the Middle East. 1865 member of the Academy, where he taught for many years; from 1878 also active as a sculptor. Belonged to the conservative academic party and became a bitter opponent of the Impressionists. In 1894 he rejected Caillebotte's legacy to the French state with the words: "If the state accepts such rubbish, then the decay of morals must be already considerably advanced".
CATALOGUE: Ackermann, G.M.: The Life and Work of J.-L.G., with a Catalogue Raisonné. London 1986.–
Ackermann, G.M.: La vie et l'œuvre de J.-L.G. Paris 1986.–
BIBLIOGRAPHY: Ackerman, G.M.: J.-L.G. Courbevoie 1985

GERVEX Henri
1852 Paris – 1929 Paris
Studied under Cabanel, at whose studio he met Forain, Regnault and Bastien-Lepage. 1873 exhibited for the first time at the Salon. Long trip to Russia, appeared at the Tsar's court. Became friends with Manet and Renoir. 1874 exhibited once again at the Salon. 1878 his nude picture "Rolla" caused a sensation and was rejected by the Salon. 1883 artistic decoration of the town hall in the 19th arrondissement and of the Opéra Comique.

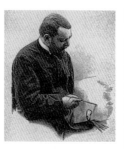

1884 invited to exhibit with Les Vingt in Brussels; organised a Manet retrospective. 1889 and 1900 Jury member at the World Fair; argued in favour of giving the Impressionists their due recognition. 1904 executed a cycle of frescoes for the town hall in Neuilly. A favourite Salon painter, whose range of subjects included female nudes, portraits and society scenes.
ILLUSTRATION:
250 The Salon Jury, 1885

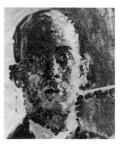

GILMAN Harold
1876 Rode Somerset – 1919 London
1896 studied at the Hastings Art School, 1897 at the Slade School in London. 1904 stayed for a year in Spain, where he copied Velázquez. Travelled in Norway and the USA. 1906 met Sickert. His initial painting style resembled that of Pissarro and Vuillard. 1911 visited Paris. Became interested in van Gogh and Cézanne. Founded the Camden Town Group, who took Continental Impressionism as their model. 1913 the group joined with others to form the London Group, with Gilman as President. His still lifes, portraits, landscapes and interiors moved increasingly towards Post-Impressionism. 1918 commissioned by the Canadian government to paint a large picture as a war memorial in Ottawa.
BIBLIOGRAPHY: Cousey, A. and R. Thomson (eds.): H.G. 1876-1919. The Arts Council of Great Britain, London 1981 (EC).– H.G. The Arts Council of Great Britain, London 1954 (EC).–Lewis, W. and L. Fergusson: H.G. An Appreciation: London 1919

ILLUSTRATION:
589 Canal Bridge, Flekkefjord, 1912

GIMENO ARASA Francisco
1858 Tortosa (Tarragona) – 1927 Barcelona
Began in the workshop of a decorative painter in Tortosa. After military service, he settled in Barcelona. 1884 became friends with de Haes, whom he visited frequently in Madrid. Between 1888 and 1904 took part in the World Fair in Barcelona and in the Nacional de Bellas Artes in Madrid. Did not receive due acclaim until 1915. His powerful brushwork created looser forms and motifs, but without becoming abstract.
ILLUSTRATION:
569 Blue Water

GIVERNY
Village at the confluence of the Epte and the Seine, about 45 miles from Paris. Monet moved here with his family in 1883. The park-like garden which he had laid out there appears in many of his pictures (pp. 362, 364, 365, 393). Artist friends, including Renoir, Sisley, Pissarro, Sargent and Rodin, and in particular foreign artists like the American Impressionists, all came to Giverny to visit Monet and to paint for themselves. (cf. p. 622).

GLEYRE Charles
1806 Chevilly (Vaud) – 1874 Paris
Swiss by birth, he studied first with his uncle in Lyons. From 1825 studied with the portrait and history painter Louis Hersent and with Bonington; attended the Ecole des Beaux-Arts and the Académie Suisse in Paris. 1829-1834 lived in Rome; met the Classical painter Léopold Robert, whose painting style influenced him considerably. Travelled with an American patron in Sicily, Greece, Egypt and the Middle East. 1837 settled for a short period in Khartoum. 1838 produced some early examples of plein-air painting. 1840 exhibited for the first time at the Salon. 1843 first notable success at the Salon. 1843 took over the studio of Delaroche and opened a popular, liberal school, the Atelier Gleyre, which had close contacts with the Ecole des Beaux-Arts and in which artists like Whistler, Monet, Renoir, Sisley and Bazille all worked. 1845 travelled to Venice, London and Madrid. 1864 closed the Atelier due to illness. Persuaded Sisley, Bazille and Renoir to follow him to Fontainebleau. Gleyre painted mythological, historical and religious pictures, many in large format, in a cool, Classical style but not without some Romantic emotion and feeling.
BIBLIOGRAPHY: Thévoz, M.: L'académisme et ses fantasmes. Le réalisme imaginaire de Charles Gleyre, Paris 1980

GOENEUTTE Norbert
1854 Paris – 1894 Auvers-sur-Oise
After training as a clerical assistant he studied painting at Pils's studio. Friendship with Frédéric-Samuel

Cordey. Regular customer in the Café de la Nouvelle-Athènes, where he met Renoir and Manet, who strongly influenced his style of painting. **1876** exhibited for the first time at the Salon. Helped organise the exhibition "Peintres graveurs". Moved to Auvers for health reasons, and was treated by Gachet. Through the support of his brother Charles, he was able to continue his artistic career without financial difficulties. He oftened modelled for Renoir's paintings: "The Swing" (p. 144), "Moulin de la Galette" (p. 153). Painted a famous portrait of Gachet (Paris, Musée d'Orsay; detail: see above).

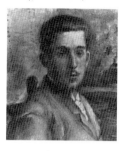

CATALOGUE: Goeneutte, N.-G.: N.G. Catalogue raisonné (in preparation)
BIBLIOGRAPHY: Knyff, G. d.: L'art libre au XIXe siècle ou la vie de N.G. Paris 1978
ILLUSTRATION:
155 The Boulevard de Clichy under Snow, 1876

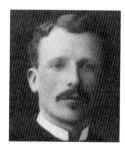

GOGH Theo van
1857 Groot-Zundert – 1891 Utrecht
Art dealer and younger brother of Vincent van Gogh. From **1878** he worked for Goupil-Boussod-Valadon. As manager of the branch on the Boulevard Montmartre 19, where Adolphe Goupil began his career, he supported the sale of Impressionist pictures. From **1884**, Vincent came to Paris and lived with him in the Rue Lepic (p. 283); his interest in Impressionism increased. He kept in close contact with his brother (from **1872** they corresponded frequently), and until Vincent's death he supported him with gifts of artistic materials

and money. Theo's sales as an art dealer include: 1 Cézanne, 23 Degas, 18 Gauguins, 5 Manets, 24 Monets, 23 Pissarros, 4 Renoirs and 7 Sisleys.

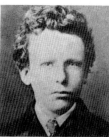

GOGH Vincent van
1853 Groot-Zundert – 1890 Auvers-sur-Oise
1869-1876 son of a parson, he worked in branches of the Paris art dealer Goupil in The Hague, Brussels and London. **1876** assistant teacher and preacher in and near London. **1877/78** trained as a lay preacher, began to draw. **1878-1880** lay preacher in the mining area of Borinage, suffered from poverty. His brother Theo, the art dealer, began to support him financially. **1880** decided on a career as an artist and studied at the academy in Brussels. **1881-1883** with the Realist painter A. Mauve in The Hague, lived with a prostitute. **1883-1885** in Drenthe (Northern Holland) and at his parent's house in Nuenen, drew and painted dark realistic scenes from the life of the poor. **1885/86** in Antwerp, for a short time at the college of art. **1886-1888** in Paris; at the Atelier Cormon he met Bernard and Toulouse-Lautrec, and through Theo the Impressionists and Neo-Impressionists; he began to employ with motifs, bright colours and style of painting. Became friends with Gauguin; impressed by the two-dimensional, decorative effects of Japanese woodcuts. **1888** in Arles; painted in a heavy style with strong colours to signify passion. A short period of artistic cooperation with Gauguin ended in a disastrous row and mental instability; in a bout of madness he cut off part of his left ear. **1889** in hospital at Arles and at the mental hospital in Saint-Rémy. Exhibited with the Indépendants in Paris. **1890** exhibited with Les Vingt in Brussels, where one of his acquaintances, the painter Anna Boch, bought the only painting he ever sold in his lifetime. Moved to Auvers-sur-Oise, where he was treated by Gachet and where, in **1890**, he shot himself. His extensive later work became a basic influence on the development of Fauvism and Expressionism.
WRITINGS, DOCUMENTS: Frank, H.: V.G. in Selbstzeugnissen und Bilddokumenten. Reinbek bei Hamburg 1976.– Gogh, V. v.: Sämtliche Briefe. Ed. by F. Erpel. 6 vols. Berlin 1965-

1968.– Gogh, V. v.: The Complete Letters of V.v.G. 3 vols. London and New York 1958.– Gogh, V. v.: Correspondance complete de V.v.G. 3 vols. Paris 1960
CATALOGUES: Faille, J.-B. de la: L'œuvre de V.v.G. Catalogue raisonné 4 vols. Paris and Brussels 1928.– Faille, J.-B. de la: The Works of V.v.G. His Paintings and Drawings. Amsterdam and New York 1970.– Hulsker, J.: V.G. en zijn weg. Het complete werk. Amsterdam 1977.– Hulsker, J.: The Complete v.G. Paintings, Drawings, Sketches. Oxford and New York 1980.– Hulsker, J.: L'opera completa di v.G. Milan 1979.– Lecaldano, P.: Tout l'œuvre peint de v.G. 2 vols. Paris 1971.– Lecaldano, P.: L'opera pittorica completa di v.G. 2 vols. Milan 1971.– Testori, G. and L. Arrigoni: V.G. Catalogo completo dei dipinti. Florence 1990.– Walther, I.F. and R. Metzger: V.v.G. Sämtliche Gemälde. 2 vols. Cologne 1989.– Walther, I.F. and R. Metzger: V.v.G. Complete Paintings. 2 vols. Cologne 1990.– Walther, I.F. and R. Metzger: V.v.G. L'œuvre compléte – peinture. Cologne 1990.– Walther, I.F. e R. Metzger: V.v.G. Tutti i dipinti. 2 vols. Cologne 1990
BIBLIOGRAPHY: Artaud, A.: V.G.: le suicidé de la société. Paris 1990.– Badt, K.: Die Farbenlehre V.G. Cologne 1961.– Bernard, B. (ed.): V.v.G. Leben und Werk in Bildern und Briefen. Munich 1987.– Bernard, B. (ed.): V.v.G. London 1988.– Boime, A.: V.G.: La nuit étoilée: l'histoire de la matière et la matière de l'histoire. Paris 1990.– Bonafoux, P.: V.G. Cologne 1990.– Bonafoux, P.: V.v.G. Paris 1990.– Cabanne, P.: V.G. Gütersloh 1961.– Cabanne, P.: V.G., l'homme et son œuvre. Paris 1961.– Cachin, F. and B. Welsh-Ovcharov (eds.): V.G. à Paris. Musée d'Orsay, Paris 1988 (EC).– Dorn, R.: Décoration. V.v.G. Werkreihe für das Gelbe Haus in Arles. Hildesheim 1990.– Elgar, F.: V.v.G. Leben und Werk. Munich and Zürich 1959.– Elgar, F.: V.v.G. Life and Work. New York 1958.– Elgar, F.: V.v.G. Paris 1958.– Erpel, F. (ed.): V.v.G. Lebensbilder, Lebenszeichen. Berlin and Munich 1989.– Hammacher, A.M. and R.: V.G. Die Biographie in Fotos, Bildern und Briefen. Stuttgart 1982.– Hammacher, A.M. and R.: V.G. A Documentary Biography. London 1982.– Lassaigne, J.: V.v.G. Munich 1973.– Lassaigne, J.: V.v.G. London 1973.– Lassaigne, J.: V.v.G. Annecy 1974.– Lassaigne, J.: V.v.G. Milan 1972.– Leymarie, J.: V.G. Paris and New York 1951.– Leymarie, J.: V.G. Geneva 1977.– Leymarie, J.: V.G. Geneva 1977.– Lövgren, S.: The Genesis of Modernism. Seurat, Gauguin, van Gogh and French Symbolism in the 1880's. Uppsala 1959, Bloomington (IN) and London 1971.– McQuillan, M.: V.G. Cologne 1990.– Mothe, A.: V.v.G. à Auvers-sur-Oise. Paris 1987.– Pickvance, R. (ed.): V.G. in Arles. Metropolitan Museum of Art, New York 1984 (EC).– Pickvance, R.: V.G. in Saint-Rémy and Auvers. The Metropolitan Museum of Art, New

York 1986 (EC).– Pollock, G. and F. Orton: V.v.G.: Artist of his Time. Oxford and New York 1978.– Roskill, M.: V.G., Gauguin and the Impressionist Circle. New York 1970.– Schapiro, M.: V.v.G. Stuttgart 1950.– Schapiro, M.: V.v.G. New York 1950.– Schapiro, M.: V.v.G. Paris 1954.– Schapiro, M.: V.v.G. Milan 1972.– Sweetman, D.: V.v.G. 1853 bis 1890. Düsseldorf 1990.– Stein, S.A. (ed.): V.G. A Retrospective. New York 1986 (EC).– Tralbaut, M.E.: V.v.G. London 1974.– Tralbaut, M.E.: V.G., le mal aimé. Lausanne 1969.– Tralbaut, M.E.: V.v.G. Milan 1969.– Tralbaut, M.E.: V.G., le mal aimé. Barcelona 1969.– Tralbaut, M.E.: V.G., le mal aimé. Amsterdam 1969.– V.G. caris. Musée d'Orsay, Paris 1988 (EC).– V.v.G.: Drawings. Rijksmuseum Kröller-Müller, Milan 1990 (EC).– V.v.G.: Paintings. Rijksmuseum Vincent van Gogh, Milan 1990 (EC).– Walther, I.F.: V.v.G. 1853-1890. Vision and Reality. Cologne 1987.– Welsh-Ovcharov, B.: V.G. in Perspective. Englewood Cliffs (NJ) 1974.– Welsh-Ovcharov, B.: V.v.G. His Paris Period 1886-1888. Utrecht and The Hague 1976.– Welsh-Ovcharov, B.: V.v.G. and the Birth of Cloisonism. Art Gallery of Ontario, Toronto 1981 (EC).– Wolk, J. v.d.: The Seven Sketchbooks of V.v.G. London 1987.– Zurcher, B.: V.G. Leben und Werk. Munich 1985.– Zurcher, B.: V.G. vie et œuvre. Fribourg 1985
ILLUSTRATIONS:
276 Le Moulin de la Galette, 1886
277 Pont de la Grande Jatte, 1887
280 View of Paris from Montmartre, 1886
282 Restaurant Rispal at Asnières, 1887
283 Paris Seen from Vincent's Room in the Rue Lepic, 1887
284 Terrace of a Café on Montmartre, 1886
287 Agostina Segatori in the Café du Tambourin, 1887
288 Fishing in Spring, Pont de Clichy, 1887
289 On the Outskirts of Paris, 1887
289 In the Jardin du Luxembourg, 1886
291 Self-Portrait in a Gray Felt Hat, 1887
292 Portrait of Père Tanguy, 1887
293 Portrait of Père Tanguy, 1887
314 The Sower, 1888
315 Vincent's House in Arles (The Yellow House), 1888

GONCOURT Edmond and Jules de
Edmond (1822 Nancy – 1896 Champrosay), Jules (1830 Paris – 1870 Paris)
French writers and art critics. Their novels, at first written together, deal with social problems, including those of the artistic milieu, in Realist, Naturalist and finally Impressionist styles. They wrote some theoretical studies on the rediscovery of painting in the 18th century. From **1888** their diaries were published ("Journal des Gon-

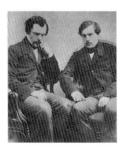

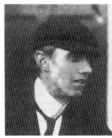

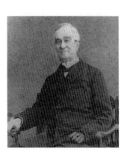

courts"), and these have become an invaluable source both for their descriptions of the life of artists in Paris and for their insights into Impressionist views, particularly those of Degas.

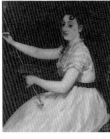

GONZALES Eva
1849 Paris – 1883 Paris
Daughter of the writer Emmanuel Gonzalès. 1865 had lessons with C. Chaplin. 1869 met Manet and became his student and model. 1870 exhibited for the first time at the Salon. Thereafter she submitted work every year to the Salon. Until 1872 she was strongly influenced by Manet but later developed her own, more personal style. Her water colours with their bright colours and soft forms achieved great success; her work was praised by both Castagnary and Zola. During the Franco-Prussian War she stayed in Dieppe. 1879 married a brother of the graphic artist Henri Guérard. Died in childbirth, five days after Manet. 1885 memorial exhibition in the rooms of "La Vie moderne", 1924 another memorial exhibition at the autumn Salon.
CATALOGUE: Sainsaulieu, M.-C. and J. de Mons: E.G. 1849-1883. Etude critique et catalogue raisonné de l'œuvre. Paris 1991
BIBLIOGRAPHY: Roger-Marx, C.: E.G. St.-Germain-en-Laye 1950
ILLUSTRATIONS:
132 A Box at the Théatre des Italiens, c. 1874
133 Morning Awakening, 1876
165 The Milliner, c. 1877

GORE Spencer Frederick
1878 Epsom – 1914 Richmond
His education – at Harrow and Slade School – finished as early as 1900. A pupil of Steer. 1903 met Lucien Pissarro and Sickert. Influenced by the landscapes of Pissarro and Degas' theatre scenes. From 1907 he belonged to the group around Sickert. 1909 became a member of the New English Art Club; co-founder of the Association des artistes alliés and President of the Camden Town Group. One of the most important exponents of Post-Impressionism in England. Under the influence of Gauguin, his painting developed after 1912 from Pointillism to a style more expressive in both colour and outline.
BIBLIOGRAPHY: Gore, F. and R. Shone (eds.): S.F.G. Anthony d'Offay Gallery, London 1983 (EC).– S.F.G. The Arts Council of Great Britain, London 1955 (EC).– S.F.G. 1878-1914. Anthony d'Offay Gallery, London 1974 (EC)
ILLUSTRATION:
590 Mornington Crescent, 1911

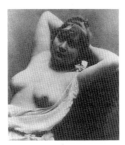

GOULUE, La
Real name: Louise Weber (1870 – 1929). Successful Parisian cancan dancer; performed in the Moulin de la Galette, the Alcazar, the Elysée-Montmartre, the Grille-d'Egout and later above all in the Moulin Rouge, often together with Valentin le Désossé. One of Toulouse-Lautrec's favourite models; he portrayed her in various paintings and posters (pp. 324, 325).

GOUPIL Adolphe
1806 Paris – 1893
Began with a small shop selling reproduction paintings, which he produced by various techniques on his own presses. He soon began trading in contemporary (but mostly academic) paintings in his own galleries in Paris, The Hague, New York, London, Brussels and Berlin. 1869 van Gogh began his apprenticeship at the branch in The Hague. His brother Theo later worked there, but no van Gogh paintings were ever exhibited.

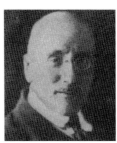

GRABAR Igor Emmanuilovich
1871 Budapest – 1960 Moscow
1880 the family moved to Russia. 1889-1893 studied law at St. Petersburg; drew caricatures and illustrations, was impressed by Serov. 1894-1896 studied with Repin at the St. Petersburg academy. Began to publish articles of art criticism. 1895 first visit to Western Europe. 1896-1901 in Munich as a student, then teacher at the private academy of Ažbè; from 1898 he began exhibiting. Travelled extensively. 1901-1903 in St. Petersburg, then in Moscow. Exhibited his Impressionist paintings at "World of Art" exhibitions. 1903 organised the permanent exhibition "Contemporary Art" in St. Petersburg, which encouraged a synthesis of painting and applied arts. 1904 member of the Federation of Russian Artists. Exhibited abroad. 1909-1914 active as an architect. 1909-1916 the first two-volume history of Russian art was published under his editorship. 1913-1925 Curator and Director of the Tretyakov Gallery in Moscow. 1914 trip to Egypt. 1917-1960 active in work-

shops for the restoration and preservation of monuments as well as at institutes of art and art history. At the same time he was a landscape, portrait and occasionally history painter. 1922 took part in the Russian exhibition in Berlin. 1924 visited the USA for the Russian exhibition. 1929 in Germany for an exhibition of icons. 1937 at the Paris World Fair. Published a long monograph on Repin. 1943 member of the Academy of Sciences of the USSR. 1947 member of the Academy of Arts.
WRITINGS, DOCUMENTS: Grabar, I.E.: My Life (Russian) Moscow and Leningrad 1937
BIBLIOGRAPHY: Andreeva, L. and T. Kaschdan (eds.): I.G., Pisma. Moscow 1974.– Azarkovich, W.G. and N.W. Egorova: I.G. Leningrad 1974.– Podobedova, O.I.: I.E.G. Moscow 1965
ILLUSTRATIONS:
507 After Lunch, 1907
509 Winter, 1904

GRENOUILLERE, La
Popular place for swimming and dining on the Seine island of Croissy (Ile-aux-Vaches) between Bougival and Chatou. From 1848 a popular meeting place for young Parisians, who gathered there to bathe, row and dance. A jetty led to a floating restaurant, while another led to a tiny island, known as "the Flower-Pot", with a single tree growing on it. La Grenouillère was one of the birthplaces of Impressionism. 1869 with the broad, horizontal strokes of their brushwork, Renoir and Monet were able to capture the atmosphere of summer, each painting a picture of the "Frog Island" on the same day (pp. 72, 73).

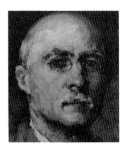

GRIGORESCU Nicolae
1838 Pitaru (near Bucharest) – 1907 Cîmpina
1848-1861 trained and worked as a religious painter of icons and churches. 1861 went to Paris on a scholarship from the principality of Moldavia. 1862 studied for a time at the Ecole des Beaux-Arts, then stayed for the first time at Barbizon. 1864 after visiting his home he returned to Barbizon and Paris. 1867 exhibited at the Paris World Fair. 1868 exhibited for the first time at the Paris Salon. 1869-1873 in Bucharest, received a gold medal at the "Exhibition of Living Artists", and became the first import-

ant Romanian painter of landscapes and rural life. **1873** exhibited for the ifrst time at exhibitions of the Society of Friends of the Arts in Bucharest. **1873/74** travelled to Italy, Athens, Constantinople. **1876** visited Paris; the doctor and art collector G. de Bellio became an avid supporter; visited Brittany. **1877/78** painted the war against Turkey. **1879-1887** several long trips to Paris and Brittany from Romania. **1889** member of the "Ileana" society for the propagation of art. **1889** exhibited at the Paris World Fair and for the first time at the Salon of the Romanian Atheneum. **1890** settled in Cîmpina (Carpathiars). **1899** first artist to become an honorary member of the Romanian Academy.
BIBLIOGRAPHY: Cârneci, M.: N.G. Bucharest 1989.– Jianu, J.: G. Bucharest n.d.– N.G. Pictura, grafica. Bucharest 1984 (EC).– Opresco, G.: G. (1838-1907). Bucharest 1961.– Popesco, M.: N.G. Bucharest 1962.– Varga, V.: N.G. Bucharest 1973.– Vasilu, A.: Marginalii la o carte despre N.G. Bucharest 1989.– Vlahuta, A.: N.J.G. Bucharest 1911
ILLUSTRATION:
526 A Clearing, c. 1885

GROHAR Ivan
1867 Spodnja Sorica – 1911 Ljubljana
1888 trained first with local painters in Agram. **1892-1895** attended drawing school in Graz. **1895** studied in museums in Munich. **1896-1900** after a short stay in Skofja Loka, he went on the advice of his friend Rihard Jakopić to study at the Ažbè school in Munich. Painted genre pictures and paintings in the style of Arnold Böcklin. **1900-1902** in Ljubljana, exhibited some Art Nouveaustyle, Neo-Romantic pictures at the 2nd Slovenian exhibition of art. **1904** organised with Jakopić the group "Save" and the group exhibition at Miethke's gallery in Vienna; took part in the 1st South Slavic exhibition of art in Belgrade. Influenced Serbian painters. He subsequently lived mostly in Skofja Loka; painted with Jakopić, Matija Jama and Matej Sternen. Changed to an Impressionist style influenced by Pointillism. **1907** stayed in Belgrade. **1908** exhibited with the group "Save" in Cracow and Warsaw. Died in **1911** of tuberculosis.
BIBLIOGRAPHY: Stelè, F.: I.G. Ljubljana 1960
ILLUSTRATION:
529 Snow in Skofja Loka, 1905

GUERBOIS → Café Guerbois

GUILBERT Yvette
1867 Paris – 1944 Aix-en-Provence
Actress in various theatres; from **1890** through her extravagant appearance and double-entendre chansons she became a famous singer at the "Eldorado". Performed also at the Moulin Rouge, Eden, Ambassadeur and Scala as well as in America and England. In Paris she became a sensation. Toulouse-Lautrec designed posters for her.

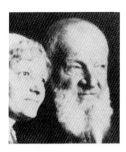

GUILLAUMIN Jean-Baptiste Armand
1841 Paris – 1927 Paris
While still at school in Moulins he met Outin and Eugène Meunier, who was to become an important collector under the name Murer. **1857** at the age of 15, he began an apprenticeship at his uncle's fashion store in Paris; at the same time, he attended evening courses at the city school of drawing with the sculptor Caillouette. **1860** employed in the administration of the Paris-Orléans railway. In his spare time he attended the Académie Suisse, where he met Pissarro and Cézanne, and began painting. **1863** exhibited at the "Salon des Refusés". A regular at the Café de Bade and later at the Café Guerbois. **1866** resigned from his position to paint with his friend Outin in the Louvre and with Pissarro in the open air. Earned his living by painting window awnings with Pissarro. He then took another administrative post in the section responsible for bridges and paths, where he only had to work at night. He painted numerous landscapes the environs of Paris and on the Seine in lively contrasting colours and broad strokes of the paintbrush. During the Franco-Prussian War he stayed with his friend Béliard in Paris. He often visited Pissarro in Pontoise and Cézanne in Auvers, where he also saw Gachet. In **1874** he took part in the 1st Impressionist exhibition. Rented an apartment in the same house as Cézanne and worked closely with him; in **1875** he rented the Daubignys' former studio. **1877-1882** exhibited at the 3rd and 5th-7th Impressionist exhibitions; rejected by Monet and Degas but defended by Pissarro. **1884** met the young Signac, but remained aloof from the new movement of Pointillism. **1884** exhibited at the Salon des Indépendants. **1886** at the last great Impressionist exhibition. Through Durand-Ruel became known in America. **1887** married his cousin, Joséphine Charreton. Became acquainted with the art dealer Portier. **1888** first one-man show. **1891** invited to Brussels by Les Vingt. **1892** after winning a large sum in the national lottery, he gave up his job and became financially indépendent, devoting himself solely to painting. **1893** rented a house in Crozant (Creuze); travelled in Brittany, Normandy and Dauphiné; these landscapes remained his major themes.

1904 spent two months in Holland.
CATALOGUE: Serret, G. and D. Fabiani: A.G. Catalogue raisonné de l'œuvre peint. Paris 1971
BIBLIOGRAPHY: Cailler, P.: A.G. Geneva 1964.– Centenaire de l'impressionnisme et hommage à Guillaumin. Petit Palais, Geneva 1974 (EC).– Courières, E. des: A.G. Paris 1924.– Gray, C.: A.G. Chester (CT) 1972.– Gros, R.: G. à Crozant. Guéret 1982.– Lecomte, G.: G. Paris 1926.– Rewald, J.: Cézanne and G. in: Châtelet, A. and N. Reynaud (eds.): Etudes d'art français offerts à Charles Sterling. Paris 1975, pp. 343-353
ILLUSTRATIONS:
69 A Path in the Snow, 1869
92 Still Life: Flowers, Faience, Books, 1872
109 Sunset at Ivry, 1873
154 Quai de la Gare, Snow (Quai de Bercy), c. 1875
205 The Seine in Winter, 1879
205 Barges in the Snow, 1881
247 The Fishermen, c. 1885
310 Outskirts of Paris, c. 1890
351 Landscape in Normandy: Apple Trees, c. 1887
351 View of Agay, 1895

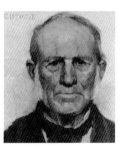

GUTHRIE James
1859 Greenock – 1930
1877 gave up his law degree to study painting at the Saint Mungo Art Club. **1879** settled in London; for a time he attended courses at the studio of John Pettie. **1882** went to Paris, where he discovered plein-air painting and changed to a freer and brighter style; influenced by Bastien-Lepage. **1884/85** decided to give up painting after plein-air studies in Berwickshire but in **1888** he was persuaded by a cousin to paint a portrait of his father; with the exception of a few landscapes in pastel, this was the start of a new and important career as a portrait painter. In his style he was influenced by his friend Whistler. **1880** member of the Glasgow Art Club; **1896-1898** President of the club. **1889** member of the New English Art Club. **1902-1919** President of the Royal Scottish Academy.
BIBLIOGRAPHY: G. and the Scottish Realists. The Fine Art Society, Glasgow 1981 (EC)
ILLUSTRATION:
582 The Morning Paper, 1890

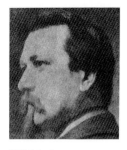

HAES Carlos de
1829 Brussels – 1898 Madrid
Son of a Belgian merchant, who had emigrated to Málaga. First lessons with the painter Luis de la Cruz y Ríos in Málaga. 1850-1855 studied with Joseph Quinaux in Belgium. 1857 returned to Spain. Won the public competition for the chair of landscape painting at the Escuela de Bellas Artes de San Fernando in Madrid. His naturalistic conception of landscape exerted a strong influence on Spanish painting (Beruete, Regoyos, Morera). 1860 became a member of the Real Academia de Bellas Artes de San Fernando. 1856-1862 received a medal at the Madrid exhibition; won awards in 1864 in Bayonne, 1876 in León, 1878 in Paris and 1882 in Vienna. Numerous study trips abroad to Spain, France and the Netherlands. He bequeathed his mostly small-format paintings to his pupils, who gave them to the Museo Nacional de Arte Moderno in Madrid.
BIBLIOGRAPHY: Puente, J. de la (ed.): Los estudios de paisaje de C. de H. (1826-1898). Oleos, dibujos y grabados. Salas de Exposiciónes de la Dirección General de Bellas Artes, Madrid 1971 (EC)
ILLUSTRATION:
557 A Stream at Pont-Aven

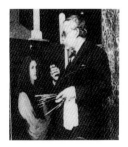

HALE Philip Leslie
1865 Boston – 1931 Boston
Brother of Ellen Day and Herbert Dudley Hale. Studied with Weir at the Art Students League in New York. Travelled in Europe and studied at the Académie Julian in Paris. Returned to the USA. Taught for thirty years at the Boston Museum

School. Art critic for the Boston Herald. Married Lilian Wescott-Hale. 1913 wrote a book on Vermeer. Exponent of the more decorative style of Impressionism often seen in the work of American artists.
WRITINGS, DOCUMENTS: Hale, P.L.: Jan Vermeer of Delft. Boston 1913
BIBLIOGRAPHY: Folts, F.P. (ed.): Paintings and Drawings by P.L.H. from the Folts Collection. Voss Galleries, Boston 1966 (EC).– Hale, N.: The Life in the Studio. Boston 1969
ILLUSTRATION:
631 The Crimson Rambler, 1908

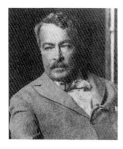

HASSAM Childe Frederick
1859 Dorchester (MA) – 1935 East Hampton (NY)
Son of a an established and well-known Puritan family. 1876 left high school in Dorchester to train as a wood carver in Boston; 1877/78 took drawing lessons at the Boston Art Club and Lowell Institute; studied with the German painter Ignaz Gaugengigl and William Rimmer. Worked in the 1880s and 1890s as an illustrator. 1883 moved to New York; travelled in England, Spain, Italy and the Netherlands. 1886-1889 lived in Paris; attended the Académie Julian under Boulanger and Lefèbvre. Lived near the Café Guerbois and met all the important French Impressionists. Monet and Pissarro became strong influences. 1889 returned to New York; founded the New York Watercolor Club. He drew his favourite motifs from the streets of New York and captured the atmosphere of the city in a unique way. Numerous exhibitions: in New York and Boston, at the Paris Salons 1887-1890, the "Exposition internationale" at G. Petit's gallery in Paris and the international art exhibitions in Munich. Spent much of his time on Appledore Island (Maine), one of the Isles of Shoals. Painted sea and landscape pictures with Metcalf and Twachtman at various locations in the USA. Travelled extensively in Europe, Cuba and the USA. 1898 with Twachtman founded The Ten American Painters and took part regularly in their exhibitions. 1913 exhibited at the Armory Show. 1916 member of the National Academy of Design in New York and 1929 the American Academy of Arts and Letters. One of the most important American expo-

nents of Impressionism on the French model.
WRITINGS, DOCUMENTS: Hassam, C.: Three Cities. New York 1899
BIBLIOGRAPHY: Adamo, A.: C.H. New York 1938.– Adams, A.: C.H. New York 1938.– Buckley, C.E. et al. (eds.): C.H. Corcoran Gallery of Art, Washington 1965 (EC).– Catalogue of the Etchings and Drypoints of C.H. San Francisco 1989.– C.H. A Retrospective Exhibition. Corcoran Gallery of Art, Washington 1965 (EC).– Curry, D.P. (ed.): C.H. An Island Garden Revisited. Yale University Art Museum, New Haven; The Denver Art Museum, Denver; The National Museum of American Art, New York 1990 (EC).– Czestochowski, J.J.: 94 Prints by C.H. New York 1980.– Eliasoph, P.: Handbook of the Complete Set of Etchings and Drypoints of C.H. New York 1933.– Fort, I.S. (ed.): The Flag Paintings of C.H. National Gallery of Art, Washington; California County Museum of Art, Los Angeles 1988 (EC).– Griffith, F.: The Lithographs of C.H.: A Catalogue. Washington 1962.– Hoopes, D.F.: C.H. New York 1979.– McGuire, J.C.: C.H. New York 1929.– Pousette-Dar, N. (ed.): C.H. New York 1972 (EC).– Steadman, W.E. (ed.): C.H. University of Arizona Museum of Art, Tucson 1972 (EC).– Wolfe, J. (ed.): C.H. Guild Hall Museum, East Hampton 1981 (EC).– Zigrosser, C.: C.H. New York 1916
ILLUSTRATIONS:
402 Fifth Avenue at Washington Square, 1891
602 Grand Prix Day, 1887
603 Une averse. Rue Bonaparte, Paris, 1887
603 Rainy Day, Columbus Avenue, Boston, 1885
618 The Little Pond, Appledore, 1890
633 Sunset at Sea, 1911
639 Allies Day, May 1917, 1917

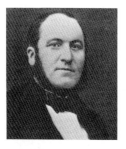

HAUSSMANN Baron Georges-Eugène
1809 Paris – 1891 Paris
Civil servant from Alsace. 1853 appointed Prefect of the Seine Département by Napoleon III and until 1870 responsible for the re-modelling of the city of Paris. At enormous cost, he pushed through the process of modernisation with its straight boulevards, large squares and extensive parks.

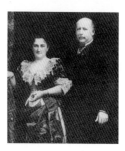

rejected an invitation to exhibit at the 8th Impressionist exhibition. 1889 exhibited at the Salon des Indépendants. 1890 invited by Les Vingt in Brussels. 1894-1897 took part in the exhibitions of the Impressionists and Symbolists at Le Barc de Boutteville. To secure a regular income, he also worked as a theatre decor painter. Frequently went his own way; quarrelled with Pissarro and Luce; in the 1890s he gave up his Neo-Impressionism in favour of a more conservative style. Experimented with various colours and paints. 1900/01 travelled in the Alps, Provence, Auvergne and the Côte d'Azur. 1908-1910 studio in La Frette. 1924 published his autobiography and in 1925 an essay on art.
CATALOGUE: Dulhon, G.: L.H. Catalogue raisonné (in preparation)
ILLUSTRATION:
294 Paris, Place de la Concorde, 1888

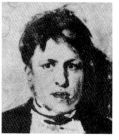

HAVEMEYER Louisine and Henry
Louisine nee Waldron Elder (1848 – 1929 New York) and husband Henry (Harry) Osborne (1847 – 1907)
Owners of the most famous collection of old and contemporary art in the USA. On the advice of Cassatt and Duret, they bought Impressionist paintings from Vollard, Durand-Ruel and other dealers and thus contributed enormously to the popularisation of the movement in America. Part of the collection is to be seen now at the Metropolitan Museum of Art in New York.

HAVRE (Le)
Important port in Normandy at the mouth of the Seine. Nearby towns include Saint-Adresse and Rouelles. As early as 1853 Couture went there with his pupils, who included Manet and Proust. Boudin and Monet spent their youth there; it was there that Monet painted the famous picture "Impression: Sunrise" that gave the name to the movement (p. 113). Many Impressionist sea pictures were painted there by such artists as Stevens, Pissarro and van de Velde.

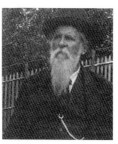

HAYET Louis
1864 Pontoise – 1940 Cormeille-en-Parisis
Son of a dealer in stained glass and other decorations in Pontoise. Although his father painted, he was not in a position to give his son an artistic training. 1878 apprenticeship with a painter-decorator. Attended courses at the Ecole des Arts décoratifs; worked with various artists. 1882 met C. and L. Pissarro in Pontoise and became friends with them. 1886 met Seurat;

Born in Sweden of Norwegian parents. Studied first in Munich. 1878 went to Paris; at the Atelier Bonnat he copied Rubens, Rembrandt and Raphael. 1878 awarded a medal at the international exhibition in Paris. 1880 visited Florence, where he met Böcklin. Returned to his home country. His light and imaginative mythological scenes became extremely popular with art collectors. Showed paintings at exhibitions organised by the Société anonyme des peintres, sculpteurs, graveurs at Georges Petit's.
CATALOGUE: Aslaksby, T.: H.H., katalog. Modums Blaafarveværk 1981
BIBLIOGRAPHY: Ostby, L.: Fra naturalisme til nyromantikk. Oslo 1934.– Thiis, J.: Edvard Munch og hans samtid. Oslo 1933
ILLUSTRATION:
469 At the Window, 1881

HEYERDAHL, Hans Olaf
1857 Dalare – 1913 Oslo

HITCHCOCK George
1850 Providence (RI) – 1913 Marken (Netherlands)
After graduating in law, he worked from 1874 as an attorney in New York. 1879 studied at Heatherly's School of Fine Arts in London, and shortly afterwards in Paris at the Académie Julian with Lefèbvre and Bouguereau. For a short period he lived in Düsseldorf, where he attended courses at the Academy. 1880 moved

to The Hague and the studio of Hendrik Mesdag. Settled in Egmond near Amsterdam. **1885** successful exhibitions at the Paris Salon and the National Academy of Design in New York. His pictures are variations on the theme of the Dutch landscape, to which he imparted a quasi-mythical and religious depth. **1887** became an honorary member of the Salon. **1889** received the gold medal at the World Fair. **1905** returned to the USA; exhibitions in New York, Detroit and Providence. **1909** received the Austrian Order of Franz-Joseph and became a member of the National Academy of Design.
ILLUSTRATION:
628 The Bride, c. 1900

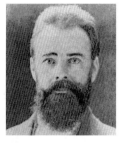

HODLER Ferdinand
1853 Berne – 1918 Geneva
Came from a poor background; helped his stepfather, a decorative painter. **1867** trained with the landscape painter and souvenir maker F. Sommer-Collier in Thun. **1871-1876** studied at the art school in Geneva under B. Menn. Became interested in Corot and the French Impressionists; his style became affected by Impressionism and Realism. Became acquainted with the philosopher Carl Vogt. **1878/79** stayed in Madrid for nine months. From **1890** he developed his own monumental style with its coloured surfaces, firm outlines and symmetrical compositions with parallel forms; mainly Symbolist in content. **1891** went to Paris and joined the Rosicrucians. **1892** exhibited at the first "Salon de la Rose-Croix" in Paris. **1897** drew a design for the armoury of the Zurich Landesmuseum, for which he won first prize; it became a subject of controversy in the press. **1901-1905** took part in the Vienna Secession. Exhibited also at the Secessions in Munich and Berlin. **1905** and **1911** trips to Italy. **1907** painted a mural for the University of Jena. **1908** met Valentine Godé-Darel; drew all the stages of her illness and death in **1915**. **1913** made an officer in the French Legion of Honour; executed murals for the city hall in Hannover. **1917** large retrospective in Zurich.
CATALOGUE: Loosli, C.A.: F.H. Leben, Werke und Nachlass. 4 vols. Berne 1921-1924
BIBLIOGRAPHY: Bätschmann, O.,

H.A. Lüthy and M. Baumgartner (ed.): F.H.: Sammlung Max Schmidheiny. Kunstmuseum des Kantons Thurgau, Frauenfeld 1989 (EC).– Burger, F.: Cézanne und Hodler. Munich 1913.– Der frühe Hodler. Das Werk 1870-1890. Kunstmuseum, Berne 1981.– Eisenmann, S.F. and O. Bätschman (ed.): F.H. Landscapes. Los Angeles, New York and Chicago 1987 (EC).– F.H. Die Mission des Künstlers. Berne 1982.– F.H. Nationalgalerie Berlin. Zurich 1983 (EC).– Guerzoni, S.: F. H. als Mensch, Maler und Lehrer. Zurich 1952.– Hirsh, S.L.: F.H. Munich 1981.– Hirsh. S.L.: F.H. London 1982.– Hugelshofer, W.: F.H. Zurich 1952.– Loosli, C.A.: F.H. Leben, Werk und Nachlass. 4 vols. Berne 1921-1924.– Mühlestein, H.: F.H. Weimar 1914.– Müller, W.Y.: Die Kunst F.H.s. Reife und Spätwerk., 1895-1918. Zurich 1941.– Roffler, T.: F.H. Frauenfeld 1926.– Schmidt, G.: F.H. Sein Leben und sein Werk. Erlenbach and Zurich 1942.– Selz, P.: F.H. University Art Museum, Berkeley (CA) 1972 (EC).– Überwasser, W.: H. Köpfe und Gestalten. Zurich 1947.– Waser, M.: Wege zu Hodler. Zurich 1927.– Weese, A.: F.H. Berne 1910
ILLUSTRATIONS:
440 Apple Tree in Blossom, c. 1890
440 Portrait of Louise-Delphine Duchosal, 1885

HONFLEUR
Small port in Normandy near Le Havre at the mouth of the Seine. Popular place for plein-air painting with the Impressionists and their predecessors. Among the first to paint there were Turner, Bonington, Corot, Daubigny and Dupré. In the second half of the 19th century the "school of Honfleur" was formed, which included Boudin (born in Honfleur), Cals, Jongkind and Troyon. They were followed by Monet, Bazille, Renoir, Sisley and others, who all tried to capture the mood of the sea and the effect of light on the water. The Neo-Impressionist Seurat also painted there (pp. 271-273).

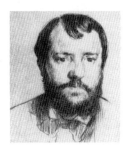

HOSCHEDE Alice and Ernest
Alice, nee Raingo (1844 Paris – 1911 Giverny), Ernest (1837 – 1891)
Collectors of Impressionist paintings (Manet, Sisley, Pissarro, Monet and others). Alice, the daughter of a rich manufacturer from Tournai, married

the department store owner E. Hoschedé in 1863 and in 1870 inherited from her father Castle Rottenbourg in Montgeron, which became a meeting place for the artists whose pictures they collected. **1876** Monet, who the couple particularly encouraged, lived in the castle. **1874** Hoschedé organised a successful exhibition and sale of Impressionist paintings. **1878** bankruptcy and auction sale of the collection; the Hoschedé family moved in with the Monets in a house in Vétheuil. Ernest lived in Paris and in **1882** published "Impressions de mon voyage au Salon". Alice lived with Monet, moving with him to Poissy in **1881** and to Giverny in **1883**. After the death of her husband she married Monet in **1892**.

HUDECEK Antonin
1872 Loučká – 1941 Častolovice
1887-1890 and **1893-1895** studied at the art academy in Prague under M. Pirner and V. Brožík. **1891-1893** studied at the Academy in Munich with O. Seitz and at the private school of Ažbè. From **1897** he painted Impressionist landscapes in Bohemia, especially mountain scenery. Became friends with Slavíček. **1900** one-man exhibition in Vienna. **1901** exhibited at the Wertheim department store in Berlin. **1902** with Preisler in Italy. **1902** exhibited for the first time with the Mánes artists' federation in Prague. **1908/09** trip to Italy. **1912-1915** three exhibitions in Berlin galleries. **1916** and **1917** in the Austrian Alps. **1923** in Yugoslavia. **1927** in Italy. Bought a house in Častolovice. **1932** travelled in Italy.
BIBLIOGRAPHY: A.H. Galerie vytv, umení Roudnici n. Labem 1966 (EC).– Boucková, J.: A.H. Oblastní galerie, Liberec 1982 (EC).– Karlíková, L.: A.H. (Czech), Prague 1983
ILLUSTRATIONS:
517 Quiet Evening, 1900
519 A Stream in Sunshine, 1897

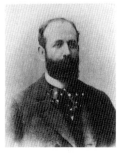

HUYSMANS Joris-Karl
1848 Paris – 1907 Paris
Real name: Charles Marie Georges Huysmans. Symbolist writer and art critic. One of the first critics to deal positively with Impressionist concepts in his writings. Recognized Cézanne's genius as early as 1877, admired Degas and drew attention to Gauguin at his first exhibition.

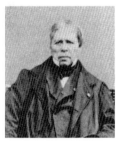

IMPRESSIONNISTE (L')
Art journal which appeared every Thursday during the 3rd Impressionist exhibition of 1877; in all, there were five issues. The office was in the Galerie Legrand, and many of the articles were written by its editor, Georges Rivière, a friend of Renoir. Rivière defended the Impressionists and attempted to popularise their views on art.

INDEPENDANTS, Salon des →
Salon des Indépendants

INGRES Jean Auguste Dominique
1780 Montauban – 1867 Paris
As early as 1791 he was a pupil at the academy in Toulon. 1797 pupil of J.-L. David in Paris. 1799-1801 studied at the college of art in Paris. 1802 exhibited for the first time at the Salon. 1806-1824 in Rome, then in Florence. His major influence was Raphael; he was a skilful draughtsman. His Classical "histories" and high-class, yet perceptive portraits were exhibited regularly in the Salon, and at first were often criticised as "Gothic". 1825-1834 member of the Academy and teacher in Paris. 1835-1841 as director of the French Academy in Rome, he became an internationally effective exponent of late Classicism. 1841 returned to Paris, became an influential and much acclaimed teacher. Ingres held strictly to the Classical ideal, in contrast to Eugène Delacroix and the other Romantics and also to Courbet's Realism; instead of the sensuality of colour effects he favoured a strictly linear composition, although he always worked carefully from nature studies. Ingres influenced Edgar

Degas, and was also admired by Renoir.

WRITINGS, DOCUMENTS: Schlenoff, N. (ed.): I., sources littéraires: Cahiers littéraires inédits. Paris 1956
CATALOGUES: Lapauze, H.: Les dessins de J.A.D.I. de Montauban. 8 vols. Paris 1901.– Wildenstein, G.: I. Œuvrekatalog. Paris and London 1954.– Zanni, A.: I. Catalogo completo dei dipinti. Florence 1992
BIBLIOGRAPHY: Alain: Ingres ou le dessin contre la couleur. Paris 1949.– Alazard, J.: I. et l'Ingrisme. Paris 1950.– Amaury-Duval, E.E.: L'atelier d'I. Paris 1878.– Cassou, J.: I. Brussels 1947.– I. Drawings from the Musée Ingres Montauban. The Arts Council of Great Britain, London 1957 (EC).– I. Zeichnungen aus dem Ingres-Museum in Montauban. Hamburger Kunsthalle, Hamburg 1961 (EC).– Lapauze, H.: I., sa vie et son œuvre (1780-1867). Paris 1911.– Lebrot, J.: Le martyre de Saint Symphrien. Dijon 1960.– Longa, R.: I. inconnu. Paris 1942.– Merson, O. and E. Bellier de la Chavignerie: I., sa vie et ses œuvres. Paris 1867.– Naef, H.: Schweizer Künstler in Bildnissen von I. Zurich 1963.– Naef, H.: I. – Rome. Zurich 1962.– Naef, H.: I. in Rome. Zurich n.d.– Picon, G.: I. Geneva 1967.– Rosenblum, R.: I. London 1985.– Toussaint, H. (ed.): Les portraits d'I. Paris 1985 (EC).– Vedute di Roma di Ingres. Rome 1958 (EC)
ILLUSTRATIONS:
14 The Bather of Valpinçon, 1808
15 Portrait of Madame Inès Moitessier, 1856
18 Angélique, 1819

INSTITUT DE FRANCE
A collective term dating from **1815** used to denote the various academies of science and arts that had existed in France since the 17th century and served as state institutions to dictate the standards and norms of cultural and scientific policy: the Académie Française, Académie des Inscriptions et Belles-Lettres, Académie des Sciences, Académie des Beaux-Arts, Académie des Sciences Morales et Politiques. The arts section had 40 members and until **1863** controlled the Paris art college (Ecole des Beaux-Arts) and the French academy in Rome. After **1863** it still had a conservative influence on the training of artists and on artistic life.

ISRAELS Isaac-Lazarus
1865 Amsterdam – 1934 The Hague
Son of Jozef Israëls, the important painter of the Hague school. **1880-1882** studied at the academy in The Hague. Influenced by the Realist plein-air painting of Bastien-Lepage. **1885** moved to Amsterdam. Formed friendships with Breitner and Bauer; turned towards Impressionism. **1903-1913** lived in Paris, impressed by Degas and Toulouse-Lautrec. **1913-1915** trips to London, **1920/21** travelled in Indonesia.
BIBLIOGRAPHY: I.I. Stedelijk Museum, Amsterdam 1959 (EC).– Reisel,

J.H.: I.I. 1967.– Wagner, A.: I.I. 1967.– Wagner, A.: I.I. Amsterdam 1969.– Wagner, A.: I.I. Venlo 1985
ILLUSTRATION:
419 In the Dance Hall, 1893

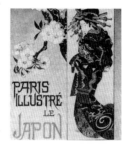

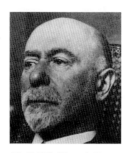

JAPONISME
The borrowing of motifs and stylistic features from Japanese art into European and American art. A successor to the "Chinoiseries" of the 18th century, a part of the "exotisme" that followed historicism, it aimed to introduce a new aesthetic stimulation to contemporary art. Japanese artefacts such as coloured woodcuts, screens and fans had become known since 1854 when Japan was forced to begin trading with the West. The formal principles of Japanese art were gradually discovered through the Japanese sections of the World Fair from 1862, through the Paris art gallery "La Porte Chinoise", which opened in the same year, and through publications and exhibitions such as the one at G. Petit's in 1883 or the exhibition organised in 1893 by S. Bing at Durand-Ruel's. Japanese art became a catalyst and inspiration to Impressionist, Symbolist, Cloissonist and art nouveau styles, which quickly seized on such features as its use of pure, strong colours and curved lines, its fleeting movement and its asymmetry, the overstepping of frames and borders, its spatial dynamics, and its use of two-dimensional surfaces. The common motifs of Japanese art were all influential: daily life, theatre, prostitution, gardens with ponds and lilies (Monet), and the grotesque (masks and demons).

JÄRNEFELT Eero Nikolai
1863 Viborg – 1937 Helsinki
1883-1886 studied at the art academy in St. Petersburg under M.P. Clodt von Jürgensburg. Knew Repin. **1886-1891** intermittent attendance at painting classes given by Bouguereau and Robert-Fleury at the Académie Julian in Paris. Influenced by the French Realists and plein-air painters, especially Jules Bastien-Lepage. In the summer months, he painted in Finland – predominantly themes of social criticism. In **1899** and **1900** he won the gold medal at the World Fair. From **1902** he worked as a teacher. **1912** appointed professor.

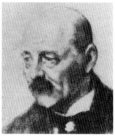

ILLUSTRATION:
478 Lefranc the Wine Merchant, Boulevard Clichy, Paris 1888

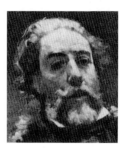

JIMENEZ Y ARANDA Luis
1845 Sevilla – 1928 Pontoise (France)
Painter of landscapes and genre pictures. Trained with his brother José and Eduardo Cano at the art school in Seville. In **1864** he achieved some success with his pictures at the National Art Exhibition. **1867-1876** lived in Rome; made numerous trips to Paris and stayed frequently in Pontoise. Took French citizenship. **1879** and **1880** exhibited at the Salon in Paris. Exhibited at the World Fair in Paris in **1889** and in Chicago in **1893**. **1864** and **1867** awards and **1893** gold medal at the Exposiciónes Nacionales de Bellas Artes in Madrid. Close observation is the key to his realistic, often highly detailed paintings.
ILLUSTRATION:
553 A Lady at the Paris World Fair, 1889

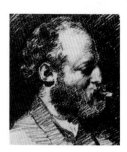

JOHANSEN Viggo
1851 Copenhagen – 1935 Copenhagen
1868 studied at the art academy in Copenhagen. **1876** first exhibition. Lived in Hornbaek, where he painted small pictures of fishermen and scenes of ports. Trip to Paris; considerably impressed by Manet. After his marriage in **1880** he painted numerous family scenes. Experimented with various techniques. **1882-1884** trips to Holland and Paris. **1885, 1887** and **1889** exhibited at the Paris Salon and received medals. Successful exhibitions at Munich, Berlin and Chicago. **1898** and **1904** travelled in Italy. **1888-1906** professor at the women's college of art in Copenhagen.
BIBLIOGRAPHY: Madsen, K.: V.J. Tilskueren 1894.– Stabell, A. (ed.): Kontrafej og Komposition. Copenhagen 1985 (EC)
ILLUSTRATION:
473 Near Skagens Østerby after a Storm, 1885

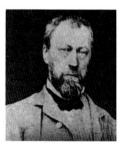

JONGKIND Johan Barthold
1819 Lattrop (Holland) – 1891 La Côte-Saint-André
Grew up in Vlaardingen near Rotterdam; worked as a solicitor's clerk. After his father's death, he studied 1836-37 at the school of drawing in The Hague as a pupil of the landscape painter A. Schelfhout. His first pictures, painted in a virtuoso but rather dry manner, reflect the traditional style of his teacher. In 1843 he received a scholarship of 200 guilders from King William II; sold a picture at the exhibition in Amsterdam. 1846-1853 settled in Paris, working at Isabey's studio and studying with Picot.

Met Israëls and Chassériau and became friends with Stevens, Courbet and Troyon. In 1847, he visited Le Havre. 1848 exhibited a picture for the first time at the Salon. 1850 went to Etretat in Normandy and in 1851 accompanied Isabey a second time to Le Havre and Normandy. Influenced by French landscape painting, he developed a sketchy style and more colourful palette. By the early 1850s, his watercolours were showing Impressionist features. In 1852 he won a third medal at the Salon. Began to paint landscapes by moonlight, which later were to become very popular. 1855 returned to Holland and lived in Rotterdam until 1860. Mental problems affected his work. 1857 travelled to Paris, where he met Courbet. 1860-1870 lived a Bohemian life in Paris in great poverty. His friends organised an auction sale of work to support him financially. He made frequent trips to Nivernais, Le Havre, Honfleur, Brussels and Holland. Met Boudin, Monet and Mme Fesser, a Dutch woman with whom he managed to overcome his unstable lifestyle. 1862 painted with Monet and Boudin in Le Havre. His financial situation improved through the success and sales of his pictures, painted in powerful colours. 1870 arrested as a spy. 1873 rejected by the Salon; decided to stop exhibiting. From 1874 he lived at La Côte-Saint-André near Grenoble where, apart from short visits to Provence and Paris, he remained until his death. His palette became increasingly brighter and his style of painting simpler. Mental imbalance and persecution mania combined with alcoholism led to his death at the mental hospital in Saint-Rambert near Grenoble. WRITINGS, DOCUMENTS: Moreau-Nélation, E.: J. raconté par lui-même. Paris 1918 CATALOGUE: Hefting, V.: J., sa vie, son œuvre, son époque. Paris 1975 BIBLIOGRAPHY: Bakker-Hefting, V.: J.B.J. Amsterdam 1964.– Boudin & J. London 1983 (EC).– Büchler-Schild, M.: J.B.J. (1819- 1891). Seine Stellung in der Landschafts- und Aquarelltradition des 19. Jahrhunderts. Berne 1979.– Colin, P.: J. Paris 1931.– Hefting, V.: L'univers de J. Paris 1976.– Hennus, M.F.: J.B.J. Amsterdam 1945.– J. and the Pre-Impressionists. Williamstown 1976 (EC).– J.B.J. 1819-1891. Dordrechts Museum et al. Tokyo 1983 (EC).– Roger-Marx, C.: J. Paris 1932.– Signac, P.: J. Paris n.d.
ILLUSTRATIONS:
409 View of Rouen, 1865
410 Dutch Landscape, 1862
411 Rue de l'Abbé-de-l'Epée and Church of Saint James, 1872

JOSEPHSON Ernst Abraham
1851 Stockholm – 1906 Stockholm
1868-1876 studied at the art academy in Stockholm. 1873 visited Paris with his friend Hill. While a student, he also travelled in France, Spain, Italy and Holland; copied Rembrandt. 1874 studied with Gérôme in Paris.

1878 trip to Rome. 1879-1888 lived in Paris, but also painted in Sweden, Norway and Brittany. 1880 exhibited for the first time at the Salon. 1884 published two articles attacking the teaching methods at the academy in Sweden; became one of the leaders of the Swedish "Opponents". 1888 in hospital with mental illness. After his recovery he worked with greater artistic freedom and began moving towards Expressionism.

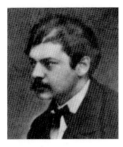

BIBLIOGRAPHY: Blomberg, E.: E.J. Gothenburg 1945.– Blomberg, E.: E.J. Stockholm 1951.– Blomberg, E.: E.J. konst. Historie–, porträtt och genremålaren. Stockholm 1956.– Blomberg, E.: E.J. konst. Från Näcken till Gåslisa. Stockholm 1959.– Hodin, J.P.: E.J. Stockholm 1942.– Jacobsson, I.: Näcken-motivet hos E. J. Gothenburg 1946.– Mesterton, I.: Vägen till försoning. Gothenburg 1956-1957.– Paulsson, G.: E.J.s teckningar 1888-1906. Stockholm 1918.– Zennström, P.O.: E.J. Stockholm 1946
ILLUSTRATION:
489 Autumn Sunlight, 1896

JULIAN → Académie Julian

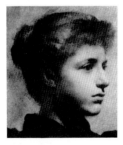

KNIGHT Laura
1877 Long Eaton (Derbyshire) – 1972 Nottingham
Encouraged to develop her artistic talent by her mother, a teacher of drawing. 1890 studied at Nottingham Art School, where she met her future husband, Harold. 1903 trip to Holland, impressed by the pictures of the school of The Hague. 1894-1906 lived with her husband at Staithes; painted country life in muted colours.

1907 moved to Newlyn; came into contact with the circle of students around Stanhope Forbes. Her landscapes from this period are characterised by brighter, shining colours. 1918 moved to London; the new subject matter of theatre, ballet and circus now dominated her work and she was regarded as a follower of Picasso. 1929 made Dame Laura Knight; from 1936 member of the Royal Academy, where she regularly exhibited after the Second World War. WRITINGS, DOCUMENTS: Knight, L.: Oil Paint and Grease Paint. 1936 BIBLIOGRAPHY: Dunbar, J.: L.K. Glasgow 1975.– Fox, C.: Dame L.K. Oxford 1988.– Grimes, T., J. Collins and O. Baddeley: Five Women Painters. Oxford 1989
ILLUSTRATIONS:
586 Flying the Kite, 1910
587 Wind and Sun, c. 1913

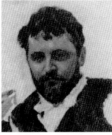

KOROVIN Constantin Alexeievich
1861 Moscow – 1939 Paris
1875-1886 studied at the School of Painting, Sculpture and Architecture in Moscow, mainly with Polenov; became friends with Levitan. 1881-1882 spent a year at the Academy in St. Petersburg. 1885-1919 stage designer in Moscow, at first for the private opera of S. Mamontov, at whose house in Abramcevo he was a frequent guest. 1885 the first of many trips to Paris and Spain. 1888 with Mamontov in Italy. Travelled widely within Russia, Caucasus and Central Asia. Exhibited with the "Wanderers". Painted in an Impressionist, and later an Art Nouveau style. 1894/95 visited Norway. 1896 joined the Moscow Association of Artists. Designed, to great acclaim, the pavilion at the All-Russian Exhibition of Arts and Crafts at Nishnii Novgorod. 1900 designed the decoration for the Central Asia section of the Paris World Fair; awarded with the Legion of Honour. 1901 took part in the exhibition "A Document of German Art" in Darmstadt. 1903 member of the new Federation of Russian Artists. 1905 received the title "Academician of Painting". 1909-1913 taught at the Moscow art school. Made regular visits to the Crimea. 1924 emigrated to Paris; supported by Shalyapin, he became a stage designer. He also became famous as a book illustrator.

WRITINGS, DOCUMENTS: Korowin, K.: Leben und Schaffen. Briefe, Dokumente, Erinnerungen. Ed. with an introduction by N.M. Moleva (Russian). Moscow 1963
BIBLIOGRAPHY: Basyrov, A.J.: K.A.K. 1861-1939. Leningrad 1985.– Kogan, D.S.: K.K. Moscow 1964.– Komarovskaya, N.J.: K.K. Leningrad 1961.– Moleva, N.M.: K.K. schisn i twortschestwo. Moscow 1963.– Moleva, N.M.: Zizn' mojazivopis? K.K. v Moskve. Moscow 1977
ILLUSTRATIONS:
510 Couple in a Boat, 1887
510 Café in Paris, c. 1890-1900
510 Boulevard des Capucines, Paris 1906

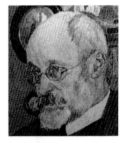

KREUGER Nils Edvard
1858 Kalmar – 1930 Stockholm
1874-1876 Attended the preparatory art course at the Stockholm Academy. Worked from 1876 to 1880 with E. Perséus. 1881-1887 lived in Paris, attending the Académie Colarossi; became a pupil of Laurens. Spent the summer of 1883 in Sweden and Holland. Began to paint in the French Impressionist style, mostly landscapes with animals. Active as a poster designer, did caricatures and illustrations. 1885 joined the "Opponents", the Swedish group of artists opposed to the Academy. 1886 participated in the founding of the Swedish Association of Artists and regularly contributed paintings to their exhibitions. 1887/88 painted with Bergh and Nordström in Varberg on the west coast of Sweden. 1888/89 short stay in Paris. 1889-1896 lived in Varberg, then moved to Stockholm. 1899 became one of the directors of the Swedish Association of Artists. BIBLIOGRAPHY: Boström K.: N.K. Stockholm 1948
ILLUSTRATIONS:
474 Gypsy on Öland, 1885
480 Snowy Weather, Paris, 1885

KROHG Christian
1852 Oslo – 1925 Oslo
1873 graduated in law and moved to Karlsruhe, where he studied figure painting at the Academy of Art under K. Gussow; in 1875 he followed his teacher to Berlin. Though he was impressed by Menzel and Liebermann, he preferred to paint in a Naturalist style. Formed a friendship with Max Klinger. 1878 returned to Norway.

Spent the summer months with friends (Thaulow, Ancher, Krøyer) at the small Danish fishing village of Skagen, where he painted the fishing and country life. **1881** won a state travel stipend and went to Paris. **1882** exhibited for the first time at the Paris Salon. He was strongly influenced by Manet and joined the Impressionist movement, painting mainly pictures of social criticism. **1884** began to exhibit regularly at the annual exhibitions in Oslo. He was one of the first exponents of Impressionism in his country. **1886** published the novel "Albertine" and in **1888** "A Duel". **1893** won the competition to exhibit a painting at the World Fair in Chicago – the painting chosen depicts the discovery of America by Leif Erikson. **1901-1909** lived mainly in Paris, and in **1902** became a teacher at the Académie Colarossi. **1907** Chairman of the Association of Norwegian Artists. **1909-1925** Director of the newly-founded Academy of Painting and Sculpture in Oslo.
WRITINGS, DOCUMENTS: Krohg, C.R.: Kampen for Tilværelsen. 4 vols. Oslo 1920-1921, 1989
BIBLIOGRAPHY: C.K. in "Kunstnere i Nasjonalgalleriet", IV, Oslo 1958.– Gauguin, P.: C.K. Oslo 1932.– Thue, O.: C.K. En bibliografi. Oslo 1968.– Thue, O.: C.K.s portretter. Oslo 1971

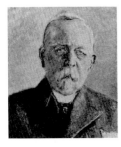

ILLUSTRATIONS:
470 Portrait of the Artist Karl Nordström at Grèz, 1882
475 Look ahead. The Harbour at Bergen, 1884
479 Portrait of the Artist Gerhard Munthe, 1885
497 Parisian Hackney Cab Driver, 1898

KRØYER Peder Severin
1851 Stavanger – 1909 Skagen
Brought up by his foster-father, the famous zoologist Henrik N. Krøyer. At the early age of ten, he was already drawing illustrations for his father's books. **1864-70** studied at the academy in Copenhagen. **1871-72** exhibited portraits in Copenhagen and in **1873** received the small gold medal; commissioned by the exhibition committee to do a portrait of the flower painter Ottesen, which attracted much attention. Spent the summer in Hornbaek. **1877** travelled via Holland and Belgium to Paris, where he studied at Bonnat's studio,

learning the rigorous techniques of French Naturalism with its precise observation of surface and light effects, its purity and brightness of colour and its large forms and simplified composition. **1878** travelled in Spain and copied Velázquez. **1879** painted at Cernay-la-Ville and Concarneau. **1880/81** tour of Italy, rejected the Romantic view of Italy all too prevalent at that time in Denmark. In **1881**, he won a medal in Paris for his Naturalist picture "Italian Village Roofers".

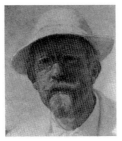

He returned to Denmark that year, spending almost every summer from then on at his house in Skagen. With the Anchers, C. Locher and Johansen in the artists' colony there he began to paint plein-air in a style influenced by Krohg. He became a leading member of the Skagen painters. His palette also brightened considerably. In **1883** he exhibited at the Paris Salon, and later also at Georges Petit's. From **1882** to **1904** he undertook periods of teaching at the school of art in Copenhagen, but in **1890** rejected the offer of a professorship at the Copenhagen academy. **1899** became ill with severe depression and paranoia.
BIBLIOGRAPHY: Bramsen, H.: P.S.K. Syv Stykker om Kunst. Copenhagen 1955.– Christensen, H.C.: P.S.K. Fortegnelse over hans Oliemalerier. 1923.– Hannover, E.: P.S.K.: Abends am Strande. Leipzig 1907 (Meister der Farbe, No. 1).– Hornung, P.M.: P.S.K. Tølløse 1987.– Lomholt, A.: Et Møde i Videnskabernes Selskab. Copenhagen 1954.– Mentze, E.: P.S.K. Kunstner af stort format – med braendte vinger. Copenhagen 1980
ILLUSTRATIONS:
476 Hip, Hip, Hooray! An Artists' Party at Skagen, c. 1884-1888
477 Artists at Breakfast, 1883
493 Bathing Children, 1892

LAMY → Franc-Lamy

LA THANGUE Henry Herbert
1859 Croydon – 1929 London
Studied at the Royal College of Art, the Lambeth School of Art and the Royal Academy School. From **1878** exhibited at the Royal Academy, where he won the gold medal in **1879**. **1879-1882** attended Gérôme's lessons at the Ecole des Beaux-Arts in Paris. Influenced by the plein-air painting of Bastien-Lepage. Travelled

in Brittany and Dauphiné. **1884** returned to England and settled in Norfolk. **1886** co-founder of the English Art Club. Tried unsuccessfully to establish an alternative exhibition to the Academy. **1891** moved to Bosham (Sussex). Trips to Italy and Provence; thereafter the Mediterranean landscape became the main subject of his paintings.

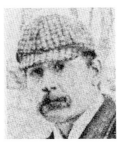

BIBLIOGRAPHY: McConkey, K. (ed.): A Painter's Harvest: Work by H.H. L.T. R.A. 1859-1929. Oldham Art Gallery, Oldham [no date of publication] (EC)
ILLUSTRATION:
583 In the Orchard, 1893

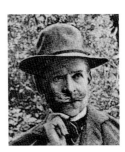

LATOUCHE Louis
1829 La Ferté-sous-Jouarre – 1884 Paris
Owner of art shop on the corner of the Rue Lafitte and the Rue Lafayette. Friendly with the young Impressionist painters (Monet, Pissarro); supported them and exhibited their paintings for sale in the rooms of his shop. His customers included Gachet and Amand Gautier. At a meeting on his premises in **1867**, Sisley, Bazille, Pissarro and Renoir decided to form a "Salon des Refusés". From **1866** he exhibited in the Salon. Took part in the 1st Impressionist Exhibition of **1874** with four works.

LAURENS Jean-Paul
1838 Fourquevaux (Haute-Garonne) – 1921 Paris
1854 Art school in Toulouse, then at the Paris School of Art. **1872** first success in the Salon with his history paintings – exciting compositions,

faithful to detail and painted in rich colours. Numerous large murals, including those of the Paris Panthéon. **1885** Professor at the Paris School of Art. **1891** joined the Academy as successor to Meissonier.

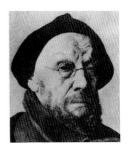

BIBLIOGRAPHY: Guitton, J.: J.-P.L. (1875-1937). Paris 1957
ILLUSTRATION:
166 The Excommunication of Robert the Pious, 1875

LA VIE MODERNE → Vie Moderne

LAWSON Ernest
1873 San Francisco – 1939 Miami Beach
1889-1891 worked as a graphic designer in Mexico. **1891** studied at the Art Students League in New York under Twachtman and Weir; attended the summer courses in Cos Cob. In **1893** moved to Paris; studied at the Académie Julian. **1894** exhibited for the first time at the Salon. Influenced heavily by the Impressionist style of Sisley. **1894** returned to the USA, settled on New York's Washington Heights. Painted numerous pictures in fresh, bright colours with motifs of Manhattan and the Harlem River.

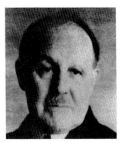

1904 met William Glackens. **1906** moved to Greenwich Village. **1907** Exhibition at the Pennsylvania Academy of the Fine Arts. In **1908** he became a member of The Eight. Exhibited in **1910** with the "Independent Artists". **1913** at the Armory Show with various Canadian groups. **1916** travelled in Spain; then in the Soviet Union and the West and South of the USA. In the 1920s he taught at

Colorado Springs and Kansas City. **1936-1939** lived for health reasons in Florida.
BIBLIOGRAPHY: Anderson, D.R. (ed.): E.L. Exhibition. ACA Galleries, New York **1976** (EC).– Berry-Hill, S. and H.: E.L., American Impressionist, **1873-1939**. Leigh-on Sea **1968**.– E.L. Whitney Museum of American Art, New York **1932** (EC).– Karpiscak, A.L. (ed.): E.L. **1878-1939**. University of Arizona Museum of Art, Tucson **1979** (EC).– O'Neal, B. (ed.): E.L., **1873-1939**. National Gallery of Canada, Ottawa **1967** (EC).– Price, F.N.: E. L., Canadian American. New York **1939**
ILLUSTRATIONS:
638 Harlem River, c. 1913-1915
638 Spring Night, Harlem River, 1913

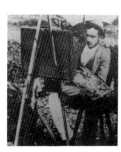

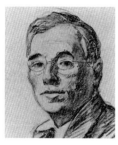

LEBASQUE Henri
1865 Champigné (Maine-et-Loire) – 1937 Cannet (Alpes-Maritimes)
Studied at the Ecole des Beaux-Arts under Bonnat. **1896** first exhibition at the Salon. Frequently visited Pissarro, whose Impressionist style overlay Bonnat's academic influence. Commissioned by the architect Perret to supply the decoration for the Théâtre des Champs-Elysées. In **1937** he contributed a significant part of his work to the exhibition "Peintres Indépendants" in the Petit Palais.
CATALOGUE: Bazetoux, D.: H.L. Catalogue raisonné (in preparation)
BIBLIOGRAPHY: Banner, L.A. and P. Fairbanks: L. San Francisco **1986**.– L. **1863-1937**. Montgomery Gallery, San Francisco **1986** (EC).– Vitry, P.: H.L. Paris **1928**
ILLUSTRATION:
385 View of Saint-Tropez, 1906

LEBEDA Otakar
1877 Prague – 1901 Malé Chuchel
1892-1897 studied at the Prague Academy of Art under Julius Marák; painted mountain landscapes. **1896** travelled in Italy. **1897** stayed in Paris. **1898** Lebeda travelled via Munich to Paris, attended the Académie Colarossi and painted landscapes in the forest of Fontainebleau, in Brittany and Normandy. Exhibited in Prague at the Mánes art federation. **1899** in Bohemia and Brittany, became neurotic and committed suicide.

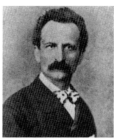

BIBLIOGRAPHY: Macková, O.: O.L. Prague **1957**
ILLUSTRATION:
517 Lilac. Village Path, 1899

LEBOURG Albert-Charles
1849 Montfort-sur-Risle – 1928 Rouen
Worked first in an architect's office in Rouen. Attended the Ecole municipale de peintre et de dessin in Rouen; took drawing lessons with Victor Delamarre. In **1867** visited Paris and was captivated by the pictures of Courbet and Manet on show at the Salon. His landscapes reveal their influence. **1872-1876** Professor of graphic art at the Société des Beaux-Arts d'Alger. As Monet and Sisley were later to do, he often painted the same motif seen in different lights. In **1873** he married in Rouen. **1877** moved to Paris and worked for two years under Laurens, as preparation for the examination of the city of Paris for teachers of drawing. **1879** and **1880** took part in the 4th and 5th Impressionist Exhibitions. **1883** first admitted to the Salon. **1884** long stay in the Auvergne. **1886-1895** lived alternately in Paris and in Normandy. Travelled in **1895/96** and again in **1896/97** to Holland; **1900** visited England and **1902** Switzerland. **1905** in Bordeaux and La Rochelle. **1900** exhibited at the World Fair. **1918** large retrospective at Georges Petit's in Paris.

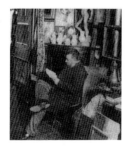

CATALOGUE: Bénédite, L.: A.L. Paris **1923**.– Walter, R.: A.L. Catalogue raisonné (in preparation)
BIBLIOGRAPHY: Bergeret, A.-M. et al. (eds.): A.L. **1849-1928**. Musée Eugène-Boudin, Honfleur; Musée de

la Chartreuse, Douai. Honfleur **1989** (EC).– Cartier, J.A.: A.L. Geneva **1955**.– Lespinasse, F.: A.L. **1849-1928**. Arras **1983**.– Melki, A. (ed.): Exposition A.L. Galerie Art Melki, Paris **1976** (EC).– Schurr, G.: A.L. Galerie Art Melki, Paris **1976** (EC)
ILLUSTRATIONS:
313 Road on the Banks of the Seine at Neuilly in Winter, c. 1888
383 Barges at Rouen, 1903

LEGA Silvestro
1826 Modigliana – 1895 Florence
1843 moved to Florence to study at the Accadémia under Servolino and Gazzarini; shortly afterwards he moved to the school of Luigi Mussini, an admirer of Ingres. **1848/49** volunteered for the Italian wars of liberation and unification. **1850** continued his studies in Florence. **1852** received the silver medal at the Concorso Triennale of the Accadémia for the picture "David playing before Saul". Frequented the Caffè Michelangiolo; in **1857** he took up plein-air painting under the influence of the Macchiaioli. **1857-1863** painted in the Church of Madonna del Cantone in Modigliana; developed into a Realist. **1861-1870** painted plein-air with other artists in the Piagentina area; this loose association became known as the "School of Piagentina". In **1870** received the silver medal for an exhibition in Parma. In **1872** he contracted an eye disease, which together with family affairs prevented him from painting. In **1875** with Borrani he opened a gallery for modern art in Florence, but it only survived for a short period. Through exhibitions of the Società Donatello he became acquainted with French Impressionism and Naturalist painting. In the 1880s he resumed painting under this new influence. From **1886** he was frequently a guest at the household of the Bandini family in Poggio Piana al Gabbro; he gave the two daughters painting lessons and also painted numerous landscapes himself.
CATALOGUE: Matteucci, G.: L. L'opera completa. 2 vols. Florence **1987**
BIBLIOGRAPHY: Daddi, G.: S.L. Spunti ed appunti. Oggiono **1978**.– Dini, P.: S.L. Gli anni di Piagentina. Turin **1984**.– Giardelli, M.: S.L. Milan **1945**.– Pepi, C. (ed.): S.L. in una raccolta privata. Villa di Poggio Piano, Il Gabbro. Livorno **1990** (EC).–

Matteucci, G.: Dipinti noti e inediti di S.L. Florence **1977**.– Signorini, T.: S.L. Florence **1895**.– S.L. Museo Civico, Bologna **1973** (EC).– S.L. Dipinti. Palazzo della Permanente, Milan; Palazzo Strozzi, Florence **1988** (EC).– Somare, E.: S.L. Milan **1926**.– Valsecchi, M.: L. Milan **1950**
ILLUSTRATIONS:
536 The Pergola, 1868
536 Giuseppe Mazzini on his Death Bed, 1873
538 Reading, 1875

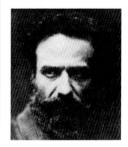

LEGROS Alphonse
1837 Dijon – 1911 Watford
Trained with a painter of devotional art. Worked with a decorative painter in Dijon, where he attended the Ecole des Beaux-Arts. **1851** at the school of drawing of Lecocq de Boisbaudran in Paris; became friends here with Fantin-Latour and Whistler. Until **1855** he attended the Ecole des Beaux-Arts in Paris. Exhibited in **1857** for the first time in the Salon. Joined the circle around Courbet. At the invitation of Whistler, he travelled in **1860** to London. In **1861** he had some success in the Salon with an ex-voto. Often with Manet in the Café de Bade or the Café Guerbois. Had difficulty finding a market for his paintings and drawings in Paris. In **1862** he travelled in Spain. Moved in **1863** to London, where he never felt fully at home. Through the intercession of Whistler, he obtained a post as teacher of drawing at the Royal College of Art; taught with success. He exhibited in **1876** at the Royal Academy. **1870-1875** supported Durand-Ruel in the setting up of exhibitions by the Society of French Artists in London. In **1876** he took part in the 2nd Impressionist Exhibition with 25 works. **1876-1892** Professor at the Slade School. **1890** individual exhibition at the gallery of Durand-Ruel. Commissioned as a sculptor by the Duke of Portland for two monumental fountains in the park of Welbeck Abbey.
BIBLIOGRAPHY: A.L. Peintre et Graveur (**1837-1911**). Musée des Beaux-Arts, Dijon **1957** (EC).– Seltzer, A.: A.L.: The Development of an Archaic Visual Vocabulary in 19th-Century Art. Doctoral thesis, State University of New York. Binghampton (NY) **1980**
ILLUSTRATION:
166 Communion, c. 1876

LEISTIKOW Walter
1865 Bromberg/Bydgoszcz – 1908
Berlin
Studied art at the Berlin Academy and with Eschke and Grube. 1890-1893 teacher at the Berlin School of Art. Friendly with the Naturalist writers G. Hauptmann, M. Halbe and A. Holz. 1892 co-founder of the literary group "Vereinigung der XI". His first novel "Auf der Schwelle" ("On the Threshold") appeared in 1896. 1898 rejection of his picture "Sunset over Lake Grunewald" (p. 448) by the Great Berlin Exhibition; formation of the Berlin Secession, of which he was a committee member until his death. In the 1880s he travelled to Denmark and Sweden. Painted impressionistic, atmospheric pictures of the Nordic landscape of forests and lakes. From 1890 he became influenced by Art Nouveau, Japanese wood cuts and Puvis de Chavannes.
ILLUSTRATION:
448 Sunset over Lake Grunewald, 1898

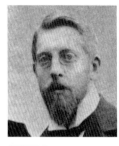

LEMMEN Georges
1865 Schaerbeek – 1916 Uccle
Attended courses for a short period at the school of drawing in St. Josse-ten-Noode. Around 1880 he became influenced by Degas and Toulouse-Lautrec. 1888 joined the group Les Vingt in Brussels; became an important supporter of "Libre Esthétique". He published articles on art in the journal of Les Vingt, "L'Art moderne", against the prevailing dogma. 1890-1893, under the influence of van Rysselberghe, he moved towards Neo-Impressionism; painted numerous portraits. Exhibited at the Salon des Indépendants in Paris. He later freed himself from Pointillism and painted in a more traditional, Belgian style. Travelled in England and became interested in artefacts. His wide-ranging work includes numerous book illustrations, posters, ceramics, carpets, drawings, pastels and gouaches.
WRITINGS, DOCUMENTS: Elslander, J.F.: Figures et souvenirs d'une belle-époque. Brussels 1950
CATALOGUE: Cardon, R.: G.L. (1865-1916). Monographie générale suivi du catalogue raisonné de l'œuvre gravé. Antwerp 1990, Cologne 1992
BIBLIOGRAPHY: G.L. Musée Horta, Brussels 1980 (EC).– G.L.: dessins et estampes. Bibliothéque Royale.

Brussels 1965 (EC).– Nyns, M.: G.L. Antwerp 1954
ILLUSTRATIONS:
424 View of the Thames, 1892
425 Self-Portrait, 1890

LEPIC Vicomte Ludovic-Napoléon
1839 Paris – 1889 Paris
Son of one of the Emperor's adjutants. At first a pupil of Cabanel, Wappers and Verlat. Studied at Gleyre's studio with Bazille and Monet, with whom he became friends. A close friendship developed, through a female cousin, with Degas, and he often went riding with the latter's brothers. With Degas he went to the opera and the horse races; in the painting "Gentlemen's Race. Before the Start" (p. 10), he is depicted as one of the amateur jockeys. Worked in Paris, in Berck and at the sea. Degas persuaded him to exhibit at the 1st Impressionist exhibition in 1874. Showed 36 landscapes at the 2nd Impressionist Exhibition at Durand-Ruel's gallery in 1876. Through his private income and influence he supported his fellow painters, but nevertheless attempted to exclude Cézanne from group exhibitions. After being banned by the Impressionists from exhibiting at the same time in the Salon, Lepic refused to take part in any of their exhibitions. He achieved surprising effects through new graphic techniques. 1872 founded the Musée d'Aix-les-Bains and became its first curator. 1879 individual exhibition at the Gallery "La vie moderne". Travelled to Egypt and Pompeii, where he took part in excavations. Exhibited in 1883 at the Musée des Arts décoratifs. Caillebotte described him in a letter to Pissarro: "Lepic, Heaven knows, has no talent". Viscount Lepic is portrayed with his daughters in Degas's painting "Place de la Concorde" (p. 169).

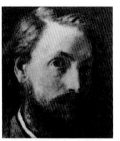

LEPINE Stanislas Victor Edouard
1835 Caen – 1892 Paris
Grew up in an artisan family. Probably studied under Corot. Influenced in his choice of themes by Jongkind. Exhibited from 1859 at the Salon. 1873 joined the Société anonyme des peintres, sculpteurs et graveurs. In 1874 he took part in the 1st Impressionist Exhibition; he exhibited in 1886 with Durand-Ruel in the USA. Mainly painted views of Paris and its

outskirts. Few people bought his pictures; organised exhibitions and sales of work at the Hôtel Drouot. Exhibited in 1889 at the World Fair. Died in poverty; friends collected money to pay the funeral costs.
BIBLIOGRAPHY: Couper, J.: S.L. (1835-1892), sa vie, son œuvre. Paris 1969.– Rostrup, H.: L., La Seine vers Rouen. In: Meddelelser fra Ny Carlsberg Glyptotek 30 (1973), pp. 7-14
ILLUSTRATIONS:
68 Banks of the Seine, 1869
202 The Seine near Argenteuil
202 Paris, Pont des Arts, c. 1878-83

LEROY Louis Joseph
1812 Paris – 1885 Paris
Painter, graphic artist, writer and critic. Exhibited 1835-1881 at the Salon in the style of the Barbizon School; wrote several successful comedies. In his critical article on the painting appeared in the "Charivari" of 25th April 1874 under the headline "Exposition des impressionnistes", Leroy first used the term "Impressionists", which was immediately taken up by the rest of the press and gave a name to the movement. In 1864 Leroy had already severely criticised Manet's painting "Bullfighters", which was exhibited in the Salon.

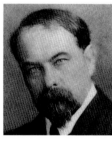

LE SIDANER Henri
1862 Port Louis (Mauritius) – 1939
Paris
In 1880 he moved to Paris and studied at the Ecole des Beaux-Arts under Cabanel. Influenced by Manet and Monet. 1882- 1887 frequently in Etaples, where he painted landscapes. He exhibited from 1887 at the Salon and in 1891 he received a medal for his picture exhibited there. Member of G. Petit's Société internationale. 1896-1900 Symbolist period; his choice of theme had literary inspiration. 1897 first individual exhibition at the Mancini gallery. 1898/99 lived in Bruges. In 1902 he settled in Gerberoy. Travelled to Holland, in 1905 to Venice and 1907/08 to London. 1929 member of the Académie Royale des Beaux-Arts in Brussels. Numerous awards: 1901 gold medal in Munich; 1908 second medal in Pittsburgh; 1914 Chevalier de la Legion d'Honneur; 1925 Carnegie award. From 1937 President of the Académie des Beaux-Arts in Paris.

CATALOGUES: Farinaux-Le-Sidaner, Y.: H.L.S. Catalogue raisonné de l'œuvre gravé et peint. Paris 1990
BIBLIOGRAPHY: H.L.S. Musée de la Ville. Dunkirk 1974 (EC).– H.L.S. Musée Marmottan. Paris 1989 (EC).– Mauclair, C.: H.L.S. Paris 1928
ILLUSTRATIONS:
386 Table beneath Lanterns, Gerberoy,1924
386 14th July, Gerberoy, 1910
387 House by the Sea at Dusk, 1927

LEVERT Jean-Baptiste-Léopold
Born 1828, active as landscape painter, graphic artist and designer of military clothing. Friends with the Rouart brothers, whom he visited regularly after the war of 1870, and with Degas, who persuaded him to join the Impressionists. 1874-1879 participated in the 1st-3rd and the 5th Impressionist exhibitions.

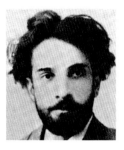

LEVITAN Isaac Ilyich
1860 Kibartai, Lithuania – 1900
Moscow
1873-1885 studied under Savrassov and Polenov at the School of Painting, Sculpture and Architecture in Moscow; as a Jew, he was from time to time refused entry to the city. He finally received a silver medal but was only given a diploma as a teacher of calligraphy. Friendship with Anton Chekhov and his brothers. Exhibited in 1884 for the first time at the "Wanderers". 1886 the first of many trips to the Crimea, mainly staying on the Volga. His poetic appreciation of the Russian landscape was highly praised. 1890-1899 trips to France, Italy, Austria, Switzerland, Finland and Germany. 1892 excluded several times from Moscow. Increasingly ill with nervous complaints and heart trouble. 1898 Teacher of landscape painting at the Moscow School of Art. In St. Petersburg he was represented for the first time at an exhibition organised by Diaghilev.
WRITINGS, DOCUMENTS: Fyodorov-Davydov, A.A. (ed.): I.I.L. Pisma, Dokumenty, vospominaniya. Moscow 1956
BIBLIOGRAPHY: Druzinin, S.N. (ed.): I.I.L. Moscow 1963.– Fyodorov-Davydov, A.A.: I.I.L. 2 vols. Moscow 1966.– Fyodorov-Davydov, A.A.: T.W. Yurova, I.I. L. Leningrad 1988.– Glagl, S. and I. Grabar: I.I.L. Moscow n.d.– Kovalenskaya, T.: I.I.L.

Moscow 1938.– Paustowski, K.: I.L. Dresden 1965

ILLUSTRATIONS:
506 Golden Autumn, 1895
506 Birch Grove, c. 1885-1889

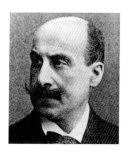

LIEBERMANN Max
1847 Berlin – 1935 Berlin
Began his studies in 1863 in the studio of Carl Steffeck. 1866 studied at the Faculty of Arts, Berlin University. 1868-1872 studied at the Weimar Academy of Art with Charles Verlat, Paul Thumann and Ferdinand Pauwels. In 1871 with the landscape painter T. Hagen he visited the Düsseldorf studio of Michael Lieb von Munkácsy; the visit made a decisive impression on him. In 1872, drawing on the tonal Realism of Leibl, he painted his first large painting "Plucking Geese", which received great acclaim, but also criticism. 1872 trip to Paris and study visit to Holland. 1873-1878 lived in Paris and followed the styles of Courbet, Millet and Ribot. Spent the summer months in Barbizon and 1876 in Amsterdam, where he imitated Franz Hals. 1878 extended visits to Berlin, Tirol and Venice; settled in Munich. At the Glaspalast in 1879 he exhibited the large painting "Christ in the Temple", which caused a scandal because of its realistic depiction of the scene. 1884 moved to Berlin. Until 1913 worked frequently in Holland. His encounter with French Impressionism in the early 1890s led to a brighter and more colourful palette. With form as his starting point, he focused on movement and rhythm as the main principle of his Impressionist style. Founded with Leistikow in 1892 the "Union of the Eleven". 1897 successful participation in a group exhibition within the Great Berlin Exhibition; awarded the gold medal and the title of Professor. 1898 appointed as member of the Academy. 1898 Co-founder of the Berlin Secession, 1899 its President. Even in old age he still painted, primarily scenes from around his country house on the Wannsee, where he lived from 1910. 1920 appointed president of the Akademie der Bildenden Künste; 1932/33 Honorary President.

WRITINGS, DOCUMENTS: Busch, G. (ed.): M.L. Die Phantasie in der Malerei. Schriften und Reden. Frankfurt am Main 1978.– Eipper, P.: Atelier-

gespräche mit L. und Corinth. Munich 1971.– Küster, B.: M.L. Ein Maler-Leben. Hamburg 1988.– Landsbergen, F. (ed.): M.L. Siebenzig Briefe. Berlin 1937.– Lichtwark, A.: Briefe an M.L. Hamburg 1947.– Liebermann, M.: Die Phantasie in der Malerei. Berlin 1916.– Liebermann, M.: Gesammelte Schriften. Berlin 1922.– Liebermann, M.: Künstlerbriefe über Kunst. Dresden 1957
CATALOGUE: Schiefler, G.: M.L. Sein graphisches Werk 1876-1923. 3 vols. Berlin 1907-1923 (Reprint: San Francisco 1991)
BIBLIOGRAPHY: Branner, L.: M.L. Berlin 1966.– Bunge, M.: M.L. als Künstler der Farbe. Berlin 1990.– Busch, G.: M.L. Maler, Zeichner, Graphiker. Frankfurt am Main 1986.– Eberle, M.(ed.): Max Liebermann in seiner Zeit. Haus der Kunst, Munich; Nationalgalerie, Berlin, Munich and Berlin 1979 (EC).– Friedländer, M.J.: M.L.s grafische Kunst. Dresden 1920.– Friedländer, M.J.: M.L. Berlin 1925.– Hancke, E.: M.L. Berlin 1923.– Küster, B.: M.L. Ein Künstler-Leben. Hamburg 1988.– Meissner, G.: M.L. Leipzig 1986.– Lenz, C.: M.L., "Münchner Biergarten", Munich 1986.– M.L. Niedersächsische Landesgalerie, Hanover 1954 (EC).– M.L. Deutsche Akademie der Künste, Berlin 1965 (EC).– Stuttmann, F.: M.L. Hannover 1961
ILLUSTRATIONS:
432 Munich Beer Garden, 1884
434 Plucking Geese, c. 1870/71
435 The Orphanage at Amsterdam, c. 1881/82
442 Woman with Goats, 1890
442 St. Steven's Foundation, Leyden, 1889
443 Boys Bathing, 1898
449 "De Oude Vinck" Restaurant, Leyden, 1905
453 Man with Parrots, 1902
453 The Parrot Walk, 1902
455 The Beach at Nordwijk, 1908
459 At the Races, 1909
462 Self-Portrait, 1911

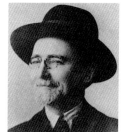

LOISEAU Gustave
1865 Paris – 1935 Paris
Son of a merchant, trained first with a decorative artist. His family enabled him to dedicate himself full-time to his art. 1888 attended the Ecole des Beaux-Arts and studied in 1889 with the painter Quignon. 1890 moved to Pont-Aven, where he met his friends

Moret and Maufra, who shared the same Impressionist style of painting, and Gauguin and Bernard. Exhibited 1891-1895 with the Neo-Impressionists at Le Barc de Boutteville, in the gallery of Durand-Ruel and at the Salon de la Nationale. His views of Paris are famous. Travelled frequently in Normandy, along the Seine, on the cliff coast of Dieppe and in the Dordogne. 1901 large single exhibition at Durand-Ruel's. Stayed often in Pontoise, where he visited Gachet. 1927 settled on the Quai d'Anjou on the Seine.
CATALOGUE: Imbert, D.: G.L. Catalogue raisonné (in preparation)
BIBLIOGRAPHY: G.L. Retrospective. Galerie des Granges, Geneva 1974 (EC).– G.L. Musée Pissarro. Pontoise 1981 (EC).– G.L. Didier Imbert Fine Arts, Paris 1985 (EC).– Melas-Kyriazi, J.: G.L. l'historiographe de la Seine. Athens 1979
ILLUSTRATIONS:
378 Orchard in Spring, c. 1899-1900
378 Banks of the Seine, 1902
379 Cap Fréhel and "La Teignouse" Cliffs, 1906

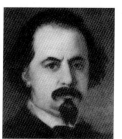

LOUVECIENNES
Village on the left bank of the Seine to the east of Paris, between Bougival and Versailles. Became popular as a place to stay and paint for many Impressionists, such as Degas, Manet, Morisot and Sisley. Renoir often went to visit his parents, who lived here. Pissarro stayed here 1869/70 and 1871/72 (pp. 82, 83, 99, 106), and Sisley lived here during the Paris Commune (pp. 84, 98, 158, 183).

LUCAS Y PADILLA Eugenio
1824 Alcalá de Henares – 1870 Madrid
Studied at the Academy in Madrid with Camarón, J. Madrazo and Tejeo. He became infamous for his

copies of Spanish masters (Goya, Velázquez) although these were not forgeries, but free imitations. Considerably influenced by Goya, he painted figures, histories and portraits. He had a talent for landscapes in small format, which, despite their indebtedness to Romanticism, have a directness and spontaneity of their own.

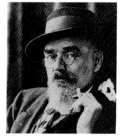

LUCE Maximilien
1858 Paris – 1941 Paris
After an initial training as a wood carver at the Ecole des Arts décoratifs, he began to study art with Hildebrand in 1872 and took evening courses with Maillart. Up to 1885 he studied at the Académie Suisse and the studio of Carolus-Duran at the Ecole des Beaux-Arts. Earned his living as a wood carver with Eugène Froment and Auguste Lançon. In his painting, he became influenced by Impressionism. 1877 travelled with Froment to London. 1879-1883 military service. 1887 exhibited at the Salon des Indépendants. 1888 first individual exhibition on the premises of the journal "La Revue indépendante". Met Pissarro, Seurat, Signac and Angrand and joined the Neo-Impressionist group. 1889 invited to exhibit in Brussels with the Twenty; exhibited 1895 and 1897 at the Libre Esthétique in Brussels and in France at Le Barc de Boutteville and at Durand-Ruel's. 1871 came under the influence of Pissarro's Anarchist ideas and formed friendships with the Anarchist writers and journalists Jules Christophe, Jean Grave, Georges Darien and Emile Pouget; 1894 became involved in the the trial of the Thirty and served a short term of imprisonment. Until 1904 he lived in Montmartre, whose streets became a favourite subject for his paintings. 1900 exhibited at the World Fair. 1904-1924 lived in Auteuil, then moved back to Paris. Besides street scenes and motifs like factories and wharfs, he painted numerous landscape paintings on his travels through the Etampes, Normandy and Brittany. During the First World War he also painted war scenes: pictures of the wounded and homecoming soldiers. 1934 elected President of the Société des Artistes Indépendants after Signac's retirement.
CATALOGUE: Bazetoux, D. and J. Bouin-Luce: M.L. Catalogue de

l'œuvre peint. 2 vols. Paris 1986
BIBLIOGRAPHY: Cazeau, P.: M.L. Lausanne and Paris 1982.– M.L. Maison de la Pensée Française. Paris 1958 (EC).– M.L. Palais des Beaux-Arts. Charleroi 1966 (EC).– M.L., un pointilliste. Musée Toulouse-Lautrec. Albi 1977 (EC).– M.L. Musée Marmottan. Paris 1983 (EC).– Tabarant, A.: M.L. Paris 1928
ILLUSTRATIONS:
295 Paris Seen from Montmartre, 1887
374 Notre-Dame, 1900
374 Notre-Dame, 1901
375 La Sainte-Chapelle, Paris, 1901

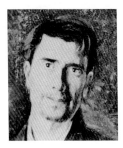

LUCHIAN Stefan
1868 Stefanesti – 1916 Bucharest
1885-1889 studied at the school of art in Bucharest, where he also exhibited his first pictures. 1889/90 studied at the Academie in Munich under Herterich. 1890-1893 at the Académie Julian in Paris, influenced by Impressionism and Symbolism. 1893 settled in Bucharest. 1894 exhibited for the first time at the "Exhibition of Living Artists". 1896 organised with others an exhibition of independent artists. 1898 exhibited at the "Ileana" society for the encouragement of art. 1902 founder member of Tinerimea Artistica ("Artistic Youth"); despite a crippling disease, he became the leading force behind modern painting in Romania. 1920 almost totally paralysed.
CATALOGUE: Jianu, I. and P. Comarnescu: S.L. (Rom.). Bucharest 1956
BIBLIOGRAPHY: Alexandru, I.: L. Bucharest 1978.– Ciuca, V.L. Bucharest 1984.– Eliasberg, N.E.: S.L. Moscow 1983.– Lassaigne, J.: S.L. Paris 1972
ILLUSTRATIONS:
525 Anemones
526 The Last Race, 1892
526 Anemones, 1908

MACCHIAIOLI
Group of Italian painters who gathered in and around Florence to paint plein-air with short brush strokes and their characteristic spots of paint (macchia) in reaction against the academic style. From 1853 the first members of the movement, including Signorini and Abbati, began to meet in the Caffè dell'Onore au Borgo della Croce; later the venue became the Caffè Michelangiolo, where they met

to discuss political and artistic freedom. The group was influenced by the Barbizon school and later by French Impressionism; its members included Fattori, De Nittis, Boldini, Lega and Zandomeneghi.

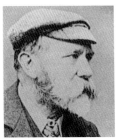

MACTAGGART William
1835 Campbelltown – 1910 Broomiekwnowie, Edinburgh
Son of a working-class family; 1852-1859 studied at the Trustee's Academy in Edinburgh under Robert Scott Lauder. 1856/57 won several prizes at the Royal Scottish Academy. His naturalistic style was influenced by the English Pre-Raphaelites, whom he met in 1857 at the Manchester Art Treasure Exhibition. Published two plays, "The Wreck of the Hesperus" (1861) and "Dora" (1868). 1870 made a member of the Royal Scottish Academy; exhibited there regularly until 1895. Made only three short trips to the Continent. His highly expressive coastal landscapes, which capture moods and dissolve forms to the point of abstraction, reveal his acquaintance with contemporary painting on the continent. He never really became known outside his native Scotland.
BIBLIOGRAPHY: Caw, J.L.: W.McT. A Biography and an Appreciation. Glasgow 1917.– Errington, L. (ed.): W.McT. 1835- 1910. National Gallery of Scotland, Edinburgh 1989 (EC).– Sir W.McT Scottish National Gallery of Modern Art, Glasgow 1968 (EC)
ILLUSTRATION:
580 The Storm, 1890

MAITLAND Paul
1863 London – 1909 London
Studied at the Government Art Training School; pupil of Roussel at the Royal College of Art. Belonged to the group of artists around Whistler. In 1888 he was made a member of the New English Art Club and 1889 of the London Impressionists. Taught drawing at the Royal College of Art. Lived in Kensington and Chelsea.
ILLUSTRATION:
583 Flower Walk, Kensington Garden, c. 1897

MAITRE Edmond
1840 Bordeaux – 1898 Bordeaux
Writer and musician. Art lover and friendly with most of the contempor-

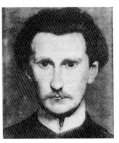

ary artists. Frequently played music with Bazille at his studio in the Rue de Furstenberg; the artist painted him as the pianist in his picture "The Artist's Studio" (p. 81); he was also painted standing next to Zola in Fantin-Latour's "Studio in the Batignolles Quarter" (p. 81). Close friends also with Baudelaire, Verlaine and Renoir, with whom he shared a love of German music, particularly Wagner.

MALEVICH Kasimir
1878 Kiev – 1935 Leningrad
Began to study art in 1895 at the art school in Kiev. The Impressionism of his early period soon gave way to Fauvism and the related styles of the Russian artists Larionov and Goncharova. Rebelled against the prevailing views on art. Developed an increasingly geometric style of figure representation, akin to Cubism and abstract painting.

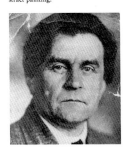

CATALOGUE: Nakov, A.: K.M. Leben und Werk. Vol. I: Œuvrekatalog, Texte und Dokumente. Landau 1992
BIBLIOGRAPHY: Nakov, A.: K.M. Leben und Werk. 3 vols. Landau 1992-1994
ILLUSTRATION:
511 Flower Girl, 1903

MALLARME Stéphane
1842 Paris – 1898 Valvins
Important Symbolist poet and writer, influential critic and proponent of Impressionist ideas. His apartment in the Rue de Rome in the Batignolles Quarter of Paris became a meeting place of the avant-garde. Became close friends with Renoir, Whistler and Degas; had a special liking for Morisot. In 1874 he wrote a highly

positive appraisal of Manet for the "Renaissance", which was well received by Manet himself; he defended Whistler and Morisot. Manet did the illustrations for Mallarmé's translation of Poe's "The Raven" and some woodcuts for "L'Aprés-midi d'un faune". After Manet's death he became interested in Gauguin's art and formed a close friendship with Redon.

MANET Edouard
1832 Paris – 1883 Paris
1844-1848 went to school at the Collège Rollin, friendship with Antonin Proust. 1848/49 trained as a sea cadet on a voyage to Brazil. 1850-1856 pupil at Couture's studio and the Académie Suisse; liaison with Suzanne Leenhoff. 1852 birth of his son Léon Koella. 1853 visited Florence and perhaps also Austria and Germany. 1856 travelled in Belgium, Holland, Germany, Austria and Italy. 1857 met Fantin-Latour. 1858 rejected by the Salon. 1860 took on apartment in the Batignolles Quarter, frequented the Café Guerbois. 1861 exhibited for the first time at the Salon – pictures in the realistic "Spanish" style – and was awarded "special mention"; began to paint subjects from "modern life". Met Degas. 1862 met Baudelaire. 1863 caused a scandal with his pictures in the Martinet gallery and the Salon des Refusés; married Suzanne Leenhoff. 1865 met Duret in Spain. 1866 became acquainted with Monet and Zola, who corresponded with him. In 1867 he staged his own exhibition during the Paris World Fair. 1868 trip to London. 1868/69 Morisot and Gonzalès became his students and models.

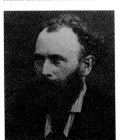

1870/71 military service in the National Guard, stayed in South West France during the Commune in Paris; Durand-Ruel bought many of his paintings. 1872 visited Holland. 1873 met Mallarmé. 1874 visited Monet at Argenteuil; began to paint plein-air in an increasingly Impressionist manner. 1875 visited Venice. 1878 rejected by the Paris World Fair. 1879 murals in the city hall in Paris. 1880 exhibition at the gallery of the journal "La vie moderne" owned by the publisher Charpentier; spent the summer at Bellevue; contracted a fatal illness. 1881 received a medal 2nd class at the Salon; received into the Legion of Honour by the Gambetta government. 1882 Chevalier of the Legion of Honour; spent the summer at Rueil. 1883 last pastels; amputation of a leg, painful death. 1884 successful memorial exhibition and auction sale. 1889/90 "Olympia" bought by donations and presented to the state. WRITINGS, DOCUMENTS: Courthion, P. and P. Cailler (eds.): M. raconté par lui-même et par ses amis. 2 vols. Geneva 1953.– Graber, H.: M. nach eigenen und fremden Zeugnissen. Basle 1941.– Manet, E.: Lettres de jeunesse 1848-1849. Voyage à Rio. Paris 1928.– Moreau-Nélaton, E. (ed.): M. raconté par lui-même. 2 vols. Paris 1926.– Tabarant, A. (ed.): Une correspondance inédite d'E.M.: Les lettres du siège de Paris (1870-1871). Paris 1935.– Valery, P.: Triomphe de M. Paris 1932.– Wilson-Bareau, J.: M. by Himself. Correspondence & Conversation. Boston 1991.– Zola, E.: M. Etude biographique et critique. Paris 1867 CATALOGUES: Guérin, M.: L'œuvre gravé de M. Paris 1944.– Harris, J.C.: E.M. The Graphic Work. A Catalogue Raisonné. New York 1970, San Francisco 1991.– Jamot, P., G. Wildenstein and M.-L. Bataille: M. 2 vols. Paris 1932.– Leiris, A. de: The Drawings of E.M. Berkeley, Los Angeles 1969.– Orienti, S.: The Complete Paintings of M. New York 1967.– Pool, P. (ed.): The Complete Paintings of M. Harmondsworth 1985.– Rouart, D. and D. Wildenstein: E.M. Catalogue raisonné de l'œuvre. 2 vols. Lausanne and Paris 1975.– Tabarant, A.: M. et ses œuvres. Paris 1947 BIBLIOGRAPHY: Adler, K.: M. Oxford 1986.– Bataille, G.: M. Lausanne 1955, Geneva 1983.– Cachin, F., C.S. Moffett et al. (eds.): M. 1832-1883. Grand Palais, Paris; Metropolitan Museum of Art, New York. Berlin 1984 (EC).– Cachin, F., C.S. Moffett et al. (eds.): M. 1832-1883. Grand Palais, Paris; Metropolitan Museum of Art, New York. Paris 1983 (EC).– Cachin, F., C.S. Moffett et al. (eds.): M. 1832-1883. Grand Palais, Paris; Metropolitan Museum of Art, New York. New York and London 1984 (EC).– Cachin, F.: M. Cologne 1991.– Cegodaev, A.D.: M. Moscow 1985.– Clark, T.J.: The Paintings of Modern Life: Paris in the Art of M. and his Followers. New York 1984.– Cogniat, R. and M. Hoog: M. Paris 1982.– Courthion, P.: E.M. London 1962, New York 1962.– Darragon, E.: M. Paris 1989.– Duret, T.: Histoire d'E.M. Paris 1902.– Florisoone, M.: M. Munich 1947.– Germer, S. and M. Fath (eds.): E.M. Naturblicke der Geschichte. Munich 1992.– Gronberg, I.A. (ed.): M. A Retrospective. New York 1988.– Hamilton, G.H.: M. and his Critics. New Haven and London 1986.– Hanson, A.C. (ed.): E.M. 1832-1883. Philadelphia Museum of Art, Philadelphia 1966 (EC).– Hanson, A.C.: M. and the Modern Tradition. New Haven (CT) and London 1976.– Hofmann, W.: Nana. Mythos und Wirklichkeit. Cologne 1973.– Hopp, G.: E.M. Farbe und Bildgestalt. Berlin 1968.– Jamot, P.

and G. Wildenstein: M. 2 vols. Paris 1932.– Jedlicka, G.: E.M. Zurich 1941.– Keller, H.: E.M. Munich 1989.– Leiris, A. de: The Drawings of E.M. Berkeley (CA) 1969.– Liebmann, K.: E.M. Dresden 1968.– Meier-Graefe, J.: E.M. und sein Kreis. Berlin 1903.– Meier- Graefe, J.: E.M. Munich 1912.– Perruchot, H.: M. Eine Biographie. Berlin, Darmstadt, Vienna 1962.– Perruchot, H.: La vie de Manet. Paris 1959.– Proust, A.: E.M., Souvenirs. Paris 1913.– Proust, A.: E.M. Erinnerungen. Berlin 1929.– Reff, T.: M.: Olympia. New York 1976.– Reff, T. (ed.): Manet and Modern Paris. The National Gallery of Art, Washington 1982 (EC).– Rewald, J.: E.M. Pastels. Oxford 1947.– Rey, R.: M. Paris 1938, New York 1938.– Richardson, J.: E.M.: Paintings and Drawings, London 1958, 1982.– Sandblad, N.G.: M. – Three Studies in Artistic Conception. Lund 1954.– Schneider, P.: The World of M., 1832-1883. New York 1968.– Schneider, P.: M. et son temps. Paris 1972.– Tabarant, A.: M.: Histoire catalographique. Paris 1931.– Tabarant, A.: M. et ses œuvres. Paris 1947.– Wilson, J. (ed.): E.M.: Das graphische Werk: Meisterwerke aus der Bibliothèque Nationale und weiteren Sammlungen. Ingelheim am Rhein 1977 (EC).– Wivel, M., J. Wilson-Bareau and H. Finsen (eds.): Ordrupgaardsamlingen, Copenhagen 1989 (EC)
ILLUSTRATIONS:
36 Le déjeuner sur l'herbe (study), 1862/63
37 Le déjeuner sur l'herbe, 1863
38 Olympia, 1863
42 The Races at Longchamp, c. 1865
42 At Longchamp Racecourse, 1864
43 Music at the Tuileries, 1862
43 Horse Race, 1864
46 Lola de Valence, 1863
47 Lola de Valence, 1862 (to post – 1867)
47 The Fifer, 1866
48 Reading, 1865-1873
48 Repose. Portrait of Berthe Morisot, 1870
62 Luncheon in the Studio, 1868
63 The Balcony, c. 1868/69
64 The Execution of Emperor Maximilian (Lithograph), 1868
65 The Execution of Emperor Maximilian (four fragments), 1867
65 The Execution of Emperor Maximilian, 1868
66 Portrait of Emile Zola, 1868
77 The Departure of the Folkestone Boat, 1869
95 The Railway, Gare Saint-Lazare, c. 1872/73
109 On the Beach, 1873
110 The Masked Ball at the Opéra, c. 1873/74
123 The Monet Family in the Garden, 1874
132 Madame Mane on a Divan, 1874
134 Argenteuil, 1874
138 Boating, 1874
139 Claude Monet and his Wife in his Studio Boat, 1874
160 Nana, 1877
165 Plum Brandy, c. 1877/78

178 Bock Drinkers, 1878
178 The Waitress, 1878/79
178 Man in a Round Hat (Alphonse Maureau), 1878
179 At the Café, 1878
179 The Waitress, 1879
179 Two Women Drinking Bocks, 1878
195 In the Garden Restaurant of Père Lathuille's, 1879
195 In the Conservatory, 1879
198 Bundle of Asparagus, 1880
200 Girl in the Garden at Bellevue, 1880
200 House at Rueil, 1882
212 Manet's Mother in the Garden at Bellevue, 1880
213 The Viennese: Portrait of Irma Brunner in a Black Hat, 1880
221 A Bar at the Folies-Bergère, c. 1881/82

MANET Eugène
1833 Paris – 1892 Paris
Painter and younger brother of Edouard Manet; 1874 married Berthe Morisot. Friends with Degas and Stevens. His own artistic endeavours fall far short of those of his wife and brother. Traces of his influence can be seen in Morisot's pictures.

MANET Julie → Rouart, Madame

MANTZ Paul
1821 Bordeaux – 1895 Paris
Began in 1841 as a critic with the journal "L'Artiste", then became the art historian and critic for the "Gazette des Beaux-Arts". At the same time he was employed as a civil servant at the Ministry of the Interior. 1882 Director-General of the Académie des Beaux-Arts. One of the first to recognize the talents of Monet and Morisot.

MANZANA → Pissarro, Georges

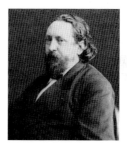

MARIS Jacob Hendricus
1837 The Hague – 1899 Karlsbad
The oldest of the Maris brothers. 1849 trained in the studio of Stroebel, an imitator of Pieter de Hooch. He then studied with J.-J. van den Berg and in 1855 with the Romantic painter Huib van Hove in Antwerp. Travelled up the Rhine to Switzerland. From 1865 in Paris as a pupil of Ernest Hébert. Influenced by the Barbizon school. From 1866 he exhibited in the Salon. From 1870 he lived in

The Hague, painting Dutch landscapes with loose brush-strokes. BIBLIOGRAPHY: Bock, T. de: J.M. Amsterdam 1902.– Croal Thomson, D.: The Brothers M. London and Paris 1907.– Maris. Een kunstenaarfamilie. Singer Museum, Laren 1991 (EC).– Maris tentoonstelling. Gemeentemuseum, The Hague; Stedelijk Museum, Amsterdam 1935 (EC).– Zilcken, P.: Les Maris: Jacob-Matthijs-Willem. Amsterdam 1896
ILLUSTRATION:
413 Allotment Gardens near The Hague, c. 1878

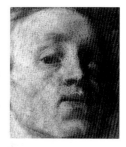

MARIS Matthijs
1837 The Hague – 1917 London
1858 trained with L. Meijer at the Academy in The Hague. A scholarship from the Queen of Holland allowed him to study in Antwerp with de Keyser. In 1859 he returned to The Hague. 1860 travelled up the Rhine as far as the Black Forest. Met Moritz von Schwindt and Wilhelm von Kaulbach and was impressed by their Romantic style. 1867-1873 lived in Paris and in 1877 settled London. Influenced by the English Pre-Raphaelites, he moved away from the styles of The Hague school. BIBLIOGRAPHY: Arondéus, W.: M.M. De tragiek van den droom. Amsterdam 1939.– Croal Thomson, D.: The Brothers M. London and Paris 1907.– Croal Thomson, D. et al.: M.M. An Illustrated Souvenir. London 1918.– Gelder, H.E. van: M.M. Amsterdam 1939.– Maris. Een kunstenaarfamilie. Singer Museum, Laren 1991 (EC).– Maris tentoonstelling. Gemeentemuseum, The Hague; Stedelijk Museum, Amsterdam 1935 (EC).– M.M. 1839-1939. Gemeentemuseum, The Hague 1939 (EC).– M.M. 1974 (EC).– Zilcken, P.: Les Maris: Jacob-Matthijs-Willem. Amsterdam 1896
ILLUSTRATION:
413 Quarry at Montmartre, c. 1871

MARIS Willem
1844 The Hague – 1910 The Hague
Became a gifted sketcher of animals as early as 1856; trained with his brothers and with P. Stortenbeker. Taught himself to paint landscapes and developed his own style in Oosterbeek and Wolfhezer, where he met Mauve in 1855. In 1863 he exhibited

for the first time in The Hague. Maris travelled with Blommers in the Rhineland 1865/66. From 1869 lived in The Hague. Willem was the most realistic of the three brothers, and his landscape paintings, reminiscent of Corot, were well received, particularly in Britain and America.

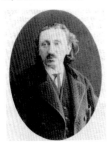

BIBLIOGRAPHY: Croal Thomson, D.: The Brothers M. London and Paris 1907.– Maris. Een kunstenaarfamilie. Singer Museum, Laren 1991 (EC).– Maris tentoonstelling. Gemeentemuseum, The Hague; Stedelijk Museum, Amsterdam 1935 (EC).– Zilcken, P.: Les Maris: Jacob-Matthijs-Willem. Amsterdam 1896
ILLUSTRATION:
412 Dusk, c. 1875

MARLOTTE
Town in the Forest of Fontainebleau, which had been used by the painters of the Barbizon school for plein-air painting. Its motifs became popular with Impressionist painters and writers, who frequently stayed there.

MARLY-LE-ROI
Viewing point on a hill overlooking the Seine in the park of the old château of Louis XIV, not far from the villages of Louveciennes, Port-Marly and L'Etang-la-Ville. In particular, Renoir and Sisley liked to paint in the forest here.

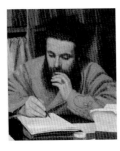

MARTELLI Diego
1838 Florence – 1896 Florence
Studied science at the University of Pisa; from 1855 a frequent customer in the Caffè Michelangiolo in Florence. Became one of the most

important critics, theorists and defenders of the Macchiaioli. 1873 founded the "Giornale Artistico"; made a considerable contribution to the spread of Impressionism in Italy.

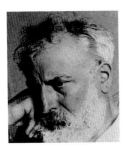

MARTIN Henri-Jean Guillaume
1860 Toulouse – 1943 La Bastide-du-Vert
Son of a carpenter; trained first in Toulouse at the Ecole des Beaux-Arts under Jules Garipuy, a pupil of Delacroix. 1879 moved to Paris and worked in the studio of Jean-Paul Laurens. 1886 exhibited for the first time at the Salon. 1885 won a scholarship for a tour of Italy, where he developed his own style with its characteristic short, divisionist brushstrokes. In 1889 he received the gold medal in the Salon and became a member of the Legion of Honour. 1895 painted some unusually large pictures for the Neo-Impressionists and won great acclaim when he exhibited them at a one-man show at the Mancini Gallery. At the World Fair in 1900 he won the Grand Prize. Commissioned to paint some important murals for the city hall in Paris (1895), for the Capitol in Toulouse (1903, 1906) and in Marseilles. Friendship with Rodin. Lived mostly in Marquairol near Bastide-du-Vert (Lot).
BIBLIOGRAPHY: H.M. Kaplan Gallery, London 1971 (EC).– Martin-Ferrières, J.: H.M., sa vie, son œuvre. Paris 1967.– Valmy-Baysse, J.: H.M., sa vie, son œuvre. Paris 1910
ILLUSTRATION:
379 The Harbour of Collioure

MARX Roger
1859 Nancy – 1913 Paris
Art collector, journalist and critic for numerous journals and newspapers and Inspector of Beaux-Arts, later Inspector-General of the provincial museums. One of the first to admire Cézanne, whom he gave preferential treatment at the World Fairs in 1900 and 1904. From 1892 friendship with Toulouse-Lautrec. On friendly terms with many contemporary artists. Important proponent of the revival of arts and crafts at the end of the 19th century.

MAUPASSANT Guy de
1850 Tourville-sur-Arques – 1893 Paris
French writer, at first also a civil servant in the Paris ministries. From

MAUFRA Maxime
1861 Nantes – 1918 Poncé (Sarthe)
Worked first in a merchant's office in England; drew in his spare time and admired the Turners in the National Gallery. Back in Nantes he was encouraged to take up art by Charles Le Roux, who initiated him into the techniques of Impressionism. After a successful exhibition at the Salon in 1886, he decided to devote himself full time to his painting. He admired Monet and Sisley and was influenced by Whistler. In 1890 he met the Pont-Aven artists (Gauguin, Sérusier, Bernard and others). He spent the subsequent summers in Pont Aven or in Pouldu. 1891 and 1893 exhibited in the Salon des Indépendants and in 1894 at Le Barc de Boutteville.
CATALOGUE: Durand-Ruel Godfroy, C.: M.M. Catalogue raisonné (in preparation).– Morane, D.: M.M., catalogue de l'œuvre gravé. Published in connection with the exhibition: M.M., du dessin à la gravure. Musée de Pont-Aven; Musée départemental du Prieuré. Saint-Germain-en-Laye 1986 (EC)

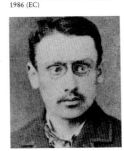

BIBLIOGRAPHY: Alexandre, A.: M.M. Paris 1926.– M.M. Galerie Durand-Ruel. Paris 1961 (EC).– M.M. Galerie Art Mel. Paris 1978 (EC).– Ramade, P.: M.M. Un ami de Gauguin en Bretagne. Le Chasse-Marré 1988
ILLUSTRATION:
338 Ile de Bréhat, 1892

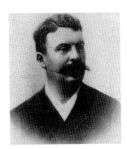

1880 Charpentier began to publish his short stories with their close observation of contemporary life, particularly the petty bourgeoisie and artists. Friends with such artists as Monet, Renoir, and Degas; their subject matter, themes, motifs and point of view is mirrored in his writings. Travelled extensively in his own yacht. Became mentally unbalanced in his old age.

MAUREAU Alphonse
Exact details of his life unknown. A friend of Degas, Manet and Desboutin; a member of the artisitic clientele in the Café de la Nouvelle-Athéns. 1877 invited by Degas to show four works at the 3rd Impressionist exhibition. In 1878, Manet did a pastel portrait of him wearing a round hat (p.178). Also friends with Nina de Callias, the musician Cabaner and the writer Duranty.
ILLUSTRATION:
289 Banks of the Seine, c. 1877

MAUS Octave
1856 Brussels – 1919 Brussels
Barrister. 1881 co-founder of the journal "L'Art moderne". As an art critic and journalist he exerted a considerable influence on the development of art in Belgium. 1883 encouraged a rejection of the Salon and the formation of the group of artists known as Les Vingt. In 1893 he founded the progressive group "Libre Esthétique", which organised concerts, conferences and especially Impressionist and Symbolist exhibitions.

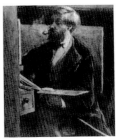

MAUVE Anton
1838 Zaandam – 1888 Arnheim
1854 trained initially as a painter of animals with P.F. van Os; 1858 a pupil of W. Verschuur for several months; in the summer he stayed at the artists' colony in Oosterbeek, where he met painters of The Hague school. Became friends with W. Maris. 1871 studio in The Hague. 1874 married the cousin of Vincent van Gogh, Ariette Sophia Jeanette Carbentus. 1873 co-founder of the "Hollandsche Teekenmaatschappij" ("Dutch Society of Draughtsmen") for the propagation of watercolour painting. 1878-1883 member of the "Pulchri studio" society of artists in The Hague. Spent the summer months of 1882 in Laren, where he moved in 1885. Painted mainly landscapes

with harmonious rich, colours and loose brushwork.
BIBLIOGRAPHY: A.M. Singer Museum, Laren 1959 (EC).– Berckenhoff, H.L.: A.M. Amsterdam 1890.– Engel, E.P.: A.M. (1838-1888). Bronnenverkenning en analyse van zijn œuvre. Utrecht 1967.– Leeman, F.: M.'s watercolours. Rijksmuseum Vincent van Gogh, Amsterdam 1988 (EC)
ILLUSTRATION:
412 Laren Woman with Goat, 1885

MCNICOLL Helen Galloway
1879 Toronto (Ontario) – 1915 Swanage (England)
Studied at the Art Association in Montreal with William Brymner, then at the Slade School of Art in London and 1906 at the art school at St. Ives in Cornwall with A. Talmage. Became interested primarily in the effects of light and atmospheric mood. Later her main work became highly expressive portraits of women and children. 1908 received the Dow Prize and 1914 the Women's Art Society Prize. 1913 elected member of the Royal Society of British Artists. 1914 member of the Royal Canadian Academy. Spent most of her life in Montreal.
ILLUSTRATION:
632 Under the Shadow of the Tent, 1914

MEDAN
Village on the Seine north-west of Paris, about 9 miles from Pontoise. Zola owned a house here from 1878 which became a meeting place for supporters of Realism. Other visitors included such Impressionist painters as Monet, Pissarro and Renoir. Cézanne spent several weeks here each year.

MEIER-GRAEFE Julius
1867 Resita (Romania) – 1935 Vevey (Switzerland)
German art historian, critic and writer. 1889 in Paris for the first time. 1890-1895 in Berlin, lived later in various places, predominantly in Paris, and travelled widely. At times edited the journals "Pan" and "Dekorative Kunst". 1899-1903 owned an Art Nouveau gallery in Paris. 1900 began a series of publications which helped to popularise the Impressionists and their predecessors in Germany, and established the German reputation of Cézanne. 1906 organised with H. von Tschudi the exhibition "A Century of German Art" in Berlin, a new re-appraisal of nineteenth-century art. The victory of modernity in art owes a great deal to his lively, subjective and sensitive analyses.

MEIFREN Y ROIG Eliseo
1859 Barcelona – 1940
Pupil of Antonio Caba at the art college in Barcelona. Specialised in Impressionist sea painting. Lived for several years in Paris and exhibited regularly at the Salon and at the Galerie Petit. Worked in Italy, the Canaries and the Balearic Islands. Director of the art school in Palma de Mallorca. Numerous awards and medals. 1916 one-man exhibition in New York.

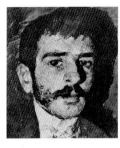

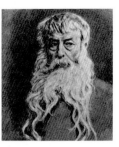

BIBLIOGRAPHY: Pantorba, B. de.: E.M. Barcelona 1942
ILLUSTRATION:
564 The Marne

MEISSONIER Jean Louis Ernest
1815 Lyon – 1891 Paris
Studied with L. Cogniet. 1834 exhibited for the first time at the Salon, from which he later remained mostly aloof. 1848 officer in the National Guard, deeply shocked by the Revolution. Painted genre scenes, mostly in the costumes of the 16th and later the 18th century, also scenes from the Napoleonic Wars; his pictures were executed with extreme precision, often in tiny format, and gained the highest awards. In 1855 Napoleon III bought his painting "La rixe". A careful observer of lighting, interested in photography. Became friends with Menzel. 1870/71 officer in the National Guard, where Manet also served; a fierce opponent of the Communards and also of Courbet. 1891 president of the Société Nationale des Beaux-Arts, a break-away group from the Indépendants. After his death he was ignored and forgotten, despised by the Impressionists, ridiculed by Degas, but re-discovered by Salvador Dalí.
BIBLIOGRAPHY: Greard, O.: M. Ses souvenirs, ses entretiens. Paris 1897
ILLUSTRATION:
27 The Reader, 1857

MENZEL Adolph Friedrich Erdmann von
1815 Breslau – 1905 Berlin
1830 trained as a lithographer with his father in Berlin. 1833 he took over the firm on the death of his father. 1833 attended the plaster cast

lessons at the Academy of Art in Berlin: achieved fame with his illustrations to Goethe's "Künstlers Erdenwallen". Came into contact with Schinkel, Rauch and Meyerheim. 1838-1845 did his most famous illustrations – to "Peter Schlemihls wundersame Geschichte" ("Peter Schlemihl's Marvellous Story") by Adalbert von Chamisso, Franz Theodor Kugler's "Geschichte Friedrichs des Grossen" ("History of Frederick the Great", Leipzig 1842) and the "Armeewerk" (1845-1857). From the 1840s he painted house interiors and portraits, which look ahead to the style of the Impressionists. 1849-1856 completion of the well-known Fridericus paintings of scenes from the life of Frederick the Great.

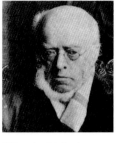

1853 member of the Prussian Academy of Arts. 1856 appointed professor. 1855, 1867 and 1868 trips to Paris, 1870 and 1873 Vienna and 1880/81 and 1883 Verona. 1875 member of the Senate at the Academy; painted his most famous picture, "The Iron Foundry". 1883 vice-chancellor of the Friedensklasse des Ordens "pour le mérite"; 1885 chancellor; 1898 received into the aristocracy: made Ritter des Schwarzen Adler-Ordens (Knight of the Order of the Black Eagle).
CATALOGUES: Bock, E.: A.M. Verzeichnis seines graphischen Werkes. San Francisco 1991
BIBLIOGRAPHY: A.M. Aus Anlaß seines 50. Todestages. Museum Dahlem, Berlin 1955 (EC).– Hochhuth, R.: M. Maler des Lichts. Frankfurt am Main 1991.– Hütt , W.: A.M. Vienna 1965.– Jensen, J.C.: A.M. Cologne 1982.– Kaiser, K.: A.M. Berlin 1956.– Vossberg, H.: Kirchliche Motive bei A.M. Berlin 1964.– Weinhold, R.: Menzel-Bibliographie. Leipzig 1959
ILLUSTRATION:
434 Departure of Kaiser Wilhelm I for the Front on 31 July 1870, 1871

METCALF Williard Leroy
1858 Lowell (MA) – 1925 New York
1875 studied with the landscape painter George Loring Brown and at the Lowell Institute; 1876-1878 studied at the Museum School of Fine Arts in Boston with Otto Grundmann. Travelled with the ethnologist Franz Cushing 1881-1883 in the

south-west of the USA; did drawings and paintings of native Americans. 1883-1888 first stay in Europe; studied at the Académie Julian in Paris under Boulanger and Lefèbvre. 1884 went to England and Pont-Aven; 1886 the first American painter in Giverny; travelled in Algeria and Tunisia. Spent the summer of 1887/88 in Giverny once more. From 1887 member of the Society of American Artists. Successful exhibition at the Paris Salon 1888. 1888 returned to the USA. 1889 his first one-man exhibition at the St. Botolph Club, Boston. 1891 taught at the Cooper Institute. 1899 mural for the the Appelate Courthouse in Madison Square, New York. 1902 visited Havana (Cuba); studies for a mural in the Havana

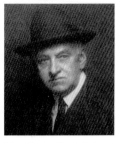

Tobacco Company Store in the St. James Building, New York City. 1903 left New York and moved to the country, settling in Clark's Cove, Maine. Despite his contacts with Giverny, it was only now that he turned to Impressionist techniques in his landscapes, done in different moods and at different times of the year. Founder member of The Ten American Painters. Travelled most of the time in New England and became an important member of the artists' colony at Old Lymne, Connecticut. Influenced in technique by Lawson, his style became a more academically-inspired version of Impressionism.
BIBLIOGRAPHY: Bolton, T. (ed.): Memorial Exhibition of Paintings by Late W.L.M. Century Association, New York 1928 (EC).– Duncan, W.J. (ed.): Paintings by W.L.M. Corcoran Gallery of Art, Washington 1925.– Murphy, F. and E. de Veer (eds.): W.L.M. Museum of Fine Arts, Springfield (MA) 1976 (EC).– Veer, E. de and R.J. Boyle: Sunlight and Shadow. The Life and Art of W.L.M. New York 1987
ILLUSTRATIONS:
621 Gloucester Harbour, 1895
630 The Poppy Garden, 1905

MEURENT Victorine Louise
1844 – c. 1885
Professional model, who posed first for the students of Couture. Became famous for sitting with the students and discussing with them. In 1862 at the age of 18 she met Manet, who spoke to her in a crowd and noted her address. For ten years she was his

favourite model, achieving fame as the woman in "Le déjeuner sur l'herbe" (p. 37) and "Olympia" (pp. 38/39). She had a relationship with Stevens, for whom she also modelled; she drew her own pictures and took lessons with the genre painter Leroy. She exhibited at the Salon in 1876, when Manet's pictures were rejected, and also in 1885. She died probably an alcoholic, in poverty.

MEYER Alfred
1832 Paris – 1904 Paris
Studied with F.E. Picot and E. Lévy. Teacher at the Bernard-Palissyschool in Paris. 1858-1871 worked at a porcelain manufacturer's in Sèvres and rediscoverd the long forgotten process of Limoges enamel painting. From 1864 exhibited at the Salon. 1866 awarded a medal. 1874 exhibited at the first Impressionist exhibition. 1895 published his book "L'Art de l'émail de Limoges".

MILICEVIC Kosta
1877 Vraka – 1920 Belgrade
1895-1898 studied drawing and painting at K. Kutlik's school in Belgrade. 1899-1901 at the private school of H. Strehblow in Vienna. 1902/03 studied with Ažbè in Munich. 1903-1910 attended the arts-and-crafts school in Belgrade. 1907 painted the icon decoration of a church. 1908 first exhibition in Belgrade. 1910 member of the Lada group of artists; painted in an Impressionist style. 1914-1916 did military service and worked as a war artist. 1916/17 and 1918 convalescence on Corfu. 1919/20 taught drawing at evening school in Belgrade.
BIBLIOGRAPHY: K.M. Muzej savremene umetnost. Belgrade 1974 (EC).– Milan Milovanicic, K.M. Narodni Mujez. Belgrade 1960 (EC).–Zivkovic, S.: K.M. Novi Sad 1970
ILLUSTRATION:
530 Spring, 1913

MILLER Richard
1875 St. Louis – 1943 St. Augustine (Florida)
1898 moved to Paris and studied at the Académie Julian under Constant and Laurens; he then worked as a teacher at the Académie Colarossi. Belongs with Frieseke to the 2nd generation of Giverny painters. Stayed for many years in France; each summer he lived and painted in Giverny, where he also gave courses to students of the Mary Wheeler School, Providence. 1901 and 1904 successes at the Paris Salon; 1909 had his own exhibition room at the Biennale in Venice. 1900-1915 exhibited in Paris, Buffalo, Liège and San Francisco. 1916 returned to the USA and taught in Pasadena at the Stickney Memorial School of Art. Became a specialist painter of decorative garden scenes.
BIBLIOGRAPHY: Ball, R. and M.W. Gottschalk: R.E.M. An Impression and Appreciation. Saint Louis 1968
ILLUSTRATION:
640 Reverie, 1913

MILLET Jean-Baptiste
1831 Gréville – 1906 Auvers-sur-Oise
Son of a Normandy peasant. Painter and graphic artist, pupil and younger brother of J.-F. Millet. The main subjects of his water colours and drawings are landscapes and peasant life. Exhibited several times at the Salon and in 1876 exhibited ten works at the 2nd Impressionist exhibition.

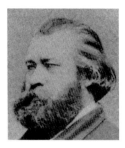

MILLET Jean-François
1814 Gruchy (Manche) – 1875 Barbizon
Son of a Normandy peasant; older brother of J.-B. Millet. 1837-39 after finishing his education in Cherbourg, he studied with Delaroche in Paris. 1840 exhibited for the first time in the Salon. Became acquainted with the Barbizon painters; chose to paint the daily life of the peasants and serious landscapes. With his friend C. Jacque he settled in Barbizon in 1849, living in poverty. 1867 won awards at the Paris World Fair. Millet was a precise and sympathetic observer, whose heavy-limbed figures of farmers and peasant children, depicted at times with almost religious sentiment, were the subject of much debate as to their significance. They clearly influenced the development of Realism in many countries, and especially influenced Pissarro and van Gogh. In 1899 his painting "The Angelus" was auctioned for the sensational price of 553,000 francs.
WRITINGS, DOCUMENTS: Moreau-Nélaton, E.: M. raconté par lui-même. 3 vols. Paris 1921
CATALOGUE: Moreau-Nélaton, E.: Monographie de référence. 3 vols. Paris 1921
BIBLIOGRAPHY: Bouchot, J.: Dessins de J.-F.M. Musée National du Louvre, Paris 1960 (EC).– Cain, J.: M. Paris 1913.– Fermigier, A.: J.-F.M. Geneva 1977.– Gay, P.: J.-F.M. 1814-1875. Paris 1951.– J.-F.M. Grand Palais, Paris 1975 (EC)
ILLUSTRATIONS:
25 Gleaners, 1857
25 The Angelus, c. 1859/60

MILOVANOVIC Milan
1876 Krusevac – 1946 Belgrad
1895 studied at K. Kutlik's art school in Belgrade. 1897-1902 studied at the private school of Ažbè in Munich. 1902-1906 at the Academy of Art in Munich under L. Herterich and C.

Marr. 1906 short period at the Académie Colorossi and the Paris art college. 1906 one-man exhibition in Belgrade. 1907 visited monasteries in Serbia, Macedonia and Mount Athos. Painted in an Impressionist style. Member of the Lada and Medulic groups. 1908 co-founder of the Serbian Association of Artists. 1914-1917 war painter with the Serbian General Staff. 1917-1937 taught at the school of art in Belgrade, but gave up painting himself.
BIBLIOGRAPHY: Duric, V.J.: M.M. Belgrade 1964.– M.M. 1876-1946. Narodni Muzej. Belgrade 1986 (EC).– M.M. Kosta Milicevic. Narodni Muzej, Belgrade 1960 (EC)
ILLUSTRATION:
531 The Blue Door, 1917

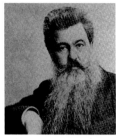

MIRBEAU Octave
1848 Trévières – 1917 Paris
Influential art and theatre critic and Romantic novelist. Acquainted with all the important Impressionist painters and contemporary writers; friends with Pissarro and Monet, for whom he wrote catalogue texts and discussed their pictures. 1889 wrote the catalogue for the large Monet exhibition at the Galerie Petit. 1891 published a study of Pissarro in "L'Art dans les deux mondes" and wrote an enthusiastic article on Gauguin. Long correspondence with Monet and Pissarro. A strong supporter of the Impressionists and the sculpture of Rodin.

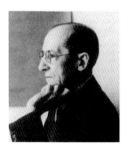

MIR TRINXET Joaquín
1873 Barcelona – 1940 Barcelona
1889 trained with Luis Graner and

for a short time at the Academy of Art in Barcelona with Antonio Caba and Arcadio Mas y Fontdevilla. 1897 failed to gain a scholarship to Rome. Imitated works by Velázquez. 1890-1893 joined the group of artists which included Nonell, Casas, Pichot and others; further developed his colourful and emotive style of Impressionism. 1898 received the bronze medal at the exhibition of arts and crafts in Barcelona and 1899 the silver medal at the Madrid exhibition of art. 1900 stayed in Mallorca. Worked in Deya with the Belgian painter William Degouve. From 1910 took part in exhibitions in Brussels, Madrid, Barcelona and won numerous awards.
BIBLIOGRAPHY: Jaürdí, E.: J.M. Barcelona 1975
ILLUSTRATION:
568 The Waters of the Maguda, 1917

MOLINS Auguste de
1821 Lausanne – 1890
Pupil of Victor Joseph Chavet in Geneva. Worked for a time in France. 1850-1870 showed in exhibitions in the Paris Salon. 1874 exhibited at the 1st Impressionist exhibition. Painted landscapes and hunting scenes. 1875 bought two pictures by Renoir. Taught drawing and painting in Lausanne.

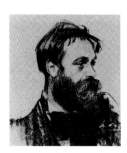

MONDRIAN Piet
1872 Amersfort – 1944 New York
Grew up in an artistic family; learnt to draw with his uncle Frits. 1892-1897 studied at the Rijksakademie in Amsterdam with A. Allebé. Impressed by Breitner and the landscape painters of the Hague and Amsterdam schools. 1904/5 in the provinces of Brabant and Overijssel; developed a more personal style, which was already beginning to move away from the idea of depiction of the visible world. 1905/6 scientific drawings for Professor Calcan in Leyden. 1908 met Toorop; became interested in Symbolism and French Pointillism. 1909 exhibited at the Stedelijk Museum in Amsterdam; his free landscape forms reminiscent of the Fauvists were heavily criticised. 1911-1914 exhibited in the Salon des Indépendants in Paris. 1912 moved to Paris. Co-founder of "De moderne kunstkring" in Amsterdam and from 1909 member of the Dutch Theosophy Society. In his philosophy and art considerably influenced by H.P.

Blavatsky's "Secret Doctrine". Gave up natural colours in favour of pure colours. From 1914 back in Holland; lived in Amsterdam, Laren, Blaricum, Scheveningen and Domburg. 1917 founded the journal "De Stijl" which gave its name to a type of art based on abstract principles.
WRITINGS, DOCUMENTS: Holtzman, H. and M.S. James (eds.): New Art, the New Life: The Collected Writings of P.M. London 1987.– Mondrian, P.: Plastic Art and Pure Plastic Art. New York 1945.– Schmidt, G.: Theorien und Ideen von P.M. Basle 1977
CATALOGUES: Blok, C.: P.M. Een catalogus van zijn werk in Nederlands bezit. Amsterdam 1974.– Ottolenghi, M.G.: L'opera completa di M. Mailand 1974.– Seuphor, M.: P.M. Paris 1970, 1987
BIBLIOGRAPHY: Champa, K.S.: Mondrian Studies. Chicago 1985.– Jaffé, H.: P.M. New York 1985.– Jaffé, H. L.C.: P.M. Paris 1970.– Lewis, D.: M., 1872-1944. London 1957.– M. and The Hague School. Whitworth Art Gallery. Manchester 1980 (EC).– Milner, J.: M. London 1992.– Seuphor, M.: P.M.: sa vie, son œuvre. Paris 1956.– Seuphor, M.: P.M.: Leben und Werk. Cologne 1957.– Sweeney, J.J. (ed.): P.M. The Museum of Modern Art, New York 1948 (EC).– Welsh, R.P.: M.'s early career, the naturalistic periods. New York and London 1977
ILLUSTRATION:
418 Idyll, c. 1900

MONET Camille
1847 Lyon – 1879 Vétheuil
Met Monet 1865 and became his favourite model. 1867 and 1878 births of their sons Jean and Michel; the couple did not marry until 1870, against the wishes of Monet's family. Camille and their sons frequently appear in Monet's pictures (pp. 118, 146, 147, 150).

MONET Claude
1840 Paris – 1926 Giverny
1845-1859 grew up in Le Havre as the son of a minor merchant. 1858 exhibited a painting he had done under the tutelage of Boudin. 1859 moved to Paris; the Barbizon painter Troyon gave help and advice. 1860 studied at the Académie Suisse; met Pissarro and Courbet. 1861 military service in Algeria. 1862 met Jongkind in Le Havre. 1862/63 studied at Gleyre's studio in Paris; friendship with Bazille, Renoir, Sisley; impressed by Manet. 1863 began plein-air painting at Chailly near Barbizon and at Honfleur. 1865 exhibited for the first time at the Salon; friendship with Zola, Cézanne, Manet; liaison with Camille Doncieux, with whom he had two sons. In Chailly he painted a plein-air figural composition that was to excel those of Manet. 1866 success at the Salon; painted in Sainte-Adresse and other localities, becoming increasingly impressive in his use of bright colours. 1867 he and Renoir were accepted by Bazille at his studio; rejected by the Salon; first broached the idea of a group exhibition. 1868 ex-

hibited at the Salon. Dire financial difficulties. Painted at Bennecourt and Fécamp; a frequent customer at the Café Guerbois. 1869 rejected by the Salon; with Renoir in Bougival on the Seine he worked out fully the formal techniques of the new Impressionist style. 1870 rejected once more by the Salon; married Camille; painted with Boudin in Trouville. When the Franco-Prussian War broke out, he moved to London, where he studied pictures by Turner and Constable. Through Daubigny he became acquainted with Durand-Ruel. 1871 exhibition organised by Durand-Ruel in London; trip to Holland. 1871-1878 lived in Argenteuil. 1872 painted in Le Havre ("Impression: Sunrise") and Holland. 1873 formed a friendship with Caillebotte; founding of a group of artists. 1874 first exhibition of the new group in Paris, referred to mockingly as the "Impressionists". 1876 met the department store owner and art collector Hoschedé; 2nd Impressionist exhibition. 1877 3rd Impressionist exhibition. 1878-1881 lived in Vétheuil with his family and with Alice Hoschedé and her six children.

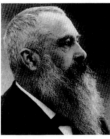

1879 death of Camille; 4th Impressionist exhibition. 1880 exhibition of a picture at the Salon. Due to a quarrel about planning arrangements he did not take part in the next two Impressionist exhibitions. Began to concentrate more and more on landscape painting; successful one-man exhibition at Charpentier's journal, "La vie moderne". 1881-1883 in Poissy, painted also on the coast of Normandy. 1882 took part for the last time in an Impressionist exhibition. 1883 finally settled in Giverny; also painted in Etretat. Large exhibition at the Durand-Ruel gallery. Travelled with Renoir to the Mediterranean; visited Cézanne. 1884 on the Riviera and in Etretat. 1885 exhibited for the first time with Durand-Ruel's competitor, G. Petit; met Maupassant in Etretat. 1886 exhibited with Les Vingt in Brussels and in New York through Durand-Ruel. Painted in Etretat, Holland and Belle-Ile (Brittany), where he met the critic Geffroy. 1888 exhibition through Theo van Gogh at the Boussod & Valadon gallery; painted in Antibes. 1889 at the century exhibition of French art at the Paris World Fair; successful joint exhibition with Rodin at Petit's; painted

in Fresselines (Creus). 1890 collected donations enabling Manet's "Olympia" to be purchased for the state; bought a house at Giverny. 1891-1912 repeatedly successful exhibitions of series paintings at the Durand-Ruel, Petit and Bernheim-Jeune galleries; became increasingly popular abroad. 1892 married Alice Hoschedé after her husband's death. 1893 began the creation of his famous garden with lily ponds at Giverny, which became the source of his most important motifs. 1895 travelled in Norway. 1897 exhibited at the Biennale in Venice. 1898 supported Zola in the Dreyfus affair. 1899-1901 made several visits to London, painted the Thames in mist. 1904 travelled in his own car to Madrid. 1908/09 two trips to Venice; his eyesight began to fail. 1911 depression after the death of his wife Alice. 1914 idea broached by his friend Clemenceau to donate a series of paintings of water lilies to the French state; worked on these until his death. 1920 rejected the offer of membership of the Institut de France.
WRITINGS, DOCUMENTS: Brive, P. (ed.): G. Clemenceau: Lettres à une amie 1923-1929. Paris 1970.– Graber, H.: Camille Pissarro, Alfred Sisley, C.M. nach eigenen und fremden Zeugnissen. Basle 1943.– Kendall, R. (ed.): C.M. par lui-même: tableaux, dessins, pastels, correspondance. Evreux 1989.– Proietti, M.L.: Lettere di C.M. Assisi and Rome 1974
CATALOGUES: Rossi Bortolotto, L.: L'opera completa di C.M. 1870-1889. Milan 1972.– Rossi Bortolotto, L. and J. Bailly-Herzberg: Tout l'œuvre peint de M. 1870-1889. Paris 1981.– Wildenstein, D.: C.M.: Biographie et catalogue raisonné. 5 vols. Lausanne and Paris 1974-1991
BIBLIOGRAPHY: Adhémar, H. et al. (eds.): Hommage à C.M. Grand Palais, Paris 1981 (EC).– Alexandre, A.: C.M. Paris 1921.– Clemenceau, G.: C.M. Les nymphéas . Paris 1928.– Bonnier, Louis: Avant-projet d'un pavillon d'exposition pour C.M. Paris 1920.– Cogniat, R.: M. and his World. London 1966.– Cogniat, R. et al. (eds.): M. et ses amis. Musée Marmottan, Paris 1971 (EC).– Elder, M.: A Giverny, chez C.M. Paris 1924.– Fels, F.: La vie de C.M. Paris 1929.– Fosca, F.: C.M. Paris 1927.– Geffroy, G.: C.M., sa vie, son temps, son œuvre. Paris 1922.– Gordon, R. and A. Forge: M. New York 1983.– Gordon, R. and A. Forge: M. Cologne 1985.– Grappe, G.: C.M. Paris 1909.– Gwynn, S.: C.M. and his Garden. London 1934.– Hamilton, G.H.: C.M.s' Paintings of the Rouen Cathedral. London 1966.– Hommage à C.M. Grand Palais, Paris 1980 (EC).– Hoschedé., J.: C.M., ce mal connu. 2 vols. Geneva 1960.– House, J.: M. Oxford 1977.– House, J.: M. Nature into Art. New Haven (CT) and London 1986.– Isaacson, J.: M.: Le déjeuner sur l'herbe. New York 1972.– Isaacson, J.: C.M., Observation and Reflection. Oxford and New York 1978.– Joyces, C. et al.: Monet at Giverny. London 1975, 1988.– Keller,

H.: Ein Garten wird Malerei. Cologne 1982.– Keller, H.: C.M. Munich 1985.– Kendall, R. (ed.): M. by Himself. London 1989.– Lévêque, J.J.: M. Paris 1980.– Levine, S.Z.: M. and his Critics. New York and London 1976.– Moffet, C.S.: M.'s Water Lilies. New York 1978.– Mount, M.: M. New York 1966.– Reutersward, O.: M. Stockholm 1948.– Rewald, J. and F. Weitzenhoffer (eds.): Aspects of M. A Symposium on the Artist's Life and Time. New York 1984.– Rouart, D.: C.M. Paris 1958.– Rouart, D. et al.: M. Nymphéas ou les miroirs du temps. Paris 1972 (EC).– Sagner-Düchting, K.: C.M.: A Feast for the Eyes. Cologne 1990.– Seiberling, G.: M.'s Series. New York and London 1981.– Seitz, W.C.: C.M. New York 1960, London 1984.– Seitz, W.C.: C.M. Seasons and Moments. New York 1970.– Spate, V.: The Colour of Time. The Life and Work of C.M. London and New York 1992.– Stucky, C.F. (ed.): M. A Retrospective. New York 1985.– Tucker, P.H.: M. at Argenteuil. New Haven (CT) and London 1982.– Tucker, P.H. (ed.): M. in the 90's. The Series Paintings. Museum of Fine Arts, Boston et al. New Haven (CT) and London 1989 (EC).– Werth, L.: C.M. Paris 1928.– Westheim, P.: C.M. Zurich 1953.– Wildenstein, D. et al. (eds.): M.'s Years at Giverny: Beyond Impressionism. Metropolitan Museum of Art, New York 1978 (EC)
ILLUSTRATIONS:
8 Monceau Park, 1878
40 The Walkers (Bazille and Camille), 1865
40 Le déjeuner sur l'herbe (left section), 1865
41 Le déjeuner sur l'herbe (study), 1865
41 Le déjeuner sur l'herbe (centre section), 1865
49 Women in the Garden, 1866
50 Quai du Louvre, 1867
51 The Garden of the Infanta, 1867
56 Angling in the Seine at Pontoise, 1882
57 The Beach at Sainte-Adresse, 1867
57 The Regatta at Sainte-Adresse, 1867
59 Terrace at Sainte-Adresse, 1867
53 La Grenouillère, 1869
76 The River, Bennecourt, 1868
91 Riverside Path at Argenteuil, 1872
91 The Harbour at Argenteuil, 1872
102 The Boulevard des Capucines, 1873
112 Red Poppies at Argenteuil, 1873
113 Impression: Sunrise, 1873
118 Monet's Garden at Argenteuil, 1873
119 The Luncheon, 1873
137 The Road Bridge at Argenteuil, 1874
137 The Bridge at Argenteuil, 1874
139 The Studio Boat, 1874
140 The Railway Bridge, Argenteuil 1873
141 The Bridge at Argenteuil, 1874
146 Lady with Parasol (facing right), 1886
146 Lady with Parasol (facing left), 1886

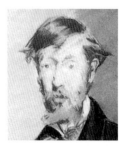

147 The Walk. Lady with Parasol, 1875
150 Madame Monet in Japanese Costume, 1875
170 Gare Saint-Lazare, Paris, 1877
170 Gare Saint-Lazare: the Train from Normandy, 1877
171 Le pont de l'Europe, Gare Saint-Lazare, 1877
176 Camille Monet on her Deathbed, 1879
177 Rue Saint-Denis, Festivities of 30 June, 1878, 1878
197 Still Life with Pears and Grapes, 1880
219 Monet's Garden at Vétheuil, 1881
230 Cliffs near Dieppe, 1882
231 Clifftop Walk at Pourville, 1882
232 Rough sea at Etretat, 1883
233 The Rocks near Pourville at Ebb Tide, 1882
233 The Beach at Etretat, 1883
245 The Rocks of Belle-Ile (Rough Sea), 1886
270 La Manneporte near Etretat, 1886
296 Young Girls in a Boat, 1887
296 Boating on the River Epte, 1890
297 The Boat, 1887
330 Poplars on the Banks of the Epte, 1891
331 Haystack in the Snow, Morning, 1890
331 Haystack in the Snow, Overcast Weather, 1891
342 Rouen Cathedral in the Morning, 1894
342 Rouen Cathedral in the Morning Sun, 1894
342 Rouen Cathedral in the Morning, 1894
342 Rouen Cathedral in Bright Sunlight, 1894
342 Rouen Cathedral in Overcast Weather, 1894
342 Rouen Cathedral. Frontal view, 1894
343 Rouen Cathedral in Bright Sunlight, 1894
362 Monet's Garden, the Irises, 1900
363 The Houses of Parliament, London, c. 1900/01
364 The Japanese Bridge, Harmony in Green, 1899
364 The Japanese Bridge, 1900
365 The Japanese Bridge, 1899
393 Waterlilies, 1914
394 Wistaria, 1919/20

MONFREID Georges-Daniel
1856 Paris – 1929 Saint-Clément
Self-taught artist and father of the novelist Henri de Monfreid. 1874 studied at the Académie Julian in Paris; friends with Schuffenecker. 1880 rejected by the Salon. Travelled by ship to Brittany, Spain and Algeria. Met Gauguin at the Académie Colarossi. 1889 contributed to the Impressionist and Synthetist exhibition at the Café Volpini, organised by Gauguin and Bernard. Exhibited at the Salon des Indépendants, the Galerie Le Barc de Boutteville, at Durand-Ruel's, and later also at the Autumn Salon. From 1892 he shared a studio with Gauguin, whom he also admired and supported financially, and kept up an extensive correspondence with him. His painting, however, was in-

spired more by Pissarro or Guillaumin. 1938 large individual exhibition at the Galerie Charpentier.

MONTICELLI Adolphe Joseph Thomas
1824 Marseilles – 1886 Marseilles
1840-1842 pupil with F. Ziem; 1842-1846 studied at the school of drawing in Marseilles with Aubert and Loubon. 1846 moved to Paris and studied in the studio of Paul Delaroche. Influenced by Delacroix and Corot; painted also at Barbizon. 1848 returned to Marseilles; until 1862 he lived alternately in Marseilles and Paris, until 1870 moved back to Paris. 1856 met Diaz and 1858 Gachet. Frequent customer in the Café Guerbois, where he met the Batignolles painters and Manet. From 1870 he lived once more in Marseilles, leaving the city only to paint in the outlying districts. A keen patron of the theatre and opera, he depicted the atmosphere of theatre and festival in his pictures; used a brush technique akin to that of van Gogh and Cézanne.
CATALOGUE: Stammegna, S.: M. 2 vols. Venice 1981-1986
BIBLIOGRAPHY: Agnel, A. d' and E. Isnard: M., sa vie, son œuvre. Paris 1926.– Alauzen, A.M. Le vrai M. Marseilles 1986.– Coquiot, G.: M. Paris 1925.– Guinaud, L.: La vie et les œuvres de M. Paris 1931

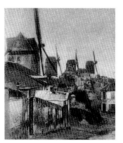

MONTMARTRE
Hill in the north of Paris, originally with four windmills, from the middle of the 19th century a quiet suburb which became a centre for the art scene. From 1876 the hill was crowned with the church of Sacré Cœur. The café in a converted windmill, "Le Moulin de la Galette", the Café de la Nouvelle-Athènes, the Place Pigalle, the "Moulin Rouge" dance hall of 1889, and the Goupil art gallery (later Boussod & Valadon) became important localities in the history of Impressionism.

MOORE Georges
1852 Moorehall Ballyglass – 1933 London
Irish art critic and writer. Attempted first to train as an artist, taking drawing lessons in London. At the age of 21, he moved to Paris and studied with Cabanel at the Ecole des Beaux-

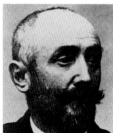

Arts and at the Académie Julian. Frequented the popular cafés and met numerous artists, especially Manet, becoming knowledgeable about their work and theories. 1879 Manet painted three portraits of him. Wrote for various journals. 1880 moved back to England and became active in the New English Art Club, a group of artists working from Impressionist principles. Moore was the only Anglo-Saxon critic to write an article on the last Impressionist exhibition of 1886.

MORET Henry
1856 Cherbourg – 1913 Paris
Studied at the Ecole des Beaux-Arts with Laurens and Gérôme. Exhibited for the first time in 1880. Soon turned away from the academic style of his teachers; influenced by Monet. 1888 met Gauguin at Pont-Aven and formed a friendship with him; also met Bernard. 1889 worked at Le Pouldu with Gauguin's adherents. 1888-1892 turned to Synthetism; established his own stylistic blend of Impressionism in the manner of Guillaumin and the style of the Pont-Aven school. From 1896 lived in the small port of Doelan in Brittany. His favourite subject was the Breton landscape. 1900 travelled in Holland.
BIBLIOGRAPHY: H.M. 1856-1913. Galerie Durand-Ruel. Paris 1959 (EC). – H.M. Aquarelles et Peintures. Musée de Pont-Aven, Pont-Aven 1988 (EC)
ILLUSTRATIONS:
382 The Village of Paulgoazec, 1906
382 Ouessant, Calm Seas, 1905

MORISOT Berthe
1841 Bourges – Paris 1895
Daughter of a top civil servant in the

Departement of Cher and a great-niece of the rococo painter Fragonard. 1857 took lessons and learned to draw. 1859 met Fantin-Latour in the Louvre. 1860-1862 a pupil of Corot with her sister Edma (later Mme Pontillon). Corot advised her to go to Auvers-sur-Oise and learn to paint plein-air. Met Daubigny there. 1864 exhibited her first landscapes in the Salon, travelled in Brittany. 1868 became friends with Manet, who gave her advice and painted her portrait ("Repose", "The Balcony", pp. 48, 63). 1872 travelled in Spain. 1874-1886 exhibited at all the Impressionist exhibitions apart from the 4th due to illness. 1874 married Manet's brother, Eugène. 1875 contributed pictures to the auction at the Hôtel Drouot. Travelled in England. 1881-1883 had a house built in Paris which became a weekly meeting place every Thursday for painters and writers such as Degas, Caillebotte, Monet, Pissarro and Whistler; Puvis de Chavannes, Duret, Renoir and Mallarmé also visited her; the latter became her closest friend and greatest admirer. 1882 exhibited at the Galerie Petit and in 1887 with Les Vingt in Brussels. 1892 widowed, bought a château in Mesnil. First single exhibition at Boussod & Valadon's. 1894 first sale of a painting to the French state. 1895 large memorial exhibition at Durand-Ruel's with 300 pictures; the catalogue introduction was written by Mallarmé. Her daughter married a son of the art collector and painter Henri Rouart; her niece Nini Gobillard married Valéry. With her fresh, bright impressions of happy domestic life, she made an important contribution to Impressionism.

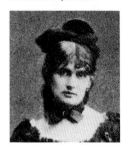

WRITINGS, DOCUMENTS: Rouart, D. (ed.): B.M.'s Correspondence with Family and Friends. London 1957 (New edition: The Correspondence of B.M. Newly introduced and edited by K. Adler and T. Garb. London 1986)
CATALOGUE: Bataille, M.L. and G. Wildenstein: B.M. Catalogue des peintures, pastels et aquarelles. Paris 1961.– Clairet, Montalan and Rouart: B.M. Catalogue raisonné (in preparation)
BIBLIOGRAPHY: Adler, K. and T. Garb: B.M. Oxford 1987.– Angoulvent, B.M. Paris 1933.– B.M. Impressionist. National Gallery of Art, Washington; The Kimbell Art Museum, Fort Worth; Mount Holyoke

College Art Museum, South Hadley (MA). New York 1987 (EC).– Edelstein, T.J. (ed.): Perspective on M. New York 1990.– Fourreau, A.: B.M. Paris 1925.– Higonnet, A.: B.M. Une biographie. Paris 1989.– Huisman, P.: B.M. Lausanne 1962.– Moskowitz, I. and E. Mongan: B.M. Zeichnungen, Pastelle, Aquarelle, Gemälde. Hamburg 1961.– Rey, J.D.: B.M. New York 1982.– Rouart, L.: B.M. Paris 1949.– Stucky, C.F. and W. Scott: B.M. Impressionistin. Stuttgart 1988.

ILLUSTRATIONS:
88 Portrait of Madame Pontillon, 1871
88 The Mother and Sister of the Artist (Reading), c. 1869/70
89 On the Balcony, c. 1871/72
89 The Cradle, 1873
95 View of Paris from the Trocadéro, 1872
108 Hide and Seek, 1873
108 In the Grass, 1874
123 Chasing Butterflies, 1874
151 At the Ball, 1875
160 Young Woman Powdering Herself, 1877
192 Summer Day (Bois de Boulogne), 1879

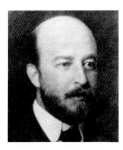

MORRICE James Wilson
1865 Montreal – 1924 Tunis
Studied law and trained as a barrister. Moved to Paris and studied at the Académie Julian. Painted with his American and British colleagues Glackens, Henri, Lawson and O'Conor in Pont-Aven and Grèz-sur-Loing. Travelled in America, Russia, Venice, Tangiers and Gibraltar. His landscapes were influenced by the restrained use of colour found in Whistler and Boudin. 1912/13 met Matisse, Marquet and Camoin in Tangiers; from then on his palette brightened and became more powerful. Financially independent, he painted mainly for his own pleasure; one of the best of the Canadian Impressionists.
BIBLIOGRAPHY: Cloutier, N. et al. (eds.): J.W.M. The Montreal Museum of Fine Arts, Montreal 1985 (EC)
ILLUSTRATION:
627 Quai des Grands-Augustins, Paris, c. 1903/04

MOULIN DE LA GALETTE, Le
Large barn in Montmartre on the Rue Lepic, surrounded by a large wooden fence. In the grounds itself stood two windmills, one of which served as a

café while the other was still used at the time to grind lily bulbs for a perfume factory. The owners of the mill, the Debrays, had extended the café to provide a dance floor and stage for the orchestra. They also baked the famous cakes which gave the mill its name (galette = a flat, round cake).

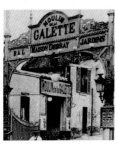

Every Sunday from 3 p.m. till midnight, Montmartre families, white-collar workers, students and artists gathered for the dance here or in the adjacent garden, lit in the evenings with Chinese lanterns. Entrance cost 25 centimes and gentlemen had to pay an extra 20 centimes for every dance. Between 1875 and 1883 Renoir looked for (and found) most of his models here (p. 153).

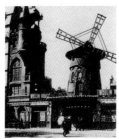

MOULIN ROUGE, Le
A dance hall, opened in October 1889 by Charles Zidler on the Boulevard de Clichy. A meeting place for Paris society high and low at the turn of the century. The red windmill on the entrance was just a façade, behind which were various sections, including a wooden elephant that transformed into a stage. The bar was decorated with mirrors, galleries and gas lamps, and brightly lit. Entrance cost 3.50 francs; the programme included various singers and artistes, plus the high point: the dancing of the quadrille and the cancan. Toulouse-Lautrec, who had reserved a table for himself from the opening night, became the artistic chronicler of the Moulin Rouge. His posters and paintings were occasionally exhibited in the foyer (see pp. 324-327).

MULOT-DURIVAGE Emilien
Born in 1838 in Granville. Painted mainly landscapes of Normandy. Member of the Société des peintres, graveurs, sculpteurs. 1874 exhibited two works at the 1st Impressionist exhibition in Nadar's rooms.

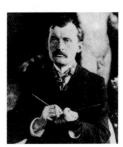

MUNCH Edvard
1863 Loten – 1944 Ekely
Came from a family of famous artists and scientists. Tragic family circumstances affected his work. 1868 death of his mother; 1877 death of his favourite sister Sophie; his father became depressive. 1880 enrolled at the technical college. 1881 studied at the Royal School of Drawing in Oslo with the sculptor Julius Middelthun. Met Krohg and under his tutelage painted light-filled, naturalistic landscapes and figural studies. 1883 attended the plein-air school of Thaulow. 1885 first visit to Paris. Development of his Persian style, in which colour and form became the expression of the mood felt. 1889 first one-man exhibition; received a state scholarship. 1889-1892 stayed in Paris. Attended Bonnat's courses on drawing; studied the Old Masters and Impressionism. The result was a series of landscapes in Pointillist style. Debate with the Pont-Aven school and the "Nabis". 1892 trip to Berlin and exhibition at the "Verein der bildenden Künstler", which caused a scandal and had to be closed; this was followed by the founding of the Berlin Secession. From 1894 he published his graphic prints; around 1900 numerous famous illustrations. In the 1890s he lived mostly abroad in France, Italy and Germany. In Berlin he came into contact with Strindberg, Meier-Graefe, Przybyszewski and others. 1896-1898 contributed to exhibitions at the Salon des Indépendants in Paris. 1902 at the Berlin Secession he exhibited the picture series "Lebensfries" ("Frieze of Life"), which he had begun in 1893. 1904 became a member of the Secession. 1905 large one-man exhibition in Prague. 1908 finally returned to Norway, after a nervous breakdown. Lived in the small fishing town of Kragerø. 1916 completed three mural decorations for the hall of Oslo University. From 1916 lived near Oslo in Ekely. 1921/22 decoration for the dining hall of the Oslo choco-

late factory Freia. In the 1930s suffered from an eye affliction.
CATALOGUES: Schiefler, G.: Verzeichnis des graphischen Werks E.M.s bis 1906. Berlin 1907.– Schiefler, G.: E.M. Das graphische Werk 1906-1926. Berlin 1928
BIBLIOGRAPHY: Benesch, O.: E.M. London 1960.– Bock, H. and Busch, G.: E.M. Probleme, Forschungen, Thesen. Munich 1973.– Boulton Smith, J.: E.M. 1863-1944. Berlin 1962.– Carlsson, A.: E.M. Leben und Werk. Stuttgart and Zurich 1984.– Deknatel, F.: E.M. New York 1950.– Eggum, A.: E.M. Paintings, Sketches and Studies. London 1984.– Eggum, A.: Munch and Photography. London 1989.– Gauguin, P.: E.M. Oslo 1946.– Gerlach, H.E. E.M. Sein Leben und sein Werk. Hamburg 1955.– Gierløff, C.: E.M. selv. Oslo 1953.– Glaser, C.: E.M. Berlin 1917.– Heller, R.: M. His Life and Work. London 1984.– Hodin, J.P.: E.M. Stockholm 1948; Berlin and Mainz 1963.– Hodin, J.P.: E.M. London 1972.– Langaard, J.H.: E.M. Modningsår Oslo 1960.– Langaard, J.H. and R. Revold: E.M. som tegner. Oslo 1958.– Langaard, J.H. and R. Revold: E.M. fra år til år. Oslo 1961.– Langaard, J.H. and R. Revold: E.M. Mesterverker i Munchmuseet. Oslo 1963.– Messer, T.: E.M. Cologne 1989.– Moen, A.: E.M. 3 vols. Oslo 1956-1958.– E.M. Haus der Kunst, Munich 1973 (EC).– E.M. 1863-1944. Museum Folkwang, Essen et al. Berne 1987.– Sarvig, O.: E.M. Grafik. Copenhagen 1948.– Stang, R.: E.M. Oslo 1972.– Stenersen, R.: E.M. Når bild av ett geni. Stockholm 1944; Oslo 1945; Zurich 1949.– Thiis, J.: E.M. og hans samtid. Oslo 1933.– Væring, R. and J.H. Langaard: E.M. selvportretter. Oslo 1947.– Willoch, S.: E.M. raderinger. Oslo 1950
ILLUSTRATIONS:
491 Rue Lafayette, 1891
492 Spring on Karl Johan, 1891

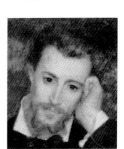

MURER Eugène
1845 Moulins – 1906 Auvers-sur-Oise
Real name: Hyacinthe Eugène Meunier. A writer, art collector and patron, and one of the most flamboyant of the characters in Impressionist circles. During a short period at the college in Moulins, he met Guillaumin and Outin. Moved to Paris and did an apprenticeship with

Eugène Gru, a confectioner and Socialist writer who frequented Bohemian and journalist circles and encouraged him to write. In **1870** he opened his own confectionery. Enthusiastic about Impressionism, he supported the painters in any way he could. His weekly meetings on Wednesdays at his flat on the Boulevard Voltaire became famous and most of the Impressionists and collectors went there. Murer was himself a painter and owned an important collection; Renoir and Pissarro both painted his portrait. **1878** co-organiser of the World Fair in Paris. From **1881** he lived in Auvers.

MUYBRIDGE, Eadweard
1830 Kingston (near London) – 1904 Kingston
Real name: Edward James Muggeridge. American photographer who, by placing a series of cameras side by side, was the first to photograph the actual positions of an animal in motion. On the basis of Muybridge's photographs of galloping horses, it was possible for Degas to make the discovery that the usual artistic formula for a "flying gallop" in which all four legs of the animal were depicted in the air did not correspond to reality (see p. 71).

NABIS
Post-Impressionist group of artists in France; the name is Hebrew for "prophets". Founded by pupils at the Académie Julian and the Ecole des Beaux Arts in **1888** under the influence of Gauguin's "Synthetist" style and Sérusier's "Talisman" (p. 320). From **1888** to **1893** various artists joined the group, including foreigners: Denis, Bonnard, Vuillard, Vallotton, Rippl-Rónai, Maillol and others. Taking the bright colours and asymmetry of the Impressionists, the Nabis favoured a more Symbolist and decorative view of art. They were influenced by Cézanne and Puvis de Chavannes, as well as by Japanese graphic art. The group first met at the studio of P. Ransons, which became known as the "Temple". From **1891** they organised exhibitions at Le Barc de Boutteville, contributed to the "Salon des Indépendants", and did work for the modern theatre. They also had connections with the journal "La Revue Blanche". In **1899** they gave a group exhibition at the Durand-Ruel gallery and in **1900** at Bernheim-Jeune's. Through Denis, Sérusier and Verkade, the group became a source of religious art in the 20th century.

NADAR
1820 Paris – 1910 Paris
Real name: Félix Tournachon. Began his career as a journalist and writer for various journals. From **1846** he became successful for his caricatures. The brunt of his witty but trenchant humour was often borne by members of the Academy. **1853/54** turned to photography; founded a photographic studio and became the first to take aerial photographs of Paris from

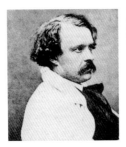

a hot-air balloon. Did the portraits of many famous personalities. Tried to raise photography to the level of a recognized art form. Supported the Impressionists and helped with the organisation of the 1st Impressionist exhibition, which took place at his studio in the Boulevard des Capucines.

NATANSON Thadée
1868 Warsaw – 1951 Paris
Important collector of Impressionist paintings; journalist and businessman. Friend of the writers Mallarmé and Anatole France and the journalists of "La Revue Blanche". In Giverny he met Monet, Pissarro and Renoir, and was acquainted with Gauguin, Redon, Rodin and Signac. He often had his portrait painted. After his death his wife donated part of his collection to the Musée National d'Art Moderne.

NEO-IMPRESSIONISM
Artistic movement started by Seurat. The application of a specific technique (Divisionism = separation of colours, or Pointillism = applying colour in small points or dashes). The result of older and contemporary physical and physiological research by Chevreul, Helmholtz, Rood and Sutter into the nature of coloured light and the processes of perception. Following this research, Seurat attempted from **1882** to find a method of rendering light in a picture as closely as possible to real perception. Thus, instead of mixing coloured paints, he juxtaposed small points or dashes of unmixed, primary colours, which at the right distance produced the desired effect on the eye of the observer. It was a kind of optical blending, using simultaneous contrasts and the heightening effect of complementary colours. This "chromoluminarism" (as Seurat called it) was seen for the first time in the picture "Bathers at Asnières" at the Salon des Indépendants in **1884**. The technique was taken over by Signac, C. Pissarro and L. Pissarro, and in **1886** it was given the name Neo-Impressionism or "scientific Impressionism" by Fénéon. This Pointillist technique was given further impetus at the 8th Impressionist exhibition and the Salon des Indépendants of **1886**, and in **1887** with Les Vingt in Brussels. It found a fluent proponent in Signac ("From Delacroix to Neo-Impressionism",

1899). The method gained temporary and more permanent adherents abroad and in **1904-1906** it became an important source for Fauvism (Matisse) and Expressionism, as well as for the later movements of Cubism and Futurism.

NIEUWERKERKE Alfred-Emilien de
1811 Paris – 1892 Gattaiola
Real name: Alfred Emilien O'Hara, Count of Nieuwerkerke. French politician of cultural affairs, of Dutch origin, originally a sculptor. **1849-1870** Director-General of the national museums. **1853** member of the Institut de France. **1863-1870** appointed by his friend Napoleon III as Superintendent of Fine Arts responsible for state policy on the arts. Chairman of the Salon jury. An opponent of realism, which he regarded as art for democrats. Despised the new Impressionism. In **1870** he was deposed; thereafter he lived in Italy.

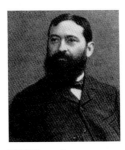

NITTIS Giuseppe De
1846 Barletta – 1884 St.-Germain-en-Laye
1861-1863 studied at the college of art in Naples, afterwards painting plein-air in Portici. **1866** contacts with the Macchiaioli in Florence. **1867-1870** living in Paris. **1872** finally settled there; travelled frequently to Italy and London. Pupil of Gérôme; sold work through the art dealer Goupil. **1869** exhibited at the Salon. Friendship with Manet and Degas, later with Toulouse-Lautrec. **1874** took part in the 1st Impressionist exhibition. **1878** awarded the Légion of Honour. **1879** turned to pastels. Very popular one-man exhibition at Charpentier's, "La Vie moderne". **1882** co-founder of Petit's "Expositions internationales". Nittis's bright, relaxed landscapes and city scenes, often in small format, and his anecdotal genre pictures of modern life are a successful compromise between Salon and Impressionism.
WRITINGS, DOCUMENTS: Cecioni, A. and E. Somaré (eds.): De N. Opere e scritti. Milan 1932.– De Nittis, G.: Notes et souvenirs. Paris 1895
CATALOGUE: Piceni, E.: De N. L'uomo e l'opera. Busto Arsizio 1979-1982
BIBLIOGRAPHY: Cassandro, M.: De N. Bari 1971.– Causa, R.: De N. Bari 1975.– De N.: dipinti 1864-1884. Palazzo della permanente,

Milan 1990 (EC).– Mantz, P.: Joseph De N. Paris 1886.– Monti, R. (ed.): G. De N. Dipinti 1864-1884. Palazzo della Permanente, Milan; Pinacoteca Provinciale, Bari. Florence 1990 (EC).– Mostra di G. De N. Società Salvator Rosa, Naples 1963 (EC).– Pica, V.: G. De N. Milan 1914.– Piceni, E.: G. De N. Milan 1955.– Piceni, E. and M. Monteverdi: I De N. di Barletta. Barletta 1971.– Piceni, E.: De N. L'uomo e l'opera. Busto Arsizio 1979.– Pittaluga, M. and E. Piceni: De N. Milan 1963
ILLUSTRATIONS:
539 The Victoria Embankment, London, 1875
540 Breakfast in the Garden, c. 1884

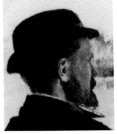

NORDSTRÖM Karl Frederik
1855 Hoga – 1923 Drottningholm (Stockholm)
1875-1878 studied at the Stockholm Royal Academy and from **1876** with E. Perséus. In **1881** moved to Paris and lived **1882-1886** mainly in Grèz-sur-Loing, a centre of Impressionist plein-air painting south-east of Paris, where he met Larsson and Krohg. At first influenced by the Barbizon school and Bastien-Lepage, he then turned to Impressionism. No success at the Salon. **1886** returned to Norway and painted Swedish (winter) landscapes. Member of the group "Kunstnärsförbundet", which opposed the Academy. **1892** moved to Varberg, where **1893-1895** he founded with Bergh and Kreuger the Varberg school, an association of Swedish Symbolists. Painted landscapes in clearly defined, separate areas of colour and dark, melancholy tones. **1920-21** travelled in France. From **1910** his palette brightened and he turned increasingly to drawing.
BIBLIOGRAPHY: Hedberg, T.: K.N. En studie. Stockholm 1905.– Högdahl, T.: Några kolteckningar av K.N. Stockholm 1923.– Svedfelt, T.: K.N.s konst. Stockholm 1939
ILLUSTRATION:
473 A Clearing in the Woods at Grèz, 1882

NOUVELLE-ATHENES → Café de la Nouvelle-Athènes

OTTIN Auguste Louis Marie
1811 Paris – 1890 Paris
Pupil of David d'Angers. **1836** won the Rome prize. **1841** exhibited for

the first time in the Salon. **1842,
1846** and **1867** won medals there.
1867 big success at the World Fair;
made Chevalier de la Légion d'Honneur. Commissioned by the state to
do the figures for the Medici fountain
in the Parc du Luxembourg. **1874**
only artist to exhibit ten sculptures at
the 1st Impressionist exhibition.
Nevertheless, there are no links between his work and that of the Impressionists.

OTTIN Léon-Auguste
**Born in Paris in 1836; date of death
unkown**
Son of the sculptor Auguste Ottin.
Pupil of Delaroche and Lecoq de Boisbaudran, at whose studio he met Fantin-Latour. **1861-1882** exhibited regularly at the Salon. **1863** and **1873** contributed to the Salon des Refusés.
With Cals, Daubigny, Lépine, Monet,
Pissarro and Sisley he signed a letter
to the Ministry of Arts demanding
that the members of the jury be selected by the artists themselves. Contributed 7 works to the 1st Impressionist
exhibition in **1874** and 22 to the 2nd
exhibition in **1876**.

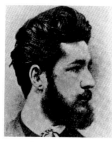

PAAL Lázló
1846 Zám – 1879 Charenton
1864-1870 studied at the Academy in
Vienna. **1870/71** stayed in Holland,
London and Düsseldorf. **1872-1879**
in Paris and Barbizon, friendship with
Munkácsy; nervous illness. A Páal Society existed **1923-1944** in honour of
his contribution to the development
of Hungarian painting.
BIBLIOGRAPHY: L. Bényi: L.P. 1846-
1879. Budapest 1979
ILLUSTRATION:
521 Path in the Woods at Fontainebleau, 1876

PANKIEWICZ Józef
1866 Lublin – 1940 Marseilles
1884 studied with W. Gerson and A.
Kaminski at the Warsaw school of
drawing; friendship with Podkowinski and Stanislawski. **1885/86** studied
at the Academy in St. Petersburg.
1886-1889 painted with Podkowinski
in Kazimierz and Warsaw. **1889**
travelled to Paris with Podkowinski;
met Slewinski and Stanislawski. **1890**
in Kazimierz, exhibited in Warsaw,
after which he mainly painted Impressionist landscapes in Warsaw.
1894 tour of Italy. **1897-1910** mem-

ber of the group "Art" (Sztuka). **1898**
travelled in western Europe. **1906-
1914** and **1919-1923** Professor at the
Academy of Arts in Cracow, in the va-
cations in France. **1908** met Bonnard.
1911/12 in Giverny, met Monet.
1914-1918 in Spain, influenced by
the Cubism of Picasso and Braque.
1925-1939 Director of the Paris
branch of the Cracow Academy. **1927**
Chevalier of the Legion of Honour.
1939 moved to Ciotat on the outbreak of war.

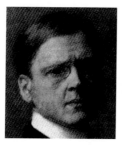

BIBLIOGRAPHY: Cybis, J.: J.P. Warsaw
1949.– Czapski, J.: J.P. Warsaw
1936.– Dmochowska, J.: W kregu P.
Cracow 1963.– Ligocki, A.: J.P. Warsaw 1973.– Pawla, J.: J.P. Warsaw
1979
ILLUSTRATION:
514 The Old City Market, Warsaw,
at Night, 1892

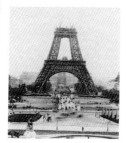

PARIS
The dominant centre of France in
politics, economics and culture; for
developments in these areas it gained
worldwide significance ("capital of
the 19th century"). During the Second Empire of Napoleon III, it was
transformed by Baron Haussmann,
Prefect of the Seine department, into
an exemplary modern city (boulevards, covered markets, railway stations); the re-structuring of the city
continued after the destructive period
of the Prussian siege and the Commune in the Third Republic. Paris
was the centre for the most important
institutions in French artistic life (Institut de France, Ecole des Beaux-
Arts, Louvre, regular art Salons). The
art trade flourished here (by 1861

there were 104 galleries) as did the
publishing of books and journals of
art. There was a rich entertainment
scene (theatre, variety shows, gastron-
omy). The World Fair was put on five
times in Paris between 1855 and
1900, which allowed the free exchange of artistic views and ideas.
The transformed city structure
brought new social, cultural and visual experiences; the view of the city,
the way of life and the change in communications all contributed to the
motifs and pictorial concepts of the
Impressionists.

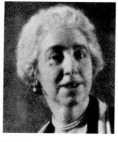

PAULI Hanna
1864 Stockholm – 1940 Stockholm
Began her artistic career at the the Au-
gust-Malström school of painting for
children in Stockholm. **1881-1885** studied at the Academy of Arts in Stockholm. **1885-1887** attended courses
with Dagnan-Bouveret, Courtois and
Collins at the Académie Colarossi in
Paris. Influenced by Manet and Bastien-Lepage; her free brushwork owes
much to her study of French plein-air
technique. In **1887** she married the
painter Georg Pauli; settled in Stockholm. Became famous as a portrait
painter; from the 1890s she also
painted genre pictures and landscapes.
ILLUSTRATION:
482 Breakfast, 1887

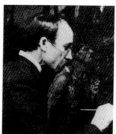

PAULSEN Julius
1860 Odense – 1940 Copenhagen
1879-1882 studied at the Academy in
Copenhagen. Protested against the
old-fashioned, traditional views of art
still held there. Followed Tuxen and
Krøyer. **1885** travelled via Holland

and Belgium to Paris with Johansen
and Krøyer; all three exhibited at the
Salon. Painted portraits and landscapes.
ILLUSTRATIONS:
481 St. John's on Tisvilde Beach,
1886
495 Under the Pont des Arts in Paris,
1910

PELLERIN Auguste
1852–1929
A rich industrialist and margarine
manufacturer, who became known
for his interest in contemporary art
and for his large collection of paintings, especially Cézannes, including
"Still Life with Onions" (p. 348). In
1910 he sold his collection for the record sum of a million francs to the art
dealers Durand-Ruel, Bernheim-Jeune
and Paul Cassirer.

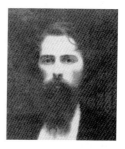

PELLIZZA DA VOLPEDO Giuseppe
1868 Volpedo – 1907 Volpedo
1883 began his studies at the Brera
Academy in Milan, then at the Academies in Florence and Rome, and in
1888 at the Carrara Academy in Bergamo. Moved away from the academic style and began his inquiries into
the phenomena of light, leading him
to a style akin to that of the Impressionists. Friends with Segantini, Previati, Nomellini, Morbelli and Grubicy,
who won him over to Divisionism.
For his first Divisionist picture he received a gold medal at Genoa in
1892. **1900** exhibited at the World
Fair in Paris. Lived alternately in
Rome, Paris and Switzerland. **1907**
committed suicide.
CATALOGUE: Scotti, A.: P.d.V. Milan
1986
BIBLIOGRAPHY: P. per il "Quarto
Stato". Città di Torino. Turin 1977
(EC).– P. da V. Palazzo Cuttica, Ales-
sandria. Milan 1980 (EC)
ILLUSTRATION:
551 Washing in the Sun, 1905

PERRY Lilla Cabot
**1848 Boston – 1933 Hancock (New
Hampshire)**
Trained with the plein-air painters
Vonnoh and Bunker. Studied in
France in the studio of Colarossi and
with Stevens. **1889** first stay in
Giverny with Monet. Bought a
country house near to Monet's which
became her summer residence for the
next ten years. Worked under the tu-

telage of Monet. **1892** received a silver medal at an exhibition in Boston. **1893** exhibited with other American Impressionists at the World Columbian Exposition in Chicago. Lived for a long period in Paris, where she met Pissarro and others. Published writings on Greek, English and German literature and in **1927** a book on Monet, "Reminiscences of Claude Monet from 1889 to 1909".

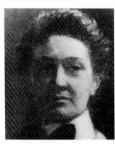

WRITINGS, DOCUMENTS: Perry, L.C.: Reminiscences of Claude Monet from 1889 to 1909. In: "American Magazine of Art" 18 1927.– Perry, L.C.: Days to Remember. Santa Fe 1983
BIBLIOGRAPHY: Feld, S. (ed.): L.C.P. A Retrospective Exhibition. Hirschl and Adler Galleries, New York 1969 (EC).– L.C.P. An American Impressionist. National Museum of Women in the Arts, Washington 1990 (EC)
ILLUSTRATION:
622 Monet's Garden at Giverny, c. 1897

PETIT Georges
1835–1900
Owner of a Café in the Rue de Sèze in Paris, founded by his father Francis Petit; Delacroix, Corot and the painters of the Barbizon school exhibited here. From 1880 he sold Impressionist works and became with Durand-Ruel one of the most important of the gallery owners. Organised numerous exhibitions for individuals and groups. The gallery was closed in 1933.

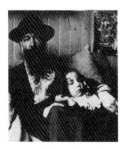

PETITJEAN Hippolyte
1854 Mâcon – 1929 Paris
Began his career as a painter-decorator.

1867-1872 attended the school of drawing in Mâcon. **1872** received a scholarship to attend the Ecole des Beaux-Arts in Paris. Studied with Cabanel. 1880-1891 exhibited regularly at the Salon. **1884** met Seurat, whose style influenced him considerably. From **1886** he painted in a Pointillist style. Up to 1898 he worked for a living as a decorator. **1898** professor of drawing at the school in the Rue de Patay and for evening courses in the Rue des Moulins-aux-près. 1892-1894 took part in several exhibitions by the Impressionists and Symbolists. 1894-1901 exhibited again in the Salon and also abroad in Brussels, Berlin and Weimar. 1903-1904 built a house in the Parc Montsouris, on the façade of which he inscribed the names of his idols, Ingres, Puvis de Chavannes and Millet. Sold very few pictures and got into financial difficulties. In **1819** he changed his style and returned to an old-fashioned type of Impressionism.
CATALOGUE: Bazalgette, L.: H.P. Catalogue raisonné (in preparation)
BIBLIOGRAPHY: Centenaire d'H.P. (1854-1954). Galerie de l'Institut, Paris 1955 (EC).– H.P. Watercolours. David B. Findley Galleries, New York (EC)
ILLUSTRATION:
375 Notre-Dame, c. 1895

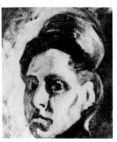

PETROVIC Nadež da
1873 Čačak – 1915 Valevo
1896-1898 attended K. Kutlik's school of drawing and painting in Belgrade. 1898-1900 studied at Ažbè's private school in Munich. 1900-1903 attended J. Exter's summer courses in and near Munich. Her paintings included landscapes in strong colours. **1900** first individual exhibition in Belgrade. 1900-1910 taught drawing in the women's school of arts in Belgrade. Painted in an Impressionist style and wrote articles of art criticism. **1904** helped with the organisation of the 1st South Slavic art exhibition in Belgrade. **1905** founded an artists' colony in Siceva. **1906** contributed works to the 1st exhibition of the Lada group. Later became a member of the Medulic group. 1910-1912 in Paris, painted views of the city; became influenced by the Fauves; exhibited at the autumn Salon. 1912/13 active in the Balkan wars. **1914** volunteer nurse in the First World War; died of typhoid.

1973 first retrospective in Belgrade.
BIBLIOGRAPHY: Ambrozić, K.: N.P. 1873-1915. Belgrade 1973.– Ambrozić, K. (ed.): N.P. 1873-1915.
Neue Pinakothek, Munich 1985 (EC)
ILLUSTRATION:
530 Lady with a White Parasol, c. 1910

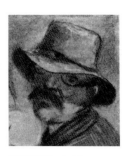

PHILIPSEN Theodor Esbern
1840 Copenhagen – 1920 Copenhagen
1862-1869 studied at the Academy in Copenhagen. 1875/76 worked in the studio of Bonnat in Paris. Impressed by Manet. 1878-1879 visited Italy, 1882-1884 Spain and Tunis. 1884/85 in Copenhagen: met Gauguin, who introduced him to Pissarro's techniques. **1889** received a bronze medal at the World Fair in Paris and took part in an exhibition of French and German Impressionists in Copenhagen. His light-filled, hazy landscapes introduced Denmark to Impressionism.
BIBLIOGRAPHY: Leth, H.: T.P. Copenhagen 1942.– Madsen, K.: Maleren T.P. Copenhagen 1912.– Madsen, K.: T.P. Copenhagen 1944
ILLUSTRATIONS:
472 Street in Tunis, 1882
486 A Lane at Kastrup, 1891

PHOTOGRAPHY
The invention was first published in 1839 and became an aid, a rival and a new branch of the arts. 1859 photographs first allowed in the Salon. Related to the Realist, Naturalist and Impressionist goal of faithfully reproducing the visible world. The Impressionists held their 1st exhibition in the recently vacated studio rooms of the Paris photographer F. Tournachon, known as Nadar, whom they had met in the Café Guerbois. Most of the Impressionist artists, for instance Courbet and Corot, and many of the Post-Impressionists used photographs of their own or others instead of sketches as the bases of their landscapes, city views, portraits, nudes and still lifes. The Impressionists were also influenced by certain peculiarities of the photograph, such as its representation of space, its partial lack of focus, and its occasional cutting-off of figures by the edge of the picture. Degas' depiction of movement was considerably influenced in the 1870s by the techno-

logy of the camera as developed by the British photographer E. Muybridge (q.v.) – the ability of the camera to record the individual stills in the motion of a galloping horse or a dancer.

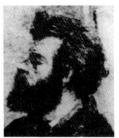

PIETTE Ludovic
1826 Niort – 1877 Paris
Pupil of Pils and Couture; met Manet in Couture's studio. Studied at the Académie Suisse, where he formed a friendship with Pissarro. Often painted with Pissarro, whose open-air technique considerably influenced him. **1864** first visit to Montfoucault in Brittany; worked frequently in Pontoise and Louveciennes. 1875 exhibited in the Salon. 1877 invited by Pissarro to exhibit at the 3rd Impressionist exhibition. After his death in 1877 his pictures were shown again at the 4th exhibition in 1879.
WRITINGS, DOCUMENTS: Piette, L.: Mon cher Pissarro. Lettres de L.P. à Camille Pissarro. Paris 1985
BIBLIOGRAPHY: C. Pissarro, C.-F. Daubigny, L.P. Musée Pissarro. Pontoise 1978 (EC).
ILLUSTRATION:
154 The Market outside Pontoise Town Hall, 1876

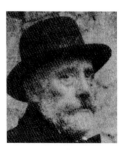

PINAZO CAMARLENCH Ignacio
1849 Valencia – 1916 Godella (Valencia)
1864 studied at the Academy of Arts in Valencia; earned a living from his hat-shop. 1873 visited Italy. 1876-1881 lived in Rome on a scholarship. 1884-1886 taught at the Escuela de Valencia. 1881-1912 awarded numerous medals. As well as land-

scapes he also painted history and genre pictures, and portraits. Did the decoration of various aristocrats' houses. His relaxed Impressionist style also uses dark browns and earth colours.
BIBLIOGRAPHY: González Martí, M.: I.P., su vida y su obra. Valencia 1920.
ILLUSTRATION:
554 The Pond

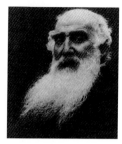

PISSARRO Camille
1830 Charlotte-Amalie (Danish Antillas) – 1903 Paris
1842-1847 in Passy near Paris, began to draw. 1847-1852 on Saint-Thomas, went into business like his French-Jewish father; his mother was Creole. 1852-1854 with the Danish painter F. Melbye in Caracas. 1855 lived as a painter in Paris and its environs. Impressed by Corot. 1859 exhibited for the first time at the Salon. 1859-1861 attended the Académie Suisse; formed friendships with Monet, Guillaumin and Cézanne. Liaison with Julie Vellay; they had eight children. 1861 and 1863 rejected by the Salon. 1863 exhibited at the "Salon des Refusés". 1864-1868 exhibited at the Salon; financial difficulties. 1866-1868 in Pontoise, painted landscapes in which he changed from Barbizon Realism to Impressionism; frequent customer in the Café Guerbois. 1869/70 in Louveciennes, exhibited at the Salon. During the Franco-Prussian War 1870/71 in London, where he married Julie. Recommended by Daubigny to the art dealer Durand-Ruel. Many of his paintings were destroyed by German troops during the occupation of Louveciennes. 1872-1878 in Pontoise, working with Cézanne; full development of his independent style of Impressionism. 1874-1886 the only artist to exhibit at all eight Impressionist exhibitions. 1876-1879 supported by the confectioner Murer. 1879 first work with Gauguin. 1881 renewed interest in depicting peasant women. 1882-1884 lived in Osny. 1883 first of several exhibitions at Durand-Ruel's; began to be interested in Socialism. His son Lucien, a graphic artist and painter, moved to London; beginning of an extensive correspondence. 1884 settled in Eragny on the Epte. 1885 became an Anarchist. 1886-1890 painted for a time in a Pointillist style. 1886 exhibition by

Durand-Ruel in New York. 1888 began to suffer from eye problems. 1889 contributed pictures to the century exhibition of the World Fair in Paris and with Les Vingt in Brussels. 1890 in London – further visits followed. 1894 fled to Belgium from the French persecution of Anarchists. 1896 and 1898 painted views of the town and harbour of Rouen, remaining faithful to the early Impressionist style. 1897-1903 mainly painted views of Paris, also Dieppe and Le Havre. 1897 through a donation, one of his paintings reached the National Gallery in Berlin. 1900 at the century exhibition of French art at the Paris World Fair.
WRITINGS, DOCUMENTS: Bailly-Herzberg, J. (ed.): Correspondance de C.P. 3 vols. Paris 1980-1988.– Bailly-Herzberg, J. (ed.): Mon cher Pissarro: Lettres de L.P. à Camille Pissarro. Paris 1985.– Graber, H.: C.P., Alfred Sisley, Claude Monet nach eigenen und fremden Zeugnissen. Basle 1943.– Pissarro, L.: Notes on the Eragny Press. London 1957.– Rewald, J. (ed.): C.P.: Letters to his Son Lucien. New York 1943 Santa Barbara and Salt Lake City 1981.– Rewald, J.: C.P. New York 1963
CATALOGUE: Pissarro, L.-R. and L. Venturi: C.P., son art, son œuvre. 2 vols. Paris 1939 (Reprint: San Francisco 1989)
BIBLIOGRAPHY: Adler, K.: C.P. A Biography. New York and London 1978.– Brettell, R., F. Cachin et al. (eds.): Pissarro 1830-1903. Hayward Gallery, London; Grand Palais, Paris; Museum of Fine Arts, Boston. Paris 1980 (EC).– Brettell, R.P.: P. and Pontoise: The Painter in a Landscape. New Haven (CT) and London 1990.– Falla, P.S.: P. Museum of Fine Arts, Boston 1980 (EC).– Günther, H.: C.P. Munich, Basle and Vienna 1954.– Jedlicka, G.: P. Bern 1950.– Kunstler, C.: C.P. Paris 1974.– Kunstler, C.: The Impressionists: C.P. London 1988.– Lachenaud, J.P. et al. (eds.): P. et Pontoise. Musée Pissarro, Pontoise 1980 (EC).– Lloyd, C. et al. (eds.): C.P. 1830-1903. The Arts Council of Great Britain et al., London 1981 (EC).– Lloyd, C.: C.P. Geneva and New York 1981.– Lloyd, C. et al. (eds.): Retrospective C.P. Isetan Museum of Fine Art (Tokyo) et al., Tokyo 1984 (EC).– Lloyd, C. (ed.): Studies on C.P. London and New York 1986.– Maillet, E. et al. (eds.): C.P., Charles-François Daubigny, Lucien Pissarro. Musée de Pontoise, Pontoise 1978 (EC).– Meier, G.: C.P. Leipzig 1975.– Natanson, T.: C.P. Lausanne 1950.– P.: Sa famille, ses amis. Musée de Pontoise, Pontoise 1976 (EC).– Recchilongo, B.: C.P. Grafiche anarchica. Rome 1981.– Reid, M.: P. London 1992.– Rewald, J. (ed.): C.P. Hayward Gallery, London; Grand Palais, Paris; Museum of Fine Arts, Boston 1981 (EC).– Rewald, J.: C.P. New York 1963, 1989.– Rewald, J.: C.P. Cologne 1963.– Roger-Marx, C.: C.P. graveur. Paris 1929.– Sérullaz, M.: C.P. Arcueil 1955.– Shikes, R.H. and P. Harper: P. His Life and Work. New York 1980.–

Shikes, R.H. and P. Harper: P. Paris 1981.– Tabarant, A.: P. London and New York 1925.– Thomson, R.: C.P. Impressionism, Landscape and Rural Labour. London 1990.– Thorold, A. (ed.): Artists, Writers, Politics: C.P. and his Friends. Ashmolean Museum, Oxford 1980 (EC)
ILLUSTRATIONS:
58 Jallais Hill, Pontoise, 1867
82 The Mailcoach at Louveciennes, 1870
83 The Road from Versailles at Louveciennes, 1870
99 Chestnut Trees at Louveciennes, c. 1872
106 Orchard in Blossom, Louveciennes, 1872
107 The Four Seasons: Spring, 1872
107 The Four Seasons: Summer, 1872
107 The Four Seasons: Autumn, 1872
107 The Four Seasons: Winter, 1872
116 Hoarfrost, 1873
127 A Cowherd on the Route du Chou, Pontoise, 1874
17 The Hermitage at Pontoise, 1874
157 Harvest at Montfoucault, 1876
157 Rye Fields at Pontoise, Côte des Mathurins, 1877
173 The Mailcoach. The Road from Ennery to the Hermitage, 1877
174 Path at "Le Chou", 1878
174 La Côte des Bœufs at the Hermitage near Pontoise, 1877
175 Vegetable Garden and Trees in Blossom, Spring, Pontoise, 1877
175 The Red Roofs, 1877
190 A Fair at the Hermitage near Pontoise, c. 1878
190 Vegetable Garden at the Hermitage near Pontoise, 1879
191 Landscape at Chaponval, 1880
191 The Woodcutter, 1879
204 The Cottage "La Garenne" at Pontoise, Snow, 1879
204 The Wheelbarrow, c. 1881
216 The Shepherdess, 1881
217 Mère Larchevêque (the Washerwoman), 1880
217 Young Peasant Girl Wearing a Hat, 1881
226 Woman and Child at a Well, 1882
226 Poultry Market at Pontoise, 1882
275 Woman in an Orchard. Spring Sunshine in a Field, Eragny, 1887
275 Apple Picking, 1886
312 View from the Artist's Window at Eragny, c. 1886-1888
337 The Chat, 1892
355 Morning, Overcast Weather, Rouen, 1896
355 Pont Boieldieu in Rouen in a Drizzle, 1896
356 The Boulevard Montmartre on a Cloudy Morning, 1897
356 The Boulevard Montmartre on a Winter Morning, 1897
357 The Boulevard Montmartre on a Sunny Afternoon, 1897
357 The Boulevard Montmartre at Night, 1897
359 The Old Market-Place in Rouen and the Rue de l'Epicerie, 1898
361 The Train, Bedford Park, 1897
361 The Tuileries Gardens in Rain, 1899

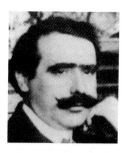

PISSARRO Georges
1871 Louveciennes – 1961 Menton
Second son of C. Pissarro, became known under the pseudonym of Manzana (the name of his grandmother on his mother's side). 1889 moved to London, where he attended the school of decoration run by the architect C.R. Ashbee. His father supported his artistic endeavours. 1891 second stay in London, where he met Sargent. After the death of his first wife he moved back to Eragny. Friendship with Luce and van Rysselberghe, with whom he worked in 1894/95 in Brussels and Hemixem. 1895 exhibited enamel works with Les Vingt in Brussels and at the Bing Gallery in Paris. Travelled in Spain and France with his brother Félix. 1898 returned to France; set up in a studio in Montmartre. Frequently worked in Moret, where he spent the holidays with Picabia. 1901 exhibited at Durand-Ruel's, 1903 for the first time at the Salon des Indépendants, and in 1906 at the autumn Salon and at the Indépendants. 1907 exhibited objets d'art and artefacts at Durand-Ruel's; from 1910 his successes grew. 1906-1936 turned to an Oriental manner influenced by Persian miniatures and Japanese painting. 1914 large one-man exhibition at the Musée d'Arts décoratifs. During the Second World War he lived in Casablanca. In his last works he returned to the techniques of plein-air painting.
BIBLIOGRAPHY: G.M.-Pissarro. Musée des Andelys 1972 (EC).– G.M.-Pissarro. Musée Pissarro, Pontoise 1987 (EC)
ILLUSTRATION:
360 The Harbour at Rouen, 1898

PISSARRO Lucien
1863 Paris – 1944 London
Oldest son of C. Pissarro, with whom he studied plein-air painting. 1880-1883 various occupations. 1883/84 stayed with relatives in London, beginning of an important correspondence with his father. 1884-1890 in Paris, worked for the printer Manzi, turned to wood-cuts and wood engravings. 1886 one of the first to join the new Neo-Impressionist movement; ten catalogue entries (paintings and graphics) at the 8th Impressionist exhibition; exhibited at the first Salon des Indépendants. 1888 exhibited with Les Vingt in Brussels. 1890 finally moved to England, contacts

with the Pre-Raphaelites and open-air painters. 1892 married Esther Bensuan. 1893 settled in Epping. 1894 founded the Eragny Press (the name comes from a place near Dieppe), which played a significant role in the development of European book art. 1895 exhibited at the Art Nouveau exhibition at the Bing Gallery in Paris. 1896 left the Indépendants. 1902 worked with his father in Eragny; thereafter settled in Stamford Brook, Hammersmith. From 1904 exhibited at the New English Art Club and in 1907 with the Fitzroy Street Group. 1911 co-founder of the Camden Town Group. 1913 first one-man exhibition in London. 1916 took British citizenship. 1919 co-founder of the Monarro group, which propagated Impressionism in England. Above all a landscape painter. 1940 moved to Hewood. The correspondence with his father is an important document of the Impressionist movement.

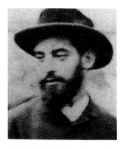

WRITINGS, DOCUMENTS: Pissarro, L. and C. Ricketts: De la typographie et de l'harmonie de la page imprimée. Paris and London 1898.- Pissarro L.: Rossetti. London and New York 1908 CATALOGUE: Thorold, A. et al. (eds.): A Catalogue of the Oil Paintings of L.P. London 1983
BIBLIOGRAPHY: Chambers, D.: L.P.: Notes on a Selection of Wood-Blocks Held at the Ashmolean Museum. Oxford 1980.– Fern, A.; L.P. Cambridge 1962.– Landscape Paintings by L.P. The Leicester Galleries, London 1963 (EC).– L.P. His Watercolours. London 1990 (EC).– Offay, A. d': L.P. 1863-1954. London 1977. – Pickvance, R. (eds.): L.P. A Centenary Exhibition. The Arts Council of Great Britain, London 1963 (EC)
ILLUSTRATIONS:
274 The Church at Gisors, 1888
274 The Deaf Woman's House, 1888

PLEIN-AIR PAINTING
The painting of landscapes and genre scenes in the open-air in order to capture the effect of light on coloration. The technique spread as part of a new striving towards naturalism and authenticity which began in Europe in the second quarter of the nineteenth century; previously, since the fifteenth century, artists working out of doors had used either water colours or the sketch pad. The development in the 1840s of portable paint in

tubes finally made it practicable to paint outside the studio. At first the technique was only used for studies, but from the middle of the century it developed as a viable method, despite opposition from academic circles. Plein-air as a preparatory stage before Impressionism, although it continued to be used by artists who did not go as far as the Impressionists in the separation of colours or the capture of the fleeting moment. It is also true to say that many Impressionist paintings were begun outside but completed in the studio.

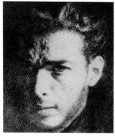

PODKOWINSKI Władisław
1866 Warsaw – 1895 Warsaw
1880-1885 studied with W. Gerson at the school of drawing in Warsaw; became friends with Pankiewicz. 1885/86 studied at the Academy in St. Petersburg. 1886-1889 with Pankiewicz in Kazimierz and Warsaw; drew realistic genre scenes for journals. 1889 with Pankiewicz in Paris; met Theo van Gogh. 1890-1895 in Warsaw, painted in an Impressionist style and then became in his last works a pioneer of Symbolism in Poland.
BIBLIOGRAPHY: Wierchowska, W.: W.P. Warsaw 1981
ILLUSTRATIONS:
512 Field of Lupins, 1891
513 Children in the Garden, 1892

POINTILLISM → Neo-Impressionism

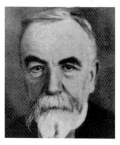

POLENOV Vassili Dimitrievich
1844 St. Petersburg – 1927 Gut Borok near Poleovo
1863-1871 during his law studies also

trained as a painter at the Academy in St. Petersburg, from which he graduated with a gold medal. 1872-1876 travelled on a scholarship to Italy and with Repin in France; did portraits and history paintings. 1876 awarded membership of the Russian Academy. 1876-1878 war painter in the war against Turkey. 1878 exhibited for the first time with the "Wanderers"; became one of their leading artists and a major influence in the development of "intimate" plein-air painting. Often visited Mamontov in Abramtsevo. 1881-1882 first of several trips to the Orient. 1882-1895 professor of landscape painting at the School of Art in Moscow; became interested in depictions of Christ and philosophical and religious questions. 1893 began to exhibit with the Moscow Association of Artists, as also Vrubel and Kandinsky were to do later. In 1905 he left the teaching staff of the Academy in protest against the massacre in St. Petersburg. 1910-1918 managed the first folk-theatre in Moscow and became active in the development of factory and village theatre. 1917-1927 lived in the studio house of his own design on the Oka; awarded the title of "Folk-Artist".
WRITINGS, DOCUMENTS: Sacharova, J.V. (eds.): V.D.P. Letters, Diaries, Memoirs (Russian). Moscow and Leningrad 1950
BIBLIOGRAPHY: Yurova, T.V.: V.D.P.: V.D.P. Moscow 1961.– Sacharova E. (ed.): V.D.P. and Y.D. Polenova. Chronicle of an Artistic Family (Russian). Moscow 1964
ILLUSTRATION:
507 A Yard in Moscow, II, 1878

PONT-AVEN
Small town in Brittany which, like the neighbouring places of Le Pouldu and Concarneau, attracted painters of landscapes and country life; one of the first artist colonies in the countryside. 1886 first visit by Gauguin, Schuffenecker and Bernard. During their second visit in 1888 they developed the "Synthetist" and Symbolist style of painting, an innovation in both form and content. Through his picture "The Talisman" (p. 320), Sérusier mediated the new style to the Nabis in Paris. 1889 the Post-Impressionist "school" of Pont-Aven held its first exhibition at the Café Volpini in Paris as a fringe event during the World Fair; they exhibited landscapes with flat areas of strong colour, genre pictures of fisherman's wives in traditional costume, portraits and religious paintings. More artists joined the movement, which also found adherents from the USA, Denmark, Holland, Poland, Sweden, Switzerland and Scotland.

PONTILLON Edma
1849 Valenciennes – 1921 Paris
Berthe Morisot's sister, also a painter. 1857 first lessons with Chocarne and Guichard. Studied plein-air with Corot. Until her marriage she lived with her sister and shared the same friends. 1862 travelled to the Pyrenees. 1864-1867 exhibited in the Salon. Her

career finished after her marriage to Adolphe Pontillon, a naval officer and friend of Manet. Morisot often painted her portrait (p.88).

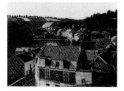

PONTOISE
Idyllic town on the Oise near Auvers, about 20 miles from Paris. Its landscape offered numerous attractive motifs for many artists, especially Pissarro with his houses built in a Roman amphitheatre. In 1866 Pissarro moved to Pontoise, where he met Cézanne in the summer of 1872 and painted with him, persuading him to join the Impressionists. Guillaumin paid him numerous visits. 1877 Cézanne again visited Pontoise while Gauguin was painting there. 1883 Pissarro moved to Osny and then to Eragny.

POST-IMPRESSIONISM
A term first used by the English painter and art critic Roger Fry and made popular by John Rewald. A loose collective idea for the various artistic movements based on Impressionism which started in the period 1884-1886: Cézanne's colour modulation (from about 1879), Pointillist Neo-Impressionism, the expressive exaggerations of van Gogh, the decorative-symbolist Synthetism of Gauguin and his disciples. The term also covers Symbolism (Redon, the Nabis, Munch and others), Art Nouveau, and Toulouse-Lautrec. To be strictly accurate, the bright palettes, sketchy style and compositional movement of many genre artists of the 1870s should also be included. It is, however, stretching the usefulness of the term to apply it to the later works of Monet and others, to the worldwide use of Impressionist technique and point of view in the art of the twentieth century, or to the direct and indirect influence of Impressionism on the early stages of modern movements such as Expressionism.

PREISLER Jan
1872 Popovice – 1918 Prague
1887-1895 studied at the School of Arts and Crafts in Prague; remained there after his studies. 1898 exhibited for the first time with the artists' federation "Mánes". An influential exponent of a Symbolism based on Impressionism; also worked as an illustrator and poster designer. Painted murals, and worked with J. Kotěra, the founder of modern Czech architecture. 1900 painted decorative pictures for the Paris World Fair. 1902-1904 travelled to Italy with Hudeček; did some murals for Kotěra's Grand Ho-

tel. 1906 stayed in Paris, influenced the Fauvists. 1913-1918 professor at the Academy of Arts in Prague.
BIBLIOGRAPHY: J.P. 1872-1918. Národní Galerie. Prague 1964 (EC).– Kotalík, J.: J.P. Prague 1968.– Wittlich, P.: J.P. Prague 1988
ILLUSTRATION:
518 Bathers, 1912

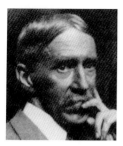

PRENDERGAST Maurice Brazil
1861 Boston – 1924 New York
Trained as a painter of advertisements in Boston. Attended evening courses at the Star King School and also painted watercolour landscapes. 1886/87 trip to England and possibly also France. 1891-1894 studied at the Académie Julian and the Académie Colarossi in Paris. Influenced by Whistler, Manet and Bonnard. 1895 returned to Boston. 1897 exhibited in Boston and rented a studio there. 1898-1900 trip to Europe, including a visit to Venice. In subsequent years he travelled repeatedly in Europe. His warm plein-air painting received great acclaim, with numerous exhibitions and awards. An active proponent of Impressionism and Post-Impressionism (Symbolists, Neo-Impressionists and Nabis); a pioneer of the style in the USA. In 1914, after a trip to Europe, settled in New York.
CATALOGUE: Clark, C. et al. (eds.): M.B.P. & Charles Prendergast. A Catalogue Raisonné. Munich and Williamstown 1989 (EC)
BIBLIOGRAPHY: Breuning, M. (ed.): M.P. Whitney Museum of American Art, New York 1931 (EC).– Langdale, C. (ed.): The Monotypes of M.P. Davis and Long Company, New York, 1979 (EC).– Pach, W. (ed.): M.P. Memorial Exhibition, Whitney Museum of American Art, New York 1934 (EC).– Rhys, H.H. (ed.) M.P. 1859-1924. Museum of Fine Arts, Boston, 1960 (EC).– Scott, D.W.: M.P. Washington 1980.– Sims, P. (ed.): M.P. Whitney Museum of American Art, New York 1980 (EC)
ILLUSTRATION:
625 Central Park, New York, 1901
625 Ponte della Paglia, Venice, 1899

PREVIATI Gaetano
1852 Ferrara – 1920 Lavagno
Studied at the School of Art in Ferrara, in Florence and in 1877 with G. Bertini at the Brera Academy in Milan. From 1875 exhibitions, 1878

first big success. Influenced by Grubicy, he turned to Impressionism. 1887-1890 illustrations for the fairy tales of Edgar Allen Poe; through this work came into contact with Symbolist themes. 1891 exhibited at the Brera Academy. 1902 showed pictures at the exhibition of the Berlin Secession. 1907 designed the "Hall of Dreams" for the Biennale in Venice.
BIBLIOGRAPHY: G.P. Galleria Nazionale d'Arte moderna, Rome 1953 (EC)
ILLUSTRATION:
545 In the Meadow, 1889/90

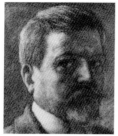

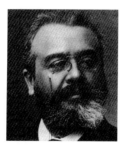

PROUST Antonin
1832 Niort – 1905 Paris
Politician and publicist. 1864 founded "La Semaine universelle". Worked as Gambetta's secretary. 1876 Republican delegate for Niort. 1881 Minister of Education, 1889 Commissar of Fine Arts for the World Fair. Frequented all the Salons; close friends with Manet, whom he knew from school days at the Collège Rollin. Due to Proust's influence, Manet was received into the Legion of Honour; his portrait was painted by Manet in 1880. Published his reminiscences of Manet in 1897.

PUVIS DE CHAVANNES Pierre
1824 Lyon – 1898 Paris
After graduation in law and two trips to Italy he became an occasional pupil of Delacroix, H. Scheffer and Couture; especially impressed by Chassériau. 1850 exhibited for the first time at the Salon, but was rejected several times thereafter. 1854/55 executed his first monumental murals, highly decorative and difficult to interpret; this

was to remain his main type of work (it includes the murals in Amiens and the Paris Panthéon). 1887 large exhibition at Durand-Ruel's. 1890 co-founder and 1891 President of the Secessionist Société Nationale des Beaux-Arts. His style was clear and calm, and oriented towards the linear forms of the Classical and Renaissance periods. Soft but bright colours. Belonged to no particular movement, but through his pictures' content and form he considerably influenced the Symbolists (Gauguin, Denis) and also Seurat and Cézanne.
BIBLIOGRAPHY: Boucher, M.-C.: Catalogue des dessins et peintures de P. de C. Paris 1879.– Foucart, J. et al. (eds.): P. de C. 1824-1898. Grand Palais, Paris 1976 (EC).– Foucart-Borville, J.: Le genèse des peintures murales de P. de C. au Musée de Picardie. Amiens 1976.– Vachon, M.: P. de C. Paris 1898.– Viéville, D.: Les peintures murales de P. de C. à Amiens. Amiens 1989.– Wattenmaker, R.J. (ed.): P. de C. and the Modern Tradition. The Art Gallery of Ontario, Toronto 1975 (EC).– Worth, L.: P. de C. 1926
ILLUSTRATION:
189 Young Women on the Seashore, 1879

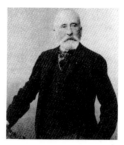

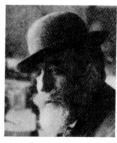

RAFFAELLI Jean-François
1850 Lyons – 1924 Paris
Lived all his life in Paris. 1868 trained initially as a singer, attending courses in the mornings at the Ecole des Beaux-Arts and studying for periods with Gérôme. 1870 exhibited for the first time at the Salon. Trips to Italy, Egypt and Spain. From 1871 rejected each time at the Salon until 1876,

when he had a big success. From the middle of the 1870s he was influenced by Monet and Sisley and changed to Impressionism. 1876 went to England. 1880 and 1881 exhibited at the 5th and 6th Impressionist exhibitions. Inventor of the Raffaëlli paint, which has the properties of both oils and watercolours. His painting is full of social criticism in his depictions of the poor areas of Paris; in their subdued tones, they are close to realism; but he also painted portraits and later also all landscapes in and around Paris. Did numerous colour illustrations, which new printing processes could reproduce cheaply. 1889 received a gold medal at the World Fair. 1891 exhibited with the Société Nationale.
BIBLIOGRAPHY: Alexandre, A.: J.-F.R. Paris 1909.– Delteil, L.: J.-F.R. Paris 1923.– Fields, B.S.: J.-F.R. (1850-1924): The Naturalist Artist. Doctoral thesis, Ann Arbor (MI) 1979.– Lecomte, G.: R. Paris 1927
ILLUSTRATION:
211 The Absinth Drinkers, 1881
240 Houses on the Banks of the Oise
240 Waiting Wedding Guests, 1884
246 Fisherman on the Bank of the Seine

RAFFAELLI Jean-Marius
Probably a graphic artist; further facts about his life unknown. 1880 exhibited six etchings at the 5th Impressionist exhibition.

RAŠKAJ Slava
1877 Ozalj – 1906 Stenjevec
1885-1893 grew up in a home for the deaf and dumb in Vienna. 1896 taught to paint by B. Čikoš in Ozalj (Croatia). 1898 exhibited at the 1st exhibition of the Society of Croatian Artists in Zagreb. 1899-1901 lived in Ozalj, Zlatar and Orahovice. 1900 showed some watercolours at the Paris World Fair. Also painted Impressionist pictures. 1901 showed 12 works at the Society of Croatian Artists; became a member. Signs of mental illness. 1902-1906 at the mental hospital in Stenjevec.
BIBLIOGRAPHY: Peić, M.: S.R. Zagreb 1985
ILLUSTRATION:
528 Trees in Snow, 1900

RAURICH Y PETRE Nicolas
1871 Barcelona – 1945 Barcelona
After training in a merchant's office, he studied art in Barcelona; travelled to Madrid, Rome, Paris, Munich and London. 1897 received a medal; began a career as a landscape and still-life painter. Had a big success at the Paris Salon in 1899, as well as in Vienna, Venice, Karlsruhe, Rome, Athens and Mexico.
ILLUSTRATION:
566 Solitude

REDON Odilon
1840 Bordeaux – 1916 Paris
Mainly self-taught in Bordeaux and Paris. 1867 exhibited an etching at the Salon. Admired Delacroix. Later met Corot, Courbet, Fantin-Latour. 1881 exhibited for the first time at the gallery of the journal "La Vie

moderne". 1884 co-founder of the Indépendants. For years he only did copper engravings. 1886 exhibited at the 8th Impressionist exhibition and with Les Vingt in Brussels. 1890 friendship with Gauguin. 1891 close contact with the poet Mallarmé; began to do Symbolist painters. 1899 exhibition in his honour by Symbolist painters at Durand-Ruel's. Began to experiment with pastels and oils in a relaxed style with intensive colours. Given a prominent place in Denis' group-portrait "Hommage à Cézanne", 1909-1916 lived a life of withdrawal and meditation at Bièvres near Paris.

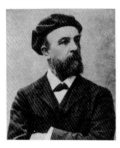

WRITINGS, DOCUMENTS: Redon, O.: Lettres d'O.R. Brussels/Paris 1923.– Redon, O.: A soi-même: Journal (1867-1915). Paris 1961.– Redon, O.: Selbstgespräch. Tagebücher und Aufzeichnungen 1867-1915. Munich 1971 CATALOGUES: Mellerio, A.: O.R. Catalogue raisonné of the Lithographs and the Etchings. New York 1968.– Wildenstein, A.: O.R. Catalogue raisonné (in preparation) BIBLIOGRAPHY: Bacou, R.: O.R. 2 vols. Geneva 1956.– Bacou, R. (ed.): O.R. Pastels. London 1987.– Berger, K.: O.R.: Phantasie und Farbe. Cologne 1964.– Cassou, J.: O.R. Munich 1974.– Hobbs, R. O.R. London and New York 1977.– Mellerio, A.: O.R.: Peintre, dessinateur et graveur. Paris 1923.– O.R.: collección Ian Woodner. Barcelona 1990 (EC).– Roger-Marx, C.: O.R. Paris 1925.– Sandstrom, S.: Le monde imaginaire d'O.R. Lund 1955.– Selz, J.: O.R. Paris, 1971
ILLUSTRATIONS:
350 Peyrelebade, c. 1896/97
376 Beatrice, c. 1905
376 Paul Gauguin, c. 1903-1905

REGOYOS VALDES Darío de
1857 Ribadesella – 1913 Barcelona
1877 studied with de Haes at the Academy of Arts in San Fernando, Madrid. 1880 travelled to Paris, where he met Luce, and 1881 to Brussels, where he met van Rysselberghe. 1881-1889 lived mostly in Brussels. 1882 showed work at the exhibitions of the group "L'Essor" in Brussels. 1882 travelled to Spain with Maus, Luce, Meunier and van Rysselberghe. 1883 co-founder of Les Vingt; 1884 first of their exhibitions, at which he was to exhibit regularly. Visited Whistler, Pissarro, Degas, Seu-

rat and Signac. 1888 travelled to Spain with Verhaeren. 1888 exhibited with Pissarro, Seurat, Signac, Cross, Anquetin and Raffaëlli in the rooms of the "Revue Blanche". His landscapes, which had a certain gloom to them despite their Impressionist style, began to be influenced by Neo-Impressionism. Exhibited in Paris at the Salon des Indépendants. 1890 exhibited for the first time but without success at the Madrid Art Exhibition. Above all he painted landscapes in which he combined an Impressionist observation of nature with a Pontillist style of painting. 1898 stayed in London, thereafter settling in San Sebastián in Spain. 1899 published his book "La España Negra". 1903 and 1906 exhibited in Paris. Became ill with cancer and in 1907 moved to Arenas (Bizcaya), then in 1910 to Granada, in 1911 to Barcelona and finally to Germany.

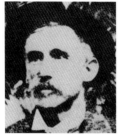

BIBLIOGRAPHY: Benet, R.: D. de R. Barcelona 1946.– D.d.R. 1857- 1913. Fundación Caja de Pensiones, Madrid 1986 (EC).– Encina, J. de la : Guiard y R. Bilbao 1921.– García Minor, A.: El pintor D. de R. y su época. Oviedo 1958
ILLUSTRATION:
563 Dolores Otaño, 1891

RENOIR Pierre-Auguste
1841 Limoges – 1919 Cagnes
Son of a poor tailor; 1844 moved to Paris. 1854-1858 trained as a porcelain painter. 1859/60 worked at a firm producing painted curtains. 1860-64 became a pupil of Gleyre; studied at the Ecole des Beaux-Arts, together with Monet, Sisley and Bazille. 1863 began painting plein-air near Barbizon, under the tutelage of N. Diaz; met Pissarro and Cézanne. 1864 and 1865 exhibited at the Salon. 1865-1872 Lise Tréhot became his model and lover. 1866 and 1867 rejected by the Salon, painted portraits in the open-air. 1867 lived at Bazille's house with Monet. 1868-1870 shared a studio with Bazille in the Batignolles quarter, frequented the Café Guerbois; met Manet; exhibited at the Salon. 1869 went with Monet at Bougival on the Seine; together they worked out the main tenets of the Impressionist method. 1870/71 military service in the war. 1872 rejected by the Salon, he called for a Salon des Refusés; Durand-Ruel exhibited one of his pictures for

the first time in London. 1873 met the critic Duret; painted with Monet at Argenteuil; a frequent customer in this period at the Café de la Nouvelle-Athènes. 1874 exhibited at the 1st Impressionist exhibition. 1875 had some pictures auctioned at the Hôtel Drouot; met the art collector Choquet. 1876 exhibited at the 2nd Impressionist exhibition; visited A. Daudet at Chaprosay; received commissions from the publisher Charpentier; his favourite themes became pictures of the middle-class at leisure and portraits. 1877 exhibited at the 3rd Impressionist exhibition; again had some pictures auctioned. 1878-1881 exhibited at the Salon but not at Impressionist exhibitions. 1879 one-man exhibition at the gallery of Charpentier's journal "La Vie moderne"; first visit to the Berard family in Wargemont (Normandy). 1880 met his future wife, Aline Charigot; broke his right arm and painted with his left hand. 1881 travelled to Algeria, later to Italy; impressed by Raphael and the Pompeii frescoes. 1882 painted a portrait of the composer Wagner at Palermo; visited Cézanne at L'Estaque. Durand-Ruel exhibited pictures by him at the 7th Impressionist exhibition and in London. 1883 one-man exhibition at the Galerie Durand-Ruel; exhibited also at the Salon and in London, Boston and Berlin. Visited Jersey, Guernsey and the Côte d'Azur. Formal characteristics of his work at this time include clearly delineated, three- dimensional human figures. 1884 formed a friendship with Morisot. 1885 exhibited for the first time at Essoyes, Aline's home village. 1886 exhibitions with the group Les Vingt in Brussels, in New York through Durand-Ruel, and in Paris through G. Petit; he did not exhibit at the last Impressionist exhibition. 1889 refused to exhibit at the World Fair in Paris. 1890 married Aline; they had three sons. Rejected the award of the Legion of Honour; exhibited for the last time at the Salon. Returned to the rich colours and free brushwork of his earlier days and painted mainly nudes and landscapes. 1892 first sale of a painting to the French state made possible by Mallarmé; large single exhibition at Durand-Ruel's; travelled in Spain and Pont-Aven. 1894 became the executor of Caillebotte's bequest of Impressionist paintings to the French state. 1896 tour of Germany; visited Bayreuth and Dresden. 1897 broke his arm after falling from a bicycle. 1898 visited Holland. 1899 due to rheumatism, moved to the South of France. 1900 exhibited at the century exhibition of French art at the World Fair in Paris; became Chevalier of the Legion of Honour. Increasing numbers of exhibitions abroad. 1902 his health deteriorated – at the end his hands were almost paralysed with arthritis. 1904 exhibited for the first time at the Autumn Salon. 1907 bought the house "Les Colettes" at Cagnes. 1910 retrospective at the 9th Biennale in Venice; visit to Munich. 1911 Officer of the Legion of Honour. 1913 began to do sculptures with the help of R. Guino.

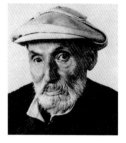

1915 death of his wife. 1919 Commander of the Legion of Honour; honoured with the hanging of one of his pictures in the Louvre.
WRITINGS, DOCUMENTS: Renoir, J.: Mein Vater A.R. Munich 1962. – Rivière, G.: R. et ses amis. Paris 1921. – Vollard, A.: R. Paris 1920
CATALOGUES: Daulte, F.: A.R.: Catalogue raisonné de l'œuvre peint. Vol. I: Figures 1860-1890. Lausanne 1971 (sole volume published). – Fezzi, E.: Das gemalte Gesamtwerk von R. aus der impressionistischen Periode 1869-1883. Lucerne 1973. – Tancock: The Sculpture of R. Philadelphia 1976. – Vollard, A.: P.-A.R. Paintings, Pastels and Drawings. San Francisco 1989

BIBLIOGRAPHY: André, A.: L'atelier de R. 2 vols. Paris 1931 (Reprint: San Francisco 1989). – André, A.: R. Dessins. Paris 1950. – Bacou, R.: P.R. 2 vols. Genova 1956. – Baudot, J.: R.: Ses amis, ses modèles. Paris 1949. – Daulte, F.: P.-A.R. Basle 1958. – Daulte, F.: P.-A.R. Watercolours, Pastels and Drawings in Colour. London 1959. – Daulte, F.: A.R. Paris 1972. – Distel, A. J. House et al. (eds.): R. Hayward Gallery, London; Grand Palais, Paris; Museum of Fine Arts, Boston. Paris 1985, London 1985 (EC). – Feist, P.H.: P.-A.R. 1841-1919. A Dream of Harmony. Cologne 1991. – Fezzi, E.: R. Paris 1972. – Florisoone, M.: R. Paris 1937. – Fosca, F.: R. London and Paris 1961. – Gaunt, W.: R. Oxford 1982. – Gowing, L.: R., Paintings. London 1947. – Haesaerts, P.: R. sculpteur. Brussels 1947. – Hoog, M. and N. Wadley: R.: un peintre, une vie, une œuvre. Paris 1989. – Meier-Graefe, J.: R. Paris 1912. – Monneret, S.: R. Cologne 1990. – Pach, W.: P.-A.R. Cologne 1958. – Perruchot, H.: La vie de R. Paris 1964. – Rewald, J. (ed.): R. Drawings. New York 1946. – Rouart, D.: R. Geneva 1954, London 1985. – White, B.E.: R. His Life, Art, and Letters. New York 1984
ILLUSTRATIONS:
2   By the Seashore, 1883
6   Mademoiselle Romaine Lacaux, 1864
11   Oarsmen at Chatou, 1879
13   The Walk, 1870
32   Alfred Sisley and his Wife, 1868
53   The Pont des Arts, Paris, 1867
73   La Grenouillère, 1869
93   Madame Monet Reading "Le Figaro", 1872

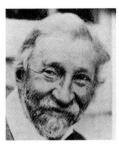

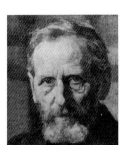

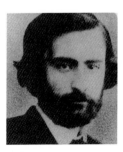

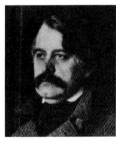

REPIN Ilya Yefimovich
1844 Chuguyevo – 1930 Kuokkala (Finland)
1864-1871 studied at the Academy in St. Petersburg, where he was awarded the distinction of a gold medal. 1871 met the art critic V. Stassov. 1873 exhibited the picture "The Volga Boatmen" at the World Fair in Vienna. 1873-1876 on a scholarship in Italy and France; met Zola. 1876/77 in Chuguyevo. Received the title of Academician of Art. 1877-82 in Moscow. 1878-1891 and again from 1897 member of the "Wanderers"; visited S. Mamontov in Abramtsevo; painted by preference portraits and genre pictures with a social theme. 1880 went with Serov to the Ukraine. 1882 moved to St. Petersburg; met Tolstoy. 1883 travelled in western Europe with Stassov; Impressionist features became increasingly apparent in his work. 1887 in Italy and Germany. 1889 went to the World Fair in Paris, and with Stassov to England, Germany and Switzerland. 1892-1907 professor at the college of the Academy in St. Petersburg. 1893/94 travelled in western Europe. 1898

travelled to Constantinople and Jerusalem. 1899 at the international exhibition of the journal "World of Art". Bought "Penaten" a country house in Kuokkala. 1900 jury member of the Paris World Fair, awarded the Legion of Honour. Exhibited in Prague. 1902 member of the Academy in Prague. 1917 moved back to Kuokkala, now part of Finland.
WRITINGS, DOCUMENTS: Repin, I.: Daljokoje bliskoje (1937), Moscow 1953. – Repin, I.: Fernes und Nahes. Erinnerungen. Berlin 1970
BIBLIOGRAPHY: Brodsky, I.: R., Pisma. Moscow 1969. – Efimowitsch, I. (ed.): I.R. Malerei. – Grabar, I.E.: I.E.R. 2 vols. Moscow 1937, 1963. – Ljaskowskaja, O.: I.E.R. Moscow 1962, 1982. – Sternin, G. et al.: I.R. Leningrad 1985. – Valkenier, E.R.: I.R. and the World of Russian Art. New York 1990
ILLUSTRATIONS:
502 Tolstoy Resting in a Wood, 1891
502 Portrait of the Artist's Daughter Vera, 1874
503 They did not expect him, 1884
504 Portrait of Sophia Mikhailovna Dragomirova, 1889
505 In the Sun, 1900

REVUE BLANCHE, La
Journal for avant-garde literature and art and an important mouthpiece for Impressionism. Founded in 1889 by Paul Leclercq and Auguste Jeunehomme. 1891 taken over by the Natanson brothers, who organised exhibitions of modern art in the rooms of the journal. Appeared for the last time in 1903.

REVUE INDEPENDANTE, La
Most important journal of the Naturalists, Symbolists and Impressionists in the last quarter of the 19th century. 1884 founded by Georges Chevier and Félix Fénéon. There were 24 issues in the period 1884-1885. After a break in publication, it resumed under Edouard Dujardin. Included on its staff Mallarmé, who wrote theatre reviews. Exhibitions of Impressionist work were held on the premises. The journal did not appear between 1893 and 1895 and in 1895 after a few issues it was discontinued.

RICO Y ORTEGA Martin
1833 Madrid – 1908 Venice
Worked as an illustrator with his

brother, a copperplate engraver. Studied at the San Fernando Academy of Arts in Madrid under Genaro Pèrez Villaamil. Extremely successful at the exhibitions in Madrid. Received medals at the World Fair in Paris in 1878 and 1888. Influenced by the painters of the Barbizon school. He was friends with Fortuny, whose light-filled style influenced him and brightened up the colours of his more Realist style as seen in his depictions of motifs and scenes from Venice, Rome and Toledo.
BIBLIOGRAPHY: Paysages d'Espagne, Aquarelles inédites de M.R. Musée Goya, Castres 1979 (EC)
ILLUSTRATION:
558 View of Venice

RING Laurits Andersen
1854 Zeeland – 1933 Roskilde
Initial training as a painter in Præstø; attended the technical school in Copenhagen; 1874 admitted to the Academy in Copenhagen, where he studied 1875-1877 and 1884. His landscapes and genre pictures frequently deal with social themes. 1889 travelled via Hamburg to Paris. Impressed by Millet and Raffaelli. The clear composition of his pictures reveals his interest in Japanese art.
ILLUSTRATION:
481 Girl Looking out of a Skylight, 1885

RIPPL-RONAI József
1861 Kaposvár – 1927 Kaposvár
1881-1883 trained as a pharmacist, then worked as a home tutor. 1884-1887 studied with Herterich and Diez at the Academy in Munich. 1887 went to Paris on a state scholarship; worked

initially with Munkácsy. 1889 visited Pont-Aven. 1890 studied at the Académie Julian; became friends with Maillol and Vuillard, later with Bonnard. 1893 travelled in England. 1894 exhibited at the Salon of the Société Nationale. Visited Gauguin; joined the Symbolist group the Nabis and the group around the "Revue Blanche". 1895 visited Cézanne; exhibited in Budapest. 1896 some of his pictures were exhibited by Gurlitt for the first time in Berlin. 1897 did an Art Nouveau design for the dining room of Count Andrássy. 1899 visited Maillol in Banyuls. 1900 silver medal for some embroidery designs at the Paris World Fair. 1900-1902 in Hungary, large one-man exhibition. 1902 travelled in Belgium and Russia; settled in Kaposvár. 1904 and 1905 trips to Italy. 1906 successful exhibition in Budapest. 1907 member of the committee of the new "Group of Hungarian Impressionists and Naturalists"; turned to decorative and Fauvist styles of painting. 1911 and 1914 stayed in Paris. 1918 on the Council for Art and Literature of the Republic. Began to have problems with his sight; drew mainly pastels. 1925 a self-portrait was commissioned in Florence.
WRITINGS, DOCUMENTS: Rippl-Rónai, J.: Emlékezései. Budapest 1957
BIBLIOGRAPHY: Fülep, L.: R.-R., Csontváry, Derkovits. Budapest 1975. – Genthon, I.: R.-R.: The Hungarian "Nabi". Budapest 1958. – Keserü, K.: J.R.-R. Berlin 1983. – R.-R. 1861-1927. Pittore, grafico, decoratore. Pinacoteca capitolina, Rome 1983 (EC). – Szabadi, J.: J.R.-R. Budapest 1978
ILLUSTRATIONS:
524 Living on Memories, 1904
524 Lady in a Polka-Dot Dress, 1889

RIVIERE Georges
1855–1943
Writer and critic. A close friend of Renoir, who painted him in his picture "Le Moulin de la Galette" (p. 153). Followed the development of Impressionism with interest and in 1877, at Renoir's prompting, founded the journal "L'Impressionniste" to defend the movement; only five issues appeared (in April). Rivière wrote almost all of the contributions himself; for many painters these were the only articles that viewed their work in a positive light. After 1920 he published books on Renoir, Cézanne and Degas.

ROBERT Léon-Paul
Born in Bagneux in 1849
Genre painter, pupil of Bonnat and Puvis de Chavannes. Founder member of the "Société des peintres, sculpteurs, graveurs". Showed two watercolours at the 1st Impressionist exhibition in 1874. 1879-1883 exhibited at the Salon.

ROBINSON Theodore
1852 Irasburg (VT) – 1896 New York
1869-1874 studied at the Art Institute in Chicago and 1874-1876 at the National Academy of Design and the Art Students League in New York. 1876-1879 tour of Europe. Studied under Carolus-Duran and Gérôme at the

Ecole des Beaux-Arts and in 1877 exhibited at the Paris Salon. In 1879 he met Whistler in Venice. 1880-1883 worked on a decorative mural for John LaFarge in Tarrytown (New York) and a mural at the Metropolitan Opera. 1884 lived at Barbizon during the summer months. 1884-1887 travelled through France, Belgium and the Netherlands. From 1888 he formed a close friendship with Monet, and was considerably influenced by his Impressionism. It is possible that his interest in photography and its relation to painting may have encouraged Monet to try similar experiments. Until 1892 he spent the winter months in New York and the summers at Giverny. 1895 became a teacher at the Pennsylvania Academy of Fine Arts.

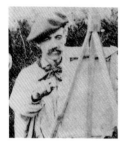

WRITINGS, DOCUMENTS: Low, W.H.: A Chronicle of Friendship. New York, 1908.– Robinson, T.: Claude Monet. In: "The Century Magazine" 44 (September 1892), pp. 696-701.
BIBLIOGRAPHY: Baur, J.I.H. (ed.): T.R. 1852-1896. Brooklyn Museum, New York 1946 (EC).– Byrd, D.G. (ed.): Paintings and Drawings by T.R. University of Wisconsin, Madison, 1964 (EC).– Clark, E.: T.R. His Life and Art. Chicago 1979.– Johnston, S. (ed.): T.R. Baltimore Museum of Art, Baltimore 1973 (EC).– Lewison, F.: T.R. and Claude Monet. In: "Apollo" 78 (September 1963), pp. 208-211.– T.R. 1852-1896. The Baltimore Museum of Art, Baltimore 1973 (EC)
ILLUSTRATIONS:
612 Two in a Boat, 1891
614 Le débâcle, 1892
615 The Wedding March, 1892

ROCHEFORT Henri de
1831 Paris – 1913 Aix-les-Bains
Civil servant and critic, Sub-Inspector of the Paris Beaux-Arts. Founded and worked for several journals. One of the most famous authors of polemical articles for "Le Figaro". Defended Gambetta in 1870 after the capitulation of Paris; supported the Commune and was accordingly deported to New Caledonia in 1873. He was much admired by the Impressionists.

ROELOFS Willem
1822 Amsterdam – 1897 Antwerp
Son of the owner of a brickworks. Pupil of E.J. van de Sande Bakhuizen in The Hague. 1848-1887 lived in

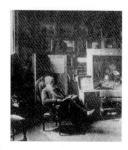

Brussels. His conception of landscape is comparable to that of Daubigny and Rousseau. Important predecessor of the Impressionists in Holland.
BIBLIOGRAPHY: Bremmer, H.P.: W.R. Amsterdam 1909.– Eere-teentoonstelling W.R. Pulchri-Studio, The Hague 1907 (EC).– Jeltes, H.F.W.: W.R. Amsterdam 1911
ILLUSTRATION:
408 Summertime, 1862

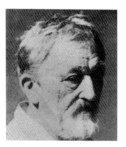

ROHLFS Christian
1849 Niendorf – 1938 Hagen
1864 a severe knee injury led later to the amputation of his leg. Began to draw and through the support of the writer Theodor Storm he was able to begin his art studies at Weimar in 1870. 1869 moved to Berlin. 1870/71 and 1874-1886 studied at the Weimar School of Art with F. Schaus, A. Struys and M. Thedy. Independently of the French Impressionists, he developed his own method of painting which was indebted to Naturalism but reminiscent of the French style; it was greeted with bitter hostility in Weimar. 1895 stayed in Berlin. 1901 given a post in Hagen at the Folkwang school planned by K.E. Osthaus, but the scheme failed and no lessons were ever taught. Met Renoir, Signac, Seurat, Cézanne and van Gogh, who influenced him. From 1900 member of the Berlin Secession. 1905/06 painted in the summer months at Soest and met Nolde. In 1910 turned to Expressionism. In 1911 he joined the New Secession and in 1914 the Free Secession. 1924 became a member of the Prussian Academy of Arts in Berlin. 1927 travelled to Ascona. 1937 all his

works were confiscated and he was dismissed from the Berlin Academy.
CATALOGUE: Vogt, P.: C.R. Œuvreka-talog der Druckgraphik. Göttingen 1950.– Vogt, P.: C.R. Aquarelle und Zeichnungen. Recklinghausen 1958 (with catalogue).– Vogt, P.: C.R. Das grafische Werk. Recklinghausen 1960.– Vogt, P.: C.R. Œuvrekatalog der Gemälde. Recklinghausen 1978
BIBLIOGRAPHY: C.R. 1849-1938. Gemälde zwischen 1918 und 1935. Museum Folkwang, Essen 1978 (EC).– C.R. Das Spätwerk. Museum Folkwang, Essen 1967 (EC).– C.R. Aquarelle und Zeichnungen. Landesmuseum Münster 1974 (EC).– Scheidig, W.: C.R. Dresden 1965.– Vogt, P.: C.R., 1849-1938: Aquarelle, Wassertemperablätter, Zeichnungen, Recklinghausen 1988 (EC)
ILLUSTRATION:
456 Birch Wood, 1907

ROLL Alfred
1846 Paris – 1919 Paris
After training as an ornamental draughtsman, he became the pupil of Gérôme, L. Bonnat and H. Harpignies at the Ecole des Beaux-Arts in Paris. Travelled in Belgium, Holland and Germany. 1870 exhibited for the first time at the Salon. Painted realistic pictures of everyday life, sometimes with a social message, and Impressionist-inspired plein-air portraits of workers. 1886 exhibited by Durand-Ruel and with the Impressionists in the USA. 1890 Co-founder of the Secession group Société Nationale des Beaux-Arts; in 1905 became their president. 1895 assisted with the painting of the town hall in Paris.

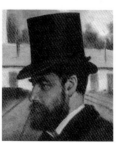

ROUART Henri
1833 Paris – 1912 Paris
Successful industrialist, art collector and painter; his achievements deserve wider recognition. Like his brother Alexis he was a school friend of Degas, with whom he kept in touch all his life; they fought together in the war of 1870/71. Painted under the tutelage of Millet and Corot. Friendship with Tillot. 1868-1872 exhibited at the Salon. 1874-1886 exhibited at all the Impressionist exhibitions except for the 7th, mostly watercolour landscapes from his many trips abroad. Took part in the discussions of the Impressionists and supported them financially. Lived in Paris and La-Queue-

en-Brie. He was a regular host and patron to the Impressionists. 1912 memorial exhibition at Durand-Ruel's. 1912 auction sale of his rich collection, which beside the Impressionists contained works by El Greco, Goya, Poussin and Breughel. His correspondence with Degas is important.
ILLUSTRATION:
203 Terrace on the Banks of the Seine at Melun, c. 1880

ROUART Julie
1879 Paris – 1967 Paris
Nee Manet. Daughter of Morisot and Eugène Manet. All her life she frequented Impressionist circles. After the deaths of her parents, Mallarmé became her guardian. In 1900 she married Ernest Rouart, the son of Henri Rouart. She was a model for Manet, Degas, Renoir, and her mother.

ROUEN
The capital of the Seine valley with an imposing Gothic cathedral. Many of the most important Impressionist pictures were painted in this city or its environs. The picturesque narrow streets had been popular motifs with the predecessors of the Impressionists (Bonington, Turner, Corot, Boudin, Jongkind and others). The Impressionists were particularly attracted to the effects of light and the changing moods and atmosphere of the town. Artists who worked here include Renoir, Sisley, Degas, van Gogh, Pissarro, Gauguin and above all Monet, who painted the famous series of paintings of the cathedral (pp. 342 and 343).

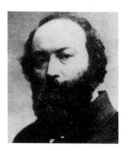

ROUSSEAU Pierre Etienne Théodore
1812 Paris – 1867 Barbizon
Studied initially with his cousin, the landscape painter Alexandre Pau, and then in 1829 with Remond, Lethière and others at the Ecole des Beaux-Arts in Paris. Completed his artistic education with open-air painting – he was probably the first to paint plein-air in the woods at Fontainebleau. 1830 painted in the Auvergne. Travelled in France and Switzerland. 1831 exhibited at the Salon but thereafter went through a period of constant rejections. 1836 in Barbizon for the first time; became the main exponent of the realistic, atmospheric landscape painting that came to be known as the "Barbizon school". 1849 received an award from the Salon. 1866

advised Monet. Durant-Ruel bought 70 pictures. **1867** president of the painting jury for the World Fair in Paris. His rather melancholy, powerful pictures reveal a very precise observation of light.
BIBLIOGRAPHY: Forges, M.T. de and H. Toussaint (eds.): T.R. Musée National du Louvre, Paris 1967 (EC).– Terrasse, A.: L'univers de T.R. Paris 1976
ILLUSTRATION:
23 Clump of Oaks, Apremont, 1852

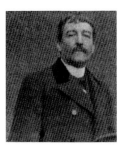

ROUSSEL Theodore
1847 Lorient – 1926 Hastings
Born in France, lived from **1874** in London. A self-taught artist. In the 1880s he was influenced by Whistler. **1887** exhibited at the Society of British Artists; joined the New English Art Club. One of the main exponents of Impressionism in England. Taught Maitland. Worked mostly in and around Chelsea.
BIBLIOGRAPHY: Rutter, F.: T.R. 1926
ILLUSTRATION:
576 The Reading Girl, 1887

RUSINOL Y PRAT Santiago
1861 Barcelona – 1931 Aranjuez
Painter, dramatist, poet and critic. Trained initially as an artist with T. Moraga. Studied in France. Exhibited at the Salon des Indépendants with the Impressionists and Symbolists. The most important Catalan landscape painter of the period. Responsible with Casas for the introduction of Western European influences into painting in Spain.

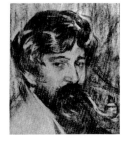

BIBLIOGRAPHY: Frances, J.: S.R. y su obra. Gerona 1945.– Pla, J.: S.R. i el

seu temps. Barcelona 1955.– Roch, H.J.: S.R. (1861-1931). Ein Beitrag zur Kunst des ausgehenden 19. Jahrhunderts in Katalonien. Doctoral thesis, Frankfurt am Main and Berlin 1983.– Rusiñol, M.: S.R. visto por su hija. Barcelona 1963
ILLUSTRATIONS:
565 A Garden in Aranjuez, 1908
567 The Kitchen of the Moulin de la Galette, c. 1890

RYSSELBERGHE Théo van
1862 Ghent – 1926 St. Clair (Var)
Studied at the Academies in Ghent and Brussels. **1881** exhibited for the first time at the Salon in Brussels. Influenced by Manet and Degas. **1883** co-founder of the group Les Vingt. Organised the exhibition with Maus and after **1893** also those of the "Libre Esthétique". **1886** travelled with the poet Emile Verhaeren to Paris. Met Seurat, admired his painting "A Sunday Afternoon at the Ile de la Grande Jatte" (pp. 260/261), and from **1887/88** turned to Pointillism, becoming the main exponent of the style in Belgium. Travelled in Spain, North Africa, the Near East and Europe. From **1897** lived in Paris. His Pointillism relaxed into a more Impressionist style of brushwork.

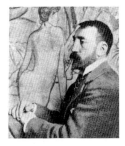

WRITINGS, DOCUMENTS: Lettres de T.v.R. à Octave Maus. In: "Bulletin des Musées Royaux de Belgique" 15 (1966), No. 1-2, pp. 55-112
BIBLIOGRAPHY: Eeckhout, P. and G. Chabot (eds): T.v.R. Museum voor Schone Kunsten, Ghent 1962 (EC).– Fierens, P.: T.v.R. Brussels 1937.– Maret, F.: T.v.R. Antwerp 1948.– Pogu, G.: T.v.R. Sa vie. (no place of publication; about 1963)
ILLUSTRATIONS:
423 Heavy Clouds, Christiania Fjord, 1893
425 Portrait of Auguste Descamps, the Painter's Uncle, 1894
426 Family in an Orchard, 1890

SAINTE-ADRESSE
Village in Normandy at the mouth of the Seine, four kilometres from Le Havre. Visited by Corot, Isabey and Jongkind. **1862** Jongkind did numerous sketches here which were to have a decisive effect on the development of Monet as an artist. **1866-1868** Monet lived here, painting the "The Beach at Sainte-Adresse" (p. 56) and the famous "Terrace at Sainte-

Adresse (p. 59). Van de Velde, Dufy and Marquet later painted beach scenes here and landscapes in the surrounding countryside.

SAINT-TROPEZ
At the end of the nineteenth century this small fishing port on the Côte d'Azur became a popular resort for sailing enthusiasts and a meeting place for writers and painters (Duran, Signac, Luce, Cross, Matisse, and others), who liked to paint in the bright light of the Mediterranean.

SALON
A regular exhibition of contemporary art, named after the Salon carré (rectangular hall) at the Royal Palace of the Louvre in Paris, where since **1667** the members of the Academy had given an annual exhibition to the king of their latest work. In 19th-century France this was the most important state-organised event for the encouragement and regularisation of artistic activity; it was imitated in other countries. The organisation and selection of the artists and their works, and the appointment or election of the jury, varied considerably. Foreign artists were also allowed to submit work.

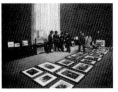

Medals and other prizes were awarded. Winners of medals were permitted to exhibit the next year without undergoing the selection process. The huge numbers of exhibits (1865: 3559, 1880: about 6000) were mostly shown in a haphazard manner, from 1857 at the Palais de l'Industrie. It was nevertheless popular with the general public (1876: c. 519,000 visitors) and was well covered in the press, for the Salon set the latest standards of artistic activity and influenced public sales and commissions, as well as the art market and the careers of individual artists. For avant-garde artists and critics the idea of "Salon painting" became a term of abuse (one still used today). **1881** the Salon was changed into the Société des artistes français. **1884** beginning of the era of Secessions in Europe, with the founding of the Indépendants with their own Salon without a jury. **1890** this movement split, with the foundation of a new Salon with jury, the Société Nationale des Beaux-Arts. **1903** founding of the Autumn Salon, which favoured the Post-Impressionists, and later the Fauves and Cubists.

SALON DES INDEPENDANTS
A French society of independent artists (Société des artistes indépendants) founded in **1884** in Paris under the

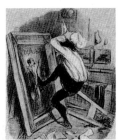

SALON
DES
ARTISTES INDÉPENDANTS
1884
Autorisé par le Ministre
des Beaux-Arts
et la Ville de Paris

BARAQUEMENT B
cour des Tuileries

du 15 Mai au 1er Juillet

presidency of Redon; organised by A. Dubois-Pillet, after an initial, chaotic exhibition without a jury. In the same year he arranged the first Salon "without a jury or prize-giving". In **1886**, shortly after the 8th Impressionist exhibition, the 2nd Salon des Indépendants was a resounding success; the Symbolists also exhibited. From then on, Salons took place every year, with increasing acclaim. The salon was opened in 1889 by the President of the city council, and in 1890 by the President of the Republic. From 1891 there were retrospectives of deceased members; foreign artists began to take part. It became an important forum for the Post-Impressionists, and later for the Fauves and Cubists etc.; imitated in other countries. Presidents: up to 1909 Valton, 1909-1934 Signac, 1934-1941 Luce.

SALON DES REFUSES
The "Salon of Rejected Artists". An exhibition set up in **1863** by Napoleon III as a liberal gesture for those artists whose work had been rejected by the Salon jury under their chairman, Count Nieuwerkerke. 1200 out of the 2300 rejected artists exhibited their work, mostly of mediocre quality, although it included pictures by Bracquemond, Cals, Cézanne, Colin, Fantin-Latour, Jongkind, Laurens, Legros, Manet, Pissarro and Whistler. Manet's "Le déjeuner sur l'herbe" (p. 36) drew over 40,000 visitors and caused a scandal, which Zola later described in his novel "L'œuvre". **1864** and **1873** this Salon was repeated, but in general it was replaced by private initiatives and group exhibitions.

SARGENT John Singer
1856 Florence – 1925 London
Son of a doctor who had emigrated
from America. First studied drawing
with the painter Carl Welsch in
Rome. 1870-1874 studied at the Accadèmia delle Belle Arti in Florence.
Continued his studies in 1874 at the
studio of Carolus-Duran in Paris.
1878 first big success at the Salon.
1879 travels in Spain, where he studied the work of Diego Velázquez.
1880-1882 lived in Holland, studied
Frans Hals. 1884 his painting "Madame Gautreau" (p. 598) caused a
scandal at the Salon. Moved to London. Formed a friendship with Whistler, whose studio he took over in
1885. 1886 co-founder of the Impressionist New English Art Club. 1888
large exhibition at the St. Botolph
Club in Boston; began in this period
to be known for his portaits. 1893-
1906 active exclusively as a portrait
painter in England and America. His
portraits have a characteristic realism,
but also follow the canons of contemporary bourgeois taste. Member in
1890 of the Legion of Honour, 1894
of the National Academy of Design in
New York and 1897 of the Royal
Academy in London. In 1907 turned
to landscape painting in water colour-
s and until 1914 painted plein-air on
the Continent. 1890-1916 series of
murals for the Boston Public Library.
1918 active as a war painter in Northern France. Drew sketches for his
monumental war painting "Gassed".
In the 1920s he executed the murals
for the Boston Museum of Fine Arts
and the Widener Library at Harvard
University.

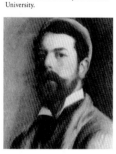

BIBLIOGRAPHY: Birnbaum, M.: J.S.S.
A Conversation Piece. New York
1941.– Charteris, E.: J.S. New York
1927.– Downes, W.H.: J.S.S. His Life
and Work. Boston 1925.– Fair-
brother, T.J.: J.S.S. and America. Doc-
toral thesis, Boston 1981.– Hills, P.
(ed.): J.S.S. Whitney Museum of
American Art, New York 1986 (EC).–
Lomax, J. and R. Ormond (eds.):
J.S.S. and the Edwardian Age. Leeds
Art Galleries, London 1979 (EC).–
McKibbin, D.: S.'s Boston. Boston
1956.– Meynell, A.: The Work of
J.S.S. London 1903.– Meynell, A.:
L'œuvre de J.S.S. Paris 1904.– Mount,
C.M.: J.S.S. A Biography. New York
1955, London 1957.– Olson, S. et al.:
S. at Broadway. The Impressionist

Years. New York and London 1986.–
Olson, S.: J.S.S. His Portrait. London
1986.– Ormond, R.: J.S.S. Oxford
1970.– Ormond, R.: J.S.S.: Paintings,
Drawings, Watercolors. New York
1970.– Ormond, R.: J.S.S. His Portraits. London 1986.– Ratcliff, C.:
J.S.S. New York 1982.– Sweet, F.A.
(ed.): S., Whistler and Mary Cassatt.
The Art Institute of Chicago, Chicago
1954 (EC)

ILLUSTRATIONS:
593 The Luxembourg Garden at Twi-
      light, 1879
597 Carnation, Lily, Lily, Rose,
      1885/86
598 Pozzi at Home, 1881
598 Portrait of Madame Gautreau
      (Study), 1884
598 Madame X (Portrait of Madame
      Gautreau), 1884
599 The Boit Daughters, 1882
604 Claude Monet Painting at the
      Edge of a Wood, 1887
608 Two Girls on a Lawn, c. 1889
609 The Boating Party, 1889
634 A Morning Walk, 1888

SCHEFFLER Karl
1869 Eppendorf – 1951 Überlingen
German art critic. Began his career as
a decorator and designer of wallpaper. 1894 started writing about the
movement for art reform as envisaged
by Ruskin and Morris; encouraged by
Meier-Graefe. 1906-1933 editor of
the journal "Kunst und Künstler"
(Art and Artists) published by B.
Cassirer. One of the most energetic
proponents of Impressionism and Secession art in Germany. Rejected Expressionism. 1944 received an honorary doctorate from the University of
Zurich.

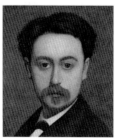

SCHUFFENECKER Claude-Emile
1851 Fresne-Saint-Mamès (Haute-
Saône) – 1934 Paris
1871 a colleague of Gauguin's – both
with the stock-broker Bertin. Attended evening courses in drawing
and took lessons with Grellet, Paul
Baudry and Carolus-Duran. Decided
to become a painter in the late 1870s.
Earned a secure living as a teacher of
art at the Lycée Michelet de Vanves.
Supported his friend Gauguin (until
1891 also financially) and introduced
him to other Impressionist painters
(Guillaumin, Pissarro). His style is
similar to that of Sisley and did not
gain the admiration of Gauguin.

1880 exhibited for the first time at
the Salon. 1883 rejected by the Salon.
1884 co-founder of the Salon des Indépendants. Friendship with Bernard.
1886 contributed to the 8th Impressionist exhibition. 1889 organised the
alternative exhibition of the Impressionists at the Café Volpini during the
World Fair. His apartment in Paris became a meeting place for the Pont-
Aven school of artists, to which his
work also belongs.
CATALOGUE: Porr, R.: C.-E.S. Catalogue raisonné (in preparation)
BIBLIOGRAPHY: C.-E.S. and the
School of Pont-Aven. Norman Mac-
kenzie Art Gallery, Regina (Saskatche-
wan) 1977 (EC).– E.S. Hirschl and
Adler Galleries, New York 1958
(EC).– E.S. Galerie des Deux-Iles,
Paris 1963 (EC).– Grossvogel, J.E.
(ed): C.-E.S., 1851-1934. State University of New York Art Gallery. Bing-
hamton (NY) 1980 (EC)
ILLUSTRATIONS:
416 A Cove at Concarneau, 1887
421 Female Nude, Seated on a Bed,
      1885

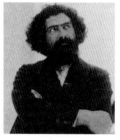

SEGANTINI Giovanni Battista
1850 Arco – 1899 Pontresina
Grew up in poverty. Trained with a
painter-decorator; 1875-1879 attended evening courses at the Brera
Academy in Milan. 1878 met Grubicy, who introduced him to Pointillism. Gave up his dark, academic
style of painting. Travelled in northern Italy. 1886 settled in Savognin.
From 1894 lived in Maloja. His favourite subjects were landscapes with
peasants, in which he combined the
close observation of nature with the
new techniques of painting. His pictures have been assigned to both Symbolism and Art Nouveau. Exhibited
in Paris, England, Germany and Austria. 1898 member of the Vienna Secession.
CATALOGUE: Arcangeli, F. and M.C.
Gozzoli: L'opera completa di G.S.
Milan 1973.– Quinsac, A.-P.: S. Catalogo generale. 2 vols. Milan 1982
BIBLIOGRAPHY: Arcangeli, F. and
M.C. Gozzoli: S. Milan 1973.– Belli,
G. (ed.): S. Palazzo delle Albere,
Milan 1987 (EC).– Budinga, L.: G.S.
Milan 1964.– Calzini, R.: S. Geneva
1947.– Nicodemi, G.: G.S. Milan
1956.– Quinsac, A.-P.: S.: Trent'
anni di vita artistica europea nei car-
teggi inediti dell'artista e dei suoi

mecenati. Oggiono 1985.– Quinsac,
A.-P.: S. Milan 1982.– Segantini, G.:
G.S. Zurich 1949.– Servaes, F.: G.S.,
sein Leben und seine Werke. Vienna
1902.– Tobler, D. and G. Magnaguagno (eds.): G.S. Kunsthaus Zürich, Zurich 1990 (EC).– Zbinden,
H.: G.S. Berne 1951
ILLUSTRATIONS:
547 Midday in the Alps (Windy
      Day), 1891
547 Ploughing, 1890

SEROV Valentin Alexandrovich
1865 St. Petersburg – 1911 Moscow
1872-1875 lived with his mother in
Munich and Paris, took art lessons
with Karl Köpping and Repin. 1875-
1880 stayed for the first time with the
Mamontow family in Abramtsevo,
went to school in Kiev and Moscow.
1880 visited and studied in Ukraine
with Repin. 1880-1885 studied at the
Academy in St. Petersburg; friendship
with Vrubel. 1885 trip to Munich
and Holland. 1886 exhibited for the
first time at an exhibition in Moscow;
stayed for the first time with his student friend Dervis in Domotkanovo.
1887 visited Vienna and Italy. 1888
received an award for the first time
from the Moscow Society for Friends
of Art. 1889 visited the World Fair in
Paris and Germany; friendship with
Korovin. 1890-1899 exhibited with
the "Wanderers" and became a member in 1894. Painted lively portraits
and landscape studies, partly plein-
air, and occasional histories; drew illustrations. 1896 exhibited for the
first time at the Munich Secession,
1898 became a member. 1897-1909
influential teacher at the Moscow
School of Art; called for the development of the "modern" in Russia.
1898 became a member of the Russian Academy. 1900-1904 worked for
the journal "World of Art" and contributed to its exhibitions. 1900 won
a distinguished award at the World
Fair in Paris for a portrait of Grand
Duke Paul. 1902 met Gorky. 1903
member of the Academy of Arts in St.
Petersburg, but refused the offer of a
teaching position; became a member
of the new Russian federation of Artists. 1904-1911 several trips to Italy,
France, Spain, England and Germany.
1905 left the Academy in St. Petersburg in protest against the shooting
of demonstrators in St. Petersburg;
drew political caricatures. 1907
visited Greece with L. Bakst; turned

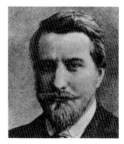

to mythological themes. **1907-1911** designed theatre sets, also in Western Europe. **1910/11** met Matisse in Paris and Moscow.
BIBLIOGRAPHY: Kopschitser, M.: V.S. Moscow 1967.– Sarabyanov, D.: V.S. Leningrad and New York 1977.– Sarabyanov, D. and G. Arbusov: V.S., Painting, Graphics and Designs of Stage Sets. Leningrad 1982.– Silberstein, E. and V. Samkov: V.S. v vospominaniyakh, dnevnikakh, i perepiske sovremennikov. Leningrad 1971
ILLUSTRATIONS:
508 The Children. Sasha and Yurra Serov, 1899
511 Girl with Peaches, 1887

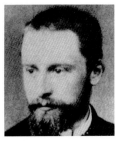

SERUSIER Paul
1864 Paris – 1927 Morlaix
1888 assistant at the private Académie Julian in Paris. At Pont-Aven, met Gauguin and the adherents of Synthetism, and mediated it to Denis, Bonnard, Vuillard. **1889** organised the Symbolist Nabis; visited Gauguin, whose depictions of Breton landscapes and peasant women influenced him considerably. **1891** under the influence of his Nabi colleague J. Verkade he began to move towards a religious and mystical conception of art. **1892** visited Pont-Aven again. **1893** with Bernard, visited Italy for the first time. **1893-1896** worked at the Lugné-Poe theatre. **1897** visited Verkade, now a monk, for the first time at Beuron monastery. **1914-1927** lived a secluded life in Brittany.
CATALOGUE: Guicheteau, M. and H. Boutaric: P.S. 2 vols. Paris 1976-1989
BIBLIOGRAPHY: Boyle-Turner, C.: P.S. Doctoral thesis, Ann Arbor (MI) 1983.– Guicheteau, P.S. Pontoise 1989
ILLUSTRATION:
320 The River Aven at Bois d'Amour (The Talisman), 1888

SEURAT Georges
1859 Paris – 1891 Paris
From a peasant family; had drawing lessons in 1875; later copied in museums. **1878/79** studied at the Ecole des Beaux-Arts; read widely on colour theory. **1880** military service; settled afterwards in Paris; concentrated for two years on dark and light drawings in chalk. **1883** accepted at the Salon; started his first large painting, an open-air scene in a new, Division-

ist and Pointillist technique. **1884** rejected by the Salon; met Signac; founded with him and others the Society of Independent Artists (Indépendants), which organised its own Salon. **1885** painted on Grand Jatte, an island in the Seine in Paris, and at Grancamp on the Normandy coast; met Pissarro, who adopted his technique of painting. **1886** won great acclaim at the 8th Impressionist exhibition; painted at Honfleur; through Durand-Ruel exhibited in New York; exhibited with Pissarro and Signac in Nantes; met the art theorist J. Henry; contacts with Symbolists and Anarchists. **1886** and subsequent years: exhibited with the Independents. **1887** exhibited with Les Vingt in Brussels, travelling there for the opening. Drew illustrations for Charpentier's journal, "La Vie moderne"; exhibited at the Théâtre Libre. **1888** painted at Port-en-Bessin, and **1889** at Crotoy beach; exhibited with Les Vingt in Brussels. **1890** painted at Gravelines; worked out his theories in writing. His arrogance threatened to split the Impressionists. **1891** exhibited once again with Les Vingt; died of diptheria. His attempt to establish a theoretical basis for painting and his strict formal discipline influenced many artists in the 20th century.
WRITINGS, DOCUMENTS: Seurat, P.: Notes sur Delacroix. Caen 1987
CATALOGUES: Chastel, A.: L'opera completa di S. Milan 1972.– Chastel, A.: Tout l'œuvre peint de S. Paris 1973.– Dorra, H. and J. Rewald: S. L'œuvre peint, biographie et catalogue critique. Paris 1959.– Grenier, C.: S. Catalogo completo dei dipinti. Florence 1990.– Grenier, C.: S. Catalogue complet des peintures. Paris 1991.– Haucke, C.-M. de: S. et son œuvre. 2 vols. Paris 1961.– Kahn, G.: Dessins. 2 vols. Paris 1920.– Minervino, F.: Das Gesamtwerk des S. Lucerne 1972.– Minervino, F.: Tout l'œuvre peint de S. Paris 1973.– Minervino, F.: L'opera completa di S. Milan 1971.– Zimmermann, M.F.: S. Sein Werk und die kunsthistorische Debatte seiner Zeit. Weinheim 1991.– Zimmermann, F.S.: S. Antwerp and London 1991.– Zimmermann, M.F.: Les mondes de S. Paris 1991
BIBLIOGRAPHY: Alexandrian, S.: G.S. New York 1980.– Bernadini, C.: S. Madrid 1982.– Broude, N. (ed.): S. in Perspective. Englewood Cliffs (NJ) 1978.– Cachin, F., R.L. Herbert et al. (eds): G.S. 1859-1891. Grand Palais, Paris; The Metropolitan Museum of Art, New York. Paris and New York 1991 (EC).– Courthion, P.: S. Cologne 1969, 1991.– Courthion, P.: S. London and New York 1968.– New York 1988.– Cousturier, L.: G.S. Paris 1969.– Cousturier, L.: G.S. Milan 1969.– Franz, E. and B. Growe (eds.): G.S. Zeichnungen. Kunsthalle Bielefeld, Munich 1983 (EC).– Fry, R. and A. Blunt: S. London 1965.– Fry, R.: S. Basle 1965.– Gould, C.: S.'s "Bathers Asnières" and the Crisis of Impressionism. London 1976.– Hautecoeur, L.: G.S. Paris 1974.– Hautecoeur, L.: G.S. Milan 1974.– Herbert, R.L.: S.'s

Drawings. New York 1962, London 1965.– Homer, W.I.: S. and the Science of Painting. Cambridge (MA) 1964, New York 1988.– Kahn, G.: The drawings of G.S. New York 1971.– Laprade, J. de: S. Paris 1951.– Lhote, A.: S. Paris 1948.– Lövgren, S.: The Genesis of Modernism. Seurat, Gauguin, van Gogh and French Symbolism in the 1880's. Uppsala 1959, Bloomington (IN) and London 1971.– Madeleine-Perdrillat, A.: S. Geneva and New York 1990.– Morris, J.: A Sunday Afternoon on the Island of La Grande Jatte, G.S. London 1979.– Perruchot, H.: La vie de S. Paris 1966.– Petránsky, L.: S. a neoimpresionizmus. Bratislava 1978.– Rewald, J.: S. New York 1943.– Rewald, J.: S. New York 1946.– Rewald, J.: S. Paris 1948.– Rewald, J.: S. A Biography. New York and London 1990.– Rich, D.C.: S. and the Evolution of "La Grande Jatte". Chicago 1935, 1969.– Rich, D.C. (ed.): S., Paintings and Drawings. The Art Institute of Chicago, Chicago 1958 (EC).– Russel, J.: S. Berlin, Darmstadt and Vienna 1968.– Russel, J.: S. London and New York 1965, 1991.– Russel, J.: S. Paris 1967.– Seligmann, G.: The Drawings of G.S. New York 1947.– Stuckey, C.F.: S. Mount Vernon and New York 1984.– Terrasse, A.: L'univers de S. Paris 1976.– Thomson, R.: S. Oxford 1985.– Wotte, H.: G.S. Wesen, Werk, Wirkung. Dresden 1988.– Zahn, L.: S. Cologne and Vienna 1967

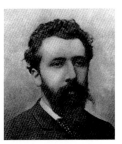

ILLUSTRATIONS:
254 Horses in the Seine (Study for "Bathers at Asnières"), c. 1883/84
254 Bather (Study for "Bathers at Asnières"), c. 1883/84
254 Bathers at Asnières, c. 1883/84
255 Echo (Study for "Bathers at Asnières"), 1883/84
255 Seated Youth with Straw Hat (Study for "Bathers at Asnières"), 1883/84
255 The Leg (Study for "Bathers at Asnières"), 1883/84
256 Watering Can, 1883
256 Houses at Le Raincy, c. 1882
258 L'Ile de la Grande Jatte, 1884
259 A Sunday Afternoon on the Ile de la Grande Jatte, 1885
259 Angler (Study for "Ile de la Grande Jatte"), 1884/85
259 Couple (Study for "Ile de la Grande Jatte"), 1884–1886

259 Woman with Parasol (Study for "Ile de la Grande Jatte"), 1884/85
260 A Sunday Afternoon at the Ile de la Grande Jatte, 1884-1886
271 The Beach at Bas-Butin near Honfleur, 1886
271 Bec du Hoc, Grandcamp, 1885
272 The Lighthouse at Honfleur, 1886
273 The "Maria", Honfleur, 1886
273 The Harbour at Honfleur, 1886
298 Seated Female Nude (Study for "The Models"), c. 1886/87
298 Woman from Behind (Study for "The Models"), c. 1886/87
299 Standing Female Nude (Study for "The Models"), 1887
299 Standing Female Nude (Study for "The Models"), 1887
300 The Circus Parade, c. 1887/88
301 The Models, 1888
318 Le Chahut, c. 1889/90
318 Dancers on Stage (Study for "Le Chahut"), 1889
319 Young Woman Powdering Herself, c. 1889/90
320 Portrait of Paul Signac, 1890
328 Study for "The Circus", 1891
329 The Circus, 1891

SECESSION
Term used for groups of artists that broke away from the established organisations to hold their own exhibitions. **1884** in France the Société des artistes indépendants broke away from the Société des artistes français and organised its own Salon. In Germany and Austria (Munich **1892**, Vienna **1897**, Berlin **1898**), the term Secession was used. Similar exhibition organisations were set up in England, Scandinavia, Belgium, Eastern and South-eastern Europe. Secession art or Secession style is an imprecise collective term for Impressionist and Post-Impressionist art in the period before Expressionism and Fauvism; it also includes architecture and arts and crafts.

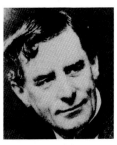

SICKERT Walter Richard
1860 Munich – 1942 Bathampton
1868 the family emigrated to London. Earned his living initially as an actor. **1881** won a scholarship to attend the Slade School of Fine Art in London. **1882** at Whistler's studio. **1883** met Degas in Paris; in Dieppe **1885** they became close friends. Influenced by Manet and Degas, who encouraged him to be meticulous in

his draughtsmanship. **1888** joined the "New English Art Club" and soon became the leading exponent of Impressionism in London. From **1885** he spent every summer in Dieppe. **1898-1905** lived permanently in Dieppe. In this period he painted almost exclusively views of either Dieppe or Venice. **1903/04** last stay in Venice. Began to paint genre scenes, which dominated his work until **1914**. From **1904** he taught at the Slade School of Fine Arts and at the Westminster Technical Institute. With Lucien Pissarro and Gore **1907-1909**, he developed a technique of painting with small, bright spots of paint applied very close to each other. **1910** rejected this method and **1913/14** developed a new technique, involving a base of two layers of paint on a coarse canvas on which areas of clear colours are then applied in layers. **1906-1914** began once again to spend regular periods in Dieppe. From **1922** he stopped travelling and stayed in England. **1934** member of the Royal Academy. His own private school developed into the "Camden Town Group", active **1911-1913**.

WRITINGS, DOCUMENTS: Stitwell, O. (ed.): A Free House: Being the Writings of W.R.S. London 1947 BIBLIOGRAPHY: Baron, W.: S. London 1973.– Bertram, A.: S. London 1955.– Browse, L.: S. London 1960.– Emmaus, R.: The Life and Opinions of W.R.S. London 1941.– Lilly, M.: S. The Painter and his Circle. London 1971.– Paintings, Drawings and Prints of W.R.S. 1860-1942. The Arts Council of Great Britain, London 1977 (EC).– Rothenstein, J.: S. London 1961.– Shone, R.: W.S. Oxford 1988.– W.R.S. Fine Art Society Ltd, London 1973 (EC).– W.R.S. Drawings and paintings 1890-1942. Liverpool 1989 (EC)

ILLUSTRATIONS:
578 Lion Comique, 1887
588 Bathers at Dieppe, c. 1902

SIGNAC Paul
1863 Paris – 1935 Paris
Son of a master harness-maker, he began to paint under the influence of Monet and Guillaumin in **1880**, instead of becoming an architect. **1883** studied at the free academy of Bing. **1884** co-founder of the Society of Independent Artists (Indépendants); friendship with Seurat, whose Divisionist, Pointillist style influenced his town and river landscapes, as well as his figural painting. Painted at Port-en-Bessin. **1886** exhibited at the 8th Impressionist exhibition, and through Durand-Ruel in New York; exhibited with Seurat and Pissarro in Nantes. He subsequently formed many new friendships, helped organise exhibitions, and wrote articles of art criticism. **1887** travelled with Seurat to Brussels and also to the Mediterranean for the first time (Collioure); drew for Charpentier's journal, "La Vie moderne", and exhibited at the Théâtre Libre. **1888** exhibited for the first time with Les Vingt in Brussels. **1889** visited van Gogh at Arles, illustrated theoretical writings by C.

Henry; politically an Anarchist. **1890** first of several trips to Italy; became the first foreign artist to join Les Vingt. **1892** married Berthe Roblès, a relative of Pissarro; sailed from Brittany to Marseilles, remaining all his life an enthusiastic sailor. His style (including watercolours), is characterised by square daubs of paint in pure, bright colours; he painted mainly views of harbours and seascapes. **1893** bought a house at Saint-Tropez, which was to become a resort and favourite of modern artists. **1896** first trip to Holland. **1899** published a book on the theory of Neo-Impressionism. **1907** trip to Constantinople. **1908** president of the Société des artistes indépendants.

WRITINGS, DOCUMENTS: Rewald, J. (ed.): P.S. Extraits du journal inédit. In: "Gazette des Beaux-Arts" 36 (1949), pp. 97- 128, 166-174, 39 (1952), 42 (1953).– Signac, P.: D'Eugène Delacroix au néo-impressionnisme. Paris 1899 (Reprint: Paris 1964, 1987)
CATALOGUE: Kornfeld, E.W. and P.A. Wick: Catalogue raisonné de l'œuvre gravé et lithographié de P.S. Berne 1974
BIBLIOGRAPHY: Besson, G.: P.S. Paris 1935.– Besson, G.: P.S. Paris 1950.– Cachin, F.: P.S. Greenwich (CT) 1971.– Cachin, F.: P.S. Paris 1971.– Cachin, F.: P.S. Milan 1970.– Cousturier, L.: P.S. Paris 1922.– Lemoyne de Forges, M.T. (ed.): Catalogue de l'exposition du centenaire de P.S. Musée du Louvre, Paris 1963 (EC).– P.S. Musée National d'Art Moderne, Paris 1951 (EC)

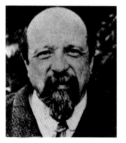

ILLUSTRATIONS:
252 Rue Caulaincourt: Mills on Montmartre, 1884
257 Outskirts of Paris: The Road to Gennevilliers, 1883
266 Two Milliners, Rue du Caire, c. 1885/86
267 The Breakfast (The Dining Room), c. 1886/87
269 The Railway at Bois-Colombes, 1886
269 Gasometers at Clichy, 1886
272 The River Bank, Petit-Andely, 1886
281 The Boulevard de Clichy under Snow, 1886
319 Woman Taking up Her Hair, 1892
321 Portrait of Félix Fénéon in Front of an Enamel of a Rhythmic

Background of Measures and Angles, Shades and Colours, 1890
366 The Papal Palace at Avignon, 1900
388 Pine Tree at Saint-Tropez, 1909

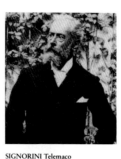

SIGNORINI Telemaco
1835 Florence – 1901 Florence
Son of the court painter to the Grand Duke of Tuscany. **1848-1852** attended the "Scuola Pié di San Giovanni degli Scolopi"; school friends included Diego Martelli and the future poet Giosué Carducci. His literary talents began to flourish in this period, and he remained active all his life as a critic, art theoretician and poet. **1852** pressurised by his father, he trained as an artist; learned to draw nudes at the Academy. **1853** became interested in landscapes and from **1854** painted plein-air with Borrani. Frequented the Caffè Michelangiolo. **1856** visited Venice, where he met Abbati. **1858** first experiments with the Macchia technique. **1859** military service in the Second War of Independence. Spent the summer of **1860** painting in the open-air at La Spezia. **1861** travelled to Paris; visited the Salon. Became very interested in the work of Corot, Décamps and Daubigny. In Florence; joined with Lega, Abbati, Borrani and Sernesi to form the Piagentina school. In the early 1870s he became friends with Degas and was influenced by him. Travelled in **1869** to Paris, **1873/74** to France, **1881** to England and Scotland, **1884** again to Paris and London. **1892** appointed professor at the "Istituto Superiore di Magistero Femminile" in Florence.

WRITINGS, DOCUMENTS: Signorini, T.: Silvestro Lega. Florence 1895
BIBLIOGRAPHY: Franchi, A.: G. Fattori, S. Lega, T.S. Milan 1953.– Masini, L.-V.: T.S. Florence 1983.– Ojetti, U.: T.S. Milan 1911, Rome 1930.– Somarè M.: T.S. Milan 1926, Bergamo 1931
ILLUSTRATIONS:
539 The Suburb of Porta Adriana, Ravenna, 1875
544 Insane Ward at San Bonifacio's, Florence, c. 1866/67

SILVESTRE Armand
1837 Paris – 1901 Toulouse
Civil servant at the Ministry of Finance, technologist, writer and journalist. On completion of his technical

studies joined the writers in Montparnasse. Frequented the Café Guerbois and the Café de la Nouvelle-Athènes and in his journals and catalogue articles became one of the first proponents of Impressionism.

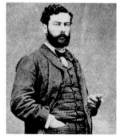

SISLEY Alfred
1839 Paris – 1899 Moret-sur-Loing
Son of well-to-do English parents in London; intended to make a career in business; **1857-1862** began to draw. **1862/63** studied at the Atelier Gleyre in Paris with Monet, Renoir and Bazille. **1863** early attempts at plein-air painting with his friends at Chailly-en-Bière near Barbizon. **1865** worked with Renoir, Monet and Pissarro at Marlotte and with Renoir on a boat on the Seine. **1866** exhibited for the first time at the Salon, married Marie Lescouezec; the couple had two children. **1867** rejected by the Salon; with others called for the founding of a "Salon des Refusés"; painted at Honfleur. **1868** spent periods with Renoir at Chailly and exhibited at the Salon. **1869** rejected by the Salon; frequented the Café Guerbois. **1870** showed Impressionist pictures at the Salon. **1871** stayed at Voisins-Louveciennes during the Commune; Durand-Ruel exhibited one of his pictures in London. **1872** Durand-Ruel began to buy regularly from him. In the following period, he painted Impressionist river landscapes and village scenes (also in the snow) at Argenteuil, Bougival and Louveciennes. **1874** exhibited at the first Impressionist exhibition; travelled to England at the expense of J.-B. Faure, the singer and art collector. **1875-1877** lived at Mary-le-Roi. **1875** a disastrous auction sale of pictures at

the Hôtel Drouot with Renoir and others. **1876** and **1877** exhibited at the 2nd and 3rd Impressionist exhibitions; auctioned more pictures. Moved to Sèvres, supported by the hotelier Murer and the publisher Charpentier. **1878/79** dire poverty; a few purchases arranged by Duret. **1879** rejected by the Salon; did not exhibit at the 4th – 6th Impressionist exhibitions. **1880-1882** lived at Veneux-Nadon with Moret. **1881** first one-man exhibition at Charpentier's journal, "La Vie moderne". **1882** exhibited at the 7th Impressionist exhibition; settled in Moret-sur-Loing. **1883** one-man exhibition without success at Durand-Ruel's; moved to Sablons. **1885** exhibited at Durand-Ruel's in London, Boston, Rotterdam and Berlin. **1887** contributed to an exhibition at G. Petit's. **1888** exhibited with Renoir and Pissarro at Durand-Ruel's. **1889** individual exhibition by Durand-Ruel in New York; moved for the last time to Moret, remaining to the end an exponent of pure Impressionist landscape painting. **1890** elected a member of the "Nationale"; subsequently exhibited in their Salon. **1893/94** painted some of his best picture series (the idea was borrowed from Monet). **1894** painted in Normandy as a guest of the art collectors Murer and Depeaux. **1897** large retrospective at G. Petit's met with little success with the critics and collectors; painted on the English coast. **1898** seriously ill with cancer; had no money to apply for French citizenship. At the posthumous auction of his work in **1899** the prices for his pictures began to rise drastically. **1911** the first memorial for an Impressionist was built for him at Moret.
WRITINGS, DOCUMENTS: Graber, H.: Camille Pissarro, A.S., Claude Monet nach eigenen und fremden Zeugnissen. Basle 1943
CATALOGUE: Daulte, F.: A.S. Catalogue raisonné de l'œuvre peint. Lausanne 1959
BIBLIOGRAPHY: Cogniat, R.: A.S. Paris 1978, 1981.– Cogniat, R.: A.S. New York 1978.– Couldrey, V.: A.S. The English Impressionist. London 1992.– Daulte, F.: Les paysages de Sisley. Lausanne 1961.– Daulte, F.: S., paysage. Paris 1961.– Daulte, F.: S. Munich 1975.– Daulte, F.: The Impressionists: A.S. London 1988.– Francastel, P.: Monet, S., Pissarro. Geneva 1974.– Gache-Patin, S. and J. Lassaigne: S. Paris 1983.– Gale, I.: S. London 1992.– Jedlicka, G.: S. Berne 1949.– Jedlicka, G.: S. Milan 1950.– Lloyd, C. et al. (eds): A.S. Isetan Museum of Art (Tokyo) et al., Tokyo 1985 (EC).– Nathason, R. (ed.): A.S. London 1981 (EC).– Scharf, A.: A.S. London 1986.– Shone, R.: S. London 1992.– Stevens, M.-A. (ed.): A.S. Royal Academy of Arts, London; Musée d'Orsay, Paris; The Walters Art Gallery, Baltimore; London 1992 (EC)
ILLUSTRATIONS:
84   First Snow at Louveciennes, c. 1870/71
84   The Saint Martin Canal in Paris, 1870

96   The Saint Martin Canal, 1872
96   The Island of Saint-Denis, 1872
97   The Bridge at Villeneuve-la-Garenne, 1872
98   The Saint Martin Canal in Paris, 1870
98   Landscape at Louveciennes, 1873
99   Villeneuve-la-Garenne on the River Seine, 1872
142   The Regatta at Molesey, 1874
158   Louveciennes, 1876
159   Flood at Port-Marly, 1876
159   Market Place at Marly, 1876
172   The Seine at Suresnes, 1877
183   Snow at Louveciennes, 1878
313   Moret-sur-Loing in Morning Sun, 1888
339   The Bridge at Moret, 1893

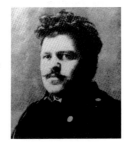

SLAVÍČEK Antonín
1870 Prague – 1910 Prague
1886/87 study trip to Munich. **1887-1889** studied with J. Mařák at the Academy of Arts in Prague. **1899** stayed at the Benedictine monastery of Gross Raigern (Moravia). **1890-1893** painted landscapes near Altbunzlau. **1891** exhibited with other pupils of Mařák in Prague. **1892-1897** joined the Association of Artists. **1894-1899** studied once again with Mařák at the Academy; painted in an Impressionist style. **1897** exhibited for the first time at the Prague Society of Fine Arts and in Vienna. **1898** began to exhibit regularly with the Mánes group of artists. **1899** became the successor of Mařák at the Academy. **1900** views of Prague became his favourite theme. **1907/08** travelled on a stipend to Paris. Became ill in **1909**, went for treatment to Dubrovnik.
BIBLIOGRAPHY: A.S. 1870-1910. Varech 1980 (EC).– Kotalík, J.: A.S., 1870-1910. Soupis díla (Czech), Prague 1965 (with catalogue).– Tomes, J.: A.S. Prague 1973
ILLUSTRATIONS:
516   Walking in the Park, 1897
518   Elizabeth Bridge, Prague, 1906

SLEVOGT Max
1868 Landshut – 1932 Neukastel
1884-1890 studied at the Academy of Fine Arts in Munich with Johann Herterich and Wilhelm Diez. Influenced by Wilhelm Leibl and Trübner. **1889** travelled to Paris and studied French Impressionism at the Académie Julian. **1890** tour of Italy. **1893** member

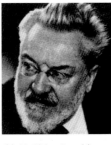

of the Munich Secession and the "Freie Vereinigung" (Free Association); **1896** worked for the journal "Simplicissimus". Through Leistikow, came into contact with the Berlin Secession. **1900** travelled to the World Fair in Paris. **1901** stayed in Frankfurt am Main, where he painted his famous brightly coloured zoo pictures. From **1901** in Berlin, working mainly as a portrait painter. Held a master class at the Academy. **1914** visited Egypt and painted landscapes in the bright sunlight. **1915** went to Belgium as a war artist. After **1918** lived in Neukastel in the Palatinate. In the 1920s returned to religious themes with his graphic cycle "Passion". Did 500 illustrations for an edition of Goethe's "Faust". **1924** murals for the concert hall at Neukastel and in Berlin, **1927** in Bremen and **1932** in the Friedenskirche Church at Ludwigshafen. **1924** did the stage design for "Don Giovanni" at the Dresden Opera.
CATALOGUE: Waldmann, E. and J. Sievers: M.S. Das druckgraphische Werk 1890-1914. Heidelberg and Berlin 1962 (Reprint: San Francisco 1992)
BIBLIOGRAPHY: Imiela, H.-J.: M.S. Karlsruhe 1967.– M.S. Saarland Museum, Saarbrücken; Rheinisches Landesmuseum, Mainz; Saarbrücken 1992 (EC).– Roland, B.: M.S. Pfälzische Landschaften. Munich 1991.– Scheffler, K.: M.S. Berlin 1940.– Voll, K.: M.S. Munich and Leipzig 1912.– Waldmann, E.: M.S. Berlin 1923.– Weber, W.: Die religiösen Werke von M.S. Kaiserslautern 1966
ILLUSTRATIONS:
447   Dance of Death, 1896
452   Man with Parrots, 1901
454   The Alster at Hamburg, 1905
458   Garden at Neu-Cladow, 1912
461   Steinbart Villa, Berlin, 1911
462   Portrait of Mrs. C., 1917

SLEWIŃSKI Władysław
1854 Białynin a.d. Pilica – 1918 Paris
1888-1905 after a short period of lessons with W. Gerson at the Warsaw School of Drawing, he studied in Paris at the Académie Julian and the Académie Colarossi. **1889** with Gauguin for the first time at Pont-Aven, began to exhibit Impressionism-inspired and Synthetist landscapes and pictures of poor and simple people at Paris and Warsaw. **1905-1910** in Cracow and Poronin (Carpathians).

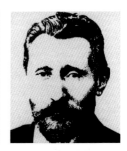

Travelled extensively, including Munich. **1910-1918** in Paris and Brittany.
CATALOGUE: Jaworska, W.: W.S., Warsaw 1983
BIBLIOGRAPHY: W.S. Museum narodowe, Warsaw 1983 (EC)
ILLUSTRATION:
515   Rough Sea at Belle-Ile, 1904

SOCIETE ANONYME DES ARTISTES
Otherwise known as Société anonyme coopérative des artistes- peintres, sculpteurs, graveurs etc. Founded on 27 December, 1873 in Paris, an officially registered society with about 30 members and a statute on the model of the Association of Bakers at Pontoise. The society was publicised in Durand-Ruel's gallery journal and in other periodicals. Its aim was to hold a group exhibition, financed by the membership fee (at least 60 francs annually) and 10% of the takings from the sale of work. It organised an exhibition, which began on 15th April 1874; this is now regarded as the first Impressionist exhibition. A financial failure, the society soon split into factions and folded on 17 December 1874.

SOMM Henry
1844 Rouen – 1907 Paris
Real name: François Clément Sommier. Pupil at the School of Drawing in Rouen with Gustave Morin and Pils. Active as a cartoonist, graphic artist and caricaturist for several journals. **1879** exhibited at the 4th Impressionist exhibition. **1890** met Toulouse-Lautrec, very impressed by his sketches of daily life. Worked for the Haviland d'Auteuil studio of which Bracquemond was artistic director.
ILLUSTRATIONS:
263   The Red Overcoat
263   Stylish Ladies in the Street

SOROLLA Y BASTIDA Joaquín
1863 Valencia – 1923 Cercedilla (Madrid)
Trained initially as a smith, then became the pupil of one of his uncles. **1875** studied at the San Carlos Academy in Valencia. **1878** and **1882** received awards. **1884** married the daughter of his patron, García, a photographer. Studied the art of Diego Velázquez. **1884/85** travelled on a stipend to Rome, Assisi and Paris. Influenced by the Realism of Morelli. In Spain in **1887** his pictures

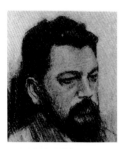

caused a scandal. Later exhibited with great success in Madrid, Berlin, Munich, Vienna and Paris. 1906 exhibited at the Galerie Petit in Paris. 1909 an exhibition in New York led to several portrait commissions in America.
BIBLIOGRAPHY: Anderson, R.M.: Costumes Painted by S. in his Provinces of Spain. Hispanic Society of America. New York 1957.– Eight Essays on J.S. y B. Hispanic Society of America. 2 vols. New York 1909.– Pantorba, B. de: La vida y la obra de J.S. Madrid 1953.– Peel, E. (ed.): The Painter J.S. y B. Instituto Valenciano de Arte Moderno, Centro Julio González, Valencia; San Diego Museum of Art, San Diego; London 1989 (EC)
ILLUSTRATIONS:
560 The Beach at Valencia
561 Selling the Catch at Valencia, 1903

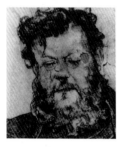

STANISLAWSKI Jan
1860 Olszany (Ukraine) – 1907 Cracow
1884/85 studied at the School of Art in Cracow, after studying mathematics and technology and attending the School of Drawing under W. Gerson in Warsaw. 1885-1888 in Paris, studied at the Academy with Carolus-Duran. 1890 at the Salon of the Société Nationale. 1896-1898 helped with the work on some panorama pictures in Russia and Germany. 1897 co-founder of the association "Art" (Sztuka). Professor of landscape painting at the College of Art in Cracow, a leading figure in the artistic life of the city and in the "Young Poland" movement. Numerous trips to Paris, Vienna, Berlin, Munich, Kiev; ex-

hibited at numerous exhibitions at home and abroad.
BIBLIOGRAPHY: W. Juszczak: J.S., Warsaw 1972.– Stepnowska, T.: J.S. Warsaw 1976
ILLUSTRATION:
513 Poplars beside the River, 1900

STARR Sidney
1857 Kingston upon Hull (Yorkshire) – 1925 New York
Studied at the Slade School of Fine Arts in London with Poynter and Legros. 1874 won a scholarship. 1882 met Whistler, whose style influenced him. From the middle of the 1870s, he exhibited at the Society of British Artists. 1882-1886 exhibitions at the Royal Academy. 1886 founder member of the New English Art Club. In the same year, elected a member of the Royal Academy. 1889 exhibited at the English Impressionist exhibition, Galerie Goupil, and at the World Fair in Paris, where he won a medal. 1892 left England due to a scandal and settled in New York. 1896 did the decorative painting for the Grace Chapel in New York and the Library of Congress, Washington.
ILLUSTRATION:
579 The City Atlas, c. 1888/89

STEER Philip Wilson
1860 Birkenhead – 1942 London
Son of a landscape and portrait painter. 1878-1881 studied at the College of Art in Gloucester and at the Art Training School. 1882/83 studied at the Académie Julian in Paris with Bouguereau and 1883/84 at the Ecole des Beaux-Arts under Cabanel. Influenced by French Impressionism (Monet, Whistler) and Pointillism. 1884 returned to England. 1886 founder member of the New English Art Club. 1889 exhibited with the English Impressionists and 1889-1894 with Les Vingt in Brussels. 1893-1930 professor at the Slade School of Fine Arts. 1894 individual exhibition at the Galerie Goupil. 1895 returned to the tradition of the English landscape painters of the early 19th century (Turner, Constable). 1918 official war painter. In the last years of the War turned to water colours.

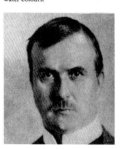

CATALOGUE: Yockney, A.: S. Catalogue Raisonné. London 1945
BIBLIOGRAPHY: Ironside, R.: W.S. London 1943.– Laughton, B.: P.W.S.

1860-1942. Oxford 1971.– MacColl, D.S.: Life, Work and Setting of P.W.S. London 1945.– Munro, J. (ed.): P.W.S. 1860-1942.– P.W.S. The Arts Council of Great Britain, London 1960 (EC)
ILLUSTRATIONS:
575 Young Woman on the Beach, Walberswick, c. 1886-1888
575 Girl Running, Walberswick Pier, c. 1890-1894
581 Summer at Cowes, 1888

STEVENS Alfred
1823 Blandford – 1906 London
Lived and worked most of his life in Paris. 1844 after an initial training in his home town with Navez, a pupil of David, he studied with Ingres at the Ecole des Beaux-Arts. 1849-1852 in Brussels, where he first exhibited in 1851. 1852 settled in Paris. Influenced by Courbet, he formed friendships with Delacroix, Baudelaire and above all Manet, in whose studio he met Bazille; frequent customer at the Café Guerbois. Had contacts at the court of Napoleon III. A successful painter of the daily life of the well-to-do bourgeoisie. Inspired compositions with a sensitive feeling for colour tone and subject matter. One of the first, with Bracquemond, to become interested in East Asian art. 1870/71 with Manet and Degas in the National Guard. Close friendship with Morisot. Gave courses in painting for ladies. 1882 co-founder of the international art exhibitions of the Petit Gallery. 1886 rejected Pointillism; published the book "Impressions sur la peinture". 1889 with H. Gervex painted the "Panorama of the 19th century" for the Paris World Fair. 1895/96 in Belgium. 1900 large retrospective in Paris. Linked to the Impressionist movement not through the treatment of light or his style of painting but rather through the unique sense of movement in his composition and his feeling for the everyday, fleeting moment.

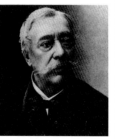

BIBLIOGRAPHY: A.S. Centenary Exhibition. Victoria and Albert Museum, London 1975 (EC).– Coles, W.A. (ed.): A.S. The University of Michigan, Museum of Art. Ann Arbor 1977 (EC).– Towndrow, K.R.: The Works of A.S., Sculptor, Painter, Designer. Tate Gallery, London 1950 (EC)
ILLUSTRATION:
199 Family Scene, c. 1880

STRYDONCK Guillaume van
1861 Namsos (Norway) – 1937 Saint-Gilles (near Brussels)
Studied at the Academy in Brussels and with E. Agneessens. Co-founder of Les Vingt. 1886 trip to Florida. His realistic style, characterised by its large brush-strokes, increasingly acquired aspects of Impressionist painting as he began to tackle the effects of light. 1887-1890 painted in Machelen und Blankenberge. 1891-1895 lived in India. 1895 settled in Weert sur l'Escaut, where the Flemish landscape became his major theme. From 1900 he taught at the Academy in Brussels.
ILLUSTRATION:
420 The Oarsmen, 1889

SUISSE → Académie Suisse

SUZOR-COTE Marc-Aurèle de Foy
1869 Arthabaska (Québec) – 1937
Initial training as a church painter. 1891 began his studies in Paris at the Ecole des Beaux-Arts under Bonnat. At first he painted mainly still lifes in the academic tradition. From 1893 came under the influence of Impressionism. His compact treatment of figures belongs in the Millet tradition. 1897-1907 second stay in Paris. Attended the Académies Colarossi and Julian. 1907 returned to Canada. Thereafter his painting remained heavily indebted to French Impressionism. Often painted the same landscape scene in varying qualities of light and at different times of the day, particularly scenes of rivers in winter. 1913 exhibited at the Canadian Art Club, where he became a member in 1914.
BIBLIOGRAPHY: Jouvancourt, H. de: S.-C. Montreal 1978.– Ostiguy, J.-R.: M.-A.d.F.S.-C. Winter Landscape. Ottawa 1978
ILLUSTRATION:
626 Port-Blanc in Brittany, 1906

SYMBOLISM
A literary (Mallarmé) and artistic movement of the last years of the nineteenth century ("Fin de siècle"), first publicised in a manifesto of 1886 by the poet J. Moréas. The movement was more a philosophical approach than a stylistic unity, a sense of crisis and a deep-felt distrust of the worship of progress and the belief in the ability of materialistic science to understand and control the natural world and human society. It led to a reaction against the realistic, naturalistic and Impressionist depiction of the visible world and to a halting, subjective concern to grasp the ineffable meaning and purpose "behind" things. There was a strong religious and mystical component to this Neo-Idealism, which included a revival of Romantic conceptions. In France, there was a simultaneous movement to combine Symbolism with decorative and primitive art. Initiated by A. Aurier in 1891, it was developed by Gauguin and the Pont-Aven school, and the Nabis; it is also seen in certain features of van Gogh's style. The movement attracted remarkable individualists such as Moreau, Puvis de Chavannes, Rops,

Redon, the English Pre-Raphaelites and Böcklin. It found a following in Belgium, Holland, Italy, Scandinavia, and German-speaking and Eastern European countries. It had a significant influence on the form and critical appreciation of Neo-Impressionism and of Monet's later works.

SZINYEI MERSE Pál
1845 Szinye-Ujfalu (Svina, Slovakia) – 1920 Jernye (Jarovnice, Slovakia)
Began to paint in 1862. 1864-1869 studied at the Munich Academy with A. Wagner and with Piloty; had contact with Leibl and G. Max. Regular stays at Jernye; finally turned to plein-air figural painting. 1869 met Courbet in Munich. From 1870 lived mostly on the family estate at Jernye. 1872/73 lived in Munich, making an independent contribution to European Impressionism. 1882/83 lived in Vienna; he then became disappointed with his lack of success and gave up painting for ten years, living as a landowner, and for a time as a parliamentary delegate. 1896 his contribution to plein-air painting was rediscovered and he was celebrated as a national hero; he began to paint again, mainly landscapes. Exhibited at the World Fair in Paris in 1900 and in St. Louis in 1904. 1905 Rector of the School of Art in Budapest. 1907 member of the committee of the new "Group of Hungarian Impressionists and Naturalists".

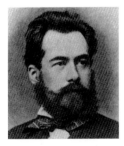

CATALOGUE: P.S.M. Budapest 1943
BIBLIOGRAPHY: Bernáth, M.: P.S.M. Budapest 1981.– Kampis, A.: P.S.M. Budapest 1975.– Kontha, S.: Páal Mészöly, Szinyei. Budapest 1975.– Pataky, D.: P.S.M. Budapest 1965.– Rajna, M.: P.S.M. Budapest 1953.– Szinyei Merse, A.: Bildgattungen und Themen im Jugendwerk von P.S.M. In: "Acta Historiae Artium" 27 (1981), No. 3-4, pp.287-361.– Végvári, L.: P.S.M. Budapest 1986
ILLUSTRATIONS:
500 A Field of Poppies, 1902
520 The Balloon, 1878
523 Luncheon on the Grass (The Picnic), 1873
523 A Field of Poppies, 1896

TANGUY Julien-François
1825 Plédran – 1894 Paris
Known as "Père Tanguy". At first a plasterer, then a butcher. 1870 moved to Paris, where he initially sold paint and then worked from 1870 as an art dealer. Took his paints to the painters, including Monet, Renoir and Pissarro, visiting them in the open-air and advising them as they painted. Anarchist and Communarde. Condemned and deported to Brest. 1873 returned to Paris and opened a shop in the Rüe Clauzel, where he also exhibited. Took pictures from the Impressionist artists in exchange for supplies of paints and canvas. Particularly supported Cézanne; exhibited the less accessible work of young Post-Impressionists. 1886 became friends with van Gogh, who painted his portrait (p.293). His shop became a meeting place for young artists, who could exchange ideas with older colleagues: Cézanne, Gauguin, Pissarro, Guillaumin, van Gogh, Seurat. He died of cancer. To raise money for his widow, the remaining paintings and other presents given him by the artists were auctioned at the Hôtel Drouot in 1894, although with only moderate results.

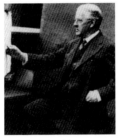

TARBELL Edmund Charles
1862 West Groton (MA) – 1938 New Castle
1877-1879 trained as a graphic artist with Forbes Lithographic Co. 1879 studied at the Boston Museum School under Otto Grundmann. Became friends with Hale; admired Fortuny. In the 1880s he travelled extensively in Europe, including Germany and Italy; stayed for a long period in Venice. 1884/85 studied at the Académie Julian in Paris. 1886 exhibited at the Salon. 1886 joined the Society of American Artists. 1888 returned to America. 1889-1912 professor at the school of the Museum of Fine Arts in Boston. 1891 first one-man show at the St. Botolph Club in Boston. 1893 exhibited at the World Fair in Chicago. 1897 member of "The Ten American Painters". 1900 a big success at the World Fair in Paris. 1906 member of the National Academy. 1918-1926 Director of the Corcoran School of Art in Washington.
BIBLIOGRAPHY: Olney, S.F. (ed.): Two American Impressionists: Frank W. Benson and E.C.T. University Art Galleries, University of New Hampshire, Durham (NH) 1979 (EC).– Pierce, P.J.: E.C.T. and The Boston School of Painting 1889-1980. Hingham (MA) 1980.– Price, L. and F. Coburn (eds):

Frank W. Benson, E.C. T. Museum of Fine Arts, Boston 1938 (EC)
ILLUSTRATION:
616 Three Sisters – A Study in June Sunlight, 1890

THORE Théophile
1824 La Flèche – 1869 Paris
Known as Wilhelm Bürger. French art critic and art historian. With views based on Romanticism, and as an admirer of Delacroix, he believed in a strong social role for art. 1848 active participant in the revolution; until 1860 in exile in Germany and Holland, writing under the pseudonym of Wilhelm Bürger. Placed the Dutch painters of the 17th century higher than Raphael and the Classicists; a proponent of the realism of the Barbizon school, of Courbet and of the young Renoir.

TILLOT Charles Victor
1825 Rouen – 1895 Rouen
1839 studied at the Ecole des Beaux-Arts in Paris. 1846 exhibited for the first time at the Salon. From 1851 also an art critic. 1860 bought a house in Barbizon; studied with Millet and Th. Rousseau. Friendship with Degas and the Rouart brothers; collected Japanese prints. 1876-1886 exhibited at all the Impressionist exhibitions except the 1st and 7th, mainly landscapes and sea scenes in the style of the Barbizon school. 1895 retrospective at the Durand-Ruel gallery.
ILLUSTRATION:
264 Still Life with Flowers

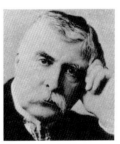

TISSOT James
1836 Nantes – 1902 Château-de-Buillon (Doubs)
1857 studied at the Ecole des Beaux-Arts in Paris; made friends with Degas, Whistler, and the writer Daudet. 1858 visited the history painter Leys in Antwerp. 1859 exhibited for the first time at the Salon – some Late Romantic-style history pictures. 1862 influenced by Japanese prints. Tour of Italy. 1863 went for a time to London, where he exhibited from 1864 at the Royal Academy. Influenced by Manet, he began to use Impressionist techniques of colour and composition. A great success with his anecdotal and detailed pictures; also influenced by the Japanese style. 1871 service in the National Guard and participation in the Com-

mune; emigrated to England. Refused to take part in Impressionist exhibitions. 1875 travelled with Manet to Venice. 1882 returned to Paris. 1883 successful exhibition, which included arts and crafts. 1883-1885 a series of 15 pictures of typical Parisian women. 1886 began to paint biblical themes. 1886/87 and 1889 travelled in Palestine. 1889 received a gold medal at the World Fair in Paris.
BIBLIOGRAPHY: J.T. Etchings, Drypoints and Mezzotints. Bury Street Gallery, London 1981 (EC).– J.T. Biblical Paintings. The Jewish Museum, New York 1982 (EC).– Matyjyszkiewicz, K. (ed.): J.T. London 1984 (EC).– Wentworth, M.: J.T. Oxford 1984.– Wood, C.: T. London 1988
ILLUSTRATIONS:
241 Berthe, 1883
241 The Newspaper, 1883
251 The Painters and their Wives, c. 1885

TOOROP Jan Theodorus
1858 Porworedjo (Java) – 1928 The Hague
Son of a Dutch official stationed on Java and the painter Charley Toorop. 1871 first lessons in drawing at The Hague. 1876-1878 studied at the technical college in Delft, 1878-1880 at the Academy in Amsterdam with A. Allébé, and 1880-1882 at the Academy in Brussels. Influenced by Courbet and Ensor. 1884 met Whistler and Matthijs Maris in London and joined the Belgian group of artists, Les Vingt; exhibited there regularly. 1885 stay in Paris; impressed by Seurat, he began to paint in the Pointillist manner. 1886 moved to The Hague. From 1891 active for the "Kunstkring" at The Hague. 1892 organised the first large van Gogh exhibition in Holland. In the 1890s he mainly painted in a Symbolist style. The most important exponent of Dutch Luminism, a technique that uses the juxtaposition of wide daubs of paint to give the effect of a mosaic. 1911 president of the "Moderne Kunstkring". Converted to Catholicism in 1905, after which he painted religious and mythical pictures.
WRITINGS, DOCUMENTS: Janssen, M.: Herinnerungen aan J.T. Amsterdam 1933
BIBLIOGRAPHY: Hefting, V: J.T. Een kennismaking. Amsterdam 1989.– Hefting, V. (ed.): J.T. 1858-1928.

Haags Gemeentemuseum 1989. The Hague 1989 (EC).– Janssen, M.: J.T. Amsterdam 1915.– J.T. 1858-1928. Impressionniste, Symboliste, Pointilliste. Institut Néerlandais. Paris 1977 (EC).– J.T. 1858-1928. Haags Gemeentemuseum. The Hague 1989 (EC).– J.T.T. De jaren 1885 tot 1919. Rijksmuseum Kröller-Müller. Otterlo 1978 (EC).– Siebelhoff, R.: The Early Development of J.T., 1879-1892. Doctoral thesis, Toronto 1973
ILLUSTRATIONS:
414 Shell Gathering on the Beach, 1891
414 The Dunes and Sea at Zoutlande, 1907
415 Three Women with Flowers, c. 1885/86

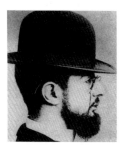

TOULOUSE-LAUTREC Henri de 1864 Albi – 1901 Castle Malromé (Gironde)
Born at Albi into an old southern French aristocratic family; already physically weak, he broke both his legs in 1878 and 1879, after which he was crippled and remained a dwarf; already active artistically. 1882-1886 studied with F. Cormon, at whose studio he met Bernard and van Gogh; painted realistic pictures of social criticism in bright Impressionist colours, and began to frequent the bars and dance halls of Montmartre and to exhibit pictures there. All his life he spent every summer by the sea. 1886 temporary liaison with the model Suzanne Valadon; first publication of his drawings in journals. 1887 contributed pictures to an exhibition at Toulouse. 1888 exhibited for the first time with Les Vingt in Brussels. Theo van Gogh from the Galerie Goupil bought a picture. 1889 exhibited for the first time at the Salon des Indépendants. Became a regular at the "Moulin Rouge". 1890 with Signac in Brussels for an exhibition of Les Vingt and then in Spain. 1891 exhibited with Impressionists and Symbolists at the art dealer's Le Barc de Boutteville; began to paint a new style of poster for bars, cabarets and publishing houses with a stylised, flat treatment of forms. 1892 visited Brussels and London. 1893 first large exhibition at the Galerie Goupil; also other exhibitions. Began to live for a time in a brothel in order to paint and draw. 1894-1897 travelled in France, Belgium, Holland, Spain, London, Lis-

bon. Exhibited at the Salon of the "Libre Esthétique" in Brussels; mixed with the circle of artists around the Nabis and the journal "La Revue Blanche"; became increasingly alcoholic. 1899 after collapsing he was taken to the the mental hospital at Neuilly, despite the protests of friends; continued to paint and to drink. 1901 became partly paralysed; died at his mother's castle.
WRITINGS, DOCUMENTS: Rodat, C. de: T.-L.; Album de famille. Fribourg 1985.– Schimmel, H.D. (ed.): The Letters of H. de T.-L. Oxford 1991
CATALOGUES: Adhémar, J.: T.-L. Lithographies. Paris 1965.– Adriani, G.: T.-L. Das graphische Werk. Cologne 1976.– Adriani, G.: T.-L. The Complete Graphic Works. London 1988.– Dortu, M.-G.: T.-L. et son œuvre. 6 vols. Paris 1971.– Sugana, G.M. and G. Caproni: The Complete Paintings of T.-L. New York 1973, Harmondsworth 1987.– Wittrock, W.: T.-L. The Complete Prints. 2 vols. London 1985
BIBLIOGRAPHY: Adriani, G.: T.-L., Gemälde und Bildstudien. Cologne 1986.– Barbier, L. (ed.): T.-L. Album de jeunesse. Berne 1985.– Bouret, J.: T.-L. London 1964.– Castleman, R. and W. Wittrock (eds): H. de T.-L. Bilder der Belle Epoque. Munich 1985 (EC).– Castleman, R. and W. Wittrock (Ed.): H. de T.-L. Images of the 1890s. The Museum of Modern Art. New York 1985 (EC).– Cooper, D.: H. de T.-L. New York 1966.– Denvir, B.: T.-L. London. 1991.– Dortu, G. and P. Huisman: L. par L. Lausanne 1964.– Jourdain, F. and J. Adhémar: T.-L. Paris 1952.– Joyant, M.: T.-L. 2 vols. Paris 1926-27.– Keller, H.: H. de T.-L. Cologne 1968.– Lassaigne, J.: T.-L. Paris 1939.– Le Targat, F.: T.-L. Paris 1988.– Natanson, Th.: Un Henri de Toulouse-Lautrec. Geneva 1951.– Perruchot, H.: La vie de T.-L. Paris 1958.– Roger-Marx, C.: T.-L. Paris 1957.– Thompson, R. et al. (eds): T.-L. Hayward Gallery, London 1991; Grand Palais, Paris 1992 (EC)
ILLUSTRATIONS:
227 Young Routy, c. 1882
243 The Laundress, 1884-1886
278 Portrait of Vincent van Gogh, 1887
324 La Goulue Entering the Moulin Rouge, 1892
325 A Dance at the Moulin Rouge, 1889/90
327 Jane Avril at the Jardin de Paris, 1893
327 Aristide Bruant at his Cabaret, 1892
344 Women in a Brothel, c. 1893/94
345 The Sofa, 1895

TROUVILLE
Town on the coast of Normandy; beside Deauville, one of the most popular resorts with the French aristocracy and rich bourgeoisie. Meeting place for writers and artists (Courbet, Jongkind, Manet, Monet etc.). The beach and the sea became favourite motifs.

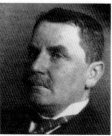

TRÜBNER Wilhelm
1851 Heidelberg – 1917 Karlsruhe
1867/68 studied with K.F. Schick at the Academy of Arts in Karlsruhe and from 1868 with A. v. Wagner at the Academy in Munich. Became acquainted with the work of the French Impressionists at the large international exhibition at the Glaspalast. 1869 became a private pupil of Hans Canon for a short time in Stuttgart. 1870 returned to Munich and studied with Wilhelm von Diez at the Academy in Munich. 1871 met Leibl, who advised him to leave the Academy; he joined the circle of Realist painters in Munich. 1872/73 travelled with Carl Schuch in Italy. 1873 went to Brussels and then to the Chiemsee; from 1890 frequently spent the summer months there. 1875-1884 lived in Munich and painted in 1876 with Schuch in Weßling and Bernried. Travelled to Paris in 1879 and to London in 1884. In the 1890s the dark tones of his palette were replaced by the brighter colours of a more Impressionist-orientated style. 1894 member of the Munich Secession. 1896 became a teacher at the Städelsches Kunstinstitut in Frankfurt. 1903-1907 professor at the Academy in Karlsruhe.
WRITINGS, DOCUMENTS: Trübner, W.: Personalien und Prinzipien. Berlin 1918
CATALOGUE: Rohrandt, K.: W.T. Kritischer und beschreibender Katalog sämtlicher Gemälde, Zeichnungen und Druckgraphik, Biographie und Studien zum Werk. Vol 1. Doctoral thesis, Kiel 1974
BIBLIOGRAPHY: Beringer, J.A.: W.T. Stuttgart and Berlin 1917.– Geissler, J.: Die Kunsttheorien von Adolf Hildebrand, W.T. and Max Liebermann. Doctoral thesis, Berlin 1963.– T. Gemälde und Zeichnungen. Berlin 1962 (EC).– T. in Heidelberg. Heidelberger Kunstverein 1967 (EC).– W.T. Gedächtnisausstellung. Kurpfälzisches Museum. Heidelberg 1951 (EC)
ILLUSTRATIONS:
449 The Pub on the Fraueninsel, 1891
461 Neuburg Gates, Heidelberg, 1913

TSCHUDI Hugo von
1851 Jakobsdorf (Austria) – 1911 Cannstadt
Swiss art historian. After graduation in law and a period of travel he be-

came an assistant at the Museum of Art and Industry in Vienna and in 1884 assistant at the museums in Berlin. 1894 professor. 1896-1907 Director of the National Gallery. 1896 with Liebermann in Paris, exhibited at Durand-Ruel's. Arranged significant donations of Impressionist pictures to the national Gallery, but this caused a difference of opinion with Kaiser Wilhelm II and he was forced to resign. 1909-1911 Director of the Pinakothek in Munich.

TURNER Joseph Mallard William
1775 London – 1851 London
1789 studied at the Royal Academy. 1790 exhibited there for the first time. 1792 study tours through Wales, England, Scotland. Painted landscapes and sea scenes, at first in watercolour; influenced by painters of the 17th and 18th centuries; later did works based on events from world history in imaginatively idyllic landscapes. 1802 made a study of Old Masters in the Louvre. 1804 first private exhibition at his own gallery. 1807 painted views of the Thames from his own boat; became professor of perspective at the Academy. 1817 second tour of the continent; many others followed. Despite his Romantic preference for literary, idealist subject matter, he influenced the Impressionists in his sensitive use of colour tone and mood, his "informal" painting style and his special feel for the optical effects of modern reality.

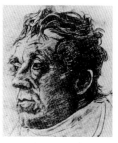

CATALOGUE: Butlin, M. and E. Joll: The Paintings of J.M.W.T. 2 vols. London 1984.– Wilton, A.: T. in his time. London 1987
BIBLIOGRAPHY: Chumbley, A. and I. Warrell (eds.): T. and the Human Figure: Studies of Contemporary Life. Tate Gallery, London 1989 (EC).– Gage, J.: J.M.W.T. A Wonderful Range of Mind. New Haven (CT) and London 1991.– Herrmann, L.: T. Paintings, Watercolours, Prints and Drawings. Oxford 1986.– Powell, C.: Turner in the South: Rome, Naples, Florence. London 1987.– Reynolds, G.: T. London 1969, 1986.– Shanes, E.: T.'s Human Landscape. London 1985.– Upstone, R. (ed.): T., The Second Decade: Watercolours and Drawings from the Turner Bequest, 1800-1810. Tate Gallery, London 1989 (EC)
ILLUSTRATIONS:
20 Cathedral Church, Lincoln, 1795

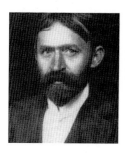

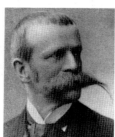

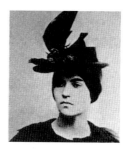

TWACHTMAN John Henry
1853 Cincinnati – 1902 Gloucester (MA)

1871-1875 studied at the Micken School of Design in Cincinnati and at Frank Duveneck's studio. 1875-1877 continued his studies in Munich with Ludwig von Löfftz. Influenced by Leibl. 1877 travelled with Duveneck and William Merritt Chase to Venice. 1878 returned to America and exhibited at the Society of American Artists; 1879 became a member there. Painted in various coastal towns of America, in New York and Cincinnati. 1880 travelled to Florence, where he gave courses at the Duveneck Studio. 1881 honeymoon in England, Belgium and Germany; painted with Weir in Holland; met Anton Mauve, who strongly influenced his Impressionist style. 1883-1885 lived in Paris and studied at the Académie Julian. 1885 moved to Connecticut near Weir. 1886 rented Holly House Farm in Cos Cob, which became a meeting place of American Impressionists. Preferred to paint snow landscapes and tried to capture their atmosphere. 1893 exhibited with Weir and Monet in New York but without much success. 1897 co-founder of The Ten American Painters. 1901 large one-man show at the Art Institute in Chicago. 1901/02 taught at summer courses in Gloucester, Massachusetts.
BIBLIOGRAPHY: Boyle, R.J.: J.T. New York 1979.– Boyle, R.J. and M.W. Baskett, (eds): A Retrospective Exhibition: J.H.T. Cincinnati Art Museum, Cincinnati 1966 (EC).– Chotner, D. et al. (eds): J.T.: Connecticut Landscapes. National Gallery of Art, Washington 1989 (EC).– Clark, E.C.: J.H.T. New York 1924 (private printing).– Hale, J.D.: The Life and Creative Development of J.H.T. 2 vols. Doctoral thesis, Ohio State University. Columbus 1957.– J.T. Connecticut Landscapes. National Gallery of Art, Washington 1989 (EC).– Tucker, A.: J.H.T. New York 1931.– Wickenden, R.J.: The Art and Etchings of J.H.T. New York 1921
ILLUSTRATIONS:
613 Winter Harmony, c. 1890-1900

UHDE Fritz von
1848 Wolkenburg – 1911 Munich

First drawing lessons while still at school; encouraged by his parents, both amateur painters. 1866 studied for three months at the Academy of Arts in Dresden. 1867-1871 military career; painted battle scenes – influenced by the war painter Ludwig Albrecht Schuster. 1876 went to Vienna, where he met Makart and was influenced by his dark, emotional style. 1879 visited Paris; pupil of M. Munkácsy. 1880 settled in Munich; became friends with Liebermann, through whose influence he discovered plein-air painting. 1882 travelled in Holland. His frequent religious themes are done in a realistic medium and reveal the influence of light-filled plein-air painting. 1892 co-founder of the Munich Secession; 1899 elected to their committee. 1907 successful showing of his pictures at the winter exhibition of the Secession.
BIBLIOGRAPHY: Brand, B.: F.v.U. Das religiöse Werk zwischen künstlerischer Intention und Öffentlichkeit. Doctoral thesis, Mainz 1983.– Keyssner, G.: U. Stuttgart and Berlin 1922.– Ostini, F. v.: F.v.U. Bielefeld and Leipzig 1902.– Rosenberger, H.: U. Stuttgart and Berlin 1908
ILLUSTRATIONS:
436 Fisher Children in Zandvoort, 1882
437 Two Daughters in the Garden, 1892
437 Big Sister, 1885
438 Walking to Bethlehem, c. 1890
439 Bavarian Drummers, 1883
460 In the Garden (The Artist's Daughters), 1906

UNION ARTISTIQUE (L')
Society for the encouragement of the arts founded in 1860 by various historians, writers, painters (including Degas and Lepic), composers and influential people. It organised literary talks, art exhibitions and concerts. Few of the Impressionists showed work at the exhibitions, which were dominated by the fashionable artists of the time such as Bastien-Lepage, Duran, Sargent, Blanche etc.

VALADON Suzanne
1867 Bourg de Bessines (near Limoges) – 1938 Paris

Real name: Marie Clémentine Valadon. Illegitimate child; had a neglected childhood in Montmartre. At age eighteen she herself had an illegitimate child; her son Maurice Valadon later became the artist Utrillo. Earned a living as a model; became the model and lover of Puvis de Chavannes and Renoir. Began to do her own painting; encouraged and instructed by the artists there (Toulouse-Lautrec, Degas and Renoir). Her favourite themes included drawings of female nudes and portraits, decorative still lifes, interiors and landscapes.
CATALOGUE: Petrides, P.: L'œuvre complet de S.V. Paris 1971

VALERY Paul
1871 Sète – 1945 Paris

Prose writer and poet. Friends with Rouart's sons; joined the circles around Degas and Morisot. 1889 began to study law at the University of Montpellier. 1894 moved to Paris and worked from 1895 as an editor at the Ministry of War. 1900 married Nini Gobillard, one of Morisot's nieces. 1900-1922 active as a private secretary. 1925 elected to the Académie Française.

VAN GOGH → Gogh

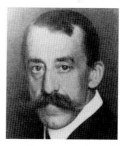

VELDE Henry van de
1863 Antwerp – 1957 Zurich

1880-1884 studied at the Academy of Arts in Antwerp and 1884/85 with Bastien-Lepage and Carolus-Duran in Paris. Influenced by J.-F. Millet and Manet. Member of "L'Art Indépend-

ant", a Belgian group of painters akin to the Barbizon school. 1888 influenced by Seurat's painting "A Sunday Afternoon at the Ile de la Grande Jatte" (pp. 260/261), he followed van Rysselberghe's advice and turned to Pointillism. Member of Les Vingt. 1894 discovered the writings of William Morris and developed the decorative, linear Art Nouveau style for which he is famous. From 1895 active as an architect. 1898 founded the "workshops for applied art" at Ixelles in Brussels, which concentrated on utilitarian art. 1902 moved to Weimar; Director of the School of Arts and Crafts until 1915 and 1926-1935 Director of the "Institut supérieur des Arts décoratifs" in Brussels. 1925-1936 professor of architecture at Ghent. From 1947 lived in Switzerland.
WRITINGS, DOCUMENTS: Velde, H. v. d.: Zum neuen Stil. Munich 1955.– Velde, H. v. d.: Geschichte meines Lebens. Munich 1962
BIBLIOGRAPHY: Curjel, H. (ed.): H.v.d.V. Kunsthaus Zürich, Zurich 1958 (EC).– Hammacher, A.M.: Die Welt H.v.d.V.s Cologne 1967.– Hammacher, A.M.: Le monde de H.v.d.V. Antwerp 1967.– H.v.d.V. 1863-1957. Palais des Beaux-Arts, Brussels; Rijksmuseum Kröller-Müller, Otterlo 1963.– H.v.d.V. (1863-1957): Schilderijen en tekeningen. Koninklijk Museum voor Schone Kunsten, Antwerp; Rijksmuseum Kröller-Müller, Otterlo; Otterlo 1988 (EC). –Hüter, K.-H.: H.v.d.V. Berlin 1967.– Sembach, K.-J.: H.v.d.V. New York 1989.– Sembach, K.-J. (ed.): H.v.d.V. Ein europäischer Künstler in seiner Zeit. Cologne 1992 (EC).– Teirlinck: H.v.d.V. Brussels 1959.– Voort, J. v.: Gedenkboek H.v.d.V. Ghent 1933
ILLUSTRATIONS:
422 Bathing Huts at Blankenberge, 1888
422 Woman at the Window, 1889

VIDAL Eugène
1847 Paris – 1907 Cagnes

Studied with Gérôme in Paris, but linked with the Impressionists. 1873 exhibited for the first time at the Salon. Travelled in Algeria. 1880 exhibited at the 5th and in 1881 at the 6th Impressionist exhibitions. 1900 a big success at the World Fair in Paris.
ILLUSTRATION:
133 Girl Resting on her Arms

VIE MODERNE, La
Illustrated weekly with large arts section, founded in 1879 by Georges Charpentier, the editor, and Emile Bergerat, the director. Silvestre and Edmond Renoir were in charge of the arts column. Exhibitions of works by the Impressionists were held in the editorial offices, while the magazine contained in-depth discussions of contemporary art, together with the latest graphics.

VIGNON Paul-Victor
1847 Villers-Cotterêts – 1909 Meulan

Pupil of Corot, who heavily influenced his style of painting. Further guidance and advice from Cals.

Painted in Pontoise, Auvers-sur-Oise and many other locations alongside Pissarro – with whom he was on friendly terms – Guillaumin and Cézanne. 1880 participation in the 5th and 1881 in the 6th Impressionist exhibitions. Despite Monet's opposition, he also exhibited 1882 in the 7th and 1886 in the 8th Impressionist exhibitions. Friends with Gachet, Murer and van Gogh's brothers. 1894 large one-man exhibition at Bernheim-Jeune's.

ILLUSTRATIONS:
202 The Crossroads
203 The Hills at Triel, c. 1881

VILLE D'AVRAY

Village near Saint-Cloud. Corot frequently stayed there; Courbet painted in the woods nearby. Monet lived there in 1860, while Renoir spent the summer of 1868 in the village.

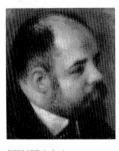

VOLLARD Ambroise
1867 Saint Denis (Réunion) – 1939 Paris

Son of a notary. One of the most important art dealers to succeed Theo van Gogh. Initially completing legal studies in Montpellier and receiving his doctorate in Paris, he then devoted himself to his hobby, art, first of all purchasing art prints from the Bouquinistes on the banks of the Seine. Thereafter, studies in the gallery of the Union Artistique. Opened his first gallery in 1893 at 41 Rue Laffitte, with an exhibition of sketches by Manet. Through Denis and Bernard, he came to know and appreciate Cézanne, organizing in 1895 the first Cézanne exhibition. Also sold pictures by Renoir, Degas and Pissarro. Moved with his gallery in 1899 to 6 Rue Laffitte. As the most important art dealer for the avant-garde, he organized the first exhibitions of works by van Gogh, Picasso (1901) and Matisse (1904). In addition, he represented unknown artists. In his role as publisher, he printed lithographs and books illustrated by artists. Published monographs on Cézanne, Degas and Renoir and, in 1937, his "Memoirs of an Art Dealer".

VONNOH Robert William
1858 Hartford (CT) – 1933 Nice

Initial artistic studies at the Massachusetts Normal Art School. 1881-1883

studies at the Académie Julian, Paris, under Boulanger and Lefèbvre. Influenced by Bastien-Lepage. 1883-1887 studies continued at the Boston Museum School and the Cowles Art School under L.C. Perry. 1887-1891 second period of residence in France. Journey to Grèz-sur-Loing; interested in Impressionism, above all in the works of Sisley and Monet. Participation in the Paris World Fair. 1891 return to America. 1891-1896 and 1918-1920 professor at the Pennsylvania Academy of the Fine Arts. 1990 member of the National Academy.

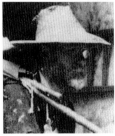

Typical representative of American Impressionism, revealing a fresh quality if with less atmosphere. His second wife, Bessie Potter Vonnoh, was also a successful painter.
WRITINGS, DOCUMENTS: Vonnoh, R.: Increasing Values in American Paintings. In: "Arts and Decoration" 2 (May 1912), pp. 254-256.– Vonnoh, R.: The Relation of Art to Existence. In: "Arts and Decoration" 17 (September 1922), p. 328f.
BIBLIOGRAPHY: Clark, E.: The Art of R.V. In: "Art in America" 16 (August 1928), pp. 223-232
ILLUSTRATION:
606 Poppies, 1888

VUILLARD Edouard
1868 Cuiseaux – 1940 La Baule

1886-1889 studies at the Paris Art High School, under Gérôme among others. Attended the free Académie Julian in 1888; friendship with Bonnard, Denis, Sérusier. 1889 one-off participation in the Salon. 1890 co-founder of the "Nabis", the Symbolist group of artists; sharing a studio

with Bonnard and Denis. 1891 one-man show at the magazine "La Revue Blanche"; long-term friendship with its editor, T. Natanson, and the latter's wife, Misia. Contact with Toulouse-Lautrec and Mallarmé, among others. Exhibition by the "Nabis" in Le Barc de Boutteville's gallery. Impressed by Japanese colour woodcuts, he began his impressive, extensively decorative, "intimate" interior scenes. 1892 first of numerous wall creations depicting decorative scenes. Contact with J. Hessel, the art dealer, the two frequently holidaying together thereafter. 1893 stage sets for the "Théâtre de l'Œuvre" of his schoolfriend Lugné-Poe. 1900 Swiss journey with F. Vallotton. Works exhibited at the Berlin Secession for the first time. 1901 exhibited with the "Indépendants". 1902 journey to Holland. 1903 co-founder of the Autumn Salon; regularly exhibiting at Bernheim-Jeune's. 1909 teaching for a time at the Académie Ranson. 1913 with Bonnard in Hamburg. 1914-1916 active military service and army painter. Later, numerous traditional portraits, interiors and urban landscapes. Died while fleeing from German troops.
CATALOGUES: Roger-Marx, C.: E.V. L'œuvre gravé. Paris 1948 (Reprint: San Francisco 1990)
BIBLIOGRAPHY: Preston, S.: V. New York 1985.– Roger-Marx, C.: V. Paris 1945.– Salomon, J.: Auprès de V. Paris 1945.– Salomon, J.: V. Paris 1968.– Thomson, B.: V. Oxford 1988
ILLUSTRATION:
340 After the Meal, c. 1890-1898

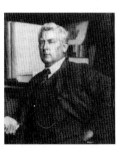

WEIR Julian Alden
1852 West Point – 1919 New York

Son of a history painter and drawing teacher at the U.S. Military Academy, West Point. Initial training from his father; later, in the 1860s, in the New York studio of his brother, John Ferguson. 1870-1872 studies at the National Academy of Design under L. Wilmarth. 1873 studies continued in Paris under Gérôme. Practising open-air painting in summer in Pont-Aven (Brittany) and Cernay-la-Ville, southwest of Paris. 1874/75 journeys to England, Spain and Holland. Friendly with Bastien-Lepage and Sargent. 1875 first work exhibited in the Paris Salon and the New York National Academy of Design. Regular partici-

pation in the Salons of the following years. 1877 return to New York; member of the Society of American Artists, engaged in the organization of exhibitions and exhibiting there himself. 1882 president of the Society. Renewed travel in Europe in the 1870s and 1880s. Close friendship with Twachtman. From 1878 teaching at the Cooper Institute. From 1885 to 1889, he took over the portrait class at the Art Students League, and conducted summer courses in Branchville in 1897-1901. 1886 member of the National Academy. Founding his career as an artist primarily on portraits and still lifes, he also painted successful history works and family scenes.
WRITINGS, DOCUMENTS: Weir, J.A.: Jules Bastien-Lepage. In: "Studio" 13 (January 1885), pp. 145-151.– Young, D.W. (ed.): The Life and Letters of J.A.W. New Haven (CT) 1960
BIBLIOGRAPHY: Blashfield, E.H.: A Commemorative Tribute to J.A.W. New York 1922.– Burke, D.B.: J.A.W. An American Impressionist. Newark (DE) 1983.– Coffin, W.A. (ed.): A Memorial Exhibition of the Works of J.A.W. Metropolitan Museum of Art, New York 1924 (EC).– Flint, J.A. (ed.): J.A.W.: American Impressionist 1852-1919. National Collection of Fine Arts, Washington 1972 (EC).– Phillips, D. et al.: J.A.W.: An Appreciation of his Life and Works. New York 1922.– Young, M.S. (ed.): J.A.W., 1852-1919: Centennial Exhibition. American Academy of Arts and Letters. New York 1952 (EC).– Young, M.S. (ed.): Paintings by J.A.W. Phillips Collection, Washington 1972 (EC)
ILLUSTRATIONS:
623 Midday Rest in New England, 1897
623 The Red Bridge, c. 1895

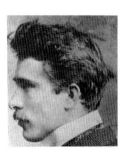

WEISGERBER Albert
1878 St. Ingbert – 1915 Fromelles (Belgium)

Attended the arts-and-crafts school in Munich. 1897-1901 studies at the Munich Academy under Franz von Stuck. 1905-1907 residing in Paris; impressed by Cézanne. From 1897 working as an illustrator for the Munich magazine "Jugend". Contact with the Matisse circle around Hans Purrmann. Experimenting with Fauvism, which replaces the pastose dark-

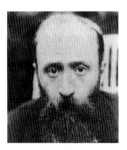

coloured application of paint with bright colours and a harmonious manner of painting; a preference for religious subjects. 1909 member of the Munich Artists' Association. 1913 president of the New Secession.
CATALOGUE: Ishikawa-Franke, S.: A.W. Leben und Werk. Saarbrücken 1978
BIBLIOGRAPHY: Christoffel, U.: A.W. St. Ingbert 1950.– Heuss, T.: Erinnerungen an A.W. Heidelberg 1962.– Weber, W.: Zum Werk A.W.s und Œuvreverzeichnis der Gemälde. Heidelberg 1962
ILLUSTRATION:
457 Riding in the English Gardens, in Munich, 1910

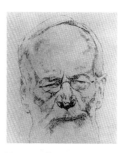

Norwegian colleagues in 1881, 1883 and 1885. Worked during 1888/89 in Bonnat's studio. Admired Manet and van Gogh. Wrote a critique in 1889 of the Copenhagen exhibition of works by French Impressionists, in which he characterized Cézanne, Guillaumin and Manet as the true Impressionists.
BIBLIOGRAPHY: Norske malere. E.W. Kristiania 1913.– Østby, L.: E.W. Tegninger og akvareller. Oslo 1977.– Svedfelt, T.: E.W. konst. Stockholm 1947
ILLUSTRATIONS:
474 Shepherds on Tåtøy, 1883
486 Autumn, 1891

WESTERHOLM Victor
1860 Åbo – 1919 Åbo
1869 start of artistic training under R.W. Ekman. 1871 with T. Waenerberg. 1878-1886 studies at the Düsseldorf Academy under E. Dücker. Work exhibited at the 1882 Paris Salon. Occupied in the summer with open-air painting in Åland. 1886 foundation of a painters' colony in Önningeby, its programme devoted to open-air painting. 1887 abandonment of idealizing style of painting, beginning of Impressionist manner. From 1888 teacher in Åbo. Influenced in the 1890s by Symbolism.
ILLUSTRATION:
487 The Seine at Paris, 1888

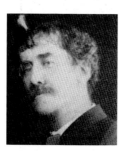

WHISTLER James Abbott McNeill
1834 Lowell (MA) – 1903 London
1843 family emigrated to Russia. 1845 initial lessons in drawing at the St. Petersburg Academy. 1849 return to America following death of his father. 1851 entered West Point Military Academy. 1855 training as painter in Paris. 1856 studies in Glyre's studio. Of greater significance for his artistic development were his encounters with Fantin-Latour, Courbet and Legros. 1858 journey to Luxembourg, northern France and the Rhine; series of 13 etchings, the "French Series". 1859 move to London following rejection by the Salon. 1864 exhibited the critically acclaimed picture "The Little White Girl: Symphony in White No. 2" (p. 573) in the Salon des Refusés. Influenced in the 1860s by Japanism. 1866 journey to Chile. Around 1870 first "Nocturnes" with the Thames landscape as subject; these works served to clearly reveal the reproduction of a poetic mood and the correspondence of pictorial and musical harmony. The subject was to occupy him all through the following decade. From the 1870s on, an increase in portraiture, which would represent his principal source of income until into the 1890s. 1874 decoration of the Peacock Room (now in the Freer Gallery of Art, Washington) for his patron, F.R. Leyland. 1878 libel action against Ruskin, which bankrupted him despite his moral victory. 1892 successful one-man exhibition in the Goupil Gallery, London. Whistler's style of painting should be compared not so much with the analytical technique of Impressionism as rather with colour impressionism, something already developed in the 17th century, the effect of which is based upon aesthetic quality. President of the Society of British Artists and the International Society of Sculptors, Painters and Gravers.
WRITINGS, DOCUMENTS: Menpes, M.: W. as I Knew Him. London 1904.– Pennell, E.R. (ed.): The W. Journal. Philadelphia 1921.– Whistler, J.A.M.: The Gentle Art of Making Enemies. New York 1953
CATALOGUES: Kennedy, E.G.: The Etched Work of W. San Francisco 1978.– Levy, M. and A. Staley: W. Lithographs. A Catalogue Raisonné. London 1975.– Lochnan, K.A.: The Etchings of J.M.W. New Haven (CT) and London 1984.– Young, A.M. et al.: The Paintings of J.M.W. 2 vols. New Haven (CT) and London 1980
BIBLIOGRAPHY: Cabanne, P.: W. Munich 1988.– Curry, D.P.: J.M.W. at the Freer Gallery of Art: Washington, New York and London 1984. Fine, R.E. (ed.): J.M.W. A Reexamination. Washington 1987.– Fleming, G.: The Young W., 1834-1866. London and Boston 1978.– Gregory, H.: The World of J.M.W. New York 1959.– J.M.W. Nationalgalerie, Berlin 1969 (EC).– Laver, J.: Paintings by J.M.W. London 1938.– McMullen, R.: Victorian Outsider. A Biography of J.M.W. New York 1973.– Pearson, H.: The Man W. London 1952, New York 1978.– Pennell, E.R. and J. Pennell: The Life of J.M.W. 2 vols. Philadelphia and London 1908.– Prideaux, T.: The World of W. New York 1970.– Spalding, F.: W. Oxford 1979.– Sutton, D.: Nocturne: The Art of J.M.W. London 1964.– Sutton, D.: J.M.W.:

Paintings, Etchings, Pastels and Watercolours. London 1966.– Sweet, F.A. (ed.): Sargent, W. and Mary Cassatt. The Art Institute of Chicago, Chicago 1954 (EC).– Taylor, H.: J.M.W. New York 1978.– Walker, J.: J.M.W. New York 1987.– Weintraub, S.: W. A Biography. New York 1974
ILLUSTRATIONS:
572 Nocturne in Blue and Gold: Old Battersea Bridge, c. 1872-1875
573 The Little White Girl: Symphony in White, No. 2, 1864
573 Rose and Silver: The Princess from the Land of Porcelain, 1864

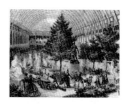

WORLD FAIRS
These representative exhibitions, organized on a country basis and embracing the latest in science, technology and culture, were intended as a means of promoting exports. They were always linked to the interests of domestic and foreign policy, for example the 100th anniversary of the French Revolution. 1851 the first in London, in the technically innovative Crystal Palace. 1855 in Paris, art for the first time given its own section, later also to encompass national retrospectives. The most important "Expositions universelles" were those of 1862 (London), 1867 (Paris), 1873 (Vienna), 1876 (Philadelphia), 1878, 1889 and 1900 (Paris), 1893 (Chicago), and 1904 (Saint Louis), the years between seeing events of a more limited nature. The competition between the nations, the possibility of international comparisons in a compressed space, and a viewing public running into millions gave the World Fairs considerable significance for artistic development, and especially for Impressionism with its interest in "modern life". In addition to the official exhibitions, excluded artists organized private one-man or group shows (Courbet in 1855 and 1867, Manet in 1867, the Pont-Aven group in 1889, Impressionist pictures belonging to American private collections in 1893). Not until 1889 and – especially – 1900 did France publicly acknowledge her Impressionists in a World Fair.

ZANDOMENEGHI Federico
1841 Venice – 1917 Paris
Scion of a well-known artistic family, his father and grandfather sculptors. 1856-1859 studies at the Venice Art Academy; training continued in Pavia. 1860-1862 participation in the national movement, following Garibaldi to Sicily. 1862-1866 residence in Florence; member of the circle around Macchiaioli. Friendly with

WEISSENBRUCH Johannes Hendrik
1824 The Hague – 1903 The Hague
1830-1846 drawing studies under J.J. Löw and evening classes at the Academy in The Hague under B.J. van Hove, the interior decorator. Copied the works of the 17th-century Flemish artists. Painting in the area surrounding The Hague, Haarlem and Arnheim. Significant open-air and watercolour painter of the "Hague School". 1866 member of the "Société Belge des Aquarellistes". Acquaintance with Roelofs. Sole journey abroad undertaken. 1900 move to Barbizon. 1901 large one-man exhibition, organized by the members of the "Pulchri Studio" and Buffa, the Amsterdam art dealer's.
BIBLIOGRAPHY: Gelder, H.E. van: J.H.W. Amsterdam 1940.– J.H.W. Schilderijen, aquarellen, grafiek. Singer Museum, Laren 1960 (EC).– Laanstra, W.: J.W., schildergraficus, 1822-1880. Amsterdam 1986
ILLUSTRATION:
408 View of Haarlem

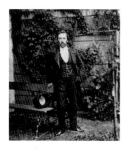

WERENSKIOLD Erik
1855 Eidskog – 1938 Oslo
1872-1876 pupil of J. Middelthun, the sculptor, and A. Ender at the Kristiania drawing school in Oslo. 1876-1880 studies at the Munich Art Academy under Löfftz and Lindenschmit. His style of painting was orientated towards the realist works of the circle around Leibl. Impressed by the exhibition of Realist works by French painters seen in Munich in 1879. Following his return to Norway, he joined Krohg, Munthe and Thaulow, travelling to Paris with his

Martelli, visiting him in Castiglion-cello. Living during **1866-1874** primarily in Venice, with visits to Rome and Florence; frequently earning his living through fashion drawings. **1874** move to Paris, where he encountered the French Impressionists. Acquaintance with Toulouse-Lautrec. Subject-matter comparable with Degas' café and street scenes, nudes and portraits. Exhibited in **1879-1881** and **1886** at the 4th, 5th, 6th and 8th Impressionism shows. Increased pastel paintings from the 1880s on. Went unacknowledged in Italy until long after his death.
CATALOGUE: Piceni, E.: Z. L'uomo e l'opera. Milan 1979

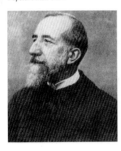

BIBLIOGRAPHY: Cinotti, M.: Z. Busto Arsizio 1960.– Dini, F.: F.Z., la vita e le opere. Florence 1989.– Dini, F.Z.: Un veneziano a Parigi. Ca' Pesaro, Venice. Milan 1988 (EC).– Piceni, E.: Z. Milan 1932, 1952, 1967
ILLUSTRATIONS:
538 Fishing on the Seine, 1878
541 Le Moulin de la Galette, 1878
542 Place d'Anvers, Paris, 1880
543 Children's Games in the Park Monceau
548 Lady in a Meadow, 1893
549 Portait of a Girl, c. 1893-1895

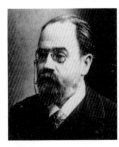

ZOLA Emile
1840 Paris – 1902 Paris
French writer and art critic; schoolfriend of Cézanne in Aix-en-Provence. Went in **1858** to Paris. **1862-1866** publicity manager for the Hachette publishing house; thereafter freelance author. **1866/67** critical defence of Manet's art. Began in **1870** to write his novel series – partly so-cially critical – about the Rougon-Macquart family, utilizing the natural-istic method of the "experimental novel"; it was published in the course of **1871-1903**, including **1880** "Nana" (cf. Manet, p. 160) and **1886** "The Masterpiece", in part a critical characterization of Impressionism. From **1877** on, second residence in Médan. Wrote art critiques, his clients including a Russian newspaper in St. Petersburg. **1896** last Salon report in "Le Figaro". **1898** journalistic involvement against antisemitism and reaction (Dreyfus Affair).

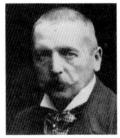

ZORN Anders Leonard
1860 Utmeland – 1920 Mora
Already studying in **1875** at the Stockholm Academy. **1881** move to Paris; thereafter leading a restless, unsettled life. **1881/82** journey to Spain; **1884** in Spain again and also in Portugal. **1882-1885** living in London, working in England exclusively as a painter of watercolours. **1885/86** journeys to Hungary, Greece and Turkey, **1887** to Spain and Algeria. **1887/88** winter spent in the international painters' colony in St. Ives, Cornwall. Thereafter living until **1896** predominantly in Paris. Preoccupation with Nordic motifs, in his early work also with those of the Orient. **1896** settled down in Mora. Founded an open-air and local-history museum, in which he also exhibited his own works (since **1939**, the public "Zornmuseet"). Well-known and successful everywhere on account of his nudes and portraits.
CATALOGUES: Asplund, K.: A.L.Z. The Engraved Work. A Descriptive Catalogue. 2 vols. San Francisco 1990.– Hjert, S. and B.: A.Z. A Complete Catalogue of the Engravings. Uppsala 1980
BIBLIOGRAPHY: Asplund, K.: A.Z. His Life and Work. London 1921.– Boëthius, G.: Z. Tecknaren, målaren, etsaren, skulptören. Stockholm 1949.– Boëthius, G.: A.Z. Stockholm 1954.– Engström, A.: Z. Stockholm 1928.– Forssmann, E.: Tecknaren A.Z. Stockholm 1959.– Forssmann, E.: Z. i Mora. Stockholm 1960.– Friedrich, P.: A.Z. Berlin 1924.– Hedberg, T.: A.Z. 2 vols. Stockholm 1923/24.– Jensen, J.C. (ed.): A.Z. Gemälde, Aquarelle, Zeichnungen. Kunsthalle der Hypo-Kulturstiftung et al. Munich 1990 (EC)

ILLUSTRATION:
488 In a Brewery, 1890

ZULOAGA Y ZABALETA Ignacio
1870 Eibar – 1945 Madrid
Son of a metal engraver, receiving his artistic training from his father. Copied works by Velázquez, Goya and El Greco in the Prado, Madrid. Exhibited at the **1887** national art exhibition for painting. **1888** residence in Rome. **1889** studies in the Paris studio of Gervex. Temporary abandonment of his austere Spanish style, painting in the manner of Monet, but also that of Renoir, Pissarro and Sisley. Friendly with Rusiñol. Exhibited in **1894** at Le Barc de Boutteville's. Regular participation in the Salon of the "Société Nationale des Beaux-Arts". Occasional residence in Bilbao, Seville and Granada. Journeys through Italy, Belgium and many European cities, where he participated in exhibitions. **1916** and **1925** journeys in the USA.

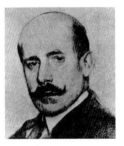

BIBLIOGRAPHY: Alonso, M.D.: Z. Madrid 1979.– Arozamena, J.M. de: I.Z. El pintor, el hombre. San Sebastián 1970.– I.Z. in America, 1909-1925. Spanish Institute. New York 1989 (EC).– Lafuente Ferrari, E.: Los retratos de Z. Pamplona 1950.– Lafuente Ferrari, E.: La vida y el arte de I.Z. Madrid 1950.– Lafuente Ferrari, E.: I.Z. y Segovia. Segovia 1950.– Lafuente Ferrari, E.: I.Z. Barcelona 1980.– Milhou, M.: I.Z. et la France. Bordeaux 1979.– Pantorba, B. de: I.Z. Madrid 1944.– Plessier, G.: Etude critique de la correspondance échangée entre Z. et Rodin de 1903 à 1917. Paris 1983
ILLUSTRATION:
562 Celestina, 1906